Advising Center Code: _____

PETERSON'S INTERNATIONAL STUDENT NETWORK
UNDERGRADUATE STUDENT SURVEY 2007-2008

Do you need help deciding which college to attend in the United States? Peterson's International Student Network Undergraduate Student Survey is a great way to make your decision easier! Complete the Survey below and give it to your adviser, or for faster service go to *www.petersons.com/internationalstudents* and complete the survey online. You may also visit *www.petersons.com/internationalstudents* to download and print additional copies of this Survey. Peterson's will take your answers and share them with all of the colleges and universities in our network that are searching for international students. The colleges and universities will send you more information, including catalogs and application forms, so you can make the right college choice. Good luck!

PRINT VERY CLEARLY. USE ENGLISH LETTERS ONLY. *INDICATES A REQUIRED FIELD   Today's Date: _____

Write your name and complete address below **EXACTLY** as if you were mailing a letter to yourself.

*Name:

*Given/First _____   *Family/Last (surname) _____

*Mailing Address: (Include *street address or post office box, city, state/province, and postal code* as if you were mailing a letter to yourself.)

_____

* Number/Street or Post Office Box Number (Required)

_____

Address Line 2 (if needed)

_____

Address Line 3 (if needed)

_____

*City, State/Province, Postal Code (Required)

*Country of Residence _____

Telephone Number (Include country code)

_____

Fax Number (Include country code)

_____

E-mail Address (in full)

Date of Birth ___ ___ / ___ ___ / ___ ___ ___ ___
Day(DD)/Month(MM)/Year(YYYY)

Gender   ❑ Male   ❑ Female

Provide the following information as completely as possible.

*1. Country of citizenship: _____

*2. I want to enter a college or university in academic year: (check one)
❑ 2007-2008   ❑ 2008-2009   ❑ 2009-2010   ❑ 2010-2011
❑ I am interested in midyear admission

*3. I am interested in the following fields of study (major): (Please use the 6-digit codes listed beside the majors on the back of this form.)

[_____] [_____] [_____]

❑ Undecided

4. I will be sponsored by:

❑ Family/Myself ❑ Government ❑ Private Organization ❑ Other

I/my sponsor will be able to contribute toward the total cost of my education (tuition & cost of living) each year: (check one)
❑ US$5000 to US$10,000   ❑ US$20,001 to US$25,000
❑ US$10,001 to US$15,000   ❑ Over US$25,000
❑ US$15,001 to US$20,000

*5. I would prefer to attend: (check one)
❑ 2-year institution (first 2 years– associate degree)
❑ 4-year institution (bachelor's degree)
❑ I have no preference

*6. I am interested in attending a college or university in the following regions of the United States: (check all that apply)
❑ I have no preference
❑ Middle Atlantic (Delaware, District of Columbia, Maryland, New Jersey, New York, Pennsylvania, Virginia, West Virginia)
❑ Midwest (Illinois, Indiana, Iowa, Kansas, Michigan, Minnesota, Missouri, Nebraska, North Dakota, Ohio, South Dakota, Wisconsin)
❑ New England (Connecticut, Maine, Massachusetts, New Hampshire, Rhode Island, Vermont)
❑ Southeast (Alabama, Florida, Georgia, Kentucky, Louisiana, Mississippi, North Carolina, South Carolina, Tennessee)
❑ Southwest (Arkansas, New Mexico, Oklahoma, Texas)
❑ West (Alaska, Arizona, California, Colorado, Hawaii, Idaho, Montana, Nevada, Oregon, Utah, Washington, Wyoming)

7. I took the TOEFL in: _____ / _____
month   year
Please select one test format below and include your score in the space provided:

Paper-Based Test: _____ (scale 310-677)
Computer-Based Test: _____ (scale 40-300)
Internet-Based Test: _____ (scale 0-120)

I will take the TOEFL in: _____ / _____
month   year

8. I took the SAT in: _____ / _____
month   year
My SAT verbal or critical reading score was: _____
My SAT math score was: _____
My SAT writing score was: _____
I will take the SAT in: _____ / _____
month   year

9. I would like information on intensive English language programs in the United States: ❑ Yes   ❑ No

10. The full name and location of my secondary/high school is:

_____ / _____
name   country

11. I will finish/finished secondary/high school in: _____
year

12. The certificate I will receive at the end of my secondary/high school studies is called: (print carefully)

_____

13. My average grade in my last year of study was: (check one)
❑ A (90-100%)   ❑ C (70-79%) ❑ F (0-59%)
❑ B (80-89%)   ❑ D (60-69%)

14. For students who have attended one or more years at a university: I have completed _____ years of university-level education at: _____
name of university

15. Check here ❑ to receive information about other Peterson's products and services related to studying in the United States.

Codes for Undergraduate Fields of Study (use these codes to fill in the boxes in number 3)

Agriculture and Natural Resources Studies

- ❏ 02.0101 Agriculture/Agricultural Sciences (general)
- ❏ 01.0101 Agricultural Business and Management
- ❏ 01.0103 Agricultural Economics
- ❏ 02.0402 Agronomy and Crop Science
- ❏ 02.0201 Animal Science
- ❏ 03.0102 Environmental Science/Studies
- ❏ 03.0391 Fish/Game Management
- ❏ 02.0301 Food Sciences and Technology
- ❏ 03.0501 Forestry
- ❏ 02.0403 Horticulture Science
- ❏ 03.0201 Natural Resources Management and Policy
- ❏ 02.0401 Plant Sciences
- ❏ 03.0601 Wildlife and Wildlands Science and Management

Architecture and Related Programs

- ❏ 04.0201 Architecture (general)
- ❏ 01.0001 City/Urban Community and Regional Planning
- ❏ 04.0401 Environmental Design/Architecture
- ❏ 04.0601 Landscape Architecture

Area, Ethnic Studies and Cultural Studies

- ❏ 05.0101 African Studies
- ❏ 05.0201 African-American/Black Studies
- ❏ 05.0202 American Indian/Native American Studies
- ❏ 05.0102 American/United States Studies
- ❏ 05.0103 Asian Studies
- ❏ 05.0200 Ethnic and Cultural Studies
- ❏ 05.0107 Latin American Studies
- ❏ 05.0291 Mexican-American/Chicano Studies
- ❏ 05.0108 Near and Middle Eastern Studies

Art and Art Related Fields

- ❏ 50.0701 Art (general)
- ❏ 50.0491 Applied Art
- ❏ 50.0703 Art History, Criticism and Conservation
- ❏ 50.0402 Commercial and Advertising Art
- ❏ 50.0492 Computer Graphics
- ❏ 50.0705 Drawing
- ❏ 50.0407 Fashion/Apparel Design
- ❏ 50.0712 Fiber, Textile and Weaving Arts
- ❏ 50.0702 Fine/Studio Arts
- ❏ 50.0404 Industrial Design
- ❏ 50.0408 Interior Design
- ❏ 51.2703 Medical Illustration
- ❏ 50.0708 Painting
- ❏ 50.0605 Photography
- ❏ 50.0709 Sculpture

Biological Sciences

- ❏ 26.0101 Biology/Biological Sciences (general)
- ❏ 26.0601 Anatomy
- ❏ 26.0202 Biochemistry
- ❏ 26.0614 Biometrics
- ❏ 26.0203 Biophysics
- ❏ 26.0301 Botany/Plant Biology
- ❏ 26.0401 Cell/Cellular Biology and Histology
- ❏ 26.0702 Entomology
- ❏ 26.0613 Genetics, Plant and Animal
- ❏ 26.0607 Marine/Aquatic Biology
- ❏ 26.0501 Microbiology/Bacteriology
- ❏ 26.0402 Molecular Biology
- ❏ 26.0608 Neuroscience
- ❏ 26.0706 Physiology, Human and Animal
- ❏ 26.9991 Wildlife Biology
- ❏ 26.0701 Zoology/Animal Biology

Business

- ❏ 52.0101 Business (general)
- ❏ 52.0301 Accounting
- ❏ 52.0802 Actuarial Science
- ❏ 52.0803 Banking and Financial Support Services
- ❏ 52.0201 Business Administration and Management
- ❏ 52.0601 Business/Managerial Economics
- ❏ 52.0801 Finance
- ❏ 52.1001 Human Resources Management
- ❏ 52.0805 Insurance and Risk Management
- ❏ 52.1101 International Business
- ❏ 52.1002 Labor and Industrial Relations
- ❏ 52.1402 Marketing Research
- ❏ 52.1501 Real Estate
- ❏ 52.1491 Retail Management
- ❏ 31.0504 Sport and Fitness Administration/Management

Communications, Journalism, Speech & Mass Communications

- ❏ 09.0101 Communications (general)
- ❏ 09.0201 Advertising
- ❏ 09.0402 Broadcast Journalism
- ❏ 09.0401 Journalism
- ❏ 09.0501 Public Relations and Organizational Communications
- ❏ 09.0491 Publishing
- ❏ 09.0701 Radio and Television
- ❏ 23.1001 Speech and Rhetorical Studies
- ❏ 09.9991 Telecommunications

Computer and Information Sciences

- ❏ 11.0101 Computer and Information Sciences (general)
- ❏ 11.0201 Computer Programming
- ❏ 11.0701 Computer Science
- ❏ 11.0401 Information Science/Studies
- ❏ 25.0101 Library Science/Librarianship
- ❏ 52.1201 Management Information Systems

Dance

- ❏ 50.0301 Dance

Education and Child Care

- ❏ 13.0101 Education (general)
- ❏ 20.0201 Child Care and Guidance
- ❏ 13.1202 Elementary Teacher Education
- ❏ 13.1307 Health Teacher Education
- ❏ 13.1314 Physical Education Teaching and Coaching
- ❏ 13.1204 Pre-Elementary/Early Childhood/Kindergarten Teacher Education
- ❏ 13.1205 Secondary Teacher Education
- ❏ 13.1001 Special Education

Engineering and Technology

- ❏ 14.0101 Engineering (general)
- ❏ 14.0201 Aerospace/Aeronautical/Astronautical Engineering
- ❏ 14.0301 Agricultural/Biological Engineering
- ❏ 14.0401 Architectural Engineering
- ❏ 15.0803 Automotive Engineering Technology
- ❏ 14.0501 Biomedical/Medical Engineering
- ❏ 14.0601 Ceramic Sciences and Engineering
- ❏ 14.0701 Chemical Engineering
- ❏ 14.0801 Civil Engineering
- ❏ 15.0201 Civil Engineering Technology
- ❏ 14.0901 Computer Engineering
- ❏ 15.0301 Computer Engineering Technology
- ❏ 15.9992 Construction Engineering
- ❏ 14.1001 Electrical/Electronics/Communications Engineering
- ❏ 15.0303 Electrical/Electronics/Communications Engineering Technology
- ❏ 15.0503 Energy Management and Systems Technology
- ❏ 14.2901 Engineering Design
- ❏ 14.3001 Engineering/Industrial Management
- ❏ 14.1401 Environmental/Environmental Health Engineering
- ❏ 14.1501 Geological Engineering
- ❏ 48.0201 Graphic and Printing Equipment Operation
- ❏ 14.1701 Industrial/Manufacturing Engineering
- ❏ 15.0603 Industrial/Manufacturing Technology
- ❏ 41.9992 Marine Technology
- ❏ 14.1801 Materials Engineering
- ❏ 14.3101 Materials Science
- ❏ 14.1901 Mechanical Engineering
- ❏ 15.0805 Mechanical Engineering/Mechanical Technology
- ❏ 14.2001 Metallurgical Engineering
- ❏ 14.2101 Mining and Mineral Engineering
- ❏ 14.2201 Naval Architecture and Marine Engineering
- ❏ 14.2301 Nuclear Engineering
- ❏ 15.0701 Occupational Safety and Health Technology
- ❏ 14.2401 Ocean Engineering
- ❏ 14.2501 Petroleum Engineering
- ❏ 11.0791 Robotics
- ❏ 15.1102 Survey Technology/Surveying
- ❏ 14.2701 Systems Engineering
- ❏ 15.9994 Transportation Technologies

Family and Consumer Sciences and Nutritional Studies

- ❏ 19.0101 Family and Consumer Sciences (general)
- ❏ 19.0503 Dietetics/Human Nutritional Services
- ❏ 19.0301 Family and Community Studies
- ❏ 19.0502 Foods and Nutrition Science

Film and Theater Arts

- ❏ 50.0501 Drama/Theater Arts (general)
- ❏ 50.0503 Acting and Directing
- ❏ 50.0602 Cinematography and Film/Video Production
- ❏ 50.0601 Film/Cinema Studies

Health Care Services and Sciences

- ❏ 51.2291 Health Sciences
- ❏ 31.0503 Athletic Training and Sports Medicine
- ❏ 51.0204 Audiology and Speech-Language Pathology
- ❏ 51.1194 Biomedical Science
- ❏ 51.0601 Dental Assistant
- ❏ 51.0602 Dental Hygienist
- ❏ 51.0603 Dental Laboratory Technician
- ❏ 51.2202 Environmental Health
- ❏ 43.0106 Forensic Science and Technology
- ❏ 51.0701 Health/Health Care Administration
- ❏ 51.1601 Nursing (R.N. Training)
- ❏ 51.2306 Occupational Therapy
- ❏ 51.1800 Ophthalmic/Optometric Services
- ❏ 51.2001 Pharmacy (B.Pharm, Pharm.D)
- ❏ 51.2308 Physical Therapy
- ❏ 51.2201 Public Health
- ❏ 51.1193 Radiological Science
- ❏ 51.2393 Rehabilitation Therapy
- ❏ 51.2394 Speech Therapy
- ❏ 51.0909 Surgical Technology

Hospitality and Recreation Careers

- ❏ 12.0503 Culinary Arts/Chef Training
- ❏ 08.0601 Food Products Retailing and Wholesaling Operations
- ❏ 08.0906 Food Sales Operations
- ❏ 52.0902 Hotel/Motel and Restaurant Management
- ❏ 31.0101 Parks, Recreation and Leisure Studies
- ❏ 08.1100 Tourism and Travel Services Marketing Operations
- ❏ 52.0903 Tourism and Travel Services Management

Humanities

- ❏ 24.0103 Humanities/Humanistic Studies (general)
- ❏ 16.1201 Classics and Classical Languages and Literatures
- ❏ 23.0301 Comparative Literature
- ❏ 23.0501 Creative Writing
- ❏ 23.0101 English Language and Literature
- ❏ 16.0102 Linguistics
- ❏ 23.9991 Literature
- ❏ 30.1301 Medieval and Renaissance Studies
- ❏ 16.0101 Non-English Languages and Literatures

- ❏ 38.0101 Philosophy
- ❏ 38.0201 Religion/Religious Studies
- ❏ 23.1101 Technical and Business Writing

Mathematics

- ❏ 27.0101 Mathematics (general)
- ❏ 27.0301 Applied Mathematics
- ❏ 27.0302 Operations Research
- ❏ 27.0501 Statistics

Music

- ❏ 50.0901 Music (general)
- ❏ 50.0992 Jazz
- ❏ 50.0902 Music History, Literature, and Theory
- ❏ 50.0904 Music Theory and Composition
- ❏ 50.0907 Piano and Organ
- ❏ 50.0901 Religious/Sacred Music
- ❏ 50.0908 Voice and Opera

Physical Sciences

- ❏ 40.0101 Physical Sciences (general)
- ❏ 40.0201 Astronomy
- ❏ 40.0301 Astrophysics
- ❏ 40.0401 Atmospheric Sciences and Meteorology
- ❏ 40.0501 Chemistry
- ❏ 40.0703 Earth and Planetary Sciences
- ❏ 40.0601 Geology/Earth Science
- ❏ 40.0603 Geophysics and Seismology
- ❏ 40.0701 Metallurgy
- ❏ 40.0806 Nuclear Physics
- ❏ 40.0702 Oceanography
- ❏ 40.0807 Optics
- ❏ 40.0801 Physics
- ❏ 40.0507 Polymer Chemistry

Pre-Professional

- ❏ 51.1101 Pre-Dentistry Studies
- ❏ 22.0102 Pre-Law Studies
- ❏ 51.1102 Pre-Medicine Studies
- ❏ 51.1104 Pre-Veterinary Studies

Psychology and Social Work

- ❏ 42.0101 Psychology (general)
- ❏ 42.9991 Behavioral Sciences
- ❏ 42.0201 Clinical Psychology
- ❏ 42.0701 Developmental and Child Psychology
- ❏ 42.0801 Experimental Psychology
- ❏ 30.1101 Gerontology
- ❏ 44.0701 Social Work

Social Sciences and History

- ❏ 45.0101 Social Sciences (general)
- ❏ 45.0201 Anthropology
- ❏ 45.0301 Archaeology
- ❏ 43.0103 Criminal Justice/Law Enforcement Administration
- ❏ 45.0601 Economics
- ❏ 45.0701 Geography
- ❏ 45.0801 History
- ❏ 45.0901 International Relations and Affairs
- ❏ 30.0501 Peace and Conflict Studies
- ❏ 45.1001 Political Science and Government
- ❏ 44.0401 Public Administration
- ❏ 44.0501 Public Policy Analysis
- ❏ 45.1101 Sociology
- ❏ 45.1201 Urban Studies/Affairs
- ❏ 45.0891 Western Civilization/Culture
- ❏ 05.0207 Women's Studies

Technical Trades, Crafts, and Aviation

- ❏ 49.0101 Aeronautics/Aviation/Aerospace Science
- ❏ 47.0609 Avionics Maintenance Technology
- ❏ 46.0400 Construction and Building Management
- ❏ 48.0101 Drafting
- ❏ 49.0309 Marine Science/Merchant Marine Officer

If submitting this form by mail, send it to:

Peterson's
Research Department
Princeton Pike Corporate Center
2000 Lenox Drive
Lawrenceville, NJ 08648
USA

Or, you can fax it to: 1-609-896-4535

For additional information on study in the U.S., visit
www.petersons.com/educationusa

Peterson's Applying to Colleges and Universities in the United States

THE INTERNATIONAL STUDENT GUIDE

18th Edition

PETERSON'S

A **nelnet** COMPANY

PETERSON'S

A nelnet COMPANY

About Peterson's, a Nelnet company
Peterson's (www.petersons.com) is a leading provider of education information and advice, with books and online resources focusing on education search, test preparation, and financial aid. Its Web site offers searchable databases and interactive tools for contacting educational institutions, online practice tests and instruction, and planning tools for securing financial aid. Peterson's serves 110 million education consumers annually.

For more information, contact Peterson's, 2000 Lenox Drive, Lawrenceville, NJ 08648; 800-338-3282; or find us on the World Wide Web at www.petersons.com

Acknowledgments
Peterson's wishes to thank the members of the International Student Network Advisory Board for their thoughtful and excellent contributions to the quality and direction of this worldwide service, which helps international undergraduate and graduate students study in the United States.

The cooperation of the Bureau of Educational and Cultural Affairs (ECA) of the United States Department of State is also gratefully acknowledged.

Editor: Linda Seghers; Production Editor: Susan W. Dilts; Copy Editors: Bret Bollmann, Michael Haines, Brooke James, Sally Ross, Pam Sullivan, Valerie Bolus Vaughan; Research Project Manager: Christine Lucas; Programmer: Phyllis Johnson; Manufacturing Manager: Ray Golaszewski; Composition Manager: Gary Rozmierski; Client Relations Representatives: Janet Clements-Garwo, Mimi Kaufman, Karen Mount, Danielle Vreeland; Contributing Editors: Kathleen Kisting Alam, Allison Hawley

ISSN 0890-3085
ISBN-13: 978-0-7689-2415-2
ISBN-10: 0-7689-2415-4

Printed in the United States of America

10 9 8 7 6 5 4 3 2 1   09 08 07

Eighteenth Edition

Contents

APPENDIXES

INDEXES

Foreword

This is a wonderful time to be working in the field of international higher education. Never have government, academia, and the private sector been more engaged in the vigorous dialogue of how to attract and welcome international students to the United States. New initiatives from the Departments of State, Education, and Commerce and other agencies have made the U.S. even more welcoming. New college programs are becoming more global and adventurous, and even the private sector has become involved, believing that it, too, may have a role as an engine for change.

Suddenly it seems that every American campus wants to "internationalize," and many vie for the honor of being recognized as the most internationalized. U.S. students, as well as international students, look carefully for indications that an institution is truly international. The creative energy that comes from the involvement of so many sectors has produced some exciting innovations.

The United States has traditionally enrolled many more of the world's students than any other nation, and it continues to do so today. According to the most recent annual survey, more than 565,000 students from other nations are currently studying in the U.S. The size, diversity, excellence, and prestige of the higher education system in the United States offer powerful incentives for you and other academically gifted young people from around the world who want to have the best educational experience possible.

It's important to note, too, that more than 200,000 U.S. students are studying abroad, a number that has increased roughly 10 percent for as many years. Destinations and fields of study have become broader with each passing year. It's good to know that study abroad flows in both directions and that many American students are contemplating studying in your home country, just as you are you now considering studying in theirs.

The U.S. higher education system is quite different from most others—largely because the federal government plays a minor role. We have a vast system of community colleges, four-year liberal arts schools, public and private institutions, and major universities granting doctoral degrees, along with a number of specialized schools at both the undergraduate and graduate levels—all a part of the U.S. higher education system.

To help you navigate through the system, the State Department offers an educational advising network providing unbiased information to all—the EducationUSA network. There are more than 450 EducationUSA advising centers in 170 countries supported by the State Department's Bureau of Educational and Cultural Affairs. Each year, they provide advice and assistance to hundreds of thousands of prospective students wishing to study in the United States. These centers actively promote U.S. higher education by offering accurate, comprehensive, objective, and timely information about educational opportunities in the United States and guidance to qualified individuals on how best to access those opportunities. EducationUSA advising centers are staffed by professional advisers, many of whom have studied in the United States and almost all of whom have received State Department–approved training about U.S. higher education and the advising process.

Here is how they can help you. First, EducationUSA advisers know the differences among the many types of U.S. colleges and universities. They can give you the tools you need to identify the best options for your educational and professional interests and choose an institution that meets your needs. Second, they know how the admission process works. They can advise you on issues such as testing, applications, essay writing, and letters of reference, and they can often assist you in identifying financial aid opportunities. EducationUSA advisers receive constant updates about U.S. visa and security requirements and can offer guidance to help you successfully negotiate the student visa application process. Finally, many EducationUSA centers also provide specialized services such as essay and resume writing workshops, academic and cultural pre-departure preparation, and translation and document verification.

Visiting an EducationUSA advising center in person is the best place to begin your college and university search. Not only will you have the opportunity to meet with an EducationUSA adviser and have your questions answered in person, but you will also be able to view the recently published books and reference materials on the full range of accredited institutions of higher learning in the United States. Many of these reference materials are written specifically for international students.

Searching for the right college or university is a difficult process, but you do not have to tackle it on your own. To find the EducationUSA center nearest you, please visit http://educationusa.state.gov/centers.

If there isn't an EducationUSA advising center near you, the EducationUSA Web site (http://educationUSA.state.gov) is a great alternative for finding valuable information. Separate pages provide information on student visas, the admission process, accreditation, financial assistance, and standardized testing. Visitors can also download *If*

You Want to Study in the United States, a set of four booklets on how to apply to and prepare for study in the U.S. It is available in several languages. And there is much more. For example, you can view profiles of international students currently studying on U.S. campuses, access the "Find-a-School" search engine developed especially for EducationUSA by Peterson's, and explore related links to other government Web sites and external resources.

U.S. colleges and universities offer the possibility of educational excellence, and we hope you choose to take advantage of this incomparable

resource. It is the best investment in your future you will ever make. We want you to come here and share your culture with the U.S. students and citizens you meet, and we want to share our society and culture with you.

Mary Thompson-Jones
Chief, Educational Information and
Resources Branch
Bureau of Educational and Cultural Affairs
United States Department of State

A Note from the Peterson's Editors

This book is made available to you through the colleges and universities that sponsor Peterson's International Student Network (listed on pages xiii–xiv). Once you have completed and submitted the survey (located in the front of the book) to Peterson's, your information will be shared with all the sponsoring institutions in the United States that are looking for students like you. In about two months, you will begin to receive, at your home address, detailed information and application materials from many colleges and universities. These schools welcome international students and are pleased that you wish to join the more than 565,000 others already pursuing undergraduate degrees in the United States.

In this guide, you will find profiles of U.S. colleges and universities that are interested in recruiting international students. You will also find narrative one-page descriptions from colleges and language academies that wish to provide more in-depth information. In addition, please take the time to read through the introductory essays so that you can learn all about higher education in the United States: the different types of U.S. institutions and the degrees they offer, the academic calendar, how the U.S. system of accreditation works, how U.S. colleges evaluate your academic credentials, and more. There is also advice on choosing the right undergraduate school, financing your education, and, most important, a step-by-step description of the application process, including advice on how to prepare your application materials. Don't forget, it is especially important to identify the tests that are required for admission to the schools that interest you and to register for them as soon as possible! Details can be obtained at your U.S. advising center. Finally, in "Tips from the Experts," you can quickly find answers to the questions most frequently asked by U.S.-bound international students just like you.

If you already have specific criteria for your college search, such as a particular major or an ESL program, the **Indexes** at the back of the book will be especially helpful. There is also an index for schools with articulation agreements, which are agreements between two schools that allow students to complete an associate degree program at one school and transfer to a related bachelor's degree program at another.

The editors at Peterson's wish you the best of luck in your U.S. college search and hope that the resources you find in this guide will help you to reach your educational goals in the United States.

Peterson's
International Student Network

Request for Application Materials from U.S. Colleges and Universities

Peterson's
International Student Network

> **To Students:**
>
> Remove this form from the guide and use it to request application materials from the colleges and universities that interest you. You may photocopy it as many times as you need. Be sure to copy both sides. Complete the form in English, using a typewriter or printing neatly in ink. Be sure to send the letter by airmail to the address listed in the college or university profile in this book. You may also send your request by fax if a fax number is included in the institution's profile. DO NOT SEND THIS FORM TO PETERSON'S. Please send it directly to the college or university.

Full Name Mr.
Mrs. _____
Miss   *Please underline your family name*

Mailing Address _____

_____

_____

Telephone Number _____   Fax Number _____
                                                                                  if available

Country of Citizenship _____   Date of Birth _____
                                                                                  month/day/year

Educational Record Please list the educational institutions you have attended. Begin with primary school and end with the educational institution that you last attended or are currently attending.

Name of Institution	Country	Field of Study	Dates Attended From – To	Name of Degree, Diploma, or Certificate Awarded

My academic rank in class at the school I currently attend or last attended:

___Top 10%   ___Top 20%   ___Top 30%   ___Top 40%   ___Top 50%   ___Bottom 50%

Request for Application Materials from U.S. Colleges and Universities

Test Record Please indicate the score(s) and date for each test taken.

☐ TOEFL _____   ☐ SAT Subject Tests _____
       Score   Date   Subject   Score   Date

☐ SAT _____   _____
       Critical   Math   Writing   Date   Subject   Score   Date
       Reading

☐ ACT _____   ☐ Other _____
       Composite Score   Date   Specify Test   Score   Date

Language spoken at home _____

Years of instruction through the medium of English _____.   Where?_____
                                                   give dates

Years of formal study of the English language _____.   Where?_____
                                             give dates

Financial Support Please indicate funds (in U.S. dollars) available each year for your education and their source.

Amount	Purpose	Source
$	Travel	
$	Room/Board/ Personal Expenses	
$	Tuition and Fees	

Will you be requesting financial aid from the college or university?   ☐ Yes   ☐ No

From other sources (government and private)?   ☐ Yes   Please specify _____   ☐ No

Education Plan

I wish to apply for admission to your institution for the term beginning _____
                                                                 month/year

as a candidate for a(n) _____ degree in _____
                        associate, bachelor's   major field

with a specialization in _____.
                                       if applicable

Date: _____   Signature _____

Comments Attach an additional page if necessary.

Peterson's International Student Network Sponsors

If a school or English language program has included an **In-Depth Description,** its name is preceded by an asterisk (*) and the page number of its **In-Depth Description** is noted after its state name.

Colleges and Universities	Location
*Adelphi University	New York (28)
*Adrian College	Michigan (29)
*Bennington College	Vermont (40)
*Berkeley College	New York (42)
*Boston University	Massachusetts (43)
*Bryant University	Rhode Island (44)
*Chapman University	California (54)
College of St. Benedict/Saint John's University	Minnesota
*Colorado State University	Colorado (61)
Columbia College Chicago	Illinois
DePauw University	Indiana
*Edgewood College	Wisconsin (73)
*Fairleigh Dickinson University	New Jersey (81)
*Florida Gulf Coast University	Florida (84)
*Florida International University	Florida (85)
*Fordham University	New York (87)
*Hawai'i Pacific University	Hawaii (97)
*Hofstra University	New York (99)
*Johnson & Wales University	Rhode Island (107)
Linfield College	Oregon
*Manhattanville College	New York (120)
*Marquette University	Wisconsin (121)
*Marymount Manhattan College	New York (123)
*Moore College of Art & Design	Pennsylvania (132)
*Mount Ida College	Massachusetts (134)
*New England Institute of Technology	Rhode Island (137)
*North Dakota State University	North Dakota (140)
Northern Arizona University	Arizona
*Nova Southeastern University	Florida (143)
*Oklahoma State University	Oklahoma (144)
*Pratt Institute	New York (152)
*St. John's College	New Mexico (166)
*Saint Louis University	Missouri (168)
*Saint Mary's College of California	California (169)
*Sam Houston State University	Texas (172)
*Santa Monica College	California (176)
*Sarah Lawrence College	New York (177)
*State University of New York at Plattsburgh	New York (195)
*State University of New York College at Geneseo	New York (196)
*Stony Brook University, State University of New York	New York (197)
*Texas Christian University	Texas (202)
*Texas Wesleyan University	Texas (204)

Colleges and Universities

Colleges and Universities	Location
*Troy University	Alabama (205)
*University of Central Missouri	Missouri (208)
*University of Southern Indiana	Indiana (225)
*The University of Tampa	Florida (228)
*University of Wyoming	Wyoming (238)
*Virginia Commonwealth University	Virginia (240)
*Washington College	Maryland (241)
*Webber International University	Florida (242)
*Wentworth Institute of Technology	Massachusetts (243)
*Western Illinois University	Illinois (244)
*Western Wyoming Community College	Wyoming (246)
*Wichita State University	Kansas (248)

The Admission Process

Applying to Colleges and Universities in the U.S.

Daniel M. Lundquist

Vice President for Admissions and Financial Aid, Union College

Robert Hunter

Director of Academic Services, World Education Services

Higher Education in the United States

More than 565,000 international students now study in more than 2,500 of 3,800 colleges and universities in the United States. The opportunity to choose from such a large range of institutions and programs is one of the greatest advantages of the U.S. educational system. American schools range from large research universities with more than 20,000 students to small colleges with fewer than 1,000 students; from universities with graduate and professional studies in medicine, law, and many other fields, to schools offering only the two-year associate degree; from urban schools in large cities to rural institutions located far from metropolitan areas.

Admission to a college or university typically follows satisfactory completion of twelve years of elementary and secondary education for students educated in the United States. The twelve-year cycle is usually broken down as follows:

- A five-year primary program beginning at about age six, generally called elementary school
- A three-year intermediate program, generally called middle school
- A four-year secondary program, generally called high school

The admission requirements for students educated outside the U.S. educational system will vary from school to school. The educational preparation that is required to apply to a university in your own country will usually enable you to apply to a U.S. college or university.

A number of secondary-level programs in other countries are seen as being at a "higher level" than the typical secondary-level program in the U.S. Some U.S. colleges and universities will give advanced-standing credit toward an undergraduate academic degree for these programs. Since U.S. colleges and universities have the authority to determine their own admission and advanced-standing policies, you should always ask each school what specific educational qualifications it requires from students educated in your country.

Types of U.S. Institutions of Higher Education

Two-year institutions, which are sometimes referred to as community or junior colleges, award the associate degree—Associate of Arts (A.A.) or Associate of Science (A.S.)—following successful completion of a specific two-year, full-time program. There are two basic types of programs at two-year institutions. Some programs are strictly academic and designed to prepare students for transfer to four-year institutions with bachelor's degree programs. Others are more practical or applied and provide career training in specific areas. This second type does not usually prepare students for transfer to a four-year institution, although some of the credits earned may still be accepted by a four-year institution. A small number of two-year institutions offer the final two years of the undergraduate program only, awarding the bachelor's degree rather than the associate degree. Most two-year institutions are publicly supported by the state and local communities, although some are private. Some private two-year colleges are proprietary, or run for a profit.

The college or university (sometimes called an institute when it emphasizes engineering or other technical courses) awards the bachelor's degree. The Bachelor of Arts (B.A.) and Bachelor of Science (B.S.) degrees are the two most frequently awarded, but a variety of bachelor's degrees by other names are also granted. Bachelor's degrees are typically awarded following successful completion of a four-year, full-time program. Bachelor's degree programs in some fields of study or at some institutions can be longer than four years. There are both public and private colleges and universities in the United States, and some have a religious affiliation.

Characteristics of U.S. Colleges

Publicly supported schools are generally state colleges or universities or two-year community colleges. These institutions receive most of their funding from the states in which they are located. Students who are residents of the sponsoring state can usually attend these schools for lower fees than students coming from other states or from outside the United States.

Private schools generally have higher costs because they do not receive the same primary funding from the state and federal government. All students at private institutions pay similar fees no matter where they are from.

Colleges and universities with religious affiliations are private. Most of them are Christian (Roman Catholic and Protestant), although there are a small number of Jewish and Islamic institutions. Many of these colleges have very active relationships with the religious institution that sponsors them, and religious life may play a large role on the campus at these schools. Others have a much looser historical affiliation, rather than an active relationship with a specific religion. You do not need to be a member of a particular church or religious group to attend a religiously affiliated college in the United States. Enrollment in these institutions will not usually interfere with your own religious views.

However, there are a few exceptions. Some colleges that emphasize in their literature that they are Christian are organized according to fundamentalist principles. Students from a Christian fundamentalist or evangelical background will be very comfortable on a campus where Bible study may be required and social life is strictly regulated. Read the literature of these colleges very carefully. They may offer the setting you seek, but they may not.

The only way that proprietary institutions are different from the other types of schools is that they are privately owned and run for a profit. They are "educational businesses" that offer services and courses similar to those at other institutions. Their programs tend to focus on technical and preprofessional courses of study.

Almost all colleges in the United States are coeducational, which means that both men and women attend. There are a small number of single-sex schools, some for men and some for women. Faculty, administration, and staff members will likely be of both sexes at any college.

The U.S. educational system is flexible in many ways. The first one to two years of most undergraduate degree programs focus primarily on basic introductory course work and general education in the arts and sciences. This exposes students to a variety of academic disciplines and shows them how these fields are related. Students entering the U.S.

system from educational systems in other countries may feel that they have completed these general education requirements at home through previous study at the secondary level. However, general and liberal arts studies at the undergraduate level in the U.S. provide international students with an understanding of the bases and values of U.S. society, a perspective that is likely missing in similar courses taught in another culture. The final two years of most undergraduate programs focus on the major subject of concentration.

In summary, the structure of the U.S. system of higher education provides students with an opportunity to take a wide variety of courses and explore different interests but also includes in-depth study in a specific field. These choices and the broadly based education they result in are among the most attractive reasons for studying in the United States.

The Academic Calendar

American colleges operate on three main types of calendars that divide the year into terms: the semester, trimester, and quarter systems. The academic year is approximately nine months long no matter how it is divided. The semester system divides that nine months in half, resulting in fall and spring semesters. Schools that use the trimester and quarter systems divide the same nine months into three 3-month terms. The summer term is the fourth quarter in the quarter system, and enrollment in classes is optional. For most institutions the academic year runs from late August or September to May or June. Many schools operate all year long, and students can often take courses over the summer term for an additional fee.

There are usually two examination periods in each term, one in the middle and one at the end. Holiday schedules vary with each school, but there are usually a number of short holidays in each term, a longer break in December and January, and a weeklong vacation period in early spring. International students who want or need to stay on campus during holiday periods should find out from the housing office if this is possible and if there is any additional charge.

Faculty Members and Methods of Instruction

Students and faculty members typically interact less formally in U.S. undergraduate programs than they do elsewhere in the world. They often develop close relationships or friendships. The size of the institution and the size of the class will be important factors. Professors sometimes ask students to join them for lunch or participate with them in community activities. Each professor has his or her own personality and style but, in general, faculty members at U.S. schools are more accessible than faculty members in many other countries.

The classroom experience is frequently characterized by discussion between the professor and the students. A portion of a student's grade for a course is often determined by the quality of participation in class discussions. It is unusual to find a course where the entire grade is based on one examination at the end of the term. International students should be prepared to participate in class discussions since classmates and professors will expect it. Most faculty members are aware that cultural factors and English language skills may initially make participation difficult for international students. With time, most international students find that this participation adds a great deal to the learning process.

There are three basic methods of instruction. Large introductory-level courses are usually taught through lectures at which several hundred students gather to hear a professor speak. The small class or seminar includes a group of 5 to 30 students. This method is generally used in more advanced courses and allows for more interaction between the students and the professor. Laboratory sections are similar to seminars and are usually required with courses in the sciences or applied fields like computer science or engineering.

Almost all colleges offer opportunities for students to work individually with professors in tutorials or independent study courses.

Academic and Personal Advising Systems

An attractive feature of U.S. higher education is the support and counseling that students receive.

International or Foreign Student Adviser. Most U.S. colleges and universities have an international office with trained professionals available to counsel students from other countries on a broad range of matters, including:

- Orientation to campus and community life
- Immigration and visa
- Employment and practical training
- Off-campus and social activities and opportunities
- Personal and health concerns
- General academic planning
- Financial problems

Faculty Adviser. At most schools, each student is assigned a faculty adviser. The assignment is usually based on the student's field of study. Faculty advising includes the following areas:

- Requirements for degrees
- Selection of academic courses
- Academic performance and progress

Peer Counselor. Many colleges have developed a system of peer counseling for students. The counselors are upperclass students and provide the student viewpoint on academic and personal matters.

Outside the Classroom

An important part of your educational experience in the U.S. will be participation in nonacademic, social, and extracurricular activities on campus. Many opportunities are available for students to become involved in sports, student government, music, drama, and other organized and individual activities. Such activities are designed to contribute to your personal growth, provide recreation, create opportunities to meet new people with similar interests, and help prepare you for future leadership roles upon graduation. Participation in these activities is not required to obtain a U.S. degree. These are optional activities, but they play a central role in campus life at U.S. colleges and universities.

How to Determine Which Colleges Are Best for You

Choosing which colleges and universities to apply to is a difficult task when you are not familiar with the U.S. and its system of education. With so many institutions to choose from, it is necessary to approach your choice in a logical way to arrive at a list of schools that would be best for you.

Begin by looking through the **Majors** index in the back of this guide to find institutions that offer the degree you seek in the subject area you wish to study. Write down the schools that match your needs. Eliminate schools that do not award the degree you wish to earn, whether associate or bachelor's. The remaining institutions constitute your first list.

Now, consider the following list. How important is each one to you? Rank them in order from one through eight, according to your own priorities.

Cost

Look for the total cost of tuition, fees, and room and board. You will need additional funds for books and other living expenses. If you need financial aid, are grants available? Compare the number of international students enrolled to the number of awards given and the average amount granted. This will give you an idea about the possibility of receiving one of these awards and how much it might help you to meet your need.

Enrollment

Look at the total and undergraduate enrollments. Is this the right size school for you? Find the percentage of international students and how many countries are represented. Does it have the blend of U.S. and international students you are looking for?

Entrance Difficulty

Find the entrance difficulty for U.S. students. Compare the number of international students who applied to the number accepted. This will tell you how difficult it is to gain admission.

Location

Consider where the institution is located. What is the climate in that area of the country? Is the campus setting urban, suburban, small-town, or rural? Would you be happy living in this type of area?

Housing

Is on-campus housing available and guaranteed? Is it available during the summer and during breaks if you need it?

Library Holdings and Facilities

Refer to the information on library holdings and other facilities, such as laboratories, computer labs, and athletic facilities, to make certain they meet your needs.

Type of Institution

Is it a two-year or four-year institution? Is it public or private? Is it religious or proprietary? These are all important factors to consider in the decision-making process.

English as a Second Language (ESL) Program

Is there an intensive English language program available (if needed)?

Decide what you want and need concerning each of the previous items. Review the profiles of the institutions on your first list. Eliminate those that do not meet the criteria that are important to you. For example, if you cannot afford more than $10,000 each year, eliminate those institutions with combined tuition and fees and room and board that come close to that amount, unless you are especially interested in a particular institution and it offers financial aid for which you are confident you will qualify. If you want to attend an institution in a particular state or area of the United States, eliminate those schools that do not fit that category. If you are sure that you want to attend a large public institution, you can eliminate the schools that do not match this criterion. You should now have a much shorter list of colleges that may be good choices for you.

Select seven to ten institutions that seem to meet your needs the best. This is your second list. Use this guide and the form in the front of the book to obtain information and an application from each school. Be sure to request application materials as early as possible. It is best to start this process sixteen months before the date you intend to enter college.

While you wait for the answers to your requests for further information, check the **Profiles of Colleges and Universities in the U.S.** in this guide for the institutions you have written to and determine which standardized admission tests you need to take. Take the necessary steps to register for them by writing to the addresses given in this guide. Most schools require the SAT® or the ACT®.

A few require SAT Subject Tests. In addition, the Test of English as a Foreign Language (TOEFL®) is generally required for international students who do not speak English as a native language. You will want to avoid having to take additional tests after receiving application materials from individual institutions because it will slow down the application process.

Review the materials that you receive and any information on these schools that is available in the advising office in your school or the center where you received this publication. Reduce your list to three to five colleges and universities by reviewing the following information:

- Detailed description of the overall academic program
- Specific course offerings and faculty information
- Academic facilities (libraries, computer, and laboratory facilities)
- Detailed description of the campus and surrounding community
- Housing, financial aid, and ESL (if needed)
- Extracurricular, cultural, and religious activities that are important to you

This is your third and final list for application purposes.

Applying

Once again, be sure to request application materials as early as possible. It is best to start this process sixteen months before the date you intend to enter college. In addition, the way you complete your application and present yourself is very important and will play a big part in determining the outcome of your efforts to gain admission. If you want to find a college or university that is able to meet your needs, it is very important for you to be completely honest and sincere in the information you provide to them.

Carefully read the application and information that you have received from each school. It will tell you how the school sees itself, its mission, philosophy, and educational goals. Once you know what a specific college values and emphasizes, you will have some idea of what aspects of your own background and goals to emphasize as you prepare your application. More important, getting a broad sense of the school will help you determine if it is a place where you would fit in and be comfortable and happy. Admission officers will be doing exactly what you did to prepare for applying. They will attempt to determine how your abilities, goals, and interests match what they have to offer and what kind of contributions you might be able to make to the college and its students. You should present yourself in your best light, but do not give incorrect information. Admission officers can usually tell when an application statement does not sound like the truth. In addition, the legal implications of giving false information about yourself can be very serious.

A complete application that is ready to be evaluated by the admission committee typically contains the following:

- Fully completed preliminary (if required) and final application forms
- Teacher recommendations (if required)
- Secondary school report (if required)
- Transcripts and academic records
- TOEFL or other English language proficiency test scores (if required and applicable)
- Standardized test scores (SAT, ACT, and SAT Subject Tests if applicable)
- Nonacademic information as requested by the college or university
- Financial aid application (if applicable)
- Application fee

Preliminary Applications

Some colleges require international applicants to complete a preliminary application. If a school uses this process, you will receive a preliminary application with the materials they send to you. The preliminary application helps admission officers determine whether or not you will be a likely candidate before you go through the more complicated process of completing the final application form.

The preliminary application will request basic information about you and may also ask for a brief statement of your goals. Your statement should indicate the reasons why you feel the school would be a good place for you and what contributions you can make to life on campus. Return the preliminary application as quickly as possible.

If the admission officer finds that your goals, abilities, and general background are compatible with what that particular college is looking for, you will be sent the final application to complete. If it is determined that you are not a competitive candidate, you will be notified of this decision and can then focus your attention and energy on the other schools you have selected.

Final Applications

It is important to complete the final application and provide all the required information and documents the college has requested as quickly as possible. The sooner the college receives your application and all the required supporting documents, the sooner they will be reviewed and evaluated. An application submitted early can only help your chance of being offered admission and will give you extra time to supply additional information if it is requested.

Personal Information

The personal information requested on an application form is an important part of the complete application package. You will likely be asked to answer a variety of questions about yourself—your abilities, goals, special talents, and why you wish to attend that particular college. Many international applicants have wonderfully rich backgrounds and experiences they can share.

Most admission officers will take into account that you are from another culture and, if applicable, that English is not your native language. Share your experiences and your enthusiasm as clearly as you can. Samples of your writing, art work, or tapes of musical performances, as applicable to the program of study you wish to pursue, may be included if you wish. If any portion of the application does not apply to you, note that on the form, along with an explanation. For example, many secondary schools in other countries have fewer school-sponsored activities than U.S. high schools. Some schools do not award academic honors. These situations should be explained.

Keep in mind that the personal information asked for on the application will provide admission officers with the information they need to get to know you as a person, not just your academic achievements and test results. Make the most of this opportunity.

Teacher Recommendations

Policies regarding teacher recommendations vary from college to college, but you should be prepared to have at least one teacher provide a reference for you. Select someone who knows you well and has taught you in a subject that is related to the course of study you are thinking of following at college. If you are undecided about a specific course of study, then it is wise to select a teacher who knows you well and has a high regard for you academically and personally.

You have the option of making these recommendations confidential between the letter writer and the college. Many teachers, headmasters, principals, and tutors will often write a more open recommendation if they know it will be confidential.

Secondary School Reports and Transcripts

The school report and the transcript of your academic record are essential to the evaluation of your academic abilities. The report form should be filled out by the official in your school who is responsible for college placement. This is usually a counselor, principal, headmaster, or careers master. This form should introduce you in the context of your whole school experience in relationship to the other students in your class. Admission committees will be interested in learning how you have performed in your own educational system. The school report should talk about your accomplishments and provide a prediction of your chances for success in university-level studies.

Your official transcript or academic record is the objective part of your application. Academic records vary greatly from one education system to the next. Systems of evaluation or grading and the formats used to present this information also differ widely. Ask your school to include a guide to the grading standards used in the educational system in your country and for your school specifically. If your school ranks students by their level of academic achievement, make certain the ranking is included with the information they send. It will provide an easily understood picture of how well you have done. If your school does not rank students, an estimate of your rank, for example top 10 percent, would be helpful. Admission officers will want to know how you have performed over time, so be sure to have records sent that describe your academic performance for the past three to four years. If there is a national school-leaving certificate examination at the end of secondary education in your country (such as the British GCSEs or British-based O and A Levels, French Baccalaureat, German Abitur, Hong Kong Certificate of Education, etc.), have official results sent as soon as they are available.

If your transcripts, academic records, and leaving-certificate examination results are not in English, make sure that you have officially certified literal English translations of all documents sent along with the official documents in the original language.

TOEFL or Other English Language Proficiency Test Scores

Your ability to speak, write, and understand English is an absolute requirement to be considered for direct admission to most degree programs in the U.S. If English is not your native language, language proficiency can be demonstrated in several ways. The Test of English as a Foreign Language (TOEFL) is the most widely accepted test of proficiency. If English is not your native language but most of your formal schooling has been in English-speaking schools, you may not be required to take an examination. The policies regarding English language proficiency vary from institution to institution. Be sure that you know the policies and requirements of each school that you are considering.

If you know that your English ability is not up to acceptable standards, you may wish to consider intensive study of English in your country or in the United States. There are many English as a second language (ESL) programs available in the United States. Entrance requirements are minimal, and students are placed at the correct level of study through testing of their ability. Programs may last from five weeks to as long as a year. Sometimes a student is admitted to a college conditionally, pending study in an intensive English language program. U.S. consular officials abroad will frequently not grant an F-1 (student) visa for admission to an ESL program in the United States unless the visa applicant also has conditional

admission to a full-time undergraduate program. For a geographical listing of schools with these programs, see the Colleges with ESL Programs index in this guide.

Many international students arriving in the U.S. for the first time are surprised to learn that they must take an additional test in English even though they had already submitted results from the TOEFL or other approved English proficiency examination. Retesting is sometimes done to enable academic counselors to make the best course placements and to determine if some additional English language training might be useful.

Standardized Test Scores

Many U.S. colleges and universities require all applicants to take either the SAT or the ACT. A few may also require three SAT Subject Tests. These examinations may present problems for some international applicants. The context and format of the tests are often unfamiliar to them, and sometimes it is difficult to find a testing center that is close enough to home. If information on these examinations is not available at your secondary school, it can be obtained by writing directly to Educational Testing Service, Rosedale Road, Princeton, New Jersey 08541 U.S.A. (SAT, SAT Subject Tests, TOEFL) or logging on to their Web site at www.ets.org. You can also write to ACT, P.O. Box 168, Iowa City, Iowa 52243-0168 U.S.A. or log on to their Web site at www.act.org.

Students often express concern over taking these tests. You should not allow these worries to grow into any unwarranted anxiety over how well you will score. Most U.S. admission officers are aware of the difficulties that tests like these present to students educated outside of the U.S. system or whose native language is not English. They will take this into account. Universities generally place greater weight on the quantitative (mathematics) sections of these tests, particularly for applicants who do not speak English as their native language. The tests are only one part of the academic evaluation, and admission committees will place the results of your examinations in the proper context.

If you are applying to a college that requires any of these standardized tests, you should make certain you know the school's requirements and expectations for level of performance. These vary from one school to the next. Another important point is that you may take the tests several times. Your performance may improve as you become more familiar and more comfortable with them. Most U.S. students begin taking these tests almost two years before they plan to enter college. If you are beginning the application process that early, it would be wise to do the same.

Nonacademic Information

While academic ability is certainly the most important factor, other factors can also play a large role and will be considered in the admission process.

Since a college education is primarily an academic experience, it is important that a candidate have the academic preparation necessary to succeed at the schools to which he or she is applying. Once a candidate has demonstrated the necessary academic ability, however, the admission officer focuses attention on the nonacademic factors that set that candidate apart from the rest of the applicants. The deciding factor in an admission decision can be the nonacademic information. (However, some candidates with extremely strong academic backgrounds may be admitted almost solely on the basis of their academic achievement and potential. This type of candidate usually has a combination of very high grades, excellent standardized test scores, and enthusiastic school support.)

Financial Aid

You must submit a financial aid application if you intend to seek financial assistance for your undergraduate studies. Unfortunately, assistance for non-U.S. citizens is generally quite limited. The policies regarding financial aid vary considerably. Find out early what the policies are at the colleges that interest you. The **Profiles of Colleges and Universities in the U.S.** indicate which colleges offer need-based and non-need-based grants to international students. You should also explore the possibilities for aid available through the government of your home country.

The Application Fee

An application fee is usually required to cover the cost of processing your application. The fee at most colleges is around $50 and is typically payable in U.S. dollars only. Some colleges will waive the fee for very needy students.

Check each college's application requirements. Complete all forms and submit the application package as early as possible.

Timing

Timing can be one of the most difficult problems that international applicants face. Make certain that you have carefully read all of the information provided by the institution. Make a list of all of the deadlines that exist for various steps in the admission process for each institution to which you are applying. The list can be used as a quick resource in the future to make sure that you do not miss any important deadlines. Send all items and correspondence by air mail, and mail them as far before the deadlines as possible. Most schools will send a card acknowledging receipt of your application and will also inform you if any required items are missing from your application package.

It's a good idea to include several mailing labels filled out with your address with your application. The admission office will appreciate your thoroughness.

Interviews

A final step in the application process may be an interview with a college representative. The interviewer may be an admission officer or a graduate of the institution who is living in your area. Many U.S. colleges send representatives abroad to meet with prospective students, and an increasing number of graduates are available to meet with international students in their home countries. These meetings provide an excellent opportunity for you to learn more about the institutions that interest you. They also give the interviewer a chance to get an impression of you and how your abilities, goals, and interests match those of the institution. The interviews are generally informal and should be viewed as an opportunity to exchange information. A written summary of the meeting is typically sent to the college, but it does not usually play a large role in the actual decision to admit or reject an applicant.

Some U.S. colleges and universities use what are called "third-party" representatives or recruiters to interview prospective students in other countries. When these representatives are not actual members of the staff, faculty, or alumni of the institution, you should be extremely careful in evaluating the information you receive. Promises of admission expressed before the college receives detailed information about your academic background may indicate that the institution has lower standards than you wish to find in a U.S. college. When you are not dealing directly with an actual faculty or staff member or an alumnus of a college or university, you should seek additional information about the institution before making a final decision concerning your application.

Be sure to check with each institution to determine its policy regarding interviews and to find out if an interviewer is available in your area.

There is one final suggestion about presenting yourself to a U.S. college or university. Most colleges are looking for a varied student population that comes from many backgrounds and represents many different academic interests and personal qualities. Don't forget to stress the unique experience you will bring to the school.

What to Do When You Have Been Accepted

Once you have received acceptances from the colleges that you applied to, there are several important steps that must be taken.

Saying Yes or No

Each college will tell you exactly what steps to follow to confirm your acceptance of their offer of admission and how to prepare for the first term. This information will be included with the letter of admission or in materials that will be sent to you shortly thereafter. You must respond with a "yes" or "no" to each offer of admission. You will usually be required to submit a financial deposit to the institution that you plan to attend. This deposit will range from about $50 to $500 (higher in a few cases) and is used to guarantee your place in the class. As soon as you decide which college you want to attend, make sure to send your replies of both yes and no to all of the colleges that accepted you. Make sure that you do not miss any deadlines.

You may receive a letter that informs you that you are on a "waiting list." This generally means that the admission office determined that you were qualified for admission but there was not enough room to admit all qualified applicants. If you are placed on a waiting list at a college you wish to attend, you will be asked to respond "yes" or "no" to the offer of staying on the waiting list. If you say yes, you may be offered admission later if space becomes available. If you have been placed on a waiting list at your first-choice college and offered admission by your second-choice school, you may wish to consider taking the following steps:

- Notify the second-choice school that you accept its offer of admission and submit any required deposit.
- Write to your first-choice school and confirm that you want to remain on the waiting list.

If you are offered a place at your first-choice college later, you can withdraw from your place at your second-choice school (but you will have to forfeit your deposit) and then attend the college you wanted to go to most. If you are not offered a place at your first-choice college, you can still attend your second-choice school when the academic term begins.

Student Visas

The rules and regulations governing the entrance of all international students into the United States are complicated. If you have any questions about matters relating to immigration rules and regulations, you should check with the international student adviser at the college you plan to attend. He or she is specially trained and kept informed of the latest information on laws, work permits, health insurance, and other matters relating to international students and their dependents. It is your responsibility, however, to maintain your status by obtaining your forms at the correct time, keeping your passport valid six months beyond the date of completion of your program, and maintaining enrollment with a full course load.

For more information on student visas, go to http://www.UnitedStatesVisas.gov/studying.html.

Fees and Other Expenses

A few U.S. institutions require international students to pay the entire year's fees in advance. U.S. consular officers in some countries have begun to ask for proof of such advance payment before issuing a visa. Many have found this necessary to protect both the student and the institution.

Problems have sometimes arisen from currency restrictions imposed by the government of the student's home country and sometimes from the actions of dishonest students. The solution for some colleges has been to institute a policy of prepayment of fees. Each institution will inform you if prepayment is required. Institutions with prepayment policies will not send the forms you need to obtain a visa until payment has been received.

Those colleges that do not require a full prepayment of fees may have several options for fee payment. Most colleges send bills twice a year, once in the summer before school begins and again in the winter to cover the second half of the year's fees. Some colleges will allow you to pay the annual fee in one large payment or to spread out your bill in monthly installments. You will be billed for the cost of tuition, general activities (to fund student organizations), health insurance if required, and housing and meal costs if you have chosen to live and eat on campus. Extra costs, such as those for books and supplies, recreational expenses, and travel will not be billed by the college, but you should make sure to include them when determining your budget for the year.

Another important item in financial planning is health and accident insurance. Most colleges require that all students be covered by a policy that will help with payment of medical or hospital bills if they are sick or injured while in the United States. There is no national health-care plan in the United States. All medical bills must be paid by the individual or through an insurance policy. Health care in the United States is very expensive, and the approximately $800 per year that students must pay to be insured is very reasonable. Information on insurance policies and how to obtain proper coverage will be supplied by the international student office at the college you choose to attend. Health insurance will not cover pre-existing conditions or dental care. Even if your college does not require you to take health insurance, you should not plan to live in the United States without it.

Housing

Each college has its own policies regarding living on campus and will usually offer a range of housing options. It is important for you to study all of the housing information you receive. This will typically be sent to you with your letter of admission or shortly afterward. Some colleges require all first-year students to live on campus in college housing. You will generally be asked to indicate your first, second, and third choices from among the options available. If the type of room you want most is not available, the housing office can then provide you with a desirable alternative from your second or third choice. A small number of colleges do not offer on-campus or college-sponsored housing. When this is the case, schools will usually help international students locate suitable housing through community organizations that are set up for this purpose.

How U.S. Colleges and Universities Evaluate Academic Credentials

Dale Edward Gough

Director, International Education Service
American Association of Collegiate Registrars and
Admissions Officers (AACRAO)

If you are a student preparing to apply for admission to colleges and universities in the United States, it is important for you to understand the procedures that most U.S. institutions follow when evaluating your academic credentials in order to decide whether or not to admit you.

In your country, it is probably the ministry of education, or some similar body, that determines the eligibility of applicants from outside your education system. In the U.S. there is no ministry of education to make such decisions. Each college or university is free to set its own standards for admission, and it is the responsibility of the institution to review your previous education and academic performance to determine if you meet those standards.

U.S. colleges and universities are generally classified as highly selective, selective, somewhat selective, or open admission (institutions that can admit students regardless of their previous academic performance). The level of selectivity that an institution follows is based on many factors, and since each college and university has its own admission criteria, your academic credentials may meet the standards at some institutions but not at others.

Many institutions have their own staff members evaluate or assess your previous education. Other institutions might require you to send your academic records to an outside agency that specializes in providing evaluations of non-U.S. education. Sometimes an institution specifies a particular agency, or it might provide you with a list of several agencies and ask you to choose one. However, these agencies do not make the decision whether or not to admit you. They assess your previous education and provide the institution with their evaluation. The institution then makes the decision regarding your admission.

Pay close attention to the instructions on each application you submit and follow the instructions carefully. If you apply to more than one institution, you will probably be required to follow different instructions for each one. Do not assume that all institutions' requirements are the same.

Here are some things to keep in mind when applying:

- You will need to have an official copy of all your previous academic records (often referred to in application materials as an "official transcript") sent to the institution (and to the reviewing agency, if one is being used). "Official" records mean that the school where you studied must send a copy of your academic record directly to the institution (and to the agency, if one is being used). You, as the applicant, should not mail such records to the institution. If you do, the records might not be considered "official."

- Academic records that are not in English need to be translated, and both the original-language records and the translation must be sent. Pay particular attention to the instructions regarding translations. Some institutions and agencies might allow you to do the translation yourself if you are sufficiently proficient in English. However, others might require an official translation or one done by an authorized or licensed translator. Follow instructions carefully to avoid unnecessary delays.

- Standardized tests are an important part of the application process for U.S. institutions. If you were educated in a system that uses external national examinations, such as the Baccalaureat from France or "Ordinary" or "Advanced" level examinations from the United Kingdom, you will need to send copies of the results of these examinations. If you are applying as a first-year student at the undergraduate (bachelor's degree) level you may also need to take certain standardized tests that are often required of U.S. applicants, such as the SAT or the ACT. Schools will instruct you as to which test(s) to take and how to make arrangements for testing.

- If English is not your native language, or if you have not been educated in a country or region where English is a native language, you may be required to submit the results of an English language proficiency test, such as the Test of English as a Foreign Language (TOEFL).

- If you need an F-1 or M-1 (student) visa or a J-1 (exchange visitor-student) visa, you will need to present evidence that you have adequate financial support for the entire period of your anticipated study. Most U.S. colleges and universities will ask you to complete a form regarding the financial support for your studies, or they will tell you what documentation is required. Usually, you will have to complete a form outlining the sources of your financial support as well as

provide verification of such support. Again, carefully follow all instructions regarding documentation.

- Deadlines are extremely important! Pay close attention to any deadlines listed on the application forms. The admission of international students to U.S. institutions does take more time than the admission of U.S. students, and most schools have an earlier international application deadline. U.S. colleges and universities receive thousands of applications from international students each year. In order to be considered for admission for the term in which you want to begin your studies, it is essential that your application and all materials be received before the deadline.

Studying in the United States will be an exciting and rewarding experience. To start off in the best possible way, carefully follow the instructions of each institution in which you are interested. If you have any questions about the application process or what materials you need to provide, contact the institution for clarification or assistance.

Understanding Accreditation

Kristine Luken

Program Specialist, U.S. Department of Education

Accreditation in the United States is a voluntary, nongovernmental process in which an institution agrees to be evaluated and/or have its programs evaluated by an accrediting agency against standards for measuring quality. The goal of accreditation is to ensure that the education provided by institutions of higher education meets acceptable levels of quality.

Accrediting agencies are nongovernmental, private educational associations that carry out the function of evaluating institutions and programs to determine their quality. Institutions and programs that request an agency's evaluation and meet its evaluation criteria are then accredited by that agency.

Having a basic understanding of accreditation — what it is and what it means—will help you to make choices that will bring you closer to meeting your career goals.

Recognized vs. Unrecognized Accrediting Agencies

Accrediting agencies fall into two categories: recognized and unrecognized. It is important to understand the difference between the two categories.

Recognized Accrediting Agencies

The U.S. Department of Education does not accredit institutions; rather, it determines which accrediting agencies receive recognition by the Department. Accrediting agencies may voluntarily seek recognition from the Secretary of Education, but it is not a requirement that they do so. Recognition by the Department is limited to those agencies that accredit institutions that need the recognition in order to participate in federal programs, such as the Federal Student Financial Aid Program. While some recognized accrediting agencies may accredit foreign institutions, those accrediting activities are outside the authority and review of the Department. An accrediting agency that meets the Department's criteria for recognition is believed to be a reliable authority on the quality of education or training provided by the institutions it accredits in the United States and its territories.

Accrediting agencies recognized by the Department of Education can have a regional or national scope: regional agencies accredit degree-granting institutions within six geographic regions of the United States, and national agencies accredit institutions or programs all across the United States. Agencies that meet these criteria are placed on the Department's List of Nationally Recognized Accrediting Agencies, available at http://www.ed.gov/admins/finaid/accred/accreditation_pg6.html#NationallyRecognized.

The Council for Higher Education Accreditation (CHEA), a private, nongovernmental agency, also recognizes organizations that accredit institutions and programs. CHEA recognizes many types of accrediting organizations, including some of the same accrediting agencies that the Department of Education recognizes. In order to be eligible for CHEA recognition, accrediting organizations must demonstrate that their mission and goals are consistent with those of CHEA and that a majority of the institutions and programs accredited by the organization award degrees. CHEA's List of Participating and Recognized Organizations can be found at http://www.chea.org/directories/index.asp.

Unrecognized Accrediting Agencies

Just as there are recognized accrediting agencies, there are unrecognized accrediting agencies. Accreditation standards of unrecognized accrediting agencies have not been reviewed by the Department of Education or CHEA. There are a variety of reasons why an agency may be unrecognized. For example, the agency may be working toward recognition with the Department or CHEA, or it may not meet the criteria for recognition by either organization.

Unrecognized accrediting agencies should be viewed with caution until their reputation can be determined. If an agency is unrecognized, this does not necessarily mean that it does not have high standards of quality. But it is important to know that many employers in the United States only recognize degrees earned from institutions accredited by an accrediting agency recognized by the Department or CHEA.

For more information about recognized and unrecognized accrediting agencies, as well as fraud and abuse related to accreditation, visit the U.S. Network for Education Information Web site at http://www.ed.gov/NLE/USNEI.

Accredited vs. Unaccredited Institutions

It is not enough to know the meaning of recognized and unrecognized accrediting agencies; it is also important to know the difference between accredited and unaccredited institutions.

Accredited Institutions

Accredited institutions have agreed to be reviewed and/or have their programs reviewed to determine the quality of education and training being provided. If an institution is accredited by an agency recognized by the Department of Education or CHEA, its teachers, course work, facilities, equipment, and supplies are reviewed on a routine basis to ensure that students receive a high-quality education and get what they pay for. Attending an accredited institution is often a requirement for employment in the United States and can be helpful if you plan to transfer academic credits to another institution, such as graduate school.

Any institution can claim to be accredited. It is important that you take the time to learn about the accrediting agency and its reputation. To find out if the institution you are interested in is accredited by an agency recognized by the Department, review the Department's database of postsecondary institutions and programs at http://www.ope.ed.gov/accreditation/.

Unaccredited Institutions

Unaccredited institutions are not reviewed against a set of standards in order to determine the quality of their education and training. This does not mean that an unaccredited institution is of poor quality, but earning a degree from an unaccredited institution may create problems for a student.

Some employers, institutions, and licensing boards only recognize degrees earned from institutions accredited by an accrediting agency recognized by the Department. With that in mind, it is recommended that a student check with other institutions regarding their transfer-of-credit policy to determine whether they would accept the degree and/or credits earned from any institution in which the student is considering enrolling.

In some states, it can even be *illegal* to use a degree from an institution that is not accredited by an accrediting agency recognized by the Department unless approved by the state licensing agency.

It is important to determine if a degree from an unaccredited institution will allow you to achieve your educational and career goals. To learn more about the issues and problems that may arise from pursuing an unaccredited degree, read over the frequently asked questions developed by Degree.net at http://www.degree.net/guides/accreditation_faqs.html.

Fake Accrediting Agencies

Fake accrediting agencies offer accreditation for a fee without doing an in-depth review of the school's programs or teachers. Their accreditation has nothing to do with ensuring that students receive a high-quality education and is worthless and meaningless.

Fake accrediting agencies may adopt names that are similar to other well-known accrediting agencies, sprinkle the names of legitimate institutions in their list of accredited members, and even use all the right-sounding words in their marketing materials to describe their accrediting standards and review process. These are just some of the ways fake accrediting agencies try to confuse students and make them believe they are legitimate.

So, do not be misled by a name or a slick marketing technique; always do your homework on any institution you want to attend. Remember, it is not enough to know that an institution is accredited. You also need to find out as much as you can about the accrediting agency. Your efforts will be worth your time.

U.S. and Foreign Diploma Mills

A familiar definition of diploma mill is "an organization that awards degrees without requiring students to meet educational standards for those degrees."

Diploma mills are not accredited by a nationally recognized agency. You will not find the institution's accrediting agency on the Department's list of Nationally Recognized Accrediting Agencies or on CHEA's List of Participating and Recognized Organizations. Instead, diploma mills often claim accreditation by a fake accrediting agency to attract more students to their degree programs and make themselves seem legitimate.

Remember: In some states it can be *illegal* to use a degree from an institution that is not accredited by a nationally recognized accrediting agency unless approved by the state licensing agency.

Not only are U.S. diploma mills a problem, but foreign diploma mills selling their degrees in the United States are a problem too. Some of these foreign diploma mills even claim to have approval from the education ministry of their country to offer degrees, when, in reality, they are operating without the knowledge of the country. Often these institutions use the name of the foreign education ministry in their marketing materials to make themselves seem legitimate. What the institution is trying to do is make students believe that its programs have been reviewed and meet some level of quality when, in fact, they do not.

Before taking the offer to enroll in a foreign institution, find out as much as you can about the accreditor and the institutions it accredits, as well as the recognition process of the foreign education ministry. This information will give you a better picture of the institution and its reputation. To review a list of agencies that license and regulate higher education in Canada and other countries, visit www.degree.net/guides/checking_out2.html.

The .edu Extension in Internet Addresses

Not all institutions in the United States that use the .edu extension as a part of their Internet address are legitimate institutions. Before the Department of Commerce created more strict requirements, some questionable institutions were approved to use .edu in their address. New requirements allow only those institutions accredited by an agency recognized by the Department of Education to use it. However, institutions that were approved to use it *before* the new requirements were put into place can still use it, which means there could still be some illegitimate institutions with .edu in their address. Whether an institution uses the .edu extension or not, it is important to know as much as possible about the institution before enrolling.

Financing Your U.S. Education

Nancy W. Keteku

Regional Educational Advising Coordinator for Africa

Education in the United States can be expensive. However, higher education is the most important investment you will ever make. You should start your financial planning at the same time you select the colleges to which you will apply; that is, about one year prior to enrollment. Most colleges have an office or a staff member assigned to assist international students with the entire process. The best place to start is usually with the Admissions Office, which can point you in the right direction.

Financing your college education is a four-pronged effort, consisting of

- assessing your personal and family funds;
- identifying financial assistance for which you are eligible;
- compiling effective applications; and
- reducing educational costs.

First, you need to confer with your parents and other family sponsors to find out how much money they can commit each year to your education. Try to raise as much money as possible from family sources, because most scholarship awards are highly competitive and cover only part of the total educational and living costs.

At the same time, conduct research in your own country to find possible funding from local government, business, or foundation sources. Although these sources are not found in all countries, you may be able to reduce your educational cost through scholarships from local organizations.

If your family and local funds do not cover the cost of a U.S. education, you will need to look for financial assistance from other sources, such as American colleges and universities. However, when searching, do not assume that all institutions award financial aid. In fact, only about 50 percent of the institutions offering bachelor's degrees provide financial assistance to students who are not citizens or permanent residents of the United States, and most of them provide only partial assistance. Keep in mind that financial aid for U.S. students is different from financial aid for international students. Be sure to inform the admissions office of your country of citizenship and request information on financial aid available to non-U.S. citizens.

Can I Afford College?

You have probably heard about scholarships and financial aid. So what's the difference? A scholarship is a financial award based on merit in areas like academics, athletics and performing arts, or community service and leadership. Financial aid is based on a student's financial need, as documented by family income, assets, and other factors. Although different in many ways, most scholarships and financial aid are extremely competitive and require an exemplary academic record. Consult with your educational adviser on how to research available financial aid for international students. You will discover that most financial awards cover only a portion of the total cost of attendance. Thus, the more money you can raise from family sources, the better your chances are of attending the college or university of your choice.

As you do your research, make a list of the colleges and universities you would like to attend. Write down the annual cost of each (tuition, fees, insurance, room and board, books, and clothing), and then enter the total financial aid award offered by each of the institutions. In this way, you can quickly see where your best chances lie, and you can eliminate the institutions where you would not stand a good chance of attending based on the financial aid you would receive. When planning your finances, consider these ways to reduce your costs:

- Look for institutions that offer the highest quality education at the lowest price.
- Try to complete a four-year bachelor's degree in three years. This will save you thousands of dollars. Students can accelerate their programs by earning transfer credit for college-level courses completed in the home country; taking courses at a nearby community college—if tuition is lower and credits are transferable; attending summer school; and taking one additional course each semester.
- Find out if the institution offers scholarship assistance based on your first-year grades. A superior academic record could save you thousands of dollars.
- Live off campus with a relative or friend.

- Attend a community college for the first two years and then transfer to a four-year institution to complete your degree.

Here are some additional pointers on financing your U.S. education:

- International students often ask about full scholarships, which cover the entire cost of education, except for airfare. These awards are both rare and competitive. The total number of full scholarships offered to incoming international students each year is about 2,000, offered by only about 200 colleges in the U.S. There are usually 20 highly qualified international students competing for each major scholarship. To compete successfully for a full scholarship, you must be one of the top students in your country, have a high grade point average (GPA), score well on the SAT and TOEFL, and demonstrate outstanding performance in other areas, such as leadership.

- International students also ask about financial assistance from foundations, organizations, and the U.S. government. These types of financial aid are rarely awarded to international students because there is very little aid available through such sources, and it is usually earmarked for advanced graduate students. Fewer than 5 percent of international undergraduates are financed through these sources. Again, your educational adviser can tell you whether or not there are special funds available for students from your country.

- Financial aid is awarded at the beginning of the academic year (August–September) and is rarely available for students entering in January. *Note: Aid is more likely to be available to first-year students than to those transferring from other institutions. If you are already enrolled in a university at home and wish to transfer to a university in the United States, ask the admission office about its policy on financial aid for international transfer students.*

- You may be able to negotiate a loan to cover part of your education. Your educational adviser will have a list of reputable loan programs for which you are eligible. These loans usually require both a creditworthy U.S. citizen to act as a cosigner and proof of enrollment in a U.S. university. Before taking a loan, make sure you know how you are going to repay it and how a loan will affect your plans for graduate study and returning home.

- Working can help pay part of your education. However, immigration regulations permit international students to work only part-time and only on campus. After your first year of study, you may apply to the Bureau of U.S. Citizenship and Immigration Services (USCIS) (formerly INS) for permission to work off campus, but there is no guarantee that this will be granted and you cannot work off campus for more than twelve months. Understanding the various regulations from the USCIS can be difficult, so you should carefully review the information found at http://uscis.gov/portal/site/uscis.

Tips from the Experts

Here are some questions that international education advisers in various countries are frequently asked about studying in the U.S.

Q When should I start the application process if I am interested in studying in the U.S.?

A You should start the application process a year and a half before your planned arrival at a U.S. college campus. The academic year generally runs from September to May or June. So if you plan to enroll in September 2009, you should begin contacting schools in March, April, or May 2008.

Q What are the best colleges in the U.S.?

A "Best" is a relative term. In the U.S., there is a very wide range of colleges offering diverse opportunities. What is best for you may not be best for another student. It is not advisable to go by so-called ranking only. You need to make a list of your own priorities, do a realistic self-assessment, and then do research in order to find the "best" colleges for you.

Q How does one select a U.S. college or university?

A Students select institutions based on some combination of the following: their academic and career goals; the type of institution they want (specialized colleges, liberal arts colleges, institutes of technology, colleges with a religious affiliation, single-gender colleges); the availability, level, and quality of programs in their fields of interest and specializations; the geographic location and setting (rural, suburban, or city-based); climate; costs; the nature of and availability of financial aid; size (number of students and student-faculty ratio); diversity on campus (including the number of international students); availability of special programs such as interdisciplinary studies and internship opportunities; and student life and campus activities.

Q What do colleges look for when making their admission decisions?

A Colleges look for a variety of factors, such as a good academic record, English language proficiency, acceptable standardized test scores, an effective statement of purpose or essay, strong letters of recommendation, proof of financial support, and other program-specific requirements.

Q Does the U.S. welcome international students?

A The U.S. is known for its diversity of peoples and cultures. U.S. universities value the perspectives brought to their classrooms and research and heartily welcome international students.

Q What attracts international students to higher education in the U.S.?

A International students are attracted to the availability of a large variety of majors and specializations, the U.S. system of accreditation, flexibility in the educational system, merit-based admission and financial assistance, and the marketability of the degree. Students enjoy their experience in a proven educational system in a country with a diverse culture and a modern outlook.

Q What is the cost of higher education in the U.S.?

A The cost of studying at a U.S. college or university is anywhere from $20,000 to more than $50,000 per year. This includes tuition, fees (including computer, lab, or other facilities usage), food, and on-campus or off-campus housing. Additional expenses include books and supplies, transportation, insurance, and personal expenses.

Q What financial aid opportunities are available for international students?

A Financial aid is very competitive at the undergraduate level. Scholarships, which are given to top students only, are very rare for international students. Financial assistance from foundations, organizations, and the U.S. government is also rarely awarded to international undergraduate students. Less than 5 percent of international undergraduates are financed through these sources. Your educational adviser will be able to tell you whether there are special funds available for students from your country.

Q What tests do I need to take and what are the minimum scores required for admission?

A Many colleges and universities require the SAT or the ACT for undergraduate admission. Also, international students whose native language is not English are required to take an English language proficiency test. The Test of English as a Foreign Language (TOEFL) is the most widely accepted test. There are many competitive colleges and universities that require SAT Subject Test scores in addition to the SAT. The Subject Tests are in subjects such as biology, math, chemistry, and physics. You need to check with the colleges and universities you are applying to and ask if they require any Subject Tests.

Each college or university has different score requirements for standardized tests. You can strengthen your application by obtaining excellent scores.

Q When should I take the tests?

A When applying for standardized tests, keep in mind the time period during which the test scores will be valid. For instance, TOEFL scores are valid for only two years. Try to take tests by October 2008 if you plan to study in the United States in September 2009. Another thing to take into consideration is that many colleges have financial aid deadlines as early as December, January, or February for enrollment in September, and if you are applying for financial aid, you must make sure that all items in your application packet, including your test scores, reach the colleges and universities of your choice before then. But do not take a test unless you feel prepared to do so. Time yourself and take a lot of practice tests to get used to the pattern of questions and the timing.

Q How important are standardized test scores?

A Standardized test scores are only one part of the application procedure and not the sole decision-making factor in the admission process. They are a valuable tool in assessing the potential of students applying from varied educational backgrounds to succeed in the higher educational system of the U.S. While the format of each test varies, most focus on measuring the verbal, analytical, problem-solving, and quantitative skills of students. The level of skills required in a particular program may vary by the field of study and by the school or department. The ability of an international student to succeed in a particular program or school is determined only after a comprehensive review of the entire application packet.

Q What is a grade point average?

A A grade point average (GPA) is the most common method of measuring a student's academic performance. For each course, grades are awarded on a scale of A to D and F. At the end of each term, letter grades are converted into numerals on a 4.0 scale (A = 4, B = 3, C = 2, D = 1, F = 0) and each numeral grade is multiplied by the number of credits each course is worth. These numbers are added together and then divided by the total number of credits taken to determine the student's GPA for that term. A GPA is calculated for each term, cumulated each year, and a final GPA is calculated. (Note: Most programs use a GPA scale of 4.0, although a few schools use a scale of 5.0.) A C average or better is generally expected of undergraduate students.

Q What are credits?

A Students receive their degree by completing a specified number of credits. One credit is roughly equivalent to one hour of class time per week. Each course earns a specified number of credits (usually 3 or 4). Sometimes the terms "semester hours," "quarter hours," or "units" are used instead of "credits" or "credit hours."

Q What is the academic year for colleges in the U.S.?

A The academic year usually runs from mid-August to the end of May. However, it varies for each college or university. It may be divided into semesters, quarters, or trimesters. In addition, many schools provide a summer term of six to eight weeks. Students sometimes take summer courses to lower their course load during the regular terms or to earn their degrees more quickly. There are at least two main breaks during the academic year: two to four weeks in December and January and about a week in the spring (called Spring Break).

Q What is the difference between applying for the fall and spring semesters?

A As stated above, the academic year begins with the fall semester, which is when most students are admitted. Orientation programs are held with this in mind, and some prerequisite courses may only be offered in the fall. However, students can apply for initial admission in the spring semester if admissions have been opened up by a particular school or department. One thing to keep in mind, though, is that since most allocations for financial aid are made for fall enrollment, those who start in the spring are less likely to receive financial assistance.

Q What is a transcript, and what does "official transcript" mean?

A A transcript is a detailed account of a student's educational record that lists courses taken and the grades received. An official transcript is issued by the school awarding the grades/degree and is certified by the designated issuing authority of that school. The official transcript must be issued in a sealed envelope with the school's stamp and the official's signature or initials across the flap.

Q What does the application packet contain?

A The application packet contains a completed application form with the application fee, official transcripts, official test scores, an essay or statement of purpose, letters of recommendation, proof of adequate financial resources, an affidavit of support, request for financial assistance (if applicable), and any supplemental materials.

Q Should I have a native speaker or a company write my application essay?

A The essay is the one section of the application that gives admission officers a chance to get to know your personality and nonacademic background. Don't waste the chance to show them how unique you are by having someone else write your essay. Only you can distinguish yourself from the hundreds of other students; at highly selective schools, the essay can be the deciding factor between two similar applicants. The essay is not a list of achievements or an autobiography. Depending on the question asked, focus on one event, book, or person that affected your view of the world. Talk about something personal, good or bad, and write so that the admission officers will remember you.

Q What should be included in recommendation letters?

A Recommendation letters can be a critical factor in the selection process and should discuss the following:

- The content of the course the student took and the methods of teaching that were used

- The student's performance in the class, including a comparison to other students in the class

- The student's attitude toward learning, including evidence of his or her motivation, commitment, curiosity, independence, and creative thinking

- The student's character, strengths, and uniqueness

- Prediction about the student's impact (academic, personal, and/or extracurricular) on a college or community

Q What are some useful tips for potential U.S.-bound students?

A Be clear about your objectives. Consult different resources to gather information. Plan well in advance. Work systematically, keeping academic strengths as priorities. Make intelligent use of available information. And while you are in the U.S., work hard, learn about the country, and promote understanding about your home country.

Q Where can I get more information about higher education in the U.S.?

A To learn more about studying in the U.S., visit

     www.petersons.com
     www.educationUSA.state.gov
     www.ed.gov
     www.edupass.org
     www.studyUSA.com

How to Use This Guide

In-Depth Descriptions of Colleges and Universities in the U.S.

This section provides full-page descriptions of colleges and universities in the United States that wish to present a greater overview of their institutions for students who are thinking of studying in the U.S. Prepared by officials at the institutions, the narratives are designed to give students a better sense of the individuality of each school. In essence, this section is an open forum for institutions, on a voluntary basis, to communicate their particular messages to prospective students. The descriptions are arranged alphabetically by the official name of the college or program. Please note the following abbreviations used in some **In-Depth Descriptions** to describe TOEFL requirements:

PBT: Paper-based test

CBT: Computer-based test

iBT: Internet-based test

Those colleges and universities that have chosen to submit **In-Depth Descriptions** have "*See In-Depth Description on page . . . .*" at the end of their **Profile.**

Profiles of Colleges and Universities in the U.S.

This section lists, in state order, accredited colleges and universities in the United States. A combination of the elements listed below makes up each **Profile.** If a college did not supply a particular data element, that element is omitted from the **Profile.**

General Information

Institutional control: This refers to the governing group of a college or university and the nature of its financial support. Private institutions are designated as independent (nonprofit), independent-religious (sponsored by or affiliated with a certain religious group or having a nondenominational or interdenominational religious orientation), or proprietary (profit making). Public institutions are designated by the source of funding, which can be federal, state, county, district (an administrative unit of public education at the local level), city, or state and local ("local" may refer to county, district, or city). A state-related institution is funded primarily by the state but is administratively autonomous.

Institutional type: Each institution is classified as one of the following. A two-year college awards associate degrees. A four-year college awards baccalaureates and may also award associate degrees, but it does not award graduate (postbaccalaureate) degrees. A five-year college awards a five-year baccalaureate in a professional field, such as architecture or pharmacy, but it does not award graduate degrees. An upper-level institution awards a baccalaureate, but entering students must have at least two years of previous college-level credit. A comprehensive institution awards baccalaureates and may also award associate degrees; graduate degree programs are offered primarily at the master's, specialist's, or professional level, although one or two doctoral programs may be offered. A university offers four years of undergraduate work plus graduate degrees through the doctorate in more than two academic or professional fields.

Student body: Institutions are listed as men's (men only—100 percent of student body), women's (women only—100 percent of student body), primarily men's, primarily women's, or coed (coeducational). A few schools are designated as undergraduate: women (or men) only; graduate: coed. Coordinate institutions have separate colleges or campuses for men and women but share facilities and courses.

Campus setting: Setting is designated as urban (located within a major city), suburban (a residential area within commuting distance of a major city), small-town (a small but compactly settled area not within commuting distance of a major city), or rural (a remote and sparsely populated area).

Degrees awarded: An associate degree program (designated by A) may be either a college-transfer program, equivalent to the first half of a bachelor's degree, or a terminal program providing training for a specific occupation. A bachelor's degree program (B) is a complete undergraduate program in a liberal arts, science, professional, or prepro-fessional field. A master's degree (M) is the first graduate degree in the liberal arts and sciences and certain professional fields. A doctoral degree (D) is the highest degree awarded in research-oriented academic disciplines. A first-professional degree (FP) is required to be academically qualified to practice in certain professions, such as law and medicine.

Entrance level for U.S. students: This is each college's own assessment of its entrance difficulty level. (Please note that criteria for international students may differ; thus these are general guidelines.) The colleges were asked to select the level that most closely corresponds to their entrance difficulty, according to the guidelines below, to assist prospective students in assessing their chances for admission. Specialized schools of art and music, upper-level schools, and other institutions for which high school class rank or standardized test scores do not apply as admission criteria were asked to select the level that best indicates their entrance difficulty as compared to other institutions of the same type that use similar admission criteria.

The five levels of entrance difficulty are as follows:

- *Most difficult:* More than 75 percent of the freshmen were in the top 10 percent of their high school class and scored higher than 1310 on the SAT (verbal and mathematical combined) or higher than 29 on the ACT (composite); about 30 percent or fewer of the applicants were accepted.

- *Very difficult:* More than 50 percent of the freshmen were in the top 10 percent of their high school class and scored above 1230 on the SAT or 26 on the ACT; about 60 percent or fewer of the applicants were accepted.

- *Moderately difficult:* More than 75 percent of the freshmen were in the top half of their high school class and scored more than 1010 on the SAT or 18 on the ACT; about 85 percent or fewer of the applicants were accepted.

- *Minimally difficult:* Most freshmen were not in the top half of their high school class and scored somewhat below 1010 on the SAT or below 19 on the ACT; up to 95 percent of the applicants were accepted.

- *Noncompetitive:* Virtually all applicants were accepted regardless of high school rank or test scores.

Enrollment: The total enrollment figure is given, including the number of undergraduates, the percentage of women, and the percentage of international students and the number of countries they come from.

Faculty: The number of faculty members teaching at the institution as of fall 2006 is given.

Library holdings: Numbers of bound volumes, current serial subscriptions, and audiovisual materials are given.

Total majors: The total number of undergraduate majors that are offered is given.

Information for International Students
Admission figures: The number of international students who applied for fall 2006 freshman (or, for upper-level institutions, entering class) entrance, the number of those accepted, and the number of those who enrolled are given.

Starting times: The terms when international students may begin taking classes are noted.

Transferring: It is indicated if international applicants are accepted as transfers—meaning that they may transfer credits—from institutions abroad.

Admission tests: These are designated either required or recommended. They can include any or all of the following: SAT, SAT Subject Tests, ACT, Test of English as a Foreign Language (TOEFL) (may include a minimum score that must be achieved to be considered for acceptance or a minimum score that must be achieved for ESL admission), Michigan Test of English Language Proficiency (MTELP), and other special tests.

Application deadline: The application deadline for fall entrance is given either as a specific date or as rolling. Rolling means that applications are processed as they are received, and qualified students are accepted as long as there are openings.

Expenses: Tuition and mandatory fees are given for full-time students for a full academic year (generally nine months). Where applicable, figures based on one academic year are also given for room and board and for room only for college-owned or -operated housing. Note: Some of the figures listed may be minimum costs.

Financial Aid: If aid is available to international students, the following information is listed: the types of need-based or non-need-based aid, the forms required, the number of students in fall 2006 who were awarded aid, and the average dollar amount received.

Housing: If housing is guaranteed for international students, this is stated. Whether it is available during the summer is also listed.

Services: Availability of an international student adviser is indicated. The availability of an English as a second language (ESL) program, either on campus or at a cooperating institution, is given, as is the type of program (full-time or part-time). This section also indicates the availability of internships and employment.

Contact: The title of the contact person is given, along with the complete mailing address, telephone and fax numbers, and e-mail and Web site addresses.

Appendixes

Glossary
This section provides definitions of the terms students are likely to encounter in the admission process at U.S. colleges and universities. However, the glossary is not an exhaustive list, so be sure to talk with a counselor or admission officer about terms and definitions that are unclear.

Map of the United States

This map is provided to offer international students a general orientation to the location of each state (with the exception of Alaska and Hawaii) and its major cities.

Institutional Changes

This is an alphabetical listing of institutions that have recently closed, merged with other institutions, or changed their name or status. For a name change, the former name appears first, followed by the new name.

Indexes

Colleges with ESL Programs

This index lists all colleges that offer English courses for students whose native language is not English (English as a second language or ESL). The colleges are listed in alphabetical order by state.

Colleges with Articulation Agreements

This index lists institutions that have articulation agreements with other schools. The articulation agreement allows a student to complete a two-year associate degree program at one school and transfer to the other school to complete a related bachelor's degree program, with a minimum loss of credit or duplication of course work.

Majors

This index lists twenty-three broad subject areas and, for each, the two- and four-year colleges that offer degrees in one or more fields in the area and have indicated an interest in enrolling international students. The areas appear in alphabetical order, each followed by an alphabetical list of the colleges (including name and location) that offer programs in that area and the degree levels (associate or bachelor's) available. The names of the majors represent their most widely used designations. However, many institutions use different terms for the same or similar fields. Readers should refer to a college's catalog for the exact terminology. In addition, while the term "major" is used in this guide, some colleges may use other terms, such as concentration, program of study, or field.

Geographical Listing of In-Depth Descriptions

This index lists those institutions that have an **In-Depth Description** in the book, along with the corresponding page number.

Alphabetical Listing of Colleges and Universities

This index provides an alphabetical listing of all the institutions in the book, along with the correspond-

ing page number of the institution's **Profile** and **In-Depth Description,** if applicable.

In the indexes at the back of this book in which the colleges are listed alphabetically, the abbreviated state name follows the college's name. The following standard abbreviations are used:

AL	Alabama	MO	Missouri
AK	Alaska	MT	Montana
AZ	Arizona	NE	Nebraska
AR	Arkansas	NV	Nevada
CA	California	NH	New Hampshire
CO	Colorado	NJ	New Jersey
CT	Connecticut	NM	New Mexico
DE	Delaware	NY	New York
DC	District of	NC	North Carolina
	Columbia	ND	North Dakota
FL	Florida	OH	Ohio
GA	Georgia	OK	Oklahoma
HI	Hawaii	OR	Oregon
ID	Idaho	PA	Pennsylvania
IL	Illinois	RI	Rhode Island
IN	Indiana	SC	South Carolina
IA	Iowa	SD	South Dakota
KS	Kansas	TN	Tennessee
KY	Kentucky	TX	Texas
LA	Louisiana	UT	Utah
ME	Maine	VT	Vermont
MD	Maryland	VA	Virginia
MA	Massachusetts	WA	Washington
MI	Michigan	WV	West Virginia
MN	Minnesota	WI	Wisconsin
MS	Mississippi	WY	Wyoming

Data Collection Procedures

The data contained in the General Information, Expenses, and Financial aid sections of the **Profiles** were collected between fall 2006 and spring 2007 through *Peterson's Annual Survey of Undergraduate Institutions* and *Peterson's Annual Survey of Undergraduate Financial Aid*. Questionnaires were sent to more than 3,800 colleges and universities that meet the criteria for inclusion. All of the data have been submitted by officials from the schools—usually admission and financial aid officers, registrars, or institutional research personnel. The information contained in the Information for International Students section of the **Profiles** was collected between February and April 2007 through a separate online survey effort. All usable information received in time for publication has been included. If a particular college did not supply a given item of data, the corresponding element is omitted from its profile. Because all material comes directly from college officials, we believe that the information presented in this guide is accurate.

Readers should be aware that changes in the data may occur after publication. For this reason, students should check with the specific college or university at the time of application to verify such figures as tuition and fees.

Criteria for Inclusion in This Book

The *Applying to Colleges and Universities in the United States* **Profiles** comprise accredited institutions in the United States that award baccalaureate and associate degrees. To be included in this guide, an institution must have full accreditation or candidate-for-accreditation (preaccreditation) status granted by an institutional or specialized accrediting body recognized by the U.S. Department of Education. Recognized institutional accrediting bodies include the following: the six regional associations of schools and colleges (Middle States, New England, North Central, Northwest, Southern,

and Western), each of which is responsible for a specified portion of the United States and its territories; the Association for Biblical Higher Education (ABHE); the Accrediting Council for Independent Colleges and Schools (ACICS); the Accrediting Commission of Career Schools and Colleges of Technology (ACCSCT); the Distance Education and Training Council (DETC); and the Transnational Association of Christian Colleges and Schools (TRACS). Program registration by the New York State Board of Regents is considered the equivalent of institutional accreditation, since the Board requires that all programs offered by an institution meet its standards before recognition is granted.

There are also recognized specialized accrediting bodies in more than forty fields, each of which is authorized to accredit specific programs in its particular field. This can serve as the equivalent of institutional accreditation for specialized institutions that offer programs in one field only (schools of art, music, optometry, theology, etc.).

In-Depth Descriptions of Colleges and Universities in the U.S.

Adelphi University

- Contact:
  Leslie Garcia
  Senior Assistant Director of International
     Admissions
  Adelphi University
  Garden City, NY 11530

  Phone: 516-877-3050
  Fax: 516-877-3039
  E-mail: intladmissions@adelphi.edu
  Web site: http://www.adelphi.edu
- Private, coed
- Suburban setting
- Enrollment: 4,758 (undergraduate)
- Student-faculty ratio: 12:1
- 2006–07 Tuition and fees: $20,900
- 2006–07 Room and board: $6350 (typical

- double room), $2800 (average meal plan)
- International students: 3.5%
- Countries represented: 37
- International students applied: 740
- International students accepted: 355
- Admissions tests:
  - TOEFL (min. score 550 PBT; 250 CBT; 80 iBT)
  - SAT or ACT: Required for new freshmen whose native language is English
- Application deadline: Fall, May 1; spring, December 1
- On-campus housing: Available
- Summer housing: Available

Area and Climate

Long Island is affected by four changes of season. The temperature ranges from a high of 85°F (29°C) in July and August to a low of 26°F (-3°C) in January and February. Rainfall is intermittent throughout the year, and it snows occasionally from November through March. Students should plan their wardrobe accordingly. Adelphi University is located 20 miles (32 kilometers) east of New York City. New York City is easily and safely accessible via the Long Island Railroad, which is a 10-minute walk from campus.

Education

Adelphi University was chartered in 1896 as a small college in Brooklyn, New York. Adelphi moved to its current location in 1929 and became a university in 1963. Today, twenty-one buildings house academic departments and classrooms, including superlative facilities to support teaching and research. Adelphi is a selective, cosmopolitan university with many of the resources of a larger institution. Adelphi's diversity of programs in the liberal arts and in the professions attracts highly qualified students from more than forty-two states and thirty-seven countries. The University, while meeting the demands of technological advances and worldwide social change, nevertheless subscribes to traditional educational values.

Campus Life

Within the Ruth S. Harley University Center, students find a Barnes & Noble bookstore and more than seventy student clubs, organizations, and activities. There are a multidenominational Chaplain's Center, a student newspaper, eight Greek-letter societies, and twenty honor societies. Elsewhere on campus, students can gather in comfort and security and get to know one another in an atmosphere of intellectual and emotional support. The University Center and Post Hall house numerous restaurants offering diverse, international dining. Meal plans are available.

For International Students

Adelphi has a strong commitment to international and intercultural education and welcomes students from all over the world. The Office of International Student Services provides the necessary assistance to keep international students in legal status with the appropriate federal agencies (Immigration and Naturalization Service, Social Security Administration, United States Information Agency, and Internal Revenue Service). The office seeks to counsel and advise international students who experience difficulties stemming from their status as noncitizens or from differences in government laws and regulations, language, customs, culture, and educational systems. Finally, the office also participates in planning cultural and social events of an international character.

Adrian College

- Contact:
   International Admissions
   Adrian College
   110 South Madison Street
   Adrian, MI 49221
   Phone: 517-265-5161 Ext. 4326
   Fax: 517-264-3878
   E-mail: admissions@adrian.edu
   Web site: http://www.adrian.edu/admissions.
      html
- Private, coed
- Small-town setting
- Enrollment: 1,100
- Student-faculty ratio: 13:1

- 2006–07 Tuition and fees: $20,000
- 2006–07 Room and board: Cost waived
- International students: 2%
- Countries represented: 7
- International students applied: 50
- International students accepted: 25
- International students enrolled: 15
- Admissions tests:
   - TOEFL (computer-based min. score 173)
   - SAT/ACT: Recommended
- Application deadline: 5/1
- On-campus housing: Guaranteed
- Summer housing: Available

Area and Climate

Adrian College's 100-acre (41-hectare) campus is situated in a safe, residential area in the southeastern corner of Michigan. Adrian, a city of approximately 22,000, is located in the center of an agricultural, industrial, and recreational area. Public transportation is available within the city limits. Highways and nearby expressways provide access to the metropolitan areas of Detroit, Toledo, Chicago, Indianapolis, and Cleveland. Changing seasons are a feature of the region, with normal temperatures in January ranging from 10°F to 30°F (-12°C to -1°C). Normal July temperatures range from 70°F to 90°F (21°C to 32°C).

Education

Adrian College, chartered in 1859 and affiliated with the United Methodist Church, awards six different bachelor's degrees. Students may select from more than forty majors and twelve preprofessional programs. Highest enrollments are in business and the sciences. The faculty has earned praise for its commitment to teaching undergraduate students. Small class size (the average is 15) allows highly active collaboration between students and faculty members. Campus facilities include twenty-one major buildings, with a planetarium, an observatory, a student center that is open 24 hours a day, and computer labs with free Internet access and e-mail for student use. Shipman Library provides print and electronic media in a quiet, comfortable setting. The academic calendar follows a semester schedule, with the fall semester running from August to December and the spring semester from January to April. May and summer terms are available at an additional cost.

Campus Life

Adrian is composed of students and faculty members with a wide variety of backgrounds from more than twenty-five states and seven countries. A majority of the students come from Michigan and the surrounding states of Ohio and Indiana. Most students live in campus residence halls. The campus atmosphere is relaxed and friendly. Students have ready access to involvement in more than fifty clubs and organizations. Dawson Auditorium, Downs Hall Theatre, an art gallery, a bookstore, a dining hall, and the Merillat Sport and Fitness Center are popular meeting places on campus. Students especially enjoy the newly renovated Caine Student Center, featuring meeting rooms, a food court, and computer access. Adrian participates in NCAA Division III athletics. Students can walk to stores or drive to movie theaters, a shopping mall, restaurants, and recreation areas. Faculty advisers help students understand the curriculum and offer advice to help them reach individual career goals.

For International Students

Each international student enrolled at Adrian receives an international student scholarship that waives the cost of room and board through the fall and spring semesters. Students earning a combined score of 860 or higher on the critical reading and math sections of the SAT also receive a $3000 International Student Achievement Scholarship. Official test scores must be received by the College no later than May 1 for admission to the August semester and by September 1 for admission to the January semester. A small number of additional scholarships are available. Orientation sessions address the specific needs of international students at the start of each semester. The College offers ESL support courses to students experiencing difficulty studying and learning in the English language. Housing is available during break periods in the fall and spring semesters. Transportation from nearby airports is offered to new students when they first arrive. Health insurance is required and may be purchased through the College.

Alverno College

- **Contact:**
  Mary Ellen Spicuzza
  International Student Counselor
  Alverno College
  3400 South 43rd Street
  P.O. Box 343922
  Milwaukee, WI 53234-3922
  Phone: 414-382-6108
  E-mail: international@alverno.edu
  Web site: http://www.alverno.edu/
- Independent, Catholic, four-year, women only (graduate program open to women and men)
- Urban setting
- Enrollment: 2,372

- **Student-faculty ratio: 13:1**
- **2006–07 Tuition and fees: $15,984–$16,728**
- **2006–07 Room and board: $5954**
- **Admissions tests:**
  - **TOEFL: Required (paper-based min. score 500; computer-based min. score 173)**
  - **SAT and ACT: Recommended**
- **Application deadline: Rolling**
- **On-campus housing: Available**
- **Summer housing: Available**

Area and Climate

The city of Milwaukee, Wisconsin, is 1 hour north of the city of Chicago on the shores of Lake Michigan. The nineteenth-largest city in the United States, Milwaukee is known for its clean and friendly communities and is composed of immigrants from around the world. This diversity is celebrated throughout the year with many festivals and special events. The wide range of recreation and cultural opportunities includes major-league baseball and basketball games, natural history and art museums, a ballet company, many live theater performances, a symphony orchestra, wonderful restaurants, and all the benefits of Lake Michigan, including beaches, sailing, and fishing. Alverno College itself is located in the Jackson Park neighborhood of Milwaukee on a 46-acre (19-hectare) parklike campus. The College provides 24-hour security and remains one of the safest college campuses in the nation.

Education

As a women's college, Alverno offers the environment and support systems that help students achieve their full potential. Founded in 1887, Alverno College offers more than sixty program areas of study (majors, minors, and associate degrees) in seven academic divisions. Alverno's unique emphasis on students learning the abilities needed

to put knowledge to use—commonly called ability-based education—has gained national praise. Surveys of American college presidents by *U.S. News & World Report* have consistently rated Alverno among the best regional liberal arts colleges in the Midwest. Eighty-nine percent of the full-time faculty members hold the highest degrees in their fields.

Campus Life

Alverno has thirty student organizations, performances by touring artists in Alverno's Pitman Theatre, a student activities center (the Pipeline), a coffeehouse (The Mug), a fitness center, a gymnasium, an outdoor volleyball pit, a basketball court, and frequent arts and cultural events. NCAA Division III intercollegiate sports include basketball, volleyball, softball, soccer, and cross-country as well as intramurals. Alverno has two residence halls, Austin Hall and Clare Hall. The former, the heart of the residence life program, offers many activities, whereas Clare Hall is a quieter environment, designed for students who wish to focus more on their studies.

For International Students

Cultural Kaleidoscope is a department-sponsored organization focused on the creation of a link between people from different cultures, celebration of the uniqueness each culture has to offer, and a support network. In order to help international students feel more a part of the community at Alverno, Cultural Kaleidoscope creates connections between them and Alverno's American students.

American Academy of Dramatic Arts

- **Contact:**
  Karen Higginbotham
  Director of Admissions
  AADA New York
  120 Madison Avenue
  New York, NY 10016-7004

  Phone: 800-463-8990
  Web site: http://www.aada.org

  Dan Justin
  Director of Admissions
  AADA Los Angeles
  1336 North LaBrea Avenue
  Hollywood, CA 90028

  Phone: 800-222-2867
  Web site: http://www.aada.org

- Private, coed
- Urban setting
- Enrollment: 300 each campus
- Student-faculty ratio: 14:1
- 2007–08 Tuition: $18,000
- International students: 20%
- Countries represented: 26
- Admissions tests:
  - Not required
  - SAT or ACT: Recommended
- Application deadline: Rolling
- On-campus housing: Not available, but off-campus options provided
- Summer housing: Not available, but off-campus options provided

Area and Climate

The American Academy of Dramatic Arts (AADA) is the only degree-granting conservatory for actors offering professional training in both of America's great centers of theatrical activity. The Academy's New York home is located in midtown Manhattan, close to all forms of public transportation and surrounded by the rich cultural life that has inspired young artists for generations. The East Coast climate is characterized by distinct seasons. AADA Los Angeles is now located in the center of the motion picture and television production capital of the world. The recently opened campus is a short walk from Hollywood Boulevard and is surrounded by film and television production companies. The California freeway system affords access to beaches, deserts, and mountains. The California climate is mild year-round.

Education

Founded in New York in 1884, the Academy was the first school in the United States to provide a professional education for actors. Since 1974, the Academy has operated an additional campus in California. The Academy remains dedicated to a single purpose: training professional actors. The love of acting, as an art and as an occupation, is the spirit that impels the school. For the serious, motivated student, the Academy offers more than a century of success; a well-balanced, carefully structured curriculum; and a vital, dedicated faculty. The Academy is a nonprofit educational institution, chartered in New York by the Board of Regents of the University of the State of New York and accredited by MSCHE, the Middle States Association of Colleges and Schools, the Western Association of Schools and Colleges, and the National Association of Schools of Theatre. Students who meet the requirements of the two-year Professional Training Program receive an associate degree. A third-year performance program is offered to selected graduates and leads to a Certificate of Advanced Studies in Actor Training. For students who desire a bachelor's degree, the Academy has articulation agreements with St. John's and Antioch Universities.

Campus Life

Academy students are diverse in their backgrounds and geographical origin; they come from every region of the United States, from Canada, and from many other countries. Approximately half of all entering students come with some college experience; the others enroll directly from secondary schools. AADA offers a variety of attractive off-campus housing options through special arrangements with local resources. The collaborative nature of the training contributes to genial relations among the student body. Students attend all types of theatrical events for free or are given the opportunity to purchase reduced-price tickets. Guest lecturers from the professional world frequently visit the Academy. Some of the Academy's most well-known alumni are Kirk Douglas, Lauren Bacall, Robert Redford, Danny DeVito, and Gena Rowlands. More recent graduates include Paul Rudd, Adrien Brody, and Kim Catrall.

For International Students

Fluency in the English language is required of a student to fully benefit from the Academy's program. English skills are assessed through the audition/interview required for admission.

American InterContinental University

- **Contact:**
  AIU Los Angeles
  12655 West Jefferson Boulevard
  Los Angeles, CA 90066
  Phone: 310-302-2000
         800-333-2652
  Fax: 310-302-2001
  Web site: http://www.aiula.com
- **Proprietary, comprehensive, coed**
- **Urban setting**
- **Enrollment: 1,000**
- **Student-faculty ratio: 15:1**

- **2005–06 Tuition and fees: $5439 (per 10-week quarter)**
- **2005–06 Room and board: $2150 (room only, per 10-week quarter)**
- **International students: 5%**
- **Countries represented: 26**
- **Admissions tests:**
  - **TOEFL: Required (min. score 173 computer-based; 500 paper-based)**
  - **SAT or ACT: Recommended**
- **On-campus housing: Not available**

Area and Climate

Situated in the heart of southern California, American InterContinental University–Los Angeles (AIU–LA) is located just minutes from beaches, mountains, and some of the world's most prestigious employers. One of the busiest manufacturing centers, Los Angeles is a community rich in cultural, geographic, and economic diversity, with residents from more than 140 countries. With about 330 sunny days a year and exceptionally mild winters, Los Angeles offers many outdoor recreational activities, including hiking, surfing, and skiing.

Education

American InterContinental University–Los Angeles is accredited by the Commission on Colleges of the Southern Association of Colleges and Schools to award associate, bachelor's, and master's degrees. AIU–LA offers undergraduate degrees in criminal justice, fashion design, fashion marketing, fashion marketing and design, information technology, interior design, international business, media production, and visual communications and graduate degrees in business administration, education, and information technology. Students have the opportunity to learn to work in teams and to use industry-current technology, and they train for rewarding careers while nurturing intellec-

tual development. A team of qualified instructors provide expert insight and instruction. Class sizes are small.

Campus Life

Though there is no on-campus housing, year-round off-campus accommodations are generally available within a 3-mile radius of the University, and the University contracts with a provider of student housing. The student activities program strengthens students' socialization skills and offers encouragement to those who are making a transition to university life. AIU-sponsored activities introduce students to many of the diverse social and cultural events held in the city. The career services department offers career placement assistance, works individually with students, and provides career fairs and resume and cover letter workshops.

For International Students

American InterContinental University offers international students a supportive and welcoming environment in which all students can succeed and thrive. Students from twenty-six countries have chosen an AIU campus for its cultural diversity, global perspective, and hands-on experience. The International Admissions Department helps students from around the world make a smooth transition to campus life. The knowledgeable international admissions staff acts as a key source of information for any questions students have regarding immigration issues, cultural adjustment, academic affairs, personal and housing issues, and employment regulations.

American University

- Contact:
  Dr. Sharon Alston
  Director of Admissions
  American University
  4400 Massachusetts Avenue NW
  Washington, D.C. 20016-8001
  Phone: 202-885-6000
  Fax: 202-885-6014
  E-mail: admissions@american.edu
  Web site: http://www.admissions.american.edu
- Private, 4-year, coed
- Suburban setting
- Enrollment: 11,279
- Student-faculty ratio: 14:1
- 2006–07 Tuition and fees: $29,673

- 2006–07 Room and board: $11,570
- International students: 1%
- Countries represented: 140
- International students applied: 801
- International students accepted: 294
- International students enrolled: 39
- Admissions tests:
  - TOEFL: Required (min. score 550 PBT; 213 CBT; 80 iBT)
  - SAT: Required
  - ACT: Not required
- Application deadline: January 15
- On-campus housing: Available
- Summer housing: Available

Area and Climate

Founded in 1893 and located in northwest Washington, D.C., at the top of "Embassy Row," American University's (AU) traditional campus is located in one of the safest suburban neighborhoods, yet is within easy access to downtown Washington, D.C. Originally planned by Frederick Law Olmsted, the noted architect of New York City's Central Park, AU's campus was designated a national arboretum and garden. Students can utilize buses, taxis, and the Metro subway system to reach downtown Washington in about 20 minutes. The city serves as an extended classroom and offers internship opportunities and job opportunities in every field, many of which are not found anywhere else in the world.

Education

Students may choose from more than 70 programs in the arts and humanities, business, education, international studies, public affairs, science, and social sciences, and preprofessional programs in law and medicine. Student may decide to double major or construct their own interdisciplinary major. Most majors offer the option of pursuing a combined bachelor's/master's program. The National Survey of Student Engagement shows that active learning is the norm at American University. Student's rated AU at the top for the "Level of Academic Challenge," "Student-Faculty Interaction," and "Enriching Educational Experiences." The five most popular majors are international service, business administration, justice, political science/government, and public communication.

Campus Life

Almost all first-year students, and about 60 percent of all students, live in recently renovated housing on campus. Laundry and cooking facilities are available on each floor. Leonard Hall is an intercultural/international hall popular with both international and U.S. students. AU has a main dining room close to the residence halls and many small cafés. Because AU is in a residential neighborhood, students have the option of finding an off-campus apartment within walking distance of campus. Students may take advantage of more than 160 student clubs, frequent on-campus speakers, and social events that include films, music, plays, and NCAA Division I and club sports.

For International Students

International Student and Scholar Services (ISS) at AU provides information and assistance to international students as they enter the University and throughout their education by affirming a sense of global community on campus; by orienting, advising, and advocating for international students; and by ensuring compliance with federal regulations governing international educational exchange. International students can work with a counselor in the Academic Support Center (ASC) to receive individual instruction in study skills and/or help in adjusting to U.S. academic culture. ASC offers ESL tutoring referrals, a writing lab with four counselors who are specially trained in working with international students, study skills workshops, and more.

Anna Maria College

- Contact:
    Admissions Office
    Anna Maria College
    Paxton, MA 01612
    Phone: 508-849-3360
    Fax: 508-849-3362
    E-mail: admission@annamaria.edu
- Private, Catholic, coed
- Small-town setting
- Enrollment: 600 (full-time)
- Student-faculty ratio: 15:1
- 2006–07 Tuition and fees: $23,234
- 2006–07 Room and board: $8410
- International students: 5%

- Countries represented: 11
- International students applied: 15
- International students accepted: 10
- International students enrolled: 5
- Admissions tests:
    - TOEFL (min. score 500 PBT to enroll)
    - SAT: Required
    - ACT: Recommended
- Application deadline: Rolling; 3/1 priority
- On-campus housing: Guaranteed to first-year students
- Summer housing: Available

Area and Climate

Anna Maria College (AMC) is located in Paxton, Massachusetts, in the northeastern corner of the United States. The town of Paxton is 8 miles (10 kilometers) north of Worcester and about 44 miles (70 kilometers) west of Boston, the capital of Massachusetts. Fields, woods, and ponds surround the peaceful campus. Students can safely walk, jog, or bike in the area. Nearby Worcester is the home of art, history, and science museums; concert halls; theater companies; fine shops; and restaurants. Paxton experiences four seasons: colorful leaves in fall, a snowy and icy winter, a late warm spring, and a hot summer.

Education

Anna Maria College is a private four-year coeducational college that provides education in the liberal arts and professional studies. Some of the most popular areas of study include business, criminal justice, education, psychology, music, art, art therapy, and social work. AMC also offers a fire science program. Many students defer their decision about a major area of study until their second year. Class sizes are kept small so that everyone can actively participate and receive individual attention from professors. Faculty and staff members stress the importance of personal values, social responsibility, and spiritual growth. AMC's focus on technology provides students with access to

exceptional computer resources. Students can cross-register for classes at twelve area colleges of the Worcester Consortium.

Campus Life

The international college community complements the school population of about 600 full-time undergraduate students. Overall, about 12 percent of the population is multicultural, with the numbers increasing with every class. International students typically live on campus with an American roommate in one of the residence halls. Living on campus allows international students the opportunity to understand English more quickly and to learn about the lifestyles of American students. Anna Maria's soccer, softball, volleyball, cross-country, basketball, baseball, and golf teams provide yearlong excitement, while student organizations and clubs offer fun activities and trips to Boston, New York City, and many other interesting places.

For International Students

Anna Maria College welcomes and appreciates the unique perspectives and valuable insights that international students bring to the campus community. Students who present outstanding academic credentials may be awarded up to $3000 per academic year, which can be renewed annually based on the student's academic performance. International students enjoy all the educational, social, recreational, and transportation services the College provides. In addition, international students receive such services as visa assistance, advisory and counseling services, vacation and housing planning, and field trip coordination.

The Art Institute of Boston at Lesley University

- **Contact:**
  Renee Webber
  International Admissions Advisor
  Office of Admissions
  The Art Institute of Boston at Lesley University
  700 Beacon Street
  Boston, MA 02215
  Phone: 617-585-6700 or 6706
  E-mail: admissions@aiboston.edu
  Web site: http://www.aiboston.edu
- **Private, coed**
- **Urban setting**
- **Enrollment: More than 500**
- **Student-faculty ratio: 14:1**
- **2006–07 Tuition and fees: $21,500**
- **2006–07 Room and board: $10,500**

- **International students: 10%**
- **Countries represented: 15**
- **International students applied: 72**
- **International students accepted: 42**
- **International students enrolled: 13**
- **Admissions tests:**
  - **TOEFL (min. score 500 paper-based) or IELTS (5.5)**
  - **SAT: Recommended**
  - **ACT: Not required**
- **Application deadline: Rolling (2/15 scholarship priority)**
- **On-campus housing: Available nearby**
- **Summer housing: Not available; assistance provided locating apartments and roommates**

Area and Climate

Boston is an extraordinary college town, with almost 250,000 students attending seventy-seven colleges and universities. Snowy winters, warm summers, and beautiful, moderate spring and fall weather characterize Boston. Students can enjoy the many exciting activities found in Boston, and the magnificent mountains and beaches of New England are within a few hours' drive.

Education

The Art Institute of Boston (AIB), founded in 1912, awards the Master of Fine Arts in visual arts and the four-year Bachelor of Fine Arts degree and diploma in animation, art history, design, fine arts, illustration, photography, and combined majors and a two-year professional certificate in illustration and design. Students may elect to earn a five-year double-major B.F.A./Diploma in fine arts/illustration, graphic design/illustration, illustration/fine arts, or illustration/ graphic design. AIB students also have the option to study for a dual B.F.A./M.Ed. in art education or B.F.A./M.A. in art/ expressive therapy. An advanced professional certificate two-year studio-intensive program is offered in animation, graphic design, or illustration. Programs are studio intensive, integrating liberal arts courses designed to broaden students' intellectual and artistic perceptions. The intimate atmosphere and small class size encourage close working relationships with faculty members and peers. Many faculty members are well-known practicing artists, designers, illustrators, and photographers. Students benefit from the talent and experi-

ence of the faculty and the extensive connections to the art and business communities that the college has nurtured. AIB's character as a private, professionally oriented college of the visual arts is now combined with the resources of a university, providing expanded educational opportunities.

Campus Life

AIB at Lesley University provides a variety of housing options for students, including residences near Harvard Square on the Cambridge campus of Lesley University (shuttle service provided). Many students live independently in apartments, and the college maintains up-to-date apartment and roommate source books. AIB students enjoy a fantastic array of cultural activities, from world-class museums to films, theaters, sporting events, and night life. Activities and opportunities for growth and learning at AIB include lectures, student exhibitions on and off campus, a visiting artist program, workshops, and field trips to galleries in New York and New England. Acclaimed artists, such as Chuck Close, Duane Michals, Edward Sorel, Andres Serrano, and Luis Gonzalez Palma, have lectured at AIB.

For International Students

AIB provides orientation for international students, and an International Student Advisor helps to ease the cultural transition to the United States. In addition to a readily available faculty, academic support is provided through tutoring and a network of faculty and peer advisers. ESL is offered, and the college has affiliations with local intensive English language programs. The college's International Student Association and the English Language Center in Boston sponsor activities specifically for international students.

Ashland University

- Contact:
  Susan Rosa, Associate Director
  Int'l Student Services
  Ashland University
  401 College Avenue
  Ashland, OH 44805
  Phone: 419-289-5935
  Fax: 419-289-5629
  E-mail: iss@ashland.edu
- Private, comprehensive, coed
- Small-town setting
- Enrollment: 2,900
- Student-faculty ratio: 16:1
- 2007–08 Tuition and fees: $22,216

- 2007–08 Room and board: $8376
- International students: 4%
- Countries represented: 33
- International students applied: 141
- International students accepted: 127
- International students enrolled: 63
- Admissions tests:
  - TOEFL (Internet-based min. score 65)
  - SAT: N/A
  - ACT: N/A
- Application deadline: Rolling
- On-campus housing: Guaranteed
- Summer housing: Available

Area and Climate

Ashland University is located in the state of Ohio in the mideastern part of the United States, below the Great Lakes system. The small city of Ashland (population 22,000) is about an hour's drive from the large cities of Cleveland and Columbus. The 120-acre (49-hectare) campus is one of the most beautiful in the state. An active symphony and theater program provides entertainment in Ashland, while professional sports, music, and theater are available in Cleveland. The area around Ashland offers summer recreation activities. Four distinct seasons provide a variety of weather; temperatures throughout the seasons average from a low of 18°F (-8°C) to a high of 80°F (27°C).

Education

Ashland University, which was founded in 1878, is a small, private university that stresses "Accent on the Individual." Its programs emphasize the liberal arts, sciences, and career-oriented programs. The University offers more than sixty majors, including business, computer science, hotel and restaurant management, environmental science, and communications. The largest number of students are enrolled in business and education. The programs are enhanced by the University Honors Program, the Ashbrook Center (political science/public affairs), and the Gill Center (economics education). The University provides extensive access to computer facilities for students, including a link to the University computer system in every residence hall room. The academic year consists of two semesters. Financial aid of $2000 to $8000 is available for students with a GPA of 2.75 or higher on a 4.0 scale.

Campus Life

Ashland's on-campus, undergraduate enrollment numbers 2,200 full-time students; 700 graduate students are enrolled in evening and weekend programs. Total enrollment, including all program centers, is 6,000. Eighty percent of on-campus students are from Ohio; others come from twenty-five states and thirty-three countries. The University offers a variety of housing options in its seven residence halls and senior apartments. All residence hall rooms are wired for Internet access. Residence halls remain open all year, including vacation periods. International students may request to live with American students. The Office of Student Activities, which won national awards for programming for several years, coordinates a wide range of activities and organizations, including academic clubs, campus services, special interest organizations, student government, religious life, media/publications, and cultural events. The University has extensive sports programs and activities and is a member of the NCAA Division II athletic program. The Student Center opened in 1996, the Patterson Technology Center opened in fall 1997, senior apartments opened in 2002, and an extraordinary business/economics building opened in 2004. A new education building, student recreation center, and science building opened in 2006.

For International Students

The University offers extensive support services for international students, including airport pickup, special advisers, and special orientation sessions. The most popular programs for international students are the International Club, the Friendship Families Program, and the World Café. Health care is provided on campus. For students who need ESL instruction before beginning academic classes, the Center for English Studies provides year-round sessions at all levels. Ashland University and the surrounding community have a very low crime rate, making this an ideal place in which to live and learn.

Barnard College

- **Contact:**
  Jennifer Gill Fondiller
  Dean of Admissions
  Barnard College
  3009 Broadway
  New York, NY 10027
  Phone: 212-854-2014
  Fax: 212-854-6220
  E-mail: admissions@barnard.edu
  Web site: http://www.barnard.edu
- Private, women's
- Urban setting
- Enrollment: 2,360
- Student-faculty ratio: 10:1
- 2006–07 Tuition and fees: $33,078
- 2006–07 Room and board: $11,392

- International students: 3%
- Countries represented: 40
- International students applied: 301
- International students accepted: 65
- International students enrolled: 27
- Admissions tests:
  - TOEFL (paper-based min. score 600; computer-based min. score 250; Internet-based min. score 100)
  - SAT Reasoning Test and 2 SAT Subject Tests or the ACT
- Application deadline: 1/1 (Early Decision 11/15)
- On-campus housing: Guaranteed
- Summer housing: Available

Area and Climate

Barnard College is located on a charming, 4-acre (2-hectare) campus in New York City, directly across the street from Columbia University. Barnard remains an independent affiliate of Columbia and offers cross-registration to its students. Barnard's upper Manhattan neighborhood, Morningside Heights, has eight major institutions of higher education and houses more than 32,800 students from around the world. The nearby streets have many bookstores, restaurants, cafés, and markets. Abounding with cultural, educational, internship, and professional opportunities, New York City is Barnard's laboratory. Excellent mass transportation provides easy access to Broadway theaters, museums, Wall Street, and hundreds of other attractions. The northeastern climate is seasonal and generally moderate.

Education

Barnard College is a selective, independent liberal arts college for women that is affiliated with Columbia University. Founded in 1889, Barnard is committed to the academic, personal, and professional success of women. It offers rigorous academic programs in nearly sixty majors leading to the Bachelor of Arts degree (A.B.). Students may also cross-register for courses at Columbia University and have access to more than 8 million volumes in Columbia's twenty-five libraries. The most popular majors at Barnard are English, psychology, political science, economics, and biology. Barnard offers double and joint degrees in coordination with other schools in the Columbia University system, including the School of International and Public Affairs, the Fu Foundation School of Engineering and Applied Science, the School of Law, the School of Dental and Oral Surgery, the Juilliard School, the Manhattan School of Music, and the Jewish Theological Seminary. Barnard operates on a two-semester calendar, with classes beginning in early September.

Campus Life

Barnard College students come from nearly every state and nearly forty countries, representing various ethnic, economic, and cultural groups. Close to 90 percent of students live on campus, and housing is guaranteed for all four years. The McIntosh Center, with student leadership offices, a cafeteria, and lounges, is the focus of student activities. Other campus facilities include a modern theater, a gym, a swimming pool, dance studios, a radio station, and a state-of-the-art greenhouse. The Barnard Center for Research on Women, a nationally recognized institute, offers numerous programs and resources in feminist scholarship. Barnard has its own student government and approximately eighty student organizations, including academic clubs, student performance groups, college publications, cultural associations, and pre-professional organizations. In addition, students have the opportunity to participate and hold leadership positions in Columbia's student organizations and coeducational social life.

For International Students

A designated dean within the Office of the Dean of Studies is available to meet with international students regarding issues that arise from their international student status, such as visas, cultural adjustment, and academic matters. Group meetings are scheduled during orientation and throughout the year to give international students the opportunity to become familiar with one another, the College, and life in the United States. While adequate proficiency in English is expected, international students who need extra English preparation take a Studies in Writing course before proceeding to other requirements. Students also benefit from Barnard's partnership with Columbia University, a school that ranks among the top five universities in the United States in the number of international students it enrolls. There are a limited number of scholarships available to international applicants. For further information, applicants should call the Office of Financial Aid at 212-854-2154.

Barry University

- Contact:

  Helen Corpuz

  Assistant Dean for Undergraduate Admissions

  Barry University

  11300 Northeast Second Avenue

  Miami Shores, FL 33161-6695

  Phone: 305-899-3100

           800-695-2279

  Fax: 305-899-2971

  E-mail: admissions@mail.barry.edu

  Web site: http://www.barry.edu/

- Private
- Urban setting
- Total enrollment: 9,400
- Student-faculty ratio: 14:1

- 2006–07 Tuition and fees: $24,000
- 2006–07 Room and board: $7850
- International students: 7.7%
- Countries represented: 70
- International students applied: 491
- International students accepted: 290
- International students enrolled: 244
- Admissions tests:
  - TOEFL: Required (min. score 550 paper-based; 213 computer-based)
  - SAT or ACT: Required
- Application deadline: Rolling
- On-campus housing: Available
- Summer housing: Available

Area and Climate

Barry University is 5 miles (8 kilometers) from the ocean in sunny, suburban Miami Shores. The hospitable climate allows for swimming, sailing, water-skiing, scuba diving, golf, tennis, soccer, and other outdoor sports year-round. Nearby, the Florida Keys, the Everglades, and living coral reefs present both recreational and educational opportunities. South Florida is an international business, tourism, and entertainment industry hub with a cosmopolitan multicultural population, offering a wide range of internship and career options as well as a vibrant cultural scene. Highlights include Urban Beach Week, the Calle Ocho street festival, the Miami International Book Fair, and the prestigious art fair, Art Basel Miami Beach. Miami also hosts the Miami Dolphins football team, the Miami Heat basketball team, the Florida Marlins baseball team, and the Florida Panthers hockey team.

Education

Barry University is an independent, coed, Catholic university offering more than seventy undergraduate and fifty graduate degrees. Founded in 1940 by the Dominican Sisters of Adrian, Michigan, the University provides a multicultural student body with an affordable, high-quality education, a caring environment, a religious dimension, and a commitment to community service. Classes are small, so students receive personal attention from distinguished faculty members and advisers. Facilities include the Monsignor William Barry Library, an extensive library network, multimedia business classrooms, and technologically advanced labs.

Campus Life

Barry students come from all compass points, age groups, ethnicities, and faiths. Barry has been ranked for seven consecutive years as the most diverse master's university in the South by *U.S. News & World Report*. Barry holds membership in twenty honor societies and hosts eighty-nine undergraduate and graduate student organizations, including Barry University Dance Theatre, the Campus Activities Board, and the *Barry Buccaneer* student newspaper as well as two fraternities and three sororities. Barry also promotes service organizations, such as Best Buddies and Habitat for Humanity. The University offers an active intramural sports program and fields twelve teams in the NCAA Division II (Sunshine State Conference), frequently winning national championships. Resident students live in eight residence halls where every room is wired for high-speed Internet access. The 78,000-square-foot R. Kirk Landon Student Union is a fully wireless facility that houses the offices of Student Services and student organizations, the University Bookstore, a platform dining room with food-cooking stations, a snack bar, a campus pub/game room, and more. A fully equipped fitness center features weight and cardio equipment. Barry hosts popular annual events such as the Festival of Nations celebration, in which students represent their native food and cultures, and Founders' Day, when the Barry community celebrates the University's history with entertainment and contests.

For International Students

Barry's Office of First-Year Programs seeks to enhance the first-year educational experience of each new student by ensuring a smooth transition into the Barry community. The Intercultural Center also gives students high-quality support, counseling, and advising with academic, financial, and personal issues. The University's nurse-directed Health Services Center is committed to promoting wellness among the Barry community and is a valuable resource to students seeking answers to questions on health issues. An ELS Language Centers program is also available for students to increase their language proficiency.

Belmont University

- **Contact:**
  Kathryn Skinner
  International Director
  Belmont University
  1900 Belmont Boulevard
  Nashville, TN 37212
  Phone: 615-460-5500
  Fax: 615-460-5539
  Web site: http://www.belmont.edu
- Private, Christian, coed
- Urban setting
- Enrollment: 4,500

- **Student-faculty ratio: 13:1**
- 2006–07 Tuition and fees: $18,420
- 2006–07 Room and board: $7100
- International students: 3%
- Countries represented: More than 30
- Admissions tests:
  - TOEFL (min. score 550 PBT; 213 CBT) or ELS level 112
- Application deadline: Rolling
- On-campus housing: Available
- Summer housing: Available

Area and Climate

Belmont University is located in Nashville, the capital of Tennessee, in the southeastern part of the United States. Nashville, with a population of 600,000, is a vibrant city full of art, music, and cultural opportunities. Nicknamed the Athens of the South for its seventeen colleges and universities and Music City, U.S.A., for being the home of country music, Nashville serves as the educational, cultural, recreational, and economic center of middle Tennessee. Ten major airlines serve Nashville, as do three interstate highways. The climate offers four distinct seasons, with temperatures ranging from 111°F (44°C) in the summer to 32°F (0°C) in the winter. Tennessee is a beautiful state full of indoor and outdoor recreational activities year-round.

Education

Founded in 1951, Belmont University, the second-largest private university in Tennessee, is a student-centered Christian community providing an academically challenging education. Seven accredited undergraduate degrees, encompassing fifty-seven majors in humanities, music, science, business administration, fine arts, nursing, and social work, are offered. Graduate degree programs include accounting, business administration, education, English, music, nursing, occupational therapy, and physical therapy. Belmont is well known for its music business degree program, one of the few programs of its kind in the world.

With a student body of 4,200 undergraduate students, close interaction between students and faculty members is part of the Belmont experience.

Campus Life

Students have a broad range of social and cultural activities with numerous student organizations, including various clubs, sororities, fraternities, concerts, honor societies, Christian organizations, music clubs, a large intramural sports program, baseball, basketball, golf, soccer, tennis, and volleyball. Weekly convocation programs provide opportunities to explore cultural, social, academic, and spiritual issues. Belmont is a beautiful historic campus dating back to 1890 in an urban setting. Coffee shops, international restaurants, and music clubs are nearby. On-campus housing is available year-round, including residence halls, language houses, and apartments.

For International Students

The Office of International Education offers a variety of special programs and support for international students from more than thirty countries. Programs include orientation, a fall retreat, host family friendship partners, International Student Association, World Fair, and many social activities. Belmont is authorized to issue F-1 and J-1 visas. The International Office helps students with admission, adjustment/cultural issues, academic advising, on-campus employment, and visa issues. Health, insurance, and travel services are also available. The ELS Language Center, which is located on Belmont's campus, enables students to study intensive English before entering the University. International students enjoy Belmont's friendly campus, where every teacher knows students by name.

Bennington College

- Contact:
    Ken Himmelman
    Dean of Admissions
    Bennington College
    Bennington, VT 05201
    Phone: 802-440-4312
        800-833-6845 (toll-free)
    Fax: 802-440-4320
    E-mail: admissions@bennington.edu
    Web site: http://www.bennington.edu
- Private, four-year, coed
- Small-town
- Enrollment: 657
- Student-faculty ratio: 7:1
- 2007–08 Tuition and fees: $36,800
- 2007–08 Room and board: $9380

- International students: 3%
- Countries represented: 13
- International students applied: 51
- International students accepted: 8
- Admissions tests:
    - TOEFL Required (min. score 577 PBT; 233 CBT; 90–91 iBT)
    - SAT or ACT: Not required (SAT, ACT, or other standardized tests are optional, but strongly encouraged to strengthen an application)
- Application deadline: January 3
- On-campus housing: Guaranteed
- Summer housing: Available

Area and Climate

Bennington College is located in the small town of Bennington, Vermont, at the foot of the Green Mountains. Just an hour by car or bus from Albany (New York) International Airport, the campus is also accessible from Boston (3 hours by bus) and New York City (4 hours by bus or train). The Vermont climate has four distinct seasons, including warm summers and snowy winters, and is renowned for its beautiful autumn colors. The area offers many outdoor activities, including hiking, rafting, and skiing, and the college campus and nearby Williamstown, Massachusetts, provide cultural activities such as films, lectures, and museums.

Education

A Bennington education is characterized by cross-disciplinary learning, the close working relationship between student and teacher, and an individualized academic planning process. Under the thoughtful guidance of faculty advisers, Bennington students learn what it means to take increasing responsibility for their own education, their own work, and their own lives. Bennington is grounded in the conviction that as a college education develops students' professional capacities, it should also prepare them to be deeply thoughtful and actively engaged citizens of the world. Each academic year includes a winter term in which students take their interests to the world beyond Bennington, where they pursue jobs and internships in areas that complement their studies. In this way,

Bennington graduates students with a well-rounded resume as well as a bachelor's degree in any area(s) of the humanities, natural sciences, social sciences, or visual and performing arts.

Campus Life

Students at Bennington College form a close-knit group of individuals representing diverse backgrounds. All undergraduates live on campus, where housing is guaranteed. Rather than traditional dormitories, Bennington students live in small houses with 25 to 30 other students. Campus activities, ranging from lectures to dance and theater productions and gallery openings to film screenings and dance parties, are attended by a majority of the students and help to build the community that makes the campus so welcoming. Each year the college hosts a number of special events, many organized by students themselves. These include distinguished lecturers, an outdoor music festival, and numerous student performances.

For International Students

Bennington welcomes international students to campus with a special International Student Orientation occurring prior to the regular undergraduate orientation. Each first-year international student is paired with an international upperclass student who acts as a peer mentor throughout the year. In addition to a regular academic adviser, the international student adviser also helps students with practical matters. Bennington also offers a Host Family Program and a student-run club called Legal Aliens. Summer and winter housing as well as on-campus employment is available to international students.

Bentley College

- **Contact:**
  Erika Vardaro
  Director of Admission
  Bentley College
  175 Forest Street
  Waltham, MA 02452-4705
  Phone: 781-891-2244
  Fax: 781-891-3414
- **Private, coed**
- **Suburban setting**
- **Enrollment: 4,250 (undergraduate)**
- **Student-faculty ratio: 12:1**
- **2006–07 Tuition: $29,810**
- **2006–07 Room and board: $10,530**

- **International students: 8%**
- **Countries represented: About 70**
- **International students applied: 628**
- **International students accepted: 199**
- **International students enrolled: 42**
- **Admissions tests:**
  - **TOEFL (paper-based min. score 550; computer-based min. score 213)**
  - **SAT or ACT: Required**
- **Application deadline: 2/1**
- **On-campus housing: Available**
- **Summer housing: Available**

Area and Climate

Bentley's suburban 163-acre (66-hectare) campus is located in the northeastern part of the United States—a region that is often referred to as New England. The school is about 10 miles (16 kilometers) west of Boston, the capital of Massachusetts and a vibrant, cosmopolitan center. Free transportation from Bentley offers easy access to the many attractions of Boston and Cambridge, including theaters, museums, nightclubs, diverse cuisine, and designer retail shops. Students at Bentley experience four distinct seasons (summer, fall, winter, and spring) while at school.

Education

Bentley focuses on educating students who are interested in business and related professions, blending the breadth and technological strength of a university with the values and student orientation of a small college. A strong curriculum focusing on business, technology, and the liberal arts provides students with many options for shaping an academic program that fits their skills, interests, and career goals.

Bachelor of Science degree programs enable students to specialize in specific business disciplines, such as accountancy, accounting information systems, computer information systems, corporate finance and accounting, economics-finance, finance, information design and corporate communication, management, managerial economics, marketing, and mathematical sciences. Bentley also offers Bachelor of Arts degree programs with majors in history, international studies, liberal arts, media and culture, and philosophy. In addition, Bentley offers students the opportunity to pursue an optional double major in business and liberal studies, so students can graduate from college prepared to work expansively, live meaningfully, and stand out to future employers. This optional major allows students to combine courses that fulfill general education requirements with related electives to pursue one of several concentrations. Students take the same number of courses but add another credential to their degree.

Bentley prepares students to meet the new demands of an information-rich, technology-driven workplace through a business curriculum that integrates technology at every level. An array of academic resources supports this curriculum, including the state-of-the-art Financial Trading Room and Center for Marketing Technology, in addition to four other specialty labs.

Bentley recognizes the differences in educational systems worldwide. International students may accelerate their individual programs by receiving advanced-standing credit upon their matriculation into Bentley. International Baccalaureate higher-level courses with examination results, Advanced Placement exam results, and A-Level results are a few examples of acceptable credit. Official records and grades are required to evaluate opportunities for advanced-standing credit.

Campus Life

About 80 percent of students, including 97 percent of freshmen, choose to live on campus. On-campus housing includes thirteen residence halls and apartment-style buildings, which are all located close to campus activities. Students choose from single-, double-, or triple-occupancy dorm rooms; apartments; or suites. Housing is guaranteed for all four years. On-campus activities include a wide range of athletic events, music and theater programs, and eighty clubs and student organizations. The Dana Athletic Center houses a new weight and fitness complex, an aerobics room, a full-service food court, a suspended track, refurbished locker rooms, and function spaces.

For International Students

Bentley offers a number of services and resources that are designed to ease international students' transition to school and the United States. The Joseph M. Cronin International Center houses International Student and Scholar Services and oversees international travel and exchange to support faculty and curriculum development. International Student and Scholar Services helps students from outside the United States adjust to living and learning at Bentley. The full-time director and staff members work with students to address academic, immigration, personal, and career issues.

Berkeley College

- **Contact:**
  Cynthia Marchese
  Vice President, Int'l Enrollment Services
  Berkeley College
  535 Fifth Avenue, 4th Floor
  New York City, NY 10017
  Phone: 212-687-3730
  Fax: 212-986-7827
  E-mail: international@berkeleycollege.edu
  Web site: http://www.berkeleycollege.edu
- **Private, coed**
- **Urban and suburban settings**
- **Enrollment: 5,200**
- **Student-faculty ratio: 25:1**

- **2006–07 Tuition and fees: $18,150**
- **2006–07 Room and board: $9000**
- **International students: 10%**
- **Countries represented: 92**
- **Admissions tests:**
  - **TOEFL (min. score 500)**
  - **SAT: N/A**
  - **ACT: N/A**
- **Application deadline: Rolling**
- **On-campus housing: Available in White Plains and Garret Mountain**
- **Summer housing: Available in White Plains and Garret Mountain**

Area and Climate

With seven campuses in or near New York City, Berkeley offers the vast resources of America's business, fashion, and cultural center. Berkeley College has a convenient campus location that is right for everyone. Whether students are looking for a small-town experience or the energy and stimulation of city living, they can find a Berkeley campus that fits their personal interests and needs. Every Berkeley location promises a close-knit community of peers and faculty members—a friendly, welcoming environment that provides a fulfilling and personal learning experience. Average temperatures range from 30°F (-1°C) to 35°F (2°C) in the winter and 70°F (21°C) to 80°F (27°C) in the summer, with beautiful fall and spring seasons.

Education

Founded in 1931, Berkeley College is proud to serve international students with an extraordinary educational program that provides a focused business curriculum. The College's reputation is well established among business and industry executives, who participate in the design of its academic programs. This corporate involvement assures Berkeley students that they will be learning exactly what employers need for the international job market. Formal internships are required for both associate and bachelor's degree programs. Students gain invaluable experience within their field of study by working for prestigious companies in internship positions. English as a second language classes are offered at the New York City location.

Campus Life

Life at Berkeley is influenced by the College's locations. In an urban-suburban environment, all have as their campus the entire New York metropolitan area. Surrounding the midtown Manhattan campus are theaters, museums, merchandising centers, and television studios, which make New York City a classroom for Berkeley students. Most campuses have nearby theaters, golf courses, tennis courts, indoor and outdoor pools, ice- and roller-skating rinks, and bowling alleys. Within easy driving distance are some of the best beaches and ski resorts in the U.S. Field trips, guest speakers, and social and cultural events in the city and suburbs combine to form the Berkeley lifestyle. On campus, Berkeley offers a wide variety of clubs and activities, including the International Club.

For International Students

The International Student Office has a staff trained to assist students. From the beginning of the process until graduation, students receive personal help with immigration procedures, housing information, orientation to the College, and adjustment to American life (including the differences in classroom protocol and practices). Students are encouraged to join the International Club. The International Student Office sponsors get-acquainted parties and other activities on and off campus, so that students can make new friends from America and around the world. Upon graduation, students are assisted with optional practical training placement.

Boston University

- **Contact:**
  Michelle Duschang, Associate Director
  Office of International Admissions
  Boston University
  121 Bay State Road
  Boston, MA 02215
  Phone: 617-353-4492
  Fax: 617-353-5334
  E-mail: intadmis@bu.edu
  Web site: http://www.bu.edu/admissions
- Private, coed
- Urban setting
- Enrollment: 30,957
- Student-faculty ratio: 12:1
- 2006–07 Tuition and fees: $33,330
- 2006–07 Room and board: $10,480

- International students: 8.1%
- Countries represented: 133
- International students applied: 2,398 (2005)
- International students accepted: 959 (2005)
- International students enrolled: 240 (2005)
- **Admissions tests:**
  - TOEFL: English language proficiency requirements are detailed at http://www.bu.edu/admissions/apply/int_language.html
  - SAT or ACT: Required
  - SAT Subject Tests: Two required
- Application deadline: 1/1
- On-campus housing: Guaranteed
- Summer housing: Available

Area and Climate

Boston University is located along the Charles River in Boston, Massachusetts, the cultural and historical capital of New England. Boston has the largest number of universities, educators, and students of any city in the United States. Students can find art, music, theater, cafés, or a park for an afternoon stroll around every corner. With four distinct seasons, Boston allows students to ski in the winter and have fun on the beach in the summer. Boston's Logan Airport serves all international carriers. Taxis, an extensive subway system, and buses make getting around the city easy.

Education

Founded in 1839, Boston University is a private, nonsectarian, coeducational research university with eleven undergraduate colleges and schools. One of the world's great academic institutions and the fourth-largest private university in the United States, Boston University offers more than 5,500 courses in more than 250 major and minor fields, including business management, communications, computer science, engineering, hospitality, humanities, medicine, performing arts, science, and the social sciences. The main University campus has 348 buildings, 489 classrooms, and 1,759 laboratories. Mugar Memorial Library, the largest of the University's twenty-three libraries, houses 1.8 million volumes and 2.8 million microform

equivalents. Academic advising, career counseling, internships, and computer facilities are available to all students. The faculty members, including three Nobel Prize winners, are accomplished, dedicated educators. Notable graduates include Martin Luther King Jr., former United States Secretary of Defense William Cohen, actress Geena Davis, and the Chairman of General Motors, John F. Smith, Jr.

Campus Life

Boston University is the embodiment of the diversity that characterizes the United States. Students come to the University from all fifty states and 133 countries. Students may choose to live in a variety of residences on campus. Specialty housing is available for students with similar academic or extracurricular interests. Nearly 400 organizations on campus keep students busy outside the classroom, including athletic, musical, cultural, and political clubs. The campus atmosphere is relaxed, friendly, and outgoing.

For International Students

Boston University is an exciting and rewarding place to get an education. International students are an important component of the community. Prior to the start of classes, the International Students and Scholars Office conducts an orientation for students to meet one another, become acquainted with the University and the city, and register for classes. The office assists students by answering questions about visas, employment, banking, and anything else of concern to the student. Intensive English preparation (ESL) is also available to students prior to enrolling in the University.

Bryant University

- **Contact:**
  Associate Director for International Admission
  Bryant University
  1150 Douglas Pike
  Smithfield, RI 02917

  Phone: 401-232-6100
  Fax: 401-232-6741
  E-mail: jeriksen@bryant.edu
  Web site: http://admission.bryant.edu
- Private, coed
- Suburban setting
- Enrollment: 3,203
- Student-faculty ratio: 16:1
- 2006–07 Tuition and fees: $27,639

- 2006–07 Room and board: $10,715
- International students: 1%
- Countries represented: 32
- International students applied: 233
- International students accepted: 105
- International students enrolled: 28
- Admissions tests:
  - **TOEFL: Required (min. score 550 paper-based; 213 computer-based)**
  - **SAT or ACT: Required**
- Application deadline: 2/1 (review begins 11/1)
- On-campus housing: Guaranteed
- Summer housing: Available (if taking classes)

Area and Climate

Bryant University is situated on 420 acres (170 hectares) of beautiful New England countryside. Bryant is only 15 minutes from the Rhode Island state capital, Providence, which offers a variety of activities and attractions, such as restaurants, concerts, museums, a nationally acclaimed repertory theater, and professional sports events. Bryant is 1 hour from Boston and 3 hours from New York City, with convenient access to all of the cultural, social, and career opportunities available in these major metropolitan areas. Public transportation is readily available. Rhode Island has four distinct seasons and a temperate climate. Temperatures during the school year generally range from 20°F (–7°C) to 71°F (22°C).

Education

Founded in 1863, Bryant is a four-year, private university in New England where students build knowledge, develop character, and achieve success—as they define it.

Throughout its 144-year history, Bryant has empowered students to achieve their personal best in life and in their chosen careers. Bryant is a great choice for individuals seeking the best integration of business and liberal arts, utilizing state-of-the-art technology. Bryant's cross-disciplinary approach provides a well-rounded education that teaches students the creative problem-solving and communication skills they need to successfully compete in a complex, global environment.

Bryant's College of Arts and Sciences offers the Bachelor of Arts degree in applied economics, applied psychology, communication, global studies, history, literary and cultural studies, politics and law, and sociology; the Bachelor of Science degree is offered in actuarial mathematics. The College of Business offers a Bachelor of Science in business administration, with concentrations in accounting, accounting information systems, computer information systems, finance, financial services, management, and marketing; a Bachelor of Science in information technology; and a Bachelor of Science in international business, with concentrations in computer information systems, finance, management, and marketing. Students can pursue one of twenty-four minors in business and liberal arts. To view additional areas of study, students should visit http://www.bryant.edu/bryant/academics/areasofstudy.jsp.

Bryant's rigorous academic programs are accredited by the New England Association of Schools and Colleges (NEASC).

The University's College of Business is accredited by AACSB International–The Association to Advance Collegiate Schools of Business, a distinction earned by only 10 percent of universities worldwide.

Campus Life

Sports and recreation play an integral role at Bryant. Students can balance their academic pursuits with overall well-being at the Elizabeth and Malcolm Chace Wellness and Athletic Center. This impressive facility features a fully equipped fitness center, a six-lane swimming pool, circuit-training equipment and free weights, and a group exercise room.

Students can compete in any of Bryant's twenty-two Division II intercollegiate varsity sports teams. In addition, students can participate in various club and intramural sports throughout the academic year. Teams play on a variety of athletic fields, and spectators can watch from the 4,000-seat Bulldog Stadium.

Bryant's seventy student clubs and organizations benefit many social causes, provide recreational enjoyment, promote intellectual exploration, and offer opportunities to develop new talents and passions. The Student Programming Board, the Intercultural Center, the Art and Culture Club, the Marketing Association, and the Student Senate are just a few of the organizations through which students can get involved in campus life. There are many places on and off campus for students to gather and enjoy music, poetry, comedy, and other kinds of entertainment. Most students (83 percent) live on campus.

For International Students

The Intercultural Center for International Education and Multicultural Affairs (ICC) at Bryant offers a range of services for international students. The center advises two major student organizations: the International Student Organization (ISO) and the Multicultural Student Union (MSU). These groups create programming and events to build greater cross-cultural understanding and foster cultural diversity. All new international students attend a special orientation program in August to learn about housing, support services, and activities on campus. They are also instructed on how to open a U.S. bank account, how to travel by bus or train, and how to adjust to American culture. The Academic Center for Excellence offers all Bryant students advising, counseling services, and access to several programs for improving grades and study skills. Bryant nurtures awareness and appreciation for diversity by bringing together community members to develop educational and social programs. An English as a second language (ESL) specialist is also available.

Bryn Mawr College

- **Contact:**
  Admissions Office
  Bryn Mawr College
  101 North Merion Avenue
  Bryn Mawr, PA 19010-2899
  Phone: 610-526-5152
  Fax: 610-526-7471
  E-mail: admissions@brynmawr.edu
  Web site: http://www.brynmawr.edu
- **Private, women only**
- **Suburban setting**
- **Student-faculty ratio: 8:1**
- **2006–07 Tuition and fees: $32,230**

- **2006–07 Room and board: $10,550**
- **International students: 11%**
- **Countries represented: 40**
- **International students applied: 364**
- **International students accepted: 45**
- **International students enrolled: 21**
- **Admissions tests:**
  - **TOEFL (min. score 600 PBT; 250 CBT)**
  - **SAT: Required**
- **Application deadline: 1/15 (regular decision)**
- **On-campus housing: Guaranteed**
- **Summer housing: Available**

Area and Climate

Bryn Mawr's 135-acre (55-hectare) suburban campus is 11 miles (18 kilometers) and 17 minutes by train from the center of Philadelphia, the nation's fifth-largest city, and all of its cultural, commercial, historical, entertainment, and transportation facilities. Philadelphia International Airport is a 30-minute ride from the Bryn Mawr campus and provides direct flights to many destinations around the world. New York City and Washington, D.C., are easily accessible by train from downtown Philadelphia. The Philadelphia metropolitan area includes many of the finest museums and important historical sites in the nation. Large stadiums and concert facilities are nearby and attract world-class athletes, musicians, and artists from around the world.

Education

A Bryn Mawr student is distinguished by a rare combination of personal characteristics: an intense intellectual commitment, a self-directed and purposeful vision of her life, and a desire to make a meaningful contribution to the world. Recognized as one of the premier liberal arts colleges in the United States, Bryn Mawr grants the Bachelor of Arts degree, with majors, minors, and concentrations in more than forty areas of study. Among the most widely chosen majors are the sciences (biology, chemistry, geology, physics, and math), English, psychology, and foreign languages. Through a cooperative arrangement with Haverford College, Swarthmore College, and the University of Pennsylvania, students have access to more than 5,000 undergraduate courses. Classes are small, many fewer than 15, and faculty members come to know their students as individuals. In fact, Bryn Mawr faculty members, world-renowned leaders in their fields, regard their students as junior colleagues, fully capable of working at a high level, developing their own ideas, and making important contributions. Facilities that enhance the learning environment include a language laboratory, with access to international

news services; networked dormitories; the new student village, Cambrian Row, a hub for student centered activities; a new $22-million science library; a new chemistry wing; and a new psychology building. The academic calendar consists of two semesters.

Campus Life

Nearly all of Bryn Mawr's undergraduates live on campus. The residence halls have been described as some of the most beautiful in the country. Diversity of every kind energizes the atmosphere and is demonstrated by the more than 100 student-run organizations on campus, including community-service organizations, cultural and ethnic groups, political groups, music and theater groups, athletic clubs, and a host of religious organizations. Students who are committed to a community that cherishes the individual find themselves in good company at Bryn Mawr. The Honor Code illustrates the mutual respect students have for one another and themselves. Bryn Mawr's Self-Government Association, the oldest of its kind in the United States, offers students the opportunity to have a voice in all aspects of the College. A modern athletic complex, tennis courts, two playing fields, an archery range, and a dance studio give students a wide range of fitness opportunities. NCAA Division III intercollegiate sports are also available and include badminton, basketball, crew, cross-country, field hockey, indoor track and field, lacrosse, outdoor track and field, soccer (football), swimming, tennis, and volleyball.

For International Students

An International Student Adviser is on staff to meet the particular needs of students studying in the U.S. A three-day orientation program for international students precedes the opening of the academic year to acquaint students with life at the College and in the U.S. The International Student Association is a student-run organization that provides both support and outreach to the community for multicultural events and programs. On the basis of need, Bryn Mawr awards a few scholarships to outstanding international applicants who cannot attend the College without financial assistance.

Bucknell University

- **Contact:**
  International Admissions Coordinator
  Bucknell University
  Lewisburg, PA 17837
  Phone: 570-577-1101
  Fax: 570-577-3538
  E-mail: ipcogan@bucknell.edu
  Web site: http://www.bucknell.edu/
- **Private, comprehensive, university**
- **Small-town/rural setting**
- **Enrollment: 3,450**
- **Student-faculty ratio: 11:1**
- **2006–07 Tuition and fees: $36,002**
- **2006–07 Room and board: $7366**

- **International students: 3% foreign national; 7%, including permanent residents and dual citizens**
- **Countries represented: 55**
- **International students applied: 375**
- **International students accepted: 63**
- **International students enrolled: 24**
- **Admissions tests:**
  - **TOEFL: Required (min. score 550 PBT; 213 CBT; 79–80 iBT)**
  - **SAT or ACT: Required**
- **Application deadline: January 1**
- **On-campus housing: Guaranteed 4 years**
- **Summer housing: Available**

Area and Climate

Bucknell students can quickly walk from the campus to downtown Lewisburg, a small, historical town about 60 miles (97 kilometers) north of the state capital of Harrisburg. Bucknell is located within a 3- to 4-hour drive of New York City; Washington, D.C.; Baltimore; Philadelphia; and Pittsburgh. The University sponsors several bus trips to these cities throughout the year. Students experience all four seasons at Bucknell. The spring and fall seasons have mild weather, while the summers can be warm and humid, with average temperatures ranging from 75°F (24°C) to 85°F (30°C). Winters are fairly cold, with temperatures dropping to 25°F (-4°C) to 40°F (4°C) or lower.

Education

Founded in 1846, Bucknell focuses its attention on undergraduate students. The University offers more than fifty majors and sixty minors, ranging from the traditional liberal arts courses to professional programs in engineering, premedicine, education, business, and music and leading to Bachelor of Arts and Bachelor of Science degrees. Half of the classes at Bucknell have 17 students or fewer, which creates a highly personal learning environment. Professors work closely with students, often helping them with special research projects. Students have access to outstanding resources and facilities, including the Writing Center, several computer labs, a comprehensive observatory, and a number of high-tech laboratories with precision instrumentation like lasers and electron scanning microscopes.

Campus Life

Bucknell's student body includes students from varied backgrounds, representing most states and fifty-five countries. With more than 150 clubs and organizations, Bucknell offers an outstanding array of choice in a strong community environment. Students can be leaders in student government, pursue artistic or musical interests, participate in athletics, perform community service, join fraternities or sororities, write for the campus newspaper, and enjoy performances and lectures by world-famous musicians and scholars such as Itzhak Perlman and Toni Morrison.

For International Students

The staff of International Student Services works closely with students to help them adjust to life in the United States, both on the campus and in the local community. The office provides international orientation, advising, academic and social support, and social and educational programming. In addition, Immigration Services provides up-to-date information regarding immigration regulations and offers individual assistance. New international students are welcomed to Bucknell by participating in a three-day international student orientation. Students are introduced to many of Bucknell's people, resources, programs, and facilities, including the Writing Center, Student Health Services, the library, the Conversation Partners Program, and the host family program, while connecting with new friends and having fun. International students are involved in activities across campus, ranging from student government to athletics to community service. If students are interested, Bucknell has more than 18 clubs that offer opportunities for them to share their home cultures and learn about other cultures. International and U.S. students come together in these organizations to plan events such as film nights, dinners, speakers, holiday celebrations, and trips.

Bunker Hill Community College

- **Contact:**
  International Center
  Bunker Hill Community College
  250 New Rutherford Avenue
  Boston, MA 02129-2925
  Phone: 617-228-2460
  Fax: 617-228-2442
  E-mail: international@bhcc.mass.edu
  Web site: http://www.bhcc.mass.edu
- Public, two-year, coed
- Urban setting
- Enrollment: 8,200
- Student-faculty ratio: 19:1
- 2006–07 Tuition and fees: $7732

- International students: 7.5%
- Countries represented: 94
- International students applied: 739
- International students accepted: 595
- Admissions tests:
  - **TOEFL:** Required (min. score 423 PBT; 113 CBT; 38 iBT, with minimum of 15 on writing session)
  - **SAT or ACT:** Not required
- Application deadline: Fall, 7/15; spring, 11/30; summer, 4/15
- On-campus housing: None

Area and Climate

Bunker Hill Community College (BHCC) is located in Boston, Massachusetts, the cultural and historical capital of New England. The school is located within minutes of downtown Boston and the city's many cultural, historical, entertainment, and athletic centers. An extensive transportation system makes it easy to get around the city. Boston has the largest number of colleges, universities, and medical centers of any city in the United States, and there are more international students in Boston than in any other city in the world. Boston has four distinct seasons, which allows students to ski in the winter and have fun on the beach and the Charles River in the summer. Temperatures range from 85°F (29°C) to 0°F (-18°C).

Education

Founded in 1973, BHCC is one of the most cosmopolitan colleges in New England. It offers nineteen Associate in Arts degree programs so students can complete the first two years of college and transfer to four-year colleges and universities throughout the country. BHCC also offers twenty-eight Associate in Science degree programs and twenty-five certificate programs that prepare students for employment. BHCC is internationally recognized for the development of individualized methods of instruction and is a leader in the application of computer-based methodologies that enhance the learning environment. It has the largest English as a second language program in Massachusetts, with many levels of instruction available. In 2005, BHCC was selected by the Ford Foundation to receive a Difficult Dialogues grant to address campus issues pertaining to race, social class, and power, joining Northeastern University, Yale University, and the University of Michigan as one of the twenty-seven recipients from an initial pool of 675 applicants nationwide. Also in 2005, BHCC ranked among the top forty community colleges in the nation for international student enrollment.

Campus Life

More than 600 students from ninety-four countries are currently enrolled at BHCC, and all report a high level of satisfaction with their experience. The College incorporates international and multicultural perspectives in its courses, programs, and institutional climate, and one of the school's goals is global learning. BHCC was honored with the 2003 Charles Kennedy Equity Award by the Associate of Community College Trustees for its commitment to women and people of color. Student organizations offer many opportunities for students to get involved on campus. International students regularly participate in student government, the Honor Society, athletics, cultural events, and more than twenty-five clubs.

For International Students

International students enjoy the exciting city of Boston, which is the home of many outstanding academic institutions to which they can transfer after graduation. They appreciate the smaller classes, individualized attention, low cost, and international environment of BHCC, where they can easily get involved in campus life and make lifelong friends. The International Center provides orientation programs and assists in obtaining host families and off-campus housing. International student advisers help students adjust to college life in the United States and provide counseling on immigration, academic, and personal concerns. They also provide assistance with transferring to four-year colleges and obtaining employment after graduation.

Butler University

- **Contact:**
  Office of International Admission
  Butler University
  4600 Sunset Avenue
  Indianapolis, IN 46208-3485
  Phone: 317-940-8100
  888-940-8100 (toll-free)
  Fax: 317-940-8150
  E-mail: intadmission@butler.edu
  Web site: http://www.butler.edu/admissions
- Private, coed
- Urban setting
- Enrollment: 4,384
- Student-faculty ratio: 14:1
- 2006–07 Tuition and fees: $24,710, undergraduate; $26,670, preprofessional pharmacy; $29,580, sixth-year pharmacy; $26,670, physician assistant program; $29,990, fifth-year physician assistant program.
- 2006–07 Room and board: $8316 (for average double room and 21-meal plan)
- Admissions tests:
  - TOEFL: Required (min. score 550 paper-based; 213 computer-based; 79 Internet-based))
  - SAT or ACT: Recommended
- Application deadlines: 7/1 (fall), 11/1 (spring)
- On-campus housing: Guaranteed
- Summer housing: Available

Area and Climate

Indianapolis, the capital of Indiana, is the twelfth-largest city in the United States, with a population of more than 1.6 million. The city is famous for the internationally known Indianapolis 500 auto racing event and Formula 1 races. Indianapolis has also become an international center for amateur athletics, hosting more than 360 national and international competitions. Indianapolis enjoys four distinct seasons. Pleasant springs are followed by warm, and sometimes humid, summers. The autumn foliage is lovely and usually lasts well into October and sometimes November. Winters can be cold, with snowfalls of 3 inches (8 centimeters) or more a few times annually.

Education

Founded in 1855, Butler University has a total enrollment representing many countries from around the world and nearly every state in the United States. Butler students commonly identify the University's strengths as academic excellence, personal attention from faculty members, a wide range of academic programs, high-quality facilities, and proven preparation for graduate school and career. Butler offers more than sixty areas of study in business, education, fine arts, liberal arts and sciences, and pharmacy and health sciences, including the AACSB-accredited business program and the ABET-accredited engineering dual-degree program with Purdue University in Indianapolis. Butler is fully accredited by the North Central Association of Colleges and Secondary Schools.

Campus Life

The majority of Butler students live on campus. Housing options include an apartment-style residence hall, a service-learning house, one all-women and two coeducational learning residence halls with optional living-learning centers, and fraternities and sororities. An upperclassman residential apartment village with a centrally located communal complex opened in fall 2006. Students can take advantage of more than 100 different student organizations, including student government; intramural sports; NCAA Division I varsity athletics; social, religious, and volunteer organizations; service clubs; honorary societies; and performance groups.

For International Students

Butler is committed to enriching and expanding its international community. The University provides comprehensive services from application to graduation, including academic advising, personal and immigration counseling, and career planning. The Office of Admission guides students from their first contact with Butler University through the completion of the application and admission process. The Office of International Student Services ensures that international students become active participants in the life of the University and the community. They provide services and programs such as airport pickup, welcome orientation, an international unit of housing in Residential College, an international club, and the Friendship Family Program.

California College of the Arts

- Contact:
  Robynne Royster
  Director of Undergraduate Admissions
  California College of the Arts
  1111 Eighth Street
  San Francisco, CA 94107-2247
  Phone: 415-703-9523
  Fax: 415-703-9539
  E-mail: enroll@cca.edu
  Web site: http://www.cca.edu
- Private, coed, visual arts
- Urban setting
- Enrollment: 1,600
- Student-faculty ratio: 18:1
- 2006–07 Tuition and fees: $27,914

- 2006–07 Room and board: $8935
- International students: 7%
- Countries represented: 25
- International students applied: 213
- International students accepted: 132
- International students enrolled: 28
- Admissions tests:
  - TOEFL: Recommended (min. score 79 iBT; 213 CBT; 550 PBT)
  - SAT and ACT: Not required
- Application deadline: Rolling (2/1 priority)
- On-campus housing: Guaranteed
- Summer housing: Not available

Area and Climate

California College of the Arts (CCA) is located in the San Francisco Bay Area, a region known for creative and technological innovation and a thriving art and design community. There are hundreds of arts venues, including major museums, galleries, and theaters. The natural environment is also an artistic inspiration. Within minutes of urban areas are many recreational opportunities, including beaches and hiking/biking trails. This area is known for its year-round mild climate. The Monterey Peninsula, Lake Tahoe, Sierra skiing, and Yosemite are all within a half-day's drive. Public transportation is easily accessible between Oakland and San Francisco.

Education

Founded in 1907, CCA is the largest regionally accredited, independent school of art and design in the western United States. It has campuses in Oakland and San Francisco and a faculty of 450 noted artists and scholars. Known for its interdisciplinary emphasis and outstanding facilities, CCA offers twenty undergraduate and seven graduate majors. CCA grants the B.F.A. in animation (new in 2007), ceramics, community arts, fashion design, glass, graphic design, illustration, industrial design, interior design, jewelry/metal arts, media arts, painting/drawing, photography, printmaking, sculpture, textiles, and wood/furniture. The B.A. is granted in visual studies and writing and literature. The B.Arch. is granted in architecture. The fine arts, B.A., and first-year programs are based in Oakland; architecture and design programs are in San Francisco. The college runs on the semester system. In addition to studio courses, CCA offers a broad liberal arts curriculum.

Campus Life

In Oakland, CCA has a historic 4-acre campus in a residential area, adjacent to an attractive shopping district and 3 miles from the University of California, Berkeley. The Oakland campus offers traditional college atmosphere with housing in Clifton Hall, where 75 percent of first-time freshmen choose to live, and CCA-owned apartments. Housing is also available at Webster Hall in downtown Oakland, 2½ miles from campus. All residences have kitchens. Housing is guaranteed for international students, but students are not required to live on campus. The San Francisco campus is in the Mission Bay area, near the design district and downtown museums and galleries. CCA runs a shuttle between the campuses and residence halls. Campus life includes exhibitions at the Wattis Institute for Contemporary Arts, talks by visiting artists, service learning opportunities through the Center for Art and Public Life, and a thriving undergraduate exhibition program.

For International Students

CCA is home to artists from across the U.S. and around the world. An international admissions counselor is available to prospective students by phone, fax, or e-mail. There is a special orientation meeting for international students before classes begin. An international student adviser provides ongoing guidance. CCA offers a special writing skills workshop for nonnative English speakers. For students who need to improve their English skills before they enroll, CCA has a partnership with ELS Language Centers (http://www.els.com). Students may fulfill CCA's language requirement by completing ELS level 112 instead of achieving a 79 (Internet-based), 213 (computer-based), or 550 (paper-based) TOEFL score. CCA issues conditional letters of acceptance to ELS students who meet all other undergraduate admissions requirements.

Calvin College

- **Contact:**
  Rosemary Etter
  Assistant Director of Admissions
  Calvin College
  3201 Burton, SE
  Grand Rapids, MI 49546
  Phone: 616-526-6106
  Fax: 616-526-6777
  E-mail: intladm@calvin.edu
  Web site: http://www.calvin.edu/international
- **Private, coed**
- **Suburban setting**
- **Enrollment: 4,199**
- **Student-faculty ratio: 12:1**

- **2006–07 Tuition and fees: $20,470**
- **2006–07 Room and board: $7040**
- **International students: 9%**
- **Countries represented: 49**
- **International students applied: 202**
- **International students accepted: 71**
- **International students enrolled: 39**
- **Admissions tests:**
  - **TOEFL (min. score 550)**
  - **SAT or ACT: Required**
- **Application deadline: June 1 (check Web site)**
- **On-campus housing: Guaranteed**
- **Summer housing: Available**

Area and Climate

Calvin College's modern campus is set amidst a sprawling, beautifully landscaped 390 acres (158 hectares) in a safe residential area in Michigan's second-largest city. Grand Rapids is within 3 hours of Chicago and Detroit. This location provides students the cultural offerings of a large city as well as access to many beaches of Lake Michigan. Calvin is within 20 minutes of the Gerald R. Ford International Airport and bus and train stations. The campus is within walking distance of three shopping malls, numerous movie theaters, and restaurants. The climate is seasonal, with warm summers and cold, snowy winters.

Education

Established in 1876, Calvin College is one of North America's oldest and largest Christian liberal arts colleges, offering nearly 100 academic options to 4,200 undergraduate students. The careful integration of faith and learning in each classroom is a hallmark of a Calvin education. Calvin College is accredited by the Commission on Institutions of Higher Education of the North Central Association of Colleges and Schools and also offers accredited programs in chemistry, computer science, engineering, music, nursing, social work, and teacher education. Calvin offers extensive academic programs in addition to internships, off-campus programs, and a variety of summer courses.

Outstanding campus facilities and resources are comparable to large universities, but personalized attention by professors is maintained in small classrooms, with a 12:1 student-faculty ratio. Computer facilities with Internet access are available to all students as is an extensive library with holdings of more than 700,000 volumes. An award-winning lecture series is held during the January Interim term.

Campus Life

Calvin students come from nearly every state and forty-nine countries. On-campus housing is guaranteed to international students throughout the year. Calvin students are involved in more than fifty student organizations and clubs, some of them especially for international students. Plays, concerts, films, dances, and sports provide an enriching social and cultural experience. An new athletic facility includes an arena, gymnasiums, swimming pool, indoor track and tennis courts, and a new fitness center. Faith, learning, and living are all integrated at Calvin College in a community that encourages academic excellence, spiritual maturity, and personal responsibility.

For International Students

International students at Calvin enjoy many levels of support. An international admissions coordinator assists with inquiries and correspondence through the application process, and the international student adviser serves students once they are on campus. Monthly meetings, dinners, and other programs for international students occur throughout the year. Professors are very accessible and provide academic advice and assistance to all students. Free tutoring is provided if requested and with the approval of the professor. Residence hall staff members help international students become acclimated to the friendly on-campus community.

The Catholic University of America

- **Contact:**
  Office of Admissions
  The Catholic University of America
  Washington, D.C. 20064
  Phone: 202-319-5305
  Fax: 202-319-6533
  E-mail: cua-admissions@cua.edu
  Web site: http://www.cua.edu
- **Private, coed**
- **Urban setting**
- **Enrollment: 3,200**
- **Student-faculty ratio: 8:1**
- **2007–08 Tuition and fees: $27,700**
- **2007–08 Room and board: $15,000**

- **International students: 6%**
- **Countries represented: 96**
- **International students enrolled: 370**
- **Admissions tests:**
  - **TOEFL: Required (min. score 550 paper-based, 213 CBT, 80 iBT with 20 in each category)**
  - **SAT or ACT: Not required if submitting TOEFL**
- **Application deadline: 2/15**
- **On-campus housing: Available for freshmen and sophomores**
- **Summer housing: Available**

Area and Climate

Catholic University of America (CUA) students enjoy the best of both worlds: a beautiful residential campus in a vibrant city. Located in the capital of the United States, CUA's 193-acre (78-hectare) landscaped campus provides the perfect combination of university and city life. Student life is enriched by a city famous for its monuments, museums, theaters, libraries, and research centers—all just minutes away via the Metro, a modern subway system that stops on the CUA campus. Home of the Cherry Blossom Festival, D.C. enjoys a mild climate in the spring and fall in addition to white winters and hot summers, with temperatures averaging 30°F (–1°C) and 85°F (29°C), respectively.

Education

CUA offers undergraduate degrees in more than seventy major areas of study in its six schools: Arts and Sciences, Architecture, Engineering, Music, Nursing, and Philosophy. With more than 360 full-time professors, students enjoy small classes and personal attention. Qualified students can take advantage of CUA's accelerated bachelor's/master's program, which takes four years to complete. CUA also offers a 3-3 law program in which a student receives a bachelor's degree and a law degree in six years. Students are invited to participate in the Honors Program. CUA provides exciting and challenging internship and research opportunities in all majors. The fall semester begins the last week of August, the spring semester begins the second week of January, and summer terms begin the second week of May.

Campus Life

CUA campus living fosters a sense of community and supports personal development. Students from all fifty states and more than ninety-six different countries live together in eighteen residence halls. Students traditionally live in double-occupancy rooms and are matched up through a questionnaire. CUA has more than 100 student organizations. Each fall, a campus fair informs students about services and social activities—from the Centerstage Theater Company to the International Students Association to the Ski Club. Students publish their own newspaper and yearbook and operate the WCUA radio station. There is something for everyone at CUA.

For International Students

The full-time staff members of the Office of International Student and Scholar Services (ISSS) are always available and sponsor many educational programs on campus. The office also holds potlucks, dinners, and special international student nights and seminars for all students to enjoy and learn from.

Centralia College

- **Contact:**
  International Programs/Dept. C
  Centralia College
  600 West Locust
  Centralia, WA 98531-4099
  Phone: 360-736-9391 Ext. 492
  Fax: 360-330-7503
  E-mail: intl@centralia.edu
  Web site: http://www.centralia.ctc.edu/
- **Public, 2-year, coed**
- **Small-town setting**
- **Enrollment: 3,862**
- **Student-faculty ratio: 24:1 (12:1 ESL)**

- **2006–07 Tuition and fees: $8042**
- **2006–07 Room and board: $4500 (approx.)**
- **International students: 1%**
- **Countries represented: 8**
- **International students applied: 81**
- **International students accepted: 78**
- **Admissions tests:**
  - **TOEFL: Not required**
  - **SAT and ACT: Not required**
- **Application deadline: 3/1; 5/1; 8/1; 12/1**
- **On-campus housing: Available**

Area and Climate

The Centralia area is a safe, friendly community of approximately 25,000 people. Located 24 miles (39 kilometers) south of the Washington State capital city of Olympia, the College is within 87 miles (140 kilometers) of the larger cities of Seattle, Washington, and Portland, Oregon. Centralia is nestled in the mild climate of the beautiful Pacific Northwest within a short distance of the majestic Cascade Mountains, spectacular Pacific Ocean beaches, golf courses, tennis courts, and outstanding ski resorts. Various recreational activities near Centralia include fishing, horseback riding, cultural events, regional shopping areas, and hiking. City transit, comfortable train service, and bus transportation are available.

Education

Founded in 1925, Centralia College leads community college education in Washington State with a mission to develop individual student potential. Comprehensive programs responsive to technological, economic, and social change are offered. Many Centralia College programs have won national awards. The latest computer technology is available to students. Numerous faculty members have earned national honors. Centralia College operates on the quarter system with classes beginning in mid-September; quarters are usually eleven weeks long. Average class size is 24, and ESL classes are much smaller. Transferable programs in forty-four disciplines and twenty-three technical programs are offered.

Campus Life

Centralia College is small, informal, and friendly, with nearly 4,000 students. Ethnic groups represent 6 percent of the student population. Currently, there are 29 international students representing eight countries. Two international houses are located near the College. Host families are available to students seeking an American family experience. Summer housing in international houses, apartments, or with host families is available with notice. Student government provides participation in various organizations and diverse areas of interest such as journalism, drama, nursing, technical areas, business, and intercollegiate sports for men and women. Previous Centralia College graduates hold prominent positions of leadership in government, performing arts, business, and international organizations.

For International Students

Centralia College provides a full-time director and specialist as well as immigration advising, personal support, academic assistance, and housing services. The ESL program provides a smooth transition to college-level classes. Tutors are available upon request. Orientation is required for all international students. Faculty advisers and the International Programs Director ensure that students have the maximum opportunity to succeed. Personable, caring faculty and staff members provide special attention to the needs of international students. Safety is a high priority, and the crime rate is low in Centralia. The College community embraces international students with interest, care, and specialized attention.

Central Michigan University

- **Contact:**
  International Admissions
  Bovee UC 106
  Central Michigan University
  Mount Pleasant, MI 48859

  Phone: 989-774-4308
  Fax: 989-774-3690
  E-mail: intlapp@cmich.edu
  Web site: http://www.cmich.edu
- Public, comprehensive, coed
- Small-town setting
- Enrollment: 20,025
- Student-faculty ratio: 22:1
- 2006–07 Tuition and fees: $14,016

- 2006–07 Room and board: $6824 (nine months)
- International students: 2%
- Countries represented: 70
- International students applied: 632
- International students accepted: 355
- International students enrolled: 157
- Admissions tests:
  - TOEFL Required (min. score 550)
  - SAT and ACT: Not required
- Application deadline: Fall, 5/1; spring, 10/1
- On-campus housing: Guaranteed
- Summer housing: Available

Area and Climate

Central Michigan University (CMU) is located in Mount Pleasant, a small town in central Michigan with a population of 28,000. The campus is bordered by both the residential and business communities. Most businesses and restaurants are within walking distance of the campus. Normal temperatures in January range from 10°F (-12°C) to 32°F (0°C); normal July temperatures range from 73°F (23°C) to 90°F (32°C). The area has an abundance of woodlands and farms and is located near many lakes and rivers.

Education

CMU, which was founded in 1892, is committed to educating students for success in a competitive global market and producing graduates who are conscious of their role in a changing society. Seven colleges offer more than fifty academic majors, with many offering specific concentrations. Business administration, computer science, teacher education, biology, music, and engineering technology are some of the more popular areas of study. CMU's English Language Institute offers all levels of English language courses. Campus facilities include new buildings for the natural sciences, industrial and engineering technology, performing arts, business administration, and health professions, in addition to a state-of-the-art library. At the heart of CMU's success is an outstanding faculty. Students often have the opportunity to present at conferences, do research, and obtain valuable internship experiences. The academic calendar is 4-4-1-1, with a fall semester from August to December and a spring semester from January to early May. The summer sessions are intensive one- or two-course sessions that are suited for first-time students attending the English Language Institute; however, due to

the limited class selection, this is not an ideal time for freshmen or transfer students to begin.

Campus Life

CMU's student body comes from all over Michigan, twenty-four states, and seventy countries. This wide diversity of backgrounds enriches the experience of the CMU student through the availability of cultural activities and multicultural student organizations. Approximately 6,500 of CMU's students live in on-campus residence halls or apartments. Rooms are typically 4-person suites with two bedrooms, a study room, and a bathroom. One residence hall remains open during holidays and spring break. The campus atmosphere is very friendly, and there are more than 200 campus organizations. The CMU International Club is very active, and programs such as International Night and International Expo have become a regular part of the University calendar. CMU's Student Activity Center also has one of the top fitness centers in the Midwest.

For International Students

The Office of International Education is a central point for CMU's 450 international students. There are full-time international student advisers and a support staff available. The Friendship Family Program is also available. Airport pick-ups are available for new students from Capital City Airport in Lansing, Michigan, or MBS International Airport in Freeland, Michigan. One week before the beginning of the fall and spring semesters, a required orientation session that includes cultural adjustment, immigration information, academic advising, and social activities is held for new international students. Career planning and placement, academic advising, academic assistance, and health services are also available on campus. International students must be enrolled full-time during the fall and spring semesters, and they are eligible to work part-time on campus.

Chapman University

- **Contact:**
  Ms. Seaby Rodriguez
  International Admission Officer
  Chapman University
  Orange, CA 92866
  Phone: 714-997-6711
  Fax: 714-997-6713
  E-mail: admit@chapman.edu
  Web site: http://www.chapman.edu
- Private, comprehensive, coed
- Suburban setting
- Enrollment: 6,000
- Student-faculty ratio: 16:1
- 2007–08 Tuition and fees: $32,622

- 2007–08 Room and board: $10,616
- International students: 6%
- Countries represented: 40
- International students applied: 162
- International students accepted: 69
- International students enrolled: 40
- Admissions tests:
  - TOEFL (min. score 550)
  - SAT or ACT: Required
- Application deadline: Fall, 1/15; spring, 11/30
- On-campus housing: Available
- Summer housing: Not available

Area and Climate

Chapman University is located in the city of Orange, in the heart of Orange County, which *Places Rated Almanac* calls the best place to live in the United States. West Coast beaches, such as Laguna Beach, Newport Beach, and Huntington Beach, are only minutes away. Orange County is home to several major attractions, including Disneyland, Knott's Berry Farm, Angel Stadium, Honda Center, and Orange County Performance Arts Center, most of which are located within a 15-minute drive of the University.

Education

Chapman is a nationally recognized, comprehensive university with a 146-year history that offers professional and liberal arts programs. The University's mission is "to provide a personalized education of distinction that leads to inquiring, ethical, and productive lives as global citizens." The strength of that mission is evident in the success of the University and its students. It is fully accredited by the Western Association of Schools and Colleges, and individual programs are accredited by the Institute of Food Technologists (the food science program), the National Association of Schools of Music (the music programs), the American Physical Therapy Association (the physical therapy program), the American Bar Association (the Law School), and AACSB International (the School of Business and Economics). Chapman is listed on the Templeton Honor Roll for character-building colleges, and *U.S. News & World Report* ranks it in the top tier of Western universities.

Campus Life

A student's personal growth is not limited to the classroom. The programs offered by Chapman's proactive student life professionals include faculty academic advising, career counseling and placement, community outreach and multicultural programs, dining services, student health and counseling, residential life, international programs, peer and health education, campus safety, student activities and organizations, and an orientation program. With more than eighty clubs and organizations, there is something for everyone. Students have the opportunity to participate in a full range of extracurricular activities, such as the international club, drama productions, academic clubs, vocal and instrumental music groups, intercollegiate and intramural athletics, the Artist-Lecture Series, and the Great Films Guild.

For International Students

The need to understand people from other cultures becomes increasingly essential in today's world. An international experience offers students the unique opportunity for immersion in another culture and country. It is also a time for adventure—to meet new people, see new things, observe different customs, eat exotic foods, and travel to exciting places.

Chapman's international students represent more than forty countries and add to the quality of life in the community. They represent a wealth of knowledge that other students cannot learn from textbooks. International students can be a part of many things while at Chapman, from listening to lectures by former President George H. Bush on cold war studies and Robert Zemekis on film directing to participating in the lu'au sponsored by the Hawaiian Club and tae kwon do by the Korean Club.

City College of San Francisco

- **Contact:**
  International Admissions
  City College of San Francisco
  50 Phelan Avenue
  San Francisco, CA 94112
  Phone: 415-239-3895
  Fax: 415-239-3804
  E-mail: international@ccsf.edu
  Web site: http://www.ccsf.edu
- Public, two-year, coed
- Urban setting
- Enrollment: 39,000 academic program, 100,000 all programs
- Student-faculty ratio: 27:1
- 2006–07 Tuition and fees: $4300 (est.)
- 2006–07 Room and board: $18,000 (est.)
- International students: 3%

- Countries represented: 85+
- International students applied: 600
- International students accepted: 500
- International students enrolled: 1,200 (total)
- Admissions tests:
  - TOEFL: TOEFL (min. score 473 PBT; 152 CBT; 52 iBT)
  - IELTS: (min. score 4.5)
  - SAT and ACT: Not required
- Application deadline: Fall: May 15; Spring: November 2
- On-campus housing: Not available; referrals to homestays and residential clubs available
- Summer housing: Available; limited off-campus, by special arrangement

Area and Climate

City College of San Francisco is located in the world-famous city of San Francisco, an important financial and international business center. The San Francisco Bay Area has a population of more than 3 million. Spectacular bridges, including the magnificent Golden Gate, connect San Francisco with the university city of Berkeley to the east and the Napa Valley wine region to the north. Outstanding wilderness areas are less than a half hour away. San Francisco is cooled in the summer by ocean breezes and stays relatively warm in the winter. The campus is easily reached by major transportation lines.

Education

City College of San Francisco (CCSF), established in 1935, serves more than 38,000 students in its academic programs. Accredited by the Western Association of Schools and Colleges (WASC), the College offers an extensive curriculum through its University Transfer Program and its Semiprofessional/Career Programs. Articulation agreements enable qualified students to successfully transfer to the University of California or the California State University system as well as numerous other private and public institutions across the United States. The top four transfer institutions for CCSF are UC Berkeley, San Francisco State University, San Jose State University, and UC Davis. Academic counselors, a Transfer Center, and a Career Development and Placement Center help students make informed choices. A Learning Assistance Center provides one-on-one tutoring. The academic calendar includes fall and spring semesters and a summer session.

Campus Life

The College community reflects the diversity of San Francisco with its wide range of racial, ethnic, and national groups. There is an active student government with more than fifty-six clubs and organizations. The library and learning resources building contains more than 80,000 volumes, 650 periodicals, and 300 computers. An on-campus cafeteria is available when classes are in session. The new Student Health Office gives first aid and emergency care to students, and a part-time physician is available by appointment. A new athletic facility, with indoor basketball and volleyball courts, a fitness room, and a swimming pool, is scheduled to open in 2008. Athletic fields for soccer, baseball, and track as well as several tennis courts are also available. The College also has a theater and horticulture center. An art film series, lecture and concert series, and performances in music, dance, and theater art are available. There is also a student-run newspaper, *The Guardsman*.

For International Students

In its academic program, City College of San Francisco serves more than 1,200 international students from more than eighty-five countries. In July and December, the international student staff offers a comprehensive orientation and counseling sessions and assistance with registration for new students. The staff includes a Support Services Coordinator for International Students ready to provide support and assistance to new and returning students. All students are invited to participate in campus activities. City College also offers an intensive English language program to prepare students to become effective and confident speakers of English in American academic institutions. The program provides TOEFL preparation. Students may call 415-239-3895 for more information or go to the College's Web site (http://www.ccsf.edu/international).

City University

- Contact:
    Sabine Csecsinovics
    Director, International Admissions
    City University
    11900 Northeast First Street
    Bellevue, WA 98005

    Phone: 425-709-5315
    Fax: 425-709-5319
    E-mail: internatladmissions@cityu.edu
    Web site: http://www.cityu.edu
- Private, not-for-profit, coed

- Suburban/urban setting
- Enrollment: 9,803
- Student-faculty ratio: 18:1
- 2005–06 Tuition and fees: $14,388
- Countries represented: 40
- Application deadline: Rolling (Fall, September 1; winter, December 1; spring, March 1; summer, June 1)
- On-campus housing: Not available

Area and Climate

City University's largest site in the Greater Seattle area is located in Bellevue, in the heart of the Pacific Northwest. The Pacific Northwest is well known for its natural beauty, safe and clean environment, and world-class companies. The region's cultural diversity and the University's cosmopolitan location make City University an ideal location to live and learn. Bellevue is located on Seattle's Eastside, on the shores of beautiful Lake Washington, and framed by Mount Rainier and the Cascade mountains.

Seattle's climate varies seasonally: October to April temperatures range from 40 to 55°F (4–13°C) with many days of rainfall; May through September temperatures range from 55 to 100°F (13–38°C). Students are advised to bring both lightweight and heavy clothing as well as rain apparel. Informal and comfortable clothing is practical for everyday occasions. Campus dress is casual.

Education

City University, founded in 1973, is a fully accredited, private, not-for-profit institution of higher learning. The University's mission is to change lives for good by offering high-quality and relevant lifelong education to anyone with the desire to learn. The mission is based on three philosophical principles: education is a lifelong process and must be relevant to the student's aspirations; education should be affordable and offered, as much as possible, at the student's convenience; and the opportunity to learn should be open to anyone with the desire to achieve.

All of City University's programs are taught in English. To assist international students, City University offers an English as a second language program as well as a Language Assisted Master of Business Administration (M.B.A.) Program in addition to its regular bachelor's and master's degree programs.

Campus Life

City University campuses are conveniently located throughout the Greater Seattle area. Locations are easy to access with ample housing available within the vicinity of the campus. The Bellevue campus houses the International Student Office, library, and computer lab. Since City University offers programs in Bulgaria, Canada, China, the Czech Republic, Greece, Mexico, Romania, Slovakia, and the United States, almost all student resources, including library services, are available online. Upon arrival, international students participate in an orientation that specifically addresses such concerns as immigration issues, health insurance, and class registration.

For International Students

City University's faculty and staff members are committed to providing one-on-one assistance to international students in all aspects of their student life, including academic and immigration advising, application assistance, orientation, prearrival and housing information, and student activities.

Applications are continuously accepted throughout the year. In most programs, students may start their studies in any quarter. Students at all levels of English are welcome to apply.

Clarion University of Pennsylvania

- **Contact:**
  Ms. Linda Heineman
  Office of Int'l Programs
  Clarion University of Pennsylvania
  Clarion, PA 16214
  Phone: 814-393-2340
  Fax: 814-393-2341
  E-mail: intlprograms@clarion.edu
  Web site: http://www.clarion.edu
- **Public coed**
- **Rural setting**
- **Enrollment: 6,591**

- **Student-faculty ratio: 20:1**
- **2006–07 Tuition and fees: $14,450**
- **2006–07 Room and board: $6546**
- **International students: 1%**
- **Countries represented: 40**
- **Admissions tests:**
  - **TOEFL: Required (min. score 500 PBT)**
  - **SAT or ACT: Not required**
- **Application deadline: Rolling**
- **On-campus housing: Available**
- **Summer housing: Available**

Area and Climate

Clarion University of Pennsylvania is located in north-western Pennsylvania, just off Interstate 80, an easy 2-hour drive from Erie and Pittsburgh. The peaceful, wooded countryside and surrounding hills offer a visually pleasing and serene atmosphere, most spectacular in autumn. Temperatures in the summer average 85°F (29°C) and in the winter, 20°F (-7°C), with pleasant fall and spring seasons. Within a few blocks of the Clarion campus are downtown Clarion and stores, restaurants, churches, pharmacies, a medical center, and all necessary services. A hospital, shopping mall, and several hotels are only 2 miles (3 kilometers) away.

Education

Clarion University, founded in 1867, is one of fourteen public institutions in the Pennsylvania State System of Higher Education. The University is committed to seeking excellence in all areas of higher education within its mission and to providing an environment that challenges students to develop their talents, to extend their intellectual capacities and interests, to expand their creative abilities, and to develop a life-long respect and enthusiasm for learning. To that end, the University offers more than ninety degree programs, including instructional programs at the associate, bachelor's, and master's levels within the Colleges of Arts & Sciences, Business Administration (accredited by AACSB International–The Association to Advance Collegiate Schools of Business), Education & Human Services, and Nursing. State-of-the-art facilities and computer technology are readily accessible to students. The fall semester begins in late August and ends in mid-December. The spring semester begins in mid-January and ends in mid-May.

Campus Life

Clarion University students come from thirty-five states and forty countries. Some choose to live on campus in one of six residence halls and take advantage of several meal plans that are available at the campus cafeteria or student center food court; others prefer to live off campus. Located very close to the campus is Reinhard Villages, offering apartments that were designed exclusively for students and provide comfortable, convenient, and carefree living. Students may choose from more than 120 organizations that include student government groups; honorary, media, speech, dramatic, and religious organizations; music performance groups; sororities and fraternities; and special interest clubs. The hub of on-campus activity is the Gemmell Student Center, which contains the University Bookstore, a convenience store, a food court, a student computer lab, the radio station, offices for campus organizations, and conference rooms of various sizes. Activity rooms include an aerobic dance studio, racquetball courts, a fitness area, and a game room. Many special events are scheduled throughout the year. Athletic opportunities include football, basketball, swimming and diving, wrestling, baseball, cross-country, track, tennis, volleyball, and golf.

For International Students

A full range of support services is provided by the Office of International Programs, including all matters related to immigration, employment requests, foreign exchange, and cultural adjustment. New students receive a weeklong orientation program before the fall semester begins. Students are encouraged to become members of the Clarion International Association, which helps build a friendly environment for all Clarion students and promotes good will and understanding among peoples and cultures. The association's activities include cultural enrichment programs, social events, and field trips to various attractions in the United States and Canada. Financial assistance in the form of partial tuition waivers is available to all international students. The international application is available on the University's Web site through the admissions home page (http://www.clarion.edu/admiss/apply.shtml). All inquiries are welcome.

Clarkson University

- **Contact:**
  Patricia Perrier
  Assistant Director of Undergraduate
      Admission
  Clarkson University
  8 Clarkson Avenue, Box 5610
  Potsdam, NY 13699-5610
  Phone: 315-268-2125
  Fax: 315-268-7647
  E-mail: intladmission@clarkson.edu
  Web site: http://www.clarkson.edu
- **Private, coed**
- **Rural/small-town setting**
- **Enrollment: 3,000**
- **Student-faculty ratio: 16:1**
- **2006–07 Tuition and fees: $26,650**
- **2006–07 Room and board: $9648**

- **International students: 2%**
- **Countries represented: 22**
- **International students applied: 252**
- **International students accepted: 72**
- **International students enrolled: 35**
- **Admissions tests:**
  - **Required: TOEFL (minimum score 213 CBT, 550 PBT, or 80 iBT) or IELTS (minimum score 6.5)**
  - **SAT or ACT: Required for first-year admission**
- **Application deadline: Fall (early decision), 12/1; spring, 3/1**
- **On-campus housing: Guaranteed**
- **Summer housing: Available**

Area and Climate

Clarkson University is located 149 miles (240 kilometers) north of Syracuse, New York, and 93 miles (150 kilometers) southwest of Montréal, Québec, Canada, in the picturesque town of Potsdam, New York. The campus is situated on 566 acres (229 hectares) of rolling woodland in the foothills of the Adirondack Mountains near the St. Lawrence River. The nearby Adirondack Park is a 6-million-acre (2.4-million-hectare) natural sanctuary offering world-class outdoor activities, such as skiing, hiking, boating, and fishing. Temperatures range from -18°F to 30°F (-26°C to 1°C) in January and from 70°F to 85°F (21°C to 30°C) in July.

Education

Clarkson stands out among America's private, nationally ranked research institutions because of its dynamic, collaborative learning environment, innovative degree and research programs, and unmatched track record for producing leaders and innovators. At Clarkson, some 3,000 high-ability undergraduate and graduate students thrive in rigorous programs in liberal arts, science, business, engineering, and health sciences. Students benefit from small classes, personal interaction with professors, and opportunities to participate in undergraduate research. Emphasis is placed on experiential learning. Students participate in group projects in the classroom and have the option of joining one of fifteen competitive design teams, such as the solar or mini-baja car teams, environmental remediation projects, and the concrete canoe team. Co-op

education and internships are available, and there is a highly competitive honors program. The academic calendar is on the semester system, with the fall semester starting in late August and the spring semester in mid-January. Two sessions of summer school are also offered.

Campus Life

The campus includes undergraduate students from thirty-four states and more than a dozen countries and features a culturally diverse faculty. Clarkson is a residential campus. First-year students are guaranteed housing and live in double rooms with a roommate. Students can bring or buy computers for use on the local network from their rooms or use those provided in numerous computer labs. Students associate not only with one another on campus but also with students from St. Lawrence University, State University of New York (SUNY) at Canton, and SUNY Potsdam. There are more than sixty professional, service, and social organizations on campus. Sports opportunities include twenty-one men's and women's intercollegiate teams and numerous intramural opportunities.

For International Students

International students receive support through the Office of the International Student Advisor and the Director of International Admission. This support includes advising, assistance with visa and immigration matters, and an orientation offered at the beginning of each semester. In addition, help is available from the writing center, computer center, academic support services center, academic advisers, or the career planning office. Tutoring on a group or individual basis is also available. Partial academic scholarships and part-time campus work-study are available on a competitive basis.

Colby-Sawyer College

- **Contact:**
  Kara Laing
  International Student Counselor
  Colby-Sawyer College
  541 Main Street
  New London, NH 03257
  Phone: 603-526-3700
  Fax: 603-526-3452
- **Private, coed**
- **Small-town setting**
- **Enrollment: 985**
- **Student-faculty ratio: 12:1**
- **2007–08 Tuition and fees: $27,910**
- **2007–08 Room and board: $9900**

- **International students: 1%**
- **Countries represented: 8**
- **International students applied: 57**
- **International students accepted: 23**
- **International students enrolled: 3**
- **Admissions tests:**
  - **TOEFL (paper-based min. score 500; computer-based min. score 173; Internet-based min. score 61)**
  - **SAT and ACT: Not required**
- **Application deadline: 5/1**
- **On-campus housing: Guaranteed**
- **Summer housing: Not available**

Area and Climate

Colby-Sawyer's 200-acre (81-hectare) campus is located in the picturesque and safe town of New London, New Hampshire. Since Boston is only 1½ hours south and Montreal 3½ hours north, students have access to major cities by College van or public bus. The seacoast at Portsmouth and the surrounding lakes, mountains, and state parks provide opportunities for outdoor activities such as hiking, swimming, sailing, canoeing, golfing, and Nordic and Alpine skiing. Arts and cultural opportunities can be found in New London as well as in nearby Manchester; Concord, the state capital; and Hanover, the home of Dartmouth College. Winter days are usually crisp and cold, with ample snow and temperatures ranging from 20°F to 40°F (-6°C to 4°C); summer temperatures range from 60°F to 90°F (15°C to 32°C).

Education

Colby-Sawyer College was founded in 1837 and provides programs of study that integrate the liberal arts and sciences with professional preparation. Bachelor's degrees are awarded in fourteen programs of study, with the highest enrollments in art, business administration, child development, nursing, psychology, and exercise and sport sciences. All students are encouraged to gain practical experiences through the internship program. Academic facilities include the newly constructed Curtis L. Ivey Science Center, the Susan Colgate Cleveland Library/Learning Center, several computer labs equipped with the latest applications, Mercer Hall, the Sawyer Fine Arts Center, and the Baker Communications Center, which houses the radio station and video studio. Colby-Sawyer offers individual Internet access and a comprehensive advising program, including academic support services. The College operates on a two-semester calendar.

Campus Life

Colby-Sawyer students come from all over the United States and six other countries, with 68 percent of the students coming from outside New Hampshire. Twelve residence halls accommodate all of the housing needs of the student body, including students participating in the English Language and American Culture Program. Colby-Sawyer is a friendly, accessible campus community where opportunities for student involvement and leadership abound. Campus activities include Student Government, Dance Club, Alpha Chi Honor Society, WSCS Colby-Sawyer Radio Station, Theatre Club, *The Courier* (student newspaper), community service, and the intercollegiate, club, and intramural athletic teams.

For International Students

Colby-Sawyer's English Language and American Culture Program assists students in improving their English language ability; in participating in the academic, cultural, and social life of Colby-Sawyer; and in understanding American culture. Orientation sessions for all new students are held in August. Upon arrival at Colby-Sawyer College, international students are given the Institutional TOEFL test. If needed, students may take an advanced ESL course while beginning regular classes in September. Health and counseling services and individualized tutorials in reading, writing, and study skills, as well as help with specific courses, are offered. Short-term homestays can be arranged for August, and students can be matched with local families for the academic year.

College of the Desert

- Contact:
  Christina M. Delgado
  Int'l Education Program Director
  College of the Desert
  43-500 Monterey Avenue
  Palm Desert, CA 92260
  Phone: 760-776-7205
  Fax: 760-862-1361
- Public, 2-year, coed
- Small-town setting
- Enrollment: 10,000
- Student-faculty ratio: 30:1
- 2006–07 Tuition and fees: $4970

- 2006–07 Room and board: $9000
- International students: 2%
- Countries represented: 38
- International students applied: 110
- International students accepted: 90
- Admissions tests:
  - TOEFL (min. score 32 iBT; 400 PBT; 97 CBT not required for Intensive English Academy)
- Application deadline: Fall, 7/15; spring, 12/15
- On-campus housing: Not available
- Summer housing: Not available

Area and Climate

College of the Desert (COD) is located in sunny southern California approximately 100 miles (161 kilometers) from Los Angeles. COD is 15 miles (24 kilometers) from the beautiful resort town of Palm Springs. This area attracts national and international cultural and athletic events throughout the year. Outdoor recreational activities are easily available due to the beautiful desert weather. The Living Desert and the Aerial Tramway are two of the many outdoor attractions in the area. Average temperatures from October to May are 75°F (24°C) to 80°F (27°C). As a small town, Palm Desert offers a safe and fun environment for study.

Education

College of the Desert is a public two-year community college dedicated to student success. Founded in 1958, COD has been providing students with fully accredited, nationally recognized academic programs for more than three decades. College of the Desert has more than eighty-five degree and certificate programs in areas such as architecture, business administration, computer science, hotel/restaurant management, liberal arts, and nursing. College services include faculty advising, university transfer assistance, and the use of the library, computer facilities, and the Academic Skills Center. Students are admitted for both the fall and spring semesters. In addition to the many academic programs, COD also offers the Intensive English Academy (IEA). The IEA is a 30-hour-per-week program of intensive English instruction. Courses are offered for both eight and sixteen weeks.

Campus Life

There are currently 10,000 students enrolled at College of the Desert. COD has a diverse student population and conducts many activities that reflect campus diversity. Currently, there are 220 international students from more than thirty-eight different countries enrolled in the College. The campus has a friendly atmosphere, and faculty and staff members are readily available to meet with students. There are many social clubs and organizations that students can join. In addition, there are events every month on campus, including the International Day celebration that is held each spring. Men's and women's athletic teams are very active on campus. Students are encouraged to get involved in all aspects of campus life.

For International Students

The International Student Office offers a range of support services to assist international students during their studies at College of the Desert. Upon arrival, students participate in the three-day Orientation Program, which assists students with immigration, cultural, housing, and registration questions. At that time, students meet their International Student Advisor, who is available for academic advising. The Housing Coordinator assists students with placement in the Host Family Program or in local apartments. There is an activities program that includes outings to southern California and local attractions. An International Student Tutor is available to assist students with their ESL needs. University transfer is a major reason why international students choose to study at a community college, and College of the Desert's International Student Counselor provides extensive services to assist in this process. Individual and group counseling sessions as well as a variety of transfer workshops help walk the student through the transfer process. The College is proud of its strong transfer rates to both the University of California and the California State University systems.

Colorado State University

- **Contact:**
  Office of Admissions
  Sprucc Hall
  1062 Campus Delivery
  Colorado State University
  Fort Collins, CO 80523-1062
  Phone: 970-491-6909
  Fax: 970-491-7799
  E-mail: admissions@colostate.edu
  Web site: http://admissions.colostate.edu/
  international
- **Public, coed**
- **Suburban setting**
- **Enrollment: 24,947**
- **Student-faculty ratio: 18:1**

- **2006–07 Tuition and fees: $16,359**
- **2006–07 Room, board, and miscellaneous: $9747**
- **International students: 3.3%**
- **Countries represented: 85**
- **International students applied: 1,385**
- **International students accepted: 529**
- **Admissions tests:**
  - **TOEFL (min. score 71 iBT, 525 PBT; 197 CBT)**
    IELTS (min. score 6)
- **Application deadline: Fall, 5/1; spring, 10/1**
- **On-campus housing: Guaranteed for freshmen**
- **Summer housing: Available**

Area and Climate

Colorado State University is located in Fort Collins, Colorado (population 134,000), 65 miles (104 kilometers) north of Denver. Shuttles run between Denver International Airport and various locations on or near the campus. The TransFort City Bus System offers free transportation for Colorado State University students. Average summer temperatures range from 82°F (28°C) to 52°F (11°C); winter temperatures, from 41°F (5°C) to 13°F (-10.5°C). Fort Collins has been nicknamed Colorado's "Choice City" for its blend of big-city advantages and small-town friendliness. This area is noted for its national parks, superb climate, and opportunities for camping, hiking, skiing, boating, and all that the majestic Rocky Mountains can offer.

Education

Colorado State is one of the top teaching and research institutions in the United States. Founded in 1870, Colorado State is a fully accredited public university recognized throughout the world for its excellence in academic programs from the baccalaureate to the postgraduate levels. The University is a premier undergraduate school for programs in the social and natural sciences, math, technology, engineering, business, and the arts and humanities, offering more than 150 programs of study in eight colleges. Each program is led by faculty members who are scholars on the cutting edge of their disciplines.

Campus Life

The enrolled students represent fifty states and eighty-five countries. On-campus housing is guaranteed for freshmen and is on a first-come, first-served basis for transfers. Summer housing on campus is available. University housing includes ten residence halls and several apartment complexes. More than 300 student clubs and organizations provide a variety of programs to meet the social, recreational, and academic needs of the diverse student population. All students have access to the sports facilities at the 100,000-square-foot (9,300-square-meter) Student Recreation Center. The campus atmosphere is student oriented and very friendly.

For International Students

An orientation prior to the beginning of the fall and spring semesters is required for international students. The Office of International Programs provides this service as well as immigration services, cross-cultural counseling, sponsored student services, and other support for international students and scholars. This office also coordinates many intercultural activities. Each November, more than thirty international student organizations sponsor International Week, celebrating cultural life around the world. The International Center and the International Friends help introduce international students to the community and promote friendships among students and local families. The Intensive English Program offers full-time English language instruction and a joint international student admissions program (GATEWAY) with the Office of Admissions. The Hartshorn Health Service is fully staffed and equipped to meet the health-care needs of students and dependents.

Columbia College

- Contact:
  Regina M. Morin
  Director of Admissions
  Columbia College
  Columbia, MO 65216
  Phone: 573-875-7352
  Fax: 573-875-7506
  E-mail: international@ccis.edu
  Web site: http://www.ccis.edu
- Private, comprehensive, coed
- Suburban setting
- Enrollment: 1037
- Student-faculty ratio: 14:1
- 2007–08 Tuition and fees: $13,034

- 2007–08 Room and board: $5320
- International students: 8%
- Countries represented: 27
- International students applied: 85
- International students accepted: 40
- International students enrolled: 25
- Admissions test:
  - TOEFL: Required (min. score 500 paper-based, 175 computer-based, 70 Web-based)
  - SAT or ACT: Recommended
- Application deadline: Rolling
- On-campus housing: Available
- Summer housing: Available

Area and Climate

Columbia College offers students an ideal blend of small-campus charm and big-city sophistication. The College is located in Columbia, Missouri, just a 2-hour drive from either St. Louis or Kansas City, Missouri. Both cities have international airports and shuttle services, making Columbia an easy destination. The city of Columbia is known as Collegetown U.S.A., because it is the home of 30,000 college students from three different higher-education institutions. With a population of 100,000 (including students), Columbia is consistently ranked in the top "Best Places to Live in the Nation" by *Money* magazine in its annual survey of the 300 largest metropolitan areas. Students enjoy the beauty of all four seasons—spring, summer, fall, and winter.

Education

Columbia College was founded in 1851 as the first women's college chartered by a state west of the Mississippi River. In 1970, the College became a coeducational, four-year liberal arts and sciences college. It offers the following degrees: Associate in Arts, Associate in Science, Bachelor of Arts, Bachelor of Arts in General Studies, Bachelor of Science, Bachelor of Fine Arts, bachelor's degree with distinction, Master of Arts in Teaching, Master of Business Administration, and Master of Science in criminal justice. The College also offers an extensive English as a second language (ESL) program, an honors program, study-abroad opportunities, internships, and international student scholarships and awards. With a student-faculty ratio of 14:1, small classes provide students with an ideal environment for personal attention. Columbia College is fully accredited by the North Central Association of Colleges and Schools.

Campus Life

The campus includes historic and contemporary buildings on 30 acres in a parklike setting that is within walking distance of downtown businesses, restaurants, and shopping. Columbia College has a diverse student body that includes students from around the United States and twenty-seven other countries. Freshmen and sophomores, as well as many juniors and seniors, live in one of three residence halls, with amenities such as individually controlled air-conditioning and heating units, cable television, e-mail, and Internet access. To help students balance academic life with fun, the College offers forty clubs and organizations, including the World Student Union and Fiesta Club for international students.

For International Students

The Coordinator of International Programs at Columbia College serves as an advocate and liaison for international students concerning their interactions with government agencies, community organizations, and campus offices. The coordinator assists international students with immigration regulations, employment, and social activities.

Columbia University, School of General Studies

- **Contact:**
  Curtis M. Rodgers
  Dean of Admissions
  408 Lewisohn Hall, MC 4101
  School of General Studies
  Columbia University
  New York, NY 10027
  Phone: 212-854-2772
  Fax: 212-854-6316
  E-mail: gs4degree@columbia.edu
  Web site: http://www.gs.columbia.edu
- Private, coed
- Urban setting
- Enrollment: 1,200
- Student-faculty ratio: 7:1
- 2005–06 Tuition and fees: $30,900
- 2005–06 Room and board: $9340

- International students: 17%
- Countries represented: 76
- International students applied: 144
- International students accepted: 58
- International students enrolled: 25
- Admissions tests:
    - TOEFL: Required (min. score 600 paper-based; 250 computer-based; 100 Internet-based) or Columbia's English Placement Test
    - SAT: Recommended
    - ACT: Not required
- Application deadline: Fall, 4/1; spring, 8/15
- On-campus housing: Available
- Summer housing: Available

Area and Climate

Located in New York City on Manhattan's Upper West Side, Columbia University is the focal point of a vibrant residential neighborhood full of bookstores, restaurants, shops, and coffee bars. With Barnard College, Teachers College, Union Theological Seminary, Jewish Theological Seminary, and the Manhattan School of Music all nearby, Morningside Heights is one of America's most dynamic academic communities. Midtown Manhattan is just 15 minutes away, and Lincoln Center for the Performing Arts, the Theater District, Museum Mile, Wall Street, Greenwich Village, Little Italy, and Chinatown are within easy reach.

Education

The School of General Studies of Columbia University is the finest liberal arts college in the country dedicated specifically to students with nontraditional backgrounds seeking a traditional education at an Ivy League university. The School of General Studies (GS) is unique among colleges of its type. Its students are fully integrated into the Columbia undergraduate curriculum, taking the same courses, with the same faculty members, and earning the same degrees as students from Columbia's three other undergraduate colleges. Students may choose from more than sixty majors in fields such as anthropology, chemistry, comparative literature, computer science, economics, psychology, and women's studies.

Campus Life

Columbia University has one of America's most distinguished urban campuses. Its 36 acres (15 hectares) include a library system that holds more than 8.6 million volumes, state-of-the-art computer facilities, a concert hall, a theater, a chapel, dining halls, a gymnasium, a health services center, and many green spaces where students can study or relax. Students may participate in any of more than 250 on-campus organizations and have the opportunity to compete athletically at the Division I level. The School of General Studies is home to international students from seventy-six countries, ranging from the Swedish 19-year-old beginning a degree in economics to the Brazilian 33-year-old completing a degree in environmental biology. While students come to the School of General Studies at different points in their academic lives, all are at Columbia because they seek a broad and rigorous liberal arts education in the University's tradition.

For International Students

As a preeminent world center of learning, Columbia University welcomes more than 4,000 students and scholars from approximately 130 countries and offers an array of services to international students through the International Students and Scholars Office (ISSO). The ISSO advisory staff assists international students with questions regarding admission and placement, adjustment to a new academic and cultural environment, personal and family services and needs, and immigration matters. In addition, the ISSO provides immigration and document services, peer advising, and a hospitality program and sponsors international student orientation as well as special social and cultural events.

Corcoran College of Art and Design

- Contact:
    Office of Admissions
    Corcoran College of Art and Design
    Washington, DC 20006-4804
    Phone: 202-639-1814
    Fax: 202-639-1830
    E-mail: admissions@corcoran.org
    Web site: http://www.corcoran.edu
- Private, coed
- Urban setting
- Enrollment: 500
- Student-faculty ratio: 5:1
- 2006–07 Tuition and fees: $24,489

- International students: 10%
- Countries represented: 24
- International students applied: 48
- International students accepted: 17
- International students enrolled: 10
- Admissions tests:
    - TOEFL (min. score 213 CBT, 79 iBT)
    - SAT: Recommended
    - ACT: Recommended
- Application deadline: Rolling
- Housing: Available (off campus)
- Summer housing: Not available

Area and Climate

The distinguished Corcoran College of Art and Design, in downtown Washington, D.C., is in the center of the nation's capital—one block from the White House and surrounded by the country's most distinguished monuments. The metropolitan location offers unparalleled inspiration for art students with dozens of public, private, and commercial galleries and cultural centers within walking distance. Washington, which is midway along the East Coast of the U.S., has a temperate climate with pleasant spring and fall seasons, temperatures near freezing in January, and humid summers. Transportation is by the modern, clean metro or by bus, bike, or foot.

Education

The historic Corcoran Museum/College complex, which opened in 1890, provides an excellent visual arts education in its Associate of Fine Arts, Bachelor of Fine Arts, and Master of Arts degree programs. Students work closely with faculty members, all of whom are practicing artists, in a friendly, studio-intensive setting. Individual studio spaces are available for fine arts majors; digital media design, graphic design, photography, and photojournalism majors complete internships with Washington businesses. Students in all majors create senior thesis projects that are exhibited in the Corcoran Museum. A library, computer lab, and faculty advisers assist with academic requirements and electives. Classes begin in early September and mid-January.

Campus Life

The student body represents a wide variety of artistic and ethnic backgrounds, nationalities, and age groups. Students visit the city's cultural centers and recreation areas and sponsor social events and art sales/shows. They get to know Washington's active arts community, attending openings at the Corcoran and other local museums and galleries.

For International Students

International students, representing a variety of artistic heritages, are welcomed into and quickly adapt to Corcoran's small but diverse student body. Supportive programs include orientation, a Tutoring Resource Center, and staff members with intercultural training. The city of Washington has embassies, international businesses and organizations, countless ethnic restaurants, and an international population. To apply, students must submit a portfolio (slides or CD) of artwork, an application form, official transcripts and test scores, and financial documentation showing proof of sufficient funds to cover the cost of attendance. Although there is no admissions deadline, international students are strongly encouraged to apply at least six months in advance. Scholarships for the first year of studies ranging from $1000 to $4000 are available for international students.

De Anza College

- **Contact:**
  International Student Coordinator
  De Anza College
  Cupertino, CA 95014
  Phone: 408-864-8826
  Fax: 408-864-5638
  E-mail: dainternational@fhda.edu
  Web site: http://www.deanza.edu/international
- **Public, 2-year, coed**
- **Urban setting**
- **Enrollment: 26,000 (approx.)**
- **Student-faculty ratio: 32.5:1**
- **2006–07 Tuition and fees: $5898 (three quarters)**

- **2006–07 Room and board: $7500 (homestay for ten months)**
- **International students: 4%**
- **Countries represented: 70+**
- **Admissions tests:**
  - **TOEFL: Required (min. score 500 paper-based, 173 computer-based, 61 iBT) or a minimum IELTS score of 5.0**
  - **SAT and ACT: Not required**
- **Application deadline: Fall, 6/30; winter, 10/31; spring, 1/31**
- **Housing: Host families and off-campus apartments**

Area and Climate

De Anza College is located on 112 acres (45 hectares) in Cupertino, in the heart of the world-renowned Silicon Valley, 45 minutes south of San Francisco and 15 minutes west of San Jose, the tenth-largest city in the U.S. De Anza was named after a famous Spanish explorer, Juan Bautista de Anza, who camped close to the campus site on March 25, 1776. The city is also home to Apple Computer. De Anza is one of the largest single-campus community colleges in the nation, with a fall enrollment that averages more than 26,000 students. There is a local transit system that provides bus service to the cities in the immediate area. Santa Clara Valley has a mild and comfortable climate year-round. The nearby cities of Sunnyvale, Santa Clara, and San Jose are consistently ranked as the country's safest.

Education

Since opening in 1967, De Anza College has emerged as one of the outstanding accredited (Western Association of Schools and Colleges) two-year colleges in the United States. In addition to Associate in Arts or Associate in Science degrees, students may earn vocational certificates of completion, achievement, and proficiency. Services are available in counseling, tutoring, career planning and placement, and financial aid. Thanks to special articulation agreements and Transfer Center assistance, DeAnza students transfer to highly selective, top-ranked, four-year universities to continue their studies. Some of the popular majors are accounting, animation, automotive technology, child development, environmental studies, film/television, graphic design, and nursing. Special programs include the honors program; Study Abroad Program, with options in eleven countries; the Internship Program; and computer-

assisted tutorial labs for writing, math, and science. The academic year consists of three 12-week quarters starting in September, January, and April.

Campus Life

De Anza has a very diverse and exciting activity program. Students have the opportunity to participate in more than forty-five college clubs, which are primarily social, educational, or service oriented in nature. De Anza offers competitive athletic programs, including baseball, basketball, cross-country, football, soccer, softball, swimming and diving, tennis, track and field, and water polo. Campus highlights include the Open Media Lab, Business and Computer Systems Lab, Advanced Technology Center, Flint Center for the Performing Arts, Euphrat Museum of Art, California History Center, Broadcast Media Center, an Olympic aquatics complex, and a planetarium.

For International Students

A special orientation session is conducted for new international students approximately three to four weeks before the start of the first quarter, with comprehensive academic, immigration, and cultural counseling. An additional class concentrates on majors and course requirements needed for transfer to four-year colleges, as well as helping students make the cultural adjustment. Students may participate in International Connection or any of the other multicultural clubs or receive free tickets to Celebrity Forum (with such speakers as Bill Cosby, Mikhail Gorbachev, and Bill Clinton). Religious organizations, such as the Muslim Student Association, are also available. Comprehensive health insurance is mandatory and is charged quarterly with the student's registration. Since there is no housing on campus, homestays ($750 per month) with carefully screened local families are offered. A housing list is maintained for students who wish to rent and share an apartment.

DeKalb Technical College

- Contact:
  Lisa Peters
  DeKalb Technical College
  495 North Indian Creek Drive
  Clarkston, GA 30021-2397
  Phone: 404-297-9522 Ext. 1154
  Fax: 404-294-6496
  E-mail: petersl@dekalbtech.edu
  Web site: http://www.dekalbtech.edu/
    studentservices/international/
    international.html
- Public, two-year, coed
- Urban setting
- Enrollment: 4,083

- Student-faculty ratio: 15:1
- 2006–07 Tuition and fees: $6340
- 2006–07 Room and board: $11,000
- Countries represented: 40
- Admissions tests:
  - TOEFL: Not required
  - SAT, ACT, CPE, ASSET, and/or COMPASS scores are accepted
- Application deadline: Fall, 8/21; winter, 11/14; spring, 2/19; summer, to be announced
- On-campus housing: Not available
- Summer housing: Not available

Area and Climate

The Clarkston campus is located in DeKalb County, Georgia, the most diverse county in the southeastern United States. More than 2,000 people live in the city of Clarkston, which sits just minutes outside Atlanta, the state capital. Summers are hot and humid, with temperatures reaching 90°F (32°C), but winters are generally mild, with little to no snowfall.

Education

Since its inception in 1961, DeKalb Technical College has been serving DeKalb, Rockdale, Newton, and Morgan counties. Students can select from more than 100 programs of study in eight general areas—business technology, computer information systems, economic development (certified specialist programs), electronics technology, electronics and computer engineering technology, health and human services, industrial technologies, and transportation technologies. Career programs are designed for students who wish to complete a technical program that prepares them to enter employment at a level of competence requiring more than a high school education but less than a four-year degree. Students receive an Associate in Applied Science degree or a diploma.

Campus Life

DeKalb Technical College is committed to meeting the educational needs of its students. Students benefit from involvement in campus organizations and student activities that enable them to participate in leadership development, exhibit social responsibility, and enjoy recreational activities, such as intramural sports, that complement their education and training. Organizations include the Association of Information Technology Professionals, Delta Epsilon Chi, the International Association of Administrative Professionals, the Inter Club Council, the International Students Club, the Machine Tool Club, Student Government Association (SGA), NOON-NET Working, Phi Beta Lambda, the DeKalb Technical College Chess Club, and SkillsUSA.

For International Students

DeKalb Technical College serves approximately 8,000 international students per year, both resident and nonresident, representing more than forty countries. DeKalb Technical College has been issuing student visas since the early 1980s. The International Student Advisor works with international students seeking or holding an F-l or M-1 student visa, keeping students informed of the regulations required for maintaining status as a visa holder. Although DeKalb Technical College does not provide, supervise, or recommend housing facilities, International Student Services maintains a list of nearby affordable housing.

DePaul University

- **Contact:**
  Karin Christoph Brown
  International Admission
  1 East Jackson Boulevard
  Suite 9100
  DePaul University
  Chicago, IL 60604
  Phone: 312-362-5620
  Fax: 312-362-8521
  E-mail: intlapp@depaul.edu
  Web site: http://www.depaul.edu/
  international
- **Private, Catholic, coed**
- **Urban setting**
- **Enrollment: 23,570**
- **Student/faculty ratio: 19:1**
- **2006–07 Tuition and fees: $22,365**
- **2006–07 Room and board: $10,000**

- **International students: 5%**
- **Countries represented: 90**
- **International students applied: 725**
- **International students accepted: 500**
- **International students enrolled: 250**
- **Admissions tests:**
  - **TOEFL: Required (min. score 550 paper-based; 80 Internet-based, with no subsection less than 17)**
  - **SAT or ACT: Not required, except for scholarship consideration**
- **Application deadline: February 1 for priority application for freshmen beginning in the fall term; all others, rolling basis with minimum of two months prior to term**
- **On-campus housing: First come, first served**
- **Summer housing: Available**

Area and Climate

DePaul University is located in the exciting urban setting of Chicago, the third-largest city in the United States. Two campuses, 3 miles (5 kilometers) apart, provide the benefits of a lovely residential neighborhood and the excitement of an internationally recognized center of commerce and trade. The Lincoln Park 30-acre (12-hectare) campus is home to the Colleges of Liberal Arts and Sciences, Music, Theatre, and Education. The downtown, or Loop, campus (six buildings in the heart of Chicago) is home to the College of Commerce; School of Computer Science, Telecommunication and Information Systems; and the Law School. The climate in Chicago is variable. The temperature falls to 14°F (-10°C) in the winter and rises to around 90°F (32°C) in the summer.

Education

For more than a century, DePaul University has built a reputation for excellence recognized throughout the United States. Founded by Vincentian Fathers in 1898, DePaul attracts students from fifty states and more than ninety countries around the world. Eight colleges and schools within the University provide more than 200 undergraduate and graduate programs reflecting the constantly changing needs of the world economy and global community. The average class size is 23 students. All classes are taught by distinguished and experienced faculty members, ensuring that the quality and scope of DePaul's academic programs reflect a commitment to education that prepares not only for a career, but for all of life. DePaul graduates are sought by internationally renowned corpora-

tions, organizations, and businesses. The academic calendar is on the quarter system; admission decisions for most programs are made on a rolling basis.

Campus Life

DePaul's campus life is as exciting as its location in Chicago. More than eighty-five student clubs and organizations, including student government, a campus newspaper, a jazz band, honor societies, ethnic clubs, political groups, a radio station, fraternities and sororities, and a literary magazine, keep the campus active and interesting. DePaul is a member of the Big East Conference and sponsors National Collegiate Athletic Association Division I varsity sports. Special events, such as concerts and theater productions, are scheduled throughout the academic year. In addition, opportunities to experience the dynamic events and activities sponsored by the city of Chicago are easily available to students.

For International Students

A comprehensive orientation is required of all international students. An International Admission Office and International Student Office ensure that students receive individual attention during the application process and throughout their careers at DePaul. English language support is available through the English Language Academy; undergraduate students who meet all academic requirements for admission except proof of English language proficiency may be eligible for conditional admission and begin in DePaul's English Language Academy. The Career Development Center, the Writing Center, and Tutoring Services provide career and academic support. International students are often hired for competitive, on-campus, part-time work opportunities throughout the year. Students of every race, nationality, and religion are welcome.

Dominican University of California

- **Contact:**
  International Student Coordinator
  Office of Admissions
  Dominican University of California
  50 Acacia Avenue
  San Rafael, CA 94901-2298
  Phone: 415-485-3204
  Fax: 415-485-3214
  E-mail: enroll@dominican.edu
- Private, Dominican heritage, coed
- Suburban setting
- Enrollment: Approximately 1,940
- Student-faculty ratio: 11:1
- 2006–07 Tuition and fees: $27,770

- **2006–07 Room and board: $10,080**
- **International students: 4%**
- **Countries represented: 23**
- **Admissions tests:**
  - **TOEFL (min. score: PBT, 550; iBT, 80) or ELS (level 112)**
  - **SAT or ACT scores may be submitted as an alternative to the TOEFL**
- **Application deadline: For international students: spring semester, November 1; fall semester, July 1**
- **On-campus housing: Available**
- **Summer housing: Available**

Area and Climate

Dominican is located on 80 wooded acres (32 hectares) in the hills of beautiful Marin County. The campus is 12 miles (27 kilometers) north of San Francisco and less than a half hour's drive from Pacific Ocean beaches. Normal temperatures in January range from 40°F (4.4°C) to 50°F (10°C); normal July temperatures range from 70°F (21°C) to 90°F (32°C). The total enrollment of the University is approximately 1,940 students. There is an excellent public transportation system throughout San Francisco and Marin County, providing service to the Dominican campus.

Education

Dominican University of California, founded in 1890, is an independent, international, learner-centered university of Dominican heritage. The international student body includes undergraduate and graduate students. A strong internship program offers students job experience in areas of their choice. Students are exposed to a variety of learning experiences that include discussions, lectures, seminars, simulations, practicums, and time for quiet reflection. The average class size is 15. There are more than thirty undergraduate and graduate majors from which to choose. Some of the more popular ones for international students are international studies, business administration, psychology, digital art, nursing, and English. Campus facilities include more than 100,000 volumes in Archbishop Alemany Library, a state-of-the-art recreation center, a computer center, an art gallery, the Science Building, the Nursing School and skills lab, and an 850-seat auditorium located in Angelico Hall. The school operates on a semester system with the fall semester beginning in late August and ending in December and the spring running from mid-January to early May.

Campus Life

The University includes students from a wide variety of backgrounds. Approximately one third of Dominican's undergraduates reside on campus. Campus housing consists of four residence halls, each with its own architectural style and personality. Housing is available for international students. There is a dining hall as well as Chilly's Café, which serves cappuccinos, snacks, and sandwiches. The University's Conlan Recreation Center features a 1,285-seat arena for basketball and volleyball, a well-equipped fitness room, and a six-lane outdoor pool. The surrounding 25-acre (10-hectare) Forest Meadows area has a soccer field, twelve tennis courts, and an outdoor amphitheater. The campus atmosphere is relaxed and friendly as well as extremely safe.

For International Students

The ELS Language Center is housed on Dominican's campus for students who are not fluent in English. The program provides intensive, high-quality English instruction to prepare international students to enter American colleges and universities. The program has an admission policy with Dominican upon the successful completion of level 112. Each student is assigned an academic adviser upon enrolling at the University. Tutoring and academic support are also available.

Drake University

- **Contact:**
  Leslie Mamoorian
  Director of International and Graduate
     Admission
  Drake University
  Des Moines, IA 50311
  Phone: 515-271-3181
  Fax: 515-271-2831
  E-mail: international@drake.edu
  Web site: http://www.choose.drake.edu
- **Private, coed**
- **Urban, residential setting**
- **Enrollment: 5,200**
- **Student-faculty ratio: 14:1**
- **2006–07 Tuition and fees: $22,682**

- **2006–07 Room and board: $6500**
- **International students: 5%**
- **Countries represented: 61**
- **International students applied: 298**
- **International students accepted: 196**
- **International students enrolled: 76**
- **Admissions tests:**
  - **TOEFL (min. score 530 PBT; 197 CBT; 76 iBT)**
  - **SAT or ACT: Recommended**
- **Application deadline: Rolling (except pharmacy)**
- **On-campus housing: Guaranteed**
- **Summer housing: Available**

Area and Climate

Drake University's safe and scenic campus is located in a residential neighborhood in Des Moines, a medium-sized city of approximately 450,000 people. As Iowa's capital and largest city, Des Moines is a metropolitan center for business (especially insurance), government, publishing, broadcasting, advertising, and the arts. The quality of life is enriched by the people of Iowa, who are noted for their friendliness, honesty, strong work ethic, and educational values. The airport, just 15 minutes by car from the campus, is served by major airlines. Because of its central U.S. location, the climate in Iowa has a cycle of four distinct seasons.

Education

Drake University is recognized nationally for teaching excellence in a student-centered learning environment. More than seventy undergraduate programs are offered in the liberal arts and sciences, business administration, journalism and mass communication, pharmacy, and education, with a diversity and depth normally found at much larger institutions. The professional programs are accredited by their corresponding professional associations. Students are admitted directly into their programs, which allows for courses required for each major to be taken as early as the first semester of enrollment. Drake also offers a variety of graduate and law degrees. All courses are taught by faculty members rather than by graduate assistants, and the advising and mentoring skills of the faculty members are valued by Drake students. Faculty members also invite undergraduates to engage in research

projects with them. This kind of interaction contributes to the fact that 93 percent of Drake graduates find employment or enter graduate or professional school within six months of receiving degrees. Overseas study programs are available in more than seventy countries throughout the world.

Campus Life

Students are encouraged to become active members of the campus community through involvement in more than 160 wide-ranging student organizations, including professional organizations, student government, Division 1 athletics and intramurals, and the International Student Association. They are also encouraged to pursue the many internship and practicum opportunities that Des Moines has to offer. The spacious campus, lined with trees and flower beds, features a variety of buildings that are architectural showplaces and historically important. The student population is drawn from forty-six states and sixty countries.

For International Students

Drake values its international student population and is pleased to offer financial assistance that can cover up to 50 percent of tuition, room, and board costs through merit scholarships and need-based programs. The Center for International Programs and Services provides a wide array of services to international students, including an airport welcome, special orientation sessions, immigration and general advising, and a host-family program. For most programs, conditional admission is available to students whose TOEFL scores are lower than 530 (paper-based test) or 197 (computer-based test). Courses to improve proficiency can be taken through the on-campus Intensive English Program.

Duquesne University

- Contact:
    Helen Auckland
    Assistant Director, International Admissions
    Duquesne University
    Pittsburgh, PA 15282-1660
    Phone: 412-396-6113
    Fax: 412-396-5178
    Web site: http://www.oip.duq.edu
- Private, coed
- Urban setting
- Enrollment: 10,184
- Student-faculty ratio: 15:1
- 2006–07 Tuition and fees: $22,665–$27,814
- 2006–07 Room and board: $8296

- International students: 5%
- Countries represented: 95
- International students applied: 431
- International students accepted: 232
- International students enrolled: 101
- Admissions test:
    - TOEFL: Recommended
    - SAT: Recommended
    - ACT: Recommended
- Application deadline: Rolling (in most programs)
- On-campus housing: Available
- Summer housing: Available

Area and Climate

Duquesne's hilltop campus, known as the Bluff, provides a quiet isolated setting for an academic experience, yet it also provides easy access to Pittsburgh, honored in recent years as one of America's most livable cities. In addition to being one of the largest sites of corporate headquarters in the nation, Pittsburgh is home to ten colleges and universities, fine medical facilities, a symphony orchestra, the opera, rock concerts, libraries, research centers, galleries, museums, and shopping. One can experience all four seasons in Pittsburgh—temperatures in the summer average 80°F (27°C) and in the winter, 25°F (-4°C).

Education

Duquesne is committed to offering an education for the mind, heart, and spirit. Whether it is in the classroom or participating in a University activity, Duquesne's goal is to develop the whole person. The College of Liberal Arts and the School of Natural and Environmental Sciences offer degrees in approximately fifty undergraduate fields of study. In addition, Duquesne offers degrees from the School of Business Administration, which is accredited by AACSB International–The Association to Advance Collegiate Schools of Business; the School of Education in early childhood, elementary, and secondary education; the School of Health Sciences in athletic training, health management systems, occupational therapy, physical therapy, and speech-language pathology; the School of Music in music education, music therapy, and six other fields; the School of Nursing; and the School of Pharmacy. The fall semester at Duquesne typically begins the last week of August, and the spring semester begins the first week of January. Duquesne also offers summer terms that start the first week of May.

Campus Life

There are students at Duquesne from more than ninety countries. Some choose to live on campus in one of five Living/Learning Centers, where campus life can be experienced to the fullest. There are numerous organizations for students, including the International Student Organization (ISO) and various other cultural organizations that help international students promote cultural identity throughout the campus. The ISO also plans socials and trips and has an annual gala affair for the entire University to promote the many cultures represented on campus.

For International Students

The mission of Duquesne University's founders (the Spiritans) has always included service to people outside the United States. Duquesne University is committed to providing an educational environment that recognizes cultural and national diversity and to developing and maintaining programs, services, and practices that promote respect for people of all backgrounds. The Office of International Programs is well staffed to meet the individual needs of the international student. There is also an excellent English as a Second Language Program for those students needing English training. Orientation is held at the beginning of each semester for all incoming international students to help them make the transition from their home country to Duquesne. In addition, scholarships and assistantships based on academic merit are available for international students.

East Carolina University

- **Contact:**
  Monika Wojciechowski, Assistant Director for
  International Student Recruitment
  The Office of International Affairs
  International House
  East Carolina University
  306 East Ninth Street
  Greenville, NC 27858-4353
  Phone: 252-328-6769
  Fax: 252-328-4813
  E-mail: intlprgm@ecu.edu
  Web site: http://www.international.ecu.edu
- Public, four-year, coed
- Small-town setting
- Enrollment: 24,351
- Student-faculty ratio: 17:1
- 2006–07 Tuition and fees: $7258.50 (per semester)
- 2006–07 Room and board: $3380 (per semester)
- International students: 1%
- Countries represented: 57
- International students applied: 88 (undergraduate)
- International students accepted: 57 (undergraduate)
- International students enrolled: 34 (undergraduate)
- Admissions tests:
  - TOEFL: Required (min. score 550 PBT, 213 CBT, 80 iBT)
- Application deadline recommended: Fall, 5/1; spring, 9/15
- On-campus housing: Available
- Summer housing: Available

Area and Climate

East Carolina University is located in Greenville, North Carolina, a city of more than 60,000 that lies equal distances between the state capital of Raleigh and the North Carolina coast beaches. Home to historic sites, parks, greenways, theaters, and museums, Greenville offers year-round activities in a usually mild climate. The city is a medical, educational, and economic hub of eastern North Carolina, and both citywide and campus transportation and services make the pace of life enjoyable in Greenville.

Education

East Carolina University (ECU) was founded in 1907 as a teacher training school and is now the fastest-growing constituent institution of the University of North Carolina system. With a mission of teaching, research, and service, East Carolina is a dynamic university seeking the challenges of the future. It leads the state in distance education, provides more teachers to the state than any other North Carolina institution, and offers high-distinction programs in business, health care, the fine and performing arts, and more. At ECU, 103 bachelor's degree programs, seventy-four master's degree programs, seventeen doctoral programs, and one first-professional M.D. program are offered.

Campus Life

East Carolina is the home of a diverse student body, with students from more than fifty foreign countries. Opportunities abound on campus, where students have a range of choices of housing, dining, clubs, and organizations. Vibrant traditions have been established through athletics, residence halls, and campus groups. Tutoring services, interest groups, and computer and technology assistance are available to assist students in their academic endeavors. Students participate in Greenville's International Festival, World Community Day, and Worldfest, and groups frequently go on cultural trips around the state and region.

For International Students

At East Carolina, international students are assisted in the transition from their home countries to campus. An orientation program offers information about campus services, social events, and immigration information. Students may also participate in cross-cultural programs to help with the transition to the United States, joining the more than 200 international students who study and conduct research on campus. General services, including health care and counseling, are also offered on campus.

Eastern Connecticut State University

- **Contact:**
  Dmitry Satsuk
  Associate Director of International
     Admissions
  Eastern Connecticut State University
  83 Windham Street
  Willimantic, CT 06226
  Phone: 860-465-5022
  Fax: 860-465-5544
  E-mail: satsukd@easternct.edu
  Web site: http://www.easternct.edu/depts/
     international/index.html
- **Public, four-year, coed**
- **Small-town setting**
- **Enrollment: 5,239**

- **Student-faculty ratio: 16:1**
- **2007–08 Tuition and fees: $15,681**
- **2007–08 Room and board: $8380**
- **International students: 0.7%**
- **Countries represented: 21**
- **Admissions tests:**
  - **TOEFL: Required**
  - **SAT or ACT: Recommended**
- **Application deadline: 5/1**
- **On-campus housing: Available**
- **Summer housing: Available**

Area and Climate

The small city of Willimantic, Connecticut, has a population of 22,000 and many convenient shopping centers. The eastern Connecticut region is famous for its rolling hills, forests, state recreational areas, nature trails, clear lakes and streams, and beaches. Skiing areas are nearby. Connecticut has a seasonal climate, with temperatures ranging above 80°F (27°C) in the summer to below freezing in the winter. Hartford is 40 minutes away, and New York City and Boston are both less than 2 hours from Willimantic by car.

Education

As a predominantly undergraduate institution, Eastern Connecticut State University develops outstanding students who integrate learning with expertise in their chosen fields of study and gain both civic and career success in a highly technological and rapidly changing world. Undergraduate degrees offered are the Associate of Science, the Bachelor of Arts, the Bachelor of General Studies, and the Bachelor of Science. Students can pursue majors in accounting, biochemistry, biology, business administration, business information systems, communication, computer science, education (early childhood, elementary, and secondary), economics, English, English/American studies, environment Earth science, general studies, history, history/ American studies, history and social science, mathematics,

the performing arts (dance, film, music, and theater), physical education, psychology, public policy and government, social work, sociology and applied social relations, Spanish, sports and leisure management, studio art, and the visual arts.

Campus Life

Most full-time students, including 90 percent of the freshmen, reside on campus in seven residence halls and five apartment complexes. There are more than fifty special-interest clubs and organizations, including a student newspaper, a yearbook, and a literary and arts magazine. Extracurricular events include concerts, dances, films, intramural sports, lectures, musical and dramatic productions, and bus trips to Boston and New York City. The University belongs to the NCAA and fields seventeen varsity teams. Varsity sports for men include baseball, basketball, cross-country, lacrosse, soccer, and track. Women participate in intercollegiate basketball, cross-country, field hockey, lacrosse, soccer, softball, swimming, track, and volleyball.

For International Students

The mission of the Office of International Programs is to assist international students in making the transition to Eastern by providing information and guidance in complying with immigration regulations and applying for related benefits. The office ensures University compliance with immigration regulations governing the enrollment of international students.

Edgewood College

- Contact:
    Office of Admissions
    Edgewood College
    1000 Edgewood College Drive
    Madison, WI 53711-1958

    Phone: 608-663-2294
    Fax: 608-663-2214
    E-mail: admissions@edgewood.edu
    Web site: http://www.edgewood.edu
- Private, comprehensive, coed
- Suburban setting
- Total enrollment: 2,500
- Student-faculty ratio: 15:1

- 2007–08 Tuition and fees: $18,050
- 2007–08 Room and board: $6200
- International students: 3%
- Countries represented: 20
- Admissions tests:
    - TOEFL: Required (paper-based min. score 525)
    - ACT: Recommended
- Application deadlines: Fall, 7/1; spring, 11/15
- On-campus housing: Available
- Summer housing: Available

Area and Climate

Edgewood College is centrally located in Madison, Wisconsin, the state's capital. Approximately 200,000 people live in this friendly, university-oriented city that has been ranked among the top places to live in the United States. Located just 1 hour west of Milwaukee and 2 hours northwest of Chicago, Edgewood College's 55-acre campus is nestled in a scenic, residential area on the shores of Lake Wingra, one of the four lakes that make up Madison's unique landscape. The safe and convenient metropolitan access provides unlimited recreational and cultural opportunities within walking and biking distance. Students enjoy the seasonal changes throughout the year.

Education

For eighty years, Edgewood College has been recognized as a leader in high-quality education. More than forty undergraduate programs are available, including business, computer information systems, and pre-engineering. The committed faculty members—nearly 85 percent of whom hold doctoral or terminal degrees—bring their knowledge and expertise to the classroom. Edgewood College's low student-faculty ratio of 15:1 ensures that students have personal interaction with professors. Through a collaborative program with the University of Wisconsin–Madison, students also have access to an incredible range of specialized classes and resources that are not usually available at a private institution of Edgewood College's size.

Campus Life

The College welcomes women and men who reflect the rich diversity of the world's cultures and perspectives. Approximately 70 students from twenty countries attend Edgewood College. New buildings and updated facilities provide students with space for academic, social, and recreational activities. Computer labs and stations throughout the campus give students ample opportunity to explore the Internet and stay in touch with family and friends via e-mail. The College offers several options for on-campus living and a wide variety of student organizations and athletics for students to explore.

For International Students

Many international students find that Edgewood College offers a friendly community with faculty and staff members and students who help with the transition to an educational experience in the United States. The International Student Office guides students through the new educational system and the American culture and helps international students to understand their rights and responsibilities as holders of nonimmigrant visas. Edgewood College works closely with the Wisconsin English as a Second Language Institute (WESLI) and the Madison English as a Second Language School (MESLS). Students attending WESLI or MESLS who meet the College's academic requirements may take classes at Edgewood College to complement their course work at the institute or the school.

Edinboro University of Pennsylvania

- **Contact:**
  Admissions Office
  Edinboro University of Pennsylvania
  Edinboro, PA 16444
  Phone: 814-732-2761
  Fax: 814-732-2420
  Web site: http://www.edinboro.edu
- **Public, comprehensive, coed**
- **Small-town setting**
- **Enrollment: 7,600**
- **Student-faculty ratio: 18:1**
- **2006–07 Tuition and fees: $11,106**

- **2006–07 Room and board: $5718**
- **International students: 1%**
- **Countries represented: 32**
- **International students enrolled: 89**
- **Admissions tests:**
  - TOEFL (min. score 500)
  - SAT and ACT: Not required
- **Application deadline: Fall, 5/1; spring, 10/1**
- **On-campus housing: Guaranteed**
- **Summer housing: Available**

Area and Climate

Edinboro University is one of the leading educational institutions in western Pennsylvania. Situated on a spacious 585-acre (237-hectare) campus in the scenic resort community of Edinboro, the University offers the relaxed atmosphere of a small town while providing the educational and cultural advantages of a large university. Located in northwestern Pennsylvania, Edinboro is within 100 miles (161 kilometers) of the famous cultural centers of Pittsburgh, Pennsylvania; Cleveland, Ohio; and Buffalo, New York, and is located only 15 miles (24 kilometers) south of Erie, the fourth-largest city in Pennsylvania. Edinboro's climate includes all four seasons. Spring and fall months are often sunny, rainy, and cool. Summers are often warm and humid. Winters are very cold, with heavy accumulations of snow.

Education

Established in 1857, Edinboro University of Pennsylvania is an institution of 7,600 undergraduate and graduate students with international representation from thirty-two countries. The University offers more than 100 associate, bachelor's, and master's degree programs. Edinboro University is one of the largest and most multipurpose universities in northwestern Pennsylvania. Edinboro has a tradition of educational excellence, matched by a distinguished faculty of more than 400 members. More than two thirds of the faculty members at Edinboro have earned doctorates. In addition, a number of faculty members have held state and national leadership roles in their professional organizations. Baron Forness Library, the largest library in northwestern Pennsylvania, has more than 480,000 holdings, 1.3 million microforms, and online computer access. Searching services are provided for more than 350 specialized databases. The student-faculty ratio of 18:1 is very conducive to individualized counseling and attention. The fall semester begins the last week in August and ends in mid-December. The spring semester begins in mid-January and ends at the beginning of May.

Campus Life

On-campus housing includes six residence halls that provide housing for approximately 2,500 students. Housing is guaranteed to international students year-round. The Student University Center is a main attraction to all students. Activities and facilities include a Friday night film series, a mini-concert series, comedians, magicians, special holiday celebrations, areas for physical fitness, a TV room, and a computer lab. A wide range of cocurricular opportunities exist for all students. More than 220 active student organizations and groups are available on campus.

For International Students

International student orientation is held one week prior to the beginning of classes in the fall semester. Classroom instruction is in English, and prospective students must demonstrate proficiency in English for admission. In order to enhance campus diversity, the University offers a tuition waiver program for international students. Upon a student's official acceptance to Edinboro University of Pennsylvania, international students qualify for an International Tuition Waiver, which reduces the cost of tuition (costs published above reflect the waiver). This award for undergraduate students continues for four years (eight semesters), as long as they achieve satisfactory academic standing, as outlined in the *University Catalogue*.

El Camino College

- Contact:

  Mr. Leonid Rachman, Program Coordinator
  El Camino College
  3400 West Manhattan Beach Boulevard
  Torrance, CA 90504

  Phone: 310-660-3431
  Fax: 310-660-6779
  E-mail: ISP@elcamino.edu
  Web site: http://www.elcamino.edu

  Ms. Destyn LaPorte, Program Manager
  El Camino Language Academy (ECLA)
  16007 Crenshaw Boulevard
  Torrance, CA 90506

  Phone: 310-660-6473
  Fax: 310-660-6470
  E-mail: dlaporte@elcamino.edu

- Public, two-year, coed
- Urban setting
- Enrollment: 25,000

- Student-faculty ratio: 24:1
- 2005–06 Tuition and fees: $5300
- 2005–06 Room and board: $7500
- International students: 3%
- Countries represented: 67
- International students applied: 300
- International students accepted: 270
- International students enrolled: 700 (total)
- Admissions tests:
  - TOEFL (paper-based min. score 450; computer-based min. score 133; Internet-based min. score 45)
  - TOEIC (min. score 620)
  - IELTS (min. score 4.5)
- Application deadline: Rolling
- On-campus housing: Limited assistance provided for homestay and apartments

Area and Climate

El Camino College (ECC) is located in Torrance, a progressive city with a population of 133,000 on the beautiful Pacific coast of California. Its central location between Los Angeles and Orange County makes it a prime business center for the South Bay. With average temperatures ranging from 50°F (10°C) to 86°F (30°C), Torrance also serves as an important tourist destination, offering year-round cultural and recreational activities and inviting sandy beaches along the shoreline. Freeways connect the city to any location in the metropolitan Los Angeles area and provide easy access to world-famous cultural and entertainment facilities.

Education

El Camino College, which was founded in 1947, offers ninety associate degree or certificate programs. A distinguished faculty and an array of student support services assist students in meeting their educational goals. Many students transfer to complete bachelor's degrees at some of the finest colleges and universities in the United States. Local universities that welcome El Camino students include UCLA, USC, and many others. Members of the Honors Transfer Program enroll in honors classes and take advantage of transfer agreements with prestigious universities in California. The campus library houses more than 110,000 volumes and an Innovation Center with the latest in computer technology. Learning support centers for math, computer technology, and writing are available.

Campus Life

Students at El Camino College are a reflection of the rich diversity of the southern California area, with a wide range of ages and ethnic and religious backgrounds represented. More than forty student-run clubs, including an International Student Club, provide a variety of social and service opportunities. The College has championship teams in men's and women's competitive sports as well as a swimming pool, racquet sports facilities, and a state-of-the-art Sports Science Center.

For International Students

The International Student Program staff is eager to assist students throughout their stay at El Camino College. An orientation program is required for incoming international students each semester. This orientation introduces students to the campus and surrounding community. Students receive individual academic counseling and assistance in creating an educational plan. For students who are not able to achieve a satisfactory English proficiency test score or who want to improve their English language skills, the El Camino Language Academy (located on the campus of ECC) prepares the ESL student to take and pass the TOEFL and transfer to the academic program at El Camino. The program is eight weeks long and is offered five times a year. Student Health Services offers a range of general medical treatment and services. ECC provides students with a variety of housing options; students may choose from an apartment locator service or homestay.

Elizabethtown College

- Contact:
  Kristin E. Smith
  Assistant Director of Admissions/
      Coordinator of International
      Recruitment
  Elizabethtown College
  Elizabethtown, PA 17022-2298
  Phone: 717-361-1400
  Fax: 717-361-1365
  E-mail: admissions@etown.edu
  Web site: http://www.etown.edu
- Private, coed
- Suburban setting
- Enrollment: 1,900

- Student-faculty ratio: 13:1
- 2006–07 Tuition and fees: $26,950
- 2006–07 Room and board: $7300
- Countries represented: 36
- International students enrolled: 80 (total)
- Admissions tests:
  - TOEFL (paper-based min. score 525; computer-based min. score 200)
  - SAT/ACT: Not required
- Application deadline: Rolling
- On-campus housing: Guaranteed

Area and Climate

Elizabethtown is a growing residential community of 20,000 in historic southeastern Pennsylvania. The city is a 10-minute drive from Hershey, the famous chocolate-making town; 25 minutes from Harrisburg, the state capital; and 25 minutes from Lancaster. Its strategic location makes it an attractive center for industry, agriculture, and education. Students enjoy a range of activities that are available in the surrounding community, including symphonies, professional athletic teams, and cultural activities. Outdoor enthusiasts enjoy skiing and fishing and exploring nearby caves. Philadelphia and Baltimore are each 1½ hours away; Washington and New York City can be reached in about 3 hours. Elizabethtown is serviced by Amtrak trains via the Philadelphia-Pittsburgh line, and Harrisburg's international airport is 10 miles away.

Education

Elizabethtown College centers learning in strong relationships, links classroom instruction with experiential learning, emphasizes international and cross-cultural perspectives, and nurtures students' capacity for lives of purpose. The College's twenty academic departments offer more than fifty majors and more than 580 courses in liberal arts and preprofessional disciplines. The faculty's primary concern is teaching, with a particular emphasis on active learning. Faculty members collaborate with students on research projects and act as contacts for internships and externships. Ninety percent of the faculty members hold the Ph.D. or other terminal degree in their field. Ninety-five percent of graduates find employment or pursue advanced degrees within eight months of graduation. The College is accredited by the Middle States Association of Colleges and Schools.

Campus Life

More than eighty clubs and organizations operate on campus. Residence halls, apartments, and houses on Elizabethtown's 192-acre (78-hectare) campus provide housing for 85 percent of students. Housing is guaranteed for four years. Recent additions to the College include the Brossman Commons student center, the Hoover Center for Business, and the Masters Center for Science, Math, and Engineering (to be completed in fall 2007). The High Library houses 180,000 volumes and 1,100 periodical subscriptions. Students can access the library, e-mail, and the Internet from their residence hall rooms through their PCs. The College's twenty intercollegiate sports teams include basketball, lacrosse, soccer, swimming, and track and field. Approximately 65 percent of students participate in intramural sports. The College sponsors trips to Philadelphia, Baltimore, New York, and Washington, D.C.

For International Students

The associate director of international programs works with students and offers advice on educational and personal matters. The student-run International Club also provides support, promoting cultural exchange and understanding on campus through a range of activities. Weeklong multicultural events sponsored by the College focus on global issues and the cultures, music, and foods of people from around the world.

Admission is selective and competitive. All applications should include a completed application form, a $30 application fee, official or attested transcripts from all institutions attended, two letters of recommendation, a personal statement, an official TOEFL score, and a certification of finances form. International applicants must provide proof of sufficient financial resources to cover the cost of living and educational expenses while at Elizabethtown. International scholarships are offered for up to half of the comprehensive fee.

Elmira College

- **Contact:**
  Dean of Admissions
  Elmira College
  One Park Place
  Elmira, NY 14901
  Phone: 607-735-1724
  Fax: 607-735-1718
  E-mail: admissions@elmira.edu
- **Private, coed**
- **Small-town setting**
- **Enrollment: 1,200**
- **Student-faculty ratio: 12:1**
- **2005–06 Tuition and fees: $28,500**
- **2005–06 Room and board: $8700**

- **International students: 5%**
- **Countries represented: 20**
- **International students applied: 248**
- **International students accepted: 81**
- **International students enrolled: 24**
- **Admissions tests:**
  - **TOEFL (paper-based min. score 500; computer-based min. score 173)**
  - **SAT and ACT: Not required**
- **Application deadline: 3/1**
- **On-campus housing: Guaranteed**
- **Summer housing: Available**

Area and Climate

Elmira College is located in the Finger Lakes region of upstate New York. The College occupies 51.7 acres (20 hectares) in a residential section of the city of Elmira, New York, which has a population of 36,000. Elmira is served by the Elmira-Corning Airport, and bus service to major cities in the northeastern United States is available. A local transit system provides excellent service within Elmira and throughout the surrounding area. Temperatures range from an average of 82°F (28°C) in the summer to 32°F (0°C) during the winter. Hiking, boating, and fishing are readily available.

Education

Founded in 1855, Elmira College is a small, private, coeducational college that emphasizes high-quality education in the liberal arts and sciences. Bachelor's degrees are available in more than thirty-five major fields of study, with international business, international studies, political science, business administration, psychology, and education particularly popular. Strong programs are offered in premedicine and prelaw as well. Close contact with faculty members and small classes provide the basis for an excellent education. Campus facilities include a library housing more than 391,000 volumes, a well-equipped computer center, a theater, a swimming pool, a gymnasium, and playing fields. Elmira College is one of fewer than 270 colleges and universities in the United States to have a chapter of the prestigious Phi Beta Kappa honor society.

Campus Life

The student body includes students from thirty-five states and twenty-three countries. All students live in dormitories on campus all four years; housing is, therefore, guaranteed to all. Housing is available for international students in the summer. Each dormitory has a Resident Life Coordinator, and each floor has a Resident Assistant. The academic year consists of two 12-week terms followed by a six-week spring term. The fall term ends before Christmas, and the winter term begins in early January and ends in mid-April (including a one-week break in late February). Term III, the spring term, begins in late April and concludes at the end of May. More than seventy student organizations are available on campus, including music, theater, student government, and intramural athletics.

For International Students

An internationally recognized orientation program precedes the fall term and is required of all students. An ESL program is available for students who need additional work in English. The International Club provides both international students and American students an opportunity to share in, and learn about, other cultures. The International Student Adviser works closely with students from other countries to assist them in their transition to Elmira College.

Embry-Riddle Aeronautical University

- Contact:
    Director of Admissions
    Embry-Riddle Aeronautical University
    Daytona Beach, FL 32114
    Phone: 386-226-6100
    Fax: 386-226-7070
    E-mail: dbadmit@erau.edu
    Web site: http://www.erau.edu/db
- Private, coed, specialized
- Urban setting
- Enrollment: 4,863
- Student-faculty ratio: 14:1
- 2007–08 Tuition and fees: $26,463
- 2007–08 Room and board: $7830

- International students: 9%
- Countries represented: 84
- International students applied: 512
- International students accepted: 233
- International students enrolled: 86
- Admissions tests:
    - TOEFL (Recommended min. score 550 PBT; 213 CBT; 79–80 iBT)
    - SAT: Recommended
    - ACT: Accepted
- Application deadline: Rolling
- On-campus housing: Available
- Summer housing: Available

Area and Climate

The Daytona Beach, Florida, residential campus of Embry-Riddle is located 10 minutes from the Atlantic shore and within an hour's drive of Orlando and the Kennedy Space Center. Palm trees, wide grass lawns, and an Olympic-size pool complement the state-of-the-art living and learning facilities of the 185-acre (74-hectare) campus. The exceptional central Florida weather allows year-round enjoyment of the 27 miles (43 kilometers) of shoreline that make up the greater Daytona Beach area, where sporting events, the arts, and festivals celebrating everything from seafood to motorcycles are presented throughout the year.

Education

The purpose of Embry-Riddle Aeronautical University, which was founded in 1926, is to provide a comprehensive education of such excellence that graduates are responsible citizens and well prepared for productive careers in aviation and aerospace. The University awards degrees at the baccalaureate and master's levels. Majors include aeronautical science (professional pilot program), aerospace electronics, aerospace engineering, air traffic management, applied meteorology, aviation maintenance science, aviation management, business administration, civil engineering, communication, computer engineering, electrical engineering, engineering physics, homeland security, human factors psychology, mechanical engineering, safety science, software engineering, and space physics. The aerospace studies program allows students to design their own major by choosing three minors, tailoring a program to meet their specific needs. The most popular programs are the engineering and aeronautical science programs.

The College of Aviation is the home of the simulation center and the fleet of aircraft. The College of Engineering is housed in the Lehman Center, which features several state-of-the-art labs. Among the library's resources is a historical aviation collection that includes materials dating from 1909 to the present. The calendar year is divided into three semesters of fifteen weeks each, with the summer session divided into two terms.

Campus Life

The international student body comprises 9 percent (437 students) of the total population and represents 84 countries. Students are required to live on campus during the first year. There is always something to do, whether it is a big event such as a concert or a comedian or a casual cookout with fellow residents. Embry-Riddle sponsors more than 100 clubs and student organizations, ranging from academically oriented groups such as the Robotics Association to recreational clubs such as skydiving, sport aviation, pep band, and crew.

For International Students

An International Student Orientation is scheduled to help arriving students adjust to the American academic system and learn to negotiate successfully in a new cultural environment. Staff members also assist with local housing, transportation, banking, and other arrangements. The International Student Services staffers plan activities throughout the year, including visits to the Kennedy Space Center, Disney theme parks, Sea World, and other attractions. For international students who have completed secondary schooling and are preparing for careers in management, flight, engineering, or the sciences, the Embry-Riddle Language Institute offers assistance. The year-round program provides preparation for university study or career training.

Emerson College

- **Contact:**
  Sara S. Ramirez
  Director of Undergraduate Admission
  Emerson College
  120 Boylston Street
  Boston, MA 02116-4624
  Phone: 617-824-8600
  Fax: 617-824-8609
  E-mail: international@emerson.edu
- Private, four-year, coed
- Urban setting
- Total enrollment: 3,000
- Student-faculty ratio: 14:1
- 2006–07 Tuition and fees: $25,248
- 2006–07 Room and board: $10,870

- **International students: 3%**
- **Countries represented: 35**
- **International students applied: 190**
- **International students accepted: 105**
- **International students enrolled: 27**
- **Admissions tests:**
  - TOEFL required (min. score 550)
  - SAT: Recommended
  - ACT: Recommended
- **Application deadline: September admission, 1/5; January admission, 11/1**
- **On-campus housing: Available**
- **Summer housing: Not available**

Area and Climate

Located on Boston Common in the heart of the city's Theatre District, Emerson's campus is within walking distance of the Massachusetts State House, historic Freedom Trail, Chinatown, the financial district, and numerous restaurants and museums. Boston is an international city with more than thirty foreign consulates, several multinational corporations, and dozens of colleges and universities. The climate has four distinct seasons with average temperatures ranging from 85°F (29°C) in summer to -20°F (-7°C) in winter.

Education

Founded in 1880, Emerson is one of the premier colleges in the United States for communication and the arts. The curriculum engages students as active participants in learning by providing unique opportunities to explore their fields of interest. Theory and experience are linked in the classroom and in applied learning settings, such as broadcast studios, stages and performance spaces, digital production and editing labs, writing workshops, and facilities in which students in communication sciences and disorders observe therapy. Undergraduate programs include acting; broadcast journalism; communication sciences and disorders; communication studies; marketing communication: advertising and public relations; media production (animation and motion media, digital postproduction, film, interactive media, radio, sound design, studio television production, writing for film and television); media studies; musical theater; political communication: leadership, politics, and social advocacy; print and multimedia journalism; stage/production management; theater design/technology; theater education; theater studies; and writing, literature and publishing. The College also sponsors an internship program in Los Angeles, study abroad in the Netherlands, and a summer film term in Prague.

Campus Life

Emerson attracts a globally diverse student body and encourages collaboration among students through course work and cocurricular activities. There are more than sixty student organizations and performance groups, fourteen intercollegiate sports, student publications, and honor societies. Approximately 1,200 students are housed on campus, some in special living/learning communities, such as the Writers' Block and Digital Culture Floor. The residence halls are air-conditioned, with cable television and Internet access. Wireless service is available in several campus locations. Emerson also has a fitness center, athletic field, and new gymnasium; a student health center; two radio stations and sound-treated television stations; an integrated digital newsroom; and an eleven-story performance and production center housing a theater design/technology center, makeup lab, and costume shop.

For International Students

International students are a vital part of the Emerson community, and Boston is home to one of the largest international student populations in the United States. The College's International Student Affairs Office provides a variety of services, such as international student orientation at the start of each semester, immigration counseling and visa paperwork processing, sponsorship of social and cultural events, and cross-cultural adjustment counseling.

Emporia State University

- Contact:
    James F. Harter
    Assistant Vice President, International
        Education
    Emporia State University
    Emporia, KS 66801-5087
    Phone: 620-341-5374
    Fax: 620-341-5918
    E-mail: oisa@emporia.edu
    Web site: http://www.emporia.edu/oie
- Public, four-year, coed
- Rural setting
- Enrollment: 6,200

- Student/faculty ratio: 20:1
- 2006–07 Tuition and fees: $11,122
- 2007–08 Room and board: $5611
- International students: 3%
- Countries represented: 40
- International students enrolled: 337
- Admissions tests: Not required
- Application deadline: Rolling
- On-campus housing: Available
- Summer housing: Available

Area and Climate

Emporia State University is located in east-central Kansas. The city of Emporia is an industrial, educational, trade, and medical center serving more than 60,000 people. Emporia enjoys an outstanding location due to its proximity and easy access to three major metropolitan areas: Wichita, Topeka, and Kansas City. The downtown area is a short walk from campus and offers convenient shopping, banking, and dining, and access to other businesses. Kansas has four colorful seasons: spring, summer, fall, and winter. The climate is always changing and includes warm, temperate summers and light snow in winter. Rain can be expected throughout the year.

Education

Emporia State University, home of the National Teachers Hall of Fame, was established in 1863 to train teachers for the state of Kansas. Today, Emporia State University is a nationally and regionally accredited university offering more than fifty majors with fifty-three areas of concentration that lead to seventeen degrees at the bachelor's, master's, and doctoral levels. In addition to the Teachers' College, there are the School of Business (accredited by AACSB International–The Association to Advance Collegiate Schools of Business) and the College of Liberal Arts and Sciences, which offer bachelor's and master's degree programs. The Library and Information Management School offers a bachelor of integrated studies along with master's and Ph.D. programs. For a complete list of degrees and majors, students should visit the Web site (http://www.emporia.edu/acadaff/departments.htm). Emporia State University also offers many Internet courses and a number of online degrees; information can be found at http://lifelong.

emporia.edu. The student-to-teacher ratio is 20:1, and the faculty members are committed to helping their students succeed. The academic year consists of two 16-week semesters and a 10-week summer session.

Campus Life

Housing in Emporia is inexpensive and plentiful. Almost 1,000 students live on campus in the three residence hall complexes. The residence halls offer study and recreational facilities as well as opportunities to meet American students. Off campus, many apartments, duplexes, and rooming houses are within walking distance. With affordable tuition and living costs, a safe and friendly campus and community, exciting athletics and special events, and outstanding academic and degree programs, international students are sure to gain a rich and varied university experience at Emporia State University. The University has more than 130 student organizations involving departmental, social, religious, and special interests, along with an active associated student government.

For International Students

International students can take advantage of Emporia State University's multilevel, intensive English programs, as well as the services and activities provided by the Office of International Education. The international programs, including the International Club, the International Choir, and many national and cultural associations, are among the most outstanding in the United States. These organizations provide international students with many opportunities to participate in academic, athletic, cultural, and social events. These special activities, along with an excellent academic program, provide students with a rich educational experience. International students find the city of Emporia a safe and friendly place in which to achieve their academic and personal goals.

Fairleigh Dickinson University

- Contact:
  Heather Augar and Barbara Heissenbuttel,
      Directors, Office of International
      Admissions
  Fairleigh Dickinson University
  1000 River Road, T-KB1-01
  Teaneck, NJ 07666
  Phone: 201-692-2205
  Fax: 201-692-2560
  E-mail: global@fdu.edu
  Web site: http://www.fdu.edu
- Private, comprehensive, multicampus, coed
- Suburban settings
- Enrollment: 12,112
- Student-faculty ratio: 16:1
- 2007–08 Tuition and fees: $27,319 (estimated)
- 2007–08 Room and board: $10,159 (estimated)

- International students: Metropolitan Campus, 23%;
  College at Florham, 8%
- Countries represented: 81
- International students applied: 532 (undergraduate)
- International students accepted: 209 (undergraduate)
- International students enrolled: 52 (undergraduate)
- Admissions tests:
  - TOEFL: Required (min. score 550 PBT; 213
    CBT; 79 iBT)
  - SAT or ACT: Recommended for all freshman
    applicants; required for all freshman applicants
    for the Col. Fairleigh S. Dickinson Scholarship
- Application deadline: Fall, July 1; spring, December 1
- On-campus housing: Available
- Summer housing: Available

Area and Climate

Fairleigh Dickinson University is located on two campuses in northern New Jersey on the east coast of the United States near New York City. Students can enjoy all the benefits of being close to a major city while studying on a safe, suburban campus. The University is close enough for weekend visits to other major U.S. cities, including Boston, Philadelphia, and Washington, D.C. The climate offers seasonal changes, with temperatures ranging from 98°F (36°C) in summer (June–September) to 23°F (–5°C) in winter (November–March).

Education

Founded in 1942, Fairleigh Dickinson University is a leader in global education, committed to serving its students. More than 12,000 students, including over 1,100 international students from eighty-one countries, are enrolled at its two campuses. There are more than 100 undergraduate programs, including biology, communications, computer science, economics, engineering, hotel and restaurant management, information technology, international business, liberal arts, and marketing. Graduate program offerings include nearly a dozen M.B.A. and graduate business degrees; M.I.S. studies; M.S. programs in biology, computer science, computer engineering, e-commerce, electrical engineering, and hospitality management; and M.A. programs in multilingual education and psychology.

Campus Life

Fairleigh Dickinson University's Metropolitan Campus is located in Teaneck, New Jersey, just 8 miles (13 kilometers) from New York City. Its university atmosphere attracts a diverse student body from the U.S. and abroad. It includes the resources of a major graduate center, access to New York City, and a wide range of professional and accelerated studies. Situated on 88 acres (36 hectares), this cosmopolitan campus is within easy walking distance of many international shops and groceries, bookstores, churches, and restaurants. For student athletics, the Metropolitan Campus offers Division I sports and intramurals.

The College at Florham, located in suburban Madison, New Jersey, about 35 miles (56 kilometers) from New York City, offers a classic experience for the contemporary world in a small college setting. It emphasizes residential living, hands-on learning, graduate and professional school preparation, and customized educational options. Students enjoy numerous activities on this 178-acre (72-hectare) countryside campus, including many fraternities and sororities, Division III athletics, and intramurals.

In addition to its two New Jersey campuses, Fairleigh Dickinson University has international campuses in England and in Canada. Wroxton College, located 75 miles from London, near Stratford-upon-Avon, is housed in a fully modernized Jacobean mansion on fifty acres of lawns, lakes, and woodlands. Students can spend a semester or summer studying at Wroxton.

FDU-Vancouver is located in Vancouver, British Columbia, one of the world's most scenic and cosmopolitan cities. Warmed by Pacific Ocean currents and surrounded by mountains, the city enjoys mild temperatures year-round. In addition to bachelor's degree programs, FDU-Vancouver offers summer-study opportunities.

For International Students

International education has been an important part of Fairleigh Dickinson University since its founding more than sixty years ago. Its location near New York City, which is a world center of culture, international business, and trade, enables the University to offer international students a broad educational and living experience in one of the world's largest international communities. International students at Fairleigh Dickinson can take advantage of a 1-Year Global M.B.A. program, which brings together international and domestic students to study international business. Since its inception in 1945, Fairleigh Dickinson has enjoyed a unique association with the United Nations, a tradition that has deepened recently through its partnership with the Ambassador's Club at the United Nations and the University's UN Pathways Program. Each semester, numerous ambassadors and diplomats visit the University's campuses for lectures and discussions with students. Interactive videoconferences also are regularly broadcast from the UN to Fairleigh Dickinson's two New Jersey campuses. Academic scholarships of up to $18,000 are available for international undergraduate students. Students may apply online at http://www.applyweb.com/apply/fdu/menu.html.

Ferris State University

- Contact:
  International Student Services
  Ferris State University
  1201 South State Street, CSS 201
  Big Rapids, MI 49307-2747
  Phone: 231-591-5444 or 3915
  Fax: 231-591-3944
  E-mail: internationaladmissions@ferris.edu
  Web site: http://www.ferris.edu/international
- Public, comprehensive, coed
- Rural setting
- Enrollment: 12,575
- 2006–07 Tuition and fees: $14,640
- 2006–07 Room and board: $7220

- Countries represented: 36
- International students applied: 519
- International students accepted: 126
- Admissions tests:
  - TOEFL: Required (min. score 500 paper-based; 173 computer-based; 61 Internet-based) or
  - IELTS (min. score 6.0) or
  - SAT: Reading score at least 450
- Application deadline: Fall, 6/15; spring, 10/15; summer, 2/15
- On-campus housing: Guaranteed
- Summer housing: Guaranteed, free

Area and Climate

Ferris State University's (FSU) campus is located in Big Rapids, a small, safe, and friendly city that is surrounded by nature and is within easy access of Chicago and Detroit. Michigan has four very distinct seasons (spring, summer, autumn, and winter), which provides opportunities for a wide array of recreational and community activities including tennis, festivals, snow skiing, golf, swimming, and intramural sports.

Education

FSU, founded in 1884, provides students with small class sizes, leadership opportunities, and the personal attention they need to achieve success. Ferris' small classes (80 percent have fewer than 25 students) are taught by professors, not graduate assistants. Ferris students may choose from more than 170 undergraduate and graduate majors in associate, bachelor's, master's, and doctoral degree programs. Colleges at FSU include Allied Health Sciences, Arts and Sciences, Business, Education and Human Services, Michigan College of Optometry, Pharmacy and Technology. Because of FSU's commitment to providing career-oriented, technological, and professional education, classes and labs take place in state-of-the-art facilities using the latest technological equipment. Many of the programs are unique in the state and in the country. The Ferris Library for Information Technology and Education (FLITE) offers a place for study and research with all the electronic media and resources that students require, including 300 computer stations.

Campus Life

Ferris students come from all over Michigan, the United States, and thirty-six countries around the world, which gives the University a very diverse and dynamic environment. Ferris offers nineteen on-campus residence halls, with all rooms furnished and complete with free Internet connections and cable TV; five on-campus dining facilities; and single- and married-student on-campus apartments, also with free Internet and cable TV. The Ferris campus offers a comprehensive student services center, more than 200 student organizations, academic support services, an on-campus 18-hole golf course, sport facilities, and a complete fitness facility.

For International Students

The International Student Advisor and the Office of International Student Services offer support services to all international students, including advising, orientation, visa assistance, and airport transportation upon arrival. Ferris State University is dedicated to helping students make the most of their education and begins with an orientation specifically for international students to familiarize them with the campus and community. Orientation includes procedures such as registration, the U.S. academic system, banking, and health care. Legal matters such as visas and work permits are also reviewed. The International Student Organization (ISO) also welcomes and assists new students as they start their academic lives at Ferris. The ISO, the Hispanic Student Organization, and the Asian Student Organization are some of the very active organizations on campus that sponsor activities such as sporting events, social gatherings, and recreational activities. A highlight of the year on campus is the International Festival of Cultures, which is held each April. The campus and community are invited to visit exhibit booths from many countries, taste ethnic food, and enjoy traditional entertainment.

FIDM/The Fashion Institute of Design & Merchandising, Los Angeles Campus

- **Contact:**
  Susan Aronson, Director of Admissions
  FIDM/The Fashion Institute of Design &
  Merchandising, Los Angeles Campus
  919 South Grand Avenue
  Los Angeles, CA 90015
  Phone: 213-624-1201
  Fax: 213-624-4799
  Web site: http://www.fidm.edu
- **Private proprietary, two-year, coed**
- **Urban setting**
- **Enrollment: 6,000**

- **Student-faculty ratio: 16:1**
- **2007–08 Tuition and fees: $20,985**
- **International students: 8%**
- **Countries represented: 30**
- **Admissions tests:**
    - **TOEFL: Required (paper-based min. score 450)**
    - **SAT and ACT: Not required**
- **Application deadline: None**
- **On-campus housing: Not available**
- **Summer housing: Off campus**

Area and Climate

FIDM/The Fashion Institute of Design & Merchandising has four California campuses. The main campus is in Los Angeles in a 180,000-square-foot facility located in the 4-acre (2-hectare) Grand Hope Park, within a few short blocks of the world-famous Garment District. The Orange County campus in Irvine was strategically built in response to the area's growing importance as a business, cultural, and residential center. At the FIDM San Francisco campus, students get an amazing view of the city and well-known retailers. Located in the hub of the city, FIDM San Diego is surrounded by a mix of turn-of-the-century architecture and contemporary high-rises.

Education

FIDM was founded in February 1969 and now has an enrollment of 6,000 full-time students. FIDM offers programs that equip students to join global communities as skilled professionals. Some of the majors offered at FIDM are apparel manufacturing management, beauty industry merchandising and marketing, digital media, fashion design, film and TV production, footwear design, graphic design, interior design, international manufacturing and product development, jewelry design, merchandise marketing (fashion merchandising or product development), textile design, theater costume, TV and film costume design, and visual communication. Graduates earn A.A.

degrees. Advanced programs and transfer programs (for students with a prior college degree) are also available. Academic counseling and peer tutoring are available for all students. Internships and apprenticeships are available for all majors. FIDM provides the opportunity for students to participate in academic study tours in Europe, Asia, and New York. Exchange programs are also available with Esmod, Paris; Instituto Artictico dell' Abbigliamento Marangoni, Milan; Accademia Intenazionale d'Alta Mode e d'Arte del Costume Koefia, Rome; and many others. FIDM is on a four-quarter academic calendar; because of rolling enrollments, students may begin their studies in any quarter throughout the year. In addition, FIDM is currently offering a Bachelor of Science degree in business management, which has candidate status with the Accreditation Commission for Senior Colleges and Universities of the Western Association of Schools and Colleges.

Campus Life

A culturally diverse student body enjoys the benefits of a variety of student organizations and activities on campus. A professional career-placement staff serves all FIDM students and graduates. The housing service helps students find suitable housing facilities. The Student Activities Committee plans and coordinates social activities, cultural events, and community projects.

For International Students

ESL classes are provided for international students. The placement office works with employers worldwide to find career positions around the world. Some FIDM international students have chosen to stay in California.

Florida Gulf Coast University

- Contact:
   Office of Admissions
   Florida Gulf Coast University
   10501 FGCU Boulevard South
   Fort Myers, FL 33965-6565
   Phone: 888-889-1095
   E-mail: admissions@fgcu.edu
   Web site: http://www.fgcu.edu/
- Public, comprehensive, coed
- Suburban setting
- Enrollment: 8,316 (fall 2006)
- Student-faculty ratio: 17:1
- 2006–07 Tuition: $15,486 (nonresident)

- 2006–07 Room and board: $7640
- International students: 1%
- Countries represented: 80
- International students applied: 69
- International students accepted: 51
- Admissions tests:
   - TOEFL: Required
   - SAT or ACT: Required
- Application deadline: Fall, 7/2; spring, 11/20; summer, 4/2
- On-campus housing: Available
- Summer housing: Available

Area and Climate

Florida Gulf Coast University (FGCU) is located on 760 acres (308 hectares) in southwest Florida. The climate is subtropical. Temperatures range from 55°F (13°C) to 80°F (26°C) in January and from 70°F (21°C) to 90°F (32°C) in July and August. The Fort Myers area and southwest Florida offer many community resources. There are beautiful beaches and natural swamps, the Everglades National Park, sailing and beaches, dolphin watching, music and theater, cultural festivals, arts and crafts fairs, and many other recreational activities as well as service and professional organizations.

Education

Florida Gulf Coast University offers forty-four undergraduate and twenty graduate programs through five colleges: the College of Arts and Sciences, which comprises the Departments of Biological Sciences, Communication and Philosophy, Language and Literature, Marine and Ecological Sciences, Physical Sciences and Mathematics, Social and Behavioral Sciences, and Visual and Performing Arts and the Bower School of Music; the Lutgert College of Business, which includes the U. A. Whitaker School of Engineering; the College of Education; the College of Health Professions, which comprises the Departments of Health Sciences, Nursing, Occupational Therapy and Community Health, and Physical Therapy and Human Performance; and the College of Professional Studies, which houses the Divisions of Justice Studies, Social Work, Public Affairs, and Resort and Hospitality Management. Opened in 1997, FGCU is in the enviable position of having facilities especially designed and built for a campus of the twenty-first century. In addition to these modern high-technology facilities, students benefit from dedicated teachers who bring to the classroom the inspiration, insights, and knowledge gained through professional affiliations and re-search in wide areas of expertise. FGCU's goal is to provide students with the competencies and skills necessary for success in life and work.

Campus Life

FGCU is a student-centered institution that is defined by academic quality, outstanding teaching, and a beautiful campus environment. The University has intentionally cultivated a diverse student population that enhances and enriches all the students' experiences, both academic and extracurricular. The Office of Student Affairs supports programs that encourage a sense of community and reflect the University's mission of total student development. It is committed to providing an environment conducive to personal, cultural, social, ethical, emotional, recreational, spiritual, and organizational development through cocurricular involvement. The University offers a wide range of clubs, organized sports teams and activities, and other extracurricular activities such as concerts, dances, lectures, movies, skating, and weekend trips. There are also many on-campus recreational facilities, such as a fitness center, pool, and lake adjacent to the apartment-style residence hall.

For International Students

The International Services Office is dedicated to providing comprehensive support services for international students at FGCU. Staff members assist students not only in successfully pursuing their academic goals but also in areas such as financial, immigration, and legal matters; employment and internships; campus life; and living in Florida. The International Services Office also sponsors the International Club, which is open to all students. The club meets regularly and sponsors activities and events, such as International Student Reception, trips to Florida sites, community projects, internationally focused programs on campus, and International Celebration. It is an excellent social and educational outlet for both international and American students and an opportunity for international students to share their cultures with FGCU, develop leadership skills, and become active members of the FGCU community.

Florida International University

- **Contact:**
  Office of Undergraduate Admissions
  Florida International University
  University Park, PC140
  Miami, FL 33199
  Phone: 305-348-2363
  Fax: 305-348-3648
  E-mail: admiss@fiu.edu
  Web site: http://admissions.FIU.edu
- **State-supported, university, coed**
- **Urban setting**
- **Enrollment: 38,000**
- **Student-faculty ratio: 18:1**
- **2006–07 Tuition and fees: $15,812**
- **2006–07 Room and board: $7566**

- **International students: 8%**
- **Countries represented: 138**
- **International students applied: 2,029 (undergraduate)**
- **International students accepted: 955**
- **International students enrolled: 495**
- **Admissions tests:**
  - **TOEFL: Required (min. score 500 paper-based; 173 computer-based; 63 Internet-based)**
  - **SAT or ACT: Required**
- **Application deadline: Fall, 4/1; spring, 9/1; summer, 2/1**
- **On-campus housing: Available**
- **Summer housing: Available**

Area and Climate

Florida International University (FIU) has two main sites: University Park in southwest Miami-Dade County, 10 miles west of downtown Miami, and the Biscayne Bay Campus, located on Biscayne Bay in North Miami. Miami, one of the most international cities in the hemisphere, is Florida's largest urban center and a major transportation and business hub of the southeastern U.S. The area is dynamic, artistically expressive, and cosmopolitan and is the gateway for Latin America and the Caribbean. The climate is subtropical. The average temperature is 76°F (24°C), with temperatures above 60°F (18°C) during the winter months and above 80°F (30°C) in the summer. The south Florida community offers a tremendous variety of recreational activities, performing arts and other cultural events, and professional sports. Disney World, the Everglades, marine and state parks, Seaquarium, Metro Zoo, Fairchild Tropical Gardens, and Parrot Jungle Island are popular student attractions. Other favorite year-round activities include swimming, waterskiing, scuba diving, sailing, tennis, golf, and horseback riding.

Education

FIU has been ranked among the top 100 public national universities in the *U.S. News & World Report* annual guide to "America's Best Colleges." Through its eighteen colleges and schools, FIU offers more than 200 baccalaureate, master's, and doctoral degree programs in more than 280 majors, including preprofessional programs in dentistry, law, medicine, and veterinary medicine. Major academic divisions are the College of Architecture and the Arts, College of Arts and Sciences, College of Business Administration, College of Education, College of Engineering and Computing, Honors College, College of Law, School of Nursing and Health Sciences, and College of Social Work, Justice, and Public Affairs. There are also the Schools of Accounting, Hospitality and Tourism Management, and Journalism and Mass Communication. In addition to the academic departments, the University's interdisciplinary centers, institutes, and special programs conduct advanced research in a wide range of areas. Sponsored research funding from outside sources is more than $75 million.

Campus Life

Students can take advantage of a diverse range of social and cultural events on and off campus. The University currently has more than 300 registered student organizations that enrich campus life and contribute to the social, cultural, and academic growth of students. University organizations sponsor concerts, films, plays, lectures, ethnic festivals, and other special events during the year. Students have opportunities to participate in student government, clubs, fraternities, sororities, and honor societies. Athletic opportunities are numerous. Students can participate in intercollegiate, intramural, and recreational sports. Both campuses offer state-of-the-art recreational facilities and apartment-style housing that provides students with the opportunity to live with others in a convenient and supportive residential setting.

For International Students

The University offers a full range of services to support international students in both their academic and personal lives. The Office of International Student and Scholar Services assists international students by providing advising services related to immigration, legal, personal, academic, cultural, social, and financial concerns. The English Language Institute (ELI) at FIU is a fully equipped, state-of-the-art language training center that is part of the University's College of Arts and Sciences. Since 1978, the ELI has taught close to 20,000 international students and professionals from more than forty-five countries to master the English language through the use of proven educational methods and the most up-to-date learning facilities.

Foothill College

- **Contact:**
  Sherri Mines
  International Admissions Coordinator
  Foothill College
  Los Altos Hills, CA 94022
  Phone: 650-949-7161
  Fax: 650-949-7080
  E-mail: foothillinternational@foothill.edu
  Web site: http://www.foothill.edu/international
- Public, 2-year, coed
- Suburban setting
- Enrollment: 18,000
- Student-faculty ratio: 25:1
- 2006–07 Tuition and fees: $5898 (three quarters)

- **2006–07 Room and board: $7500 (homestay for ten months)**
- International students: 4%
- Countries represented: 70+
- Admissions tests:
  - **TOEFL: Required (min. score 500 paper-based, 173 computer-based, or 61 iBT) or a minimum IELTS score of 5.0**
  - SAT and ACT: Not required
- Application deadline: Fall, 6/30; winter, 10/31; and spring, 1/31
- Housing: Host families and off-campus apartments

Area and Climate

Foothill College is located on 122 acres in the rolling foothills of Los Altos Hills, in the heart of the world-renowned Silicon Valley, 45 minutes south of San Francisco and 20 minutes west of San Jose, the tenth-largest city in the U.S. Foothill College has been called "the most beautiful community college ever built" for its distinctive Pacific-style architecture. With 300 sunny days and average temperature of 21°C all year round, Foothill offers a truly California lifestyle: a short drive will bring you to the Pacific coast beaches with some of the best surfing, golfing, and sightseeing in the country. The Valley is served by inexpensive bus, train, and light rail public transportation systems and two bus lines that directly enter the Foothill campus. Foothill is close to headquarters of such companies as Google and Yahoo! in neighboring Mountain View, as well as to Apple, Adobe, eBay, Cisco Systems, and many others. The nearby cities of Sunnyvale, Santa Clara, and San Jose are consistently ranked as the country's safest.

Education

Since opening in 1958, Foothill College has emerged as one of the outstanding accredited (Western Association of Schools and Colleges) two-year colleges in the United States. Foothill's academic programs lead to Associate in Arts or Associate in Science degrees and parallel requirements for the first two years of university study. Students can choose from more than 100 university transfer majors and professional certificate programs, from business and film to prelaw and enterprise networking. They can get a competitive edge by studying the hottest fields of the future, such as biotechnology, informatics, GIS, video game development, and travel careers. Thanks to special articulation agreements and Transfer Center assistance, students transfer to highly selective, top-ranked, four-year universities to continue their studies. Special programs include the honors program; Study Abroad Program, with options in eleven countries; the Internship Pro-

gram; and computer-assisted tutorial labs for writing, math, and science. The academic year consists of three 12-week quarters starting in September, January, and April.

Campus Life

Foothill offers outstanding campus living and facilities. Highlights include leading-edge computer and multimedia labs, dental clinic, stadiums, golf and tennis complex, Olympic-size swimming pool, Krause Center for Innovation, Bamboo Garden, and an observatory. A new chapter will be launched in 2007–08 with the construction of a modern Campus Center and Life Sciences and Performing Arts Centers. Foothill inspires students to engage, learn, and lead. The campus has more than fifty dynamic clubs, student government, intercollegiate athletics, a newspaper, a radio station, and unique cultural heritage months. Athletics include basketball, football, golf, soccer, softball, swimming, tennis, volleyball, and water polo.

For International Students

International students participate in a mandatory four-day orientation, three to four weeks before the start of the first quarter, with comprehensive academic, immigration, and cultural counseling. Extensive staff support with 6 full-time counselors ensures student success and well-being, from class registration help to career search and tax-filing assistance. Special activities are monthly coffee hours, free tickets to Celebrity Forum (with such speakers as Bill Cosby, Mikhail Gorbachev, and Bill Clinton), an annual ice-skating trip, International Film Festival, and Thanksgiving and Valentine's Day dinners. The International Student Connection Club engages all students in celebrating diversity and organizing the annual International Night celebration. All students receive the interactive electronic newsletter. Foothill offers a comprehensive English as a second language program at six levels of proficiency. Individual tutoring in English and in all academic areas is available through the Tutorial Center. Comprehensive health insurance is mandatory and is charged quarterly with the student's registration. Since there is no housing on campus, homestays ($750 per month) with carefully screened local families are offered.

Fordham University

- Contact:
    Monica Esser
    Associate Director for International
        Admission
    Office of Undergraduate Admission–Duane
        Library
    Fordham University
    441 East Fordham Road
    Bronx, NY 10458
    Phone: 718-817-5204
    Fax: 718-817-2424
    E-mail: esscr@fordham.edu
    Web site: http://www.fordham.edu/
        admissions/entry_requirements/
        rose_hill__lincoln_c/
        international_studen_2093.asp
- Independent, Roman Catholic, coed
- Urban setting
- Enrollment: 15,814

- Student-faculty ratio: 11:1
- 2007–08 Tuition and fees: $31,800
- 2007–08 Room and board: $12,540
- International students: 1%
- Countries represented: 44
- International students applied: 653
- International students accepted: 236
- International students enrolled: 38
- Admissions tests:
    - TOEFL
    - SAT: Recommended
    - ACT: Recommended
- Application deadline: January 15
- On-campus housing: Available
- Summer housing: Available

Area and Climate

During the summer (June through September), the weather is often hot and humid, with temperatures ranging between 70°F (21°C) and the 90s (above 32°C). The winter season (late November through March) is marked by sudden and extreme weather changes; several days of cold weather may be followed by days of moderate temperatures. As an international center of both culture and commerce, New York City has no equal. Fordham University has been a vital part of this dynamic city, offering its students a campus that functions as an urban classroom that is unique in its combination of cultural, commercial, and educational experiences.

Education

The eleven graduate, undergraduate, and professional schools at Fordham University reside on its two major campuses in New York City and two in Westchester County. Each school is among the most highly rated in the country. More than sixty-five academic programs are available, and all students take courses in a common core curriculum. Fordham University Libraries own more than 2 million volumes and subscribe to nearly 16,000 periodicals and serials. The libraries are a depository for U.S. government documents. The Fordham University faculty includes about 650 full-time members; more than 93 percent hold a

doctorate or other terminal degree. In addition, 12 percent are members of minority groups.

Campus Life

Fordham undergraduates support and participate in about 120 student clubs and organizations. Student activity fees that are collected from all full-time day students are used to develop a lively student activities program, which provides leadership training, social events, entertainment, and out-of-class cocurricular experiences for students. Activities include student-run businesses, entertainment committees, club sports teams, and academic and cultural groups. With twenty-two men's and women's varsity sports teams, the Fordham Rams are members of the NCAA Division I and compete in the Atlantic 10 conference in all sports except football. The Rams were the 2003 Patriot League (NCAA Division I-AA) champions in football.

For International Students

Fordham University welcomes international students and currently enrolls students from about 100 different countries. The Office of International Students serves as a resource center for international students and facilitates their adjustment to life in the United States. The office assists students in matters concerning immigration, such as visas and SEVIS I-20 or DS-2019 forms or employment and travel authorizations. This office also provides personal counseling, information on health insurance requirements and banking, and programs to promote cross-cultural and international understanding.

Full Sail Real World Education

- Contact:
  Jessica Aloi-Smith
  International Liaison
  Full Sail Real World Education
  Winter Park, FL 32792
  Phone: 407-679-6333
  Fax: 407-215-9486
  E-mail: admissions@fullsail.com
  Web site: http://www.fullsail.com
- Private, coed
- Suburban setting
- Enrollment: 5,219
- Student-faculty ratio: 10:1

- 2006–07 Tuition and fees: $40,005 to $61,775 per degree program
- International students: 2%
- Countries represented: 35
- International students enrolled: 100
- Admissions test:
  - TOEFL: Required (min. score 550 PBT, 213 CBT, 79 iBT)
  - SAT or ACT: Optional
- Application deadline: 3 months prior to program start date
- On-campus housing: Not available

Area and Climate

Full Sail's campus is situated on 90 acres (36 hectares) in the city of Winter Park, Florida, which is in the southeastern United States. Entertainment, restaurants, and shopping are plentiful in Central Florida. The school is 20 minutes from downtown Orlando, 35 minutes from Disney World and Universal Studios, 1 hour from Cape Canaveral and the Atlantic beaches, and 2 hours from the Gulf of Mexico. Central Florida typically experiences warm weather year-round. Summer temperatures range from 70° to 95°F (21° to 35°C), and winter temperatures are slightly cooler, from 50° to 70°F (10° to 21°C).

Education

Established in 1979, Full Sail Real World Education is a private, coeducational college offering extensive training in entertainment media production and entertainment technology. Associate of Science degrees are offered in recording arts and in show production and touring. Bachelor of Science degrees are offered in computer animation, digital arts and design, entertainment business, film, and game development. Hands-on experience and solid, practical knowledge combine to provide an education where learning meets the real world. Students receive an introduction to many job opportunities in each career field and an overview of what each position requires.

Full Sail's facilities include recording consoles, digital video editing workstations, cameras, concert sound systems, computerized moving lights, and computer/graphic workstations used to create Web sites, animation sequences, 3-D graphics, computer-generated models, characters, visual effects, and interactive games. Full Sail provides extensive hands-on instruction in all of these areas and more, offering a unique style of training that puts students right in the middle of the entertainment and media production industry while in school.

At Full Sail, tuition ranges from $40,005 to $61,775 (US) per degree program. These tuition costs include books, lab fees, course materials, career development assistance, and lifetime auditing.

Campus Life

Full Sail is home to more than 5,000 students, representing fifty states and thirty-five countries worldwide. The student body is primarily men (89 percent). The International Student Society provides a chance to meet students from around the world. Full Sail employs a full-time Housing Manager, who is dedicated to providing information about affordable accommodations in one of the many apartment complexes near the school. The Housing Manager can also help with information regarding roommates (other incoming Full Sail students), utilities, phones, furniture, and helpful community programs in the Central Florida area.

For International Students

Full Sail warmly welcomes applications from international students interested in the entertainment media fields. The current student body represents over thirty-five countries worldwide. An International Student Liaison is available to assist international students with matters regarding visa status. Full Sail's liaisons and other administrative staff members work closely to answer questions and ensure a smooth transition for international students.

Genesee Community College

- **Contact:**
  Meryll Pentz, International Advisor
  International Admissions
  Genesee Community College
  1 College Road
  Batavia, NY 14020
  Phone: 585-345-0055 Ext. 6457
  Fax: 585-345-6810
  E-mail: mapentz@genesee.edu
  Web site: http://www.genesee.edu/depts/
       admissions/international/
- Public, two-year, coed
- Small-town setting
- Enrollment: 6,400
- Student-faculty ratio: 20:1
- 2005–06 Tuition and fees: $3540

- 2005–06 Room and board: $4100
- International students: 2%
- Countries represented: 18
- International students applied: 131
- International students accepted: 131
- International students enrolled: 131
- Admissions tests:
  - TOEFL (paper-based min. score 460; computer-based min. score 140; Internet-based min. score 48)
  - SAT and ACT: Recommended
- Application deadline: Rolling
- On-campus housing: Available
- Summer housing: Available

Area and Climate

Genesee Community College (GCC) is located just outside the city of Batavia in upstate New York, centered between the greater metropolitan areas of Buffalo and Rochester. The 240-acre (97-hectare) Batavia campus and College Village, the student residence community adjacent to the main campus, are nestled amid the scenic hills and farmland of the quiet Genesee County countryside. Yet less than 40 minutes away are two urban areas teeming with cultural, sporting, and civic opportunities. In addition to the main campus in Batavia, Genesee Community College also has five Campus Centers located in Livingston, Orleans, and Wyoming Counties.

Education

With six campus locations in four counties and more than 6,000 students, GCC has become one of the most highly respected community colleges in the United States. Since its founding in 1966, GCC has become an important part of the prestigious State University of New York (SUNY) education system. More than fifty-eight academic programs of study are designed to fill a wide variety of interests. Associate degrees and certificates are offered in business and commerce, computers and technology, creative arts, health care, human services, law and criminal justice, liberal arts, math and science, office technology and support, sports and physical education, and teaching and education.

Campus Life

At Genesee, more than 1,000 students every year participate in activities sponsored by student clubs, intercollegiate athletic teams, the student government, and the Student Activities Council.

The College offers concerts throughout the year, comedy showcases, blockbuster movies, performing arts, travel excursions, and leadership training programs. Lunchtime Live hosts professional comedians, musicians, magicians, hypnotists, or novelty groups twice monthly during the academic year. In addition, the Student Activities Council sponsors many social events, such as Up All Night, dances, festivals, and a spring break trip. The student government hosts the Student Development Series, which provides opportunities to experience interactive and group learning activities while enhancing interpersonal and team-building skills.

For International Students

Thanks in part to available housing nearby, a growing number of international students have chosen to make Genesee part of their educational career. GCC can help international students transfer to a four-year institution once they have completed their two-year degree. Although no financial aid is available, the art department and the athletic department do offer some support in their programs. Further information can be obtained from each area.

Georgia College and State University

- **Contact:**
  Jason Wynn
  International Admissions Counselor
  Campus Box 49
  Georgia College and State University
  Milledgeville, GA 31061
  Phone: 478-445-4789
  Fax: 478-445-2623
  E-mail: intladm@gcsu.edu
  Web site: http://www.gcsu.edu/international
- **Public, comprehensive, coed**
- **Small-town setting**
- **Enrollment: 5,000**
- **Student-faculty ratio: 15:1**
- **2006–07 Tuition and fees: $15,352**

- **2006–07 Room and board: $7116**
- **International students: 2%**
- **Countries represented: 45**
- **International students applied: 199**
- **International students accepted: 67**
- **International students enrolled: 42**
- **Admissions test:**
  - **TOEFL: Required (min. score 500 PBT, 173 CBT, 61 iBT)**
  - **SAT and ACT: Not required**
- **Application deadline: April 1, September 1**
- **On-campus housing: Available**
- **Summer housing: Available**

Area and Climate

The University is located in the beautiful historic district of Milledgeville (population 25,000), conveniently located in the center of Georgia and within easy driving distance of all major cities in the state, including Atlanta (95 miles/153 kilometers northwest). This friendly and attractive small town is surrounded by gently rolling hills and forests, and its sunny and mild year-round climate makes the University a perfect place to study. International flights land at Hartsfield-Jackson Airport in Atlanta. Nearby Macon has its own commercial airport and interstate bus service.

Education

Founded in 1889, the University has been designated the public liberal arts university for the state of Georgia and houses the fully accredited Schools of Liberal Arts and Sciences, Business, Education, and Health Sciences. *Kaplan/ Newsweek College Catalog 2002* recognized the University as one of the Southeast's most academically challenging, and *U.S. News & World Report* ranks the school among the top twenty master's universities in the South. The highly qualified faculty offers more than eighty undergraduate and graduate programs of study in a supportive environment of small classes and individual advisement. Accounting, biology, business, computer science, economics, education, information systems, nursing, and various preprofessional programs are popular majors with international students, and scholarships and assistantships are available to assist with tuition costs. Fall semester runs from mid-August to mid-December; spring semester from early January to early May.

Campus Life

The University offers an extensive array of extracurricular activities, including more than 100 student organizations and a dozen intercollegiate and intramural sports for its diverse student body. The residential campus is one of the safest, according to U.S. Department of Education statistics, and offers a number of on-campus housing choices, from the traditional-style residence hall to apartment-style living. All university residence halls and apartments are newly built and come furnished with full amenities, including high-speed Internet and cable television access, laundry facilities and kitchens. Many students choose to live in "Casa Mondo: The Cross-Cultural Living Experience," where students from different cultural backgrounds live together and participate in special programs.

For International Students

The more than 100 international students from forty-five countries are an important part of the University. They enjoy the support of both the University and Milledgeville community, as well as the friendships they develop among U.S. students and the diverse international student group. Many belong to the International Club, which organizes weekend trips, activities, and campus-wide international programs, such as the annual International Week and International Dinner. The International Education Center provides information and counseling to international students, assists them with group medical insurance and health care, and organizes community and campus activities, such as the International Host Family Program, International Student Orientation, and Atlanta airport pickups for new students. The Career Center works closely with international students in identifying job opportunities in the U.S. and abroad.

Georgia State University

- **Contact:**
  International Student and Scholar Services
  Room 252-Sparks Hall
  Georgia State University
  30 Gilmer Street SE
  Atlanta, GA 30303
  Phone: 404-463-9073
  Fax: 404-463-9077
  E-mail: international@gsu.edu
  Web site: http://www.gsu.edu/isss
- State-supported, comprehensive, coed
- Urban setting
- Enrollment: 27,000
- Student-faculty ratio: 17:1

- 2006–07 Tuition and fees: $8248 per semester
- 2006–07 Room and board: $2797 to $4668 per semester
- International students: 5%
- Countries represented: 145
- Admissions tests:
  - TOEFL: Required (min. score 550 PBT; 213 CBT; 79–80 iBT)
  - SAT or ACT: Required
- Application deadline: Fall, 3/1; spring, 10/1
- On-campus housing: Available
- Summer housing: Available

Area and Climate

The city of Atlanta is the capital of Georgia and the cultural and economic center of the nation's fastest-growing region. Atlanta is a thriving international city with a diverse population, flourishing business and industry, and exceptional educational and research universities. Georgia State University is located in the heart of Atlanta's central business district. All the cultural advantages and conveniences of big city living are a short walk or shuttle ride away.

Atlanta is situated in the foothills of the Southern Appalachian range and is within 5 hours' driving distance of the Great Smoky Mountains and the Atlantic and Gulf coasts. Numerous large lakes, state parks, and national parks are within easy driving distance of the city. Atlanta also has professional basketball, baseball, football, and hockey teams.

The climate is moderate. The average temperature is 72°F (22°C), with summer highs in the mid-90s (34° to 36°C) and winter lows in the 30s (-1° to 4°C).

Education

Georgia State University offers a vibrant learning atmosphere where traditional education is enhanced through hands-on learning, internships, guest lectures, and employment in the region's thriving financial, legal, communications, entertainment, hospitality, and business centers. The University offers more than fifty undergraduate and graduate programs covering some 250 fields of study through the Colleges of Arts and Sciences, Business, Education, Health and Human Services, and Law and the School of Policy Studies. Georgia State University is responsive to students' career goals and provides educational and research programs relevant to the practical needs of both the students and the community.

Campus Life

With thirty buildings, Georgia State University is a prominent fixture in the downtown community. Georgia State's more than 255 acres (103 hectares) (24 acres located downtown and more than 200 acres elsewhere in the metropolitan area) include centers for recreation, research, and academic instruction. There are three options for on-campus living: Georgia State Village, which consists of four residence halls; University Lofts—231 apartments in eight floor plans; and University Commons, a complex of four apartment buildings built around a large landscaped courtyard. While the University is recognized for its statewide, regional, and national contributions, students worldwide are drawn by the school's international focus. Students from 145 countries and all fifty states come each year to take part in the multicultural experience of living and learning at Georgia State.

For International Students

Georgia State University welcomes students and scholars from other countries. The University's philosophy of education recognizes the value of cultural exchange, which fosters better cooperation, friendship, and understanding among the peoples of the world. The office of International Student and Scholar Services provides international students with a wide range of services, including pre-admission/arrival services, orientation programs, immigration and personal advising, advocacy, educational programs, student program support and leadership development, nonresident tax compliance programming, insurance support, and postcompletion immigration services. In addition, students in need of additional English language assistance may enroll in Georgia State's Intensive English Program (IEP), which provides English classes ranging from basic levels to advanced levels. Georgia State University is authorized to offer I-20s for the Intensive English Program and for all graduate and undergraduate programs.

Glendale Community College (California)

- **Contact:**
  Mr. David J. Nelson, Director
  Int'l Recruitment and Outreach
  Glendale Community College
  1500 North Verdugo Road
  Glendale, CA 91208-2894

  Phone: 818-240-1000 Ext. 5439 or 5887
  Fax: 818-240-1345
  E-mail: gcciso@glendale.edu
         dnelson@glendale.edu
  Web site: http://www.glendale.edu

- **Public, two-year, coed**
- **Urban/suburban setting**
- **Enrollment: 15,000**
- **Student-faculty ratio: 25:1**
- **2006–07 Tuition and fees: $4340**
- **2006–07 Room and board: $11,000 (off-campus estimate)**
- **International students: 4% (550 total)**
- **Countries represented: 50**
- **International students applied: 300 (fall 2005)**
- **International students accepted: 250 (fall 2005)**
- **International students enrolled: 165 (fall 2005)**
- **Admissions tests:**
  - **TOEFL: Required (min. score 450 paper-based; 133 computer-based; 45 Internet-based)**
  - **SAT or ACT: Not required**
- **Application deadline: Fall, 7/1; winter, 11/1; spring, 12/1; and summer 4/15**
- **On-campus housing: Off-campus available**
- **Summer housing: Off-campus available**

Area and Climate

Glendale Community College (GCC) is located in a safe and suburban residential community about 10 miles (16 kilometers) northeast of Los Angeles. GCC offers a scenic hillside campus on the slopes of the San Rafael Mountains overlooking the valleys in Glendale and parts of the Los Angeles skyline. The location provides easy access to the various entertainment, social, and recreational attractions of southern California. Glendale has a population of 200,000. The weather is generally dry and warm year-round, with average temperatures ranging from 59°F (15°C) in the winter to 95°F (35°C) in the summer.

Education

GCC has served Glendale and the surrounding area since 1927, earning a strong reputation for academic excellence that meets the needs of a changing world. It is fully accredited by the Western Association of Schools and Colleges (WASC) and provides a variety of academic, vocational, and short-term course programs. Seventy-five academic majors are offered leading to the Associate in Arts and Associate in Science degrees. Popular majors include arts and animation design, aviation (with flight attendant studies), business administration, communications, computer science/information systems, culinary arts, hotel/restaurant management, music, nursing, theater, television production, and visual arts. The College also offers a wide selection of general education courses, allowing students to complete requirements for the first two years of study and then transfer to a university with full junior standing. GCC has one of the highest transfer rates within the California Community College system. Academic instruction at Glendale is highlighted by small, personalized classes, along with state-of-the-art technology, equipment, lab facilities, and teaching methods.

Campus Life

Approximately 15,000 students from diverse backgrounds attend day and evening classes for credit, including more than 500 international visa students from fifty countries. Facilities and services include the new student center/bookstore, cafeteria, and culinary arts building. Other features include a renovated library, student health center, transfer center, math/science center, advanced technology center, auditorium for the performing arts, fitness center, athletic track, and various computer labs. The College has an active Student Government Association and other multicultural organizations.

For International Students

Full support services, academic and immigration advising, and a flexible admission policy are available in the International Student Program department. The College welcomes applications from all over the world. All new international students are required to attend orientation before the start of the semester classes for counseling, placement testing, and academic course planning. Glendale also provides a comprehensive English as a second language program for academic credit.

Golden Gate University

- **Contact:**
  International Admissions and Advising
      Services
  536 Mission Street, First Floor
  San Francisco, CA 94105-2968
  Phone: 415-442-7800
  Fax: 415-442-7807
  E-mail: info@ggu.edu
  Web site: http://www.ggu.edu/student_services/
      international_admissions_advising
- Private, four-year, coed
- Urban setting
- Enrollment: 6,115
- Student-faculty ratio: 14:1

- 2006–07 Tuition and fees: $11,520
- 2006–07 Room and board: $16,950
- International students: 12%
- Countries represented: 83
- Admissions tests:
  - TOEFL: Required (min. score 197 (undergraduate) or 213 (graduate) computer-based)
  - SAT and ACT: Not required
- Application deadline: Fall, 5/15; spring, 9/15; summer, 1/15
- On-campus housing: Not available
- Summer housing: Not available

Area and Climate

Located in the heart of the Bay Area, in the center of downtown San Francisco, California, Golden Gate University (GGU) has San Francisco's legal and financial districts on one side and the growing "South of Market" corporate corridor on the other. One of the most beautiful cities in the world, San Francisco is made up of immigrants from every region. The University has close ties with businesses across the region, including Silicon Valley, and there is always something to do, from shopping to movies, sports, sightseeing, and the arts. GGU has convenient regional sites in northern California (Sacramento, San Jose, Monterey, and Walnut Creek), offering a range of undergraduate and graduate programs in business management and information technology, and in Seattle and Los Angeles, offering graduate taxation programs.

Education

GGU has been helping students build successful careers in business and management, taxation, and law for more than 100 years. GGU knows that the right learning environment can make all the difference, and students have the opportunity to share ideas and experiences, make new contacts, and gain practical insights from instructors who are also working professionals. Classes are small and the focus is on practical application in real-world situations.

GGU offers the B.A., B.B.A., B.S., M.A., M.B.A., M.S., D.B.A., J.D., LL.M., and S.J.D. degrees in areas such as accounting, business administration, finance, human resources, information technology, international business, law, marketing, organizational psychology, and taxation. Programs start throughout the year, with evening, weekend, and online classes available.

Campus Life

Life at GGU is defined by three features—information, involvement, and networking. Students are encouraged to play an active role in their education by staying informed in both the academic and administrative aspects of the University. Through the student newsletter, students can learn and contribute information about classes, the administration, teachers, fellow students, and alumni, as well as a variety of other topics. Through the student government, students can involve themselves in the policies, goals, and objectives that affect the student body by promoting student development and properly allocating student funds. Through the student organizations, students can network, learn team-building and leadership skills, and participate in social events through a variety of academic, professional, and cultural clubs offered at GGU. The University generally does not encourage applicants who are just graduating from high school. The average GGU student is in his or her late 20s and early 30s, so younger students are encouraged to seek admission to a good two-year community college and then transfer to Golden Gate once they have completed the general education course requirements.

For International Students

The International Admissions and Advising Office is staffed by professional counselors who help students from admissions through graduation. Services provided include visa assistance, temporary housing assistance, new student orientation, and registration. GGU's international students also benefit from personal and academic counseling, program-related internships, and career placement assistance for postgraduate education. Continuing students may apply for endowed and gift scholarships. Undergraduate transfer students from recognized U.S. or international institutions are eligible for automatic scholarships at the time of admission.

Goldey-Beacom College

- Contact:
    Kevin Barrett
    International Admissions Representative
    Goldey-Beacom College
    4701 Limestone Road
    Wilmington, DE 19808
    Phone: 302-225-6383
    Fax: 302-996-5408
    E-mail: barrett@gbc.edu
- Private, coed
- Suburban setting
- Enrollment: 1,600
- Student-faculty ratio: 30:1
- 2007–08 Tuition and fees: $17,170

- 2007–08 Room only: $4620 (board optional)
- International students: 22%
- Countries represented: 72
- International students applied: 119
- International students accepted: 50
- International students enrolled: 21
- Admissions tests:
    - TOEFL: Required (min. score 60 iBT)
    - SAT: Recommended
    - ACT: Not required
- Application deadline: Rolling
- On-campus housing: Guaranteed
- Summer housing: Available

Area and Climate

Goldey-Beacom College (G-BC) is located in beautiful Pike Creek Valley, a suburb of Wilmington, Delaware's largest city. The College is situated on 27 acres (11 hectares) and is within easy reach of the major cities Philadelphia, Baltimore, and Washington, D.C., as well as the beaches of Delaware and New Jersey. The area is accessible via Amtrak trains and Interstate 95. Philadelphia International Airport is a 30-minute drive away. Many cultural and recreational activities are available in the area.

Education

Goldey-Beacom is a private college that provides high-quality education for successful careers in business. For more than 120 years, the College has been responsive to the needs of the business community by giving its students a thorough understanding of the dynamics of business technology and theory. The College is a teaching-oriented institution nationally accredited by the Association of Collegiate Business Schools and Programs (ACBSP). Bachelor's and associate degrees are offered in accounting, business administration, computer information systems, human resource management, international business management, management, management information systems, and marketing. Campus facilities include computer labs, a Learning Resource Center, and an excellent library. The College operates on a semester calendar; limited winter and summer sessions are also available. The College also offers a five-year B.S./M.B.A. degree. Students can complete their undergraduate and graduate degrees in as quickly as five years.

Campus Life

Students at Goldey-Beacom represent many states as well as seventy-two countries. Twenty-two percent of the students currently enrolled are members of minority groups. The ratio of women to men is 2:1. The majority of the students at the College range in age from 18 to 22 years. Students are housed in four apartment-style residence halls. Resident students may cook their meals in their apartments or purchase a meal plan. Opportunities for leadership and involvement are provided by many clubs and organizations, including an active International Student Association, Honor Society, Student Government Association, professional clubs, and two sororities and fraternities. The College offers NCAA Division II intercollegiate men's basketball, cross-country, golf, and soccer and women's, basketball, cross-country, soccer, softball, tennis, and volleyball. The annual International Night offers students the opportunity to enjoy foods and entertainment, representing countries all over the world.

For International Students

Since 1979, students from all over the world have shared the campus of G-BC, pursuing degrees in business. International students make up more than 22 percent of the student population, coming from more than seventy-two countries. The diverse enrollment reflects the global economy of the twenty-first century. The Goldey-Beacom education reflects the international, interlocking nature of today's business world. At the start of each semester, a separate orientation program is held for international students. Counseling and support services are provided by the International Admission Office, the Academic Advisement Department, and the Student Affairs Office. A buddy program pairs new students with current international students to assist with the adjustment to life in the United States. A limited number of academic scholarships and on-campus, part-time employment opportunities exist. Additional career guidance and counseling services are provided by the Career Services Office, which also assists with locating off-campus employment. Instruction in basic English and tutorial services are provided by the College's Academic Resource Center.

Grand Valley State University

- Contact:
  Jim Crawley
  Assoc. Dir. for Int'l Recruitment
  Grand Valley State University
  1 Campus Drive
  Allendale, MI 49401-9403

  Phone: 616-331-2025
  Fax: 616-331-2000
  E-mail: global@gvsu.edu
  Web site: http://admissions.gvsu.edu
- Public, comprehensive, coed
- Rural setting
- Enrollment: 23,295
- 2006–07 Tuition and fees: $13,000

- 2006–07 Room and Board: $7000
- Countries represented: 45
- International students applied: 471
- International students accepted: 160
- Admissions tests:
  - TOEFL: Required (paper-based min. score 550; computer-based min. score 213; Internet-based min. score 79)
- Application deadline: 5/1 (2/1 for scholarship consideration)
- On-campus housing: Available
- Summer housing: Available

Area and Climate

Grand Valley State University (GSVU) is in Allendale, a rural community located midway between the city of Grand Rapids and the beaches of Lake Michigan. This is the residential campus, while certain bachelor's-level programs and all master's programs are offered on the new downtown Grand Rapids campus. Transportation is provided between the campuses. The Grand Rapids area offers a full schedule of sporting events, concerts, cultural events, and many other attractions. Michigan offers four seasons of weather, providing many outdoor activities to enjoy.

Education

Grand Valley State University is a teaching institution dedicated to providing the highest level of instruction. With more than seventy bachelor's and twenty-six master's degree offerings, GVSU offers students many of the most desirable areas of study. At the undergraduate level, students can choose from such majors as international business, international relations, computer science, computer information systems, biological sciences, hospitality and tourism management, engineering, and communication. Some of the available master's degrees include the M.B.A., computer information systems, public administration, and communication. Grand Valley enables its students to participate in student-faculty research opportunities across the curriculum, using some of the most modern equipment available. All classes are taught by faculty members, not graduate assistants. The average class size is 27. The Zumberge Library holds more than 500,000 books and thousands of periodicals. Online research opportunities allow students to search for sources not found in the library.

Campus Life

Students may choose from many different styles of living centers, as well as on-campus apartments. In addition, there are many off-campus apartments that are within walking distance. Each on-campus living facility is equipped with an online computer connection in each room for each resident. More than 200 organizations are active on campus, including volunteer groups, artistic organizations, and social clubs. Student services include tutoring, advising, counseling, and low-cost health care. GVSU's Recreation Center offers students the opportunity to maintain health and fitness through the use of modern facilities. Athletic opportunities are open to all students.

For International Students

GVSU is committed to the recruitment and retention of international students. The campus community is very welcoming and its location provides an ideal learning environment. International students are required to provide original academic documents, an essay, proof of competency in the English language, and verification of financial support as part of the application process. Typically, admissions decisions for international applicants are made within two weeks of receipt of a complete application. Requests and questions may be sent via e-mail for the quickest response.

Partial scholarships may be available to international students who have the equivalent of an A or B average (GPA of at least 3.5 on a 4.0 scale). Complete application files must be submitted by February 1 of each year. This scholarship is only available for fall-semester entry.

Harrington College of Design

- **Contact:**
  Wendi Franczyk
  Vice President of Admissions
  Harrington College of Design
  Chicago, IL 60605
  Phone: 877-939-4975
  Fax: 312-697-8032
  E-mail: admissions@harringtoncollege.com
  Web site: http://www.harringtoncollege.com
- Private, coed
- Urban setting
- Enrollment: 1,506

- **Student-faculty ratio:** 13:1
- **2006–07 Tuition:** $575 per credit hour plus fees
- **International students:** 1.8%
- **Countries represented:** 18
- **International students enrolled:** 27
- **Admissions tests:**
  - TOEFL (min. score 500 paper-based)
  - SAT and ACT: Recommended
- **Application deadline:** Rolling
- **On-campus housing:** Not available

Area and Climate

Harrington College of Design's location in the heart of Chicago allows access to world-class cultural institutions, outstanding professional and educational enrichment experiences, and four-season recreational opportunities. Harrington's location is of inestimable value; students can see every design principle described in the classroom come to life in the design and culture of this vibrant city, and they are part of a unique college "campus" in Chicago's Loop and South Loop neighborhoods, where over 50,000 students attend more than 20 institutions of higher education. Students can run and bike along the miles of lakefront, sunbathe or play volleyball at Oak Street Beach, visit galleries in the River North neighborhood, shop the Magnificent Mile, dine in a world of ethnic restaurants, and enjoy the nightlife offered by this great city.

Education

Harrington College of Design, committed to creating the next generation of design professionals to lead and serve the global community, is a four-year college that offers flexible scheduling for a Bachelor of Fine Arts degree in interior design, an Associate of Applied Science degree in interior design or digital photography, and a new Bachelor of Fine Arts in communication design.

Fast-paced yet thorough, the dynamic programs provide education-through-application under the tutelage of proven industry specialists. Evidence-based research in the interior design program helps students make informed choices for the built environment; the communication design program teaches them to apply and deliver messages through various media, and the digital photography program helps answer the demand for a rapidly expanding division of commercial photography.

Harrington is accredited by the Accrediting Council for Independent Colleges and Schools (ACICS) and is an accredited institutional member of the National Association of Schools of Art and Design (NASAD). Harrington is recognized as a private college by the Illinois Board of Higher Education, which authorizes it to confer baccalaureate and associate degrees. Harrington's B.F.A. program in interior design is accredited by the Council for Interior Design Accreditation, formerly known as the Foundation for Interior Design Education and Research (FIDER).

Campus Life

There is no typical Harrington student. From varied backgrounds, life experiences, and parts of the world, Harrington students share a common desire to be creative and successful. Students may be women or men, recent high school graduates or returning students who have been in the workplace for a while. Some may already have degrees in other fields, but for many, this is their first design experience. Students feel connected at Harrington. Through academic collaborations and extracurricular activities, they begin lifelong friendships and professional relationships. Teamwork in the studio classrooms can be developed into successful business partnerships, and Harrington students can benefit from the larger alumni network after graduation. The common bond among Harrington students is the desire to excel in the field of interior design, photography, and communication design. A wide array of services and opportunities are available to students through professional organizations, such as the American Society of Interior Designers (ASID), International Interior Design Association (IIDA), American Society of Media Photographers (ASMP), and American Institute of Graphic Arts (AIGA), where they can network, engage in continuing education, and advocate for their profession.

Harrington's six-story vertical campus within a glass-and-granite high-rise serves as a learning laboratory. A unique three-story display space connects floors designed to hold a mix of classrooms, galleries, offices, and spaces for conversation and collaboration on projects. Student research is supported by a specialized design library with extensive traditional archival holdings and continuously updated digital resources. Harrington's technology delivers a flexible and innovative education in studio, computer, and lecture classrooms while its faculty of practicing professionals expands the learning experience to the rich design and cultural community of Chicago.

For International Students

International students are encouraged to apply for admission and must meet the same admission requirements as U.S. citizens. Original documents must be presented for copying to the student file. All documents must be accompanied by an evaluation for U.S. equivalency from an approved credential evaluation service, and non-English documents must be translated by a qualified professional. Students whose native language is not English may be required to take the TOEFL or IELTS, or demonstrate English proficiency through other measures established by the College. A minimum TOEFL score of 500 on the paper version or 173 on the computer-based test, or a minimum score of 5.5 on the IELTS, is required. An affidavit of financial support must be submitted. A DVD of Harrington College of Design is available upon request.

Hawai'i Pacific University

- **Contact:**
  Office of International Admissions
  Hawaii Pacific University
  1164 Bishop Street, Suite 1100
  Honolulu, HI 96813
  Phone: 808-543-8088
  Fax: 808-543-8065
- Private, coed
- Urban and rural settings
- Enrollment: 8,500
- Student-faculty ratio: 18:1
- 2007–08 Tuition and fees: $13,000
- 2007–08 Room and board: $10,560

- **International students: 14%**
- **Countries represented: 100+**
- **International students applied: 547**
- **International students accepted: 481**
- **International students enrolled: 285**
- **Admissions tests:**
  - TOEFL
  - SAT/ACT: Optional
- **Application deadline: Rolling**
- **On-campus housing: Available**
- **Summer housing: Available**

Area and Climate

With three campuses linked by shuttle, Hawai'i Pacific University (HPU) combines the excitement of an urban, downtown campus with the serenity of the windward Hawai'i Loa residential campus, which is set in the lush foothills of the Ko'olau mountains. The main campus is located in downtown Honolulu, the business and financial center of the Pacific. Eight miles away, situated on 135 acres in Kaneohe, the windward Hawai'i Loa campus is the site of the School of Nursing, the marine science program, and a variety of other course offerings. The third campus, Oceanic Institute, is an applied aquaculture research facility located on a 56-acre site at Makapuu Point on the windward coast of Oahu, Hawaii, with facilities on the Big Island of Hawaii as well. The beautiful weather, for which Hawai'i is famous, allows unlimited opportunities for recreation year-round. However, the emphasis on a career-related curriculum keeps students focused on their academic goals. Hawai'i Pacific University enjoys a mild year-round climate. The average temperature is 77°F (25°C).

Education

Hawai'i Pacific's dedicated professors put a priority on teaching; there are no teaching assistants. Students get to know their professors as colleagues and mentors. The HPU faculty members are actively involved in their academic fields and bring this experience to the classroom. Many of them are renowned leaders in their particular disciplines. Hawai'i Pacific has a staff of professional academic advisers whose primary responsibility is to assist students with academic programs and guide students toward their individual goals. Students meet with an adviser prior to every semester's registration. Hawai'i Pacific offers the Bachelor of Arts (B.A.) degree, with majors in advertising,

anthropology, applied sociology, communication (concentrations in speech and visual communication), East-West classical studies, economics, engineering (3-2 program), English, environmental studies, history, human resource development, human services, international relations, international studies (concentrations in American, Asian, comparative, European, and Pacific studies), justice administration, political science, psychology, social sciences, and teaching English as a second language.

Campus Life

Students at HPU come from every state in the United States and more than 100 countries around the world. The diversity of the student body stimulates learning about other cultures both in and out of the classroom. There is no majority population at HPU. Students are encouraged to examine the values, customs, traditions, and principles of others to gain a clearer understanding of their own perspectives. HPU students develop friendships with students from throughout the United States and the world—important connections for success in the global economy of the twenty-first century.

For International Students

The University offers one of the largest and most comprehensive English language programs in the United States. TOEFL scores are not required; the University can accommodate students at any English level. Upon successful completion of the English Foundations Program (EFP), students are eligible for regular degree programs. The International Student Advisor and staff assist students with orientation, visa issues, and work authorization and assist the Council of Countries, one of the largest and most active groups on campus. Every year, the Council of Countries holds Intercultural Day. This event includes a parade, country booths, and performances by various student groups, attracting thousands of students, faculty and staff members, and members of the Honolulu community.

Hillsdale College

- **Contact:**
    Jeffrey S. Lantis
    Director of Admissions
    Hillsdale College
    Hillsdale, MI 49242

    Phone: 517-607-2327
    Fax: 517-607-2223
- **Private, coed**
- **Small-town setting**
- **Enrollment: 1,300**
- **Student-faculty ratio: 10:1**
- **2007–08 Tuition and fees: $18,600**
- **2007–08 Room and board: $7340**

- **International students: 2%**
- **Countries represented: 13**
- **International students applied: 40**
- **International students accepted: 20**
- **International students enrolled: 6**
- **Admissions tests:**
    - **TOEFL (min. score 550)**
    - **SAT and ACT: Recommended**
- **Application deadline: 2/15**
- **On-campus housing: Guaranteed**
- **Summer housing: Not available**

Area and Climate

Hillsdale College is located in the Irish Hills area of south-central Michigan, approximately 2 hours from Detroit and 3 hours from Chicago. Centered in Hillsdale, which has a population of 10,000, the 200-acre (81-hectare) campus offers the Sage Center for the Arts, the Hillsdale Academy (a K–12 private school run by the College), a 60,000-square-foot (5,580-square-meter) sports facility, two 30,000-square-foot (2,790-square-meter) science facilities, and a newly opened, 32,800-square-foot (3,050-square-meter) music hall. The College provides a shuttle service to local airports for a nominal fee. Students are certain to see all four seasons on campus, with average temperatures ranging from 80°F (27°C) in the summer to 25°F (-4°C) in the winter.

Education

Hillsdale College, which was founded in 1844, is a selective, coeducational college of liberal arts that pursues the founders' intent "to furnish all persons who wish, irrespective of nation, color, or sex, a literary and scientific education." To remain truly independent, the College accepts no federal funding. Degrees offered are the Bachelor of Science and Bachelor of Arts in thirty major fields of study. The most popular programs include premedicine, prelaw, education, and business. Qualified freshmen can join the Honors Program, which provides a challenge above the regular course work. A recent library addition has provided space for up to 400,000 volumes and 15,000 periodicals; a new computer system provides in-house library and Internet access. The student-faculty ratio of 10:1 and a faculty advising system ensure the students close contact with professors.

Campus Life

The student body includes students from forty-seven states and thirteen other countries. Approximately 50 percent of the students are from Michigan. Students can become involved in more than forty clubs and organizations on campus, including NCAA Division II athletics, the fine arts (including music, dance, and theater), Inter-Varsity Christian Fellowship, volunteerism associations, and academic honor societies. The school year consists of two 15-week semesters separated by a 4-week Christmas vacation; two 3-week sessions of summer school are also offered. Eighty-five percent of the students live in ten single-sex dorms and six sorority and fraternity houses. Each residence provides a full-time house mother or father and student resident assistants. One central cafeteria managed by Saga Inc., DBA Hillsdale Dining Service, serves the student body.

For International Students

International students may apply for fall and spring terms and both summer school sessions. A specific international student application is required and can be obtained through the Hillsdale College Admissions Office. Since Hillsdale College does not offer an ESL program, international students must demonstrate adequate command of both written and spoken English. Those whose primary language is not English must achieve a minimum TOEFL score of 550, and they join all new students in the College's orientation programs. Many international students become involved with the International Club, along with a wide range of other campus activities.

Hofstra University

- **Contact:**
  Jessica Eads
  Dean of Admission and Financial Aid
  100 Hofstra University
  Hempstead, NY 11549-1000
  Phone: 516-463-6700
  Fax: 516-463-5100
- Private, university, coed
- Suburban setting
- Enrollment: 7,762(full-time undergraduates)
- Student-faculty ratio: 14:1
- 2006–07 Tuition and fees: $24,830
- 2006–07 Room and board: $9800

- **International students: 2%**
- **Countries represented: 65**
- **International students applied: 315**
- **International students accepted: 186**
- **International students enrolled: 28**
- **Admissions tests:**
  - **TOEFL (min. score PBT 550; CBT 213)**
  - **SAT and ACT: Not required**
- **Application deadline: Rolling**
- **On-campus housing: Available**
- **Summer housing: Available**

Area and Climate

Hofstra University's lush, 240-acre (97 hectare) campus, an accredited arboretum, is located just 25 miles (40 kilometers) from New York City and all of its cultural and business opportunities. With New York City just a short ride by train or car, students can take advantage of the city's many internship possibilities in areas such as finance, business, media, advertising, and entertainment. Students can also experience the city's many cultural riches. Broadway shows, The Metropolitan Museum of Art, Madison Square Garden, Chinatown and Little Italy, and Wall Street all are within easy reach of the Hofstra campus. The surrounding Long Island area offers world-class beaches and parks; the Hamptons; sports fishing and boating; Nassau Coliseum, home of the New York Islanders hockey team; and conveniently located shopping malls. Long Island has a moderate climate, with average winter temperatures around 30°F (-1°C) and average summer temperatures around 80°F (27°C).

Education

Hofstra University is a dynamic, private institution where students find their edge to succeed in more than 140 undergraduate and 155 graduate programs in liberal arts and sciences, business, communication, education and allied human services, and honors studies, as well as a school of law. With an outstanding faculty, advanced technological resources, and state-of-the-art facilities, Hofstra has a growing national reputation. Yet the average class size is kept small, at just 23, and the student-to-faculty ratio is 14:1 to ensure that students get the personal attention they need.

Hofstra University is composed of the Hofstra College of Liberal Arts and Sciences, Frank G. Zarb School of Business, School of Communication, School of Education and Allied Human Services, the School of Law, Honors College, New College, and School for University Studies. Honors College is a program for high-achieving students; New College offers interdisciplinary study and innovative block scheduling; and School for University Studies was developed for students with academic challenges. Within these schools are many innovative programs designed to meet the needs of the diverse student body. These include the Legal Education Accelerated Program, which allows students to earn both a B.A. and a J.D. in six years, and Connections, an academic and social program that helps first-year students connect to all of the resources and opportunities of the University.

Campus Life

Hofstra has a dynamic campus life, with more than 150 student clubs and organizations, including about thirty fraternities and sororities; eighteen varsity sports; and more than 500 cultural events each year. Students can choose from organizations as diverse as French Club, Danceworks, and the National Broadcasting Society. Hofstra's Division I athletic program includes baseball, field hockey, football, softball, volleyball, and wrestling and men's and women's basketball, cross-country, golf, lacrosse, soccer and tennis. Students who are not Division I athletes can join the student section "Lion's Den" or participate with more than 25 percent of Hofstra's students in numerous intramural sports. Students can also attend debates, lectures, and readings by the many scholars, business leaders, writers, and celebrities who visit campus each year. Some great series include Great Writers, Great Readings; the Day of Dialogue; and Distinguished Faculty Lectures.

For International Students

Hofstra's student body is geographically, ethnically, and culturally diverse. Students attending Hofstra come from forty-six states and sixty-five countries. The Hofstra campus is easily accessible by plane and train or car. J.F. Kennedy and La-Guardia International Airports are located within 30 minutes of the campus, and the Long Island Railroad stops within 2 miles. International students can find help with immigration and other student-related issues at the Office of Multicultural and International Student Programs, which also coordinates a wide range of social and cultural programs that celebrate the diversity of the Hofstra community.

The Illinois Institute of Art–Chicago

- **Contact:**
  Janis Anton
  Vice President, Director of Admissions
  The Illinois Institute of Art–Chicago
  350 North Orleans Street
  Chicago, IL 60654
  Phone: 312-280-3500
  Fax: 312-280-8562
  E-mail: janton@aii.edu
  Web site: http://www.ilic.artinstitutes.edu
- **Proprietary, coed**
- **Urban setting**
- **Enrollment: 2,850**
- **Student-faculty ratio: 20:1**

- **2006–07 Tuition and fees: $19,968**
- **2006–07 Room and board: $9066**
- **International students: 4%**
- **Countries represented: 24**
- **International students enrolled: 70**
- **Admissions tests:**
  - TOEFL (min. score 500 paper-based; 173 computer-based; 61 iBT); or SAT (min. score 500); or ACT (min. score 19) required
- **Application deadline: Rolling**
- **On-campus housing: Available**
- **Summer housing: Available**

Area and Climate

Chicago, located in the midwestern United States alongside Lake Michigan on the east, is a diverse city filled with endless artistic inspiration. From world-class art museums to year-round sports, music, food, entertainment, shopping, and culture, the nation's second-largest city has something to offer everyone. The Institute's main campus is located in the vibrant River North area, which is known for its exquisite art galleries. Chicago residents enjoy all four seasons.

Education

The Illinois Institute of Art–Chicago is America's leader in creative education, preparing students for careers in the visual and media arts, fashion, and culinary arts. It is a member of the Art Institutes, with locations in more than thirty cities in the United States. The Institute offers programs leading to the Bachelor of Fine Arts in digital film and video production, fashion design, game art and design, interactive media design, interior design, media arts and animation, visual communication, and visual effects and motion graphics. In addition, the Institute offers a Bachelor of Arts in advertising and fashion marketing and management and a Bachelor of Applied Science in culinary management. The Institute's associate degree programs include culinary arts, fashion merchandising, fashion production, graphic design, and interactive multimedia production. All programs are conducted on a year-round basis, allowing students, if they desire, to study and progress without interruption. The Institute is accredited by the Higher Learning Commission of the North Central Association of Colleges and Schools. It is also accredited by the Accrediting Commission of Career Schools and Colleges of Technology (ACCSCT), an accrediting agency recognized by the United States Department of Education. The college's bachelor's degree program in interior design is accredited by the Council for Interior Design Accreditation (CIDA), and the A.A.S. in culinary arts degree program is accredited by the American Culinary Federation (ACF).

Campus Life

The 105,000-square-foot campus is located in the heart of Chicago, in the Apparel Center and Merchandise Mart Complex, an area within walking distance of many of the city's cultural offerings. Classrooms, studios, computer labs with Internet access, administration buildings, galleries, and a resource center make up the main facility. Located eight blocks away, additional facilities have 75,000 square feet of kitchen space, classrooms, computer labs, a video studio, an editing studio, a sound studio, and a student-operated bistro.

Students participate in a variety of campus groups and professional organizations. One leading organization is the International Student Association, which organizes an annual Culture Festival that highlights the Institute's diverse student body.

For International Students

The Institute has made available a limited number of special scholarships to international students throughout the course of the program. This program provides students pursuing a bachelor's degree with a one-time scholarship of $2500 or $5000 and those pursuing an associate degree with $2500. Applicants must demonstrate strong academic ability. Each scholarship applicant is required to submit the following: a scholarship entry form; a typewritten essay explaining their goals and motivation for enrolling; three letters of recommendation from an arts-related instructor, guidance counselor, or school official; complete secondary school transcripts; bank verification of ability to cover expenses not fulfilled by the scholarship; and proof of citizenship. All documents must be submitted in the original language (if not English), with official English translations of all documents.

Illinois Institute of Technology

- Contact:
  Gerald Doyle, Associate Vice President of
      Undergraduate Admission
  Illinois Institute of Technology
  Chicago, IL 60616
  Phone: 312-567-3025
  Fax: 312-567-6939
  E-mail: admission@iit.edu
  Web site: http://www.iit.edu
- Private
- Urban setting
- Enrollment: 2,089 undergraduates
- Student-faculty ratio: 13:1
- 2006–07 Tuition and fees: $23,329

- 2006–07 Room and board: $8050
- International students: 16%
- Countries represented: More than 60
- International students applied: 770
- International students accepted: 354
- International students enrolled: 147
- Admissions tests:
  - TOEFL (paper-based min. score 550; computer-based min. score 213)
  - SAT or ACT: Required
- Application deadlines: Fall, 5/15; spring, 10/15
- On-campus housing: Available
- Summer housing: Available

Area and Climate

Illinois Institute of Technology (IIT) stands in the midst of a developing urban area in Chicago, one of the largest cities in the United States. IIT is located 1 mile west of Lake Michigan and 3 miles south of the Chicago Loop, offering students unlimited opportunities to enjoy art, music, drama, films, museums, entertainment, and recreation. Chicago has four distinct seasons, with hot summers and cold winters. The campus is easily accessible to the rest of Chicago via two major expressways, bus, and elevated trains. The free campus shuttle bus provides transportation to local stores, downtown Chicago, and train stations.

Education

Illinois Institute of Technology was formed in 1940 when Armour Institute (1890) merged with Lewis Institute (1895). IIT is a private, Ph.D.-granting research institute with programs in aerospace engineering, applied mathematics, architectural engineering, architecture, biomedical engineering, business administration, chemical engineering, civil engineering, computer engineering, computer information systems, computer science, electrical engineering, humanities, Internet communication, journalism, mechanical engineering, materials science and engineering, molecular biochemistry and biophysics, physics, political science, professional and technical communication, and psychology. IIT's mission is to educate and prepare students for complex professional roles in a challenging world and to advance knowledge through research and scholarship. Through committed faculty members, close personal attention, and its signature interprofessional programs, Illinois Institute of Technology provides a challenging academic program focused on the integration of education and the professional world. Cooperative education is encouraged. The University operates on a semester calendar.

Campus Life

Students are encouraged to participate in many social, cultural, and athletic opportunities. Student activities include the campus newspaper, the WIIT radio station, special interest clubs, theater and music groups, intramural and varsity athletics, fraternities and sororities, honor and professional societies, student government, residence hall organizations, and the student-run Union Board. IIT has more than 100 student organizations on campus. Counseling, job placement, and student health services are included in the various campus services. The library has access to more than 22 million volumes. Recreational activities include weekly movies, intramural sports, a swimming pool, a recreation center, and discount tickets to area events. More than half of IIT's undergraduates live on campus in residence halls or fraternity/sorority housing. All students have access to e-mail and the Internet.

For International Students

The international student population enriches the diversity and sense of community at Illinois Institute of Technology. All incoming students are required to participate in orientation the week before classes begin each semester. The International Center offers support to students through workshops and assists students with travel, employment, and immigration issues. The International Student Organization offers membership to all students, and many other international, ethnic, and religious clubs welcome new members. Each year, international students organize and participate in the International Fest, in which the campus and surrounding community are invited to sample cuisine from around the world and witness traditional dance, song, and musical performances.

Illinois Wesleyan University

- Contact:
  Paul J. Schley
  Director of International Admissions
  Illinois Wesleyan University
  1312 Park Street
  Bloomington, IL 61701-1773
  Phone: 309-556-3031
  Fax: 309-556-3820
  E-mail: international@iwu.edu
  Web site: http://www.iwu.edu
- Private, coed
- Urban setting
- Enrollment: 2,100
- Student-faculty ratio: 12:1

- 2005–06 Tuition and fees: $27,654
- 2005–06 Room and board: $6426
- International students: 2%
- Countries represented: 15
- International students applied: 215
- International students accepted: 59
- International students enrolled: 19
- Admissions tests:
  - TOEFL (min. score 550 paper-based)
  - SAT or ACT: Required
- Application deadline: 2/1
- On-campus housing: Guaranteed
- Summer housing: Available

Area and Climate

Illinois Wesleyan University is located on a 79-acre (32 hectares) parklike campus in Bloomington's historic Northside residential district. The twin cities of Bloomington/Normal, with a combined population of more than 110,000, are centers for county government; insurance, retail, and manufacturing concerns; and higher education. The cities are located midway between Chicago and St. Louis, interesting metropolitan areas easily accessed by auto, train, or bus within 2 to 3 hours. The climate exhibits all four seasons. Cold months are from November through February, and spring and fall are moderate seasons.

Education

Illinois Wesleyan University is a private, coeducational school that selectively enrolls 2,100 undergraduates. Founded in 1850, Illinois Wesleyan consists of a College of Liberal Arts, School of Nursing, and College of Fine Arts with professional Schools of Art, Music, and Theatre Arts. The 4-4-1 academic calendar provides challenging opportunities to learn in small classes averaging 18 students, participate in work-related internships off campus, and conduct research or study/travel internationally. All students have individual faculty advisers. Additional counseling is available for career and graduate school placement. Illinois Wesleyan is a nationally recognized liberal arts university dedicated to personalized undergraduate education.

Campus Life

The campus atmosphere is relaxed and friendly; dress is casual. More than 80 percent of the students live on campus. Thirty-four states and fifteen nations are represented. On-campus activities include an International Society, Model UN, student senate, professional and honorary societies, intramural and intercollegiate sports, national social fraternities and sororities, political and religious groups, service groups, activities in the arts, a radio station, and several publications.

For International Students

Four-year, merit-based scholarships are available to exceptional international students. An extensive orientation program for international students is provided one week prior to the beginning of classes. Housing for international students is available on the campus over holiday breaks and summer vacation. Illinois Wesleyan University welcomes the interest of international students.

Indiana University South Bend

- Contact:
  Julie Marie Williams
  Director, International Student Services
  Administration Building A166X
  Indiana University South Bend
  1700 Mishawaka Avenue
  P.O. Box 7111
  South Bend, IN 46634-7111
  Phone: 574-520-4419
  Fax: 574-520-4590
  E-mail: jwilliam@iusb.edu
  Web site: http://www.iusb.edu/~oiss/
- Public, four-year, coed
- Suburban setting
- Enrollment: 7,501

- 2006–07 Tuition and fees: $12,600
- 2006–07 Room and board: $5700
- International students: 2%
- Admissions tests:
  - TOEFL: Required (min. score 197 computer-based)
  - SAT or ACT: Recommended
- Application deadline: Fall, 7/1; spring, 11/1; summer 4/1
- On-campus housing: Available
- Summer housing: Available

Area and Climate

The Indiana University (IU) South Bend campus borders the St. Joseph River. Like the river, IU South Bend is a focal point for the region. The campus provides academic and professional programs and community services for nearly a dozen north-central Indiana and southwestern Michigan counties within a 50-mile (80-kilometer) radius. South Bend's proximity to Lake Michigan means that winters see some lake-effect snow, with temperatures averaging around 34°F (1°C). Summertime temperatures hover around 80°F (27°C).

Education

The third-largest of the eight Indiana University campuses, IU South Bend offers more than 100 academic programs at the undergraduate and graduate levels. The University is developing new academic programs and new strengths in interdisciplinary inquiry, linking disciplines and students with professions that will advance research, professional service, and learning. IU South Bend is accredited by the Higher Learning Commission of the North Central Association of Colleges and Schools. Students can earn associate, bachelor's, master's, and doctoral degrees and earn certificates through the College of Liberal Arts and Sciences, the Ernestine M. Raclin School of the Arts, the School of Business and Economics, the School of Education, the School of Public and Environmental Affairs, the School of Social Work, the Division of Labor Studies, the Division of Nursing and Health Professions, and the Division of Extended Learning Services.

Campus Life

The student body is rich in diversity, including a mix of traditional and adult students and more than 200 international students. The vibrant campus life program features more than seventy student organizations, a student newspaper, intramural and club sports, student theater and musical productions, and more. NAIA Division I sports are men's and women's basketball. Intramural sports include basketball, flag football, soccer, softball, racquetball, and many more.

For International Students

The Office of International Student Services provides admission and immigration services for all international students. Trained staff members help international students adjust to life at the University and in the community. International students with fewer than 26 credit hours must take placement exams in English and mathematics. All international students attend an International Student Orientation, providing them a chance to meet new people, enjoy fun activities, and find out more about the University before classes begin. Students can pick a date that works for them; a list of upcoming orientation dates is available from the Office of International Student Services.

International College of Hospitality Management

- **Contact:**
  Office of Admissions
  International College of Hospitality
      Management
  1760 Mapleton Avenue
  Suffield, CT 06078
  Phone: 860-668-3515
  Fax: 860-668-7369
  E-mail: admissions@ichm.edu
  Web site: http://www.ichm.edu
- **Private, 2-year, coed**
- **Small-town setting**
- **Enrollment: 50**

- **Student-faculty ratio: 10:1**
- **2007–08 Tuition and fees: $19,970**
- **2007–08 Room and board: $5000**
- **International students: 50%**
- **Countries represented: 38**
- **Admissions test:**
  - **TOEFL (min. score 500) or sufficient documentation of English instruction**
  - **SAT: Recommended**
  - **ACT: Not required**
- **Application deadline: Rolling**
- **On-campus housing: Available**

Area and Climate

The International College of Hospitality Management is located in the rolling hills of the northwestern part of Connecticut, midway between New York City and Boston. The area is noted for its scenic beauty, shopping, and year-round recreation. Cultural and sightseeing opportunities are abundant in the area. Temperatures range from 95°F (35°C) in summer to 1°F (-17°C) in winter. There are four seasons: spring, summer, fall, and winter.

Education

The International College of Hospitality Management (ICHM) is a private, international two-year college of hospitality management. The College's unique program combines the art of European hospitality, emphasizing service and professionalism, with American management techniques, incorporating state-of-the-art computer technology, marketing strategies, and liberal arts. The curriculum emphasizes the international aspects of the industry. Students complete four 11-week academic terms followed by a six-month paid internship in the industry. Internship sites are typically 4- or 5-star properties. Academic terms

begin in February, April, August, and November. The College's placement rate is 100 percent.

Campus Life

Although some ICHM students choose to commute, most live on campus in multiple-occupancy dormitories. The building features wireless broadband Internet connectivity throughout, and there are three computer labs for those who prefer a hardwired environment. There is a large gymnasium adjacent to an exercise facility for student use. Student lounges feature large-screen televisions, pool tables, air hockey, computer games, etc. The Six Flags New England Amusement Park is located within walking distance, as are a selection of stores and restaurants. The campus is within easy reach of major cities such as Hartford, New York, and Boston. Students are actively involved in campus activities and community events.

For International Students

The students' average age is early twenties, although many students enroll directly from high school. The College provides an orientation program for incoming students. Graduates hold impressive and important positions in prominent hospitality properties in more than fifty countries.

Jacksonville State University

- **Contact:**
  Dr. John J. Ketterer, Director
  International Programs
  Jacksonville State University
  Jacksonville, AL 36265
  Phone: 256-782-5674
  Fax: 256-782-8344
  E-mail: intprog@jsu.edu
  Web site: http://www.jsu.edu
- **Public, coed**
- **Small-town setting**
- **Enrollment: 9,300**
- **Student-faculty ratio: 30:1**

- **2006–07 Tuition and fees: $338 per credit hour, approximately $9464 per year (28 credit hours)**
- **2006–07 Room: $1620**
- **International students: 3%**
- **Countries represented: 70**
- **International students enrolled: 240**
- **Admissions tests:**
  - **TOEFL (min. score 500 PBT; 173 CBT)**
  - **SAT or ACT: Recommended (accepted as alternatives to TOEFL)**
- **Application deadline: Rolling**
- **Summer housing: Available**

Area and Climate

Jacksonville, Alabama, is located in the Southeastern part of the United States. The city has about 11,000 residents. The region has very mild winters, a long autumn, and hot summers. Compared with larger American cities, Jacksonville is quieter, more relaxed, friendlier, and safer. Jacksonville is about the same latitude as Casablanca, Beirut, Islamabad, and Shanghai. It is 1½ hours' driving distance from Birmingham, Alabama, and 2 hours from Atlanta, Georgia. For weekend recreation, people drive 6 hours to the Gulf of Mexico beaches, New Orleans, Savannah, or the Smoky Mountains.

Education

Jacksonville State University was created in 1883. The campus now covers 318 acres (129 hectares) with fifty-eight air-conditioned buildings. The school is committed to high-quality education by integrating traditional academic studies with career-oriented programs at reasonable costs. There are approximately 250 faculty members; 70 percent have the Ph.D. degree. Graduate assistants do not teach classes. A full range of undergraduate degree programs is offered. Master's-level degrees are offered in business, public administration, education, and humanities and social sciences. Computer science and business are popular programs of study. Students have free access to more than ten modern computer labs to complete assignments and

obtain Internet access. A full range of services is available to students, including tutoring, career counseling, and personal counseling.

Campus Life

Students come from thirty-five states and sixty-six countries. Most students live in the region and commute by car. Students may live on campus in dormitories or apartments or off campus in apartments. An international dormitory available on campus never closes, has cooking facilities, and has reasonable costs. University housing requires a reservation and a deposit in advance of arrival. The University supports a wide range of honor societies, social clubs, athletic events, recreational opportunities, and social activities. Other activities include a student-run radio station and newspaper, a film series, plays, concerts, and lecture series.

For International Students

International students play an important part in campus life. International students have a permanent representative in the Student Government Association, are key figures in the University tennis and golf teams, and have a strong International Student Organization. Each year the International Student Organization holds International Week, which includes a well-received Taster's Fair and Talent Show. International students are provided support by the Office of International Programs and Services. Students visit or call the office to receive assistance related to all aspects of their lives in the United States, including questions on law, health, travel, and taxes. Student rights and responsibilities are explained in orientations, personal meetings, and newsletters.

Jacksonville University

- Contact:
  Yvonne Martel
  Associate Director of Admissions,
      International
  Jacksonville University
  Jacksonville, FL 32211
  Phone: 904-256-7000
  Fax: 904-256-7012
  E-mail: ymartel@ju.edu
  Web site: http://www.ju.edu
- Private, coed
- Suburban setting
- Enrollment: 3,093
- Student-faculty ratio: 14:1
- 2007–08 Tuition and fees: $22,500
- 2007–08 Room and board: $8560

- International students: 3%
- Countries represented: 50
- International students applied: 116
- International students accepted: 49
- International students enrolled: 26
- Admissions tests:
  - TOEFL (min. score 540 (paper-based) or 207 (computer-based) for university-level courses) or IELTS (minimum band 6.0)
  - SAT or ACT: Required of applicants from English-speaking countries
- Application deadline: Fall, 6/1; spring, 11/1; summer, 2/1
- On-campus housing: Available
- Summer housing: Available

Area and Climate

Jacksonville University is located on 198 acres (80 hectares) of beautiful suburban riverfront land in Jacksonville, a city of more than 1 million people in northeast Florida. Jacksonville is nationally known as a center for technology, business, medical, and industrial commerce. It also has a professional symphony orchestra, theaters, science and art museums and galleries, a national jazz festival, a professional football team, and numerous Fortune 500 companies. Average temperatures range from 54°F (12°C) in winter to 86°F (30°C) in summer. The University is just 20 minutes from several Atlantic Ocean beaches and Jacksonville International Airport. The oldest city in the United States, St. Augustine, is 40 miles (64 kilometers) south of Jacksonville, and NASA's Kennedy Space Center and the Walt Disney World Resort are 2 hours south.

Education

Jacksonville University, which was founded in 1934, is a private, independent, coeducational institution that awards bachelor's and master's degrees in more than fifty areas. The University grants bachelor's degrees in liberal arts, fine arts, natural and applied sciences, education, business, aviation, nursing, and social sciences. Preprofessional studies and honors programs are available. The academic calendar includes a fall and spring semester and summer terms. Jacksonville University is accredited by the Commission on Colleges of the Southern Association of Colleges and Schools (1866 Southern Lane, Decatur, Georgia 30033-4097; phone: 404-679-4501) to award bachelor's and

master's degrees. A few of Jacksonville's educational resources include centers for advising, writing, reading, math, study skills, and career services.

Campus Life

Computerized library holdings and a concerned faculty are readily accessible to students. Computers are available in the University's residence facilities, and Internet access is provided in every dormitory room and every bedroom of the campus apartments. Several computer labs are found throughout the campus, as are an FM radio station, a museum, a cyber café, a wellness and fitness center, and numerous athletic facilities. Students participate in more than fifty organizations and seventeen NCAA Division I intercollegiate sports. Concerts and other entertainment are regularly held on campus and in the nearby city. The campus is located in a safe, residential area, and the sunny, warm climate encourages outdoor living and recreational activities.

For International Students

The Office of Student Life provides excellent support services for international students, beginning with a required orientation that is designed to assist new students with the transition to Jacksonville University by exposing them to the opportunities available on campus and in the United States. The program includes registering students for classes, arranging bank accounts, obtaining necessary government documents and health insurance information, arranging tours of the local area, shopping, and meeting new and interesting people from other countries. The office also provides other services, such as immigration advising, housing assistance, and cross-cultural and financial counseling. The International Student Association sponsors popular programs throughout the year.

Johnson & Wales University

- **Contact:**
  International Admission Office
  Johnson & Wales University
  Providence, RI 02903
  Phone: 401-598-1074
  Fax: 401-598-4773
  E-mail: admissions.intl@jwu.edu
        admissions.grad@jwu.edu
  Web site: http://www.jwu.edu
- **Private, comprehensive, coed**
- **Urban setting**
- **Enrollment: 16,000**

- **Student-faculty ratio: 20:1**
- **2006–07 Tuition and fees: $19,875**
- **2006–07 Room and board: $9300**
- **International students: 7%**
- **Countries represented: 94**
- **International students enrolled: 1,105**
- **Admissions tests:**
  - **TOEFL (min. score: PBT, 550; iBT, 80)**
  - **SAT and ACT: Not required**
- **Application deadline: Rolling**
- **On-campus housing: Guaranteed**

Area and Climate

Johnson & Wales University (JWU) has locations in Providence, Rhode Island; Denver, Colorado; North Miami, Florida; and Charlotte, North Carolina. By car, Providence is 1 hour from Boston and 3 hours from New York City. Popular nearby tourist spots such as Cape Cod and Newport have excellent beaches and recreational areas. The downtown location enables students to take advantage of a wealth of cultural, educational, and recreational facilities. Rhode Island's moderate climate is influenced by the ocean. Autumn and spring are often rainy but usually quite comfortable, with temperatures ranging from 50°F (10°C) to 70°F (21°C). Winter temperatures range from below 0°F (-18°C) to 40°F (4°C). Denver is near the scenic Rocky Mountains and enjoys 300 days of sunshine. The historic 25-acre campus is minutes from downtown and is located in a beautiful residential area. North Miami has year-round tropical weather, and the campus is close to popular entertainment, fine dining, shopping, and sunny beaches. Charlotte is one of the fastest-growing cities in the southeast U.S. Its mild year-round climate, outdoor activity, and Southern charm attract tourists and newcomers.

Education

Founded in 1914, Johnson & Wales University is a private, career-oriented institution offering programs that are geared to the success of the students. Students represent fifty states and ninety-four countries. The academic focus of the University is on two- and four-year programs in business, food service, hotel and restaurant management, and technology, with accelerated one- and two-year M.B.A. programs in accounting, marketing, management, international business, and hospitality administration. The academic calendar is divided into three 11-week sessions, which enables students to take four or five classes at a time. The University offers flex-

ible enrollment periods: September, December, March, and June (ESL only). Classes generally meet Monday through Thursday. Student services include academic counseling and testing, a tutorial center, and health services. Johnson & Wales University is accredited by the New England Association of Schools and Colleges.

Campus Life

The Providence location of Johnson & Wales consists of two major campuses. The Weybosset Hill Campus, located in and around downtown Providence, is home to students in the College of Business, the Hospitality College, and the School of Technology. The Harborside Park Campus is for students in the College of Culinary Arts and the Graduate School. Residential facilities are located throughout Providence, Cranston, and Warwick. The University provides free shuttle-bus service between the various campuses and residence halls. The campus atmosphere is relaxed and friendly. T. F. Green Airport is nearby, as is bus and train service. Students also arrive at Logan Airport in Boston.

The other JWU locations offer similar amenities, with intercollegiate and intramural sports, myriad clubs and cultural and recreational activities, area sports teams, academic societies, and public transportation.

For International Students

The International Center at Johnson & Wales in Providence is located in downtown Providence within walking distance of many of the academic buildings. The International Center assists with a variety of services for international students: arrival assistance, temporary housing, general orientation, host-family program, and legal advice on U.S. employment as well as general guidance throughout enrollment at the University. Students arriving at the Providence campus are met at the airport and bus or train station and receive complimentary overnight stays at the Radisson Airport Hotel.

The other JWU locations provide an equal number of special services and programs for international students, including ESL programs and assistance with immigration matters.

Juniata College

- Contact:
  Mr. Brett Basom
  Director of Int'l Admissions
  Juniata College
  1700 Moore Street
  Huntingdon, PA 16652
  Phone: 814-641-3427
  Fax: 814-641-3100
  E-mail: usastudy@juniata.edu
  Web site: http://www.juniata.edu
- Private, four-year, coed
- Small-town setting
- Enrollment: 1,460
- Student-faculty ratio: 13:1
- 2006–07 Tuition and fees: $27,590

- 2006–07 Room and board: $7680
- International students: 6.5%
- Countries represented: 36
- International students applied: 102
- International students accepted: 39
- International students enrolled: 18
- Admissions tests:
  - TOEFL: Recommended (min. score 550 PBT; 213 CBT; 80 iBT)
  - SAT: Required for some
  - ACT: Not required
- Application deadline: 3/1
- On-campus housing: Guaranteed
- Summer housing: Available

Area and Climate

Juniata College is located in a small town in the mountains of central Pennsylvania. Huntingdon, a quiet, friendly town of 9,000 people, is a place where students can feel safe and secure. The beautiful surrounding countryside is ideal for a variety of outdoor recreational opportunities. The Juniata River runs through Huntingdon, and Raystown Lake, a major resort area, is only 15 minutes away. Pittsburgh; Washington, D.C.; Baltimore; and Philadelphia are all within 4 hours of Huntingdon, and the town of State College, home of Penn State University, is just 45 minutes away. Juniata students enjoy four distinct seasons with average temperatures ranging from 86°F (30°C) in summer to about 32°F (0°C) in winter. Snow can be expected in January and February.

Education

Founded in 1876, Juniata offers bachelor's degrees in more than sixty majors. A Juniata education is characterized by the personalized attention given to each student by a distinguished faculty, 91 percent of whom hold a Ph.D. or equivalent degree. Classes are small, and each student has 2 faculty advisers. Particularly popular fields of study include traditional majors in the sciences, education, and business as well as innovative programs in such fields as international studies, environmental science, peace studies, and information technology. The success of graduates is reflected by high rates of acceptance to graduate school programs. The Juniata academic calendar includes two semesters (late August–early May) and a limited course offering in the summer.

Campus Life

The Juniata community, composed of students and faculty and staff members, is a friendly, closely-knit community with an extended family atmosphere. Nearly all students live on campus in residence halls, normally with 2 students in each room. Students also eat their meals together in the Juniata dining hall. The campus is well equipped for the needs of both academic study and social and recreational pursuits. Juniata offers students a full range of activities, including concerts, dances, movies, plays, art exhibitions, lectures from visiting dignitaries, and an extensive program of athletics. In addition, more than ninety student organizations and clubs permit students to explore a wide variety of interests.

For International Students

Juniata is committed to increasing the presence of international students on its campus and believes that the goal of a liberal arts education for the twenty-first century should be to prepare students for life in a multicultural global society. The College's Center for International Education offers a full range of services to international students and helps to ensure that they become fully integrated into the campus community. Juniata's ESL program prepares students for successful university-level study and provides assistance to degree-program students as needed. Credit is given for ESL and advanced-level ESL program students, who may begin part-time degree-program study while still enrolled in ESL. Students with AP, IB, or A-level course work may be eligible for transfer credit at Juniata.

Kapiolani Community College

- Contact:
  International Admissions
  Honda International Center
  Kapi'olani Community College
  4303 Diamond Head Road
  Honolulu, HI 96816
  Phone: 808-734-9312
  Fax: 808-734-9454
  E-mail: HIC@hawaii.edu
  Web site: http://www.kcc.hawaii.edu/object/
      applyf1.htm
- Public, two-year, coed
- Suburban setting
- Total enrollment: 7,303
- Student-faculty ratio: 20:1
- 2006–07 Tuition and fees: $5976
- 2006–07 Room and board: $12,192

- Countries represented: 40
- International students applied: 248 (fall 2006 and spring 2007)
- International students accepted: 208 (fall 2006 and spring 2007)
- Admissions tests:
  - TOEFL (paper-based min. score 400 for ESOL Intensive Transition Program, 500 for academic courses), STEP, IELTS, TOEIC, Cambridge Exams, MELAB
  - SAT and ACT: Not required
- Application deadlines: Six weeks before the start of fall, spring, or summer term
- On-campus housing: Limited space available; assistance provided in locating off-campus housing

Area and Climate

Kapi'olani Community College (KCC) is situated on the slopes of Diamond Head Crater in Honolulu on the island of O'ahu. The lush campus is 10 minutes from Waikiki and major shopping areas. The entire island is accessible by convenient public transportation. O'ahu offers access to stunning natural beauty and the cultural attractions of a multicultural metropolis, including museums, symphonies, and international festivals.

Education

As the largest of the seven community colleges in the University of Hawai'i (UH) System, KCC is a fully accredited institution and provides a wide range of academic, professional, occupational, and technical programs. KCC offers a transferable Associate of Arts degree in liberal arts and two-year Associate of Science degrees and certificates in business education, culinary arts, health sciences, prenursing, and travel and tourism. Students develop a firm academic foundation for becoming global citizens through KCC's small classes, diverse student body, extensive noncredit programs, and cross-curricular emphases, such as Asia-Pacific, information technology, mathematics, service learning, and writing and critical thinking.

Campus Life

More than 7,000 students from many cultures and countries enroll each semester at KCC. The pleasant, open tropical design of the campus reflects the aloha spirit that is central to Hawaiian culture and embraces all who come there. KCC students become well-rounded individuals through publication of student artwork and writing, access to study-abroad programs, and access to UH System libraries, guest speakers, and other cultural activities. KCC has more than a dozen student clubs, including an active International Café, that organize hiking, sports, and community service activities.

For International Students

The Intensive Transition Program in ESOL serves as a vehicle to transition students into the College. After successfully completing one semester of the Intensive Transition Program, students are eligible to take a range of credit courses offered by the College. Typically, students who successfully complete the Intensive Transition Program are eligible for freshman-level university course work (100-level) within one academic year. International students may qualify for tuition waivers after completing one semester of credit study. Full-time advisers and staff members in the Honda International Center assist international students with visa issues, admission, orientation, financial aid, employment, banking, health insurance, and academic counseling. In addition to academic services, students have the opportunity to showcase their own cultures through the annual weeklong International Festival. KCC values international students and their participation in the multicultural campus community.

Keystone College

- Contact:
  Sarah Keating
  Director of Admissions
  Keystone College
  One College Green
  La Plume, PA 18440-1099
  Phone: 570-945-8111
  Fax: 570-945-7916
  E-mail: admissions@keystone.edu
  Web site: http://www.keystone.edu
- Private, coed
- Rural setting
- Enrollment: 1,600 full-time students
- Student-faculty ratio: 13:1
- 2006–07 Tuition and fees: $15,916

- 2006–07 Room and board: $8110
- International students: 3%
- Countries represented: 7
- International students applied: 26
- International students accepted: 16
- International students enrolled: 9
- Admissions tests:
  - TOEFL: Required (min. score 550 paper-based)
  - SAT: Recommended (English-speaking)
  - ACT: Recommended (U.S.-based only)
- Application deadline: Rolling
- On-campus housing: Guaranteed
- Summer housing: Available

Area and Climate

Keystone College is nestled in the wooded foothills of northeastern Pennsylvania. The 270-acre (109-hectare) campus is scenic, safe, and peaceful. Normal temperatures in January range from 10°F (-12°C) to 30°F (-1°C); normal July temperatures range from 70°F (21°C) to 90°F (32°C). The area is noted for its lakes, rivers, parks, woodlands, and famous Pocono resorts. Both Philadelphia and New York City are less than a 2½-hour drive from the campus, and every major city in the Northeast is within a day's drive. Keystone is easily reached by bus or plane from the Wilkes-Barre/Scranton International Airport, 30 minutes from the campus.

Education

Keystone College, founded in 1868, is dedicated to excellence in the liberal arts tradition that prepares students to achieve success in their careers and personal lives. Keystone College offers the best of all worlds: a beautiful campus with a mix of modern technology and a sense of the College's history and an enrollment large enough to make education a stimulating experience but small enough that students maintain their identity. Keystone College offers forty majors and maintains transfer agreements with numerous colleges and universities. Some of the most popular majors are art, communications, culinary arts, early childhood education, environmental science, forensic biology, health sciences, and hotel/restaurant management. Bachelor's degrees are offered in accounting, art, biology, business, communications, criminal justice, early childhood education, elementary education, environmental resource management, forensic biology, information technology, sport and recreation management, teaching: art education, teaching: math education, and teaching: social studies education.

Campus Life

At Keystone College, opportunities for membership and leadership roles in clubs and organizations occur from the day classes begin. Campus organizations include Student Senate, Commuter Council, Art Society, Computer Club, Keystone Drama Guild, Ski Club, and WKCV Radio. Fourteen NCAA Division III varsity sports programs and an extensive intramural program are offered.

For International Students

An orientation program prior to the beginning of each semester is required. The Office of International Student Services and Programs provides year-round academic advisement as well as activity programming. Supportive campus programs include placement and career services, academic advising, residential programs, and computer labs. Although the College requires a minimum score of 550 on the paper-based version of the TOEFL for full-time admission, individuals may be granted conditional admission. Keystone offers a minimal "bridge" program for these students, allowing them one semester to achieve a minimum score of 550 on the paper-based version of the TOEFL.

Kilgore College

- Contact:
    Brenda Thornhill, Director
    International Student Programs
    Kilgore College
    1100 Broadway
    Kilgore, TX 75662
    Phone: 903-983-8204
    Fax: 903-983-8607
    E-mail: bthornhill@kilgore.edu
    Web site: http://www.kilgore.edu
- Public, two-year, coed
- Enrollment: 8,800

- Student-faculty ratio: 18:1
- 2006–07 Tuition and fees: $12,000 (9 months)
- 2006–07 Room and board, mandatory health insurance, books: $3000 per semester
- International students: 3%
- Countries represented: 35
- International students applied: 200
- International students enrolled: 140
- Application deadline: Rolling
- On-campus housing: Available
- Summer housing: Available

Area and Climate

Kilgore College is located in Kilgore, Texas, a city of 10,000 people located in the northeast section of the state referred to as the Piney Woods. Pine and hardwood forests, lakes, rivers, streams, and hills characterize the area. Kilgore is in the middle of what was once one of the most productive oil fields in the continental U.S. A small, quiet, safe community, Kilgore is located 2 miles (3.22 kilometers) off Interstate 20, 2 hours east of Dallas, Texas, and 1 hour west of Shreveport, Louisiana. The climate varies with the turn of the four seasons, with temperatures ranging from 35°F (1.7°C) to 55°F (12.8°C) in the winter and from 70°F (21.1°C) to 98°F (36.7°C) in the summer. Winter is mild, with little or no snow, and summers are hot and humid. Fall and spring are beautiful with the changing color of the foliage and cool temperatures.

Education

Kilgore College, founded in 1935, is an open-door, student-centered institution characterized by excellence in teaching and learning and by leadership in cultural and economic endeavors. Kilgore College believes in the worth and dignity of the individual, meets the needs of a diverse student population, and has a vision of community as a place to be served and a climate to be created. The student body is a microcosm of the communities served by the College and is diverse in ethnic origin, social background, age, and goals. Associate degrees and certificates of completion are available in subjects as diverse as art, business, computer science, engineering, physical therapy, nursing, journalism, and technology. Academic courses transfer to universities all across the U.S. and may be applied toward a bachelor's degree. Students

with acceptable GPAs are guaranteed that they can transfer all their Core Curriculum courses to any university in the state of Texas.

Campus Life

The Office of Student and Residential Life coordinate some thirty clubs and organizations for individual and group opportunities to explore interests outside the classroom, develop social skills and relationships, and participate in intramural sports. Approximately 520 students reside in three residence halls. All students have access to a new student center that houses all the major offices, bookstore, a cafeteria, snack bar, ball room, TV rooms, a piano room, and a game room. Other facilities include a full-service fitness center with a swimming pool, track, weights, racquetball, and workout machines; three computerized study labs with Internet connections; a full-service library; and ESOL classes and labs.

For International Students

Students are tested in English and math proficiency for placement in ESOL (English for speakers of other languages) or academic classes. ESOL students can enroll in academic classes once they reach the reading level while completing the ESOL series of classes. An international student adviser assists students with transition to a new culture and with the required immigration, local, and college rules and regulations. Monthly activities and cultural trips of interest to international students are planned monthly. Student support services available include tutoring, math, and English skill labs; residential life activities; and a health clinic. On-campus employment opportunities are very limited for international students. Kilgore College is a small, safe, inexpensive community for international students interested in completing the first two years of study toward a bachelor's degree. Twelve years of education in the student's home country are required. First-semester tuition, fees, room, and board ($5000) must be wired to Kilgore College prior to arrival; instructions are given in the orientation packet after the F1 student visa is granted.

Lakeland College

- Contact:
  Patrick Liu
  Director of International Admissions
  Lakeland College
  P.O. Box 359
  Sheboygan, WI 53082-0359
  Phone: 920-565-1337
  Fax: 920-565-1556
  E-mail: liup@lakeland.edu
  Web site: http://www.lakeland.edu
- Independent, comprehensive, coed
- Rural setting
- Enrollment: Approximately 1,000 (on-campus, undergraduate)

- Student-faculty ratio: 18:1
- 2006–07 Tuition and fees: $16,795
- 2006–07 Room and board: $2758
- International students: 11%
- Countries represented: 20
- International students enrolled: 110
- Admissions tests:
  - TOEFL: Required (min. score 173 CBT; 65 iBT)
  - SAT, ACT, or IELTS could replace TOEFL
- Application deadline: Rolling
- On-campus housing: Available
- Summer housing: Available

Area and Climate

Lakeland College takes great pride in its traditions and opportunities. All the positive elements of a small, growing town contribute to this community's compelling sense of self. Lakeland is just 11 miles (18 kilometers) from Sheboygan, located on Lake Michigan's western shore, halfway between Milwaukee and Green Bay. This city of more than 50,000 was recently named the third-safest city of its size in the country by *Money* magazine. Citizens are proud of their community and work diligently to keep it attractive and livable. Fine schools, delightful residential neighborhoods, diverse cultural opportunities, extremely low crime rates, and a robust local economy are all present in this bustling metropolitan area.

Education

Lakeland College was founded in 1862 and is fully accredited. As a liberal arts college offering both undergraduate and graduate degrees, Lakeland provides students with an education that is broad in scope, comprehensive in spirit, and focused in at least one area of study. Lakeland offers a wide variety of academic programs—something of interest for everyone. Majors and programs include accounting, art, biochemistry, biology, business education, business management, chemistry, computer science, criminal justice, education, English, fitness studies, German, history, international business, marketing, mathematics, music, nonprofit organization management, psychology, religion, resort management, sociology, Spanish, and writing, and there is an English Language Institute for those who do not have the required English language proficiency. Lakeland's undergraduate day curriculum is organized around six academic divisions, and students major in one or more disciplines, usually within one of these divisions. The College's general studies requirements ensure that all students experience some of the same course work. Many academic majors also offer international students internship opportunities.

Campus Life

Many international students, who make up more than 15 percent of the resident undergraduate population, find an inviting academic home at Lakeland College. Lakeland is a fun and exciting place to be. With vibrant student activities, campus organizations, and award-winning athletics teams, there is a lot of action on the Lakeland campus throughout the year. Lakeland offers the kind of small-town atmosphere that allows anyone to be involved in anything of interest, whether it be writing a column for the student newspaper or campaigning with the Student Association for an officer's position to make Lakeland a better place. The College offers a variety of on-campus living facilities, including nine traditional residence halls, all of which are wired for Internet access.

For International Students

Lakeland offers need- and merit-based college grants, ranging from $1000 to full tuition per year, to qualified undergraduate day program international applicants. Each semester, shortly before the general orientation for all new students, the International Student Office conducts a special orientation program for new international students. During this required orientation, students take part in programs designed to help them adjust to life on campus and to familiarize them with the community and the services provided by the College.

Laramie County Community College

- Contact:
  Sara Fleenor
  International Student Advisor
  Laramie County Community College
  Cheyenne, WY 82007
  Phone: 307-778-1221
  Fax: 307-778-1282
  E-mail: diversity@lccc.wy.edu
  Web site: http://www.lccc.wy.edu/intl_stu/
- Public, two-year, coed
- Small-town setting
- Enrollment: 4,158
- Student-faculty ratio: 21:1
- 2006–07 Tuition and fees: $6000
- 2006–07 Room and board: $6600 (not including summer)
- International students: 1%
- Countries represented: 13
- International students applied: 35
- International students accepted: 30
- International students enrolled: 25
- Admissions tests:
  - TOEFL (paper-based min. score 500; computer-based min. score 173)
  - SAT and ACT: Not required
- Application deadline: Rolling
- On-campus housing: Available
- Summer housing: Available

Area and Climate

Laramie County Community College (LCCC) is in Cheyenne, Wyoming, the state capital. With a population of 50,000, Cheyenne is in the southeast corner of Wyoming, 100 miles (161 kilometers) from Denver, Colorado. Outdoor, cultural, and entertainment activities include fishing, hiking, rock climbing, skiing, camping, theater, concerts, museums, and rodeo. Winter weather is cold, often sunny, and occasionally snowy, with an average temperature of about 28°F (-2°C). Summers have warm days and cool nights, with afternoon thundershowers common. The average summer temperature is about 65°F (18°C). Low humidity and brisk winds are found year-round. The city is safe and welcomes international students. Cheyenne is easily reached by airplane or bus.

Education

Founded in 1968, LCCC offers students an opportunity to study in a dynamic learning environment with instructors who are dedicated to providing high-quality education. The College has fifty academic and vocational/technical programs intended either for transfer to four-year institutions or to prepare students for immediate employment. The computer technology, business, agriculture, and health occupations are among the most popular. Through an online catalog, students have access to thousands of books, periodicals, and other materials in the LCCC library and other Wyoming libraries. Most full-time instructors have master's degrees, and more than 10 have doctoral degrees. The academic year includes two 16-week semesters and a summer session.

Campus Life

Although most LCCC students come from the Cheyenne area, students are enrolled from around Wyoming and the region. Modern on-campus housing featuring 4-person suites is available during the fall and spring semesters. Student life at LCCC includes a variety of student clubs and teams as well as fun activities. Organizations include the Across Cultures Club, groups for people with special interests, Phi Theta Kappa international honor society, and clubs for students in particular majors. Dances, workshops, contests, intramural sports, and more take place on and off campus. The newly refurbished physical education facility includes a swimming pool, a weight room, an aerobic center, indoor ball courts, and a climbing wall. Athletics include intercollegiate men's basketball, women's volleyball, and men's and women's soccer. The campus has twenty modern buildings situated on 271 acres (110 hectares).

For International Students

Before arriving at LCCC, international students can participate in a pen-pal program that allows them to correspond with LCCC students during the application process. Once on campus, an orientation acquaints international students with campus life and facilities. Students take placement tests to ensure that they enroll in the appropriate level of courses. Precollege courses in reading, math, and English are offered for students who need additional preparation before taking college-level courses. LCCC's intensive English as a second language (ESL) program is available to students who do not meet the English language requirement for admission to the College and wish to improve their English language skills. TOEFL scores are not required for students enrolling in this program. An international student adviser is available on a part-time basis to assist students with problems or concerns. Students who need help with course work or tutoring can find both in the Student Success Center. Every effort is made to ensure that international students are successful in obtaining an excellent education at Laramie County Community College.

Lawrence University

- Contact:
  Steven T. Syverson
  Dean of Admissions and Financial Aid
  Lawrence University
  Appleton, WI 54911
  Phone: 920-832-6500
  Fax: 920-832-6782
  E-mail: excel.international@lawrence.edu
- Private, coed
- Urban setting
- Enrollment: 1,400
- Student-faculty ratio: 9:1
- 2006–07 Tuition and fees: $29,388
- 2006–07 Room and board: $6382 (avg.)

- International students: 12%
- Countries represented: 54
- International students applied: 317
- International students accepted: 103
- International students enrolled: 47
- Admissions tests:
  - TOEFL (recommended paper-based min. score 575, computer-based min. score 233) or IELTS (recommended min. score 6.5)
  - SAT and ACT: Optional
- Application deadline: 1/15
- On-campus housing: Guaranteed
- Summer housing: Available

Area and Climate

Lawrence University is located on an 84-acre (34-hectare) campus in Appleton, Wisconsin, which has a metropolitan-area population of 250,000 and is located in the heartland of the United States. Appleton is located in the area of the state that enjoys both the fastest rate of growth and the highest rate of employment; it has been identified as one of the safest cities of its size in the United States. It consistently appears among the top fifty communities in the United States considered to have the finest quality of life. The campus itself is adjacent to the downtown area of the city and is bordered by the Fox River and residential neighborhoods. Summers in Wisconsin are typically warm and humid; fall brings cooler temperatures and colorful leaves; winter brings snow as well as clear, bright, cold weather; and spring offers warmer temperatures, occasional rain, and colorful flowering trees. Four major airlines fly into Appleton from Chicago, Detroit, Minneapolis, Cincinnati, and Milwaukee.

Education

Founded in 1847, Lawrence was among the first colleges in the nation to be founded coeducational. It offers more than 500 courses in nearly forty academic disciplines in the natural sciences, humanities, social sciences, and fine arts, culminating in the Bachelor of Arts degree. The Conservatory of Music, which awards the Bachelor of Music degree as well as a five-year B.A./B.Mus. double degree, offers professional training in music performance, music education, and theory-composition. Conservatory concerts, recitals, guest artists, and faculty artists provide more than 200 performances each year for all students to enjoy.

Campus Life

Students at Lawrence participate in approximately 100 clubs and organizations, twenty-three varsity sports, and more than a dozen music ensembles. On-campus housing is available for all students, with more than 95 percent living on campus all four years of attendance. Lawrence International, the largest club on campus, enjoys members from the United States as well as all international students. The International Cabaret, an annual dinner with food chosen and prepared by the international students and entertainment reflecting their heritages, celebrates the diversity on campus. It is attended by students, faculty members, and the Appleton community.

For International Students

An international student adviser assists students in making the transition to Lawrence even before they arrive on campus in the fall. The International House provides satellite television programming from around the world; newspapers from more than twenty countries; a place to meet, relax, and study; and a kitchen to make favorite meals from home. The Health and Counseling Center provides medical care and counseling for a variety of issues; the Center for Teaching and Learning's Writing Lab offers peer tutoring and faculty assistance in writing and research skills; and one-on-one faculty advising for every student guarantees excellent curricular support and guidance. While it is expected that non-U.S. students support the majority of their expenses to attend Lawrence, a number of partial-tuition scholarships are available to such students. One full-tuition scholarship, which is renewable for four years, is awarded to a student who demonstrates exceptional need. The Lawrence community welcomes international students warmly and values the perspective international students add to the campus.

Leeward Community College

- **Contact:**
  International Programs Office
  University of Hawaii—Leeward Community
    College
  96-045 Ala Ike
  Pearl City, HI 96782
  Phone: 808-455-0510
  Fax: 808-455-0640
  E-mail: isa@lcc.hawaii.edu
  Web site: http://www.lcc.hawaii.edu/ipo
- **Public two-year coed**
- **Suburban setting**
- **Enrollment: 6,000**
- **Student-faculty ratio: 18:1**

- **2006–07 Tuition and fees: $5833**
  (two semesters)
- **2006–07 Room and board: $9600 (off-campus**
  average for twelve months)
- **International students: 2%**
- **Countries represented: 26**
- **International students enrolled: 70**
- **Admissions tests:**
    - **TOEFL (paper-based min. score 500;**
      computer-based min. score 173)
    - **SAT/ACT: Not required**
- **Application deadline: Rolling**
- **On-campus housing: Not available**

Area and Climate

Leeward Community College is located on the island of O'ahu, in the suburb of Pearl City, just 20 minutes from downtown Honolulu and famous Waikiki Beach. Oahu is the main population base for the state of Hawai'i and is home to 902,700 people. Honolulu is one of the most beautiful cities in the country and is routinely ranked among the top ten healthiest cities in which to live in the United States. The Leeward campus sits on 49 acres (20 hectares) of mildly sloping land in the suburb of Pearl City, with a commanding and magnificent view of Pearl Harbor. Hawai'i is well known for its tropical climate, year-round outdoor lifestyle, and beautiful natural scenery. The average daytime winter temperature is 78°F (25.6°C), while in the summer, the average is 85°F (29.4°C). Temperatures at night drop approximately 10°F. There is a local transit system that provides bus service anywhere on the island.

Education

As one of ten campuses of the world-renowned, nationally ranked University of Hawaii system, Leeward Community College is a fully accredited, public, two-year institution offering a variety of programs and dedicated to student success. In addition to the Associate in Arts (A.A.), the Associate in Science (A.S.), and the Associate in Applied Sciences (A.A.S.) degrees, students may earn Certificates of Achievement, Completion, Academic Subject, and Competence. Programs of study are available in the arts and sciences, business, culinary arts, digital media, human services, information and computer science, pre-engineering, and television production. Guaranteed admission and transfer is available within the University of Hawaii system, which includes three 4-year universities in the state. Students may also transfer to other four-year universities

across the United States. International student services are available in immigration and academic counseling, tutoring, career planning, and university transfer.

Campus Life

Leeward students get involved in a wide variety of clubs, organizations, and events on campus, including a student-run newspaper, Student Government, International Club, Astronomy Club, Information Technology Club, Japanese Circle, Phi Beta Lambda, Phi Theta Kappa, International Week, and musical performances, to name a few. Campus facilities include a bookstore, a student center, a cafeteria, a library, computer labs, a health center, and a theater that offers a variety of performances year-round.

For International Students

The International Programs Office offers a range of support services to assist international students during their studies at Leeward Community College. A new-student orientation is conducted for international students every semester to familiarize them with the campus and the community. The English Language Institute offers an Intensive English Program for students who need to improve their English before enrolling in credit classes. The TOEFL is not required for admission to the Intensive English Program; upon completion, students can enter the degree programs without further admission requirements. For more information, students should e-mail eli@ hawaii.edu. Leeward provides academic counseling, including university transfer, immigration, and visa counseling, and assistance with housing placement by referral. A housing list is maintained for students who wish to rent or share an apartment. Leeward also works with a homestay agency for students who want to experience life in an American home. Social activities for international students are planned by the International Programs Office and include excursions to local events, outdoor activities, and visits to local museums and places of interest.

Long Beach City College

- **Contact:**
  Denise Kinsella
  International Student Program Manager
  Long Beach City College
  4901 East Carson Street
  Long Beach, CA 90808
  Phone: 562-938-4745
  Fax: 562-938-4747
  E-mail: dkinsella@lbcc.edu
  Web site: http://intl.lbcc.edu
- **Public, 2-year, coed**
- **Urban setting**
- **Enrollment: 25,000**
- **Student-faculty ratio: 20:1**

- **2006–07 Tuition and fees: $4536**
- **2006–07 Room and board: $8400**
- **International students: 1%**
- **Countries represented: 60**
- **International students applied: 210**
- **International students accepted: 176**
- **Admissions tests:**
  - **TOEFL: Required (min. score 500 PBT; 173 CBT; 61 iBT)**
- **Application deadline: Fall, 6/1; spring, 10/1**
- **On-campus housing: Not available**
- **Summer housing: Through homestay**

Area and Climate

Long Beach City College (LBCC) is ideally located in the international port city of Long Beach. The city has a population of nearly 800,000 and is centrally located on the coast in southern California. As a result, it has a mild climate year-round. Its location near highways, airports, and public transportation make it easy to access many attractions and cultural hubs in the area. Disneyland and Hollywood are 30 minutes away by car, and San Diego and mountain resorts are less than 2 hours away. In between there are countless attractions and activities, including universities and major shopping centers. In addition to its well known beaches, the city of Long Beach hosts one of the largest ports in the United States and offers a vibrant and active downtown area as well.

Education

LBCC was founded in 1927 and is accredited by the Western Association of Schools and Colleges. The College has two campuses. The Liberal Arts Campus is situated in a lovely residential neighborhood and primarily houses the academic programs of the College. The Pacific Coast Campus offers both academic as well as vocational programs. The College offers more than 100 degree and certificate programs in both academic and vocational fields. It is perhaps best known as being a leader in transfer to universities in the region, including UC, Irvine; UCLA; USC; and CSU, Long Beach. The College is well known for several of its programs, including business, marketing, radio/television and film, music recording, electronics, aviation, hotel and tourism, nursing, and the sciences. In addition, the College has an excellent intensive English language training program, which allows students who do not meet the TOEFL admission requirement to be conditionally admitted and begin their studies at the College.

Campus Life

The Long Beach City College campuses reflect the diversity of the city of Long Beach (known as the "International City") with not only F1 international students but people from the community. There are many active clubs, including the International Student Club, which has weekly meetings, events, and trips. In addition there are many special interest clubs and a great intramural athletic program. Student athletes attend LBCC for its long tradition in athletic and academic excellence, and the College is regularly honored nationally as a leader for its endeavors. The campus facilities include a stadium and track, student activities center, game room, lounge, pool, tennis courts, and fitness center. Housing for students is ample as the campus is located in a residential neighborhood. Homestays with an American family can be arranged, and apartments are also available and close by.

For International Students

Orientation is required for all new international students prior to each semester. This involves testing students for their placement; informing them about the college, its services, and the area; counseling them individually; registering them for classes; and meeting new friends. There are two ESL programs at the College. The regular program allows students to refine their English over the course of the semester while taking other academic courses. There is also an intensive English program that offers nine-week terms for students who need to become proficient enough to take regular classes as soon as possible. There is an International Student Center where students can find special resources and services.

Long Island University, C.W. Post Campus

- Contact:
    Beth Carson
    Admissions Office (Attn: International)
    Long Island University, C.W. Post Campus
    720 Northern Boulevard
    Brookville, NY 11548-1300

    Phone: 516-299-2900
    Fax: 516-299-2418
    E-mail: enroll@cwpost.liu.edu
    Web site: http://www.liu.edu/cwpost
- Private, four-year, coed
- Suburban setting
- Enrollment: 4,900
- Student-faculty ratio: 15:1
- 2007–08 Tuition and fees: $25,750

- 2007–08 Room and board: $9320
- International students: 5%
- Countries represented: 48
- International students applied: 981
- International students accepted: 656
- International students enrolled: 285
- Admissions tests:
    - TOEFL (min. score 527 PBT; 197 CBT; 71 iBT)
    - SAT or ACT: Recommended
- Application deadline: Fall, 7/1; spring, 11/1
- On-campus housing: Yes
- Summer housing: Yes

Area and Climate

The 307-acre suburban campus, located only 20 miles from Manhattan, is considered one of the most beautiful college settings in North America. The campus is located in the community of Brookville, on the north shore of Long Island, and features rolling green lawns, tree-lined paths and gardens, and several historic mansions as well as modern buildings such the Kahn Discovery Center, the Pratt Recreation Center and Winnick Student Center. New York City is just a 50-minute car or train ride from the campus. Weather on Long Island is seasonal, with flower-filled springs, hot and hazy summers, picturesque autumns, and snowy winters.

Education

C.W. Post is one of six campuses of Long Island University, one of the largest private universities in the United States. Serving a population of 8,500 full- and part-time students, the C.W. Post campus is distinguished by programs of excellence with small classes in accountancy, business, computer science, education, liberal arts and sciences, library and information science, health professions and nursing, public service, and visual and performing arts. C.W. Post offers 106 undergraduate degrees, 75 graduate degrees, several accelerated 5-year bachelor's/master's degree programs, and doctoral programs in clinical psychology and information studies. Most of the University's academic programs hold accreditation by the most prestigious organizations in their fields.

Campus Life

C.W. Post offers students a rich and vibrant campus life, with more than eighty clubs and organizations, athletic teams, sororities, and fraternities. This high-tech campus includes more than 500 computers for student use as well as wireless Internet connectivity in classrooms, study lounges, dining halls, and even outdoors on the campus's Great Lawn. The Student Technology Center offers free printing services, software assistance, and laptop rentals. Students enjoy excellent sports, fitness, and recreation facilities at the modern Pratt Recreation Center and top notch academic resources at the campus library—one of the largest research libraries in New York. The campus offers a wide range of cultural events at its respected art museum, galleries, and world-renowned Tilles Center for the Performing Arts.

For International Students

The Office of International Student Services (ISS) at C.W. Post provides international students with orientation, immigration and employment information, personal counseling, and workshops on adjusting to life in the United States. The ISS office assists students with both college life in America and campus life at C.W. Post. The campus is also the home of The English Language Institute, where students who speak English as a second language can improve their listening, speaking, reading, and writing skills. All C.W. Post students receive individual academic counseling and are encouraged to utilize C.W. Post's nationally recognized office of Professional Experience and Career Planning.

Loyola University Chicago

- Contact:
    Undergraduate Admission
    Loyola University Chicago
    Chicago, IL 60610
    Phone: 312-915-6500
    E-mail: admission@luc.edu
    Web site: http://www.luc.edu/undergrad/
- Private, comprehensive, coed
- Suburban setting
- Total enrollment: 15,194
- Student-faculty ratio: 14:1
- 2007–08 Tuition and fees: $27,200
- 2007–08 Room and board: $9930 (average)

- International students: 1%
- Countries represented: 82
- International students applied: 587 (total, undergraduate and graduate)
- International students accepted: 165
- Admissions tests:
    - TOEFL: Required (min. score 550 PBT; 213 CBT; 79–80 iBT)
    - SAT and ACT: Required
- Application deadline: Rolling
- On-campus housing: Available
- Summer housing: Available

Area and Climate

Loyola University Chicago gives students the best of campus and city life with diverse living and learning opportunities in world-class Chicago. Students at Loyola benefit from Chicago's exceptional cultural and economic resources. In addition to providing an unparalleled setting for educational opportunities, Chicago is also one of the most prestigious cities in the world in terms of recreation and entertainment. Public transportation is available near both of Loyola's city campuses. Chicago enjoys four changes of season, with temperatures averaging -6°C (21°F) in January and 23°C (73°F) in July.

Education

Loyola University Chicago offers a total of 185 programs of study—sixty-nine undergraduate, seventy-seven graduate, thirty-six doctoral, and three professional. All undergraduate programs focus on a solid liberal arts education, encouraging students to think and question, communicate creatively, and discover the meaning and purpose in existence. In addition, all undergraduate students must complete Loyola's Core Curriculum, which focuses on developing the values and skills needed to build a successful future. Loyola's student-faculty ratio of 14:1', well below the national average of 19:1, ensures personal attention. Nearly all of Loyola's 940 full-time faculty

members hold Ph.D.s. Five campus libraries and hundreds of networked computers provide students with unlimited access to resources and technology.

Campus Life

Loyola's 45-acre Lake Shore Campus, home to most undergraduate programs, includes more than fifty buildings on the shore of Lake Michigan. The Water Tower campus, located in the heart of the city, just off Chicago's Magnificent Mile, provides easy access to the city's business and cultural center. More than 3,200 students choose to live on campus in traditional residence halls or apartment-style living facilities like Baumhart Hall, a new twenty-five story building located at the Water Tower Campus. Recreational facilities at Loyola include an outdoor track and playing fields, indoor racquetball courts, a swimming pool, and fitness equipment. Students may participate in more than 125 student clubs and organizations, including academic/honorary, cultural/ethnic, political/social, service/spiritual, and media organizations.

For International Students

With a student body representing eighty-two nations, Loyola University Chicago is committed to international education and cultural diversity. The Office of International Programs works to ease international students' transition into the University community, offering services that include prearrival information, orientation, immigration advising, immigration document production, workshops, social events, and more.

Manchester College

- Contact:
  David McFadden
  Executive Vice President
  Manchester College
  604 East College Avenue
  North Manchester, IN 46962
  Phone: 260-982-5055
  Fax: 260-982-5239
  E-mail: international@manchester.edu
  Web site: http://www.manchester.edu
- Private, coed
- Small-town setting
- Enrollment: 1,050
- Student-faculty ratio: 14:1

- 2007–08 Tuition and fees: $21,640
- 2007–08 Room and board: $7610
- International students: 5%
- Countries represented: 22
- International students applied: 185
- International students accepted: 70
- International students enrolled: 9
- Admissions tests:
  - TOEFL (paper-based min. score 550)
- Application deadline: 5/1
- On-campus housing: Guaranteed
- Summer housing: Available

Area and Climate

Manchester College is located in northern Indiana, 37 miles (60 kilometers) from Fort Wayne, a city of 175,000 people; 124 miles (200 kilometers) from Indianapolis; and 186 miles (300 kilometers) from Chicago. Fort Wayne offers excellent cultural activities, movies, shopping centers, restaurants, and an international airport. The town of North Manchester, with 6,000 residents, is a friendly and safe place to study. The beautiful 94-acre (38-hectare) campus has many trees and large open spaces. The weather varies from cold winters with snow to warm summers.

Education

Manchester College was founded in 1889. Manchester offers bachelor's degrees in forty-five areas of study. Accounting, athletic training, biology, business, chemistry, corporate finance, environmental studies, premedicine, and physics are especially strong programs. Classes are small and students get individual attention from teachers. International students are eligible to apply for the honors program. All students use the campus computer network, and computers are available to students in a computer lab and the residence halls. The academic calendar has two semesters (fall and spring), with a special January session that lasts three weeks.

Campus Life

Manchester has students from all over the world and half of the United States. Students live in five residence halls; one is for women only and four are coed. Meals are provided on campus. All students must live on campus for three years; after one year, they can choose the hall in which they live. Summer jobs and summer and holiday housing are available. Students play in seventeen different sports for both men and women, including soccer, basketball, track, and cross-country. There are many organizations and clubs on campus, including a very active Manchester College International Association. Jobs are easily available on campus.

For International Students

Manchester College welcomes students of all religious and national backgrounds. International students especially like the friendly people at Manchester. Limited international student scholarships are available. Special activities for international students include an international student organization, an international fair where students can display materials from their home countries, and a host-family program. International student orientation is held just before school begins, and students receive help applying for campus jobs, setting up a bank account, and shopping for essentials. Airport pick-up from Fort Wayne is provided. An international student adviser meets with each new student during orientation, and a program director works with international students all year long.

Manhattanville College

- **Contact:**
  José Flores
  Vice President, Enrollment Management
  Manhattanville College
  2900 Purchase Street
  Purchase, NY 10577
  Phone: 914-323-5464
  Fax: 914-694-1732
  E-mail: admissions@manhattanville.edu
  Web site: http://www.manhattanville.edu
- **Private, comprehensive, coed**
- **Suburban setting**
- **Enrollment: 1,600**
- **Student-faculty ratio: 12:1**

- **2006–07 Tuition and fees: $28,000**
- **2006–07 Room and board: $11,550**
- **International students: 11%**
- **Countries represented: 59**
- **International students applied: 287**
- **International students accepted: 134**
- **Admissions tests:**
  - **TOEFL: Required (min. score 550 PBT; 213 CBT; 80 iBT)**
  - **SAT or ACT: Required**
- **Application deadline: March 1**
- **On-campus housing: Guaranteed**
- **Summer housing: Available**

Area and Climate

Manhattanville's 100-acre (41 hectares) campus lies in the heart of Westchester County, bordered on the east by Long Island Sound and on the west by the Hudson River. From the roof of the castle that serves as the campus' main hall, the skyline of Manhattan is clearly visible. This proximity to one of the world's leading cultural and financial centers is one of Manhattanville's many assets. Located in the Northeastern region of the United States, Manhattanville enjoys four distinct seasons with spectacular bursts of fall foliage and bright summer sun.

Education

Manhattanville College is a private, four-year liberal arts college with a curriculum that nurtures intellectual curiosity and independent thinking. A student-faculty ratio of 12:1 allows for an individualized education within the structure of a diverse curriculum. Manhattanville offers the unique Portfolio requirement for students, where each student must present a collection of academic and cocurricular experiences. Freshmen are asked to complete the Preceptorial, an interdisciplinary survey of the liberal arts taught by faculty members who also serve as academic advisers. Art, chemistry, computer science, economics, history, literature, music, and psychology are a few of the more than fifty choices of academic concentration. The College's mission is to educate ethically and socially responsible leaders for the global community.

Campus Life

On its 100-acre campus 30 miles (48 km) north of New York City, Manhattanville has created a small global village. Its 1,600 students come from fifty-nine nations and thirty-nine states. They have backgrounds in diverse cultures, religions, and ethnicities. The majority of students decide to live in one of the College's four residence halls, and every night of the week (especially weekends) there are many campus events, such as lectures by UN ambassadors or museum curators or performances by the college's dance and theater department. The campus lends itself to outdoor activities. Manhattanville is only 30 minutes from New York City, one of the world's most exciting cultural centers. The College provides transportation to the city on weekends and to Manhattan-bound commuter trains during the week so that students can take advantage of all New York City has to offer.

For International Students

Manhattanville College welcomes applications from qualified international applicants for any of its semesters. A minimum TOEFL score of 550 on the paper-based version (213 on the computer-based and 80 on the Internet-based versions) and ability to meet the cost of attendance, along with a strong academic background, serve as requirements for admission. The College also offers the Manhattanville College English Language Institute for students who wish to improve their English skills prior to their matriculation. The College provides a separate orientation for international students, as well as a campus adviser who assists with visa issues, work authorizations, and more. Scholarships and other forms of financial assistance may be available for qualified international students.

Marquette University

- **Contact:**
  Office of International Education
  Alumni Memorial Union 425-S
  Marquette University
  P.O. Box 1881
  Milwaukee, WI 53201-1881
  Phone: 414-288-7289
  Fax: 414-288-3701
  E-mail: welcome27@ask.mu.edu
  Web site: http://www.marquette.edu/oie
- Private (Roman Catholic), university, coed
- Urban setting
- Enrollment: 11,500

- Student-faculty ratio: 15:1
- 2007–08 Tuition and fees: $26,270
- 2007–08 Room and board: $9100
- International students: 5%
- Countries represented: 80
- Admissions tests:
  - **TOEFL, IELTS, or APIEL: Required for some**
  - **SAT: Recommended for freshmen**
- Application deadline: Rolling
- On-campus housing: Guaranteed
- Summer housing: Available

Area and Climate

Marquette University, in Milwaukee, Wisconsin, is located on the west shore of beautiful Lake Michigan in the north-central United States. With 1.5 million residents, the Milwaukee metropolitan area is the largest urban center in the state and the nineteenth-largest city in the U.S. Milwaukee offers the advantages of metropolitan life without the major problems of large cities. Milwaukee is a clean and friendly city with many outstanding recreational and cultural activities, including museums, theaters, ethnic festivals, a horticultural conservatory, and a zoo. In addition, professional baseball, basketball, soccer, and ice-hockey teams play in Milwaukee. Wisconsin is well known for the natural beauty of its open countryside, forests, rivers, parks, wildlife, and recreation areas. The area offers the changes of the four seasons, with summer greenery and temperatures sometimes above 90°F (31°C) and winter snows and temperatures sometimes below 0°F (-18°C). Milwaukee is easily accessed by plane, bus, and train. Students can fly directly to Milwaukee's General Mitchell International Airport or Chicago's O'Hare International Airport, which is located 90 miles (145 kilometers) south of Milwaukee.

Education

Marquette University is a highly accredited university offering more than seventy-three undergraduate fields of study in six colleges—Arts and Sciences, Business Administration, Communication, Engineering, Health Sciences, and Nursing—as well as postgraduate programs in dentistry and law. Courses are taught by caring faculty members who are scholars at the top of their fields and are dedicated to helping students reach their potential in the classroom and beyond. The Marquette community, which focuses on care for each student, includes more than 550 international students from eighty countries. Merit scholarships and transfer credit for AP, I.B., and university-level work are available.

Campus Life

Marquette's beautiful 80-acre (32-hectare) campus houses state-of-the-art academic, recreational, and cultural facilities, including the Haggerty Museum of Art, Helfaer Theatre, St. Joan of Arc Chapel, and a 13-acre (5-hectare) outdoor athletic complex. Students can choose from more than 160 student organizations, a broad variety of on-campus activities, and NCAA Division I intercollegiate, club, and intramural sports. Residence halls offer free voice mail, free cable TV, Internet connection, 24-hour front desk service, helpful staff members, and specialty living options. The campus is located adjacent to the downtown area and allows easy access to the city's most interesting places, including museums, theaters, restaurants, trendy coffeehouses, major-league sports, clubs, and abundant internship opportunities.

For International Students

Specialized orientation and housing programs for international students are held prior to each semester, and ongoing orientation sessions are held throughout the year. Marquette University's Office of International Education (OIE) assists students from other countries throughout their Marquette experience and promotes international activities for all students. OIE coordinates admission for undergraduates who are not U.S. citizens or permanent residents. Each student has full-time advisers to help maintain U.S. legal status, plan an effective academic program, participate in campus and community life, arrange for health care and insurance, and discuss issues of concern. OIE offers cross-cultural advising, social and educational activities, and credited courses in English as a second language. The International Program Center, which is administered by OIE, promotes interaction among students from around the world. All members of the Marquette community are invited to share in the activities of the center, participate in its operation, and plan on-site international events. A variety of campus departments and student groups use the center for their meetings, dinners, films, lectures, and other activities.

Marshall University

- **Contact:**
  Dr. Clark Egnor
  Executive Director, Center for International
    Programs
  Marshall University
  Old Main 320
  One John Marshall Drive
  Huntington, WV 25755
  Phone: 304-696-6265
  Fax: 304-696-6353
  E-mail: cip@marshall.edu
  Web site: http://www.marshall.edu
- **Public, four-year, coed**
- **Urban setting**
- **Enrollment: 14,000**
- **Student-faculty ratio: 19:1**
- **2006–07 Tuition and fees: $11,104**

- **2006–07 Room and board: $6492**
- **International students: 3%**
- **Countries represented: 70**
- **International students applied: 359 (fall 2006)**
- **International students accepted: 168 (fall 2006)**
- **International students enrolled: 146 (fall 2006)**
- **Admissions tests:**
  - **TOEFL: Required (min. score 500 paper-based; 173 computer-based; 61 Internet-based)**
  - **SAT or ACT: Required (19 ACT or 910 SAT, verbal and math combined)**
- **Application deadline: Rolling**
- **On-campus housing: Available**
- **Summer housing: Available**

Area and Climate

The Marshall University main campus lies within the small, safe city of Huntington, West Virginia, on the banks of the Ohio River, bordering eastern Kentucky and southern Ohio. Huntington, with a population of 55,000 is the second-largest urban center in West Virginia. The campus is within walking distance of hotels, shopping malls, restaurants, movie theaters, supermarkets, and banks. The city is served by a regional airport and rail and bus lines. The South Charleston campus is located just outside the state capital, the political center of West Virginia, with excellent restaurants, museums, and cultural centers. West Virginia experiences four seasons, with mild winters and warm summers.

Education

The University offers forty-four baccalaureate program degrees that include the Bachelor of Arts (B.A.), Bachelor of Business Administration (B.B.A.), Bachelor of Fine Arts (B.F.A.), Bachelor of Science (B.S.), Bachelor of Science in Medical Technology (B.S.M.T.), Bachelor of Science in Nursing (B.S.N.), and Bachelor of Social Work (B.S.W.). Bachelor's programs include biological sciences, botany, chemistry, communication disorders, communication studies, computer science, counseling, criminal justice, cytotechnology, dietetics, economics, education (elementary and secondary), English, environmental biology, family and consumer science, finance, French, geography, geology, German, history, integrated science and technology, international affairs, journalism and mass communications, Latin, management, management information systems, management technology, marketing, mathematics, microbiology, multidisciplinary studies, music, park resources and leisure services, physics, physiology/ molecular biology, political science, psychology, safety technology, sociology, Spanish, theater, visual arts, women's studies, and zoology. In addition to the Associate of Science in

Nursing (A.S.N.) degree, Marshall offers Associate of Applied Science (A.A.S.) programs that include banking and finance, electronics technology, health information technology, hospitality management, information technology, interior design, legal assistant studies, management technology, medical assistant studies, medical lab technology, physical therapist assistant studies, police science, radiologic technology, respiratory therapy assistant studies, and technical studies. The University is accredited by the North Central Association of Colleges and Schools, and the business administration program is accredited by AACSB International–The Association to Advance Collegiate Schools of Business. The University also offers forty-six graduate programs, including doctorates in biomedical science, education, medicine, and psychology.

Campus Life

More than 100 student organizations and intramural athletics provide excellent opportunities for extracurricular involvement, including the International Student Organization, Chinese Students and Scholars Association, Latino Club, Indian Students Association, African Student Association, Muslim Students Association, and International Students Women's Club. Events and activities, such as the Language Buffet—an evening foreign-language program where the international students teach their language—and the annual International Festival in November bring international students into contact with the community.

For International Students

Student services provided for international students by the Center for International Programs include airport pickup for new arrivals, recreational and cultural activities, a homestay program, immigration and academic advising, and many other services that add to an international student's life. There is no TOEFL requirement for students who complete the advanced level of the LEAP Intensive English Program, which prepares international students for university study through 18 hours of year-round instruction in reading, writing, speaking, and listening.

Marymount Manhattan College

- Contact:
  Office of Admissions
  Marymount Manhattan College
  221 East 71st Street
  New York, NY 10021
  Phone: 212-517-0430
  Fax: 212-517-0448
  E-mail: admissions@mmm.edu
  Web site: http://www.mmm.edu
- Private, coed, liberal arts
- Urban setting
- Total enrollment: 2,100
- Student-faculty ratio: 12:1

- 2006–07 Tuition and fees: $19,638
- 2006–07 Room and board: $12,090
- International students: 5%
- International students enrolled: 100
- Admissions tests:
  - TOEFL (paper-based min. score 550; computer-based min. score 213)
  - SAT or ACT: Required (if English is the native language)
- Application deadline: Rolling
- On-campus housing: Available
- Summer housing: Not available

Area and Climate

Marymount Manhattan College (MMC) is situated in Manhattan at 221 East 71st Street, between Second and Third Avenues on the Upper East Side. Subway and bus lines are nearby, as is Central Park. Countless museums, cultural attractions, historic points of interest, and shopping, all of which are world-class, are within easy reach. The New York City climate is temperate, featuring hot summers and mild springs and autumns. Winter features some cold weather and snow, but nothing that is not dealt with easily.

Education

Marymount Manhattan College is a four-year, private, coeducational institution that offers preprofessional development within the context of strong programs in the liberal arts and sciences. MMC offers sixteen majors, twenty-nine minors, several honor societies, and many internship opportunities. The library has an extensive collection of publications, videos, and electronic databases, in addition to two computer labs and more than 100 laptop computers. The Theresa Lang Theatre provides students with training and work experience in a professionally equipped facility for exhibiting the work of students. The Freeman Center for Science Education, which is equipped with new biology, chemistry, and physics laboratories, enhances the educational experience of all students. The Theresa Lang Center for Producing comprises a digital media lab, an experimental video studio, a "smart" classroom, a digital sound-design suite, and nonlinear digital-editing suites. Marymount Manhattan has new, state-of-the-art facilities for the psychology and communication sciences and disorders departments.

Campus Life

Marymount Manhattan College has approximately 2,100 students. There is a student club, organization, or activity that meets the interests and needs of every student. The Student Government and the LEAD Team (Leadership, Excellence, and Development) are voluntary student groups that are open to all interested members of the student body. These groups help govern the student body and plan and support such activities as orientation, homecoming, and other events throughout the year. Every month, there are cultural activities to represent MMC's diverse population. The College has three residence halls, housing approximately 750 students.

For International Students

Marymount Manhattan College has students from more than thirty-six countries worldwide; 5 percent of the student body are international students. The International Student Office provides support in obtaining and maintaining F-1 student status. It offers orientation for new students and guides them through their first semester. Thereafter, the office acts as an advocate for international students, referring them to appropriate offices and staff members. On-campus events give students the chance to meet others and become involved in campus activities. MMC also has an intensive ESL program that is offered during the academic year.

Marywood University

- Contact:
  Robert Reese
  Director of Admissions
  Marywood University
  2300 Adams Avenue
  Scranton, PA 18509
  Phone: 866-279-9663
  Fax: 570-961-4763
  E-mail: yourfuture@marywood.edu
  Web site: http://www.mymarywood.com
- Private, coed
- Suburban setting
- Enrollment: 3,164

- Student-faculty ratio: 12:1
- 2006–07 Tuition and fees: $21,840
- 2006–07 Room and board: $9700
- International students: 2%
- Countries represented: 25
- Admissions tests:
  - TOEFL (paper-based min. score 500; computer-based min. score 173)
  - SAT: Required (English-speaking students)
- Application deadline: Rolling, preferred dates March 1 (fall), October 1 (spring)
- On-campus housing: Available

Area and Climate

Marywood University is located in Scranton, in the northeastern section of Pennsylvania near the scenic Pocono Mountains. Scranton has a four-season climate, with average summer temperatures between 59°F (15°C) and 80°F (27°C) and average winter temperatures between 20°F (-7°C) and 35°F (2°C). Marywood's 115-acre (47-hectare) campus is in a safe, residential neighborhood. Students enjoy sports, special events, music, theater, art, and parks in a friendly community that is located 120 miles (193 kilometers) west of New York City and 115 miles (47 kilometers) north of Philadelphia. Marywood is easily accessible by car, bus, and airplane. The Wilkes-Barre/Scranton International Airport is a 15-minute ride by car from Marywood's campus.

Education

Marywood is committed to integrating liberal arts and professional studies in the context of ethical and religious values. Founded in 1915 by the Congregation of the Sisters, Servants of the Immaculate Heart of Mary, Marywood enrolls more than 3,000 graduate and undergraduate students. Marywood provides an educational framework that enables students to fully develop and master the professional and leadership skills necessary to meet human need on local, regional, and global levels. Its sixty undergraduate programs include art, biology, business, communication arts, communication sciences and disorders, education, English, foreign languages, health and physical education, mathematical sciences, music, nursing, nutrition and dietetics, physician assistant studies, psychol-

ogy, religious studies, science, social science, and special education and several preprofessional programs. Nineteen buildings on campus, including the student residence halls, are wired for access to the Internet and the World Wide Web.

Campus Life

Marywood welcomes women and men of all faiths and backgrounds. Many come from Pennsylvania and surrounding states; others have come from nations around the world, including Brazil, Bulgaria, Chile, China, the Czech Republic, Ghana, Israel, Japan, Kenya, Liberia, Mongolia, Nepal, Poland, Russia, Slovakia, South Korea, Spain, Syria, Taiwan, Tanzania, and Venezuela. Diverse student interests are enriched by more than fifty student organizations, including performing groups, honor societies, academic-interest clubs, and service-related organizations. Concerts, lectures, films, plays, dances, art exhibits, and other activities take place on campus. Marywood students interact extensively with students at nearby colleges and universities.

For International Students

Citizens of other nations are welcome at Marywood and should contact the Office of Admissions for special guidance. International candidates are required to meet the academic standards for admission, demonstrate proficiency in the use of the English language, and submit documentation of sufficient funds to cover educational and living expenses for the duration of study. To certify English proficiency, applicants whose native language is not English must submit their scores from the Test of English as a Foreign Language (TOEFL). An Intensive English Program is available to students who score 300 to 500 on TOEFL. The Director of International Programs advises international students.

McNeese State University

- **Contact:**
  Preble Girard
  International Student Affairs Officer
  McNeese State University
  Lake Charles, LA 70611
  Phone: 337-475-5243
  Fax: 337-475-5151
  E-mail: intinfo@mcneese.edu
  Web site: http://www.mcneese.edu/international
- Public, four-year, university
- Small-town setting
- Enrollment: 8,992
- Student-faculty ratio: 23:1
- 2006–07 Tuition and fees: Approx. $4600 per semester

- 2006–07 Room and board: Approx. $2025 per semester
- International students: 3%
- Countries represented: 52
- International students applied: 622
- International students accepted: 260
- International students enrolled: 146
- Admissions tests:
  - TOEFL (paper-based min. score 500; computer-based min. score 173)
  - SAT: Required (min. scores 450 verbal, 430 math)
  - ACT: Required (min. scores 18 English, 18 math)
- Application deadlines: 4/15, 9/15, 2/15
- On-campus housing: Available
- Summer housing: Available

Area and Climate

Lake Charles and southwest Louisiana are historically and culturally rich. The year 2003 marked the bicentennial of the Louisiana Purchase, and Cajun culture is still very much alive in this region. The area has a mixed heritage, with French, Spanish, Native American, and African roots. Lake Charles has a population of 75,000 and important petrochemical, entertainment, and shipping industries. Contraband Days, the second-largest festival in Louisiana, is held annually in May, and Mardi Gras is also a festive time during the spring. Perhaps the greatest local attraction is the Cajun food, which is the pride of southwest Louisiana. The climate in Lake Charles is very temperate, with average temperatures ranging from 51°F (11°C) in winter to 82°F (28°C) in summer. Lake Charles lies along the I-10 corridor, with Houston and Baton Rouge just over 2 hours away and New Orleans almost 4 hours away. The area offers a variety of outdoor activities, cultural events, and entertainment opportunities for students attending McNeese.

Education

Founded in 1939, McNeese State University is a comprehensive institution that awards undergraduate and graduate degrees. Named after John McNeese, a pioneer southwest Louisiana educator, the University is committed to providing its students with outstanding academic opportunities that prepare them to pursue their educational and career goals. At McNeese, more than 8,000 students can choose from more than eighty degree programs offered by seven colleges. As one of the top-ranked schools in the nation for the individual attention students receive from their instructors, McNeese features an international faculty that is devoted to meeting students' academic needs. The University is home to the English as a Second Language International (ESLI) program, which provides international students with intensive English training. Students also have access to state-of-the-art computer labs located throughout the campus with convenient hours.

Campus Life

McNeese has a growing international student population, with nearly 200 students from forty-two countries. New residence halls provide comfortable and affordable housing for McNeese students and are available year-round. The new Recreational Sports Center offers an Olympic-size swimming pool, free weights, an indoor track, and state-of-the-art exercise equipment that is free to all students. Students may participate in a wide range of organizations, including student government, newspaper and yearbook staffs, social fraternities and sororities, religious organizations, and numerous honor societies. On-campus dining options range from homemade meals at Rowdy's cafeteria to international fare to fast-food chains, such as Blimpie and Chick-fil-A. The campus also features a convenience store, coffee shop, bookstore, post office, and ATM.

For International Students

McNeese provides excellent advising and student services in order to make international students as comfortable and successful as possible. All international students benefit from a special orientation session, advising workshops, and the services of the International Student Affairs Officer. A newsletter is sent out monthly to keep students involved and informed. Each fall, students are invited to a welcome back picnic as well as to a monthly international coffee hour. The International Student Association is active on campus and hosts sponsored events. McNeese has a variety of scholarships and nonresident fee waivers that are available to qualified international applicants. Special consideration is given to scholarship applicants with SAT scores over 1060 or composite ACT scores over 23 and at least a 2.5 GPA.

Menlo College

- **Contact:**
  Greg Smith, Ph.D., Vice President for Enrollment
  Menlo College
  1000 El Camino Real
  Atherton, CA 94027
  Phone: 650-543-3753
  Fax: 650-543-4496
  E-mail: admissions@menlo.edu
  Web site: http://www.menlo.edu
- **Private, four-year, coed**
- **Suburban setting**
- **Enrollment: 779**
- **Student-faculty ratio: 15:1**
- **2006–07 Tuition and fees: $26,220**

- **2006–07 Room and board: $9800**
- **International students: 20%**
- **Countries represented: 30**
- **International students applied: 150**
- **International students accepted: 80**
- **International students enrolled: 65**
- **Admissions tests:**
  - **TOEFL: Required (min. score 500, PBT; 173, CBT; 61, iBT)**
  - **SAT or ACT: Recommended**
- **Application deadline: Rolling (February 1 priority date)**
- **On-campus housing: July 1 deadline**
- **Summer housing: Available**

Area and Climate

Menlo College is located on the San Francisco peninsula in the town of Atherton, a quiet, tree-lined community near the cities of Menlo Park and Palo Alto. The area ranks among the most attractive and exciting in the world. Menlo students take advantage of wonderful learning and leisure opportunities in one of the world's most important cultural, financial, and high-technology locations. The temperate climate of northern California is ideal for outdoor sightseeing and activities. Exploring beautiful and cosmopolitan San Francisco, snow skiing in the Sierra Nevada Mountains at Lake Tahoe, hiking in Yosemite National Park, and surfing at Pacific Ocean beaches are popular pastimes. Bus or train service provides excellent transportation around the Bay Area.

Education

Menlo College, an independent, coeducational institution, is devoted to preparing students for distinguished careers and for useful and fulfilling lives. Founded in 1927, Menlo's mission is to promote the traditional subjects of humanities, sciences, mathematics, and social sciences in a professional curriculum designed for career success. Bachelor of Arts or Bachelor of Science degrees are offered in business management, mass communications, and liberal arts, with concentrations in general business management, history, humanities, international management, management information systems, marketing communication, media management, media studies, psychology, and sports management. A Menlo education is characterized by close faculty-student interaction and outside learning opportunities. Menlo is on the semester system. Prominent Menlo graduates include Dan Crown, President and CEO of Crown Theaters, and S. T. Jack Brigham III, Senior Vice President, Corporate Affairs General Counsel, Hewlett-Packard Corporation.

Campus Life

The 60-acre (24-hectare) campus at Menlo is a true microcosm of the world. Menlo's diverse student body includes people from all over the United States and all around the world. Approximately 60 percent of all students live in on-campus residence halls, which offer a safe and secure environment in which to reside and study. Menlo students enjoy on-campus dances, dinners, concerts, and special events, including the annual Spring Fest. Participation in intercollegiate athletics and more than thirty clubs, organizations, and honor societies is open to all students. The Menlo College International Club sponsors International Week, a celebration of Menlo's student cultures, featuring cuisine, music, dancing, and exhibits. The College also sponsors a student-run newspaper and television and radio stations.

For International Students

Menlo provides international students with individual counseling through the Office of International Student Services. Here, international students find social and cultural programming, a mentor program for new students, immigration advising, and personal and cross-cultural counseling. Menlo offers scholarships of up to $12,000 per year to many international students; and each year, 10 outstanding students receive scholarships of up to $17,000 each.

Mesa Community College

- **Contact:**
    Office of International Education
    Mesa Community College
    1833 West Southern Avenue
    Mesa, AZ 85202

    Phone: 480-461-7758
    Fax: 480-461-7139
    E-mail: ie@mcmail.maricopa.edu
- **Public, two-year, coed**
- **Urban setting**
- **Enrollment: 27,179**
- **Student-faculty ratio: 20:1**
- **2006–07 Tuition and fees: $6800**
- **2006–07 Room and board: $9,250**
- **International students: .8%**

- **Countries represented: More than 50**
- **International students applied: 142 (fall 2006)**
- **International students accepted: 97**
- **Admissions tests:**
    - **TOEFL: Required (For academic admission, min. score 500 paper-based, 133 computer-based, 61 Internet-based; for Intensive English Program, min. score 400 paper-based, 97 computer-based, 32 Internet-based), or six years of English instruction, or letter of recommendation**
    - **SAT or ACT: Not required**
- **Application deadlines: Year-round**
- **On-campus housing: Not available**
- **Summer housing: Not available**

Area and Climate

Mesa Community College (MCC) is located in Mesa, Arizona, which is part of the metropolitan Phoenix area. With a population of more than 450,000 residents, Mesa has a history full of interesting pioneer traditions and ancient folklore. There are legends of vanished Indian tribes, battles fought along the Apache Trail, and gold hidden in the Superstition Mountains. Mesa averages 306 sunny days per year, with temperatures ranging from about 43°F (6°C) to 65°F (18°C) during the winter and about 81°F (27°C) to 104°F (40°C) during the summer. The location and climate encourage outdoor activities in the nearby mountains and on the many rivers and lakes.

Education

Founded in 1965, MCC is part of the Maricopa Community College District. With more than 27,000 students, MCC is one of the largest community colleges in the United States. The campus sits on 160 acres and has easy access to Phoenix. The College is state and locally supported. It is the largest provider of transfer students to Arizona State University. Through its twenty-three departments, MCC offers Associate of Applied Science occupational degree programs and more than sixty certificate programs. The ethnic and racial composition of MCC mirrors that of the local community, with more than 18 percent of the students identifying themselves as a member of a minority group. MCC has a strong commitment to international education.

Campus Life

The world is the home that all cultures, nations, and people must share. Mesa Community College serves a diverse student population from more than 100 countries. Although MCC does not provide housing for students, there are many apartment complexes within walking distance. The International Student Association (ISA), the Asian Pacific Islander Coalition (APIC), and the Movimiento Estudiantil Chicano de Aztlan (MECHA) are examples of the many clubs and organizations providing excellent opportunities to students for involvement on campus.

For International Students

The International Education Office offers counseling and advisement to international students who may need special assistance. All students on F1 visas are encouraged to meet with the student adviser. The multicultural and multilingual staff members at the International Education Office offer guidance in the transition to college life in the United States and act as counselors on immigration, academic, personal, and cultural concerns. For further information, students should contact the Office of International Education, Mesa Community College, 1833 West Southern Avenue, Mesa, Arizona 85202 (telephone: 480-461-7758; fax: 480-461-7139; e-mail: ie@mcmail.maricopa.edu). The Intensive English Program (IEP) provides comprehensive English language training to students who need to improve their English skills for academic, professional, and personal purposes. The ESL program helps international students make a smooth transition to academic programs.

Miami Dade College

- **Contact:**
  District Admissions
  Miami Dade College
  300 N.E. Second Avenue
  Miami, FL 33132

  Phone: 305-237-8888
  Fax: 305-237-2964
  Web site: http://www.mdc.edu
- Public, primarily 2-year, coed
- Urban setting
- Enrollment: 165,000
- Student-faculty ratio: 24:1
- 2006–07 Tuition and fees: $228.76 per credit hour

- **Room and board:** N/A
- **International students:** 1.4%
- **Countries represented:** 157
- **International students applied:** 700
- **International students accepted:** 680
- **Admissions test:**
  - TOEFL: Required
  - SAT and ACT: Not required
- **Application deadline:** 60 days prior to term
- **On-campus housing:** Not available
- **Summer housing:** Not available

Area and Climate

Miami Dade College (MDC) has eight campuses and numerous outreach centers located throughout the greater Miami area in southeastern Florida. Because of its sunny and subtropical climate, beautiful beaches, and diverse international culture, the area has been a mecca for students and tourists for decades. With a population of more than 2.3 million, greater Miami offers a variety of year-round exciting cultural, sporting, and intellectual activities. Students can explore unique settings, such as the historic Miami Beach Art Deco District or the Everglades National Park. Miami is a gateway city with easy access to most countries.

Education

Founded in 1960, Miami Dade College is the largest community college and institution of higher education in the United States. It has received national and international awards for excellence in providing high-quality education. It offers undergraduate study in more than 200 academic areas and professions. The College has an open-door admissions policy, which provides educational opportunities to all who are interested in enrolling. The Associate in Arts degree prepares students to enter the junior year at four-year and upper-division colleges and universities. The Associate in Science degree is awarded to students who successfully complete one of the occupational education, allied health, or nursing programs designed to prepare students for immediate employment. The College also offers college-credit certificate programs and vocational-credit certificate programs. In 2003, the School of Education began offering four-year bachelor's degree programs leading to teacher certification in the areas of exceptional student education, secondary mathematics, and secondary science. The College offers a Bachelor of Applied Science in public safety management through the School of Justice; the program provides ten areas of specialization, including the option to obtain law enforcement certification. In 2008, the College plans to offer a four-year bachelor's degree in nursing. Special student services include academic advisement and counseling, career planning and placement, services for disabled students, honors programs, and independent study. The campus libraries have a combined book collection of more than 342,000 titles and 17,000 periodicals. Some 25,000 audiovisual materials,

as well as online databases, are available. Computers for student use are available in computer labs, learning resource centers, labs, classrooms, and the library.

Miami Dade College is a leader in working proactively to assist students with disabilities. Each campus has a ground floor ACCESS office to provide to the guidance and technological accommodations required. Some 2,368 students with disabilities were enrolled at MDC during 2005. Of these, 348 were physically challenged and 94 were visually impaired. Computers equipped with voice synthesizer programs are available as are note-takers to attend classes with physically challenged students.

Campus Life

The diversity of the student body at the College contributes to the exciting atmosphere and varied activities. Students from 157 countries add diversity to a student population of credit students that is 66 percent Hispanic, 21 percent African American, and 10 percent white non-Hispanic. More than 100 organizations offer opportunities for students to participate in student government, student publications, music ensembles, dramatic productions (in English and Spanish), religious activities, social and service clubs, professional organizations, honor societies, and formidable debate and chess teams. In addition, its athletic program is nationally renowned. The Lady Sharks volleyball team has captured the national championship numerous times, most recently in 2004. MDC hosts the annual Miami Book Fair International and Miami International Film Festival, which have become celebrated cultural events of national significance. In addition, MDC celebrates Black History Month, Women's History Month, and Hispanic Heritage Month presentations. Out-of-town students are responsible for making their own housing arrangements; however, there is an abundant supply of housing convenient to the school's campuses.

For International Students

Each campus has an international student adviser or international student office. Orientations to the College and immigration regulations are provided. The College has a strong English as a second language (ESL) program that offers six levels of instruction. International students who do not present a minimum score of 550 on the TOEFL are tested and placed in the appropriate level of ESL. Special activities and international clubs are available. International students are required to have adequate financial resources to cover full tuition costs and to provide evidence of health insurance.

MiraCosta College

- Contact:
  Institute for International Perspectives
  MiraCosta College
  One Barnard Drive
  Oceanside, CA 92056
  Phone: 760-795-6897
  Fax: 760-757-8209
  E-mail: iip@miracosta.edu
  Web site: http://www.miracosta.edu/iip
- Public, two-year, coed
- Suburban setting
- Total enrollment: 9,800
- 2005–06 Tuition and fees: $4700
- 2005–06 Room and board: $7650
- International students: 2.5%

- Countries represented: 32
- International students applied: 127
- International students accepted: 100
- International students newly enrolled: 89
- Admissions tests:
  - TOEFL: Required (min. score 450 paper-based; 133 computer-based; 46 Internet-based)
  - SAT and ACT: Not required
- Application deadline: Fall, 7/1 priority; spring, 11/15 priority; summer intersession, 5/15 priority
- On-campus housing: Not available

Area and Climate

Founded in 1934, MiraCosta has two beautiful campuses in northern San Diego County, California. The Oceanside and Cardiff-by-the-Sea campuses are located approximately 30 miles north of the San Diego airport in a safe, suburban area. MiraCosta is within driving distance of Los Angeles, Mexico, Disneyland, Hollywood, La Jolla, San Diego Zoo, SeaWorld, and other world famous attractions in Southern California. The sunny climate and ocean views make MiraCosta a great place to live and study.

Education

MiraCosta College is a fully accredited California community college offering associate degrees and certificate programs in more than ninety-eight subject areas. Students receive personal attention through small class sizes, free tutoring services, and extensive computer facilities. Most classes have fewer than 30 students. The college's most popular majors include travel and tourism, business administration, hospitality management, child development, record production and recording arts, and biotechnology. Academic counselors support international students planning to transfer to four-year institutions. MiraCosta has the highest transfer rate to University of California campuses compared to all other San Diego community colleges. International students transfer to UC San Diego, San Diego State University, UC Berkeley, and many other universities across the United States.

Campus Life

MiraCosta College is rich with activities, events, and sports that enhance the experience of international students. MiraCosta's Surf Team is ranked top in the nation. MiraCosta College offers more than fifty student clubs, including the International Club, religious clubs, Anthropology Club, Soccer Club, and many more. International students also take leadership roles with the Associated Student Government. Facilities include a new library and technology center, student computer labs, cafeteria and patio, an outdoor amphitheater, tennis courts, track, gymnasium, on-campus health center and fitness center. Housing options include host family placement and nearby private apartments.

For International Students

The international student office and the English Language and College Skills Institute are committed to helping international students meet their academic and professional goals. MiraCosta provides on-going services to new international students to help them select classes and adjust to life in the MiraCosta community. TOEFL preparation and English language courses are offered through the English Language and College Skills Institute (EL&CSI). EL&CSI offers academic preparation in reading, listening, speaking, grammar, and U.S. culture. Academic planning, immigration advising, and workshops are provided throughout the year from academic counselors and international student advisers. International students can also participate in on-campus and off-campus work opportunities.

Monmouth University

- Contact:
   Mr. Andre Richburg
   Assistant Director of Undergraduate Admission
   Office of Undergraduate Admission
   Monmouth University
   400 Cedar Avenue
   West Long Branch, NJ 07764-1898
   Phone: 732-571-3456
   Fax: 732-263-5166
   E-mail: admission@monmouth.edu
   Web site: http://www.monmouth.edu
- Private, comprehensive, coed
- Suburban setting
- Enrollment: approximately 6,000
- Student-faculty ratio: 15:1
- 2006–07 Tuition and fees: $21,868
- 2006–07 Room and board: $8472

- International students: 2.1%
- Countries represented: 28
- International students applied (2006): 78
- International students accepted (2006): 22
- International students enrolled (2006): 11
- Admissions tests:
   - TOEFL: (min. scores: iBT 79, CBT 213, PBT 550)
   - SAT: Recommended
   - IELTS: (no subscore below 5.5)
   - MELAB: (min. score 77)
   - CAE: (min. score B2)
- Application deadlines: June 1 (fall semester); November 1 (spring semester)
- On-campus housing: Space available
- Summer housing: Available

Area and Climate

Monmouth University is located in a safe, suburban area less than 1 mile (1.6 kilometers) from the scenic New Jersey shoreline of the Atlantic Ocean, halfway between New York City and Philadelphia. The University's 155-acre (63-hectare) campus, which is considered to be one of the most beautiful in New Jersey, offers numerous recreational, entertainment, and research opportunities for international students. The New Jersey shore area experiences four distinct weather seasons each year. Temperatures range from 91°F (33°C) in summer to 10°F (-12°C) in winter, with warm days and cool nights in the spring and fall.

Education

Monmouth University, which was founded in 1933, is a private, medium-sized, coeducational, accredited institution that offers undergraduate and graduate degrees in more than forty-five majors and concentrations. Professional, liberal arts, and graduate programs are offered within the School of Business Administration; the School of Education; the Wayne D. McMurray School of Humanities and Social Sciences; the Marjorie K. Unterberg School of Nursing and Health Studies; the School of Science, Technology and Engineering; and the Graduate School. Some of the more popular majors include business administration, education, psychology, and communication. There are unique academic program opportunities within the School of Science, Technology and Engineering, including software engineering (one of ten accredited programs in the U.S.), medical technology, marine and environmental biology and policy, and computer science. Regardless of major, highly qualified students may also be invited to join the Honors School. A dedicated, distinguished faculty and a ratio of 15 students to each professor ensure small classes and active learning. Academic programs are supported by state-of-the-art computer hardware, software, and classroom/laboratory facilities. The academic year consists of two semesters and three summer sessions, which facilitates flexibility in course scheduling and accelerated learning.

Campus Life

Monmouth's diverse student body is made up of undergraduate and graduate students representing twenty-five states and twenty-eight countries. The University offers a variety of housing options in its ten residence halls and three garden-style apartment complexes. On-campus housing for all first-year undergraduate students is not guaranteed; it is available on a first-come, first-served basis. However, a number of spaces are reserved for international undergraduates. Residence halls have traditional rooms and suite-style arrangements. More than sixty-seven student organizations are recognized by the Student Government Association. They include academic honor societies, departmental clubs, and the University newspaper, radio station, and yearbook. The International Club sponsors the annual International Festival and assists with such programs as the Model United Nations competition and other cultural events on campus. Monmouth also has an active and competitive NCAA Division I athletics program.

For International Students

Monmouth University provides an international student adviser to assist international students in adjusting to life on campus and in the U.S. The Office of International Student Services provides an orientation program for new students at the beginning of each semester. The office also provides assistance with immigration issues, guidance on how to obtain health insurance, and help with understanding academic and cultural issues.

Montclair State University

- **Contact:**
  Admissions Office
  Montclair State University
  1 Normal Avenue
  Montclair, NJ 07043
  Phone: 973-655-7801
  Fax: 973-655-7700
  E-mail: msuadm@mail.montclair.edu
  Web site: http://www.montclair.edu/
- **Public, four-year, coed**
- **Suburban setting**
- **Enrollment: 16,076**
- **Student-faculty ratio: 17:1**

- **2006–07 Comprehensive fee: $27,500**
- **International students: 4%**
- **Countries represented: 98**
- **International students enrolled: 737 (total)**
- **Admissions tests:**
  - **TOEFL (min. score 213 computer-based; 80 Internet-based)**
  - **SAT or ACT: Recommended, but not required for international applicants**
- **Application deadline: Fall, 3/1; spring, 11/1**
- **On-campus housing: Available**
- **Summer housing: Available**

Area and Climate

Montclair State University (MSU) sits on a 275-acre (111 hectares) suburban campus, only 14 miles (23 kilometers) west of New York City. This proximity to the city gives students the opportunity to take advantage of the unusually rich cultural, social, and educational environment of the metropolitan area. The University has its own train station offering direct access to New York City. Montclair (pop. 38,000), with its beautiful homes and tree-lined streets, offers top-notch opportunities for eating, shopping, culture, and recreation. The town has its own art museum and many performance spaces, as well as eighteen public parks and two nature reserves. Mountain resorts and ocean beaches are also nearby. New Jersey has a variable climate—cold winters with periodic snowfalls and hot, humid summers.

Education

Founded in 1908, MSU has evolved into a four-year comprehensive public institution that provides a broad range of educational and cultural opportunities. The University offers forty-eight undergraduate majors through six schools. Through its diverse programs and services, Montclair State seeks to develop educated men and women who are inquiring, creative, and responsible contributors to society. MSU's general education program consists of a collection of courses that all undergraduate students are required to take in addition to course work in their major. These 51–57 credits are spread across ten main areas of study—writing and speech; the arts, world languages, and humanities; math, science, and computer science; physical education; and the social sciences. The University also offers master's and doctoral programs.

Campus Life

International students participate in every aspect of campus life, including more than 115 campus organizations such as the Student Government Association, theater, music and arts programming, and classes and seminars in every academic major department. The International Student Organization (ISO) is one of the highest ranking and most highly respected student organizations on campus. It welcomes both American and international student to participate in meetings, activities, and cultural excursions. The Montclair State Athletic Department offers seventeen sports for men and women, with most teams competing in the highly regarded New Jersey Athletic Conference. MSU also is a member of the largest athletic conference in the country—the Eastern College Athletic Conference—and all sports are designated in the NCAA as Division III.

For International Students

The mission of International Services (IS) at Montclair State University is to be responsible for the general growth, development, and welfare of all international students and scholars on campus. International students are required to attend the International Student Orientation, held at the beginning of each semester, and are eligible to participate in a range of programs and services. The International Living Community is a unique apartment-style residential community for international and American students offering social and cultural programs and excursions. MSU offers English as a second language (ESL) courses for non-native speakers of English. Students are eligible to enroll in ESL courses based on the results of a University ESL exam that is arranged after their acceptance to the University.

Moore College of Art & Design

- **Contact:**
  Lori Hoffman
  Assistant Director of Admissions
  Moore College of Art & Design
  20th Street and The Parkway
  Philadelphia, PA 19103
  Phone: 215-965-4014
  Fax: 215-568-3547
  E-mail: enroll@moore.edu
  Web site: http://www.moore.edu
- **Private, women only**
- **Urban setting**
- **Enrollment: 503**
- **Student-faculty ratio: 9:1**

- **2005–06 Tuition and fees: $24,788**
- **2005–06 Room and board: $9346**
- **International students: 5%**
- **Countries represented: 14**
- **International students applied: 30**
- **International students accepted: 22**
- **International students enrolled: 14**
- **Admissions tests:**
  - **TOEFL (min. score 527 paper-based; 197 computer-based; 71 Internet-based)**
- **Application deadline: Rolling**
- **On-campus housing: Guaranteed**

Area and Climate

Moore is located in Philadelphia, Pennsylvania, in the northeastern United States. New York City, Baltimore, and Washington, D.C., are within an easy one- to two-hour trip by car or train. Moore's campus is in the heart of Philadelphia's Museum District, central to the city's arts and culture scene, fine restaurants, galleries, shopping areas, clubs, theaters, and other attractions. Moore is also steps away from the Schuylkill River and the boathouses, trails, and playing fields of Fairmount Park, one of the largest municipal park systems in the U.S. As the home of Independence National Historical Park, Philadelphia is rich in historic venues. This, combined with its vitality as the fifth-largest American city, means Moore students have access to a dazzling array of artistic and cultural resources. The region's nearly eighty colleges and universities form one of the largest higher-education communities in the nation, second only to New York City. The fall and spring are mild and pleasant. The winter brings cool temperatures of 26°F (-3°C) to 50°F (10°C), usually with moderate snowfall, and summer temperatures average 80°F (27°C) to 89°F (32°C). The Philadelphia International Airport is accessible by public transportation.

Education

Moore is dedicated to setting the standard of excellence in educating women for careers in art and design. As the first and only women's college of the visual arts in the nation, founded in 1848, Moore students enjoy an accessible, supportive small-college community and learn from a dedicated faculty of award-winning artists, designers, and scholars. With an average of 500 students and a 9:1 student-to-faculty member ratio, Moore offers Bachelor of Fine Arts majors in art education, art history, curatorial studies, fashion design, graphic design, illustration, interior design, photography and digital arts, textile design, and fine arts (with 2-D and/or 3-D emphasis). Career and leadership skills are emphasized throughout the academic program, with each major providing extensive career preparation for their respective field.

The Locks Career Center for Women in the Arts facilitates and provides exciting professional internships and a broad range of career resources and opportunities. Moore's campus includes Sarah Peter Hall, Wilson Hall, and two residence halls—Stahl Residence Hall and Sartain Halls. There are expansive classrooms and studios, Mac and PC computer labs, abundant exhibition space, lounges, and outdoor courtyards. The Connolly Library's holdings feature 40,000 monographs, Internet access, 185 art journals, a slide collection of more than 123,000 images, and picture files of more than 300,000 images.

Campus Life

Forty-one percent of the students live in on-campus housing or in nearby apartments. Located in the heart of Philadelphia, Moore plays a significant role in the cultural life of this vibrant city. Students live, study, work, and create in a rich environment of arts and cultural organizations, galleries, and nearby institutions like the Philadelphia Museum of Art and the Rodin Museum. The city itself becomes an extension of the classroom. Student Services provides a gym membership, group excursions, free access to the Roxy Cinema, and free or discounted tickets for students to local art, theater, music, and sporting events. Moore also has an active student government, leadership, and mentoring program.

For International Students

Moore College of Art & Design is proud of its increasing cultural diversity. Recent students have come from China, Germany, India, Indonesia, Japan, Korea, Luxembourg, Malaysia, Poland, Sweden, Taiwan, and Thailand. One week prior to the start of classes, international students attend an orientation that pairs them with a student mentor. An International Student Handbook provides pertinent information regarding the College and the Philadelphia area. A full range of support is offered through the Student Services office and ESS (Educational Support Services). Scholarships up to $6000 per year are available to qualified international students who attend Moore on a full-time basis, as long as they remain in good standing. Interested students can receive application materials from the Admissions Office or can apply online at the Web site (http://www.moore.edu).

Mount Holyoke College

- **Contact:**
  Diane Anci
  Dean of Admission
  Mount Holyoke College
  South Hadley, MA 01075
  Phone: 413-538-2023
  Fax: 413-538-2409
  E-mail: admission@mtholyoke.edu
  Web site: http://www.mtholyoke.edu
- Private, women only
- Small-town setting
- Enrollment: 2,100
- Student-faculty ratio: 10:1
- 2006–07 Tuition and fees: $34,256
- 2006–07 Room and board: $10,040

- International students: 17%
- Countries represented: 70
- International students applied: 751
- International students accepted: 189
- International students enrolled: 80
- Admissions tests:
  - **TOEFL:** Recommended (paper-based mean score 639; computer-based mean score 275)
  - **SAT and ACT:** Optional
- Application deadline: 1/15
- On-campus housing: Available
- Summer housing: Available

Area and Climate

Located in South Hadley, Massachusetts, a small town in the western portion of the state, Mount Holyoke is about 1½ hours from Boston and 2½ hours from New York City. The area is known for its semirural New England charm and diversity of landscape. The region is also home to several historic landmarks. Typical of New England, summer weather is often warm and humid, ranging from 75°F (25°C) to 90°F (32°C), while winter is generally cold and snowy, with temperatures ranging between below 0°F (-17°C) and 40°F (5°C). Both autumn and spring are sometimes rainy, but the average temperatures (50° to 70°F, or 10° to 20°C) are quite comfortable.

Education

Mount Holyoke was founded in 1837 and is the oldest continuing institution for women's education in the United States. Long distinguished for the quality of its curricular and cocurricular life, the diversity of its student body, and the success of its alumnae, Mount Holyoke is a private, nonsectarian, highly selective college of the liberal arts and sciences for women. Situated on an 800-acre (324-hectare) campus, the College offers forty-nine majors and the option of a self-designed major. The College's student-faculty ratio is 10:1. Most students pursue interdisciplinary courses, some taught by teams of faculty members from different fields. Critical thinking, the use of computers, and proficiency in foreign languages are stressed throughout the curriculum. Mount Holyoke participates in the Five College Consortium, which also includes Amherst, Hamp-shire, and Smith Colleges and the University of Massachusetts Amherst. Students enrolled at any of the Five Colleges can take part in the academic, cultural, and social offerings of the other four.

Campus Life

The residence halls complement the liberal arts experience, coordinating cultural and social events and providing a home away from home for all students. Almost all students live on campus in the residence halls, each of which accommodates between 65 and 130 students. Forming a vital part of Mount Holyoke's offerings are diverse cocurricular opportunities—concerts, conferences, exhibitions, films, and social events. A comprehensive sports complex has indoor and outdoor facilities, including tennis, volleyball, squash, and racquetball courts; a 200-meter track; and an eight-lane swimming pool with a separate diving tank. The 20-acre (8-hectare) Equestrian Center provides a sixty-stall barn and large indoor and outdoor riding arenas.

For International Students

The College endeavors to meet the needs of its international students, beginning with a program of orientation. The McCulloch Center for Global Initiatives helps to facilitate students' transition to life in the United States. During the year, its staff provides sessions on health, visas, work permits, and cross-cultural awareness. The International Big Sister/Little Sister Program pairs second- or third-year students with new arrivals, providing a ready source of support and information. The Career Development Center assists by furnishing information and advice on employment, careers, and internships that may be of special interest.

Mount Ida College

- **Contact:**
  Elizabeth Storinge
  Dean of Admissions
  Mount Ida College
  Newton, MA 02459
  Phone: 617-928-4553
  Fax: 617-928-4507
  E-mail: admissions@mountida.edu
  Web site: http://www.mountida.edu
- Private, coed
- Suburban setting
- Enrollment: Approx. 1,300
- 2006–07 Tuition and fees: $19,800
- 2006–07 Room and board: $10,225

- International students: 8%
- Countries represented: 28
- International students applied: 120
- International students accepted: 75
- International students enrolled: 25
- Admissions tests:
  - TOEFL: Required (min. score 525 paper-based; 197 computer-based)
  - SAT: Required
  - ACT: Required
- Application deadline: Rolling
- On-campus housing: Available, limited
- Summer housing: Not available

Area and Climate

Mount Ida College is located on a secure 72-acre residential campus in Newton Centre, a suburban city located in the northeast region of the United States approximately 8 miles (13 kilometers) from downtown Boston, Massachusetts. A regularly scheduled College bus provides transportation to the Newton Centre train station, which offers service to downtown Boston. With its reputation as a center of American higher education, Boston offers college students endless opportunities for cultural activities, sports, recreation, and a varied social life. Temperatures average 90°F (32°C) in the summer and 23°F (-5°C) in the winter, with pleasant fall and spring seasons.

Campus Life

The student body is diverse and comes from twenty-three states and approximately thirty countries. Housing is available to international students during the academic year. Residence halls are staffed with trained Residence Directors and Resident Assistants. The campus atmosphere is relaxed and friendly; dress is informal. The College offers a number of student activities as well as a study-abroad program. Students can join a number of on-campus organizations, such as student government, drama club, student newspaper, yearbook, outdoors club, and fashion design.

Mount Ida College is located in a safe suburban neighborhood and is only 8 miles from downtown Boston, the greatest college town in America. The College provides campus security on a 24-hour basis.

Education

Founded in 1899, Mount Ida College has developed into a comprehensive baccalaureate institution that also offers a number of associate degree majors. The College is committed to achieving a balanced and integrated approach to the liberal arts and to professional and career studies. Faculty members are available after class and have office hours on a regular basis. Campus facilities include the College library, a technology center, an athletic center, computer facilities, general laboratories, a licensed pre-school and day-care facility, and five residence halls. Most programs offer opportunities for students to participate in internships related to their studies and the career they wish to pursue. The academic year consists of two semesters: fall semester begins in September and ends before Christmas; spring semester begins mid-January and ends in mid-May.

For International Students

An orientation program prior to the beginning of the fall semester is required for all newly enrolled international students. The College provides an International Student Advisor to help with cultural adjustment, orientation issues, and immigration procedures.

The SAT and ACT admissions test requirement may be waived at the discretion of the Dean.

Mount Ida offers an ESL Plus program. ESL Plus allows students, based upon their TOEFL test score, to study English part-time as well as enroll in some courses in their major. Students who receive a TOEFL test score of 525 (197 computer-based) or higher may be eligible for full-time study at Mount Ida College. Applicants should contact the admissions office for more information about TOEFL score requirements for admission to the College.

New College of Florida

- **Contact:**
  Kathleen M. Killion
  Dean of Admissions and Financial Aid
  New College of Florida
  5800 Bay Shore Road
  Sarasota, FL 34243-2109
  Phone: 941-487-5000
  Fax: 941-487-5010
  Web site: http://www.ncf.edu
- **Public, coed**
- **Suburban setting**
- **Enrollment: 761**
- **Student-faculty ratio: 11:1**
- **2006–07 Tuition and fees: $3616 (Florida residents), $19,374 (nonresidents)**

- **2006–07 Room and board: $6213**
- **International students: 5%**
- **Countries represented: 28**
- **International students applied: 32**
- **International students accepted: 7**
- **International students enrolled: 3**
- **Admissions tests:**
  - **TOEFL (paper-based min. score 560; computer-based min. score 220)**
  - **SAT or ACT: Required**
- **Application deadline: 12/1, 2/15, 4/15**
- **On-campus housing: Available**

Area and Climate

Southwest Florida's climate is subtropical. Temperatures average from about 82°F (28°C) in summer to about 58°F (14°C) in the winter. New College's 144-acre campus is located along the Gulf of Mexico in Sarasota. Access by air is through Sarasota Bradenton International Airport and Tampa International Airport.

Education

New College opened in 1964 as a private liberal arts college for academically talented students; it joined the State University System of Florida in 1975. As the state of Florida's officially designated "honors college for the arts and sciences," New College of Florida offers the rigorous program and intimate environment of a highly competitive private school but at the modest cost of a state-sponsored university.

Average class size is 18 students (64 percent of classes are under 20). Students plan their work closely with professors; faculty members in turn assess student work through narrative evaluations, providing direct feedback for individual success and areas of improvement. Students pursue annual independent-study projects; a tutorial system provides students the opportunity to design individualized research that addresses each student's educational goals and objectives. Each year, nearly 260 courses are offered, 500 independent-study projects are arranged, and 600 to 700 tutorials are undertaken. The final requirement in each major is a senior thesis project, with an oral baccalaureate exam administered before a faculty committee.

Four Fulbright Fellowship winners were among the graduating class of 2006, adding to the College's impressive

success in producing Fulbright scholars. During the past twelve years, 24 New College students have received Fulbright awards, thus placing the College among the nation's leaders in per capita production of Fulbright winners. In addition, New College is a leading per capita producer of alumni who go on to obtain doctoral degrees. Graduates include Gregory Dubois-Felsmann (experimental particle physicist and former Rhodes Scholar), Lincoln Diaz-Balart (U.S. Representative, Miami, Florida), William Thurston (Fields Medal winner in mathematics), Esther Barazzone (President, Chatham College), Dennis Saver (President, Florida Academy of Family Physicians), Anita Allen (Professor of Law and Philosophy, University of Pennsylvania), Carol Flint (former Executive Producer for the television shows *ER* and *L.A. Law*), and Thomas Bell (Senior Research Scientist, NASA).

New College offers more than thirty majors. With faculty permission, students also may create self-designed program majors.

Campus Life

The Student Allocations Committee approves funding for more than ninety different groups and functions per year, including social justice events, parties, concerts, religious organizations, and athletic teams. Sports are informal and inclusive; for most, anyone may play regardless of athletic talent.

For International Students

Students from all countries are welcome to apply. The Assistant Registrar advises international students concerning Immigration and Naturalization Service regulations. The Diversity and Gender Center works with students to arrange educational events celebrating different cultures, inviting all to take part.

New England College

- **Contact:**
  Paul Miller, Director of Admission and
  Financial Aid
  New England College
  Henniker, NH 03242
  Phone: 603-428-2223
  Fax: 603-428-3155
  E-mail: admission@nec.edu
  Web site: http://www.nec.edu
- Private, 4-year, coed
- Small-town setting
- Enrollment: 1,000
- Student-faculty ratio: 13:1
- 2006–07 Tuition and fees: $23,010

- 2006–07 Room and board: $8456
- International students: 9%
- Countries represented: 20
- International students applied: 86
- International students accepted: 80
- International students enrolled: 36
- Admissions tests:
  - TOEFL (Required for ESL: min. score 450 PBT, 133 CBT, 45 iBT)
- Application deadline: Rolling
- On-campus housing: Available
- Summer housing: Not available

Area and Climate

Located in Henniker, New Hampshire, New England College (NEC) is situated in a small town of 4,700 on the Contoocook River. This location provides numerous opportunities for enjoying the outdoors. The shopping, restaurants, and cultural events of New Hampshire's capital of Concord are a short 20-minute drive away. Henniker is 150 kilometers, or a 90-minute drive, from Boston, Massachusetts. New Hampshire enjoys a seasonal climate. Fall brings the changing color of leaves, which attracts tourists from all over the world. The winter is cold, allowing for skating, skiing, and snowboarding at Pat's Peak, which is 3 kilometers away. Average temperatures are 16°C to 28°C in summer and -4°C to 7°C in winter.

Education

Founded in 1946, New England College balances two vital educational roles, a fundamental liberal arts education and career preparation. The College awards the Bachelor of Arts and Bachelor of Science degrees. General education courses in areas such as cultural diversity and human rights help students gain a deep appreciation for the world in which they live. Internships are available in most majors; for example, marketing students have worked for Velcro International, while communications majors have worked with New Hampshire Public Radio. The library holds more than 104,000 volumes, 650 periodical subscriptions, 36,000 microfilms, 2,000 audiovisual materials, and 3,200 separate government documents. IBM and Macintosh PCs, laser printers, flatbed and slide scanners, and color printers are available for student use.

Campus Life

Students come from all areas of the United States and twenty countries. The campus encompasses thirty-three buildings and 225 acres (91 hectares). Housing includes traditional residences (rooms extending off a long hallway and a shared bath), modern buildings or restored homes, and smoking and nonsmoking rooms. Occupancy is based on 2 people per room. Direct-dial, long-distance telephone and high-speed Internet hook-up services are available in student rooms. The Fitness Center, the Simon Center, and the Lee Clement Ice Arena help promote cocurricular programs such as students clubs and organizations, intercollegiate athletics, social programs, outdoor leadership adventures, and community service projects. The College sponsors varsity competition in men's and women's basketball, cross-country, ice hockey, lacrosse, and soccer; women's field hockey and softball; and men's baseball.

For International Students

An International Student Adviser provides academic, immigration, and social services to international students. The International Student Orientation is held two days before the start of the fall new-student orientation in August. The Adviser, with the International Student Association and the ESL Director, sponsors a yearly International Week, with speakers and guests from many nations and films and music representing different cultures. All students are required to purchase NEC health insurance. The on-campus health center is staffed by nurses, with a physician's clinic three days a week and a doctor on call for emergencies. The ESL transition program provides ESL instruction with academic course work for graduation credit.

New England Institute of Technology

- Contact:
  Mark Seltzer
  Director of International Admissions
  New England Institute of Technology
  2500 Post Road
  Warwick, RI 02886

  Phone: 401-467-7744 Ext. 3489
  Fax: 401-738-5122
  E-mail: MSeltzer@neit.edu
  Web site: http://www.neit.edu
- Private, comprehensive, coed

- Small-town setting
- Enrollment: 3,200
- Student-faculty ratio: 15:1
- 2007–08 Tuition and fees: $16,150
- 2007–08 Room and board: $10,000
- International students: 5%
- Countries represented: 20+
- Admissions tests:
  - TOEFL and SAT: Not required
- Application deadline: Rolling

Area and Climate

Warwick, Rhode Island, is 10 minutes from the capital city of Providence; 1 hour south of Boston, Massachusetts; and 3 hours north of New York City. There are numerous beaches along the Rhode Island coast, and Cape Cod is less than an hour's drive from the campus.

Rhode Island enjoys four distinct seasons per year. Winter temperatures average around 37°F (3°C), both fall and spring temperatures average 60°F (16°C), and summer temperatures average 80°F (27°C).

Education

For more than sixty years, New England Institute of Technology (NEIT) has been the leader in technical career education in southeastern New England. New England Tech is a private, nonprofit college offering more than thirty associate and bachelor's degree programs in technical areas. Each program is taught with a powerful combination of technical expertise and hands-on training. Students learn by doing. Upon graduation, they have the experience necessary for a rewarding career. Associate degrees can be earned in as little as eighteen months and bachelor's degrees can be earned in as little as three years. New England Tech's programs are designed by industry leaders, ensuring that they reflect the needs and requirements of today's employers. The programs are taught by faculty members with years of industry experience.

New England Tech is accredited by the New England Association of Schools and Colleges, Inc. (NEASC), and many of its programs maintain individual accreditation. For example, the Electronics Engineering Technology program at the bachelor's level is accredited by the Technology Accreditation Commission (TAC) of the Accreditation Board for Engineering and Technology (ABET).

Classes start four times per year. Both day and evening classes are offered.

Campus Life

New England Tech assists international students and those who reside beyond commuting distance in finding housing. To ease expenses, shared living arrangements are also available with other New England Tech students. Clubs are open to all students from any technology. Participation in some technical club activities may require that a student possess certain technical proficiencies in order to participate fully. NEIT has recently completed construction of a building dedicated solely to the training of automotive technicians. This hi-tech automotive facility includes glass skylights, a 24,000-square-foot hands-on training laboratory, and an attached 29,000-square-foot three-story classroom building.

For International Students

New England Tech has a growing community of international students who are seeking a career education from one of the leading technical colleges in the United States. The International Student Office assists students with all of their needs. Students are enrolled from over twenty countries from around the world.

New York School of Interior Design

- **Contact:**
  Office of Admissions
  New York School of Interior Design
  New York, NY 10021
  Phone: 212-472-1500 Ext. 204
  Fax: 212-472-1867
  E-mail: admissions@nysid.edu
  Web site: http://www.nysid.edu
- Private, coed
- Urban setting
- Enrollment: 750
- Student-faculty ratio: 9:1
- 2007–08 Tuition: $620 per credit
- International students: 10%

- Countries represented: 30
- International students applied: 101
- International students accepted: 60
- Admissions tests:
  - TOEFL (paper-based min. score 550; computer-based min. score 213; Internet-based min. score 79–80)
  - SAT: Recommended
  - ACT: Recommended
- Application deadline: Rolling
- On-campus housing: Not available
- Summer housing: Not available

Area and Climate

Manhattan experiences all four seasons, with high summer and fall temperatures, snowfall in winter months, and cool, crisp weather during the spring. The New York School of Interior Design (NYSID) is located on the Upper East Side of Manhattan in New York City, New York. The School is within walking distance of museums and buildings with significant architectural interiors and is surrounded by show-rooms, stores, and popular restaurants. It is also convenient to all forms of public transportation.

Education

Established in 1916 by architect Sherrill Whiton, the New York School of Interior Design is a NASAD-accredited, independent, nonprofit, coeducational institution providing comprehensive interior design education. The Bachelor of Fine Arts (132 credits), associate degree (66 credits), nondegree Basic Interior Design Program (24 credits), and Master of Fine Arts in interior design are offered. NYSID's Bachelor of Fine Arts degree program is accredited by the Council for Interior Design Accreditation (formerly FIDER). Programs are presented in a broad cultural perspective. Architectural and decorative styles are viewed from social, personal, economic, and aesthetic viewpoints. Special activities include visits to showrooms, museum tours, summer workshops, summer study tours, and trips to historical sites. The School maintains an active career placement service for all current students and graduates. The fall semester runs from early September to late December and the spring semester from January to mid-May. A summer session is also offered.

Campus Life

Students of all backgrounds and ages find that NYSID offers a lively, stimulating academic and social environment as well as a unique cooperative spirit among students and faculty and staff members. Close contact is maintained with students throughout the school year through academic counseling and career guidance. The School maintains a list of nearby hotels and residences with reasonable rates where students may live. A student chapter of the American Society of Interior Designers (ASID) organizes lectures, tours, workshops, and other events throughout the school year, providing an inside view of the interior design industry. Lectures have featured renowned designers, including Barbara Barry, Eric Cohler, Mark Hampton, Albert Hadley, Mariette Himes Gomez, and Vladimir Kagan.

For International Students

The New York School of Interior Design offers comprehensive interior design programs to international students. For those students needing additional instruction in English language skills, the School offers a special writing course featuring small classes to teach and reinforce the four basic skills: listening, reading, writing, and speaking. International students also have an opportunity to learn the specialized language used by interior designers. Students gain experience in the technical, aesthetic, and management areas of the interior design field. Graduates of NYSID are prepared for careers in design firms, auction houses, galleries, hotel chains, and a variety of design-related areas. International students find a wealth of cultural, educational, and artistic resources at the School and in the city of New York, and they are warmly welcomed at the New York School of Interior Design.

North Central College

- **Contact:**
  Megan Otermat
  International Admission Counselor
  North Central College
  30 North Brainard Street
  Naperville, IL 60540-4690
  Phone: 630-637-5800
  Fax: 630-637-5819
  E-mail: msotermat@noctrl.edu
  Web site: http://www.northcentralcollege.edu
- **Private, coed**
- **Suburban setting**
- **Enrollment: 2,500**
- **Student-faculty ratio: 14:1**
- **2006–07 Tuition and fees: $23,115**

- **2006–07 Room and board: $7440**
- **International students: 2%**
- **Countries represented: 24**
- **International students applied: 23**
- **International students accepted: 12**
- **International students enrolled: 8**
- **Admissions tests:**
  - **TOEFL: Required (min. score 520 PBT; 190 CBT; 68 iBT) or IELTS (min. score 6)**
  - **SAT and ACT: Recommended**
- **Application deadline: 90 days before new term**
- **On-campus housing: Available**
- **Summer housing: Available**

Area and Climate

North Central College is located in a safe, residential area of Naperville, Illinois, a suburban city of more than 140,000. Naperville is located 29 miles (47 kilometers) west of Chicago, the nation's third-largest city, and offers a rich variety of cultural and recreational resources. The College's Midwest location makes travel convenient to either coast from O'Hare International Airport. The Illinois Research and Development Corridor, two national labs, and many multinational corporate headquarters are nearby. Temperatures vary from –9°F (–23°C) in winter to 93°F (34°C) in summer.

Education

North Central College, founded in 1861 by the United Methodist Church, is committed to recognizing the individual needs of a diverse student body by offering programs in the traditional liberal arts, business, preprofessional, and graduate programs. B.A. and B.S. degrees are awarded in fifty-five majors; the highest enrollments are in business, psychology, education, and computer science. Honors programs and special independent study/travel awards are available. All students have individual faculty advisers and receive personal attention from professors in small classes. The calendar consists of 3 ten-week terms, a six-week December interim, and an eight-week summer program. An intensive ESL program is available in August and one advanced ESL course is available in the fall, winter, and spring terms.

Campus Life

North Central students come from a variety of backgrounds. About 92 percent claim Illinois as home; others come from thirty-four states and twenty-four other countries. Approximately 1,100 of the 2,000 full-time students live on campus; evening and weekend programs include another 215 part-time students in addition to students enrolled in six graduate programs. Campus housing is available through Interim (three weeks in December) and summer school (eight weeks from late June to early August). At other vacation times, students are assisted in finding other housing or in making travel plans. The campus offers activities each weekend; special events include fall culture weeks, interim international study tours, winter cultural days, and spring arts festivals.

For International Students

An extended orientation program during the first weeks of the fall term is provided for all new international students. The Office of International Programs provides advising for both academic and immigration matters. Each student is assigned a faculty adviser and a student mentor. Host family visits are available, and an active International Club arranges events and trips to Chicago and surrounding areas. Scholarships, based on academic merit and financial need, are available for up to $10,000 annually.

North Dakota State University

- **Contact:**
  Office of International Programs
  North Dakota State University
  P.O. Box 5582
  Fargo, ND 58105-5582
  Phone: 701-231-7895
  Fax: 701-231-1014
  E-mail: ndsu.international@ndsu.edu
  Web site: http://www.ndsu.edu/International
- **State-supported, university, coed**
- **Urban setting**
- **Enrollment: 12,258**
- **Student-faculty ratio: 19:1**
- **2006–07 Tuition and fees: $12,747**

- **2006–07 Room and board: $5477**
- **International students: 5%**
- **Countries represented: 70**
- **Admissions tests:**
  - **TOEFL: Required (paper-based min. score 525; computer-based min. score 193; Internet-based min. score 70); IELTS (min. score 5.5)**
  - **SAT: Not required**
  - **ACT: Not required**
- **Application deadline: Fall, 5/1; spring, 10/1**
- **On-campus housing: Guaranteed**
- **Summer housing: Available**

Area and Climate

North Dakota is in the north-central United States. It is bounded by Minnesota to the east, South Dakota to the south, Montana to the west, and Canada to the north. North Dakota has cold winters and hot summers. January, the coldest month, has an average temperature of 9°F (-13°C), and July, the warmest month, averages 80°F (27°C). With a metropolitan-area population of about 180,000, Fargo is the largest city in North Dakota and is the commercial, financial, cultural, and medical center of a rich farming and livestock-producing area. The Fargo area is friendly, safe, and easy to get around. Area attractions include movie theaters, shopping malls, concerts, museums, theatrical productions, professional baseball, and indoor and outdoor recreation areas.

Education

North Dakota State University (NDSU) was established in 1890 as a land-grant university. It serves and educates the people of North Dakota, the nation, and the international community through the discovery, communication, application, and preservation of knowledge. With about 600 faculty members, NDSU offers 100 majors through the Colleges of Agriculture, Food Systems, and Natural Resources; Arts, Humanities, and Social Sciences; Business Administration; Engineering and Architecture; Human Development and Education; Pharmacy; Science and Mathematics; and University Studies. NDSU students get individual attention and experience working directly with faculty members in all academic programs. Many faculty members receive a significant number of grants and fellowships in support of their research, allowing opportu-

nities for students to work closely with their professors on important studies. Members of the faculty also serve as academic advisers and help students plan their academic programs.

Campus Life

NDSU has eleven residence halls and offers a wide variety of living arrangements, ranging from apartment-style living to freshmen-only halls. Campus facilities include a state-of-the-art Wellness Center, featuring cardiovascular and strength equipment; an indoor three-lane, twelve-lap-per-mile running/walking track; and a group exercise studio. The newly remodeled student union serves as a gathering place for students to study, visit, and relax between classes. Students have access to computers throughout the campus, and the University's wireless network is rapidly expanding. The campus is home to 200 student organizations that students can join to network and meet new people.

For International Students

The Office of International Programs is devoted to helping students have a successful university experience. The office coordinates many support services for international students, including arrival assistance such as airport pickup, orientation for new international students, and advice on immigration issues. The International Student Association also welcomes new students to the campus, provides advice and support, helps new students adjust to campus life, organizes social activities, and plans community outreach events.

An Intensive English Language Program (IELP) is available during the academic year and the summer to help students develop skills needed for academic study and general use of the language in the United States. IELP is a full-time, noncredit program that emphasizes speaking, listening, reading, and writing.

Northeastern University

- **Contact:**
    International Admissions
    150 Richards Hall
    Northeastern University
    360 Huntington Avenue
    Boston, MA 02115

    Phone: 617-373-2200
    Fax: 617-373-8780
    E-mail: internationaladmissions@neu.edu
    Web site: http://www.northeastern.edu/
    admissions
- **Private, coed**
- **Urban setting**
- **Enrollment: 14,698 (undergraduate)**
- **Student-faculty ratio: 16:1**
- **2006–07 Tuition and fees: $29,910**

- **2006–07 Room and board: $10,580**
- **International students: 7%**
- **Countries represented: 127**
- **International students applied: 1,128 (fall 2006 freshmen)**
- **International students accepted: 669**
- **International students enrolled: 103**
- **Admissions test:**
    - **TOEFL: (min. score 550 PBT; 213 CBT; 79–80 iBT)**
    - **SAT or ACT: Required**
- **Application deadline: 11/15 (early action); 1/15 (regular)**
- **On-campus housing: Available**
- **Summer housing: Available**

Area and Climate

Located near the Back Bay section of Boston, Northeastern University offers all the cultural amenities of a big city and the charm of a colonial European-like city. Boston's quality of life is outstanding. The city is known for having the largest concentration of colleges, universities, and medical research centers in the nation. In fact, there is no other place in the world with more international students. Boston offers sports and cultural activities, including the Boston Symphony, the Museum of Fine Arts, and water activities on the Charles River. During the winter, skiing is only an hour away. Temperatures range from 85°F (29°C) to 25°F (-4°C). Travel to New York City takes 4 hours by car and travel to Washington, D.C., or Montreal, Canada, takes only 9 hours.

Education

Founded more than 100 years ago, Northeastern University integrates rigorous classroom studies with experiential learning opportunities anchored by the nation's largest, most innovative cooperative (co-op) education program. Students participate in opportunities such as research, study abroad, and community service projects. The co-op program offers students the opportunity to alternate periods of classroom experience with full-time work, often paid, in their chosen field.

Northeastern's six undergraduate schools, eight graduate schools, and two part-time divisions offer bachelor's, master's, and doctoral degrees in a wide variety of academic disciplines and professional areas. Faculty members infuse undergraduate and graduate classrooms alike with the spirit of discovery, and students in all degree programs have ample opportunities to participate in research.

Campus Life

The University remains (among private schools) one of the most diverse international campuses in the United States, with 127 nations represented. Students have freedom to choose living arrangements according to their lifestyle, staying in dormitories by theme or school or residing in nearby private, rented apart-

ments. More than 240 student organizations represent academic interests, sports, and other intellectual or social activities. Northeastern offers a truly serious and challenging academic environment with a relaxed attitude outside the classroom, fostering understanding and promoting the advantages offered by individual contributions to an international atmosphere. The University's dynamic campus offers modern academic, residential, and recreational facilities, including Snell Library and the state-of-the-art Marino Recreation Center.

For International Students

International students are required to submit TOEFL, APIEL, or ELPT scores if English is not their native language. The SAT is required of international applicants who attend a high school in the United States, or who will graduate from an international school that follows a U.S. curriculum, or specified student athletes or Canadian nationals, unless the student has completed at least 27 transferable credits, which transfer into the student's major. Through the International Student & Scholar Institute (ISSI), international students are welcomed to campus with several weeks of orientation and acculturation programming that comprises OASIS (Orientation Assistance for International Students), which is designed to help them adjust to studying and living in the United States. Topics covered include academic support, campus life, cultural adjustment, and the logistics of attending an educational institution in the United States. The ISSI also organizes educational and immigration-related workshops to ensure compliance with federal regulations and SEVIS requirements. In addition, the ISSI sponsors an array of cultural enrichment programming and excursions in Boston and throughout New England. International students on specified nonimmigrant visas may be eligible to engage in employment at co-op jobs in their field of study, pending authorization from the ISSI. Co-op is not required in all colleges. As part of its programs and services, the ISSI also organizes a two-month celebration of cultural diversity (International Carnevale), an intercultural dialogue series, peer mentoring and student leadership programs, an international spouse network, and an honor society for international scholars, among other initiatives. For more details, candidates may also visit the Northeastern University Web site.

Northern Kentucky University

- **Contact:**
  International Student Affairs
  Northern Kentucky University
  University Center 336
  Highland Heights, KY 41099
  Phone: 859-572-6517
  Fax: 859-572-6178
  E-mail: isa@nku.edu
  Web site: http://www.nku.edu/~isa
- Public, four-year, coed
- Suburban setting
- Enrollment: 14,000
- Student-faculty ratio: 17:1

- 2006–07 Tuition and fees: $22,010
- 2006–07 Room and board: $8500
- International students: 2%
- Countries represented: 72
- Admissions tests:
  - TOEFL: Required (min. score 500 PBT, 173 CBT, 61 iBT)
  - SAT or ACT: Recommended
- Application deadline: June 1
- On-campus housing: Available
- Summer housing: Available

Area and Climate

Northern Kentucky University (NKU) is located in Highland Heights, Kentucky, on 300 acres (121 hectares) of rolling countryside just 7 miles (11 kilometers) from downtown Cincinnati, Ohio. The campus has earned industry commendations for its level of handicapped-accessibility. Northern Kentucky and metropolitan Cincinnati offer a wide selection of leisure-time activities and entertainment. The many cultural and recreational opportunities include theaters, restaurants, art galleries, museums, parks, and outdoor festivals. Many state and county parks for camping and hiking are within an easy drive. NKU's proximity to major national corporations offers opportunities to extend learning beyond the classroom and laboratory through internships, cooperative learning experiences, and community involvement.

Education

NKU awards the Bachelor of Arts, Bachelor of Fine Arts, Bachelor of Music, Bachelor of Science, Bachelor of Science in Nursing, and Bachelor of Social Work degrees as well as the Associate of Applied Science degree. NKU also offers preprofessional programs and secondary education teacher certification. To receive a bachelor's degree, students must complete a minimum of 128 credit hours. At least 64 credit hours are required for the associate degree. All classes are taught by full- or part-time faculty members—not by graduate teaching assistants. About 80 percent of instructors hold the highest degrees in their fields.

Campus Life

There are more than 120 campus clubs and organizations, including WNKU, the campus radio station, and the independent student-run newspaper, *The Northerner*. A member of the NCAA II Great Lakes Valley Conference, NKU sponsors intercollegiate competition in thirteen varsity sports, six for men (baseball, basketball, cross-country, golf, soccer, and tennis) and seven for women (basketball, cross-country, golf, soccer, softball, tennis, and volleyball).

For International Students

The International Student Affairs department is specifically designed to address the needs of all international students and permanent residents attending NKU. Staff members are committed to assisting students achieve their academic objectives and to advising students on cultural adjustment and financial, academic, employment, and personal matters. The office organizes workshops on immigration regulations and practical and cross-cultural training, potluck dinners, the International Friendship Program, newsletters that announce activities and immigration updates, and, along with the International Student Union, ongoing programs and activities. The international student orientation begins two weeks prior to the first day of the semester.

Nova Southeastern University

- **Contact:**
  Nova Southeastern University
  Fort Lauderdale, FL 33314
  Phone: 954-262-8000
      800-338-4723 Ext. 8000
  Fax: 954-262-3811
  E-mail: admissions@nova.edu
  Web site: http://www.nova.edu
- **Private, university, coed**
- **Suburban setting**
- **Enrollment: 4,100 (undergraduates)**
- **Student-faculty ratio: 12:1**
- **2007–08 Tuition and fees: $18,900**
- **International students: 13%**

- **Countries represented: 42**
- **International students applied: 166**
- **International students accepted: 84**
- **International students enrolled: 37**
- **Admissions tests:**
  - **TOEFL: Required (paper-based min. score 550; computer-based min. score 213)**
  - **SAT and ACT: Not required**
- **Application deadline: Rolling**
- **On-campus housing: Required for most new students**
- **Summer housing: Available**

Area and Climate

The main campus of Nova Southeastern University (NSU) is located on a 300-acre (121-hectare) site in Broward County, Florida. The county is a rapidly growing community for international business, banking and finance, communication, high-technology industries, and health-care-related services. The average year-round temperature is 75°F (24°C). Natural areas for boating, fishing, golf, tennis, and swimming surround the University. Fort Lauderdale provides the best in shopping, dining, and cultural offerings.

Education

Founded just forty years ago, NSU has enjoyed tremendous growth and success, which continues to this day. There are now more than 25,000 students enrolled, from the main campus to NSU locations in twenty-four states and nine countries. Nova Southeastern University is a not-for-profit, independent, coeducational institution that is accredited by the Commission on Colleges of the Southern Association of Colleges and Schools to award associate, bachelor's, master's, education specialist, and doctoral degrees.

Unusual among institutions of higher education, NSU is a university for all ages. The University School for children, numerous undergraduate and graduate degree programs in a variety of fields, and nondegree continuing education programs are all available at NSU. The traditional population in the undergraduate program comprises approximately 4,100 students. With students from all fifty states and forty-two other countries, NSU is a university of national and international scope.

Campus Life

Students enrolled in academic programs at Nova Southeastern University have numerous academic facilities available to them. Computer labs provide courses and programs in applied microcomputer technology. The University Computing Center provides data processing facilities and services to meet the instructional, research, and administrative needs of the University and is available to students for computer-oriented course work. Other facilities within the University include the University School (prekindergarten through grade 12), the Family Center, the Shepard Broad Law School, the Oceanography Center, the Health Professions Division, and the Center for Psychological Studies. The NSU Alvin Sherman Library, Research, Information, and Technology Center offers twenty electronic classrooms, 700 workstations, and 1,000 user seats equipped with Internet access and the 500-seat Rose and Alfred Miniaci Performing Arts Center. The library has the capacity to house 1.4 million volumes of reference materials, making it the largest in Florida. In addition, the new University Center houses an arena for sports, concerts, and major conferences; a place for the academic community and the south Florida community to meet; a wellness center that promotes good health and personal fitness; the NSU Student Union; and a place to learn about and enjoy the performing arts.

Student activities include more than fifty faculty-sponsored clubs; events sponsored by the student government; NCAA Division II sports such as baseball, basketball, cross-country, golf, soccer, softball, and volleyball; a newspaper; a radio station; intramurals; five national fraternities and six national sororities; an International Student Club; and a variety of sport clubs.

For International Students

All admissions counselors have been trained to work with international students and assist with any admission, I-20, or other questions students have. All new students who do not plan to live with immediate family members in south Florida are required to live in NSU's on-campus dormitory. The Office of Residential Life provides advisement, activities, and social events for international students.

Oklahoma State University

- **Contact:**
    Office of Undergraduate Admissions
    219 Student Union
    Oklahoma State University
    Stillwater, OK 74078

    Phone: 405-744-5358
    Fax: 405-744-7092
    E-mail: admissions@okstate.edu
- Public, comprehensive, coed
- Small-town setting
- Enrollment: 23,307 (fall 2006)
- Student-faculty ratio: 19:1
- 2006–07 Tuition and fees: $12,389
- 2006–07 Room and board: $5848 (9 mos.)

- International students: 7%
- Countries represented: 113
- International students applied: 397 (undergraduate)
- International students accepted: 216
- International students enrolled: 145
- Admissions tests:
    - TOEFL (min. score 500 PBT, 173 CBT, 61 iBT) or IELTS (min. score 6.0)
    - SAT and ACT: Not required
- Application deadline: Fall, May 15; spring, October 1; summer, March 1
- On-campus housing: Guaranteed
- Summer housing: Available

Area and Climate

Oklahoma State University (OSU) is located in Stillwater, a small city in north-central Oklahoma, approximately 59 miles (95 kilometers) north of Oklahoma City and 62 miles (100 kilometers) west of Tulsa. Both of these cities have major airports only 75 minutes by car from Stillwater. OSU emphasizes academic excellence and career preparation in the friendly and safe environment of a university community. The 840-acre (340-hectare) campus is recognized for the beauty of its modified Georgian architecture and attractive landscaping. Although temperatures are usually mild, they occasionally drop below 32°F (0°C) in the winter months and may reach 100°F (38°C) during the summer months.

Education

Founded in 1890, Oklahoma State University offers bachelor's, master's, and doctoral degrees in more than 200 degree programs and options. OSU's programs in accounting, agricultural sciences, biological and environmental sciences, engineering, fire protection and safety technology, hotel and restaurant management, integrated design and manufacturing, lasers, materials science, and mathematics are rated among the best in the nation. OSU's Edmon Low Library contains more than 5 million books, documents, and microforms and over 90,000 print and electronic serials that support the research projects at the University at both the undergraduate and graduate levels. More than 1,100 full-time faculty members are employed, with approximately 90 percent having doctorates or comparable advanced degrees.

Campus Life

A total of 1,645 undergraduate and graduate international students who enrolled for the 2006 fall semester bring a diversity to the campus seldom seen in this part of the United States. With more than 400 registered student organizations available, students grow and develop culturally and personally as well as intellectually. Crime rates for both the campus and the community are among the lowest in the nation for cities of comparable size. Recreational activities include one of the most successful intramural programs in the U.S., clubs for almost every sport, outdoor adventure programs, film series, theater productions, concerts, and art exhibits. In the heart of the campus is the Student Union, which has more than 500,000 square feet (46,500 square meters) of shops, restaurants, meeting rooms, and auditoriums and an 81-room hotel.

For International Students

OSU's long history of involvement with international education, spanning more than five decades, illustrates its understanding and commitment to a global community. OSU is dedicated to helping students from around the world feel comfortable with the campus, faculty members, and services. Orientation prior to the beginning of the fall and spring semesters is required for all new international students and offers a wide variety of timely and important information. In addition, international student organizations represent countries and geographic areas around the world. OSU also offers an intensive English language program designed to assist students at any level to attain the proficiency necessary to enter a degree program.

Oregon State University

- **Contact:**
  Julie Walkin
  Interim Assistant Director of International
      Admissions
  104 Kerr Administration Building
  Oregon State University
  Corvallis, OR 97331-2106

  Phone: 541-737-4411
  Fax: 541-737-2482
  E-mail: osuadmit@oregonstate.edu
  Web site: http://oregonstate.edu
- **Public, four-year, coed**
- **Small-town setting**
- **Total enrollment: 19,362**
- **Student-faculty ratio: 28:1**
- **2007–08 Tuition and fees: $18,090**

- **2007–08 Room and board: $7300**
- **International students: 4.6%**
- **Countries represented: 93**
- **International students applied: 2,158**
- **International students accepted: 904**
- **International students enrolled: 481**
- **Admissions tests:**
  - **TOEFL (paper-based min. score 550; computer-based min. score 213; Internet-based min. score 80)**
  - **SAT: Not required**
  - **ACT: Not required**
- **Application deadline: 6/15**
- **On-campus housing: Available**
- **Summer housing: Available**

Area and Climate

Oregon State University (OSU) is located in Corvallis, Oregon (population 53,000), a university-oriented, friendly, and safe community that is situated in a green valley between the Pacific Ocean and the Cascade Mountains. Free bus service makes it easy for students to get around the city. Miles of bike lanes create opportunities to explore the community and its beautiful surroundings. Within a couple of hours of the University are countless opportunities for outdoor recreation (skiing, hiking, and camping) and urban diversions (museums, entertainment, and shopping). Portland, the largest city in Oregon, is within easy driving distance of the University. The climate is moderate—winters are cool and rainy and summers are warm and sunny.

Education

Founded in 1868, OSU offers close, personal attention to its students in a wide range of undergraduate, graduate, and professional programs. Academic programs prepare students for careers and leadership positions in business and industry, government, engineering and computer-related fields, science, teaching, natural resources and the environment, pharmacy, health and sports management, liberal arts, and other professions. Designated as a Carnegie Research University, OSU is recognized for education and research, which is an important part of many academic programs. OSU also has several unique programs, such as the Honors College and the International Degree program. OSU has earned the distinction as one of America's 100 most wired colleges and is committed to providing electronic services to students.

Campus Life

OSU students come from every state in the United States and from ninety-three countries around the world. New students interact with faculty members and students in special courses and activities that are designed to ease their adjustment to college life. A wide range of housing and dining options are available on campus and in the community. All rooms in campus residences are wired for high-speed access to the Internet. Students have more than 300 campus clubs and organizations to meet their needs for leadership, social, cultural, recreational, or academic activities. Through the International Degree and international internships, OSU students can create study, work, and research opportunities almost anywhere in the world. OSU has been named one of the friendliest campuses in the U.S.

For International Students

OSU has a long tradition of welcoming international students and providing personal support for them. Crossroads International, a volunteer community organization, offers a three-day homestay for new students, arranges conversation partners, creates opportunities for students to visit community families, provides a language school for wives of students, and hosts social events throughout the year. International Student Advisers provide an orientation program that is integrated into the University-wide program, help with adjustment needs, advise on U.S. government regulations that affect students, and assist with other personal matters. The English Language Institute offers intensive language instruction for pre-academic students as well as for students who receive conditional admission to the University. It also provides a wide range of cultural and social activities.

Otterbein College

- **Contact:**
  Kristen Messenheimer
  Admission Counselor
  Otterbein College
  Westerville, OH 43081-2006
  Phone: 614-823-1500
  Fax: 614-823-1200
  E-mail: kmessenheimer@otterbein.edu
- **Private, coed**
- **Suburban setting**
- **Enrollment: 3,090**
- **Student-faculty ratio: 12:1**
- **2006–07 Tuition and fees: $23,871 (academic)**

- **2006–07 Room and board: $6789**
- **International students: 1%**
- **Countries represented: 22**
- **International students applied: 46**
- **International students accepted: 10**
- **International students enrolled: 6**
- **Admissions tests:**
    - **TOEFL (min. score 523)**
    - **SAT: Recommended**
- **Application deadline: 3 months prior to term**
- **On-campus housing: Available**
- **Summer housing: Available**

Area and Climate

Otterbein College is located in Westerville, Ohio, a town of 36,000 and a suburb of Columbus, the thriving state capital. Its small-town setting and its proximity to a large metropolitan area provide students with a wide variety of opportunities. Central Ohio experiences different seasons and temperatures, ranging from warm to hot days in the spring and summer (52°F/11°C in April, 77°F/25°C in July) to cool and cold days in fall and winter (57°F/14°C in October, 32°F/0°C in January). Autumn foliage in the nearby hills is breathtaking.

Education

Founded in 1847, Otterbein was the first liberal arts college in the United States to begin as a coeducational institution and the first to include women on its faculty. Its doors have always been open to people of all races and religious convictions. Otterbein offers a bachelor's degree in thirty-eight fields of study, including business administration, speech communication, education (teacher training), theater, music, equine science, preprofessional programs, and engineering (dual degree). Campus facilities include a 325,000-volume library, an instructional media center, a television studio, a radio station, a completely equipped sports and recreation center, and extensive computer facilities.

Campus Life

Otterbein has a wide variety of organizations: clubs, honoraries, service groups, religious organizations, varsity and intramural athletic teams, committees, sororities, fraternities, artistic organizations, and musical groups. As members of the International Students Association, one of the most active organizations on campus, U.S. and international students participate in social and cultural events and travel to points of interest in Ohio and out of state as well. International students live with an American roommate in residence halls on campus. Each hall has a full-time director and several student assistants, each assigned to a small group of residents.

For International Students

Recognizing the increasing need for understanding and good will among people of all nations, Otterbein College welcomes international students. Newly enrolled international students are required to attend a complete orientation prior to the beginning of the fall term. The International Student Programs office provides services that are specifically designed to meet the needs of international students, including transportation, immigration counseling, and a host-family program.

Pace University

- Contact:
  Office of Undergraduate Admission
  Pace University
  1 Pace Plaza
  New York, NY 10038
  Phone: 212-346-1323 (New York City campus)
  914-773-3746 (Westchester campus)
  Fax: 212-346-1821
  Web site: http://www.pace.edu
- Private, comprehensive, coed
- Setting varies by campus
- Enrollment: 13,500

- Student-faculty ratio: 15:1
- 2006–07 Tuition and fees: $29,500 (approx.)
- 2006–07 Room and board: $9000 (approx.)
- Countries represented: 128
- Admissions tests:
  - TOEFL (min. score 570 PBT; 230 CBT; 88 iBT) or IELTS (6.0 or higher)
  - SAT and ACT: Not required (except for scholarship consideration)
- Application deadline: April 30
- On-campus housing: Available
- Summer housing: Available

Area and Climate

Pace University is a multicampus institution with undergraduate campuses in both New York City and Pleasantville, New York. The downtown Manhattan campus is adjacent to the financial district and City Hall. Lincoln Center, Broadway theaters, museums, and many world-famous attractions are minutes away. The Pleasantville campus, 35 miles north of New York City, is located in the suburb of Westchester, New York. It houses an environmental center, riding stables, and a new athletic center. Towns and villages hosting gifted resident artisans, local musical and theater groups, and museums surround the campus. Pleasantville is within easy reach of resort and ski areas and close to New York City. Both campuses are accessible by University shuttle bus service, car, and public transportation. Average temperatures range from 32°F (0°C) in the winter to 81°F (27°C) in the summer.

Education

Pace University was founded by brothers Homer and Charles Pace in 1906. Their vision is reflected in Pace's motto, Opportunitas. A comprehensive, diversified, coeducational institution, Pace offers more than eighty majors and 3,000 individual courses of study through five undergraduate schools and colleges: the Lubin School of Business, the Dyson College of Arts and Sciences, the Ivan G. Seidenberg School of Computer Science and Information Systems, the School of Education, and the Lienhard School of Nursing. All campus locations are equipped with computers, laboratories, libraries, and videoconferencing facilities. Programs of special interest include the nationally recognized Cooperative Education Internship Program, the English Language Institute, and the Pforzheimer Honors College. The academic year consists of fall and spring semesters as well as two summer terms.

Campus Life

More than eighty clubs and organizations are active on campus, including the Model United Nations, the Black Student Organization, the Chinese Club, the Caribbean Students Association, and the Collegiate Italian American Organization. Pace offers many campus activities, including student government associations, fraternities, sororities, two literary magazines, two yearbooks, and two campus radio broadcasting systems. Athletic facilities are available for students, and intercollegiate Division II sports in Pleasantville include baseball, basketball, cross-country, equestrian, football, golf, lacrosse, women's soccer, softball, tennis, track and field, and volleyball. Students represent forty-eight states and come from eighty countries.

For International Students

International Student Advisors are available for consultation on both campuses, and international student orientation is offered at the beginning of each semester. The English Language Institute offers courses for students whose native language is not English. Students should submit a completed Undergraduate Student Application, two letters of recommendation, and official TOEFL or IELTS scores (if English is not the first language). Freshman applicants must submit official secondary school transcripts and matriculation exam results where applicable. Transfer students must also submit official postsecondary transcripts. Certified English translations are required. Students who wish to be considered for a merit-based scholarship are required to submit SAT scores.

Parsons The New School for Design

- **Contact:**
  Admissions Office
  Parsons The New School for Design
  65 Fifth Avenue, ground floor
  New York, NY 10003
  Phone: 212-229-8989
  Fax: 212-229-5611
  E-mail: parsadm@newschool.edu
  Web site: http://www.parsons.newschool.edu
- **Private, independent, comprehensive, coed**
- **Urban setting**
- **Enrollment: 3,180**

- **Student-faculty ratio: 8:1**
- **2006–07 Tuition and fees: $30,207**
- **2006–07 Room and board: $13,100**
- **International students: 34.5%**
- **Countries represented: 70**
- **Admissions tests:**
  - **TOEFL: Required**
  - **SAT: Required**
- **Application deadline: Fall, 2/1; spring, 10/15**
- **On-campus housing: Guaranteed**
- **Summer housing: Available**

Area and Climate

Part of The New School, a distinctive New York City university, Parsons' main campus is located downtown in Greenwich Village, a historic neighborhood with a distinct style and atmosphere. The Village is home to design and art studios, galleries, and shops and restaurants as well as avant-garde artists, musicians, and writers. New York City is a vibrant environment that has inspired and challenged artists and designers throughout its history. It is home to more than eighty museums. The weather in the area changes with the four seasons. Summer temperatures sometimes reach above 90°F (31°C), and winter temperatures average in the 30s (-1°C to 4°C).

Education

Parsons The New School for Design has been a forerunner in the field of art and design since its founding in 1896. Parsons focuses on creating engaged citizens and outstanding artists, designers, scholars, and business leaders through a design-based professional and liberal arts education. Areas of study include architecture, art, art education, commercial and advertising art, drawing, environmental design/architecture, fashion/apparel design, fashion merchandising, industrial design, interior design, photography, and sculpture. The School embraces curricular innovation, pioneering uses of technology, collaborative methods, and global perspectives on the future of design. In recent years, Parsons has strongly promoted technological skills development. By mastering computer graphics, computer-assisted design, interactive multimedia, digital imaging, and a host of other technological tools, Parsons graduates are on the leading edge of an ever-evolving design world. To Parsons faculty members, the city is an extension of the classroom and is incorporated into the basic fabric of the curriculum. The faculty members use New York City as an urban design

laboratory, teaching the architecture of the city, the fabric of its populations, and the language of its commercial and private communication. One of eight schools that made up The New School, Parsons, in collaboration with Eugene Lang College The New School for Liberal Arts, offers a five-year program in which undergraduate students simultaneously complete both the professional Bachelor of Fine Arts (B.F.A.) degree at Parsons and the Bachelor of Arts (B.A.) in liberal arts degree at Lang.

Campus Life

More than 1,100 students live in university housing in the Greenwich Village and Wall Street areas. In addition to the myriad social, recreational, and cultural opportunities that New York City provides, The New School Residence Life Program provides exciting social and educational programs and activities for the students. The residential communities are comfortable and inclusive. The New School Office of Student Development and Activities also facilitates meaningful interaction outside the classroom. Through social, cultural, leadership, educational, and recreational experiences, students are encouraged to form a community that includes students from every academic division and program and to become active participants in university life.

For International Students

The New School considers its international students an invaluable resource. International Student Services is dedicated to serving the special needs of international students and helping create a supportive environment for living and studying. In cooperation with other departments, faculty and staff members, and students themselves, International Student Services seeks to encourage international students to become active participants in classes, extracurricular activities, dorms, and life in New York City. From the point students are accepted to completion of studies, International Student Services provides support and comprehensive advising as well as cultural, social, and cocurricular programming.

Peninsula College

- Contact:
    Ge-Yao Liu, Director of International
        Programs
    Peninsula College
    Port Angeles, WA 98362
    Phone: 360-417-6491
    Fax: 360-417-6482
    E-mail: gliu@ctc.edu
    Web site: http://www.pc.ctc.edu
- Public, coed
- Small-town setting
- Enrollment: 5,500
- 2006–07 Tuition and fees (plus books): $8481

- 2006–07 Room and board: $4500
- International students: 6%
- Countries represented: 10
- International students applied: 140
- International students accepted: 140
- Admissions tests:
    - TOEFL: Required (paper-based min. score 500; computer-based min. score 173)
- Application deadline: Rolling
- On-campus housing: Not available
- Summer housing: Not available

Area and Climate

Peninsula College is located on the Olympic Peninsula of Washington State in the small seaport city of Port Angeles. The Olympic Mountains, a United Nations World Heritage National Park, the Strait of Juan de Fuca, the Pacific Ocean, and temperate rain forests provide a unique educational environment. The climate is moderate. Temperatures average 70°F (21°C) in the summer and 35°F to 40°F (2°C to 4°C) in the winter, with an occasional light dusting of snow. Nearby cities include Seattle, Washington, and the Canadian cities of Victoria and Vancouver, British Columbia. The Fairchild International Airport provides important transportation links to Seattle and elsewhere.

Education

Peninsula College was founded in 1961 as a student-oriented institution that believes that teaching and learning are at the center of its mission. The College offers four degrees: Associate of Arts Honors, Associates of Arts, Associate of Science Transfer, and Associate of Applied Science. The highest-enrolled majors are in arts and sciences. Library holdings include 28,416 books, 191 periodicals, eleven newspapers, and films and electronic media. Peninsula College has walk-in access to computers in its library, PUB, and computer labs; several computerized classrooms; and computers in the residence hall. Many faculty members hold doctorates and receive honors for their teaching. The College operates on the quarter system.

Campus Life

Peninsula College's small, friendly campus is home to students from throughout the United States and several international countries and Native Americans from five local tribes. The residence hall, which is moments from the center of the campus, is open year-round. Students participate in several campus-based clubs; join varsity basketball, soccer, and softball teams; hear weekly guest speakers and performers through the Studium Generale program; listen to visiting writers read their own works; attend weekly films; catch well-known singers and other performers several times each quarter; and enjoy the Art Gallery. In 2003, a member of the alumni was named an Outstanding Alumni member by the American Association of Community Colleges.

For International Students

A new international student orientation is held a few days prior to the beginning of each academic term. The orientation mainly focuses on U.S. immigration regulations, cross-cultural issues, and the U.S. educational system. All new students are required to take a placement test upon arrival. After the test, students see an adviser for appropriate class selections. Those whose English is not yet proficient are required to enroll in the ESL program, which has four levels. Homestay is available for new students upon request; off-campus apartments are also available. Airport pickup is free for new international students on the recommended arrival date each quarter.

Philadelphia University

- **Contact:**
  Colleen Duffey
  Assistant Director of Admissions
  Philadelphia University
  Philadelphia, PA 19144
  Phone: 215-951-2800
  Fax: 215-951-2907
  Web site: http://www.PhilaU.edu
- **Private, coed**
- **Suburban setting**
- **Enrollment: 2,500**
- **Student-faculty ratio: 13:1**
- **2006–07 Tuition and fees: $23,748**
- **2006–07 Room and board: $7936**

- **International students: 4.5%**
- **Countries represented: 37**
- **International students applied: 261**
- **International students accepted: 91**
- **International students enrolled: 14**
- **Admissions tests:**
  - **TOEFL (min. score 500 PBT; 170 CBT; 59 iBT)**
  - **SAT and ACT: Not required**
- **Application deadline: Rolling**
- **On-campus housing: Available**
- **Summer housing: Available, not guaranteed**

Area and Climate

Philadelphia University is located in a residential neighborhood of Philadelphia, Pennsylvania—the fifth-largest city in the United States. The tree-lined, 100-acre (41-hectare) campus is adjacent to Fairmount Park, the largest city park in the United States. The campus is just minutes from the entertainment, cultural events, and 300 years of American history in Center City Philadelphia. New York City is situated approximately 99 miles (160 kilometers) to the north, and Washington, D.C., is just 149 miles (240 kilometers) to the south. The Philadelphia International Airport is within 30 minutes of the campus. Philadelphia has an excellent public transportation system. Temperatures range from 5°F (-15°C) to 50°F (10°C) in January and from 70°F (21°C) to 95°F (35°C) in July.

Education

Philadelphia University is a private, independent, four-year college for students with high motivation and academic promise. Founded in 1884, the University offers programs in graphic design, business, engineering, fashion, textiles, psychology, and the sciences, achieving an extremely high placement rate of more than 90 percent in these fields. The University offers fully accredited programs in architecture, interior design, and physician's assistant studies. The University operates on a semester system, with the fall semester beginning in late August and the spring semester beginning in mid-January. Students benefit from small classes, personalized advising, membership in the prestigious National Textile Center, and a internship program ranked in the top 1 percent. A recently completed $5-million technology initiative brings universal access to sophisticated information technology from anywhere on or off campus.

Campus Life

Philadelphia University has a long history of educating students from all over the world. At present, there are thirty countries represented and more than 110 international students. Contributing to the excitement that pervades the campus are nationally ranked athletic teams, movies, concerts, dances, and more than fifty student clubs and organizations. Fourteen varsity teams compose the intercollegiate athletics program, and an extensive intramural sports program is available to all students. There is a variety of housing options, including residence halls and town houses.

For International Students

Philadelphia University has a long-standing commitment to the internationalization of the campus. An International Student Advisor is available to serve the needs of the international students, such as providing orientation assistance, counseling, referral to language classes, and administrative liaison with governmental and immigration agencies. International students who wish to enter the University must submit an application for admission along with official transcripts. TOEFL and/or SAT scores must accompany the application. International Student Merit Scholarships are available to qualified students.

Pierce College

- **Contact:**
  Director of International Programs
  Pierce College
  Lakewood, WA 98498-1999
  Phone: 253-964-7327
  Fax: 253-964-6256
  E-mail: international@pierce.ctc.edu
  Web site: http://www.pierce.ctc.edu/
    international
- **Public, 2-year, coed**
- **Suburban setting**
- **Enrollment: 8,000**
- **Student-faculty ratio: 27:1**
- **2005–06 Tuition and fees: $7908 (15 credits);
  for intensive English, $6450**

- **International students: 2%**
- **Countries represented: 18**
- **International students applied: 190**
- **International students accepted: 180**
- **International students enrolled: 155**
- **Admissions tests:**
    - **TOEFL (paper-based min. score 500;
      computer-based min. score 173)**
    - **SAT: Not required**
    - **ACT: Not required**
- **Application deadline: 9/1, 12/1, 3/1, 5/1**
- **On-campus housing: Homestay only**
- **Summer housing: Homestay only**

Area and Climate

Pierce College District consists of two colleges, Pierce College Fort Steilacoom and Pierce College Puyallup. The Colleges are located 32 miles (52 kilometers) apart and are about 40 minutes and 30 minutes, respectively, from Seatac International Airport. Snowy mountains are visible to the east and west, and Puget Sound is close by. The area has a mild climate and is rarely very cold or very hot. Seattle, Vancouver, and Portland, Oregon, are within easy reach. In the winter season, ski slopes are only about 1 hour to the east.

Education

Pierce College is a two-year community college founded in 1967. It has a well-known college-preparation Intensive English Program. Most international students come to Pierce College to complete their general education requirements for transfer to a four-year university program. Many students return home after completing a two-year associate program, and some take a one-year certificate program. Some students attend simply to improve their English skills. In addition to the Associate in Arts and Sciences degree, the College offers associate programs in accounting, business, business management, computer information systems, computer programming, criminal justice, dental hygiene, early childhood education, electronic engineering technology, fashion merchandising, general office management, international business secretary studies, social service/mental health, and veterinary technology. Classes are small and instructors are focused exclusively on teaching. Advising is provided at every stage of the student's career at the College, and advisers and instructors are readily available to help students succeed. Students wishing to transfer to universities receive advice and support in deciding on their future plans and in making their applications.

Campus Life

International students enjoy meeting students from a wide cross-section of American society. Both campuses have libraries, computer labs, and many other facilities. There are active International Clubs and many other clubs and student activities at both campuses.

For International Students

The international education office is a district-wide operation and supports international students in all aspects of their college activities. The office staff helps students with orientation, advising, registration, and visa issues. Assistance with placement in host families and with accommodation questions in general is provided by Abode Homestay, Inc. (Web site: http://www.abodehomestay.org).

Pratt Institute

- Contact:
  Heidi Metcalf
  Director of Admissions
  Pratt Institute
  200 Willoughby Avenue
  Brooklyn, NY 11205
  Phone: 718-636-3514
  Fax: 718-636-3670
  E-mail: admissions@pratt.edu
  Web site: http://www.pratt.edu
- Private, coed
- Urban setting
- Enrollment: 4,762
- Student-faculty ratio: 12:1

- 2006–07 Tuition and fees: $28,100
- 2006–07 Room and board: $8752
- International students: 15%
- Countries represented: 58
- International students applied: 1,291
- International students accepted: 617
- International students enrolled: 263
- Admissions tests:
  - TOEFL (min. score 530)
- Application deadline: 1/1; 2/1
- On-campus housing: Guaranteed for incoming students who apply by 5/1
- Summer housing: Available

Area and Climate

Pratt Institute has a 25-acre (10-hectare) campus with grassy plazas, century-old trees, and historic buildings in the landmark residential neighborhood of Clinton Hill in Brooklyn, New York. Since Pratt is located just 25 minutes from downtown Manhattan, students have easy access to Manhattan's SoHo galleries, museums, and cultural events. Subway and bus stops are within a 5-minute walking distance of the campus. Pratt also has a Manhattan campus on 14th Street in Chelsea. Mountains, lakes, and the ocean are within a 2-hour drive from Pratt. Temperatures average 41°F (5°C) in winter and 76°F (24°C) in summer.

Education

Pratt Institute has educated professionals for productive careers in artistic and technical fields since its founding in 1887. Pratt offers one of the best professional architecture, art, and design educations in the world with an outstanding faculty of practicing professionals and exceptional state-of-the-art facilities. Pratt offers baccalaureate degrees in architecture, art history, art and design education, computer graphics, construction management, critical and visual studies, fashion design, film/video, fine arts, graphic design, illustration, industrial design, interior design, photography, and writing for publication, art and media. Pratt also offers master's degrees in more than fifteen programs in its Schools of Art and Design, Architecture, and Information and Library Science.

Campus Life

In 2006–07, the Institute educated 4,762 undergraduate and graduate students from forty-eight states and fifty-eight countries. Approximately 90 percent of freshmen and 79 percent of all Pratt undergraduates live on campus in one of five residence halls. The campus atmosphere is friendly and relaxed. Pratt has more than sixty student activities, including professional organizations, fraternities and sororities, honor societies, special interest groups, and student-run publications. In addition, the campus houses the largest enclosed athletic and recreational facility in Brooklyn. Pratt has several men's and women's NCAA and intramural sports teams.

For International Students

With 15 percent of Pratt's student body from abroad, there is truly an international atmosphere on campus. To support the needs of international students, Pratt has an Office of International Students, which provides counseling on cross-cultural differences, financial matters, and family concerns. All new students whose first language is not English are required to take Pratt's Intensive English Proficiency Exam (regardless of TOEFL scores). Students who score below the exempt level are required to enroll in Pratt's Intensive English Program, which helps to strengthen their English reading, writing, and speaking skills.

Quality College of Culinary Careers

- **Contact:**
  Admissions Office
  Quality College of Culinary Careers
  1776 North Fine Avenue
  Fresno, CA 93727
  Phone: 559-497-5050
  866-373-CHEF (toll-free)
  E-mail: john.moore@qualitycollege.edu
  Web site: http://www.qualitycollege.edu/
  Culinary%20Arts/food.htm
- **Proprietary, two-year, coed**
- **Urban setting**
- **Enrollment: 100**

- **Student-faculty ratio: 20:1**
- **2006–07 Tuition and fees: $500 to $36,000 per certificate**
- **International students: 0%**
- **International students enrolled: 0**
- **Admissions tests:**
  - **TOEFL: Recommended**
- **Application deadline: Rolling**
- **On-campus housing: No**
- **Summer housing: Yes**

Area and Climate

Fresno, California, lies in central California and, with more than 1 million residents, has the state's sixth-largest population. Located near Highways 41 and 99, Fresno is easily accessible. Many concerts, museums, and professional sports teams offer a variety of entertainment. The city has numerous parks, and Yosemite National Park is just a 60-minute drive away. During the winter, Fresno is generally rainy and cool, with low temperatures ranging in the upper 30s and lower 40s Fahrenheit (3–7°C). Summers are hot and dry; temperatures can soar near 100°F (38°C).

Education

Quality College of Culinary Careers (QCCC) is a private vocational college and accredited member of the Accrediting Commission of Career Schools and Colleges of Technology (ACCSCT). In an environment that encourages free expression, leadership, and responsible decision-making, curricula are taught by faculty members who are, or have been, working professionals. The curricula and methods of instruction are intended to provide students with a broad understanding of the demands of the occupation of their choice; develop the student's creative, technical, and analytical skills; introduce the practical aspects of business; and develop a keen awareness of the professional responsibilities of the chosen vocation.

The custom culinary curriculum is developed by and for the College Food Service Program. It takes the student on a structured day-by-day journey into the world of food service. Lessons are reinforced with reference texts that include *On Cooking* and *The Art and Science of Culinary Preparation*. Students can enroll in the culinary arts, culinary chef, food and beverage manager, professional baking and pastry chef, or professional cooking and culinary arts tracks. Programs can be taken in modules together or separately.

Campus Life

Students gain hands-on culinary experience by working in the College's restaurant, the California Bistro & Grille.

For International Students

International students must assume personal responsibility with regard to immigration and visa law. QCCC staff members, however, provide assistance and advisement where possible.

Quinnipiac University

- **Contact:**
  Joan Isaac Mohr
  V.P./Dean of Admissions
  Quinnipiac University
  Hamden, CT 06518
  Phone: 203-582-8600
  Fax: 203-582-8906
  E-mail: admissions@quinnipiac.edu
  Web site: http://www.quinnipiac.edu/
- **Private, coed**
- **Suburban setting**
- **Enrollment: 7,341**
- **Student-faculty ratio: 16:1**
- **2006–07 Tuition and fees: $26,280**
- **2006–07 Room and board: $10,700**
- **International students: 2%**

- **Countries represented: 19**
- **International students applied: 80**
- **International students accepted: 60**
- **International students enrolled: 23**
- **Admissions tests:**
  - **TOEFL: Required (min. score 550 PBT; 213 CBT)**
  - **SAT: Recommended (if English is the first language; otherwise it is not needed)**
  - **ACT: Not required (can be substituted for the SAT)**
- **Application deadline: Rolling (3/1 recommended)**
- **On-campus housing: Guaranteed for three years**
- **Summer housing: Limited**

Area and Climate

Connecticut is the third-smallest state in the United States. Students can travel from campus to any part of Connecticut, as well as to Boston and New York City (by train or car), within 2 hours. The 500-acre (204-hectare) scenic campus is adjacent to Sleeping Giant State Park, which has 1,700 acres (689 hectares) of trails for hiking, picnicking, jogging, or other outdoor activities. New England has moderately cool winters, with some snowfall usual from January through early March. Summers range from 70°F (21°C) to 90°F (32°C). The area near the campus is suburban, the town of Hamden offers shopping and entertainment, and nearby New Haven and Hartford, the state capital, are known for a wide variety of ethnic restaurants, concerts, and off-Broadway theater and dance. Most students from overseas fly into John F. Kennedy Airport (JFK) in New York and take the Connecticut Limousine Service to New Haven, ending with a 15-minute taxi ride to campus. Students in the U.S. may choose to fly into Bradley Airport (BDL), north of Hartford, which is also serviced by Connecticut (CT) Limousine Service.

Education

Founded in 1929, Quinnipiac offers bachelor's degrees (undergraduate programs) in business, communications, health sciences, and liberal arts and graduate programs in business, education, interactive communications, health sciences, journalism, and law. Major programs are focused toward career preparation and offer clinical experiences or internships as part of each program, as well as study-abroad opportunities. The core curriculum gives students a broad basis in several areas of the liberal arts, math, and social sciences. The most popular majors are accounting, athletic training, biology, communications, computer science, criminal justice, entrepreneurship, international business, marketing, nursing, physical and occupational therapy, political science, and psychology. Quinnipiac's philosophy and practice stress the importance of maintaining high-quality academic programs, a student-oriented environment, and a sense of community. The University has a 16:1 student-faculty ratio and excellent campus facilities that include the computerized, state-of-the-art, $12-million Arnold Bernhard Library; the Terry Goodwin '67 Financial Technology Center; a clinical-care lab facility; a motion analysis lab for athletic training; a fully digital, high-definition production studio and news technology center in the Ed McMahon Center for Communications; a recreation center with an extensive weight room and suspended indoor track; and an artificial-turf field for lacrosse.

Campus Life

Students attend Quinnipiac from twenty-four states and nineteen countries and become involved in their choice of more than seventy clubs, student government, publications, recreation, athletics (NCAA Division I), community service, and on- and off-campus internships. Seventy percent of students live on campus. Housing is currently guaranteed for three years to incoming freshmen. Quinnipiac is adding 1,800 additional residence beds to provide housing for all undergraduates by 2009–10. On-campus housing is not available for married or graduate students, but there are ample rental facilities in nearby communities such as Cheshire, Hamden, New Haven, North Haven, and Wallingford.

For International Students

Through the efforts of the Office of International Education, an International Club, Foreign Student Advisor, orientation and registration, and International Student Handbook are available. Faculty members act as advisers for academic programming, and the small campus atmosphere makes becoming a part of the campus community an easy transition.

Radford University

- Contact:
    Amy Jarich
    Associate Director of Admissions
    Radford University
    Radford, VA 24142
    Phone: 540-831-5371
    Fax: 540-831-5038
    E-mail: awjarich@radford.edu
    Web site: http://www.radford.edu
- Public, comprehensive, coed
- Small-town setting
- Enrollment: 9,221
- Student-faculty ratio: 21:1
- 2006–07 Tuition and fees: $13,494

- 2006–07 Room and board: $6218
- International students: 10%
- Countries represented: 43
- International students applied: 75
- International students accepted: 30
- International students enrolled: 18
- Admissions tests:
    - TOEFL: Required (min. score 520 PTB; 190 CBT for full-time academics)
    - SAT or ACT: Required
- Application deadline: 4/1 fall, 8/1 spring
- On-campus housing: Guaranteed
- Summer housing: Available

Area and Climate

Radford University (RU) is located in a small town in southwestern Virginia. The medium-sized secure campus is situated on 175 acres (71 hectares) and is 267 miles (430 kilometers) from Washington, D.C. Since Radford is located near the Blue Ridge Mountains, the summers are moderate and the winters can be quite cool. Generally the climate is pleasant and permits outdoor activities throughout most of the year. Average temperatures for the various seasons are as follows: fall, 65°F (18°C); winter, 43°F (6°C); spring, 53°F (12°C); and summer, 81°F (27°C).

Education

Radford University was founded in 1910 and is a comprehensive, residential university committed to individualized instruction in medium-sized classes offering high academic standards and excellence in teaching. Degree options include 106 undergraduate and thirty-eight graduate programs through the Colleges of Arts and Sciences, Business and Economics, Education and Human Development, Information Science and Technology, Visual and Performing Arts, Health and Human Services, and Graduate and Extended Studies. The McConnell Library offers students access to textual material, periodicals, and information recorded on film, microfilm, records, compact audio discs, and tapes.

Campus Life

Radford University is home to students from forty-five states and forty-three countries. The diverse student body enhances the campus and surrounding area. RU offers more than 200 student organizations, guest speakers, theatrical productions, concerts, films, student publications, intramural sports, and other cultural, social, and leisure opportunities. RU's intercollegiate teams participate in nineteen sports and are members of NCAA Division I. Fifteen residence halls, housing from 120 to 950 students each, offer a variety of options to the 3,150 students who live on campus. Students live in two-room suites that share one private bathroom.

For International Students

International Student Services provides a wide range of programs to facilitate the acculturation of international students. A comprehensive International Student Orientation Program is held at the beginning of each semester. Other programs conducted for international students include the International Friendship Program, which matches international students with families from the community; the International Speakers Bureau; International Coffee Hours; and International Week. Immigration services, a campus Health Center, a Learning Assistance and Resource Center, and tutors, as well as a variety of international clubs and organizations, are available to students.

Randolph College

- Contact:
  Joy McGrath
  Associate Director of Admissions for
    International Students
  Randolph College
  Lynchburg, VA 24503
  Phone: 434-947-8100
  Fax: 434-947-8996
- Private, coed
- Suburban setting
- Enrollment: 750
- Student-faculty ratio: 9:1

- 2006–07 Tuition and fees: $24,410
- 2006–07 Room and board: $8000
- International students: 13%
- Countries represented: More than 45
- Admissions tests:
  - TOEFL (min. score 550)
  - SAT: Recommended
  - ACT: Not required
- Application deadline: 3/1
- On-campus housing: Guaranteed
- Summer housing: Not available

Area and Climate

Randolph College (RC) is located in the foothills of the Blue Ridge Mountains in Virginia. The College occupies 100 acres (41 hectares) in a residential section of the city of Lynchburg, which has a population of 70,000. Hiking, rafting, and other outdoor activities are available, as are cultural events, which include visual arts, theater, and music. Lynchburg's location is convenient to many historical sites, including Appomattox and Monticello. The area is served by Lynchburg Airport and a local bus system. Students can also travel to and from other cities by bus and train. Temperatures range from an average of 82°F (35°C) in the summer to 39°F (4°C) in the winter.

Education

Randolph College, founded as Randolph-Macon Woman's College in 1891, has always been committed to excellence in providing a liberal arts and sciences education for women. Its purpose is to prepare students for meaningful professional and personal lives. The College will begin enrolling men in fall 2007. Randolph College is accredited by the Commission of Colleges of the Southern Association of Colleges and Schools to award bachelor's and master's degrees. More than sixty majors, concentrations (minors), and fields of study are offered, the most popular of which are psychology and biology. Ninety-two percent of the faculty members hold Ph.D.'s or the appropriate terminal degree in their field. Students are assigned a faculty adviser to assist them in course scheduling and other planning until they declare a major, at which time they are assigned a major adviser. Randolph College is fully connected to the Internet, including access from the several computer laboratories and all residence hall rooms and classrooms. Students enjoy the campus portal system and numerous wireless locations. RC uses a two-semester calendar year.

Campus Life

The College enrolls approximately 715 students from forty-four states and more than forty-five countries. Randolph College is a residential campus; therefore, it is required that all students live in the residence halls for all four years. Housing is not available during the summer. Students are active in organizations and activities, such as campus publications, performing arts, volunteer service groups, religious life, and athletics. One of the most popular events on campus is the Pan World Coffeehouse, which is sponsored by international students and students who are interested in global issues. Traditions such as Pumpkin Parade, Ring Night, and the Odd/Even Class rivalry are important features of student life. Campus life is governed by the observance of the Honor Code.

For International Students

Randolph College offers merit scholarships ranging from $5000 to $13,000 per year to international students. These scholarships are based on academic achievement and extracurricular involvement. Admissions requirements for international students include a minimum TOEFL score of 550 (paper-based) or 213 (computer-based) or an SAT verbal or critical reading score of at least 500. Orientation takes place during the summer to acquaint new international students with the College, and the International Student Services Committee is available to address questions and concerns. Macon Intercultural Exchange (MIX) is a residential program in which U.S. students are housed with international students for the academic year. Randolph College also manages a Friendship Family program to enable international students to become acquainted with a local American family.

Rensselaer Polytechnic Institute

- **Contact:**
  James G. Nondorf
  Vice President for Enrollment
  Rensselaer Polytechnic Institute
  Troy, NY 12180-3590
  Phone: 518-276-6216
  Fax: 518-276-4072
- Highly selective, coeducational, private, nonsectarian
- Parklike setting in urban metropolitan area
- Enrollment: 7,433
- Student-faculty ratio: 15:1
- 2006–07 Tuition and fees: $32,600
- 2006–07 Room and board: $9915 (first year)

- International students: 12%
- Countries represented: 67
- International students applied: 337
- International students accepted: 139
- International students enrolled: 19 (freshmen)
- Admissions tests:
  - **TOEFL:** (min. score 570 paper-based; 230 computer-based)
  - **SAT or ACT:** Required
- Application deadline: 1/15
- On-campus housing: Available
- Summer housing: Available

Area and Climate

Rensselaer's 110-hectare (275-acre) campus offers the best of both worlds: the beauty and grandeur of the nearby Adirondack Mountains and the excitement of New York's Capital District, a metropolitan area of 750,000 people. The region is famed for its snowy winters, lush green springs and summers, and brilliantly colorful autumns. Overlooking the Hudson River, Rensselaer blends a cluster of classical brick buildings with modern, technology-rich infrastructure. Extensive renovation has equipped the campus with wireless computing, superb laboratories, and comfortable accommodations while preserving the traditional elegance of its historic buildings. Students enjoy easy access to Boston (3 hours), New York City (2½ hours), and Montreal (4 hours). Rensselaer is accessible via Albany International Airport, the Albany/Rensselaer Amtrak rail station, the Albany bus station, and interstate highways.

Education

Ranked among the world's elite technological research universities, Rensselaer was founded in 1824 to instruct students "in the application of science to the common purposes of life." More than 100 programs and 1,000 courses lead to bachelor's, master's, and doctoral degrees. Undergraduates pursue their studies in the Schools of Architecture, Engineering, Humanities and Social Sciences, Management and Technology, and Science and in the interdisciplinary degree program in information technology (IT). The undergraduate experience features close collaboration with faculty members, studio class-rooms, undergraduate research, and a rigorous curriculum. Accelerated programs in medicine and law are offered in cooperation with other universities. Rensselaer is at the forefront among universities in computing capability and capacity. All state-of-the-art teaching and research facilities are available to undergraduate students. The Folsom Library houses more than 520,000 publications and participates in a library consortium that makes thousands of additional materials available to students.

Campus Life

Rensselaer is a residential campus where students from forty-eight states and sixty-seven nations enjoy a rich diversity of extracurricular activities. Administering a budget of $8.5 million, elected student leaders oversee more than 160 clubs, multicultural and special interest groups, professional societies, sports offerings, and organizations, including a weekly newspaper, an FM radio station, and musical ensembles. Rensselaer students participate in eighteen intramural sports, and twenty-three varsity teams are in NCAA competition. Summer housing is provided for those who choose to enjoy the beauty of upstate New York in all of its splendor.

For International Students

The Office of International Services for Students and Scholars (ISSS) begins assisting international students before they arrive, with information on visas, banking, housing, health care, and more. A fall orientation program provides a perfect introduction to Rensselaer and to living in the United States. Other services include immigration counseling, tax seminars, career workshops, and social events. Academic counseling and tutoring are available for all students, and there is special help for those who wish to improve their command of English.

Rider University

- **Contact:**
  Director of Undergraduate Admissions
  Rider University
  2083 Lawrenceville Road
  Lawrenceville, NJ 08648-3099
  Phone: 609-896-5042
  E-mail: admissions@rider.edu
  Web site: http://www.rider.edu
- **Independent, comprehensive, coed**
- **Suburban setting**
- **Enrollment: 5,790**
- **Student-faculty ratio: 13:1**
- **2006–07 Tuition and fees: $24,790**

- **2006–07 Room and board: $9280**
- **International students: 3%**
- **Countries represented: 53**
- **Admissions tests:**
  - **TOEFL: Required (min. score 550 PBT; 213 CBT; 80 iBT)**
  - **SAT: Recommended**
  - **ACT: Not required**
- **Application deadline: Fall, 6/1; spring, 11/1**
- **On-campus housing: Guaranteed for all four years**
- **Summer housing: Available**

Area and Climate

Rider University is located in the suburban community of Lawrenceville, New Jersey, midway between Princeton and Trenton, New Jersey. It is approximately 35 miles (56 kilometers) northeast of Philadelphia and 65 miles (105 kilometers) southwest of New York City. The location combines the advantages of accessibility to the cultural and recreational facilities of major urban areas and to the peaceful surroundings of a suburban community. The climate offers seasonal changes, with temperatures ranging from 98°F (36°C) in summer (June-September) to 23°F (-5°C) in winter (November-March).

Education

Founded in 1865, Rider University is an independent, coeducational, nonsectarian institution. Rider offers sixty undergraduate and seventeen graduate programs through four academic schools and colleges: the College of Business Administration; the College of Liberal Arts, Education, and Sciences; the College of Continuing Studies; and Westminster Choir College, which is located in neighboring Princeton, New Jersey. Rider is a student-centered university that emphasizes high-quality teaching and learning and a supportive community of dedicated faculty and staff members who are committed to students' success. Primarily a teaching institution, Rider University selects instructors who are committed to imparting the knowledge and skills of a particular discipline. Full professors teach at all levels, and 96 percent of Rider's full-time faculty members hold a doctorate or other appropriate advanced degree. Rider's rich history has emphasized purposeful connections between academic study and education for the professions—creating meaningful linkages between the classroom and a variety of other learning experiences that help students build leadership skills and achieve success in life and work. Student internships or field experiences, community service-learning placements, and undergraduate research fellowships are offered. For 2007–08, merit-

based freshman scholarships range from $5000 to $15,000 per year and merit-based transfer scholarships range from $2500 to $7,500 per year. Need-based financial aid is not available for transfer students.

Campus Life

To facilitate the total development of the student while at Rider, the student affairs program and services supplement and complement the academic mission of the College. Rider offers hundreds of activities, from intramural sports to Division I NCAA men's and women's athletics, from student government to a wide variety of student clubs and organizations, from internships to service learning opportunities—all of which give students opportunities to become involved, enhance their educational experiences, and stretch their minds and imagination. On-campus housing options at the Lawrenceville campus are varied; twelve residence halls and six Greek houses provide opportunities for students to live among their peers in well-kept, secure, and supportive environments that promote their well-being and their educational experience. Residence halls offer both single-sex and coeducational housing that varies in size and scope. All residence halls are equipped with voice, video, and data service.

For International Students

The Office of International Programs plays a crucial role in insuring that international students get the most from their experience at Rider. The Office of International Programs is a place students feel comfortable coming to for help and advice on everything from visa problems and obtaining a driver's license to handling academic and personal adjustment problems. It is an office dedicated to meeting international students' needs. At the Office of International Programs, students find expert advice on immigration regulations and knowledgeable referrals to the resources of the surrounding community. They also find staff members who have traveled extensively and who understand what it is like to move halfway around the world to an unfamiliar culture and environment. Students can obtain more information at http://www.rider.edu/international.

Riverside Community College

- Contact:
    Marylin V. Jacobsen
    Director, Center for Int'l. Students and
        Programs
    Riverside Community College District
    4800 Magnolia Avenue
    Riverside, CA 92506-1299
    Phone: 951-222-8160
    Fax: 951-222-8376
    E-mail: internationalcenter@rcc.edu
    Web site: http://www.rcc.edu/international
- Public, 2-year, coed
- Suburban setting
- Enrollment: 32,400
- Student-faculty ratio: 35:1
- 2006–07 Tuition and fees: $4800 (approx.)

- 2006–07 Room and board: $10,000 (approx.)
- International students: 2.5% (approx.)
- Countries represented: 60
- International students enrolled: 300 (total)
- Admissions test:
    - TOEFL: Required (min. score 450 PBT; 45 iBT)
    - SAT and ACT: Not required
- Application deadline: Fall, 6/1; spring, 11/1; summer, 4/1
- On-campus housing: Available through homestays and apartments
- Summer housing: Available through homestays and apartments

Area and Climate

Riverside Community College (RCC) is located in southern California, an hour's drive east of Los Angeles. RCC opened two additional campuses in 1991 in nearby Norco and Moreno Valley. Riverside is a traditional southern California community. Art and history museums, libraries, a symphony orchestra, and theater companies add to the cultural life of the region. More than twenty-five colleges and universities are located within 30 miles (48 kilometers) of Riverside. Newport Beach, Laguna Beach, the San Bernardino Mountains, and the Palm Springs desert resort region are close. Disneyland is also within an hour's drive, and Las Vegas is about a four-hour drive. The weather is mild, with a Mediterranean climate. Westerly breezes create balmy evenings even when summer days are warm.

Education

The RCC District, which has three colleges, enrolls approximately 32,400 people. Part of the California Community College system, RCC offers the first two years of a four-year education in preparation for transfer to four-year universities. More than 2,000 classes are offered each semester in more than seventy majors. In addition to courses that prepare students for transfer, the Associate of Arts degree is awarded after two years (or 60 units) of study. Certificate programs in many occupational fields are also available. Transfer admission is guaranteed to California State University and University of California campuses upon completion of required classes.

Campus Life

With more than 300 young people from sixty countries attending each semester, RCC maintains a Center for International Students and Programs. The center assists students in becoming acquainted with American college life, meeting other students and faculty members on campus, touring Riverside and southern California points of interest, and receiving academic tutoring when needed. Housing is not provided. However, the Center keeps lists of home-stay families and apartment houses as well as lists of students who are seeking someone to share an apartment.

For International Students

The RCC Center for International Students and Programs has 2 full-time staff members to assist students with admissions, registration, advising on academic and career goals, immigration, and transfer to universities to complete bachelor's degrees. A minimum TOEFL score of 450 (paper-based) or 45 (Internet-based) or an IELTS score of at least 4.5 is required for students to benefit from instruction at the college level. Students on an F-1 Visa must present evidence of financial resources to meet all costs for tuition, books, insurance, and personal living expenses. International students must be at least 18 years of age unless they are graduates of a U.S. high school. Health and accident insurance is required. Students must purchase health insurance through the College. Applications should be submitted as early as possible. The RCC Center for International Students and Programs is located on the Riverside campus, but students may take classes in Moreno Valley or Norco.

Rochester Institute of Technology

- Contact:
  Coordinator of International Admissions
  Rochester Institute of Technology
  60 Lomb Memorial Drive
  Rochester, NY 14623-5604
  Phone: 585-475-6631
  Fax: 585-475-7424
  E-mail: admissions@rit.edu
- Private, coed
- Suburban setting
- Enrollment: 15,200
- Student-faculty ratio: 13:1
- 2006–07 Tuition and fees: $25,011
- 2006–07 Room and board: $8748

- International students: 5%
- Countries represented: 90
- International students applied: 1013
- International students accepted: 490
- International students enrolled: 147
- Admissions tests:
  - TOEFL: Required (min. score 550 paper-based)
  - SAT or ACT: Recommended
- Application deadline: Rolling
- On-campus housing: Guaranteed (first year)
- Summer housing: Available

Area and Climate

Rochester Institute of Technology (RIT) is located on 1,300 acres (527 hectares) in suburban Rochester, the third-largest city in New York State. RIT's suburban setting and modern facilities provide a quiet, attractive, and safe environment for academic and social activities. Rochester is the world center of photography, the largest producer of optical goods in the United States, and is among the leaders in graphic arts and in production of electronic equipment and precision instruments. There are four distinct seasons each year. In the summer, temperatures average 68°F (20°C) to 82°F (28°C); in the winter, many days are below 32°F (0°C). Spring and autumn are pleasant and moderate.

Education

Rochester Institute of Technology was founded in 1829 and is recognized internationally as a leader in professional and career-oriented education. RIT offers more than 200 academic programs in business, engineering, engineering technology, art and design, science, mathematics, computing, information sciences, liberal arts, photography, hospitality, and many other areas. Students may choose from more than fifty different minors to develop personal and professional interests that complement their academic program. Opportunities to participate in cooperative education, internships, study abroad, and undergraduate research are also available. As home to the National Technical Institute for the Deaf (NTID), RIT is a leader in providing access services for deaf and hard-of-hearing students.

Campus Life

Close to 70 percent of RIT's full-time students live on the campus in residence halls or campus apartments. RIT offers a variety of housing options, including residence halls and apartments. The residence halls have a number of special-interest houses, including one for international students. The diversity of the student body is reflected in the variety of activities on campus. There are more than 175 different student clubs and organizations in the following categories: career-related, hobby and special interest, music, fraternities and sororities, sports, ethnic, and religious.

For International Students

There are more than a dozen student organizations on campus designed to promote interaction and understanding among students of different cultures through social, cultural, and recreational programs. A few examples are the Global Union, Organization of the Alliance of Students from the Indian Subcontinent, the Asian Culture Society, the Latin American Student Association, and the Society of European Affairs. International House, a special-interest residence hall, provides accommodations for men and women undergraduates, both international and American, where students can share their cultural heritages. Staff members of the Office of Student Transition and Support are available to assist international students with such issues as orientation and cross-cultural training as well as advising students concerning immigration regulations.

Roger Williams University

- **Contact:**
  Mr. Didier Bouvet
  Director of International & Transfer Admission
  Mr. Saad Z. Sait
  Assistant Director of International Admission
  Office of Undergraduate Admission
  Roger Williams University
  Bristol, RI 02809-2921

  Phone: 401-254-3500
  Fax: 401-254-3557
  E-mail: intadmit@rwu.edu
  Web site: http://www.rwu.edu
- **Private, coed**
- **Suburban setting**
- **Enrollment: 3,775**

- **Student-faculty ratio: 16:1**
- **2006–07 Tuition and fees: $23,040 (architecture: $26,400)**
- **2006–07 Room and board: $10,422**
- **International students: 3%**
- **Countries represented: 41**
- **Admissions tests:**
    - **TOEFL: Strongly recommended**
    - **SAT: Recommended**
- **Application deadline: Rolling**
- **On-campus housing: Available**
- **Summer housing: Available**

Area and Climate

Roger Williams University (RWU) is located in Rhode Island, in the historic seacoast town of Bristol. The beautiful and modern campus is a living and learning laboratory, spread over 140 acres (57 hectares) of waterfront property. RWU is ideally situated near major cities like Providence (RI), Boston (MA), and New York (NY). The Atlantic coastal area of Rhode Island experiences all four seasons. The temperature changes from an average high of 81°F (27°C) in July and August to 37°F (3°C) in January and February, with occasional snowfall from December to March. In the fall (September through November) and spring (April through June), temperatures are mild, averaging 60°F (16°C).

Education

U.S. News & World Report has ranked RWU among the top ten best Northern comprehensive colleges. The University is accredited by the New England Association of Schools and Colleges (NEASC). The AACSB-accredited Gabelli School of Business is ranked among the top 10 percent of business schools worldwide.

As a leading comprehensive university, RWU is dedicated to challenging students with academic programs that merge the traditional with the innovative, while focusing on global studies. Students can choose from more than thirty-five liberal arts and science majors or professional programs, including architecture, business, education, engineering, justice studies, and law. RWU is a midsized university with an average class size of 21 students. Students receive personal attention from faculty members, all of whom are distinguished in their fields and dedicated to research and teaching. Students have access to the latest resources, including media-equipped classrooms, two state-of-the-art libraries, an advanced computer network, and a well-developed Academic Support Center.

Campus Life

On a peninsula that extends between Mount Hope Bay and Narragansett Bay, this scenic location is a safe and ideal setting for students from across the U.S. and around the world. RWU offers a diverse environment, where students come to learn and share ideas, cultures, and experiences. In addition to nurturing a student's mind, RWU also helps to promote a healthy lifestyle by offering students the opportunity to participate in several sports, eat healthy foods, and exercise at the state-of-the-art recreation center, which includes an indoor heated Olympic-style swimming pool, weight-lifting and cardio room, squash courts, a Jacuzzi, and a sauna. In addition to more than seventy different student clubs and organizations, students also have the opportunity to participate in a variety of NCAA Division III athletic teams, intramural teams, and club teams.

For International Students

Several developments in the international arena at RWU include the Initiative to Educate Afghan Women and the inauguration of the Phi Beta Delta, an honor society dedicated to scholarly achievement in international education.

RWU welcomes international students and is dedicated to providing a safe, nurturing environment. The Intercultural Center, dedicated to serving the needs of international students, encompasses all aspects of international student life at RWU, including personal and academic adjustment to living and studying in the U.S., immigration advising, tax preparation, and social programming. Intercultural Center staff members continuously strive to bring international students together and to promote cultural awareness among the members of the University community.

RWU offers the RWU ESL Bridge Program and intensive English language program at the ELS Language Center for those who qualify. Students with a TOEFL score equal to or greater than 550 (paper-based) or 213 (computer-based) can be admitted directly into the undergraduate program.

RWU offers qualified and selected international students merit-based scholarships ranging from $10,000 to $16,000 per year.

Roosevelt University

- Contact:
  Rubee Li Fuller
  Director, Office of International Programs
  Roosevelt University
  430 South Michigan Avenue
  Chicago, IL 60605
  Phone: 312-341-3531
  Fax: 312-341-6377
  E-mail: internat@roosevelt.edu
- Private nondenominational, university, coed
- Urban setting
- Enrollment: 7,400
- Student-faculty ratio: 16:1
- 2006–07 Tuition and fees: $15,314

- 2006–07 Room and board: $8200
- International students: 4% (2005)
- Countries represented: 65 (2005)
- International students applied: 345 (2005)
- International students accepted: 156 (2005)
- International students enrolled: 90 (2005)
- Admissions tests:
  - TOEFL: Not required with proof of English proficiency
  - SAT and ACT: Not required
- Application deadline: Fall, 6/1; spring, 10/1
- On-campus housing: Available
- Summer housing: Available

Area and Climate

Roosevelt University has two full-service campuses. The Chicago campus is located in the National Historic Landmark Auditorium Building, designed by Adler & Sullivan in 1890. The second campus is in suburban Schaumburg, approximately 30 miles (48 kilometers) northwest of Chicago. The metropolitan city of Chicago experiences seasonal temperature fluctuations from 14°F (-10°C) to 95°F (35°C). Its 7 million inhabitants have access to an extraordinary range of museums, galleries, theaters, orchestras, and cuisine of the highest caliber, all accessible by excellent public transportation systems. Many venues are within walking distance of the Chicago campus.

Education

The mission of the University, founded in 1945, is to provide equal educational opportunities to students of all backgrounds who are able to benefit from higher education. Based on this founding ideal, Roosevelt provides access to higher education to a diverse student population and actively seeks out underserved populations. The faculty and administration of the University recognize a responsibility to serve as a major educational and cultural resource to the citizens of a metropolitan society. Through teaching and advising, Roosevelt fulfills its commitment to the individual learner's personal and intellectual growth. The academic calendar includes fall and spring semesters, with multiple summer sessions also available. A number of partial scholarships are available to qualified students, especially in the fields of music and theater. Roosevelt University offers four-year bachelor's degrees, two-year master's degrees, and two doctoral programs. The five colleges offer fifty undergraduate and forty graduate degrees. Business, computer science, hospitality management, music, psychology, and other liberal arts disciplines currently have the highest enrollments. Students benefit from small class sizes. Roosevelt University's library has access to ILLINET Online in addition to linkages to other relevant databases.

Campus Life

Students at Roosevelt University represent a wide range of age groups and ethnic and religious backgrounds and enjoy two on-campus living opportunities. University Center, a newly constructed 18-story, state-of-the-art, multi-university residence hall is only one block from the Roosevelt University Auditorium Building. Located in the heart of Chicago's South Loop, the hall includes a roof-top garden; full dining services; music, art, and meeting rooms; and a fitness center. University Center houses students from Roosevelt, DePaul University, and Columbia College Chicago, providing a diverse community of fellow learners. It is located in an exciting neighborhood, teeming with cultural and artistic entertainments. The 17-story Herman Crown Center (HCC), located right next to the Auditorium Building, has only thirteen rooms on each floor. Together with full dining services, the fully furnished, double- and single-occupancy rooms make residence life exclusive and hospitable. HCC contains the Marvin Moss Student Center (a free recreational facility complete with fitness center, game room, basketball courts, and locker rooms); a bookstore; multiple computer labs; a community TV room; and the offices of Residence Life, Student Activities, and International Programs. The on-campus O'Malley Theater, historic Ganz Hall, and the University-based Chicago College of Performing Arts provide forums for plays, concerts, and recitals. Roosevelt University's active student body is involved in the international Student Union; Student Senate; the University newspaper, *The Torch*; and additional on-site student clubs.

For International Students

The Office of International Programs consists of 4 full-time staff members who provide individual and group advising regarding U.S. immigration regulations and assistance with cross-cultural concerns. Students participate in a required orientation program designed to facilitate adjustment to Roosevelt and life in the United States. Students who can prove their proficiency in English are not required to submit TOEFL scores; details are available at http://www.roosevelt.edu/admission/int/admiss.edu. Roosevelt offers a comprehensive English Language Program to prepare students for successful study. On-campus housing and student activities provide international students with the opportunity to fully experience college life in the U.S. Many students participate in the International Student Union or other clubs of particular interest to international students.

Sacred Heart University

- **Contact:**
    Karen N. Guastelle
    Dean of Undergraduate Admissions
    Sacred Heart University
    Fairfield, CT 06825
    Phone: 203-371-7880
    Fax: 203-365-7607
- **Private, Catholic, coed**
- **Suburban setting**
- **Enrollment: 3,100**
- **Student-faculty ratio: 12:1**
- **2006–07 Tuition and fees: $23,750**
- **2006–07 Room and board: $9694**

- **International students: 4%**
- **Countries represented: 48**
- **International students applied: 70**
- **International students accepted: 40**
- **International students enrolled: 25**
- **Admissions tests:**
    - **TOEFL: Required (min. score 550 paper-based)**
    - **SAT or ACT: Required**
- **Application deadline: Rolling**
- **On-campus housing: Guaranteed**
- **Summer housing: Available**

Area and Climate

Sacred Heart University in Fairfield, Connecticut, is located in the northeastern United States, 2½ hours from Boston and 1 hour from New York City. The 56-acre (23-hectare) suburban campus is bordered by a thirty-six-hole golf course. Connecticut is one of the seven states recognized as New England. The region is known for its four seasons. The campus is readily accessible by plane, train, or automobile. The nearest major airport is John F. Kennedy Airport in New York City. The region features major shopping malls, entertainment centers, restaurants, and museums close to campus.

Education

The University was founded in 1963. It offers bachelor's and master's degrees in thirty-one different academic programs in the fields of health sciences, arts and sciences, business, and education. Popular programs include biology, business, computer science, education, physical therapy, and psychology. Students can take accelerated graduate courses to achieve both bachelor's and master's degrees in business, chemistry, computer science, education, occupational therapy, physical therapy, or religious studies. A work experience to supplement classroom study is a critical component of the University's educational philosophy. The campus is located near numerous American corporations and health-care agencies as well as public and private organizations that offer students opportunities for internships. In addition, the University was one of the first Catholic colleges to introduce a Student Mobile Computing Program, providing new first-year students with a Dell notebook computer within the University's wireless campus. Classroom study, library research, e-mail, and international network access are built into the curriculum,

guaranteeing that students are technologically literate before they graduate. The University offers a comprehensive Learning Center to assist students with their classwork. With a 12:1 student-faculty ratio, students receive personal attention in and out of the classroom.

Campus Life

The undergraduate student body represents thirty-four states and forty-eight countries. The population is equally divided between men and women. Seventy-two percent of the undergraduate student body lives in University residence halls. The University has built ten new residence halls on campus in the last ten years. Four apartment-style residence halls are operated within a short distance of campus. Three new residence halls will open in fall 2004. The University sponsors eighty-eight different clubs and organizations, including the International Students Club. The club sponsors trips to New York City, international coffee houses, and an annual gala dinner and dance on campus. The University features thirty-two NCAA Division I men's and women's varsity athletic teams in baseball, basketball, bowling, crew, cross-country, equestrian events, fencing, field hockey, football, golf, lacrosse, soccer, softball, swimming, tennis, track and field (indoor and outdoor), volleyball, and wrestling. A $17-million health and recreation complex, which houses four multipurpose basketball courts, a three-lane running track, and a dedicated fitness center is available for all students. This building also houses a faculty-operated physical therapy clinic, one of only a few such facilities nationwide.

For International Students

International student orientation is held just before the start of classes in September each year. The comprehensive English as a Second Language Program is offered for credit during the academic year; an intensive program is offered during the summer.

St. Ambrose University

- **Contact:**
  International Student Services
  St. Ambrose University
  518 West Locust Street
  Davenport, IA 52803
  Phone: 563-333-6309
  Fax: 563-333-6256
  E-mail: global@sau.edu
- Private, Roman Catholic, comprehensive, coed
- Urban setting
- Enrollment: 3,780
- Student-faculty ratio: 15:1
- 2006–07 Tuition and fees: $19,460
- 2006–07 Room and board: $7525

- **International students: 1%**
- **Countries represented: 22**
- **International students applied: 40**
- **International students accepted: 12**
- **International students enrolled: 11**
- **Admissions tests:**
  - TOEFL: Required (paper-based min. score 500; computer-based min. score 173; Internet-based min. score 61)
  - SAT and ACT: Accepted
- **Application deadline: Rolling**
- **On-campus housing: Available**
- **Summer housing: Available**

Area and Climate

St. Ambrose University is located on 11 acres (4.5 hectares) in a residential neighborhood of Davenport, Iowa, which is part of a group of cities known as the Quad Cities (total population of 400,000). It is situated 183 miles (294 kilometers) west of Chicago, Illinois, and is easily reached via the Quad City International Airport in Moline, Illinois. Located on the banks of the Mississippi River, the Quad Cities offer a variety of cultural and entertainment activities, such as blues and jazz music festivals, the Quad-City Symphony, Figge Art Museum, professional athletic teams, and walking and biking trails. Davenport has four distinct seasons. February's average low temperature is 16°F (-9°C), and the average annual snowfall is 35 inches (89 centimeters). August's average high temperature is 84°F (29°C).

Education

St. Ambrose is a coeducational liberal arts university where students develop intellectually, spiritually, ethically, socially, artistically, and physically to enrich their own lives and the lives of others. St. Ambrose is small enough to provide students with individual assistance when they want it but large enough to allow for individual freedom. Students can choose from more than fifty-five undergraduate majors and professional programs, twelve master's degrees, and two doctoral degrees. Undergraduate programs include accounting, art and graphic design, astronomy, biology, business and marketing, chemistry, communications, computer science, criminal justice, economics, education, English, history, industrial engineering, journalism, kinesiology, languages, management science, mathematics, music, nursing, occupational therapy, philosophy, physics, political science, psychology, public administration, sociology, theater, and theology.

Students are assigned academic advisers and are encouraged to interact with faculty members outside the classroom.

Some curricular learning takes place outside the classroom in the form of internships. To support students in reaching their educational goals, free tutoring and assistance with writing papers are offered in the Student Success Center.

Campus Life

With more than 3,700 students, St. Ambrose prides itself on creating a caring and friendly community where individual attention is given to every student.

On-campus housing facilities include traditional residence halls, apartment-style town houses, and two suite-style residence halls. Affordable and convenient living accommodations are available for those who prefer to live off campus. O'Keefe Library provides students with abundant, comfortable study areas. Students have free access to numerous computer labs, in addition to recreational facilities that include a gym, indoor pool, and weight room. The Galvin Fine Arts Center hosts a season series of plays, live performances, and concerts, which are free to students. In 2005, the Rogalski Student Center was completed. It houses the campus post office and health-care services and offers dining, recreation, and programming facilities. Students can get involved in campus TV, radio, and newspapers or the more than forty-five student organizations.

For International Students

International Student Services was established to provide specialized support to international students. This office helps students with immigration compliance, the application process, and orientation to the U.S. and campus cultures. The international student adviser advocates for international students and assists them when dealing with other campus offices. To encourage and support international initiatives, St. Ambrose University sponsors an international organization called BeeGlobal that hosts social and cultural activities. In the admission process, all international students are considered for academic, athletic, and fine arts scholarships that are available to qualified international students.

Saint Anselm College

- **Contact:**
  Nancy Griffin
  Dean of Admission
  Saint Anselm College
  Manchester, NH 03102
  Phone: 603-641-7500
  Fax: 603-641-7550
- **Private, Catholic, coed**
- **Suburban setting**
- **Enrollment: 1,900**
- **Student-faculty ratio: 13:1**
- **2006–07 Tuition and fees: $25,430**

- **2006–07 Room and board: $9620**
- **International students: 3%**
- **Countries represented: 28**
- **Admissions tests:**
  - **TOEFL (paper-based min. score 550; computer-based min. score 250)**
  - **SAT: Recommended**
  - **ACT: Recommended**
- **Application deadline: 2/1**
- **On-campus housing: Guaranteed**
- **Summer housing: Not available**

Area and Climate

Saint Anselm College is located just 2 miles (3 kilometers) from downtown Manchester, the largest city in the three northern New England states. It has a reputation as one of the most attractive campuses in New England. Its harmonious blend of traditional and modern facilities, surrounded by the natural beauty of the New Hampshire countryside, creates a distinctive environment for learning and growth. Approximately 1 hour from Boston and 4 hours from New York City, Saint Anselm attracts students for its accessibility to a wide array of attractions: the excitement and culture found in both Manchester and Boston; skiing and hiking in some of the finest mountains in the East; the beaches of the Atlantic; and the spectacular beauty of southern New Hampshire. The average temperature for the area ranges from 15°F (-9°C) in January to 70°F (21°C) in July. Manchester airport is located conveniently within 10 minutes of the campus.

Education

Founded in 1889, Saint Anselm College offers a core curriculum that reaffirms the importance of liberal arts as the best way to prepare graduates for a life of vision, moral commitment, and bold, risk-taking enterprise. The majority of students enter undecided about their majors. The sciences, economics and business, nursing, psychology, criminal justice, politics, history, and English continue to be the most popular of the thirty-one majors. The Geisel Library houses more than 215,000 volumes and maintains a collection of more than 4,000 periodical titles and 18,000 microforms. The College continues to maintain a commitment to integrating new technology into the student experience.

Campus Life

Students enjoy a rich variety of extracurricular, athletic, social, and entertainment opportunities. The campus is an ideal size for everyone to be involved, and the College is vibrant with spirit and activity, offering more than eighty campus organizations and twenty-five different club sports, intramural leagues, recreational activities, and El Club Hispanico. Included among these is "My Collage," a multicultural organization that helps to support the College's aim of promoting diversity on campus. All students are guaranteed the opportunity to live on campus in dormitories, apartments, or townhouses during their time as a student. Part of the special flavor and family spirit of Saint Anselm College comes from the presence of the Benedictine monks, who are always available as teachers, administrators, counselors, advisers, and friends.

For International Students

Saint Anselm College has recently inaugurated a support network for international students. This includes admissions counseling, new student orientation, a local host network, and academic and social mentoring. The new program features English as a second language in an innovative format that integrates international students into the general English curriculum, thus creating true exchange. Individual tutoring is available in all subjects. On-campus employment is available part-time during the academic year. A number of scholarships are available for international students.

St. John's College

- **Contact:**
  Larry Clendenin, Director of Admissions
  St. John's College
  1160 Camino Cruz Drive
  Santa Fe, NM 87505
  Phone: 505-984-6060
        800-331-5232 (toll-free)
  Fax: 505-984-6162
  E-mail: admissions@sjcsf.edu
  John Christensen, Director of Admissions
  St. John's College
  P.O. Box 2800
  Annapolis, MD 21404
  Phone: 410-626-2522
        800-727-9238 (toll-free)
  Fax: 410-269-7916
  E-mail: admissions@sjca.edu
  Web site: http://www.stjohnscollege.edu
- **Private coed**

- **Enrollment: 900**
- **Student-faculty ratio: 8:1**
- **2007–08 Tuition and fees: $36,346**
- **2007–08 Room and board: $8684**
- **International students: 1%**
- **Countries represented: 24**
- **International students applied: 15**
- **International students accepted: 8**
- **International students enrolled: 4**
- **Admissions test:**
  - **TOEFL: Required (min. score 550 PBT; 213 CBT)**
  - **SAT: Required**
  - **ACT: Not required**
- **Application deadline: 3/1 (preferred)**
- **On-campus housing: Available**
- **Summer housing: Available**

Area and Climate

The climate in Annapolis is temperate, with average daily temperatures in the fall and spring of 22°C (72°F). Winters bring periodic snowfalls and average daily temperatures of 7°C (44°F). Summers in Annapolis are hot and humid. The Santa Fe campus offers the high-desert climate of the American Southwest. Average daily temperatures in fall and spring are about 16°C (60°F) during the day and 5°C (41°F) at night. Summers are generally warm with little humidity. Both campuses enjoy four distinct seasons and the changing natural scenery they bring.

Education

St. John's College is a coeducational, private, residential liberal arts college with no religious affiliation and two campuses. The College traces its origins to King William's School, founded in Annapolis, Maryland, in 1696. The College adopted its new program, based on the great works of Western civilization, in 1937. A second campus in Santa Fe, New Mexico, opened in 1964. The curriculum is unique in American higher education. The College has no majors, no departments, and no elective courses. Instead, all students follow the same course of study, reading and discussing seminal works from the Western tradition. Students study from the classics of literature, philosophy, theology, psychology, political science, economics, history, mathematics, laboratory science, and music.

Campus Life

Each campus offers a wide range of extracurricular activities, including student government, sports, theater and music groups, fine arts, and informal study groups. Sailing, crew, sweep-oar rowing, and sculling are available in Annapolis, which is situated on the Chesapeake Bay. Students can enjoy the easy access to the historic and cultural attractions of Washington, D.C., and Baltimore. Skiing, kayaking, rock climbing, and wilderness exploration are popular in Santa Fe, which offers the natural beauty and the cultural attractions of the Southwest. Intramural sports, such as soccer and basketball, are popular on both campuses. Students may transfer between the two campuses at the end of any academic year.

For International Students

Because both St. John's campuses are small, cohesive, and supportive communities, there is no separate office for international student services. Instead, the Office of the Assistant Dean handles all aspects of student life and provides counseling and guidance on an individual basis. Each new student participants in a two-day orientation program at the time of registration. The College's Registrar acts as adviser to all international students with respect to visa requirements and related matters. Informal F-1 clubs have been formed by international students together with other students and faculty and staff members for special social events. In general, international students fit comfortably into the mainstream of campus academic and social life.

Saint Leo University

- Contact:
  Office of Admission
  Marion Hall
  Saint Leo University
  33701 State Road 52
  MC–2008 P.O. Box 6665
  Saint Leo, FL 33574-6665
  Phone: 352-588-8283
  E-mail: admission@saintleo.edu
  Web site: http://www.saintleo.edu
- Independent, Roman Catholic, comprehensive, coed
- Rural setting
- Enrollment: 1,514
- Student-faculty ratio: 16:1
- 2007–08 Tuition and fees: $16,420

- 2007–08 Room and board: $8102
- International students: 11%
- Countries represented: 45
- Admissions tests:
  - TOEFL: Required (min. score 550 PBT; 213 CBT) or IELTS (min. score 6.0)
  - SAT or ACT: Required for academic scholarships
- Application deadline: Rolling, with fall (3/1) and spring (10/1) priority deadlines
- On-campus housing: Guaranteed to those meeting deposit deadline of May 1
- Summer housing: May be available by special arrangement

Area and Climate

Saint Leo University is nestled in the rolling hills of west central Florida in a small, friendly, and safe community. The climate is temperate year-round. The University's campus is within 30 minutes of Tampa, which is known for its exciting nightlife, excellent ethnic restaurants, professional sports teams, and fine arts and concert venues. Clearwater, home to some of Florida's best beaches and outdoor recreation activities, is just 45 minutes away. Orlando, the home of Walt Disney World, Universal Studios, SeaWorld, and a whole host of other unforgettable thrills, is only 90 minutes from campus.

Education

Throughout its history, Saint Leo has provided a solid liberal arts education rooted in the 1,500-year-old tradition of Benedictine values. By reaching out to students both near and far, Saint Leo lives up to its mission to be a leading Catholic teaching university of international consequence. Saint Leo University's academic programs integrate values into a strong liberal arts foundation. Students enjoy small classes (the average class size is 18) and develop close relationships with experienced, well-qualified professors (84 percent of full-time instructional faculty members hold the terminal degree in their fields). There are more than forty undergraduate majors and specializations from which to choose, including popular and respected programs in business administration (including several specializations), criminal justice (offering both bachelor's and master's degrees), education, sport business, and international hospitality and tourism. Highly qualified students may be eligible to participate in the nationally recognized honors program.

Campus Life

The University takes pride in serving a diverse student body—students come from thirty-eight states and U.S. territories and forty five countries, with 30 percent minority representation. Campus life at Saint Leo University is fun and exciting. Students are able to take advantage of outdoor recreational activities year-round, including enjoying the golf course, lake, and Olympic-sized outdoor swimming pool on campus. Students can also participate in a variety of intramurals, and Saint Leo competes in NCAA Division II intercollegiate sports. There are more than fifty different clubs and organizations on campus, including national fraternities and sororities. Various campus organizations also sponsor movies, lectures, dances, and other special events throughout the academic year.

For International Students

Comprehensive support services are provided to international students at Saint Leo University, beginning with the required International Student Orientation. Orientation includes a detailed discussion of academic, cultural, and immigration issues, while social activities enhance the experience. This orientation dovetails into New Student Orientation, so that once the international students have gotten to know one another, they are also able to get to know new U.S. students.

The Intercultural Student Association (ISA), which is open to all students, organizes and cosponsors events throughout the year, such as the International Signature Week, which includes an international food festival; international movie nights and speakers on international topics; monthly Food for Thought trips to various ethnic restaurants; signature weeks during the year that showcase various minority groups and themes; and trips to various tourist attractions.

Saint Louis University

- **Contact:**
  International Center
  Saint Louis University
  221 North Grand Boulevard DB 149
  St. Louis, MO 63103
  Phone: 314-977-2490
  Fax: 314-977-3412
  E-mail: icadmit@slu.edu
  Web site: http://www.slu.edu/centers/
  international
- **Private, Catholic, coed**
- **Urban setting**
- **Enrollment: 11,145**
- **Student-faculty ratio: 12:1**

- **2006–07 Tuition: $26,250 (ESL tuition: $10,130)**
- **2006–07 Room and board: $10,350**
- **International students: 5%**
- **Countries represented: 88**
- **Admissions tests:**
  - **TOEFL (min. score 525 paper-based; 194 computer-based), recommended but not required**
  - **SAT and ACT: Recommended**
- **Application deadline: Fall, 10/1 to 3/1; spring, 5/1 to 9/1**
- **On-campus housing: Available**
- **Summer housing: Available**

Area and Climate

Saint Louis University is located in the heart of St. Louis, Missouri, a metropolitan area of more than 2 million people that offers a wealth of educational, cultural, social, and recreational opportunities. Temperatures range from 32°F (0°C) in the winter to 90°F (32°C) in the summer.

Education

Founded in 1818 as the second Jesuit university in the nation, Saint Louis University offers more than 2,600 courses each semester with an average class size of 22 students. The University welcomes students of all backgrounds, countries, races, and religions. There are approximately 11,145 students and 1,301 faculty members. More than eighty academic programs are offered in thirteen colleges and schools: the College of Arts and Sciences, the College of Philosophy and Letters, the College of Public Service, Parks College of Engineering and Aviation, the John Cook School of Business and Administration, the School of Social Service, the School of Law, the School for Professional Studies, the Graduate School, the School of Public Health, the School of Medicine, the School of Nursing, and the School of Allied Health Professions. The academic calendar has two semesters (fifteen weeks each), starting in late August and early January, and six- and eight-week summer sessions, both ending in late July.

English as a second language (ESL) is available to students who have been admitted into an academic program. The ESL program has been preparing students for more than thirty years. The program has three levels, from intermediate through advanced, to prepare students for full-time academic studies.

Campus Life

Saint Louis University includes students from all fifty states and eighty-five countries. The campus atmosphere is relaxed and very friendly. There are more than 100 student organizations, including a drama/theater group, student newspaper, a campus radio station, the International Student Federation, eight fraternities, four sororities, a campus film service, a campus theater, and an extensive intramural and club sports program. Recreational facilities include an 86,000-square-foot indoor Recreational Sports Center, which houses a standard 25-meter pool.

For International Students

Saint Louis University has an International Center that provides the following services: initial airport pickup, shopping trips, city tours, orientation programs, welcome reception, issuance of I-20/IAP-66, travel authorizations, immigration regulation advising and workshops, visa and passport information, international ambassadors, handbook and periodic online newsletter, and additional social and cultural activities. The International Student Federation is the largest student-run organization on campus. To look at their Web site, students should visit http://pages.slu.edu/org/isf/Site/About_ISF.html.

Saint Mary's College of California

- Contact:
  Lin Larson, Senior Assistant Director of
      Admissions
  Coordinator of International Recruitment
  Saint Mary's College
  P.O. Box 4800
  Moraga, CA 94575-4800
  Phone: 925-631-4224, 800-800-4SMC
  Fax: 925-376-7193
  E-mail: international@stmarys-ca.edu
  Web site: http://www.stmarys-ca.edu
- Private, Roman Catholic, comprehensive, coed
- Suburban setting
- Enrollment: 2,500
- Student-faculty ratio: 13:1
- 2006–07 Tuition and fees: $28,900

- 2006–07 Room and board: $10,575
- International students: 3%
- Countries represented: 40
- International students applied: 115
- International students accepted: 72
- International students enrolled: 34
- Admissions tests:
    - TOEFL: Required (paper-based min. score 525; computer-based min. score 197)
    - SAT and ACT: Not required for admission purposes
- Application deadline: Fall, 5/1; spring, 1/1; January term, 12/1
- On-campus housing: Available

Area and Climate

Saint Mary's beautiful 420-acre (170-hectare) campus is located in the rolling hills of Moraga, California, just 20 miles (32 kilometers) east of San Francisco and 12 miles (20 kilometers) from Berkeley, so it offers the dual benefits of a pastoral setting and proximity to major metropolitan centers. The climate is temperate. Temperatures range from 50°F (10°C) to 70°F (21°C) in the summer to 45°F (7°C) to 60°F (16°C) in the winter.

Education

Saint Mary's offers twenty-five outstanding degree programs and was recently ranked by *U.S. News & World Report* and *Princeton Review* as one of America's best colleges. Saint Mary's personalized education gives students the opportunity to make connections with their professors, fellow students, and chosen academic disciplines. The average class size is 20 students. The faculty members are experts in their respective fields and are absolutely dedicated to their primary role as teachers. They sincerely care about their students, which is evident in the hours they spend with them outside of class during office hours, at campus events, and, occasionally, over dinner at their homes. The collaborative classroom environment fosters shared ideas and in-depth exploration. Saint Mary's offers conditional admission for undergraduate students.

Campus Life

Saint Mary's is small enough to provide a personal education (2,500 undergraduate and 2,000 graduate students) and big enough to include many extras (NCAA Division I athletics, a diverse student body, more than 60 international students, science and technology resources, study-abroad programs, and career and graduate school services). At Saint Mary's, students become involved in a wide variety of social and extracurricular activities. The residential campus, clubs, athletic opportunities, and vibrant student body ensure that a student's free time is exciting and fun-filled. The College's size and sense of community help to create a warm and friendly atmosphere in which everyone belongs.

For International Students

The Center for International Programs helps coordinate programs and activities, assists students with matters relating to their immigration status, and provides support for international students during their stay at Saint Mary's.

Saint Mary's College does offer merit-based scholarships to international students. Freshmen must have SAT scores of 1200 or higher on the critical reading and math sections and a GPA of at least 3.7. Transfer students must have at least 30 transferable academic units with a GPA of at least 3.5. Scholarship awards require freshman students to sit for the SAT exam.

St. Mary's University of San Antonio

- **Contact:**
  Nelson Delgado
  International Admission Counselor
  St. Mary's University of San Antonio
  One Camino Santa Maria
  San Antonio, TX 78228
  Phone: 210-436-3126
         800-367-7868 (toll-free)
  Fax: 210-431-6742
  E-mail: ndelgado@stmarytx.edu
  Web site: http://www.stmarytx.edu
- Private, four-year comprehensive, coed
- Urban setting
- Enrollment: 3,904
- Student-faculty ratio: 13:1
- 2006–07 Tuition and fees: $19,334 (undergraduate, 12–18 hours, w/notebook computer)

- 2006–07 Room and board: $5740–$6100 (based on residence hall and meal plan selection)
- International students: 3%
- Countries represented: 41
- International students applied: 97
- International students accepted: 25
- International students enrolled: 16
- Admissions tests:
  - TOEFL (min. score 550 paper-based; 213 computer-based; 79 Internet-based for regular admission)
  - SAT or ACT: Recommended
- Application deadline: Rolling
- On-campus housing: Available
- Summer housing: Available

Area and Climate

St. Mary's is located in charming, historic San Antonio, Texas, the seventh largest city in the United States. San Antonio, a multicultural city, is famous for the Alamo and other Spanish colonial missions. The picturesque downtown River Walk is lined with shops and restaurants. Art museums, high-tech movie theaters, a nationally renowned zoo, and the Sea World and Fiesta Texas theme parks are other remarkable attractions.

Shaded by tall oak, pecan, and palm trees, and always blooming with flowers, the campus reflects San Antonio's natural beauty. From there, students can discover Mexico, explore the Hill Country, or sunbathe on the beaches of the Gulf of Mexico. With more than 300 sunny days a year, the average yearly temperature is 19°C (67°F).

Education

Founded by the Society of Mary in 1852, St. Mary's University, a Catholic and Marianist liberal arts institution, is a nationally recognized master's level school ranked among the top colleges in the West for best value and academic reputation by *U.S. News & World Report.*

St. Mary's offers forty-four academic programs in addition to preprofessional programs in allied health, dentistry, engineering, law, medicine, nursing, and pharmacy. The Bill Greehey School of Business prepares business leaders who learn technical content, enhance their ethical values, and develop knowledge, skills, and abilities. A student-faculty ratio of 13:1 assures personal attention from some 200 full-time faculty members, 92 percent of whom hold doctorate or terminal degrees. St. Mary's University integrates liberal arts and professional studies in each student's degree plan to develop creativity, analytical skills, and an understanding of humanity.

All St. Mary's students are issued Dell laptops to enhance their studies.

Campus Life

Service is woven into student life at St. Mary's. For 155 years, St. Mary's has been a strong force, serving the community and making a difference in the world. Students who live on campus become a part of more than just the campus community as organizations offer academic, political, cultural, social, and community service activities. Students also actively participate in sixty University-sponsored clubs and organizations or in programs such as Emerging Leaders, Intramural Athletics, and Coffee and Politics.

For International Students

Through its office of International Student Services (ISS), St. Mary's provides an array of services from assisting with visas to hosting a special orientation for new international students. ISS acts as an advocate on behalf of international students in their academic, cultural, and social lives at St. Mary's and in South Texas. St. Mary's staff will help students new to the U.S. with necessities like opening a bank account, learning where to shop and obtain health care, and how to get around San Antonio.

The Intensive English Program (IEP) offers a nine-week summer program to provide the necessary proficiency in English to pursue undergraduate or graduate studies at St. Mary's. With a focus on English for Academic Purposes (EAP), classes and individualized tutoring concentrate on listening, speaking, reading, and writing skills for 20 hours per week. Students will also be encouraged to participate in campus events and cultural excursions. IEP applicants must submit their TOEFL scores (minimum 450 PBT, 133 CBT, 45 iBT). TOEFL can be waived under certain conditions, and a minimum score of 112 on the English Language Skills (ELS) test is accepted in lieu of TOEFL results. More information about IEP is available on the Web at http://www.stmarytx.edu/intensive_english/.

St. Thomas University

- Contact:
  Christina Torres
  St. Thomas University
  16401 NW 37th Avenue
  Miami Gardens, FL 33054
  Phone: 305-628-6709
  Fax: 305-628-6591
  E-mail: cjtorres@stu.edu
  Web site: http://www.stu.edu/
- Private Catholic coed
- Suburban setting
- Enrollment: 2,600
- Student-faculty ratio: 18:1
- 2006–07 Tuition and fees: $18,950

- 2006–07 Room and board: $5910
- International students: 20%
- Countries represented: 65
- International students applied: 227
- International students accepted: 50
- International students enrolled: 33
- Admissions tests:
  - TOEFL (min. score 197)
  - SAT: Recommended
  - ACT: Recommended
- Application deadline: Rolling
- On-campus housing: Guaranteed

Area and Climate

St. Thomas University is located in suburban Miami, Florida, a vibrant metropolitan area of more than 2 million people. South Florida's pleasant climate and the open spaces and unique botanical features of the St. Thomas campus combine to create a relaxed learning environment. The location of St. Thomas offers students the advantages of a modern cosmopolitan city plus several offerings that many cities cannot offer, such as beautiful beaches, recreational areas, museums, and an assortment of natural attractions: the Florida Keys, Everglades National Park, and numerous state and county parks. Miami's Coconut Grove and South Beach are famous for their unique shops and incredible people-watching.

Education

The University was founded by the Order of the Augustinian Friars in 1961 as Biscayne College. It traces its roots to the Universidad Santo Tomas Villanueva in Havana, Cuba. In recognition of expanding graduate programs and the founding of its Law School, university status was attained in 1984. Sponsorship was passed to the Archdiocese of Miami in 1988. The mission of St. Thomas University is to teach and prepare its students in a setting where faculty members and students can work under Catholic auspices with competence, objectivity, and respect for freedom. Twenty-five undergraduate programs lead to

the bachelor's degree, while the Graduate Studies Program offers twelve master's degrees. The Juris Doctor is offered at Morley School of Law.

Campus Life

St. Thomas offers a wide range of cultural, governmental, and social activities, including more than twenty clubs and organizations. Those include Student Government Association, Resident Council, Political Action Club, and International Student Organization. St. Thomas fields intercollegiate men's varsity baseball, basketball, cross-country, golf, soccer, and tennis and women's basketball, cross-country, fast-pitch softball, soccer, and tennis. Facilities include six tennis courts, a swimming pool, fitness and weight-training equipment, two basketball courts, baseball fields, a soccer field, and softball fields. When students decide to venture off campus for excitement, they don't have to go far. The main campus of St. Thomas is just 10 miles (16 kilometers) from downtown Miami and 15 miles (24 kilometers) from Fort Lauderdale. Every imaginable activity or event, cultural or recreational, can be found on Florida's Gold Coast.

For International Students

International Student Services, administered through the Office of Student Affairs, coordinates the University's program for international students and serves as an advocate to those students. Various administrative and departmental offices, agencies of the United States, international governments, and private organizations represent the international students. St. Thomas is enriched by a large international student body, a vital commercial center, and a dynamic marketplace of ideas.

Sam Houston State University

- Contact:
  Mr. Trevor Thorn
  Undergraduate Admissions
  Box 2418
  Huntsville, TX 77341-2418

  Phone: 936-294-1584
          866-232-7528 (toll-free)
  Fax: 936-294-3758
  E-mail: admissions@shsu.edu
  Web site: http://www.shsu.edu
          http://www.shsu.edu/admissions
- Public, university, coed
- Rural setting
- Enrollment: 14,350
- Student-faculty ratio: 22:1
- 2006–07 Tuition and fees: $9942
- 2006–07 Room and board: $4960

- Countries represented: 55
- International students applied: 235 (undergraduate)
- International students accepted: 124 (undergraduate)
- International students enrolled: 47 (undergraduate)
- Admissions test:
  - TOEFL: Required (min. score 550 paper-based; 213 computer-based)
  - SAT or ACT: Required
- Application deadline: Sixty days before the semester
- On-campus housing: Available
- Summer housing: Available

Area and Climate

Sam Houston State University is located between Houston and Dallas in a small city of 35,000 residents. Although only 70 miles (113 kilometers) from downtown Houston, Huntsville is surrounded by forests, lakes, and ranch lands. The combination of students and faculty from metropolitan and local areas creates a unique community atmosphere. This warm-weather city retains its small-town friendliness while offering intellectual and cultural stimulation. Huntsville is the home and burial place of General Sam Houston, "Texas' greatest hero." It offers shopping and food in the historic, revitalized downtown area, which is the home of antique stores, specialty shops, and museums. Huntsville offers the best of both worlds and is ranked as the best small city in Texas by *Life in America's Small Cities*. Huntsville was also one of two towns in Texas with a population of 10,000 to 50,000 named a "dream town" by an online publication that rated small American cities.

Education

Founded in 1879, Sam Houston State has a long-standing tradition of personalized education. Students of all backgrounds, countries, races, and religions are welcome. The University consists of five colleges offering more than eighty undergraduate programs, more than fifty graduate programs, and four doctoral programs within the Colleges of Arts and Sciences, Business Administration, Criminal Justice, Education, and Humanities and Social Sciences.

Professors interact with students in small classes that average just 30–35 students. The University is committed to its major goal of giving students a productive, challenging, and exciting educational experience.

Campus Life

Sam Houston State University provides general computing access 24 hours a day. Students are encouraged to create their own Web pages, and they may register on the Web. Beyond academics, SHSU offers student government, career planning, tutoring and study skills, museums, live entertainment, and movies. The Student Activities Office coordinates more than 150 student organizations. The students operate a cable television station, a radio station, and a campus newspaper. Students have numerous opportunities to develop leadership and social skills. Housing choices encompass thirty-two different residence halls, including men's, women's, coed, family, academic, sorority, and apartment-style housing. The University employs its own campus police force and has a comfortable and safe environment that gives it a relaxed and friendly atmosphere.

For International Students

International students should contact the Office of International Programs (Ms. Pat Herrington; telephone: 936-294-3892; fax: 936-294-4620). A special orientation program is held for international students at the start of each semester. Students receive detailed instructions and assistance in the registration process and in immigration requirements. There is also an English Language Institute (ELI). Students should contact Lea Cornelius, Director, at 936-294-1028 for further ELI information.

San Diego State University

- Contact:
  International Student Center
  San Diego State University
  5500 Campanile Drive
  San Diego, CA 92182-5101
  Phone: 619-594-0770
  Fax: 619-594-1973
  E-mail: intl_admissions@sdsu.edu
  Web site: http://www.sdsu.edu/isc
- Public, four-year
- Urban setting
- Enrollment: 34,000
- Student-faculty ratio: 19:1
- 2006–07 Tuition and fees: $11,500
- 2006–07 Room and board: $9450 (12 months)

- International students: 4%
- Countries represented: 90
- International students applied: 2,988
- International students accepted: 1,318
- International students enrolled: 722
- Admissions tests:
    - TOEFL: Min. score 550, paper-based; 213, computer-based; 80, Internet-based
    - SAT: Required for students attending a U.S.-accredited high school
    - ACT: Not required
- Application deadline: May 1
- On-campus housing: Available
- Summer housing: Available

Area and Climate

San Diego State University (SDSU) is a leading public state university located at the southern tip of California, just north of the Mexican border. The campus is located within 10 miles (17 kilometers) of the beach and the downtown area. The San Diego Trolley, which has a transit station on the campus, enables students to travel all the way from the campus to downtown to the Mexican border. The sixth-largest city in the United States, San Diego is fondly called "America's Finest City" for its hospitality, excellent climate, and picturesque sandy beaches. San Diego has beautiful weather year-round, with an average daily temperature of 70.5°F (21.4°C).

Education

San Diego State University, founded in 1879, is the flagship campus of the California State University system. It is an academically rich urban university that provides endless opportunities for students. SDSU offers eighty-one bachelor's, seventy-eight master's, and sixteen doctoral degrees within seven colleges. The undergraduate international business program was recently ranked number 10 in the nation in U.S. News & World Report's "America's Best Colleges 2007." With more than 34,000 students, award-winning professors, top-notch research facilities, and locally thriving biotech and telecommunications industries, students have the resources to expand their knowledge and potential both inside and outside the classroom.

Campus Life

SDSU's urban, cosmopolitan campus reflects the healthy diversity of Southern California and its unique location as the gateway to Latin America and the Pacific Rim. Whether students are interested in playing NCAA or intramural sports, joining one of nearly 200 clubs and organizations, leading a community service project, running for student government office, or writing for the student newspaper, they will find something outside the classroom to round out their college experience. The campus also offers numerous recreational facilities, which include a 76,000-square-foot fitness and recreational facility featuring a weight-training room, a fitness room, exercise classes, and a rock-climbing wall. The most recent addition to the campus is the Aztec Aquaplex, with a 50-meter pool, a recreation pool, and a hydrotherapy spa.

For International Students

The International Student Center (ISC) serves as the international students' point of contact at SDSU and offers a variety of services, including assistance in applying to the University, immigration advising, cross-cultural advising, employment advising, and special events. The International Student Center offers scholarships for new undergraduate students. Details and applications can be found on the International Student Center Web site. Located on the campus is the American Language Institute (ALI), one of the most internationally renowned university-based ESL programs. TOEFL waivers are available for advanced ALI students applying to SDSU graduate degree programs.

San Francisco Art Institute

- Contact:
  Director of Admissions
  San Francisco Art Institute
  800 Chestnut Street
  San Francisco, CA 94133
  Phone: 415-749-4500
  Fax: 415-749-4592
  E-mail: admissions@sfai.edu
  Web site: http://www.sfai.edu
- Private, coed
- Urban setting
- Total enrollment: 650
- Student-faculty ratio: 5:1

- 2006–07 Tuition and fees: $27,200
- 2006–07 Room and board: $10,800
- International students: 9%
- Countries represented: 20
- International students enrolled: 59
- Admissions tests:
  - TOEFL: Required (min. score 80 Internet-based)
  - SAT and ACT: Not required
- Application deadline: Rolling
- On-campus housing: Available
- Summer housing: Not available

Area and Climate

San Francisco has a population of about 740,000. It is located on the tip of the San Francisco Peninsula, surrounded by the Pacific Ocean and San Francisco Bay. San Francisco is renowned for its steep rolling hills, an eclectic mix of architecture, a broad ethnic diversity, and its liberal cultural and political identity. The Bay Area is home to an exciting art scene that includes museums, galleries, and alternative spaces; opera; dance; traditional and experimental theater; and a wide range of music and cinema. San Francisco has a remarkably mild climate with little seasonal temperature variation. Average summer high temperatures in San Francisco are 70°F (21°C). Winters are mild, with daytime highs near 60°F (15°C).

Education

Founded in 1871, SFAI has consistently offered one of the most open, innovative, and interdisciplinary environments in higher education.

SFAI is fully accredited by the Western Association of Schools and Colleges (WASC) and by the National Association of Schools of Art and Design (NASAD). SFAI consists of two schools: the School of Studio Practice and the School of Interdisciplinary Studies. The School of Studio Practice offers B.F.A., M.F.A., and low-residency summer M.F.A. degree programs, and post-baccalaureate certificates in design+technology, film, new genres, painting, photography, printmaking, and sculpture. The School of Interdisciplinary Studies offers degree programs in history and theory of contemporary art (B.A., M.A.), urban studies (B.A., M.A.), and exhibition and museum studies (M.A.). Students at SFAI receive a broad education that informs and enhances their primary area of study, choosing electives and fulfilling curriculum requirements from both schools.

Campus Life

The campus is located on Russian Hill, overlooking San Francisco Bay, within walking distance of downtown museums and galleries. In addition to working with SFAI's esteemed full- and part-time faculty members, students are introduced to a spectrum of visiting artists and scholars. SFAI provides an extensive roster of lectures, film screenings, symposia, and panel discussions that engage students in contemporary issues and ideas. Two large student-run galleries show weekly exhibitions of student work. Among SFAI's distinguished alumni are Devendra Banhart, Karen Finley, Don Ed Hardy, Toba Khedoori, Annie Liebovitz, Paul McCarthy, Barry McGee, Jason Rhoades, Kehinde Wiley, and many others

For International Students

The U.S. Department of Homeland Security has approved SFAI for enrollment of non-immigrant students. SFAI offers a thorough orientation program that focuses on important issues facing international students. An international student adviser supports international students during the course of their studies and directs students to supportive campus services, including career services, academic advising, and English as a second language (ESL) courses. Competitive scholarships, need-based grants, and on-campus employment are available to international students.

San Francisco State University

- **Contact:**
  Patrice Mulholland
  Assistant Director
  San Francisco State University
  San Francisco, CA 94132
  Phone: 415-338-1293
  Fax: 415-338-6234
  E-mail: world@sfsu.edu
  Web site: http://www.sfsu.edu
- Public, comprehensive, coed
- Urban setting
- Enrollment: 29,000
- Student-faculty ratio: 25:1
- 2005–06 Tuition and fees: $11,280
- 2005–06 Room and board: $10,450

- **International students: 6%**
- **Countries represented: 112**
- **International students applied: 1,600**
- **International students accepted: 855**
- **Admissions tests:**
  - **TOEFL: Required (paper-based min. score 500, computer-based min. score 173; undergraduate)**
  - **SAT and ACT: Not required**
- **Application deadline: 5/1 (fall), 8/31 (spring); deadlines may be extended**
- **On-campus housing: Available**
- **Summer housing: Available**

Area and Climate

San Francisco State University (SFSU) is located in a safe residential area of the city, next to Lake Merced. SFSU is just a 20-minute streetcar ride from downtown San Francisco and less than 1 mile (1.5 kilometers) from the beach. Major ski areas and Silicon Valley are easily accessible by car, bus, or train. San Francisco is one of the world's most internationally and culturally diverse cities. SFSU's urban location affords students access to numerous employment and internship opportunities and recreational events and activities. The city experiences a temperate climate and enjoys mild weather year-round.

Education

San Francisco State University, which was founded in 1899, is one of the nation's preeminent public, urban universities. It is known for its commitment to excellent teaching, and students enjoy close contact with senior professors beginning in their freshman year. SFSU professors win international and national awards, solve community problems, and do cutting-edge research, often while working side by side with their students. The University offers choice and flexibility. Students are allowed to change their majors throughout their course of study. SFSU offers more than 210 majors leading to a bachelor's or master's degree. Three joint doctoral degrees and short-term certificate programs are also available. Two 16-week semesters are offered each school year, along with winter and summer sessions.

Campus Life

More than 200 student clubs and organizations help students explore their interests and connect with others. Fully furnished residence halls and apartments on the campus offer free cable TV hookup, telephone service, and high-speed Internet connection. On-campus housing also provides proximity to 24-hour computer labs, the library (with more than 4 million items), the Media Access Center, study and support groups, and the different departments' cultural and social events. University Park, which is directly across from the campus, offers apartments and town houses for students and families. The on-campus Student Health Center provides high-quality medical care to all students, including low-cost health insurance. The athletic facilities include an indoor pool, a weight room, tennis courts, soccer/baseball fields, and an all-weather track. SFSU sponsors sixteen varsity sports, intramural sports, and open recreation activities throughout the year.

For International Students

The Office of International Programs (OIP) serves more than 2,000 international students from more than 110 countries. The multilingual staff helps students adjust to SFSU, beginning with an intensive orientation program at the start of the semester. OIP continues to offer assistance and services to international students year-round, with a variety of workshops, fun activities, and advising appointments covering visa and immigration issues, personal/financial matters, and employment regulations. The on-campus American Language Institute (ALI) offers international students a four-level intensive English program that emphasizes university preparation and academic skills as well as TOEFL preparation. Students are encouraged to enroll in ALI before applying to SFSU if the required TOEFL score has not been obtained. ALI offers conditional letters of admission for qualified students.

Santa Monica College

- **Contact:**
    Dr. Elena M. Garate
    Dean, International Education
    Santa Monica College
    Santa Monica, CA 90405
    Phone: 310-434-4217
    Fax: 310-434-3651
    E-mail: intled@smc.edu
    Web site: http://www.smc.edu
- Public, coed
- Urban setting
- Enrollment: 27,700
- Student-faculty ratio: 40:1
- 2006–07 Tuition and fees: $5688
- 2006–07 Room and board: $9812 (est.)

- International students: 9%
- Countries represented: 105
- International students applied: 1,600
- International students accepted: 896
- International students enrolled: 2,628 (total)
- Admissions tests:
    - TOEFL (min. score 450 PBT; 133 CBT; 45–46 iBT)
    - SAT: Not required
    - ACT: Not required
- Application deadline: Rolling
- Housing: Assistance provided for homestays and shared apartments

Area and Climate

Santa Monica College (SMC) is located on a 44-acre (18-hectare) campus in a residential area of Santa Monica, a city with a population of 100,000 on the Pacific Ocean in southern California. Because of its nearness to the ocean and the Santa Monica Mountains, the city has clear air and a mild climate with Fahrenheit temperatures in the 70s (21°C–27°C) all year long. The campus is only a few minutes from the downtown shopping center, with its variety of restaurants, theaters, and art galleries. Outstanding theater, music, and museum facilities are available in Los Angeles.

Education

Santa Monica College is a two-year community college, founded in 1929. For the past five years, more students have transferred from Santa Monica to UCLA and other campuses of the University of California than from any of the 106 community colleges in California. Santa Monica College awards an Associate of Arts degree in more than sixty fields of study. The College has a new library and a learning resource center that provides media-assisted individual instruction and free tutoring. The academic calendar includes a fall semester, winter session, spring semester, and a summer session.

Campus Life

Students at Santa Monica College represent a wide range of age groups, ethnic backgrounds, and religions. The residential neighborhoods of Santa Monica make home-stays or shared apartments readily available within a short commuting distance of the campus. A student lounge, cafeteria, and bookstore are available to students, along with athletic facilities that include a swimming pool and a gymnasium with a fitness room. A theater, amphitheater, music auditorium, and art gallery provide venues for student-produced plays, symphonies, operas, and art shows. In addition, a state-of-the-art science building provides students with a strong curriculum of science courses.

For International Students

International Education at SMC provides a complete range of student services, including international admissions, registration, academic counseling, housing assistance, nonimmigration matters (F-1), study abroad, short-term programs, the Intensive ESL Program, international programs, and the office of the Dean. The International Education Center and the International Education Counseling Center at Santa Monica College consist of 11 counselors and 13 staff members who are committed to assisting international students. Before each semester and session, information seminars are held to provide information about SMC and to determine the English and math levels of international students. In addition, all new international students are required to enroll in an Orientation to Higher Education course that assists them in adjusting to campus life. Many students participate in the International Speakers' Club.

Sarah Lawrence College

- **Contact:**
  Shirley Bé
  Director of International Admission
  Sarah Lawrence College
  Bronxville, NY 10708-5999
  Phone: 914-395-2505
  Fax: 914-395-2515
  E-mail: slcadmit@slc.edu
  Web site: http://www.sarahlawrence.edu
- **Private, coed**
- **Suburban setting**
- **Enrollment: 1,391**
- **Student-faculty ratio: 6:1**
- **2007–08 Tuition and fees: $37,230**

- **2007–08 Room and board: $12,720**
- **International students: 3%**
- **Countries represented: 42**
- **International students applied: 225**
- **International students accepted: 50**
- **International students enrolled: 20**
- **Admissions tests:**
  - **TOEFL: Required (paper-based min. score 600)**
  - **SAT: Not required**
- **Application deadline: 1/1**
- **On-campus housing: Guaranteed**
- **Summer housing: Not available**

Area and Climate

Just 15 miles (24 kilometers) north of midtown Manhattan in New York City, Sarah Lawrence College offers its students both the social and cultural riches of America's major metropolis and the gracious environment of its own 40-acre (16-hectare) campus. The setting resembles a rural English village, with Tudor houses and converted mansions providing classroom and dormitory facilities. More recent buildings house the science, computer, and sports centers and offer a full complement of technologically sophisticated equipment in each area. A 60,000-square-foot visual arts center opened in fall 2004. Nearly 90 percent of the College's undergraduate students live on campus, where they enjoy the changing seasons of the northeastern United States.

Education

Sarah Lawrence College opened in 1928 and has since served as the model for individualized education. The College's distinctive pedagogy invites students to pursue diverse academic interests in depth while working toward the Bachelor of Arts degree. Seminars enroll up to 15 students, who also conduct related independent projects in regular individual conference meetings with their professors. The student-faculty ratio is 6:1, one of the lowest in the country. The exceptional faculty includes some of the country's leading intellectuals, scholars, writers, artists, and performers. The College's nationally acclaimed programs in the creative and performing arts rely on the same combination of intellect and imagination that stimulates the entire Sarah Lawrence education.

Campus Life

Sarah Lawrence draws its students from across the United States and thirty other countries. Although the student body is diverse, there are special qualities that distinguish Sarah Lawrence students. They are inventive and enthusiastic, believe learning can be a personal and passionate activity, and desire an extracurricular life that complements the freedom and vitality they find in their classes. The College is an active community, offering many opportunities for involvement in clubs, organizations, dramatic productions, literary societies, student publications, student government, and intramural athletics. There are no sororities or fraternities. The vast majority of students live on campus in shared rooms, single rooms, or small group houses. Many Sarah Lawrence students choose to spend some part of their four undergraduate years studying abroad, and the College offers its own prestigious programs at Oxford as well as in London, Paris, Florence, Catania (Sicily), and Havana, Cuba.

For International Students

Sarah Lawrence is a diverse community whose members realize the intellectual and creative benefits of international perspectives. International students have the opportunity to make their diverse backgrounds part of their formal study at the College through the independent conference work that is central to the curriculum. Since extensive reading, writing, and discussion form the foundation of the Sarah Lawrence education, the College welcomes students whose language skills in English can support higher learning. Limited need-based financial aid is available.

Savannah College of Art and Design

- Contact:
  Admission Department
  Savannah College of Art and Design
  P.O. Box 2072
  Savannah, GA 31402-2072
  Phone: 912-525-5100
         800-869-7223 (toll-free in the U.S.)
  Fax: 912-525-5986
- Private, coed
- Urban setting
- Enrollment: 8,236
- Student-faculty ratio: 16:1
- 2007–08 Tuition and fees: $24,390

- 2007–08 Room and board: $10,765
- International students: 10%
- Countries represented: More than 95
- International students applied: 1,183
- International students accepted: 569
- International students enrolled: 271
- Admissions tests:
  - TOEFL: Required
  - SAT and ACT: Recommended
- Application deadline: Rolling
- On-campus housing: Available
- Summer housing: Available

Area and Climate

The College has locations in Savannah and Atlanta, Georgia, and in Lacoste, France. The Savannah location offers a full university experience in one of the largest National Historic Landmark districts in the United States. The Atlanta facility is strictly state-of-the-art, situated in the fast-paced professional marketplace of a major metropolitan hub for business, the arts, and transportation. The Lacoste campus is nestled in a picturesque hillside setting amid a medieval village in Provence. Students take classes at any time of day or night, from anywhere in the world, through SCAD e-Learning.

Education

Named "Hottest for Studying Art" among "America's 25 Hottest Colleges" by *Kaplan/Newsweek*, the Savannah College of Art and Design is a private nonprofit institution that has locations in Atlanta and Savannah, Georgia, and in Lacoste, France. Founded in 1978, the College prepares talented students for careers in the visual and performing arts, design, the building arts, and the history of art and architecture. It emphasizes learning through individual attention in a positively oriented environment. The College offers Bachelor of Arts, Bachelor of Fine Arts, Master of Architecture, Master of Arts, Master of Fine Arts, and Master of Urban Design degrees. Accredited degree programs also are offered online through SCAD e-Learning.

Campus Life

The students at the Savannah College of Art and Design represent all fifty states and more than ninety-five different countries. This diversity creates an exciting atmosphere and encourages open exchange of ideas. Alumni are pursuing successful careers in New York, Los Angeles, Chicago, Europe, Asia, and South America and throughout the world. An annual spring highlight is the International Student Festival, where students from many countries share their cultures with the local community through their native food, clothing, customs, music, and dances. Housing is available year-round in attractive residence halls with meals provided or in apartment-style residences furnished with kitchens.

For International Students

International students receive extensive orientation and ongoing assistance through the International Student Services Office, which helps them adjust to life and education in another culture. A health clinic attends to the medical needs of students so that they may fully enjoy their educational experience. An active Intercultural Student Association involves students in many social activities, including trips and art festivals. A strong English as a Second Language Program equips students to successfully complete their education in the United States and learn new technologies designed to make them more competitive and marketable in the global marketplace.

Schiller International University

- **Contact:**
  Markus Leibrecht
  Director of Admissions
  Schiller International University
  300 East Bay Drive
  Largo, FL 33770
  Phone: 727-736-5082
         800-336-4133 (toll-free)
  Fax: 727-734-0359
  E-mail: admissions@schiller.edu
  Web site: http://www.schiller.edu
- **Private, comprehensive, coed**
- **Suburban setting**
- **Enrollment: 355 (Florida campus only)**

- **Student-faculty ratio: 16:1**
- **2006–08 Tuition and fees: $17,920 per year**
- **2006–08 Room and board: $3800 per semester**
- **International students: 70%**
- **Countries represented: 140**
- **International students enrolled: 1,200 (total)**
- **Admissions tests: Not required**
- **Application deadline: Rolling**
- **On-campus housing: Available**
- **Summer housing: Available**

Area and Climate

Schiller International University's (SIU) home campus in Florida, in the Clearwater-Tampa-St. Petersburg metropolitan area, is near the beautiful Gulf of Mexico, one of the most beautiful coastal regions in America with one of its fastest-growing economies. Famous for its mild semitropical climate, the area has a thriving hotel and tourism industry as well as the cultural and recreational facilities of three major cities within a 15-mile (24-kilometer) radius of the SIU campus. Museums of art and culture, state parks with unique nature preserves, and the unparalleled fishing, sailing, and swimming of Florida's Gulf Coast have drawn a cosmopolitan mixture of inhabitants to the area from all over the United States and the world. A bus system links the area's population.

Education

SIU was founded in 1964 and is dedicated to the encouragement and development of international understanding and cooperation through its educational program. SIU places emphasis upon professional education and the ability to communicate competently in two or more languages. The largest programs are in international business and hotel and hospitality management. Degrees are also offered in information technology, international tourism management, club management, liberal arts, international relations and diplomacy, psychology, and interdepartmental studies. SIU provides students with a highly qualified faculty with credentials from some of the most prestigious American universities. Campus facilities include limited student accommodations, a library with thousands of holdings as well as access to many library networks and computer facilities. Independent study projects are available. Some degrees are available through distance learning.

Campus Life

The student body is multinational and features a friendly atmosphere, which aids students in adjusting to a different country and culture. Students are housed in residence facilities and nearby apartments. Overall, SIU has alumni from more than 140 countries. There is an active Office of Alumni Affairs that helps SIU graduates keep in touch with each other and opens up important networking opportunities to them. Campus activities include a student government, field trips, and organized semester-break trips.

For International Students

At the beginning of every semester, the campus conducts an orientation program specially designed to assist incoming students in adjusting to life in a new country. All students for whom English is not the native language must take the English Placement Exam before enrolling for classes. SIU offers English as a Foreign Language courses on six levels for those needing to improve their English. Students may transfer to SIU's other campuses located in England, France, Germany, Switzerland, and Spain without losing any credit. Students are required to carry their own health and accident insurance. Students requiring visas should apply at least two months before the beginning of the semester for which they wish to enroll.

School of the Art Institute of Chicago

- **Contact:**
  Saskia Hofman
  Director of International Affairs
  The School of the Art Institute of Chicago
  36 South Wabash Avenue, 12th Floor
  Chicago, IL 60603

  Phone: 312-629-6830
  Fax: 312-629-6831
  E-mail: intaff@saic.edu
  Web site: http://www.saic.edu/international
- Private, comprehensive, coed
- Urban setting
- Enrollment: 2,873
- Student-faculty ratio: 11:1

- 2007–08 Tuition and fees: $30,750
- 2007–08 Room and board: $8900
- International students: 18%
- Countries represented: 42
- International students applied: 534
- International students accepted: 364
- Admissions tests:
  - TOEFL: Required (min. score 550 paper-based; 213 computer-based)
  - SAT and ACT: Not required
- Application deadline: Rolling
- On-campus housing: Available
- Summer housing: Available

Area and Climate

The School of the Art Institute of Chicago (SAIC) is located in the heart of the exciting urban setting of Chicago, the third-largest city in the United States. Culturally diverse, it is a city of neighborhoods, each with its own atmosphere, customs, and cuisine. Chicago's energy and pride have produced ninety-five institutions of higher learning, the Chicago Symphony Orchestra, fine opera and ballet companies, jazz, blues, improvisational comedy, experimental theater, and international restaurants. Lake Michigan and its beaches, parks with outdoor concerts, exhibitions and festivals, zoos, museums, and galleries are all part of the city. The climate in Chicago is variable. The temperature falls to 14°F (-10°C) in the winter and rises to around 90°F (32°C) in the summer.

Education

The Art Institute of Chicago was founded by a small group of artists in 1866 to provide an excellent education in the studio arts in conjunction with exhibition opportunities. The collections now constitute some of the finest museum holdings in the world. SAIC is one of the largest accredited independent schools of art and design in the U.S. and since 1976 has occupied its own modern facilities adjoining the museum and overlooking Grant Park and Lake Michigan. SAIC offers a broad and dynamic spectrum of undergraduate, graduate, and postbaccalaureate study, including architecture and designed objects; art and technology; art education and art therapy; art history, theory, and criticism; arts administration; exhibition studies; fashion design; fiber and materials study; film, video, and new media; historic preservation and interior architecture; painting and drawing; performance; photography; printmedia; sculptural practices; sculpture; sound; visual and critical studies; visual communication; and writing. A comprehensive program in liberal arts emphasizes the pivotal role that humanities, mathematics, and sciences play in artists' development. SAIC also serves as a national resource for issues related to the position and importance of the arts in society.

Campus Life

Chicago offers a wide variety of housing choices to serve the diverse needs of students at SAIC. Many students spend their first few years living in one of two beautiful residence halls. As residents, students can truly immerse themselves in a community of fellow artists, live right in the heart of Chicago's Loop, and enjoy conveniences they do not find in most student apartments. Both halls of residence are just minutes away from classes and have controlled building access and 24-hour security staff. The Student Life staff plans activities and programs to foster a sense of community and to support the individual and artistic development of the students. Some of these programs include faculty/student dinners, trips throughout the city using public transportation, All-School BBQ, Thanksgiving Dinner, Halloween Ball, and the annual holiday and spring art sales.

For International Students

International students make up 18 percent of SAIC's enrollment. A comprehensive orientation is provided for all international students, covering immigration issues, cross-cultural adjustment, and social activities around the campus and city. The International Affairs Office ensures that students receive individualized attention through specialized programming, workshops, and advising from the time of enrollment through graduation. Examples of annual programs include Life After F-1, Career Café, International Culture Week, and International Graduation Lunch. Intensive English language courses are available, including a summer language program. Academic Advising, Career Development, Cooperative Education, the Learning Center, and Counseling and Health Services provide international students with personal, professional, and academic support.

School of the Museum of Fine Arts, Boston

- **Contact:**
  Susan Clain
  Dean of Admissions
  School of the Museum of Fine Arts, Boston
  230 The Fenway
  Boston, MA 02115

  Phone: 617-369-3626, 800-643-6078
  Fax: 617-369-3679
  E-mail: admissions@smfa.edu
  Web site: http://www.smfa.edu
- Private, coed
- Urban setting
- Enrollment: 775 undergraduate and graduate; 650 nonmatriculated
- Student-faculty ratio: 9:1
- 2006–07 Tuition and fees: $25,280

- 2006–07 Room and board: $16,000
- International students: 9.6%
- Countries represented: 32
- International students applied: 130
- International students accepted: 118
- International students enrolled: 24
- Admissions tests:
  - **TOEFL: Required (paper-based min. score 550; computer-based min. score 213; Internet-based min. score 79)**
  - **SAT: Recommended**
  - **ACT: Not required**
- Application deadline: 2/1
- On-campus housing: Limited amount available
- Summer housing: Limited amount available

Area and Climate

The School of the Museum of Fine Arts (SMFA), Boston, is located in the city of Boston, the state capital of Massachusetts, on the northeast Atlantic coast of the United States. The city is an environment that is rich in educational, cultural, historical, and recreational resources. The climate in Boston can vary from 5°F (-15°C) in winter to 100°F (38°C) in the summer, making very lightweight as well as very warm clothing necessary.

Education

The School of the Museum of Fine Arts, Boston, or Museum School, is a division of the Museum of Fine Arts (MFA), Boston, and affiliated with Tufts University. In partnership with Tufts, the School offers the following degree programs: the Bachelor of Fine Arts, the Bachelor of Fine Arts in art education, the five-year combined-degree program (B.A./B.F.A. or B.S./B.F.A.), the Master of Fine Arts, and the Master of Arts in Teaching in art education. All students in degree programs are fully enrolled at the School of the Museum of Fine Arts and Tufts University and graduate with a degree from Tufts University. The School also offers the all-studio Diploma program and the one-year Fifth Year and Post-Baccalaureate Certificate programs.

As in an artists' colony, the Museum School's focus is on creative investigation, risk taking, and the exploration of an individual vision. A truly interdisciplinary institution, the School does not have a mandatory foundations program, nor does it have majors. Students are given the freedom to design a program of study that best suits their needs and goals. This freedom comes with strong support and guidance from faculty advisers.

Campus Life

Students at the Museum School have the city of Boston as their campus, where a short walk can span many different landscapes, including Copley Square, Fenway Park, Newbury Street, and Chinatown. The more than sixty colleges and universities in Boston make this coastal city a mecca for students. The city is devoted to the arts. Along with the Museum of Fine Arts (which is adjacent to the School) are the Isabella Stewart Gardner Museum, the newly reopened Institute of Contemporary Art, and the Photographic Resource Center. Across the Charles River in Cambridge are the List Center, which is associated with the Massachusetts Institute of Technology, and the many museums associated with Harvard University, including the Fogg Museum, the Busch-Reisinger Museum, the Sackler Museum, the Semitic Museum, the Carpenter Center, and the Harvard University Museum. Boston also has a lively gallery scene, with spaces ranging from the traditional to the most avant-garde.

For International Students

International student advising is offered through the Office of Student Affairs. In addition, students are tutored in specific areas that pertain to language that is essential to communication within an artistic community. For those students needing additional help, Boston has numerous reputable programs for study of the English language, including an ELS Language Center located adjacent to the Museum School.

School of Visual Arts

- Contact:
  Office of Admissions
  School of Visual Arts
  209 East 23rd Street
  New York, NY 10010
  Phone: 212-592-2100
  Fax: 212-592-2116
  E-mail: admissions@sva.edu
  Web site: http://www.sva.edu
- Private, coed
- Urban setting
- Enrollment: 3,003 full-time undergraduate
- Student-faculty ratio: 9:1
- 2006–07 Tuition and fees: $22,080
- 2006–07 Room and board: $8100–$10,800

- International students: 11%
- Countries represented: 40
- International students applied: 343
- International students accepted: 175
- International students enrolled: 105
- Admissions tests:
  - TOEFL: Required (min. score 79 Internet-based)
  - SAT and ACT: Required
- Application deadline: Rolling admission; February 1 for scholarship; May 1 for fall semester; October 1 for spring semester
- On-campus housing: Available but not guaranteed
- Summer housing: Available

Area and Climate

The School of Visual Arts (SVA), New York City, offers students the opportunity to become involved in one of America's largest and most vibrant cities, the art capital of the world. The city is rich with visual arts culture that is reflected virtually everywhere—from the world's foremost museums, to the Chelsea and SoHo galleries, to the many well-known design firms and advertising agencies, to the innovative people who work, study, reside in, and are New York.

Education

Undergraduate degree programs include advertising, animation, cartooning, computer art, film and video, fine arts, graphic design, illustration, interior design, photography, and visual and critical studies. The four-year curriculum remains responsive to the needs and demands of the industry and is designed to allow students greater freedom of choice in electives and requirements with each succeeding year. The first year of each program, a foundation year, ensures the mastery of basic skills in each chosen discipline, as well as in art history and writing. After the first year, students focus on specific areas of concentration and, under the guidance of academic advisers and faculty members, pursue their own individual goals. The College provides students with studios that continually mirror the standards of the professional art world.

Campus Life

Students are encouraged to take advantage of all New York City has to offer through a diverse range of campus life–sponsored activities, such as theatrical performances, poetry readings, concerts, and gallery openings. Students may also choose to join a number of different clubs and organizations on campus. SVA students enjoy a range of living alternatives, from campus dormitories to shared apartments to independent living.

For International Students

Applicants who meet the academic and creative requirements for admission to SVA and have a good grasp on English but do not yet meet the English proficiency requirements for undergraduate study may qualify for the ESL/Studio Program. This is a unique three-semester program that offers extensive English as a second language (ESL) study and studio course work.

Seton Hall University

- **Contact:**
  Bryan Terry, Ph.D.
  AVP Enrollment Services
  Seton Hall University
  South Orange, NJ 07079-2680

  Phone: 800-THE-HALL (toll-free in U.S.)
  Fax: 973-275-2040
  E-mail: thehall@shu.edu
  Web site: http://www.shu.edu
- **Private, Roman Catholic, coed**
- **Suburban setting**
- **Enrollment: 5,200**

- **Student-faculty ratio: 15:1**
- **2006–07 Tuition and fees: $25,529**
- **2006–07 Room and board: $9358**
- **International students: 3%**
- **Countries represented: 60**
- **Admissions tests:**
  - **TOEFL (min. score 550)**
  - **SAT or ACT: Required**
- **Application deadline: Rolling**
- **On-campus housing: Available**
- **Summer housing: Available**

Area and Climate

Seton Hall University is located in northeastern New Jersey, in the scenic village of South Orange, a suburban residential area with a population of 16,390. The campus covers 58 acres (23 hectares) and is 14 miles (23 kilometers) from one of America's most famous cosmopolitan centers, New York City. The weather in New Jersey and along the northeast coast of the United States varies tremendously, depending on the season. During the summer (June–September) temperatures can reach 99°F (37°C) and in the winter (November–March) can drop below 5°F (–15°C). Because of the variable temperatures, students need both warm-weather and cold-weather clothing.

Education

Seton Hall University is a private, four-year, coeducational Catholic institution founded in 1856. In addition to its high-quality academic reputation, the University is distinguished by its attention to the critical, moral, ethical, and social issues. Seton Hall comprises eight schools and colleges: the College of Arts and Sciences, the Stillman School of Business, the College of Education and Human Services, the College of Nursing, the Whitehead School of Diplomacy and International Relations, the Immaculate Conception Seminary School of Theology, the School of Graduate Medical Education, and the School of Law (located in Newark). Campus facilities include an art gallery, TV and radio studios, theater-in-the-round, a modern recreation center, indoor pool and track, the Walsh Library, several computer labs, wireless technology, Trading Room, Sport Polling Center, and a new science and technology center is under construction.

Campus Life

Seton Hall has six residence halls and two off-campus apartment building, each fully staffed by resident advisers and a resident hall director. Many social events are organized within the residence halls. Most of the more than 100 student clubs and organizations meet in the University Center, which is a central meeting place. Seton Hall University has seventeen varsity sports teams that compete in the most competitive college division. Intramural and club sports are also popular activities. The University's proximity to New York City allows for social trips and internship opportunities.

For International Students

The Office of International Programs (OIP) is responsible for assisting international students with all aspects of student life at Seton Hall. Personal or academic concerns may be discussed privately. International student orientation takes place in August and is also organized by the OIP. International students who need to improve their English skills may enroll in the University's ESL Institute. Students may study ESL full-time and may qualify to obtain the I-20 form. The International Students Association strives to promote better understanding, greater friendship, and more unity among students of all nations. It also provides opportunities for educational, social, and cultural exchange among all students at Seton Hall.

Shorter College

- **Contact:**
  John Head
  Vice President of Enrollment Management
  Shorter College
  Rome, GA 30165
  Phone: 706-233-7319
          800-868-6980
  Fax: 706-233-7224
  E-mail: admissions@shorter.edu
  Web site: http://www.shorter.edu
- **Private, coed**
- **Small-town setting**
- **Enrollment: 1,048**

- **Student-faculty ratio: 13:1**
- **2005–06 Tuition and fees: $14,300**
- **2005–06 Room and board: $6600**
- **International students: 5%**
- **Countries represented: 22**
- **Admissions tests:**
  - **TOEFL (min. score 500 PBT; 173 CBT)**
  - **SAT and ACT: Accepted**
- **Application deadline: May 30**
- **On-campus housing: Guaranteed**
- **Summer housing: Available**

Area and Climate

Shorter College is located in Rome, Georgia, a community of approximately 93,000 that is located in the northwestern corner of the state. The average temperature is 72°F (22°C), with summer highs in the mid-90s (34°C to 36°C) and winter lows in the 30s (-1°C to 4°C). The area experiences occasional snowfall in the winter months and occasional spring rain. Shorter College is conveniently located within an hour's drive of the South's international city, Atlanta, Georgia. Students can easily find international flights into Hartsfield International Airport and take advantage of the hourly shuttle service to and from Rome.

Education

Shorter College was founded in 1873. Currently, Shorter is the home of 967 students, who live and work in its seventeen buildings. With state-of-the-art facilities and highly qualified faculty members, Shorter provides an exceptional educational experience for its students, who reap the benefits of an 13:1 student-teacher ratio and small class sizes. With nationally recognized, award-winning programs in all areas of the liberal arts, performing arts, sciences, and medicine, Shorter graduates continue to excel in many professional fields. Shorter offers its students a global perspective while remaining true to its mission of challenging students to grow intellectually, spiritually, and socially.

Campus Life

With organizations such as the Student Government Association, the Fitton Activities Board, and several religious, Greek, and student professional organizations on campus, Shorter provides a variety of different avenues for socializing, leading, and learning. Active involvement in student organizations greatly enhances students' experience at Shorter College. Students are encouraged to become involved with one of the three student-staffed publications, student council, and intramural and varsity-level sports. Students thrive inside Shorter's gates in an atmosphere of safety and educational, spiritual, and social support.

For International Students

Shorter College is now home to a growing international community, representing twenty-one different nations. Support services for international students are managed by the Director of Programming for Campus Globalization, who conducts programs and activities that provide information and enjoyment and assist with immigration matters before and after students arrive. On request, students receive assistance with other U.S. government agencies, such as Social Security and the Internal Revenue Service. International students must purchase the school's health insurance or provide proof of equivalent coverage. Shorter College provides a limited number of partial scholarships to international students. In addition, music and athletic scholarships are available on an audition or tryout basis.

Sierra College

- **Contact:**
  Patricia S. Efseaff
  International Students Office
  Sierra College
  5000 Rocklin Road
  Rocklin, CA 95677
  Phone: 916-789-2903
  Fax: 916-789-2922
  E-mail: internationalstudents@sierracollege.edu
  Web site: http://www.sierracollege.edu/int
- **Public, two-year**
- **Suburban setting**
- **Total enrollment: 18,000**

- **Student-faculty ratio: 25:1**
- **2005–06 Tuition and fees: $4400**
- **International students: .003%**
- **Countries represented: 45**
- **International students applied: 155**
- **International students enrolled: 217 (total)**
- **Admissions tests:**
  - **TOEFL: required (min. score 450 PBT, 133 CBT, 45 iBT) or enroll in ESL**
- **Application deadlines: Fall, 7/1; spring, 12/1**
- **On-campus housing: Available**
- **Summer housing: Available**

Area and Climate

Sierra College is located in the foothills of the beautiful Sierra Nevada Mountains of California, which is 100 miles (160 kilometers) east of San Francisco. The main campus is located in Rocklin, just minutes from Sacramento, the state capital of California. The climate is moderate, with an annual rainfall of approximately 18 inches (46 centimeters). Close to the campus, there are many recreational opportunities, with nearby golf courses, river systems, and lakes. In 1 hour by car, students can be in the beautiful Lake Tahoe region, which offers skiing, hiking, horseback riding, and boating, or can go sightseeing in San Francisco, the Napa Valley, or the northern California coast.

Education

Sierra College is a public, two-year community college founded in 1936. Sierra has a national reputation of excellence and offers more than seventy associate degrees. Certificates of Achievement are offered in a variety of technical-vocational areas. Once they are proficient in English, students may complete their first two years of university study at Sierra College and then transfer to a university for their final two years. All Sierra College students benefit from supportive services such as academic advising, career and professional preparation, tutoring, and health services. In addition, math and writing centers and computer labs are available to students. Students may begin their study during the fall or spring semesters. If the student is transferring from an American college or coming from a country where English is the primary language in its educational system, they may begin during

the summer. An excellent faculty, smaller classes, and lower tuition fees are great advantages for international students.

Campus Life

With an enrollment of around 18,000 students and a small percentage of international students, a great opportunity awaits students wishing to improve their English skills. Sierra students may participate in an active Student Government and many campus clubs, intercollegiate athletics, and intramural sports. Sports facilities include a pool, a gymnasium, a fitness/cardio room, and fields for soccer and football. There are also a theater, an art gallery, and a science museum. Sierra College is one of the few community colleges in California to have residence halls on campus. A homestay program and assistance in renting apartments are also available. For students wishing to live off campus, Sierra College has a homestay program and provides rental information.

For International Students

Sierra College offers international students a wide range of advantages, including transfer programs to other colleges and universities; a safe, friendly environment in which to study; affordable tuition rates; a variety of supportive services; and a beautiful campus location. Sierra College offers an English as a second language (ESL) program for students who wish to improve their English skills before entering regular academic studies. Enrollment in the ESL program also provides a fine opportunity for students to be admitted to Sierra College with TOEFL scores of less than 45 on the Internet-based test, 450 on the paper-based test, or 133 on the computer-based test. The International Students Office provides a variety of individualized support services, including admissions, registration, counseling, student visa information, and international student orientation.

Simmons College

- Contact:
  Simmons College
  300 The Fenway
  Boston, MA 02115
  Phone: 617-521-2051
        800-345-8468 (toll-free)
  Fax: 617-521-3190
  E-mail: ugadm@simmons.edu
  Web site: http://www.simmons.edu
- Private, women's
- Urban setting
- Enrollment: 1,938 undergraduate women
- Student-faculty ratio: 12:1
- 2006–07 Tuition and fees: $26,708

- 2006–07 Room and board: $10,710
- International students: 6%
- Countries represented: more than 40
- Admissions tests:
  - TOEFL or IELTS required if English is not applicant's first language; other English proficiency exams accepted on case-by-case basis
  - SAT or ACT: Required
- Application deadline: February 1
- On-campus housing: Available
- Summer housing: Not available

Area and Climate

Boston, Massachusetts (pop. 600,000), is situated approximately 200 miles (320km) northeast of New York City, on the Atlantic seaboard. Often called "America's best college town," Boston has more than fifty colleges and universities—attracting international students from every country in the world. Its leading industries include finance, health care, computer research and development, biotechnology, and multimedia services. Historic, charming, compact, and clean, Boston offers a good mix of culturally diverse neighborhoods that are easy to explore via foot or public transportation. Centrally located, the beautiful Simmons campus is within walking distance of many other colleges as well as shops, cafes, museums, movie theaters, parks, and public transportation. With four distinct seasons, Boston's weather ranges from hot and humid in the summer (83°F/28°C) to cold and snowy in the winter (19°F/-7°C). Autumn and spring temperatures are moderate.

Education

In 1899, Simmons College was founded to educate women so that they could "lead meaningful lives and earn independent livelihoods." Today, Simmons provides a strong liberal arts education for undergraduate women that is integrated with career preparation, interdisciplinary study, and global perspectives. Simmons offers more than 40 majors and programs, including 14 accelerated and integrated undergraduate-to-graduate degree programs. In 2006, the top five majors were psychology, nursing, biology, political science, and communications. Students fulfill an independent learning requirement—and gain professional experience—through internships, fieldwork, or research projects. Simmons offers exceptional laboratory, library, and computer facilities. Students say small classes, intellectual focus, individual attention from faculty mentors, and a collaborative environment contribute to their confidence and success. Simmons also offers renowned graduate programs for women and men, and the world's only M.B.A. designed specifically for women.

Campus Life

Simmons has more than fifty student organizations and academic liaisons—including eight NCAA Division III varsity teams, honor societies, cultural organizations, volunteer programs, a literary magazine, and more. Annual international-student events include a Boston Harbor evening cruise and a traditional New England Thanksgiving. Organizations such as the International Multicultural Student Association provide community and resources for international students, including cultural awareness programs, lectures on international issues, performances, and outings around Boston. Simmons has two dining halls with a wide range of meal options, including vegetarian and kosher. On the residence campus, nine brick residence halls enclose a private, landscaped quad. Students say they love the fact that they can easily access Boston's rich social and cultural opportunities—and then return home to a safe, quiet, comfortable campus when it's time to eat, sleep, and study.

For International Students

A special orientation program for international students takes place at the start of the fall semester. In addition to the international admission coordinator, Simmons's foreign student adviser helps students with personal, academic, employment, and visa issues. Support services include academic advising, writing and course-specific tutors, technology training, career education, and comprehensive English as a second language services. Part-time, paid campus work positions are available for international students.

Skagit Valley College

- **Contact:**
  Visakan Ganeson, B.B.A., M.B.A.
  Director, International Programs
  Skagit Valley College
  Mount Vernon, WA 98273
  Phone: 360-416-7734
  Fax: 360-416-7868
  E-mail: internationaladmissions@skagit.edu
  Web site: http://www.skagit.edu
- Public, two-year, coed
- Small-town setting
- Enrollment: 5,908
- Student-faculty ratio: 20:1
- 2006–07 Tuition and fees: $8164.80

- 2006–07 Room and board: $7086
- International students: 2%
- Countries represented: 19
- International students applied: 170
- International students accepted: 140
- International students enrolled: 98
- Admissions tests:
  - **TOEFL: required (min. score 450 PBT; 133 CBT; 45 iBT)**
  - **SAT and ACT: Not required**
- Application deadline: Rolling
- On-campus housing: Available
- Summer housing: Available

Area and Climate

Skagit Valley College, in Mount Vernon, Washington, is located in the northwest portion of Washington State between Seattle, Washington, and Vancouver, B.C., Canada. The majestic Cascade Mountains stand to the east, overlooking a fertile valley boasting a variety of agricultural crops. Running through the valley is the powerful Skagit River, flowing westward toward the beautiful San Juan Islands. World famous tulip fields blanket the valley in the spring. Flocks of Canada geese, snow geese, and trumpeter swans can be seen in the winter. Bald eagles soar overhead year-round, and great blue herons stand along the shorelines. Mount Vernon is located adjacent to the city of Burlington; they are separated only by a bridge across the Skagit River. Mount Vernon, Washington, was voted "Best Small City in America" by the *New Rating Guide to Life in America's Small Cities*. The city of Burlington has established itself as a shopper's mecca, drawing shoppers from Canada, Seattle, and beyond with several large and small mall complexes that feature many of the biggest names in retail sales. Together, both cities boast a population of approximately 35,000 and serve Skagit County, with a total population of 103,000 people.

Education

Skagit Valley College is recognized by the League of Innovation as being a Learning College Champion. The College has a deep commitment to putting learning first and providing the student with challenging and affordable educational opportunities. Skagit Valley College strives to create a learning environment that encourages collaborative learning; challenges students to think critically; promotes thinking and discussion on cultural pluralism; develops writing, math, reading, and speaking skills; develops decision-making and research skills; involves students in the natural world, culture, and the arts; and helps students put their learning into action.

Campus Life

The College has on-campus housing (apartments) located next to campus. Student apartments feature four private bedrooms, a bath, and a living/dining/kitchen area. Located within a three-minute walk of campus, the apartments (Campus View Village) is just steps away from classrooms, the gymnasium, jogging trails, and other campus services. It offers excellent value for international students who can get to know one another in a friendly, relaxed atmosphere.

For International Students

International students are welcome to join any student club or college-sponsored activity. There are more than twenty-five campus clubs in which the student can get involved and make connections with new friends. Many international students have enjoyed an active student life by joining these clubs.

A student from Indonesia said, "The faculty and staff are really concerned about student achievement."

"It's a friendly place with helpful teachers. I like the small classes too," said a student from Japan.

Another student from Japan stated, "For the first few quarters, I was just struggling and faced many high walls which I needed to get over, such as improving my writing skills. However, those struggles brought me some tips to survive the battlefield which is called 'college.'"

A student in the advanced level said, "You will be surprised with the improvements in your English and understand more about American culture and communications."

Slippery Rock University of Pennsylvania

- **Contact:**
  Pamela J. Frigot
  Slippery Rock University of Pennsylvania
  Slippery Rock, PA 16057
  Phone: 724-738-2605
  Fax: 724-738-2289
  E-mail: kelly.slogar@sru.edu
  Web site: http://www.sru.edu
- **Public coed**
- **Rural setting**
- **Enrollment: 8,200**
- **Student-faculty ratio: 19:1**
- **2006–07 Tuition and fees: $13,986**
- **2006–07 Room and board: $4998**

- **International students: 2%**
- **Countries represented: 46**
- **International students applied: 226**
- **International students accepted: 96**
- **International students enrolled: 52**
- **Admissions test:**
  - **TOEFL (min. score 500 paper-based, 173 computer-based; 61 Internet-based)**
  - **SAT and ACT: Recommended**
- **Application deadline: 4/1 (fall), 10/1 (spring)**
- **On-campus housing: Guaranteed**
- **Summer housing: Available**

Area and Climate

Slippery Rock University's expansive 250-hectare campus includes more than thirty major buildings as well as woods, streams, ponds, and wide-open spaces. The rural, quiet setting in western Pennsylvania, only 1 hour north of Pittsburgh, is ideal for study, yet close to the major eastern North American metropolitan and tourist areas, including Washington, D.C.; Niagara Falls; Toronto; and New York City. The region has four distinct seasons each year, with temperatures ranging from -18°C in January and February to 32°C in July and August.

Education

Founded in 1889, Slippery Rock University is one of fourteen state-owned institutions in the Pennsylvania State System of Higher Education. More than eighty programs are offered at the bachelor's, master's, and doctoral levels in the Colleges of Business Information and Social Sciences; Education; Health, Environment, and Science; Humanities, Fine and Performing Arts; and Graduate Studies. Programs in computers, business, and the sciences are traditionally the most popular with international students and open doors for them into premier graduate programs worldwide as well as employment in both the public and private sectors in the U.S. and at home. In addition to the challenging yet nurturing classroom environment, students are encouraged to take advantage of domestic and international internships, study-abroad oppor-

tunities in twenty-one different countries, an exceptional honors program, and state-of-the-art computer and technological facilities, including free e-mail and Internet access.

Campus Life

With students from forty states and forty different countries, campus activities are diverse and extensive. More than 100 different clubs and organizations, fifteen sports teams, and an extensive selection of concerts, lectures, movies, and special events complement the academic component on campus. The annual Internations Week and International Dinner highlight the cuisines, cultures, and talents of the international students and are traditionally the most popular events on campus each fall. On-campus housing is required for all first-year students and is also available during the summer months. New international students share this living and learning environment with American students.

For International Students

Of all the accolades and special recognitions that Slippery Rock University has received, it is most proud of its reputation as a caring and friendly university. Special full-time services provided by the International Services staff members include an extensive weeklong orientation program prior to the start of classes; advisement on academic, legal, cultural, and social issues; and publication of the international students' newsletter, *Longitudes & Latitudes*. A host family program welcoming students into American homes for meals, holidays, and sightseeing is also offered. Financial aid in the form of partial tuition waivers is available to all international students.

South Dakota State University

- **Contact:**
  Donna Raetzman, International Student
  Adviser
  International Student Affairs
  Box 2201
  Admin. Bldg. 101
  South Dakota State University
  Brookings, SD 57007-1098
  Phone: 605-688-4122
  Fax: 605-688-6540
  E-mail: sdsu_intlstud@sdstate.edu
  Web site: http://www3.sdstate.edu/
  Admissions/InternationalAdmissions
  /Index.cfm
- **Public, four-year, coed**
- **Small-town setting**
- **Enrollment: 11,377**

- **Student-faculty ratio: 16:1**
- **2006–07 Comprehensive fee: $11,516**
- **International students: 2%**
- **Countries represented: 50**
- **International students applied: 577**
- **International students accepted: 132**
- **International students enrolled: 87**
- **Admissions tests:**
  - **TOEFL: Required (min. score 500 PBT)**
  - **SAT or ACT: Not required**
- **Application deadline: Fall, 4/15; spring,8/15**
- **On-campus housing: Available**
- **Summer housing: Available**

Area and Climate

South Dakota State University (SDSU) is located in Brookings, South Dakota. This small but lively town of nearly 19,000 people is just miles from the Minnesota border and less than an hour's drive from the state's largest city, Sioux Falls. In the winter, temperatures range from –2° to 39°F (–19° to 4°C); in the summer, the temperature averages 75°F (24°C).

Education

Founded in 1881, SDSU has more than 200 majors, minors, and options of study, with more than 6,000 course offerings. It is accredited by the North Central Association of Colleges and Secondary Schools. Degrees are offered through eight colleges—the College of Agriculture and Biological Sciences, the College of Arts and Science, the College of Education and Counseling, the College of Engineering, the College of Family and Consumer Sciences, the College of General Studies, the College of Nursing, and the College of Pharmacy. The College of Engineering is accredited by the Engineering Accreditation Commission of the Accreditation Board of Engineering and Technology (EAC/ABET).

Campus Life

In addition to academics, SDSU has hundreds of activities to participate in, including academic and sports clubs, intramurals, theater, music, art, student government, student publications, multicultural events, and more. South Dakota State University is a Division I, National Collegiate Athletic Association member and offers competition in eleven sports for women and ten sports for men. The National Collegiate Athletic Association (NCAA) governs competition for both women and men. Women compete in basketball, cross-country, equestrian, golf, soccer, softball, swimming, tennis, indoor and outdoor track and field, and volleyball. Men compete in baseball, basketball, cross-country, football, golf, swimming, tennis, indoor and outdoor track and field, and wrestling.

For International Students

The Office of International Student Affairs was established in 1988. The New International Student Orientation Program introduces students to the campus and community, easing the transition to SDSU. Attendees build connections with other students, become familiar with campus resources, tour the University, meet with an academic adviser, and register for classes.

Southeast Missouri State University

- Contact:
  International Education & Services
  Southeast Missouri State University
  One University Plaza MS 2000
  Cape Girardeau, MO 63701
  Phone: 573-986-6863
  Fax: 573-986-6866
  E-mail: intadmit@semo.edu
  Web site: http://www2.semo.edu/intadmit
- Public, coed
- Small-town setting
- Enrollment: 10,477
- Student-faculty ratio: 18:1
- 2006–07 Tuition and fees: $305.30 per credit hour
- 2005–06 Room and board: $5647

- International students: 235
- Countries represented: 35
- International students applied: 450
- International students accepted: 342
- International students enrolled: 235 (total)
- Admissions tests:
  - TOEFL: Required (min. score 500 paper-based, 61 iBT, or IEP enroll) or IELTS (min. score 5.0 or IEP enroll)
  - SAT: 860 (old) or 1290 (new), optional
  - ACT: 18, recommended
- Application deadline: fall, 7/1; spring, 10/1; summer, 4/1
- On-campus housing: Guaranteed
- Summer housing: Available

Area and Climate

Cape Girardeau is approximately 120 miles (200 kilometers) south of St. Louis on the Mississippi River, the largest river in North America. Southeast draws students from across the United States and around the world, creating a variety of cultures and experiences. "Friendly" and "safe" are words that describe Southeast Missouri State University. Established more than 200 years ago, Cape Girardeau has evolved from a tiny French trading post to a thriving, culturally rich community on the world's only inland cape. The climate is moderate, with an average daily temperature of 57°F (14°C).

Education

Founded in 1873, nationally recognized Southeast Missouri State University offers a wide range of challenging programs of study. Premed, business, education, the sciences, technology, nursing, pre-engineering, computer technology, health, and the arts are included, and more than 150 programs are offered. The University is composed of five colleges and a school of polytechnic studies and is accredited by AACSB International—The Association to Advance Collegiate Schools of Business. More than 90 percent of majors offer clinical or intern experiences. The only two-time winner of the prestigious Christa McAuliffe Award for Excellence in teacher education and in science and math teaches at the University. Class sizes average 25 to 30 students, and more than 95 percent of classes are taught by full-time faculty members.

Campus Life

Southeast provides on-campus activities, including concerts, plays, movies, games, sports, and lectures. From the Chess Club to cave exploration to an active Muslim Student Association, Southeast students have many interests. From juried art shows and major theater productions to award-winning debates, music concerts, and literary magazines, Southeast provides outlets for talent. Complete exercise and workout equipment is available in the Recreation Center, a facility that has been expanded and updated to meet the needs of an increasingly active student body. A 7,000-seat events facility—the Show Me Center—brings talent from around the U.S. to Cape Girardeau. Southeast is an NCAA Division I school, which places it at the highest level of collegiate athletic competition in the United States. Athletes from Southeast not only win national championships but also go on to compete in the Olympics.

For International Students

The Office of International Education & Services provides an orientation designed to meet the needs of international students, as well as immigration counseling and special activities. The center holds yearly events in which international students share their cultures and interests with other Southeast students. The center also offers and coordinates various seminars and programs of interest. Students who need additional English skills may study in the Intensive English Program (IEP).

Southern Illinois University Carbondale

- **Contact:**
  Dr. Christine L. Svec
  International Programs and Services
  Southern Illinois University
  Carbondale, IL 62901-6831
  Phone: 618-453-2056
  Fax: 618-453-3085
  E-mail: intlinfp@siu.edu
  Web site: http://www.siuc.edu/~ips/INTLP/
  IntlDimP.html
- **Public, coed**
- **Small-town setting**
- **Enrollment: 21,003**
- **Student-faculty ratio: 17:1**
- **2007–08 Tuition and fees: $15,242 (9 mos., 12 hrs.)**

- **2007–08 Room and board: $5500 (9 mos., higher on campus)**
- **International students: 6%**
- **Countries represented: 104**
- **International students applied: 1,275**
- **International students accepted: 973**
- **International students enrolled: 402**
- **Admissions tests:**
  - TOEFL: Required (min. score 520 paper-based; 190 computer-based; 68 Internet-based)
  - SAT or ACT: Recommended for some scholarships
- **Application deadline: Rolling**
- **On-campus housing: Available**
- **Summer housing: Available**

Area and Climate

Carbondale is a friendly, small city with a population of around 27,000 located in southern Illinois. The large and beautiful rural campus is within driving distance of urban areas such as St. Louis, Missouri (96 miles/155 kilometers); Memphis, Tennessee (213 miles/343 kilometers); and Chicago, Illinois (329 miles/530 kilometers). Within minutes of campus are the Mississippi and Ohio Rivers and the spectacular 270,000-acre (109,350-hectare) Shawnee National Forest. The mid-South climate is ideal for year-round outdoor activities. Carbondale, which has been rated the best small city in Illinois, supports one large enclosed mall, several mini-malls, theaters, and restaurants. Free year-round bus service is available to students.

Education

Chartered in 1869, SIUC is nationally and internationally recognized for its instructional, research, and service programs. Carnegie-classified as a Research University-High, SIUC is one of the most comprehensive public universities in Illinois and is fully accredited. SIUC offers more than 200 undergraduate majors, specializations, and minors; sixty master's and postbaccalaureate certificates; and more than twenty-five doctoral degrees. Dual degrees are offered in several areas. All are offered through SIUC's various schools and colleges. Morris Library's total holdings number approximately 2.8 million volumes, with 43,083 current journals, including nearly 16,000 journals in electronic format that can be accessed across the campus, in residence halls, and off-campus through network authentication. Students have access to nearly 1,800 public and dedicated microcomputers plus significant indoor and outdoor wireless coverage. The faculty is dedicated to excellence in teaching and to the advancement of knowledge. Many are well-known nationally and internationally. SIUC's academic year consists of two semesters and an eight-week summer term.

Campus Life

Where can students be involved in internationally recognized research in the morning and go camping in the afternoon or study finance with a state-of-the-art trading floor in the morning and go rappelling in the afternoon? There is only one place—Southern Illinois University Carbondale. SIUC integrates scenic beauty, community, diversity, culture, research, traditions, nature, discovery, and success for students. The SIUC Student Recreation Center is easily accessible to all students and includes an Olympic-size pool, several gyms, aerobics facilities, racquetball courts, weight rooms, martial arts rooms, a climbing wall, a base camp where students may check out camping facilities, a complete indoor track, and saunas. Students enjoy swimming or boating in the lake on campus and intramural sporting activities, including a very strong soccer program. The Student Center is one of the largest in the United States without a hotel. Facilities include the bookstore, several restaurants, a bowling alley, TV lounges, and study areas. Students can also participate in one or more of more than 400 registered student organizations.

For International Students

As a result of the sixty-year history of serving international students, SIUC has developed an overall campus climate supportive of visitors and students from around the world. International students are exceptionally well served by the office of International Programs and Services (IPS). Through IPS, students begin orientation to the campus before arrival and participate in Friday afternoon coffee hour with the community, join English in Action, share their culture with local schools, join one of several international student organizations, obtain assistance with immigration issues, and obtain work referrals. IPS serves international students to help them achieve their first priority goal—a high-quality education at an outstanding U.S. university. SIUC also offers English language from beginner to advanced through its Center for English as a Second Language.

Southern Illinois University Edwardsville

- Contact:
  Todd Burrell, Director of Admissions
  Southern Illinois University Edwardsville
  Edwardsville, IL 62026
  Phone: 618-650-3705
  Fax: 618-650-5013
  E-mail: intladm@siue.edu
  Web site: http://www.siue.edu
- Public, coed
- Suburban setting
- Enrollment: 13,449
- Student-faculty ratio: 17:1
- 2006–07 Tuition and fees: $10,609 (12 hours)
- 2006–07 Room and board: $6500
- International students: 2.6%

- Countries represented: 46
- International students applied: 1,296
- International students accepted: 518
- International students enrolled: 355
- Admissions tests:
  - TOEFL: Required (min. score 550 paper-based; 213 computer-based; 80 Internet-based)
  - SAT and ACT: Recommended
  - IELTS: Required 6.5 overall band score
- Application deadlines: Fall, 6/1; spring, 10/1; summer, 3/1
- On-campus housing: Available
- Summer housing: Available

Area and Climate

Southern Illinois University Edwardsville (SIUE) is located in southwestern Illinois in the town of Edwardsville, which has a population of 21,500. Because SIUE's 2,660-acre (1,077-hectare) campus is located just a ½-hour drive from St. Louis, students have the opportunity to experience the benefits of a culturally diverse, major American city while living and studying in a friendly, small-town university community. SIUE students experience four distinct seasons, with winter temperatures averaging 32°F (0°C) and summer temperatures averaging 80°F (27°C).

Education

Established in 1957, SIUE is part of a modern, comprehensive, multicampus university and provides forty-three undergraduate programs and sixty-three graduate/professional programs. SIUE's seven academic units include Arts and Sciences, Business, Dental Medicine, Education, Engineering (includes computer science), Nursing, and Pharmacy. SIUE's facilities include a new pharmacy classroom and laboratory building and a state-of-the-art engineering building. The Career Development Center's Cooperative Education Program allows students to work for a U.S. business in a job related to their academic program. SIUE's programs, faculty, location, and affordability make it an outstanding choice for a successful academic career.

Campus Life

The SIUE campus provides a wealth of social, recreational, and educational opportunities that enhance and broaden the university experience. SIUE offers a Student Fitness Center, a beautiful campus lake and swimming pool, bike trails, theatrical productions in the on-campus theater, modern computer labs, and more than 190 student organizations, including eight international student organizations. SIUE's apartment complex includes computer labs, athletic courts, and a small grocery and restaurant. Although the on-campus apartments are within walking distance of the academic buildings, a year-round transportation service is available to the central campus as well as to surrounding communities.

For International Students

Ongoing assistance and support are provided by the Office of International Student Services (ISS), which makes every effort to ensure that each international student's experience at SIUE is enjoyable and productive. Services provided by ISS include assistance with U.S. immigration regulations and procedures, work eligibility clearance, and visa information. International Student Orientation is held the week before the start of classes. The office also provides various programs, workshops, and tours designed to ease the adjustment into a new environment. The International Hospitality Program, a community volunteer organization, provides additional support and the opportunity to interact with local families.

Southern Utah University

- **Contact: Trudy Smith**
  International Admissions
  Southern Utah University
  351 West University Boulevard
  Cedar City, UT 84720
  Phone: 435-586-7740
  Fax: 435-865-8223
  E-mail: international@suu.edu
  Web site: http://www.suu.edu/you
- **Public, comprehensive, coed**
- **Small-city setting**
- **Enrollment: 7,000**
- **Student-faculty ratio: 23:1**
- **2006–07 Tuition and fees: $10,602**

- **2006–07 Room and board: $6420**
- **International students: 60**
- **Countries represented: 40**
- **Admissions tests:**
  - **TOEFL or IELTS: Required (TOEFL min. score 500 PBT; 173 CBT; 61 iBT; IELTS min. score 5)**
  - **SAT: Optional**
- **Application deadline: Eight weeks prior to start of semester**
- **On-campus housing: Available**
- **Summer housing: Available**

Area and Climate

Southern Utah University (SUU) is located in Cedar City, Utah, in the heart of southern Utah and just a 2½-hour drive from Las Vegas, Nevada, and a 3½-hour drive from Salt Lake City, Utah, where the 2002 winter Olympics were held. Cedar City enjoys the best of the four seasons. The temperatures range from an average high of 95°F (35°C) in the summer to an average low of 35°F (2°C) in winter. Students can find many activities outside the classroom, from skiing at local resorts to playing golf at one of the region's top golf courses to exploring the magnificent vistas of nearby national parks such as Zion, Bryce Canyon, and Grand Canyon. Cedar City offers a wide variety of restaurants, shopping venues, and cultural activities. It is home to the Tony-Award-Winning Utah Shakespearean Festival, and there are concerts by orchestras and choirs and fairs and community events in addition to the variety of campus activities at SSU.

Education

One of SUU's hallmarks is academic quality. In 2004 SUU was ranked in the top ten in the nation for quality and value by *Consumer Digest*. In addition, SUU was named by Princeton Review as one of America's "Best Value Colleges" for 2007.

The achievements of SUU graduates attest to its high academic standards. In the last ten years, SUU graduates have had a 90 percent acceptance rate into accredited law schools. There has been an 86 percent acceptance rate at pharmaceutical schools. Acceptance by medical schools and dental schools averages 80 percent and 84 percent, respectively. There are 127 programs of study in a wide range of areas, including business, chemistry, computer science, performing arts, the sciences, teacher education, nursing, and engineering, to name a few. Due to the size of

the University, 83 percent of classes have fewer than 30 students, and over 50 percent of the classes have fewer than 20.

Campus Life

SUU is a friendly student-focused campus. There are over 100 clubs that students can join, including the International Student Association. In addition, the University holds a number of student activities every month, which are a great way to make new friends and have some fun. Activities range from a Mardi Gras party and movie nights to dances and performances by local bands.

Southern Utah University competes in sixteen NCAA-sanctioned sports. Students have opportunities to play on one of the many intramural or club teams, which include basketball, football, and soccer. There is also a state-of-the-art physical education building on campus with racquetball/squash courts, basketball courts, an indoor track, and an Olympic-size swimming pool.

For International Students

SUU is a culturally diverse university with 60 international students from over 40 countries. There is an English as a Second Language program housed on campus. International students are met at the airport and brought to the campus. Southern Utah University is centrally located in the United States in Cedar City, Utah. With flights coming from two International Airports (Las Vegas and Salt Lake City) getting to SUU is easy.

International students also have access to all the support systems of the University, such as the Student Success Center, which offers services that help students adjust to college life, select college courses, and identify academic and career options. The center also provides academic advisement, information and registration opportunities for a variety of tests, and free tutoring. International students have the opportunity for part-time employment on campus, and there are limited scholarships for incoming international freshmen.

South Puget Sound Community College

- **Contact:**
  International Student Services
  South Puget Sound Community College
  2011 Mottman Road SW
  Olympia, WA 98512-6292
  Phone: 360-596-5396
  Fax: 360-596-5708
  E-mail: internationalstudents@spscc.ctc.edu
  Web site: http://www.spscc.ctc.edu
- Public, two-year, coed
- Suburban setting
- Enrollment: 6,000
- Student-faculty ratio: 20:1
- 2007–08 Tuition and fees: $7950

- 2007–08 Room and board: $4500
- International students: 2%
- Countries represented: 15
- International students applied: 95
- International students accepted: 80
- Admissions tests:
  - College admission placement test; TOEFL not required
  - SAT and ACT: Not required
- Application deadline: Rolling
- Housing: Homestay
- Summer housing: Homestay

Area and Climate

South Puget Sound Community College is located minutes from downtown Olympia, the capital of Washington State, with a total population of 150,000. On the southern tip of the Puget Sound, Olympia is known for its unique blend of small-town friendliness, business and political activities, and natural beauty. It is only a short drive to Seattle, the Pacific Ocean, and the Cascade ski slopes. Set in a lush wooded area, the campus is well-kept, attractive, and secure. Olympia has a mild climate that provides for cool summers and temperate winters. Normal temperatures range from 41°F (5°C) in January to 77°F (25°C) in July.

Education

Founded in 1962, South Puget Sound Community College is one of the fastest-growing colleges in Washington State. It is a fully accredited, public, two-year college, offering a complete college transfer program (Associate of Arts and Associate of Science) as well as more than thirty vocational/technical programs (Associate of Technical Arts). A full-time ESL program is available. The College has an up-to-date library collection, a theater, a bookstore, a counseling and career center, a computer lab, and a cafeteria. Free tutoring and transfer assistance are available through the International Student Office. The academic calendar is based on the quarter (ten weeks) system, with the summer quarter being only eight weeks. Classes begin in September, January, April, and June.

Campus Life

The student population represents the community, with a wide range of age groups, ethnic backgrounds, and religions. There is an active homestay program, and apartments are available within a short commuting distance of the College. All are easily accessible by public bus service, which is free for all full-time students. Some of the College's available activities include field trips, student clubs, student government and newspaper, a gymnasium with training room, intercollegiate and intramural sports, and campus performances by comedians, musicians, and noted speakers.

For International Students

An orientation is given to provide information about the College and community. A proficiency exam is given to determine math and English placement levels of all students. The International Student Office helps students find housing and provides visa assistance and academic counseling, which includes class selection and free tutoring services. The Counseling and Career Center can help students explore career options, research four-year colleges/universities, and assist with personal issues. One of the many student clubs is the International Student Association (ISA), which brings together American and international students to share their experiences and cultures. ISA sponsors trips, social events, and community service activities. Some of the trips ISA has taken this past year are to the Olympic National Rainforest, the Cascade Mountain range (skiing), Seattle, the Oregon Coast, and Vancouver and Victoria, Canada.

State University of New York at Plattsburgh

- Contact:
    Ms. Jacqueline G. Vogl
    Director, International Student Services
    SUNY Plattsburgh
    Plattsburgh, NY 12901
    Phone: 518-564-3287
    Fax: 518-564-3292
    E-mail: iss@plattsburgh.edu
    Web site: http://www.plattsburgh.edu/
        international
- Public, comprehensive, coed
- Small-town setting
- Enrollment: 6,000
- Student-faculty ratio: 17:1
- 2007–08 Tuition and fees: $12,350

- 2007–08 Room and board: $5580
- International students: 6%
- Countries represented: 50
- International students applied: 394
- International students accepted: 253
- International students enrolled: 126
- Admissions test:
    - TOEFL (min. score 540 paper-based; 207 computer-based; 45 Internet-based)
    - SAT or ACT: Recommended
- Application deadline: Fall, 6/1; spring, 11/1
- On-campus housing: Available
- Summer housing: Available

Area and Climate

SUNY Plattsburgh enjoys a spectacular location in northern New York State between the Adirondack Mountains and Lake Champlain. The average temperature ranges from a high of 85°F (29°C) in July to a low of 16°F (-9°C) in January. Popular activities in the winter include skiing, snowboarding, and ice skating, while in spring and fall, people enjoy activities such as hiking, sailing, and swimming. The campus is located in a small city, with shopping malls, movie theaters, restaurants, and hotels all located near the campus. The University is easily reached by bus, rail, and air (with a small airport nearby and three larger airports in Montreal, Canada, and Burlington, Vermont).

Education

SUNY Plattsburgh, founded in 1889, prepares students for a wide range of professional careers by providing them with a strong foundation in the liberal arts. The University offers nearly sixty bachelor's degree programs. Biochemistry, biology, business, communication (radio and television), environmental science, hotel-restaurant-tourism management, nursing, and psychology are popular majors. The Division of Library and Information Services at Plattsburgh offers many services, including electronic databases, high-speed Internet access, e-mail, specialized software, and instruction in information and computer literacy. The library houses more than 300,000 volumes and subscribes to more than 1,400 magazines.

Campus Life

SUNY Plattsburgh has a very diverse student body that includes approximately 350 international students. There are twelve residence halls (also known as dormitories) on campus, housing about 2,900 students. On-campus housing is available to all degree-seeking students throughout the entire calendar year, including vacation periods. The campus environment is friendly, safe, and comfortable. Walking across the campus, students see both modern and traditional architecture. Among other things, these buildings house art galleries, a state-of-the-art planetarium, and a fully equipped and staffed fitness center. Academic, social, and cultural activities for students are plentiful on campus and occur seven days a week.

For International Students

When newly enrolling international students arrive for a three-day interactive orientation before beginning classes, they are introduced to many individuals on campus who can help them, including staff members in Student Health Services and the Learning Center. The staff in International Student Services is committed to supporting the academic and social well-being of each student. Students whose English-language proficiency does not allow full-time academic admission can enroll through the English Bridge Program. Furthermore, all accepted international students are considered for financial aid based on family income and resources, as well as academic achievement.

State University of New York College at Geneseo

- **Contact:**
    Mary B. Hope
    Director, Int'l Student Services
    SUNY College at Geneseo
    Geneseo, NY 14454
    Phone: 585-245-5404
    Fax: 585-245-5405
    E-mail: iss@geneseo.edu
    Web site: http://iss.geneseo.edu
- **Public, coed**
- **Small-town setting**
- **Enrollment: 5,306**
- **Student-faculty ratio: 17:1**
- **2006–07 Tuition and fees: $11,820**
- **2006–07 Room and board: $8128**

- **International students: 2%**
- **Countries represented: 30**
- **International students applied: 146**
- **International students accepted: 82**
- **International students enrolled: 41**
- **Admissions tests:**
    - **TOEFL: Required (min. score 525 PBT; 197 CBT; 71 iBT)**
    - **SAT and ACT: Not required**
- **Application deadline: Fall, 6/1; January intake, 11/1**
- **On-campus housing: Guaranteed**
- **Summer housing: Available**

Area and Climate

Founded in 1871, SUNY College at Geneseo overlooks the Genesee River Valley—one of the most beautiful regions of New York State. The village of Geneseo, a friendly community of 7,000, is located 30 miles (48 km) south of Rochester (New York's third-largest city). Rochester has major sporting events, shopping, museums, and nightspots. Geneseo has a thriving Main Street with small shops and restaurants nestled among many Victorian homes. The College's shady oak trees and ivy-covered buildings add to an idyllic atmosphere for learning. Winter temperatures normally range between 21°F and 36°F (-6°C and 2°C). Summer temperatures rise to 68°F to 77°F (20°C to 25°C). Each season provides a variety of activities, from skiing in the winter to golf and water sports in the summer.

Education

The *New York Times* describes SUNY College at Geneseo as "one of the country's most highly regarded public colleges." *Kiplinger's Personal Finance* magazine (February 2006) rates Geneseo as the best value in the United States for international students. *Kiplinger's* staff looked at more than 500 public colleges and universities and concluded Geneseo's high quality of education and its low cost made it the number one best value. Geneseo's primary mission is undergraduate education, offering bachelor's degrees with fifty-four available majors. Popular studies include accounting, business, communication, computer science, economics, international relations, premed biology, and psychology. Geneseo's emphasis on personal attention allows many students to supplement their studies by assisting in faculty research projects or with off-campus internships. Modern facilities, including a new, $55-million integrated science building, broadcast studios, computer labs, and a wireless campus network for laptop PCs support the classroom experience.

Campus Life

Geneseo is a safe, residential campus community. Students find the campus and their fellow students friendly and approachable. Students may live in corridor-style, suite-style, or town-house-style residence halls. A professional Residence Director lives in each hall. Student rooms have free access to cable TV and the Internet. More than 180 student activity clubs, nineteen intercollegiate sports for men and women, intramural sports, and strong music/theater programs provide a variety of weekly activities. A shuttle bus runs to shopping malls and movies daily, with weekend shuttles to Rochester's entertainment districts. Geneseo is 90 minutes from Niagara Falls, 3 hours from Toronto, and an 8-hour drive from New York City.

For International Students

Geneseo has a dedicated International Student Services (ISS) office and professional staff. The ISS office offers support services from prearrival planning and airport pickup to advising on legal status, travel, employment, or internships. Orientation covers cultural norms, faculty expectations, U.S. banking, and shopping. English as a second language courses in writing, speaking, and listening are offered for credit. Merit scholarships are given to outstanding students and are renewable for up to four years. Applications for admission are reviewed as soon as they become complete.

Stony Brook University, State University of New York

- **Contact:**
  International Undergraduate Admissions
  Administration 118
  Stony Brook University, SUNY
  Stony Brook, NY 11794-1901

  Phone: 631-632-6146
  Fax: 631-632-9898
  E-mail: enrollintl@stonybrook.edu
  Web site: http://www.stonybrook.edu/
  admissions
- **State-supported, university, coed**
- **Small-town setting**
- **Enrollment: 22,000**

- **Student-faculty ratio: 17:1**
- **2006–07 Tuition and fees: $11,835**
- **2006–07 Room and board: $8450**
- **International students: 4%**
- **Countries represented: 110**
- **Admissions tests:**
  - **TOEFL: Required for some**
  - **SAT: Required for some**
- **Application deadline: Fall, 4/1; spring, 10/1**
- **On-campus housing: Available**
- **Summer housing: Available**

Area and Climate

Stony Brook University is set among 1,100 wooded acres (445 hectares) on Long Island's North Shore. The town of Stony Brook is a quaint, colonial village with some forty-five specialty shops, restaurants, and services. From the campus, it's an easy bicycle ride to other picturesque villages and the harbors of the North Shore of Long Island and a short drive to spectacular Atlantic beaches, the vineyards of the North Fork, and the elegant resorts of the Hamptons. In addition, it is just a 90-minute train ride to New York City. The area has four distinct seasons. Temperatures range from 40°F to 90°F (4.5°C to 32°C) in the summer and from 0°F to 45°F (-18°C to 7°C) in the winter.

Education

The University offers 128 undergraduate majors and minors and more than 170 graduate programs. Stony Brook offers exceptional strength in the sciences, mathematics, computer science, humanities, fine arts, social sciences, engineering, marine sciences, and health professions. The major academic units of the University consist of the College of Arts and Sciences, the College of Engineering and Applied Science, the College of Business, the Marine Sciences Research Center, the School of Journalism, the School of Professional Development and Continuing Studies, and the Health Sciences Center's Schools of Basic Health Sciences and Health Technology and Management. The distinguished international faculty of 1,962 members attracts more than $150 million in external research

support, and Stony Brook is one of ten universities given a National Science Foundation recognition award for integrating research and education.

Campus Life

Stony Brook has a blend of people, activities, interest groups, and sports that takes its students' college experience far beyond the academic. The fun begins with Opening Week and is sustained throughout the year. A wide variety of lectures, seminars, concerts, exhibits, theatrical performances, movies, and sporting events are scheduled regularly throughout the academic year.

For International Students

Stony Brook offers comprehensive services and support for international students. International Services provides advisement for international students in areas such as immigration, taxes, financial problems, employment, cross-cultural issues, and other matters related to the U.S. and the U.S. system of education, including orientation and instructional programs for new and continuing students. An International Student Adviser meets with each international student during the first two weeks of classes and is available throughout the year to address any concerns that may arise. Each student is assigned an academic adviser to assist in the planning of an academic program that is consistent with his or her educational aspirations and career objectives. The Intensive English Center offers a program of courses and activities designed to meet the special needs and interests of people from other countries who want to study at universities in the United States or improve their English to meet personal and professional goals.

Suffolk University

- Contact:
  John Hamel, Director of Undergraduate
    Admission
  Suffolk University
  Boston, MA 02108
  Phone: 617-573-8460
  Fax: 617-557-1574
  E-mail: admission@suffolk.edu
  Web site: http://www.suffolk.edu
- Private, coed
- Urban setting
- Enrollment: 6,600 undergraduate and graduate
- Student-faculty ratio: 12:1
- 2006–07 Tuition and fees: $21,140
- 2006–07 Room and board: $11,700

- International students: 13%
- Countries represented: 102
- International students enrolled: 671 (Boston campus)
- Admissions tests:
  - TOEFL: Required (min. score 525 PBT; 197 CBT)
  - SAT: Required for all applicants whose first language is English
- Application deadline: 3/15, freshmen (preferred); 6/30, transfer and international students
- On-campus housing: First come, first served, based on date admission deposit is received
- Summer housing: Available

Area and Climate

Suffolk University is located in the heart of Boston, a cosmopolitan city in the northeastern United States. Known for its history and culture, Boston is a popular tourist destination, featuring world-class museums, concert halls, theaters, and shopping. Boston is known worldwide as a premier center for academics, research, and business. Suffolk's campus is in historic Beacon Hill, a secure residential neighborhood of brick homes and the grand state capitol building. Boston's public transportation system makes it easy to travel around the city. Spectacular beaches and snow-covered mountains are within driving distance of the campus. Boston and New England enjoy four distinct seasons each year—fall, winter, spring, and summer—with temperatures ranging from 60°F (16°C) to 90°F (23°C) in the warmer months and from 0°F (-18°C) to 40°F (4°C) in the colder months.

Education

Suffolk University is a comprehensive university offering a wide range of undergraduate and graduate degrees in the College of Arts and Sciences, Sawyer Business School, and Law School. The University's excellent academic programs emphasize high-quality teaching, small class size, and real-world career applications. Suffolk's faculty members are of the highest caliber. Ninety-four percent of the faculty members hold Ph.D.'s and many are practicing professionals in their fields. However, their first priority is teaching

and mentoring. The undergraduate academic program offers more than seventy majors and 1,000 courses. Suffolk was selected to the first tier of "Best Universities–Master's in the North" by *U.S. News & World Report*, as one of the "Best 361 Colleges" by the *Princeton Review*, to *Barron's Best Buys in College Education*, and, most recently, as a College of Distinction by an independent committee of high school guidance counselors and college admissions professionals.

Campus Life

Suffolk offers more than seventy-five active student clubs and organizations, a nationally ranked debate team, three student-run publications, a strong performing arts program, and numerous special events, dances, lectures, and community service activities. A variety of intercollegiate and intramural athletics for both men and women are available. Suffolk has two residence halls, a new state-of-the-art undergraduate library, and a new theater. Modern dormitory facilities provide Internet, cable, and telephone access and beautiful views of the city. The University has campuses in Boston; Madrid, Spain; and Dakar, Senegal.

For International Students

Suffolk is a diverse university. There are nearly 1,000 international students enrolled at the Boston, Madrid, and Dakar campuses. The University is committed to helping international students adjust to life in the United States. The Center for International Education assists students and advises them on immigration, administrative, and cultural adjustment issues. Special social and cultural activities are offered to all international students. Courses in English as a second language, writing, and tutoring are also offered.

Sullivan University

- **Contact:**
    Greg Cawthon
    Director of Admissions
    Sullivan University
    3101 Bardstown Road
    Louisville, KY 40205
    Phone: 502-456-6505
    Fax: 502-456-0040
    Web site: http://www.sullivan.edu
- **Private, coed**
- **Suburban setting**
- **Enrollment: 4,899**
- **Student-faculty ratio: 19:1**
- **2005–06 Tuition and fees: $13,800**

- **2005–06 Room: $4320**
- **International students: 1%**
- **Countries represented: N/A**
- **International students applied: 96**
- **International students accepted: 80**
- **International students enrolled: 80**
- **Admissions tests:**
    - **TOEFL (min. score 500 PBT; 197 CBT)**
    - **SAT and ACT: Accepted**
- **Application deadline: Rolling**
- **On-campus housing: Not available**
- **Summer housing: Guaranteed**

Area and Climate

Situated on the banks of the Ohio River, Louisville is the home of the main campus of Sullivan University. Louisville is a major city contrasting the modern with the traditional. The city enjoys a colorful history as an old river city with deep bluegrass traditions dating back to the pre–Civil War era. In recent years, Louisville has become one of the world's leading medical treatment and research centers. The city is also proud of its long-standing interest in the arts and music. As Kentucky's largest financial center, Louisville is a major transportation hub for several large corporate headquarters and attracts visitors from all over the world. It has a dynamic cultural flavor due to its dedication to local artists, exhibits, worldwide entertainment events, and attractions offered throughout the year. Louisville, with its people and many diverse opportunities, is the perfect community for Sullivan University students to study, work, and enjoy.

Education

Sullivan University has grown to be the largest independent college or university in Kentucky. The University is acclaimed as one of the most successful universities in the United States and offers students a unique opportunity to prepare for a successful career in today's professional world. Sullivan University is unique among institutions of higher education. With its innovative "career first" curriculum, students have the opportunity not only to obtain a diploma in a year or less but also to earn both an associate degree and a bachelor's degree in as little as three years after entry. They are able to accept employment as a graduate at each level. The Master of Business Administration (M.B.A.) degree, the Master of Science in Managing Information Technology (M.S.M.I.T.) degree, the Executive M.B.A. degree, the Master of Science degree in Dispute Resolution, and the dual Master of Business Administration/Master of Science in Managing Information Technology (M.B.A./M.S.M.I.T.) degree programs are offered through the graduate school.

Campus Life

From informal breaks between classes to planned school-wide special events, Sullivan University offers students a positive social experience both on and off campus. A favorite event among students is the annual fall cruise aboard the historic *Belle of Louisville*. This excursion, in the grand riverboat tradition, is the perfect way to meet new classmates. Picnic-style food, music, and dancing are all part of this fun cruise on the Ohio River. Students take advantage of the popular camping and ski areas in southern Indiana and northern Kentucky. Special group trips give students the opportunity to socialize while enjoying the benefits of fun and exciting extracurricular activities. Throughout the year, students participate in a variety of intramural sports such as coed softball, volleyball, bowling, and soccer. Information regarding intramural sports can be obtained through the Student Services Department.

For International Students

Sullivan University encourages international understanding through intercultural exchange derived from the admission of qualified international students from countries throughout the world. Applications received from international students are reviewed on a competitive basis. Fulfillment of the minimum requirements does not guarantee admission to the University. An effort is made to admit students from a variety of countries. International students readily adapt to the University's career-first curriculum.

Syracuse University

- **Contact:**
  Susan E. Donovan
  Dean of Admissions
  Syracuse University
  Syracuse, NY 13244-2130
  Phone: 315-443-3611
  Fax: 315-443-4226
- Private, independent, university, coed
- Urban setting
- Enrollment: 11,400
- Student-faculty ratio: 13:1
- 2006–07 Tuition and fees: $29,970
- 2006–07 Room and board: $10,604
- International students: 3%

- Countries represented: 106
- International students applied: 766
- International students accepted: 424
- International students enrolled: 113
- Admissions tests:
  - **TOEFL: Required** (min. score 550 paper-based; 213 computer-based; 80 Internet-based)
  - **SAT: Required**
  - **ACT: Optional**
- Application deadline: 1/1
- On-campus housing: Required for the first two years
- Summer housing: Available

Area and Climate

Syracuse University is located on a hilltop overlooking the city of Syracuse. There are 700,000 people living in the Syracuse metropolitan area, a center of business, medical, and cultural activities. The city has a symphony orchestra, an opera company, a professional theater company, museums, and very good shopping centers and restaurants. The countryside around Syracuse is quite beautiful, filled with mountains and lakes, and it is a popular vacation area. Syracuse has four distinct seasons. During the summer the temperature may go as high as 90°F (32°C). There is snow on the ground most of the winter, and temperatures are usually about 15°F (-9°C). Many students take advantage of the winter weather to ski and ice skate.

Education

Syracuse has a long tradition of educating international students and welcomes applications from them. The University has found that international students bring a fresh outlook both to the classroom and to life on campus. Syracuse is a private research university where educating students is the primary focus. There are 11,400 undergraduate students (those working toward their first degrees) and approximately 4,600 postgraduate students at Syracuse. Syracuse University is divided into nine different colleges: Architecture, Arts and Sciences, Education, Engineering and Computer Science, Human Services and Health Professions, Information Studies, Management (Business), Public Communications, and Visual and Performing Arts. There are more than 200 programs of study taught at Syracuse.

Campus Life

The Syracuse University campus is beautiful. It covers 200 acres (81 hectares) and is filled with lawns, trees, and sculptures. The campus center is a large grassy area called the Quad. The student housing offered by Syracuse is impressive in its quality and diversity. More than 65 percent of the students take advantage of it. The Schine Student Center, one block from the Quad, is the center of student activity and houses a restaurant, auditorium, bookstore, and meeting rooms and offices for student organizations. There are many student clubs at Syracuse. Some are academically oriented while others are for those with special interests. The University sponsors a very large sports program in which thousands of students participate.

For International Students

There are several offices and groups on campus to advise and assist international students. The Slutzker Center for International Services (SCIS) offers services ranging from immigration to personal counseling and a place to study. Among the many different programs offered through the SCIS are English-language conversation groups, international support groups, an American Family Dinner Program, a Fulbright Speakers Bureau, and cultural outings in the city of Syracuse. The English Language Institute helps students who must improve their language skills. The International Living Center (ILC) is a small living center for international and U.S. students.

Tennessee Tech University

- Contact:
    Charles Wilkerson, Director of International
        Student Affairs
    Derryberry Hall Room 103
    1 William L. Jones Drive
    Tennessee Tech University
    Box 5093
    Cookeville, TN 38505
    Phone: 931-372-3634
    Fax: 931-372-3674
    E-mail: cwilkerson@tntech.edu
    Web site: http://www.tntech.edu/international/
            http://www.tntech.edu/graduatestudies
            (graduate admission requirements)
- Public, four-year, coed
- Rural setting
- Enrollment: 9,733
- Student-faculty ratio: 20:1
- 2006–07 Tuition and fees: $7308 per semester

- 2006–07 Room and board: $3082 per semester
- International students: 3.2%
- Countries represented: 65
- International students applied: 250
- International students accepted: 100
- International students enrolled: 325 (total)
- Admissions tests:
    - TOEFL (paper-based min. score 500;
      computer-based min. score 173; Internet-
      based min. score 61); IELTS (min. score 5.5);
      TOEIC (min. score 580); or STEPS-EIKEN
      (min. pre–1st grade) (undergraduate)
    - SAT or ACT: Recommended
- Application deadline: Fall, 6/1; spring, 11/1;
  summer, 3/1
- On-campus housing: Available
- Summer housing: Available

Area and Climate

Although Tennessee Tech University (TTU) is located in some of Tennessee's most beautiful countryside, the campus is only a little more than an hour from three of the state's metropolitan areas—82 miles east of Nashville, 109 miles west of Knoxville, and 96 miles north of Chattanooga. The region offers placid lakes, waterfalls, quiet woodland trails, and spectacular mountain vistas. It is a place to relax and reflect, to become acquainted with the real Tennessee. Antiques, arts and crafts, festivals, golf, historic sites, shopping, symphony, theater, house boating, whitewater rafting, hunting and fishing—there is something for everyone in this scenic center of the state.

Education

Tennessee Tech is a public, coeducational, comprehensive university located in Cookeville, a town of about 25,000 residents. Tennessee Tech is known as Tennessee's technological university, but it houses seven strong academic divisions—the College of Agriculture and Human Ecology, the College of Arts and Sciences, the College of Business Administration, the College of Education, the College of Engineering, the School of Nursing, and the School of Interdisciplinary Studies and Extended Education. Tennessee Tech is ranked among the Top Public Schools in the South and among the top forty Best Universities–Master's in *U.S. News & World Report's* 2007 edition of *America's Best Colleges*. TTU was also ranked among the Top Public Schools in the South in the 2002, 2003, 2005, 2006, and 2007 college guides. The Princeton Review named TTU as a "Best Southeastern College" for the third year in a row. This year, TTU has also been named one of *America's 100 Best College Buys*. The University offers forty-four bachelor's degrees; twenty-three graduate programs, including an M.B.A., an Ed.S., and Ph.D. programs in education, engineering, and environmental sciences; and online degree programs. More than 75 percent of TTU's faculty members hold Ph.D.'s. With an enrollment of 9,733, strong faculty-student relationships are a hallmark of a TTU educational experience; more than 50 percent of the University's classes enroll 20 or fewer students. Tennessee Tech University offers students a welcoming campus, an affordable education, preparation for a successful career, and a challenging environment.

Campus Life

Home to nearly 200 clubs and organizations, including sororities, fraternities, honor societies, and religious groups, TTU provides a rich extracurricular campus experience. Its Campus Recreation staff members coordinate eleven intramural and club sports: basketball, bowling, flag football, golf, racquetball, rugby, soccer, softball, tennis, volleyball, and wrestling. TTU's Fitness Center is a free, full-service health club for students. It houses a fully equipped weight room, a 25-meter indoor pool, cardiovascular equipment, and an indoor track.

For International Students

Upon arrival at TTU, all undergraduate and graduate international students find a home in the Office of International Student Affairs (ISA). The TTU Office of International Student Affairs is the center for all international applicants. ISA is responsible for all international and permanent resident undergraduate applications. ISA also provides international students and visiting scholars with immigration services and community programming. In addition, ISA coordinates study-abroad programs for all TTU students. The ISA provides personalized admission assistance, academic and registration advising, new student orientation, visa counseling, and issuance of I-20s. Tennessee Tech University encourages the enrollment of qualified international students in suitable programs and seeks to attract students whose academic potential has already been recognized in their home countries. Students who do not meet the University's test requirements may receive conditional letters of acceptance. An international student is classified for educational purposes as a person who is a citizen or permanent resident of a country other than the United States. Tennessee Tech is authorized under federal law to enroll nonimmigrant students.

Texas Christian University

- **Contact:**
  Karen Scott
  Director of Int'l Admission
  Texas Christian University
  2800 South University Drive
  Fort Worth, TX 76129
  Phone: 817-257-7871
  Fax: 817-257-5256
  E-mail: frogworld@tcu.edu
  Web site: http://www.tcu.edu
- **Private, coed**
- **Suburban setting**
- **Enrollment: 8,865**
- **Student-faculty ratio: 14:1**
- **2006–07 Tuition and fees: $22,980**

- **2006–07 Room and board: $7414**
- **International students: 5%**
- **Countries represented: 80**
- **International students enrolled: 425**
- **Admissions tests:**
  - **TOEFL (min. score PBT 550; CBT 213; iBT 80)**
  - **SAT: Required for scholarship consideration; required of applicants in schools where English is the language of instruction**
- **Application deadline: 3/1**
- **On-campus housing: Available**
- **Summer housing: Available**

Area and Climate

Texas Christian University (TCU) is located 4 miles from downtown Fort Worth and 40 miles west of Dallas. The campus is spread over 260 beautifully landscaped acres (105 hectares) in an established residential neighborhood. Situated in a temperate climate zone, the winters are typically mild, and there is plenty of sunshine. Students find an uncommon blend of Southwestern friendliness and metropolitan culture and class in this city of 600,000 people. World-class museums, theaters, performance halls, restaurants, a booming downtown, and professional sporting events are all a short distance from the campus. A local shuttle service is available from the Dallas/Fort Worth Airport, and the city's public transportation system is offered for students to use, free of charge.

Education

Founded in 1873, TCU's mission is "to educate individuals to think and act as ethical leaders and responsible citizens in the global community." It is independent and self-governing, offering the strengths, choices, and research opportunities of a major university, balanced by the individual attention of a smaller college. TCU offers bachelor's degrees in nearly 100 areas of study, a ranked M.B.A. program, and other master's and Ph.D. degree programs. Undergraduate majors include art, biology, business, chemistry, computer science, dance, education, engineering, journalism, language, music, nursing, psychology, radio/TV/film, and theater. The University features facilities and equipment on the cutting edge of technology, renovated classrooms and labs, and newly opened academic buildings. Faculty and professional advisers assist in selecting courses, and the Writing Center helps refine writing skills. More than a third of TCU students study or participate in other programs abroad. Internships in locations such as

London and Washington, D.C., are also available. TCU works to develop the talents of each student and provides a liberal arts core that exposes students to the world around them.

Campus Life

The University encourages personal growth and leadership in both academic and extracurricular activities. Outside of class, students can lead or participate in student government, work for the school newspaper, attend concerts and other cultural events, or play on an intramural sports team. TCU competes in NCAA Division I athletics in modern facilities and sporting venues that enhance the experience for both athletes and students. Facilities and services include a new athletic center, post office, health center, counseling center, career services office, nine dining facilities, sixteen residence halls, and a student center. While TCU is related to the Christian Church (Disciples of Christ), students and faculty members come from diverse faith backgrounds, and participation in religious activities is voluntary.

For International Students

TCU has an active International Student Association and an international friendship program that introduces students to local Fort Worth families. Multicultural activities are designed to encourage U.S. and international students to interact. TCU is known for its First Year Experience, which offers an extensive orientation program and an off-campus retreat that helps students learn TCU traditions while forging lasting bonds and friendships. Once classes begin, freshmen take part in Connections, a program designed to build relationships and develop the leadership skills that help students thrive on campus. The International Student Services Office also helps new students make a successful transition to TCU through international orientation. Partial academic scholarships and financial aid are available on a competitive basis. A technologically advanced Intensive English Program is available for those with TOEFL scores below 550.

Texas State University–San Marcos

- Contact:
    Dianelle Ritter
    Head Admissions Processor for Undergraduate
        International Students
    Undergraduate Admissions
    Texas State University–San Marcos
    San Marcos, TX 78666
    Phone: 512-245-2759
    Fax: 512-245-9020
    E-mail: DR05@txstate.edu
    Web site: http://www.txstate.edu
- Public, comprehensive, coed
- Suburban setting
- Enrollment: 27,485 (fall 2006)
- Student-faculty ratio: 24:1
- 2007–08 Tuition and fees: $12,096 (fall and spring, 12 hours per semester)

- 2007–08 Room and board: $13,390 (twelve months)
- International students: 2%
- International students applied: 266
- Admissions tests:
    - TOEFL (min. score 550 PBT; 213 CBT; 78 iBT with minimum section scores of 19 on Reading, 19 on Listening, 19 on Speaking, and 18 on Writing); undergraduates only: IELTS (minimum overall band of 6.5)
- Application deadline: Fall, 6/1 (business and communication design, 3/15); spring, 10/1 (business and communication design, 10/15); summer I, 5/1 (business, 3/15); summer II, 6/15 (business, 3/15)
- On-campus housing: Available
- Summer housing: Available

Area and Climate

Centrally located in the beautiful Texas Hill Country, San Marcos is a small, friendly city with a population of 41,600. The average summer daytime temperature is 91°F (34°C), while the average winter daytime temperature is 62°F (17°C). It is less than 1-hour's drive from the two larger cities of Austin and San Antonio. Austin is the capital of Texas and San Antonio is a center of culture, tourism, and entertainment.

Education

Texas State University–San Marcos (Texas State) has been named by the *Princeton Review* as one of America's Best Value Colleges for 2007 and is ranked in the top tier of master's universities in the fifteen-state western region of the *U.S. News & World Report* ranking system. With an enrollment of more than 27,000 students, Texas State is the largest institution in the nine-member Texas State University system. The University's growth is evidenced by the construction of a new science building, a new Student Health Center, and new student housing. Established in 1899, Texas State is accredited by the Southern Association of Colleges and Schools and offers more than 100 undergraduate majors, numerous master's programs, and six Ph.D. programs. Outstanding programs include computer science, business administration, technology, manufacturing and industrial engineering, education, and health professions. The ratio of students to faculty members is 24:1. Faculty members in the fields of geography, speech communication, business, mathematics, and mass communication have been recognized as some of the best in the United States. The geography program is consistently among the largest in the U.S.

Campus Life

Texas State offers a variety of campus housing facilities with food service options to suit a variety of budgets and tastes.

Twenty-four residence halls offer single-gender and coeducational housing options. Texas State also manages three apartment complexes adjacent to the campus, which are reserved for older students, students with families, and upper-level students. There are approximately 200 student organizations in which to participate. Several of the organizations are specifically international in nature. Texas State has a recreation center, an indoor swimming pool, tennis courts, athletic fields, and a nine-hole golf course.

For International Students

Texas State strives to accommodate international students in every way possible. Transportation to the campus from the Austin-Bergstrom and San Antonio International Airports is provided for new students. New Student Orientation is provided for all undergraduate students. It is designed to prepare students for academic and social life on campus. The International Office assists new students in succeeding within the U.S. culture and academic environment. In addition to specialized orientations for all new international students, it provides counseling and assistance related to nonimmigrant U.S. government regulations, serving as an advocate for international students during their academic program. Academic intensive English language study is offered through the Texas State Intensive English Program (TSIE). Academically eligible students lacking the full admission TOEFL or IELTS scores may qualify for conditional admission through the Bridge Program. Students take a reduced load of academic study with intensive English classes. Bridge language requirements: TOEFL 500–547 (PBT), 173–210 (CBT), 59–77 (iBT) with minimum scores of 14 on each subsection, or IELTS 5.5 to 6.0. In addition, there is Pre-Bridge conditional admission. Students take at least one semester of full-time intensive English study before academic study. Pre-Bridge Program language requirements: TOEFL 450–497 (PBT), 133–170 (CBT), or 45–58 (iBT).

Texas Wesleyan University

- **Contact:**
  Ashley Austin
  International Student Advisor
  Texas Wesleyan University
  1201 Wesleyan
  Fort Worth, Texas 76105
  Phone: 817-531-4934
  Fax: 817-531-4499
  E-mail: 1world@txwes.edu
  Web site: http://www.international.txwes.edu
- **Private, coed**
- **Urban setting**
- **Enrollment: 2,600**
- **Student-faculty ratio: 16:1**

- **2007–08 Tuition and fees: $15,775**
- **2007–08 Room and board: $5610**
- **International students: 2%**
- **Countries represented: 30**
- **International students applied: 44**
- **International students accepted: 27**
- **International students enrolled: 22**
- **Admissions tests:**
  - **TOEFL: Not required (see description)**
  - **SAT or ACT: Not required**
- **Application deadline: Rolling**
- **On-campus housing: Available**
- **Summer housing: Available**

Area and Climate

Texas Wesleyan University is located in a small community just minutes from downtown Fort Worth. Together with Dallas and the surrounding cities, Fort Worth is part of the Metroplex, an urban area spanning 9,650 square miles (25,000 square kilometers) that is home to more than 5.2 million people. Yet Texas Wesleyan is a small university in an old residential neighborhood, with easy access to big-city attractions and the DFW International Airport. Public transportation is convenient and available within Fort Worth and Dallas and also between the two cities. Fort Worth is the home of many cultural sites, including world-renowned art museums, science museums, performance halls, theaters, professional sports stadiums, amusement parks, restaurants, and shopping malls. Winters in north Texas are mild, with an average temperature of 50°F (10°C) and plenty of sunshine. Summers are hot, with temperatures averaging between 90°F and 97°F (32°C and 36°C).

Education

Founded in 1890, Texas Wesleyan is a private institution that is committed to the principle that each student deserves personal attention and that all members of the academic community must have freedom to pursue independent thought and exercise intellectual curiosity. Texas Wesleyan offers more than twenty-five undergraduate degrees in the Schools of Arts and Sciences, Business, and Education. Six graduate degrees are offered in business, counseling, education, and nurse anesthesia. There are also other special programs, and the School of Law offers a Doctor of Jurisprudence. The University is truly student centered, with small classes and faculty members who are available and helpful to students. Faculty and staff members provide a strong supportive network to assist students in achieving their goals. The mission of the University is to help students achieve their dreams of becoming educated members of the world community. The University follows a traditional semester calendar of fall, spring, and summer sessions.

Campus Life

Texas Wesleyan is a small school where big things are happening. There are exciting programs and activities on campus, and the campus infrastructure is expanding as new buildings are completed each year. The majority of Texas Wesleyan's students are nontraditional students, and the campus is a small, comfortable place where students meet others from a variety of backgrounds. There is a welcoming family feel on the friendly campus, and living on campus is safe and convenient. On-campus housing is available year-round in traditional dormitories as well as new on-campus apartments. Several student organizations are active on campus, hosting events in the Student Union Building or on the quad. Sports play a big part in campus life, with national-champion basketball and table tennis teams and top-ranked teams in soccer, golf, and other sports. International students often play on the varsity or intramural teams.

For International Students

The Office of International Programs (IP) provides information and counseling to international students on admission to the University, immigration regulations and procedures, medical insurance, housing, and financial matters. Upon arrival, a two-day orientation helps students settle in and acquire the information they need for a successful education in the U.S. IP provides social services such as monthly shopping trips and maintains close ties with various University offices, the community, and the region to ensure that students have the opportunity to experience the unique blend of Texas cultures. Most international students belong to the International Club, which hosts a variety of monthly activities, such as dinner club at restaurants, field trips, and lunch meetings, along with special fundraising events and the University's annual fall International Week and spring International Sports Day.

For admission, applicants must show English proficiency. Depending on the applicant's background, this may be accomplished through the TOEFL (minimum score 520 (paper-based), 190 (computer-based), or 68 (Internet-based)), IELTS (minimum score 5.5), or another approved manner. Also, applicants must complete the application form, have official school transcripts sent directly to the University, and provide proof of financial support. Scholarships are available to qualified students based on entrance status and qualifications. IP works with the applicant to complete the process.

Troy University

- **Contact:**
  International Programs
  Troy University
  Troy, AL 36082
  Phone: 334-670-3335
  Fax: 334-670-3735
  E-mail: intlprog@troy.edu
- Public, coed
- Small-town setting
- Enrollment: 5,000
- Student/faculty ratio: 20:1
- 2006–07 Tuition and fees: $8000

- 2006–07 Room and board: $4800
- Countries represented: 60
- International students accepted: 630
- Admissions tests:
  - TOEFL: Required (min. score 500)
  - SAT and ACT: Not required
- Application deadlines: 7/1, 9/1, 11/1, 2/1, 4/1
- On-campus housing: Guaranteed, 365 days per year
- Summer housing: Available

Area and Climate

Troy University is located on a tree-lined campus in Troy, a city of about 15,000 in southeast Alabama. The campus is less than an hour's drive from Alabama's capital city of Montgomery and only about 2 hours north of the white sand beaches of the Gulf of Mexico. Moderate temperatures invite outdoor activities all year. The mean temperature in January is 10°C (43°F); the mean July temperature is 25°C (79°F). The beautiful residential campus, with thirty-five major buildings and excellent recreation facilities, provides a safe and attractive environment. This, together with the famous hospitality of the South and the warm climate and low cost of living, attracts students from more than forty states and thirty nations around the globe.

Education

Founded in 1887, Troy University has been recognized for the quality of its academic programs and its focus on the individual student. Troy University is a worldwide system, committed to international education at Troy and throughout the world. The main campus is located in Troy, Alabama. Named one of the top traditional Southern regional universities, Troy offers a variety of undergraduate curriculum choices, including business, computer science, journalism, marine biology, and fine arts, as well as the M.B.A., M.S. in environmental management, and other graduate degrees. Small classes combined with faculty advising ensure success for the international student.

Campus Life

Troy provides numerous recreational facilities on its beautiful 600-acre (243-hectare) campus, including a health and fitness center, a food court, tennis courts, a golf course, a weight room, indoor and outdoor pools, and dining facilities. Student services include academic advising, comprehensive counseling, health services, and career planning and placement. A well-rounded program of student activities includes movies, concerts, plays, and athletics. Student clubs and social organizations complement the academic programs. Students are encouraged to take advantage of learning opportunities and resources available in the computer laboratories and the arboretum (which covers more than 100 acres (41 hectares)) as well as in the classrooms and library.

For International Students

The professional staff in the Center for International Programs serves a growing number of international students. Transportation from the nearest airport is provided upon request. An orientation session and student mentors assist the international population with adjustment to college life. The International Center, as part of University housing, provides a home away from home for both American and international students. The center promotes cultural exchange, understanding, and appreciation between nations. The American English Group offers a full program of ESL course work in preparation for University admission and meeting the TOEFL requirement. The International Students Cultural Organization (ISCO) plans and implements activities that foster friendship between American and international students.

University at Buffalo, the State University of New York

- **Contact:**
  Mr. Joseph Hindrawan
  International Enrollment Management
  411 Capen Hall
  University at Buffalo, the State University of New York
  Buffalo, NY 14260-1604
  Phone: 716-645-2368
  Fax: 716-645-2528
  E-mail: intiem@buffalo.edu
  Web site: http://www.buffalo.edu
- **Public, coed**
- **Suburban setting**
- **Total enrollment: 26,168**
- **Student-faculty ratio: 19:1**

- **2006–07 Tuition and fees: $13,370**
- **2006–07 Room and board: $8672**
- **International students: 12.05%**
- **Countries represented: 109**
- **International students applied: 1,314**
- **International students accepted: 868**
- **International students enrolled: 322**
- **Admissions tests:**
  - **TOEFL (min. score 550)**
  - **SAT: Recommended**
- **Application deadline: Rolling (recommended by April 1)**
- **On-campus housing: Guaranteed (by May 1)**
- **Summer housing: Available**

Area and Climate

Buffalo is the second-largest city in New York State, having a metropolitan population of more than 1 million. Buffalo is 450 miles (725 kilometers) northwest of New York City, 20 miles (32 kilometers) from Niagara Falls, and 100 miles (161 kilometers) south of Toronto, Canada. Buffalo enjoys four distinct seasons, and students should prepare for weather of all types. Winter temperatures range between 15°F (-9°C) and 32°F (0°C), while summers are pleasant and moderate, with the temperature rarely rising above 90°F (32°C). Buffalo is a city of friendly neighborhoods with big-city recreation for all tastes: professional sports teams, the Buffalo Philharmonic Orchestra, the renowned twentieth-century art collection in the Albright-Knox Art Gallery, and a lively club scene.

Education

The University at Buffalo (UB) is a full-spectrum public university where undergraduate education is enriched and intensified by its close association with graduate programs and cutting-edge research. The University at Buffalo offers more academic choices—ninety-three bachelor's degree programs and more than sixty undergraduate minors, 112 master's and ninety-eight doctoral degree programs, and more than 3,000 courses—than any other public university in New York and New England. In addition to its College of Arts and Sciences, with twenty-eight departments, the University at Buffalo has schools of architecture, dental medicine, education, engineering, library studies, law, management, medicine, nursing, pharmacy, public health and health professions, and social work. The University's library system contains more than 3 million volumes and subscribes to more than 21,000 journals, all electronically cataloged. The University's computing facilities can support research on any scale, and its campuses are thoroughly wired for easy student computer access.

Campus Life

UB's two campuses combine the charms of vintage buildings on the South Campus with the latest in educational architecture on the newer North Campus. The North Campus, the University's primary campus, is located on a 1,200-acre (486-hectare) site in suburban Amherst. It has ample open green space and includes a 60-acre (24-hectare) lake yet is only 15 minutes from the city. The South Campus is an oasis of ivy-covered buildings in the midst of a vital city. On campus, students enjoy more than 375 clubs and organizations and a first-rate athletic facility that serves extensive intramural programs in addition to UB's intercollegiate NCAA Division I athletic teams. The residence halls house 5,500 students with a variety of room sizes and accommodations.

For International Students

International Student and Scholar Services (ISSS) is the central reference point for all international student concerns, immigration and visa-related requirements that affect study in the U.S., educational and cocurricular activities, and general advisement on personal and academic matters. ISSS cooperates with the Faculty Student Association to implement the health insurance program for international students.

University of Central Florida

- **Contact:**
  Talia Cerrone
  Senior Admissions Specialist
  International Services Center
  University of Central Florida
  P.O. Box 160130
  Orlando, FL 32816-0130

  Phone: 407-823-1845
  Fax: 407-823-2176
  E-mail: tcerrone@mail.ucf.edu
  Web site: http://www.intl.ucf.edu/
- **Public, university, coed**
- **Suburban setting**
- **Enrollment: 45,000**

- **Student-faculty ratio: 27:1**
- **2006–07 Tuition and fees: $14,790**
- **2006–07 Room and board: $12,010**
- **International students: 1%**
- **Countries represented: 131**
- **Admissions tests:**
  - **TOEFL: Required for some (min. score 550 PBT; 213 CBT)**
  - **SAT or ACT: Required for some**
- **Application deadline: Fall, 3/1; spring, 9/1**
- **On-campus housing: Available**

Area and Climate

The University of Central Florida is located on 1,415 acres (573 hectares) approximately 13 miles (21 kilometers) east of downtown Orlando. Metropolitan Orlando is a growing, dynamic area of more than 2.5 million people. Cultural and recreational activities and facilities are abundant. Although best known for its various tourist attractions, Orlando also has an extremely broad technical and industrial base. Central Florida has an ideal climate, with an average temperature of 72°F (22°C), which makes it possible to enjoy outdoor activities during the whole year. The Atlantic Ocean is an hour's drive east of campus.

Education

The University of Central Florida (UCF), formerly known as Florida Technological University, was founded in 1963. A youthful, dynamic institution, UCF is part of the State University System of Florida. UCF is known for world-class research, the integration of technology and learning, and innovative community partnerships that provide students with exceptional research and learning experiences through co-op and internship programs. Bachelor's degrees are offered in ninety-two areas. International scholars and students at UCF make significant contributions to campus learning, community diversity, research, and the global partnerships necessary for advancement through the twenty-first century. The University offers educational and research programs that complement the economy, with strong components in aerospace engineering, business, education, film, health, hospitality management, nursing, and social sciences. UCF's programs in communication and the fine arts help to meet the cultural and recreational needs of a growing metropolitan area.

Campus Life

As one of the nation's fastest-growing universities and the seventh largest in the nation, UCF enrolls a diverse student body representing all fifty states and more than 130 countries. Students participate in more than 350 organizations, including special interest clubs, multicultural associations, fraternities and sororities, honor societies, and academic and preprofessional organizations. The Office of Student Life and the Office of Student Activities schedule a wide array of extracurricular programs, including concerts, movies, and guest speakers. The on-campus and campus-affiliated housing facilities, which include traditional residence halls, apartment-style options, and Greek housing, accommodate approximately 9,000 students, and the planned construction of new residential facilities will make it possible to accommodate additional students. Several thousand students live in apartments located within walking distance of the campus. Approximately 400 students live in on-campus Greek housing.

For International Students

The University actively recruits and welcomes international scholars and students. The University's International Services Center (ISC) offers a wide-range of workshops, activities, and events specifically designed for new and currently enrolled international students. Its main functions are to serve as a source of information, advocacy, and support; to provide assistance in adjusting to a new academic environment and culture; and to provide immigration, admission, and other advising to prospective, new, and currently enrolled international students at UCF. Excellent English language programs are offered to meet various levels of need.

University of Central Missouri

- **Contact:**
  Charles W. Petentler
  Director of International Admissions
  University of Central Missouri
  Warrensburg, MO 64093
  Phone: 660-543-4762
  Fax: 660-543-4201
  E-mail: intladmit@cmsu1.cmsu.edu
  Web site: http://www.cmsu.edu/international
- **Public, comprehensive, coed**
- **Enrollment: 10,604**
- **Student-faculty ratio: 18:1**
- **2006–07 Tuition: $9000**
- **2006–07 Room and board: $5412**

- **International students: 4%**
- **Countries represented: 51**
- **International students applied: 468**
- **International students accepted: 369**
- **International students enrolled: 188**
- **Admissions tests:**
  - **TOEFL: Required (min. score 500 paper-based)**
- **Application deadline: Fall (August), 5/1; spring (January), 10/1**
- **On-campus housing: Available**
- **Summer housing: Available**

Area and Climate

The University of Central Missouri (UCM) is located in Warrensburg, Missouri, in the heart of the United States. Warrensburg is a safe community of 15,000 that is conveniently located 50 miles (81 kilometers) southeast of Kansas City, Missouri, and combines the urban and rural influences of life in the United States. The community is easily accessible via the interstate highway system, the Amtrak railway system, and an international airport in Kansas City. Missouri is well known for its wide range of weather patterns. Summer temperatures range from 77°F (25°C) to 98.6°F (37°C), and winter temperatures may fall below freezing. Spring and fall offer comfortable temperatures and the beauty of Missouri's natural foliage and geography.

Education

Founded in 1871, UCM is an acknowledged leader in program-specific accreditations among Missouri's public universities. Students may choose from more than 150 areas of study leading to associate, bachelor's, master's, and doctoral degrees. Central is accredited by the North Central Association of Colleges and Schools. Programs in actuarial science, art, aviation, business administration, chemistry, construction science, design–drafting technology, dietetics, industrial hygiene, industrial technology–manufacturing management, library science, music, nursing, occupational safety and health, social work, speech pathology and audiology, sports education, and teacher education are accredited by independent national accreditation organizations. Central's statewide mission in professional technology has allowed the University to expand its traditional emphasis on preparing students for career challenges in a wide variety of fields. It is committed to integrating the latest real-world technologies throughout its curriculum. The campus contains many exceptional learning facilities to support its varied academic programs.

Campus Life

UCM's residence halls are located within two blocks of the campus and house more than 3,000 students. Most residents share facilities in a suite arrangement, with two residents to a room and two rooms sharing a bathroom. Students may participate in the many social, cultural, and athletic opportunities that Central has to offer, most of which are available at little or no cost. Dozens of nationally known musicians, lecturers, comedians, and actors visit each year. The Department of Music sponsors numerous concerts during the school year that feature Central musicians. For many students, health, fitness, and competition are important components of the University experience. The Multipurpose Building has facilities for basketball, handball, racquetball, running, swimming, tennis, volleyball, and weight training. Nearby Pertle Springs contains 300 acres (121.5 hectares) of rolling hills and woods and an eighteen-hole golf course.

For International Students

UCM welcomes international students and the diversity they bring to the campus and the surrounding community. The International Center provides services to students and scholars through orientation and advocacy for all international concerns. Other areas of service include immigration and student status certification matters, coordination and sponsorship of campus and community multicultural activities, sponsorship of the International Student Organization, and promotion of the role of international education at Central. Academic excellence is recognized through Phi Beta Delta, the Honorary Society for International Scholars. The Intensive English Program at Central offers concentrated, full-time instruction in English-language study, including a core academic preparation curriculum of reading, writing, grammar, communication skills, and American culture.

University of Charleston

- **Contact:**
  Office of Admissions
  University of Charleston
  2300 MacCorkle Avenue, SE
  Charleston, WV 25304
  Phone: 304-357-4750
  Fax: 304-357-4781
  E-mail: admissions@ucwv.edu
  Web site: http://www.ucwv.edu
- **Private, comprehensive, coed**
- **Urban setting**
- **Enrollment: 1,000**

- **Student-faculty ratio: 15:1**
- **2006–07 Tuition and fees: $21,000**
- **2005–06 Room and board: $7600**
- **International students: 7%**
- **Countries represented: 27**
- **Admissions tests:**
  - **TOEFL (min. score 550 PBT; 173 CBT)**
  - **SAT or ACT: Required**
- **Application deadline: 7/15**
- **On-campus housing: Guaranteed**
- **Summer housing: Available**

Area and Climate

The University of Charleston (UC) is located in the state capital of West Virginia, one of the safest states in America. Charleston is the largest city in West Virginia, with a surrounding metropolitan population of more than 200,000. The 40-acre (16-hectare) campus is located on the banks of the Kanawha River overlooking the state capitol complex. Many students become active participants in the daily life of the Charleston community by taking advantage of an impressive array of work, cultural, and entertainment options in this exciting city, and breathtaking natural mountain vistas, rivers, and parks are only minutes away. White-water rafting, skiing, mountain climbing, and mountain biking are available within a one-hour drive from the campus.

West Virginia weather is characterized by four distinct seasons. Winters are mild and summers are warm but pleasant. In autumn, there are brilliant fall foliage colors.

Education

UC offers undergraduate degrees in twenty-nine major areas of study in its three divisions (Morris Harvey Division of Arts and Sciences, the Herbert Jones Division of Business, and the Bert Bradford Division of Health Sciences) and the Robert C. Byrd School of Pharmacy. Students enjoy small classes and personal attention; the average class size is 15 students. The University of Charleston has been recognized as a national model for the freshman-year experience, which includes faculty mentoring, University Transitions, and Living/Learning Communities. The Collegiate Learning Assessment also recognizes the University for its outstanding commitment to student learning. The UC educational program focuses on "learning your way." The focus is on students, allowing them to demonstrate what they have learned in order to earn the credits necessary for graduation. Students are expected to demonstrate knowledge and skills in the areas of communication, critical thinking, citizenship, ethical practice, science, and creativity. These attributes are integrated with knowledge and skills in a chosen field of study.

Campus Life

Because the University believes that students learn from their involvement in community and campus activities, students are strongly encouraged to participate in one or more of the forty cocurricular organizations found at the University. There are academic clubs, publications, fraternities, sororities, religious organizations, intramural sports, honorary societies, drama clubs, cheerleading, chorus and band programs, and many student leadership organizations. The University sponsors many events, including plays, concerts, lectures, and movies, and UC participates in the NCAA Division II in both men's and women's varsity sports. The University's Welch Colleague program integrates student involvement, the academic curriculum, community service, and leadership. The Community Service program provides opportunities for students to participate both on campus and in the Charleston area. In addition, there are numerous civic, political, social, and charitable organizations easily accessible in the community.

For International Students

International students are an integral part of UC. The Office of International Student Programs coordinates advising and orientation for all international students, including assistance in the transition to American culture and college life. Services provided by International Student Programs include advising on personal, immigration, and legal matters; assistance with completing tax and immigration forms; airport transportation; programming of activities; and a host family program. Concurrent ESL instruction is available to undergraduate students whose first language is not English. International scholarships and on-campus work opportunities are available.

International students at the University have organized an International Student Organization (ISO). The organization promotes cultural awareness on the campus and throughout the local community. Worldfest, the annual international student festival, is held in February. At this event, students from approximately twenty-seven countries present information about their culture, dress, and country. Samples of favorite traditional recipes are also available. The event is free and open to the public.

University of Cincinnati

- Contact:
  Office of Admissions
  University of Cincinnati
  2624 Clifton Avenue
  Cincinnati, OH 45221-0091
  Phone: 513-556-1100
  E-mail: admissions@uc.edu
  Web site: http://www.admissions.uc.edu/
  international
- Public, comprehensive, coed
- Urban setting
- Enrollment: 35,000

- Student-faculty ratio: 15:1
- 2006–07 Tuition and fees: $23,922
- 2006–07 Room and board: $8286
- International students: .05%
- Countries represented: 100
- Admissions tests:
  - SAT, TOEFL, or IELTS: Required
- Application deadline: Rolling (January 15 priority)
- On-campus housing: Required freshman year
- Summer housing: Available

Area and Climate

Cincinnati offers all the benefits of a large metropolis with the charm, security, and welcoming atmosphere of a small town. Recently named one of the top 10 cities in the U.S. (cityrating.com), it is a wonderful city in which to live and experience American culture. Cincinnati is a city of theater, concerts, restaurants, festivals, amusement parks, and professional sports. It is also the home of many multinational corporations, including Procter & Gamble, GE Aircraft Engines, and Fifth Third Bank, which provide students with a wide array of opportunities for co-op employment, internships, and careers after graduation.

Cincinnati is centrally located in the U.S., and there is an international airport just 15 minutes from campus. The area's climate changes with the seasons. In spring and fall, temperatures are moderate. Summer temperatures of 90°F (33°C) are not unusual, and winter can get very cold and snowy (10°F/24°C).

Education

The University of Cincinnati (UC), a major comprehensive university, is ranked among the top 100 public universities in the U.S. and, with more than $330 million in research funding, stands among the top 25 public research universities. Students choose from hundreds of undergraduate and graduate programs, including some of the most highly ranked in the nation, offered through fourteen colleges, including the College of Applied Science; College of Arts and Sciences; College of Business; College of Design, Architecture, Art, and Planning; and the College of Engineering. Students work with nationally recognized faculty members and enjoy state-of-the-art research facilities. UC's sixteen libraries are ranked in the top 50 research libraries in the U.S. Alliances with major computing vendors such as SAP, Microsoft, Oracle, Dell, and IBM ensure that students always have access to the latest software and hardware, and most of UC's campus is wireless.

UC offers students a balance of educational excellence and real-world experience, providing many opportunities to enhance their learning experiences through practical applications of their studies. These opportunities include field work, internships, research projects, and service learning as well as the University's unique Cooperative Education (Co-op) program. Co-op is the practice of alternating students' studies with paid work related to their major. Not only does Co-op education provide students with invaluable practical experience in their fields, it also substantially contributes to paying for their education.

Campus Life

UC is a thriving center of learning and living, with spectacular buildings, open green spaces, fountains, and pedestrian walkways. It is often compared to a small town, and the campus has what every small town should have: a MainStreet. MainStreet includes the One-Stop Student Service Center, MainStreet Cinema, Catskellar Game Room & Sports Lounge, a food court, and a full-service bank and ATMs. The University just completed a $1-billion construction project that included the new Campus Recreation Center, a huge full-service health club. UC residence halls offer a variety of hall styles, floor plans, and room types with air-conditioning, high-speed Internet access, and cable television. UC also has its own cell phone plan, which allows students to get free phones and discounted service plans. The University supports hundreds of student organizations and activities for every possible interest, including thirty-three sports and recreation clubs, leadership opportunities, special-interest clubs, diversity education, and fraternity and sorority life.

For International Students

UC enjoys the enrollment of about 2,000 international students from virtually every country in world and takes great pride in successfully meeting their needs. In the most recent International Student Barometer survey, international students gave UC the highest marks for student satisfaction among participating universities in eight different categories, including welcome activities, International Services, and academic registration. UC International Services (http://www.isso.uc.edu) strives to integrate international students into all aspects of campus and community life and offers programs designed to advise students on such issues as immigration regulations, social and cultural adjustment, and personal and financial concerns. They also sponsor special events, including Welcome Day, International Education Week, the WorldFest Celebration, and the International Friendship program. In addition, UC has many International Student Organizations whose purpose is to promote education and understanding among cultures and to create a network of friendship for students from all over the world.

The University of Cincinnati welcomes international students to apply and has a growing network of official representatives around the world to provide students with personalized service. Their locations can be found at http://www.admissions.uc.edu/travel. Students can also apply directly to the University (http://www.admissions.uc.edu/international) if no representative is available in their country. UC offers scholarships for international students, including the new UC Global Scholarship (up to $7000 per year, renewable for up to four years). Scholarships are awarded based on SAT scores, and students are automatically considered for them upon applying.

University of Dayton

- **Contact:**
  Beverly T. Jenkins
  Associate Director of International Recruitment
  Office of Admission
  University of Dayton
  300 College Park
  Dayton, OH 45469-1300

  Phone: 937-229-4464
  E-mail: beverly.jenkins@notes.udayton.edu
  Web site: http://international.udayton.edu
- **Independent Roman Catholic, coed**
- **Suburban setting**
- **Enrollment: 10,000+**
- **Student-faculty ratio: 13:1**

- **2006–07 Tuition and fees: $23,970**
- **2006–07 Room and board: $7190**
- **International students: 1%**
- **Countries represented: 25**
- **Admissions tests:**
  - **TOEFL: Required (min. score 523 PBT; 193 CBT; 70 iBT for full admission)**
  - **SAT or ACT: Not required, but should be submitted if available**
- **Application deadline: Fall, 5/1; winter, 8/1**
- **On-campus housing: Guaranteed**
- **Summer housing: Available**

Area and Climate

The University's campus is located on 259 acres (104 hectares), 2 miles (3 kilometers) from the city of Dayton in the Midwestern United States. The Dayton metropolitan area is a vibrant, growing community of approximately 950,000 people. It is an affordable city—housing, food, transportation, and entertainment cost considerably less in Dayton than in other U.S. cities. Top cultural, recreational, sports, and entertainment programs are available throughout the year, and varied business, industrial, research, and educational enterprises provide students with extensive work opportunities related to their academic disciplines. Dayton is also a diverse community of many religions and cultures; international students are likely to find a local group that represents their home culture.

The climate in Dayton offers four distinct seasons. The temperature ranges from 60° to 82°F (15° to 28°C) in the summer and from 19° to 35°F (-12.5° to 1.6°C) in winter.

Education

Nationally recognized as a top-tier university, the University of Dayton (UD) is a vibrant learning community that offers the resources of a large university and the personal attention of a small college. More than seventy undergraduate programs and over fifty graduate programs are available in the College of Arts and Sciences and in the Schools of Business Administration, Education and Allied Professions, Engineering, and Law. Founded by the Society of Mary (the Marianists) in 1850, the University of Dayton focuses on educating the whole person through a community of challenge and support. A University of Dayton education is transformative. Students are prepared for both life and work and learn skills in building community.

Campus Life

The residential nature of the campus encourages active extracurricular involvement. More than 180 clubs and organizations exist on campus, including more than thirty service organizations, forty academic/professional clubs, fifteen honor societies, recreation/sports clubs, theatrical and musical performance groups, and fraternities and sororities. NCAA Division I intercollegiate athletics as well as intramural sports are also prevalent. The John F. Kennedy Memorial Union offers a variety of services for the University community, including numerous cultural, educational, recreational, and social activities. The facility includes a theater; an art gallery; a food court containing a pizzeria, bakery, grill, and delicatessen; Flyer TV, a student-run television station; the commuter lounge; The Galley, a student-operated snack shop; and The Hanger, a game room that provides bowling lanes, billiards, a cyber café, video games, and lounge and performance spaces. First-year students are required to live in the University residence halls. Sophomore students are also required to live in University housing.

For International Students

The University's Center for International Programs supports a diverse and multicultural environment on campus and beyond, and help for international students begins from the time they begin the application process and continues to the moment they earn their degrees. International Student and Scholar Services (ISSS) staff members assist international students in a wide variety of areas such as immigration issues, counseling, personal advising, extracurricular activities, and emergencies. The office also serves as a link between international students and the rest of the University and the surrounding community. ISSS sponsors social events that are of particular interest to international students, such as the International Festival each spring, as well as other events throughout the academic year that are designed to introduce international students to the American culture and way of life

Through the University of Dayton's Intensive English Program, students benefit from a concentrated and intense language program combined with a true American-university experience. UD's Intensive English Program aims to introduce language learners to the American culture through continuous interaction with American and international students on campus. Through field trips, a conversation partner program, intercultural living communities, and involvement in student clubs on campus, students develop strong English skills to prepare them for the University classroom or the work place. As University of Dayton students, they have access to the leading technology in higher education, including technology for language learning.

University of Denver

- **Contact:**
  Office of Admission
  2197 South University Boulevard
  Denver, CO 80208
  Phone: 303-871-2790
          800-525-9495
  Fax: 303-871-3301
  E-mail: intladm@du.edu
  Web site: http://www.du.edu/admission/
          international
- **Private, coed**
- **Urban setting**
- **Enrollment: 10,076**
- **Student-faculty ratio: 10:1**
- **2006–07 Tuition and fees: $30,372**

- **2006–07 Room and board: $8351**
- **International students: 7%**
- **Countries represented: 83**
- **International students applied: 340**
- **International students accepted: 154**
- **International students enrolled: 40**
- **Admissions tests:**
  - **TOEFL: Required (min. score 525 paper-based; 193 computer-based; 70 Internet-based)**
  - **SAT and ACT: Not required**
- **Application deadline: January 15**
- **On-campus housing: Available**
- **Summer housing: Limited**

Area and Climate

With rainfall averaging only 15.5 inches (394 millimeters) annually, Denver enjoys a semiarid climate characterized by 300 days of sunshine a year. In fall, winter, and spring, Denver occasionally gets short-lived snowstorms of just a few inches. Temperatures range from a high of about 104°F (40°C) in midsummer to a low of about -10°F (-23°C) in winter. Because temperatures can fluctuate dramatically in a few hours, students should plan a wardrobe conducive to layering.

Denver is located on Colorado's high plains just a few kilometers from the base of the Rocky Mountains. World-class ski resorts and recreation areas are a 90-minute drive from the University of Denver (DU) campus.

Education

Founded in 1864, the University of Denver is the premier private university in the Rocky Mountain region, blending the friendliness and personal attention of a small college with the resources and intellectual diversity of a large research institution. Undergraduates pursue studies in everything from the arts and social sciences to business and engineering. In the last decade, DU has invested nearly $500 million in new and renovated facilities, including a performing arts center; a hall for the arts, humanities, and social sciences; a state-of-the-art science building; and new homes for the Daniels College of Business; the School of Hotel, Restaurant, and Tourism Management; and the Sturm College of Law.

Campus Life

DU's welcoming community offers diverse opportunities for students to develop as leaders: a student senate, more than 100 student organizations, and a student programming board that books speakers, arranges film screenings, and schedules entertainment. Many DU students participate in club sports, everything from kayaking to volleyball, and all students can take advantage of a new recreation center and indoor, Olympic-size swimming pool.

Most first-year and sophomore students are required to live on campus. Modern residence halls typically include common areas and kitchens. DU also offers a choice of themed living and learning communities, in which individuals with common interests benefit from a common residence space and related programming.

For International Students

DU welcomes students from all over the world and provides services to help international students adapt to campus life. The International Student and Scholar Services office conducts an orientation program and offers immigration advising, cross-cultural adjustment assistance, advocacy, and general support. In addition, the English Language Center offers comprehensive language instruction for students who need extra preparation for classroom success. At the University's hospitable International House, students can mingle, share ideas, and feel at home. In addition, an annual Festival of Nations allows students to celebrate the many cultures represented by the student population.

University of Hartford

- **Contact:**
  Samuel N. Skinner
  Director of International Admissions
  University of Hartford
  West Hartford, CT 06117

  Phone: 860-768-4981
  Fax: 860-768-4961
  E-mail: iua@hartford.edu
  Web site: http://admission.hartford.edu/intl
- **Private, comprehensive, coed**
- **Suburban setting**
- **Enrollment: 4,600 (undergraduate)**
- **Student-faculty ratio: 12:1**
- **2006–07 Tuition and fees: $25,736**
- **2006–07 Room and board: $10,382**

- **International students: 7%**
- **Countries represented: 62**
- **International students applied: 425**
- **International students accepted: 300**
- **International students enrolled: 110**
- **Admissions tests:**
  - **TOEFL: Accepted (min. score 550 paper-based; 213 computer-based; 72 Internet-based) or IELTS: Accepted (min. score 6.5)**
  - **SAT or ACT: Optional**
- **Application deadline: Rolling**
- **On-campus housing: Available**
- **Summer housing: Available**

Area and Climate

The University of Hartford is situated on a scenic 320-acre campus in an attractive residential section of West Hartford, Connecticut. Within a 2-hour drive are the great American cities of Boston and New York. The University campus is easily accessible to all major forms of transportation. Hartford's climate offers students the opportunity to enjoy four different seasons: spring (March–May, flowers come into bloom, average temperature 37°F to 59°F (3°C to 15°C)), summer (June–August, beach weather, 59°F to 95°F (15°C to 35°C)), autumn (September–November, trees change color, 46°F to 59°F (8°C to 15°C)), and winter (time for making snow sculptures, 0°F to 27°F (−18°C to −3°C)).

Education

Cited as one of the finest Eastern comprehensive universities, the University of Hartford's nine schools and colleges offer bachelor's degrees in more than 100 disciplines (majors). Professors teach in classes that average 25 students. Professors are available to meet with students outside of class to assist them in planning their course of study. Once students apply for an undergraduate degree, they are considered for merit-based scholarships. International grants range in value from $2000 to $6000 and can be renewed if the student maintains satisfactory academic progress. Students applying to study either music or fine arts are considered for scholarships that have a value of up to full tuition. Students applying as student athletes are considered for awards that have a value of up to the full cost of academic and living fees.

Campus Life

In addition to a high-quality education, the University of Hartford also offers students many cultural, social, and athletic activities. Students may participate in one of more than 150 fitness and leisure classes, compete in sports, and take advantage of the swimming, fitness, and athletic facilities at the Sports Center. Ninety percent of the undergraduate students choose to live in housing provided by the University. The University offers a choice of living arrangements that include the Residential College for the Arts (for students interested in music and art) and Honors Residential College (for students interested in independent study beyond the classroom). Two apartment-style housing options, the Village and Park-River Apartments, are also available.

For International Students

The staff at the International Center is well qualified to assist international students with visa issues and cultural and personal concerns. The University helps international students learn about their new home with an orientation program. This program was created to help students learn about the American educational system and to introduce them to the University campus. For further information about the International Center, prospective students should visit the Web site at http://uhaweb.hartford.edu/intcenter/. Staff members at the English Language Institute offer courses and full programs to any students who are still developing their English. For further information about the English Language Institute, students should visit the Web site at http://www.hartford.edu/eli.

University of Hawaii at Manoa

- **Contact:**
  Admissions Office
  2600 Campus Road, Room 1
  University of Hawaii at Manoa
  Honolulu, HI 96822
  Phone: 808-956-8975
  Fax: 808-956-4148
  E-mail: ar-info@hawaii.edu
  Web site: http://www.hawaii.edu/admrec
- **Public, comprehensive, coed**
- **Urban setting**
- **Enrollment: 20,307**
- **Student-faculty ratio: 15:1**

- **2006–07 Tuition and fees: $12,394.40**
- **2006–07 Room and board: $6800**
- **International students: 8.1%**
- **Countries represented: 93**
- **International students enrolled: 1,648**
- **Admissions tests:**
  - **TOEFL (min. score 500 paper-based; 173 computer-based)**
  - **SAT or ACT: Required**
- **Application deadline: Fall, 2/1; spring, 9/1**
- **On-campus housing: Available, but limited**
- **Summer housing: Available, but limited**

Area and Climate

The University of Hawaii at Manoa (UHM), which is located in Honolulu, is situated on a modern 320-acre (130-hectare) campus in Manoa Valley, a safe and quiet residential neighborhood minutes by public transport from cultural, recreational, and shopping areas. Although Honolulu is a major American city, its multiethnic culture and close ties to Asia give the city a unique international and cosmopolitan character. With a reputation as a world-class travel destination, Honolulu is also a mid-Pacific center for commercial, cultural, artistic, and scientific endeavors, many of which are centered on the University of Hawaii. Hawaii has a semitropical climate and mild temperatures averaging 77°F (25°C).

Education

The University of Hawaii, which was founded in 1907, is a major public research university with an outstanding national and international reputation for teaching and research. The University is fully accredited by the Western Association of Schools and Colleges, and its professional programs are also accredited by appropriate organizations, such as the AACSB International–The Association to Advance Collegiate Schools of Business. The faculty members are experts in their field and eager to share their knowledge, research methods, and results. Degrees are offered in eighty-eight fields of study. UHM is widely recognized for its excellent programs of study relating to the Asian and Pacific region, foreign languages, marine sciences and geosciences, international business, tropical agriculture, electrical engineering, and computer science. To complement their learning, students have access to computing services, including free e-mail and Internet access; a research library with more than 3 million volumes;

up-to-date science, engineering, and foreign language laboratories; art, music, and dance studios; and fully equipped theaters and concert halls. The academic year is divided into a fall and spring semester, with an optional summer session.

Campus Life

The University's motto, "Above all nations is humanity," reflects the belief that a significant part of a college education is studying other cultures and living and learning with students from other ethnic and racial backgrounds. The 20,000 students come from all across the United States and from ninety-three countries. On-campus housing is available in dormitories and shared apartments. Other amenities include dining halls and snack bars (serving an array of international cuisines), a bookstore, extensive sports facilities for student use, student lounges, a student newspaper and radio station, a full range of recreational activities, and more than 200 student clubs (academic, religious, political, professional, and social). Students can attend theater performances and concerts, view an art exhibit, participate in a community service project, or cheer for UHM's athletic teams.

For International Students

The International Student Services Office provides international students with a full range of services, including orientation, immigration advising, adjustment counseling, social activities, and assistance in applying for available scholarship aid. International students, who must obtain health insurance, are offered reasonably priced services by the University Health Services clinic. Students wishing to improve their English language proficiency may enroll in the University's Hawaii English Language Program (HELP). The University of Hawaii is fully authorized to issue student I-20s for the HELP program as well as for all undergraduate and graduate degree programs.

University of Kansas

- **Contact:**
  Daphne Johnston, Associate Director, ISSS
  International Undergraduate Admissions
  University of Kansas
  Lawrence, KS 66045-7535
  Phone: 785-864-2616
  Fax: 785-864-3404
  E-mail: issapps@ku.edu
  Web site: http://www.ku.edu/students/
  international/
- **Public, comprehensive, coed**
- **Suburban setting**
- **Enrollment: 26,934**
- **Student-faculty ratio: 13:1**
- **2006–07 Tuition and fees: $15,170**
- **2006–07 Room and board: $5411**

- **International students: 5.8%**
- **Countries represented: 107**
- **International students enrolled: 1,579**
- **Admissions tests:**
  - **TOEFL: Not required for undergraduate admission (on-site English proficiency testing and intensive English courses provided)**
  - **SAT: Recommended (required for some majors)**
  - **ACT: Recommended (required for some majors)**
- **Application deadline: Fall and summer, 4/1; spring, 10/15**
- **On-campus housing: Available**
- **Summer housing: Available**

Area and Climate

Located in the Midwestern state of Kansas, the University of Kansas (KU) is famous for its beautiful, hilly woodland campus. Lawrence, a community of 80,000, is about 40 miles (64 kilometers) west of the major metropolitan area of Kansas City and 20 miles (32 kilometers) east of Topeka, the state capital. Lawrence is a small city with a friendly atmosphere, a lower cost of living, and a much lower crime rate than major U.S. cities. An attractive downtown area with unique shops, restaurants, and cultural and recreational facilities is within walking distance of the campus. The weather in Kansas has four distinct seasons, with warm autumns, mild springs, hot summers, and cold winters. A wardrobe for changing seasons is recommended.

Education

Founded in 1866, KU is a major comprehensive teaching and research institution with fourteen academic schools offering bachelor's, master's, and doctoral degrees in more than 175 fields and programs for intensive English study. The Carnegie Foundation identifies KU as a Doctoral/ Research University–Extensive institution, the classification given to top research universities. KU is a member of the Association of American Universities, a select group of leading higher education institutions in the U.S. and Canada. KU consistently ranks among the top 100 research universities in research grant awards. According to America's Best Colleges, a *U.S. News & World Report* guidebook, KU is among the top fifty public universities in the U.S.

Campus Life

KU has several convenient on-campus housing options, including eleven residence halls, eight scholarship halls, and two apartment complexes. Conveniently located and safe, the halls provide meals, laundry rooms, social activities, and opportunities to meet other students. More than 400 student clubs and organizations are available, offering a variety of academic, professional, social, and recreational options. KU is proud of its champion sports teams, and students can enjoy sporting events on campus. Cultural activities include theater presentations, musical events, lectures, and performances by nationally and internationally recognized individuals and groups. The Student Recreation Fitness Center features state-of-the-art facilities for a variety of health-promoting and intramural sports programs.

For International Students

The Office of International Student and Scholar Services (ISSS) offers a comprehensive range of services, including the admission of international undergraduate students, immigration advising, and special programming. A special weeklong international student orientation program is offered each semester. Advisers are skilled in cross-cultural communication and are sensitive to the unique needs of international students. ISSS coordinates many activities to encourage friendship and understanding among international and U.S. students and sponsors the International Student Association. ISSS facilitates friendship with local families through visits and organized activities, including the opportunity for holiday homestays.

University of Missouri–St. Louis

- Contact:
    Leonard Trudo
    International Admissions Officer
    University of Missouri–St. Louis
    One University Boulevard
    St. Louis, MO 63121-4400
    Phone: 314-516-5229
    Fax: 314-516-5636
    E-mail: iss@umsl.edu
    Web site: http://www.umsl.edu
- State-supported, coed
- Suburban setting
- Enrollment: 15,500
- Student-faculty ratio: 10:1

- 2006–07 Tuition and fees: $14,810
- 2006–07 Room and board: $6500
- International students: 2.5%
- Countries represented: 113
- International students applied: 660
- International students accepted: 324
- Admissions tests:
    - TOEFL (min. score 500 PBT; 173 CBT; 61 iBT)
    - SAT or ACT: Not required
- Application deadline: Rolling
- On-campus housing: Available
- Summer housing: Available

Area and Climate

The largest university in the region, University of Missouri–St. Louis (UM–St. Louis), is known for academic excellence and its reputation for attention to the individual student. St. Louis is a 300-year-old city located on the historic Mississippi River. It is the nineteenth-largest population center in the United States. The area provides students with both urban and suburban settings. The campus is a short distance from downtown and just minutes from the airport. Students benefit from inexpensive bus and train (MetroLink) transportation as well as a free campus shuttle system. The region has four distinct seasons, with summer temperatures averaging 87°F (31°C) and winter temperatures averaging 39°F (4°C). Snow falls a few days each winter.

Education

The University of Missouri System was founded in 1839. The University of Missouri–St. Louis campus opened in 1963 and offers a full university experience: forty-eight undergraduate programs, thirty-one master's degree programs, twelve doctoral programs, and one professional degree program. Academic programs are enriched through advanced technologies and partnerships that link UM–St. Louis to institutions and businesses locally, regionally, nationally, and internationally. UM–St. Louis has a strong international focus for its teaching, research, and public service, along with a rich tradition of fostering student learning through excellent teaching. More than 90 percent of the full-time faculty members hold doctoral degrees. All students have personal academic advisers to assist them in planning their programs. The campus has more than 1,000 computer systems available in the labs and classrooms available for student use. The campus also has several areas on the campus with secured wireless Internet access. The Honors College offers special courses and housing for exceptional students. In 2005, *U.S. News & World Report*'s "America's Best Colleges" ranked UM–St. Louis tenth in the U.S. for its undergraduate international business program. Semesters begin in August, January, and June.

Campus Life

The Millennium Student Center is the hub of the UM–St. Louis campus and welcomes students, alumni, and visitors. Of the more than 100 student organizations, fifteen are internationally focused or oriented. Students can participate in activities on campus and in the local area such as concerts, film series, day trips, plays, movies, swimming, soccer, tennis, professional and amateur sports events, and informal gatherings. Students come from more than 100 countries and nearly every state in the U.S. to study at UM–St. Louis. On-campus residence halls and apartments, as well as off-campus housing, are available year round. A friendly and safe campus environment adds to students' enjoyment of the university experience.

For International Students

The Office of International Student and Scholar Services (ISSS) provides a full range of services including admissions, immigration advising, housing assistance, help with cross-cultural adjustment, academic assistance, health insurance support, and transfer credit guidance. A one-week orientation program prior to the start of classes helps students become familiar with the campus and community. This program includes adapting to life in the United States, arranging bank accounts, obtaining necessary government documents, tours of the local area, shopping, registering for classes, and meeting new and interesting people.

University of Nebraska–Lincoln

- **Contact:**
  Assistant Director for International
  Admissions
  Office of Admissions
  University of Nebraska–Lincoln
  Lincoln, NE 68588-0417
  Phone: 402-472-2023
  Fax: 402-472-0670
  E-mail: admissions@unl.edu
  Web site: http://www.unl.edu
- **Public, comprehensive, coed**
- **Urban setting**
- **Enrollment: 21,675**
- **Student-faculty ratio: 16:1**

- **2006–07 Tuition and fees: $15,506**
- **2006–07 Room and board: $6306**
- **International students: 6%**
- **Countries represented: 110**
- **Admissions tests:**
  - **TOEFL: Required (paper-based min. score 523)**
  - **SAT: Recommended**
  - **ACT: Recommended**
- **Application deadline: Fall, 5/1; spring, 10/1; summer, 4/1**
- **On-campus housing: Available**
- **Summer housing: Available**

Area and Climate

The University of Nebraska–Lincoln (UNL) is located in the north-central Great Plains region of the United States. The city of Lincoln—home to the University—is the capital and second-largest city in Nebraska, with a population of 250,000. Lincoln combines the safe, friendly ambiance of a small town with the amenities of a much larger city. It is often mentioned on lists of "most livable" cities in the United States. Nebraska experiences all weather seasons—winter, spring, summer, and fall—with an average temperature in the winter of 24°F (-4.4°C) and an average temperature in the summer of 75°F (24°C).

Education

The University of Nebraska, which was established in 1869, is recognized by *U.S. News & World Report* as one of the top fifty public institutions in the U.S. UNL is also recognized for offering a best value in education, most recently by *Consumers Digest* and Kiplinger's. A founding member of the prestigious Association of American Universities (AAU), UNL continues to be one of the sixty-two member universities chosen on the basis of their national significance in research and graduate studies. The University offers 150 undergraduate majors, twenty-one preprofessional programs, and 120 graduate degree programs as well as a 2.5-million-volume library, 24-hour computer labs, and Internet access in every residence hall room.

Campus Life

In learning communities and in living communities, students feel at home. Nebraska's sixteen residence halls have dining facilities, computer labs, 24-hour study areas, laundry facilities, recreation areas, and vending machines. Each room has high-speed Internet access, cable television, air conditioning, and local phone service. With more than twenty international student organizations and nearly 400 student-involvement organizations, students connect with each other. These organizations include professional, volunteer, mentoring, religious, political, and social groups. Students seek health and fitness in the Campus Recreation Center, which includes an extensive exercise facility, an indoor athletic practice field, wellness services and classes, and extensive intramural sports programs.

For International Students

UNL is known for the merit-based scholarships it offers to international students at the time of admission. Scholarships range between $2100 and $8900. New students learn about UNL and the community at the International Student Orientation, which includes tours, meeting peer advisers, social gatherings, and discussions about the academic system. The Intensive English Program (IEP) offers two 8-week sessions during both the fall and spring semesters and an eight-week session and a four-week session during the summer. Intensive English instruction is provided at several proficiency levels. The sessions are designed to get students up to speed in English so they can be successful in UNL's classrooms.

University of New Mexico

- **Contact:**
  Terry Babbitt
  Associate Vice President, Enrollment
     Management
  University of New Mexico
  Albuquerque, NM 87131-0001
  Phone: 505-277-5829
  Fax: 505-277-6686
  E-mail: goglobal@unm.edu
  Web site: http://www.unm.edu
- **Public**
- **Urban setting**
- **Enrollment: 25,000**
- **Student-faculty ratio: 19:1**
- **2006–07 Tuition and fees: $14,177**

- **2006–07 Room and board: $4500–$7900**
- **International students: 4%**
- **Countries represented: 90**
- **Admissions tests:**
  - **TOEFL: Required (min. score 520 paper-based; 190 computer-based; 68 Internet-based)**
  - **IELTS: Required (min. score 6.4)**
  - **SAT or ACT: Not required for international students**
- **Application deadline: Fall, 3/1; spring, 8/1; summer, 1/1**
- **On-campus housing: Available**
- **Summer housing: Available**

Area and Climate

Nestled in the heart of the American Southwest, the state of New Mexico is a land of haunting beauty, where prehistoric man hunted bison in the shadow of snowcapped mountains, where the ancestors of Pueblo Indians built the most impressive dwellings of their era, and where several cultures have blended into a rich tapestry. New Mexico today is no less a treasure. Minutes away from the metropolitan city of Santa Fe is a largely rural high-desert landscape dotted with small towns and Native American pueblos. The Old West brushes up against Los Alamos, the birthplace of the Nuclear Age. New Mexico is truly the Land of Enchantment, and Albuquerque, home of the University of New Mexico (UNM), provides an ideal climate where students can live and learn.

Education

The University of New Mexico (UNM) offers more than 225 degree programs and majors and has New Mexico's only Schools of Architecture and Planning, Medicine, Law, and Pharmacy. The General Library system has more than 2 million volumes and is the largest in the state. Programs such as primary care and family medicine, clinical law, photography, printmaking, art and art history, and engineering have attained national rankings. UNM's diverse faculty is distinguished by a Nobel laureate, MacArthur fellows, Fulbright scholars, and members of the national academics. The low 19:1 student-faculty ratio means that most classes are small, and students take advantage of faculty mentorship. Last year, UNM received more than $247 million in contracts and grants for support of research, instruction, training, and public service. Many

UNM students work on cutting-edge research in the most sophisticated facilities. UNM provides an acclaimed faculty, progressive courses of study, state-of-the-art facilities, and abundant learning resources, each contributing to the value of students' education.

Campus Life

The University of New Mexico campus is a vibrant center of activity, with clubs, sports, 240 student organizations, and a completely renovated, state-of-the-art Student Union Building. Arts and entertainment are also foundations of campus life. Musical and dance performances, theater and concerts, film and cultural events, speakers, lecturers, and stand-up comedy all pack UNM's entertainment calendar, along with the Lobos, UNM's Division I athletic teams. New Mexico is a mecca for those who crave the great outdoors. Snow skiing, hiking, white-water rafting, and year-round biking are just some of the activities available a few minutes and a few miles from the UNM campus.

For International Students

UNM's Office of International Programs and Studies (OIPS) provides international students with valuable services, which begin with an orientation program upon their arrival on campus and continue until they return to their home country. OIPS offers support in five basic areas: help in maintaining legal immigration status while in the U.S.; academic and personal advising; liaison with sponsoring agencies, consulates, the U.S. government, businesses, and other UNM offices and departments; community and campus activities; and assistance with work permission and transition from school to work upon graduation. More information can be found at the OIPS Web site at http://www.unm.edu/oips. Students can submit applications online at http://www.unm.edu/preview/na_online. htm. For inquiries, students should send e-mail to the address listed above.

University of New Orleans

- **Contact:**
  Mr. Jorge Franco
  Assistant Director of Admissions
  University of New Orleans
  New Orleans, LA 70148
  Phone: 504-280-6595
  Fax: 504-280-5522
  E-mail: admissions@uno.edu
  Web site: http://www.uno.edu
- Public, comprehensive, coed
- Urban setting
- Enrollment: 11,800
- Student-faculty ratio: 17:1
- 2006–07 Tuition and fees: $10,336
- 2006–07 Room and board: $3775

- **International students: 5%**
- **Countries represented: 102**
- **International students applied: 1,300**
- **International students accepted: 504**
- **International students enrolled: 160**
- **Admissions tests:**
  - **TOEFL: Required (min. score 525 paper-based; 195 computer-based)**
  - **SAT or ACT: Recommended**
- **Application deadline: Fall, 7/1; spring, 11/1; summer, 4/1**
- **On-campus housing: Available**
- **Summer housing: Available**

Area and Climate

The University of New Orleans's (UNO) 195-acre (79-hectare) main campus is set in one of the most beautiful residential areas on the southern shore of Lake Pontchartrain in the southeastern United States. Renowned for Creole and Cajun cuisine, Mardi Gras, and the Jazz and Heritage Festival, New Orleans culture offers a unique environment for students to grow both socially and academically. The city's semitropical climate and thousands of acres of parks, lakes, rivers, and bayous allow for year-round outdoor activities. The city is easily accessible by public transit from UNO main campus.

Education

Established in 1958, UNO offers fifty-one bachelor's and forty-two graduate degree programs. UNO derives its strength from its urban setting and strives to enhance the economic, social, and cultural amenities of New Orleans through its numerous research projects, outreach programs, and special cooperative agreements. Other academic enhancements include an honors program; the UNO Library, which houses a 1.5-million-volume collection; and six on-campus computer labs with Internet connections, including wireless Internet access in selected buildings. Academic advising within each department is available to all students. Eighty percent of the faculty members hold doctorates or terminal degrees in their field of study; the UNO faculty is dedicated to and deeply involved in student affairs and campus life.

Campus Life

The University of New Orleans attracts students from forty-nine states and 102 countries, with the majority of students being Louisiana residents. UNO offers three unique styles of year-round on-campus housing: Bienville Hall, a coeducational dormitory; Privateer Place Apartments, which overlooks Lake Pontchartrain; and a new student-housing development that is planned to feature suite-style units as well as TV and recreation rooms, study lounges, laundry facilities, and a convenience store. UNO has more than 100 student organizations, including academic, professional, Greek, political, and religious groups. In addition, UNO students can participate in several recreational and intramural sports as well as NCAA Division I sports. Students can also enjoy year-round lecture and musical series, concerts, and theatrical events.

For International Students

The Office of International Students and Scholars (OISS) provides immigration advisory and documentation services, such as issuance of forms I-20 and DS 2019, school transfer procedures, employment, housing, and maintenance of status while in the United States. OISS offers support on such matters as cross-cultural adjustment, family and financial concerns, academic difficulties, and personal concerns. An intensive English language program is located on campus for students who need language training prior to entering an academic program. International undergraduate students who are interested in partial scholarships are encouraged to apply as soon as possible due to limited availability.

University of Northern Iowa

- Contact:
  Kristi Marchesani
  Assistant Director of Admissions/International
  University of Northern Iowa
  Cedar Falls, IA 50614-0018
  Phone: 319-273-2281
  Fax: 319-273-6103
  E-mail: kristi.marchesani@uni.edu
  Web site: http://www.uni.edu/intladm
- Public, comprehensive, coed
- Enrollment: 12,513
- Student-faculty ratio: 17:1
- 2006–07 Tuition and fees: $13,828

- 2006–07 Room and board: $5537
- International students: 3%
- Countries represented: 78
- International students enrolled: 442 (total)
- Admissions test:
  - TOEFL: Required (min. score 550 PBT; 213 CBT)
  - SAT and ACT: Not required
- Application deadline: Rolling
- On-campus housing: Guaranteed
- Summer housing: Available

Area and Climate

The University of Northern Iowa (UNI) is located in Cedar Falls, a pleasant college town in northeast Iowa. The metropolitan area of Cedar Falls and the neighboring town of Waterloo have a population of more than 110,000. The UNI/Cedar Falls community was recently named the safest of 467 campus communities in the nation. The area offers a host of opportunities and activities, including art galleries and museums; theatrical and musical performances; places of worship, including an Islamic center; movie theaters and shopping centers; ethnic restaurants; ethnic grocery stores; and parks and nature reserves that feature hiking, biking, and cross-country skiing trails.

Education

UNI is a liberal arts institution with special emphasis on teaching. Classes are taught by faculty members who include Fulbright Scholars, top-quality researchers, former Fortune 500 executives, and authors who are accessible outside the classroom. There are opportunities for research participation at the undergraduate level. The classes are small and take place in modern facilities, and the academic support services are excellent. *U.S. News & World Report* recently ranked UNI second among Midwest regional public universities for the tenth year in a row. More than 12,500 students from forty-six states and seventy-eight countries come to earn undergraduate and graduate degrees in more than 120 undergraduate and seventy graduate majors. At the undergraduate level, the University offers five baccalaureate degrees.

Campus Life

UNI is a medium-sized university with a small-college atmosphere. The 840-acre (340-hectare) parklike campus is a walk-ing campus—any building can be reached in about 10 minutes. The buildings combine the grandeur of early 1900s architecture with striking, modern designs resulting from a recent period of growth. Students have a host of extracurricular activities from which to choose, such as international student association; international host families; art, music, and drama; academic honor groups; intramural sports and wellness programs; fraternities and sororities; student publications; religious fellowship; student government; and pre-professional clubs. Currently, more than 390 international students attend UNI.

For International Students

The International Services Office at UNI exists for the sole support of international students and scholars. The International Services Office assists students in their transition to campus from their home countries and in their daily campus activities while they are enrolled. International students find a full complement of services especially for them. Each semester, the International Services Office provides the Orientation and Registration Program for all new students. The mandatory program provides important information about UNI, campus resources, and other issues concerning international students. Throughout the year, International Services hosts social and cultural events to bring students together and provide new experiences. The International Student Association (ISA), a cultural and social club for international and American students, provides opportunities for them to share cultural experiences and learn from others. The club plans many social events throughout the school year including picnics, movie nights, and other fun activities. The Culture and Intensive English Program (CIEP) of the University of Northern Iowa emphasizes practical use of spoken and written English.

University of North Texas

- **Contact:**
  International Admissions Advisor
  University of North Texas
  P.O. Box 311067
  Denton, TX 76203
  Phone: 940-565-2442
  Fax: 940-565-4822
  E-mail: international@unt.edu
  Web site: http://www.international.unt.edu
- **Public, comprehensive, coed**
- **Suburban setting**
- **Enrollment: 32,000**
- **Student-faculty ratio: 19:1 (approx.)**
- **2007–08 Tuition and fees (per semester): $5783 (12 undergraduate credit hours)**

- **2007–08 Room and board: $2400–$3400 per semester**
- **International students: 5%**
- **Countries represented: 110**
- **International students applied: 1,200**
- **International students accepted: 800**
- **International students enrolled: 1,820 (total)**
- **Admissions tests:**
  - **TOEFL: Required (min. score 550 PBT; 213 CBT; 80 iBT)**
  - **SAT and ACT: Not required**
- **Application deadline: Fall, 3/1; spring, 8/1**
- **On-campus housing: Available**
- **Summer housing: Available**

Area and Climate

Denton, Texas, is a small, safe southern city with a warm climate. It is home to two major universities, University of North Texas (UNT) and Texas Woman's University, and has a population of nearly 100,000. Because it is a university city, people in Denton have easy access to concerts, art exhibits, lectures, and sports events. Denton is about 30 minutes from the Dallas/Fort Worth International Airport and 45 minutes from Dallas and Fort Worth, which provide the cuisine, entertainment, shopping, culture, and medical centers of major cities. North and west of Denton are large horse ranches and rolling, grassy hills. Summer temperatures range from 79°F to 100°F (26°C to 38°C), and winter temperatures range from 32°F to 50°F (0°C to 10°C).

Education

The University of North Texas is recognized for education, research, creative activities, and public service. UNT is an inclusive and diverse institution with an international perspective. UNT commits to creating an informed citizenry, high-quality graduates, and a workforce well prepared for the global economy. UNT's nearly 31,000 students enroll in eleven colleges and schools, which offer 100 bachelor's, 125 master's, and fifty doctoral degree programs. A fully accredited university system that includes the Denton campus, the South Dallas campus, and the Fort Worth Health Sciences Center, UNT is designated a Doctoral/Research University–Extensive by the Carnegie Foundation. Many undergraduate and graduate courses and select degree programs are available on the Internet.

Campus Life

UNT offers a rich and culturally diverse experience for students from every U.S. state and 110 countries. More than 250 student organizations provide activities for all interests. About 5,000 students live in twelve residence halls, all within a 5- to 10-minute walk of dining halls and the majestic fountain at the campus center. UNT buses provide free transportation to and from nearby student apartments. Students have access to libraries and computer labs that are open 24 hours a day as well as a state-of-the-art Student Recreation Center, the Student Health and Wellness Center, concerts, and athletic competition in major university-level sports. Incoming freshmen participate in a first-year program that combines a comprehensive introduction to college life with ongoing mentoring to ensure academic and social success at UNT.

For International Students

UNT is a great place for international students. Diversity is welcomed. Nearly 2,000 students from 110 countries are enrolled in undergraduate and graduate degree programs and in the Intensive English Language Institute (IELI). IELI's seven-level intensive academic preparatory English language program provides a smooth transition into UNT. No TOEFL score is required for admission to UNT for IELI graduates. Conditional admission is available for undergraduate and graduate students. UNT offers a unique program for graduate students who struggle with the verbal portion of the TOEFL. Completion of this rigorous Graduate Preparation Course substitutes for the GRE/GMAT verbal score requirements for many graduate programs. International students are eligible to apply for competitive scholarships that may include in-state tuition. Students are eligible for paid internships—on campus and off campus in the Denton or Dallas-Fort Worth communities—and for nearly 3,000 on-campus jobs.

University of Rochester

- **Contact:**
  Director of International Admissions
  University of Rochester
  Rochester, NY 14627-0251
  Phone: 585-275-3221
  　　　888-822-2256 (toll-free)
  Fax: 585-461-4595
  E-mail: admit@admissions.rochester.edu
  Web site: http://www.enrollment.rochester.
  　　　edu/admissions
- Private, comprehensive, four-year
- Suburban setting
- Total enrollment: 4,353
- Student-faculty ratio: 8:1
- 2006–07 Tuition and fees: $33,426
- 2006–07 Room and board: $10,192

- International students: 4%
- Countries represented: 11
- International students applied: 532
- International students accepted: 230
- International students enrolled: 51
- Admissions tests:
  - TOEFL: Required for nonnative speakers attending international schools
  - SAT: Required for native speakers or students attending international or American schools
- Application deadline: Freshman: fall, 12/1; spring, 10/1. Transfer: fall, 6/15; spring, 10/1 (recommended dates)
- On-campus housing: Available
- Summer housing: Available

Area and Climate

Rochester is ranked among the nation's best metropolitan areas with respect to quality of life. The greater Rochester area, with a population of 1 million, is rich in educational, cultural, and recreational resources. Fortune 500 companies that include Bausch & Lomb, Kodak, and Xerox offer Rochester students options for research in business and industry. Cultural attractions abound. The school stages more than 700 concerts and recitals throughout the year. Summer is sunny, warm, and lush with greenery; autumn is crisp and abundantly colorful; winter is the season of sledding, ice-skating, and downhill and cross-country skiing; and spring is a delight in "The Flower City."

Education

The University of Rochester was founded in 1850 and is comprised of six colleges and schools: the College, including programs in the arts and sciences and the School of Engineering and Applied Sciences; the Eastman School of Music; the School of Medicine and Dentistry; the School of Nursing; the William E. Simon Graduate School of Business Administration; and the Margaret Warner School of Education and Human Development. The University of Rochester is a high-quality research university that is modest in size and is among the best private institutions in the United States. Class sizes tend to be small and students interact with faculty members on a more informal basis while at the same time having access to the finest research facilities. The College is the heart of undergraduate and graduate education in the arts, sciences, and engineering at the University of Rochester.

Campus Life

Rochester students relax at Wilson Commons, the University's light-filled student union designed by I.M. Pei; exercise at the Goergen Athletic Complex; or bicycle, jog, or canoe through nearby Genesee Valley Park and on the Genesee River. Films, performances, lectures, sporting events, conferences, and innumerable special events are held at the University year round. The Eastman School of Music presents hundreds of concerts that feature distinguished faculty members, visiting artists, and students. For the sports enthusiast, there are professional baseball, hockey, and soccer franchises, one of the nation's finest collections of urban park environments, and nearby wilderness. In the winter, jogging trails are used extensively for cross-country skiing. The University also has a 400-meter outdoor track; a four-lane, 200-meter oval indoor track; squash and racquetball courts, and extensive exercise and weight-training facilities.

For International Students

The University values the diversity of ideas and cultures brought by international students to the Rochester community. The International Services Office (ISO) at the University of Rochester is an excellent resource for international students. Faculty and staff members at the University of Rochester are committed to providing international students with the services they need to be successful. The ISO coordinates a two-day International Student Orientation Program (ISOP). Here, advisers assist students with their adjustment to life in the United States and to the University of Rochester. The ISOP also addresses the topics of banking, securing a driver's license, the American educational system, American customs, transportation, immigration, tax information, safety, health care in the United States, and employment.

University of San Francisco

- Contact:
  Mike Hughes
  Director of Undergraduate Admission
  University of San Francisco
  2130 Fulton Street
  San Francisco, CA 94117
  Phone: 415-422-6563
  Fax: 415-422-2217
- Private Catholic, university, coed
- Urban setting
- Enrollment: 4,274 (undergraduate)
- Student-faculty ratio: 14:1
- 2006–07 Tuition and fees: $28,420
- 2006–07 Room and board: $10,530

- International students: 8%
- Countries represented: 82
- International students applied: 395
- International students enrolled: 39
- Admissions tests:
  - TOEFL: Required (min. score 550 paper-based; 213 computer-based)
  - SAT and ACT: Recommended, but not required
- Application deadline: Fall, February 1 (priority); spring, November 1
- On-campus housing: Guaranteed for first- and second-year students
- Summer housing: Available

Area and Climate

The University of San Francisco (USF) is located in a beautiful residential neighborhood in the center of San Francisco. The hilltop campus, bordering Golden Gate Park, is 3 miles (5 kilometers) from the downtown financial district and offers panoramic views of the city. San Francisco serves as an exciting and diverse urban environment where students can benefit from the educational, cultural, and professional opportunities that few cities can match. San Francisco's temperature is moderate year-round, ranging from 50°F to 70°F (10°C to 21°C).

Education

Founded in 1855, University of San Francisco has grown and developed over the past 150 years into one of the premier private universities in California. Throughout its history, USF has remained faithful to its Jesuit mission of preparing men and women as leaders in service to others. It is committed to academic programs that offer intellectual traditions and tools to understand the past, clarify the present, and anticipate the future. Students can choose from more than forty majors in the College of Arts and Sciences, McLaren College of Business, and School of Nursing. Popular majors among the international students include business, communications, computer science, economics, psychology, and the visual arts. Regardless of their major, small class sizes provide USF's students with an intimate learning experience and an opportunity to work closely with its distinguished teaching faculty.

Campus Life

USF is one of the most diverse university campuses in the United States. Living and studying with students from all fifty states and more than eighty countries greatly enhances the learning experience. Outside of class, students can choose to get involved in more than eighty clubs and organizations. Among their many other options, USF students participate in student government, journalism, the performing arts, culturally-focused clubs, and professional associations. Students have access to the spectacular Koret Health and Recreation Center, where they can exercise, participate in intramural sports leagues, or join off-campus excursions. USF is a residential campus, and housing is available throughout the four years of study.

For International Students

Upon arrival, international students participate in New Student Orientation, a program that helps them get acquainted with campus resources, meet other new students, and explore San Francisco. International student advisers help the students make the adjustment to living and studying in the United States. International student clubs provide camaraderie and an opportunity for cultural exchange. Students needing additional English training can take advantage of the on-campus Intensive English Program.

University of South Carolina Upstate

- **Contact:**
  Donette Stewart
  Office of Admissions
  University of South Carolina Upstate
  800 University Way
  Spartanburg, SC 29303
  Phone: 864-503-5280
  Fax: 864-503-5727
  E-mail: admissions@uscupstate.edu
  Web site: http://www.uscupstate.edu/
      enrollment_services/
      international/International.asp
- **Public, four-year, coed**
- **Suburban setting**
- **Enrollment: 4,409**

- **Student-faculty ratio: 18:1**
- **2006–07 Comprehensive fee: $18,900**
- **Countries represented: 71**
- **Admissions tests:**
    - **TOEFL (min. score 500 paper-based; 173 computer-based)**
    - **SAT or ACT: Required**
- **Application deadline: Fall, 7/15; spring, 12/1; summer, 3/15**
- **On-campus housing: Available**
- **Summer housing: Available**

Area and Climate

The University of South Carolina Upstate (USC Upstate), set in the picturesque foothills of the Blue Ridge Mountains, is conveniently located along the thriving I-85 economic corridor between Atlanta and Charlotte, just a few hours' drive from the beaches and mountains. Upstate South Carolina is a dynamic international hub, and Spartanburg County is home to the highest per-capita concentration of international business in the United States.

The average summer temperature is 97°F (36°C). In January, temperatures hover around 40°F (4°C), and the area sees less than 6 inches (15 centimeters) of snowfall a year.

Education

As a senior comprehensive public institution of the University of South Carolina, the University's primary responsibilities are to offer baccalaureate education to the citizens of Upstate South Carolina and to offer selected master's degrees in response to regional demand. USC Upstate offers bachelor's degree programs in the liberal arts, sciences, business administration, nursing, and teacher education and master's degrees in education. The five most popular majors at USC Upstate are nursing, elementary education, interdisciplinary studies, business, and psychology. For the bachelor's degree, all students must complete a set of courses in the general education requirement, in the department, and in the cognate or minor, as well as several electives.

Campus Life

Students can participate in an array of campus groups, including community service groups, fraternities and sororities, honor societies, leadership programs, performing groups, religious organizations, and special-interest organizations. USC Upstate joins the Atlantic Sun Conference as the league's twelfth member in the 2007–08 season. Men's sports include baseball, basketball, cross-country, golf, soccer, tennis, and track and field. Women compete in basketball, cross-country, golf, soccer, softball, tennis, track and field, and volleyball. USC Upstate also offers a full campus-recreation program that includes free aerobics classes and intramural sports such as badminton, basketball, bowling, flag football, soccer, softball, running, and tennis, among others.

For International Students

USC Upstate is proud to be home to many international students from more than seventy nations, including Canada, Czech Republic, France, Korea, Norway, Peru, South Africa, Tanzania, and many others. International students are among the school's most academically and socially successful, leading many of the social and honors organizations on campus. Open to all students, the International Club promotes understanding and appreciation of the cultural diversities that exist in the world and in the community and attempts to provide related educational experiences. English as a second language (ESL) continuing education courses are offered.

University of Southern Indiana

- **Contact:**
  Heidi Gregori-Gahan, Director
  International Programs and Services
  University of Southern Indiana
  Evansville, IN 47712

  Phone: 812-465-1248
  Fax: 812-465-1057
  E-mail: intlprog@usi.edu
  Web site: http://www.usi.edu
- **Public, comprehensive, coed**
- **Suburban setting**
- **Enrollment: 10,050**
- **Student-faculty ratio: 18:1**
- **2006–07 Tuition and fees: $10,450**

- **2006–07 Room and board: $6370**
- **International students: 1%**
- **Countries represented: 30**
- **International students accepted: 73**
- **International students enrolled: 34**
- **Admissions tests:**
    - **TOEFL: Required (min. score 525 paper-based)**
    - **SAT and ACT: Recommended**
- **Application deadline: Rolling**
- **On-campus housing: Available**
- **Summer housing: Available**

Area and Climate

The 300-acre (122-hectare) wooded campus is situated in beautiful rolling hills on the edge of Evansville, Indiana's third-largest city. A cultural and economic hub for the region, Evansville is located in the southwestern tip of Indiana, on the banks of the Ohio River. Evansville's moderate size of approximately 130,000 residents provides the activity and accessibility of a large metropolitan city while maintaining the special charm of a small river town. Numerous recreational activities are available in the city, including live concerts throughout the year, theatrical productions, and sports. Evansville is a comfortable drive to metropolitan areas such as Chicago, St. Louis, Cincinnati, and Indianapolis. The climate of the region is moderate, offering four distinct seasons throughout the year.

Education

Founded in 1965, the University of Southern Indiana (USI) is a broad-based institution offering programs of instruction, research, and service. More than seventy academic programs are offered through the Colleges of Business, Education and Human Services, Liberal Arts, Nursing and Health Professions, and Science and Engineering. The University strives to maintain a low student-faculty ratio to enhance learning; the average class size is 25 students. University facilities include nine major classroom buildings and the Rice Library, which houses nearly 200,000 volumes and 1,500 newspapers and periodicals. The academic calendar consists of two 15-week semesters and three summer terms. A full-time ESL program is also available throughout the year.

Campus Life

The University has more than eighty clubs and organizations. An active Student Government Association serves as the voice of the students. The Activities Programming Board organizes major campus events, films, lecture series, and other entertainment throughout the year. Numerous athletic and health-related activities are offered through the intramural program and the Recreational Fitness Center. Approximately 2,500 students live in campus apartments or suite-style residence halls that feature laundry facilities, computer labs, and e-mail access. Apartments consist of two bedrooms and two bathrooms, a living room, a dining area, and a fully equipped kitchen. The suite-style halls combine the benefits of a traditional residence hall with the popular apartment-style housing at USI. Housing is available during the academic year and summer terms. A full meal plan is available in the campus dining center when classes are in session.

For International Students

The Office of International Programs and Services provides a comprehensive range of services designed to meet the unique needs of international students. An international orientation program is held before the beginning of each semester. Ongoing programs include the Host Family Program, Conversation Partners, and the International Outreach Program. The Global Community Floor in Ruston Hall offers students the opportunity to interact with American and international students in a comfortable, cross-cultural setting. The International Club sponsors numerous social and cultural events throughout the year.

University of Southern Maine

- Contact:
  Dee Gardner
  Director of Undergraduate Admission
  University of Southern Maine
  Portland, Gorham, and Lewiston, Maine
  Phone: 207-780-5670
  Fax: 207-780-5640
  E-mail: usmadm@usm.maine.edu
  Web site: http://www.usm.maine.edu/
- Public, comprehensive, coed
- Urban setting
- Enrollment: 4,788 (full-time undergraduate)
- Student-faculty ratio: 13:1
- 2006–07 Tuition and fees: $15,581
- 2006–07 Room and board: $6341

- International students: 1%
- Countries represented: 39
- International students applied: 43
- International students accepted: 9
- International students enrolled: 6
- Admissions tests:
  - TOEFL: Required (paper-based min. score 550; computer-based min. score 213; Internet-based min. score 79)
  - SAT and ACT: Recommended, but not required
- Application deadline: Fall, 2/15 (priority); spring, 10/1
- On-campus housing: Available
- Summer housing: Available

Area and Climate

The University of Southern Maine's (USM) location is an ideal place to be a college student. Portland, Maine, which is conveniently located along the New England coast, less than 2 hours north of Boston, Massachusetts, is nationally rated for outdoor recreation and is considered to be one of the best and safest cities in which to live in the United States. This vibrant seaport, with a thriving visual and performing arts scene, is a gathering place for the 35,000 students who attend college within an hour of the city. Its proximity to the Atlantic Ocean, mountains, and lakes provides students with the recreational opportunities associated with the four distinct seasons. Portland International Jetport is located within minutes of the campus. Train and bus service to Boston's Logan International Airport is also available.

Education

Since its founding in 1878, USM has evolved into a selective, comprehensive, regional, residential public university. USM undergraduates learn from exceptional professors who give personal attention to students. The average class size is 22 students. Students enjoy the friendly atmosphere of a small, residential New England college campus combined with many opportunities that are typically available only at large, national, urban universities. USM offers forty-seven bachelor's degrees, twenty-six master's degrees, and three doctoral degrees through its College of Arts and Sciences, Lewiston-Auburn College, and six professional schools: the College of Education and Human Development; the School of Business; the School of Applied Science, Engineering and Technology; the College of Nursing and Health Professions; the Muskie School of Public Service; and the School of Law. In addition, many students take advantage of opportunities to participate in research projects with their professors, the National and International Exchange Programs, study tours, internships, and cooperative education.

Campus Life

USM offers a unique blend of academic and residential life opportunities on two distinct campuses (Portland, an urban setting, and Gorham, a small New England town) only 8 miles apart. The diverse student body of 4,700 full-time undergraduates represents students from thirty-four states and thirty-nine countries. Students choose from more than 100 clubs and organizations and twenty-three men's and women's NCAA Division III intercollegiate athletic teams. Social life on campus includes concerts, dances, performances, and special events. Off campus, students enjoy the city life of Portland as well as the outdoor activities of the region, including downhill skiing, hiking, white-water rafting, and sea kayaking. Organized trips to Boston, Montreal, and New York City are popular.

For International Students

A special orientation program for international students is held prior to the beginning of each semester. Assistance with transportation from the Portland International Jetport is provided. The Office of International Exchange works directly with students and assists them with their transition to USM and the region. Residence halls are open throughout the academic year and summer. USM's English Language Bridge Program provides assistance to students who need additional work with their language skills.

University of South Florida

- **Contact:**
  International Admissions
  University of South Florida
  4202 East Fowler Avenue, CPR 107
  Tampa, FL 33620
  Phone: 813-974-8790
  Fax: 813-974-8044
  E-mail: ia@iac.usf.edu
  Web site: http://web.usf.edu/iac/admissions
- **State-supported, comprehensive, coed**
- **Urban setting**
- **Enrollment: 44,000**
- **Student-faculty ratio: 17:1**

- **2007–08 Tuition and fees: $16,040**
- **2007–08 Room and board: $7590**
- **International students: 3%**
- **Countries represented: 133**
- **Admissions tests:**
  - **TOEFL: Required (min. score 550 PBT, 213 CBT, 79 iBT)**
  - **SAT or ACT: Required**
- **Application deadline: Fall, 1/2; spring, 7/1**
- **On-campus housing: Available**
- **Summer housing: Available**

Area and Climate

Those who choose to join the University of South Florida (USF) family have an even bigger community to explore: the Tampa Bay area. With 2.5 million residents, the Tampa Bay area is one of the world's most desirable locations in which to live, offering a booming employment rate, year-round festivals and activities, and a climate that is consistently pleasant and sunny (annual temperatures range from 50°F (10°C) to 95°F (35°C)). Situated off the Gulf of Mexico, on the west coast of the central portion of the Florida peninsula, it is only 1 hour west of Orlando's famous theme parks and minutes from beautiful local beaches. Busch Gardens, Lowry Park Zoo, Florida Aquarium, and the historic Ybor City district are some of the many attractions in the area. Tampa hosts national professional baseball, football, and hockey teams. Tampa's cultural offerings include the Museum of Science and Industry, the Tampa Bay Performing Arts Center, Ruth Eckerd Hall, the Tampa Museum of Art, the Salvador Dalí Museum in St. Petersburg, and the Ringling Brothers Museum in Sarasota.

Education

The University of South Florida awards the Bachelor of Arts and Bachelor of Science degrees and a variety of graduate and doctoral degrees through the Colleges of Architecture, Arts and Sciences, Business, Education, Engineering, Marine Science, Medicine, Nursing, Public Health, and Visual and Performing Arts and the Honors College. USF, one of America's top sixty Research 1 universities, offers more than 200 majors and programs, including accounting, biotechnology, business, education, engineering, health sciences, and mass communications. USF offers a broad-based liberal arts curriculum that produces graduates who have a well-rounded education and are prepared to pursue employment or further study at the graduate level. The prestigious Honors College is the largest in the state of Florida and requires a minimum SAT score of 1270 for international applicants. It attracts highly motivated, bright undergraduate students and provides them annual scholarships of $500 per year for up to four years, personal mentoring by senior faculty members, research opportunities with professors, and support to attend professional conferences. USF is accredited by SACS and has professional accreditation in more than thirty disciplines/fields, including accounting, business (AACSB International–The Association to Advance Collegiate Schools of Business), engineering (ABET, Inc.), and others.

Campus Life

USF has more than 300 student clubs and organizations, thirty-nine of which are international student organizations. There are seventeen national fraternities and thirteen national sororities. A wide array of extracurricular programs are scheduled, including concerts, movies, and a lecture series. USF is a member of the NCAA and Conference USA; all teams compete on the NCAA Division I level. Club and intramural sports and outdoor adventures are also offered. The Tampa campus features an eighteen-hole championship golf course, four swimming pools, sand volleyball courts, tennis courts, and a state-of-the-art recreation center. Sixty-four percent of freshmen live on campus. On-campus housing, which includes residence halls, suites, apartments, and special-interest and honors housing, is wired for telephone, cable TV, and high-speed Internet access.

For International Students

The International Affairs Center provides excellent service to the approximately 2,100 international students and 200 research scholars at the University, including the issuance and maintenance of visa documentation, SEVIS compliance, and enrollment and expense letters. The mission of International Student and Scholar Services (ISSS) is to support and enhance the academic, cultural, and social experience of all international students and scholars at the University of South Florida. ISSS is dedicated to offering excellence in service and serves as the primary link between international students/scholars and the University, the community, and the federal government. The staff is trained and experienced in cross-cultural counseling and advises students in immigration, adjustment to life in the U.S., and personal and academic issues. ISSS collaborates with other USF departments to promote cross-cultural understanding and to provide high-quality service to international students and scholars. In addition, ISSS provides orientation and cultural programs, immigration workshops, and social activities and is also a liaison with several community service programs, including the Friends of Internationals. International students can study abroad and volunteer for USF's new Global Ambassadors Program, which places students who are interested in international education in volunteer summer internships around the world. An Intensive English Program is offered through the University's English Language Institute. USF offers provisional acceptance to qualified students who enroll in the institute's program.

The University of Tampa

- **Contact:**
  International Admissions
  The University of Tampa
  West Kennedy Boulevard
  Tampa, FL 33606-1490
  Phone: 813-253-6211
  Fax: 813-258-7398
  E-mail: admissions@ut.edu
  Web site: http://ut.edu
- Private, coed
- Urban setting
- Enrollment: 5,202
- Student-faculty ratio: 17:1

- 2005–06 Tuition and fees: $19,628
- 2005–06 Room and board: $7252
- International students: 315
- Countries represented: 100
- Admissions tests:
  - TOEFL (min. score 550, PBT; 213, CBT; 79–80 iBT)
  - SAT: Required for English speakers
- Application deadline: Rolling, with priority dates
- On-campus housing: Available
- Summer housing: Available

Area and Climate

Home to 2.3 million people in the southeastern part of the United States, Tampa is one of the most exciting growth areas in the country. The University's 100-acre (40-hectare) parklike campus is just across the river (two blocks) from downtown Tampa. The campus has forty-five buildings, including nine residence halls, a student center, the John H. Sykes College of Business, a library, computer and science labs, theaters, an art gallery, a museum, and sports facilities. The main classroom and administration building is a National Historic Landmark and one of the finest examples of Moorish architecture in the Western Hemisphere. Tampa's airport is just 15 minutes away and is served by major airlines with connecting flights to cities around the world. The University is 1 hour from Orlando, where Disney World theme parks are located. Florida is warm and sunny year-round, and beautiful Gulf beaches are only 30 minutes away.

Education

Fully accredited by the Southern Association of Colleges and Schools and AACSB International–The Association to Advance Collegiate Schools of Business, the University offers more than 100 areas of study in two colleges, the College of Business and the College of Liberal Arts and Sciences. At the graduate level, the University offers graduate programs in business, nursing, and teaching. Popular undergraduate majors include international business, management, marketing, computer information systems, finance, sciences, psychology, communication, and the fine arts. Excellent students participate in the Honors Program, with expanded instruction and research. Hundreds of internships are also available. Professors value the relationships they develop with their students in classes where enrollments average 21. Faculty members are also involved in research, and students serve as research assistants.

Campus Life

Extracurricular activities include more than 120 interest and honors clubs and fraternities and sororities. Many athletic teams rank among the top ten in NCAA Division II. Intercollegiate sports for men and women include basketball, cross-country, soccer, and swimming. Also offered are men's baseball and golf and women's crew, softball, tennis, and volleyball. Campus housing is available, and 80 percent of all residence halls are new since 1998. The campus, which employs its own security personnel, has a comfortable and safe environment. Students attend concerts, art exhibitions, theater and dance performances, and special lectures and films on campus and nearby. Just across the river are the Museum of Art, Performing Arts Center, Convention Center, and Aquarium.

For International Students

Every international student is assigned an academic adviser. A full-time International Student Coordinator also works with the Dean of Students to provide special assistance to international students. The International Student Organization sponsors social and professional activities. Students may pursue a degree or enroll for just one semester or for a one-year study program.

University of Texas at San Antonio

- **Contact:**
  Rebecca Underwood
  Assistant Director of Admissions
  University of Texas at San Antonio
  One UTSA Circle
  San Antonio, TX 78249-0616
  Phone: 210-458-6065
  Fax: 210-458-7564
  E-mail: IntlAdmissions@utsa.edu
  Web site: http://www.utsa.edu/admissions/international.htm
- **Public, comprehensive, coed**
- **Urban setting**
- **Enrollment: 27,291**
- **Student-faculty ratio: 23.6:1**
- **2006–07 Tuition and fees: $12,468**
- **2006–07 Room and board: $5900**

- **International students: 3%**
- **Countries represented: 85**
- **International students applied: 867**
- **International students accepted: 545**
- **International students enrolled: 251 (total on campus: 823)**
- **Admissions tests:**
  - TOEFL (paper-based min. score 500; computer-based min. score 173; Internet-based min. score 61)
  - IELTS: min. score 5
  - SAT or ACT: Recommended
- **Application deadline: Fall, 6/1; spring, 10/15; summer, 3/1**
- **On-campus housing: Available**
- **Summer housing: Available**

Area and Climate

The multicultural city of San Antonio serves as the gateway to the Texas hill country and the Gulf Coast. The winters are mild and the summers are usually hot; the annual rainfall is 28 inches (71 centimeters). VIA Metropolitan Transit provides affordable public transportation throughout the city of more than a million people. The San Antonio art museums, theaters, and symphony are among the state's finest. Famous for the Alamo, the Spanish missions, and two large theme parks (Six Flags Fiesta Texas and Sea World), San Antonio is not only the most historic city in Texas but also among its most playful.

Education

Established in 1969 as a component of the University of Texas System, the University of Texas at San Antonio (UTSA) is the city's only comprehensive, four-year public university, with 27,291 students enrolled in bachelor's, master's, and doctoral degree programs. Seven colleges form the backbone of the curricula: Business, Education and Human Development, Engineering, Liberal and Fine Arts, Public Policy, Sciences, and the School of Architecture. UTSA offers fifty-eight undergraduate, forty-two master's, and thirteen Ph.D. degrees. Biology, business, engineering, psychology, and computer science are among the most popular freshman majors. Ninety-nine percent of the faculty members have earned Ph.D.'s or terminal degrees in their academic field; 51 have earned prestigious

Fulbright fellowships. Ninety-five percent of the full-time faculty members teach undergraduate courses.

Campus Life

UTSA is now composed of two campuses, the main campus on the northwest side of the city and a new campus downtown. The student body is one of the most diverse in the country. More than 56 percent are from underrepresented groups, and 54 percent are women. The average age of the student body is 24; the average age of freshmen is 18. On-campus housing options include residence halls that house 3,000 students in spacious 1- and 2-person rooms and suites and a gated apartment complex with one-, two-, and four-bedroom plans.

For International Students

Orientation for new international students is held the week before classes begin. This orientation includes information necessary to adjust to a new school and a new city. Some of the topics covered include how to open a bank account, where shopping centers are located, and off-campus activities available to University students. During this week, students also participate in the English language placement program, consult with their academic advisers, and register for classes. Tutors for all subjects are available through the Tomas Rivera Center for Student Success. A Shopping Shuttle provides free transportation to a local shopping center one day a week for students who wish to patronize the grocery store, shops, restaurants, or theater. The UTSA Intensive English Program is available for any student whose TOEFL/IELTS score does not meet the admission requirements; a separate application is not necessary for this program.

University of the Incarnate Word

- **Contact:**
  Office of Admissions
  University of the Incarnate Word
  4301 Broadway, Box 285
  San Antonio, TX 78209
  Phone: 210-829-6005
       800-749-9673
  Fax: 210-829-3921
  E-mail: admis@uiwtx.edu
  Web site: http://www.uiw.edu
- **Private, coed**
- **Enrollment: 5,500**
- **Student-faculty ratio: 14:1**
- **2006–07 Tuition and fees: $18,370 (with laptop, $19,870)**

- **2006–07 Room and board: $3205**
- **International students: 6%**
- **Countries represented: 37**
- **International students applied: 129 (fall 2006)**
- **International students accepted: 97 (fall 2006)**
- **International students enrolled: 324 (current total)**
- **Admissions tests:**
  - **TOEFL (min. score 550, paper-based test)**
  - **SAT and ACT: Recommended**
- **Application deadline: Rolling**
- **On-campus housing: Available**
- **Summer housing: Available**

Area and Climate

The University of the Incarnate Word (UIW) is located on a beautiful tree-lined campus in the north central district of San Antonio that is adjacent to Brackenridge Park and the suburb of Alamo Heights. San Antonio is a beautiful city that is known for its many civic celebrations, including Fiesta. The city is rich in educational offerings and fosters a flourishing arts community. An assortment of museums are located nearby, in addition to a number of restaurants, shops, cultural attractions, recreational facilities, and the famous Paseo del Rio, or River Walk. San Antonio has more than 300 sunny days each year and is mild in winter and warm in summer, with an average yearly temperature of 19°C (67°F). San Antonio has an annual rainfall of 70 cm. (27.5 in.)

Education

Founded in 1881, UIW offers educational diversity that incorporates a global outlook and offers a wide range of undergraduate programs, including business administration; education; humanities, arts, and social sciences; interactive media and design; math, science, and engineering; nursing and health professions, as well as prepharmacy. Graduate programs are in administration, biology, business administration; communication arts, education, English, health informatics, kinesiology, math, multidisciplinary studies, nursing, nutrition, religious studies, sciences, and sport management. The University offers the Doctor of Philosophy (Ph.D.) degree in the School of Education, which has three concentrations: international education and entrepreneurship, mathematics education,

and organizational leadership. The Doctor of Pharmacy (Pharm.D.) program began in 2006; UIW is one of six schools in Texas to offer this professional program. The UIW library is located on campus, offering all the information that students need as well as a variety of information online. UIW also has a laptop program to provide all students with Gateway laptops to aid study. UIW also conducts a number of programs online. UIW promotes education and cultural exchange with more than ninety sister schools with whom UIW has exchange agreements.

Campus Life

UIW is a residential campus and houses more than 800 students in several residence halls. UIW hosts a multitude of sporting activities, including baseball, basketball, golf, soccer, softball, swimming, synchronized swimming, tennis, various track and field events, and volleyball. The Wellness Center, a state-of-the-art gymnasium that includes a spa, a sauna, and a basketball court, is located on campus. UIW's Natatorium, which opened in 2002, has an Olympic-size swimming pool.

For International Students

The International Students Association plans a wide range of activities and trips. The International Conference Center buildings on campus house, among residential and state-of-the-art conference facilities, the Office of International Programs and Initiatives. Staff members come from a wide range of nationalities and coordinate student study abroad, student exchanges, ESL classes, the Learning Resource Center activities, and conference and housing facilities and assist in the general well-being of the UIW international student. An Intensive English Program is available on campus, which is administered by the Berlitz Company.

University of Tulsa

- **Contact:**
  International Student Services
  University of Tulsa
  600 South College Avenue
  Tulsa, OK 74104
  Phone: 918-631-2329
  Fax: 918-631-3322
  E-mail: inst@utulsa.edu
  Web site: http://www.utulsa.edu
- **Private, coed**
- **Urban setting**
- **Enrollment: 4,084**
- **Student-faculty ratio: 11:1**
- **2006–07 Tuition and fees: $20,658**

- **2006–07 Room and board: $7796**
- **International students: 11%**
- **Countries represented: 61**
- **International students applied: 662**
- **International students accepted: 345**
- **International students enrolled: 107**
- **Admissions tests:**
  - **TOEFL (paper-based min. score 500; computer-based min. score 173)**
  - **SAT and ACT: Not required**
- **Application deadline: Fall, 7/15; spring, 11/15**
- **On-campus housing: Guaranteed**
- **Summer housing: Available**

Area and Climate

The University of Tulsa (TU) is a major southwestern university located in Oklahoma. TU's 200-acre (81-hectare) campus lies in a suburban setting 2 miles (3 kilometers) from downtown Tulsa, a safe, friendly city with a population of approximately 550,000. Tulsa International Airport is 10 minutes from the campus, and bus service is available to major cities throughout the Southwest. Although the city has four distinct seasons, the climate is mild. Snow falls occasionally during the winter, but warm days extend from March through October. The favorable weather allows for a variety of activities at the city's hundreds of parks and nearby lakes.

Education

The University of Tulsa, which was founded in 1894, is a private coed university with an academically strong student body, a distinguished faculty, comprehensive library holdings, and state-of-the-art facilities. Bachelor's degrees are offered in nearly ninety fields of study in the Colleges of Engineering, Business Administration, and Arts and Sciences. TU also offers thirty master's and ten doctoral degree programs as well as a law degree program and several joint-degree programs. Some of the more popular undergraduate majors include petroleum engineering, computer science, marketing, management, mechanical engineering, accounting, MIS, finance, psychology, and

communication. TU's professors are recognized worldwide for their writing and research, but their emphasis is on undergraduate teaching.

Campus Life

Students at the University of Tulsa come from forty-six states and sixty-one countries. For those students who choose to live on campus, residence hall housing is designed to provide not only a comfortable home away from home but also a fulfilling social environment. Professionally trained residence directors work with student hall officers and staff members to schedule programs and activities each semester and are available for counseling and referral assistance. Student life is enhanced by more than 160 student organizations reflecting a wide range of interests and an extensive intramural and recreational sports program.

For International Students

The University of Tulsa has a tradition of providing personal attention to all of its students, and international students can look forward to a warm reception upon reaching the TU campus. International students have the opportunity to take advantage of services designed specifically to assist them in achieving their educational goals. The Office of International Student Services provides assistance in the areas of undergraduate admission, immigration matters, and adjusting to life in the United States. An ESL program is also available for those needing additional instruction in English.

University of Wisconsin–Eau Claire

- **Contact:**
  Phillip J. Huelsbeck
  International Student Advisor
  Center for International Education
  105 Garfield Avenue
  Eau Claire, WI 54702-4004

  Phone: 715-836-4411
  Fax: 715-836-4948
  E-mail: huelsbpj@uwec.edu
  Web site: http://www.uwec.edu
- Public, comprehensive, coed
- Small-town setting
- Enrollment: 10,395
- Student-faculty ratio: 20:1

- **2007–08 Tuition and fees: $16,444**
- **2007–08 Room and board: $5508**
- **International students: 1%**
- **Countries represented: 45**
- **International students enrolled: 140**
- **Admissions tests:**
  - **TOEFL (paper-based min. score 525; computer-based min. score 197)**
  - **SAT and ACT: Not required**
- **Application deadlines: 7/1, 11/1**
- **On-campus housing: Guaranteed**
- **Summer housing: Available for students taking summer classes**

Area and Climate

The city of Eau Claire offers students small-town charm and security along with ready access to larger urban areas. Eau Claire is a community of 60,000 people located 90 minutes east of the Minneapolis–St. Paul metropolitan area and 290 miles (467 kilometers) northwest of Chicago. It is an educational, commercial, medical, and cultural center for west-central Wisconsin. Clean air and water quality make the area one of great natural beauty. Eau Claire has a "northern temperate" climate with four distinct seasons. Most students adjust well to the climate and enjoy year-round outdoor recreation, including boating, hiking, fishing, and skiing.

Education

The University of Wisconsin–Eau Claire (UWEC) was founded in 1916 and seeks to foster the intellectual, personal, cultural, and social development of each student. *U.S. News & World Report* ranked UWEC third among all public regional universities in the Midwest and in the top tier of all regional Midwestern universities, both public and private. UWEC offers more than eighty majors and areas of concentration, including accounting, biology, business, computer science, education, nursing, and management information systems; an M.B.A. degree is also available. UWEC is designated as a Center of Excellence for Faculty–Undergraduate Student Research Collaboration. With more than 900 computers available at no charge to students, the University has a ratio of one computer for every 11 students. The McIntyre Library is a leading center for traditional and electronic resources and is open 24 hours per day at peak study times.

Campus Life

UWEC is known as one of the most beautiful, safe, and friendly campuses in Wisconsin. More than 10,000 students enroll each year, including approximately 125 international students from forty-five countries. Student clubs and associations are an integral part of student life. The University is a major athletic, cultural, and entertainment center for the Chippewa Valley's 143,000 residents. Highlights include concerts, recitals, theater productions, and many dance, music, film, lecture, and sports activities. Housing is guaranteed for international students in one of the nine coed and two single-sex residence halls on campus; each is equipped with computer labs, social rooms, fitness rooms, a reception desk, food sales, and large TV lounges. Approximately 4,000 students live in the residence halls.

For International Students

The Center for International Education (CIE) provides a full range of services to international students, beginning with an outstanding orientation program. During orientation, the CIE staff and Peer Guides (student assistants) assist students with every step of adjustment to life in Eau Claire. An English as a Second Language Program is available for students who need further English training. ESL programs are offered year-round, and intensive summer programs are available. Information on the English Language Academy can be found on the Web at http://www.uwec.edu/esl or http://www.uwec.edu/CE/iep.htm. A Host Family/Friend program is available, enabling international students to experience American family life. All international students are considered for partial-tuition scholarships when applying for admission.

University of Wisconsin–La Crosse

- Contact:
  Mr. Danny Wan
  International Admissions Specialist
  Office of International Education
  University of Wisconsin–La Crosse
  La Crosse, WI 54601
  Phone: 608-785-8016
  Fax: 608-785-8923
  E-mail: uwlworld@uwlax.edu
  Web site: http://www.uwlax.edu/oie
- Public, comprehensive, coed
- Suburban setting
- Enrollment: 8,750
- Student-faculty ratio: 22:1

- 2006–07 Tuition and fees: $13,280
- 2006–07 Room and board: $4820
- International students: 2%
- Countries represented: 43
- International students applied:216
- International students accepted: 188
- International students enrolled: 160
- Admissions tests:
  - TOEFL: Recommended
  - SAT and ACT: Not required
- Application deadline: Fall, 5/1; spring, 11/1
- On-campus housing: Limited
- Summer housing: Available

Area and Climate

The University of Wisconsin–La Crosse (UW–La Crosse) is located in the safe, friendly community of La Crosse in scenic southwestern Wisconsin. The city, located on the banks of the Mississippi River, is home to more than 52,000 people and is a regional center for education, health care, industry, recreation, and business. Residents enjoy a distinctive four-season climate. La Crosse is located within 5 hours' driving distance from Chicago, Illinois, and 3 hours of Minneapolis, Minnesota.

Education

The University of Wisconsin–La Crosse, established in 1909 as a teachers' college, has grown to become a fully accredited comprehensive university. It is one of thirteen universities in the highly respected University of Wisconsin system. In addition to more than eighty-five high-quality undergraduate programs and twenty-five distinctive graduate programs, the University also offers an English as a Second Language (ESL) Program. Undergraduate programs include business, computer science, communications, allied health programs, recreation and health, sport science, archeology, and physics/engineering. Many of the academic programs have received national and regional recognition. Average class size is 30 students, and all classes are taught by faculty members. UW–La Crosse has been consistently ranked by two national magazines, *Kiplinger's* and *U.S. News & World Reports,* as one of the best universities in the U.S.

Campus Life

The parklike UW–La Crosse campus is a safe, friendly place to live and learn. More than 150 student organizations, including student government; sports, music, and theater groups; and social and professional fraternities, provide students with the opportunities to meet new friends and become active members of the campus community. Students make great use of the campus facilities, which include the multipurpose student life center, the Center for the Arts, the recreational activity center, the exercise and sport science complex, a newly expanded library, and numerous computer labs. Other important services include the Student Health Center, a confidential counseling service, and the Career Services Office.

For International Students

International student admissions and advising services work cooperatively in the Office of International Education to provide students with the best assistance possible. The office also works closely with the University's English as a Second Language Program. All new students receive a prearrival packet, which includes information about transportation, class registration, and orientation that is conducted the week before classes begin. Many students become involved in the International Student Organization, Global Link (a volunteer speakers bureau), La Crosse Friends of International Students (a community organization of friendship families), and L.I.F.E. (a program that matches international students with an American student partner). Application instructions and forms are available via the Web at http://www.uwlax.edu/oie.

University of Wisconsin– Stevens Point

- **Contact:**
  Foreign Student Office
  University of Wisconsin–Stevens Point
  1108 Fremont Street , #020 SSC
  Stevens Point, WI 54481-3897
  Phone: 715-346-3849
  Fax: 715-346-3819
  E-mail: fso@uwsp.edu
  Web site: http://www.uwsp.edu
- Public, university
- Small-town setting
- Enrollment: 8,700
- Student-faculty ratio: 19:1

- 2006–07 Tuition and fees: $13,000
- 2006–07 Room and board: $4715
- International students: 2%
- Countries represented: 40
- International students enrolled: 185
- Admissions tests:
    - TOEFL: Required (min. score 523 paper-based, 193 computer-based, 70 Internet-based)
- Application deadline: Fall semester, July 1; spring semester, November 15
- On-campus housing: Available

Area and Climate

Located on the Wisconsin River in the heart of Wisconsin, Stevens Point is a safe, friendly city of about 25,000 in a metropolitan area of nearly 60,000. Stevens Point offers students and visitors many recreational and cultural activities. The city is served by several airlines through the Central Wisconsin Airport (airport code CWA). Central Wisconsin enjoys four seasons. Summers are warm and pleasant. Winters are cold, but all buildings are heated. The average summer temperature is 72°F (22°C), and the average winter temperature is 16°F (-9°C).

Education

University of Wisconsin–Stevens Point (UWSP) is one of thirteen universities in the University of Wisconsin System. Founded in 1894, UWSP has a long and proud tradition and offers some of the most diverse curricula in the region to 8,700 students, including international students from forty countries. Many UWSP programs are not only regionally famous but also have both a national and international reputation. UWSP offers baccalaureate degrees in more than fifty subjects in the College of Letters and Science, College of Professional Studies, College of Fine Arts and Communication, and College of Natural Resources. UWSP offers an environment that emphasizes teaching excellence. More than 90 percent of the more than 400 full-time professors have doctoral or equivalent degrees. The University is large enough to offer a diversity of programs yet small enough to offer individualized educational experiences. Since UWSP is a state-supported institution, tuition is very reasonable. In addition, qualified students may be awarded partial tuition waivers and scholarships. *U.S. News & World Report* called UWSP a "best buy" that offers a high-quality education at a sensible cost and ranked it the sixth-best public university in the Midwest. It is ranked among the 100 best state universities in the nation by *Kiplinger's Personal Finance* magazine. There are ninety-five program choices within forty-eight majors, plus seventy-five minors and sixteen graduate programs. Fall semester runs from August through December; spring semester runs from January through May. The North Central Association of Colleges and Schools fully accredits all the undergraduate and graduate programs at UWSP.

Campus Life

Students attend classes in seven academic buildings and live in one of the thirteen residence halls. The Health Enhancement Center, which features an indoor track, an Olympic-size pool, and a therapeutic pool, is open for exercise. Personal and professional opportunities are extended through residence life programs that offer studying, socializing, and learning, as well as through more than 150 student organizations, one of the largest and most active being the International Club.

For International Students

The Foreign Student Office serves the special needs of all international students. It provides opportunities for developing friendships and for personal growth through the International Friendship Program, International Club, Speakers' Bureau, International Dinner and Entertainment, and Community Cultural Festival. Students who are not yet proficient in English may study at the Intensive English Program, which offers four levels of instruction in five 8-week sessions each year.

University of Wisconsin–Stout

- Contact:
    Vickie Kuester, Associate Director
    Office of International Education
    University of Wisconsin–Stout
    Menomonie, WI 54751
    Phone: 715-232-2132
    Fax: 715-232-2500
    E-mail: kuesterv@uwstout.edu
    Web site: http://www.uwstout.edu/
- Public, comprehensive, coed
- Small-town setting
- Enrollment: 8,257
- Student-faculty ratio: 20:1
- 2007–08 Tuition and fees: $14,613

- 2007–08 Room and board: $5500
- International students: 1%
- Countries represented: 30
- International students applied: 150
- International students enrolled: 138
- Admissions tests:
    - TOEFL: Required (min. score 500 PBT, 173 CBT, 61 iBT)
    - SAT and ACT: Not required
- On-campus housing: Guaranteed
- Summer housing: Available for students taking summer courses

Area and Climate

The University of Wisconsin–Stout (UW–Stout) is located near the Red Cedar River in Menomonie, Wisconsin, a safe, quiet community of 15,000 residents. Menomonie offers the friendliness and ease of a small town while being only an hour from the large metropolitan area of St. Paul, Minnesota. Because the campus is located in the center of the city, restaurants and shopping are within walking distance. Northwestern Wisconsin enjoys four distinct and beautiful seasons. Students may enjoy snow-time recreational activities and summer experiences.

Education

The University of Wisconsin–Stout is a member of the University of Wisconsin System, one of the largest educational systems in the world. Founded in 1891, UW–Stout is a special-mission university recognized nationally and internationally for its programs leading to professional careers in industry, commerce, education, and human services through the study of technology, applied mathematics and science, art, business, industrial management, human behavior, family and consumer sciences, and manufacturing-related engineering and technologies. UW–Stout offers twenty-nine undergraduate and nineteen graduate programs. The University has excellent computer and library facilities. The academic calendar has two semesters (September–December and January–May) and a summer session (June–August).

Campus Life

The UW–Stout campus is both beautiful and welcoming. There are many campus activities for students that provide international students the opportunity to participate in active learning and social experiences. Campus activities include clubs and organizations, such as the International Relations Club, that promote interaction between international students and American students through educational and social activities. International Week is a special event for international students to share their cultures and customs with the UW–Stout community. Recreational athletics are open to all students, and special entertainers often visit the campus. On-campus residence halls are available for year-round housing, and the student life staff plans a variety of activities for students.

For International Students

The Office of International Education works with students from thirty countries. The office staff members provide advisement and referrals for foreign nationals at the University in such areas as housing, finances, academics, social customs, and personal concerns. The office also provides a link between the international students and the greater area community. An orientation program for all newly arrived international students is held prior to the start of classes in the fall and spring semesters. International student tuition reductions are available. In addition, part-time work on campus is available.

University of Wisconsin–Superior

- **Contact:**
  Mark MacLean, International Student
  Services Specialist
  Office of International Programs
  University of Wisconsin–Superior
  Main 337
  Belknap & Catlin, P.O. Box 2000
  Superior, WI 54880-4500
  Phone: 715-394-8052
  Fax: 715-394-8363
  E-mail: international@uwsuper.edu
  Web site: http://www.uwsuper.edu/OIP/
- **Public, four-year, coed**
- **Small-town/regional city setting**
- **Enrollment: 2,800**

- **Student-faculty ratio: 17:1**
- **2006–07 Comprehensive fee: $17,825**
- **International students: 5%**
- **Countries represented: 32**
- **International students applied: 80**
- **International students accepted: 42**
- **International students enrolled: 32**
- **Admissions tests:**
  - **TOEFL: Required (min. score 61 iBT; 500 PBT; 173 CBT)**
  - **SAT and ACT: Recommended**
- **Application deadline: Fall, 7/1; spring, 11/1**
- **On-campus housing: Available**
- **Summer housing: Available**

Area and Climate

The University of Wisconsin–Superior (UW–Superior) is located in the city of Superior in the northwestern tip of the state of Wisconsin. On a residential campus set in a quiet neighborhood, the University is within the Duluth, Minnesota/Superior, Wisconsin, metropolitan area (population 240,000). It is also just minutes away from the beauty of the largest freshwater lake in the word, Lake Superior, and the surrounding lakes, forests, and outdoor activities. The weather in northern Wisconsin offers something for all tastes, whether it's the blossoming flowers of spring, the brilliantly colored leaves of fall, the pleasantly sunny weather of summer, or the snowy wonderland of winter. Fall and spring temperatures range from 41°F to 75°F (5°C to 24°C), with summer temperatures between 70°F and 81°F (21°C and 27°C), and winter temperatures between 32°F and −26°F (0°C and −32°C). Snow is common from December to March.

Education

Selected as one of nineteen nationwide members of the Council of Public Liberal Arts Colleges, the University offers more than thirty majors and many more minors and preprofessional programs, including medicine, engineering, and law. Individually designed majors and minors enable students to work with an academic adviser to design a specialized study program. Many students use this option to create majors for their specific career goals or personal interests. All faculty members are required to hold office hours each week. The average class size is 23 students.

Campus Life

Students take part in a wide variety of organizations, sports, and recreational opportunities on campus and within the Duluth-Superior community. International students are encouraged to live on campus in order to get to know their fellow American students, as well as students from many other countries. All residence halls have twenty-four-hour computer rooms, study areas, exercise rooms, telephones in all rooms, VCR rental, cable TV in lounges, and laundry facilities. Options include a women-only residence hall.

For International Students

As part of its mission, the Office of International Programs (OIP) welcomes to campus approximately 120 international students from more than thirty countries each year. International students at UW–Superior have a long history of high academic achievement, leadership, involvement on campus, athletic excellence, and success in the job market. The OIP provides services related to international students, including support and assistance concerning visas and related immigration issues. It also conducts new-student orientations and offers guidance regarding social, cultural, and academic issues. The OIP serves as a resource center for and about international students.

The University of Wisconsin–Superior actively promotes diversity on its campus. To this end, the University has established the Tuition Award Program (TAP), which grants qualified nonresident degree-seeking students—including international students—a partial waiver on their out-of-state tuition expenses.

University of Wisconsin–Whitewater

- **Contact:**
  Steve McKellips
  Executive Director of Admissions
  University of Wisconsin–Whitewater
  Whitewater, WI 53190
  Phone: 262-472-1440
  Fax: 262-472-1515
  E-mail: uwwadmit@uww.edu
  Web site: http://www.uww.edu
- Public, comprehensive, coed
- Small-town setting
- Enrollment: 10,654
- Student-faculty ratio: 30:1
- 2006–07 Tuition and fees: $17,630
- 2006–07 Room and board: $5005

- International students: 1.3%
- Countries represented: 36
- International students applied: 65
- International students accepted: 60
- International students enrolled: 120
- Admissions tests:
  - **TOEFL: Required (paper-based min. score 500; computer-based min. score 173; Internet-based min. score 61)**
  - **SAT or ACT: Not required**
- Application deadline: Fall, 4/15; spring, 10/15
- On-campus housing: Guaranteed
- Summer housing: Available

Area and Climate

The UW–Whitewater campus is located in southeastern Wisconsin. The city of Whitewater has a population of about 12,500 residents. The community is 50 miles (81 kilometers) southwest of Milwaukee (population 629,800) and 100 miles (161 kilometers) northwest of Chicago (population 8,066,000). Its location combines the advantages of small-city living in one of Wisconsin's famed recreational areas with access to the theaters, art galleries, and other cultural offerings of nearby cities. Whitewater has restaurants, shops, pharmacies, travel agencies, banks, and other businesses. There are four distinct seasons, and the temperature ranges from below 0°F (-18°C) during the winter to more than 90°F (32°C) during the summer.

Education

Founded in 1868, UW–Whitewater offers forty-three undergraduate majors in four colleges: Arts and Communication, Business and Economics, Education, and Letters and Science. The University's outstanding programs, innovations, and reputation for personalized service and caring have made it a popular choice for both domestic and international students. UW–Whitewater maintains its tier-one ranking of twenty top Midwestern regional colleges in the *College Guide of America's Best Colleges* and is ranked as having the number one four-year computing degree in the United States and Canada.

Campus Life

UW–Whitewater has an enrollment of 10,654 students, including international students representing thirty-six countries. More than 140 student organizations are available, including an International Student Association (ISA), an International Business Association, and a Chinese Student Association. The ISA sponsors several cultural and social programs on campus, such as the International Week and the International Dinner. Opportunities are available to participate in sports (including soccer). Students may choose to become involved in student government, the campus radio station, cable TV, the campus newspaper, or speaker's bureau.

For International Students

Special orientation programs for international students are held before the beginning of each semester. The Office of International Education assists international students in their day-to-day activities. The office provides individual and group advising services and assists students with personal, academic, financial, housing, food, and immigration needs. The Host Family Program in Whitewater serves international students by providing opportunities for interaction with an American family. Academic Support Services provides free tutorial and learning services for students. It assists students in the areas of mathematics, note-taking, college-level reading assignments, study skills, word processing, and all stages of the writing process. IBM and Macintosh computer labs are available. Two courses in English for international students are offered on campus for students who need additional assistance in the English language.

University of Wyoming

- Contact:
  Brooke Culver
  Admissions Representative
  Dept. 3435, 1000 University Avenue
  University of Wyoming
  Laramie, WY 82071-3435

  Phone: 307-766-5160
  Fax: 307-766-4042
  Web site: http://www.uwyo.edu
- Public, coed
- Small-town setting
- Enrollment: 13,126
- Student-faculty ratio: 15:1

- 2007–08 Tuition and fees: $9750 (14-credit-hour average class load)
- 2007–08 Room and board: $7274, based on double occupancy and unlimited meal plan
- International students: 4%
- Countries represented: 64
- Admissions tests:
  - TOEFL (min. score 525 paper-based)
  - SAT and ACT: Required for freshmen
- Application deadline: March 1 (priority deadline)
- On-campus housing: Available
- Summer housing: Available

Area and Climate

The University of Wyoming, known as UW, is located in the southeast corner of Wyoming. This safe and welcoming Rocky Mountain state encompasses 97,914 square miles (253,598 square kilometers) and has a population of 493,782. Wyoming is known for its wide-open spaces, mountains, ranches, mineral resources, and cowboy legends as well as its outdoor recreation opportunities. Yellowstone and Grand Teton National Parks are located in the northwest corner of the state, about 400 miles (643 kilometers) from Laramie. Laramie is easily accessible by automobile, bus, and commuter airline and is an easy 2-hour drive from the metropolitan area of Denver, Colorado. Summer temperatures can range from 50°F to 90°F (10°C to 32°C), while the winter months are usually cold. However, the winter weather is changeable, and there are periods when the temperature climbs to nearly 60°F (15°C). The annual precipitation average is 14.36 inches (36.83 centimeters).

Education

UW was founded in 1886 and offers more than eighty undergraduate degree programs in agriculture, arts and sciences, business, education, engineering, and health sciences. UW is committed to undergraduate education and offers undergraduates opportunities to do research with nationally and internationally recognized faculty members. University of Wyoming students also receive academic recognition. UW proudly claims 2 Rhodes scholars since 1994, being one of only fourteen schools in the U.S. to have 2 Rhodes scholars from the same institution in the last seven years. The library system consists of three major libraries and several satellite locations and holds more than 1.1 million books and periodicals. Computers are available in all major buildings for student use. The University of Wyoming operates on a semester system and offers an extensive summer term. The most popular majors are engineering, pharmacy, nursing, psychology, education, and business.

Campus Life

UW's total enrollment is 13,126, representing all fifty states and almost seventy other countries, and includes more than 300 international students. Nearby mountains offer outdoor recreation, but there are also cultural events and sports and activities available on campus and in the community. The International Student Association is just one of more than 200 clubs and organizations available. On-campus housing is available year-round in six residence halls and one-, two-, and three-bedroom apartments. Priority for University apartments is given to students who are married or have children. Arrangements for housing should be made well in advance of the student's arrival.

For International Students

Many services for international students are provided by the International Services Office, which gives assistance to international students with immigration, personal, and nonacademic problems. They also offer a variety of programs and activities, including the American Conversation Club, International Student Orientation, Friendship Family Program, International Neighbors Program, International Student Association, International Week, and the Chinese New Year Festival. The UW Student Health Service provides excellent health care to students. All international students are required to have health insurance. In addition, all UW students born in 1957 or after must provide proof of immunity to measles, mumps, and rubella before they may register for classes.

Utica College

- **Contact:**

  Mrs. Kate Cominsky
  Office of International Admissions
  1600 Burrstone Road
  Utica, NY 13502

  Phone: 315-792-5290
  Fax: 315-223-2515
  E-mail: ccominsky@utica.edu
  Web site: http://www.utica.edu/enrollment/
  admission/international.htm
  http://www.utica.edu

- Private, comprehensive, coed
- Suburban setting
- Enrollment: 2,465
- Student-faculty ratio: 18:1
- 2006–07 Tuition and fees: $23,130
- 2006–07 Room and board: $9720

- International students: 4%
- Countries represented: 35
- International students applied: 135
- International students accepted: 51
- International students enrolled: 46
- Admissions tests:
  - **TOEFL:** Required (min. score 195 computer-based); not required for international students transferring from U.S. colleges.
  - **SAT and ACT:** Not required
- Application deadline: Rolling
- On-campus housing: Guaranteed (if requested at least two months prior to start of semester)
- Summer housing: Guaranteed (if requested at least two months prior to start of classes)

Area and Climate

Utica College (UC) is located in the geographical center of New York State, approximately 4 hours by car, train, or bus from New York City, Boston, Philadelphia, and Montreal. The College offers an ideal combination—a safe, convenient 128-acre (52-hectare) campus located within a lively small city. The Utica area is home to 300,000 people of many ethnicities. As a result, there are a variety of places of worship, ethnic restaurants, and social and cultural activities. The picturesque Mohawk Valley is known for its spectacular resources and a four-season climate, which provides unlimited recreational activities. The campus is also close to theaters, a major art museum, a sports arena, and several shopping malls.

Education

For the past four years, *U.S. News & World Report* has ranked Utica College in the top tier for among similar colleges in the Northeast. UC's academic offerings rival those of much larger universities. At Utica College, the liberal arts, a broad-based study of major areas of knowledge, and professional studies, the development of career-specific employment skills and opportunities for experiential learning, are interwoven. As a result, UC graduates are prepared for success in their personal and professional lives.

Utica College offers a broad curriculum, with thirty undergraduate majors and twenty-four minors in both liberal arts and professional studies. In addition, there are accelerated programs, independent-study opportunities, cooperative education, field placements, and internships. International students often choose to study management, computer science, communications, psychology, and health sciences. The College grants the Bachelor of Arts and Bachelor of Science degrees from the prestigious Syracuse University. Utica College graduate degrees are offered in twelve different areas, including business administration, economic crime management, education, liberal studies, occupational therapy, and physical therapy.

Campus Life

Utica College ranks as one of the most diverse campuses in New York State. Students from more than forty countries and myriad backgrounds, races, and religions attend UC each year. The College's current enrollment includes students from Angola, Armenia, Bosnia, Canada, El Salvador, Finland, France, Georgia, Germany, Ghana, Greece, Hong Kong, Japan, Kenya, Korea, Kosovo, Nepal, Pakistan, the Philippines, Spain, Sweden, Taiwan, Trinidad, and the United Kingdom.

On its modern campus, Utica College students gather in the academic complex where classes are held, the Frank E. Gannett Memorial Library, the seven residence halls, and the athletic center, which includes a large gymnasium, racquetball courts, a swimming pool, saunas, a free-weight room, and a fully equipped fitness room. There are also numerous playing fields and courts and a multisport stadium. Ice hockey is played at the Utica Memorial Auditorium and has become a popular student and community event. Housing is guaranteed for all students throughout the year. Campus dining services offer a wide variety of options to students throughout the day and evening.

Utica College has something for everyone. There are more than eighty student clubs and organization on campus, and students are encouraged to try new activities, meet new people, and develop new skills. There are sports activities at many different levels, including nineteen varsity sports for men and women. Eighty percent of Utica College students participate in a sports activity, either for the competition, to stay fit, or to just have fun.

For International Students

The Office of International Programs provides incoming international and exchange students with information about the campus and its services. Staff members can assist students with immigration, health care and insurance, academics, banking, communications, employment, campus housing, and a number of other areas related to life and study at Utica College. Each semester, the Office of International Programs presents an informative orientation program for all incoming international students.

Limited financial assistance is available for international students who are non-U.S. citizens. These grants, which are awarded on the basis of outstanding academic achievement, range from $2000 to $12,000 per year and do not require a separate application. Private loans are available to students with either a U.S. citizen or permanent resident as a cosigner. Limited student employment positions are also available on campus.

Virginia Commonwealth University

- Contact:
  Executive Director
  Office of International Education
  916 West Franklin Street, Room 203
  Virginia Commonwealth University
  Richmond, VA 23284
  Phone: 804-828-8471
  Fax: 804-828-2552
  E-mail: vcuia@vcu.edu
  Web site: http://www.vcu.edu/oie
- Public, comprehensive, coed
- Urban setting
- Enrollment: 30,000
- Student-faculty ratio: 13:1
- 2005–06 Tuition and fees: $17,000 (est.)

- 2005–06 Room and board: $7800 (est.)
- International students: 3.8%
- Countries represented: 114
- International students enrolled: 1,128 (total)
- Admissions tests:
  - TOEFL: Required (paper-based min. score 550)
  - SAT: Recommended
  - ACT: Not required
- Application deadline: 2 months prior to orientation
- On-campus housing: Limited
- Summer housing: Available

Area and Climate

Richmond is located on the James River in the central part of Virginia. It is a 2-hour drive south of Washington, D.C., and approximately the same distance from the Atlantic coast. Richmond is the political, economic, and cultural focal point of Virginia. More than 1 million people live in the metropolitan region. Historically, Richmond was the capital city for the Confederate States of America during the Civil War and is rich in Colonial and Revolutionary War history. Known as the City of Monuments, Richmond is home to many museums, theaters, and other places where the arts can be enjoyed. Average temperatures in Richmond range from 95°F (35°C) in the summer to 39°F (4°C) in the winter.

Education

Virginia Commonwealth University (VCU) and the VCU Medical Center are located on two downtown campuses in Richmond, Virginia. Virginia Commonwealth University is ranked nationally by the Carnegie Foundation as a top research institution and enrolls nearly 30,000 students in more than 170 certificate, undergraduate, graduate, professional, and doctoral programs in the arts, sciences, and humanities in fifteen schools and one college. Forty of the University's programs are unique in Virginia, and twenty graduate and professional programs have been ranked by *U.S. News & World Report* as among the best of their kind. MCV Hospitals, clinics, and the health sciences schools of Virginia Commonwealth University make up the VCU Medical Center, one of the leading academic medical centers in the country. For more information, students should visit http://www.vcu.edu.

Campus Life

VCU comprises two campuses. The medical campus is in the heart of the financial, governmental, and retail district. The academic campus is in a historic residential district. Combined, the University's 151 buildings sit on more than 100 acres (41 hectares) of land. There are approximately 160 student clubs and organizations. Free concerts, plays, and lectures are frequently given and feature students, faculty members, and guests. VCU's recreational sports facilities include tennis courts, a soccer field, basketball courts, and three modern, well-equipped gymnasiums. Student recreational programs offer informal recreation, fitness, and sport club activities. The University library collections include more than 1 million books and 8,200 journal subscriptions. Students have access to two major research libraries and two media resource centers. More than 6,500 personal computers are available for student use. More than 2,300 students live in University-operated housing, which includes high-rise residence halls, suites of dormitory rooms, and apartments on campus. Private housing is available nearby.

For International Students

The Office of International Education provides assistance and information to make a student's stay in the United States a pleasant and rewarding experience. In the fall and spring semesters, orientation programs help new international students become acquainted with the University and the city. Academic advising, class registration, and social activities are part of the program. Ongoing activities bring international and local students together at a weekly coffee hour and for excursions to interesting and important sites in and around Richmond. An international student adviser interprets relevant immigration rules and regulations and counsels students with personal, cultural, and financial concerns. The English Language Program (ELP) offers language classes that prepare students for university study so that they can be successful in the classroom. ELP has five entry points each year: January, March, May, August, and October.

Washington College

- **Contact:**
  Tony Littlefield
  Coordinator, Int'l Admissions
  Washington College
  Chestertown, MD 21620-1197

  Phone: 410-778-7700
  Fax: 410-778-7287
  E-mail: tlittlefield2@washcoll.edu
  Web site: http://www.washcoll.edu
- **Private, coed**
- **Small-town setting**
- **Enrollment: 1,300**
- **Student-faculty ratio: 12:1**
- **2006–07 Tuition and fees: $30,200**

- **2006–07 Room and board: $6250**
- **International students: 3%**
- **Countries represented: 30**
- **International students applied: 75**
- **International students accepted: 27**
- **International students enrolled: 10**
- **Admissions tests:**
  - **TOEFL (min. score 550)**
  - **SAT: Recommended**
  - **ACT: Optional**
- **Application deadline: 2/15**
- **On-campus housing: Guaranteed**
- **Summer housing: Not available**

Area and Climate

Washington College is located in Chestertown, Maryland, a community of 4,000 on the Eastern Shore of the Chesapeake Bay, just a short drive (75 miles/121 kilometers) from three major cities: Philadelphia, Baltimore, and Washington, D.C. Chestertown reflects the quiet grace and friendly spirit of rural America, in a setting surrounded by the waters of the Bay and the Chester River. When international students visit the campus with sufficient advance notice, the College provides free ground transportation to and from the airports in Philadelphia or Baltimore. The climate is temperate, with daytime highs averaging 86°F (30°C) in summer and 41°F (5°C) in winter.

Education

Founded in 1782, Washington College is the tenth-oldest college in the United States and remains committed to a traditional liberal arts and sciences curriculum. Within the academic program, the more notable strengths are in literature and creative writing, international studies, political science, business management, psychology, chemistry, and preprofessional preparation for law and medicine. Among the significant benefits that are inherent in this small, residential college—1,300 undergraduate students—are small classes, individual academic advising, and modern academic facilities.

Campus Life

Washington College students come from more than thirty states and forty other nations. Eighty percent (all who wish to do so) live in campus residence halls, usually sharing space with one roommate. Housing includes one residence that is specifically available to international students, guaranteed during the fall (late August to mid-December) and spring (mid-January to early May). There is no summer session. Student life on the 120-acre (49-hectare) campus is informal and includes student government, drama, music, publications, recreational and fitness activities, and competitive athletic teams in soccer, field hockey, volleyball, swimming, basketball, tennis, sailing, and rowing.

For International Students

Students must demonstrate proficiency in English before admission. The College does not offer ESL instruction. Merit-based scholarships and campus employment are available to international students. Financial affidavits provided by Washington College must be completed by admitted international citizens who require student visas before immigration documentation can be completed. All international students must be in Chestertown to attend a three-day orientation in late August. Various Washington College staff members serve as individual and group advisers to international students. Campus and community health services are readily available. Washington College welcomes students of every race, nationality, and creed.

Webber International University

- **Contact:**
  Admissions Office
  Webber International University
  Babson Park, FL 33827-9990
  Phone: 800-741-1844
  Fax: 863-638-1591
  Web site: http://www.webber.edu
- Private, coed
- Small-town setting
- Enrollment: 640
- Student-faculty ratio: 22:1
- 2007–08 Tuition and fees: $16,760 per year
- 2007–08 Room and board: $5690 per year
- International students: 16%

- Countries represented: 33
- International students applied: 104
- International students accepted: 97
- International students enrolled: 96
- Admissions tests:
  - **TOEFL:** Required (min. score 500 paper-based; 273 computer-based)
  - **SAT:** Required (min. score 870)
  - **ACT:** Required (min. score 18)
- Application deadline: Fall, 8/1; spring, 12/1
- On-campus housing: Available
- Summer housing: Available

Area and Climate

Webber International University (WIU) is located in Babson Park, Florida, a small community located just 45 minutes south of the Orlando area theme parks of Disney World, Universal Studios, and Sea World and less than 90 minutes from either the Gulf or Atlantic beaches. The temperature ranges from winter highs of 64°F (18°C) to summer highs of 93°F (34°C). The nighttime lows rarely drop below 41°F (5°C).

Education

Founded in 1927, Webber International University is an accredited coeducational business university. Associate and bachelor's degrees are available in the following areas: accounting, finance, general business studies, global business management, hospitality business management, international tourism management, management, marketing, prelaw, and sport management. Master of Business Administration (M.B.A.) degrees are offered with options in accounting, management, and sport management. Webber International University's Career Services Office has more than an 85 percent placement record.

Campus Life

Out of Webber's 600 full-time students, 90 are international students. They represent thirty-eight countries on six continents. Students may not find one of their neighbors studying at Webber, but they will find new friends from far-off places. Many of the international students live in the men's and women's dormitories on campus.

For International Students

Claudia Ponce, La Paz, Bolivia: "Webber International University is a home away from home. It's a place where the students, faculty members, and staff members are all your friends. Being on a one-on-one basis with teachers makes learning so much easier and fun."

Johanna de Verteuil, Port of Spain, Trinidad and Tobago: "At WIU, one really feels at home. The warm and friendly atmosphere created allows me to grow and develop academically as well as individually, acquiring knowledge that will assist me in all areas of my life. The faculty members and staff really care about my success in life. WIU has played an important role in my life, and here I have created wonderful memories and lasting friendships."

Natalie Patihk, Port of Spain, Trinidad: "Webber is like one big family. Everyone helps each other. When you have problems there is always someone there to lend a helping hand.... We are so close to Orlando to go to Disney or sample the night life."

Hiromi Tamura, Tokyo, Japan: "Webber International University is located in a most beautiful setting. The sunsets across the lake are just incredible.... One of the advantages of a small college is that it is easy to get information about what is going on."

Malin Andreasson, Gothenburg, Sweden: "I appreciate the teachers. They know the students by name and are willing to help you become successful in their class. Many have worked within their field and therefore really know what they are talking about.... The students are from all over the world, and this provides the opportunity to learn about other cultures."

Wentworth Institute of Technology

- **Contact:**
  Admissions Office
  Wentworth Institute of Technology
  550 Huntington Avenue
  Boston, MA 02115
  Phone: 617-989-4000
  Fax: 617-989-4010
  E-mail: admissions@wit.edu
  Web site: http://www.wit.edu
- Private, coed
- Urban setting
- Enrollment: 3,000 (3,636 total)
- Student-faculty ratio: 25:1
- 2006–07 Tuition and fees: $19,300
- 2006–07 Room and board: $9300

- International students: 150
- Countries represented: 50
- International students applied: 126
- International students accepted: 93
- International students enrolled: 35
- Admissions tests:
  - **TOEFL (paper-based min. score 525; computer-based min. score 197; Internet-based min. score 71)**
  - **SAT: Not required for international admission**
  - **ACT: Not required for international admission**
- Application deadline: Rolling
- On-campus housing: Not guaranteed
- Summer housing: Available

Area and Climate

Boston is one of America's most beautiful and historical cities and the original center of higher education in the United States. Its fifty colleges and universities bring in a quarter of a million students every year. A thriving, multicultural city with a metropolitan area that is home to a population of 5 million, Boston is a hub for technology, business, and medicine that gives students many opportunities. Wentworth's location makes it easy to get from one end of the city to the other. The public transportation system, which is known locally as the T, is accessible, as are major attractions ranging from Fenway Park (home of the Boston Red Sox baseball team) to the Museum of Fine Arts to the trendy shops of Newbury Street, which are only a short walk away. Boston's climate has four distinct seasons, so students can experience New England's famed fall foliage along with winter snow, spring breezes, and warm summer days. Average temperatures range from 80°F (27°C) in the summer to 30°F (–1°C) in the winter.

Education

Founded in 1904, Wentworth Institute of Technology is a private, coeducational college located in the heart of Boston, Massachusetts. Wentworth enrolls 3,636 students and offers on-campus housing on its 35-acre (15-hectare), fully equipped campus. Students benefit from a small class size (approximately 22 students) and individual attention from a dedicated teaching faculty with professional industry experience. There are more than eighty on-campus laboratories and studios, which are an integral component of all majors at Wentworth. Wentworth is also one of the most affordable full-time baccalaureate options in Boston, offering programs in the fields of architecture, computer science, design, engineering, engineering technology, environmental science, and management of technology. Wentworth offers one of the largest and most comprehensive cooperative education (Co-op) programs in the United States. For more than thirty years,

Wentworth has been opening career doors and helping students gain professional, paid work experience. Co-op is an important feature of Wentworth's career-focused education. All students are required to work for two semesters before graduation in a paid position that is directly related to their major. Co-op provides valuable practical experience that serves students well in their search for employment after graduation. A Co-op coordinator helps students find and secure the perfect Co-op position. In addition, Wentworth sponsors workshops on resume writing, job search strategies, and interviewing techniques. Employment has included positions such as facilities manager, game tester, product designer, and software engineer at companies such as the Gillette Company, Sikorsky Aircraft, and Pratt & Whitney.

Campus Life

Students very quickly find themselves feeling at home, because the college is committed to creating a comfortable yet vibrant living and learning community. Some of the qualities that make Wentworth so attractive to on-campus students are a traditional campus surrounding a tree-lined quad nestled in the heart of Boston; modern residence halls, including a new, state-of-the-art coed hall with amenities that include a study area, computer and game rooms, a lounge, a laundry facility, and a fitness center; student activities, including more than forty clubs and organizations; resources of a major university because of the school's membership in the Colleges of the Fenway, in which six neighboring colleges collaborate to sponsor events and activities, share facilities, and offer cross-registration; and full-time security staff 24 hours a day, every day.

For International Students

Wentworth evaluates all admission applications on a rolling basis. Wentworth strongly suggests that students apply as early as possible to ensure a place in the program as well as in on-campus housing. The Admissions Committee evaluates an application when all the necessary documentation has been submitted. Students must submit official transcripts, English proficiency test results (TOEFL, IELTS), declaration and certification of finances, an essay, and a recommendation.

Western Illinois University

- Contact:
  Center for International Studies
  1 University Circle, Seal Hall 211
  Western Illinois University
  Macomb, IL 61455
  Phone: 309-298-2501
  Fax: 309-298-2405
  E-mail: international-ed@wiu.edu
  Web site: http://www.wiu.edu/international/
           announce/topAnnouncements.do
- Public, four-year, coed
- Small-town setting
- Enrollment: 13,600
- Student-faculty ratio: 17:1
- 2006–07 Tuition and fees (comprehensive):
  approx. $10,000 per academic year

- 2006–07 Room and board: $6500 (double occupancy, ala carte) per academic year
- International students: 2.5%
- Countries represented: 56
- International students applied: 563
- International students accepted: 378
- International students enrolled: 143
- Admissions tests:
  - TOEFL: Required (min. score 550 PBT; 213 CBT)
  - SAT or ACT: Recommended
- Application deadline: Fall, 5/1; spring, 10/1; summer, 2/1
- On-campus housing: Available
- Summer housing: Available

Area and Climate

The main campus is located in Macomb, the McDonough County seat, 40 miles (64 kilometers) east of the Mississippi River. Macomb is a welcoming, small-town community with a population of about 20,000. Two U.S. highways, 136 and 67, intersect at Macomb and provide direct access to Interstates 74, 80, and 55. Rail passenger service is available from Quincy and Chicago to Macomb.

Education

Established April 24, 1899, Western Illinois University (WIU) has been recognized as one of the "Best in the Midwest Colleges" by the *Princeton Review* and selected as one of just twenty-four public universities ranked as a Tier 1 Midwestern Masters Institution by *U.S. News & World Report*. The University offers fifty-seven undergraduate degree programs and thirty-six graduate degree programs. Programs are offered in the humanities, social sciences, fine arts, business, education, and a number of preprofessional and technical fields of study. Undergraduate degrees include the Bachelor of Arts (B.A.), the Bachelor of Business (B.B.), the Bachelor of Fine Arts (B.F.A.), the Bachelor of Music (B.M.), the Bachelor of Science (B.S.), the Bachelor of Science in Education (B.S.Ed.), and the Bachelor of Social Work (B.S.W.). WIU also offers post baccalaureate certificates and master's degree programs.

Campus Life

Students can participate in a wide variety of activities, including clubs and sports. The University is a member of the NCAA Division I, with programs in baseball, basketball, cross-country running, golf, soccer, softball, swimming and diving, tennis, track and field, and volleyball; football is a Division I-AA sport. Several organizations on campus represent the University's spectrum of cultural diversity, including the African Student Association, the Chinese Student Association, the Latin American Student Association, the Nepalese Student Association, the Taiwanese Student Association, and the Turkmen Student Association—all of which are officially recognized by the University—and the International Friendship Club, which represents all international students and has as an objective to promote cultural awareness, respect, and understanding among all students through various cultural, educational, and social activities.

For International Students

The Center for International Studies (CIS) provides a centralized source of information for all internationally-related programs and activities. Through the efforts of the various units that make up the Center, the CIS staff seeks to facilitate, from the application process for international applicants through to when the student arrives on campus to enroll in classes. Assistance is given with visa and immigration issues, cross-cultural concerns, and adjustment to life in the United States. In addition, Western Illinois University offers a comprehensive English as a second language program to prepare international students for success in their academic studies. The University has developed the International House for those students from all corners of the world who want to live and work together while learning from one another while attending Western Illinois University. During the week prior to the start of the semester, there is an orientation for newly enrolling international students, and various activities and programs are offered throughout the semester.

Western New England College

- Contact:
    Admissions Office
    Western New England College
    1215 Wilbraham Road
    Springfield, MA 01119-7111
    Phone: 413-782-1321
    Fax: 413-782-1777
    E-mail: ugradmis@wnec.edu
    Web site: http://www.wnec.edu
- Private, four-year, coed
- Suburban setting
- Enrollment: Approximately 4,100 (2,400 undergraduates)
- Student-faculty ratio: 15:1

- 2007–08 Comprehensive fee: $35,940 (engineering, $37,032)
- International students applied: 37
- International students accepted: 13
- International students enrolled: 2
- Admissions tests:
    - TOEFL (min. score 500 paper-based; 173 computer-based)
    - SAT or ACT: Recommended
- Application deadline: Rolling
- On-campus housing: Available
- Summer housing: Not available

Area and Climate

Western New England College was developed in a residential section of Springfield, Massachusetts, about 4 miles (6 kilometers) from downtown Springfield. The picturesque, 215-acre (87 hectares) campus is located 150 miles (241 kilometers) north of New York City, 86 miles (138 kilometers) west of Boston, and 24 miles (39 kilometers) from Bradley International Airport in Hartford, Connecticut. The College is also just an hour from the beautiful Berkshire Mountains and 2 hours from the beaches of Cape Cod. The region has four distinct seasons. In December through February, the average temperature is 29°F (−1.67°C); the average high temperature in the summer is around 80°F (26.67°C).

Education

Founded in 1919, Western New England College is a private, coeducational institution offering more than thirty undergraduate majors at the baccalaureate level in the Schools of Arts and Sciences, Business, and Engineering. The College prepares students for success in graduate school or their chosen profession, and professors take a personal interest in each student's success. Throughout their education, students gain hands-on practical experience—including through the Learning Beyond the Classroom Program and internships—that lets them put their knowledge and understanding to work. In many courses, students work as part of a team for projects and assignments.

Campus Life

With more than sixty clubs and organizations available, there is something of interest for every student. Preprofessional programs, such as the Accounting Association, complement a student's major, and special-interest clubs like the Outing Club allow students to enjoy a hobby. As active members of NCAA Division III, the Eastern Collegiate Athletic Conference (ECAC), and the Great Northeast Athletic Conference (GNAC), the Golden Bear teams strive for athletic excellence. Nineteen teams are fielded: baseball, basketball, cross-country, football, golf, ice hockey, lacrosse, soccer, tennis, and wrestling for men, and basketball, cross-country, field hockey, lacrosse, soccer, softball, swimming, tennis, and volleyball for women.

For International Students

A full-time international student adviser helps students with immigration, academic, and personal issues. The First-Year Program pairs upperclassmen with international students to help them learn their way around campus and adapt to college life in the United States. The College also provides limited English as a second language (ESL) support services to non-native English-speaking students. International Student Scholarships of $9000 are awarded to students with outstanding academic records. These are only partial scholarships, and they are offered to a limited number of students.

Western Wyoming Community College

- **Contact:**
  Laurie Watkins
  Director of Admissions
  Western Wyoming Community College
  2500 College Drive
  Rock Springs, WY 82902
  Phone: 307-382-1600
  Fax: 307-382-1636
  E-mail: admissions@wwcc.wy.edu
  Web site: http://www.wwcc.wy.edu
- Public, two-year, coed
- Small-town setting
- Enrollment: 3,500
- Student-faculty ratio: 18:1
- 2006–07 Tuition and fees: $4804
- 2006–07 Room and board: $3394
- International students: 2%

- Countries represented: 25
- International students applied: 80
- International students accepted: 80
- International students enrolled: 72
- Admissions tests:
  - TOEFL (min. score 500 PBT; 173 CBT; 61 iBT), STEP Eiken (Grade Pre-1 level), Cambridge ESOL exam, or IELTS (level 5) for regular College program. Students with lower scores or no scores are accepted for ESL.
  - SAT and ACT: Required only for academic scholarships
- Application deadline: Rolling
- On-campus housing: Guaranteed
- Summer housing: Available

Area and Climate

Western Wyoming Community College (WWCC) is located on a high-desert plateau overlooking southwestern Wyoming in Rock Springs, a town with 23,000 residents. The closest cities are Salt Lake City, Utah (180 miles, 290 kilometers), and Denver, Colorado (350 miles, 560 kilometers). Opened in 1959 as a public, comprehensive community college, WWCC offers a 10-acre (4 hectare) campus and comfortable on-campus housing. The student-faculty ratio is 18:1, offering small classes (average class size is 20) and individual attention. WWCC welcomes students from thirty-two states and twenty-five countries. The area offers many outdoor activities, such as hiking, fishing, and snowboarding. Winter weather is cold with some snow (11° to 40°F, –12° to 5°C) and summers are beautiful (70° to 82°F, 17° to 27°C). The community is safe and welcoming to international students. The Rock Springs Airport has connecting flights from Denver, Colorado, and bus service is available from Salt Lake City, Utah.

Education

More than 80 transfer degree and occupational programs are offered in art, business, health professions, humanities, science, social sciences, and technology. Popular majors include education, business, engineering, nursing, computer science, and social work. Small classes taught by experienced, qualified instructors allow for individual attention and help as needed to ensure academic success. Students transfer successfully to four year colleges and universities across the United States after completing their studies at WWCC.

Campus Life

WWCC's facility is spectacular—a unique architectural design. The modern, enclosed campus includes well-equipped classrooms and laboratories. Over 350 computers in five labs and wireless Internet access are available to students. Recreation facilities include an aquatic center, wellness center, weight room, soccer and softball fields, walking track, and tennis and basketball courts. Students participate in competitive sports (men's basketball, soccer, and wrestling and women's basketball, club soccer, and volleyball) and other activities (campus newspaper, radio station, cheerleading, dance team, student government, intramurals, and several campus clubs). Comfortable on-campus housing offers apartments and residence hall rooms. A new residence hall is planned to open for the 2007–08 academic year.

For International Students

WWCC offers ESL, an honors program, free tutoring, career and personal counseling, internships, job placement services, and disability support services. Many students participate in the Host Family Program and Students Without Borders international club. Scholarships may be available to qualified international students.

Westminster Choir College of Rider University

- **Contact:**
  Joseph MacAde
  Director, Office of International Programs
  Westminster Choir College of Rider
     University
  101 Walnut Lane
  Princeton, New Jersey 08540
  Phone: 609-921-7100
  Fax: 609-921-2538
  E-mail: wccadmission@rider.edu
  Web site: http://www.rider.edu/westminster
- Private, four-year, coed
- Suburban setting
- Enrollment: 454
- Student-faculty ratio: 6:1

- 2006–07 Tuition and fees: $24,790
- 2006–07 Room and board: $9640
- International students: 9%
- Countries represented: 14
- International students applied: 41
- International students accepted: 26
- International students enrolled: 19
- Admissions tests:
  - TOEFL: Required (min. score 550 PBT)
  - SAT and ACT: Recommended
- Application deadline: Rolling
- On-campus housing: Available
- Summer housing: Available

Area and Climate

Located in the culturally rich town of Princeton, New Jersey, Westminster is a 40-minute train ride from the cosmopolitan cultural centers of New York City and Philadelphia, offering Westminster students a wealth of educational and recreational activities. Princeton University, a short walk from Westminster, offers lectures, art exhibits, recitals, and concerts. Through a cooperative agreement, Westminster students may enroll in courses at Princeton University. Near the Westminster campus, the Tony Award–winning Mc-Carter Theatre stages several major productions each year and hosts guest artists and musical performers. Average temperatures range from 22°F (-6°C) in the winter to 85°F (29°C) in the summer.

Education

Westminster grants the Bachelor of Music degree with majors in music education, music theater, organ performance, piano (with emphases in accompanying, pedagogy, and performance), sacred music, theory and composition, and voice performance. The Bachelor of Arts in Music degree is offered with concentrations in organ, piano, and voice. A minor in arts management, music theater, or piano pedagogy may be combined with any of the undergraduate programs. Westminster offers programs leading to the Master of Music degree in choral conducting, composition, music education, organ performance, piano accompanying and vocal coaching, piano performance, piano performance and pedagogy, sacred music, and voice performance and pedagogy. Other programs include the Master of Music

Education and Master of Voice Pedagogy. All Westminster students perform in professional concerts each year. The 200-voice Westminster Symphonic Choir sings and records on a regular basis with the New York Philharmonic under world-class conductors at Lincoln Center and Carnegie Hall. The Westminster Symphonic Choir has performed and recorded with Bernstein, Ormandy, Masur, Toscanini, Walter, Leinsdorf, Mehta, Ozawa, and Muti. Students may also perform in seven additional choirs, including the Westminster Choir, Westminster Kantori, Chapel Choir, Westminster Concert Bell Choir, Jubilee Singers, Williamson Voices, and Schola Cantorum. The Westminster choirs tour nationally and internationally. Westminster also offers students opportunities to perform in ensembles, and young composers' works are often showcased on campus and in community concerts.

Campus Life

Westminster offers housing in three residence halls, each of which provides a unique living environment for its residents. All residence halls have practice rooms. Rider University offers all of its students many extracurricular activities, including opportunities to participate in theatrical productions, intramural athletics, and intercollegiate athletic teams in several sports.

For International Students

The Office of International Programs is dedicated to meeting the needs of international students. It offers help and advice on everything from visa problems and obtaining a driver's license to handling academic and personal adjustment problems. Staff members have traveled extensively throughout the world and understand student issues in an unfamiliar culture and environment.

Wichita State University

- Contact:
    Vince Altum
    Associate Director
    Wichita State University
    Wichita, KS 67260-0122
    Phone: 316-978-3232
    Fax: 316-978-3777
- Public, coed
- Urban setting
- Enrollment: 15,000
- Student-faculty ratio: 14:1
- 2006–07 Tuition and fees: $9478
- 2006–07 Room and board: $5276

- International students: 9%
- Countries represented: 113
- International students accepted: 525
- International students enrolled: 300
- Admissions tests:
    - TOEFL: Required (min. score 530 paper-based)
    - SAT and ACT: Not required
- Application deadline: Rolling
- On-campus housing: Guaranteed
- Summer housing: Available

Area and Climate

Wichita State University is located in Wichita, Kansas, near the geographic center of the United States. With a population of 400,000, Wichita offers the advantages of a metropolitan environment but is small enough to be a safe and friendly city. Wichita is known as a high-technology center and as the aviation capital of the world. It is home to Boeing, Cessna, Raytheon (Beech), and Learjet as well as many businesses that manufacture computers and software, electronic equipment, chemicals, and agricultural products. A World Trade Center and Foreign Trade Zone make the city an important center for international commerce. The climate is temperate as compared to the winter cold of northern states and the summer heat of southern states.

Education

Wichita State University was established in 1895. The campus has eighty-one buildings on 346 acres (140 hectares). An accelerated study program allows students in many majors to complete a bachelor's degree in three years instead of the usual four. Many students find jobs through the University's cooperative education program. Excellent programs include engineering, business, computer science, fine arts, and liberal arts. Students are served by a library with nearly 2 million items, a new computing center with a supercomputer, campuswide computer laboratories, and science and engineering laboratories. Access to e-mail, the Internet, and the World Wide Web is free of charge. There

are two 16-week semesters and an eight-week summer session. Students may enter in August, January, or June.

Campus Life

Wichita State University has a friendly and helping environment where students are challenged to do their best. There are many opportunities for academic and personal growth. Nearly 200 student and academic organizations fulfill varied interests. Students may live in apartments on campus or in modern University residence halls with dining halls, computer terminals, and recreational facilities. Advisers provide for the welfare of international students and promote interaction between international and U.S. students. Housing is guaranteed for the academic year and the summer session. A modern sports complex offers indoor swimming, tennis, badminton, volleyball, and other sports.

For International Students

International students feel welcome and at home at Wichita State University. They become familiar with the campus and the U.S. educational system through the orientation program of the Office of International Programs. Services include airport pick-up, help with housing, assistance with immigration documents, a host-family program, and academic, personal, and financial counseling. The International Student Union offers cultural and social programs. Students who require English language instruction may enroll in the University's Intensive English Program during any of five sessions each year. Undergraduate students without a TOEFL score may receive conditional admission to the University. These students take a proficiency test after arrival on campus and then either enter academic classes or Intensive English.

Widener University

- **Contact:**
  Erik Hyde
  Assistant Dean of International and
      Undergraduate Admissions
  Widener University
  One University Place
  Chester, PA 19013
  Phone: 610-499-4595
  Fax: 610-499-4676
  E-mail: admissions.office@widener.edu
  Web site: http://www.widener.edu
- **Private, comprehensive, coed**
- **Urban setting**
- **Enrollment: 2,465 (full-time undergraduates)**
- **Student-faculty ratio: 12:1**

- **2006–07 Tuition and fees: $26,350**
- **2006–07 Room and board: $9640**
- **International students: 2.2%**
- **Countries represented: 32**
- **International students enrolled: 147**
- **Admissions tests:**
  - **TOEFL (paper-based min. score 500; computer-based min. score 173) or IELTS (min. score 5)**
  - **SAT and ACT: Recommended**
- **Application deadline: Rolling**
- **On-campus housing: Guaranteed for undergraduate students**
- **Summer housing: Available**

Area and Climate

Widener is a metropolitan university in the Northeast, located on a beautiful, spacious campus in Chester, Pennsylvania. Philadelphia, the fifth-largest city in the United States, is only 20 minutes from Widener by car or public transportation. The campus is only 10 minutes from the Philadelphia International Airport and less than 3 hours from New York City or Washington, D.C., by bus, train, or car. The New Jersey beaches and the Pocono Mountains can be reached within 1½ hours by car. The climate offers seasonal changes, with average temperatures ranging from 23°F (-5°C) in the winter to 95°F (35°C) in the summer.

Education

Founded in 1821, Widener offers fully accredited undergraduate and graduate degree programs in a variety of disciplines, including engineering, law, education, business, arts and sciences, hospitality management, psychology, social work, physical therapy, and nursing. The key to students' success in all programs is the supportive environment Widener offers. Faculty members and students interact closely, and talented students participate in the Honors Program, which enriches their learning experiences through challenging discussions. Academic support services for all students are available through the Math, Writing, and Reading Centers. Other academic facilities include state-of-the-art computing labs; a brand-new, $50-million addition to Kirkbride Hall, Widener's science and engineering building; and the Wolfgram Memorial Library, which holds more than 240,000 volumes. Widener's academic year consists of two semesters—the fall semester runs from early September through mid-

December, and the spring semester begins in mid-January and ends in mid-May. Many programs also offer summer courses.

Campus Life

With a diverse body of students from all over the United States and thirty-two countries and a range of social and cultural activities to choose from, Widener's campus is always lively. There are more than eighty student clubs and organizations, including several with an international focus. Regular campus events include concerts, movies, guest lectures, and athletic events. Students who are interested in athletics can participate in twenty-two intercollegiate sports—including soccer, swimming, and baseball—and several intramural sports. The Main Campus provides ultramodern sports facilities, including an athletics stadium, Olympic-size pool, fitness center, and playing fields.

For International Students

The Office of International Student Services assists students with all aspects of their lives on the Widener campus. Its staff provides assistance with all immigration needs, including filing for allowable employment, and offers a variety of special programs during the year. The Community Resource Network, which is made up of local families, invites international students to dinners and holiday celebrations. In addition, peer orientation volunteer students assist international students during the first few weeks of the first semester and are available for informal meetings and conversation throughout the year. Interaction with these resource groups gives international students a chance to share information about their cultures as they gain an understanding of the traditions in the United States. Another valuable resource is the Pennsylvania Language Institute, which provides intensive English courses to students.

Worcester Polytechnic Institute

- **Contact:**
  Aleksandra Fedorovich
  Coordinator of International Admissions
  Worcester Polytechnic Institute
  Worcester, MA 01524
  Phone: 508-831-5286
  Fax: 508-831-5875
  Web site: http://admissions.wpi.edu
- **Independent, coed**
- **Suburban setting**
- **Enrollment: 2,851**
- **Student-faculty ratio: 13:1**
- **2006–07 Tuition and fees: $33,318**
- **2006–07 Room and board: $9960**

- **International students: 10%**
- **Countries represented: 70**
- **International students applied: 471**
- **International students enrolled: 86**
- **Admissions tests:**
  - **TOEFL (min. score 79 iBT; 550 PBT; 213 CBT) or**
  - **IELTS (min. score 6.5, with no band less than 6.0)**
  - **SAT or ACT: Required**
- **Application deadline: 2/1 for August**
- **On-campus housing: Guaranteed first year**
- **Summer housing: Available**

Area and Climate

Worcester Polytechnic Institute's (WPI) 80-acre (32-hectare) hilltop campus, bordered by public parks and residential areas, is only a short walk from downtown Worcester, the second-largest city in Massachusetts (population 184,000). Home to fourteen colleges and universities, Worcester is a dynamic city offering cultural, educational, and commercial opportunities. The city is serviced by regional air, rail, and bus transportation. Boston is within an hour's drive, New York City is within 3 hours, and the New England seashore and the mountain ranges of New Hampshire and Vermont are within a 2-hour drive. Hiking, biking, and skiing are just some of the recreational opportunities available. The climate changes with the seasons. Average daytime temperatures range from 25°F (-4°C) in winter to 80°F (27°C) in summer.

Education

Founded in 1865, WPI, the third-oldest private technological university in the United States, is committed to academic excellence. The university offers bachelor's, master's, and doctoral degrees. An innovative curriculum, which provides real-life project experience combined with classroom learning, provides students with teamwork and professional skills. More than thirty-five areas of study in engineering, science, management, and the liberal arts allow many academic options, from molecular biology to music. The highest enrollments of students are in the fields of engineering, computer science, natural science, and management. Campus facilities include a library, research and computer labs, classroom buildings, gymnasiums, a performing arts center, residence halls and apartments, a bookstore, and dining areas. A fiber-optic LAN links every lab, classroom, office, and residence hall on campus to one another and to the Internet. In addition, all residence halls and campus buildings have wireless connections. Students benefit from small classes (average size is 15 to 25) and one-to-one faculty interaction. WPI's global program is the most extensive of any technological university in the nation, sending more engineering students abroad than any other program. The academic calendar consists of four 7-week terms and one summer session.

Campus Life

WPI is dedicated to creating an atmosphere that encourages diversity in all aspects of campus life. Students at WPI come from forty-one states and seventy other countries. Housing is guaranteed for first-year students. The campus atmosphere is lively and friendly. More than 200 student organizations, including musical and theater groups, ensure all student interests are addressed.

For International Students

International student services are coordinated by the Office of International Students and Scholars, which assists international students with their transition to WPI. A special two-day pre-orientation program is highly recommended for all international students before the standard academic and social orientation program begins. WPI's ESL Summer Institute provides an intensive five-week English language program. Support programs for students who wish to improve their English language skills are also available. WPI's International House is home to the Center for International Students and Scholars, which provides cultural programming and activities, career service workshops, speakers, and meeting and storage space as well as other support services. The International Student Council provides programs to meet the needs of the international student community and helps to coordinate activities for all international student organizations.

Profiles of Colleges and Universities in the U.S.

ALABAMA

ALABAMA AGRICULTURAL AND MECHANICAL UNIVERSITY, HUNTSVILLE

General Information State-supported, coed university. Suburban setting. *Awards:* B, M, D. *Entrance level for U.S. students:* Minimally difficult. *Enrollment:* 6,076 total; 4,978 undergraduates (53% women) including 3% international students from 45 foreign countries. *Faculty:* 391. *Library holdings:* 507,500 books, 2,500 current serial subscriptions. *Total majors:* 36. *Expenses:* (2007–08) $7800; room and board, $4770 (on campus); room only, $2756 (on campus). *Financial aid:* Non-need financial aid available.

ALABAMA STATE UNIVERSITY, MONTGOMERY

General Information State-supported, coed institution. Urban setting. *Awards:* A, B, M, D. *Entrance level for U.S. students:* Minimally difficult. *Enrollment:* 5,565 total; 4,584 undergraduates (59% women) including 0.4% international students from 9 foreign countries. *Faculty:* 409. *Library holdings:* 417,404 books, 2,082 current serial subscriptions, 43,318 audiovisual materials. *Total majors:* 49. *Expenses:* (2007–08) $8016; room and board, $3400 (on campus); room only, $1980 (on campus). *Financial aid:* Non-need-based athletic awards, on-campus employment. Forms required: International Student's Certification of Finances. For fall 2006 (estimated), 22 international students on campus received college administered financial aid ($7830 average).

ATHENS STATE UNIVERSITY, ATHENS

General Information State-supported, coed institution. Small town setting. *Awards:* B. *Entrance level for U.S. students:* Noncompetitive. *Enrollment:* 2,777 total. *Undergraduate faculty:* 177. *Library holdings:* 137,233 books, 250 current serial subscriptions. *Total majors:* 29. *Expenses:* (2006–07) $7200; room only, $900 (on campus).

AUBURN UNIVERSITY, AUBURN UNIVERSITY

General Information State-supported, coed university. Small town setting. *Awards:* B, M, D, FP. *Entrance level for U.S. students:* Moderately difficult. *Enrollment:* 23,547 total; 19,367 undergraduates (49% women) including 1% international students from 59 foreign countries. *Faculty:* 1,292. *Library holdings:* 3.7 million books, 29,355 current serial subscriptions, 14,760 audiovisual materials. *Total majors:* 138. *Expenses:* (2006–07) $15,496; room and board, $7564 (on campus); room only, $3250 (on campus).

AUBURN UNIVERSITY MONTGOMERY, MONTGOMERY

General Information State-supported, coed institution. Suburban setting. *Awards:* B, M, D. *Entrance level for U.S. students:* Moderately difficult. *Enrollment:* 5,079 total; 4,300 undergraduates (63% women) including 0.2% international students. *Faculty:* 346. *Library holdings:* 347,044 books, 2,303 current serial subscriptions. *Total majors:* 24. *Expenses:* (2006–07) $14,020; room and board, $3050 (on campus); room only, $2890 (on campus). *Financial aid:* Forms required: International Student's Financial Aid Application.

BEVILL STATE COMMUNITY COLLEGE, SUMITON

General Information State-supported, 2-year, coed college. Rural setting. *Awards:* A. *Entrance level for U.S. students:* Noncompetitive. *Enrollment:* 4,327 total (63% women). *Undergraduate faculty:* 335. *Library holdings:* 31,690 books, 192 current serial subscriptions. *Total majors:* 12. *Financial aid:* Forms required: International Student's Certification of Finances.

BIRMINGHAM-SOUTHERN COLLEGE, BIRMINGHAM

General Information Independent Methodist, coed institution. Urban setting. *Awards:* B, M. *Entrance level for U.S. students:* Moderately difficult. *Enrollment:* 1,256 total; 1,207 undergraduates (59% women) including 0.2% international students from 23 foreign countries. *Faculty:* 131. *Library holdings:* 232,330 books, 949 current serial subscriptions, 31,471 audiovisual materials. *Total majors:* 43. *Expenses:* (2007–08) $24,300; room and board, $8062 (on campus); room only, $5000 (on campus). *Financial aid:* Need-based college/university scholarships/grants from institutional funds, loans from outside sources, on-campus employment. Non-need-based college/university scholarships/grants from institutional funds, loans from outside sources, on-campus employment. Forms required: International Student's Certification of Finances. For fall 2006 (estimated), 19 international students on campus received college administered financial aid ($18,768 average).

CALHOUN COMMUNITY COLLEGE, DECATUR

General Information State-supported, 2-year, coed college. Suburban setting. *Awards:* A. *Entrance level for U.S. students:* Noncompetitive. *Enrollment:* 9,452 total including 0.2% international students from 16 foreign countries. *Undergraduate faculty:* 424. *Library holdings:* 36,699 books, 202 current serial subscriptions, 23,948 audiovisual materials. *Total majors:* 46.

Information for International Students For fall 2006: 45 international students applied, 27 were accepted, 27 enrolled. Students can start in fall, spring, or summer. *Admission tests:* Required: TOEFL (minimum score: iBT 61; paper-based 500; computer-based 173), placement test. *Application deadline:* 6/29. *Expenses:* (2006–07) $5312. *Services:* International student adviser on campus. ESL program at cooperating institution. *Contact:* Transcript Specialist/International Student Advisor, Calhoun Community College, PO Box 2216, Decatur, AL 35609-2216. Telephone: 256-306-2599. Fax: 256-306-2941. E-mail: bjt@calhoun.edu. URL: http://www.calhoun.edu.

CONCORDIA COLLEGE, SELMA

General Information Independent Lutheran, 4-year, coed college. Small town setting. *Awards:* A, B. *Entrance level for U.S. students:* Minimally difficult. *Enrollment:* 902 total (66% women) including 3% international students from 6 foreign countries. *Undergraduate faculty:* 49. *Library holdings:* 60,000 books, 183 current serial subscriptions, 4,000 audiovisual materials. *Total majors:* 4.

Information for International Students For fall 2006: 11 international students applied, 11 were accepted, 7 enrolled. Students can start in fall or spring. Transfers accepted from institutions abroad. *Admission tests:* Required: TOEFL (minimum score: paper-based 500; computer-based 173), ELS. Recommended: SAT. TOEFL can be waived under certain conditions. *Application deadline:* 6/1. *Expenses:* (2006–07) $6246; room and board, $3600 (on campus); room only, $1600 (on campus). *Financial aid:* Need-based financial aid available. Forms required: institution's own financial aid form. *Housing:* Guaranteed. *Services:* International student adviser on campus. Employment opportunities (on-campus) available. *Contact:* Director of Enrollment Management and Placement, Concordia College, 1804 Green Street, Selma, AL 36701. Telephone: 334-874-5700 Ext. 171. Fax: 334-874-3728. E-mail: epickens@concordiaselma.edu. URL: http://www.concordiaselma.edu.

FAULKNER UNIVERSITY, MONTGOMERY

General Information Independent, coed institution, affiliated with Church of Christ. Urban setting. *Awards:* A, B, M, FP. *Entrance level for U.S. students:* Minimally difficult. *Enrollment:* 2,625 total; 2,212 undergraduates (64% women) including 1% international students from 3 foreign countries. *Faculty:* 147. *Library holdings:* 170,577 books, 3,233 current serial subscriptions, 2,300 audiovisual materials. *Total majors:* 48. *Expenses:* (2007–08) $11,565; room and board, $5400 (on campus); room only, $2500 (on campus). *Financial aid:* Non-need-based college/university scholarships/grants from institutional funds.

GADSDEN STATE COMMUNITY COLLEGE, GADSDEN

General Information State-supported, 2-year, coed college. Small town setting. *Awards:* A. *Entrance level for U.S. students:* Noncompetitive. *Enrollment:* 5,204 total (61% women) including 4% international students from 32 foreign countries. *Undergraduate faculty:* 263. *Library holdings:* 109,568 books, 234 current serial subscriptions, 12,030 audiovisual materials. *Total majors:* 21. *Expenses:* (2006–07) $3864; room and board, $3750 (on campus).

HERITAGE CHRISTIAN UNIVERSITY, FLORENCE

General Information Independent, coed, primarily men's institution, affiliated with Church of Christ. Small town setting. *Awards:* A, B, M. *Entrance level for U.S. students:* Noncompetitive. *Enrollment:* 112 total; 93 undergraduates (18% women) including 4% international students from 5 foreign countries. *Faculty:* 21. *Library holdings:* 63,000 books, 365 current serial subscriptions, 12,981 audiovisual materials. *Total majors:* 1. *Expenses:* (2007–08) $9076; room only, $3000 (on campus). *Financial aid:* Need-based loans from outside sources. Non-need-based college/university scholarships/grants from institutional funds, loans from outside sources.

HERZING COLLEGE, BIRMINGHAM

General Information Proprietary, primarily 2-year, coed college. Urban setting. *Awards:* A, B. *Entrance level for U.S. students:* Minimally difficult. *Enrollment:* 600 total (29% women). *Undergraduate faculty:* 27. *Total majors:* 9.

HUNTINGDON COLLEGE, MONTGOMERY

General Information Independent United Methodist, 4-year, coed college. Suburban setting. *Awards:* A, B. *Entrance level for U.S. students:* Moderately difficult. *Enrollment:* 731 total (50% women) including 2% international students. *Undergraduate faculty:* 61.

Library holdings: 97,436 books, 443 current serial subscriptions, 1,811 audiovisual materials. *Total majors:* 50.

Information for International Students Students can start in fall or spring. Transfers accepted from institutions abroad. *Admission tests:* Required: SAT or ACT, TOEFL (minimum score: paper-based 500; computer-based 173). TOEFL can be waived under certain conditions. *Application deadline:* 7/1. *Financial aid:* Non-need financial aid available. Forms required: International Student's Certification of Finances. international students on campus received college administered aid averaging $10,967. *Housing:* Guaranteed. *Services:* International student adviser on campus. Internships and employment opportunities (on-campus) available. *Contact:* Director of Admissions, Huntingdon College, 1500 East Fairview Avenue, Montgomery, AL 36106. Telephone: 334-833-4398. Fax: 334-833-4347. E-mail: joseph.miller@huntingdon.edu. URL: http://www.huntingdon.edu.

JACKSONVILLE STATE UNIVERSITY, JACKSONVILLE

General Information State-supported, coed institution. Small town setting. *Awards:* B, M. *Entrance level for U.S. students:* Minimally difficult. *Enrollment:* 8,957 total; 7,311 undergraduates (57% women) including 1% international students from 70 foreign countries. *Faculty:* 450. *Library holdings:* 685,991 books, 14,376 current serial subscriptions. *Total majors:* 58.

Information for International Students Students can start in fall, winter, spring, or summer. Transfers accepted from institutions abroad. *Admission tests:* Required: TOEFL (minimum score: paper-based 500; computer-based 173), SAT or ACT may be substituted for TOEFL. *Application deadline:* Rolling. *Expenses:* (2006–07) $10,140; room and board, $3764 (on campus). *Financial aid:* Non-need-based college/university scholarships/grants from institutional funds, tuition waivers, athletic awards, loans from institutional funds, on-campus employment, graduate assistantship, small stipend. Forms required: institution's own financial aid form, International Student's Certification of Finances. For fall 2005, 10 international students on campus received college administered financial aid ($1000 average). *Housing:* Available during summer. *Services:* International student adviser on campus. ESL program at cooperating institution. Employment opportunities (on-campus) available. *Contact:* Director, International Programs, Jacksonville State University, Jacksonville, AL 36265. Telephone: 256-782-5674. Fax: 256-782-8057. E-mail: intprog@jsucc.jsu.edu. URL: http://www.jsu.edu.

See In-Depth Description on page 105.

JEFFERSON STATE COMMUNITY COLLEGE, BIRMINGHAM

General Information State-supported, 2-year, coed college. Suburban setting. *Awards:* A. *Entrance level for U.S. students:* Noncompetitive. *Enrollment:* 7,173 total (62% women) including 2% international students from 61 foreign countries. *Undergraduate faculty:* 397. *Library holdings:* 77,015 books, 242 current serial subscriptions, 3,349 audiovisual materials. *Total majors:* 23.

LAWSON STATE COMMUNITY COLLEGE, BIRMINGHAM

General Information State-supported, 2-year, coed college. Urban setting. *Awards:* A. *Entrance level for U.S. students:* Noncompetitive. *Enrollment:* 3,141 total (63% women) including 0.03% international students. *Undergraduate faculty:* 222. *Library holdings:* 48,903 books, 243 current serial subscriptions. *Total majors:* 44. *Expenses:* (2007–08) $4860; room and board, $3000 (on campus); room only, $2000 (on campus). *Financial aid:* Forms required: institution's own financial aid form.

NORTHEAST ALABAMA COMMUNITY COLLEGE, RAINSVILLE

General Information State-supported, 2-year, coed college. Rural setting. *Awards:* A. *Entrance level for U.S. students:* Noncompetitive. *Enrollment:* 2,015 total (65% women). *Undergraduate faculty:* 136. *Library holdings:* 45,000 books, 142 current serial subscriptions. *Total majors:* 18. *Expenses:* (2006–07) $4980.

NORTHWEST-SHOALS COMMUNITY COLLEGE, MUSCLE SHOALS

General Information State-supported, 2-year, coed college. Small town setting. *Awards:* A. *Entrance level for U.S. students:* Noncompetitive. *Enrollment:* 2,077 total (60% women) including 0.05% international students from 1 foreign country. *Undergraduate faculty:* 217. *Library holdings:* 66,986 books, 262 current serial subscriptions, 1,401 audiovisual materials. *Total majors:* 41. *Expenses:* (2007–08) $5010; room only, $1675 (on campus). *Financial aid:* Need-based loans from outside sources, on-campus

employment. Non-need-based college/university scholarships/grants from institutional funds, tuition waivers, athletic awards.

SAMFORD UNIVERSITY, BIRMINGHAM

General Information Independent Baptist, coed university. Suburban setting. *Awards:* A, B, M, D, FP. *Entrance level for U.S. students:* Moderately difficult. *Enrollment:* 4,478 total; 2,882 undergraduates (64% women) including 1% international students from 18 foreign countries. *Faculty:* 407. *Library holdings:* 439,760 books, 3,724 current serial subscriptions. *Total majors:* 68. *Expenses:* (2006–07) $16,000; room and board, $6060 (on campus); room only, $2970 (on campus). *Financial aid:* Non-need financial aid available. For fall 2005, 8 international students on campus received college administered financial aid ($11,069 average).

SOUTH UNIVERSITY, MONTGOMERY

General Information Proprietary, coed institution. Urban setting. *Awards:* A, B, M. *Entrance level for U.S. students:* Minimally difficult. *Enrollment:* 446 total; 435 undergraduates (77% women) including 0.2% international students. *Faculty:* 37. *Library holdings:* 17,270 books, 82 current serial subscriptions. *Total majors:* 12. *Expenses:* (2007–08) $15,800. *Financial aid:* Forms required: institution's own financial aid form, International Student's Certification of Finances.

SPRING HILL COLLEGE, MOBILE

General Information Independent Roman Catholic (Jesuit), coed institution. Suburban setting. *Awards:* A, B, M. *Entrance level for U.S. students:* Moderately difficult. *Enrollment:* 1,446 total; 1,218 undergraduates (65% women) including 1% international students from 10 foreign countries. *Faculty:* 147. *Library holdings:* 185,868 books, 2,200 current serial subscriptions, 1,201 audiovisual materials. *Total majors:* 43. *Expenses:* (2006–07) $22,000; room and board, $8120 (on campus); room only, $4200 (on campus). *Financial aid:* Non-need-based college/university scholarships/grants from institutional funds, athletic awards, loans from outside sources, on-campus employment. Forms required: institution's own financial aid form, International Student's Certification of Finances. For fall 2006 (estimated), 9 international students on campus received college administered financial aid ($15,147 average).

TROY UNIVERSITY, TROY

General Information State-supported, coed institution. Small town setting. *Awards:* A, B, M. *Entrance level for U.S. students:* Moderately difficult. *Enrollment:* 27,938 total; 20,069 undergraduates (55% women) including 2% international students from 51 foreign countries. *Faculty:* 1,489. *Library holdings:* 504,716 books, 3,263 current serial subscriptions, 19,532 audiovisual materials. *Total majors:* 50.

Information for International Students For fall 2006: 1419 international students applied, 636 were accepted, 221 enrolled. Students can start in fall, spring, or summer. Transfers accepted from institutions abroad. *Admission tests:* Recommended: TOEFL (minimum score: paper-based 500; computer-based 173). *Application deadline:* Rolling. *Expenses:* (2006–07) $8108; room and board, $5491 (on campus); room only, $2863 (on campus). *Financial aid:* International transfer students are eligible to apply for aid. *Housing:* Guaranteed, also available during summer. *Services:* International student adviser on campus. Full-time ESL program on campus. ESL program available during the academic year and the summer. Employment opportunities (on-campus) available. *Contact:* Director of International Admissions, Troy University, 128 International Center, Troy, AL 36082. Telephone: 334-670-3335. Fax: 334-670-3735. E-mail: intladm@troy.edu. URL: http://www.troy.edu.

See In-Depth Description on page 205.

TUSKEGEE UNIVERSITY, TUSKEGEE

General Information Independent, coed institution. Small town setting. *Awards:* B, M, D, FP. *Entrance level for U.S. students:* Moderately difficult. *Enrollment:* 2,842 total; 2,420 undergraduates (55% women) including 3% international students from 30 foreign countries. *Faculty:* 256. *Library holdings:* 623,824 books, 81,157 current serial subscriptions. *Total majors:* 43. *Expenses:* (2007–08) $14,615; room and board, $6783 (on campus).

THE UNIVERSITY OF ALABAMA, TUSCALOOSA

General Information State-supported, coed university. Suburban setting. *Awards:* B, M, D, FP. *Entrance level for U.S. students:* Moderately difficult. *Enrollment:* 23,838 total; 19,471 undergraduates (53% women) including 1% international students from 62 foreign countries. *Faculty:* 1,168. *Library holdings:* 2.6 million books, 34,461 current serial subscriptions. *Total majors:* 78.

Information for International Students For fall 2006: 307 international students applied, 137 were accepted, 100 enrolled.

The University of Alabama (continued)

Students can start in fall, spring, or summer. Transfers accepted from institutions abroad. *Admission tests:* Required: TOEFL (minimum score: iBT 61; paper-based 500; computer-based 173), completion of Level 5 at institution's language institute may be substituted for TOEFL, IELTS also accepted. TOEFL can be waived under certain conditions. *Application deadline:* 5/1. *Expenses:* (2006–07) $15,294; room and board, $5380 (on campus); room only, $3400 (on campus). *Housing:* Available during summer. *Services:* International student adviser on campus. Full-time and part-time ESL programs on campus. ESL program available during the academic year and the summer. Internships and employment opportunities (on-campus) available. *Contact:* Assistant Director of Undergraduate International Admissions, The University of Alabama, Box 870132, Tuscaloosa, AL 35487-0132. Telephone: 205-348-5924. Fax: 205-354-9046. E-mail: edwina.crawford@ua.edu. URL: http://www.ua.edu.

THE UNIVERSITY OF ALABAMA AT BIRMINGHAM, BIRMINGHAM

General Information State-supported, coed university. Urban setting. *Awards:* B, M, D, FP. *Entrance level for U.S. students:* Moderately difficult. *Enrollment:* 16,561 total; 11,284 undergraduates (61% women) including 2% international students from 69 foreign countries. *Faculty:* 915. *Library holdings:* 853,445 books, 3,934 current serial subscriptions. *Total majors:* 48. *Expenses:* (2006–07) $10,732; room and board, $7111 (on campus); room only, $3427 (on campus).

THE UNIVERSITY OF ALABAMA IN HUNTSVILLE, HUNTSVILLE

General Information State-supported, coed university. Suburban setting. *Awards:* B, M, D. *Entrance level for U.S. students:* Moderately difficult. *Enrollment:* 7,091 total; 5,719 undergraduates (49% women) including 3% international students from 64 foreign countries. *Faculty:* 469. *Library holdings:* 334,684 books, 926 current serial subscriptions. *Total majors:* 29.

Information for International Students For fall 2006: 45 international students applied, 44 were accepted, 37 enrolled. Students can start in fall, spring, or summer. Transfers accepted from institutions abroad. *Admission tests:* Required: SAT or ACT, TOEFL (minimum score: iBT 62; paper-based 500; computer-based 173; minimum score for ESL admission: iBT 45). *Application deadline:* Rolling. *Expenses:* (2006–07) $10,224; room and board, $5110 (on campus); room only, $4560 (on campus). *Financial aid:* Need-based college/university scholarships/grants from institutional funds, athletic awards, loans from institutional funds, loans from outside sources, on-campus employment. Non-need-based college/university scholarships/grants from institutional funds, athletic awards, loans from outside sources, on-campus employment. International transfer students are eligible to apply for aid. For fall 2006 (estimated), 18 international students on campus received college administered financial aid ($2408 average). *Housing:* Available during summer. *Services:* International student adviser on campus. Full-time and part-time ESL programs on campus. ESL program available during the academic year and the summer. Internships and employment opportunities (on-campus and off-campus) available. *Contact:* Director of Admissions Processing, The University of Alabama in Huntsville, Office of Undergraduate Admissions, 301 Sparkman Drive, Huntsville, AL 35899. Telephone: 256-824-2744. Fax: 256-824-7780. E-mail: williams@uah.edu. URL: http://www.uah.edu.

UNIVERSITY OF MOBILE, MOBILE

General Information Independent Southern Baptist, coed institution. Suburban setting. *Awards:* A, B, M. *Entrance level for U.S. students:* Moderately difficult. *Enrollment:* 1,639 total; 1,445 undergraduates (66% women) including 3% international students from 20 foreign countries. *Faculty:* 146. *Library holdings:* 81,852 books, 401 current serial subscriptions, 1,680 audiovisual materials. *Total majors:* 30. *Expenses:* (2007–08) $13,390; room and board, $7140 (on campus); room only, $4260 (on campus).

UNIVERSITY OF MONTEVALLO, MONTEVALLO

General Information State-supported, coed institution. Small town setting. *Awards:* B, M. *Entrance level for U.S. students:* Moderately difficult. *Enrollment:* 2,895 total; 2,463 undergraduates including 0.1% international students from 20 foreign countries. *Faculty:* 216. *Library holdings:* 260,463 books, 4,495 audiovisual materials. *Total majors:* 49. *Expenses:* (2006–07) $11,124; room and board, $4084 (on campus).

UNIVERSITY OF NORTH ALABAMA, FLORENCE

General Information State-supported, coed institution. Urban setting. *Awards:* B, M. *Entrance level for U.S. students:* Minimally difficult. *Enrollment:* 6,810 total; 5,600 undergraduates (57% women) including 9% international students from 44 foreign countries. *Faculty:* 375. *Library holdings:* 380,361 books, 3,760 current serial subscriptions, 11,869 audiovisual materials. *Total majors:* 38.

Information for International Students Students can start in fall, spring, or summer. Transfers accepted from institutions abroad. *Admission tests:* Required: SAT or ACT, TOEFL (minimum score: iBT 61; paper-based 500; computer-based 173). *Application deadline:* 7/13. *Expenses:* (2006–07) $8419; room and board, $4372 (on campus); room only, $2060 (on campus). *Financial aid:* Non-need-based college/university scholarships/grants from institutional funds, athletic awards, loans from outside sources, on-campus employment. Forms required: International Student's Certification of Finances. *Housing:* Guaranteed, also available during summer. *Services:* International student adviser on campus. Full-time ESL program on campus. ESL program available during the academic year and the summer. Employment opportunities (on-campus) available. *Contact:* International Student Services Specialist, Office of Admissions, University of North Alabama, One Harrison Plaza, UNA Box 5058, Florence, AL 35632-0001. Telephone: 256-765-4626. Fax: 256-765-5404. E-mail: mrnelson@una.edu. URL: http://www.una.edu.

UNIVERSITY OF SOUTH ALABAMA, MOBILE

General Information State-supported, coed university. Suburban setting. *Awards:* B, M, D, FP. *Entrance level for U.S. students:* Moderately difficult. *Enrollment:* 13,090 total; 10,078 undergraduates (60% women) including 5% international students from 98 foreign countries. *Faculty:* 992. *Library holdings:* 1.1 million books, 7,344 current serial subscriptions. *Total majors:* 47. *Expenses:* (2006–07) $8312; room and board, $4428 (on campus); room only, $2468 (on campus).

THE UNIVERSITY OF WEST ALABAMA, LIVINGSTON

General Information State-supported, coed institution. Small town setting. *Awards:* A, B, M. *Entrance level for U.S. students:* Minimally difficult. *Enrollment:* 3,633 total; 1,821 undergraduates (56% women) including 1% international students from 10 foreign countries. *Faculty:* 100. *Library holdings:* 161,991 books, 30,000 current serial subscriptions, 3,072 audiovisual materials. *Total majors:* 19. *Expenses:* (2007–08) $8164; room and board, $3438 (on campus); room only, $1746 (on campus).

ALASKA

ALASKA PACIFIC UNIVERSITY, ANCHORAGE

General Information Independent, coed institution. Suburban setting. *Awards:* A, B, M. *Entrance level for U.S. students:* Moderately difficult. *Enrollment:* 733 total; 510 undergraduates (66% women) including 1% international students from 3 foreign countries. *Faculty:* 110. *Library holdings:* 788,708 books, 3,434 current serial subscriptions. *Total majors:* 12.

Information for International Students For fall 2006: 15 international students applied, 3 were accepted, 3 enrolled. Students can start in fall or spring. Transfers accepted from institutions abroad. *Admission tests:* Required: TOEFL (minimum score: iBT 79; paper-based 550; computer-based 213). Recommended: SAT or ACT, SAT Subject Tests. *Application deadline:* 6/1. *Expenses:* (2007–08) $19,610; room and board, $7000 (on campus). *Financial aid:* Need-based college/university scholarships/grants from institutional funds, tuition waivers, on-campus employment. Non-need-based college/university scholarships/grants from institutional funds, tuition waivers, on-campus employment. Forms required: International Student's Financial Aid Application. International transfer students are eligible to apply for aid. 2 international students on campus received college administered financial aid ($4962 average). *Services:* International student adviser on campus. Internships and employment opportunities (on-campus) available. *Contact:* International Admissions Counselor, Alaska Pacific University, Office of Admissions, 4101 University Drive, Anchorage, AK 99508. Telephone: 907-564-8248. Fax: 907-564-8317. E-mail: admissions@alaskapacific.edu. URL: http://www.alaskapacific.edu.

SHELDON JACKSON COLLEGE, SITKA

General Information Independent, 4-year, coed college, affiliated with Presbyterian Church (U.S.A.). Small town setting. *Awards:* A, B. *Entrance level for U.S. students:* Noncompetitive. *Enrollment:* 274 total (67% women). *Undergraduate faculty:* 38. *Library holdings:* 46,000 books, 150 current serial subscriptions. *Total majors:* 10.

UNIVERSITY OF ALASKA ANCHORAGE, ANCHORAGE
General Information State-supported, coed institution. Urban setting. *Awards:* A, B, M. *Entrance level for U.S. students:* Noncompetitive. *Enrollment:* 17,023 total; 16,242 undergraduates (60% women) including 2% international students from 41 foreign countries. *Faculty:* 1,199. *Library holdings:* 894,080 books, 3,833 current serial subscriptions. *Total majors:* 67. *Expenses:* (2006–07) $11,970; room and board, $8030 (on campus). *Financial aid:* Need-based college/university scholarships/grants from institutional funds, tuition waivers, athletic awards. Non-need-based college/university scholarships/grants from institutional funds, tuition waivers, athletic awards. Forms required: institution's own financial aid form.

UNIVERSITY OF ALASKA ANCHORAGE, MATANUSKA-SUSITNA COLLEGE, PALMER
General Information State-supported, 2-year, coed college. Small town setting. *Awards:* A. *Entrance level for U.S. students:* Noncompetitive. *Enrollment:* 1,326 total (68% women) including 0.2% international students from 18 foreign countries. *Undergraduate faculty:* 96. *Library holdings:* 50,000 books, 280 current serial subscriptions, 1,840 audiovisual materials. *Total majors:* 8. *Expenses:* (2006–07) $9826.

UNIVERSITY OF ALASKA FAIRBANKS, FAIRBANKS
General Information State-supported, coed university. Small town setting. *Awards:* A, B, M, D. *Entrance level for U.S. students:* Minimally difficult. *Enrollment:* 8,341 total; 7,274 undergraduates (60% women) including 2% international students from 34 foreign countries. *Faculty:* 658. *Library holdings:* 620,760 books, 144,583 current serial subscriptions, 729,494 audiovisual materials. *Total majors:* 68. *Expenses:* (2007–08) $12,678; room and board, $6030 (on campus); room only, $3440 (on campus). *Financial aid:* Non-need-based college/university scholarships/grants from institutional funds, tuition waivers, athletic awards, on-campus employment. Forms required: International Student's Certification of Finances. For fall 2006 (estimated), 39 international students on campus received college administered financial aid ($11,535 average).

UNIVERSITY OF ALASKA SOUTHEAST, JUNEAU
General Information State-supported, coed institution. Small town setting. *Awards:* A, B, M. *Entrance level for U.S. students:* Noncompetitive. *Enrollment:* 2,965 total; 2,753 undergraduates (64% women) including 4% international students from 5 foreign countries. *Faculty:* 239. *Library holdings:* 176,312 books, 438 current serial subscriptions. *Total majors:* 17. *Expenses:* (2006–07) $12,766; room and board, $5790 (on campus). *Financial aid:* Need-based college/university scholarships/grants from institutional funds, tuition waivers. Non-need-based college/university scholarships/grants from institutional funds, tuition waivers. Forms required: institution's own financial aid form, International Student's Certification of Finances. For fall 2005, 8 international students on campus received college administered financial aid ($9009 average).

ARIZONA

ARIZONA STATE UNIVERSITY, TEMPE
General Information State-supported, coed university. Suburban setting. *Awards:* B, M, D, FP. *Entrance level for U.S. students:* Moderately difficult. *Enrollment:* 51,234 total; 41,815 undergraduates (51% women) including 3% international students from 96 foreign countries. *Faculty:* 1,974. *Library holdings:* 3.9 million books, 30,839 current serial subscriptions, 1.5 million audiovisual materials. *Total majors:* 86.
Information for International Students For fall 2006: 1500 international students applied, 850 were accepted, 250 enrolled. Students can start in fall or spring. Transfers accepted from institutions abroad. *Admission tests:* Required: TOEFL (minimum score: iBT 61; paper-based 500; computer-based 173). Recommended: IELTS. TOEFL can be waived under certain conditions. *Application deadline:* 5/1. *Expenses:* (2006–07) $15,847; room and board, $6900 (on campus); room only, $4200 (on campus). *Financial aid:* Non-need financial aid available. Forms required: ASU Estimate of Expenses and Financial Guarantee. For fall 2005, 490 international students on campus received college administered financial aid ($7742 average). *Housing:* Available during summer. *Services:* International student adviser on campus. Full-time and part-time ESL programs on campus. ESL program available during the academic year and the summer. Employment opportunities (on-campus) available. *Contact:* Director of Undergraduate International Admissions, Arizona State University, PO Box 870112, Tempe, AZ 85287-0112. Telephone: 480-965-2688. Fax: 480-965-3610. E-mail: zohreh.sotoodeh@asu.edu. URL: http://www.asu.edu.

ARIZONA STATE UNIVERSITY WEST, PHOENIX
General Information State-supported, coed institution. Urban setting. *Awards:* B, M. *Entrance level for U.S. students:* Moderately difficult. *Enrollment:* 8,211 total; 6,941 undergraduates (65% women) including 0.5% international students from 15 foreign countries. *Faculty:* 462. *Library holdings:* 348,697 books, 2,422 current serial subscriptions. *Total majors:* 23. *Expenses:* (2006–07) $15,794; room only, $4200 (on campus). *Financial aid:* Non-need financial aid available. 6 international students on campus received college administered financial aid ($11,191 average).

ARIZONA WESTERN COLLEGE, YUMA
General Information State and locally supported, 2-year, coed college. Rural setting. *Awards:* A. *Entrance level for U.S. students:* Noncompetitive. *Enrollment:* 6,579 total (61% women) including 12% international students from 27 foreign countries. *Undergraduate faculty:* 349. *Library holdings:* 94,116 books, 402 current serial subscriptions, 4,486 audiovisual materials. *Total majors:* 43. *Expenses:* (2006–07) $5760; room and board, $4468 (on campus); room only, $1790 (on campus). *Financial aid:* Forms required: institution's own financial aid form, International Student's Certification of Finances.

CENTRAL ARIZONA COLLEGE, COOLIDGE
General Information County-supported, 2-year, coed college. Rural setting. *Awards:* A. *Entrance level for U.S. students:* Noncompetitive. *Enrollment:* 6,471 total including 0.4% international students from 6 foreign countries. *Undergraduate faculty:* 332. *Library holdings:* 99,480 books, 494 current serial subscriptions. *Total majors:* 26. *Expenses:* (2007–08) $7112; room and board, $4670 (on campus). *Financial aid:* Non-need financial aid available.

COCHISE COLLEGE, DOUGLAS
General Information State and locally supported, 2-year, coed college. Rural setting. *Awards:* A. *Entrance level for U.S. students:* Noncompetitive. *Enrollment:* 4,436 total (61% women) including 0.03% international students from 3 foreign countries. *Undergraduate faculty:* 381. *Library holdings:* 65,000 books, 7,000 current serial subscriptions, 4,000 audiovisual materials. *Total majors:* 49. *Expenses:* (2007–08) $7020; room and board, $3910 (on campus).

COCHISE COLLEGE, SIERRA VISTA
General Information State and locally supported, 2-year, coed college. Small town setting. *Awards:* A. *Entrance level for U.S. students:* Noncompetitive. *Enrollment:* 4,446 total (57% women) including 0.5% international students from 8 foreign countries. *Undergraduate faculty:* 394. *Library holdings:* 67,317 books, 305 current serial subscriptions, 3,124 audiovisual materials. *Total majors:* 34.
Information for International Students For fall 2006: 102 international students enrolled. Students can start in fall, spring, or summer. *Admission tests:* Required: ELS, ACCUPLACER. *Application deadline:* Rolling. *Expenses:* (2006–07) $6360; room and board, $3562 (on campus). *Housing:* Available during summer. *Services:* International student adviser on campus. Full-time and part-time ESL programs on campus. ESL program available during the academic year and the summer. Employment opportunities (on-campus) available. *Contact:* Administrative Assistant, Student Development Center, Cochise College, 4190 West Highway 80, Douglas, AZ 85607. Telephone: 520-417-4038. Fax: 520-417-4192. E-mail: martins@cochise.edu. URL: http://www.cochise.cc.az.us.

DEVRY UNIVERSITY, PHOENIX
General Information Proprietary, coed institution. Urban setting. *Awards:* A, B, M. *Entrance level for U.S. students:* Minimally difficult. *Enrollment:* 1,185 total; 1,006 undergraduates (22% women) including 1% international students from 4 foreign countries. *Faculty:* 70. *Library holdings:* 22,500 books, 7,230 current serial subscriptions. *Total majors:* 11. *Expenses:* (2007–08) $13,220.

EASTERN ARIZONA COLLEGE, THATCHER
General Information State and locally supported, 2-year, coed college. Small town setting. *Awards:* A. *Entrance level for U.S. students:* Noncompetitive. *Enrollment:* 5,239 total (59% women) including 1% international students. *Undergraduate faculty:* 298. *Total majors:* 50. *Expenses:* (2006–07) $6460; room and board, $4320 (on campus). *Financial aid:* Non-need-based college/university scholarships/grants from institutional funds,

Eastern Arizona College (continued)
athletic awards, on-campus employment. Forms required: institution's own financial aid form.

EMBRY-RIDDLE AERONAUTICAL UNIVERSITY, PRESCOTT

General Information Independent, coed institution. Suburban setting. *Awards:* B, M. *Entrance level for U.S. students:* Moderately difficult. *Enrollment:* 1,674 total; 1,630 undergraduates (17% women) including 4% international students from 29 foreign countries. *Faculty:* 124. *Total majors:* 11. *Expenses:* (2007–08) $26,130; room and board, $7214 (on campus); room only, $3990 (on campus). *Financial aid:* Need-based loans from outside sources, on-campus employment. Non-need-based college/university scholarships/grants from institutional funds, athletic awards, on-campus employment. For fall 2006 (estimated), 56 international students on campus received college administered financial aid ($7806 average).

EVEREST COLLEGE, PHOENIX

General Information Proprietary, primarily 2-year, coed college. Urban setting. *Awards:* A, B. *Entrance level for U.S. students:* Noncompetitive. *Enrollment:* 1,187 total (83% women) including 0.3% international students. *Undergraduate faculty:* 77. *Library holdings:* 17,515 books, 48 current serial subscriptions, 514 audiovisual materials. *Total majors:* 5. *Expenses:* (2007–08) $13,156. *Financial aid:* Forms required: institution's own financial aid form, International Student's Financial Aid Application.

GATEWAY COMMUNITY COLLEGE, PHOENIX

General Information State and locally supported, 2-year, coed college. Urban setting. *Awards:* A. *Entrance level for U.S. students:* Noncompetitive. *Enrollment:* 9,377 total (47% women) including international students from 26 foreign countries. *Undergraduate faculty:* 259. *Library holdings:* 50,000 books, 300 current serial subscriptions. *Total majors:* 39.
Information for International Students For fall 2006: 100 international students applied, 90 were accepted, 25 enrolled. Students can start in fall, spring, or summer. Transfers accepted from institutions abroad. *Admission tests:* Required: TOEFL (minimum score: paper-based 500; computer-based 173). TOEFL can be waived under certain conditions. *Application deadline:* Rolling. *Expenses:* (2006–07) $6750. *Services:* International student adviser on campus. ESL program at cooperating institution. ESL program available during the academic year and the summer. Employment opportunities (on-campus) available. *Contact:* Director of Admissions and Records, GateWay Community College, 108 North 40th Street, Phoenix, AZ 85034. Telephone: 602-286-8052. Fax: 602-286-8072. E-mail: gibson@gwc.maricopa.edu. URL: http://www.gwc.maricopa.edu.

GLENDALE COMMUNITY COLLEGE, GLENDALE

General Information State and locally supported, 2-year, coed college. Suburban setting. *Awards:* A. *Entrance level for U.S. students:* Noncompetitive. *Enrollment:* 20,070 total (56% women) including 1% international students. *Undergraduate faculty:* 912. *Library holdings:* 79,006 books, 406 current serial subscriptions, 3,807 audiovisual materials. *Total majors:* 28.
Information for International Students For fall 2006: 200 international students applied, 150 were accepted, 45 enrolled. Students can start in fall or spring. Transfers accepted from institutions abroad. *Admission tests:* Recommended: TOEFL (minimum score: iBT 80; paper-based 500; computer-based 173; minimum score for ESL admission: paper-based 400; computer-based 97), ELS, IELTS. TOEFL can be waived under certain conditions. *Application deadline:* 7/1. *Expenses:* (2006–07) $6750. *Services:* International student adviser on campus. Full-time ESL program on campus. ESL program available during the academic year. Employment opportunities (on-campus) available. *Contact:* Director, International Education Program, Glendale Community College, 6000 West Olive Avenue, Glendale, AZ 85302. Telephone: 623-845-3136. Fax: 623-845-3541. E-mail: isc@gcmail.maricopa.edu. URL: http://www.gc.maricopa.edu.

GRAND CANYON UNIVERSITY, PHOENIX

General Information Independent Southern Baptist, coed institution. Urban setting. *Awards:* B, M. *Entrance level for U.S. students:* Moderately difficult. *Enrollment:* 10,297 total; 2,693 undergraduates (69% women) including 1% international students from 10 foreign countries. *Faculty:* 1,683. *Total majors:* 55. *Expenses:* (2007–08) $14,420; room and board, $7500 (on campus). *Financial aid:* Need-based college/university scholarships/grants from institutional funds, athletic awards. Forms required: International Student's Certification of Finances.

INTERNATIONAL BAPTIST COLLEGE, TEMPE

General Information Independent Baptist, coed institution. Suburban setting. *Awards:* A, B, M, D. *Entrance level for U.S. students:* Difficulty N/R. *Enrollment:* 76 total; 75 undergraduates (49% women) including 3% international students. *Faculty:* 13. *Total majors:* 2. *Expenses:* (2006–07) $6570; room and board, $4300 (on campus).

MESA COMMUNITY COLLEGE, MESA

General Information State and locally supported, 2-year, coed college. Urban setting. *Awards:* A. *Entrance level for U.S. students:* Noncompetitive. *Enrollment:* 28,000 total. *Undergraduate faculty:* 1,065. *Library holdings:* 56,224 books, 794 current serial subscriptions. *Total majors:* 36.
Information for International Students For fall 2006: 142 international students applied, 97 were accepted, 71 enrolled. Students can start in fall or spring. Transfers accepted from institutions abroad. *Admission tests:* Required: TOEFL (minimum score: iBT 61; paper-based 500; computer-based 173; minimum score for ESL admission: iBT 32; paper-based 400; computer-based 97). Recommended: ELS, COMPASS, ASSET, ACCUPLACER. TOEFL can be waived under certain conditions. *Application deadline:* Rolling. *Financial aid:* Need-based college/university scholarships/grants from institutional funds, tuition waivers, athletic awards, loans from institutional funds, loans from outside sources, on-campus employment. Non-need-based college/university scholarships/grants from institutional funds. Forms required: institution's own financial aid form, International Student's Certification of Finances. *Services:* International student adviser on campus. Full-time and part-time ESL programs on campus. ESL program available during the academic year and the summer. Employment opportunities (on-campus) available. *Contact:* International Education Office, Mesa Community College, 1833 West Southern Avenue, Mesa, AZ 85202. Telephone: 480-461-7758. Fax: 480-461-7139. E-mail: ie@mcmail.maricopa.edu. URL: http://www.mc.maricopa.edu.

See In-Depth Description on page 127.

NORTHCENTRAL UNIVERSITY, PRESCOTT

General Information Proprietary, coed institution. *Awards:* B, M, D (offers only distance learning programs). *Entrance level for U.S. students:* Minimally difficult. *Enrollment:* 1,401 total; 166 undergraduates (58% women). *Faculty:* 301. *Total majors:* 4.

NORTHERN ARIZONA UNIVERSITY, FLAGSTAFF

General Information State-supported, coed university. Small town setting. *Awards:* B, M, D, FP. *Entrance level for U.S. students:* Moderately difficult. *Enrollment:* 20,562 total; 14,526 undergraduates (60% women) including 2% international students from 66 foreign countries. *Faculty:* 1,492. *Library holdings:* 687,456 books, 29,526 current serial subscriptions, 34,118 audiovisual materials. *Total majors:* 113.
Information for International Students Students can start in fall or spring. *Admission tests:* TOEFL can be waived under certain conditions. *Application deadline:* Rolling. *Expenses:* (2006–07) $13,486; room and board, $6260 (on campus); room only, $3452 (on campus). *Financial aid:* Non-need-based college/university scholarships/grants from institutional funds, tuition waivers, athletic awards, on-campus employment. For fall 2006 (estimated), 61 international students on campus received college administered financial aid ($4734 average). *Contact:* Center for International Education, Northern Arizona University, PO Box 5598, Flagstaff, AZ 86011. Telephone: 928-523-2409. Fax: 928-523-9489. E-mail: cie@nau.edu. URL: http://www.nau.edu.

PIMA COMMUNITY COLLEGE, TUCSON

General Information State and locally supported, 2-year, coed college. Urban setting. *Awards:* A. *Entrance level for U.S. students:* Noncompetitive. *Enrollment:* 32,532 total (56% women) including 1% international students from 52 foreign countries. *Undergraduate faculty:* 1,471. *Library holdings:* 219,346 books, 984 current serial subscriptions. *Total majors:* 49. *Expenses:* (2007–08) $7230.

PRESCOTT COLLEGE, PRESCOTT

General Information Independent, coed institution. Small town setting. *Awards:* B, M, D. *Entrance level for U.S. students:* Moderately difficult. *Enrollment:* 1,053 total; 758 undergraduates (61% women). *Faculty:* 77. *Library holdings:* 26,169 books, 248 current serial subscriptions. *Total majors:* 49.
Information for International Students For fall 2006: 12 international students applied, 6 were accepted, 4 enrolled. Students can start in fall or spring. Transfers accepted from institutions abroad. *Admission tests:* Required: TOEFL (minimum score: paper-based 500; computer-based 173; minimum score for ESL admission: iBT 61). TOEFL can be waived under certain

conditions. *Application deadline:* Rolling. *Expenses:* (2006–07) $18,711; room only, $1560 (on campus). *Financial aid:* International transfer students are eligible to apply for aid. *Services:* International student adviser on campus. Internships and employment opportunities (on-campus) available. *Contact:* Associate Director of Admissions, Admissions Office, Prescott College, 220 Grove Avenue, Prescott, AZ 86301. Telephone: 928-350-2104. Fax: 928-776-5242. E-mail: mgetzin@prescott.edu. URL: http://www.prescott.edu.

SCOTTSDALE COMMUNITY COLLEGE, SCOTTSDALE
General Information State and locally supported, 2-year, coed college. Urban setting. *Awards:* A. *Entrance level for U.S. students:* Noncompetitive. *Enrollment:* 10,884 total (55% women) including 1% international students from 48 foreign countries. *Undergraduate faculty:* 629. *Total majors:* 25. *Expenses:* (2007–08) $8430. *Financial aid:* Non-need financial aid available.

UNIVERSITY OF ADVANCING TECHNOLOGY, TEMPE
General Information Proprietary, coed institution. Urban setting. *Awards:* A, B, M. *Entrance level for U.S. students:* Difficulty N/R. *Enrollment:* 1,227 total; 1,178 undergraduates (6% women) including 1% international students. *Faculty:* 64. *Library holdings:* 27,500 books, 92 current serial subscriptions, 1,200 audiovisual materials. *Total majors:* 7. *Expenses:* (2007–08) $16,400; room and board, $8400 (on campus); room only, $6360 (on campus). *Financial aid:* Non-need financial aid available.

THE UNIVERSITY OF ARIZONA, TUCSON
General Information State-supported, coed university. Urban setting. *Awards:* B, M, D, FP. *Entrance level for U.S. students:* Moderately difficult. *Enrollment:* 36,805 total; 28,442 undergraduates (53% women) including 3% international students from 135 foreign countries. *Faculty:* 1,455. *Library holdings:* 4.4 million books, 23,790 current serial subscriptions, 51,136 audiovisual materials. *Total majors:* 128. *Expenses:* (2006–07) $14,972; room and board, $7850 (on campus); room only, $4350 (on campus).

UNIVERSITY OF PHOENIX ONLINE CAMPUS, PHOENIX
General Information Proprietary, coed institution. *Awards:* A, B, M, D. *Entrance level for U.S. students:* Noncompetitive. *Enrollment:* 160,150 total; 113,387 undergraduates (64% women) including 6% international students. *Faculty:* 6,237. *Library holdings:* 1,759 books, 692 current serial subscriptions. *Total majors:* 11. *Expenses:* (2006–07) $14,180.

UNIVERSITY OF PHOENIX–PHOENIX CAMPUS, PHOENIX
General Information Proprietary, coed institution. Urban setting. *Awards:* B, M. *Entrance level for U.S. students:* Noncompetitive. *Enrollment:* 8,497 total; 4,910 undergraduates (57% women) including 5% international students. *Faculty:* 784. *Library holdings:* 1,759 books, 692 current serial subscriptions. *Total majors:* 26. *Expenses:* (2006–07) $9630.

UNIVERSITY OF PHOENIX–SOUTHERN ARIZONA CAMPUS, TUCSON
General Information Proprietary, coed institution. Urban setting. *Awards:* B, M. *Entrance level for U.S. students:* Noncompetitive. *Enrollment:* 2,839 total; 2,096 undergraduates (60% women) including 11% international students. *Faculty:* 610. *Library holdings:* 1,759 books, 692 current serial subscriptions. *Total majors:* 12. *Expenses:* (2006–07) $9990.

WESTERN INTERNATIONAL UNIVERSITY, PHOENIX
General Information Proprietary, coed institution. Urban setting. *Awards:* A, B, M. *Entrance level for U.S. students:* Moderately difficult. *Enrollment:* 2,229 total; 1,649 undergraduates (67% women) including 2% international students from 52 foreign countries. *Faculty:* 385. *Library holdings:* 7,500 books, 125 current serial subscriptions. *Total majors:* 12. *Expenses:* (2006–07) $7992.

YAVAPAI COLLEGE, PRESCOTT
General Information State and locally supported, 2-year, coed college. Small town setting. *Awards:* A. *Entrance level for U.S. students:* Noncompetitive. *Enrollment:* 7,422 total (62% women) including 0.02% international students. *Undergraduate faculty:* 372. *Library holdings:* 81,144 books, 1,091 current serial subscriptions. *Total majors:* 25.
Information for International Students For fall 2006: 10 international students enrolled. Students can start in fall, spring, or summer. Transfers accepted from institutions abroad. *Admission tests:* Required: TOEFL (minimum score: iBT 45; paper-based 450;

computer-based 133). TOEFL can be waived under certain conditions. *Application deadline:* 4/1. *Expenses:* (2006–07) $6880. *Financial aid:* Need-based college/university scholarships/grants from institutional funds. Non-need-based college/university scholarships/grants from institutional funds, athletic awards. Forms required: institution's own financial aid form. *Housing:* Available during summer. *Services:* International student adviser on campus. Employment opportunities (on-campus) available. *Contact:* International Student Admissions Advisor, Yavapai College, Admissions and Registration, 1100 East Sheldon Street, Prescott, AZ 86301. Telephone: 928-776-2144. Fax: 928-776-2151. E-mail: marianne_doyle@yc.edu. URL: http://www2.yc.edu.

ARKANSAS

ARKANSAS STATE UNIVERSITY, JONESBORO
General Information State-supported, coed institution. Small town setting. *Awards:* A, B, M, D (specialist). *Entrance level for U.S. students:* Minimally difficult. *Enrollment:* 10,727 total; 9,340 undergraduates (59% women) including 1% international students from 30 foreign countries. *Faculty:* 619. *Library holdings:* 604,568 books, 1,712 current serial subscriptions, 18,949 audiovisual materials. *Total majors:* 80. *Expenses:* (2006–07) $12,760; room and board, $4440 (on campus).

ARKANSAS STATE UNIVERSITY–BEEBE, BEEBE
General Information State-supported, 2-year, coed college. Small town setting. *Awards:* A. *Entrance level for U.S. students:* Noncompetitive. *Enrollment:* 3,976 total (57% women) including 0.1% international students. *Undergraduate faculty:* 97. *Library holdings:* 90,000 books, 500 current serial subscriptions, 10 audiovisual materials. *Total majors:* 17.

ARKANSAS STATE UNIVERSITY–MOUNTAIN HOME, MOUNTAIN HOME
General Information State-supported, 2-year, coed college. Small town setting. *Awards:* A. *Entrance level for U.S. students:* Noncompetitive. *Enrollment:* 960 total (65% women) including 0.1% international students. *Undergraduate faculty:* 57. *Library holdings:* 33,573 books, 15,360 current serial subscriptions, 2,212 audiovisual materials. *Total majors:* 11. *Expenses:* (2007–08) $3900. *Financial aid:* Non-need-based college/university scholarships/grants from institutional funds, tuition waivers.

ARKANSAS TECH UNIVERSITY, RUSSELLVILLE
General Information State-supported, coed institution. Small town setting. *Awards:* A, B, M (Educational Specialist's). *Entrance level for U.S. students:* Moderately difficult. *Enrollment:* 7,038 total; 6,435 undergraduates (53% women) including 3% international students from 34 foreign countries. *Faculty:* 372. *Library holdings:* 278,540 books, 1,069 current serial subscriptions, 6,975 audiovisual materials. *Total majors:* 53. *Expenses:* (2006–07) $9350; room and board, $4422 (on campus); room only, $2412 (on campus). *Financial aid:* Non-need-based tuition waivers, athletic awards, loans from outside sources, on-campus employment. Forms required: institution's own financial aid form. For fall 2005, 63 international students on campus received college administered financial aid ($4737 average).

EAST ARKANSAS COMMUNITY COLLEGE, FORREST CITY
General Information State-supported, 2-year, coed college. Small town setting. *Awards:* A. *Entrance level for U.S. students:* Minimally difficult. *Enrollment:* 1,477 total (67% women) including 0.1% international students. *Undergraduate faculty:* 91. *Library holdings:* 21,908 books, 109 current serial subscriptions. *Total majors:* 7. *Expenses:* (2006–07) $2220.

HARDING UNIVERSITY, SEARCY
General Information Independent, coed institution, affiliated with Church of Christ. Small town setting. *Awards:* B, M. *Entrance level for U.S. students:* Moderately difficult. *Enrollment:* 6,085 total; 4,029 undergraduates (53% women) including 4% international students from 53 foreign countries. *Faculty:* 391. *Library holdings:* 230,499 books, 16,582 current serial subscriptions, 9,153 audiovisual materials. *Total majors:* 96.
Information for International Students Students can start in fall, winter, spring, or summer. Transfers accepted from institutions abroad. *Admission tests:* Required: TOEFL (minimum score: paper-based 500; computer-based 173). Recommended: SAT or ACT. TOEFL can be waived under certain conditions. *Application deadline:* Rolling. *Expenses:* (2006–07) $11,650; room and board, $5442 (on campus); room only, $2700 (on campus). *Financial aid:*

Harding University (continued)

Need-based college/university scholarships/grants from institutional funds, tuition waivers, athletic awards, loans from institutional funds, loans from outside sources, on-campus employment. Non-need-based college/university scholarships/grants from institutional funds, tuition waivers, athletic awards, loans from institutional funds, loans from outside sources, on-campus employment. Forms required: institution's own financial aid form. International transfer students are eligible to apply for aid. 104 international students on campus received college administered financial aid ($7085 average). *Housing:* Guaranteed. *Services:* International student adviser on campus. ESL program at cooperating institution. Internships and employment opportunities (on-campus) available. *Contact:* Assistant Vice President for Enrollment Management, Harding University, HU Box 12255, Searcy, AR 72149-2255. Telephone: 501-279-4407. Fax: 501-279-4129. E-mail: admissions@harding.edu. URL: http://www.harding.edu.

HENDERSON STATE UNIVERSITY, ARKADELPHIA

General Information State-supported, coed institution. Small town setting. *Awards:* A, B, M. *Entrance level for U.S. students:* Moderately difficult. *Enrollment:* 3,664 total; 2,939 undergraduates (56% women) including 2% international students from 15 foreign countries. *Faculty:* 229. *Total majors:* 41. *Expenses:* (2006–07) $7758; room and board, $4176 (on campus). *Financial aid:* Non-need financial aid available. 151 international students on campus received college administered financial aid ($2890 average).

HENDRIX COLLEGE, CONWAY

General Information Independent United Methodist, coed institution. Suburban setting. *Awards:* B, M. *Entrance level for U.S. students:* Very difficult. *Enrollment:* 1,095 total; 1,088 undergraduates (55% women) including 1% international students from 6 foreign countries. *Faculty:* 126. *Library holdings:* 219,843 books, 37,162 current serial subscriptions, 2,161 audiovisual materials. *Total majors:* 26. *Expenses:* (2006–07) $22,916; room and board, $6738 (on campus); room only, $3008 (on campus). *Financial aid:* Non-need-based college/university scholarships/grants from institutional funds, on-campus employment. Forms required: institution's own financial aid form, International Student's Financial Aid Application. For fall 2006 (estimated), 8 international students on campus received college administered financial aid ($14,715 average).

JOHN BROWN UNIVERSITY, SILOAM SPRINGS

General Information Independent interdenominational, coed institution. Small town setting. *Awards:* B, M. *Entrance level for U.S. students:* Moderately difficult. *Enrollment:* 1,882 total; 1,682 undergraduates (51% women) including 6% international students from 45 foreign countries. *Faculty:* 145. *Library holdings:* 102,031 books, 751 current serial subscriptions, 11,097 audiovisual materials. *Total majors:* 59. *Expenses:* (2006–07) $16,158; room and board, $5956 (on campus). *Financial aid:* Need-based college/university scholarships/grants from institutional funds, tuition waivers, athletic awards, loans from institutional funds, loans from outside sources, on-campus employment. Non-need-based college/university scholarships/grants from institutional funds, tuition waivers, athletic awards, loans from institutional funds, loans from outside sources, on-campus employment. For fall 2005, 36 international students on campus received college administered financial aid ($8441 average).

MID-SOUTH COMMUNITY COLLEGE, WEST MEMPHIS

General Information State-supported, 2-year, coed college. Suburban setting. *Awards:* A. *Entrance level for U.S. students:* Noncompetitive. *Enrollment:* 1,467 total (65% women) including 0.4% international students from 2 foreign countries. *Undergraduate faculty:* 99. *Library holdings:* 14,672 books, 88 current serial subscriptions, 2,151 audiovisual materials. *Total majors:* 5. *Expenses:* (2006–07) $3360. *Financial aid:* Need-based college/university scholarships/grants from institutional funds, on-campus employment. Non-need-based college/university scholarships/grants from institutional funds, tuition waivers.

NORTH ARKANSAS COLLEGE, HARRISON

General Information State and locally supported, 2-year, coed college. Small town setting. *Awards:* A. *Entrance level for U.S. students:* Noncompetitive. *Enrollment:* 2,047 total (61% women) including 0.1% international students from 1 foreign country. *Undergraduate faculty:* 148. *Library holdings:* 28,751 books, 219 current serial subscriptions, 1,235 audiovisual materials. *Total majors:* 24. *Expenses:* (2007–08) $4470. *Financial aid:* Forms required: institution's own financial aid form, FAFSA.

NORTHWEST ARKANSAS COMMUNITY COLLEGE, BENTONVILLE

General Information State and locally supported, 2-year, coed college. Urban setting. *Awards:* A. *Entrance level for U.S. students:* Noncompetitive. *Enrollment:* 5,732 total (60% women). *Undergraduate faculty:* 400. *Library holdings:* 15,500 books, 159 current serial subscriptions. *Total majors:* 17.

Information for International Students For fall 2006: 74 international students applied, 73 were accepted, 70 enrolled. Students can start in fall, spring, or summer. Transfers accepted from institutions abroad. *Admission tests:* Required: TOEFL (minimum score: paper-based 500; computer-based 173), or IELTS. Recommended: ACT. TOEFL can be waived under certain conditions. *Application deadline:* Rolling. *Expenses:* (2007–08) $4195. *Services:* International student adviser on campus. Part-time ESL program on campus. ESL program available during the academic year. Employment opportunities (on-campus) available. *Contact:* Director of International Student Services, NorthWest Arkansas Community College, 1 College Drive, Bentonville, AR 72712. Telephone: 479-619-4234. Fax: 479-619-4346. E-mail: dmontgom@nwacc.edu. URL: http://www.nwacc.edu.

OUACHITA TECHNICAL COLLEGE, MALVERN

General Information State-supported, 2-year, coed college. Small town setting. *Awards:* A. *Entrance level for U.S. students:* Noncompetitive. *Enrollment:* 1,590 total (51% women) including 0.3% international students from 2 foreign countries. *Undergraduate faculty:* 99. *Library holdings:* 8,000 books, 100 current serial subscriptions, 1,200 audiovisual materials. *Total majors:* 18. *Expenses:* (2007–08) $3630. *Financial aid:* Need-based financial aid available.

PULASKI TECHNICAL COLLEGE, NORTH LITTLE ROCK

General Information State-supported, 2-year, coed college. Urban setting. *Awards:* A. *Entrance level for U.S. students:* Noncompetitive. *Enrollment:* 8,455 total (69% women) including 0.1% international students. *Undergraduate faculty:* 477. *Library holdings:* 35,406 books, 276 current serial subscriptions, 1,994 audiovisual materials. *Total majors:* 8. *Expenses:* (2007–08) $3168.

SOUTHERN ARKANSAS UNIVERSITY–MAGNOLIA, MAGNOLIA

General Information State-supported, coed institution. Small town setting. *Awards:* A, B, M. *Entrance level for U.S. students:* Moderately difficult. *Enrollment:* 3,057 total; 2,803 undergraduates (57% women) including 5% international students from 37 foreign countries. *Faculty:* 184. *Library holdings:* 151,166 books, 1,065 current serial subscriptions. *Total majors:* 45.

Information for International Students For fall 2006: 300 international students applied, 200 were accepted, 180 enrolled. Students can start in fall or spring. Transfers accepted from institutions abroad. *Admission tests:* Required: TOEFL (minimum score: iBT 61; paper-based 500; computer-based 173). Recommended: SAT or ACT, ELS, 550 on IELTS. TOEFL can be waived under certain conditions. *Application deadline:* 7/1. *Expenses:* (2006–07) $6840; room and board, $3970 (on campus); room only, $2024 (on campus). *Financial aid:* Need-based college/university scholarships/grants from institutional funds, athletic awards. Non-need-based on-campus employment. Forms required: scholarship application form. For fall 2006 (estimated), 181 international students on campus received college administered financial aid ($3947 average). *Housing:* Guaranteed, also available during summer. *Services:* International student adviser on campus. ESL program at cooperating institution. Internships and employment opportunities (on-campus) available. *Contact:* Director of International Student Services, Southern Arkansas University–Magnolia, 100 East University, PO Box 9224, Magnolia, AR 71754-9224. Telephone: 870-235-4082. Fax: 870-235-5096. E-mail: cjlyons@saumag.edu. URL: http://www.saumag.edu.

SOUTHERN ARKANSAS UNIVERSITY TECH, CAMDEN

General Information State-supported, 2-year, coed college. Rural setting. *Awards:* A. *Entrance level for U.S. students:* Noncompetitive. *Enrollment:* 1,767 total (43% women). *Undergraduate faculty:* 81. *Library holdings:* 17,389 books, 115 current serial subscriptions, 960 audiovisual materials. *Total majors:* 15.

Information for International Students For fall 2006: 105 international students applied, 105 were accepted, 105 enrolled. Students can start in fall, spring, or summer. Transfers accepted from institutions abroad. *Admission tests:* Required: TOEFL (minimum score: paper-based 500; computer-based 173). Recommended: SAT or ACT, SAT Subject Tests. TOEFL can be waived under certain conditions. *Application deadline:* 6/1.

Expenses: (2006–07) $2758; room and board, $3413 (on campus); room only, $2100 (on campus). *Financial aid:* Need-based loans from outside sources, on-campus employment. Non-need-based college/university scholarships/grants from institutional funds, tuition waivers. Forms required: none available/not applicable. *Housing:* Guaranteed, also available during summer. *Services:* International student adviser on campus. Internships and employment opportunities (on-campus and off-campus) available. *Contact:* Vice Chancellor for Student Services, Southern Arkansas University Tech, Post Office Box 3499, 100 Carr Road, East Camden, AR 71711-1599. Telephone: 870-574-4504. Fax: 870-574-4478. E-mail: rcooper@sautech.edu. URL: http://www.sautech.edu.

UNIVERSITY OF ARKANSAS, FAYETTEVILLE

General Information State-supported, coed university. Suburban setting. *Awards:* B, M, D, FP. *Entrance level for U.S. students:* Moderately difficult. *Enrollment:* 17,926 total; 14,350 undergraduates (50% women) including 2% international students from 103 foreign countries. *Faculty:* 863. *Library holdings:* 1.8 million books, 18,173 current serial subscriptions. *Total majors:* 75.

Information for International Students For fall 2006: 356 international students applied, 203 were accepted, 139 enrolled. Students can start in fall, spring, or summer. Transfers accepted from institutions abroad. *Admission tests:* Required: TOEFL (minimum score: iBT 80; paper-based 550; computer-based 213). Recommended: SAT or ACT, IELTS (6.5 minimum). TOEFL can be waived under certain conditions. *Application deadline:* 5/31. *Expenses:* (2006–07) $13,942; room and board, $6522 (on campus); room only, $3904 (on campus). *Financial aid:* Need-based college/university scholarships/grants from institutional funds, loans from outside sources, on-campus employment. Non-need-based college/university scholarships/grants from institutional funds, tuition waivers, athletic awards, loans from outside sources, on-campus employment. Forms required: International Student's Certification of Finances. International transfer students are eligible to apply for aid. For fall 2006 (estimated), 105 international students on campus received college administered financial aid ($7472 average). *Housing:* Guaranteed, also available during summer. *Services:* International student adviser on campus. Full-time ESL program on campus. ESL program available during the academic year and the summer. Internships and employment opportunities (on-campus) available. *Contact:* Assistant Director, International Admissions Office, University of Arkansas, 747 West Dickson Street, #8, 180 DICX, Fayetteville, AR 72701. Telephone: 479-575-6246. Fax: 479-575-5055. E-mail: iao@uark.edu. URL: http://www.uark.edu.

UNIVERSITY OF ARKANSAS AT FORT SMITH, FORT SMITH

General Information State and locally supported, 4-year, coed college. Suburban setting. *Awards:* A, B. *Entrance level for U.S. students:* Minimally difficult. *Enrollment:* 6,767 total (60% women) including 0.1% international students from 6 foreign countries. *Undergraduate faculty:* 368. *Library holdings:* 85,358 books, 1,750 current serial subscriptions. *Total majors:* 34.

Information for International Students For fall 2006: 12 international students applied, 12 were accepted, 10 enrolled. Students can start in fall, spring, or summer. Transfers accepted from institutions abroad. *Admission tests:* Required: TOEFL (minimum score: iBT 61; paper-based 500; computer-based 173), COMPASS. Recommended: ACT. TOEFL can be waived under certain conditions. *Application deadline:* 6/15. *Expenses:* (2006–07) $8170; room only, $2880 (on campus). *Financial aid:* Need-based athletic awards. Non-need-based athletic awards. Forms required: institution's own financial aid form, International Student's Certification of Finances. *Housing:* Available during summer. *Services:* International student adviser on campus. ESL program at cooperating institution. Employment opportunities (on-campus) available. *Contact:* Director, Academic Programs Support, University of Arkansas at Fort Smith, 5210 Grand Avenue, PO Box 3649, Fort Smith, AR 72913-3649. Telephone: 479-788-7409. Fax: 479-788-7016. E-mail: amccaleb@uafortsmith.edu. URL: http://www.uafortsmith.edu.

UNIVERSITY OF ARKANSAS AT LITTLE ROCK, LITTLE ROCK

General Information State-supported, coed university. Urban setting. *Awards:* A, B, M, D, FP. *Entrance level for U.S. students:* Minimally difficult. *Enrollment:* 11,905 total; 9,325 undergraduates including 2% international students from 43 foreign countries. *Faculty:* 749. *Library holdings:* 3,998 current serial subscriptions. *Total majors:* 55. *Expenses:* (2006–07) $12,726; room only, $3100 (on campus).

UNIVERSITY OF ARKANSAS AT MONTICELLO, MONTICELLO

General Information State-supported, coed institution. Small town setting. *Awards:* A, B, M. *Entrance level for U.S. students:* Noncompetitive. *Enrollment:* 3,179 total; 3,064 undergraduates (61% women) including 0.3% international students from 2 foreign countries. *Faculty:* 208. *Library holdings:* 241,822 books, 956 current serial subscriptions. *Total majors:* 33. *Expenses:* (2006–07) $8080; room and board, $3440 (on campus); room only, $1400 (on campus). *Financial aid:* Non-need-based athletic awards, on-campus employment. Forms required: scholarship application.

UNIVERSITY OF ARKANSAS AT PINE BLUFF, PINE BLUFF

General Information State-supported, coed institution. Urban setting. *Awards:* A, B, M. *Entrance level for U.S. students:* Minimally difficult. *Enrollment:* 3,128 total; 3,051 undergraduates (57% women) including 1% international students from 17 foreign countries. *Faculty:* 225. *Library holdings:* 287,857 books, 3,041 current serial subscriptions. *Total majors:* 52.

Information for International Students For fall 2006: 10 international students applied, 5 were accepted, 1 enrolled. Students can start in fall, spring, or summer. Transfers accepted from institutions abroad. *Admission tests:* Required: SAT or ACT, TOEFL (minimum score: paper-based 525; computer-based 195). TOEFL can be waived under certain conditions. *Application deadline:* Rolling. *Expenses:* (2006–07) $8864; room and board, $5940 (on campus). *Financial aid:* Need-based college/university scholarships/grants from institutional funds, athletic awards. Non-need-based college/university scholarships/grants from institutional funds, athletic awards. For fall 2005, 15 international students on campus received college administered financial aid. *Housing:* Guaranteed, also available during summer. *Services:* International student adviser on campus. Internships and employment opportunities (on-campus) available. *Contact:* Registrar, University of Arkansas at Pine Bluff, 1200 North University Drive, PO Box 4983, Pine Bluff, AR 71601. Telephone: 870-575-8487. Fax: 870-575-4608. E-mail: fultone@uapb.edu. URL: http://www.uapb.edu.

UNIVERSITY OF ARKANSAS COMMUNITY COLLEGE AT BATESVILLE, BATESVILLE

General Information State-supported, 2-year, coed college. Small town setting. *Awards:* A. *Entrance level for U.S. students:* Noncompetitive. *Enrollment:* 1,317 total (69% women) including 0.1% international students. *Undergraduate faculty:* 96. *Library holdings:* 8,000 books, 149 current serial subscriptions, 1,500 audiovisual materials. *Total majors:* 13. *Financial aid:* Non-need-based college/university scholarships/grants from institutional funds, tuition waivers, on-campus employment. Forms required: institution's own financial aid form.

UNIVERSITY OF ARKANSAS COMMUNITY COLLEGE AT MORRILTON, MORRILTON

General Information State-supported, 2-year, coed college. Rural setting. *Awards:* A. *Entrance level for U.S. students:* Noncompetitive. *Enrollment:* 1,763 total (61% women) including 0.1% international students from 1 foreign country. *Undergraduate faculty:* 105. *Library holdings:* 15,621 books, 45 current serial subscriptions, 197 audiovisual materials. *Total majors:* 17. *Expenses:* (2007–08) $3474.

UNIVERSITY OF CENTRAL ARKANSAS, CONWAY

General Information State-supported, coed institution. Small town setting. *Awards:* A, B, M, D. *Entrance level for U.S. students:* Moderately difficult. *Enrollment:* 12,330 total; 10,637 undergraduates (58% women) including 3% international students from 65 foreign countries. *Faculty:* 651. *Library holdings:* 505,000 books, 2,000 current serial subscriptions. *Total majors:* 58. *Expenses:* (2006–07) $10,707; room and board, $4320 (on campus); room only, $2460 (on campus). *Financial aid:* Forms required: International Student's Certification of Finances.

CALIFORNIA

ACADEMY OF ART UNIVERSITY, SAN FRANCISCO

General Information Proprietary, coed institution. Urban setting. *Awards:* A, B, M. *Entrance level for U.S. students:* Noncompetitive. *Enrollment:* 9,483 total; 7,438 undergraduates (51% women) including 15% international students from 75 foreign countries. *Faculty:* 1,047. *Library holdings:* 36,000 books, 476 current serial subscriptions, 3,500 audiovisual materials. *Total majors:* 26. *Expenses:* (2007–08) $14,680; room and board, $12,600 (on campus).

ALLAN HANCOCK COLLEGE, SANTA MARIA

General Information State and locally supported, 2-year, coed college. Small town setting. *Awards:* A. *Entrance level for U.S. students:* Noncompetitive. *Enrollment:* 10,387 total (55% women) including 0.1% international students from 12 foreign countries. *Undergraduate faculty:* 594. *Library holdings:* 47,370 books, 397 current serial subscriptions, 2,463 audiovisual materials. *Total majors:* 50. *Expenses:* (2006–07) $5748.

ALLIANT INTERNATIONAL UNIVERSITY, SAN DIEGO

General Information Independent, coed university. Suburban setting. *Awards:* B, M, D. *Entrance level for U.S. students:* Difficulty N/R. *Enrollment:* 3,521 total; 178 undergraduates (52% women) including 30% international students from 38 foreign countries. *Faculty:* 288. *Library holdings:* 212,394 books, 674 current serial subscriptions. *Total majors:* 10. *Expenses:* (2007–08) $14,770. *Financial aid:* Non-need-based college/university scholarships/grants from institutional funds, tuition waivers, athletic awards, loans from outside sources, on-campus employment. For fall 2006 (estimated), 100 international students on campus received college administered financial aid ($1400 average).

AMERICAN ACADEMY OF DRAMATIC ARTS/HOLLYWOOD, HOLLYWOOD

General Information Independent, 2-year, coed college. Suburban setting. *Awards:* A. *Entrance level for U.S. students:* Moderately difficult. *Enrollment:* 308 total (54% women) including 10% international students from 3 foreign countries. *Undergraduate faculty:* 27. *Library holdings:* 7,700 books, 24 current serial subscriptions, 320 audiovisual materials. *Total majors:* 1. *Expenses:* (2006–07) $17,400. *Financial aid:* Forms required: international scholarship application form.

AMERICAN INTERCONTINENTAL UNIVERSITY, LOS ANGELES

General Information Proprietary, coed institution. Urban setting. *Awards:* A, B, M. *Entrance level for U.S. students:* Noncompetitive. *Enrollment:* 1,405 total; 1,304 undergraduates including 2% international students from 21 foreign countries. *Faculty:* 133. *Library holdings:* 20,000 books, 228 current serial subscriptions. *Total majors:* 11.
Information for International Students For fall 2006: 120 international students applied, 60 were accepted, 48 enrolled. Students can start in fall, winter, spring, or summer. Transfers accepted from institutions abroad. *Admission tests:* TOEFL can be waived under certain conditions. *Application deadline:* 9/30. *Financial aid:* Non-need financial aid available. *Housing:* Guaranteed, also available during summer. *Services:* International student adviser on campus. ESL program at cooperating institution. ESL program available during the academic year and the summer. Internships and employment opportunities (on-campus) available. *Contact:* International Student Advisor, American InterContinental University, 12655 West Jefferson Boulevard, Los Angeles, CA 90066-5603. Telephone: 310-302-2461. Fax: 310-302-2001. E-mail: rdiviccaro@la.aiuniv.edu. URL: http://www.aiuniv.edu.

See In-Depth Description on page 32.

ANTIOCH UNIVERSITY LOS ANGELES, CULVER CITY

General Information Independent, coed institution. Urban setting. *Awards:* B, M. *Entrance level for U.S. students:* Moderately difficult. *Enrollment:* 495 total; 139 undergraduates (68% women). *Faculty:* 172. *Total majors:* 1.
Information for International Students Students can start in fall, winter, or spring. Transfers accepted from institutions abroad. *Admission tests:* TOEFL can be waived under certain conditions. *Application deadline:* 8/1. *Expenses:* (2007–08) $15,498. *Services:* International student adviser on campus. ESL program at cooperating institution. *Contact:* Director of Enrollment Management, Antioch University Los Angeles, 400 Corporate Pointe, Culver City, CA 90230. Telephone: 310-578-1080 Ext. 411. Fax: 310-821-6032. E-mail: admissions@antiochla.edu. URL: http://www.antiochla.edu.

ANTIOCH UNIVERSITY SANTA BARBARA, SANTA BARBARA

General Information Independent, coed institution. Small town setting. *Awards:* B, M. *Entrance level for U.S. students:* Difficulty N/R. *Enrollment:* 284 total; 94 undergraduates (69% women) including 1% international students from 1 foreign country. *Faculty:* 71. *Total majors:* 1.
Information for International Students Students can start in fall, winter, spring, or summer. Transfers accepted from institutions abroad. *Admission tests:* Required: TOEFL (minimum score: paper-based 550; computer-based 213). *Application deadline:* 7/30.

Expenses: (2006–07) $13,983. *Services:* International student adviser on campus. *Contact:* Admissions Counselor, Antioch University Santa Barbara, 801 Garden Street, Suite 101, Santa Barbara, CA 93101. Telephone: 805-962-8179. Fax: 805-962-4786. E-mail: admissions@antiochsb.edu. URL: http://www.antiochsb.edu.

ART CENTER COLLEGE OF DESIGN, PASADENA

General Information Independent, coed institution. Suburban setting. *Awards:* B, M. *Entrance level for U.S. students:* Very difficult. *Enrollment:* 1,631 total; 1,485 undergraduates (40% women) including 16% international students from 28 foreign countries. *Faculty:* 407. *Library holdings:* 93,038 books, 450 current serial subscriptions. *Total majors:* 19.
Information for International Students For fall 2006: 223 international students applied, 140 were accepted, 83 enrolled. Students can start in fall, spring, or summer. Transfers accepted from institutions abroad. *Admission tests:* Required: TOEFL (minimum score: iBT 80; paper-based 550; computer-based 213; minimum score for ESL admission: iBT 80; paper-based 550; computer-based 213). *Application deadline:* Rolling. *Expenses:* (2006–07) $27,910. *Financial aid:* Need-based college/university scholarships/grants from institutional funds, on-campus employment. Non-need-based on-campus employment. Forms required: International Student's Certification of Finances. International transfer students are eligible to apply for aid. For fall 2005, 55 international students on campus received college administered financial aid ($2500 average). *Services:* International student adviser on campus. Internships and employment opportunities (on-campus) available. *Contact:* Vice President, Student Services, Art Center College of Design, 1700 Lida Street, Pasadena, CA 91103. Telephone: 626-396-2373. Fax: 626-795-0578. E-mail: admissions@artcenter.edu. URL: http://www.artcenter.edu.

AZUSA PACIFIC UNIVERSITY, AZUSA

General Information Independent nondenominational, coed institution. Small town setting. *Awards:* B, M, D, FP. *Entrance level for U.S. students:* Moderately difficult. *Enrollment:* 8,128 total; 4,722 undergraduates (63% women) including 2% international students from 47 foreign countries. *Faculty:* 334. *Library holdings:* 185,708 books, 14,031 current serial subscriptions. *Total majors:* 37. *Expenses:* (2006–07) $23,750; room and board, $7328 (on campus); room only, $3690 (on campus). *Financial aid:* Need-based college/university scholarships/grants from institutional funds. Forms required: institution's own financial aid form. For fall 2005, 55 international students on campus received college administered financial aid ($6654 average).

BERKELEY CITY COLLEGE, BERKELEY

General Information State and locally supported, 2-year, coed college. Urban setting. *Awards:* A. *Entrance level for U.S. students:* Noncompetitive. *Enrollment:* 5,100 total including 5% international students. *Undergraduate faculty:* 164. *Total majors:* 21. *Expenses:* (2007–08) $5944. *Financial aid:* Need-based college/university scholarships/grants from institutional funds, tuition waivers, loans from outside sources, on-campus employment. Forms required: institution's own financial aid form, International Student's Certification of Finances.

BETHANY UNIVERSITY, SCOTTS VALLEY

General Information Independent Assemblies of God, coed institution. Small town setting. *Awards:* A, B, M. *Entrance level for U.S. students:* Minimally difficult. *Enrollment:* 547 total; 474 undergraduates (59% women) including 1% international students from 5 foreign countries. *Faculty:* 72. *Library holdings:* 59,453 books, 858 current serial subscriptions. *Total majors:* 18. *Expenses:* (2007–08) $17,275; room and board, $6760 (on campus); room only, $3360 (on campus). *Financial aid:* Need-based and non-need-based financial aid available. Forms required: institution's own financial aid form. 8 international students on campus received college administered financial aid ($4455 average).

BIOLA UNIVERSITY, LA MIRADA

General Information Independent interdenominational, coed university. Suburban setting. *Awards:* B, M, D, FP. *Entrance level for U.S. students:* Moderately difficult. *Enrollment:* 5,752 total; 3,924 undergraduates (60% women) including 4% international students from 42 foreign countries. *Faculty:* 444. *Library holdings:* 301,956 books, 17,876 current serial subscriptions, 18,712 audiovisual materials. *Total majors:* 39. *Expenses:* (2007–08) $25,143; room and board, $7370 (on campus); room only, $3850 (on campus). *Financial aid:* Need-based college/university scholarships/grants from institutional funds, athletic awards, loans from institutional funds, loans from outside sources. Non-need-based college/university scholarships/grants from institutional funds, athletic awards, loans from institutional funds, loans from outside sources. Forms required: institution's own financial aid form, International Student's Certification of Finances. 54 international students on campus received college administered financial aid ($4568 average).

CALIFORNIA BAPTIST UNIVERSITY, RIVERSIDE

General Information Independent Southern Baptist, coed institution. Suburban setting. *Awards:* B, M. *Entrance level for U.S. students:* Minimally difficult. *Enrollment:* 3,409 total; 2,623 undergraduates (64% women) including 3% international students from 27 foreign countries. *Faculty:* 285. *Library holdings:* 180,946 books, 11,166 current serial subscriptions, 3,633 audiovisual materials. *Total majors:* 32. *Expenses:* (2006–07) $18,900; room and board, $6810 (on campus); room only, $2800 (on campus). *Financial aid:* Non-need-based college/university scholarships/grants from institutional funds, athletic awards. Forms required: International Student's Certification of Finances. For fall 2005, 17 international students on campus received college administered financial aid ($8029 average).

CALIFORNIA CHRISTIAN COLLEGE, FRESNO

General Information Independent religious, 4-year, coed college. Urban setting. *Awards:* A, B. *Entrance level for U.S. students:* Noncompetitive. *Enrollment:* 32 total (38% women). *Undergraduate faculty:* 10. *Library holdings:* 13,154 books, 7 current serial subscriptions, 430 audiovisual materials. *Total majors:* 2.

Information for International Students Students can start in fall or spring. Transfers accepted from institutions abroad. *Admission tests:* Required: SAT, ACT, TOEFL (minimum score: paper-based 423; computer-based 173), in-house placement tests instead of SAT/ACT. *Application deadline:* Rolling. *Expenses:* (2006–07) $9500. *Contact:* Registrar, California Christian College, 4881 East University Avenue, Fresno, CA 93703. Telephone: 559-251-4215. Fax: 559-251-4231. E-mail: cccregistrar@sbcglobal.net. URL: http://www.calchristiancollege.org.

CALIFORNIA COLLEGE OF THE ARTS, SAN FRANCISCO

General Information Independent, coed institution. Urban setting. *Awards:* B, M. *Entrance level for U.S. students:* Moderately difficult. *Enrollment:* 1,622 total; 1,310 undergraduates (59% women) including 7% international students from 26 foreign countries. *Faculty:* 375. *Library holdings:* 39,000 books, 340 current serial subscriptions. *Total majors:* 17.

Information for International Students For fall 2006: 234 international students applied, 135 were accepted, 25 enrolled. Students can start in fall or spring. Transfers accepted from institutions abroad. *Admission tests:* Required: TOEFL (minimum score: iBT 79; paper-based 550; computer-based 213; minimum score for ESL admission: iBT 79; paper-based 550; computer-based 213). TOEFL can be waived under certain conditions. *Application deadline:* Rolling. *Expenses:* (2006–07) $27,914; room and board, $8615 (on campus). *Financial aid:* Need-based loans from outside sources. Non-need-based college/university scholarships/grants from institutional funds, loans from outside sources, on-campus employment. Forms required: International Student's Certification of Finances. 2 international students on campus received college administered financial aid ($3000 average). *Housing:* Guaranteed. *Services:* International student adviser on campus. ESL program at cooperating institution. ESL program available during the academic year and the summer. Internships and employment opportunities (on-campus) available. *Contact:* Assistant Director of International Admissions, California College of the Arts, 1111 8th Street, San Francisco, CA 94107. Telephone: 415-703-9520. Fax: 415-703-9539. E-mail: enroll@cca.edu. URL: http://www.cca.edu.

See In-Depth Description on page 49.

CALIFORNIA INSTITUTE OF TECHNOLOGY, PASADENA

General Information Independent, coed university. Suburban setting. *Awards:* B, M, D. *Entrance level for U.S. students:* Most difficult. *Enrollment:* 2,086 total; 864 undergraduates (29% women) including 8% international students from 28 foreign countries. *Faculty:* 311. *Library holdings:* 3.2 million books, 3,500 current serial subscriptions. *Total majors:* 26. *Expenses:* (2007–08) $32,835; room and board, $9540 (on campus); room only, $5370 (on campus). *Financial aid:* Need-based college/university scholarships/grants from institutional funds, loans from institutional funds, on-campus employment. Non-need-based college/university scholarships/grants from institutional funds, on-campus employment. Forms required: institution's own financial aid form, International Student's Financial Aid Application. For fall 2006 (estimated), 31 international students on campus received college administered financial aid ($37,191 average).

CALIFORNIA INSTITUTE OF THE ARTS, VALENCIA

General Information Independent, coed institution. Suburban setting. *Awards:* B, M. *Entrance level for U.S. students:* Very difficult. *Enrollment:* 1,349 total; 839 undergraduates (43% women) including international students from 33 foreign countries. *Faculty:* 287. *Library holdings:* 98,415 books, 324 current serial subscriptions. *Total majors:* 23.

Information for International Students For fall 2006: 72 international students enrolled. Students can start in fall or spring. Transfers accepted from institutions abroad. *Admission tests:* Required: TOEFL (minimum score: iBT 80; paper-based 550; computer-based 213). TOEFL can be waived under certain conditions. *Application deadline:* 1/5. *Expenses:* (2007–08) $31,855; room and board, $8000 (on campus); room only, $4530 (on campus). *Financial aid:* Need-based college/university scholarships/grants from institutional funds, on-campus employment. Non-need-based college/university scholarships/grants from institutional funds. Forms required: institution's own financial aid form, International Student's Certification of Finances. International transfer students are eligible to apply for aid. 41 international students on campus received college administered financial aid ($9124 average). *Services:* International student adviser on campus. ESL program at cooperating institution. ESL program available during the academic year and the summer. Internships and employment opportunities (on-campus) available. *Contact:* International Student Advisor, California Institute of the Arts, 24700 McBean Parkway, Valencia, CA 91355-2397. Telephone: 661-253-7845. Fax: 661-291-3049. E-mail: pweston@calarts.edu. URL: http://www.calarts.edu.

CALIFORNIA LUTHERAN UNIVERSITY, THOUSAND OAKS

General Information Independent Lutheran, coed institution. Suburban setting. *Awards:* B, M, D. *Entrance level for U.S. students:* Moderately difficult. *Enrollment:* 3,298 total; 2,128 undergraduates (53% women) including 3% international students from 21 foreign countries. *Faculty:* 283. *Library holdings:* 132,744 books, 1,497 current serial subscriptions. *Total majors:* 51.

Information for International Students For fall 2006: 250 international students applied, 100 were accepted, 25 enrolled. Students can start in fall or spring. Transfers accepted from institutions abroad. *Admission tests:* Required: TOEFL (minimum score: iBT 79; paper-based 550; computer-based 213), IELTS. Recommended: SAT or ACT. TOEFL can be waived under certain conditions. *Application deadline:* 6/1. *Expenses:* (2007–08) $25,990; room and board, $9230 (on campus). *Financial aid:* Need-based college/university scholarships/grants from institutional funds, loans from outside sources, on-campus employment. Non-need-based college/university scholarships/grants from institutional funds, loans from outside sources, on-campus employment. Forms required: International Student's Certification of Finances. International transfer students are eligible to apply for aid. 20 international students on campus received college administered financial aid ($8908 average). *Housing:* Guaranteed. *Services:* International student adviser on campus. ESL program at cooperating institution. ESL program available during the academic year and the summer. Internships and employment opportunities (on-campus and off-campus) available. *Contact:* Coordinator of International Admission, California Lutheran University, 60 West Olsen Road, #1350, Thousand Oaks, CA 91360-2787. Telephone: 805-493-3135. Fax: 805-493-3114. E-mail: admissions@callutheran.edu. URL: http://www.callutheran.edu.

CALIFORNIA POLYTECHNIC STATE UNIVERSITY, SAN LUIS OBISPO, SAN LUIS OBISPO

General Information State-supported, coed institution. Small town setting. *Awards:* B, M. *Entrance level for U.S. students:* Moderately difficult. *Enrollment:* 18,722 total; 17,777 undergraduates (43% women) including 1% international students from 39 foreign countries. *Faculty:* 1,170. *Library holdings:* 763,651 books, 5,529 current serial subscriptions. *Total majors:* 60.

Information for International Students For fall 2006: 539 international students applied, 216 were accepted, 101 enrolled. Students can start in fall, winter, spring, or summer. Transfers accepted from institutions abroad. *Admission tests:* Required: TOEFL (minimum score: paper-based 550; computer-based 213). *Application deadline:* 11/30. *Expenses:* (2006–07) $18,870; room and board, $8453 (on campus); room only, $4766 (on campus). *Services:* International student adviser on campus. Full-time and part-time ESL programs on campus. ESL program available during the academic year. *Contact:* Director, International Education and Programs, Admissions Office, California Polytechnic State University, San Luis Obispo, San Luis Obispo, CA 93407. Telephone: 805-756-5837. Fax: 805-756-5484. E-mail: bandre@calpoly.edu. URL: http://www.calpoly.edu.

CALIFORNIA STATE POLYTECHNIC UNIVERSITY, POMONA, POMONA

General Information State-supported, coed institution. Urban setting. *Awards:* B, M. *Entrance level for U.S. students:* Moderately difficult. *Enrollment:* 20,510 total; 18,650 undergraduates (43% women) including 5% international students from 46 foreign countries. *Faculty:* 1,289. *Library holdings:* 748,154 books, 4,603 current serial subscriptions, 6,062 audiovisual materials. *Total majors:* 88.

Information for International Students Students can start in fall, winter, spring, or summer. Transfers accepted from institutions abroad. *Admission tests:* Required: TOEFL (minimum score: iBT 71; paper-based 525; computer-based 195), English Placement Test and Math Placement Test. Recommended: SAT or ACT, ELS. TOEFL can be waived under certain conditions. *Application deadline:* 7/15. *Expenses:* (2006–07) $13,185; room and board, $7908 (on campus). *Housing:* Available during summer. *Services:* International student adviser on campus. Full-time and part-time ESL programs on campus. ESL program available during the academic year and the summer. Internships and employment opportunities (on-campus) available. *Contact:* Coordinator, International Admissions, California State Polytechnic University, Pomona, Office of Admissions and Outreach, 3801 West Temple Avenue, Pomona, CA 91768. Telephone: 909-869-2107. Fax: 909-869-4529. E-mail: kevinmartin@csupomona.edu. URL: http://www.csupomona.edu.

CALIFORNIA STATE UNIVERSITY, BAKERSFIELD, BAKERSFIELD

General Information State-supported, coed institution. Urban setting. *Awards:* B, M. *Entrance level for U.S. students:* Moderately difficult. *Enrollment:* 7,549 total; 5,960 undergraduates (66% women) including 2% international students from 48 foreign countries. *Faculty:* 515. *Library holdings:* 354,016 books, 2,260 current serial subscriptions. *Total majors:* 30. *Financial aid:* Non-need financial aid available. Forms required: scholarship application form.

CALIFORNIA STATE UNIVERSITY, CHICO, CHICO

General Information State-supported, coed institution. Small town setting. *Awards:* B, M. *Entrance level for U.S. students:* Moderately difficult. *Enrollment:* 16,250 total; 14,927 undergraduates (53% women) including 2% international students from 36 foreign countries. *Faculty:* 965. *Library holdings:* 957,181 books, 24,244 current serial subscriptions, 28,500 audiovisual materials. *Total majors:* 120. *Expenses:* (2006–07) $16,102; room and board, $8314 (on campus); room only, $5772 (on campus). *Financial aid:* Need-based tuition waivers, athletic awards, on-campus employment. Non-need-based athletic awards, loans from institutional funds, loans from outside sources, on-campus employment. Forms required: scholarship application form.

CALIFORNIA STATE UNIVERSITY, DOMINGUEZ HILLS, CARSON

General Information State-supported, coed institution. Urban setting. *Awards:* B, M. *Entrance level for U.S. students:* Moderately difficult. *Enrollment:* 12,068 total; 8,925 undergraduates (69% women) including 1% international students from 46 foreign countries. *Faculty:* 687. *Library holdings:* 428,840 books, 49,130 current serial subscriptions, 4,999 audiovisual materials. *Total majors:* 70. *Expenses:* (2007–08) $16,272; room and board, $8690 (on campus); room only, $5990 (on campus).

CALIFORNIA STATE UNIVERSITY, EAST BAY, HAYWARD

General Information State-supported, coed institution. Suburban setting. *Awards:* B, M. *Entrance level for U.S. students:* Moderately difficult. *Enrollment:* 12,535 total; 9,129 undergraduates (62% women) including 5% international students from 86 foreign countries. *Faculty:* 741. *Library holdings:* 908,577 books, 2,210 current serial subscriptions, 28,416 audiovisual materials. *Total majors:* 91.

CALIFORNIA STATE UNIVERSITY, FRESNO, FRESNO

General Information State-supported, coed institution. Urban setting. *Awards:* B, M, D. *Entrance level for U.S. students:* Minimally difficult. *Enrollment:* 22,098 total; 18,951 undergraduates (58% women) including 2% international students from 69 foreign countries. *Faculty:* 1,251. *Library holdings:* 2,617 current serial subscriptions. *Total majors:* 87. *Expenses:* (2006–07) $16,248; room and board, $6880 (on campus); room only, $3700 (on campus).

CALIFORNIA STATE UNIVERSITY, FULLERTON, FULLERTON

General Information State-supported, coed institution. Suburban setting. *Awards:* B, M. *Entrance level for U.S. students:* Moderately difficult. *Enrollment:* 35,921 total; 30,606 undergraduates (58% women) including 4% international students from 58 foreign countries. *Faculty:* 2,031. *Library holdings:* 1.2 million books, 29,888 current serial subscriptions. *Total majors:* 88. *Expenses:* (2006–07) $13,200; room only, $4408 (on campus).

CALIFORNIA STATE UNIVERSITY, LONG BEACH, LONG BEACH

General Information State-supported, coed institution. Suburban setting. *Awards:* B, M. *Entrance level for U.S. students:* Moderately difficult. *Enrollment:* 35,574 total; 29,576 undergraduates (60% women) including 5% international students from 85 foreign countries. *Faculty:* 2,227. *Library holdings:* 1.5 million books, 18,749 current serial subscriptions. *Total majors:* 149.

Information for International Students For fall 2006: 805 international students applied, 364 were accepted, 278 enrolled. Students can start in fall or spring. Transfers accepted from institutions abroad. *Admission tests:* Required: TOEFL (minimum score: iBT 60; paper-based 500; computer-based 173), IELTS. Recommended: SAT or ACT. TOEFL can be waived under certain conditions. *Application deadline:* 3/1. *Expenses:* (2007–08) $13,286; room and board, $7536 (on campus). *Housing:* Available during summer. *Services:* International student adviser on campus. Full-time and part-time ESL programs on campus. ESL program available during the academic year and the summer. *Contact:* Director, International Admissions, California State University, Long Beach, Center for International Education, 1250 North Bellflower Boulevard, BH 210, Long Beach, CA 90840-0109. Telephone: 562-985-5476. Fax: 562-985-1725. E-mail: cie-admission@csulb.edu. URL: http://www.csulb.edu.

CALIFORNIA STATE UNIVERSITY, LOS ANGELES, LOS ANGELES

General Information State-supported, coed institution. Urban setting. *Awards:* B, M, D. *Entrance level for U.S. students:* Moderately difficult. *Enrollment:* 20,565 total; 15,352 undergraduates (62% women) including 6% international students from 64 foreign countries. *Faculty:* 1,184. *Library holdings:* 1.2 million books, 31,366 current serial subscriptions, 2,545 audiovisual materials. *Total majors:* 63. *Expenses:* (2006–07) $14,296; room and board, $7866 (on campus).

CALIFORNIA STATE UNIVERSITY, MONTEREY BAY, SEASIDE

General Information State-supported, coed institution. Small town setting. *Awards:* B, M. *Entrance level for U.S. students:* Minimally difficult. *Enrollment:* 3,577 total; 3,376 undergraduates (56% women) including 1% international students from 19 foreign countries. *Faculty:* 291. *Library holdings:* 65,000 books, 3,800 current serial subscriptions, 1,250 audiovisual materials. *Total majors:* 16. *Expenses:* (2007–08) $13,205; room and board, $7696 (on campus); room only, $5196 (on campus).

CALIFORNIA STATE UNIVERSITY, NORTHRIDGE, NORTHRIDGE

General Information State-supported, coed institution. Urban setting. *Awards:* B, M. *Entrance level for U.S. students:* Moderately difficult. *Enrollment:* 34,560 total; 28,281 undergraduates (59% women) including 5% international students from 7 foreign countries. *Faculty:* 1,941. *Library holdings:* 1.4 million books, 1,779 current serial subscriptions, 10,046 audiovisual materials. *Total majors:* 47. *Expenses:* (2006–07) $14,220; room and board, $9328 (on campus); room only, $5155 (on campus).

CALIFORNIA STATE UNIVERSITY, SACRAMENTO, SACRAMENTO

General Information State-supported, coed institution. Urban setting. *Awards:* B, M, D. *Entrance level for U.S. students:* Moderately difficult. *Enrollment:* 28,529 total; 23,615 undergraduates (57% women) including 1% international students from 142 foreign countries. *Faculty:* 1,719. *Library holdings:* 1.3 million books, 2,918 current serial subscriptions, 23,880 audiovisual materials. *Total majors:* 84.

Information for International Students For fall 2006: 901 international students applied, 301 were accepted, 133 enrolled. Students can start in fall or spring. Transfers accepted from institutions abroad. *Admission tests:* Required: TOEFL (minimum score: iBT 64; paper-based 510; computer-based 180). Recommended: SAT or ACT. *Application deadline:* 4/1. *Expenses:* (2006–07) $15,974; room and board, $7966 (on campus); room only, $5250 (on campus). *Financial aid:* Non-need-based college/university scholarships/grants from institutional funds, tuition waivers, athletic awards, loans from outside sources, on-campus employment. *Services:* International student adviser on campus. Full-time ESL program on campus. ESL program available during the academic year and the summer. Internships and employment opportunities (on-campus) available. *Contact:* Coordinator of International Admissions, California State University, Sacramento, 6000 J Street, Sacramento, CA 95819-6012. Telephone: 916-278-7772. Fax: 916-278-7471. E-mail: intlinfo@csus.edu. URL: http://www.csus.edu.

CALIFORNIA STATE UNIVERSITY, SAN BERNARDINO, SAN BERNARDINO

General Information State-supported, coed institution. Suburban setting. *Awards:* B, M. *Entrance level for U.S. students:* Moderately difficult. *Enrollment:* 16,479 total; 12,926 undergraduates (65% women) including 3% international students from 43 foreign countries. *Faculty:* 633. *Library holdings:* 731,259 books, 2,028 current serial subscriptions. *Total majors:* 51. *Expenses:* (2006–07) $11,534; room and board, $5886 (on campus); room only, $4376 (on campus).

CALIFORNIA STATE UNIVERSITY, SAN MARCOS, SAN MARCOS

General Information State-supported, coed institution. Suburban setting. *Awards:* B, M. *Entrance level for U.S. students:* Moderately difficult. *Enrollment:* 6,956 total; 6,327 undergraduates (61% women) including 3% international students. *Faculty:* 501. *Library holdings:* 233,445 books, 2,043 current serial subscriptions. *Total majors:* 23. *Expenses:* (2006–07) $11,228; room only, $5600 (on campus). *Financial aid:* Forms required: institution's own financial aid form.

CALIFORNIA STATE UNIVERSITY, STANISLAUS, TURLOCK

General Information State-supported, coed institution. Small town setting. *Awards:* B, M. *Entrance level for U.S. students:* Difficulty N/R. *Enrollment:* 8,374 total; 6,671 undergraduates (66% women) including 1% international students from 46 foreign countries. *Faculty:* 511. *Library holdings:* 369,047 books, 17,612 current serial subscriptions, 4,593 audiovisual materials. *Total majors:* 35.

Information for International Students For fall 2006: 137 international students applied, 49 were accepted, 18 enrolled. Students can start in fall, winter, spring, or summer. Transfers accepted from institutions abroad. *Admission tests:* Required: TOEFL (minimum score: iBT 61; paper-based 500; computer-based 173). TOEFL can be waived under certain conditions. *Application deadline:* Rolling. *Expenses:* (2006–07) $13,213; room and board, $7178 (on campus); room only, $4278 (on campus). *Financial aid:* Need-based college/university scholarships/grants from institutional funds. Non-need-based college/university scholarships/grants from institutional funds, athletic awards. Forms required: FAFSA (for state aid only). For fall 2006 (estimated), 17 international students on campus received college administered financial aid ($1858 average). *Housing:* Available during summer. *Services:* International student adviser on campus. Employment opportunities (on-campus and off-campus) available. *Contact:* Acting Director, Global Affairs, California State University, Stanislaus, 801 West Monte Vista Avenue, Turlock, CA 95382. Telephone: 209-667-3117. Fax: 209-667-3791. E-mail: hheath@csustan.edu. URL: http://www.csustan.edu.

CAÑADA COLLEGE, REDWOOD CITY

General Information State and locally supported, 2-year, coed college. Suburban setting. *Awards:* A. *Entrance level for U.S. students:* Noncompetitive. *Enrollment:* 6,230 total including 1% international students from 32 foreign countries. *Undergraduate faculty:* 250. *Library holdings:* 53,417 books, 414 current serial subscriptions. *Total majors:* 49.

Information for International Students For fall 2006: 51 international students applied, 34 were accepted, 12 enrolled. Students can start in fall or spring. Transfers accepted from institutions abroad. *Admission tests:* Required: TOEFL (minimum score: paper-based 480; computer-based 157; minimum score for ESL admission: paper-based 480; computer-based 157). TOEFL can be waived under certain conditions. *Application deadline:* 4/15. *Expenses:* (2007–08) $6168. *Financial aid:* Need-based college/university scholarships/grants from institutional funds, college has annual scholarship program each spring. Non-need-based college/university scholarships/grants from institutional funds, on campus employment, college has annual scholarship program each spring. *Services:* International student adviser on campus. Full-time and part-time ESL programs on campus. ESL program available during the academic year and the summer. Internships and employment opportunities (on-campus) available. *Contact:* International Student Admissions Coordinator, Cañada College, 4200 Farm Hill Boulevard, Redwood City, CA 94061-1099. Telephone: 650-306-3494. Fax: 650-306-3113. E-mail: Urena@smccd.edu. URL: http://www.canadacollege.net.

CERRO COSO COMMUNITY COLLEGE, RIDGECREST

General Information State-supported, 2-year, coed college. Small town setting. *Awards:* A. *Entrance level for U.S. students:* Noncompetitive. *Enrollment:* 5,020 total (61% women) including 0.4% international students. *Undergraduate faculty:* 214. *Library holdings:* 25,000 books, 800 current serial subscriptions. *Total majors:* 30.

Information for International Students For fall 2006: 12 international students applied, 12 were accepted, 12 enrolled. Students can start in fall, spring, or summer. Transfers accepted from institutions abroad. *Admission tests:* Required: TOEFL (minimum score: paper-based 500; computer-based 173). Recommended: college placement exam. TOEFL can be waived under certain conditions. *Application deadline:* 7/27. *Expenses:* (2006–07) $6630. *Services:* International student adviser on campus. Employment opportunities (off-campus) available. *Contact:* Vice President of Student Services, Cerro Coso Community College, 3000 College Heights Boulevard, Ridgecrest, CA 93555. Telephone: 760-384-6354. Fax: 760-384-6377. E-mail: jboard@cerrocoso.edu. URL: http://www.cerrocoso.edu.

CHABOT COLLEGE, HAYWARD

General Information State-supported, 2-year, coed college. Suburban setting. *Awards:* A. *Entrance level for U.S. students:* Noncompetitive. *Enrollment:* 15,075 total including international students from 78 foreign countries. *Undergraduate faculty:* 512. *Library holdings:* 100,000 books, 160 current serial subscriptions. *Total majors:* 90.

Information for International Students For fall 2006: 40 international students were accepted, 30 enrolled. Students can start in fall or spring. Transfers accepted from institutions abroad. *Admission tests:* Required: TOEFL (minimum score: iBT 61; paper-based 500; computer-based 173). TOEFL can be waived under certain conditions. *Application deadline:* 6/30. *Financial aid:* Forms required: institution's own financial aid form. *Services:* International student adviser on campus. ESL program at cooperating institution. ESL program available during the academic year and the summer. Employment opportunities (on-campus) available. *Contact:* DSO/Coordinator, International Student Program, Chabot College, 25555 Hesperian Boulevard, Hayward, CA 94545. Telephone: 510-723-6715. Fax: 510-723-7510. E-mail: intladms@chabotcollege.edu. URL: http://www.chabotcollege.edu.

CHAFFEY COLLEGE, RANCHO CUCAMONGA

General Information District-supported, 2-year, coed college. Suburban setting. *Awards:* A. *Entrance level for U.S. students:* Noncompetitive. *Enrollment:* 17,930 total. *Undergraduate faculty:* 683. *Library holdings:* 72,000 books, 232 current serial subscriptions. *Total majors:* 63.

Information for International Students For fall 2006: 200 international students enrolled. Students can start in fall, spring, or summer. Transfers accepted from institutions abroad. *Admission tests:* Required: TOEFL (minimum score: paper-based 450; computer-based 133), on-site assessment tests required prior to enrollment. TOEFL can be waived under certain conditions. *Application deadline:* Rolling. *Financial aid:* Need-based college/university scholarships/grants from institutional funds, tuition waivers, on-campus employment. Non-need-based college/university scholarships/grants from institutional funds, on-campus employment. *Services:* International student adviser on campus. Full-time and part-time ESL programs on campus. ESL program available during the academic year. Internships and employment opportunities (on-campus) available. *Contact:* Coordinator, International Student Office, Chaffey College, 5885 Haven Avenue, Rancho Cucamonga, CA 91737-3002. Telephone: 909-941-2352. Fax: 909-466-2805. E-mail: intlstudents@chaffey.edu. URL: http://www.chaffey.edu.

CHAPMAN UNIVERSITY, ORANGE

General Information Independent, coed institution, affiliated with Christian Church (Disciples of Christ). Suburban setting. *Awards:* B, M, FP. *Entrance level for U.S. students:* Moderately difficult. *Enrollment:* 5,908 total; 4,086 undergraduates (59% women) including 2% international students from 32 foreign countries. *Faculty:* 538. *Library holdings:* 220,759 books, 1,731 current serial subscriptions. *Total majors:* 54.

Information for International Students For fall 2006: 162 international students applied, 69 were accepted, 40 enrolled. Students can start in fall or spring. Transfers accepted from institutions abroad. *Admission tests:* Required: SAT or ACT, TOEFL

Chapman University (continued)

(minimum score: paper-based 550; computer-based 213). TOEFL can be waived under certain conditions. *Application deadline:* 1/15. *Expenses:* (2006–07) $30,748; room and board, $10,500 (on campus). *Financial aid:* Need-based college/university scholarships/grants from institutional funds. Non-need-based college/university scholarships/grants from institutional funds. For fall 2005, 11 international students on campus received college administered financial aid ($10,531 average). *Services:* International student adviser on campus. Full-time ESL program on campus. ESL program available during the academic year and the summer. Internships and employment opportunities (on-campus and off-campus) available. *Contact:* International Admission Officer, Chapman University, Orange, CA 92866. Telephone: 714-997-6711. Fax: 714-997-6713. E-mail: admit@chapman.edu. URL: http://www.chapman.edu.

See In-Depth Description on page 54.

CITRUS COLLEGE, GLENDORA

General Information State and locally supported, 2-year, coed college. Small town setting. *Awards:* A. *Entrance level for U.S. students:* Noncompetitive. *Enrollment:* 11,576 total (59% women) including 4% international students. *Undergraduate faculty:* 447. *Library holdings:* 45,091 books, 133 current serial subscriptions. *Total majors:* 43. *Expenses:* (2006–07) $5164.

CITY COLLEGE OF SAN FRANCISCO, SAN FRANCISCO

General Information State and locally supported, 2-year, coed college. Urban setting. *Awards:* A. *Entrance level for U.S. students:* Noncompetitive. *Enrollment:* 106,480 total including 3% international students. *Undergraduate faculty:* 2,317. *Library holdings:* 93,518 books, 774 current serial subscriptions. *Total majors:* 69.
Information for International Students Students can start in fall or spring. *Admission tests:* Required: TOEFL (minimum score: iBT 52; paper-based 473; computer-based 152). Recommended: IELTS (minimum score 4.5). TOEFL can be waived under certain conditions. *Application deadline:* 5/15. *Expenses:* (2007–08) $4966. *Financial aid:* Forms required: institution's own financial aid form. *Services:* International student adviser on campus. Full-time and part-time ESL programs on campus. ESL program available during the academic year and the summer. Employment opportunities (on-campus and off-campus) available. *Contact:* International Admissions, City College of San Francisco, 50 Phelan Avenue, San Francisco, CA 94112. Telephone: 415-239-3895. Fax: 415-239-3804. E-mail: international@ccsf.edu. URL: http://www.ccsf.edu.

See In-Depth Description on page 55.

CLAREMONT MCKENNA COLLEGE, CLAREMONT

General Information Independent, 4-year, coed college. Small town setting. *Awards:* B. *Entrance level for U.S. students:* Most difficult. *Enrollment:* 1,153 total (46% women) including 4% international students from 25 foreign countries. *Undergraduate faculty:* 146. *Library holdings:* 2 million books, 6,028 current serial subscriptions. *Total majors:* 83. *Expenses:* (2006–07) $34,850; room and board, $10,740 (on campus); room only, $5420 (on campus). *Financial aid:* Need-based college/university scholarships/grants from institutional funds, loans from institutional funds, loans from outside sources, on-campus employment. Non-need-based college/university scholarships/grants from institutional funds, tuition waivers, loans from institutional funds, loans from outside sources. Forms required: CSS PROFILE, International Student's Financial Aid Application, International Student's Certification of Finances. For fall 2006 (estimated), 530 international students on campus received college administered financial aid ($20,733 average).

CLEVELAND CHIROPRACTIC COLLEGE-LOS ANGELES CAMPUS, LOS ANGELES

General Information Independent, coed institution. Urban setting. *Awards:* A, B, FP. *Entrance level for U.S. students:* Minimally difficult. *Enrollment:* 379 total; 108 undergraduates (34% women) including 2% international students from 2 foreign countries. *Faculty:* 38. *Library holdings:* 23,937 books, 152 current serial subscriptions, 2,323 audiovisual materials. *Total majors:* 1. *Expenses:* (2006–07) $5720.

COLLEGE OF ALAMEDA, ALAMEDA

General Information State and locally supported, 2-year, coed college. Urban setting. *Awards:* A. *Entrance level for U.S. students:* Noncompetitive. *Enrollment:* 5,500 total including international students from 9 foreign countries. *Undergraduate faculty:* 166. *Library holdings:* 40,000 books, 200 current serial subscriptions. *Total majors:* 31.

COLLEGE OF THE CANYONS, SANTA CLARITA

General Information State and locally supported, 2-year, coed college. Suburban setting. *Awards:* A. *Entrance level for U.S. students:* Noncompetitive. *Enrollment:* 19,023 total (41% women) including 1% international students. *Undergraduate faculty:* 597. *Library holdings:* 55,559 books, 160 current serial subscriptions, 20,436 audiovisual materials. *Total majors:* 46.
Information for International Students For fall 2006: 118 international students applied, 91 were accepted, 73 enrolled. Students can start in fall, winter, spring, or summer. Transfers accepted from institutions abroad. *Admission tests:* Required: TOEFL (minimum score: iBT 45; paper-based 450; computer-based 133). TOEFL can be waived under certain conditions. *Application deadline:* 6/15. *Expenses:* (2007–08) $5138. *Financial aid:* Need-based and non-need-based financial aid available. *Services:* International student adviser on campus. Part-time ESL program on campus. ESL program available during the academic year and the summer. Internships and employment opportunities (on-campus) available. *Contact:* DSO/Student Services Technician, International Students Program, College of the Canyons, 26455 Rockwell Canyon Road, Santa Clarita, CA 91355. Telephone: 661-362-3580. Fax: 661-362-5539. E-mail: isp@canyons.edu. URL: http://www.canyons.edu.

COLLEGE OF THE DESERT, PALM DESERT

General Information State and locally supported, 2-year, coed college. Small town setting. *Awards:* A. *Entrance level for U.S. students:* Noncompetitive. *Enrollment:* 9,946 total. *Undergraduate faculty:* 338. *Library holdings:* 58,000 books, 260 current serial subscriptions. *Total majors:* 64.
Information for International Students For fall 2006: 60 international students applied, 55 were accepted, 40 enrolled. Students can start in fall or spring. Transfers accepted from institutions abroad. *Admission tests:* Required: TOEFL (minimum score: iBT 32; paper-based 400; computer-based 97). TOEFL can be waived under certain conditions. *Application deadline:* 7/15. *Expenses:* (2007–08) $5498. *Financial aid:* Forms required: institution's own financial aid form. *Services:* International student adviser on campus. Full-time ESL program on campus. ESL program available during the academic year and the summer. Internships and employment opportunities (on-campus) available. *Contact:* International Education Program Director, College of the Desert, 43-500 Monterey Avenue, Palm Desert, CA 92260. Telephone: 760-776-7205. Fax: 760-862-1361. E-mail: cdelgado@collegeofthedesert.edu. URL: http://desert.cc.ca.us.

See In-Depth Description on page 60.

COLLEGE OF THE SISKIYOUS, WEED

General Information State and locally supported, 2-year, coed college. Rural setting. *Awards:* A. *Entrance level for U.S. students:* Noncompetitive. *Enrollment:* 2,998 total including 1% international students from 6 foreign countries. *Undergraduate faculty:* 151. *Library holdings:* 34,708 books, 148 current serial subscriptions, 9,433 audiovisual materials. *Total majors:* 30. *Financial aid:* Forms required: International Student's Financial Aid Application, International Student's Certification of Finances.

COLUMBIA COLLEGE, SONORA

General Information State and locally supported, 2-year, coed college. Rural setting. *Awards:* A. *Entrance level for U.S. students:* Noncompetitive. *Enrollment:* 2,670 total (58% women) including 0.04% international students. *Undergraduate faculty:* 163. *Library holdings:* 34,892 books, 320 current serial subscriptions. *Total majors:* 32. *Expenses:* (2007–08) $4840; room only, $7550 (on campus). *Financial aid:* Need-based college/university scholarships/grants from institutional funds, tuition waivers, on-campus employment.

CONCORDIA UNIVERSITY, IRVINE

General Information Independent, coed institution, affiliated with Lutheran Church–Missouri Synod. Suburban setting. *Awards:* B, M (associate's degree for international students only). *Entrance level for U.S. students:* Difficulty N/R. *Enrollment:* 2,317 total; 1,348 undergraduates (62% women) including 2% international students from 10 foreign countries. *Faculty:* 199. *Library holdings:* 80,300 books, 7,144 current serial subscriptions, 1,365 audiovisual materials. *Total majors:* 23. *Expenses:* (2006–07) $21,130; room and board, $7060 (on campus); room only, $4380 (on campus). *Financial aid:* Non-need-based athletic awards, athletic. Forms required: institution's own financial aid form. For fall 2005, international students on campus received college administered aid averaging $568.

CONTRA COSTA COLLEGE, SAN PABLO

General Information State and locally supported, 2-year, coed college. Small town setting. *Awards:* A. *Entrance level for U.S.

students: Noncompetitive. *Enrollment:* 8,834 total (62% women) including 2% international students from 21 foreign countries. *Undergraduate faculty:* 415. *Library holdings:* 57,017 books, 333 current serial subscriptions, 4,976 audiovisual materials. *Total majors:* 46. *Expenses:* (2006–07) $4512. *Financial aid:* Forms required: institution's own financial aid form.

COSUMNES RIVER COLLEGE, SACRAMENTO
General Information District-supported, 2-year, coed college. Rural setting. *Awards:* A. *Entrance level for U.S. students:* Noncompetitive. *Enrollment:* 19,284 total including international students from 30 foreign countries. *Undergraduate faculty:* 550. *Library holdings:* 55,447 books, 375 current serial subscriptions. *Total majors:* 61.
Information for International Students For fall 2006: 10 international students applied, 10 were accepted, 10 enrolled. Students can start in fall, spring, or summer. Transfers accepted from institutions abroad. *Admission tests:* Required: TOEFL (minimum score: paper-based 450; computer-based 133). *Application deadline:* 5/1. *Services:* International student adviser on campus. Full-time ESL program on campus. ESL program available during the academic year. Employment opportunities (on-campus) available. *Contact:* DSO/Administrative Assistant to the Vice President of Student Services, Cosumnes River College, 8401 Center Parkway, Sacramento, CA 95823. Telephone: 916-691-7469. Fax: 916-691-7375. E-mail: kimuraj@crc.losrios.edu. URL: http://www.crc.losrios.edu.

CUYAMACA COLLEGE, EL CAJON
General Information State-supported, 2-year, coed college. Suburban setting. *Awards:* A. *Entrance level for U.S. students:* Noncompetitive. *Enrollment:* 7,690 total including 2% international students from 8 foreign countries. *Undergraduate faculty:* 280. *Library holdings:* 32,129 books, 130 current serial subscriptions, 2,588 audiovisual materials. *Total majors:* 33. *Expenses:* (2006–07) $6240. *Financial aid:* Need-based college/university scholarships/grants from institutional funds, tuition waivers, loans from outside sources, on-campus employment. Non-need-based college/university scholarships/grants from institutional funds, loans from outside sources. Forms required: institution's own financial aid form.

DE ANZA COLLEGE, CUPERTINO
General Information State and locally supported, 2-year, coed college. Suburban setting. *Awards:* A. *Entrance level for U.S. students:* Noncompetitive. *Enrollment:* 23,344 total (53% women) including 6% international students from 79 foreign countries. *Undergraduate faculty:* 812. *Library holdings:* 80,000 books, 927 current serial subscriptions. *Total majors:* 65.
Information for International Students Students can start in fall, winter, or spring. Transfers accepted from institutions abroad. *Admission tests:* Required: TOEFL (minimum score: iBT 61; paper-based 500; computer-based 173), IELTS (score of 5.0). TOEFL can be waived under certain conditions. *Application deadline:* 6/30. *Expenses:* (2006–07) $4454. *Services:* International student adviser on campus. ESL program at cooperating institution. ESL program available during the summer. Internships and employment opportunities (on-campus and off-campus) available. *Contact:* International Student Coordinator, De Anza College, Cupertino, CA 95014. Telephone: 408-864-8826. Fax: 408-864-5638. E-mail: dainternational@fhda.edu. URL: http://www.deanza.fhda.edu.
See In-Depth Description on page 65.

DEEP SPRINGS COLLEGE, DEEP SPRINGS
General Information Independent, 2-year, men's college. Rural setting. *Awards:* A. *Entrance level for U.S. students:* Most difficult. *Enrollment:* 27 total including 4% international students from 3 foreign countries. *Undergraduate faculty:* 9. *Library holdings:* 20,000 books, 60 current serial subscriptions. *Total majors:* 1.

DEVRY UNIVERSITY, FREMONT
General Information Proprietary, coed institution. Suburban setting. *Awards:* A, B, M. *Entrance level for U.S. students:* Minimally difficult. *Enrollment:* 1,581 total; 1,421 undergraduates (29% women) including 1% international students from 9 foreign countries. *Faculty:* 124. *Library holdings:* 40,000 books, 3,060 current serial subscriptions. *Total majors:* 10. *Expenses:* (2007–08) $14,640.

DEVRY UNIVERSITY, LONG BEACH
General Information Proprietary, coed institution. Urban setting. *Awards:* A, B, M. *Entrance level for U.S. students:* Minimally difficult. *Enrollment:* 1,098 total; 892 undergraduates (30% women) including 0.1% international students from 11 foreign countries.

Faculty: 94. *Library holdings:* 15,500 books, 85 current serial subscriptions. *Total majors:* 9. *Expenses:* (2007–08) $14,020.

DEVRY UNIVERSITY, POMONA
General Information Proprietary, coed institution. Urban setting. *Awards:* A, B, M. *Entrance level for U.S. students:* Minimally difficult. *Enrollment:* 1,706 total; 1,541 undergraduates (28% women) including 1% international students from 19 foreign countries. *Faculty:* 93. *Library holdings:* 17,000 books, 77 current serial subscriptions. *Total majors:* 11. *Expenses:* (2007–08) $14,020.

DEVRY UNIVERSITY, SHERMAN OAKS
General Information Proprietary, coed institution. *Awards:* A, B, M. *Entrance level for U.S. students:* Difficulty N/R. *Enrollment:* 635 total; 525 undergraduates (24% women) including 1% international students. *Faculty:* 93. *Total majors:* 7. *Expenses:* (2007–08) $14,020.

DEVRY UNIVERSITY, WEST HILLS
General Information Proprietary, coed institution. Suburban setting. *Awards:* A, B, M. *Entrance level for U.S. students:* Minimally difficult. *Enrollment:* 769 total; 671 undergraduates (26% women) including 3% international students from 13 foreign countries. *Faculty:* 61. *Library holdings:* 16,177 books, 130 current serial subscriptions, 597 audiovisual materials. *Total majors:* 11. *Expenses:* (2006–07) $12,650.

DIABLO VALLEY COLLEGE, PLEASANT HILL
General Information State and locally supported, 2-year, coed college. Suburban setting. *Awards:* A. *Entrance level for U.S. students:* Noncompetitive. *Enrollment:* 20,476 total. *Undergraduate faculty:* 831. *Library holdings:* 88,286 books, 298 current serial subscriptions. *Total majors:* 1.
Information for International Students For fall 2006: 407 international students applied, 263 were accepted, 240 enrolled. Students can start in fall or spring. Transfers accepted from institutions abroad. *Admission tests:* Required: TOEFL (minimum score: iBT 61; paper-based 500; computer-based 173), ELS, IELTS accepted in lieu of TOEFL. TOEFL can be waived under certain conditions. *Application deadline:* 7/1. *Expenses:* (2006–07) $5490. *Services:* International student adviser on campus. ESL program at cooperating institution. ESL program available during the academic year and the summer. Internships and employment opportunities (on-campus and off-campus) available. *Contact:* Supervisor, Diablo Valley College, 321 Golf Club Road, Pleasant Hill, CA 94523. Telephone: 925-685-1230 Ext. 2075. Fax: 925-691-9503. E-mail: gzaraboz@dvc.edu. URL: http://www.dvc.edu.

DOMINICAN SCHOOL OF PHILOSOPHY AND THEOLOGY, BERKELEY
General Information Independent Roman Catholic, coed institution. Urban setting. *Awards:* B, M, FP. *Entrance level for U.S. students:* Moderately difficult. *Enrollment:* 89 total; 5 undergraduates (40% women). *Faculty:* 24. *Library holdings:* 409,592 books, 1,466 current serial subscriptions. *Total majors:* 1.
Information for International Students Students can start in fall, spring, or summer. Transfers accepted from institutions abroad. *Admission tests:* Required: TOEFL (minimum score: iBT 68; paper-based 550; computer-based 213; minimum score for ESL admission: iBT 68; paper-based 550; computer-based 213). *Application deadline:* 3/15. *Expenses:* (2007–08) $11,666. *Housing:* Available during summer. *Services:* International student adviser on campus. ESL program at cooperating institution. ESL program available during the academic year and the summer. *Contact:* Director of Admissions, Dominican School of Philosophy and Theology, 2301 Vine Street, Berkeley, CA 94708. Telephone: 510-883-2073. Fax: 510-849-1372. E-mail: admissions@dspt.edu. URL: http://www.dspt.edu.

DOMINICAN UNIVERSITY OF CALIFORNIA, SAN RAFAEL
General Information Independent, coed institution, affiliated with Roman Catholic Church. Suburban setting. *Awards:* B, M. *Entrance level for U.S. students:* Moderately difficult. *Enrollment:* 2,045 total; 1,468 undergraduates (76% women) including 2% international students from 16 foreign countries. *Faculty:* 306. *Library holdings:* 93,207 books, 415 current serial subscriptions, 2,011 audiovisual materials. *Total majors:* 28.
Information for International Students Students can start in fall or spring. Transfers accepted from institutions abroad. *Admission tests:* Required: TOEFL (minimum score: iBT 80; paper-based 550; computer-based 213; minimum score for ESL admission: paper-based 550; computer-based 213). Recommended: SAT or ACT, ELS. TOEFL can be waived under certain conditions. *Application deadline:* 7/1. *Expenses:* (2007–08) $30,780; room and board, $12,000 (on campus); room only, $6980 (on campus).

Dominican University of California (continued)

Financial aid: Need-based college/university scholarships/grants from institutional funds, tuition waivers, athletic awards, loans from outside sources, on-campus employment, private scholarship and grants. Non-need-based college/university scholarships/grants from institutional funds, tuition waivers, athletic awards, loans from outside sources, on-campus employment, private scholarship and grants. Forms required: institution's own financial aid form, International Student's Certification of Finances. For fall 2005, 28 international students on campus received college administered financial aid ($6911 average). *Services:* International student adviser on campus. Full-time ESL program on campus. ESL program available during the academic year and the summer. Internships and employment opportunities (on-campus) available. *Contact:* Undergraduate Admissions Counselor, Dominican University of California, 50 Acacia Avenue, San Rafael, CA 94901. Telephone: 415-257-1369. Fax: 415-485-3214. E-mail: rchrisostomo@dominican.edu. URL: http://www.dominican.edu.

See In-Depth Description on page 68.

EAST LOS ANGELES COLLEGE, MONTEREY PARK

General Information State and locally supported, 2-year, coed college. Urban setting. *Awards:* A. *Entrance level for U.S. students:* Noncompetitive. *Enrollment:* 24,015 total (60% women). *Undergraduate faculty:* 619. *Library holdings:* 102,000 books, 228 current serial subscriptions. *Total majors:* 60.

Information for International Students For fall 2006: 205 international students applied, 171 were accepted, 85 enrolled. Students can start in fall or spring. Transfers accepted from institutions abroad. *Admission tests:* Required: TOEFL (minimum score: iBT 45; paper-based 450; computer-based 133). Recommended: IELTS if no TOEFL. TOEFL can be waived under certain conditions. *Application deadline:* 7/15. *Expenses:* (2006–07) $4966. *Services:* International student adviser on campus. Full-time ESL program on campus. ESL program available during the academic year. *Contact:* International Student Advisor, East Los Angeles College, 1301 Avenida Cesar Chavez, Monterey Park, CA 91754-6033. Telephone: 323-265-8801. Fax: 323-260-8192. E-mail: allredjp@elac.edu. URL: http://www.elac.edu.

EL CAMINO COLLEGE, TORRANCE

General Information State-supported, 2-year, coed college. Urban setting. *Awards:* A. *Entrance level for U.S. students:* Noncompetitive. *Enrollment:* 24,000 total including international students from 30 foreign countries. *Undergraduate faculty:* 645. *Library holdings:* 116,051 books, 864 current serial subscriptions. *Total majors:* 73.

Information for International Students For fall 2006: 315 international students applied, 275 were accepted, 175 enrolled. Students can start in fall or spring. Transfers accepted from institutions abroad. *Admission tests:* Required: TOEFL (minimum score: iBT 45; paper-based 450; computer-based 133; minimum score for ESL admission: iBT 45; paper-based 450; computer-based 133). TOEFL can be waived under certain conditions. *Application deadline:* 7/15. *Expenses:* (2007–08) $4710. *Services:* International student adviser on campus. Full-time and part-time ESL programs on campus. ESL program available during the academic year and the summer. Employment opportunities (on-campus) available. *Contact:* Coordinator, International Student Program, El Camino College, 16207 Crenshaw Boulevard, Torrance, CA 90506. Telephone: 310-660-3431. Fax: 310-660-6779. E-mail: isp@elcamino.edu. URL: http://www.elcamino.edu.

See In-Depth Description on page 75.

EVERGREEN VALLEY COLLEGE, SAN JOSE

General Information State and locally supported, 2-year, coed college. Urban setting. *Awards:* A. *Entrance level for U.S. students:* Noncompetitive. *Enrollment:* 11,751 total including 1% international students from 11 foreign countries. *Undergraduate faculty:* 301. *Library holdings:* 42,782 books, 368 current serial subscriptions. *Total majors:* 27. *Expenses:* (2006–07) $5536.

FASHION CAREERS COLLEGE, SAN DIEGO

General Information Proprietary, 2-year, coed, primarily women's college. Urban setting. *Awards:* A. *Entrance level for U.S. students:* Minimally difficult. *Enrollment:* 101 total (88% women) including 2% international students from 3 foreign countries. *Undergraduate faculty:* 9. *Library holdings:* 800 books, 14 current serial subscriptions, 175 audiovisual materials. *Total majors:* 2.

Information for International Students For fall 2006: 5 international students applied, 5 were accepted, 5 enrolled. Students can start in fall, winter, spring, or summer. Transfers accepted from institutions abroad. *Admission tests:* Required: Wonderlic. Recommended: ELS. *Application deadline:* Rolling.

Expenses: (2006–07) $16,225. *Services:* International student adviser on campus. ESL program at cooperating institution. Internships available. *Contact:* International Student Advisor, Fashion Careers College, 1923 Morena Boulevard, San Diego, CA 92110. Telephone: 619-275-4700 Ext. 314. Fax: 619-275-0635. E-mail: karen@fashioncareerscollege.com. URL: http://www.fashioncollege.com.

FEATHER RIVER COLLEGE, QUINCY

General Information State and locally supported, 2-year, coed college. Rural setting. *Awards:* A. *Entrance level for U.S. students:* Noncompetitive. *Enrollment:* 1,714 total (56% women) including 1% international students from 6 foreign countries. *Undergraduate faculty:* 93. *Library holdings:* 20,782 books, 4,122 current serial subscriptions, 1,762 audiovisual materials. *Total majors:* 19. *Expenses:* (2006–07) $6574; room only, $3920 (on campus).

FIDM/THE FASHION INSTITUTE OF DESIGN & MERCHANDISING, LOS ANGELES CAMPUS, LOS ANGELES

General Information Proprietary, primarily 2-year, coed college. Urban setting. *Awards:* A, B (also includes Orange County Campus). *Entrance level for U.S. students:* Moderately difficult. *Enrollment:* 4,143 total (90% women) including 7% international students from 25 foreign countries. *Undergraduate faculty:* 292. *Library holdings:* 21,099 books, 462 current serial subscriptions. *Total majors:* 9.

Information for International Students For fall 2006: 284 international students enrolled. Students can start in fall, winter, spring, or summer. Transfers accepted from institutions abroad. *Admission tests:* TOEFL can be waived under certain conditions. *Application deadline:* Rolling. *Expenses:* (2007–08) $18,785. *Housing:* Guaranteed. *Services:* International student adviser on campus. Full-time and part-time ESL programs on campus. ESL program available during the academic year and the summer. Internships and employment opportunities (on-campus and off-campus) available. *Contact:* Executive Director of Admissions, FIDM/The Fashion Institute of Design & Merchandising, Los Angeles Campus, 919 South Grand Avenue, Los Angeles, CA 90015. Telephone: 213-624-1201. Fax: 213-624-4799. E-mail: info@fidm.com. URL: http://www.fidm.edu.

See In-Depth Description on page 83.

FIDM/THE FASHION INSTITUTE OF DESIGN & MERCHANDISING, SAN DIEGO CAMPUS, SAN DIEGO

General Information Proprietary, 2-year, coed college. Urban setting. *Awards:* A. *Entrance level for U.S. students:* Moderately difficult. *Enrollment:* 288 total (94% women) including 1% international students from 2 foreign countries. *Undergraduate faculty:* 27. *Library holdings:* 2,959 books, 178 current serial subscriptions, 58 audiovisual materials. *Total majors:* 7. *Expenses:* (2007–08) $18,785. *Financial aid:* Need-based and non-need-based financial aid available.

FIDM/THE FASHION INSTITUTE OF DESIGN & MERCHANDISING, SAN FRANCISCO CAMPUS, SAN FRANCISCO

General Information Proprietary, 2-year, coed, primarily women's college. Urban setting. *Awards:* A. *Entrance level for U.S. students:* Moderately difficult. *Enrollment:* 983 total (93% women) including 3% international students from 20 foreign countries. *Undergraduate faculty:* 90. *Library holdings:* 5,592 books, 252 current serial subscriptions, 328 audiovisual materials. *Total majors:* 8. *Expenses:* (2007–08) $18,785. *Financial aid:* Need-based and non-need-based financial aid available.

FOOTHILL COLLEGE, LOS ALTOS HILLS

General Information State and locally supported, 2-year, coed college. Suburban setting. *Awards:* A. *Entrance level for U.S. students:* Noncompetitive. *Enrollment:* 18,342 total (51% women) including 7% international students from 74 foreign countries. *Undergraduate faculty:* 633. *Library holdings:* 70,000 books, 450 current serial subscriptions. *Total majors:* 52.

Information for International Students Students can start in fall, winter, or spring. Transfers accepted from institutions abroad. *Admission tests:* Required: TOEFL (minimum score: iBT 61; paper-based 500; computer-based 173; minimum score for ESL admission: paper-based 500; computer-based 173), IELTS in lieu of TOEFL (score of 5.0). *Application deadline:* 6/30. *Expenses:* (2007–08) $5508. *Services:* International student adviser on campus. ESL program at cooperating institution. Internships and employment opportunities (on-campus) available. *Contact:* International Admissions Coordinator, Foothill College, Los Altos

Hills, CA 94022. Telephone: 650-949-7161. Fax: 650-949-7080.
E-mail: foothillinternational@foothill.edu.
URL: http://www.foothill.edu.

See In-Depth Description on page 86.

FRESNO CITY COLLEGE, FRESNO

General Information District-supported, 2-year, coed college.
Urban setting. *Awards:* A. *Entrance level for U.S. students:*
Noncompetitive. *Enrollment:* 22,812 total including 1%
international students. *Undergraduate faculty:* 1,476. *Library
holdings:* 67,500 books. *Total majors:* 62.

Information for International Students For fall 2006: 65
international students applied, 55 were accepted, 50 enrolled.
Students can start in fall or spring. Transfers accepted from
institutions abroad. *Admission tests:* Required: TOEFL (minimum
score: paper-based 500; computer-based 173; minimum score for
ESL admission: iBT 61). TOEFL can be waived under certain
conditions. *Application deadline:* 5/1. *Services:* International student
adviser on campus. ESL program at cooperating institution. ESL
program available during the academic year and the summer.
Employment opportunities (on-campus and off-campus) available.
Contact: International Admissions Specialist, Fresno City College,
1101 East University Avenue, Fresno, CA 93741.
Telephone: 559-442-8224. Fax: 559-442-8243.
E-mail: mary.alfieris@scccd.com.
URL: http://www.fresnocitycollege.com.

FRESNO PACIFIC UNIVERSITY, FRESNO

General Information Independent, coed institution, affiliated
with Mennonite Brethren Church. Suburban setting. *Awards:* A, B,
M. *Entrance level for U.S. students:* Moderately difficult.
Enrollment: 2,324 total; 1,565 undergraduates (68% women)
including 2% international students from 36 foreign countries.
Faculty: 238. *Library holdings:* 196,000 books, 16,000 current serial
subscriptions. *Total majors:* 42.

Information for International Students For fall 2006: 53
international students applied, 29 were accepted, 20 enrolled.
Students can start in fall or spring. Transfers accepted from
institutions abroad. *Admission tests:* Required: TOEFL (minimum
score: iBT 61; paper-based 500; computer-based 173).
Recommended: SAT or ACT. TOEFL can be waived under certain
conditions. *Application deadline:* 7/13. *Expenses:* (2006–07) $20,790;
room and board, $5990 (on campus); room only, $3400 (on campus).
Financial aid: Need-based college/university scholarships/grants
from institutional funds, athletic awards, loans from outside
sources, on-campus employment. Non-need-based college/university
scholarships/grants from institutional funds, tuition waivers. Forms
required: institution's own financial aid form. International transfer
students are eligible to apply for aid. For fall 2005, 52 international
students on campus received college administered financial aid
($15,211 average). *Housing:* Available during summer. *Services:*
International student adviser on campus. Full-time and part-time
ESL programs on campus. ESL program available during the
academic year and the summer. Internships and employment
opportunities (on-campus and off-campus) available. *Contact:*
International Student Counselor, International Programs and
Services Office, Fresno Pacific University, 1717 South Chestnut
Avenue, #2003, Fresno, CA 93702. Telephone: 559-453-2069.
Fax: 559-453-7147. E-mail: ipso@fresno.edu.
URL: http://www.fresno.edu.

FULLERTON COLLEGE, FULLERTON

General Information State and locally supported, 2-year, coed
college. Suburban setting. *Awards:* A. *Entrance level for U.S.
students:* Noncompetitive. *Enrollment:* 19,862 total including
international students from 21 foreign countries. *Undergraduate
faculty:* 835. *Library holdings:* 113,236 books, 600 current serial
subscriptions. *Total majors:* 68.

Information for International Students For fall 2006: 161
international students applied, 112 were accepted, 78 enrolled.
Students can start in fall, spring, or summer. Transfers accepted
from institutions abroad. *Admission tests:* Required: TOEFL
(minimum score: iBT 61; paper-based 500; computer-based 173;
minimum score for ESL admission: iBT 61; paper-based 500;
computer-based 173), students currently in U.S. may take Fullerton
College ESL Test in place of TOEFL, STEP test scores also
accepted. TOEFL can be waived under certain conditions.
Application deadline: 6/1. *Financial aid:* Need-based
college/university scholarships/grants from institutional funds,
tuition waivers, athletic awards, loans from outside sources,
on-campus employment. Non-need-based loans from outside
sources, on-campus employment. Forms required: institution's own
financial aid form, International Student's Certification of Finances,
FAFSA. *Services:* International student adviser on campus. ESL
program at cooperating institution. Internships and employment
opportunities (on-campus and off-campus) available. *Contact:*

International Student Center Staff, Fullerton College, 321 East
Chapman Avenue, Fullerton, CA 92832-2095.
Telephone: 714-992-7580. Fax: 714-992-7308.
E-mail: isc@fullcoll.edu. URL: http://www.fullcoll.edu.

GAVILAN COLLEGE, GILROY

General Information State and locally supported, 2-year, coed
college. Rural setting. *Awards:* A. *Entrance level for U.S. students:*
Noncompetitive. *Enrollment:* 6,064 total including 0.1%
international students from 11 foreign countries. *Undergraduate
faculty:* 164. *Library holdings:* 55,440 books, 205 current serial
subscriptions. *Total majors:* 38. *Expenses:* (2006–07) $5476.

GLENDALE COMMUNITY COLLEGE, GLENDALE

General Information State and locally supported, 2-year, coed
college. Urban setting. *Awards:* A. *Entrance level for U.S. students:*
Noncompetitive. *Enrollment:* 14,265 total (58% women) including
26% international students from 121 foreign countries.
Undergraduate faculty: 854. *Library holdings:* 91,371 books, 312
current serial subscriptions, 1,893 audiovisual materials.
Total majors: 61.

Information for International Students For fall 2006: 280
international students applied, 220 were accepted, 155 enrolled.
Students can start in fall, winter, spring, or summer. Transfers
accepted from institutions abroad. *Admission tests:* Required:
TOEFL (minimum score: iBT 45; paper-based 450; computer-based
133; minimum score for ESL admission: iBT 45; paper-based 450;
computer-based 133). Recommended: IELTS band score of 4.5.
TOEFL can be waived under certain conditions. *Application
deadline:* 7/1. *Expenses:* (2006–07) $4960. *Financial aid:* Need-based
college/university scholarships/grants from institutional funds,
tuition waivers, on-campus employment. Non-need-based
college/university scholarships/grants from institutional funds,
on-campus employment. International transfer students are eligible
to apply for aid. *Services:* International student adviser on campus.
Full-time ESL program on campus. ESL program available during
the academic year. Employment opportunities (on-campus)
available. *Contact:* Director, International Recruitment and
Outreach, Glendale Community College, 1500 North Verdugo Road,
International Student Office, Glendale, CA 91208-2894.
Telephone: 818-240-1000 Ext. 5887. Fax: 818-240-1345.
E-mail: dnelson@glendale.edu. URL: http://www.glendale.edu.

See In-Depth Description on page 92.

GOLDEN GATE UNIVERSITY, SAN FRANCISCO

General Information Independent, coed university. Urban setting.
Awards: B, M, D, FP. *Entrance level for U.S. students:* Moderately
difficult. *Enrollment:* 3,891 total; 567 undergraduates including 8%
international students from 50 foreign countries. *Faculty:* 489.
Library holdings: 79,204 books, 3,335 current serial subscriptions.
Total majors: 8.

Information for International Students For fall 2006: 1200
international students applied, 1150 were accepted, 877 enrolled.
Students can start in fall, spring, or summer. Transfers accepted
from institutions abroad. *Admission tests:* Required: TOEFL
(minimum score: iBT 71; paper-based 525; computer-based 197;
minimum score for ESL admission: iBT 61; paper-based 475;
computer-based 153). TOEFL can be waived under certain
conditions. *Application deadline:* Rolling. *Expenses:* (2006–07)
$11,520. *Financial aid:* Non-need financial aid available. Forms
required: International Student's Financial Aid Application,
International Student's Certification of Finances. International
transfer students are eligible to apply for aid. 63 international
students on campus received college administered financial aid
($1000 average). *Services:* International student adviser on campus.
Full-time ESL program on campus. ESL program available during
the academic year and the summer. Internships and employment
opportunities (on-campus and off-campus) available. *Contact:*
Associate Director of Admissions for International Recruitment,
Golden Gate University, 536 Mission Street, San Francisco, CA
94105-2968. Telephone: 415-442-7800. Fax: 415-442-7807.
E-mail: info@ggu.edu. URL: http://www.ggu.edu.

See In-Depth Description on page 93.

GOLDEN WEST COLLEGE, HUNTINGTON BEACH

General Information State and locally supported, 2-year, coed
college. Suburban setting. *Awards:* A. *Entrance level for U.S.
students:* Noncompetitive. *Enrollment:* 13,091 total including
international students from 28 foreign countries. *Undergraduate
faculty:* 440. *Library holdings:* 95,000 books, 410 current serial
subscriptions. *Total majors:* 35.

Information for International Students For fall 2006: 108
international students applied, 53 were accepted, 45 enrolled.
Students can start in fall, spring, or summer. Transfers accepted
from institutions abroad. *Admission tests:* Required: TOEFL
(minimum score: iBT 61; paper-based 500; computer-based 173).

Golden West College (continued)

Recommended: STEP Eiken, IELTS. TOEFL can be waived under certain conditions. *Application deadline:* 7/15. *Financial aid:* Need-based financial aid available. *Services:* International student adviser on campus. Part-time ESL program on campus. ESL program available during the academic year and the summer. Employment opportunities (on-campus and off-campus) available. *Contact:* Supervisor, International Student Program, Golden West College, 15744 Golden West Street, PO Box 2748, Huntington Beach, CA 92647-2748. Telephone: 714-895-8146 Ext. 3. Fax: 714-895-8973. E-mail: jleighton@gwc.cccd.edu. URL: http://www.gwc.cccd.edu.

HARVEY MUDD COLLEGE, CLAREMONT

General Information Independent, 4-year, coed college. Suburban setting. *Awards:* B, M. *Entrance level for U.S. students:* Most difficult. *Enrollment:* 729 total (29% women) including 4% international students from 20 foreign countries. *Faculty:* 89. *Library holdings:* 3.2 million books, 16,308 current serial subscriptions. *Total majors:* 6.
Information for International Students For fall 2006: 178 international students applied, 33 were accepted, 10 enrolled. Students can start in fall. Transfers accepted from institutions abroad. *Admission tests:* Recommended: TOEFL. *Application deadline:* 1/15. *Expenses:* (2007–08) $34,670; room and board, $11,412 (on campus); room only, $5729 (on campus). *Financial aid:* Need-based college/university scholarships/grants from institutional funds, loans from outside sources, on-campus employment. Non-need-based college/university scholarships/grants from institutional funds, loans from outside sources, on-campus employment. Forms required: International Student's Financial Aid Application, International Student's Certification of Finances. For fall 2006 (estimated), 14 international students on campus received college administered financial aid ($35,281 average). *Housing:* Guaranteed. *Services:* International student adviser on campus. Employment opportunities (on-campus) available. *Contact:* Harvey Mudd College, 301 Platt Boulevard, Claremont, CA 91711. Telephone: 909-621-8011. Fax: 909-607-7046. E-mail: judy_givigliano@hmc.edu. URL: http://www.hmc.edu.

HOLY NAMES UNIVERSITY, OAKLAND

General Information Independent Roman Catholic, coed, primarily women's institution. Urban setting. *Awards:* B, M. *Entrance level for U.S. students:* Moderately difficult. *Enrollment:* 1,048 total; 620 undergraduates (75% women) including 4% international students from 13 foreign countries. *Faculty:* 136. *Library holdings:* 109,297 books, 8,003 current serial subscriptions, 5,078 audiovisual materials. *Total majors:* 26. *Expenses:* (2006–07) $22,710; room and board, $8000 (on campus); room only, $4200 (on campus). *Financial aid:* Need-based college/university scholarships/grants from institutional funds. Non-need-based college/university scholarships/grants from institutional funds, athletic awards. Forms required: institution's own financial aid form, International Student's Certification of Finances.

HOPE INTERNATIONAL UNIVERSITY, FULLERTON

General Information Independent, coed institution, affiliated with Christian Churches and Churches of Christ. Suburban setting. *Awards:* A, B, M. *Entrance level for U.S. students:* Moderately difficult. *Enrollment:* 903 total; 660 undergraduates (52% women) including 3% international students from 22 foreign countries. *Faculty:* 211. *Library holdings:* 100,000 books, 500 current serial subscriptions. *Total majors:* 19.
Information for International Students For fall 2006: 20 international students applied, 14 were accepted, 10 enrolled. Students can start in fall, winter, spring, or summer. Transfers accepted from institutions abroad. *Admission tests:* Required: TOEFL (minimum score: paper-based 500; computer-based 173; minimum score for ESL admission: paper-based 420; computer-based 110). Recommended: SAT, ACT, native English speakers may take the ACT or SAT instead of TOEFL. TOEFL can be waived under certain conditions. *Application deadline:* 6/1. *Expenses:* (2006–07) $18,820; room and board, $7250 (on campus); room only, $4200 (on campus). *Financial aid:* Need-based and non-need-based financial aid available. Forms required: institution's own financial aid form, International Student's Certification of Finances. International transfer students are eligible to apply for aid. 30 international students on campus received college administered financial aid ($2988 average). *Housing:* Guaranteed, also available during summer. *Services:* International student adviser on campus. Full-time and part-time ESL programs on campus. ESL program available during the academic year and the summer. Internships and employment opportunities (on-campus) available. *Contact:* International Student Programs Director, Hope International University, 2500 East Nutwood Avenue, Fullerton, CA

92831. Telephone: 714-879-3901 Ext. 1407. Fax: 714-681-7478. E-mail: nfeinwaechter@hiu.edu. URL: http://www.hiu.edu.

HUMBOLDT STATE UNIVERSITY, ARCATA

General Information State-supported, coed institution. Rural setting. *Awards:* B, M. *Entrance level for U.S. students:* Moderately difficult. *Enrollment:* 7,435 total; 6,466 undergraduates (54% women) including 1% international students from 12 foreign countries. *Faculty:* 551. *Library holdings:* 1 million books, 1,737 current serial subscriptions, 20,962 audiovisual materials. *Total majors:* 78.

JOHN F. KENNEDY UNIVERSITY, PLEASANT HILL

General Information Independent, coed institution. Suburban setting. *Awards:* B, M, D, FP. *Entrance level for U.S. students:* Noncompetitive. *Enrollment:* 1,653 total; 197 undergraduates. *Faculty:* 728. *Library holdings:* 96,366 books, 823 current serial subscriptions, 2,147 audiovisual materials. *Total majors:* 6.
Information for International Students For fall 2006: 4 international students applied, 4 were accepted, 4 enrolled. Students can start in fall, winter, spring, or summer. Transfers accepted from institutions abroad. *Admission tests:* Required: TOEFL (minimum score: iBT 79; paper-based 550; computer-based 213; minimum score for ESL admission: paper-based 550; computer-based 213). TOEFL can be waived under certain conditions. *Application deadline:* Rolling. *Financial aid:* Need-based college/university scholarships/grants from institutional funds. Non-need-based tuition waivers. *Services:* International student adviser on campus. ESL program at cooperating institution. ESL program available during the academic year and the summer. Employment opportunities (on-campus) available. *Contact:* International Student Advisor, John F. Kennedy University, Admissions, 100 Ellinwood Way, Pleasant Hill, CA 94523-4817. Telephone: 925-969-3339. Fax: 925-969-3331. E-mail: ssermeno@jfku.edu. URL: http://www.jfku.edu.

LANEY COLLEGE, OAKLAND

General Information State and locally supported, 2-year, coed college. Urban setting. *Awards:* A. *Entrance level for U.S. students:* Noncompetitive. *Enrollment:* 13,463 total (58% women). *Undergraduate faculty:* 451. *Library holdings:* 78,054 books, 209 current serial subscriptions. *Total majors:* 42.
Information for International Students Students can start in fall, spring, or summer. Transfers accepted from institutions abroad. *Admission tests:* Required: TOEFL (minimum score: paper-based 480; computer-based 157). TOEFL can be waived under certain conditions. *Application deadline:* 6/1. *Services:* International student adviser on campus. Full-time and part-time ESL programs on campus. ESL program available during the academic year and the summer. Internships and employment opportunities (on-campus and off-campus) available. *Contact:* Laney College, 333 East 8th Street, Oakland, CA 94606. Telephone: 510-466-7380. Fax: 510-465-3257. E-mail: globaled@peralta.edu. URL: http://www.peralta.cc.ca.us.

LA SIERRA UNIVERSITY, RIVERSIDE

General Information Independent Seventh-day Adventist, coed institution. Suburban setting. *Awards:* B, M, D. *Entrance level for U.S. students:* Moderately difficult. *Enrollment:* 1,896 total; 1,578 undergraduates (56% women) including 10% international students from 27 foreign countries. *Faculty:* 178. *Library holdings:* 261,629 books, 1,072 current serial subscriptions, 10,702 audiovisual materials. *Total majors:* 33. *Expenses:* (2007–08) $21,846; room and board, $6330 (on campus). *Financial aid:* Need-based college/university scholarships/grants from institutional funds, loans from outside sources, on-campus employment. Non-need-based college/university scholarships/grants from institutional funds, loans from outside sources. Forms required: International Student's Certification of Finances. For fall 2005, 160 international students on campus received college administered financial aid ($7022 average).

LAS POSITAS COLLEGE, LIVERMORE

General Information State-supported, 2-year, coed college. Suburban setting. *Awards:* A. *Entrance level for U.S. students:* Noncompetitive. *Enrollment:* 8,044 total. *Total majors:* 23.
Information for International Students Students can start in fall or spring. Transfers accepted from institutions abroad. *Admission tests:* Required: TOEFL (minimum score: iBT 45; paper-based 450; computer-based 133). TOEFL can be waived under certain conditions. *Application deadline:* 8/1. *Services:* International student adviser on campus. Full-time and part-time ESL programs on campus. ESL program available during the academic year and the summer. Internships and employment opportunities (on-campus) available. *Contact:* International Student Program Coordinator, Las Positas College, 3033 Collier Canyon Road,

Livermore, CA 94551. Telephone: 925-424-1548. Fax: 925-424-1877. E-mail: cbalero@laspositascollege.edu. URL: http://www.clpccd.cc.ca.us/lpc.

LIFE PACIFIC COLLEGE, SAN DIMAS

General Information Independent, 4-year, coed college, affiliated with International Church of the Foursquare Gospel. Suburban setting. *Awards:* A, B. *Entrance level for U.S. students:* Minimally difficult. *Enrollment:* 528 total (46% women) including 1% international students from 2 foreign countries. *Undergraduate faculty:* 39. *Library holdings:* 40,022 books, 1,954 current serial subscriptions, 1,563 audiovisual materials. *Total majors:* 3.

Information for International Students For fall 2006: 2 international students applied, 1 was accepted. Students can start in fall or spring. Transfers accepted from institutions abroad. *Admission tests:* Required: TOEFL (minimum score: paper-based 550; computer-based 213). *Application deadline:* 5/1. *Financial aid:* Need-based college/university scholarships/grants from institutional funds. Non-need-based college/university scholarships/grants from institutional funds. 1 international student on campus received college administered financial aid ($5800 average). *Housing:* Guaranteed. *Services:* ESL program at cooperating institution. Internships and employment opportunities (on-campus) available. *Contact:* Admissions Director, Life Pacific College, 1100 Covina Boulevard, San Dimas, CA 91773. Telephone: 909-599-5433 Ext. 314. Fax: 909-706-3070. E-mail: admissions@lifepacific.edu. URL: http://www.lifepacific.edu.

LINCOLN UNIVERSITY, OAKLAND

General Information Independent, coed institution. Urban setting. *Awards:* B, M. *Entrance level for U.S. students:* Minimally difficult. *Enrollment:* 227 total; 54 undergraduates (50% women) including international students from 12 foreign countries. *Faculty:* 35. *Library holdings:* 17,752 books, 762 current serial subscriptions. *Total majors:* 6.

Information for International Students For fall 2006: 235 international students applied, 228 were accepted, 88 enrolled. Students can start in fall, spring, or summer. Transfers accepted from institutions abroad. *Admission tests:* Required: TOEFL (minimum score: iBT 60; paper-based 500; computer-based 173), English Placement Test. TOEFL can be waived under certain conditions. *Application deadline:* 8/28. *Expenses:* (2007–08) $7720. *Services:* International student adviser on campus. Full-time ESL program on campus. ESL program available during the academic year and the summer. Employment opportunities (on-campus) available. *Contact:* Acting Admission Officer, Lincoln University, 401 15th Street, Oakland, CA 94612. Telephone: 510-628-8010. Fax: 510-628-8012. E-mail: admission@lincolnuca.edu. URL: http://www.lincolnuca.edu.

LOMA LINDA UNIVERSITY, LOMA LINDA

General Information Independent Seventh-day Adventist, coed institution. Small town setting. *Awards:* A, B, M, D, FP (associate degree and nursing students may enter at the sophomore level). *Entrance level for U.S. students:* Difficulty N/R. *Enrollment:* 3,972 total; 1,212 undergraduates (75% women) including 7% international students from 30 foreign countries. *Faculty:* 155. *Library holdings:* 338,418 books, 1,671 current serial subscriptions. *Total majors:* 14. *Expenses:* (2007–08) $27,320; room only, $2460 (on campus).

LONG BEACH CITY COLLEGE, LONG BEACH

General Information State-supported, 2-year, coed college. Urban setting. *Awards:* A. *Entrance level for U.S. students:* Noncompetitive. *Enrollment:* 26,296 total (56% women). *Undergraduate faculty:* 1,133. *Library holdings:* 151,367 books, 471 current serial subscriptions, 3,150 audiovisual materials. *Total majors:* 69.

Information for International Students For fall 2006: 309 international students applied, 235 were accepted, 179 enrolled. Students can start in fall, spring, or summer. Transfers accepted from institutions abroad. *Admission tests:* Required: TOEFL (minimum score: iBT 61; paper-based 500; computer-based 173). Recommended: ELS, STEP accepted in place of TOEFL. TOEFL can be waived under certain conditions. *Application deadline:* Rolling. *Expenses:* (2006–07) $4532. *Financial aid:* Forms required: institution's own financial aid form. *Services:* International student adviser on campus. Full-time ESL program on campus. ESL program available during the academic year and the summer. Internships and employment opportunities (on-campus and off-campus) available. *Contact:* Admissions Assistant, International Student Office, Long Beach City College, 4901 East Carson Street, Long Beach, CA 90808. Telephone: 562-938-4452. Fax: 562-938-4747. E-mail: international_staff@lbcc.edu. URL: http://www.lbcc.edu.

See In-Depth Description on page 116.

LOS ANGELES HARBOR COLLEGE, WILMINGTON

General Information State and locally supported, 2-year, coed college. Suburban setting. *Awards:* A. *Entrance level for U.S. students:* Noncompetitive. *Enrollment:* 9,469 total (61% women). *Undergraduate faculty:* 270. *Library holdings:* 82,790 books, 302 current serial subscriptions. *Total majors:* 23.

Information for International Students For fall 2006: 31 international students applied, 31 were accepted, 16 enrolled. Students can start in fall or spring. Transfers accepted from institutions abroad. *Admission tests:* Required: TOEFL (minimum score: iBT 45; paper-based 450; computer-based 133; minimum score for ESL admission: iBT 45; paper-based 450; computer-based 133), ELS (minimum score: 109), IELTS or college's ESL Assessment Test. TOEFL can be waived under certain conditions. *Application deadline:* Rolling. *Expenses.* (2007–08) $4320. *Services:* International student adviser on campus. Full-time ESL program on campus. ESL program available during the academic year. *Contact:* International (Foreign) Student Advisor, Los Angeles Harbor College, 1111 Figueroa Place, Wilmington, CA 90744. Telephone: 310-233-4111. Fax: 310-233-4223. E-mail: gradyp@lahc.edu. URL: http://www.lahc.edu.

LOS ANGELES MISSION COLLEGE, SYLMAR

General Information State and locally supported, 2-year, coed college. Small town setting. *Awards:* A. *Entrance level for U.S. students:* Noncompetitive. *Enrollment:* 7,617 undergraduates including international students from 8 foreign countries. *Undergraduate faculty:* 270. *Library holdings:* 40,000 books, 450 current serial subscriptions. *Total majors:* 38.

Information for International Students For fall 2006: 55 international students enrolled. Students can start in fall or spring. *Admission tests:* Required: college assessment test. Recommended: TOEFL (minimum score: paper-based 400; computer-based 97; minimum score for ESL admission: paper-based 400; computer-based 97). TOEFL can be waived under certain conditions. *Application deadline:* Rolling. *Financial aid:* Need-based college/university scholarships/grants from institutional funds, tuition waivers, loans from institutional funds, loans from outside sources. Forms required: institution's own financial aid form. *Services:* International student adviser on campus. Full-time ESL program on campus. ESL program available during the academic year. *Contact:* Director of International Students, Los Angeles Mission College, 13356 Eldridge Avenue, Sylmar, CA 91342-3245. Telephone: 818-364-7741. Fax: 818-833-3304. E-mail: Moralev@laccd.edu. URL: http://www.lamission.cc.ca.us.

LOS ANGELES PIERCE COLLEGE, WOODLAND HILLS

General Information State and locally supported, 2-year, coed college. Suburban setting. *Awards:* A. *Entrance level for U.S. students:* Noncompetitive. *Enrollment:* 16,255 total including international students from 48 foreign countries. *Undergraduate faculty:* 558. *Library holdings:* 106,122 books, 395 current serial subscriptions. *Total majors:* 34.

Information for International Students For fall 2006: 230 international students enrolled. Students can start in fall or spring. Transfers accepted from institutions abroad. *Admission tests:* Required: TOEFL (minimum score: iBT 45; paper-based 450; computer-based 133), IELTS and STEP Eiken are accepted in lieu of TOEFL. TOEFL can be waived under certain conditions. *Application deadline:* 5/15. *Expenses:* (2007–08) $5382. *Services:* International student adviser on campus. ESL program at cooperating institution. Internships and employment opportunities (on-campus) available. *Contact:* International Admissions, Los Angeles Pierce College, 6201 Winnetka Avenue, PMB 304, Woodland Hills, CA 91371-0002. Telephone: 818-710-2511. Fax: 818-347-8704. E-mail: intlstu@piercecollege.edu. URL: http://www.lapc.cc.ca.us.

LOS ANGELES SOUTHWEST COLLEGE, LOS ANGELES

General Information State and locally supported, 2-year, coed college. Urban setting. *Awards:* A. *Entrance level for U.S. students:* Noncompetitive. *Enrollment:* 6,000 total including international students from 4 foreign countries. *Undergraduate faculty:* 223. *Library holdings:* 60,000 books, 600 current serial subscriptions. *Total majors:* 34.

Information for International Students For fall 2006: 33 international students applied, 29 were accepted, 14 enrolled. Students can start in fall or spring. *Admission tests:* Required: TOEFL (minimum score: iBT 45; paper-based 450; computer-based 133; minimum score for ESL admission: iBT 45; paper-based 450; computer-based 133). TOEFL can be waived under certain conditions. *Application deadline:* 7/30. *Services:* International student adviser on campus. ESL program at cooperating institution. ESL program available during the academic year and the summer. Employment opportunities (on-campus) available. *Contact:* International Student Advisor, Los Angeles Southwest College, 1600

Los Angeles Southwest College (continued)
West Imperial Highway, Los Angeles, CA 90047.
Telephone: 323-241-5277. Fax: 323-242-5577.
E-mail: LarsonL@lasc.edu. URL: http://www.lasc.cc.ca.us.

LOS ANGELES TRADE-TECHNICAL COLLEGE, LOS ANGELES

General Information State and locally supported, 2-year, coed college. Urban setting. *Awards:* A. *Entrance level for U.S. students:* Noncompetitive. *Enrollment:* 13,194 total (51% women) including 1% international students from 20 foreign countries. *Undergraduate faculty:* 443. *Library holdings:* 98,000 books, 367 current serial subscriptions. *Total majors:* 34.

LOS MEDANOS COLLEGE, PITTSBURG

General Information District-supported, 2-year, coed college. Suburban setting. *Awards:* A. *Entrance level for U.S. students:* Noncompetitive. *Enrollment:* 7,152 total including international students from 15 foreign countries. *Undergraduate faculty:* 244. *Library holdings:* 15,439 books, 205 current serial subscriptions. *Total majors:* 29.

LOYOLA MARYMOUNT UNIVERSITY, LOS ANGELES

General Information Independent Roman Catholic, coed institution. Suburban setting. *Awards:* B, M, D, FP. *Entrance level for U.S. students:* Very difficult. *Enrollment:* 8,903 total; 5,746 undergraduates (58% women) including 2% international students from 38 foreign countries. *Faculty:* 1,154. *Library holdings:* 495,920 books, 10,057 current serial subscriptions. *Total majors:* 48. *Expenses:* (2006–07) $29,834; room and board, $11,290 (on campus); room only, $7890 (on campus). *Financial aid:* Need-based college/university scholarships/grants from institutional funds, athletic awards, loans from institutional funds, loans from outside sources, on-campus employment. Non-need-based college/university scholarships/grants from institutional funds, athletic awards, loans from institutional funds, loans from outside sources, on-campus employment. Forms required: CSS PROFILE.

MARYMOUNT COLLEGE, PALOS VERDES, CALIFORNIA, RANCHO PALOS VERDES

General Information Independent Roman Catholic, 2-year, coed college. Suburban setting. *Awards:* A. *Entrance level for U.S. students:* Minimally difficult. *Enrollment:* 652 total (54% women) including 10% international students from 21 foreign countries. *Undergraduate faculty:* 91. *Library holdings:* 42,104 books, 328 current serial subscriptions. *Total majors:* 1.
Information for International Students For fall 2006: 177 international students applied, 121 were accepted, 40 enrolled. Students can start in fall or spring. Transfers accepted from institutions abroad. *Admission tests:* Recommended: SAT or ACT, TOEFL. TOEFL can be waived under certain conditions. *Application deadline:* Rolling. *Expenses:* (2007–08) $21,551; room and board, $9894 (on campus). *Financial aid:* Need-based college/university scholarships/grants from institutional funds, athletic awards. Non-need-based college/university scholarships/grants from institutional funds, athletic awards. Forms required: institution's own financial aid form. *Housing:* Guaranteed, also available during summer. *Services:* International student adviser on campus. Full-time and part-time ESL programs on campus. ESL program available during the academic year and the summer. Employment opportunities (on-campus) available. *Contact:* Associate Director of Admission, Marymount College, Palos Verdes, California, 30800 Palos Verdes Drive East, Rancho Palos Verdes, CA 90275-6299. Telephone: 310-377-5501 Ext. 311. Fax: 310-265-0962. E-mail: admission@marymountpv.edu. URL: http://www.marymountpv.edu.

THE MASTER'S COLLEGE AND SEMINARY, SANTA CLARITA

General Information Independent nondenominational, coed institution. Suburban setting. *Awards:* B, M, D, FP. *Entrance level for U.S. students:* Moderately difficult. *Enrollment:* 1,521 total; 1,130 undergraduates (50% women) including 3% international students from 24 foreign countries. *Faculty:* 188. *Library holdings:* 178,337 books, 12,867 current serial subscriptions, 7,413 audiovisual materials. *Total majors:* 47. *Expenses:* (2006–07) $20,770; room and board, $6900 (on campus); room only, $3860 (on campus). *Financial aid:* Need-based college/university scholarships/grants from institutional funds, athletic awards, on-campus employment. Non-need-based college/university scholarships/grants from institutional funds, athletic awards, on-campus employment. Forms required: institution's own financial aid form, International Student's Financial Aid Application, International Student's Certification of Finances. For fall 2005, 27 international students on campus received college administered financial aid ($18,119 average).

MENLO COLLEGE, ATHERTON

General Information Independent, 4-year, coed college. Small town setting. *Awards:* B. *Entrance level for U.S. students:* Moderately difficult. *Enrollment:* 769 total (40% women) including 10% international students from 34 foreign countries. *Undergraduate faculty:* 71. *Library holdings:* 64,700 books, 175 current serial subscriptions. *Total majors:* 3.
Information for International Students For fall 2006: 44 international students applied, 42 were accepted, 27 enrolled. Students can start in fall or spring. Transfers accepted from institutions abroad. *Admission tests:* Required: TOEFL (minimum score: paper-based 500; computer-based 173; minimum score for ESL admission: paper-based 500; computer-based 173). Recommended: SAT or ACT, STEP alternative to TOEFL. *Application deadline:* Rolling. *Expenses:* (2006–07) $26,220; room and board $9800 (on campus). *Financial aid:* Non-need-based college/university scholarships/grants from institutional funds. Forms required: International Student's Certification of Finances. International transfer students are eligible to apply for aid. For fall 2006 (estimated), 55 international students on campus received college administered financial aid ($10,115 average). *Housing:* Guaranteed, also available during summer. *Services:* International student adviser on campus. ESL program at cooperating institution. ESL program available during the academic year and the summer. Internships and employment opportunities (on-campus) available. *Contact:* Senior Associate Director of Admission, Menlo College, 1000 El Camino Real, Atherton, CA 94027-4301. Telephone: 650-543-3753. Fax: 650-543-4496. E-mail: admissions@menlo.edu. URL: http://www.menlo.edu.
See In-Depth Description on page 126.

MERRITT COLLEGE, OAKLAND

General Information State and locally supported, 2-year, coed college. Urban setting. *Awards:* A. *Entrance level for U.S. students:* Noncompetitive. *Enrollment:* 7,984 total (70% women) including international students from 12 foreign countries. *Undergraduate faculty:* 201. *Library holdings:* 80,000 books, 200 current serial subscriptions. *Total majors:* 33.
Information for International Students Students can start in fall, spring, or summer. Transfers accepted from institutions abroad. *Admission tests:* Required: TOEFL (minimum score: paper-based 480; computer-based 157). TOEFL can be waived under certain conditions. *Application deadline:* 6/1. *Services:* International student adviser on campus. Full-time and part-time ESL programs on campus. ESL program available during the academic year and the summer. Internships and employment opportunities (on-campus and off-campus) available. *Contact:* Merritt College, 333 East 8th Street, Oakland, CA 94606. Telephone: 510-466-7380. Fax: 510-465-3257. E-mail: globaled@peralta.cc.ca.us. URL: http://www.merritt.edu.

MILLS COLLEGE, OAKLAND

General Information Independent, undergraduate: women only; graduate: coed institution. Urban setting. *Awards:* B, M, D. *Entrance level for U.S. students:* Moderately difficult. *Enrollment:* 1,410 total; 927 undergraduates (100% women) including 3% international students from 6 foreign countries. *Faculty:* 189. *Library holdings:* 254,351 books, 13,211 current serial subscriptions, 7,640 audiovisual materials. *Total majors:* 38.
Information for International Students For fall 2006: 35 international students applied, 22 were accepted, 4 enrolled. Students can start in fall or spring. Transfers accepted from institutions abroad. *Admission tests:* Required: SAT or ACT, TOEFL (minimum score: iBT 80; paper-based 550; computer-based 213; minimum score for ESL admission: iBT 80; paper-based 500; computer-based 173). Recommended: SAT Subject Tests. TOEFL can be waived under certain conditions. *Application deadline:* 2/1. *Expenses:* (2006–07) $33,024; room and board, $10,240 (on campus); room only, $5460 (on campus). *Financial aid:* Non-need financial aid available. Forms required: International Student's Financial Aid Application, International Student's Certification of Finances. International transfer students are eligible to apply for aid. 15 international students on campus received college administered financial aid ($8742 average). *Housing:* Guaranteed. *Services:* International student adviser on campus. Full-time ESL program on campus. ESL program available during the academic year. Internships available. *Contact:* Associate Dean of Admission, Mills College, 5000 MacArthur Boulevard, Oakland, CA 94613. Telephone: 510-430-2135. Fax: 510-430-3298. E-mail: admission@mill.edu. URL: http://www.mills.edu.

MIRACOSTA COLLEGE, OCEANSIDE

General Information State-supported, 2-year, coed college. Suburban setting. *Awards:* A. *Entrance level for U.S. students:* Noncompetitive. *Enrollment:* 10,252 total including international students from 44 foreign countries. *Undergraduate faculty:* 529. *Library holdings:* 113,810 books, 272 current serial subscriptions, 5,340 audiovisual materials. *Total majors:* 54.

Information for International Students For fall 2006: 148 international students applied, 113 were accepted, 97 enrolled. Students can start in fall, spring, or summer. Transfers accepted from institutions abroad. *Admission tests:* Required: TOEFL (minimum score: paper-based 450; computer-based 133). TOEFL can be waived under certain conditions. *Application deadline:* 6/1. *Expenses:* (2006–07) $5604. *Services:* International student adviser on campus. Full-time ESL program on campus. ESL program available during the academic year and the summer. Internships and employment opportunities (on-campus and off-campus) available. *Contact:* Coordinator, MiraCosta College, One Barnard Drive, Oceanside, CA 92056. Telephone: 760-795-6897. Fax: 760-757-8209. E-mail: iip@miracosta.edu. URL: http://www.miracosta.edu.

See In-Depth Description on page 129.

MODESTO JUNIOR COLLEGE, MODESTO

General Information State and locally supported, 2-year, coed college. Urban setting. *Awards:* A. *Entrance level for U.S. students:* Noncompetitive. *Enrollment:* 18,240 total. *Undergraduate faculty:* 534. *Library holdings:* 69,865 books, 4,161 audiovisual materials. *Total majors:* 87.

Information for International Students For fall 2006: 60 international students applied, 34 were accepted, 24 enrolled. Students can start in fall or spring. Transfers accepted from institutions abroad. *Admission tests:* Required: TOEFL (minimum score: iBT 45; paper-based 450; computer-based 133; minimum score for ESL admission: iBT 45; paper-based 450; computer-based 133). TOEFL can be waived under certain conditions. *Application deadline:* Rolling. *Expenses:* (2006–07) $4504. *Financial aid:* Forms required: institution's own financial aid form. *Services:* International student adviser on campus. Part-time ESL program on campus. ESL program available during the academic year. Employment opportunities (on-campus) available. *Contact:* Coordinator of International Student Program, Modesto Junior College, 435 College Avenue, Modesto, CA 95350. Telephone: 209-575-6012. Fax: 209-575-6720. E-mail: sturbainb@mjc.edu. URL: http://www.mjc.edu.

MONTEREY PENINSULA COLLEGE, MONTEREY

General Information State-supported, 2-year, coed college. Small town setting. *Awards:* A. *Entrance level for U.S. students:* Noncompetitive. *Enrollment:* 14,074 total including international students from 47 foreign countries. *Undergraduate faculty:* 317. *Library holdings:* 52,000 books, 281 current serial subscriptions, 2,623 audiovisual materials. *Total majors:* 70.

Information for International Students For fall 2006: 30 international students applied, 30 were accepted, 28 enrolled. Students can start in fall, spring, or summer. Transfers accepted from institutions abroad. *Admission tests:* Required: TOEFL (minimum score: iBT 48; paper-based 460; computer-based 140). TOEFL can be waived under certain conditions. *Application deadline:* Rolling. *Financial aid:* Forms required: institution's own financial aid form, FAFSA. *Services:* International student adviser on campus. Part-time ESL program on campus. ESL program available during the academic year and the summer. Internships and employment opportunities (on-campus and off-campus) available. *Contact:* Director, International Student Programs, Monterey Peninsula College, 980 Fremont Street, Monterey, CA 93940-4799. Telephone: 831-645-1357. Fax: 831-645-1390. E-mail: international_center@mpc.edu. URL: http://www.mpc.edu.

MOORPARK COLLEGE, MOORPARK

General Information County-supported, 2-year, coed college. Small town setting. *Awards:* A. *Entrance level for U.S. students:* Noncompetitive. *Enrollment:* 15,266 total including international students from 50 foreign countries. *Undergraduate faculty:* 590. *Library holdings:* 50,000 books, 100 current serial subscriptions. *Total majors:* 38.

MOUNT ST. MARY'S COLLEGE, LOS ANGELES

General Information Independent Roman Catholic, coed, primarily women's institution. Suburban setting. *Awards:* A, B, M. *Entrance level for U.S. students:* Moderately difficult. *Enrollment:* 2,384 total; 1,921 undergraduates (94% women) including 0.2% international students. *Faculty:* 327. *Library holdings:* 140,000 books, 750 current serial subscriptions. *Total majors:* 40. *Expenses:* (2006–07) $24,150; room and board, $8747 (on campus).

MT. SAN ANTONIO COLLEGE, WALNUT

General Information District-supported, 2-year, coed college. Suburban setting. *Awards:* A. *Entrance level for U.S. students:* Noncompetitive. *Enrollment:* 29,079 total (54% women) including 1% international students. *Undergraduate faculty:* 1,330. *Library holdings:* 64,291 books, 753 current serial subscriptions. *Total majors:* 72. *Expenses:* (2006–07) $4852.

MT. SAN JACINTO COLLEGE, SAN JACINTO

General Information State and locally supported, 2-year, coed college. Suburban setting. *Awards:* A. *Entrance level for U.S. students:* Noncompetitive. *Enrollment:* 12,592 total. *Undergraduate faculty:* 421. *Library holdings:* 28,000 books, 330 current serial subscriptions. *Total majors:* 29. *Financial aid:* Non-need financial aid available.

MUSICIANS INSTITUTE, HOLLYWOOD

General Information Proprietary, 4-year, coed college. *Awards:* A, B. *Entrance level for U.S. students:* Minimally difficult. *Enrollment:* 650 total. *Total majors:* 1.

NATIONAL UNIVERSITY, LA JOLLA

General Information Independent, coed institution. Urban setting. *Awards:* A, B, M. *Entrance level for U.S. students:* Minimally difficult. *Enrollment:* 25,992 total; 7,068 undergraduates (58% women) including 1% international students from 76 foreign countries. *Faculty:* 3,195. *Library holdings:* 250,000 books, 18,889 current serial subscriptions, 17,884 audiovisual materials. *Total majors:* 45. *Expenses:* (2006–07) $9132. *Financial aid:* Forms required: institution's own financial aid form.

NEW COLLEGE OF CALIFORNIA, SAN FRANCISCO

General Information Independent, coed institution. Urban setting. *Awards:* B, M. *Entrance level for U.S. students:* Minimally difficult. *Enrollment:* 1,316 total; 681 undergraduates (50% women) including 0.4% international students from 5 foreign countries. *Faculty:* 192. *Library holdings:* 24,000 books, 50 current serial subscriptions. *Total majors:* 9.

Information for International Students Students can start in fall, winter, spring, or summer. Transfers accepted from institutions abroad. *Admission tests:* Required: TOEFL (minimum score: iBT 90; paper-based 500; computer-based 173; minimum score for ESL admission: iBT 90; paper-based 500; computer-based 173). TOEFL can be waived under certain conditions. *Application deadline:* Rolling. *Expenses:* (2007–08) $13,530. *Financial aid:* Need-based financial aid available. *Services:* International student adviser on campus. Internships available. *Contact:* Dean of International Students, New College of California, 777 Valencia Street, San Francisco, CA 94110. Telephone: 415-437-3400. Fax: 415-626-5174. E-mail: Intl@newcollege.edu. URL: http://www.newcollege.edu.

NORTHWESTERN POLYTECHNIC UNIVERSITY, FREMONT

General Information Independent, coed institution. Urban setting. *Awards:* B, M, D. *Entrance level for U.S. students:* Difficulty N/R. *Enrollment:* 439 total; 132 undergraduates (38% women) including 61% international students from 10 foreign countries. *Faculty:* 56. *Library holdings:* 12,000 books, 200 current serial subscriptions. *Total majors:* 4.

Information for International Students For fall 2006: 104 international students applied, 93 were accepted, 51 enrolled. Students can start in fall, spring, or summer. Transfers accepted from institutions abroad. *Admission tests:* Required: on-campus assessment tests. Recommended: SAT, TOEFL (minimum score: iBT 79; paper-based 550; computer-based 213; minimum score for ESL admission: paper-based 400; computer-based 97), ELS. TOEFL can be waived under certain conditions. *Application deadline:* Rolling. *Expenses:* (2006–07) $6740; room only, $3600 (on campus). *Housing:* Guaranteed, also available during summer. *Services:* International student adviser on campus. Full-time and part-time ESL programs on campus. ESL program available during the academic year. Employment opportunities (on-campus) available. *Contact:* Admission Officer, Northwestern Polytechnic University, 47671 Westinghouse Drive, Fremont, CA 94539. Telephone: 510-657-5913. Fax: 510-657-8975. E-mail: catherine@npu.edu. URL: http://www.npu.edu.

NOTRE DAME DE NAMUR UNIVERSITY, BELMONT

General Information Independent Roman Catholic, coed institution. Suburban setting. *Awards:* B, M. *Entrance level for U.S. students:* Minimally difficult. *Enrollment:* 1,583 total; 857 undergraduates (64% women) including 4% international students from 11 foreign countries. *Faculty:* 156. *Library holdings:* 90,702 books, 15,000 current serial subscriptions, 9,122 audiovisual materials. *Total majors:* 37.

Notre Dame de Namur University (continued)

Information for International Students For fall 2006: 45 international students applied, 45 were accepted, 7 enrolled. Students can start in fall or spring. Transfers accepted from institutions abroad. *Admission tests:* Required: TOEFL (minimum score: paper-based 450; computer-based 133; minimum score for ESL admission: paper-based 450; computer-based 133). Recommended: SAT or ACT. TOEFL can be waived under certain conditions. *Application deadline:* Rolling. *Expenses:* (2007–08) $24,650; room and board, $10,580 (on campus); room only, $7000 (on campus). *Financial aid:* Non-need financial aid available. *Housing:* Guaranteed, also available during summer. *Services:* International student adviser on campus. Internships and employment opportunities (on-campus) available. *Contact:* Dean of Enrollment, Undergraduate Admissions Office, Notre Dame de Namur University, 1500 Ralston Avenue, Belmont, CA 94002-1908. Telephone: 650-508-3600. Fax: 650-508-3426. E-mail: admiss@ndnu.edu. URL: http://www.ndnu.edu.

OCCIDENTAL COLLEGE, LOS ANGELES

General Information Independent, coed institution. Urban setting. *Awards:* B, M. *Entrance level for U.S. students:* Very difficult. *Enrollment:* 1,825 total; 1,804 undergraduates (56% women) including 2% international students from 21 foreign countries. *Faculty:* 220. *Library holdings:* 497,161 books, 903 current serial subscriptions. *Total majors:* 31. *Expenses:* (2007–08) $35,333; room and board, $9500 (on campus). *Financial aid:* Need-based college/university scholarships/grants from institutional funds. Non-need-based college/university scholarships/grants from institutional funds. Forms required: International Student's Financial Aid Application, International Student's Certification of Finances. For fall 2005, 30 international students on campus received college administered financial aid ($32,301 average).

ORANGE COAST COLLEGE, COSTA MESA

General Information State and locally supported, 2-year, coed college. Suburban setting. *Awards:* A. *Entrance level for U.S. students:* Noncompetitive. *Enrollment:* 22,412 total (50% women) including 2% international students from 76 foreign countries. *Undergraduate faculty:* 940. *Library holdings:* 84,447 books, 420 current serial subscriptions. *Total majors:* 102.
Information for International Students For fall 2006: 230 international students applied, 170 were accepted, 155 enrolled. Students can start in fall or spring. Transfers accepted from institutions abroad. *Admission tests:* Required: TOEFL (minimum score: paper-based 500; computer-based 173). *Application deadline:* Rolling. *Expenses:* (2007–08) $5338. *Services:* International student adviser on campus. *Contact:* Director, International Center, Orange Coast College, International Center, 2701 Fairview Road, Costa Mesa, CA 92628-5005. Telephone: 714-432-5940. Fax: 714-432-5191. E-mail: intctr@cccd.edu. URL: http://www.orangecoastcollege.com.

OTIS COLLEGE OF ART AND DESIGN, LOS ANGELES

General Information Independent, coed institution. Urban setting. *Awards:* B, M. *Entrance level for U.S. students:* Moderately difficult. *Enrollment:* 1,125 total; 1,073 undergraduates (67% women) including 12% international students from 13 foreign countries. *Faculty:* 257. *Library holdings:* 42,000 books, 150 current serial subscriptions. *Total majors:* 10.
Information for International Students For fall 2006: 253 international students applied, 105 were accepted, 42 enrolled. Students can start in fall or spring. Transfers accepted from institutions abroad. *Admission tests:* Required: TOEFL (minimum score: iBT 79; paper-based 550; computer-based 213). Recommended: SAT or ACT. TOEFL can be waived under certain conditions. *Application deadline:* Rolling. *Expenses:* (2007–08) $28,346. *Financial aid:* Need-based college/university scholarships/grants from institutional funds, loans from outside sources, on-campus employment. Non-need-based loans from outside sources, on-campus employment. Forms required: institution's own financial aid form. For fall 2005, 16 international students on campus received college administered financial aid ($5100 average). *Services:* International student adviser on campus. Full-time ESL program on campus. ESL program available during the academic year. Internships and employment opportunities (on-campus) available. *Contact:* Dean of Admissions, Otis College of Art and Design, 9045 Lincoln Boulevard, Los Angeles, CA 90045. Telephone: 310-665-6820. Fax: 310-665-6821. E-mail: admissions@otis.edu. URL: http://www.otis.edu.

OXNARD COLLEGE, OXNARD

General Information State-supported, 2-year, coed college. Urban setting. *Awards:* A. *Entrance level for U.S. students:* Noncompetitive. *Enrollment:* 6,379 total (58% women) including 0.4% international students from 30 foreign countries.

Undergraduate faculty: 267. *Library holdings:* 31,500 books, 107 current serial subscriptions. *Total majors:* 44. *Expenses:* (2007–08) $4722.

PACIFIC OAKS COLLEGE, PASADENA

General Information Independent, coed, primarily women's institution. Small town setting. *Awards:* B, M. *Entrance level for U.S. students:* Difficulty N/R. *Enrollment:* 1,028 total; 257 undergraduates (96% women). *Faculty:* 125. *Library holdings:* 36,000 books, 87 current serial subscriptions, 125 audiovisual materials. *Total majors:* 6. *Expenses:* (2007–08) $19,140.

PACIFIC STATES UNIVERSITY, LOS ANGELES

General Information Independent, coed institution. Urban setting. *Awards:* B, M. *Entrance level for U.S. students:* Minimally difficult. *Enrollment:* 68 total; 44 undergraduates (18% women). *Faculty:* 16. *Library holdings:* 15,000 books, 108 current serial subscriptions. *Total majors:* 3. *Expenses:* (2006–07) $8860.

PACIFIC UNION COLLEGE, ANGWIN

General Information Independent Seventh-day Adventist, coed institution. Rural setting. *Awards:* A, B, M. *Entrance level for U.S. students:* Moderately difficult. *Enrollment:* 1,397 total; 1,394 undergraduates (54% women) including 7% international students from 24 foreign countries. *Faculty:* 95. *Library holdings:* 173,839 books, 812 current serial subscriptions. *Total majors:* 67. *Expenses:* (2006–07) $20,265; room and board, $5652 (on campus); room only, $3447 (on campus).

PALOMAR COLLEGE, SAN MARCOS

General Information State and locally supported, 2-year, coed college. Suburban setting. *Awards:* A. *Entrance level for U.S. students:* Noncompetitive. *Enrollment:* 28,597 total. *Undergraduate faculty:* 1,089. *Library holdings:* 108,000 books. *Total majors:* 78.
Information for International Students For fall 2006: 105 international students applied, 81 were accepted, 71 enrolled. Students can start in fall, spring, or summer. Transfers accepted from institutions abroad. *Admission tests:* Required: TOEFL (minimum score: iBT 47; paper-based 470; computer-based 150). TOEFL can be waived under certain conditions. *Application deadline:* 5/1. *Expenses:* (2006–07) $5932. *Services:* International student adviser on campus. Full-time ESL program on campus. ESL program available during the academic year and the summer. Internships and employment opportunities (on-campus) available. *Contact:* International Admissions Assistant, Palomar College, Office of International Education, 1140 West Mission Road, San Marcos, CA 92069-1487. Telephone: 760-744-1150 Ext. 2167. Fax: 760-761-3592. E-mail: rbonner@palomar.edu. URL: http://www.palomar.edu.

PEPPERDINE UNIVERSITY, MALIBU

General Information Independent, coed university, affiliated with Church of Christ. Small town setting. *Awards:* B, M, D, FP. *Entrance level for U.S. students:* Very difficult. *Enrollment:* 7,593 total; 3,297 undergraduates (57% women) including 6% international students from 61 foreign countries. *Faculty:* 707. *Library holdings:* 1.5 million books, 103,654 current serial subscriptions. *Total majors:* 43. *Expenses:* (2006–07) $32,740; room and board, $9500 (on campus).

PITZER COLLEGE, CLAREMONT

General Information Independent, 4-year, coed college. Suburban setting. *Awards:* B. *Entrance level for U.S. students:* Moderately difficult. *Enrollment:* 958 total (59% women) including 2% international students from 8 foreign countries. *Undergraduate faculty:* 95. *Library holdings:* 2.5 million books, 16,000 current serial subscriptions. *Total majors:* 53.
Information for International Students Students can start in fall or spring. Transfers accepted from institutions abroad. *Admission tests:* Required: TOEFL (minimum score: iBT 70; paper-based 520; computer-based 190). Recommended: SAT. *Application deadline:* 1/1. *Expenses:* (2006–07) $34,038; room and board, $9670 (on campus); room only, $6120 (on campus). *Housing:* Guaranteed, also available during summer. *Services:* International student adviser on campus. ESL program available during the academic year. Internships and employment opportunities (on-campus) available. *Contact:* Associate Director, International Programs, Pitzer College, 1050 North Mills Avenue, Claremont, CA 91711. Telephone: 909-621-8308. Fax: 909-621-0518. E-mail: todd_sasaki@pitzer.edu. URL: http://www.pitzer.edu.

PLATT COLLEGE SAN DIEGO, SAN DIEGO

General Information Proprietary, primarily 2-year, coed college. Suburban setting. *Awards:* A, B. *Entrance level for U.S. students:* Difficulty N/R. *Enrollment:* 264 total (27% women). *Undergraduate*

faculty: 37. *Library holdings:* 750 books, 27 current serial subscriptions, 403 audiovisual materials. *Total majors:* 9.
Information for International Students Students can start in fall, winter, spring, or summer. *Admission tests:* Required: Wonderlic. Recommended: SAT or ACT, SAT Subject Tests, TOEFL, ELS. *Application deadline:* Rolling. *Expenses:* (2007–08) $19,324. *Contact:* Director of International Education, Platt College San Diego, 6250 El Cajon Boulevard, San Diego, CA 92115. Telephone: 619-265-0107. Fax: 619-308-0570. E-mail: info@platt.edu. URL: http://www.platt.edu.

POINT LOMA NAZARENE UNIVERSITY, SAN DIEGO
General Information Independent Nazarene, coed institution. Suburban setting. *Awards:* B, M. *Entrance level for U.S. students:* Moderately difficult. *Enrollment:* 3,437 total; 2,383 undergraduates (61% women) including 1% international students from 14 foreign countries. *Library holdings:* 152,377 books, 25,505 current serial subscriptions. *Total majors:* 55. *Expenses:* (2007–08) $23,730; room and board, $7470 (on campus). *Financial aid:* Non-need financial aid available. Forms required: institution's own financial aid form. For fall 2006 (estimated), 8 international students on campus received college administered financial aid ($19,541 average).

PORTERVILLE COLLEGE, PORTERVILLE
General Information State-supported, 2-year, coed college. Rural setting. *Awards:* A. *Entrance level for U.S. students:* Noncompetitive. *Enrollment:* 5,024 total including international students from 4 foreign countries. *Undergraduate faculty:* 140. *Library holdings:* 31,557 books, 297 current serial subscriptions. *Total majors:* 34.

PROFESSIONAL GOLFERS CAREER COLLEGE, TEMECULA
General Information Independent, 2-year, coed, primarily men's college. *Awards:* A. *Entrance level for U.S. students:* Difficulty N/R. *Enrollment:* 318 total including international students from 13 foreign countries. *Undergraduate faculty:* 23. *Library holdings:* 2,291 books, 45 current serial subscriptions, 115 audiovisual materials. *Expenses:* (2006–07) $9820; room only, $5200 (on campus).

QUALITY COLLEGE OF CULINARY CAREERS, FRESNO
General Information Proprietary, 2-year, coed college. *Awards:* A. *Entrance level for U.S. students:* Difficulty N/R. *Total majors:* 2.
Information for International Students Students can start in fall, winter, spring, or summer. *Application deadline:* Rolling. *Contact:* Admissions Office, Quality College of Culinary Careers, 1776 North Fine Avenue, Fresno, CA 93727. Telephone: 559-497-5050. Fax: 559-764-4454. E-mail: john.moore@qualitycollege.edu. URL: http://www.qualityschool.com/Culinary%20Arts/food.htm.
See In-Depth Description on page 153.

REEDLEY COLLEGE, REEDLEY
General Information State and locally supported, 2-year, coed college. Rural setting. *Awards:* A. *Entrance level for U.S. students:* Noncompetitive. *Enrollment:* 11,782 total (61% women) including 0.04% international students. *Undergraduate faculty:* 534. *Library holdings:* 36,000 books, 217 current serial subscriptions. *Total majors:* 39. *Expenses:* (2007–08) $4856.

RIVERSIDE COMMUNITY COLLEGE DISTRICT, RIVERSIDE
General Information State and locally supported, 2-year, coed college. Suburban setting. *Awards:* A. *Entrance level for U.S. students:* Noncompetitive. *Enrollment:* 30,709 total (57% women). *Undergraduate faculty:* 1,453. *Library holdings:* 101,243 books, 911 current serial subscriptions. *Total majors:* 22.
Information for International Students For fall 2006: 133 international students applied, 93 were accepted, 61 enrolled. Students can start in fall, winter, spring, or summer. Transfers accepted from institutions abroad. *Admission tests:* Required: TOEFL (minimum score: iBT 45; paper-based 450; computer-based 133; minimum score for ESL admission: iBT 45; paper-based 450; computer-based 133), ELS (minimum score: 109), IELTS , Eiken STEP. TOEFL can be waived under certain conditions. *Application deadline:* 6/1. *Expenses:* (2006–07) $4320. *Services:* International student adviser on campus. ESL program at cooperating institution. ESL program available during the academic year and the summer. Internships and employment opportunities (on-campus) available. *Contact:* Director, Center for International Students and Programs, Riverside Community College District, Center for International Students and Programs, 4800 Magnolia Avenue, Riverside, CA

92506. Telephone: 951-222-8160. Fax: 951-222-8376. E-mail: internationalcenter@rcc.edu. URL: http://www.rcc.edu.
See In-Depth Description on page 159.

SACRAMENTO CITY COLLEGE, SACRAMENTO
General Information State and locally supported, 2-year, coed college. Urban setting. *Awards:* A. *Entrance level for U.S. students:* Noncompetitive. *Enrollment:* 21,890 total. *Undergraduate faculty:* 554. *Library holdings:* 68,462 books, 415 current serial subscriptions. *Total majors:* 49.
Information for International Students For fall 2006: 203 international students enrolled. Students can start in fall or spring. Transfers accepted from institutions abroad. *Admission tests:* Required: TOEFL (minimum score: iBT 45; paper-based 450; computer-based 133; minimum score for ESL admission: iBT 45; paper-based 450; computer-based 133). Recommended: ELS, college assessment ESL/English and Essay and Math tests (for transfer in/visiting international students). TOEFL can be waived under certain conditions. *Application deadline:* 5/1. *Services:* International student adviser on campus. Full-time ESL program on campus. ESL program available during the academic year. Internships and employment opportunities (on-campus) available. *Contact:* International Admissions, Sacramento City College, SCC International Student Center (#P), 3835 Freeport Boulevard, Sacramento, CA 95822-1386. Telephone: 916-558-2486. Fax: 916-650-2909. E-mail: intlctr@scc.losrios.edu. URL: http://www.scc.losrios.edu.

SADDLEBACK COLLEGE, MISSION VIEJO
General Information State and locally supported, 2-year, coed college. Suburban setting. *Awards:* A. *Entrance level for U.S. students:* Noncompetitive. *Enrollment:* 18,351 total including 1% international students from 23 foreign countries. *Undergraduate faculty:* 754. *Library holdings:* 109,000 books, 132 current serial subscriptions. *Total majors:* 84.

SAINT MARY'S COLLEGE OF CALIFORNIA, MORAGA
General Information Independent Roman Catholic, coed institution. Suburban setting. *Awards:* B, M, D. *Entrance level for U.S. students:* Moderately difficult. *Enrollment:* 3,962 total; 2,835 undergraduates (63% women) including 2% international students from 28 foreign countries. *Faculty:* 539. *Library holdings:* 220,337 books, 15,000 current serial subscriptions, 5,670 audiovisual materials. *Total majors:* 69.
Information for International Students For fall 2006: 75 international students applied, 46 were accepted, 6 enrolled. Students can start in fall, winter, or spring. Transfers accepted from institutions abroad. *Admission tests:* Required: TOEFL (minimum score: iBT 71; paper-based 525; computer-based 199). TOEFL can be waived under certain conditions. *Application deadline:* 5/1. *Expenses:* (2006–07) $29,050; room and board, $10,566 (on campus); room only, $5926 (on campus). *Financial aid:* Non-need-based college/university scholarships/grants from institutional funds, tuition waivers, athletic awards, on-campus employment. For fall 2006 (estimated), 20 international students on campus received college administered financial aid ($34,494 average). *Housing:* Guaranteed. *Services:* International student adviser on campus. ESL program at cooperating institution. ESL program available during the academic year and the summer. Internships and employment opportunities (on-campus) available. *Contact:* Senior Assistant Director of Admission/Coordinator, Saint Mary's College of California, 1928 Saint Mary's Road, Moraga, CA 94556. Telephone: 925-631-4224. Fax: 925-376-7193. E-mail: ll4@stmarys-ca.edu. URL: http://www.stmarys-ca.edu.
See In-Depth Description on page 169.

THE SALVATION ARMY COLLEGE FOR OFFICER TRAINING AT CRESTMONT, RANCHO PALOS VERDES
General Information Independent religious, 2-year, coed college. Suburban setting. *Awards:* A. *Entrance level for U.S. students:* Noncompetitive. *Enrollment:* 27 total (52% women) including 7% international students from 1 foreign country. *Undergraduate faculty:* 35. *Library holdings:* 35,700 books, 125 current serial subscriptions. *Total majors:* 1. *Expenses:* (2006–07) $2350; room and board, $8250 (on campus).

SAMUEL MERRITT COLLEGE, OAKLAND
General Information Independent, coed, primarily women's institution. Urban setting. *Awards:* B, M, D, FP (bachelor's degree offered jointly with Saint Mary's College of California). *Entrance level for U.S. students:* Moderately difficult. *Enrollment:* 1,178 total; 403 undergraduates (88% women) including 0.3% international students from 1 foreign country. *Faculty:* 171. *Library holdings:*

Samuel Merritt College (continued)

36,995 books, 2,970 current serial subscriptions, 1,947 audiovisual materials. *Total majors:* 1. *Expenses:* (2006–07) $29,576; room only, $5903 (on campus).

SAN BERNARDINO VALLEY COLLEGE, SAN BERNARDINO

General Information State and locally supported, 2-year, coed college. *Awards:* A. *Entrance level for U.S. students:* Noncompetitive. *Enrollment:* 1,540 total. *Undergraduate faculty:* 375. *Library holdings:* 122,802 books, 657 current serial subscriptions. *Total majors:* 64.

Information for International Students For fall 2006: 10 international students applied, 10 were accepted, 5 enrolled. Students can start in fall, spring, or summer. Transfers accepted from institutions abroad. *Admission tests:* Required: TOEFL (minimum score: iBT 45; paper-based 450; computer-based 133; minimum score for ESL admission: iBT 45; paper-based 450; computer-based 133). TOEFL can be waived under certain conditions. *Application deadline:* 5/1. *Services:* International student adviser on campus. Part-time ESL program on campus. ESL program available during the academic year. Employment opportunities (on-campus) available. *Contact:* International Student Counselor, San Bernardino Valley College, 701 South Mount Vernon Avenue, San Bernardino, CA 92410. Telephone: 909-384-8980. Fax: 909-381-4368. E-mail: wwhitney@valleycollege.edu. URL: http://www.valleycollege.edu.

SAN DIEGO CITY COLLEGE, SAN DIEGO

General Information State and locally supported, 2-year, coed college. Urban setting. *Awards:* A. *Entrance level for U.S. students:* Noncompetitive. *Enrollment:* 15,475 total. *Undergraduate faculty:* 485. *Library holdings:* 73,000 books, 337 current serial subscriptions. *Total majors:* 68.

Information for International Students For fall 2006: 31 international students applied, 18 were accepted, 15 enrolled. Students can start in fall, winter, spring, or summer. *Admission tests:* Required: TOEFL (minimum score: iBT 61; paper-based 500; computer-based 173). *Application deadline:* 5/1. *Expenses:* (2007–08) $4872. *Financial aid:* Need-based college/university scholarships/grants from institutional funds, tuition waivers, loans from outside sources, on-campus employment. Non-need-based loans from outside sources. Forms required: institution's own financial aid form. *Services:* International student adviser on campus. Employment opportunities (on-campus) available. *Contact:* International Student Specialist/DSO, San Diego City College, 1313 Park Boulevard, San Diego, CA 92101. Telephone: 619-388-3476. Fax: 619-388-3505. E-mail: dmeza@sdccd.edu. URL: http://www.sdcity.edu.

SAN DIEGO MIRAMAR COLLEGE, SAN DIEGO

General Information State and locally supported, 2-year, coed college. Suburban setting. *Awards:* A. *Entrance level for U.S. students:* Noncompetitive. *Enrollment:* 8,080 total. *Undergraduate faculty:* 284. *Library holdings:* 19,301 books, 135 current serial subscriptions, 901 audiovisual materials. *Total majors:* 35.

SAN DIEGO STATE UNIVERSITY, SAN DIEGO

General Information State-supported, coed university. Urban setting. *Awards:* B, M, D. *Entrance level for U.S. students:* Moderately difficult. *Enrollment:* 34,305 total; 28,527 undergraduates (58% women) including 2% international students from 64 foreign countries. *Faculty:* 1,725. *Library holdings:* 1.3 million books, 8,245 current serial subscriptions. *Total majors:* 106.

Information for International Students For fall 2006: 556 international students applied, 228 were accepted, 120 enrolled. Students can start in fall. Transfers accepted from institutions abroad. *Admission tests:* Required: TOEFL (minimum score: iBT 80; paper-based 550; computer-based 213). Recommended: SAT/ACT required only from graduates of U.S. accredited high schools. TOEFL can be waived under certain conditions. *Application deadline:* 5/1. *Expenses:* (2006–07) $13,330; room and board, $10,093 (on campus). *Financial aid:* Need-based and non-need-based financial aid available. For fall 2006 (estimated), 60 international students on campus received college administered financial aid ($11,900 average). *Housing:* Available during summer. *Services:* International student adviser on campus. Full-time ESL program on campus. ESL program available during the academic year and the summer. Internships and employment opportunities (on-campus) available. *Contact:* International Student Advisor and Outreach Coordinator, San Diego State University, International Student Center, 5500 Campanile Drive, San Diego, CA 92182-5101. Telephone: 619-5940770. Fax: 619-5941973. E-mail: intl_admissions@sdsu.edu. URL: http://www.sdsu.edu.

See In-Depth Description on page 173.

SAN FRANCISCO ART INSTITUTE, SAN FRANCISCO

General Information Independent, coed institution. Urban setting. *Awards:* B, M. *Entrance level for U.S. students:* Moderately difficult. *Enrollment:* 652 total; 420 undergraduates (50% women) including 8% international students from 12 foreign countries. *Faculty:* 121. *Library holdings:* 35,500 books, 210 current serial subscriptions, 1,250 audiovisual materials. *Total majors:* 8.

Information for International Students For fall 2006: 59 international students enrolled. *Admission tests:* Required: TOEFL (minimum score: iBT 80). *Application deadline:* Rolling. *Expenses:* (2006–07) $27,235; room only, $7200 (on campus). *Financial aid:* Need-based loans from institutional funds. Non-need-based college/university scholarships/grants from institutional funds, loans from outside sources, on-campus employment. Forms required: institution's own financial aid form. For fall 2006 (estimated), 10 international students on campus received college administered financial aid ($17,980 average). *Services:* International student adviser on campus. Employment opportunities (on-campus) available. *Contact:* Director of Admissions, San Francisco Art Institute, 800 Chestnut Street, San Francisco, CA 94133. Telephone: 415-749-4500. Fax: 415-749-4592. E-mail: admissions@sfai.edu. URL: http://www.sfai.edu.

See In-Depth Description on page 174.

SAN FRANCISCO CONSERVATORY OF MUSIC, SAN FRANCISCO

General Information Independent, coed institution. Urban setting. *Awards:* B, M. *Entrance level for U.S. students:* Moderately difficult. *Enrollment:* 374 total; 220 undergraduates (52% women) including 26% international students from 19 foreign countries. *Faculty:* 104. *Library holdings:* 60,000 books, 80 current serial subscriptions, 15 audiovisual materials. *Total majors:* 7. *Expenses:* (2007–08) $29,980. *Financial aid:* Need-based financial aid available. Forms required: institution's own financial aid form, International Student's Financial Aid Application, International Student's Certification of Finances. 14 international students on campus received college administered financial aid ($12,707 average).

SAN FRANCISCO STATE UNIVERSITY, SAN FRANCISCO

General Information State-supported, coed institution. Urban setting. *Awards:* B, M, D. *Entrance level for U.S. students:* Moderately difficult. *Enrollment:* 29,628 total; 23,843 undergraduates (59% women) including 6% international students from 129 foreign countries. *Faculty:* 1,807. *Library holdings:* 1.2 million books, 15,644 current serial subscriptions, 192,862 audiovisual materials. *Total majors:* 91.

Information for International Students For fall 2006: 2056 international students applied, 490 were accepted, 368 enrolled. Students can start in fall or spring. Transfers accepted from institutions abroad. *Admission tests:* Required: TOEFL (minimum score: iBT 61; paper-based 500; computer-based 173). TOEFL can be waived under certain conditions. *Application deadline:* Rolling. *Expenses:* (2006–07) $13,336; room and board, $9544 (on campus); room only, $6202 (on campus). *Financial aid:* Non-need-based on-campus employment. *Services:* International student adviser on campus. Full-time ESL program on campus. ESL program available during the academic year and the summer. Internships and employment opportunities (on-campus and off-campus) available. *Contact:* Assistant Director, Office of International Programs, San Francisco State University, 1600 Holloway Avenue, San Francisco, CA 94132. Telephone: 415-338-1293. Fax: 415-338-6234. E-mail: oip@sfsu.edu. URL: http://www.sfsu.edu.

See In-Depth Description on page 175.

SAN JOAQUIN DELTA COLLEGE, STOCKTON

General Information District-supported, 2-year, coed college. Urban setting. *Awards:* A. *Entrance level for U.S. students:* Noncompetitive. *Enrollment:* 18,800 total including 1% international students. *Undergraduate faculty:* 633. *Library holdings:* 92,398 books, 605 current serial subscriptions. *Total majors:* 82. *Expenses:* (2007–08) $5790.

SAN JOSE STATE UNIVERSITY, SAN JOSE

General Information State-supported, coed institution. Urban setting. *Awards:* B, M. *Entrance level for U.S. students:* Difficulty N/R. *Enrollment:* 29,604 total; 22,521 undergraduates (51% women) including 3% international students. *Library holdings:* 1.8 million books, 35,390 current serial subscriptions, 32,270 audiovisual materials. *Total majors:* 89. *Expenses:* (2006–07) $13,466; room and board, $9096 (on campus); room only, $5640 (on campus). *Financial aid:* Need-based financial aid available. Non-need-based college/university scholarships/grants from institutional funds. For fall 2005, 52 international students on campus received college administered financial aid ($506 average).

SANTA BARBARA CITY COLLEGE, SANTA BARBARA

General Information State and locally supported, 2-year, coed college. Small town setting. *Awards:* A. *Entrance level for U.S. students:* Noncompetitive. *Enrollment:* 16,043 total (54% women) including 7% international students from 58 foreign countries. *Undergraduate faculty:* 751. *Library holdings:* 131,918 books, 6,832 current serial subscriptions, 40 audiovisual materials. *Total majors:* 79.

Information for International Students For fall 2006: 362 international students applied, 358 were accepted, 252 enrolled. Students can start in fall, spring, or summer. Transfers accepted from institutions abroad. *Admission tests:* TOEFL can be waived under certain conditions. *Application deadline:* 7/1. *Expenses:* (2007–08) $5243. *Services:* International student adviser on campus. Full-time ESL program on campus. ESL program available during the academic year and the summer. Internships and employment opportunities (on-campus) available. *Contact:* Administrative Assistant, Santa Barbara City College, 721 Cliff Drive, Santa Barbara, CA 93109-2394. Telephone: 805-965-0581 Ext. 2240. Fax: 805-965-0781. E-mail: flores@sbcc.edu. URL: http://www.sbcc.edu.

SANTA CLARA UNIVERSITY, SANTA CLARA

General Information Independent Roman Catholic (Jesuit), coed university. Suburban setting. *Awards:* B, M, D, FP. *Entrance level for U.S. students:* Moderately difficult. *Enrollment:* 7,952 total; 4,613 undergraduates (54% women) including 3% international students from 21 foreign countries. *Faculty:* 766. *Library holdings:* 786,360 books, 4,459 current serial subscriptions, 10,493 audiovisual materials. *Total majors:* 43. *Expenses:* (2006–07) $30,900; room and board, $10,380 (on campus).

SANTA MONICA COLLEGE, SANTA MONICA

General Information State and locally supported, 2-year, coed college. Urban setting. *Awards:* A. *Entrance level for U.S. students:* Noncompetitive. *Enrollment:* 24,497 total (54% women) including 14% international students from 101 foreign countries. *Undergraduate faculty:* 1,238. *Library holdings:* 101,317 books, 389 current serial subscriptions. *Total majors:* 64.

Information for International Students For fall 2006: 1600 international students applied, 896 were accepted. Students can start in fall, winter, spring, or summer. Transfers accepted from institutions abroad. *Admission tests:* Required: TOEFL (minimum score: paper-based 450; computer-based 133). TOEFL can be waived under certain conditions. *Application deadline:* Rolling. *Expenses:* (2006–07) $5494. *Financial aid:* Need-based and non-need-based financial aid available. *Services:* International student adviser on campus. Full-time ESL program on campus. ESL program available during the academic year. Internships and employment opportunities (on-campus and off-campus) available. *Contact:* Dean, International Education, Santa Monica College, Santa Monica, CA 90405. Telephone: 310-434-4217. Fax: 310-434-3651. E-mail: intled@smc.edu. URL: http://www.smc.edu.

See In-Depth Description on page 176.

SANTA ROSA JUNIOR COLLEGE, SANTA ROSA

General Information State and locally supported, 2-year, coed college. Urban setting. *Awards:* A. *Entrance level for U.S. students:* Noncompetitive. *Enrollment:* 25,031 total including 0.3% international students. *Undergraduate faculty:* 1,486. *Library holdings:* 123,068 books, 389 current serial subscriptions, 10,600 audiovisual materials. *Total majors:* 83.

Information for International Students For fall 2006: 44 international students applied, 34 were accepted, 20 enrolled. Students can start in fall, spring, or summer. *Admission tests:* Required: TOEFL (minimum score: iBT 53; paper-based 475; computer-based 153). *Application deadline:* 6/11. *Expenses:* (2007–08) $4660. *Financial aid:* Forms required: International Student's Certification of Finances. *Services:* International student adviser on campus. Employment opportunities (on-campus) available. *Contact:* Admissions Specialist, Admissions Office, Santa Rosa Junior College, 1501 Mendocino Avenue, Santa Rosa, CA 95401. Telephone: 707-524-1751. Fax: 707-527-4798. E-mail: khunt@santarosa.edu. URL: http://www.santarosa.edu.

SCRIPPS COLLEGE, CLAREMONT

General Information Independent, 4-year, women's college. Suburban setting. *Awards:* B. *Entrance level for U.S. students:* Very difficult. *Enrollment:* 890 total; 869 undergraduates including 1% international students from 6 foreign countries. *Undergraduate faculty:* 95. *Library holdings:* 2.5 million books, 35,033 current serial subscriptions, 3,578 audiovisual materials. *Total majors:* 57.

Information for International Students For fall 2006: 55 international students applied, 12 were accepted, 2 enrolled. Students can start in fall or spring. Transfers accepted from institutions abroad. *Admission tests:* Required: SAT or ACT, TOEFL (minimum score: paper-based 600; computer-based 250; minimum score for ESL admission: paper-based 600; computer-based 250). Recommended: SAT Subject Tests. *Application deadline:* 1/1. *Expenses:* (2006–07) $33,700; room and board, $10,100 (on campus); room only, $5400 (on campus). *Financial aid:* Need-based college/university scholarships/grants from institutional funds, loans from institutional funds. Non-need-based college/university scholarships/grants from institutional funds, loans from institutional funds. Forms required: International Student's Financial Aid Application, International Student's Certification of Finances. For fall 2006 (estimated), 3 international students on campus received college administered financial aid ($15,533 average). *Housing:* Guaranteed. *Services:* International student adviser on campus. ESL program at cooperating institution. ESL program available during the summer. Internships and employment opportunities (on-campus and off-campus) available. *Contact:* Dean of Admission, Office of Admissions, Scripps College, 1030 Columbia Avenue, PB 1265, Claremont, CA 91711. Telephone: 909-621-8149. Fax: 909-607-7508. E-mail: admission@scrippscollege.edu. URL: http://www.scrippscollege.edu.

SHASTA BIBLE COLLEGE, REDDING

General Information Independent nondenominational, coed institution. Small town setting. *Awards:* A, B, M. *Entrance level for U.S. students:* Noncompetitive. *Enrollment:* 109 total; 94 undergraduates (52% women) including 4% international students from 3 foreign countries. *Faculty:* 34. *Library holdings:* 30,321 books, 103 current serial subscriptions. *Total majors:* 3. *Expenses:* (2007–08) $7580; room only, $1650 (on campus). *Financial aid:* Need-based on-campus employment. Non-need-based on-campus employment.

SIERRA COLLEGE, ROCKLIN

General Information State-supported, 2-year, coed college. Suburban setting. *Awards:* A. *Entrance level for U.S. students:* Noncompetitive. *Enrollment:* 19,416 total (57% women) including 1% international students. *Undergraduate faculty:* 870. *Library holdings:* 69,879 books, 189 current serial subscriptions. *Total majors:* 51.

Information for International Students For fall 2006: 150 international students applied, 120 were accepted, 71 enrolled. Students can start in fall, spring, or summer. Transfers accepted from institutions abroad. *Admission tests:* Required: TOEFL (minimum score: iBT 45; paper-based 450; computer-based 133; minimum score for ESL admission: iBT 45; paper-based 450; computer-based 133). TOEFL can be waived under certain conditions. *Application deadline:* 7/1. *Expenses:* (2006–07) $5100. *Services:* International student adviser on campus. Full-time ESL program on campus. ESL program available during the academic year. Internships and employment opportunities (on-campus) available. *Contact:* International Students Office, Sierra College, 5000 Rocklin Road, Rocklin, CA 95677. Telephone: 916-789-2903. Fax: 916-789-2922. E-mail: internationalstudents@sierracollege.edu. URL: http://www.sierracollege.edu.

See In-Depth Description on page 185.

SIMPSON UNIVERSITY, REDDING

General Information Independent, coed institution, affiliated with The Christian and Missionary Alliance. Suburban setting. *Awards:* A, B, M. *Entrance level for U.S. students:* Moderately difficult. *Enrollment:* 1,015 total; 862 undergraduates (64% women) including 1% international students from 5 foreign countries. *Faculty:* 104. *Library holdings:* 116,871 books, 12,235 current serial subscriptions, 2,548 audiovisual materials. *Total majors:* 20. *Expenses:* (2007–08) $18,600; room and board, $6400 (on campus). *Financial aid:* Need-based and non-need-based financial aid available. Forms required: institution's own financial aid form. For fall 2005, 12 international students on campus received college administered financial aid ($12,500 average).

SONOMA STATE UNIVERSITY, ROHNERT PARK

General Information State-supported, coed institution. Small town setting. *Awards:* B, M. *Entrance level for U.S. students:* Moderately difficult. *Enrollment:* 7,749 total; 6,599 undergraduates (63% women) including 1% international students from 29 foreign countries. *Faculty:* 542. *Library holdings:* 636,613 books, 21,115 current serial subscriptions. *Total majors:* 64. *Expenses:* (2006–07) $13,818.

SOUTHERN CALIFORNIA INSTITUTE OF ARCHITECTURE, LOS ANGELES

General Information Independent, coed institution. Urban setting. *Awards:* B, M, FP. *Entrance level for U.S. students:*

Southern California Institute of Architecture (continued)

Moderately difficult. *Enrollment:* 438 total; 232 undergraduates (32% women) including 16% international students from 18 foreign countries. *Faculty:* 80. *Library holdings:* 30,000 books, 109 current serial subscriptions. *Total majors:* 1.

Information for International Students For fall 2006: 176 international students applied, 115 were accepted, 67 enrolled. Transfers accepted from institutions abroad. *Admission tests:* Required: TOEFL (minimum score: iBT 83; paper-based 550; computer-based 250; minimum score for ESL admission: iBT 83; paper-based 550; computer-based 250). TOEFL can be waived under certain conditions. *Application deadline:* 5/1. *Expenses:* (2007–08) $10,696. *Financial aid:* Need-based college/university scholarships/grants from institutional funds, tuition waivers. Non-need-based loans from outside sources, on-campus employment. Forms required: institution's own financial aid form, International Student's Financial Aid Application, International Student's Certification of Finances, I-20 Form (certificate of Eligibility for Nonimmigrant Student Status). For fall 2005, 8 international students on campus received college administered financial aid ($31,000 average). *Services:* International student adviser on campus. Employment opportunities (on-campus) available. *Contact:* Director of Admissions, Southern California Institute of Architecture, 960 East Third Street, Los Angeles, CA 90013. Telephone: 213-356-5321. Fax: 213-613-2260. E-mail: jj@sciarc.edu. URL: http://www.sciarc.edu.

STANFORD UNIVERSITY, STANFORD

General Information Independent, coed university. Suburban setting. *Awards:* B, M, D, FP. *Entrance level for U.S. students:* Most difficult. *Enrollment:* 17,747 total; 6,422 undergraduates (48% women) including 6% international students from 68 foreign countries. *Faculty:* 1,041. *Library holdings:* 8.2 million books, 75,000 current serial subscriptions, 1.5 million audiovisual materials. *Total majors:* 68.

Information for International Students For fall 2006: 96 international students enrolled. Students can start in fall. Transfers accepted from institutions abroad. *Admission tests:* Required: SAT or ACT. Recommended: SAT Subject Tests, TOEFL. *Application deadline:* 1/1. *Expenses:* (2006–07) $32,994; room and board, $10,367 (on campus); room only, $5571 (on campus). *Financial aid:* Need-based college/university scholarships/grants from institutional funds, loans from institutional funds, loans from outside sources, on-campus employment. Non-need-based athletic awards, loans from institutional funds, loans from outside sources. Forms required: International Student's Financial Aid Application, International Student's Certification of Finances. International transfer students are eligible to apply for aid. For fall 2005, 196 international students on campus received college administered financial aid ($28,080 average). *Housing:* Guaranteed, also available during summer. *Services:* International student adviser on campus. Internships and employment opportunities (on-campus) available. *Contact:* Coordinator of International Admission, Office of Undergraduate Admission, Stanford University, Office of Undergraduate Admission, Montag Hall - 355 Galvez Street, Stanford, CA 94305-3005. Telephone: 650-723-2091. Fax: 650-725-2846. E-mail: intl.admission@stanford.edu. URL: http://www.stanford.edu.

THOMAS AQUINAS COLLEGE, SANTA PAULA

General Information Independent Roman Catholic, 4-year, coed college. Rural setting. *Awards:* B. *Entrance level for U.S. students:* Very difficult. *Enrollment:* 351 total (50% women) including 8% international students from 8 foreign countries. *Undergraduate faculty:* 37. *Library holdings:* 62,000 books, 85 current serial subscriptions. *Total majors:* 4.

Information for International Students For fall 2006: 35 international students enrolled. Students can start in fall. *Admission tests:* Required: SAT. Recommended: TOEFL (minimum score: paper-based 550; computer-based 213). *Application deadline:* Rolling. *Expenses:* (2007–08) $20,400; room and board, $6600 (on campus). *Financial aid:* Need-based college/university scholarships/grants from institutional funds, on-campus employment. Forms required: institution's own financial aid form, International Student's Financial Aid Application, income tax returns. For fall 2006 (estimated), 23 international students on campus received college administered financial aid ($16,937 average). *Housing:* Guaranteed. *Contact:* Director of Admission, Thomas Aquinas College, 10000 North Ojai Road, Santa Paula, CA 93060. Telephone: 805-525-4417. Fax: 805-525-9342. E-mail: admissions@thomasaquinas.edu. URL: http://www.thomasaquinas.edu.

UNIVERSITY OF CALIFORNIA, BERKELEY, BERKELEY

General Information State-supported, coed university. Urban setting. *Awards:* B, M, D, FP. *Entrance level for U.S. students:* Very

difficult. *Enrollment:* 33,933 total; 23,863 undergraduates (54% women) including 3% international students from 87 foreign countries. *Faculty:* 2,026. *Library holdings:* 15.2 million books, 192,030 current serial subscriptions, 125,734 audiovisual materials. *Total majors:* 93. *Expenses:* (2006–07) $25,338; room and board, $13,074 (on campus). *Financial aid:* Need-based and non-need-based financial aid available.

UNIVERSITY OF CALIFORNIA, DAVIS, DAVIS

General Information State-supported, coed university. Suburban setting. *Awards:* B, M, D, FP. *Entrance level for U.S. students:* Moderately difficult. *Enrollment:* 29,628 total; 23,458 undergraduates (55% women) including 2% international students from 101 foreign countries. *Faculty:* 1,888. *Library holdings:* 4.4 million books, 44,020 current serial subscriptions, 14,944 audiovisual materials. *Total majors:* 83. *Expenses:* (2006–07) $25,761; room and board, $11,354 (on campus). *Financial aid:* Need-based and non-need-based financial aid available. Forms required: FAFSA. For fall 2005, 47 international students on campus received college administered financial aid ($11,356 average).

UNIVERSITY OF CALIFORNIA, IRVINE, IRVINE

General Information State-supported, coed university. Suburban setting. *Awards:* B, M, D, FP. *Entrance level for U.S. students:* Difficulty N/R. *Enrollment:* 25,229 total; 20,719 undergraduates (51% women) including 2% international students. *Faculty:* 1,925. *Total majors:* 66. *Expenses:* (2006–07) $24,825; room and board, $9815 (on campus). *Financial aid:* Non-need-based fee waivers.

UNIVERSITY OF CALIFORNIA, LOS ANGELES, LOS ANGELES

General Information State-supported, coed university. Urban setting. *Awards:* B, M, D, FP. *Entrance level for U.S. students:* Very difficult. *Enrollment:* 38,218 total; 25,432 undergraduates (56% women) including 4% international students from 59 foreign countries. *Faculty:* 2,505. *Library holdings:* 8.2 million books, 77,509 current serial subscriptions, 291,664 audiovisual materials. *Total majors:* 150. *Expenses:* (2006–07) $25,970; room and board, $11,141 (on campus). *Financial aid:* Need-based college/university scholarships/grants from institutional funds, loans from outside sources, on-campus employment. Non-need-based loans from outside sources. Forms required: International Student's Financial Aid Application, International Student's Certification of Finances. 156 international students on campus received college administered financial aid ($10,716 average).

UNIVERSITY OF CALIFORNIA, RIVERSIDE, RIVERSIDE

General Information State-supported, coed university. Urban setting. *Awards:* B, M, D. *Entrance level for U.S. students:* Very difficult. *Enrollment:* 16,875 total; 14,792 undergraduates (52% women) including 2% international students from 26 foreign countries. *Faculty:* 857. *Library holdings:* 2.4 million books, 29,941 current serial subscriptions, 27,313 audiovisual materials. *Total majors:* 59. *Expenses:* (2006–07) $25,275; room and board, $10,200 (on campus).

UNIVERSITY OF CALIFORNIA, SANTA BARBARA, SANTA BARBARA

General Information State-supported, coed university. Suburban setting. *Awards:* B, M, D. *Entrance level for U.S. students:* Very difficult. *Enrollment:* 21,062 total; 18,212 undergraduates (55% women) including 1% international students from 112 foreign countries. *Faculty:* 1,067. *Library holdings:* 3.3 million books, 36,902 current serial subscriptions, 125,324 audiovisual materials. *Total majors:* 71. *Expenses:* (2006–07) $25,961; room and board, $11,178 (on campus); room only, $8798 (on campus).

UNIVERSITY OF CALIFORNIA, SANTA CRUZ, SANTA CRUZ

General Information State-supported, coed university. Small town setting. *Awards:* B, M, D. *Entrance level for U.S. students:* Very difficult. *Enrollment:* 15,364 total; 13,961 undergraduates (53% women) including 1% international students from 12 foreign countries. *Faculty:* 759. *Library holdings:* 1.5 million books, 25,486 current serial subscriptions, 36,585 audiovisual materials. *Total majors:* 76.

Information for International Students For fall 2006: 773 international students applied, 492 were accepted, 104 enrolled. Students can start in fall. Transfers accepted from institutions abroad. *Admission tests:* Required: TOEFL (minimum score: paper-based 550; computer-based 220). TOEFL can be waived under certain conditions. *Application deadline:* 11/30. *Expenses:* (2006–07) $26,130; room and board, $11,805 (on campus). *Housing:*

Guaranteed. *Services:* International student adviser on campus. ESL program at cooperating institution. ESL program available during the academic year and the summer. Internships and employment opportunities (on-campus) available. *Contact:* International Admissions Specialist, Office of Admissions, University of California, Santa Cruz, 1156 High Street, Office of Admissions, Santa Cruz, CA 95064. Telephone: 831-459-2131. Fax: 831-459-4163. E-mail: admissions@ucsu.edu. URL: http://www.ucsc.edu.

UNIVERSITY OF LA VERNE, LA VERNE
General Information Independent, coed university. Suburban setting. *Awards:* A, B, M, D, FP (also offers continuing education program with significant enrollment not reflected in profile). *Entrance level for U.S. students:* Moderately difficult. *Enrollment:* 3,876 total; 1,685 undergraduates (64% women) including 2% international students from 5 foreign countries. *Faculty:* 402. *Library holdings:* 195,488 books, 531,006 current serial subscriptions, 1,720 audiovisual materials. *Total majors:* 48.
Information for International Students For fall 2006: 92 international students applied, 58 were accepted, 30 enrolled. Students can start in fall or spring. Transfers accepted from institutions abroad. *Admission tests:* Required: TOEFL (minimum score: paper-based 500; computer-based 173; minimum score for ESL admission: paper-based 500, computer-based 173), English Placement Test. TOEFL can be waived under certain conditions. *Application deadline:* Rolling. *Expenses:* (2007–08) $25,590; room and board, $9750 (on campus); room only, $5100 (on campus). *Financial aid:* Non-need-based college/university scholarships/grants from institutional funds. Forms required: International Student's Certification of Finances, bank statement, financial statement. International transfer students are eligible to apply for aid. *Housing:* Guaranteed. *Services:* International student adviser on campus. Part-time ESL program on campus. ESL program available during the academic year and the summer. Internships and employment opportunities (on-campus) available. *Contact:* Associate Director, Undergraduate Admissions, University of La Verne, 1950 Third Street, La Verne, CA 91750-4443. Telephone: 909-593-3511 Ext. 4029. Fax: 909-392-2714. E-mail: mckinney@ulv.edu. URL: http://www.ulv.edu.

UNIVERSITY OF PHOENIX–BAY AREA CAMPUS, PLEASANTON
General Information Proprietary, coed institution. Urban setting. *Awards:* A, B, M. *Entrance level for U.S. students:* Noncompetitive. *Enrollment:* 3,139 total; 2,249 undergraduates (61% women) including 11% international students. *Faculty:* 1,426. *Library holdings:* 1,759 books, 692 current serial subscriptions. *Total majors:* 24. *Expenses:* (2006–07) $13,390.

UNIVERSITY OF PHOENIX–CENTRAL VALLEY CAMPUS, FRESNO
General Information Proprietary, coed institution. Urban setting. *Awards:* B, M. *Entrance level for U.S. students:* Noncompetitive. *Enrollment:* 2,145 total; 1,780 undergraduates (68% women) including 4% international students. *Faculty:* 652. *Library holdings:* 1,759 books, 692 current serial subscriptions. *Total majors:* 8. *Expenses:* (2006–07) $12,350.

UNIVERSITY OF PHOENIX–SACRAMENTO VALLEY CAMPUS, SACRAMENTO
General Information Proprietary, coed institution. Urban setting. *Awards:* B, M. *Entrance level for U.S. students:* Noncompetitive. *Enrollment:* 4,585 total; 3,480 undergraduates (66% women) including 15% international students. *Faculty:* 1,303. *Library holdings:* 1,759 books, 692 current serial subscriptions. *Total majors:* 28. *Expenses:* (2006–07) $12,900.

UNIVERSITY OF PHOENIX–SAN DIEGO CAMPUS, SAN DIEGO
General Information Proprietary, coed institution. Urban setting. *Awards:* B, M. *Entrance level for U.S. students:* Noncompetitive. *Enrollment:* 3,781 total; 2,780 undergraduates (55% women) including 10% international students. *Faculty:* 978. *Library holdings:* 1,759 books, 692 current serial subscriptions. *Total majors:* 12. *Expenses:* (2006–07) $12,450.

UNIVERSITY OF PHOENIX–SOUTHERN CALIFORNIA CAMPUS, COSTA MESA
General Information Proprietary, coed institution. Urban setting. *Awards:* B, M. *Entrance level for U.S. students:* Noncompetitive. *Enrollment:* 14,760 total; 11,166 undergraduates (65% women) including 9% international students. *Faculty:* 3,228. *Library holdings:* 1,759 books, 692 current serial subscriptions. *Total majors:* 11. *Expenses:* (2006–07) $13,710.

UNIVERSITY OF REDLANDS, REDLANDS
General Information Independent, coed institution. Small town setting. *Awards:* B, M. *Entrance level for U.S. students:* Moderately difficult. *Enrollment:* 2,407 total; 2,313 undergraduates (57% women) including 2% international students from 10 foreign countries. *Faculty:* 316. *Library holdings:* 268,387 books, 11,800 current serial subscriptions, 7,134 audiovisual materials. *Total majors:* 42. *Expenses:* (2006–07) $28,776; room and board, $9360 (on campus); room only, $5221 (on campus). *Financial aid:* Need-based college/university scholarships/grants from institutional funds. Non-need-based college/university scholarships/grants from institutional funds. Forms required: International Student's Certification of Finances. For fall 2006 (estimated), 8 international students on campus received college administered financial aid ($12,342 average).

UNIVERSITY OF SAN DIEGO, SAN DIEGO
General Information Independent Roman Catholic, coed university. Urban setting. *Awards:* B, M, D, FP. *Entrance level for U.S. students:* Very difficult. *Enrollment:* 7,483 total; 4,962 undergraduates (60% women) including 2% international students. *Faculty:* 723. *Library holdings:* 714,082 books, 10,451 current serial subscriptions. *Total majors:* 35.
Information for International Students For fall 2006: 390 international students applied, 149 were accepted, 31 enrolled. Students can start in fall or spring. Transfers accepted from institutions abroad. *Admission tests:* Required: SAT or ACT, TOEFL (minimum score: iBT 78; paper-based 550; computer-based 213). Recommended: SAT. TOEFL can be waived under certain conditions. *Application deadline:* 1/15. *Expenses:* (2007–08) $32,564; room and board, $10,960 (on campus). *Financial aid:* Non-need-based athletic awards, loans from outside sources, on-campus employment. *Housing:* Guaranteed. *Services:* International student adviser on campus. Full-time ESL program on campus. ESL program available during the academic year and the summer. Internships and employment opportunities (on-campus) available. *Contact:* Assistant Director of International Admissions, University of San Diego, Office of Admissions, 5998 Alcala Park, San Diego, CA 92110-2492. Telephone: 619-260-4506. Fax: 619-260-6836. E-mail: msmalloy@SanDiego.edu. URL: http://www.sandiego.edu.

UNIVERSITY OF SAN FRANCISCO, SAN FRANCISCO
General Information Independent Roman Catholic (Jesuit), coed university. Urban setting. *Awards:* B, M, D, FP. *Entrance level for U.S. students:* Moderately difficult. *Enrollment:* 8,549 total; 5,384 undergraduates (64% women) including 7% international students from 62 foreign countries. *Faculty:* 871. *Library holdings:* 1.1 million books, 5,560 current serial subscriptions. *Total majors:* 64.
Information for International Students For fall 2006: 395 international students applied, 39 enrolled. Students can start in fall or spring. Transfers accepted from institutions abroad. *Admission tests:* Required: TOEFL (minimum score: paper-based 550; computer-based 213; minimum score for ESL admission: paper-based 460; computer-based 140). Recommended: SAT or ACT. TOEFL can be waived under certain conditions. *Application deadline:* 2/1. *Expenses:* (2007–08) $31,180; room and board, $10,730 (on campus); room only, $7230 (on campus). *Financial aid:* Non-need-based athletic awards. *Services:* International student adviser on campus. Full-time and part-time ESL programs on campus. ESL program available during the academic year and the summer. Employment opportunities (on-campus) available. *Contact:* Director of International Admission, University of San Francisco, 2130 Fulton Street, San Francisco, CA 94117. Telephone: 415-422-6563. Fax: 415-422-2217. URL: http://www.usfca.edu.

See In-Depth Description on page 223.

UNIVERSITY OF SOUTHERN CALIFORNIA, LOS ANGELES
General Information Independent, coed university. Urban setting. *Awards:* B, M, D, FP. *Entrance level for U.S. students:* Most difficult. *Enrollment:* 33,389 total; 16,729 undergraduates (50% women) including 9% international students from 114 foreign countries. *Faculty:* 2,570. *Library holdings:* 4 million books, 60,718 current serial subscriptions, 59,824 audiovisual materials. *Total majors:* 111. *Expenses:* (2006–07) $33,892; room and board, $10,144 (on campus); room only, $5580 (on campus). *Financial aid:* Non-need-based college/university scholarships/grants from institutional funds, loans from outside sources. For fall 2005, 225 international students on campus received college administered financial aid ($23,669 average).

UNIVERSITY OF THE PACIFIC, STOCKTON
General Information Independent, coed university. Suburban setting. *Awards:* B, M, D, FP. *Entrance level for U.S. students:*

University of the Pacific (continued)

Moderately difficult. *Enrollment:* 6,251 total; 3,535 undergraduates (56% women) including 3% international students from 18 foreign countries. *Faculty:* 656. *Library holdings:* 373,759 books, 1,826 current serial subscriptions, 10,755 audiovisual materials. *Total majors:* 55. *Expenses:* (2006–07) $27,350; room and board, $8700 (on campus); room only, $4350 (on campus).

VANGUARD UNIVERSITY OF SOUTHERN CALIFORNIA, COSTA MESA

General Information Independent, coed institution, affiliated with Assemblies of God. Suburban setting. *Awards:* B, M. *Entrance level for U.S. students:* Moderately difficult. *Enrollment:* 2,146 total; 1,854 undergraduates (63% women) including 1% international students from 17 foreign countries. *Faculty:* 204. *Library holdings:* 157,500 books, 2,000 current serial subscriptions, 6,900 audiovisual materials. *Total majors:* 37.

Information for International Students For fall 2006: 10 international students applied, 7 were accepted, 5 enrolled. Students can start in fall or spring. Transfers accepted from institutions abroad. *Admission tests:* Required: TOEFL (minimum score: paper-based 550; computer-based 213). Recommended: SAT or ACT. TOEFL can be waived under certain conditions. *Application deadline:* 7/1. *Expenses:* (2006–07) $21,564; room only, $3568 (on campus). *Housing:* Guaranteed, also available during summer. *Services:* International student adviser on campus. Internships and employment opportunities (on-campus) available. *Contact:* Director of Undergraduate Admissions, Vanguard University of Southern California, 55 Fair Drive, Costa Mesa, CA 92626. Telephone: 714-556-3610 Ext. 4102. Fax: 714-966-5471. E-mail: awolf@vanguard.edu. URL: http://www.vanguard.edu.

VENTURA COLLEGE, VENTURA

General Information State and locally supported, 2-year, coed college. Suburban setting. *Awards:* A. *Entrance level for U.S. students:* Noncompetitive. *Enrollment:* 11,757 total (58% women) including 1% international students. *Undergraduate faculty:* 504. *Library holdings:* 63,529 books, 341 current serial subscriptions. *Total majors:* 29. *Expenses:* (2006–07) $5466. *Financial aid:* Forms required: institution's own financial aid form.

WEST HILLS COMMUNITY COLLEGE, COALINGA

General Information State-supported, 2-year, coed college. Small town setting. *Awards:* A. *Entrance level for U.S. students:* Noncompetitive. *Enrollment:* 6,088 total (61% women) including 2% international students from 5 foreign countries. *Undergraduate faculty:* 263. *Library holdings:* 32,000 books, 210 current serial subscriptions. *Total majors:* 29. *Expenses:* (2007–08) $4320; room and board, $5296 (on campus).

WESTMONT COLLEGE, SANTA BARBARA

General Information Independent nondenominational, 4-year, coed college. Suburban setting. *Awards:* B. *Entrance level for U.S. students:* Moderately difficult. *Enrollment:* 1,337 total; 1,332 undergraduates (60% women) including 1% international students from 10 foreign countries. *Undergraduate faculty:* 142. *Library holdings:* 174,246 books, 380 current serial subscriptions, 11,375 audiovisual materials. *Total majors:* 43.

Information for International Students For fall 2006: 32 international students applied, 15 were accepted, 1 enrolled. Students can start in fall, spring, or summer. Transfers accepted from institutions abroad. *Admission tests:* Required: SAT or ACT, TOEFL (minimum score: paper-based 560; computer-based 220), ELS. Recommended: SAT Subject Tests. TOEFL can be waived under certain conditions. *Application deadline:* 2/15. *Expenses:* (2006–07) $29,470; room and board, $9232 (on campus); room only, $5672 (on campus). *Financial aid:* Need-based college/university scholarships/grants from institutional funds, athletic awards. Non-need-based college/university scholarships/grants from institutional funds, athletic awards. International transfer students are eligible to apply for aid. For fall 2006 (estimated), 8 international students on campus received college administered financial aid ($12,557 average). *Housing:* Guaranteed. *Services:* International student adviser on campus. Internships and employment opportunities (on-campus) available. *Contact:* International Student Advisor, Westmont College, 955 La Paz Road, Santa Barbara, CA 93108-1089. Telephone: 805-565-6226. Fax: 805-565-6234. E-mail: slyon@westmont.edu. URL: http://www.westmont.edu.

WEST VALLEY COLLEGE, SARATOGA

General Information State and locally supported, 2-year, coed college. Small town setting. *Awards:* A. *Entrance level for U.S. students:* Noncompetitive. *Enrollment:* 11,000 total including

international students from 20 foreign countries. *Undergraduate faculty:* 560. *Library holdings:* 82,959 books, 491 current serial subscriptions. *Total majors:* 40.

Information for International Students For fall 2006: 15 international students applied, 14 were accepted, 14 enrolled. Students can start in fall and spring. Transfers accepted from institutions abroad. *Admission tests:* Required: TOEFL (minimum score: iBT 61; paper-based 500; computer-based 173; minimum score for ESL admission: iBT 61; paper-based 500; computer-based 173), STEP Eiken Pre-1 level. TOEFL can be waived under certain conditions. *Application deadline:* 5/7. *Services:* International student adviser on campus. Part-time ESL program on campus. ESL program available during the academic year and the summer. Employment opportunities (on-campus) available. *Contact:* International Student Counselor, West Valley College, 14000 Fruitvale Avenue, Saratoga, CA 95070-5698. Telephone: 408-741-2694. Fax: 408-741-4076. E-mail: sara_patterson@westvalley.edu. URL: http://www.westvalley.edu.

WESTWOOD COLLEGE–ANAHEIM, ANAHEIM

General Information Proprietary, primarily 2-year, coed college. Suburban setting. *Awards:* A, B. *Entrance level for U.S. students:* Difficulty N/R. *Enrollment:* 674 total (23% women) including 0.1% international students. *Undergraduate faculty:* 52. *Total majors:* 13.

WESTWOOD COLLEGE–SOUTH BAY CAMPUS, LONG BEACH

General Information Proprietary, primarily 2-year, coed college. Urban setting. *Awards:* A, B. *Entrance level for U.S. students:* Moderately difficult. *Enrollment:* 265 total (34% women) including 0.4% international students. *Undergraduate faculty:* 19. *Total majors:* 8.

WHITTIER COLLEGE, WHITTIER

General Information Independent, coed institution. Suburban setting. *Awards:* B, M, FP. *Entrance level for U.S. students:* Moderately difficult. *Enrollment:* 1,307 total (57% women) including 4% international students from 20 foreign countries. *Faculty:* 127. *Library holdings:* 225,337 books, 1,357 current serial subscriptions. *Total majors:* 25. *Expenses:* (2006–07) $28,206; room and board, $8542 (on campus). *Financial aid:* Non-need-based college/university scholarships/grants from institutional funds, loans from institutional funds, on-campus employment. Forms required: International Student's Certification of Finances. For fall 2005, 17 international students on campus received college administered financial aid ($8020 average).

WOODBURY UNIVERSITY, BURBANK

General Information Independent, coed institution. Suburban setting. *Awards:* B, M. *Entrance level for U.S. students:* Moderately difficult. *Enrollment:* 1,485 total; 1,310 undergraduates (56% women) including 6% international students from 39 foreign countries. *Faculty:* 237. *Library holdings:* 69,515 books, 363 current serial subscriptions, 2,035 audiovisual materials. *Total majors:* 17.

Information for International Students For fall 2006: 31 international students applied, 22 were accepted, 18 enrolled. Students can start in fall, spring, or summer. Transfers accepted from institutions abroad. *Admission tests:* Required: SAT or ACT, TOEFL (minimum score: paper-based 500; computer-based 173). *Application deadline:* Rolling. *Expenses:* (2006–07) $23,572; room and board, $8104 (on campus); room only, $4952 (on campus). *Housing:* Available during summer. Internships and employment opportunities (on-campus) available. *Contact:* Director of Admissions, Woodbury University, 7500 Glenoaks Boulevard, Burbank, CA 91510-7846. Telephone: 818-767-0888 Ext. 221. Fax: 818-767-7520. E-mail: admissions@woodbury.edu. URL: http://www.woodbury.edu.

WYOTECH, FREMONT

General Information Proprietary, 2-year, coed, primarily men's college. Urban setting. *Awards:* A. *Entrance level for U.S. students:* Difficulty N/R. *Enrollment:* 1,554 total including 0.1% international students. *Undergraduate faculty:* 62. *Library holdings:* 1,000 audiovisual materials. *Total majors:* 3. *Expenses:* (2007–08) $25,066.

COLORADO

ADAMS STATE COLLEGE, ALAMOSA

General Information State-supported, coed institution. Small town setting. *Awards:* A, B, M. *Entrance level for U.S. students:* Moderately difficult. *Enrollment:* 4,899 total; 2,308 undergraduates (57% women) including 0.05% international students from 2 foreign countries. *Faculty:* 217. *Library holdings:* 469,783 books, 19,979 current serial subscriptions, 2,576 audiovisual materials. *Total majors:* 31. *Expenses:* (2006–07) $9351; room and board, $6160 (on campus); room only, $3290 (on campus). *Financial aid:* Non-need financial aid available. Forms required: institutional scholarship application form.

AIMS COMMUNITY COLLEGE, GREELEY

General Information District-supported, 2-year, coed college. Urban setting. *Awards:* A. *Entrance level for U.S. students:* Noncompetitive. *Enrollment:* 5,098 total (55% women). *Undergraduate faculty:* 321. *Library holdings:* 39,129 books, 258 current serial subscriptions. *Total majors:* 18.

Information for International Students For fall 2006: 50 international students applied, 50 were accepted, 35 enrolled. Students can start in fall, spring, or summer. Transfers accepted from institutions abroad. *Admission tests:* Recommended: TOEFL (minimum score: paper-based 500; computer-based 173; minimum score for ESL admission: paper-based 500; computer-based 173), ELS. TOEFL can be waived under certain conditions. *Application deadline:* 8/13. *Financial aid:* Need-based and non-need-based financial aid available. *Services:* International student adviser on campus. Full-time and part-time ESL programs on campus. ESL program available during the academic year and the summer. *Contact:* Director of International Education, Aims Community College, 5401 West 20th Street, Greeley, CO 80634. Telephone: 970-339-6675. Fax: 970-506-6947. E-mail: alan.hendrickson@aims.edu. URL: http://www.aims.edu.

ARAPAHOE COMMUNITY COLLEGE, LITTLETON

General Information State-supported, 2-year, coed college. Suburban setting. *Awards:* A. *Entrance level for U.S. students:* Noncompetitive. *Enrollment:* 7,560 total (63% women) including 1% international students from 35 foreign countries. *Undergraduate faculty:* 414. *Library holdings:* 45,000 books, 441 current serial subscriptions. *Total majors:* 48. *Expenses:* (2006–07) $8081.

THE ART INSTITUTE OF COLORADO, DENVER

General Information Proprietary, 4-year, coed college. Urban setting. *Awards:* A, B. *Entrance level for U.S. students:* Minimally difficult. *Enrollment:* 2,765 total (51% women) including international students from 5 foreign countries. *Undergraduate faculty:* 137. *Library holdings:* 13,100 books, 200 current serial subscriptions, 500 audiovisual materials. *Total majors:* 10.

Information for International Students For fall 2006: 9 international students applied, 9 were accepted, 9 enrolled. Students can start in fall, winter, spring, or summer. Transfers accepted from institutions abroad. *Admission tests:* Required: TOEFL (minimum score: paper-based 500; computer-based 173; minimum score for ESL admission: paper-based 500; computer-based 173), ELS (minimum score: 109). Recommended: MTELP. TOEFL can be waived under certain conditions. *Application deadline:* Rolling. *Financial aid:* Need-based college/university scholarships/grants from institutional funds, tuition waivers, loans from institutional funds, loans from outside sources, on-campus employment. Non-need-based college/university scholarships/grants from institutional funds, tuition waivers, loans from outside sources. *Housing:* Available during summer. *Services:* International student adviser on campus. ESL program at cooperating institution. ESL program available during the academic year. Internships and employment opportunities (on-campus and off-campus) available. *Contact:* Associate Director of International Admissions, The Art Institute of Colorado, 1200 Lincoln Street, Denver, CO 80203-2903. Telephone: 303-824-4716. Fax: 303-860-8520. E-mail: brocrcm@aii.edu. URL: http://www.aic.artinstitutes.edu.

COLORADO CHRISTIAN UNIVERSITY, LAKEWOOD

General Information Independent interdenominational, coed institution. Suburban setting. *Awards:* A, B, M. *Entrance level for U.S. students:* Moderately difficult. *Enrollment:* 2,221 total; 1,897 undergraduates (61% women) including 0.5% international students from 9 foreign countries. *Faculty:* 46. *Library holdings:* 71,565 books, 1,192 current serial subscriptions. *Total majors:* 26. *Expenses:* (2007–08) $18,350; room and board, $7625 (on campus); room only, $4415 (on campus). *Financial aid:* Need-based college/university scholarships/grants from institutional funds, tuition waivers, athletic awards. Non-need-based college/university scholarships/grants from institutional funds, tuition waivers, athletic awards. Forms required: International Student's Certification of Finances. 3 international students on campus received college administered financial aid ($5732 average).

THE COLORADO COLLEGE, COLORADO SPRINGS

General Information Independent, coed institution. Urban setting. *Awards:* B, M (master's degree in education only). *Entrance*

level for U.S. students: Very difficult. *Enrollment:* 1,998 total; 1,970 undergraduates (55% women) including 2% international students from 17 foreign countries. *Faculty:* 195. *Library holdings:* 532,793 books, 4,649 current serial subscriptions, 22,830 audiovisual materials. *Total majors:* 46.

Information for International Students For fall 2006: 214 international students applied, 16 were accepted, 5 enrolled. Students can start in fall. Transfers accepted from institutions abroad. *Admission tests:* Required: SAT or ACT, TOEFL (minimum score: paper-based 550; computer-based 213). Recommended: SAT. TOEFL can be waived under certain conditions. *Application deadline:* 1/15. *Expenses:* (2006–07) $32,124; room and board, $8052 (on campus); room only, $4368 (on campus). *Financial aid:* Need-based college/university scholarships/grants from institutional funds, on-campus employment. Non-need-based college/university scholarships/grants from institutional funds, on-campus employment. Forms required: International Student's Financial Aid Application, International Student's Certification of Finances. International transfer students are eligible to apply for aid. For fall 2006 (estimated), 16 international students on campus received college administered financial aid ($39,875 average). *Housing:* Guaranteed. *Services:* International student adviser on campus. Internships and employment opportunities (on-campus) available. *Contact:* Associate Director of Admission, The Colorado College, 14 East Cache La Poudre Street, Colorado Springs, CO 80903. Telephone: 719-389-6345. Fax: 719-389-6816. E-mail: mbonser@coloradocollege.edu. URL: http://www.coloradocollege.edu.

COLORADO MOUNTAIN COLLEGE, GLENWOOD SPRINGS

General Information District-supported, 2-year, coed college. Rural setting. *Awards:* A. *Entrance level for U.S. students:* Noncompetitive. *Enrollment:* 2,238 total including 0.4% international students. *Library holdings:* 36,000 books, 186 current serial subscriptions. *Total majors:* 24. *Expenses:* (2007–08) $7110; room and board, $6866 (on campus); room only, $3570 (on campus).

COLORADO MOUNTAIN COLLEGE, ALPINE CAMPUS, STEAMBOAT SPRINGS

General Information District-supported, 2-year, coed college. Rural setting. *Awards:* A. *Entrance level for U.S. students:* Noncompetitive. *Enrollment:* 1,809 total including 0.2% international students. *Library holdings:* 17,000 books, 192 current serial subscriptions. *Total majors:* 21. *Expenses:* (2007–08) $7110; room and board, $6866 (on campus); room only, $3570 (on campus).

COLORADO NORTHWESTERN COMMUNITY COLLEGE, RANGELY

General Information State-supported, 2-year, coed college. Rural setting. *Awards:* A. *Entrance level for U.S. students:* Noncompetitive. *Enrollment:* 2,242 total (51% women) including 0.3% international students from 3 foreign countries. *Undergraduate faculty:* 277. *Library holdings:* 20,063 books, 230 current serial subscriptions, 3,559 audiovisual materials. *Total majors:* 40.

COLORADO SCHOOL OF HEALING ARTS, LAKEWOOD

General Information Proprietary, 2-year, coed college. *Awards:* A. *Entrance level for U.S. students:* Noncompetitive. *Enrollment:* 240 total (86% women) including 1% international students. *Undergraduate faculty:* 35. *Total majors:* 1. *Expenses:* (2006–07) $10,161.

COLORADO SCHOOL OF MINES, GOLDEN

General Information State-supported, coed university. Small town setting. *Awards:* B, M, D, FP. *Entrance level for U.S. students:* Very difficult. *Enrollment:* 4,056 total; 3,223 undergraduates (22% women) including 4% international students from 52 foreign countries. *Faculty:* 299. *Library holdings:* 150,000 books, 4,883 current serial subscriptions. *Total majors:* 16. *Expenses:* (2006–07) $21,546; room and board, $6880 (on campus); room only, $3600 (on campus).

COLORADO SCHOOL OF TRADES, LAKEWOOD

General Information Proprietary, 2-year, coed college. *Awards:* A. *Entrance level for U.S. students:* Difficulty N/R. *Enrollment:* 125 total (2% women). *Total majors:* 1. *Expenses:* (2006–07) $16,354.

COLORADO STATE UNIVERSITY, FORT COLLINS

General Information State-supported, coed university. Urban setting. *Awards:* B, M, D, FP. *Entrance level for U.S. students:* Moderately difficult. *Enrollment:* 26,723 total; 21,283 undergraduates (52% women) including 1% international students

Colorado State University (continued)

from 50 foreign countries. *Faculty:* 892. *Library holdings:* 2.1 million books, 31,372 current serial subscriptions, 5,932 audiovisual materials. *Total majors:* 118.

Information for International Students For fall 2006: 789 international students enrolled. Students can start in fall, spring, or summer. Transfers accepted from institutions abroad. *Admission tests:* Required: TOEFL (minimum score: iBT 71; paper-based 525; computer-based 197; minimum score for ESL admission: iBT 44; paper-based 450; computer-based 130). Recommended: IELTS (minimum score of 6). TOEFL can be waived under certain conditions. *Application deadline:* 5/1. *Expenses:* (2006–07) $16,245; room and board, $6602 (on campus); room only, $2980 (on campus). *Services:* International student adviser on campus. Full-time and part-time ESL programs on campus. ESL program available during the academic year and the summer. Internships and employment opportunities (on-campus and off-campus) available. *Contact:* Assistant Director of Admissions, Office of Admissions, Colorado State University, 1062 Campus Delivery, Fort Collins, CO 80523-1062. Telephone: 970-491-6909. Fax: 970-491-7799. E-mail: admissions@colostate.edu. URL: http://www.colostate.edu.

See In-Depth Description on page 61.

COLORADO STATE UNIVERSITY-PUEBLO, PUEBLO

General Information State-supported, coed institution. Suburban setting. *Awards:* B, M. *Entrance level for U.S. students:* Moderately difficult. *Enrollment:* 6,205 total; 5,087 undergraduates (60% women) including 3% international students from 22 foreign countries. *Faculty:* 315. *Library holdings:* 265,062 books, 8,404 current serial subscriptions, 12,902 audiovisual materials. *Total majors:* 65. *Expenses:* (2006–07) $14,758; room and board, $5810 (on campus); room only, $2960 (on campus). *Financial aid:* Need-based college/university scholarships/grants from institutional funds, on-campus employment. Non-need-based college/university scholarships/grants from institutional funds, on-campus employment. Forms required: institution's own financial aid form. For fall 2006 (estimated), 99 international students on campus received college administered financial aid ($4286 average).

COMMUNITY COLLEGE OF AURORA, AURORA

General Information State-supported, 2-year, coed college. Suburban setting. *Awards:* A. *Entrance level for U.S. students:* Noncompetitive. *Enrollment:* 5,477 total (61% women) including 2% international students. *Undergraduate faculty:* 347. *Library holdings:* 7,440 books, 126 current serial subscriptions. *Total majors:* 15. *Expenses:* (2006–07) $10,480. *Financial aid:* Need-based financial aid available. Forms required: institution's own financial aid form.

COMMUNITY COLLEGE OF DENVER, DENVER

General Information State-supported, 2-year, coed college. Urban setting. *Awards:* A. *Entrance level for U.S. students:* Noncompetitive. *Enrollment:* 8,909 total (63% women) including 6% international students. *Undergraduate faculty:* 441. *Library holdings:* 683,045 books, 3,233 current serial subscriptions, 16,821 audiovisual materials. *Total majors:* 19. *Expenses:* (2006–07) $10,991.

DEVRY UNIVERSITY, BROOMFIELD

General Information Proprietary, coed institution. *Awards:* A, B. *Entrance level for U.S. students:* Minimally difficult. *Enrollment:* 460 total (23% women) including 2% international students from 4 foreign countries. *Undergraduate faculty:* 62. *Library holdings:* 5,037 books, 46,172 current serial subscriptions, 446 audiovisual materials.

DEVRY UNIVERSITY, COLORADO SPRINGS

General Information Proprietary, coed institution. Urban setting. *Awards:* A, B, M. *Entrance level for U.S. students:* Minimally difficult. *Enrollment:* 275 total; 216 undergraduates (35% women) including 0.5% international students from 1 foreign country. *Faculty:* 42. *Total majors:* 5. *Expenses:* (2006–07) $12,650.

FORT LEWIS COLLEGE, DURANGO

General Information State-supported, 4-year, coed college. Small town setting. *Awards:* B. *Entrance level for U.S. students:* Moderately difficult. *Enrollment:* 3,907 total (48% women) including 1% international students from 10 foreign countries. *Undergraduate faculty:* 240. *Library holdings:* 187,642 books, 17,551 current serial subscriptions, 4,046 audiovisual materials. *Total majors:* 56.

Information for International Students For fall 2006: 41 international students applied, 30 were accepted, 23 enrolled. Students can start in fall, winter, or summer. Transfers accepted from institutions abroad. *Admission tests:* Required: TOEFL (minimum score: paper-based 500; computer-based 173).

Recommended: SAT or ACT. *Application deadline:* 6/1. *Expenses:* (2006–07) $14,061; room and board, $6468 (on campus); room only, $3420 (on campus). *Financial aid:* Non-need-based college/university scholarships/grants from institutional funds, athletic awards. For fall 2005, 8 international students on campus received college administered financial aid ($9608 average). *Housing:* Guaranteed, also available during summer. *Services:* International student adviser on campus. Internships and employment opportunities (on-campus and off-campus) available. *Contact:* Director of Admission, Fort Lewis College, 1000 Rim Drive, Durango, CO 81301-3999. Telephone: 970-247-7180. Fax: 970-247-7179. E-mail: burns_a@fortlewis.edu. URL: http://www.fortlewis.edu.

FRONT RANGE COMMUNITY COLLEGE, WESTMINSTER

General Information State-supported, 2-year, coed college. Suburban setting. *Awards:* A. *Entrance level for U.S. students:* Noncompetitive. *Enrollment:* 14,749 total (59% women) including 0.2% international students. *Undergraduate faculty:* 991. *Total majors:* 25. *Expenses:* (2006–07) $8562.

MESA STATE COLLEGE, GRAND JUNCTION

General Information State-supported, coed institution. Small town setting. *Awards:* A, B, M. *Entrance level for U.S. students:* Minimally difficult. *Enrollment:* 5,938 total; 5,854 undergraduates (59% women) including 0.3% international students. *Faculty:* 396. *Library holdings:* 260,784 books, 31,992 current serial subscriptions, 12,248 audiovisual materials. *Total majors:* 67.

Information for International Students For fall 2006: 16 international students enrolled. Students can start in fall, spring, or summer. Transfers accepted from institutions abroad. *Admission tests:* Required: SAT or ACT. Recommended: TOEFL (minimum score: paper-based 525; computer-based 190), ELS, MELAB. TOEFL can be waived under certain conditions. *Application deadline:* 3/1. *Expenses:* (2007–08) $11,419; room and board, $7214 (on campus); room only, $3708 (on campus). *Financial aid:* Need-based college/university scholarships/grants from institutional funds, tuition waivers, athletic awards, loans from outside sources, on-campus employment. Non-need-based college/university scholarships/grants from institutional funds, tuition waivers, athletic awards, loans from outside sources, on-campus employment. Forms required: contact financial aid office. *Services:* International student adviser on campus. Internships and employment opportunities (on-campus) available. *Contact:* International Admissions Counselor, Office of Admission and Records, Mesa State College, 1100 North Avenue, Grand Junction, CO 81501. Telephone: 970-248-1875 Ext. 1613. Fax: 970-248-1973. E-mail: intladmissions@mesastate.edu. URL: http://www.mesastate.edu.

METROPOLITAN STATE COLLEGE OF DENVER, DENVER

General Information State-supported, 4-year, coed college. Urban setting. *Awards:* B. *Entrance level for U.S. students:* Minimally difficult. *Enrollment:* 20,761 total (56% women) including 1% international students from 58 foreign countries. *Undergraduate faculty:* 1,141. *Library holdings:* 607,971 books, 2,380 current serial subscriptions, 16,309 audiovisual materials. *Total majors:* 49. *Expenses:* (2006–07) $10,841.

NAROPA UNIVERSITY, BOULDER

General Information Independent, coed institution. Urban setting. *Awards:* B, M, FP. *Entrance level for U.S. students:* Moderately difficult. *Enrollment:* 1,136 total; 473 undergraduates (59% women) including 3% international students from 7 foreign countries. *Faculty:* 206. *Library holdings:* 27,500 books, 75 current serial subscriptions. *Total majors:* 11. *Expenses:* (2006–07) $19,426; room and board, $6894 (on campus); room only, $4050 (on campus). *Financial aid:* Need-based college/university scholarships/grants from institutional funds, on-campus employment. Forms required: institution's own financial aid form, International Student's Certification of Finances. For fall 2006 (estimated), 5 international students on campus received college administered financial aid ($6200 average).

NAZARENE BIBLE COLLEGE, COLORADO SPRINGS

General Information Independent, 4-year, coed college, affiliated with Church of the Nazarene. Urban setting. *Awards:* A, B. *Entrance level for U.S. students:* Noncompetitive. *Enrollment:* 808 total (37% women) including 0.5% international students from 1 foreign country. *Undergraduate faculty:* 79. *Library holdings:* 64,651 books, 1,756 current serial subscriptions, 8,580 audiovisual materials. *Total majors:* 6. *Expenses:* (2007–08) $8400.

OTERO JUNIOR COLLEGE, LA JUNTA

General Information State-supported, 2-year, coed college. Rural setting. *Awards:* A. *Entrance level for U.S. students:* Noncompetitive. *Enrollment:* 1,636 total (61% women) including 0.4% international students. *Undergraduate faculty:* 78. *Library holdings:* 36,701 books, 183 current serial subscriptions. *Total majors:* 25. *Expenses:* (2006–07) $6810; room and board, $4512 (on campus).

PIKES PEAK COMMUNITY COLLEGE, COLORADO SPRINGS

General Information State-supported, 2-year, coed college. Urban setting. *Awards:* A. *Entrance level for U.S. students:* Noncompetitive. *Enrollment:* 10,917 total (57% women) including 1% international students from 90 foreign countries. *Undergraduate faculty:* 673. *Library holdings:* 34,332 books, 311 current serial subscriptions, 3,832 audiovisual materials. *Total majors:* 31.
Information for International Students For fall 2006: 30 international students applied, 26 were accepted, 24 enrolled. Students can start in fall, spring, or summer. Transfers accepted from institutions abroad. *Admission tests:* Required: TOEFL (minimum score: iBT 45; paper-based 450; computer-based 133; minimum score for ESL admission: iBT 45; paper-based 450; computer-based 133), college placement test. TOEFL can be waived under certain conditions. *Application deadline:* 7/15. *Services:* International student adviser on campus. Full-time and part-time ESL programs on campus. ESL program available during the academic year and the summer. *Contact:* DSO, Enrollment Services, Pikes Peak Community College, 5675 South Academy Boulevard, C27, Colorado Springs, CO 80906. Telephone: 719-502-2035. Fax: 719-502-2069. E-mail: vicki.furaus@ppcc.edu. URL: http://www.ppcc.edu.

REGIS UNIVERSITY, DENVER

General Information Independent Roman Catholic (Jesuit), coed institution. Suburban setting. *Awards:* B, M, D. *Entrance level for U.S. students:* Moderately difficult. *Enrollment:* 16,004 total; 8,119 undergraduates (63% women) including 1% international students. *Faculty:* 1,342. *Library holdings:* 350,000 books, 20,800 current serial subscriptions. *Total majors:* 33. *Expenses:* (2007–08) $26,900; room and board, $8830 (on campus); room only, $5050 (on campus). *Financial aid:* Non-need-based college/university scholarships/grants from institutional funds. Forms required: International Student's Certification of Finances.

TRINIDAD STATE JUNIOR COLLEGE, TRINIDAD

General Information State-supported, 2-year, coed college. Small town setting. *Awards:* A. *Entrance level for U.S. students:* Noncompetitive. *Enrollment:* 1,732 total (56% women) including 0.1% international students from 1 foreign country. *Undergraduate faculty:* 154. *Library holdings:* 54,255 books, 105 current serial subscriptions, 1,574 audiovisual materials. *Total majors:* 46. *Expenses:* (2006–07) $8740; room and board, $4298 (on campus); room only, $1048 (on campus). *Financial aid:* Forms required: institution's own financial aid form.

UNIVERSITY OF COLORADO AT BOULDER, BOULDER

General Information State-supported, coed university. Suburban setting. *Awards:* B, M, D, FP. *Entrance level for U.S. students:* Moderately difficult. *Enrollment:* 31,399 total; 26,163 undergraduates (47% women) including 2% international students from 115 foreign countries. *Faculty:* 1,845. *Library holdings:* 3.6 million books, 26,152 current serial subscriptions, 450,928 audiovisual materials. *Total majors:* 60.
Information for International Students For fall 2006: 276 international students applied, 156 were accepted, 60 enrolled. Students can start in fall, spring, or summer. Transfers accepted from institutions abroad. *Admission tests:* Required: SAT or ACT, TOEFL (minimum score: iBT 61; paper-based 500; computer-based 173). TOEFL can be waived under certain conditions. *Application deadline:* 1/15. *Expenses:* (2006–07) $23,539; room and board, $8300 (on campus). *Financial aid:* Need-based financial aid available. Non-need-based college/university scholarships/grants from institutional funds, athletic awards, loans from institutional funds, loans from outside sources, on-campus employment. Forms required: institution's own financial aid form, bank statement. For fall 2006 (estimated), 52 international students on campus received college administered financial aid ($10,250 average). *Housing:* Guaranteed. *Services:* International student adviser on campus. Full-time ESL program on campus. ESL program available during the academic year. Employment opportunities (on-campus) available. *Contact:* Assistant Director of Admissions, University of Colorado at Boulder, Office of Admissions, 65 UCB, Boulder, CO 80309-0065. Telephone: 303-492-6301. Fax: 303-735-2501. E-mail: thomas.naumann@colorado.edu. URL: http://www.colorado.edu.

UNIVERSITY OF COLORADO AT COLORADO SPRINGS, COLORADO SPRINGS

General Information State-supported, coed institution. Suburban setting. *Awards:* B, M, D. *Entrance level for U.S. students:* Moderately difficult. *Enrollment:* 8,583 total; 6,296 undergraduates (59% women) including 0.3% international students from 26 foreign countries. *Faculty:* 556. *Library holdings:* 391,638 books, 2,201 current serial subscriptions. *Total majors:* 34.
Information for International Students Students can start in fall, spring, or summer. Transfers accepted from institutions abroad. *Admission tests:* Required: SAT or ACT, TOEFL (minimum score: paper-based 550; computer-based 213). *Application deadline:* 6/1. *Expenses:* (2006–07) $23,997; room and board, $7662 (on campus). *Financial aid:* Need-based college/university scholarships/grants from institutional funds, loans from outside sources. Non-need-based college/university scholarships/grants from institutional funds, loans from outside sources. For fall 2005, 4 international students on campus received college administered financial aid ($3175 average). *Housing:* Available during summer. *Services:* International student adviser on campus. Employment opportunities (on-campus) available. *Contact:* Office of Admissions and Records, University of Colorado at Colorado Springs, PO Box 7150, Colorado Springs, CO 80933-7150. Telephone: 719-262-3383. Fax: 719-262-3116. E-mail: admrec@mail.uccs.edu. URL: http://www.uccs.edu.

UNIVERSITY OF COLORADO AT DENVER AND HEALTH SCIENCES CENTER - DOWNTOWN DENVER CAMPUS, DENVER

General Information State-supported, coed university. Urban setting. *Awards:* B, M, D, FP. *Entrance level for U.S. students:* Moderately difficult. *Enrollment:* 19,766 total; 10,387 undergraduates (57% women) including 2% international students from 57 foreign countries. *Faculty:* 1,362. *Library holdings:* 927,468 books, 88,134 current serial subscriptions, 15,366 audiovisual materials. *Total majors:* 30. *Expenses:* (2007–08) $17,047. *Financial aid:* Non-need financial aid available. 1 international student on campus received college administered financial aid ($375 average).

UNIVERSITY OF DENVER, DENVER

General Information Independent, coed university. Suburban setting. *Awards:* B, M, D, FP. *Entrance level for U.S. students:* Moderately difficult. *Enrollment:* 10,374 total; 4,877 undergraduates (55% women) including 4% international students from 54 foreign countries. *Faculty:* 1,050. *Library holdings:* 1.2 million books, 6,283 current serial subscriptions. *Total majors:* 68.
Information for International Students For fall 2006: 485 international students applied, 198 were accepted, 47 enrolled. Students can start in fall. Transfers accepted from institutions abroad. *Admission tests:* Recommended: SAT or ACT, TOEFL (minimum score: iBT 70; paper-based 525; computer-based 193; minimum score for ESL admission: iBT 20; paper-based 350; computer-based 60). TOEFL can be waived under certain conditions. *Application deadline:* 1/15. *Expenses:* (2006–07) $30,372; room and board, $9228 (on campus); room only, $5676 (on campus). *Financial aid:* Need-based college/university scholarships/grants from institutional funds. Non-need-based tuition waivers, athletic awards, loans from outside sources, on-campus employment. International transfer students are eligible to apply for aid. For fall 2005, 120 international students on campus received college administered financial aid ($20,705 average). *Housing:* Guaranteed, also available during summer. *Services:* International student adviser on campus. Full-time ESL program on campus. ESL program available during the academic year and the summer. Internships and employment opportunities (on-campus) available. *Contact:* International Admission Counselor, University of Denver, 2197 South University Boulevard, University Hall 114, Denver, CO 80208-0132. Telephone: 303-871-2790. Fax: 303-871-3522. E-mail: INTLADM@du.edu. URL: http://www.du.edu.

See In-Depth Description on page 212.

UNIVERSITY OF NORTHERN COLORADO, GREELEY

General Information State-supported, coed university. Suburban setting. *Awards:* B, M, D (specialist). *Entrance level for U.S. students:* Moderately difficult. *Enrollment:* 12,981 total; 10,799 undergraduates (61% women) including 0.5% international students. *Faculty:* 632. *Library holdings:* 1 million books, 3,417 current serial subscriptions. *Total majors:* 42. *Expenses:* (2006–07) $12,532; room and board, $6832 (on campus); room only, $3260 (on campus). *Financial aid:* Need-based financial aid available. Non-need-based college/university scholarships/grants from institutional funds, athletic awards, loans from institutional funds, on-campus employment. Forms required: International Student's Certification of Finances, financial statement for International Student form. For fall 2005, 18 international students on campus received college administered financial aid ($5173 average).

UNIVERSITY OF PHOENIX–SOUTHERN COLORADO CAMPUS, COLORADO SPRINGS

General Information Proprietary, coed institution. Urban setting. *Awards:* B, M. *Entrance level for U.S. students:* Noncompetitive. *Enrollment:* 1,090 total; 618 undergraduates (54% women) including 20% international students. *Faculty:* 431. *Library holdings:* 1,759 books, 692 current serial subscriptions. *Total majors:* 18. *Expenses:* (2006–07) $9750.

WESTWOOD COLLEGE–DENVER NORTH, DENVER

General Information Proprietary, primarily 2-year, coed college. Suburban setting. *Awards:* A, B. *Entrance level for U.S. students:* Moderately difficult. *Enrollment:* 1,423 total (32% women) including 0.1% international students from 2 foreign countries. *Undergraduate faculty:* 97. *Library holdings:* 2,000 books, 90 current serial subscriptions, 120 audiovisual materials. *Total majors:* 22. *Expenses:* (2006–07) $12,810.

CONNECTICUT

ALBERTUS MAGNUS COLLEGE, NEW HAVEN

General Information Independent Roman Catholic, coed institution. Suburban setting. *Awards:* A, B, M. *Entrance level for U.S. students:* Moderately difficult. *Enrollment:* 2,186 total; 1,769 undergraduates (69% women) including 0.2% international students from 4 foreign countries. *Faculty:* 217. *Library holdings:* 538 current serial subscriptions. *Total majors:* 56.

Information for International Students For fall 2006: 7 international students applied, 4 were accepted, 3 enrolled. Students can start in fall or spring. Transfers accepted from institutions abroad. *Admission tests:* Required: SAT or ACT, TOEFL (minimum score: paper-based 550; computer-based 213). TOEFL can be waived under certain conditions. *Application deadline:* 7/15. *Expenses:* (2006–07) $19,390; room and board, $8403 (on campus). *Financial aid:* Need-based and non-need-based financial aid available. Forms required: institution's own financial aid form. *Housing:* Guaranteed. Internships available. *Contact:* Assistant Director of Admission, Albertus Magnus College, 700 Prospect Street, New Haven, CT 06511. Telephone: 203-773-8501. Fax: 203-773-5248. E-mail: admissions@albertus.edu. URL: http://www.albertus.edu.

BRIARWOOD COLLEGE, SOUTHINGTON

General Information Proprietary, primarily 2-year, coed college. Small town setting. *Awards:* A, B. *Entrance level for U.S. students:* Minimally difficult. *Enrollment:* 647 total (74% women) including 1% international students from 2 foreign countries. *Undergraduate faculty:* 95. *Library holdings:* 11,500 books, 154 current serial subscriptions. *Total majors:* 22.

Information for International Students For fall 2006: 2 international students applied, 2 were accepted, 2 enrolled. Students can start in fall or spring. Transfers accepted from institutions abroad. *Admission tests:* Recommended: TOEFL. TOEFL can be waived under certain conditions. *Application deadline:* Rolling. *Expenses:* (2007–08) $16,620; room only, $3600 (on campus). *Financial aid:* Non-need-based college/university scholarships/grants from institutional funds, loans from outside sources. International transfer students are eligible to apply for aid. *Housing:* Guaranteed. *Services:* International student adviser on campus. Internships and employment opportunities (on-campus) available. *Contact:* Senior Director of Admissions, Briarwood College, Southington, CT 06489. Telephone: 860-628-4751 Ext. 214. Fax: 860-628-6444. E-mail: brennanv@briarwood.edu. URL: http://www.briarwood.edu.

CAPITAL COMMUNITY COLLEGE, HARTFORD

General Information State-supported, 2-year, coed college. Urban setting. *Awards:* A. *Entrance level for U.S. students:* Noncompetitive. *Enrollment:* 3,573 total (72% women) including 1% international students. *Library holdings:* 46,760 books, 359 current serial subscriptions, 2,409 audiovisual materials. *Total majors:* 20. *Expenses:* (2006–07) $7376. *Financial aid:* Need-based loans from outside sources. Non-need-based loans from outside sources.

CENTRAL CONNECTICUT STATE UNIVERSITY, NEW BRITAIN

General Information State-supported, coed institution. Suburban setting. *Awards:* B, M, D. *Entrance level for U.S. students:* Moderately difficult. *Enrollment:* 12,144 total; 9,644 undergraduates (50% women) including 1% international students from 64 foreign countries. *Faculty:* 850. *Library holdings:* 688,604 books, 2,705 current serial subscriptions, 8,169 audiovisual

materials. *Total majors:* 53. *Expenses:* (2007–08) $16,618; room and board, $8348 (on campus); room only, $4250 (on campus).

CONNECTICUT COLLEGE, NEW LONDON

General Information Independent, coed institution. Suburban setting. *Awards:* B, M. *Entrance level for U.S. students:* Very difficult. *Enrollment:* 1,886 total; 1,872 undergraduates (60% women) including 6% international students from 45 foreign countries. *Faculty:* 248. *Library holdings:* 496,817 books, 2,279 current serial subscriptions. *Total majors:* 56.

Information for International Students For fall 2006: 447 international students applied, 73 were accepted, 22 enrolled. Students can start in fall. Transfers accepted from institutions abroad. *Admission tests:* Required: ACT, TOEFL (minimum score: iBT 100; paper-based 650; computer-based 250). TOEFL can be waived under certain conditions. *Application deadline:* 12/15. *Expenses:* (2006–07) $44,240. *Financial aid:* Need-based college/university scholarships/grants from institutional funds. Forms required: International Student's Financial Aid Application. For fall 2006 (estimated), 74 international students on campus received college administered financial aid ($40,758 average). *Housing:* Guaranteed. *Services:* International student adviser on campus. Internships and employment opportunities (on-campus) available. *Contact:* Associate Director of Admission, Admission Office, Connecticut College, Horizon Building, 270 Mohegan Avenue, New London, CT 06320. Telephone: 860-439-2200. Fax: 860-439-4301. E-mail: scott.alexander@conncoll.edu. URL: http://www.connecticutcollege.edu.

EASTERN CONNECTICUT STATE UNIVERSITY, WILLIMANTIC

General Information State-supported, coed institution. Small town setting. *Awards:* A, B, M. *Entrance level for U.S. students:* Moderately difficult. *Enrollment:* 5,239 total; 4,898 undergraduates (57% women) including 1% international students from 43 foreign countries. *Faculty:* 404. *Library holdings:* 239,218 books, 1,729 current serial subscriptions. *Total majors:* 29.

Information for International Students Students can start in fall or spring. Transfers accepted from institutions abroad. *Admission tests:* Required: TOEFL (minimum score: iBT 79; paper-based 550; computer-based 213). TOEFL can be waived under certain conditions. *Application deadline:* Rolling. *Expenses:* (2006–07) $13,570; room and board, $8020 (on campus); room only, $4470 (on campus). *Financial aid:* Non-need financial aid available. *Services:* International student adviser on campus. ESL program at cooperating institution. Internships and employment opportunities (on-campus) available. *Contact:* Associate Director of International Admissions, Eastern Connecticut State University, Office of Admissions, 83 Windham Street, Willimantic, CT 06226. Telephone: 860-465-5022. Fax: 860-465-5544. E-mail: satsukd@easternct.edu. URL: http://www.easternct.edu.

See In-Depth Description on page 72.

FAIRFIELD UNIVERSITY, FAIRFIELD

General Information Independent Roman Catholic (Jesuit), coed institution. Suburban setting. *Awards:* B, M. *Entrance level for U.S. students:* Moderately difficult. *Enrollment:* 5,091 total; 4,008 undergraduates (58% women) including 1% international students from 27 foreign countries. *Faculty:* 450. *Library holdings:* 347,244 books, 1,614 current serial subscriptions, 10,757 audiovisual materials. *Total majors:* 35.

Information for International Students For fall 2006: 96 international students applied, 37 were accepted, 5 enrolled. Students can start in fall or spring. Transfers accepted from institutions abroad. *Admission tests:* Required: TOEFL (minimum score: paper-based 550; computer-based 213; minimum score for ESL admission: paper-based 550; computer-based 213). Recommended: SAT or ACT. TOEFL can be waived under certain conditions. *Application deadline:* 1/15. *Expenses:* (2006–07) $31,955; room and board, $9980 (on campus); room only, $5980 (on campus). *Financial aid:* Need-based college/university scholarships/grants from institutional funds, tuition waivers, loans from institutional funds, loans from outside sources, on-campus employment. Non-need-based college/university scholarships/grants from institutional funds, athletic awards, loans from outside sources. Forms required: CSS PROFILE, International Student's Certification of Finances, FAFSA. For fall 2006 (estimated), 24 international students on campus received college administered financial aid ($21,535 average). *Housing:* Guaranteed, also available during summer. *Services:* International student adviser on campus. Internships and employment opportunities (on-campus) available. *Contact:* Assistant Director of Admission, Fairfield University, 1073 North Benson Road, Fairfield, CT 06824-5195. Telephone: 203-254-4000 Ext. 4100. Fax: 203-254-4199. E-mail: foreign@mail.fairfield.edu. URL: http://www.fairfield.edu.

GATEWAY COMMUNITY COLLEGE, NEW HAVEN

General Information State-supported, 2-year, coed college. Urban setting. *Awards:* A. *Entrance level for U.S. students:* Noncompetitive. *Enrollment:* 5,824 total (64% women) including 1% international students from 38 foreign countries. *Undergraduate faculty:* 329. *Library holdings:* 54,802 books, 532 current serial subscriptions. *Total majors:* 33. *Expenses:* (2007–08) $7820.

HOLY APOSTLES COLLEGE AND SEMINARY, CROMWELL

General Information Independent Roman Catholic, coed institution. Suburban setting. *Awards:* A, B, M, FP. *Entrance level for U.S. students:* Noncompetitive. *Enrollment:* 270 total; 57 undergraduates (39% women) including 7% international students from 2 foreign countries. *Faculty:* 23. *Library holdings:* 85,000 books, 250 current serial subscriptions, 400 audiovisual materials. *Total majors:* 6.

Information for International Students For fall 2006: 3 international students applied, 3 were accepted, 3 enrolled. Students can start in fall, spring, or summer. Transfers accepted from institutions abroad. *Admission tests:* Required: SAT. *Application deadline:* Rolling. *Expenses:* (2007–08) $7440. *Services:* Full-time ESL program on campus. ESL program available during the academic year. *Contact:* Registrar, Holy Apostles College and Seminary, 33 Prospect Hill Road, Cromwell, CT 06416. Telephone: 860-632-3033. Fax: 860-632-3075. E-mail: registrar@holyapostles.edu. URL: http://www.holyapostles.edu.

INTERNATIONAL COLLEGE OF HOSPITALITY MANAGEMENT, SUFFIELD

General Information Proprietary, 2-year, coed college. Small town setting. *Awards:* A. *Entrance level for U.S. students:* Minimally difficult. *Enrollment:* 116 total (59% women) including 51% international students from 34 foreign countries. *Undergraduate faculty:* 13. *Library holdings:* 10,000 books, 50 current serial subscriptions. *Total majors:* 2.

Information for International Students Students can start in fall, winter, spring, or summer. Transfers accepted from institutions abroad. *Admission tests:* Required: TOEFL (minimum score: paper-based 500; computer-based 173; minimum score for ESL admission: paper-based 400; computer-based 200). Recommended: SAT. TOEFL can be waived under certain conditions. *Application deadline:* Rolling. *Expenses:* (2006–07) $15,900; room and board, $4978 (on campus). *Financial aid:* Forms required: institution's own financial aid form. *Services:* International student adviser on campus. Internships available. *Contact:* Office of Admissions, International College of Hospitality Management, 1760 Mapleton Avenue, Suffield, CT 06078. Telephone: 860-668-3515. Fax: 860-668-7369. E-mail: admissions@ichm.edu. URL: http://www.ichm.edu.

See In-Depth Description on page 104.

MANCHESTER COMMUNITY COLLEGE, MANCHESTER

General Information State-supported, 2-year, coed college. Small town setting. *Awards:* A. *Entrance level for U.S. students:* Noncompetitive. *Enrollment:* 6,135 total (56% women) including 1% international students. *Undergraduate faculty:* 353. *Library holdings:* 45,265 books, 493 current serial subscriptions, 2,481 audiovisual materials. *Total majors:* 31. *Expenses:* (2006–07) $7056. *Financial aid:* Forms required: FAFSA.

MIDDLESEX COMMUNITY COLLEGE, MIDDLETOWN

General Information State-supported, 2-year, coed college. Suburban setting. *Awards:* A. *Entrance level for U.S. students:* Noncompetitive. *Enrollment:* 2,474 total (63% women) including 0.3% international students. *Undergraduate faculty:* 178. *Library holdings:* 45,000 books, 180 current serial subscriptions. *Total majors:* 25.

Information for International Students For fall 2006: 15 international students applied, 15 were accepted, 10 enrolled. Students can start in fall or spring. Transfers accepted from institutions abroad. *Admission tests:* Required: ELS (minimum score: 3), ACCUPLACER. TOEFL can be waived under certain conditions. *Application deadline:* 7/1. *Expenses:* (2007–08) $7376. *Financial aid:* Forms required: FAFSA. *Services:* International student adviser on campus. Part-time ESL program on campus. ESL program available during the academic year. *Contact:* Director of Admissions, Middlesex Community College, 100 Training Hill Road, Middletown, CT 06457-4889. Telephone: 860-343-5719. Fax: 860-344-3055. E-mail: mshabazz@mxcc.commnet.edu. URL: http://www.mxcc.commnet.edu.

MITCHELL COLLEGE, NEW LONDON

General Information Independent, 4-year, coed college. Suburban setting. *Awards:* A, B. *Entrance level for U.S. students:* Minimally difficult. *Enrollment:* 727 total (51% women) including 1% international students from 5 foreign countries. *Undergraduate faculty:* 71. *Library holdings:* 80,000 books, 120 current serial subscriptions, 300 audiovisual materials. *Total majors:* 20.

Information for International Students For fall 2006: 15 international students applied, 8 were accepted, 2 enrolled. Students can start in fall or spring. Transfers accepted from institutions abroad. *Admission tests:* Required: TOEFL (minimum score: paper-based 500; computer-based 190). Recommended: ELS. TOEFL can be waived under certain conditions. *Application deadline:* Rolling. *Expenses:* (2006–07) $21,767; room and board, $9795 (on campus); room only, $5093 (on campus). *Financial aid:* Non-need-based college/university scholarships/grants from institutional funds. Forms required: International Student's Certification of Finances. *Housing:* Guaranteed. *Services:* International student adviser on campus. Full-time and part-time ESL programs on campus. ESL program available during the academic year and the summer. Internships and employment opportunities (on-campus) available. *Contact:* Vice President of Enrollment Management and Marketing, Mitchell College, Henry Hall, 437 Pequot Avenue, New London, CT 06320. Telephone: 860-701-5002. Fax: 860-444-1209. E-mail: mayne_k@mitchell.edu. URL: http://www.mitchell.edu.

NORWALK COMMUNITY COLLEGE, NORWALK

General Information State-supported, 2-year, coed college. Suburban setting. *Awards:* A. *Entrance level for U.S. students:* Noncompetitive. *Enrollment:* 6,036 total including international students from 30 foreign countries. *Undergraduate faculty:* 349. *Library holdings:* 66,080 books, 221 current serial subscriptions, 2,988 audiovisual materials. *Total majors:* 32.

Information for International Students For fall 2006: 105 international students applied, 105 were accepted, 82 enrolled. Students can start in fall, winter, spring, or summer. Transfers accepted from institutions abroad. *Admission tests:* Required: ESL and math placement test. *Application deadline:* Rolling. *Expenses:* (2006–07) $7376. *Services:* International student adviser on campus. Full-time and part-time ESL programs on campus. ESL program available during the academic year and the summer. Internships and employment opportunities (on-campus) available. *Contact:* International Student Advisor, Norwalk Community College, 188 Richards Avenue, Norwalk, CT 06854-1655. Telephone: 203-857-7282. Fax: 203-857-6948. E-mail: dbogusky@ncc.commnet.edu. URL: http://www.ncc.commnet.edu.

PAIER COLLEGE OF ART, INC., HAMDEN

General Information Proprietary, 4-year, coed college. Suburban setting. *Awards:* A, B. *Entrance level for U.S. students:* Minimally difficult. *Enrollment:* 248 total (68% women) including 4% international students from 9 foreign countries. *Undergraduate faculty:* 39. *Library holdings:* 12,000 books, 72 current serial subscriptions. *Total majors:* 14.

Information for International Students For fall 2006: 2 international students applied, 2 were accepted, 2 enrolled. Students can start in fall or summer. Transfers accepted from institutions abroad. *Admission tests:* Required: TOEFL (minimum score: paper-based 500; computer-based 300). Recommended: ELS. *Application deadline:* Rolling. *Expenses:* (2006–07) $12,380. *Financial aid:* Need-based and non-need-based financial aid available. Forms required: FAFSA. 2 international students on campus received college administered financial aid ($5000 average). *Services:* International student adviser on campus. ESL program at cooperating institution. *Contact:* Registrar, Paier College of Art, Inc., 20 Gorham Avenue, Hamden, CT 06514-3902. Telephone: 203-287-3032. Fax: 203-287-3021. E-mail: paier.admin@snet.net. URL: http://www.paiercollegeofart.edu.

POST UNIVERSITY, WATERBURY

General Information Independent, 4-year, coed college. Suburban setting. *Awards:* A, B. *Entrance level for U.S. students:* Minimally difficult. *Enrollment:* 1,101 total (60% women) including 3% international students from 15 foreign countries. *Undergraduate faculty:* 122. *Library holdings:* 85,000 books, 500 current serial subscriptions, 1,027 audiovisual materials. *Total majors:* 23. *Expenses:* (2006–07) $21,500; room and board, $8400 (on campus). *Financial aid:* Need-based college/university scholarships/grants from institutional funds, athletic awards. Non-need-based college/university scholarships/grants from institutional funds, athletic awards. Forms required: institution's own financial aid form, International Student's Financial Aid Application,

Post University (continued)

International Student's Certification of Finances. 6 international students on campus received college administered financial aid ($11,850 average).

QUINNIPIAC UNIVERSITY, HAMDEN

General Information Independent, coed institution. Suburban setting. *Awards:* B, M, D, FP. *Entrance level for U.S. students:* Moderately difficult. *Enrollment:* 7,341 total; 5,821 undergraduates (61% women) including 1% international students from 20 foreign countries. *Faculty:* 778. *Library holdings:* 285,000 books, 5,500 current serial subscriptions. *Total majors:* 60.

Information for International Students For fall 2006: 90 international students applied, 40 were accepted, 21 enrolled. Students can start in fall or spring. Transfers accepted from institutions abroad. *Admission tests:* Required: TOEFL (minimum score: paper-based 550; computer-based 213). Recommended: SAT. TOEFL can be waived under certain conditions. *Application deadline:* 2/15. *Expenses:* (2007–08) $28,720; room and board, $11,200 (on campus). *Financial aid:* Need-based college/university scholarships/grants from institutional funds. Non-need-based college/university scholarships/grants from institutional funds, athletic awards, on-campus employment. Forms required: International Student's Financial Aid Application, International Student's Certification of Finances. International transfer students are eligible to apply for aid. 62 international students on campus received college administered financial aid ($24,616 average). *Housing:* Guaranteed. *Services:* International student adviser on campus. ESL program at cooperating institution. ESL program available during the academic year and the summer. Internships and employment opportunities (on-campus and off-campus) available. *Contact:* Vice President and Dean of Admissions, Quinnipiac University, 275 Mount Carmel Avenue, Hamden, CT 06518. Telephone: 203-582-8600. Fax: 203-582-8906. E-mail: admissions@quinnipiac.edu. URL: http://www.quinnipiac.edu.

See In-Depth Description on page 154.

SACRED HEART UNIVERSITY, FAIRFIELD

General Information Independent Roman Catholic, coed institution. Suburban setting. *Awards:* A, B, M, D (also offers part-time program with significant enrollment not reflected in profile). *Entrance level for U.S. students:* Moderately difficult. *Enrollment:* 5,756 total; 4,203 undergraduates (62% women) including 1% international students from 41 foreign countries. *Faculty:* 497. *Library holdings:* 134,348 books, 860 current serial subscriptions, 1,797 audiovisual materials. *Total majors:* 67.

Information for International Students For fall 2006: 70 international students applied, 40 were accepted, 25 enrolled. Students can start in fall or spring. Transfers accepted from institutions abroad. *Application deadline:* Rolling. *Expenses:* (2006–07) $25,400; room and board, $10,320 (on campus); room only, $7638 (on campus). *Financial aid:* Need-based college/university scholarships/grants from institutional funds, athletic awards, loans from institutional funds, loans from outside sources, on-campus employment. Non-need-based college/university scholarships/grants from institutional funds, athletic awards, loans from outside sources, on-campus employment. Forms required: CSS PROFILE. For fall 2006 (estimated), 24 international students on campus received college administered financial aid ($27,326 average). *Housing:* Guaranteed, also available during summer. *Services:* International student adviser on campus. Full-time and part-time ESL programs on campus. ESL program available during the academic year. Internships and employment opportunities (on-campus and off-campus) available. *Contact:* Dean of Undergraduate Admissions, Sacred Heart University, Fairfield, CT 06825. Telephone: 203-371-7880. Fax: 203-365-7607. E-mail: guastellek@sacredheart.edu. URL: http://www.sacredheart.edu.

See In-Depth Description on page 163.

SAINT JOSEPH COLLEGE, WEST HARTFORD

General Information Independent Roman Catholic, undergraduate: women only; graduate: coed institution. Suburban setting. *Awards:* B, M. *Entrance level for U.S. students:* Difficulty N/R. *Enrollment:* 1,803 total; 1,042 undergraduates (98% women) including 0.1% international students from 1 foreign country. *Faculty:* 212. *Total majors:* 34. *Expenses:* (2006–07) $23,490; room and board, $11,500 (on campus); room only, $6220 (on campus).

SOUTHERN CONNECTICUT STATE UNIVERSITY, NEW HAVEN

General Information State-supported, coed institution. Urban setting. *Awards:* B, M, D. *Entrance level for U.S. students:* Moderately difficult. *Enrollment:* 12,326 total; 8,577

undergraduates (62% women) including 1% international students from 46 foreign countries. *Faculty:* 1,024. *Library holdings:* 495,660 books, 3,549 current serial subscriptions. *Total majors:* 42. *Expenses:* (2007–08) $14,076; room and board, $8432 (on campus); room only, $4668 (on campus).

TRINITY COLLEGE, HARTFORD

General Information Independent, coed institution. Urban setting. *Awards:* B, M. *Entrance level for U.S. students:* Very difficult. *Enrollment:* 2,528 total; 2,353 undergraduates (50% women) including 2% international students from 22 foreign countries. *Faculty:* 243. *Library holdings:* 1 million books, 1,813 current serial subscriptions, 2,349 audiovisual materials. *Total majors:* 44.

Information for International Students For fall 2006: 509 international students applied, 44 were accepted, 13 enrolled. Students can start in fall. Transfers accepted from institutions abroad. *Admission tests:* Recommended: SAT or ACT, SAT Subject Tests, TOEFL (minimum score: paper-based 550; computer-based 210; minimum score for ESL admission: paper-based 550; computer-based 210). TOEFL can be waived under certain conditions. *Application deadline:* 1/4. *Expenses:* (2006–07) $35,130; room and board, $8970 (on campus). *Financial aid:* Need-based college/university scholarships/grants from institutional funds, loans from institutional funds. Forms required: International Student's Financial Aid Application, International Student's Certification of Finances. International transfer students are eligible to apply for aid. For fall 2005, 56 international students on campus received college administered financial aid ($40,626 average). *Services:* International student adviser on campus. Internships and employment opportunities (on-campus and off-campus) available. *Contact:* Admissions Outreach Coordinator, Trinity College, 300 Summit Street, Hartford, CT 06106-3100. Telephone: 860-297-2180. Fax: 860-297-2287. E-mail: admissions.office@mail.trincoll.edu. URL: http://www.trincoll.edu.

TUNXIS COMMUNITY COLLEGE, FARMINGTON

General Information State-supported, 2-year, coed college. Suburban setting. *Awards:* A. *Entrance level for U.S. students:* Noncompetitive. *Enrollment:* 3,894 total (61% women) including 1% international students. *Undergraduate faculty:* 234. *Library holdings:* 33,866 books, 285 current serial subscriptions, 3,571 audiovisual materials. *Total majors:* 23. *Expenses:* (2006–07) $7376.

UNIVERSITY OF BRIDGEPORT, BRIDGEPORT

General Information Independent, coed institution. Urban setting. *Awards:* A, B, M, D, FP. *Entrance level for U.S. students:* Moderately difficult. *Enrollment:* 4,018 total; 1,694 undergraduates (65% women) including 15% international students from 62 foreign countries. *Faculty:* 380. *Library holdings:* 272,430 books, 2,117 current serial subscriptions. *Total majors:* 33. *Expenses:* (2006–07) $21,710; room and board, $9600 (on campus); room only, $5000 (on campus). *Financial aid:* Non-need-based college/university scholarships/grants from institutional funds, tuition waivers, athletic awards, loans from outside sources, on-campus employment. For fall 2006 (estimated), 140 international students on campus received college administered financial aid ($7828 average).

UNIVERSITY OF CONNECTICUT, STORRS

General Information State-supported, coed university. Rural setting. *Awards:* A, B, M, D, FP. *Entrance level for U.S. students:* Moderately difficult. *Enrollment:* 23,557 total; 16,347 undergraduates (51% women) including 1% international students from 64 foreign countries. *Faculty:* 1,308. *Library holdings:* 3 million books, 17,378 current serial subscriptions, 61,417 audiovisual materials. *Total majors:* 96. *Expenses:* (2007–08) $22,786; room and board, $8850 (on campus); room only, $4698 (on campus).

UNIVERSITY OF HARTFORD, WEST HARTFORD

General Information Independent, coed institution. Suburban setting. *Awards:* A, B, M, D. *Entrance level for U.S. students:* Moderately difficult. *Enrollment:* 7,308 total; 5,602 undergraduates (51% women) including 7% international students from 53 foreign countries. *Faculty:* 787. *Library holdings:* 473,115 books, 2,425 current serial subscriptions. *Total majors:* 90.

Information for International Students For fall 2006: 425 international students applied, 300 were accepted, 110 enrolled. Students can start in fall, spring, or summer. Transfers accepted from institutions abroad. *Admission tests:* Required: TOEFL (minimum score: iBT 72; paper-based 550; computer-based 213; minimum score for ESL admission: paper-based 450; computer-based 133). TOEFL can be waived under certain conditions. *Application deadline:* Rolling. *Expenses:* (2007–08)

$26,996; room and board, $10,418 (on campus); room only, $6424 (on campus). *Financial aid:* Non-need-based college/university scholarships/grants from institutional funds, athletic awards. Forms required: International Student's Certification of Finances. International transfer students are eligible to apply for aid. For fall 2005, 99 international students on campus received college administered financial aid ($14,151 average). *Services:* International student adviser on campus. Full-time ESL program on campus. ESL program available during the academic year and the summer. Internships and employment opportunities (on-campus) available. *Contact:* Director of International Admissions, University of Hartford, West Hartford, CT 06117. Telephone: 860-768-4981. Fax: 860-768-4961. E-mail: iua@hartford.edu. URL: http://www.hartford.edu.

See In-Depth Description on page 213.

UNIVERSITY OF NEW HAVEN, WEST HAVEN

General Information Independent, coed institution. Suburban setting. *Awards:* A, B, M. *Entrance level for U.S. students:* Moderately difficult. *Enrollment:* 4,649 total; 2,877 undergraduates (48% women) including 2% international students from 33 foreign countries. *Faculty:* 444. *Total majors:* 48. *Expenses:* (2006–07) $24,645; room and board, $10,130 (on campus); room only, $6170 (on campus). *Financial aid:* Non-need financial aid available. For fall 2006 (estimated), 7 international students on campus received college administered financial aid ($3000 average).

WESLEYAN UNIVERSITY, MIDDLETOWN

General Information Independent, coed university. Small town setting. *Awards:* B, M, D. *Entrance level for U.S. students:* Most difficult. *Enrollment:* 3,220 total; 2,813 undergraduates (50% women) including 6% international students from 45 foreign countries. *Faculty:* 365. *Library holdings:* 1.3 million books, 6,789 current serial subscriptions. *Total majors:* 48.
Information for International Students For fall 2006: 754 international students applied, 100 were accepted, 43 enrolled. Students can start in fall. Transfers accepted from institutions abroad. *Admission tests:* Required: TOEFL (minimum score: iBT 100; paper-based 600; computer-based 250), SAT or ACT. TOEFL can be waived under certain conditions. *Application deadline:* 1/1. *Expenses:* (2006–07) $35,144; room and board, $9540 (on campus); room only, $5808 (on campus). *Financial aid:* Need-based college/university scholarships/grants from institutional funds, loans from institutional funds, on-campus employment. Forms required: International Student's Financial Aid Application. For fall 2005, 49 international students on campus received college administered financial aid ($42,634 average). *Housing:* Guaranteed, also available during summer. *Services:* International student adviser on campus. ESL program at cooperating institution. ESL program available during the summer. Internships and employment opportunities (on-campus) available. *Contact:* Associate Dean of Admissions, Wesleyan University, 70 Wyllys Avenue, Middletown, CT 06459-0260. Telephone: 860-685-3000. Fax: 860-685-3001. E-mail: toverton@wesleyan.edu. URL: http://www.wesleyan.edu.

WESTERN CONNECTICUT STATE UNIVERSITY, DANBURY

General Information State-supported, coed institution. Urban setting. *Awards:* A, B, M, D. *Entrance level for U.S. students:* Moderately difficult. *Enrollment:* 6,086 total; 5,384 undergraduates (55% women) including 0.4% international students from 19 foreign countries. *Faculty:* 481. *Library holdings:* 182,915 books, 1,273 current serial subscriptions. *Total majors:* 40. *Expenses:* (2006–07) $13,859; room and board, $7784 (on campus); room only, $4516 (on campus).

YALE UNIVERSITY, NEW HAVEN

General Information Independent, coed university. Urban setting. *Awards:* B, M, D, FP. *Entrance level for U.S. students:* Most difficult. *Enrollment:* 11,416 total; 5,333 undergraduates (49% women) including 8% international students from 74 foreign countries. *Faculty:* 1,559. *Library holdings:* 11.1 million books, 61,649 current serial subscriptions. *Total majors:* 67. *Expenses:* (2006–07) $33,030; room and board, $10,020 (on campus). *Financial aid:* Need-based college/university scholarships/grants from institutional funds, loans from institutional funds, loans from outside sources, on-campus employment. Non-need-based on-campus employment. Forms required: CSS PROFILE, International Student's Financial Aid Application, International Student's Certification of Finances. For fall 2006 (estimated), 277 international students on campus received college administered financial aid ($44,203 average).

DELAWARE

DELAWARE COLLEGE OF ART AND DESIGN, WILMINGTON

General Information Independent, 2-year, coed college. Urban setting. *Awards:* A. *Entrance level for U.S. students:* Moderately difficult. *Enrollment:* 194 total (51% women) including 1% international students. *Undergraduate faculty:* 20. *Library holdings:* 8,000 books, 76 current serial subscriptions, 500 audiovisual materials. *Total majors:* 6. *Expenses:* (2006–07) $14,070; room only, $5490 (on campus).

DELAWARE STATE UNIVERSITY, DOVER

General Information State-supported, coed institution. Small town setting. *Awards:* B, M, D. *Entrance level for U.S. students:* Moderately difficult. *Enrollment:* 3,657 total; 3,278 undergraduates (59% women) including 0.2% international students from 31 foreign countries. *Faculty:* 328. *Library holdings:* 360,616 books. *Total majors:* 85. *Expenses:* (2006–07) $12,054; room and board, $8658 (on campus); room only, $5778 (on campus).

DELAWARE TECHNICAL & COMMUNITY COLLEGE, JACK F. OWENS CAMPUS, GEORGETOWN

General Information State-supported, 2-year, coed college. Small town setting. *Awards:* A. *Entrance level for U.S. students:* Noncompetitive. *Enrollment:* 3,936 total (67% women) including 6% international students from 9 foreign countries. *Undergraduate faculty:* 280. *Library holdings:* 72,657 books, 514 current serial subscriptions. *Total majors:* 36.
Information for International Students For fall 2006: 100 international students applied, 80 were accepted, 67 enrolled. Students can start in fall or spring. Transfers accepted from institutions abroad. *Admission tests:* Required: CPT, Levels of English Proficiency Test. Recommended: ACT, SAT Subject Tests, TOEFL (minimum score: paper-based 550; computer-based 213; minimum score for ESL admission: paper-based 550; computer-based 213). TOEFL can be waived under certain conditions. *Application deadline:* 6/15. *Expenses:* (2006–07) $5392. *Services:* International student adviser on campus. Full-time and part-time ESL programs on campus. ESL program available during the academic year and the summer. Employment opportunities (on-campus) available. *Contact:* Foreign Student Advisor, Office of Student Services, Delaware Technical & Community College, Jack F. Owens Campus, Route 18, PO Box 610, Georgetown, DE 19947. Telephone: 302-856-5400 Ext. 1661. Fax: 302-856-5454. E-mail: derney@college.dtcc.edu. URL: http://www.dtcc.edu.

DELAWARE TECHNICAL & COMMUNITY COLLEGE, STANTON/WILMINGTON CAMPUS, NEWARK

General Information State-supported, 2-year, coed college. *Awards:* A. *Entrance level for U.S. students:* Noncompetitive. *Enrollment:* 7,473 total (63% women) including 2% international students from 45 foreign countries. *Undergraduate faculty:* 525. *Library holdings:* 60,066 books, 793 current serial subscriptions. *Total majors:* 43. *Expenses:* (2006–07) $5392.

DELAWARE TECHNICAL & COMMUNITY COLLEGE, TERRY CAMPUS, DOVER

General Information State-supported, 2-year, coed college. Small town setting. *Awards:* A. *Entrance level for U.S. students:* Noncompetitive. *Enrollment:* 2,569 total (71% women) including 1% international students from 10 foreign countries. *Undergraduate faculty:* 184. *Library holdings:* 9,663 books, 245 current serial subscriptions. *Total majors:* 25. *Expenses:* (2006–07) $5392.

GOLDEY-BEACOM COLLEGE, WILMINGTON

General Information Independent, coed institution. Suburban setting. *Awards:* A, B, M. *Entrance level for U.S. students:* Moderately difficult. *Enrollment:* 1,223 total; 940 undergraduates (55% women) including 0.2% international students. *Faculty:* 44. *Library holdings:* 29,700 books, 817 current serial subscriptions. *Total majors:* 7.
Information for International Students For fall 2006: 119 international students applied, 50 were accepted, 21 enrolled. Students can start in fall, spring, summer, or winter. Transfers accepted from institutions abroad. *Admission tests:* Required: TOEFL (minimum score: iBT 60; paper-based 500; computer-based 173). Recommended: SAT. TOEFL can be waived under certain conditions. *Application deadline:* Rolling. *Expenses:* (2007–08) $17,510; room only, $4600 (on campus). *Financial aid:* Need-based college/university scholarships/grants from institutional funds, athletic awards, loans from outside sources, on-campus employment. Non-need-based college/university scholarships/grants from institutional funds, loans from outside sources. Forms required: International Student's Certification of Finances.

Goldey-Beacom College (continued)

International transfer students are eligible to apply for aid. *Housing:* Guaranteed, also available during summer. *Services:* International student adviser on campus. Internships and employment opportunities (on-campus and off-campus) available. *Contact:* International Admissions Representative, Goldey-Beacom College, Wilmington, DE 19808. Telephone: 302-225-6383. Fax: 302-996-5408. E-mail: barrett@gbc.edu. URL: http://goldey.gbc.edu.

See In-Depth Description on page 94.

UNIVERSITY OF DELAWARE, NEWARK

General Information State-related, coed university. Small town setting. *Awards:* A, B, M, D. *Entrance level for U.S. students:* Moderately difficult. *Enrollment:* 19,742 total; 16,296 undergraduates (58% women) including 1% international students from 100 foreign countries. *Faculty:* 1,421. *Library holdings:* 2.7 million books, 12,532 current serial subscriptions, 19,294 audiovisual materials. *Total majors:* 133. *Expenses:* (2006–07) $18,450; room and board, $7366 (on campus); room only, $4336 (on campus).

WESLEY COLLEGE, DOVER

General Information Independent United Methodist, coed institution. Small town setting. *Awards:* A, B, M. *Entrance level for U.S. students:* Moderately difficult. *Enrollment:* 2,306 total; 2,128 undergraduates (54% women) including 1% international students from 7 foreign countries. *Faculty:* 157. *Library holdings:* 104,636 books, 252 current serial subscriptions, 946 audiovisual materials. *Total majors:* 18. *Expenses:* (2007–08) $17,579; room and board, $7800 (on campus). *Financial aid:* Need-based college/university scholarships/grants from institutional funds, on-campus employment. Non-need-based academic. Forms required: institution's own financial aid form.

DISTRICT OF COLUMBIA

AMERICAN UNIVERSITY, WASHINGTON

General Information Independent Methodist, coed university. Suburban setting. *Awards:* A, B, M, D, FP. *Entrance level for U.S. students:* Very difficult. *Enrollment:* 11,279 total; 5,921 undergraduates (62% women) including 6% international students from 117 foreign countries. *Faculty:* 941. *Library holdings:* 1 million books, 23,955 current serial subscriptions, 48,300 audiovisual materials. *Total majors:* 53.

Information for International Students For fall 2006: 801 international students applied, 294 were accepted, 39 enrolled. Students can start in fall or spring. Transfers accepted from institutions abroad. *Admission tests:* Required: TOEFL (minimum score: iBT 80; paper-based 550; computer-based 213); minimum score for ESL admission: iBT 61; paper-based 510; computer-based 180), ELS (minimum score: 112), SAT (verbal) or IELTS scores may substitute for TOEFL; students who have not yet met English language proficiency requirement may receive conditional admission and study intensive ELS. TOEFL can be waived under certain conditions. *Application deadline:* 1/15. *Expenses:* (2006–07) $29,673; room and board, $11,570 (on campus); room only, $7350 (on campus). *Financial aid:* Need-based financial aid available. Non-need-based college/university scholarships/grants from institutional funds, athletic awards. Forms required: institution's own financial aid form. International transfer students are eligible to apply for aid. *Housing:* Guaranteed, also available during summer. *Services:* International student adviser on campus. Full-time ESL program on campus. ESL program available during the academic year and the summer. Internships and employment opportunities (on-campus and off-campus) available. *Contact:* Director, International Admissions, American University, 4400 Massachusetts Avenue, NW, Washington, DC 20016-8001. Telephone: 202-885-6000. Fax: 202-885-1025. E-mail: admissions@american.edu. URL: http://www.american.edu.

See In-Depth Description on page 33.

THE CATHOLIC UNIVERSITY OF AMERICA, WASHINGTON

General Information Independent, coed university, affiliated with Roman Catholic Church. Urban setting. *Awards:* B, M, D, FP. *Entrance level for U.S. students:* Moderately difficult. *Enrollment:* 6,148 total; 3,123 undergraduates (56% women) including 2% international students from 38 foreign countries. *Faculty:* 691. *Library holdings:* 1.6 million books, 10,448 current serial subscriptions, 40,697 audiovisual materials. *Total majors:* 77.

Information for International Students For fall 2006: 218 international students applied, 85 were accepted, 45 enrolled. Students can start in fall, spring, or summer. Transfers accepted from institutions abroad. *Admission tests:* Required: TOEFL (minimum score: iBT 80; paper-based 550; computer-based 213). Recommended: SAT or ACT. TOEFL can be waived under certain conditions. *Application deadline:* 2/15. *Expenses:* (2007–08) $28,990; room and board, $10,808 (on campus); room only, $6224 (on campus). *Financial aid:* Forms required: Immigration and Naturalization Service Document (1-141, I-92, or I-688). *Housing:* Guaranteed, also available during summer. *Services:* International student adviser on campus. Full-time and part-time ESL programs on campus. ESL program available during the academic year and the summer. Internships and employment opportunities (on-campus and off-campus) available. *Contact:* Director of International Admissions, The Catholic University of America, 102 McMahon Hall, Office of Admissions, Washington, DC 20064. Telephone: 202-319-5305. Fax: 202-319-6533. E-mail: cua-admissions@cua.edu. URL: http://www.cua.edu.

See In-Depth Description on page 51.

CORCORAN COLLEGE OF ART AND DESIGN, WASHINGTON

General Information Independent, coed institution. Urban setting. *Awards:* A, B, M. *Entrance level for U.S. students:* Moderately difficult. *Enrollment:* 592 total; 459 undergraduates (67% women) including 12% international students from 25 foreign countries. *Faculty:* 213. *Library holdings:* 29,413 books, 167 current serial subscriptions. *Total majors:* 10.

Information for International Students For fall 2006: 43 international students applied, 20 were accepted, 11 enrolled. Students can start in fall or spring. Transfers accepted from institutions abroad. *Admission tests:* Required: TOEFL (minimum score: iBT 79; paper-based 550; computer-based 213). Recommended: SAT or ACT. TOEFL can be waived under certain conditions. *Application deadline:* Rolling. *Expenses:* (2006–07) $24,489; room and board, $10,795 (on campus); room only, $8476 (on campus). *Financial aid:* Need-based college/university scholarships/grants from institutional funds, tuition waivers, loans from outside sources. Non-need-based loans from outside sources. Forms required: institution's own financial aid form. For fall 2005, international students on campus received college administered aid averaging $9067. *Housing:* Guaranteed. *Services:* International student adviser on campus. ESL program at cooperating institution. Employment opportunities (on-campus) available. *Contact:* Director of Admissions, Corcoran College of Art and Design, 500 17th Street, NW, Washington, DC 20006-4804. Telephone: 202-639-1814. Fax: 202-639-1830. E-mail: admissions@corcoran.org. URL: http://www.corcoran.edu.

See In-Depth Description on page 64.

GEORGETOWN UNIVERSITY, WASHINGTON

General Information Independent Roman Catholic (Jesuit), coed university. Urban setting. *Awards:* B, M, D, FP. *Entrance level for U.S. students:* Most difficult. *Enrollment:* 14,148 total; 6,853 undergraduates (54% women) including 4% international students from 71 foreign countries. *Faculty:* 1,215. *Library holdings:* 2.5 million books, 31,099 current serial subscriptions, 37,661 audiovisual materials. *Total majors:* 48. *Expenses:* (2007–08) $35,568; room and board, $12,146 (on campus); room only, $8092 (on campus). *Financial aid:* Need-based college/university scholarships/grants from institutional funds, athletic awards, loans from outside sources, on-campus employment. Non-need-based athletic awards, loans from outside sources, on-campus employment. Forms required: International Student's Financial Aid Application. For fall 2006 (estimated), 23 international students on campus received college administered financial aid ($32,200 average).

THE GEORGE WASHINGTON UNIVERSITY, WASHINGTON

General Information Independent, coed university. Urban setting. *Awards:* A, B, M, D, FP. *Entrance level for U.S. students:* Very difficult. *Enrollment:* 24,531 total; 10,813 undergraduates (55% women) including 4% international students from 101 foreign countries. *Faculty:* 2,062. *Library holdings:* 2 million books, 15,365 current serial subscriptions, 171,397 audiovisual materials. *Total majors:* 82. *Expenses:* (2007–08) $39,240; room and board, $11,520 (on campus); room only, $8020 (on campus). *Financial aid:* Need-based and non-need-based financial aid available. For fall 2005, 136 international students on campus received college administered financial aid ($21,363 average).

SOUTHEASTERN UNIVERSITY, WASHINGTON

General Information Independent, coed institution. Urban setting. *Awards:* A, B, M. *Entrance level for U.S. students:* Noncompetitive. *Enrollment:* 935 total; 665 undergraduates (74% women) including 9% international students from 40 foreign countries. *Faculty:* 110. *Library holdings:* 32,000 books, 200 current serial subscriptions, 250 audiovisual materials. *Total majors:* 8. *Expenses:* (2006–07) $10,230.

TRINITY (WASHINGTON) UNIVERSITY, WASHINGTON

General Information Independent Roman Catholic, undergraduate: women only; graduate: coed institution. Urban setting. *Awards:* B, M. *Entrance level for U.S. students:* Moderately difficult. *Enrollment:* 1,672 total; 968 undergraduates (98% women) including 1% international students. *Faculty:* 158. *Library holdings:* 207,000 books, 498 current serial subscriptions, 13,760 audiovisual materials. *Total majors:* 27.

Information for International Students For fall 2006: 60 international students applied, 40 were accepted, 20 enrolled. Students can start in fall, spring, or summer. Transfers accepted from institutions abroad. *Admission tests:* Required: TOEFL (minimum score: paper-based 550; computer-based 213; minimum score for ESL admission: paper-based 550; computer-based 213). Recommended: SAT or ACT, SAT Subject Tests. *Application deadline:* Rolling. *Housing:* Guaranteed. *Services:* International student adviser on campus. ESL program at cooperating institution. Internships and employment opportunities (on-campus and off-campus) available. *Contact:* Director, Office of International Student Services, Office of Admissions, Trinity (Washington) University, 125 Michigan Avenue, NE, Washington, DC 20017. Telephone: 202-884-9019. Fax: 202-884-9241. E-mail: peppind@trinitydc.edu. URL: http://www.trinitydc.edu.

FLORIDA

ATI HEALTH EDUCATION CENTER, MIAMI

General Information Proprietary, 2-year, coed college. Urban setting. *Awards:* A. *Entrance level for U.S. students:* Minimally difficult. *Enrollment:* 275 total including international students from 5 foreign countries. *Undergraduate faculty:* 19. *Library holdings:* 20 current serial subscriptions. *Total majors:* 3. *Financial aid:* Forms required: institution's own financial aid form.

BARRY UNIVERSITY, MIAMI SHORES

General Information Independent Roman Catholic, coed university. Suburban setting. *Awards:* B, M, D, FP. *Entrance level for U.S. students:* Moderately difficult. *Enrollment:* 8,885 total; 5,355 undergraduates (68% women) including 4% international students from 81 foreign countries. *Faculty:* 845. *Library holdings:* 233,938 books, 2,880 current serial subscriptions. *Total majors:* 58.

Information for International Students For fall 2006: 466 international students applied, 196 were accepted, 56 enrolled. Students can start in fall, spring, or summer. Transfers accepted from institutions abroad. *Admission tests:* Required: TOEFL (minimum score: paper-based 550; computer-based 213). TOEFL can be waived under certain conditions. *Application deadline:* Rolling. *Expenses:* (2006–07) $24,000; room and board, $7850 (on campus). *Financial aid:* Need-based college/university scholarships/grants from institutional funds, tuition waivers, athletic awards, loans from institutional funds, loans from outside sources, on-campus employment. Non-need-based college/university scholarships/grants from institutional funds, tuition waivers, athletic awards, loans from institutional funds, loans from outside sources, on-campus employment. Forms required: International Student's Certification of Finances. International transfer students are eligible to apply for aid. 161 international students on campus received college administered financial aid ($11,022 average). *Housing:* Available during summer. *Services:* International student adviser on campus. Full-time and part-time ESL programs on campus. ESL program available during the academic year. *Contact:* Director of Undergraduate Admissions, Barry University, 11300 NE Second Avenue, Miami Shores, FL 33161-6695. Telephone: 305-899-3100. Fax: 305-899-2971. E-mail: admissions@mail.barry.edu. URL: http://www.barry.edu. *See In-Depth Description on page 38.*

BREVARD COMMUNITY COLLEGE, COCOA

General Information State-supported, 2-year, coed college. Suburban setting. *Awards:* A. *Entrance level for U.S. students:* Noncompetitive. *Enrollment:* 13,670 total (60% women) including 1% international students from 79 foreign countries. *Undergraduate faculty:* 1,016. *Library holdings:* 213,873 books, 904 current serial subscriptions. *Total majors:* 37. *Expenses:* (2006–07) $5928.

BROWARD COMMUNITY COLLEGE, FORT LAUDERDALE

General Information State-supported, 2-year, coed college. Urban setting. *Awards:* A. *Entrance level for U.S. students:* Noncompetitive. *Enrollment:* 31,030 total (60% women) including 8% international students from 4 foreign countries. *Undergraduate faculty:* 1,561. *Library holdings:* 200,000 books, 600 current serial subscriptions. *Total majors:* 48. *Expenses:* (2006–07) $6,938.

CENTRAL FLORIDA COMMUNITY COLLEGE, OCALA

General Information State and locally supported, 2-year, coed college. Small town setting. *Awards:* A. *Entrance level for U.S. students:* Noncompetitive. *Enrollment:* 5,825 total (63% women) including 0.4% international students. *Undergraduate faculty:* 485. *Library holdings:* 82,112 books, 412 current serial subscriptions, 6,244 audiovisual materials. *Total majors:* 19.

Information for International Students For fall 2006: 23 international students applied, 19 were accepted, 17 enrolled. Students can start in fall, winter, spring, or summer. Transfers accepted from institutions abroad. *Admission tests:* Required: TOEFL (minimum score: iBT 61; paper-based 500; computer-based 173; minimum score for ESL admission: iBT 37; paper-based 420; computer-based 110). Recommended: LOEP. TOEFL can be waived under certain conditions. *Application deadline:* 5/20. *Expenses:* (2006–07) $7382; room and board, $5562 (on campus). *Housing:* Available during summer. *Services:* International student adviser on campus. Full-time and part-time ESL programs on campus. ESL program available during the academic year. Employment opportunities (on-campus) available. *Contact:* International Education Specialist, Central Florida Community College, 3001 SW College Road, Ocala, FL 34474. Telephone: 352-854-2322 Ext. 1386. Fax: 352-873-5882. E-mail: trexlerj@cf.edu. URL: http://www.cf.edu.

CLEARWATER CHRISTIAN COLLEGE, CLEARWATER

General Information Independent nondenominational, 4-year, coed college. Suburban setting. *Awards:* A, B. *Entrance level for U.S. students:* Minimally difficult. *Enrollment:* 582 total (49% women) including international students from 15 foreign countries. *Undergraduate faculty:* 53. *Library holdings:* 106,000 books, 700 current serial subscriptions. *Total majors:* 25.

Information for International Students For fall 2006: 7 international students enrolled. Students can start in fall or spring. *Admission tests:* Required: SAT or ACT, TOEFL (minimum score: paper-based 500; computer-based 173). *Application deadline:* 6/1. *Expenses:* (2006–07) $12,500; room and board, $5330 (on campus). *Financial aid:* Need-based college/university scholarships/grants from institutional funds, loans from outside sources, on-campus employment. Non-need-based college/university scholarships/grants from institutional funds, loans from outside sources, on-campus employment. Forms required: institution's own financial aid form. For fall 2006 (estimated), 1 international student on campus received college administered financial aid ($1700 average). *Services:* International student adviser on campus. Employment opportunities (on-campus) available. *Contact:* Director of Admissions, Clearwater Christian College, 3400 Gulf to Bay Boulevard, Clearwater, FL 33759. Telephone: 727-726-1153 Ext. 220. Fax: 727-726-8597. E-mail: admissions@clearwater.edu. URL: http://www.clearwater.edu.

DEVRY UNIVERSITY, MIRAMAR

General Information Proprietary, coed institution. *Awards:* A, B, M. *Entrance level for U.S. students:* Minimally difficult. *Enrollment:* 960 total; 834 undergraduates (35% women) including 6% international students from 5 foreign countries. *Faculty:* 80. *Library holdings:* 1,700 books, 75 current serial subscriptions. *Total majors:* 10. *Expenses:* (2007–08) $14,020.

DEVRY UNIVERSITY, ORLANDO

General Information Proprietary, coed institution. Urban setting. *Awards:* A, B, M. *Entrance level for U.S. students:* Minimally difficult. *Enrollment:* 1,295 total; 1,134 undergraduates (33% women) including 2% international students. *Faculty:* 101. *Library holdings:* 11,000 books, 60 current serial subscriptions. *Total majors:* 12. *Expenses:* (2007–08) $14,020.

ECKERD COLLEGE, ST. PETERSBURG

General Information Independent Presbyterian, 4-year, coed college. Suburban setting. *Awards:* B. *Entrance level for U.S. students:* Moderately difficult. *Enrollment:* 1,845 total (57% women) including 4% international students from 33 foreign countries. *Undergraduate faculty:* 167. *Library holdings:* 165,717 books, 1,738 current serial subscriptions, 2,140 audiovisual materials. *Total majors:* 36.

Information for International Students For fall 2006: 173 international students applied, 32 were accepted, 12 enrolled.

Eckerd College (continued)

Students can start in fall, winter, or spring. Transfers accepted from institutions abroad. *Admission tests:* Required: TOEFL (minimum score: iBT 79; paper-based 550; computer-based 213). Recommended: SAT, ACT, ELS. TOEFL can be waived under certain conditions. *Application deadline:* Rolling. *Expenses:* (2006–07) $27,618; room and board, $7868 (on campus); room only, $4072 (on campus). *Financial aid:* Need-based financial aid available. Non-need-based college/university scholarships/grants from institutional funds, athletic awards, loans from institutional funds, on-campus employment. International transfer students are eligible to apply for aid. For fall 2005, 150 international students on campus received college administered financial aid ($12,540 average). *Housing:* Guaranteed, also available during summer. *Services:* International student adviser on campus. Full-time and part-time ESL programs on campus. ESL program available during the academic year and the summer. Internships and employment opportunities (on-campus) available. *Contact:* Assistant Director of Admissions, Eckerd College, 4200 54th Avenue South, St. Petersburg, FL 33711. Telephone: 727-864-8331. Fax: 727-866-2304. E-mail: cruzcl@eckerd.edu. URL: http://www.eckerd.edu.

EDISON COLLEGE, FORT MYERS

General Information State and locally supported, 2-year, coed college. Urban setting. *Awards:* A. *Entrance level for U.S. students:* Noncompetitive. *Enrollment:* 10,642 total including 3% international students from 45 foreign countries. *Undergraduate faculty:* 417. *Library holdings:* 181,085 books, 10,297 audiovisual materials. *Total majors:* 29.

Information for International Students For fall 2006: 83 international students applied, 83 were accepted, 75 enrolled. Students can start in fall, winter, spring, or summer. Transfers accepted from institutions abroad. *Admission tests:* Required: TOEFL (minimum score: iBT 79; paper-based 550; computer-based 213; minimum score for ESL admission: iBT 61; paper-based 500; computer-based 173). Recommended: SAT or ACT, Florida College Entry Level Placement Test if no SAT or ACT. *Application deadline:* 7/1. *Services:* International student adviser on campus. Full-time ESL program on campus. ESL program available during the academic year and the summer. Internships and employment opportunities (on-campus) available. *Contact:* District Director of Student Development, Edison College, PO Box 60210, 8099 College Parkway, Fort Myers, FL 33906-6210. Telephone: 239-489-9362. Fax: 239-489-9040. E-mail: bsilva@edison.edu. URL: http://www.edison.edu.

EMBRY-RIDDLE AERONAUTICAL UNIVERSITY, DAYTONA BEACH

General Information Independent, coed institution. Suburban setting. *Awards:* B, M. *Entrance level for U.S. students:* Moderately difficult. *Enrollment:* 4,863 total; 4,473 undergraduates (16% women) including 8% international students from 84 foreign countries. *Faculty:* 328. *Library holdings:* 138,327 books, 741 current serial subscriptions, 7,030 audiovisual materials. *Total majors:* 19.

Information for International Students For fall 2006: 512 international students applied, 233 were accepted, 86 enrolled. Students can start in fall, spring, or summer. Transfers accepted from institutions abroad. *Admission tests:* Required: TOEFL (minimum score: paper-based 550; computer-based 213). TOEFL can be waived under certain conditions. *Application deadline:* Rolling. *Expenses:* (2007–08) $26,496; room and board, $9150 (on campus); room only, $4750 (on campus). *Financial aid:* Non-need-based college/university scholarships/grants from institutional funds, athletic awards, loans from outside sources, on-campus employment. For fall 2006 (estimated), 245 international students on campus received college administered financial aid ($5071 average). *Housing:* Available during summer. *Services:* International student adviser on campus. Full-time ESL program on campus. ESL program available during the academic year and the summer. Internships and employment opportunities (on-campus) available. *Contact:* Director of Admissions, Embry-Riddle Aeronautical University, Daytona Beach, FL 32114. Telephone: 386-226-6100. Fax: 386-226-7070. E-mail: dbadmit@erau.edu. URL: http://www.embryriddle.edu.

See In-Depth Description on page 78.

EVERGLADES UNIVERSITY, BOCA RATON

General Information Independent, coed institution. Suburban setting. *Awards:* B, M. *Entrance level for U.S. students:* Difficulty N/R. *Enrollment:* 711 total; 644 undergraduates including 1% international students. *Faculty:* 118. *Total majors:* 6. *Expenses:* (2006–07) $11,120.

FLAGLER COLLEGE, ST. AUGUSTINE

General Information Independent, 4-year, coed college. Small town setting. *Awards:* B. *Entrance level for U.S. students:*

Moderately difficult. *Enrollment:* 2,253 total (61% women) including 2% international students from 23 foreign countries. *Undergraduate faculty:* 170. *Library holdings:* 130,201 books, 549 current serial subscriptions. *Total majors:* 23.

Information for International Students Students can start in fall or spring. Transfers accepted from institutions abroad. *Admission tests:* Required: TOEFL (minimum score: paper-based 550; computer-based 213). *Application deadline:* 3/1. *Expenses:* (2007–08) $11,200; room and board, $6800 (on campus). *Financial aid:* Need-based college/university scholarships/grants from institutional funds. Non-need-based college/university scholarships/grants from institutional funds, athletic awards, loans from outside sources, on-campus employment, private scholarships. Forms required: institution's own financial aid form. For fall 2006 (estimated), 20 international students on campus received college administered financial aid ($5202 average). *Services:* International student adviser on campus. Internships and employment opportunities (on-campus and off-campus) available. *Contact:* Senior Assistant Director of Admissions and International Coordinator, Flagler College, 74 King Street, PO Box 1027, St. Augustine, FL 32084. Telephone: 904-829-6481. Fax: 904-829-6838. E-mail: flaglerc@flagler.edu. URL: http://www.flagler.edu.

FLORIDA ATLANTIC UNIVERSITY, BOCA RATON

General Information State-supported, coed university. Suburban setting. *Awards:* A, B, M, D. *Entrance level for U.S. students:* Moderately difficult. *Enrollment:* 25,385 total; 21,139 undergraduates (60% women) including 3% international students from 144 foreign countries. *Faculty:* 1,260. *Library holdings:* 1.3 million books, 12,811 current serial subscriptions. *Total majors:* 62.

Information for International Students For fall 2006: 987 international students enrolled. Students can start in fall, spring, or summer. Transfers accepted from institutions abroad. *Admission tests:* Required: SAT or ACT, TOEFL (minimum score: iBT 80; paper-based 550; computer-based 213; minimum score for ESL admission: iBT 80; paper-based 550; computer-based 213). *Application deadline:* 4/1. *Expenses:* (2006–07) $16,391; room and board, $8280 (on campus). *Financial aid:* Need-based financial aid available. Non-need-based college/university scholarships/grants from institutional funds, tuition waivers, athletic awards, loans from institutional funds, loans from outside sources, on-campus employment. Forms required: FAFSA. *Housing:* Available during summer. *Services:* International student adviser on campus. Full-time ESL program on campus. ESL program available during the academic year and the summer. Internships and employment opportunities (on-campus) available. *Contact:* Assistant Director of International Admissions, Florida Atlantic University, 777 Glades Road, Boca Raton, FL 33431. Telephone: 561-297-2627. Fax: 561-297-2758. E-mail: eklimcza@fau.edu. URL: http://www.fau.edu.

FLORIDA GULF COAST UNIVERSITY, FORT MYERS

General Information State-supported, coed institution. Suburban setting. *Awards:* A, B, M. *Entrance level for U.S. students:* Moderately difficult. *Enrollment:* 8,292 total; 7,121 undergraduates (61% women) including 1% international students from 77 foreign countries. *Faculty:* 490. *Library holdings:* 312,132 books, 7,119 current serial subscriptions, 10,078 audiovisual materials. *Total majors:* 25.

Information for International Students For fall 2006: 69 international students applied, 51 were accepted, 35 enrolled. Students can start in fall or spring. Transfers accepted from institutions abroad. *Admission tests:* Required: SAT or ACT, TOEFL (minimum score: paper-based 550; computer-based 213; minimum score for ESL admission: paper-based 550; computer-based 213). TOEFL can be waived under certain conditions. *Application deadline:* 5/1. *Expenses:* (2006–07) $16,440; room and board, $7740 (on campus); room only, $4240 (on campus). *Financial aid:* Need-based financial aid available. Non-need-based college/university scholarships/grants from institutional funds, tuition waivers, athletic awards. Forms required: institution's own financial aid form, International Student's Certification of Finances, I-20 Form (certificate of Eligibility for Nonimmigrant Student Status). 14 international students on campus received college administered financial aid ($13,504 average). *Services:* ESL program at cooperating institution. Internships and employment opportunities (on-campus and off-campus) available. *Contact:* Admissions Coordinator, Florida Gulf Coast University, 10501 FGCU Boulevard South, Fort Myers, FL 33965-6565. Telephone: 239-590-7878. Fax: 239-590-7894. E-mail: oar@fgcu.edu. URL: http://www.fgcu.edu.

See In-Depth Description on page 84.

FLORIDA INSTITUTE OF TECHNOLOGY, MELBOURNE

General Information Independent, coed university. Small town setting. *Awards:* B, M, D. *Entrance level for U.S. students:*

Moderately difficult. *Enrollment:* 4,741 total; 2,365 undergraduates (31% women) including 16% international students from 80 foreign countries. *Faculty:* 416. *Library holdings:* 290,582 books, 18,051 current serial subscriptions, 5,964 audiovisual materials. *Total majors:* 47.

Information for International Students For fall 2006: 900 international students applied, 607 were accepted, 127 enrolled. Students can start in fall, spring, or summer. Transfers accepted from institutions abroad. *Admission tests:* Recommended: SAT or ACT, TOEFL (minimum score: paper-based 550; computer-based 213; minimum score for ESL admission: paper-based 450; computer-based 133). TOEFL can be waived under certain conditions. *Application deadline:* Rolling. *Expenses:* (2006–07) $27,540; room and board, $7400 (on campus); room only, $4200 (on campus). *Financial aid:* Non-need-based college/university scholarships/grants from institutional funds, athletic awards, loans from outside sources, on-campus employment. Forms required: International Student's Certification of Finances. For fall 2006 (estimated), 185 international students on campus received college administered financial aid ($9506 average). *Housing:* Guaranteed, also available during summer. *Services:* International student adviser on campus. Full-time and part-time ESL programs on campus. ESL program available during the academic year and the summer. Internships and employment opportunities (on-campus) available. *Contact:* Associate Director of International Admissions, Florida Institute of Technology, 150 West University Boulevard, Melbourne, FL 32901-6975. Telephone: 321-674-8030. Fax: 321-723-9468. E-mail: senstice@fit.edu. URL: http://www.fit.edu.

FLORIDA INTERNATIONAL UNIVERSITY, MIAMI
General Information State-supported, coed university. Urban setting. *Awards:* B, M, D, FP. *Entrance level for U.S. students:* Moderately difficult. *Enrollment:* 37,997 total; 31,712 undergraduates (56% women) including 3% international students from 115 foreign countries. *Faculty:* 1,495. *Library holdings:* 2 million books, 40,813 current serial subscriptions, 159,978 audiovisual materials. *Total majors:* 91.

Information for International Students For fall 2006: 2029 international students applied, 955 were accepted, 495 enrolled. Students can start in fall, spring, or summer. Transfers accepted from institutions abroad. *Admission tests:* Required: SAT or ACT, TOEFL (minimum score: iBT 63; paper-based 500; computer-based 173; minimum score for ESL admission: paper-based 500; computer-based 173). TOEFL can be waived under certain conditions. *Application deadline:* 4/1. *Expenses:* (2006–07) $15,529; room and board, $9740 (on campus); room only, $6520 (on campus). *Housing:* Available during summer. *Services:* Full-time and part-time ESL programs on campus. ESL program available during the academic year and the summer. Internships and employment opportunities (on-campus) available. *Contact:* Office of Undergraduate Admissions, Florida International University, University Park, PC 140, Miami, FL 33199. Telephone: 305-348-2363. Fax: 305-348-3648. E-mail: admiss@fiu.edu. URL: http://www.fiu.edu.

See In-Depth Description on page 85.

FLORIDA KEYS COMMUNITY COLLEGE, KEY WEST
General Information State-supported, 2-year, coed college. Small town setting. *Awards:* A. *Entrance level for U.S. students:* Noncompetitive. *Enrollment:* 1,551 total. *Undergraduate faculty:* 138. *Library holdings:* 29,402 books, 330 current serial subscriptions, 1,001 audiovisual materials. *Total majors:* 8.

Information for International Students For fall 2006: 2 international students applied, 2 were accepted. Students can start in fall, spring, or summer. Transfers accepted from institutions abroad. *Admission tests:* Required: TOEFL (minimum score: iBT 83; paper-based 560; computer-based 220). TOEFL can be waived under certain conditions. *Application deadline:* 7/1. *Financial aid:* Forms required: International Student's Certification of Finances. *Services:* International student adviser on campus. Part-time ESL program on campus. ESL program available during the academic year. *Contact:* Assistant Director, Office of Enrollment Services/International Student Advisor, Florida Keys Community College, 5901 College Road, Key West, FL 33040. Telephone: 305-809-3278. Fax: 305-292-5163. E-mail: campion_j@firn.edu. URL: http://www.fkcc.edu.

FLORIDA METROPOLITAN UNIVERSITY–POMPANO BEACH CAMPUS, POMPANO BEACH
General Information Proprietary, coed institution. Urban setting. *Awards:* A, B, M. *Entrance level for U.S. students:* Minimally difficult. *Enrollment:* 1,377 total; 1,282 undergraduates including 12% international students from 60 foreign countries. *Faculty:* 61. *Library holdings:* 14,500 books, 61 current serial subscriptions. *Total majors:* 9. *Expenses:* (2006–07) $28,884.

FLORIDA NATIONAL COLLEGE, HIALEAH
General Information Proprietary, 2-year, coed college. Urban setting. *Awards:* A. *Entrance level for U.S. students:* Noncompetitive. *Enrollment:* 1,884 total (67% women) including 2% international students. *Undergraduate faculty:* 69. *Library holdings:* 28,754 books, 123 current serial subscriptions, 2,348 audiovisual materials. *Total majors:* 34. *Expenses:* (2007–08) $11,445.

FLORIDA SOUTHERN COLLEGE, LAKELAND
General Information Independent, coed institution, affiliated with United Methodist Church. Suburban setting. *Awards:* B, M. *Entrance level for U.S. students:* Moderately difficult. *Enrollment:* 1,873 total; 1,753 undergraduates (61% women) including 4% international students from 31 foreign countries. *Faculty:* 180. *Library holdings:* 182,765 books, 939 current serial subscriptions, 15,567 audiovisual materials. *Total majors:* 57. *Expenses:* (2007–08) $21,190; room and board, $7500 (on campus); room only, $4140 (on campus). *Financial aid:* Non-need-based college/university scholarships/grants from institutional funds, athletic awards, on-campus employment. Forms required: complex admissions requirements. For fall 2005, 58 international students on campus received college administered financial aid ($7981 average).

FLORIDA STATE UNIVERSITY, TALLAHASSEE
General Information State-supported, coed university. Suburban setting. *Awards:* A, B, M, D, FP. *Entrance level for U.S. students:* Very difficult. *Enrollment:* 39,973 total; 31,347 undergraduates (56% women) including 0.5% international students from 118 foreign countries. *Faculty:* 1,654. *Library holdings:* 2.9 million books, 58,093 current serial subscriptions, 251,340 audiovisual materials. *Total majors:* 157.

Information for International Students For fall 2006: 328 international students applied, 105 were accepted, 39 enrolled. Students can start in fall, spring, or summer. Transfers accepted from institutions abroad. *Admission tests:* Required: SAT or ACT, TOEFL (minimum score: iBT 80; paper-based 550; computer-based 213). *Application deadline:* 2/14. *Expenses:* (2006–07) $16,439; room and board, $7078 (on campus); room only, $3780 (on campus). *Housing:* Available during summer. *Services:* International student adviser on campus. Full-time ESL program on campus. ESL program available during the academic year and the summer. Internships and employment opportunities (on-campus) available. *Contact:* Associate Director of Admissions, Office of Admissions-2400, Florida State University, A2500 University Center, Tallahassee, FL 32306-2400. Telephone: 850-644-1389. Fax: 850-644-2514. E-mail: intladms@admin.fsu.edu. URL: http://www.fsu.edu.

FULL SAIL REAL WORLD EDUCATION, WINTER PARK
General Information Proprietary, primarily 2-year, coed, primarily men's college. Suburban setting. *Awards:* A, B. *Entrance level for U.S. students:* Noncompetitive. *Enrollment:* 5,219 total (11% women) including 1% international students from 6 foreign countries. *Library holdings:* 2,531 books, 84 current serial subscriptions, 784 audiovisual materials. *Total majors:* 7.

Information for International Students Students can start in fall, winter, spring, or summer. Transfers accepted from institutions abroad. *Admission tests:* Required: TOEFL (minimum score: iBT 79; paper-based 213), ELS (minimum score: 109), IELTS (score of 6). TOEFL can be waived under certain conditions. *Application deadline:* Rolling. *Financial aid:* Forms required: International Student's Certification of Finances. *Services:* International student adviser on campus. Internships and employment opportunities (on-campus) available. *Contact:* International Liaison, Full Sail Real World Education, 3300 University Boulevard, Winter Park, FL 32792. Telephone: 407-679-6333. Fax: 407-678-0070. E-mail: admissions@fullsail.com. URL: http://www.fullsail.com.

See In-Depth Description on page 88.

GULF COAST COMMUNITY COLLEGE, PANAMA CITY
General Information State-supported, 2-year, coed college. Suburban setting. *Awards:* A. *Entrance level for U.S. students:* Noncompetitive. *Enrollment:* 6,058 total (60% women) including 1% international students from 8 foreign countries. *Undergraduate faculty:* 494. *Library holdings:* 80,000 books, 521 current serial subscriptions, 32,041 audiovisual materials. *Total majors:* 44.

Information for International Students For fall 2006: 22 international students applied, 8 were accepted, 8 enrolled. Students can start in fall, spring, or summer. Transfers accepted from institutions abroad. *Admission tests:* Required: TOEFL (minimum score: iBT 79; paper-based 550; computer-based 213; minimum score for ESL admission: iBT 79; paper-based 550; computer-based 213), college placement test. TOEFL can be waived

Gulf Coast Community College (continued)

under certain conditions. *Application deadline:* 7/15. *Expenses:* (2006–07) $7208. *Financial aid:* Forms required: any required by the USDOE to complete financial aid file. *Services:* International student adviser on campus. Part-time ESL program on campus. ESL program available during the academic year and the summer. Employment opportunities (on-campus) available. *Contact:* International Student Representative, Gulf Coast Community College, 5230 West US Highway 98, Panama City, FL 32401. Telephone: 850-872-3892 Ext. 4894. Fax: 850-913-3308. E-mail: dshoffer@gulfcoast.edu. URL: http://www.gulfcoast.edu.

INTERNATIONAL ACADEMY OF DESIGN & TECHNOLOGY, TAMPA

General Information Proprietary, coed institution. Urban setting. *Entrance level for U.S. students:* Noncompetitive. *Enrollment:* 2,405 total (65% women) including 0.5% international students from 9 foreign countries. *Undergraduate faculty:* 167. *Library holdings:* 6,000 books, 150 current serial subscriptions, 50 audiovisual materials. *Total majors:* 6.

INTERNATIONAL COLLEGE, NAPLES

General Information Independent, coed institution. Suburban setting. *Awards:* A, B, M. *Entrance level for U.S. students:* Minimally difficult. *Enrollment:* 1,640 total; 1,454 undergraduates (70% women) including 2% international students. *Faculty:* 111. *Library holdings:* 29,711 books, 230 current serial subscriptions. *Total majors:* 13. *Expenses:* (2006–07) $13,130.

JACKSONVILLE UNIVERSITY, JACKSONVILLE

General Information Independent, coed institution. Suburban setting. *Awards:* B, M. *Entrance level for U.S. students:* Moderately difficult. *Enrollment:* 3,093 total; 2,699 undergraduates (58% women) including 3% international students from 50 foreign countries. *Faculty:* 232. *Library holdings:* 385,016 books, 686 current serial subscriptions, 24,919 audiovisual materials. *Total majors:* 58.

Information for International Students For fall 2006: 116 international students applied, 49 were accepted, 26 enrolled. Students can start in fall, spring, or summer. Transfers accepted from institutions abroad. *Admission tests:* Required: TOEFL (minimum score: iBT 76; paper-based 540; computer-based 207). Recommended: SAT or ACT. TOEFL can be waived under certain conditions. *Application deadline:* 6/1. *Expenses:* (2006–07) $21,200; room and board, $6780 (on campus); room only, $3180 (on campus). *Financial aid:* Non-need financial aid available. Forms required: institution's own financial aid form. For fall 2005, 63 international students on campus received college administered financial aid ($12,902 average). *Services:* International student adviser on campus. Internships and employment opportunities (on-campus) available. *Contact:* Associate Director of Admissions, College of Arts and Sciences, Jacksonville University, Office of Admission, 2800 University Boulevard North, Jacksonville, FL 32211. Telephone: 904-256-7000 Ext. 7006. Fax: 904-256-7012. E-mail: ymartel@ju.edu. URL: http://www.ju.edu.

See In-Depth Description on page 106.

JOHNSON & WALES UNIVERSITY, NORTH MIAMI

General Information Independent, 4-year, coed college. Suburban setting. *Awards:* A, B. *Entrance level for U.S. students:* Minimally difficult. *Enrollment:* 2,215 total (53% women) including 7% international students from 49 foreign countries. *Undergraduate faculty:* 86. *Library holdings:* 12,721 books, 200 current serial subscriptions, 2,165 audiovisual materials. *Total majors:* 16.

Information for International Students For fall 2006: 375 international students applied, 250 were accepted, 80 enrolled. Students can start in fall, winter, or spring. Transfers accepted from institutions abroad. *Admission tests:* Required: TOEFL (minimum score: iBT 80; paper-based 550; computer-based 210). Recommended: SAT or ACT, ELS. TOEFL can be waived under certain conditions. *Application deadline:* Rolling. *Expenses:* (2007–08) $21,460; room and board, $9600 (on campus). *Financial aid:* Non-need-based college/university scholarships/grants from institutional funds. Forms required: International Student's Certification of Finances. For fall 2005, 206 international students on campus received college administered financial aid ($2761 average). *Housing:* Guaranteed, also available during summer. *Services:* International student adviser on campus. ESL program at cooperating institution. Internships and employment opportunities (on-campus and off-campus) available. *Contact:* International Admissions Officer, Johnson & Wales University, 1701 NE 127th Street, North Miami, FL 33181. Telephone: 305-892-7001. Fax: 305-892-7020. E-mail: treisinger@jwu.edu. URL: http://www.jwu.edu.

JONES COLLEGE, JACKSONVILLE

General Information Independent, 4-year, coed college. Urban setting. *Awards:* A, B. *Entrance level for U.S. students:* Noncompetitive. *Enrollment:* 623 total (80% women). *Undergraduate faculty:* 61. *Library holdings:* 34,000 books, 161 current serial subscriptions. *Total majors:* 7.

Information for International Students Students can start in fall, winter, spring, or summer. Transfers accepted from institutions abroad. *Admission tests:* Required: TOEFL (minimum score: paper-based 450; computer-based 133), CPAt. *Application deadline:* 8/10. *Expenses:* (2006–07) $6690. *Services:* International student adviser on campus. *Contact:* President/PDSO, Jones College, 5353 Arlington Expressway, Jacksonville, FL 32211-5588. Telephone: 904-743-1122 Ext. 105. Fax: 904-743-4446. E-mail: fmccaffe@jones.edu. URL: http://www.jones.edu.

KEISER UNIVERSITY, MIAMI

General Information Proprietary, primarily 2-year, coed college. Suburban setting. *Awards:* A, B. *Entrance level for U.S. students:* Difficulty N/R. *Enrollment:* 812 total (64% women) including 0.2% international students from 2 foreign countries. *Undergraduate faculty:* 49. *Total majors:* 12. *Expenses:* (2007–08) $12,040.

LAKE CITY COMMUNITY COLLEGE, LAKE CITY

General Information State-supported, 2-year, coed college. Small town setting. *Awards:* A. *Entrance level for U.S. students:* Noncompetitive. *Enrollment:* 2,736 total (64% women) including 1% international students from 7 foreign countries. *Undergraduate faculty:* 165. *Library holdings:* 42,000 books, 180 current serial subscriptions. *Total majors:* 19. *Expenses:* (2006–07) $7290; room and board, $4535 (on campus). *Financial aid:* Forms required: institution's own financial aid form.

LAKE-SUMTER COMMUNITY COLLEGE, LEESBURG

General Information State and locally supported, 2-year, coed college. Suburban setting. *Awards:* A. *Entrance level for U.S. students:* Noncompetitive. *Enrollment:* 3,641 total (66% women) including 1% international students. *Undergraduate faculty:* 183. *Library holdings:* 74,858 books, 284 current serial subscriptions, 980 audiovisual materials. *Total majors:* 14. *Expenses:* (2006–07) $7582.

LYNN UNIVERSITY, BOCA RATON

General Information Independent, coed institution. Suburban setting. *Awards:* B, M, D. *Entrance level for U.S. students:* Moderately difficult. *Enrollment:* 2,715 total; 2,300 undergraduates (50% women) including 12% international students from 82 foreign countries. *Faculty:* 238. *Library holdings:* 173,000 books, 455 current serial subscriptions, 13,500 audiovisual materials. *Total majors:* 15.

Information for International Students For fall 2006: 327 international students applied, 191 were accepted, 70 enrolled. Students can start in fall or spring. Transfers accepted from institutions abroad. *Admission tests:* Required: SAT or ACT, TOEFL (minimum score: iBT 61; paper-based 500; computer-based 173). TOEFL can be waived under certain conditions. *Application deadline:* Rolling. *Expenses:* (2007–08) $28,850; room and board, $9650 (on campus). *Financial aid:* Non-need-based college/university scholarships/grants from institutional funds, athletic awards, on-campus employment. Forms required: institution's own financial aid form, International Student's Certification of Finances. International transfer students are eligible to apply for aid. 113 international students on campus received college administered financial aid ($15,481 average). *Housing:* Guaranteed, also available during summer. *Services:* International student adviser on campus. Internships and employment opportunities (on-campus) available. *Contact:* Director of International Admissions, Lynn University, 3601 North Military Trail, Boca Raton, FL 33431-5598. Telephone: 561-237-7900. Fax: 561-237-7100. E-mail: admission@lynn.edu. URL: http://www.lynn.edu.

MANATEE COMMUNITY COLLEGE, BRADENTON

General Information State-supported, 2-year, coed college. Suburban setting. *Awards:* A. *Entrance level for U.S. students:* Noncompetitive. *Enrollment:* 9,080 total (63% women) including 2% international students from 40 foreign countries. *Undergraduate faculty:* 463. *Library holdings:* 65,386 books, 378 current serial subscriptions. *Total majors:* 96.

Information for International Students Students can start in fall, winter, spring, or summer. Transfers accepted from institutions abroad. *Admission tests:* Required: TOEFL (minimum score: iBT 61; paper-based 500; computer-based 173). Recommended: SAT or ACT, ELS, FPT, CPT. TOEFL can be waived under certain conditions. *Application deadline:* Rolling. *Expenses:* (2007–08) $9052. *Services:*

International student adviser on campus. ESL program at cooperating institution. ESL program available during the academic year and the summer. Employment opportunities (on-campus) available. *Contact:* Coordinator of Admissions and International Student Services, Manatee Community College, 5840 26th Street West, Bradenton, FL 34207. Telephone: 941-752-5418. Fax: 941-727-6024. E-mail: hekkinw@mccfl.edu. URL: http://www.mccfl.edu.

MIAMI DADE COLLEGE, MIAMI

General Information State and locally supported, primarily 2-year, coed college. Urban setting. *Awards:* A, B. *Entrance level for U.S. students:* Noncompetitive. *Enrollment:* 54,169 total (62% women) including 3% international students from 160 foreign countries. *Undergraduate faculty:* 2,103. *Library holdings:* 327,417 books, 4,916 current serial subscriptions, 17,186 audiovisual materials. *Total majors:* 136.

Information for International Students For fall 2006: 420 international students applied, 356 were accepted, 343 enrolled. Students can start in fall, spring, or summer. Transfers accepted from institutions abroad. *Admission tests:* Required: TOEFL (minimum score: iBT 79; paper-based 550; computer-based 213). TOEFL can be waived under certain conditions. *Application deadline:* 5/24. *Expenses:* (2006–07) $6577. *Financial aid:* Forms required: Scholarships and Institutional Grants Application. *Services:* International student adviser on campus. Full-time ESL program on campus. ESL program available during the academic year and the summer. Internships and employment opportunities (on-campus and off-campus) available. *Contact:* Director, International Student Services, Miami Dade College, Wolfson Campus, 300 NE 2nd Avenue, Room 3113, Miami, FL 33132. Telephone: 305-237-3485. Fax: 305-237-7596. E-mail: pepstein@mdc.edu. URL: http://www.mdc.edu.

See In-Depth Description on page 128.

MIAMI INTERNATIONAL UNIVERSITY OF ART & DESIGN, MIAMI

General Information Proprietary, coed institution. Urban setting. *Awards:* A, B, M. *Entrance level for U.S. students:* Moderately difficult. *Enrollment:* 1,406 total; 1,328 undergraduates (64% women) including 1% international students from 60 foreign countries. *Faculty:* 110. *Library holdings:* 22,000 books, 158 current serial subscriptions. *Total majors:* 11. *Expenses:* (2006–07) $18,960; room only, $6150 (on campus).

NEW COLLEGE OF FLORIDA, SARASOTA

General Information State-supported, 4-year, coed college. Suburban setting. *Awards:* B. *Entrance level for U.S. students:* Very difficult. *Enrollment:* 746 total (59% women) including 1% international students from 25 foreign countries. *Undergraduate faculty:* 84. *Library holdings:* 268,305 books, 953 current serial subscriptions, 4,774 audiovisual materials. *Total majors:* 38.

Information for International Students For fall 2006: 60 international students applied, 5 were accepted, 1 enrolled. Students can start in fall or spring. Transfers accepted from institutions abroad. *Admission tests:* Required: SAT or ACT, TOEFL (minimum score: iBT 83; paper-based 560; computer-based 220). TOEFL can be waived under certain conditions. *Application deadline:* 4/15. *Expenses:* (2007–08) $20,575; room and board, $7080 (on campus); room only, $4590 (on campus). *Financial aid:* Need-based college/university scholarships/grants from institutional funds, loans from outside sources, on-campus employment, state grants. Non-need-based college/university scholarships/grants from institutional funds, tuition waivers, loans from outside sources. Forms required: International Student's Certification of Finances. For fall 2006 (estimated), 9 international students on campus received college administered financial aid ($5152 average). *Services:* International student adviser on campus. Internships and employment opportunities (on-campus) available. *Contact:* Director of Transfer and Multicultural Recruitment, New College of Florida, 5800 Bay Shore Road, Sarasota, FL 34243. Telephone: 941-487-5000. Fax: 941-487-5010. E-mail: swu@ncf.edu. URL: http://www.ncf.edu.

See In-Depth Description on page 135.

NEW ENGLAND INSTITUTE OF TECHNOLOGY AT PALM BEACH, WEST PALM BEACH

General Information Proprietary, 2-year, coed college. Urban setting. *Awards:* A. *Entrance level for U.S. students:* Noncompetitive. *Enrollment:* 1,200 total. *Undergraduate faculty:* 46. *Total majors:* 13. *Financial aid:* Forms required: institution's own financial aid form.

NOVA SOUTHEASTERN UNIVERSITY, FORT LAUDERDALE

General Information Independent, coed university. Suburban setting. *Awards:* A, B, M, D, FP. *Entrance level for U.S. students:*

Moderately difficult. *Enrollment:* 25,960 total; 5,413 undergraduates (73% women) including 6% international students. *Faculty:* 1,553. *Library holdings:* 725,000 books, 22,295 current serial subscriptions, 23,738 audiovisual materials. *Total majors:* 32.

Information for International Students For fall 2006: 166 international students applied, 84 were accepted, 37 enrolled. Students can start in fall or winter. Transfers accepted from institutions abroad. *Admission tests:* Required: TOEFL (minimum score: paper-based 550; computer-based 213). *Application deadline:* Rolling. *Expenses:* (2006–07) $18,650; room and board, $6012 (on campus); room only, $3612 (on campus). *Financial aid:* Non-need-based college/university scholarships/grants from institutional funds, athletic awards, loans from outside sources, on-campus employment. Forms required: institution's own financial aid form, International Student's Financial Aid Application, letter of application. For fall 2006 (estimated), 88 international students on campus received college administered financial aid ($8048 average). *Services:* International student adviser on campus. Full-time ESL program on campus. ESL program available during the academic year and the summer. Internships and employment opportunities (on-campus) available. *Contact:* Admissions, Nova Southeastern University, Fort Lauderdale, FL 33314. Telephone: 954-262-8000. Fax: 954-262-3811. E-mail: admissions@nova.edu. URL: http://www.nova.edu.

See In-Depth Description on page 143.

PALM BEACH ATLANTIC UNIVERSITY, WEST PALM BEACH

General Information Independent nondenominational, coed institution. Urban setting. *Awards:* A, B, M, FP. *Entrance level for U.S. students:* Moderately difficult. *Enrollment:* 3,264 total; 2,524 undergraduates (63% women) including 3% international students from 10 foreign countries. *Faculty:* 274. *Library holdings:* 147,514 books, 332 current serial subscriptions, 4,540 audiovisual materials. *Total majors:* 46. *Expenses:* (2006–07) $18,740; room and board, $6780 (on campus); room only, $3750 (on campus). *Financial aid:* Need-based financial aid available. Non-need-based college/university scholarships/grants from institutional funds, tuition waivers, athletic awards. Forms required: International Student's Certification of Finances. For fall 2005, 41 international students on campus received college administered financial aid ($1984 average).

PALM BEACH COMMUNITY COLLEGE, LAKE WORTH

General Information State-supported, 2-year, coed college. Urban setting. *Awards:* A. *Entrance level for U.S. students:* Noncompetitive. *Enrollment:* 21,938 total (62% women) including 3% international students from 138 foreign countries. *Undergraduate faculty:* 1,272. *Library holdings:* 151,000 books, 1,474 current serial subscriptions. *Total majors:* 67. *Expenses:* (2006–07) $5708.

PASCO-HERNANDO COMMUNITY COLLEGE, NEW PORT RICHEY

General Information State-supported, 2-year, coed college. Small town setting. *Awards:* A. *Entrance level for U.S. students:* Noncompetitive. *Enrollment:* 7,547 total (65% women) including 1% international students from 9 foreign countries. *Undergraduate faculty:* 350. *Library holdings:* 69,903 books, 231 current serial subscriptions. *Total majors:* 19. *Expenses:* (2006–07) $7388. *Financial aid:* Non-need financial aid available. Forms required: scholarship application form.

PENSACOLA JUNIOR COLLEGE, PENSACOLA

General Information State-supported, 2-year, coed college. Urban setting. *Awards:* A. *Entrance level for U.S. students:* Noncompetitive. *Enrollment:* 11,000 total including international students from 21 foreign countries. *Undergraduate faculty:* 747. *Total majors:* 64. *Expenses:* (2006–07) $7,423.

POLK COMMUNITY COLLEGE, WINTER HAVEN

General Information State-supported, 2-year, coed college. Suburban setting. *Awards:* A. *Entrance level for U.S. students:* Noncompetitive. *Enrollment:* 6,964 total (65% women) including 1% international students from 49 foreign countries. *Undergraduate faculty:* 534. *Library holdings:* 181,000 books, 325 current serial subscriptions, 2,500 audiovisual materials. *Total majors:* 21. *Expenses:* (2006–07) $7393. *Financial aid:* Forms required: PCC Foundation Application.

REMINGTON COLLEGE–TAMPA CAMPUS, TAMPA

General Information Proprietary, primarily 2-year, coed college. Urban setting. *Awards:* A, B. *Entrance level for U.S. students:* Noncompetitive. *Enrollment:* 685 total including 3% international students. *Undergraduate faculty:* 26. *Library holdings:* 4,100 books,

Remington College–Tampa Campus (continued)
124 current serial subscriptions, 340 audiovisual materials.
Total majors: 6. *Financial aid:* Forms required: personal data sheet.

ROLLINS COLLEGE, WINTER PARK

General Information Independent, coed institution. Suburban setting. *Awards:* B, M. *Entrance level for U.S. students:* Very difficult. *Enrollment:* 2,454 total; 1,720 undergraduates (60% women) including 3% international students from 33 foreign countries. *Faculty:* 233. *Library holdings:* 303,519 books, 17,874 current serial subscriptions, 5,406 audiovisual materials. *Total majors:* 32. *Expenses:* (2006–07) $30,860; room and board, $9626 (on campus); room only, $5650 (on campus). *Financial aid:* Need-based college/university scholarships/grants from institutional funds, loans from institutional funds, loans from outside sources, on-campus employment. Non-need-based college/university scholarships/grants from institutional funds, tuition waivers, athletic awards, loans from outside sources, on-campus employment. Forms required: institution's own financial aid form. For fall 2006 (estimated), 29 international students on campus received college administered financial aid ($24,451 average).

SAINT LEO UNIVERSITY, SAINT LEO

General Information Independent Roman Catholic, coed institution. Rural setting. *Awards:* A, B, M. *Entrance level for U.S. students:* Moderately difficult. *Enrollment:* 2,774 total; 1,514 undergraduates (54% women) including 8% international students from 45 foreign countries. *Faculty:* 129. *Library holdings:* 208,110 books, 890 current serial subscriptions, 6,542 audiovisual materials. *Total majors:* 26.
Information for International Students For fall 2006: 484 international students applied, 172 were accepted, 41 enrolled. Students can start in fall or spring. Transfers accepted from institutions abroad. *Admission tests:* Required: TOEFL (minimum score: paper-based 550; computer-based 213), SAT required for academic scholarships. *Application deadline:* Rolling. *Expenses:* (2007–08) $16,420; room and board, $8102 (on campus). *Financial aid:* Need-based loans from outside sources, on-campus employment. Non-need-based college/university scholarships/grants from institutional funds, athletic awards, loans from outside sources, on-campus employment. International transfer students are eligible to apply for aid. For fall 2006 (estimated), 121 international students on campus received college administered financial aid ($8059 average). *Services:* International student adviser on campus. Full-time and part-time ESL programs on campus. ESL program available during the academic year. Internships and employment opportunities (on-campus) available. *Contact:* Office of Admission, Saint Leo University, 33701 State Road 52, MC-2008, PO Box 6665, Saint Leo, FL 33574-6665. Telephone: 352-588-8283. Fax: 352-588-8257. E-mail: admission@saintleo.edu. URL: http://www.saintleo.edu.
See In-Depth Description on page 167.

ST. PETERSBURG COLLEGE, ST. PETERSBURG

General Information State and locally supported, primarily 2-year, coed college. Suburban setting. *Awards:* A, B. *Entrance level for U.S. students:* Noncompetitive. *Enrollment:* 24,102 total (63% women) including 1% international students from 30 foreign countries. *Undergraduate faculty:* 1,912. *Library holdings:* 222,990 books, 1,393 current serial subscriptions, 16,543 audiovisual materials. *Total majors:* 66.
Information for International Students For fall 2006: 180 international students applied, 180 were accepted, 95 enrolled. Students can start in fall, spring, or summer. Transfers accepted from institutions abroad. *Admission tests:* Required: TOEFL (minimum score: iBT 61; paper-based 500; computer-based 173; minimum score for ESL admission: iBT 61; paper-based 500; computer-based 173). TOEFL can be waived under certain conditions. *Application deadline:* 7/7. *Services:* International student adviser on campus. Full-time and part-time ESL programs on campus. ESL program available during the academic year. Internships and employment opportunities (on-campus and off-campus) available. *Contact:* International Student Officer, St. Petersburg College, St. Petersburg/Gibbs Campus, PO Box 13489, St. Petersburg, FL 33733. Telephone: 727-341-4370. Fax: 727-341-3510. E-mail: berger.judy@spcollege.edu. URL: http://www.spjc.edu.

ST. THOMAS UNIVERSITY, MIAMI GARDENS

General Information Independent Roman Catholic, coed institution. Suburban setting. *Awards:* B, M, FP. *Entrance level for U.S. students:* Moderately difficult. *Enrollment:* 2,517 total; 1,155 undergraduates (60% women) including 8% international students

from 58 foreign countries. *Faculty:* 231. *Library holdings:* 154,017 books, 898 current serial subscriptions, 7,894 audiovisual materials. *Total majors:* 28.
Information for International Students For fall 2006: 226 international students applied, 49 were accepted, 31 enrolled. Students can start in fall, spring, or summer. Transfers accepted from institutions abroad. *Admission tests:* Required: TOEFL (minimum score: paper-based 527; computer-based 197). Recommended: SAT, ACT. *Application deadline:* Rolling. *Expenses:* (2006–07) $18,750; room and board, $5910 (on campus). *Financial aid:* Need-based and non-need-based financial aid available. For fall 2005, 78 international students on campus received college administered financial aid ($6500 average). *Services:* International student adviser on campus. Full-time and part-time ESL programs on campus. ESL program available during the academic year and the summer. Employment opportunities (on-campus) available. *Contact:* Admissions Officer/International Recruiter, St. Thomas University, 16401 NW 37th Avenue, Miami, FL 33054. Telephone: 305-628-6709. Fax: 305-628-6591. E-mail: cjtorres@stu.edu. URL: http://www.stu.edu.
See In-Depth Description on page 171.

SANTA FE COMMUNITY COLLEGE, GAINESVILLE

General Information State and locally supported, 2-year, coed college. Suburban setting. *Awards:* A (offers bachelor's degrees in conjunction with Saint Leo College). *Entrance level for U.S. students:* Noncompetitive. *Enrollment:* 13,806 total (53% women) including 3% international students from 80 foreign countries. *Undergraduate faculty:* 782. *Library holdings:* 81,832 books, 624 current serial subscriptions. *Total majors:* 38.

SCHILLER INTERNATIONAL UNIVERSITY, LARGO

General Information Independent, coed institution. Suburban setting. *Awards:* A, B, M. *Entrance level for U.S. students:* Minimally difficult. *Enrollment:* 246 total including 81% international students from 50 foreign countries. *Faculty:* 34. *Library holdings:* 1,918 books, 34 current serial subscriptions. *Total majors:* 7.
Information for International Students For fall 2006: 265 international students applied, 255 were accepted, 201 enrolled. Students can start in fall, spring, or summer. Transfers accepted from institutions abroad. *Admission tests:* Required: TOEFL (minimum score: paper-based 500; computer-based 173), ELS. TOEFL can be waived under certain conditions. *Application deadline:* Rolling. *Expenses:* (2006–07) $16,880; room and board, $7600 (on campus). *Services:* International student adviser on campus. Full-time and part-time ESL programs on campus. ESL program available during the academic year and the summer. Internships and employment opportunities (on-campus) available. *Contact:* Associate Director of Admissions, Schiller International University, 300 East Bay Drive, Largo, FL 33770. Telephone: 727-736-5082. Fax: 727-734-0359. E-mail: admissions@schiller.edu. URL: http://www.schiller.edu.
See In-Depth Description on page 179.

SEMINOLE COMMUNITY COLLEGE, SANFORD

General Information State and locally supported, 2-year, coed college. Small town setting. *Awards:* A. *Entrance level for U.S. students:* Noncompetitive. *Enrollment:* 11,747 total (59% women) including 5% international students from 96 foreign countries. *Undergraduate faculty:* 807. *Library holdings:* 112,000 books, 373 current serial subscriptions, 6,550 audiovisual materials. *Total majors:* 50. *Expenses:* (2006–07) $6613.

SOUTH UNIVERSITY, WEST PALM BEACH

General Information Proprietary, coed institution. Suburban setting. *Awards:* A, B, M. *Entrance level for U.S. students:* Minimally difficult. *Enrollment:* 649 total; 635 undergraduates (80% women) including 2% international students from 4 foreign countries. *Faculty:* 62. *Library holdings:* 29,879 books, 86 current serial subscriptions, 1,195 audiovisual materials. *Total majors:* 15. *Expenses:* (2007–08) $11,850. *Financial aid:* Forms required: institution's own financial aid form, International Student's Certification of Finances.

STETSON UNIVERSITY, DELAND

General Information Independent, coed institution. Small town setting. *Awards:* B, M, FP. *Entrance level for U.S. students:* Moderately difficult. *Enrollment:* 3,762 total; 2,273 undergraduates (58% women) including 3% international students from 31 foreign countries. *Faculty:* 259. *Library holdings:* 395,069 books, 20,000 current serial subscriptions, 17,260 audiovisual materials. *Total majors:* 60. *Expenses:* (2007–08) $28,780; room and board, $7968 (on campus); room only, $4548 (on campus). *Financial aid:* Non-need-based college/university scholarships/grants from institutional funds, athletic awards, loans from outside sources, on-campus employment. Forms required: institution's own financial aid form. For fall 2006 (estimated), 54 international students on campus received college administered financial aid ($17,120 average).

TALLAHASSEE COMMUNITY COLLEGE, TALLAHASSEE

General Information State and locally supported, 2-year, coed college. Suburban setting. *Awards:* A. *Entrance level for U.S. students:* Noncompetitive. *Enrollment:* 13,493 total (56% women) including 1% international students from 37 foreign countries. *Undergraduate faculty:* 581. *Library holdings:* 108,282 books, 179 current serial subscriptions, 9,283 audiovisual materials. *Total majors:* 30. *Expenses:* (2006–07) $6705. *Financial aid:* Forms required: institution's own financial aid form, FAFSA.

TALMUDIC COLLEGE OF FLORIDA, MIAMI BEACH

General Information Independent Jewish, men's institution. Urban setting. *Awards:* B, M, D. *Entrance level for U.S. students:* Moderately difficult. *Enrollment:* 35 total; 30 undergraduates including 20% international students from 5 foreign countries. *Faculty:* 6. *Library holdings:* 25,000 books, 10,000 audiovisual materials. *Total majors:* 5. *Expenses:* (2007–08) $7500; room and board, $5000 (on campus); room only, $2500 (on campus). *Financial aid:* Need-based and non-need-based financial aid available. Forms required: institution's own financial aid form. 4 international students on campus received college administered financial aid ($3800 average).

TRINITY BAPTIST COLLEGE, JACKSONVILLE

General Information Independent Baptist, coed institution. Urban setting. *Awards:* A, B, M. *Entrance level for U.S. students:* Moderately difficult. *Enrollment:* 366 total; 319 undergraduates (51% women) including 1% international students from 6 foreign countries. *Faculty:* 53. *Library holdings:* 35,070 books, 191 current serial subscriptions. *Total majors:* 6. *Expenses:* (2007–08) $7070; room and board, $4550 (on campus); room only, $2260 (on campus). *Financial aid:* Non-need financial aid available. Forms required: institution's own financial aid form.

TRINITY COLLEGE OF FLORIDA, NEW PORT RICHEY

General Information Independent nondenominational, 4-year, coed college. Small town setting. *Awards:* A, B. *Entrance level for U.S. students:* Minimally difficult. *Enrollment:* 182 total (38% women) including 2% international students from 3 foreign countries. *Undergraduate faculty:* 23. *Library holdings:* 45,664 books, 173 current serial subscriptions, 213 audiovisual materials. *Total majors:* 8.

Information for International Students For fall 2006: 6 international students applied, 1 was accepted, 1 enrolled. Students can start in fall or spring. Transfers accepted from institutions abroad. *Admission tests:* Required: SAT or ACT, TOEFL (minimum score: paper-based 500; computer-based 173; minimum score for ESL admission: paper-based 500; computer-based 173). Recommended: ELS. TOEFL can be waived under certain conditions. *Application deadline:* 5/31. *Expenses:* (2007–08) $9656; room and board, $5620 (on campus). *Financial aid:* Need-based college/university scholarships/grants from institutional funds, loans from outside sources, on-campus employment. Non-need-based college/university scholarships/grants from institutional funds, on-campus employment. Forms required: institution's own financial aid form. 5 international students on campus received college administered financial aid ($500 average). *Housing:* Available during summer. *Services:* International student adviser on campus. Internships and employment opportunities (on-campus) available. *Contact:* Assistant Director of Enrollment, Trinity College of Florida, 2430 Welbilt Boulevard, Trinity, FL 34655. Telephone: 727-376-6911 Ext. 309. Fax: 727-569-1410. E-mail: kbonsignore@trinitycollege.edu. URL: http://www.trinitycollege.edu.

UNIVERSITY OF CENTRAL FLORIDA, ORLANDO

General Information State-supported, coed university. Suburban setting. *Awards:* A, B, M, D. *Entrance level for U.S. students:* Moderately difficult. *Enrollment:* 46,719 total; 39,545 undergraduates (55% women) including 1% international students from 129 foreign countries. *Faculty:* 1,664. *Library holdings:* 1.4 million books, 16,368 current serial subscriptions, 42,610 audiovisual materials. *Total majors:* 81.

Information for International Students Students can start in fall, spring, or summer. Transfers accepted from institutions abroad. *Admission tests:* Required: SAT, TOEFL (minimum score: iBT 80; paper-based 550; computer-based 213; minimum score for ESL admission: iBT 80). *Application deadline:* 3/1. *Expenses:* (2006–07) $17,017; room and board, $8000 (on campus); room only,

$4600 (on campus). *Financial aid:* Non-need-based tuition waivers, athletic awards, loans from outside sources. For fall 2005, 30 international students on campus received college administered financial aid ($972 average). *Housing:* Available during summer. *Services:* International student adviser on campus. Full-time and part-time ESL programs on campus. ESL program available during the academic year and the summer. Internships and employment opportunities (on-campus and off-campus) available. *Contact:* Senior Admissions Specialist, University of Central Florida, PO Box 160130, Orlando, FL 32816-0130. Telephone: 407-823-0061. Fax: 407-823-2176. E-mail: tcerrone@mail.ucf.edu. URL: http://www.ucf.edu.

See In-Depth Description on page 207.

UNIVERSITY OF FLORIDA, GAINESVILLE

General Information State-supported, coed university. Suburban setting. *Awards:* B, M, D, FP. *Entrance level for U.S. students:* Very difficult. *Enrollment:* 50,822 total; 35,110 undergraduates (54% women) including 1% international students from 128 foreign countries. *Faculty:* 2,311. *Library holdings:* 5.3 million books, 25,342 current serial subscriptions, 25,953 audiovisual materials. *Total majors:* 98. *Expenses:* (2006–07) $17,790; room and board, $6590 (on campus); room only, $4170 (on campus). *Financial aid:* Forms required: International Student's Certification of Finances.

UNIVERSITY OF MIAMI, CORAL GABLES

General Information Independent, coed university. Suburban setting. *Awards:* B, M, D, FP. *Entrance level for U.S. students:* Very difficult. *Enrollment:* 15,670 total; 10,509 undergraduates (55% women) including 5% international students from 90 foreign countries. *Faculty:* 1,292. *Library holdings:* 3 million books, 45,953 current serial subscriptions, 66,094 audiovisual materials. *Total majors:* 125.

Information for International Students For fall 2006: 1328 international students applied, 630 were accepted, 125 enrolled. Students can start in fall, spring, or summer. Transfers accepted from institutions abroad. *Admission tests:* Required: TOEFL (minimum score: iBT 59; paper-based 550; computer-based 213). TOEFL can be waived under certain conditions. *Application deadline:* 1/15. *Expenses:* (2007–08) $33,070; room and board, $9606 (on campus); room only, $5762 (on campus). *Financial aid:* Non-need-based college/university scholarships/grants from institutional funds, athletic awards. For fall 2006 (estimated), 184 international students on campus received college administered financial aid ($20,334 average). *Housing:* Guaranteed, also available during summer. *Services:* International student adviser on campus. Full-time and part-time ESL programs on campus. ESL program available during the academic year and the summer. Internships and employment opportunities (on-campus) available. *Contact:* Director of International Admissions, Office of International Admission, University of Miami, PO Box 248025, Coral Gables, FL 33124-2230. Telephone: 305-284-2271. Fax: 305-284-6811. E-mail: mreid@miami.edu. URL: http://www.miami.edu.

UNIVERSITY OF NORTH FLORIDA, JACKSONVILLE

General Information State-supported, coed institution. Urban setting. *Awards:* A, B, M, D (doctoral degree in education only). *Entrance level for U.S. students:* Very difficult. *Enrollment:* 15,954 total; 14,124 undergraduates (58% women) including 1% international students from 63 foreign countries. *Faculty:* 696. *Library holdings:* 798,321 books, 3,101 current serial subscriptions, 26,885 audiovisual materials. *Total majors:* 50. *Expenses:* (2006–07) $14,995; room and board, $6268 (on campus); room only, $3866 (on campus). *Financial aid:* Non-need financial aid available. Forms required: scholarship application form. For fall 2006 (estimated), 63 international students on campus received college administered financial aid ($2330 average).

UNIVERSITY OF PHOENIX–CENTRAL FLORIDA CAMPUS, MAITLAND

General Information Proprietary, coed institution. Urban setting. *Awards:* B, M. *Entrance level for U.S. students:* Noncompetitive. *Enrollment:* 2,072 total; 1,562 undergraduates (63% women) including 15% international students. *Faculty:* 525. *Library holdings:* 1,759 books, 692 current serial subscriptions. *Total majors:* 15. *Expenses:* (2006–07) $10,058.

UNIVERSITY OF PHOENIX–FORT LAUDERDALE CAMPUS, FORT LAUDERDALE

General Information Proprietary, coed institution. Urban setting. *Awards:* B, M. *Entrance level for U.S. students:* Noncompetitive. *Enrollment:* 3,121 total; 2,343 undergraduates (71% women) including 17% international students. *Faculty:* 264. *Library holdings:* 1,759 books, 692 current serial subscriptions. *Total majors:* 14. *Expenses:* (2006–07) $10,058.

UNIVERSITY OF PHOENIX–NORTH FLORIDA CAMPUS, JACKSONVILLE

General Information Proprietary, coed institution. Urban setting. *Awards:* B, M. *Entrance level for U.S. students:* Noncompetitive. *Enrollment:* 2,211 total; 1,632 undergraduates (62% women) including 6% international students. *Faculty:* 255. *Library holdings:* 1,759 books, 692 current serial subscriptions. *Total majors:* 16. *Expenses:* (2006–07) $10,058.

UNIVERSITY OF PHOENIX–WEST FLORIDA CAMPUS, TEMPLE TERRACE

General Information Proprietary, coed institution. Urban setting. *Awards:* B, M. *Entrance level for U.S. students:* Noncompetitive. *Enrollment:* 2,659 total; 1,983 undergraduates (62% women) including 7% international students. *Faculty:* 359. *Library holdings:* 1,759 books, 692 current serial subscriptions. *Total majors:* 10. *Expenses:* (2006–07) $10,058.

UNIVERSITY OF SOUTH FLORIDA, TAMPA

General Information State-supported, coed university. Urban setting. *Awards:* A, B, M, D, FP. *Entrance level for U.S. students:* Moderately difficult. *Enrollment:* 43,636 total; 34,438 undergraduates (59% women) including 2% international students from 131 foreign countries. *Faculty:* 1,937. *Library holdings:* 2.1 million books, 20,440 current serial subscriptions. *Total majors:* 84.

Information for International Students For fall 2006: 753 international students applied, 310 were accepted, 183 enrolled. Students can start in fall, spring, or summer. Transfers accepted from institutions abroad. *Admission tests:* Required: SAT or ACT, TOEFL (minimum score: iBT 79; paper-based 550; computer-based 213). TOEFL can be waived under certain conditions. *Application deadline:* 1/2. *Expenses:* (2006–07) $16,189; room and board, $7180 (on campus); room only, $3648 (on campus). *Financial aid:* Need-based tuition waivers, athletic awards, on-campus employment. Non-need-based tuition waivers, athletic awards, on-campus employment. For fall 2005, 55 international students on campus received college administered financial aid ($9065 average). *Housing:* Available during summer. *Services:* International student adviser on campus. Full-time ESL program on campus. ESL program available during the academic year and the summer. Internships and employment opportunities (on-campus) available. *Contact:* International Admissions, University of South Florida, 4202 East Fowler Avenue, CPR 107, Tampa, FL 33620-5550. Telephone: 813-974-8790. Fax: 813-974-8044. E-mail: ia@iac.usf.edu. URL: http://www.usf.edu.

See In-Depth Description on page 227.

THE UNIVERSITY OF TAMPA, TAMPA

General Information Independent, coed institution. Urban setting. *Awards:* A, B, M. *Entrance level for U.S. students:* Moderately difficult. *Enrollment:* 5,381 total; 4,745 undergraduates (61% women) including 6% international students from 100 foreign countries. *Faculty:* 435. *Library holdings:* 288,857 books, 24,122 current serial subscriptions, 7,103 audiovisual materials. *Total majors:* 45.

Information for International Students For fall 2006: 412 international students applied, 241 were accepted, 87 enrolled. Students can start in fall, winter, spring, or summer. Transfers accepted from institutions abroad. *Admission tests:* Required: TOEFL (minimum score: paper-based 550; computer-based 213), SAT or ACT required for English speaking students only. *Application deadline:* Rolling. *Expenses:* (2006–07) $19,628; room and board, $7254 (on campus); room only, $3354 (on campus). *Financial aid:* Non-need-based college/university scholarships/grants from institutional funds, athletic awards. Forms required: International Student's Certification of Finances. For fall 2006 (estimated), 12 international students on campus received college administered financial aid ($4166 average). *Housing:* Guaranteed, also available during summer. *Services:* International student adviser on campus. ESL program at cooperating institution. ESL program available during the academic year and the summer. Internships and employment opportunities (on-campus) available. *Contact:* Director of International Admissions, The University of Tampa, 401 West Kennedy Boulevard, Box F, Tampa, FL 33606-1490. Telephone: 813-253-6211. Fax: 813-258-7398. E-mail: admissions@ut.edu. URL: http://www.utampa.edu.

See In-Depth Description on page 228.

UNIVERSITY OF WEST FLORIDA, PENSACOLA

General Information State-supported, coed institution. Suburban setting. *Awards:* A, B, M, D (specialists). *Entrance level for U.S. students:* Moderately difficult. *Enrollment:* 9,819 total; 8,254 undergraduates (60% women) including 1% international students from 78 foreign countries. *Faculty:* 575. *Library holdings:* 792,733 books, 5,122 current serial subscriptions, 10,061 audiovisual materials. *Total majors:* 55.

Information for International Students For fall 2006: 109 international students applied, 48 were accepted, 16 enrolled. Students can start in fall, spring, or summer. Transfers accepted from institutions abroad. *Admission tests:* Required: SAT or ACT, TOEFL (minimum score: paper-based 525; computer-based 193). TOEFL can be waived under certain conditions. *Application deadline:* 5/15. *Expenses:* (2006–07) $15,878; room and board, $6600 (on campus). *Services:* International student adviser on campus. Full-time and part-time ESL programs on campus. ESL program available during the academic year. Employment opportunities (on-campus) available. *Contact:* Director of Admissions, University of West Florida, 11000 University Parkway, Building 18, Pensacola, FL 32514-5750. Telephone: 850-474-2230. Fax: 850-474-3360. E-mail: admissions@uwf.edu. URL: http://uwf.edu.

VALENCIA COMMUNITY COLLEGE, ORLANDO

General Information State-supported, 2-year, coed college. Urban setting. *Awards:* A. *Entrance level for U.S. students:* Noncompetitive. *Enrollment:* 30,245 total (58% women) including 3% international students from 84 foreign countries. *Undergraduate faculty:* 1,215. *Library holdings:* 183,264 books, 2,196 current serial subscriptions, 23,140 audiovisual materials. *Total majors:* 41. *Expenses:* (2006–07) $6287.

WARNER SOUTHERN COLLEGE, LAKE WALES

General Information Independent, coed institution, affiliated with Church of God. Rural setting. *Awards:* A, B, M. *Entrance level for U.S. students:* Minimally difficult. *Enrollment:* 970 total; 921 undergraduates (58% women) including 2% international students from 17 foreign countries. *Faculty:* 99. *Library holdings:* 56,419 books, 224 current serial subscriptions, 14,935 audiovisual materials. *Total majors:* 24. *Financial aid:* Need-based college/university scholarships/grants from institutional funds, athletic awards, loans from outside sources, on-campus employment. Non-need-based college/university scholarships/grants from institutional funds, athletic awards, loans from outside sources, on-campus employment. Forms required: International Student's Certification of Finances. 26 international students on campus received college administered financial aid ($8868 average).

WEBBER INTERNATIONAL UNIVERSITY, BABSON PARK

General Information Independent, coed institution. Small town setting. *Awards:* A, B, M. *Entrance level for U.S. students:* Moderately difficult. *Enrollment:* 617 total; 560 undergraduates (42% women) including 16% international students from 34 foreign countries. *Faculty:* 47. *Library holdings:* 15,000 books, 55 current serial subscriptions. *Total majors:* 11.

Information for International Students Students can start in fall or spring. Transfers accepted from institutions abroad. *Admission tests:* Required: TOEFL (minimum score: iBT 61; paper-based 500; computer-based 173). Recommended: ACT, ELS. *Application deadline:* 8/1. *Expenses:* (2006–07) $15,900; room and board, $4990 (on campus); room only, $2900 (on campus). *Financial aid:* Need-based on-campus employment. Non-need-based college/university scholarships/grants from institutional funds, tuition waivers, athletic awards, on-campus employment. For fall 2006 (estimated), 83 international students on campus received college administered financial aid ($8598 average). *Housing:* Guaranteed, also available during summer. *Services:* International student adviser on campus. Full-time and part-time ESL programs on campus. ESL program available during the academic year and the summer. Employment opportunities (on-campus) available. *Contact:* Admissions Assistant, Webber International University, 1201 North Scenic Highway, Babson Park, FL 33827. Telephone: 863-638-2911. Fax: 863-638-1591. E-mail: admissions@webber.edu. URL: http://www.webber.edu.

See In-Depth Description on page 242.

GEORGIA

ABRAHAM BALDWIN AGRICULTURAL COLLEGE, TIFTON

General Information State-supported, 2-year, coed college. Small town setting. *Awards:* A. *Entrance level for U.S. students:* Noncompetitive. *Enrollment:* 3,423 total (58% women) including 1% international students. *Undergraduate faculty:* 154. *Library holdings:* 69,986 books, 431 current serial subscriptions. *Total majors:* 57. *Financial aid:* Non-need-based tuition waivers, athletic awards.

AGNES SCOTT COLLEGE, DECATUR

General Information Independent, undergraduate: women only; graduate: coed institution, affiliated with Presbyterian Church (U.S.A.). Urban setting. *Awards:* B, M. *Entrance level for U.S. students:* Very difficult. *Enrollment:* 902 total; 886 undergraduates (99% women) including 5% international students from 26 foreign countries. *Faculty:* 106. *Library holdings:* 218,046 books, 1,842 current serial subscriptions, 19,989 audiovisual materials. *Total majors:* 27.

Information for International Students For fall 2006: 121 international students applied, 28 were accepted, 6 enrolled. Students can start in fall or spring. Transfers accepted from institutions abroad. *Admission tests:* Required: SAT or ACT, TOEFL (minimum score: paper-based 577; computer-based 233), either TOEFL or ELPT is required. *Application deadline:* 3/1. *Expenses:* (2006–07) $25,785; room and board, $8990 (on campus); room only, $4495 (on campus). *Financial aid:* Need-based college/university scholarships/grants from institutional funds, on-campus employment. Non-need-based college/university scholarships/grants from institutional funds, tuition waivers, on-campus employment. Forms required: International Student's Financial Aid Application, International Student's Certification of Finances. International transfer students are eligible to apply for aid. For fall 2006 (estimated), 33 international students on campus received college administered financial aid ($15,644 average). *Housing:* Guaranteed, also available during summer. *Services:* International student adviser on campus. Internships and employment opportunities (on-campus) available. *Contact:* Dean of Admission, Agnes Scott College, 141 East College Avenue, Decatur, GA 30030-3797. Telephone: 404-471-6285. Fax: 404-471-6414. E-mail: admission@agnesscott.edu. URL: http://www.agnesscott.edu.

AMERICAN INTERCONTINENTAL UNIVERSITY, ATLANTA

General Information Proprietary, coed institution. Urban setting. *Awards:* A, B, M. *Entrance level for U.S. students:* Noncompetitive. *Enrollment:* 1,152 total; 1,138 undergraduates (55% women) including 1% international students from 2 foreign countries. *Faculty:* 69. *Library holdings:* 30,699 books, 245 current serial subscriptions, 2,716 audiovisual materials. *Total majors:* 7.

Information for International Students For fall 2006: 120 international students applied, 36 were accepted, 36 enrolled. Students can start in fall, winter, spring, or summer. Transfers accepted from institutions abroad. *Admission tests:* Required: TOEFL (minimum score: paper-based 500; computer-based 173), ELS. Recommended: SAT, ACT. TOEFL can be waived under certain conditions. *Application deadline:* Rolling. *Services:* International student adviser on campus. ESL program at cooperating institution. Internships and employment opportunities (on-campus and off-campus) available. *Contact:* International Admissions Advisor, American InterContinental University, 3330 Peachtree Road, NE, Atlanta, GA 30326. Telephone: 404-965-5931. Fax: 404-965-5997. E-mail: Shane.Corrodus@buckhead.aiuniv.edu. URL: http://www.aiuniv.edu.

ARMSTRONG ATLANTIC STATE UNIVERSITY, SAVANNAH

General Information State-supported, coed institution. Suburban setting. *Awards:* A, B, M. *Entrance level for U.S. students:* Minimally difficult. *Enrollment:* 6,728 total; 6,086 undergraduates (68% women) including 4% international students from 75 foreign countries. *Faculty:* 372. *Library holdings:* 227,439 books, 990 current serial subscriptions. *Total majors:* 34. *Expenses:* (2007–08) $10,756; room only, $6000 (on campus). *Financial aid:* Need-based college/university scholarships/grants from institutional funds, tuition waivers, athletic awards, loans from outside sources, on-campus employment. Non-need-based college/university scholarships/grants from institutional funds, tuition waivers, athletic awards, loans from outside sources, on-campus employment. Forms required: institutional scholarship application form. For fall 2005, 14 international students on campus received college administered financial aid ($2143 average).

ATHENS TECHNICAL COLLEGE, ATHENS

General Information State-supported, 2-year, coed college. Suburban setting. *Awards:* A. *Entrance level for U.S. students:* Noncompetitive. *Enrollment:* 3,961 total (68% women) including 0.03% international students. *Undergraduate faculty:* 289. *Library holdings:* 33,891 books, 538 current serial subscriptions, 3,279 audiovisual materials. *Total majors:* 28. *Expenses:* (2006–07) $2475.

ATLANTA CHRISTIAN COLLEGE, EAST POINT

General Information Independent Christian, 4-year, coed college. Suburban setting. *Awards:* A, B. *Entrance level for U.S. students:* Moderately difficult. *Enrollment:* 443 total. *Library holdings:* 50,000 books, 187 current serial subscriptions. *Total majors:* 9. *Expenses:* (2006–07) $13,160; room and board, $5040 (on campus).

ATLANTA METROPOLITAN COLLEGE, ATLANTA

General Information State-supported, 2-year, coed college. Urban setting. *Awards:* A. *Entrance level for U.S. students:* Minimally difficult. *Enrollment:* 1,748 total (64% women) including 3% international students from 39 foreign countries. *Undergraduate faculty:* 72. *Library holdings:* 48,719 books, 113 current serial subscriptions, 3,874 audiovisual materials. *Total majors:* 31. *Expenses:* (2006–07) $6600.

AUGUSTA STATE UNIVERSITY, AUGUSTA

General Information State-supported, coed institution. Urban setting. *Awards:* A, B, M. *Entrance level for U.S. students:* Minimally difficult. *Enrollment:* 6,552 total; 5,707 undergraduates (65% women) including 1% international students from 32 foreign countries. *Faculty:* 359. *Library holdings:* 478,420 books, 29,468 current serial subscriptions, 4,738 audiovisual materials. *Total majors:* 33. *Expenses:* (2006–07) $10,748; room only, $4920 (on campus). *Financial aid:* Forms required: International Student's Certification of Finances.

AUGUSTA TECHNICAL COLLEGE, AUGUSTA

General Information State-supported, 2-year, coed college. Urban setting. *Awards:* A. *Entrance level for U.S. students:* Noncompetitive. *Enrollment:* 4,445 total (63% women) including 0.1% international students. *Undergraduate faculty:* 376. *Library holdings:* 70,816 books, 445 current serial subscriptions, 7,733 audiovisual materials. *Total majors:* 24. *Expenses:* (2006–07) $2487.

BEACON UNIVERSITY, COLUMBUS

General Information Independent religious, coed institution. Urban setting. *Awards:* A, B, M, D. *Entrance level for U.S. students:* Difficulty N/R. *Enrollment:* 229 total; 126 undergraduates. *Library holdings:* 85,000 books, 67 current serial subscriptions. *Total majors:* 3.

Information for International Students For fall 2006: 8 international students applied, 4 were accepted, 4 enrolled. Students can start in fall, spring, or summer. Transfers accepted from institutions abroad. *Admission tests:* Recommended: SAT or ACT, TOEFL (minimum score: paper-based 500; computer-based 173; minimum score for ESL admission: paper-based 500; computer-based 173), COMPASS. *Application deadline:* Rolling. *Housing:* Available during summer. *Services:* International student adviser on campus. *Contact:* Admissions Officer, Beacon University, 6003 Veterans Parkway, Columbus, GA 31909. Telephone: 706-323-5364 Ext. 258. Fax: 706-323-5891. E-mail: cindy.winkles@beacon.edu. URL: http://www.beacon.edu.

BERRY COLLEGE, MOUNT BERRY

General Information Independent interdenominational, coed institution. Suburban setting. *Awards:* B, M. *Entrance level for U.S. students:* Moderately difficult. *Enrollment:* 1,842 total; 1,718 undergraduates (66% women) including 2% international students from 16 foreign countries. *Faculty:* 193. *Library holdings:* 203,522 books, 2,082 current serial subscriptions, 3,596 audiovisual materials. *Total majors:* 39. *Expenses:* (2006–07) $18,950; room and board, $7164 (on campus); room only, $4024 (on campus). *Financial aid:* Non-need-based college/university scholarships/grants from institutional funds, athletic awards, on-campus employment. Forms required: institution's own financial aid form. For fall 2006 (estimated), 34 international students on campus received college administered financial aid ($20,413 average).

BRENAU UNIVERSITY, GAINESVILLE

General Information Independent, undergraduate: women only; graduate: coed institution. Small town setting. *Awards:* B, M (also offers coed evening and weekend programs with significant enrollment not reflected in profile). *Entrance level for U.S. students:* Moderately difficult. *Enrollment:* 846 total; 807 undergraduates (100% women) including 6% international students from 11 foreign countries. *Faculty:* 97. *Total majors:* 35. *Expenses:* (2007–08) $17,700; room and board, $8950 (on campus). *Financial aid:* Need-based college/university scholarships/grants from institutional funds, athletic awards, loans from outside sources, on-campus employment. Non-need-based college/university scholarships/grants from institutional funds, athletic awards, loans from outside sources, on-campus employment. Forms required: International Student's Certification of Finances. For fall 2006 (estimated), 25 international students on campus received college administered financial aid ($19,008 average).

BREWTON-PARKER COLLEGE, MT. VERNON

General Information Independent Southern Baptist, 4-year, coed college. Rural setting. *Awards:* A, B. *Entrance level for U.S. students:* Minimally difficult. *Enrollment:* 1,119 total (64% women) including 1% international students from 2 foreign countries. *Undergraduate faculty:* 189. *Library holdings:* 82,366 books, 320 current serial subscriptions, 5,592 audiovisual materials. *Total majors:* 31. *Expenses:* (2006–07) $13,360; room and board, $4750 (on campus); room only, $2250 (on campus). *Financial aid:* Need-based college/university scholarships/grants from institutional funds, athletic awards, on-campus employment. Non-need-based college/university scholarships/grants from institutional funds, athletic awards, on-campus employment. Forms required: copy of Social Security card. 30 international students on campus received college administered financial aid ($7732 average).

CENTRAL GEORGIA TECHNICAL COLLEGE, MACON

General Information State-supported, 2-year, coed college. Suburban setting. *Awards:* A. *Entrance level for U.S. students:* Noncompetitive. *Enrollment:* 4,898 total (66% women) including 0.04% international students from 1 foreign country. *Undergraduate faculty:* 484. *Library holdings:* 16,500 books, 300 current serial subscriptions, 1,800 audiovisual materials. *Total majors:* 28. *Expenses:* (2006–07) $2475.

CHATTAHOOCHEE TECHNICAL COLLEGE, MARIETTA

General Information State-supported, 2-year, coed college. Suburban setting. *Awards:* A. *Entrance level for U.S. students:* Noncompetitive. *Enrollment:* 5,994 total (54% women) including 2% international students. *Undergraduate faculty:* 300. *Library holdings:* 22,127 books, 292 current serial subscriptions, 1,826 audiovisual materials. *Total majors:* 23.

Information for International Students Students can start in fall, winter, spring, or summer. Transfers accepted from institutions abroad. *Admission tests:* Required: SAT or ACT, TOEFL (minimum score: iBT 61; paper-based 500; computer-based 173), ASSET or COMPASS required if no SAT or ACT. Recommended: SAT. TOEFL can be waived under certain conditions. *Application deadline:* Rolling. *Expenses:* (2006–07) $2496. *Financial aid:* Need-based college/university scholarships/grants from institutional funds, on-campus employment. Non-need-based college/university scholarships/grants from institutional funds. *Services:* International student adviser on campus. ESL program at cooperating institution. ESL program available during the academic year and the summer. Employment opportunities (on-campus and off-campus) available. *Contact:* Director, International Students, Chattahoochee Technical College, 980 South Cobb Drive, Marietta, GA 30060-3398. Telephone: 770-528-4528. Fax: 770-528-5817. E-mail: gmoor@chattcollege.com. URL: http://www.chattcollege.com.

CLAYTON STATE UNIVERSITY, MORROW

General Information State-supported, coed institution. Suburban setting. *Awards:* A, B. *Entrance level for U.S. students:* Minimally difficult. *Enrollment:* 6,081 total; 6,068 undergraduates (70% women) including 2% international students from 44 foreign countries. *Undergraduate faculty:* 353. *Library holdings:* 77,043 books, 4,250 current serial subscriptions. *Total majors:* 93. *Expenses:* (2006–07) $11,370. *Financial aid:* Non-need financial aid available.

COASTAL GEORGIA COMMUNITY COLLEGE, BRUNSWICK

General Information State-supported, 2-year, coed college. Small town setting. *Awards:* A. *Entrance level for U.S. students:* Noncompetitive. *Enrollment:* 3,054 total (67% women) including 0.5% international students from 11 foreign countries. *Undergraduate faculty:* 148. *Library holdings:* 535 current serial subscriptions, 1,151 audiovisual materials. *Total majors:* 35.

Information for International Students For fall 2006: 8 international students applied, 5 were accepted, 4 enrolled. Students can start in fall, winter, spring, or summer. Transfers accepted from institutions abroad. *Admission tests:* Recommended: COMPASS. TOEFL can be waived under certain conditions. *Application deadline:* Rolling. *Expenses:* (2006–07) $6772. *Financial aid:* Non-need financial aid available. *Services:* International student adviser on campus. Employment opportunities (on-campus) available. *Contact:* Admissions Clerk, Coastal Georgia Community College, 3700 Altama Avenue, Brunswick, GA 31520-3644. Telephone: 912-264-7253. Fax: 912-262-3072. E-mail: cltoler@cgcc.edu. URL: http://www.cgcc.edu.

COLUMBUS STATE UNIVERSITY, COLUMBUS

General Information State-supported, coed institution. Suburban setting. *Awards:* A, B, M. *Entrance level for U.S. students:* Minimally difficult. *Enrollment:* 7,597 total; 6,764 undergraduates (62% women) including 1% international students from 34 foreign countries. *Faculty:* 449. *Library holdings:* 387,026 books, 1,400 current serial subscriptions, 10,864 audiovisual materials. *Total majors:* 60. *Expenses:* (2006–07) $10,870; room and board, $6284 (on campus); room only, $4320 (on campus). *Financial aid:* Need-based financial aid available. Non-need-based college/university scholarships/grants from institutional funds, tuition waivers, loans from institutional funds. Forms required: institutional scholarship application. For fall 2006 (estimated), 46 international students on campus received college administered financial aid ($3769 average).

COLUMBUS TECHNICAL COLLEGE, COLUMBUS

General Information State-supported, 2-year, coed college. Urban setting. *Awards:* A. *Entrance level for U.S. students:* Noncompetitive. *Enrollment:* 3,327 total (64% women) including 0.1% international students. *Undergraduate faculty:* 230. *Library holdings:* 26,072 books, 49 current serial subscriptions, 533 audiovisual materials. *Total majors:* 24. *Expenses:* (2006–07) $2478.

DEKALB TECHNICAL COLLEGE, CLARKSTON

General Information State-supported, 2-year, coed college. Suburban setting. *Awards:* A. *Entrance level for U.S. students:* Noncompetitive. *Enrollment:* 3,641 total (63% women) including 0.03% international students. *Undergraduate faculty:* 459. *Total majors:* 28.

Information for International Students Students can start in fall, winter, spring, or summer. *Admission tests:* Required: SAT, ACT, CPE, ASSET, and/or COMPASS. *Application deadline:* 8/21. *Expenses:* (2006–07) $2523. *Contact:* International Student Admission, DeKalb Technical College, 495 North Indian Creek Drive, Clarkston, GA 30021-2397. Telephone: 404-297-9522 Ext. 1154. Fax: 404-294-6496. E-mail: petersl@dekalbtech.edu. URL: http://www.dekalbtech.edu.

See In-Depth Description on page 66.

DEVRY UNIVERSITY, ALPHARETTA

General Information Proprietary, coed institution. Suburban setting. *Awards:* A, B, M. *Entrance level for U.S. students:* Minimally difficult. *Enrollment:* 743 total; 577 undergraduates (41% women) including 2% international students. *Faculty:* 89. *Library holdings:* 7,659 books, 73 current serial subscriptions. *Total majors:* 11. *Expenses:* (2007–08) $13,220.

DEVRY UNIVERSITY, DECATUR

General Information Proprietary, coed institution. Suburban setting. *Awards:* A, B, M. *Entrance level for U.S. students:* Minimally difficult. *Enrollment:* 2,279 total; 1,954 undergraduates (50% women) including 1% international students. *Faculty:* 160. *Library holdings:* 18,849 books, 80 current serial subscriptions. *Total majors:* 15. *Expenses:* (2007–08) $12,900.

EMORY UNIVERSITY, ATLANTA

General Information Independent Methodist, coed university. Suburban setting. *Awards:* A, B, M, D, FP (enrollment figures include Emory University, Oxford College; application data for main campus only). *Entrance level for U.S. students:* Most difficult. *Enrollment:* 12,338 total; 6,646 undergraduates (58% women) including 5% international students from 57 foreign countries. *Faculty:* 1,459. *Library holdings:* 3.2 million books, 51,500 current serial subscriptions, 54,000 audiovisual materials. *Total majors:* 57.

Information for International Students For fall 2006: 1061 international students applied, 301 were accepted, 107 enrolled. Students can start in fall, spring, or summer. Transfers accepted from institutions abroad. *Admission tests:* Required: SAT or ACT. Recommended: TOEFL (minimum score: iBT 95; paper-based 600; computer-based 250). *Application deadline:* 1/15. *Expenses:* (2007–08) $34,336; room and board, $11,020 (on campus). *Financial aid:* Need-based college/university scholarships/grants from institutional funds, on-campus employment. Non-need-based college/university scholarships/grants from institutional funds, on-campus employment. Forms required: CSS PROFILE. For fall 2006 (estimated), 34 international students on campus received college administered financial aid ($25,081 average). *Housing:* Guaranteed, also available during summer. *Services:* International student adviser on campus. ESL program at cooperating institution. ESL program available during the academic year. Internships available. *Contact:* Associate Dean of Admission, Office of Admission, Emory University, 200 B. Jones Center, Atlanta, GA 30322. Telephone: 404-727-6036. Fax: 404-727-4303. E-mail: admiss@learnlink.emory.edu. URL: http://www.emory.edu.

EMORY UNIVERSITY, OXFORD COLLEGE, OXFORD

General Information Independent Methodist, 2-year, coed college. Small town setting. *Awards:* A. *Entrance level for U.S. students:*

Moderately difficult. *Enrollment:* 554 total (59% women) including 3% international students from 7 foreign countries. *Undergraduate faculty:* 54. *Library holdings:* 80,099 books, 240 current serial subscriptions, 656 audiovisual materials. *Total majors:* 1. *Financial aid:* Non-need-based college/university scholarships/grants from institutional funds.

FORT VALLEY STATE UNIVERSITY, FORT VALLEY
General Information State-supported, coed institution. Small town setting. *Awards:* A, B, M, D, FP. *Entrance level for U.S. students:* Moderately difficult. *Enrollment:* 2,174 total; 1,997 undergraduates (55% women) including 1% international students from 21 foreign countries. *Faculty:* 121. *Library holdings:* 186,365 books, 1,213 current serial subscriptions. *Total majors:* 36. *Expenses:* (2006–07) $13,456; room and board, $4720 (on campus); room only, $2310 (on campus). *Financial aid:* Non-need financial aid available. Forms required: institution's own financial aid form.

GAINESVILLE COLLEGE, OAKWOOD
General Information State-supported, primarily 2-year, coed college. Small town setting. *Awards:* A, B. *Entrance level for U.S. students:* Noncompetitive. *Enrollment:* 5,985 total (54% women) including 2% international students from 12 foreign countries. *Undergraduate faculty:* 131. *Library holdings:* 70,000 books, 398 current serial subscriptions. *Total majors:* 35. *Financial aid:* Forms required: institution's own financial aid form.

GEORGIA COLLEGE & STATE UNIVERSITY, MILLEDGEVILLE
General Information State-supported, coed institution. Small town setting. *Awards:* B, M. *Entrance level for U.S. students:* Moderately difficult. *Enrollment:* 6,041 total; 5,141 undergraduates (60% women) including 2% international students from 45 foreign countries. *Faculty:* 405. *Library holdings:* 175,299 books, 22,955 current serial subscriptions, 5,306 audiovisual materials. *Total majors:* 39.
Information for International Students For fall 2006: 99 international students applied, 35 were accepted, 18 enrolled. Students can start in fall or spring. Transfers accepted from institutions abroad. *Admission tests:* Required: TOEFL (minimum score: iBT 61; paper-based 500; computer-based 173). TOEFL can be waived under certain conditions. *Application deadline:* 4/1. *Expenses:* (2006–07) $15,352; room and board, $7116 (on campus); room only, $3800 (on campus). *Financial aid:* Non-need-based tuition waivers, athletic awards. Forms required: institution's own financial aid form. International transfer students are eligible to apply for aid. For fall 2005, 27 international students on campus received college administered financial aid ($4372 average). *Housing:* Guaranteed, also available during summer. *Services:* International student adviser on campus. Internships and employment opportunities (on-campus) available. *Contact:* International Admissions Counselor, Georgia College & State University, Campus Box 49, Milledgeville, GA 31061. Telephone: 478-445-4789. Fax: 478-445-2623. E-mail: intladm@gcsu.edu. URL: http://www.gcsu.edu.
See In-Depth Description on page 90.

GEORGIA HIGHLANDS COLLEGE, ROME
General Information State-supported, 2-year, coed college. Small town setting. *Awards:* A. *Entrance level for U.S. students:* Noncompetitive. *Enrollment:* 3,933 total (64% women) including 1% international students. *Undergraduate faculty:* 251. *Library holdings:* 65,090 books, 267 current serial subscriptions, 9,964 audiovisual materials. *Total majors:* 40.
Information for International Students For fall 2006: 106 international students applied, 66 were accepted. Students can start in fall, spring, or summer. Transfers accepted from institutions abroad. *Admission tests:* Required: SAT or ACT, TOEFL (minimum score: iBT 80; paper-based 550; computer-based 213). TOEFL can be waived under certain conditions. *Application deadline:* 7/20. *Expenses:* (2006–07) $6614. *Financial aid:* Need-based and non-need-based financial aid available. *Contact:* Admissions Specialist, Georgia Highlands College, 3175 Cedartown Highway, SE, Rome, GA 30161. Telephone: 706-295-6339. Fax: 706-295-6341. E-mail: cgraham@highlands.edu. URL: http://www.highlands.edu.

GEORGIA INSTITUTE OF TECHNOLOGY, ATLANTA
General Information State-supported, coed university. Urban setting. *Awards:* B, M, D. *Entrance level for U.S. students:* Very difficult. *Enrollment:* 17,936 total; 12,361 undergraduates (29% women) including 4% international students from 71 foreign countries. *Faculty:* 859. *Library holdings:* 2.4 million books, 34,576 current serial subscriptions, 6,958 audiovisual materials. *Total majors:* 34. *Expenses:* (2006–07) $20,272; room and board,

$7094 (on campus); room only, $4192 (on campus). *Financial aid:* Forms required: International Student's Certification of Finances.

GEORGIA SOUTHERN UNIVERSITY, STATESBORO
General Information State-supported, coed institution. Small town setting. *Awards:* B, M, D. *Entrance level for U.S. students:* Moderately difficult. *Enrollment:* 16,425 total; 14,483 undergraduates (49% women) including 1% international students from 80 foreign countries. *Faculty:* 738. *Library holdings:* 588,997 books, 2,690 current serial subscriptions, 29,118 audiovisual materials. *Total majors:* 79.
Information for International Students For fall 2006: 57 international students applied, 35 were accepted, 23 enrolled. Students can start in fall, spring, or summer. Transfers accepted from institutions abroad. *Admission tests:* Required: TOEFL (minimum score: iBT 61; paper-based 500; computer-based 173). Recommended: SAT or ACT. TOEFL can be waived under certain conditions. *Application deadline:* 5/1. *Expenses:* (2007–08) $12,954; room and board, $6860 (on campus); room only, $4340 (on campus). *Financial aid:* Need-based tuition waivers, athletic awards. Non-need-based tuition waivers, athletic awards, loans from outside sources. Forms required: out of country waiver application. For fall 2005, 17 international students on campus received college administered financial aid ($5889 average). *Housing:* Available during summer. *Services:* International student adviser on campus. Full-time ESL program on campus. ESL program available during the academic year and the summer. Internships and employment opportunities (on-campus) available. *Contact:* International Student Recruitment Manager, Georgia Southern University, PO Box 8024, Statesboro, GA 30460. Telephone: 912-681-5836. Fax: 912-486-7240. E-mail: rjones@georgiasouthern.edu. URL: http://www.georgiasouthern.edu.

GEORGIA SOUTHWESTERN STATE UNIVERSITY, AMERICUS
General Information State-supported, coed institution. Small town setting. *Awards:* A, B, M. *Entrance level for U.S. students:* Moderately difficult. *Enrollment:* 2,457 total; 2,222 undergraduates (63% women) including 2% international students from 31 foreign countries. *Faculty:* 143. *Library holdings:* 428,197 books, 516 current serial subscriptions. *Total majors:* 64. *Expenses:* (2006–07) $10,770; room and board, $4956 (on campus); room only, $2700 (on campus). *Financial aid:* Non-need financial aid available. Forms required: institution's own financial aid form.

GEORGIA STATE UNIVERSITY, ATLANTA
General Information State-supported, coed university. Urban setting. *Awards:* B, M, D, FP. *Entrance level for U.S. students:* Moderately difficult. *Enrollment:* 26,134 total; 19,122 undergraduates (61% women) including 3% international students from 143 foreign countries. *Faculty:* 1,514. *Library holdings:* 1.5 million books, 7,788 current serial subscriptions, 22,551 audiovisual materials. *Total majors:* 54.
Information for International Students Students can start in fall, spring, or summer. Transfers accepted from institutions abroad. *Admission tests:* Required: SAT or ACT, TOEFL (minimum score: paper-based 550; computer-based 213). *Application deadline:* 3/1. *Expenses:* (2006–07) $16,206; room and board, $7264 (on campus); room only, $5594 (on campus). *Financial aid:* Non-need financial aid available. *Housing:* Available during summer. *Services:* International student adviser on campus. Full-time and part-time ESL programs on campus. ESL program available during the academic year and the summer. Internships and employment opportunities (on-campus and off-campus) available. *Contact:* International Student and Scholar Services, Office of Admissions, Georgia State University, Room 252, Sparks Hall, 30 Gilmer Street, SE, Atlanta, GA 30303. Telephone: 404-463-9073. Fax: 404-463-9077. E-mail: international@gsu.edu. URL: http://www.gsu.edu.
See In-Depth Description on page 91.

GORDON COLLEGE, BARNESVILLE
General Information State-supported, 2-year, coed college. Small town setting. *Awards:* A. *Entrance level for U.S. students:* Minimally difficult. *Enrollment:* 3,595 total (64% women) including 1% international students from 19 foreign countries. *Undergraduate faculty:* 161. *Library holdings:* 122,918 books, 6,682 current serial subscriptions, 5,463 audiovisual materials. *Total majors:* 25. *Expenses:* (2007–08) $6817; room only, $2300 (on campus).

GRIFFIN TECHNICAL COLLEGE, GRIFFIN
General Information State-supported, 2-year, coed college. Small town setting. *Awards:* A. *Entrance level for U.S. students:* Noncompetitive. *Enrollment:* 3,287 total (65% women) including 0.04% international students from 1 foreign country. *Undergraduate*

Griffin Technical College (continued)

faculty: 240. *Library holdings:* 12,493 books, 188 current serial subscriptions, 1,326 audiovisual materials. *Total majors:* 23. *Expenses:* (2006–07) $2475.

HEART OF GEORGIA TECHNICAL COLLEGE, DUBLIN

General Information State-supported, 2-year, coed college. Small town setting. *Awards:* A. *Entrance level for U.S. students:* Noncompetitive. *Enrollment:* 1,588 total (55% women) including 0.1% international students. *Undergraduate faculty:* 186. *Total majors:* 9. *Expenses:* (2006–07) $2487.

HERZING COLLEGE, ATLANTA

General Information Proprietary, primarily 2-year, coed college. Urban setting. *Awards:* A, B. *Entrance level for U.S. students:* Moderately difficult. *Enrollment:* 276 total. *Undergraduate faculty:* 25. *Library holdings:* 6,000 books, 25 current serial subscriptions. *Total majors:* 6. *Expenses:* (2006–07) $11,325. *Financial aid:* Forms required: institution's own financial aid form, International Student's Certification of Finances.

KENNESAW STATE UNIVERSITY, KENNESAW

General Information State-supported, coed institution. Suburban setting. *Awards:* B, M. *Entrance level for U.S. students:* Moderately difficult. *Enrollment:* 19,854 total; 17,708 undergraduates (61% women) including 3% international students from 136 foreign countries. *Faculty:* 1,003. *Library holdings:* 630,614 books, 4,410 current serial subscriptions, 10,000 audiovisual materials. *Total majors:* 44.

Information for International Students For fall 2006: 500 international students applied, 350 were accepted, 346 enrolled. Students can start in fall, spring, or summer. Transfers accepted from institutions abroad. *Admission tests:* Required: SAT, TOEFL (minimum score: iBT 75; paper-based 527; computer-based 197; minimum score for ESL admission: iBT 75; paper-based 527; computer-based 197). *Application deadline:* Rolling. *Expenses:* (2006–07) $10,948; room only, $4620 (on campus). *Housing:* Available during summer. *Services:* International student adviser on campus. Internships and employment opportunities (on-campus and off-campus) available. *Contact:* Director of International Student Admissions, Kennesaw State University, 1000 Chastain Road, Kennesaw, GA 30144-5591. Telephone: 770-423-6336. Fax: 770-499-3430. E-mail: jespana@ksumail.kennesaw.edu. URL: http://www.kennesaw.edu.

LAGRANGE COLLEGE, LAGRANGE

General Information Independent United Methodist, coed institution. Small town setting. *Awards:* A, B, M. *Entrance level for U.S. students:* Moderately difficult. *Enrollment:* 1,136 total; 1,058 undergraduates (57% women) including 2% international students from 14 foreign countries. *Faculty:* 126. *Library holdings:* 116,300 books, 374 current serial subscriptions, 116,929 audiovisual materials. *Total majors:* 33. *Expenses:* (2007–08) $18,575; room and board, $7598 (on campus). *Financial aid:* Forms required: institution's own financial aid form.

LIFE UNIVERSITY, MARIETTA

General Information Independent, coed institution. Suburban setting. *Awards:* A, B, M, FP. *Entrance level for U.S. students:* Minimally difficult. *Enrollment:* 1,662 total; 495 undergraduates (44% women) including 11% international students from 25 foreign countries. *Faculty:* 128. *Library holdings:* 56,199 books, 22,816 current serial subscriptions, 8,533 audiovisual materials. *Total majors:* 5. *Expenses:* (2006–07) $5823; room and board, $12,000 (on campus). *Financial aid:* Non-need-based college/university scholarships/grants from institutional funds, athletic awards, tuition discounts. Forms required: International Student's Financial Aid Application, International Student's Certification of Finances. For fall 2006 (estimated), 1 international student on campus received college administered financial aid ($1000 average).

MEDICAL COLLEGE OF GEORGIA, AUGUSTA

General Information State-supported, coed institution. Urban setting. *Awards:* B, M, D, FP. *Entrance level for U.S. students:* Moderately difficult. *Enrollment:* 2,227 total; 648 undergraduates (86% women) including 1% international students from 20 foreign countries. *Faculty:* 790. *Library holdings:* 164,138 books, 2,429 current serial subscriptions. *Total majors:* 10. *Expenses:* (2007–08) $15,748; room only, $2556 (on campus). *Financial aid:* Need-based college/university scholarships/grants from institutional funds, loans from institutional funds, loans from outside sources, on-campus employment. Non-need-based loans from institutional funds, loans from outside sources. Forms required: institution's own

financial aid form, FAFSA. For fall 2006 (estimated), 19 international students on campus received college administered financial aid ($10,674 average).

MERCER UNIVERSITY, MACON

General Information Independent Baptist, coed institution. Suburban setting. *Awards:* B, M, D, FP. *Entrance level for U.S. students:* Moderately difficult. *Enrollment:* 5,090 total; 2,301 undergraduates (54% women) including 2% international students from 34 foreign countries. *Faculty:* 591. *Library holdings:* 692,225 books, 28,163 current serial subscriptions, 64,319 audiovisual materials. *Total majors:* 49. *Expenses:* (2006–07) $25,256; room and board, $7710 (on campus); room only, $3710 (on campus). *Financial aid:* Non-need financial aid available. Forms required: institution's own financial aid form. For fall 2006 (estimated), 61 international students on campus received college administered financial aid ($10,520 average).

MIDDLE GEORGIA COLLEGE, COCHRAN

General Information State-supported, 2-year, coed college. Small town setting. *Awards:* A. *Entrance level for U.S. students:* Minimally difficult. *Enrollment:* 2,677 total (59% women) including 0.4% international students. *Undergraduate faculty:* 129. *Library holdings:* 110,000 books, 147 current serial subscriptions, 5,119 audiovisual materials. *Total majors:* 15. *Expenses:* (2006–07) $6786; room and board, $4500 (on campus); room only, $2200 (on campus). *Financial aid:* Need-based college/university scholarships/grants from institutional funds. Non-need-based college/university scholarships/grants from institutional funds.

NORTH GEORGIA COLLEGE & STATE UNIVERSITY, DAHLONEGA

General Information State-supported, coed institution. Small town setting. *Awards:* A, B, M. *Entrance level for U.S. students:* Moderately difficult. *Enrollment:* 4,922 total; 4,356 undergraduates (60% women) including 1% international students from 46 foreign countries. *Faculty:* 327. *Library holdings:* 146,888 books, 2,548 current serial subscriptions, 3,151 audiovisual materials. *Total majors:* 48. *Expenses:* (2006–07) $11,134; room and board, $4780 (on campus); room only, $2384 (on campus). *Financial aid:* Need-based financial aid available. Forms required: institution's own financial aid form.

NORTH METRO TECHNICAL COLLEGE, ACWORTH

General Information State-supported, 2-year, coed college. *Awards:* A. *Entrance level for U.S. students:* Noncompetitive. *Enrollment:* 1,928 total (65% women) including 0.1% international students. *Undergraduate faculty:* 110. *Total majors:* 10. *Expenses:* (2006–07) $2475.

OGLETHORPE UNIVERSITY, ATLANTA

General Information Independent, coed institution. Suburban setting. *Awards:* B, M. *Entrance level for U.S. students:* Very difficult. *Enrollment:* 1,030 total; 985 undergraduates (65% women) including 5% international students from 21 foreign countries. *Faculty:* 102. *Library holdings:* 150,000 books, 710 current serial subscriptions. *Total majors:* 33. *Expenses:* (2006–07) $23,510; room and board, $8000 (on campus). *Financial aid:* Need-based college/university scholarships/grants from institutional funds, tuition waivers, on-campus employment. Non-need-based college/university scholarships/grants from institutional funds, tuition waivers, on-campus employment. Forms required: institution's own financial aid form, International Student's Financial Aid Application, International Student's Certification of Finances. For fall 2005, 47 international students on campus received college administered financial aid ($10,607 average).

PIEDMONT COLLEGE, DEMOREST

General Information Independent, coed institution, affiliated with United Church of Christ. Rural setting. *Awards:* B, M. *Entrance level for U.S. students:* Moderately difficult. *Enrollment:* 2,118 total; 949 undergraduates (64% women) including 0.3% international students from 20 foreign countries. *Faculty:* 217. *Library holdings:* 115,400 books, 365 current serial subscriptions, 2,500 audiovisual materials. *Total majors:* 32. *Expenses:* (2007–08) $16,500; room and board, $6000 (on campus). *Financial aid:* Need-based and non-need-based financial aid available. Forms required: institution's own financial aid form, International Student's Certification of Finances. For fall 2006 (estimated), 12 international students on campus received college administered financial aid ($6863 average).

REINHARDT COLLEGE, WALESKA

General Information Independent, 4-year, coed college, affiliated with United Methodist Church. Rural setting. *Awards:* A, B. *Entrance level for U.S. students:* Moderately difficult. *Enrollment:*

1,060 total (59% women) including 1% international students from 8 foreign countries. *Undergraduate faculty:* 122. *Library holdings:* 59,204 books, 371 current serial subscriptions, 2,600 audiovisual materials. *Total majors:* 22. *Expenses:* (2007–08) $14,970; room and board, $6018 (on campus). *Financial aid:* Need-based and non-need-based financial aid available. Forms required: institution's own financial aid form, CSS PROFILE. For fall 2006 (estimated), 12 international students on campus received college administered financial aid ($9700 average).

SAVANNAH COLLEGE OF ART AND DESIGN, SAVANNAH

General Information Independent, coed institution. Urban setting. *Awards:* B, M. *Entrance level for U.S. students:* Moderately difficult. *Enrollment:* 8,236 total; 6,913 undergraduates (53% women) including 4% international students from 95 foreign countries. *Faculty:* 508. *Library holdings:* 170,909 books, 948 current serial subscriptions, 5,710 audiovisual materials. *Total majors:* 21.

Information for International Students For fall 2006: 412 international students applied, 198 were accepted, 98 enrolled. Students can start in fall, winter, spring, or summer. Transfers accepted from institutions abroad. *Admission tests:* Required: TOEFL (minimum score: iBT 45; paper-based 450; computer-based 133; minimum score for ESL admission: iBT 45; paper-based 450; computer-based 133). Recommended: SAT or ACT. TOEFL can be waived under certain conditions. *Application deadline:* Rolling. *Expenses:* (2007–08) $24,890; room and board, $10,015 (on campus); room only, $6460 (on campus). *Financial aid:* Need-based college/university scholarships/grants from institutional funds, athletic awards, on-campus employment. Non-need-based college/university scholarships/grants from institutional funds, athletic awards, on-campus employment. Forms required: institution's own financial aid form, International Student's Certification of Finances. International transfer students are eligible to apply for aid. For fall 2006 (estimated), 268 international students on campus received college administered financial aid ($8136 average). *Housing:* Available during summer. *Services:* International student adviser on campus. Full-time ESL program on campus. ESL program available during the academic year and the summer. Internships and employment opportunities (on-campus) available. *Contact:* Director of International Recruitment, Savannah College of Art and Design, PO Box 2072, Savannah, GA 31402-2072. Telephone: 912-525-5100. Fax: 912-525-5986. E-mail: admission@scad.edu. URL: http://www.scad.edu.

See In-Depth Description on page 178.

SAVANNAH STATE UNIVERSITY, SAVANNAH

General Information State-supported, coed institution. Suburban setting. *Awards:* B, M. *Entrance level for U.S. students:* Minimally difficult. *Enrollment:* 3,188 total; 3,056 undergraduates (56% women) including international students from 20 foreign countries. *Faculty:* 167. *Library holdings:* 187,916 books, 812 current serial subscriptions. *Total majors:* 28.

Information for International Students For fall 2006: 40 international students applied, 29 were accepted, 6 enrolled. Students can start in fall or spring. Transfers accepted from institutions abroad. *Admission tests:* Required: SAT or ACT, TOEFL (minimum score: paper-based 550; computer-based 213). TOEFL can be waived under certain conditions. *Application deadline:* 5/1. *Expenses:* (2006–07) $10,860; room and board, $5010 (on campus); room only, $2300 (on campus). *Financial aid:* Non-need financial aid available. Forms required: International Student's Certification of Finances. *Housing:* Available during summer. *Services:* International student adviser on campus. Internships and employment opportunities (on-campus) available. *Contact:* Associate Director of Admissions, Savannah State University, PO Box 20209, Savannah, GA 31404. Telephone: 912-356-2181. Fax: 912-356-2256. E-mail: admissions@savstate.edu. URL: http://www.savstate.edu.

SAVANNAH TECHNICAL COLLEGE, SAVANNAH

General Information State-supported, 2-year, coed college. Urban setting. *Awards:* A. *Entrance level for U.S. students:* Noncompetitive. *Enrollment:* 3,965 total (67% women) including 1% international students. *Undergraduate faculty:* 290. *Library holdings:* 20,804 books, 160 current serial subscriptions, 3,150 audiovisual materials. *Total majors:* 16. *Expenses:* (2006–07) $2475.

SHORTER COLLEGE, ROME

General Information Independent Baptist, coed institution. Small town setting. *Awards:* B. *Entrance level for U.S. students:* Moderately difficult. *Enrollment:* 1,044 total (50% women) including 5% international students from 20 foreign countries. *Undergraduate faculty:* 124. *Library holdings:* 134,201 books, 596 current serial subscriptions. *Total majors:* 38.

Information for International Students Students can start in fall, spring, or summer. Transfers accepted from institutions abroad. *Admission tests:* Required: TOEFL (minimum score: paper-based 500; computer-based 173). *Application deadline:* 5/30. *Expenses:* (2006–07) $14,300; room and board, $6600 (on campus); room only, $3600 (on campus). *Financial aid:* Non-need financial aid available. Forms required: institution's own financial aid form, International Student's Certification of Finances. International transfer students are eligible to apply for aid. For fall 2005, 43 international students on campus received college administered financial aid ($15,503 average). *Housing:* Guaranteed, also available during summer. *Services:* International student adviser on campus. Internships and employment opportunities (on-campus) available. *Contact:* Vice President of Enrollment Management, Shorter College, Rome, GA 30165. Telephone: 706-233-7319. Fax: 706-233-7224. E-mail: admissions@shorter.edu. URL: http://www.shorter.edu.

See In-Depth Description on page 184.

SOUTHERN POLYTECHNIC STATE UNIVERSITY, MARIETTA

General Information State-supported, coed institution. Suburban setting. *Awards:* A, B, M. *Entrance level for U.S. students:* Moderately difficult. *Enrollment:* 4,206 total; 3,680 undergraduates (17% women) including 6% international students from 89 foreign countries. *Faculty:* 226. *Library holdings:* 119,917 books, 1,124 current serial subscriptions, 85 audiovisual materials. *Total majors:* 23. *Expenses:* (2006–07) $11,683; room and board, $5610 (on campus); room only, $3210 (on campus). *Financial aid:* Need-based tuition waivers, athletic awards, on-campus employment. Non-need-based tuition waivers, athletic awards, on-campus employment.

SOUTH GEORGIA COLLEGE, DOUGLAS

General Information State-supported, 2-year, coed college. Small town setting. *Awards:* A. *Entrance level for U.S. students:* Minimally difficult. *Enrollment:* 1,504 total (64% women) including 1% international students from 2 foreign countries. *Undergraduate faculty:* 60. *Library holdings:* 79,190 books, 327 current serial subscriptions. *Total majors:* 53.

Information for International Students For fall 2006: 8 international students applied, 6 were accepted, 5 enrolled. Students can start in fall, spring, or summer. Transfers accepted from institutions abroad. *Admission tests:* Required: TOEFL (minimum score: iBT 70; paper-based 523; computer-based 193; minimum score for ESL admission: iBT 70; paper-based 523; computer-based 193). TOEFL can be waived under certain conditions. *Application deadline:* 5/31. *Expenses:* (2006–07) $10,047; room and board, $8475 (on campus); room only, $3900 (on campus). *Housing:* Guaranteed, also available during summer. *Services:* International student adviser on campus. ESL program at cooperating institution. Employment opportunities (on-campus) available. *Contact:* Director of Enrollment Services, South Georgia College, 100 West College Park Drive, Douglas, GA 31533. Telephone: 912-389-4263. Fax: 912-383-4388. E-mail: amy.prodan@sga.edu. URL: http://www.sga.edu.

THOMAS UNIVERSITY, THOMASVILLE

General Information Independent, coed institution. Small town setting. *Awards:* A, B, M. *Entrance level for U.S. students:* Noncompetitive. *Enrollment:* 684 total; 594 undergraduates (74% women) including 4% international students from 13 foreign countries. *Faculty:* 82. *Library holdings:* 41,467 books, 451 current serial subscriptions, 560 audiovisual materials. *Total majors:* 23. *Expenses:* (2006–07) $10,570; room only, $2500 (on campus). *Financial aid:* Non-need-based college/university scholarships/grants from institutional funds. 2 international students on campus received college administered financial aid ($13,905 average).

UNIVERSITY OF GEORGIA, ATHENS

General Information State-supported, coed university. Suburban setting. *Awards:* A, B, M, D, FP. *Entrance level for U.S. students:* Moderately difficult. *Enrollment:* 33,959 total; 25,437 undergraduates (57% women) including 1% international students from 131 foreign countries. *Faculty:* 2,159. *Library holdings:* 4 million books, 67,268 current serial subscriptions. *Total majors:* 144. *Expenses:* (2006–07) $18,040; room and board, $6848 (on campus); room only, $3704 (on campus). *Financial aid:* Need-based tuition waivers. Non-need-based tuition waivers, athletic awards.

UNIVERSITY OF WEST GEORGIA, CARROLLTON

General Information State-supported, coed institution. Small town setting. *Awards:* B, M, D. *Entrance level for U.S. students:* Minimally difficult. *Enrollment:* 10,163 total; 8,475 undergraduates (60% women) including 1% international students from 75 foreign

University of West Georgia (continued)

countries. *Faculty:* 490. *Library holdings:* 563,677 books, 14,884 current serial subscriptions, 11,048 audiovisual materials. *Total majors:* 51. *Expenses:* (2006–07) $11,142; room and board, $5162 (on campus); room only, $2458 (on campus). *Financial aid:* Need-based college/university scholarships/grants from institutional funds. Non-need-based college/university scholarships/grants from institutional funds, tuition waivers, athletic awards, on-campus employment.

VALDOSTA STATE UNIVERSITY, VALDOSTA

General Information State-supported, coed university. Small town setting. *Awards:* A, B, M, D. *Entrance level for U.S. students:* Moderately difficult. *Enrollment:* 10,888 total; 9,489 undergraduates (59% women) including 2% international students from 55 foreign countries. *Faculty:* 563. *Library holdings:* 499,501 books, 2,786 current serial subscriptions, 23,003 audiovisual materials. *Total majors:* 49. *Expenses:* (2007–08) $11,172; room and board, $5680 (on campus); room only, $2880 (on campus). *Financial aid:* Need-based college/university scholarships/grants from institutional funds, on-campus employment. Non-need-based college/university scholarships/grants from institutional funds, athletic awards, loans from outside sources, on-campus employment.

WESLEYAN COLLEGE, MACON

General Information Independent United Methodist, undergraduate: women only; graduate: coed institution. Suburban setting. *Awards:* B, M. *Entrance level for U.S. students:* Moderately difficult. *Enrollment:* 636 total; 540 undergraduates (99% women) including 9% international students from 22 foreign countries. *Faculty:* 80. *Library holdings:* 117,547 books, 630 current serial subscriptions, 3,927 audiovisual materials. *Total majors:* 31. *Expenses:* (2007–08) $15,200; room and board, $7600 (on campus). *Financial aid:* Non-need-based college/university scholarships/grants from institutional funds, tuition waivers, on-campus employment. Forms required: institution's own financial aid form, International Student's Certification of Finances. For fall 2005, 72 international students on campus received college administered financial aid ($12,770 average).

YOUNG HARRIS COLLEGE, YOUNG HARRIS

General Information Independent United Methodist, 2-year, coed college. Rural setting. *Awards:* A. *Entrance level for U.S. students:* Moderately difficult. *Enrollment:* 606 total (48% women) including 2% international students from 9 foreign countries. *Undergraduate faculty:* 53. *Library holdings:* 90,000 books, 130 current serial subscriptions, 3,000 audiovisual materials. *Total majors:* 36.
Information for International Students For fall 2006: 25 international students applied, 14 were accepted, 11 enrolled. Students can start in fall, spring, or summer. Transfers accepted from institutions abroad. *Admission tests:* Required: TOEFL (minimum score: paper-based 550; computer-based 220; minimum score for ESL admission: paper-based 550; computer-based 220), SAT or ELS (minimum score 109) may substitute for TOEFL. TOEFL can be waived under certain conditions. *Application deadline:* 6/1. *Expenses:* (2007–08) $15,636; room and board, $4864 (on campus); room only, $1870 (on campus). *Financial aid:* Non-need financial aid available. International transfer students are eligible to apply for aid. *Housing:* Guaranteed, also available during summer. *Services:* International student adviser on campus. Employment opportunities (on-campus) available. *Contact:* Director of Institutional Research, Young Harris College, PO Box 116, Young Harris, GA 30582. Telephone: 706-379-3111 Ext. 5192. Fax: 706-379-3108. E-mail: rosemary@yhc.edu. URL: http://www.yhc.edu.

GUAM

GUAM COMMUNITY COLLEGE, BARRIGADA

General Information Territory-supported, 2-year, coed college. Suburban setting. *Awards:* A. *Entrance level for U.S. students:* Noncompetitive. *Enrollment:* 2,841 total (64% women) including 2% international students from 10 foreign countries. *Undergraduate faculty:* 120. *Library holdings:* 15,806 books, 375 current serial subscriptions, 1,567 audiovisual materials. *Total majors:* 29. *Expenses:* (2006–07) $3094.

UNIVERSITY OF GUAM, MANGILAO

General Information Territory-supported, coed institution. Suburban setting. *Awards:* B, M. *Entrance level for U.S. students:* Noncompetitive. *Enrollment:* 3,176 total; 2,923 undergraduates (62% women) including 1% international students from 7 foreign countries. *Faculty:* 249. *Library holdings:* 386,539 books, 2,276 current serial subscriptions. *Total majors:* 36.
Information for International Students For fall 2006: 11 international students applied, 7 were accepted, 7 enrolled. Students can start in fall, spring, or summer. Transfers accepted from institutions abroad. *Admission tests:* Required: TOEFL (minimum score: iBT 61; paper-based 500; computer-based 173). TOEFL can be waived under certain conditions. *Application deadline:* 4/23. *Expenses:* (2007–08) $13,540; room and board, $7785 (on campus); room only, $3668 (on campus). *Financial aid:* Non-need financial aid available. *Housing:* Available during summer. *Services:* Full-time ESL program on campus. ESL program available during the academic year. Internships and employment opportunities (on-campus) available. *Contact:* Admissions Supervisor, University of Guam, Admissions and Records Office, UOG Station, Mangilao, GU 96923. Telephone: 671-735-2201. Fax: 671-735-2203. E-mail: akanthon@uog9.uog.edu. URL: http://www.uog.edu.

HAWAII

CHAMINADE UNIVERSITY OF HONOLULU, HONOLULU

General Information Independent Roman Catholic, coed institution. Urban setting. *Awards:* A, B, M. *Entrance level for U.S. students:* Minimally difficult. *Enrollment:* 1,810 total; 1,106 undergraduates (69% women) including 2% international students from 11 foreign countries. *Faculty:* 131. *Library holdings:* 78,000 books, 6,730 current serial subscriptions, 566 audiovisual materials. *Total majors:* 22. *Expenses:* (2006–07) $14,960; room and board, $9380 (on campus); room only, $4980 (on campus). *Financial aid:* Non-need-based loans from institutional funds. 19 international students on campus received college administered financial aid ($4053 average).

HAWAII COMMUNITY COLLEGE, HILO

General Information State-supported, 2-year, coed college. Small town setting. *Awards:* A. *Entrance level for U.S. students:* Noncompetitive. *Enrollment:* 2,409 total (64% women) including 3% international students from 32 foreign countries. *Undergraduate faculty:* 260. *Total majors:* 17.
Information for International Students For fall 2006: 19 international students applied, 17 were accepted, 15 enrolled. Students can start in fall, spring, or summer. Transfers accepted from institutions abroad. *Admission tests:* Required: TOEFL (minimum score: iBT 45; paper-based 450; computer-based 133; minimum score for ESL admission: paper-based 470; computer-based 150). Recommended: COMPASS. *Application deadline:* 4/15. *Housing:* Available during summer. *Services:* Full-time and part-time ESL programs on campus. ESL program available during the academic year and the summer. Employment opportunities (on-campus and off-campus) available. *Contact:* Admissions Specialist, Hawaii Community College, 200 West Kawili Street, Admissions Office, Hilo, HI 96720-4091. Telephone: 808-974-7661. Fax: 808-974-7692. E-mail: dorinna@hawaii.edu. URL: http://www.hawcc.hawaii.edu.

HAWAI'I PACIFIC UNIVERSITY, HONOLULU

General Information Independent, coed institution. Urban setting. *Awards:* A, B, M. *Entrance level for U.S. students:* Moderately difficult. *Enrollment:* 8,080 total; 6,856 undergraduates (61% women) including 10% international students from 103 foreign countries. *Faculty:* 618. *Library holdings:* 162,000 books, 12,000 current serial subscriptions, 8,700 audiovisual materials. *Total majors:* 55.
Information for International Students For fall 2006: 566 international students applied, 547 were accepted, 285 enrolled. Students can start in fall, winter, spring, or summer. Transfers accepted from institutions abroad. *Admission tests:* Recommended: TOEFL (minimum score: iBT 80; paper-based 550; computer-based 213). TOEFL can be waived under certain conditions. *Application deadline:* Rolling. *Expenses:* (2007–08) $13,080; room and board, $10,560 (on campus). *Financial aid:* Need-based financial aid available. Non-need-based college/university scholarships/grants from institutional funds, tuition waivers, athletic awards, loans from outside sources, on-campus employment. Forms required: institution's own financial aid form, International Student's Certification of Finances. For fall 2006 (estimated), 118 international students on campus received college administered financial aid ($6069 average). *Services:* International student adviser on campus. Full-time ESL program on campus. ESL program available during the academic year and the summer. Internships and employment opportunities (on-campus and

off-campus) available. *Contact:* Director, International Center, Hawai'i Pacific University, International Center, 1164 Bishop Street, Suite 1100, Honolulu, HI 96813. Telephone: 808-543-8088. Fax: 808-543-8065. E-mail: international@hpu.edu. URL: http://www.hpu.edu.

See In-Depth Description on page 97.

HAWAII TOKAI INTERNATIONAL COLLEGE, HONOLULU

General Information Independent, 2-year, coed college. Urban setting. *Awards:* A. *Entrance level for U.S. students:* Noncompetitive. *Enrollment:* 54 total (46% women) including international students from 3 foreign countries. *Undergraduate faculty:* 24. *Library holdings:* 7,000 books, 100 current serial subscriptions, 500 audiovisual materials. *Total majors:* 2.

Information for International Students For fall 2006: 8 international students applied, 8 were accepted, 8 enrolled. Students can start in fall, winter, spring, or summer. Transfers accepted from institutions abroad. *Admission tests:* Required: TOEFL (minimum score: paper-based 450; computer-based 130). TOEFL can be waived under certain conditions. *Application deadline:* Rolling. *Financial aid:* Need-based financial aid available. Forms required: institution's own financial aid form. *Housing:* Guaranteed, also available during summer. *Services:* International student adviser on campus. Full-time ESL program on campus. ESL program available during the academic year and the summer. *Contact:* Admissions Officer, Hawaii Tokai International College, 2241 Kapiolani Boulevard, Honolulu, HI 96826. Telephone: 808-983-4187. Fax: 808-983-4107. E-mail: dkerr@tokai.edu. URL: http://www.tokai.edu.

HONOLULU COMMUNITY COLLEGE, HONOLULU

General Information State-supported, 2-year, coed college. Urban setting. *Awards:* A. *Entrance level for U.S. students:* Noncompetitive. *Enrollment:* 4,238 total (47% women) including 1% international students from 39 foreign countries. *Undergraduate faculty:* 183. *Library holdings:* 54,902 books, 1,280 current serial subscriptions, 858 audiovisual materials. *Total majors:* 22. *Financial aid:* Need-based college/university scholarships/grants from institutional funds. Non-need-based college/university scholarships/grants from institutional funds. Forms required: institution's own financial aid form.

KAPIOLANI COMMUNITY COLLEGE, HONOLULU

General Information State-supported, 2-year, coed college. Urban setting. *Awards:* A. *Entrance level for U.S. students:* Noncompetitive. *Enrollment:* 7,174 total (58% women) including 7% international students from 59 foreign countries. *Undergraduate faculty:* 344. *Library holdings:* 50,000 books, 600 current serial subscriptions. *Total majors:* 17.

Information for International Students For fall 2006: 248 international students applied, 208 were accepted. Students can start in fall, spring, or summer. Transfers accepted from institutions abroad. *Admission tests:* Required: TOEFL (minimum score: paper-based 500; computer-based 173; minimum score for ESL admission: paper-based 400; computer-based 97). *Application deadline:* Rolling. *Expenses:* (2006–07) $6036. *Financial aid:* Non-need financial aid available. *Services:* International student adviser on campus. Full-time ESL program on campus. ESL program available during the academic year. Employment opportunities (on-campus) available. *Contact:* International Admissions, College Information Office, Kapiolani Community College, 4303 Diamond Head Road, Honolulu, HI 96816. Telephone: 808-734-9312. Fax: 808-734-9454. E-mail: HIC@hawaii.edu. URL: http://www.kcc.hawaii.edu.

See In-Depth Description on page 109.

LEEWARD COMMUNITY COLLEGE, PEARL CITY

General Information State-supported, 2-year, coed college. Suburban setting. *Awards:* A. *Entrance level for U.S. students:* Noncompetitive. *Enrollment:* 6,201 total. *Undergraduate faculty:* 236. *Library holdings:* 62,000 books, 358 current serial subscriptions, 1,009 audiovisual materials. *Total majors:* 12.

Information for International Students For fall 2006: 41 international students applied, 41 were accepted, 39 enrolled. Students can start in fall, spring, or summer. Transfers accepted from institutions abroad. *Admission tests:* Required: TOEFL (minimum score: iBT 61; paper-based 500; computer-based 173). TOEFL can be waived under certain conditions. *Application deadline:* Rolling. *Financial aid:* Need-based college/university scholarships/grants from institutional funds, tuition waivers, loans from institutional funds, loans from outside sources, on-campus employment. Non-need-based tuition waivers, loans from institutional funds, loans from outside sources, on-campus employment. *Services:* International student adviser on campus.

Full-time ESL program on campus. ESL program available during the academic year and the summer. Employment opportunities (on-campus and off-campus) available. *Contact:* International Admissions Officer, Leeward Community College, 96-045 Ala Ike, Pearl City, HI 96782. Telephone: 808-455-0570. Fax: 808-455-0568. E-mail: isa@lcc.hawaii.edu. URL: http://www.lcc.hawaii.edu.

See In-Depth Description on page 115.

MAUI COMMUNITY COLLEGE, KAHULUI

General Information State-supported, 2-year, coed college. Rural setting. *Awards:* A. *Entrance level for U.S. students:* Noncompetitive. *Enrollment:* 2,779 total including 4% international students from 15 foreign countries. *Undergraduate faculty:* 92. *Library holdings:* 49,812 books, 631 current serial subscriptions, 1,333 audiovisual materials. *Total majors:* 17.

Information for International Students For fall 2006: 10 international students applied, 10 were accepted, 10 enrolled. Students can start in fall, spring, or summer. Transfers accepted from institutions abroad. *Admission tests:* Required: TOEFL (minimum score: paper-based 450; computer-based 133; minimum score for ESL admission: paper-based 400; computer-based 97), COMPASS. TOEFL can be waived under certain conditions. *Application deadline:* 7/1. *Expenses:* (2007–08) $7756; room only, $3210 (on campus). *Financial aid:* Non-need financial aid available. *Services:* International student adviser on campus. Full-time and part-time ESL programs on campus. ESL program available during the academic year and the summer. Internships and employment opportunities (on-campus and off-campus) available. *Contact:* Director of Admissions and Records, Student Services Office, Maui Community College, 310 Kaahumanu Avenue, Kahului, HI 96732. Telephone: 808-984-3517. Fax: 808-242-9618. E-mail: kameda@mccada.mauicc.hawaii.edu. URL: http://mauicc.hawaii.edu.

TRANSPACIFIC HAWAII COLLEGE, HONOLULU

General Information Independent, 2-year, coed, primarily women's college. Suburban setting. *Awards:* A (majority of students are from outside of U.S. and participate in intensive ESL program in preparation for transfer to a 4-year institution). *Entrance level for U.S. students:* Minimally difficult. *Enrollment:* 240 total (60% women) including 100% international students from 3 foreign countries. *Undergraduate faculty:* 45. *Library holdings:* 606 books, 6 current serial subscriptions, 50 audiovisual materials. *Total majors:* 1. *Expenses:* (2006–07) $16,250.

UNIVERSITY OF HAWAII AT HILO, HILO

General Information State-supported, coed institution. Small town setting. *Awards:* B, M. *Entrance level for U.S. students:* Moderately difficult. *Enrollment:* 3,507 total; 3,276 undergraduates (60% women) including 9% international students from 38 foreign countries. *Faculty:* 377. *Library holdings:* 250,000 books, 2,500 current serial subscriptions. *Total majors:* 29. *Expenses:* (2006–07) $9700; room and board, $6292 (on campus); room only, $3190 (on campus). *Financial aid:* Non-need-based college/university scholarships/grants from institutional funds, tuition waivers, athletic awards, on-campus employment. For fall 2006 (estimated), 5 international students on campus received college administered financial aid ($3306 average).

UNIVERSITY OF HAWAII AT MANOA, HONOLULU

General Information State-supported, coed university. Urban setting. *Awards:* B, M, D, FP. *Entrance level for U.S. students:* Moderately difficult. *Enrollment:* 20,357 total; 14,037 undergraduates (55% women) including 6% international students from 86 foreign countries. *Faculty:* 1,272. *Library holdings:* 3.3 million books, 28,705 current serial subscriptions, 63,942 audiovisual materials. *Total majors:* 87.

Information for International Students For fall 2006: 1760 international students applied, 879 were accepted, 608 enrolled. Students can start in fall or spring. Transfers accepted from institutions abroad. *Admission tests:* Required: SAT or ACT, TOEFL (minimum score: iBT 61; paper-based 500; computer-based 173; minimum score for ESL admission: iBT 61; paper-based 500; computer-based 173). TOEFL can be waived under certain conditions. *Application deadline:* 2/1. *Expenses:* (2007–08) $14,654; room and board, $7185 (on campus); room only, $4527 (on campus). *Financial aid:* Need-based and non-need-based financial aid available. International transfer students are eligible to apply for aid. For fall 2006 (estimated), 559 international students on campus received college administered financial aid ($4989 average). *Housing:* Available during summer. *Services:* International student adviser on campus. Full-time and part-time ESL programs on campus. ESL program available during the academic year. Internships and employment opportunities (on-campus and off-campus) available. *Contact:* Admissions Office, Office of Admissions and Records, University of Hawaii at Manoa, 2600

University of Hawaii at Manoa (continued)

Campus Road, Room 001, Honolulu, HI 96822.
Telephone: 808-956-8975. Fax: 808-956-4148.
E-mail: ar-info@hawaii.edu. URL: http://www.uhm.hawaii.edu.
See In-Depth Description on page 214.

UNIVERSITY OF HAWAII–WEST OAHU, PEARL CITY

General Information State-supported, coed institution. Small town setting. *Awards:* B. *Entrance level for U.S. students:* Moderately difficult. *Enrollment:* 866 total (69% women) including 0.2% international students from 1 foreign country. *Undergraduate faculty:* 53. *Library holdings:* 25,000 books, 132 current serial subscriptions. *Total majors:* 13. *Expenses:* (2007–08) $10,186. *Financial aid:* Non-need financial aid available.

UNIVERSITY OF PHOENIX–HAWAII CAMPUS, HONOLULU

General Information Proprietary, coed institution. Urban setting. *Awards:* B, M (courses conducted at 121 campuses and learning centers in 25 states). *Entrance level for U.S. students:* Noncompetitive. *Enrollment:* 1,730 total; 796 undergraduates (68% women) including 31% international students. *Faculty:* 430. *Library holdings:* 1,759 books, 692 current serial subscriptions. *Total majors:* 30. *Expenses:* (2006–07) $11,700.

IDAHO

ALBERTSON COLLEGE OF IDAHO, CALDWELL

General Information Independent, coed institution. Suburban setting. *Awards:* B, M. *Entrance level for U.S. students:* Moderately difficult. *Enrollment:* 822 total; 793 undergraduates (59% women) including 1% international students from 9 foreign countries. *Faculty:* 93. *Library holdings:* 183,308 books, 703 current serial subscriptions. *Total majors:* 26. *Expenses:* (2007–08) $17,680; room and board, $6325 (on campus); room only, $2850 (on campus). *Financial aid:* Non-need-based college/university scholarships/grants from institutional funds, athletic awards. Forms required: institution's own financial aid form. 10 international students on campus received college administered financial aid ($9966 average).

BOISE STATE UNIVERSITY, BOISE

General Information State-supported, coed institution. Urban setting. *Awards:* A, B, M, D. *Entrance level for U.S. students:* Minimally difficult. *Enrollment:* 188,265 total; 17,040 undergraduates (54% women) including 1% international students from 47 foreign countries. *Faculty:* 1,073. *Library holdings:* 838,932 books, 5,575 current serial subscriptions, 58,047 audiovisual materials. *Total majors:* 97.
Information for International Students For fall 2006: 353 international students applied, 149 were accepted, 102 enrolled. Students can start in fall, spring, or summer. Transfers accepted from institutions abroad. *Admission tests:* Required: TOEFL (minimum score: iBT 61; paper-based 500; computer-based 173). Recommended: SAT or ACT. TOEFL can be waived under certain conditions. *Application deadline:* 6/1. *Expenses:* (2006–07) $9262; room and board, $5778 (on campus). *Financial aid:* Need-based college/university scholarships/grants from institutional funds. Non-need-based college/university scholarships/grants from institutional funds, tuition waivers, athletic awards, on-campus employment. Forms required: International Student's Certification of Finances. International transfer students are eligible to apply for aid. For fall 2006 (estimated), 322 international students on campus received college administered financial aid ($6056 average). *Housing:* Guaranteed, also available during summer. *Services:* International student adviser on campus. Full-time and part-time ESL programs on campus. ESL program available during the academic year and the summer. Internships and employment opportunities (on-campus) available. *Contact:* International Admissions Coordinator, Boise State University, 1910 University Drive, Boise, ID 83725-1320. Telephone: 208-426-1757. Fax: 208-426-3765. E-mail: interntl@boisestate.edu. URL: http://www.boisestate.edu.

COLLEGE OF SOUTHERN IDAHO, TWIN FALLS

General Information State and locally supported, 2-year, coed college. Small town setting. *Awards:* A. *Entrance level for U.S. students:* Noncompetitive. *Enrollment:* 7,105 total (64% women) including 4% international students from 27 foreign countries. *Undergraduate faculty:* 205. *Library holdings:* 62,556 books, 374 current serial subscriptions, 4,216 audiovisual materials.

Total majors: 73. *Expenses:* (2006–07) $5600; room and board, $3980 (on campus). *Financial aid:* Forms required: institution's own financial aid form.

IDAHO STATE UNIVERSITY, POCATELLO

General Information State-supported, coed university. Small town setting. *Awards:* B, M, D, FP. *Entrance level for U.S. students:* Minimally difficult. *Enrollment:* 12,679 total; 10,640 undergraduates (56% women) including 2% international students from 65 foreign countries. *Faculty:* 908. *Library holdings:* 1.2 million books, 444 current serial subscriptions, 2,204 audiovisual materials. *Total majors:* 101.
Information for International Students For fall 2006: 623 international students applied, 332 were accepted, 63 enrolled. Students can start in fall or spring. Transfers accepted from institutions abroad. *Admission tests:* Required: TOEFL (minimum score: iBT 69; paper-based 500; computer-based 173), ELS. Recommended: IELTS. TOEFL can be waived under certain conditions. *Application deadline:* 6/1. *Expenses:* (2007–08) $12,460; room and board, $4950 (on campus); room only, $2250 (on campus). *Financial aid:* Non-need-based college/university scholarships/grants from institutional funds, tuition waivers, athletic awards, loans from outside sources, on-campus employment. Forms required: International Student's Financial Aid Application, International Student's Certification of Finances. International transfer students are eligible to apply for aid. For fall 2005, 61 international students on campus received college administered financial aid ($3077 average). *Housing:* Guaranteed, also available during summer. *Services:* International student adviser on campus. Full-time and part-time ESL programs on campus. ESL program available during the academic year and the summer. Internships and employment opportunities (on-campus and off-campus) available. *Contact:* International Admissions Coordinator, Idaho State University, Museum Building 319, International Admissions, Pocatello, ID 83209-8270. Telephone: 208-282-2314. Fax: 208-282-4511. E-mail: intl@isu.edu. URL: http://www.isu.edu.

LEWIS-CLARK STATE COLLEGE, LEWISTON

General Information State-supported, 4-year, coed college. Small town setting. *Awards:* A, B. *Entrance level for U.S. students:* Minimally difficult. *Enrollment:* 3,394 total (62% women) including 4% international students from 31 foreign countries. *Library holdings:* 139,499 books, 1,612 current serial subscriptions. *Total majors:* 50.
Information for International Students For fall 2006: 112 international students applied, 62 were accepted, 31 enrolled. Students can start in fall, spring, or summer. Transfers accepted from institutions abroad. *Admission tests:* Required: TOEFL (minimum score: iBT 61; paper-based 500; computer-based 173). TOEFL can be waived under certain conditions. *Application deadline:* 6/1. *Expenses:* (2006–07) $10,841; room and board, $4670 (on campus); room only, $2200 (on campus). *Financial aid:* Non-need-based college/university scholarships/grants from institutional funds, tuition waivers, athletic awards, on-campus employment. Forms required: Supplemental Scholarship Application. International transfer students are eligible to apply for aid. For fall 2005, 146 international students on campus received college administered financial aid ($3250 average). *Services:* International student adviser on campus. Full-time and part-time ESL programs on campus. ESL program available during the academic year and the summer. Internships and employment opportunities (on-campus and off-campus) available. *Contact:* Director of International Programs, Lewis-Clark State College, International Programs, 500 8th Avenue, Lewiston, ID 83501. Telephone: 208-792-2210. Fax: 208-792-2824. E-mail: intloff@lcsc.edu. URL: http://www.lcsc.edu.

NORTHWEST NAZARENE UNIVERSITY, NAMPA

General Information Independent, coed institution, affiliated with Church of the Nazarene. Rural setting. *Awards:* B, M. *Entrance level for U.S. students:* Moderately difficult. *Enrollment:* 1,749 total; 1,225 undergraduates (60% women) including 1% international students from 7 foreign countries. *Faculty:* 93. *Library holdings:* 100,966 books, 821 current serial subscriptions. *Total majors:* 64. *Expenses:* (2007–08) $19,970; room and board, $5300 (on campus). *Financial aid:* Need-based college/university scholarships/grants from institutional funds, athletic awards. Non-need-based college/university scholarships/grants from institutional funds, athletic awards, on-campus employment. Forms required: institution's own financial aid form. For fall 2006 (estimated), 10 international students on campus received college administered financial aid ($13,476 average).

UNIVERSITY OF IDAHO, MOSCOW

General Information State-supported, coed university. Small town setting. *Awards:* B, M, D, FP. *Entrance level for U.S. students:*

Moderately difficult. *Enrollment:* 11,739 total; 9,127 undergraduates (45% women) including 2% international students from 73 foreign countries. *Faculty:* 590. *Library holdings:* 1.4 million books, 14,230 current serial subscriptions, 8,717 audiovisual materials. *Total majors:* 109. *Expenses:* (2006–07) $13,800; room and board, $5696 (on campus). *Financial aid:* Need-based financial aid available. Non-need-based college/university scholarships/grants from institutional funds, tuition waivers, athletic awards, on-campus employment. Forms required: International Student's Certification of Finances. For fall 2005, 52 international students on campus received college administered financial aid ($4500 average).

UNIVERSITY OF PHOENIX–IDAHO CAMPUS, MERIDIAN

General Information Proprietary, coed institution. Urban setting. *Awards:* B, M. *Entrance level for U.S. students:* Noncompetitive. *Enrollment:* 659 total; 532 undergraduates (53% women) including 28% international students. *Faculty:* 113. *Library holdings:* 1,759 books, 692 current serial subscriptions. *Total majors:* 23. *Expenses:* (2006–07) $10,200.

ILLINOIS

AMERICAN ACADEMY OF ART, CHICAGO

General Information Proprietary, coed institution. Urban setting. *Awards:* B, M. *Entrance level for U.S. students:* Moderately difficult. *Enrollment:* 410 total; 396 undergraduates (39% women) including 0.2% international students from 3 foreign countries. *Faculty:* 35. *Library holdings:* 1,730 books, 62 current serial subscriptions, 101 audiovisual materials. *Total majors:* 10. *Expenses:* (2006–07) $20,930.

AUGUSTANA COLLEGE, ROCK ISLAND

General Information Independent, 4-year, coed college, affiliated with Evangelical Lutheran Church in America. Suburban setting. *Awards:* B. *Entrance level for U.S. students:* Moderately difficult. *Enrollment:* 2,463 total including 1% international students from 23 foreign countries. *Undergraduate faculty:* 235. *Library holdings:* 190,641 books, 1,705 current serial subscriptions, 2,019 audiovisual materials. *Total majors:* 67. *Expenses:* (2006–07) $24,924; room and board, $6807 (on campus); room only, $3447 (on campus). *Financial aid:* Need-based college/university scholarships/grants from institutional funds, on-campus employment. Non-need-based college/university scholarships/grants from institutional funds, on-campus employment. Forms required: International Student's Financial Aid Application, International Student's Certification of Finances. For fall 2006 (estimated), 19 international students on campus received college administered financial aid ($14,300 average).

AURORA UNIVERSITY, AURORA

General Information Independent, coed institution. Suburban setting. *Awards:* B, M, D. *Entrance level for U.S. students:* Moderately difficult. *Enrollment:* 3,791 total; 1,974 undergraduates (67% women) including 0.1% international students from 2 foreign countries. *Faculty:* 293. *Library holdings:* 92,025 books, 210 current serial subscriptions, 7,621 audiovisual materials. *Total majors:* 32. *Expenses:* (2007–08) $16,850; room and board, $7034 (on campus); room only, $3080 (on campus). *Financial aid:* Non-need-based college/university scholarships/grants from institutional funds. Forms required: International Student's Certification of Finances.

BENEDICTINE UNIVERSITY, LISLE

General Information Independent Roman Catholic, coed institution. Suburban setting. *Awards:* A, B, M, D. *Entrance level for U.S. students:* Moderately difficult. *Enrollment:* 3,900 total; 2,657 undergraduates (57% women) including 1% international students from 9 foreign countries. *Faculty:* 353. *Library holdings:* 201,190 books, 14,177 current serial subscriptions, 2,500 audiovisual materials. *Total majors:* 51. *Expenses:* (2006–07) $20,310; room and board, $6700 (on campus).

BRADLEY UNIVERSITY, PEORIA

General Information Independent, coed institution. Suburban setting. *Awards:* B, M, FP. *Entrance level for U.S. students:* Moderately difficult. *Enrollment:* 6,126 total; 5,315 undergraduates (55% women) including 1% international students from 26 foreign countries. *Faculty:* 547. *Library holdings:* 518,000 books, 3,529 current serial subscriptions. *Total majors:* 75. *Expenses:* (2006–07) $20,060; room and board, $6750 (on campus); room only, $3900 (on campus).

CHICAGO STATE UNIVERSITY, CHICAGO

General Information State-supported, coed institution. Urban setting. *Awards:* B, M, D. *Entrance level for U.S. students:* Minimally difficult. *Enrollment:* 7,035 total; 5,167 undergraduates (73% women) including 1% international students from 13 foreign countries. *Faculty:* 453. *Library holdings:* 426,691 books, 1,654 current serial subscriptions, 1,688 audiovisual materials. *Total majors:* 63. *Expenses:* (2006–07) $12,748; room and board, $6492 (on campus). *Financial aid:* Non-need financial aid available. Forms required: institution's own financial aid form.

CITY COLLEGES OF CHICAGO, HAROLD WASHINGTON COLLEGE, CHICAGO

General Information State and locally supported, 2-year, coed college. Urban setting. *Awards:* A. *Entrance level for U.S. students:* Noncompetitive. *Enrollment:* 8,434 total (58% women). *Undergraduate faculty:* 231. *Library holdings:* 65,926 books, 360 current serial subscriptions, 2,695 audiovisual materials. *Total majors:* 50.

Information for International Students For fall 2006: 318 international students enrolled. Students can start in fall, spring, or summer. Transfers accepted from institutions abroad. *Admission tests:* Required: TOEFL (minimum score: iBT 45; paper-based 450; computer-based 133; minimum score for ESL admission: iBT 45; paper-based 450; computer-based 133). TOEFL can be waived under certain conditions. *Application deadline:* 7/15. *Services:* International student adviser on campus. Full-time and part-time ESL programs on campus. ESL program available during the academic year and the summer. Internships and employment opportunities (on-campus) available. *Contact:* Administrative Assistant for Office of Admissions, City Colleges of Chicago, Harold Washington College, 30 East Lake Street, Chicago, IL 60601. Telephone: 312-553-6004. Fax: 312-553-3107. E-mail: ytownsend@ccc.edu. URL: http://hwashington.ccc.edu.

CITY COLLEGES OF CHICAGO, KENNEDY-KING COLLEGE, CHICAGO

General Information State and locally supported, 2-year, coed college. Urban setting. *Awards:* A. *Entrance level for U.S. students:* Noncompetitive. *Enrollment:* 3,054 total. *Undergraduate faculty:* 147. *Library holdings:* 45,000 books, 200 current serial subscriptions, 2,500 audiovisual materials. *Total majors:* 33.

Information for International Students For fall 2006: 8 international students applied, 6 were accepted, 4 enrolled. Students can start in fall, spring, or summer. Transfers accepted from institutions abroad. *Admission tests:* Required: TOEFL (minimum score: paper-based 450; computer-based 133). TOEFL can be waived under certain conditions. *Application deadline:* Rolling. *Services:* International student adviser on campus. ESL program at cooperating institution. ESL program available during the academic year. *Contact:* Project Coordinator of Admissions and Recruitment, City Colleges of Chicago, Kennedy-King College, 6800 South Wentworth Avenue, Chicago, IL 60621-3798. Telephone: 773-602-5062. Fax: 773-602-5247. E-mail: wmurphy@ccc.edu. URL: http://kennedyking.ccc.edu.

COLLEGE OF DUPAGE, GLEN ELLYN

General Information State and locally supported, 2-year, coed college. Suburban setting. *Awards:* A. *Entrance level for U.S. students:* Noncompetitive. *Enrollment:* 26,032 total (55% women). *Undergraduate faculty:* 1,167. *Library holdings:* 203,300 books, 6,005 current serial subscriptions. *Total majors:* 84.

Information for International Students For fall 2006: 125 international students enrolled. Students can start in fall, spring, or summer. *Admission tests:* Required: TOEFL (minimum score: iBT 79; paper-based 550; computer-based 213). *Application deadline:* 5/15. *Expenses:* (2007–08) $11,122. *Services:* International student adviser on campus. Full-time ESL program on campus. ESL program available during the academic year. Employment opportunities (on-campus) available. *Contact:* International Student Admission Specialist, College of DuPage, 425 Fawell Boulevard, IC 2046-H, Glen Ellyn, IL 60137. Telephone: 630-942-2979. Fax: 630-790-2686. E-mail: intladm@cod.edu. URL: http://www.cod.edu.

COLLEGE OF LAKE COUNTY, GRAYSLAKE

General Information District-supported, 2-year, coed college. Suburban setting. *Awards:* A. *Entrance level for U.S. students:* Noncompetitive. *Enrollment:* 15,558 total (57% women) including 1% international students from 31 foreign countries. *Undergraduate faculty:* 832. *Library holdings:* 106,842 books, 766 current serial subscriptions. *Total majors:* 40.

Information for International Students Students can start in fall, spring, or summer. Transfers accepted from institutions abroad. *Admission tests:* Recommended: SAT or ACT, TOEFL

College of Lake County (continued)

(minimum score: iBT 70; paper-based 525; computer-based 197), basic skills assessment test. TOEFL can be waived under certain conditions. *Application deadline:* 7/1. *Expenses:* (2007–08) $8280. *Services:* International student adviser on campus. Full-time ESL program on campus. ESL program available during the academic year and the summer. Employment opportunities (on-campus) available. *Contact:* International Admissions Specialist, International Education, College of Lake County, 19351 West Washington Street, Grayslake, IL 60030-1198. Telephone: 847-543-2733. Fax: 847-543-3733. E-mail: ssmith2@clcillinois.edu. URL: http://www.clcillinois.edu.

COLUMBIA COLLEGE CHICAGO, CHICAGO

General Information Independent, coed institution. Urban setting. *Awards:* B, M. *Entrance level for U.S. students:* Noncompetitive. *Enrollment:* 11,499 total; 10,771 undergraduates (50% women) including 1% international students from 36 foreign countries. *Faculty:* 1,477. *Library holdings:* 258,883 books, 1,232 current serial subscriptions, 21,257 audiovisual materials. *Total majors:* 42.

Information for International Students Students can start in fall, winter, spring, or summer. Transfers accepted from institutions abroad. *Admission tests:* Required: proof of English proficiency. *Application deadline:* Rolling. *Expenses:* (2006–07) $16,788; room and board, $9765 (on campus); room only, $8265 (on campus). *Financial aid:* Need-based college/university scholarships/grants from institutional funds, tuition waivers, loans from outside sources, on-campus employment. Non-need-based college/university scholarships/grants from institutional funds, tuition waivers, loans from outside sources, on-campus employment. Forms required: International Student's Certification of Finances. *Contact:* International Undergraduate Counselor, Columbia College Chicago, 600 South Michigan Avenue, Chicago, IL 60605. Telephone: 312-344-7458. E-mail: intladmissions@colum.edu. URL: http://www.colum.edu.

CONCORDIA UNIVERSITY, RIVER FOREST

General Information Independent, coed institution, affiliated with Lutheran Church–Missouri Synod. Suburban setting. *Awards:* B, M, D. *Entrance level for U.S. students:* Moderately difficult. *Enrollment:* 3,710 total; 1,074 undergraduates (61% women) including international students from 1 foreign country. *Faculty:* 349. *Library holdings:* 140,000 books, 235 current serial subscriptions, 2,250 audiovisual materials. *Total majors:* 54.

Information for International Students Students can start in fall, winter, spring, or summer. Transfers accepted from institutions abroad. *Admission tests:* Required: SAT or ACT, TOEFL (minimum score: paper-based 525; computer-based 195). Recommended: ELS. *Application deadline:* 7/1. *Expenses:* (2007–08) $21,320; room and board, $6992 (on campus). *Financial aid:* Non-need financial aid available. Forms required: institution's own financial aid form. For fall 2005, 4 international students on campus received college administered financial aid ($2000 average). *Services:* International student adviser on campus. ESL program at cooperating institution. Employment opportunities (on-campus) available. *Contact:* International Counselor, Concordia University, 7400 Augusta Street, River Forest, IL 60305-1499. Telephone: 708-209-3100. Fax: 708-209-3176. URL: http://www.curf.edu.

DANVILLE AREA COMMUNITY COLLEGE, DANVILLE

General Information State and locally supported, 2-year, coed college. Small town setting. *Awards:* A. *Entrance level for U.S. students:* Noncompetitive. *Enrollment:* 3,000 total. *Undergraduate faculty:* 121. *Library holdings:* 50,000 books, 2,487 audiovisual materials. *Total majors:* 52.

DEPAUL UNIVERSITY, CHICAGO

General Information Independent Roman Catholic, coed university. Urban setting. *Awards:* B, M, D, FP. *Entrance level for U.S. students:* Moderately difficult. *Enrollment:* 23,149 total; 14,893 undergraduates (56% women) including 1% international students from 74 foreign countries. *Faculty:* 1,697. *Library holdings:* 897,564 books, 28,514 current serial subscriptions, 27,242 audiovisual materials. *Total majors:* 100.

Information for International Students Students can start in fall, winter, spring, or summer. Transfers accepted from institutions abroad. *Admission tests:* Required: TOEFL (minimum score: iBT 80; paper-based 550; computer-based 213). Recommended: SAT or ACT. *Application deadline:* Rolling. *Expenses:* (2006–07) $22,575; room and board, $10,392 (on campus); room only, $6771 (on campus). *Financial aid:* International transfer students are eligible to apply for aid. *Services:* International student adviser on campus. ESL program available during the academic year and the summer. Employment opportunities (on-campus) available. *Contact:*

International Recruiter, DePaul University, 1 East Jackson Boulevard, Suite 9100, Chicago, IL 60604. Telephone: 312-362-8300. Fax: 312-362-8521. E-mail: intlapp@depaul.edu. URL: http://www.depaul.edu.

See In-Depth Description on page 67.

DEVRY UNIVERSITY, ADDISON

General Information Proprietary, 4-year, coed college. Suburban setting. *Awards:* A, B. *Entrance level for U.S. students:* Minimally difficult. *Enrollment:* 1,440 total (29% women) including 4% international students. *Undergraduate faculty:* 106. *Library holdings:* 18,500 books, 4,000 current serial subscriptions. *Total majors:* 10. *Expenses:* (2007–08) $13,220.

DEVRY UNIVERSITY, CHICAGO

General Information Proprietary, coed institution. Urban setting. *Awards:* A, B. *Entrance level for U.S. students:* Minimally difficult. *Enrollment:* 2,055 total (39% women) including 7% international students. *Undergraduate faculty:* 103. *Library holdings:* 16,573 books, 79 current serial subscriptions. *Total majors:* 10. *Expenses:* (2007–08) $13,220.

DEVRY UNIVERSITY, TINLEY PARK

General Information Proprietary, coed institution. Suburban setting. *Awards:* A, B, M. *Entrance level for U.S. students:* Minimally difficult. *Enrollment:* 1,261 total; 1,023 undergraduates (29% women) including 1% international students. *Faculty:* 120. *Library holdings:* 17,500 books, 82 current serial subscriptions. *Total majors:* 11. *Expenses:* (2007–08) $13,220.

DEVRY UNIVERSITY ONLINE, OAKBROOK TERRACE

General Information Proprietary, coed institution. *Awards:* A, B, M. *Entrance level for U.S. students:* Difficulty N/R. *Enrollment:* 6,569 total; 4,427 undergraduates (60% women) including 0.3% international students. *Faculty:* 791. *Total majors:* 2. *Expenses:* (2006–07) $12,650; room and board, $9598 (on campus); room only, $7310 (on campus).

DOMINICAN UNIVERSITY, RIVER FOREST

General Information Independent Roman Catholic, coed institution. Suburban setting. *Awards:* B, M. *Entrance level for U.S. students:* Moderately difficult. *Enrollment:* 3,292 total; 1,462 undergraduates (71% women) including 1% international students from 18 foreign countries. *Faculty:* 315. *Library holdings:* 255,840 books, 14,089 current serial subscriptions, 4,635 audiovisual materials. *Total majors:* 46. *Expenses:* (2006–07) $21,250; room and board, $6620 (on campus). *Financial aid:* Need-based financial aid available. Non-need-based college/university scholarships/grants from institutional funds, on-campus employment. Forms required: International Student's Financial Aid Application, International Student's Certification of Finances. For fall 2006 (estimated), 5 international students on campus received college administered financial aid ($8000 average).

EASTERN ILLINOIS UNIVERSITY, CHARLESTON

General Information State-supported, coed institution. Small town setting. *Awards:* B, M. *Entrance level for U.S. students:* Difficulty N/R. *Enrollment:* 12,349 total; 10,592 undergraduates (58% women) including 1% international students from 22 foreign countries. *Faculty:* 770. *Library holdings:* 1 million books, 14,714 current serial subscriptions, 14,129 audiovisual materials. *Total majors:* 42. *Expenses:* (2006–07) $17,482; room and board, $6660 (on campus).

EAST-WEST UNIVERSITY, CHICAGO

General Information Independent, 4-year, coed college. Urban setting. *Awards:* A, B. *Entrance level for U.S. students:* Minimally difficult. *Enrollment:* 1,040 total including 7% international students from 12 foreign countries. *Undergraduate faculty:* 70. *Library holdings:* 32,000 books, 3,450 current serial subscriptions. *Total majors:* 17. *Expenses:* (2006–07) $12,645.

ELGIN COMMUNITY COLLEGE, ELGIN

General Information State and locally supported, 2-year, coed college. Suburban setting. *Awards:* A. *Entrance level for U.S. students:* Noncompetitive. *Enrollment:* 10,072 total (56% women) including 0.01% international students from 2 foreign countries. *Undergraduate faculty:* 476. *Library holdings:* 58,413 books, 458 current serial subscriptions. *Total majors:* 49. *Expenses:* (2007–08) $13,117.

ELMHURST COLLEGE, ELMHURST

General Information Independent, coed institution, affiliated with United Church of Christ. Suburban setting. *Awards:* B, M. *Entrance level for U.S. students:* Moderately difficult. *Enrollment:*

3,107 total; 2,841 undergraduates (65% women) including 1% international students from 21 foreign countries. *Faculty:* 313. *Library holdings:* 222,441 books, 2,010 current serial subscriptions. *Total majors:* 67. *Expenses:* (2007–08) $24,660; room and board, $7164 (on campus); room only, $4200 (on campus). *Financial aid:* Non-need-based college/university scholarships/grants from institutional funds, loans from outside sources, on-campus employment. Forms required: International Student's Certification of Finances. For fall 2006 (estimated), 27 international students on campus received college administered financial aid ($8989 average).

EUREKA COLLEGE, EUREKA

General Information Independent, 4-year, coed college, affiliated with Christian Church (Disciples of Christ). Small town setting. *Awards:* B. *Entrance level for U.S. students:* Moderately difficult. *Enrollment:* 516 total (56% women) including 1% international students from 2 foreign countries. *Undergraduate faculty:* 69. *Library holdings:* 75,000 books, 330 current serial subscriptions, 500 audiovisual materials. *Total majors:* 42. *Expenses:* (2006–07) $14,180; room and board, $6220 (on campus). *Financial aid:* Need-based college/university scholarships/grants from institutional funds. Non-need-based college/university scholarships/grants from institutional funds, on-campus employment. Forms required: financial certificate, supporting documentation, deposit balance statement. For fall 2006 (estimated), 5 international students on campus received college administered financial aid ($3500 average).

GOVERNORS STATE UNIVERSITY, UNIVERSITY PARK

General Information State-supported, coed institution. Suburban setting. *Awards:* B, M. *Entrance level for U.S. students:* Difficulty N/R. *Enrollment:* 5,405 total; 2,632 undergraduates including 1% international students from 20 foreign countries. *Faculty:* 212. *Library holdings:* 260,000 books, 2,200 current serial subscriptions, 2,700 audiovisual materials. *Total majors:* 35. *Expenses:* (2006–07) $12,316.

GREENVILLE COLLEGE, GREENVILLE

General Information Independent Free Methodist, coed institution. Small town setting. *Awards:* B, M. *Entrance level for U.S. students:* Moderately difficult. *Enrollment:* 1,451 total; 1,322 undergraduates (55% women) including 1% international students from 15 foreign countries. *Faculty:* 152. *Library holdings:* 134,569 books, 490 current serial subscriptions, 3,711 audiovisual materials. *Total majors:* 51.
Information for International Students For fall 2006: 41 international students applied, 14 were accepted, 3 enrolled. Students can start in fall or spring. Transfers accepted from institutions abroad. *Admission tests:* TOEFL can be waived under certain conditions. *Application deadline:* Rolling. *Expenses:* (2006–07) $17,932; room and board, $6136 (on campus); room only, $2904 (on campus). *Financial aid:* Need-based college/university scholarships/grants from institutional funds, on-campus employment. Non-need-based college/university scholarships/grants from institutional funds, on-campus employment. Forms required: International Student's Certification of Finances. International transfer students are eligible to apply for aid. For fall 2005, 14 international students on campus received college administered financial aid ($7728 average). *Housing:* Guaranteed, also available during summer. *Services:* International student adviser on campus. ESL program at cooperating institution. ESL program available during the academic year and the summer. Employment opportunities (on-campus) available. *Contact:* Admissions Counselor, Greenville College, 315 East College Avenue, Greenville, IL 62246. Telephone: 618-664-7100. Fax: 618-664-9841. E-mail: admissions@greenville.edu. URL: http://www.greenville.edu.

HARPER COLLEGE, PALATINE

General Information State and locally supported, 2-year, coed college. Suburban setting. *Awards:* A. *Entrance level for U.S. students:* Noncompetitive. *Enrollment:* 15,053 total (56% women) including 1% international students from 17 foreign countries. *Undergraduate faculty:* 843. *Library holdings:* 141,124 books, 6,606 current serial subscriptions, 37,973 audiovisual materials. *Total majors:* 70.
Information for International Students For fall 2006: 88 international students applied, 57 were accepted, 39 enrolled. Students can start in fall, spring, or summer. Transfers accepted from institutions abroad. *Admission tests:* Required: TOEFL (minimum score: iBT 79; paper-based 550; computer-based 210). TOEFL can be waived under certain conditions. *Application deadline:* 6/15. *Expenses:* (2006–07) $9138. *Financial aid:* Forms required: scholarship application form. *Services:* International student adviser on campus. Full-time and part-time ESL programs on campus. ESL program available during the academic year and the summer. Employment opportunities (on-campus) available. *Contact:* International Student Specialist, Harper College, 1200

West Algonquin Road, Palatine, IL 60067. Telephone: 847-925-6226. Fax: 847-925-6082. E-mail: jizumika@harpercollege.edu. URL: http://www.harpercollege.edu.

HARRINGTON COLLEGE OF DESIGN, CHICAGO

General Information Proprietary, 4-year, coed, primarily women's college. Urban setting. *Awards:* A, B. *Entrance level for U.S. students:* Noncompetitive. *Enrollment:* 1,563 total (87% women). *Undergraduate faculty:* 142. *Library holdings:* 22,000 books, 149 current serial subscriptions, 450 audiovisual materials. *Total majors:* 2.
Information for International Students Students can start in fall, winter, spring, or summer. Transfers accepted from institutions abroad. *Admission tests:* Required: TOEFL (minimum score: paper-based 500; computer-based 173). Recommended: ELS. *Application deadline:* Rolling. *Expenses:* (2007–08) $20,520; room only, $2600 (on campus). *Services:* International student adviser on campus. ESL program at cooperating institution. Employment opportunities (on-campus) available. *Contact:* Director of Admissions, Harrington College of Design, 200 West Madison, 6th Floor, Chicago, IL 60606. Telephone: 877-9394975 Ext. 1183. Fax: 312-697-8115. E-mail: dpeitz@harringtoncollege.com. URL: http://www.interiordesign.edu.

See In-Depth Description on page 96.

HIGHLAND COMMUNITY COLLEGE, FREEPORT

General Information State and locally supported, 2-year, coed college. Rural setting. *Awards:* A. *Entrance level for U.S. students:* Noncompetitive. *Enrollment:* 2,406 total (63% women) including 0.2% international students. *Undergraduate faculty:* 190. *Library holdings:* 47,000 books, 3,980 current serial subscriptions, 2,776 audiovisual materials. *Total majors:* 43. *Expenses:* (2006–07) $3000. *Financial aid:* Forms required: institution's own financial aid form.

ILLINOIS CENTRAL COLLEGE, EAST PEORIA

General Information State and locally supported, 2-year, coed college. Suburban setting. *Awards:* A. *Entrance level for U.S. students:* Noncompetitive. *Enrollment:* 12,343 total including 1% international students from 20 foreign countries. *Undergraduate faculty:* 658. *Library holdings:* 82,492 books, 563 current serial subscriptions. *Total majors:* 37. *Expenses:* (2006–07) $4960; room only, $3978 (on campus). *Financial aid:* Need based college/university scholarships/grants from institutional funds, tuition waivers, athletic awards, on-campus employment. Non-need-based college/university scholarships/grants from institutional funds, tuition waivers, athletic awards.

ILLINOIS COLLEGE, JACKSONVILLE

General Information Independent interdenominational, 4-year, coed college. Small town setting. *Awards:* B. *Entrance level for U.S. students:* Moderately difficult. *Enrollment:* 1,023 total (53% women) including 2% international students from 14 foreign countries. *Undergraduate faculty:* 90. *Library holdings:* 163,810 books, 10,234 current serial subscriptions. *Total majors:* 44.
Information for International Students For fall 2006: 50 international students applied, 34 were accepted, 8 enrolled. Students can start in fall or spring. Transfers accepted from institutions abroad. *Admission tests:* Required: TOEFL (minimum score: iBT 79; paper-based 550; computer-based 213; minimum score for ESL admission: iBT 79; paper-based 550; computer-based 213). Recommended: SAT or ACT, SAT Subject Tests. TOEFL can be waived under certain conditions. *Application deadline:* 6/1. *Expenses:* (2006–07) $17,100; room and board, $6730 (on campus); room only, $2800 (on campus). *Financial aid:* Need-based on-campus employment. Non-need-based college/university scholarships/grants from institutional funds, on-campus employment. Forms required: International Student's Financial Aid Application, International Student's Certification of Finances. International transfer students are eligible to apply for aid. For fall 2006 (estimated), 16 international students on campus received college administered financial aid ($7956 average). *Housing:* Guaranteed, also available during summer. *Services:* International student adviser on campus. Internships and employment opportunities (on-campus) available. *Contact:* Associate Director of Admission, Office of Admissions, Illinois College, 1101 West College Avenue, Jacksonville, IL 62650. Telephone: 217-245-3030. Fax: 217-245-3034. E-mail: rlbystry@ic.edu. URL: http://www.ic.edu.

ILLINOIS EASTERN COMMUNITY COLLEGES, OLNEY CENTRAL COLLEGE, OLNEY

General Information State and locally supported, 2-year, coed college. Rural setting. *Awards:* A. *Entrance level for U.S. students:* Noncompetitive. *Enrollment:* 1,737 total (62% women) including 0.1% international students. *Undergraduate faculty:* 122. *Library holdings:* 22,917 books, 28,036 current serial subscriptions, 1,081

*Illinois Eastern Community Colleges, Olney Central
College (continued)*

audiovisual materials. *Total majors:* 19. *Expenses:* (2007–08) $7365.
Financial aid: Forms required: institution's own financial aid form.

ILLINOIS EASTERN COMMUNITY COLLEGES, WABASH VALLEY COLLEGE, MOUNT CARMEL

General Information State and locally supported, 2-year, coed
college. Rural setting. *Awards:* A. *Entrance level for U.S. students:*
Noncompetitive. *Enrollment:* 4,840 total (47% women) including
0.1% international students. *Undergraduate faculty:* 168. *Library
holdings:* 31,988 books, 85 current serial subscriptions, 1,374
audiovisual materials. *Total majors:* 19. *Expenses:* (2007–08) $7365.
Financial aid: Forms required: institution's own financial aid form.

THE ILLINOIS INSTITUTE OF ART–CHICAGO, CHICAGO

General Information Proprietary, 4-year, coed college. Urban
setting. *Awards:* A, B. *Entrance level for U.S. students:* Minimally
difficult. *Enrollment:* 2,680 total (61% women) including 0.04%
international students from 24 foreign countries. *Undergraduate
faculty:* 175. *Library holdings:* 11,324 books, 264 current serial
subscriptions. *Total majors:* 14.

Information for International Students For fall 2006: 70
international students enrolled. Students can start in fall, winter,
spring, or summer. Transfers accepted from institutions abroad.
Admission tests: Required: TOEFL, SAT, or ACT. *Application
deadline:* Rolling. *Expenses:* (2007–08) $20,284; room only, $11,512
(on campus). *Services:* International student advisor on campus.
ESL program at cooperating institution. ESL program available
during the academic year and the summer. Internships and
employment opportunities (on-campus) available. *Contact:* Vice
President/Director of Admissions, The Illinois Institute of
Art–Chicago, 350 North Orleans Street, Chicago, IL 60654.
Telephone: 312-280-3500. Fax: 312-280-8562.
E-mail: janton@aii.edu. URL: http://www.ilic.artinstitutes.edu.

See In-Depth Description on page 100.

ILLINOIS INSTITUTE OF TECHNOLOGY, CHICAGO

General Information Independent, coed university. Urban setting.
Awards: B, M, D, FP. *Entrance level for U.S. students:* Very difficult.
Enrollment: 6,795 total; 2,353 undergraduates (25% women)
including 14% international students from 74 foreign countries.
Faculty: 631. *Library holdings:* 1.1 million books, 21,498 current
serial subscriptions, 3,266 audiovisual materials. *Total majors:* 31.

Information for International Students Students can start in
fall or spring. Transfers accepted from institutions abroad.
Admission tests: Required: SAT or ACT, TOEFL (minimum score:
iBT 80; paper-based 550; computer-based 213). TOEFL can be
waived under certain conditions. *Application deadline:* 5/15.
Expenses: (2006–07) $24,113; room and board, $8049 (on campus);
room only, $4212 (on campus). *Financial aid:* Non-need-based
college/university scholarships/grants from institutional funds,
tuition waivers, loans from outside sources, on-campus employment.
International transfer students are eligible to apply for aid. For fall
2005, 316 international students on campus received college
administered financial aid ($9616 average). *Housing:* Guaranteed,
also available during summer. *Services:* International student
adviser on campus. Internships and employment opportunities
(on-campus and off-campus) available. *Contact:* Coordinator of
International Admission, Office of Admissions, Illinois Institute of
Technology, Office of Undergraduate Admission, 10 West 33rd
Street, PH101, Chicago, IL 60616-3793. Telephone: 312-567-3025.
Fax: 312-567-6939. E-mail: admission@iit.edu.
URL: http://www.iit.edu.

See In-Depth Description on page 101.

ILLINOIS STATE UNIVERSITY, NORMAL

General Information State-supported, coed university. Urban
setting. *Awards:* B, M, D. *Entrance level for U.S. students:*
Moderately difficult. *Enrollment:* 20,521 total; 17,885
undergraduates (57% women) including 1% international students
from 38 foreign countries. *Faculty:* 1,113. *Library holdings:* 1.6
million books, 14,166 current serial subscriptions. *Total majors:* 61.
Expenses: (2006–07) $14,730; room and board, $6148 (on campus);
room only, $3200 (on campus).

ILLINOIS WESLEYAN UNIVERSITY, BLOOMINGTON

General Information Independent, 4-year, coed college. Suburban
setting. *Awards:* B. *Entrance level for U.S. students:* Very difficult.
Enrollment: 2,144 total (58% women) including 2% international
students from 19 foreign countries. *Undergraduate faculty:* 224.
Library holdings: 313,495 books, 12,238 current serial
subscriptions, 13,084 audiovisual materials. *Total majors:* 53.

Information for International Students For fall 2006: 332
international students applied, 70 were accepted, 18 enrolled.
Students can start in fall. Transfers accepted from institutions
abroad. *Admission tests:* Required: SAT or ACT, TOEFL (minimum
score: iBT 80; paper-based 550; computer-based 213). TOEFL can
be waived under certain conditions. *Application deadline:* 3/1.
Expenses: (2007–08) $30,750; room and board, $7030 (on campus);
room only, $4330 (on campus). *Financial aid:* Need-based
college/university scholarships/grants from institutional funds,
loans from institutional funds, on-campus employment.
Non-need-based college/university scholarships/grants from
institutional funds, on-campus employment. Forms required:
International Student's Certification of Finances. International
transfer students are eligible to apply for aid. For fall 2006
(estimated), 37 international students on campus received college
administered financial aid ($24,701 average). *Housing:* Guaranteed,
also available during summer. *Services:* International student
adviser on campus. Internships and employment opportunities
(on-campus) available. *Contact:* Director of International
Admissions, Illinois Wesleyan University, 1312 Park Street,
Bloomington, IL 61701. Telephone: 309-556-3031.
Fax: 309-556-3820. E-mail: international@iwu.edu.
URL: http://www.iwu.edu.

See In-Depth Description on page 102.

JOHN WOOD COMMUNITY COLLEGE, QUINCY

General Information District-supported, 2-year, coed college.
Small town setting. *Awards:* A. *Entrance level for U.S. students:*
Noncompetitive. *Enrollment:* 2,516 total (63% women) including
0.5% international students from 3 foreign countries.
Undergraduate faculty: 192. *Library holdings:* 18,000 books, 160
current serial subscriptions. *Total majors:* 35. *Expenses:* (2007–08)
$5880. *Financial aid:* Need-based college/university
scholarships/grants from institutional funds, tuition waivers.
Non-need-based college/university scholarships/grants from
institutional funds, tuition waivers, athletic awards, on-campus
employment.

JOLIET JUNIOR COLLEGE, JOLIET

General Information State and locally supported, 2-year, coed
college. Suburban setting. *Awards:* A. *Entrance level for U.S.
students:* Noncompetitive. *Enrollment:* 12,924 total (59% women)
including 0.1% international students. *Undergraduate faculty:* 554.
Library holdings: 60,364 books, 360 current serial subscriptions.
Total majors: 51.

Information for International Students For fall 2006: 30
international students applied, 13 were accepted, 13 enrolled.
Students can start in fall, spring, or summer. Transfers accepted
from institutions abroad. *Admission tests:* Required: TOEFL
(minimum score: iBT 61; paper-based 500; computer-based 173;
minimum score for ESL admission: paper-based 500;
computer-based 173). TOEFL can be waived under certain
conditions. *Application deadline:* 7/2. *Expenses:* (2007–08) $8280.
Financial aid: Forms required: institution's own financial aid form.
Housing: Available during summer. *Services:* ESL program at
cooperating institution. Internships and employment opportunities
(on-campus and off-campus) available. *Contact:* Administrative
Supervisor, Admissions Office, Joliet Junior College, 1215 Houbolt
Road, Joliet, IL 60431-8938. Telephone: 815-280-2247.
Fax: 815-280-6740. E-mail: admissions@jjc.cc.il.us.
URL: http://www.jjc.edu.

JUDSON COLLEGE, ELGIN

General Information Independent Baptist, coed institution.
Suburban setting. *Awards:* B, M. *Entrance level for U.S. students:*
Moderately difficult. *Enrollment:* 1,243 total; 1,180 undergraduates
(59% women) including 4% international students from 28 foreign
countries. *Faculty:* 133. *Library holdings:* 104,331 books, 450
current serial subscriptions, 12,500 audiovisual materials.
Total majors: 48.

Information for International Students For fall 2006: 14
international students applied, 14 were accepted, 11 enrolled.
Students can start in fall or spring. Transfers accepted from
institutions abroad. *Admission tests:* Required: SAT or ACT, TOEFL
(minimum score: paper-based 550; computer-based 213; minimum
score for ESL admission: paper-based 450; computer-based 133).
Recommended: ELS. *Application deadline:* 7/31. *Expenses:*
(2007–08) $20,420; room and board, $7200 (on campus). *Financial
aid:* Need-based college/university scholarships/grants from
institutional funds, tuition waivers, athletic awards, on-campus
employment. Non-need-based college/university scholarships/grants
from institutional funds, tuition waivers, athletic awards. Forms
required: International Student's Certification of Finances.
International transfer students are eligible to apply for aid. For fall
2005, 46 international students on campus received college
administered financial aid ($8000 average). *Housing:* Guaranteed,

also available during summer. *Services:* International student adviser on campus. Internships and employment opportunities (on-campus) available. *Contact:* International and Intercultural Advisor, Judson College, 1151 North State Street, Elgin, IL 60123. Telephone: 847-628-1572. Fax: 847-628-2526. E-mail: glongjohn@judsoncollege.edu. URL: http://www.judsoncollege.edu.

KANKAKEE COMMUNITY COLLEGE, KANKAKEE

General Information State and locally supported, 2-year, coed college. Small town setting. *Awards:* A (also offers continuing education program with significant enrollment not reflected in profile). *Entrance level for U.S. students:* Noncompetitive. *Enrollment:* 3,353 total (65% women) including 0.2% international students from 5 foreign countries. *Undergraduate faculty:* 193. *Library holdings:* 48,239 books, 245 current serial subscriptions, 2,308 audiovisual materials. *Total majors:* 28.

Information for International Students For fall 2006: 10 international students applied, 3 were accepted, 3 enrolled. Students can start in fall, spring, or summer. Transfers accepted from institutions abroad. *Admission tests:* Required: TOEFL, COMPASS. *Application deadline:* 7/1. *Expenses:* (2007–08) $9275. *Financial aid:* Forms required: institution's own financial aid form, International Student's Certification of Finances. *Services:* International student adviser on campus. Full-time ESL program on campus. ESL program available during the academic year. Employment opportunities (on-campus) available. *Contact:* Director, Admissions and Registration, Kankakee Community College, 100 College Drive, Kankakee, IL 60901. Telephone: 815-802-8524. Fax: 815-802-8101. E-mail: mdriscoll@kcc.edu. URL: http://www.kcc.cc.il.us.

KASKASKIA COLLEGE, CENTRALIA

General Information State and locally supported, 2-year, coed college. Rural setting. *Awards:* A. *Entrance level for U.S. students:* Noncompetitive. *Enrollment:* 4,742 total (58% women) including 0.2% international students from 2 foreign countries. *Undergraduate faculty:* 246. *Library holdings:* 23,685 books, 165 current serial subscriptions, 480 audiovisual materials. *Total majors:* 21. *Expenses:* (2006–07) $8349.

KNOX COLLEGE, GALESBURG

General Information Independent, 4-year, coed college. Small town setting. *Awards:* B. *Entrance level for U.S. students:* Very difficult. *Enrollment:* 1,351 total (56% women) including 7% international students from 44 foreign countries. *Undergraduate faculty:* 127. *Library holdings:* 316,886 books, 519 current serial subscriptions, 7,461 audiovisual materials. *Total majors:* 33.

Information for International Students For fall 2006: 291 international students applied, 147 were accepted, 43 enrolled. Students can start in fall, winter, or spring. Transfers accepted from institutions abroad. *Admission tests:* Required: TOEFL (minimum score: iBT 80; paper-based 550; computer-based 213). TOEFL can be waived under certain conditions. *Application deadline:* 2/1. *Expenses:* (2006–07) $27,900; room and board, $5925 (on campus); room only, $2865 (on campus). *Financial aid:* Need-based college/university scholarships/grants from institutional funds, loans from outside sources, on-campus employment. Non-need-based college/university scholarships/grants from institutional funds, loans from outside sources, on-campus employment. Forms required: institution's own financial aid form. International transfer students are eligible to apply for aid. For fall 2006 (estimated), 88 international students on campus received college administered financial aid ($16,778 average). *Housing:* Guaranteed, also available during summer. *Services:* International student adviser on campus. ESL program at cooperating institution. ESL program available during the academic year and the summer. Internships and employment opportunities (on-campus) available. *Contact:* Coordinator of International Recruitment, Knox College, 2 East South Street, Galesburg, IL 61401-4999. Telephone: 309-341-7100. Fax: 309-341-7070. E-mail: admission@knox.edu. URL: http://www.knox.edu.

LAKE FOREST COLLEGE, LAKE FOREST

General Information Independent, coed institution. Suburban setting. *Awards:* B, M. *Entrance level for U.S. students:* Very difficult. *Enrollment:* 1,448 total; 1,422 undergraduates (58% women) including 7% international students from 54 foreign countries. *Faculty:* 155. *Library holdings:* 263,918 books, 1,798 current serial subscriptions, 5,800 audiovisual materials. *Total majors:* 32. *Expenses:* (2006–07) $29,164; room and board, $6960 (on campus); room only, $3500 (on campus). *Financial aid:* Need-based college/university scholarships/grants from institutional funds, loans from institutional funds, loans from outside sources, on-campus employment. Non-need-based college/university scholarships/grants from institutional funds, loans from outside

sources, on-campus employment. Forms required: institution's own financial aid form, International Student's Certification of Finances. For fall 2006 (estimated), 101 international students on campus received college administered financial aid ($21,462 average).

LAKE LAND COLLEGE, MATTOON

General Information State and locally supported, 2-year, coed college. Rural setting. *Awards:* A. *Entrance level for U.S. students:* Noncompetitive. *Enrollment:* 7,431 total including 1% international students from 14 foreign countries. *Undergraduate faculty:* 191. *Library holdings:* 28,000 books, 225 current serial subscriptions, 1,939 audiovisual materials. *Total majors:* 37.

Information for International Students For fall 2006: 115 international students applied, 45 were accepted, 30 enrolled. Students can start in fall, spring, or summer. Transfers accepted from institutions abroad. *Admission tests:* Required: TOEFL (minimum score: iBT 61; paper-based 500; computer-based 173). TOEFL can be waived under certain conditions. *Application deadline:* Rolling. *Expenses:* (2007–08) $9355. *Financial aid:* Forms required: institution's own financial aid form. *Housing:* Guaranteed, also available during summer. *Services:* International student adviser on campus. Full-time and part-time ESL programs on campus. ESL program available during the academic year and the summer. Internships and employment opportunities (on-campus) available. *Contact:* Director, International Studies Program, Lake Land College, 5001 Lake Land Boulevard, Mattoon, IL 61938. Telephone: 217-234-5382. Fax: 217-234-5390. E-mail: klotz@lakelandcollege.edu. URL: http://www.lakelandcollege.edu.

LEWIS UNIVERSITY, ROMEOVILLE

General Information Independent, coed institution, affiliated with Roman Catholic Church. Suburban setting. *Awards:* A, B, M, D. *Entrance level for U.S. students:* Moderately difficult. *Enrollment:* 5,289 total; 3,850 undergraduates (60% women) including 3% international students from 26 foreign countries. *Faculty:* 499. *Library holdings:* 149,870 books, 1,990 current serial subscriptions. *Total majors:* 66. *Expenses:* (2007–08) $20,450; room and board, $7800 (on campus); room only, $5200 (on campus).

LINCOLN COLLEGE–NORMAL, NORMAL

General Information Independent, primarily 2-year, coed college. Suburban setting. *Awards:* A, B. *Entrance level for U.S. students:* Minimally difficult. *Enrollment:* 520 total (62% women) including 1% international students from 3 foreign countries. *Undergraduate faculty:* 50. *Library holdings:* 1.8 million books, 25,000 audiovisual materials. *Total majors:* 21. *Expenses:* (2006–07) $15,810; room only, $3200 (on campus). *Financial aid:* Non-need financial aid available.

LINCOLN LAND COMMUNITY COLLEGE, SPRINGFIELD

General Information District-supported, 2-year, coed college. Suburban setting. *Awards:* A. *Entrance level for U.S. students:* Noncompetitive. *Enrollment:* 6,532 total (59% women) including 0.2% international students. *Undergraduate faculty:* 372. *Library holdings:* 65,000 books, 10,000 current serial subscriptions. *Total majors:* 29.

Information for International Students Students can start in fall, spring, or summer. Transfers accepted from institutions abroad. *Admission tests:* Required: TOEFL (minimum score: paper-based 500; computer-based 173; minimum score for ESL admission: paper-based 500; computer-based 173). *Application deadline:* 5/31. *Expenses:* (2007–08) $6780. Employment opportunities (on-campus) available. *Contact:* Director of Admissions, Lincoln Land Community College, 5250 Shepherd Road, PO Box 19256, Springfield, IL 62794-9256. Telephone: 217-786-2243. Fax: 217-786-2492. E-mail: ron.gregoire@llcc.edu. URL: http://www.llcc.edu.

LOYOLA UNIVERSITY CHICAGO, CHICAGO

General Information Independent Roman Catholic (Jesuit), coed university. Urban setting. *Awards:* B, M, D, FP (also offers adult part-time program with significant enrollment not reflected in profile). *Entrance level for U.S. students:* Moderately difficult. *Enrollment:* 15,194 total; 9,725 undergraduates (65% women) including 1% international students from 60 foreign countries. *Faculty:* 1,143. *Library holdings:* 1.4 million books, 136,663 current serial subscriptions, 16,486 audiovisual materials. *Total majors:* 51.

Information for International Students Students can start in fall, winter, spring, or summer. Transfers accepted from institutions abroad. *Admission tests:* Required: SAT, ACT, TOEFL (minimum score: paper-based 550; computer-based 213; minimum score for ESL admission: paper-based 500; computer-based 190). *Application deadline:* Rolling. *Expenses:* (2007–08) $27,966; room and board, $9930 (on campus); room only, $6680 (on campus). *Financial aid:* Non-need-based college/university scholarships/grants from

Loyola University Chicago (continued)

institutional funds, athletic awards, loans from outside sources. Forms required: International Student's Certification of Finances. International transfer students are eligible to apply for aid. *Services:* International student adviser on campus. Full-time and part-time ESL programs on campus. ESL program available during the academic year and the summer. Internships and employment opportunities (on-campus) available. *Contact:* Undergraduate Admission, Undergraduate Admissions Office, Loyola University Chicago, Chicago, IL 60610. Telephone: 312-915-6500. Fax: 773-915-6414. E-mail: admission@luc.edu. URL: http://www.luc.edu.

See In-Depth Description on page 118.

MCKENDREE COLLEGE, LEBANON

General Information Independent, coed institution, affiliated with United Methodist Church. Small town setting. *Awards:* B, M. *Entrance level for U.S. students:* Moderately difficult. *Enrollment:* 3,212 total; 2,399 undergraduates (56% women) including 3% international students from 24 foreign countries. *Faculty:* 215. *Library holdings:* 109,000 books, 450 current serial subscriptions, 6,637 audiovisual materials. *Total majors:* 50. *Expenses:* (2006–07) $18,900; room and board, $7380 (on campus); room only, $3900 (on campus). *Financial aid:* Need-based college/university scholarships/grants from institutional funds. Non-need-based college/university scholarships/grants from institutional funds. For fall 2006 (estimated), 61 international students on campus received college administered financial aid ($19,318 average).

MIDSTATE COLLEGE, PEORIA

General Information Proprietary, 4-year, coed, primarily women's college. Urban setting. *Awards:* A, B. *Entrance level for U.S. students:* Moderately difficult. *Enrollment:* 478 total (80% women) including 0.2% international students. *Undergraduate faculty:* 45. *Library holdings:* 8,724 books, 104 current serial subscriptions. *Total majors:* 13.

Information for International Students For fall 2006: 2 international students applied, 2 were accepted, 2 enrolled. Students can start in fall or spring. Transfers accepted from institutions abroad. *Admission tests:* Required: TOEFL (minimum score: paper-based 500; computer-based 300), entrance exam, admissions testing. *Application deadline:* Rolling. *Expenses:* (2006–07) $10,680. *Financial aid:* Need-based and non-need-based financial aid available. Forms required: institution's own financial aid form. Employment opportunities (on-campus) available. *Contact:* Director of Enrollment Management, Midstate College, 411 West Northmoor Road, Peoria, IL 61614. Telephone: 309-692-4092 Ext. 1090. Fax: 309-692-3893. E-mail: jhancock2@midstate.edu. URL: http://www.midstate.edu.

MILLIKIN UNIVERSITY, DECATUR

General Information Independent, coed institution, affiliated with Presbyterian Church (U.S.A.). Suburban setting. *Awards:* B, M. *Entrance level for U.S. students:* Moderately difficult. *Enrollment:* 2,488 total; 2,453 undergraduates (59% women) including 0.4% international students from 9 foreign countries. *Faculty:* 267. *Library holdings:* 215,096 books, 478 current serial subscriptions, 2,632 audiovisual materials. *Total majors:* 51. *Expenses:* (2007–08) $23,845; room and board, $7210 (on campus); room only, $4010 (on campus). *Financial aid:* Need-based and non-need-based financial aid available. Forms required: International Student's Financial Aid Application, International Student's Certification of Finances.

MONMOUTH COLLEGE, MONMOUTH

General Information Independent, 4-year, coed college, affiliated with Presbyterian Church. Small town setting. *Awards:* B. *Entrance level for U.S. students:* Moderately difficult. *Enrollment:* 1,345 total (53% women) including 2% international students from 14 foreign countries. *Undergraduate faculty:* 155. *Library holdings:* 176,470 books, 514 current serial subscriptions, 3,975 audiovisual materials. *Total majors:* 38. *Expenses:* (2006–07) $20,200; room and board, $5750 (on campus); room only, $3240 (on campus). *Financial aid:* Need-based and non-need-based financial aid available. Forms required: International Student's Financial Aid Application, International Student's Certification of Finances. 24 international students on campus received college administered financial aid ($9036 average).

MORAINE VALLEY COMMUNITY COLLEGE, PALOS HILLS

General Information State and locally supported, 2-year, coed college. Suburban setting. *Awards:* A. *Entrance level for U.S. students:* Noncompetitive. *Enrollment:* 15,693 total (58% women) including 2% international students from 36 foreign countries.

Undergraduate faculty: 749. *Library holdings:* 74,091 books, 464 current serial subscriptions. *Total majors:* 28. *Expenses:* (2006–07) $7412.

MORRISON INSTITUTE OF TECHNOLOGY, MORRISON

General Information Independent, 2-year, coed, primarily men's college. Small town setting. *Awards:* A. *Entrance level for U.S. students:* Noncompetitive. *Enrollment:* 126 total. *Undergraduate faculty:* 11. *Library holdings:* 7,946 books, 39 current serial subscriptions. *Total majors:* 6. *Expenses:* (2006–07) $12,660; room only, $2600 (on campus). *Financial aid:* Need-based college/university scholarships/grants from institutional funds, loans from outside sources, on-campus employment. Non-need-based college/university scholarships/grants from institutional funds, loans from outside sources, on-campus employment.

NORTH CENTRAL COLLEGE, NAPERVILLE

General Information Independent United Methodist, coed institution. Suburban setting. *Awards:* B, M. *Entrance level for U.S. students:* Moderately difficult. *Enrollment:* 2,556 total; 2,236 undergraduates (58% women) including 1% international students from 33 foreign countries. *Faculty:* 225. *Library holdings:* 145,918 books, 2,243 current serial subscriptions, 3,578 audiovisual materials. *Total majors:* 63.

Information for International Students For fall 2006: 17 international students applied, 13 were accepted, 8 enrolled. Students can start in fall, winter, or spring. Transfers accepted from institutions abroad. *Admission tests:* Required: TOEFL (minimum score: iBT 79; paper-based 520; computer-based 190). TOEFL can be waived under certain conditions. *Application deadline:* Rolling. *Expenses:* (2006–07) $23,115; room and board, $7440 (on campus). *Financial aid:* Need-based college/university scholarships/grants from institutional funds, loans from outside sources, on-campus employment. Non-need-based college/university scholarships/grants from institutional funds, tuition waivers, loans from institutional funds, loans from outside sources, on-campus employment. International transfer students are eligible to apply for aid. For fall 2006 (estimated), 27 international students on campus received college administered financial aid ($10,573 average). *Housing:* Guaranteed, also available during summer. *Services:* International student adviser on campus. Part-time ESL program on campus. ESL program available during the summer. Internships and employment opportunities (on-campus and off-campus) available. *Contact:* International Admission Counselor, North Central College, 30 North Brainard Street, Naperville, IL 60540. Telephone: 630-637-5800. Fax: 630-637-5819. E-mail: msotermat@noctrl.edu. URL: http://www.noctrl.edu.

See In-Depth Description on page 139.

NORTHEASTERN ILLINOIS UNIVERSITY, CHICAGO

General Information State-supported, coed institution. Urban setting. *Awards:* B, M. *Entrance level for U.S. students:* Minimally difficult. *Enrollment:* 12,056 total; 9,257 undergraduates (61% women) including 1% international students from 45 foreign countries. *Faculty:* 701. *Library holdings:* 718,536 books, 2,919 current serial subscriptions, 8,222 audiovisual materials. *Total majors:* 42. *Expenses:* (2006–07) $11,511. *Financial aid:* Non-need-based college/university scholarships/grants from institutional funds, tuition waivers. Forms required: institution's own financial aid form, International Student's Certification of Finances. For fall 2006 (estimated), 2 international students on campus received college administered financial aid ($2000 average).

NORTHERN ILLINOIS UNIVERSITY, DE KALB

General Information State-supported, coed university. Small town setting. *Awards:* B, M, D, FP. *Entrance level for U.S. students:* Moderately difficult. *Enrollment:* 25,313 total; 18,816 undergraduates (52% women) including 1% international students from 105 foreign countries. *Faculty:* 1,193. *Library holdings:* 3.1 million books, 24,696 current serial subscriptions. *Total majors:* 61. *Expenses:* (2006–07) $12,555; room and board, $6848 (on campus). *Financial aid:* Need-based and non-need-based financial aid available.

NORTHWESTERN UNIVERSITY, EVANSTON

General Information Independent, coed university. Suburban setting. *Awards:* B, M, D, FP. *Entrance level for U.S. students:* Most difficult. *Enrollment:* 17,460 total; 8,153 undergraduates (53% women) including 5% international students from 48 foreign countries. *Faculty:* 1,192. *Library holdings:* 4.7 million books, 45,259 current serial subscriptions. *Total majors:* 112.

Information for International Students For fall 2006: 849 international students applied, 281 were accepted, 94 enrolled. Students can start in fall. Transfers accepted from institutions abroad. *Admission tests:* Required: SAT or ACT, TOEFL (minimum score: iBT 100; paper-based 600; computer-based 250). Recommended: SAT Subject Tests, TOEFL may be waived if SAT verbal score is greater than 650. TOEFL can be waived under certain conditions. *Application deadline:* 1/1. *Expenses:* (2006–07) $33,559; room and board, $10,266 (on campus); room only, $5838 (on campus). *Financial aid:* Need-based financial aid available. Forms required: International Student's Financial Aid Application, International Student's Certification of Finances, parent and student federal or foreign tax returns. For fall 2005, 10 international students on campus received college administered financial aid ($39,300 average). *Services:* International student adviser on campus. Internships and employment opportunities (on-campus) available. *Contact:* Senior Associate Director of Admissions, Northwestern University, 1801 Hinman Avenue, Evanston, IL 60204-3060. Telephone: 847-491-7271. E-mail: international@northwestern.edu. URL: http://www.northwestern.edu.

OLIVET NAZARENE UNIVERSITY, BOURBONNAIS

General Information Independent, coed institution, affiliated with Church of the Nazarene. Small town setting. *Awards:* A, B, M. *Entrance level for U.S. students:* Minimally difficult. *Enrollment:* 4,364 total; 2,633 undergraduates (60% women) including 1% international students from 15 foreign countries. *Faculty:* 123. *Library holdings:* 160,039 books, 925 current serial subscriptions, 6,818 audiovisual materials. *Total majors:* 77. *Expenses:* (2006–07) $17,590; room and board, $6400 (on campus); room only, $3200 (on campus). *Financial aid:* Need-based college/university scholarships/grants from institutional funds, tuition waivers, athletic awards, loans from outside sources. Non-need-based college/university scholarships/grants from institutional funds, tuition waivers, athletic awards, loans from outside sources, on-campus employment. Forms required: International Student's Certification of Finances.

PRAIRIE STATE COLLEGE, CHICAGO HEIGHTS

General Information State and locally supported, 2-year, coed college. Suburban setting. *Awards:* A. *Entrance level for U.S. students:* Noncompetitive. *Enrollment:* 5,083 total (62% women) including 0.2% international students. *Undergraduate faculty:* 363. *Library holdings:* 45,000 books, 515 current serial subscriptions, 4,000 audiovisual materials. *Total majors:* 24. *Expenses:* (2006–07) $8084. *Financial aid:* Need-based college/university scholarships/grants from institutional funds, athletic awards, loans from outside sources, on-campus employment. Non-need-based college/university scholarships/grants from institutional funds, loans from outside sources.

PRINCIPIA COLLEGE, ELSAH

General Information Independent Christian Science, 4-year, coed college. Rural setting. *Awards:* B. *Entrance level for U.S. students:* Moderately difficult. *Enrollment:* 542 total (52% women) including 13% international students from 24 foreign countries. *Undergraduate faculty:* 66. *Library holdings:* 211,460 books, 11,876 current serial subscriptions, 7,792 audiovisual materials. *Total majors:* 28.
Information for International Students For fall 2006: 59 international students applied, 30 were accepted, 21 enrolled. Students can start in fall. Transfers accepted from institutions abroad. *Admission tests:* Required: SAT or ACT, TOEFL (minimum score: iBT 79; paper-based 550; computer-based 213). Recommended: SAT. TOEFL can be waived under certain conditions. *Application deadline:* 2/16. *Expenses:* (2006–07) $21,450; room and board, $7896 (on campus); room only, $3831 (on campus). *Financial aid:* Need-based college/university scholarships/grants from institutional funds, loans from institutional funds. Non-need-based college/university scholarships/grants from institutional funds, loans from institutional funds. Forms required: institution's own financial aid form, International Student's Financial Aid Application, International Student's Certification of Finances, bank statements. International transfer students are eligible to apply for aid. For fall 2005, 57 international students on campus received college administered financial aid ($24,925 average). *Housing:* Guaranteed, also available during summer. *Services:* International student adviser on campus. ESL program at cooperating institution. Internships and employment opportunities (on-campus) available. *Contact:* International Student Admissions Counselor, Principia College, 1 Maybeck Place, Elsah, IL 62028-9703. Telephone: 618-374-5179. Fax: 618-374-4000. E-mail: intladmissions@prin.edu. URL: http://www.prin.edu/college.

QUINCY UNIVERSITY, QUINCY

General Information Independent Roman Catholic, coed institution. Small town setting. *Awards:* A, B, M. *Entrance level for U.S. students:* Moderately difficult. *Enrollment:* 1,250 total; 1,005 undergraduates (58% women) including 1% international students

from 9 foreign countries. *Faculty:* 130. *Library holdings:* 204,557 books, 365 current serial subscriptions, 9,293 audiovisual materials. *Total majors:* 40.
Information for International Students Students can start in fall, spring, or summer. Transfers accepted from institutions abroad. *Admission tests:* Required: TOEFL (minimum score: paper-based 500; computer-based 250; minimum score for ESL admission: paper-based 500; computer-based 250). Recommended: ACT. *Application deadline:* 4/1. *Expenses:* (2007–08) $19,600; room and board, $7390 (on campus); room only, $3990 (on campus). *Financial aid:* Non-need-based college/university scholarships/grants from institutional funds, athletic awards, on-campus employment. Forms required: International Student's Certification of Finances. International transfer students are eligible to apply for aid. 6 international students on campus received college administered financial aid ($14,441 average). *Housing:* Guaranteed. *Services:* International student adviser on campus. Internships available. *Contact:* International Students Coordinator, Quincy University, 1800 College Avenue, Quincy, IL 62301-2499. Telephone: 217-228-5215. Fax: 217-228-5479. E-mail: admissions@quincy.edu. URL: http://www.quincy.edu.

RICHLAND COMMUNITY COLLEGE, DECATUR

General Information District-supported, 2-year, coed college. Small town setting. *Awards:* A. *Entrance level for U.S. students:* Noncompetitive. *Enrollment:* 3,152 total (63% women) including 0.2% international students. *Undergraduate faculty:* 217. *Library holdings:* 39,452 books, 275 current serial subscriptions. *Total majors:* 27. *Expenses:* (2006–07) $10,377.

ROCKFORD COLLEGE, ROCKFORD

General Information Independent, coed institution. Suburban setting. *Awards:* B, M. *Entrance level for U.S. students:* Moderately difficult. *Enrollment:* 1,426 total; 880 undergraduates (65% women) including 1% international students from 5 foreign countries. *Faculty:* 152. *Library holdings:* 140,000 books, 831 current serial subscriptions. *Total majors:* 47. *Expenses:* (2007–08) $22,950; room and board, $6750 (on campus); room only, $3850 (on campus). *Financial aid:* Need-based and non-need-based financial aid available. Forms required: International Student's Financial Aid Application, International Student's Certification of Finances. 14 international students on campus received college administered financial aid ($14,694 average).

ROCK VALLEY COLLEGE, ROCKFORD

General Information District-supported, 2-year, coed college. Suburban setting. *Awards:* A. *Entrance level for U.S. students:* Noncompetitive. *Enrollment:* 8,145 total (59% women) including 0.3% international students from 3 foreign countries. *Undergraduate faculty:* 291. *Library holdings:* 67,168 books. *Total majors:* 23. *Expenses:* (2006–07) $12,304.

ROOSEVELT UNIVERSITY, CHICAGO

General Information Independent, coed institution. Urban setting. *Awards:* B, M, D. *Entrance level for U.S. students:* Moderately difficult. *Enrollment:* 7,186 total; 3,975 undergraduates (66% women) including 2% international students from 44 foreign countries. *Faculty:* 621. *Library holdings:* 186,944 books, 1,195 current serial subscriptions. *Total majors:* 86.
Information for International Students For fall 2006: 90 international students applied, 47 were accepted, 31 enrolled. Students can start in fall or spring. Transfers accepted from institutions abroad. *Admission tests:* Required: ELS. Recommended: TOEFL (minimum score: iBT 80; paper-based 550; computer-based 213), Test of Written English (minimum score 4.5). TOEFL can be waived under certain conditions. *Application deadline:* 6/1. *Expenses:* (2007–08) $16,980; room and board, $8750 (on campus); room only, $6100 (on campus). *Financial aid:* Forms required: students recommended for institutional scholarships by the Director of International Admissions on a case-by-case basis. International transfer students are eligible to apply for aid. *Housing:* Available during summer. *Services:* International student adviser on campus. Full-time and part-time ESL programs on campus. ESL program available during the academic year. Internships and employment opportunities (on-campus and off-campus) available. *Contact:* Assistant Director, Roosevelt University, Office of International Programs, 430 South Michigan Avenue, Chicago, IL 60605-1394. Telephone: 312-341-3531. Fax: 312-341-6377. E-mail: dhougland@roosevelt.edu. URL: http://www.roosevelt.edu.
See In-Depth Description on page 162.

SAINT XAVIER UNIVERSITY, CHICAGO

General Information Independent Roman Catholic, coed institution. Urban setting. *Awards:* B, M. *Entrance level for U.S. students:* Moderately difficult. *Enrollment:* 5,657 total; 3,316 undergraduates (72% women) including 0.4% international students

Saint Xavier University (continued)

from 2 foreign countries. *Faculty:* 405. *Library holdings:* 170,753 books, 717 current serial subscriptions. *Total majors:* 39. *Expenses:* (2006–07) $19,860; room and board, $7414 (on campus); room only, $4230 (on campus). *Financial aid:* Need-based college/university scholarships/grants from institutional funds. Non-need-based college/university scholarships/grants from institutional funds, tuition waivers, athletic awards, on-campus employment. 12 international students on campus received college administered financial aid ($2708 average).

SAUK VALLEY COMMUNITY COLLEGE, DIXON

General Information District-supported, 2-year, coed college. Rural setting. *Awards:* A. *Entrance level for U.S. students:* Noncompetitive. *Enrollment:* 2,745 total (62% women). *Undergraduate faculty:* 157. *Library holdings:* 55,000 books, 268 current serial subscriptions. *Total majors:* 52.

Information for International Students For fall 2006: 15 international students applied, 15 were accepted, 15 enrolled. Students can start in fall, spring, or summer. *Admission tests:* Required: TOEFL (minimum score: paper-based 500; computer-based 173; minimum score for ESL admission: paper-based 500; computer-based 173), on-campus placement test. Recommended: ACT. TOEFL can be waived under certain conditions. *Application deadline:* Rolling. *Expenses:* (2006–07) $10,688. *Services:* International student adviser on campus. Full-time and part-time ESL programs on campus. ESL program available during the academic year. *Contact:* Director of Admissions, Counseling, and Records, Sauk Valley Community College, 173 IL Route 2, Dixon, IL 61021. Telephone: 815-288-5511 Ext. 297. Fax: 815-288-3190. E-mail: breedt@svcc.edu. URL: http://www.svcc.edu.

SCHOOL OF THE ART INSTITUTE OF CHICAGO, CHICAGO

General Information Independent, coed institution. Urban setting. *Awards:* B, M. *Entrance level for U.S. students:* Moderately difficult. *Enrollment:* 2,873 total; 2,274 undergraduates (65% women) including 17% international students from 27 foreign countries. *Faculty:* 468. *Library holdings:* 72,490 books, 334 current serial subscriptions, 4,067 audiovisual materials. *Total majors:* 36.

Information for International Students For fall 2006: 534 international students applied, 387 were accepted, 136 enrolled. Students can start in fall, spring, or summer. Transfers accepted from institutions abroad. *Admission tests:* Required: TOEFL (minimum score: iBT 80; paper-based 550; computer-based 213; minimum score for ESL admission: iBT 80; paper-based 550; computer-based 213). TOEFL can be waived under certain conditions. *Application deadline:* Rolling. *Expenses:* (2007–08) $31,020; room only, $8900 (on campus). *Financial aid:* Non-need-based college/university scholarships/grants from institutional funds, loans from outside sources, on-campus employment. International transfer students are eligible to apply for aid. 70 international students on campus received college administered financial aid ($4239 average). *Housing:* Available during summer. *Services:* International student adviser on campus. Part-time ESL program on campus. ESL program available during the academic year and the summer. Internships and employment opportunities (on-campus and off-campus) available. *Contact:* Director of International Affairs, School of the Art Institute of Chicago, 36 South Wabash Avenue, Chicago, IL 60603. Telephone: 312-629-6830. Fax: 312-629-6831. E-mail: intaff@saic.edu. URL: http://www.artic.edu/saic.

See In-Depth Description on page 180.

SHIMER COLLEGE, CHICAGO

General Information Independent, 4-year, coed college. Urban setting. *Awards:* B. *Entrance level for U.S. students:* Moderately difficult. *Enrollment:* 138 total; 126 undergraduates (33% women) including 4% international students from 4 foreign countries. *Undergraduate faculty:* 15. *Library holdings:* 200,000 books, 200 current serial subscriptions. *Total majors:* 7. *Expenses:* (2006–07) $21,000; room and board, $8049 (on campus). *Financial aid:* Need-based college/university scholarships/grants from institutional funds, tuition waivers, loans from outside sources, on-campus employment. Non-need-based college/university scholarships/grants from institutional funds, tuition waivers, loans from outside sources, on-campus employment. Forms required: institution's own financial aid form. For fall 2005, 2 international students on campus received college administered financial aid ($20,000 average).

SOUTHEASTERN ILLINOIS COLLEGE, HARRISBURG

General Information State-supported, 2-year, coed college. Rural setting. *Awards:* A. *Entrance level for U.S. students:*

Noncompetitive. *Enrollment:* 2,559 total including 0.3% international students from 2 foreign countries. *Undergraduate faculty:* 253. *Library holdings:* 58,030 books, 300 current serial subscriptions, 1,059 audiovisual materials. *Total majors:* 25. *Expenses:* (2006–07) $3270; room and board, $3655 (on campus).

SOUTHERN ILLINOIS UNIVERSITY CARBONDALE, CARBONDALE

General Information State-supported, coed university. Rural setting. *Awards:* A, B, M, D, FP. *Entrance level for U.S. students:* Moderately difficult. *Enrollment:* 21,003 total; 16,294 undergraduates (43% women) including 2% international students from 107 foreign countries. *Faculty:* 1,097. *Library holdings:* 4.2 million books, 18,271 current serial subscriptions, 371,180 audiovisual materials. *Total majors:* 89.

Information for International Students For fall 2006: 1275 international students applied, 973 were accepted, 402 enrolled. Students can start in fall, spring, or summer. *Admission tests:* Required: TOEFL (minimum score: iBT 68; paper-based 520; computer-based 190). Recommended: SAT or ACT recommended for some scholarships. *Application deadline:* Rolling. *Expenses:* (2007–08) $16,783; room and board, $6666 (on campus); room only, $3650 (on campus). *Financial aid:* Need-based college/university scholarships/grants from institutional funds, tuition waivers, athletic awards, on-campus employment. Non-need-based college/university scholarships/grants from institutional funds, tuition waivers, athletic awards, on-campus employment. Forms required: International Student's Certification of Finances. For fall 2006 (estimated), 117 international students on campus received college administered financial aid ($19,653 average). *Services:* International student adviser on campus. Full-time and part-time ESL programs on campus. ESL program available during the academic year and the summer. Internships and employment opportunities (on-campus) available. *Contact:* International Programs and Services, New Student Admissions Office, Southern Illinois University Carbondale, Carbondale, IL 62901-6831. Telephone: 618-453-2056. Fax: 618-453-3085. E-mail: intlinfp@siu.edu. URL: http://www.siu.edu/siuc.

See In-Depth Description on page 191.

SOUTHERN ILLINOIS UNIVERSITY EDWARDSVILLE, EDWARDSVILLE

General Information State-supported, coed institution. Suburban setting. *Awards:* B, M, FP. *Entrance level for U.S. students:* Moderately difficult. *Enrollment:* 13,449 total; 10,960 undergraduates (55% women) including 1% international students from 48 foreign countries. *Faculty:* 815. *Library holdings:* 847,631 books, 24,530 current serial subscriptions, 30,078 audiovisual materials. *Total majors:* 43.

Information for International Students For fall 2006: 74 international students applied, 31 were accepted, 26 enrolled. Students can start in fall, spring, or summer. Transfers accepted from institutions abroad. *Admission tests:* Required: TOEFL (minimum score: iBT 80; paper-based 550; computer-based 213), IELTS (6.5 overall band score). TOEFL can be waived under certain conditions. *Application deadline:* 6/1. *Expenses:* (2007–08) $14,255; room and board, $6500 (on campus); room only, $3970 (on campus). *Financial aid:* Non-need-based tuition waivers. *Housing:* Available during summer. *Services:* International student adviser on campus. Internships and employment opportunities (on-campus and off-campus) available. *Contact:* International Student Advisor, Southern Illinois University Edwardsville, Campus Box 1616, Edwardsville, IL 62026. Telephone: 618-650-3785. Fax: 618-650-5099. E-mail: rschaef@siue.edu. URL: http://www.siue.edu.

See In-Depth Description on page 192.

SOUTHWESTERN ILLINOIS COLLEGE, BELLEVILLE

General Information District-supported, 2-year, coed college. Suburban setting. *Awards:* A. *Entrance level for U.S. students:* Noncompetitive. *Enrollment:* 14,479 total (57% women) including 0.1% international students from 19 foreign countries. *Undergraduate faculty:* 829. *Library holdings:* 82,537 books, 638 current serial subscriptions, 2,688 audiovisual materials. *Total majors:* 43. *Expenses:* (2006–07) $8070.

SPOON RIVER COLLEGE, CANTON

General Information State-supported, 2-year, coed college. Rural setting. *Awards:* A. *Entrance level for U.S. students:* Noncompetitive. *Enrollment:* 2,333 total including 0.1% international students. *Undergraduate faculty:* 142. *Library holdings:* 34,799 books, 121 current serial subscriptions, 3,213 audiovisual materials. *Total majors:* 41. *Expenses:* (2006–07) $5160. *Financial aid:* Forms required: institution's own financial aid form, International Student's Certification of Finances.

SPRINGFIELD COLLEGE IN ILLINOIS, SPRINGFIELD

General Information Independent, 2-year, coed college, affiliated with Roman Catholic Church. Urban setting. *Awards:* A (the college partners with Benedictine University, offering baccalaureate and master degree programs at Springfield College's campus). *Entrance level for U.S. students:* Moderately difficult. *Enrollment:* 552 total (68% women) including 1% international students from 8 foreign countries. *Undergraduate faculty:* 71. *Library holdings:* 19,951 books, 146 current serial subscriptions, 2,490 audiovisual materials. *Total majors:* 16. *Expenses:* (2006–07) $9480; room and board, $5920 (on campus). *Financial aid:* Forms required: institution's own financial aid form.

TRINITY INTERNATIONAL UNIVERSITY, DEERFIELD

General Information Independent, coed university, affiliated with Evangelical Free Church of America. Suburban setting. *Awards:* B, M, D, FP. *Entrance level for U.S. students:* Moderately difficult. *Enrollment:* 2,855 total; 1,247 undergraduates (59% women) including 0.2% international students. *Faculty:* 381. *Library holdings:* 245,320 books, 1,176 current serial subscriptions. *Total majors:* 39. *Expenses:* (2006–07) $20,106; room and board, $6550 (on campus); room only, $3620 (on campus). *Financial aid:* Need-based college/university scholarships/grants from institutional funds, tuition waivers, athletic awards, loans from outside sources, on-campus employment. Non-need-based college/university scholarships/grants from institutional funds, tuition waivers, athletic awards. Forms required: institution's own financial aid form, International Student's Certification of Finances. For fall 2006 (estimated), 3 international students on campus received college administered financial aid ($15,300 average).

TRITON COLLEGE, RIVER GROVE

General Information State-supported, 2-year, coed college. Suburban setting. *Awards:* A. *Entrance level for U.S. students:* Noncompetitive. *Enrollment:* 11,021 total (55% women) including 0.2% international students from 26 foreign countries. *Undergraduate faculty:* 597. *Library holdings:* 70,859 books, 1,247 current serial subscriptions. *Total majors:* 66. *Expenses:* (2006–07) $6920.

UNIVERSITY OF CHICAGO, CHICAGO

General Information Independent, coed university. Urban setting. *Awards:* B, M, D, FP. *Entrance level for U.S. students:* Most difficult. *Enrollment:* 11,730 total; 4,807 undergraduates (50% women) including 7% international students. *Faculty:* 1,630. *Library holdings:* 7 million books, 47,000 current serial subscriptions. *Total majors:* 75. *Expenses:* (2006–07) $34,005; room and board, $10,608 (on campus). *Financial aid:* Need-based financial aid available. Forms required: institution's own financial aid form, International Student's Financial Aid Application.

UNIVERSITY OF ILLINOIS AT CHICAGO, CHICAGO

General Information State-supported, coed university. Urban setting. *Awards:* B, M, D, FP. *Entrance level for U.S. students:* Moderately difficult. *Enrollment:* 24,654 total; 15,006 undergraduates (54% women) including 1% international students from 49 foreign countries. *Faculty:* 1,519. *Library holdings:* 3 million books, 38,392 current serial subscriptions, 28,670 audiovisual materials. *Total majors:* 76. *Expenses:* (2006–07) $22,132; room and board, $7446 (on campus).

UNIVERSITY OF ILLINOIS AT SPRINGFIELD, SPRINGFIELD

General Information State-supported, coed institution. Suburban setting. *Awards:* B, M, D. *Entrance level for U.S. students:* Moderately difficult. *Enrollment:* 4,761 total; 2,758 undergraduates (59% women) including 1% international students from 15 foreign countries. *Faculty:* 334. *Library holdings:* 550,249 books, 39,357 current serial subscriptions, 41,839 audiovisual materials. *Total majors:* 19.

Information for International Students For fall 2006: 189 international students applied, 140 were accepted, 65 enrolled. Students can start in fall, spring, or summer. Transfers accepted from institutions abroad. *Admission tests:* Required: SAT or ACT, TOEFL (minimum score: iBT 61; paper-based 500; computer-based 173). *Application deadline:* 6/20. *Expenses:* (2006–07) $16,394; room and board, $7495 (on campus); room only, $3400 (on campus). *Financial aid:* Need-based tuition waivers, athletic awards, loans from outside sources, on-campus employment. Non-need-based college/university scholarships/grants from institutional funds, tuition waivers, athletic awards, loans from institutional funds, loans from outside sources, on-campus employment. Forms required: institution's own financial aid form. 3 international students on campus received college administered financial aid ($9723 average). *Housing:* Available during summer. *Services:* International student adviser on campus. Part-time ESL program

on campus. ESL program available during the academic year and the summer. Internships and employment opportunities (on-campus and off-campus) available. *Contact:* Admissions and Records Officer, Office of Enrollment Services, F 20, University of Illinois at Springfield, One University Plaza, MS UHB 1080, Springfield, IL 62703-5407. Telephone: 217-206-4847. Fax: 217-206-6620. E-mail: jberr1@uis.edu. URL: http://www.uis.edu.

UNIVERSITY OF ILLINOIS AT URBANA–CHAMPAIGN, CHAMPAIGN

General Information State-supported, coed university. Urban setting. *Awards:* B, M, D, FP. *Entrance level for U.S. students:* Very difficult. *Enrollment:* 42,728 total; 31,472 undergraduates (47% women) including 5% international students from 62 foreign countries. *Faculty:* 2,051. *Library holdings:* 10.4 million books, 63,413 current serial subscriptions, 4,245 audiovisual materials. *Total majors:* 155. *Expenses:* (2007–08) $25,216; room and board, $8196 (on campus). *Financial aid:* Need-based college/university scholarships/grants from institutional funds, tuition waivers, athletic awards, loans from institutional funds, loans from outside sources, on-campus employment. Non-need-based college/university scholarships/grants from institutional funds, tuition waivers, athletic awards, loans from outside sources, on-campus employment. For fall 2005, 1,262 international students on campus received college administered financial aid ($1935 average).

UNIVERSITY OF PHOENIX–CHICAGO CAMPUS, SCHAUMBURG

General Information Proprietary, coed institution. Urban setting. *Awards:* B, M. *Entrance level for U.S. students:* Noncompetitive. *Enrollment:* 1,590 total; 1,320 undergraduates (60% women) including 7% international students. *Faculty:* 437. *Library holdings:* 1,756 books, 692 current serial subscriptions. *Total majors:* 9. *Expenses:* (2006–07) $11,190.

UNIVERSITY OF ST. FRANCIS, JOLIET

General Information Independent Roman Catholic, coed institution. Suburban setting. *Awards:* B, M. *Entrance level for U.S. students:* Moderately difficult. *Enrollment:* 2,060 total; 1,289 undergraduates (68% women) including 3% international students. *Faculty:* 206. *Library holdings:* 111,546 books, 24,985 current serial subscriptions, 3,214 audiovisual materials. *Total majors:* 43. *Expenses:* (2006–07) $19,540; room and board, $7280 (on campus). *Financial aid:* Need-based loans from outside sources. Non-need-based college/university scholarships/grants from institutional funds, athletic awards, loans from outside sources. Forms required: institution's own financial aid form, International Student's Certification of Finances. For fall 2006 (estimated), 15 international students on campus received college administered financial aid ($9482 average).

VANDERCOOK COLLEGE OF MUSIC, CHICAGO

General Information Independent, coed institution. Urban setting. *Awards:* B, M. *Entrance level for U.S. students:* Moderately difficult. *Enrollment:* 227 total; 150 undergraduates (48% women) including 2% international students from 2 foreign countries. *Total majors:* 1.

Information for International Students Students can start in fall, spring, or summer. Transfers accepted from institutions abroad. *Admission tests:* Required: SAT or ACT, TOEFL (minimum score: paper-based 500; computer-based 173; minimum score for ESL admission: paper-based 500; computer-based 173). TOEFL can be waived under certain conditions. *Application deadline:* 4/1. *Expenses:* (2006–07) $17,890; room and board, $8050 (on campus). *Financial aid:* Non-need financial aid available. Forms required: International Student's Certification of Finances. International transfer students are eligible to apply for aid. Employment opportunities (on-campus) available. *Contact:* Director of Admissions and Retention, VanderCook College of Music, 3140 South Federal Street, Chicago, IL 60616. Telephone: 312-225-6288 Ext. 230. Fax: 312-225-5211. E-mail: admissions@vandercook.edu. URL: http://www.vandercook.edu.

WAUBONSEE COMMUNITY COLLEGE, SUGAR GROVE

General Information District-supported, 2-year, coed college. Rural setting. *Awards:* A. *Entrance level for U.S. students:* Noncompetitive. *Enrollment:* 8,834 total (57% women) including 0.05% international students from 2 foreign countries. *Undergraduate faculty:* 877. *Library holdings:* 53,679 books, 562 current serial subscriptions, 6,388 audiovisual materials. *Total majors:* 46. *Expenses:* (2006–07) $7200.

WESTERN ILLINOIS UNIVERSITY, MACOMB

General Information State-supported, coed institution. Small town setting. *Awards:* B, M, D. *Entrance level for U.S. students:* Moderately difficult. *Enrollment:* 13,602 total; 11,334

Illinois

Western Illinois University (continued)

undergraduates (48% women) including 1% international students from 50 foreign countries. *Faculty:* 731. *Library holdings:* 998,041 books, 3,200 current serial subscriptions. *Total majors:* 53.
Information for International Students For fall 2006: 563 international students applied, 378 were accepted, 143 enrolled. Students can start in fall, spring, or summer. Transfers accepted from institutions abroad. *Admission tests:* Required: TOEFL (minimum score: paper-based 550; computer-based 213). Recommended: SAT or ACT. TOEFL can be waived under certain conditions. *Application deadline:* 5/1. *Expenses:* (2006–07) $10,130; room and board, $6446 (on campus); room only, $3876 (on campus). *Financial aid:* Non-need-based college/university scholarships/grants from institutional funds, tuition waivers, athletic awards, on-campus employment. For fall 2006 (estimated), 29 international students on campus received college administered financial aid ($7055 average). *Services:* International student adviser on campus. Full-time and part-time ESL programs on campus. ESL program available during the academic year and the summer. Employment opportunities (on-campus) available. *Contact:* Center for International Studies, Western Illinois University, 1 University Circle, Seal Hall 211, Macomb, IL 61455. Telephone: 309-298-2501. Fax: 309-298-2405. E-mail: international-ed@wiu.edu. URL: http://www.wiu.edu.

See In-Depth Description on page 244.

WHEATON COLLEGE, WHEATON

General Information Independent nondenominational, coed institution. Suburban setting. *Awards:* B, M, D. *Entrance level for U.S. students:* Very difficult. *Enrollment:* 2,924 total; 2,365 undergraduates (51% women) including 1% international students from 18 foreign countries. *Faculty:* 295. *Library holdings:* 461,249 books, 4,012 current serial subscriptions, 30,142 audiovisual materials. *Total majors:* 38. *Expenses:* (2006–07) $22,450; room and board, $7040 (on campus); room only, $4160 (on campus). *Financial aid:* Need-based financial aid available. Non-need-based on-campus employment. Forms required: institution's own financial aid form. For fall 2006 (estimated), 11 international students on campus received college administered financial aid ($13,782 average).

INDIANA

ANCILLA COLLEGE, DONALDSON

General Information Independent Roman Catholic, 2-year, coed college. Rural setting. *Awards:* A. *Entrance level for U.S. students:* Noncompetitive. *Enrollment:* 624 total (73% women) including 0.2% international students. *Undergraduate faculty:* 50. *Library holdings:* 27,859 books, 152 current serial subscriptions, 1,499 audiovisual materials. *Total majors:* 34.
Information for International Students Students can start in fall, winter, spring, or summer. Transfers accepted from institutions abroad. *Admission tests:* Required: SAT, TOEFL (minimum score: paper-based 550; computer-based 213; minimum score for ESL admission: paper-based 550; computer-based 213), ELS, ACCUPLACER. Recommended: SAT or ACT. *Application deadline:* Rolling. *Expenses:* (2006–07) $11,030. *Financial aid:* Forms required: institution's own financial aid form, International Student's Financial Aid Application, International Student's Certification of Finances. *Services:* International student adviser on campus. ESL program at cooperating institution. ESL program available during the academic year and the summer. *Contact:* Assistant Director of Admissions, Ancilla College, 9601 Union Road, PO Box 1, Donaldson, IN 46513-0001. Telephone: 574-936-8898. Fax: 574-935-1773. E-mail: tara.minix@ancilla.edu. URL: http://www.ancilla.edu.

ANDERSON UNIVERSITY, ANDERSON

General Information Independent, coed institution, affiliated with Church of God. Suburban setting. *Awards:* A, B, M, D, FP. *Entrance level for U.S. students:* Moderately difficult. *Enrollment:* 2,730 total; 2,199 undergraduates (58% women) including 2% international students from 23 foreign countries. *Faculty:* 250. *Library holdings:* 247,966 books, 728 current serial subscriptions, 5,867 audiovisual materials. *Total majors:* 58. *Expenses:* (2006–07) $19,990; room and board, $6460 (on campus); room only, $3940 (on campus). *Financial aid:* Need-based college/university scholarships/grants from institutional funds, loans from outside sources, on-campus employment. Non-need-based college/university scholarships/grants from institutional funds, loans from outside sources, on-campus employment. Forms required: International Student's Certification of Finances. For fall 2006 (estimated), 56 international students on campus received college administered financial aid ($15,000 average).

BALL STATE UNIVERSITY, MUNCIE

General Information State-supported, coed university. Suburban setting. *Awards:* A, B, M, D. *Entrance level for U.S. students:* Moderately difficult. *Enrollment:* 17,082 total (52% women) including 0.1% international students from 47 foreign countries. *Faculty:* 1,148. *Library holdings:* 1.1 million books, 2,937 current serial subscriptions, 516,000 audiovisual materials. *Total majors:* 124.
Information for International Students For fall 2006: 300 international students applied, 150 were accepted, 98 enrolled. Students can start in fall, spring, or summer. Transfers accepted from institutions abroad. *Admission tests:* Required: TOEFL (minimum score: iBT 79; paper-based 550; computer-based 213; minimum score for ESL admission: iBT 45; paper-based 450; computer-based 133), IELTS or STEPS. TOEFL can be waived under certain conditions. *Application deadline:* 5/15. *Expenses:* (2006–07) $17,186; room and board, $6898 (on campus). *Financial aid:* International transfer students are eligible to apply for aid. *Housing:* Guaranteed, also available during summer. *Services:* International student adviser on campus. Full-time and part-time ESL programs on campus. ESL program available during the academic year and the summer. Internships and employment opportunities (on-campus) available. *Contact:* Director of International Services, Ball State University, Rinker Center for International Programs, 2000 West University Avenue, Sc-102, Muncie, IN 47306. Telephone: 765-285-5422. Fax: 765-285-3710. E-mail: intadmit@bsu.edu. URL: http://www.bsu.edu.

BETHEL COLLEGE, MISHAWAKA

General Information Independent, coed institution, affiliated with Missionary Church. Suburban setting. *Awards:* A, B, M. *Entrance level for U.S. students:* Minimally difficult. *Enrollment:* 2,093 total; 1,934 undergraduates (65% women) including 2% international students from 13 foreign countries. *Faculty:* 184. *Library holdings:* 106,584 books, 450 current serial subscriptions, 3,926 audiovisual materials. *Total majors:* 59. *Expenses:* (2006–07) $17,450; room and board, $5380 (on campus). *Financial aid:* Non-need financial aid available. Forms required: institution's own financial aid form, International Student's Certification of Finances. For fall 2006 (estimated), 32 international students on campus received college administered financial aid ($7125 average).

BUTLER UNIVERSITY, INDIANAPOLIS

General Information Independent, coed institution. Urban setting. *Awards:* B, M, FP. *Entrance level for U.S. students:* Moderately difficult. *Enrollment:* 4,437 total; 3,652 undergraduates (62% women) including 3% international students from 53 foreign countries. *Faculty:* 454. *Library holdings:* 346,805 books, 13,441 current serial subscriptions, 15,268 audiovisual materials. *Total majors:* 52.
Information for International Students For fall 2006: 458 international students applied, 213 were accepted, 25 enrolled. Students can start in fall or spring. Transfers accepted from institutions abroad. *Admission tests:* Required: TOEFL (minimum score: iBT 79; paper-based 550; computer-based 213). Recommended: SAT or ACT. TOEFL can be waived under certain conditions. *Application deadline:* 7/1. *Expenses:* (2006–07) $25,414; room and board, $8530 (on campus); room only, $4180 (on campus). *Financial aid:* Need-based college/university scholarships/grants from institutional funds, on-campus employment. Non-need-based college/university scholarships/grants from institutional funds. Forms required: International Student's Certification of Finances. International transfer students are eligible to apply for aid. *Housing:* Guaranteed, also available during summer. *Services:* International student adviser on campus. Internships and employment opportunities (on-campus and off-campus) available. *Contact:* Coordinator for International Admission, Butler University, 4600 Sunset Avenue, Indianapolis, IN 46208. Telephone: 317-940-8100. Fax: 317-940-8150. E-mail: intadmission@butler.edu. URL: http://www.butler.edu.

See In-Depth Description on page 48.

CALUMET COLLEGE OF SAINT JOSEPH, WHITING

General Information Independent Roman Catholic, coed institution. Urban setting. *Awards:* A, B, M. *Entrance level for U.S. students:* Noncompetitive. *Enrollment:* 1,252 total; 1,091 undergraduates (55% women) including 0.2% international students. *Faculty:* 142. *Library holdings:* 106,000 books, 21,850 current serial subscriptions, 1,000 audiovisual materials. *Total majors:* 28. *Expenses:* (2006–07) $10,650. *Financial aid:* Need-based college/university scholarships/grants from institutional funds. Non-need-based college/university scholarships/grants from institutional funds, athletic awards.

DEPAUW UNIVERSITY, GREENCASTLE

General Information Independent, 4-year, coed college, affiliated with United Methodist Church. Small town setting. *Awards:* B.

Entrance level for U.S. students: Moderately difficult. *Enrollment:* 2,326 total (56% women) including 2% international students from 32 foreign countries. *Undergraduate faculty:* 265. *Library holdings:* 333,346 books, 2,030 current serial subscriptions, 22,491 audiovisual materials. *Total majors:* 45.

Information for International Students For fall 2006: 148 international students applied, 46 were accepted, 15 enrolled. Students can start in fall. *Admission tests:* Required: SAT or ACT. Recommended: TOEFL (minimum score: iBT 83; paper-based 560; computer-based 220). TOEFL can be waived under certain conditions. *Application deadline:* 2/1. *Expenses:* (2006–07) $27,780; room and board, $7800 (on campus); room only, $4100 (on campus). *Financial aid:* Need-based college/university scholarships/grants from institutional funds, tuition waivers, loans from institutional funds, loans from outside sources, on-campus employment. Non-need-based college/university scholarships/grants from institutional funds, tuition waivers, loans from institutional funds, loans from outside sources, on-campus employment. Forms required: International Student's Financial Aid Application, International Student's Certification of Finances. For fall 2005, 35 international students on campus received college administered financial aid ($27,092 average). *Housing:* Guaranteed, also available during summer. *Services:* International student adviser on campus. Internships and employment opportunities (on-campus) available. *Contact:* Senior Associate Director of International Admission, Office of Admission, DePauw University, 101 East Seminary Street, Office of Admission, Greencastle, IN 46135-0037. Telephone: 765-658-4006. Fax: 765-658-4007. E-mail: intladmission@depauw.edu. URL: http://www.depauw.edu.

DEVRY UNIVERSITY, INDIANAPOLIS

General Information Proprietary, coed institution. *Awards:* A, B, M. *Entrance level for U.S. students:* Minimally difficult. *Enrollment:* 246 total; 143 undergraduates (52% women) including 1% international students. *Faculty:* 14. *Total majors:* 4. *Expenses:* (2007–08) $13,020.

EARLHAM COLLEGE, RICHMOND

General Information Independent, coed institution, affiliated with Society of Friends. Small town setting. *Awards:* B, M, FP. *Entrance level for U.S. students:* Very difficult. *Enrollment:* 1,410 total; 1,248 undergraduates (57% women) including 8% international students from 61 foreign countries. *Faculty:* 111. *Library holdings:* 406,699 books, 22,571 current serial subscriptions, 6,855 audiovisual materials. *Total majors:* 32. *Expenses:* (2006–07) $29,320; room and board, $6200 (on campus); room only, $3060 (on campus). *Financial aid:* Need-based and non-need-based financial aid available. Forms required: International Student's Financial Aid Application, International Student's Certification of Finances. 55 international students on campus received college administered financial aid ($16,605 average).

GOSHEN COLLEGE, GOSHEN

General Information Independent Mennonite, 4-year, coed college. Small town setting. *Awards:* B. *Entrance level for U.S. students:* Moderately difficult. *Enrollment:* 951 total (60% women) including 7% international students from 28 foreign countries. *Undergraduate faculty:* 110. *Library holdings:* 136,550 books, 496 current serial subscriptions. *Total majors:* 48.

Information for International Students For fall 2006: 58 international students applied, 19 were accepted, 10 enrolled. Students can start in fall or spring. Transfers accepted from institutions abroad. *Admission tests:* Required: TOEFL (minimum score: iBT 79; paper-based 550; computer-based 213; minimum score for ESL admission: iBT 79; paper-based 550; computer-based 213). TOEFL can be waived under certain conditions. *Application deadline:* Rolling. *Expenses:* (2007–08) $21,300; room and board, $7000 (on campus); room only, $3750 (on campus). *Financial aid:* Need-based college/university scholarships/grants from institutional funds, athletic awards, on-campus employment. Non-need-based college/university scholarships/grants from institutional funds, athletic awards, on-campus employment. Forms required: International Student's Financial Aid Application, International Student's Certification of Finances. International transfer students are eligible to apply for aid. For fall 2005, 60 international students on campus received college administered financial aid ($13,790 average). *Housing:* Guaranteed. *Services:* International student adviser on campus. ESL program at cooperating institution. ESL program available during the academic year and the summer. Internships and employment opportunities (on-campus and off-campus) available. *Contact:* Executive Director of Enrollment, Goshen College, Admission Office, 1700 South Main Street, Goshen, IN 46526. Telephone: 574-535-7535. Fax: 574-535-7609. E-mail: international@goshen.edu. URL: http://www.goshen.edu.

GRACE COLLEGE, WINONA LAKE

General Information Independent, coed institution, affiliated with Fellowship of Grace Brethren Churches. Small town setting. *Awards:* A, B, M, D, FP. *Entrance level for U.S. students:* Moderately difficult. *Enrollment:* 1,291 total; 1,179 undergraduates (46% women) including 1% international students from 6 foreign countries. *Faculty:* 53. *Library holdings:* 156,637 books, 23,972 current serial subscriptions, 3,806 audiovisual materials. *Total majors:* 39. *Expenses:* (2006–07) $17,350; room and board, $6360 (on campus); room only, $3280 (on campus).

HOLY CROSS COLLEGE, NOTRE DAME

General Information Independent Roman Catholic, primarily 2-year, coed college. Urban setting. *Awards:* A, B. *Entrance level for U.S. students:* Moderately difficult. *Enrollment:* 430 total (35% women) including 2% international students from 7 foreign countries. *Undergraduate faculty:* 38. *Library holdings:* 15,000 books, 160 current serial subscriptions. *Total majors:* 1. *Expenses:* (2007–08) $16,660; room and board, $8000 (on campus).

HUNTINGTON UNIVERSITY, HUNTINGTON

General Information Independent, coed institution, affiliated with Church of the United Brethren in Christ. Small town setting. *Awards:* A, B, M. *Entrance level for U.S. students:* Moderately difficult. *Enrollment:* 1,084 total; 997 undergraduates (55% women) including 4% international students from 15 foreign countries. *Faculty:* 84. *Library holdings:* 166,122 books. *Total majors:* 58.

Information for International Students For fall 2006: 20 international students applied, 5 were accepted, 5 enrolled. Students can start in fall or spring. Transfers accepted from institutions abroad. *Admission tests:* Required: SAT or ACT, TOEFL (minimum score: iBT 71; paper-based 535; computer-based 200). Recommended: SAT Subject Tests, ELS. TOEFL can be waived under certain conditions. *Application deadline:* 5/1. *Expenses:* (2007–08) $19,430; room and board, $6730 (on campus). *Financial aid:* Need-based college/university scholarships/grants from institutional funds. Non-need-based college/university scholarships/grants from institutional funds, athletic awards. Forms required: institution's own financial aid form. International transfer students are eligible to apply for aid. For fall 2006 (estimated), 24 international students on campus received college administered financial aid ($11,279 average). *Housing:* Guaranteed. Internships and employment opportunities (on-campus) available. *Contact:* Vice President of Enrollment Management, Huntington University, 2303 College Avenue, Huntington, IN 46750. Telephone: 260-359-4000. Fax: 260-358-3699. E-mail: admissions@huntington.edu. URL: http://www.huntington.edu.

INDIANA STATE UNIVERSITY, TERRE HAUTE

General Information State-supported, coed university. Small town setting. *Awards:* A, B, M, D. *Entrance level for U.S. students:* Moderately difficult. *Enrollment:* 10,568 total; 8,537 undergraduates (51% women) including 1% international students from 47 foreign countries. *Faculty:* 641. *Library holdings:* 1.3 million books, 43,464 current serial subscriptions, 32,843 audiovisual materials. *Total majors:* 76. *Expenses:* (2006–07) $13,852; room and board, $6294 (on campus); room only, $3339 (on campus).

INDIANA TECH, FORT WAYNE

General Information Independent, coed institution. Urban setting. *Awards:* A, B, M. *Entrance level for U.S. students:* Moderately difficult. *Enrollment:* 3,405 total; 3,035 undergraduates (53% women) including 0.3% international students from 3 foreign countries. *Faculty:* 251. *Library holdings:* 20,000 books, 80 current serial subscriptions, 102 audiovisual materials. *Total majors:* 18.

Information for International Students Students can start in fall or spring. Transfers accepted from institutions abroad. *Admission tests:* Required: TOEFL (minimum score: iBT 53; paper-based 477; computer-based 173). Recommended: SAT or ACT. *Application deadline:* Rolling. *Expenses:* (2007–08) $19,460; room and board, $7300 (on campus). *Financial aid:* Non-need financial aid available. *Contact:* Director of Admissions, Indiana Tech, 1600 East Washington Boulevard, Admissions, Fort Wayne, IN 46803. Telephone: 260-422-5561 Ext. 12348. Fax: 260-422-7696. E-mail: mlladig@indianatech.edu. URL: http://www.indianatech.edu.

INDIANA UNIVERSITY BLOOMINGTON, BLOOMINGTON

General Information State-supported, coed university. Small town setting. *Awards:* A, B, M, D, FP. *Entrance level for U.S. students:* Moderately difficult. *Enrollment:* 38,247 total; 29,828 undergraduates (52% women) including 4% international students

Indiana University Bloomington (continued)

from 135 foreign countries. *Faculty:* 2,233. *Library holdings:* 6.5 million books, 60,019 current serial subscriptions. *Total majors:* 141.

Information for International Students For fall 2006: 1794 international students applied, 1170 were accepted, 423 enrolled. Students can start in fall, spring, or summer. Transfers accepted from institutions abroad. *Admission tests:* Required: SAT or ACT, published TOEFL score requirement only for undergraduate music majors, TOEFL recommended for undergraduate business majors, TOEFL not required for all other undergraduate majors, English Language Skills test administered to all non-English speakers upon arrival. Recommended: TOEFL. *Application deadline:* Rolling. *Expenses:* (2006–07) $20,472; room and board, $6352 (on campus); room only, $3872 (on campus). *Financial aid:* Need-based college/university scholarships/grants from institutional funds, tuition waivers, athletic awards, loans from institutional funds, loans from outside sources. Non-need-based college/university scholarships/grants from institutional funds, tuition waivers, athletic awards, loans from institutional funds, loans from outside sources. For fall 2006 (estimated), 603 international students on campus received college administered financial aid ($4291 average). *Housing:* Guaranteed, also available during summer. *Services:* International student adviser on campus. Full-time and part-time ESL programs on campus. ESL program available during the academic year and the summer. Internships and employment opportunities (on-campus) available. *Contact:* Associate Director of International Admissions, Indiana University Bloomington, Office of Admissions, 300 North Jordan Avenue, Bloomington, IN 47405-1106. Telephone: 812-855-4306. Fax: 812-856-5378. E-mail: steajohn@indiana.edu. URL: http://www.iub.edu.

INDIANA UNIVERSITY KOKOMO, KOKOMO

General Information State-supported, coed institution. Small town setting. *Awards:* A, B, M. *Entrance level for U.S. students:* Minimally difficult. *Enrollment:* 2,734 total; 2,604 undergraduates (70% women) including 0.4% international students. *Faculty:* 174. *Library holdings:* 132,424 books, 1,513 current serial subscriptions. *Total majors:* 18. *Expenses:* (2006–07) $12,026. *Financial aid:* Need-based college/university scholarships/grants from institutional funds, tuition waivers, loans from institutional funds, loans from outside sources. Non-need-based college/university scholarships/grants from institutional funds, tuition waivers, loans from institutional funds, loans from outside sources. For fall 2006 (estimated), 2 international students on campus received college administered financial aid ($200 average).

INDIANA UNIVERSITY NORTHWEST, GARY

General Information State-supported, coed institution. Urban setting. *Awards:* A, B, M. *Entrance level for U.S. students:* Minimally difficult. *Enrollment:* 4,819 total; 4,229 undergraduates (70% women) including 0.2% international students. *Faculty:* 367. *Library holdings:* 251,508 books, 1,541 current serial subscriptions. *Total majors:* 45. *Expenses:* (2006–07) $12,086. *Financial aid:* Need-based college/university scholarships/grants from institutional funds, tuition waivers, athletic awards, loans from institutional funds, loans from outside sources. Non-need-based college/university scholarships/grants from institutional funds, tuition waivers, athletic awards, loans from institutional funds, loans from outside sources. For fall 2006 (estimated), 2 international students on campus received college administered financial aid ($2000 average).

INDIANA UNIVERSITY–PURDUE UNIVERSITY FORT WAYNE, FORT WAYNE

General Information State-supported, coed institution. Urban setting. *Awards:* A, B, M. *Entrance level for U.S. students:* Minimally difficult. *Enrollment:* 11,672 total; 10,890 undergraduates (56% women) including 1% international students from 67 foreign countries. *Faculty:* 798. *Library holdings:* 478,091 books, 24,872 current serial subscriptions, 6,527 audiovisual materials. *Total majors:* 97. *Expenses:* (2006–07) $12,452; room only, $4940 (on campus). *Financial aid:* Non-need-based tuition waivers, athletic awards. 48 international students on campus received college administered financial aid ($5658 average).

INDIANA UNIVERSITY–PURDUE UNIVERSITY INDIANAPOLIS, INDIANAPOLIS

General Information State-supported, coed university. Urban setting. *Awards:* A, B, M, D, FP. *Entrance level for U.S. students:* Moderately difficult. *Enrollment:* 29,764 total; 21,193 undergraduates (59% women) including 2% international students from 122 foreign countries. *Faculty:* 3,091. *Library holdings:* 1.5 million books, 14,673 current serial subscriptions. *Total majors:* 78. *Expenses:* (2006–07) $17,366; room and board, $4834 (on campus); room only, $2434 (on campus). *Financial aid:* Need-based

college/university scholarships/grants from institutional funds, tuition waivers, athletic awards, loans from institutional funds, loans from outside sources. Non-need-based college/university scholarships/grants from institutional funds, tuition waivers, athletic awards, loans from institutional funds, loans from outside sources. Forms required: International Student's Certification of Finances. For fall 2006 (estimated), 140 international students on campus received college administered financial aid ($5013 average).

INDIANA UNIVERSITY SOUTH BEND, SOUTH BEND

General Information State-supported, coed institution. Suburban setting. *Awards:* A, B, M. *Entrance level for U.S. students:* Moderately difficult. *Enrollment:* 7,420 total; 6,371 undergraduates (61% women) including 2% international students. *Faculty:* 523. *Library holdings:* 300,202 books, 1,937 current serial subscriptions. *Total majors:* 54.

Information for International Students Students can start in fall, spring, or summer. Transfers accepted from institutions abroad. *Admission tests:* Required: TOEFL (minimum score: paper-based 530; computer-based 197). Recommended: SAT or ACT. *Application deadline:* 7/1. *Expenses:* (2006–07) $13,018. *Financial aid:* Need-based college/university scholarships/grants from institutional funds, tuition waivers, athletic awards, loans from institutional funds, loans from outside sources. Non-need-based college/university scholarships/grants from institutional funds, tuition waivers, athletic awards, loans from institutional funds, loans from outside sources. For fall 2006 (estimated), 34 international students on campus received college administered financial aid ($5083 average). *Housing:* Available during summer. *Services:* International student adviser on campus. *Contact:* Director, International Student Services, Indiana University South Bend, 1700 Mishawaka Avenue, PO Box 7111, South Bend, IN 46634-7111. Telephone: 574-520-4419. Fax: 574-520-4590. E-mail: jwilliam@iusb.edu. URL: http://www.iusb.edu.

See In-Depth Description on page 103.

INDIANA UNIVERSITY SOUTHEAST, NEW ALBANY

General Information State-supported, coed institution. Suburban setting. *Awards:* A, B, M. *Entrance level for U.S. students:* Minimally difficult. *Enrollment:* 6,183 total; 5,365 undergraduates (63% women) including 0.3% international students. *Faculty:* 425. *Library holdings:* 215,429 books, 962 current serial subscriptions. *Total majors:* 38.

Information for International Students For fall 2006: 10 international students enrolled. Students can start in fall, winter, spring, or summer. Transfers accepted from institutions abroad. *Admission tests:* Required: SAT or ACT, TOEFL (minimum score: iBT 75; paper-based 530; computer-based 197). TOEFL can be waived under certain conditions. *Application deadline:* 7/1. *Expenses:* (2006–07) $12,075. *Financial aid:* Need-based college/university scholarships/grants from institutional funds, tuition waivers, athletic awards, loans from institutional funds, loans from outside sources. Non-need-based college/university scholarships/grants from institutional funds, tuition waivers, athletic awards, loans from institutional funds, loans from outside sources. For fall 2006 (estimated), 4 international students on campus received college administered financial aid ($1863 average). *Services:* International student adviser on campus. ESL program at cooperating institution. ESL program available during the academic year and the summer. Internships and employment opportunities (on-campus and off-campus) available. *Contact:* Admissions Counselor/Coordinator of International Student Recruitment, Indiana University Southeast, 4201 Grant Line Road, US 102, New Albany, IN 47150-6405. Telephone: 812-941-2212. Fax: 812-941-2595. E-mail: intladm@indiana.edu. URL: http://www.ius.edu.

INDIANA WESLEYAN UNIVERSITY, MARION

General Information Independent Wesleyan, coed institution. Small town setting. *Awards:* A, B, M, D (also offers adult program with significant enrollment not reflected in profile). *Entrance level for U.S. students:* Moderately difficult. *Enrollment:* 2,935 total (62% women) including 1% international students from 14 foreign countries. *Faculty:* 265. *Library holdings:* 141,236 books, 76,011 current serial subscriptions, 11,321 audiovisual materials. *Total majors:* 61.

Information for International Students Students can start in fall, spring, or summer. Transfers accepted from institutions abroad. *Admission tests:* Required: SAT or ACT, TOEFL (minimum score: iBT 79; paper-based 550; computer-based 213). *Application deadline:* 5/1. *Expenses:* (2007–08) $18,284; room and board, $6368 (on campus); room only, $3072 (on campus). *Financial aid:* International transfer students are eligible to apply for aid. *Housing:* Available during summer. *Services:* International student adviser on campus. Internships and employment opportunities (on-campus) available. *Contact:* International Student Advisor,

Indiana Wesleyan University, 4201 South Washington Street, Marion, IN 46953. Telephone: 765-677-2254. Fax: 765-677-2333. E-mail: tony.stevens@indwes.edu. URL: http://www.indwes.edu.

IVY TECH COMMUNITY COLLEGE–BLOOMINGTON, BLOOMINGTON

General Information State-supported, 2-year, coed college. *Awards:* A. *Entrance level for U.S. students:* Noncompetitive. *Enrollment:* 3,565 total (61% women) including 0.1% international students. *Undergraduate faculty:* 275. *Library holdings:* 5,516 books, 97 current serial subscriptions, 1,281 audiovisual materials. *Total majors:* 27. *Expenses:* (2006–07) $5435.

IVY TECH COMMUNITY COLLEGE–CENTRAL INDIANA, INDIANAPOLIS

General Information State-supported, 2-year, coed college. Urban setting. *Awards:* A. *Entrance level for U.S. students:* Noncompetitive. *Enrollment:* 11,590 total (59% women) including 0.2% international students. *Undergraduate faculty:* 662. *Library holdings:* 20,247 books, 138 current serial subscriptions, 2,135 audiovisual materials. *Total majors:* 42. *Expenses:* (2006–07) $5435.

IVY TECH COMMUNITY COLLEGE–COLUMBUS, COLUMBUS

General Information State-supported, 2-year, coed college. Small town setting. *Awards:* A. *Entrance level for U.S. students:* Noncompetitive. *Enrollment:* 2,216 total (71% women) including 0.1% international students. *Undergraduate faculty:* 193. *Library holdings:* 7,855 books, 13,382 current serial subscriptions, 989 audiovisual materials. *Total majors:* 32. *Expenses:* (2006–07) $5435.

IVY TECH COMMUNITY COLLEGE–EAST CENTRAL, MUNCIE

General Information State-supported, 2-year, coed college. Suburban setting. *Awards:* A. *Entrance level for U.S. students:* Noncompetitive. *Enrollment:* 5,943 total (65% women) including 0.02% international students. *Undergraduate faculty:* 445. *Library holdings:* 5,779 books, 145 current serial subscriptions, 6,266 audiovisual materials. *Total majors:* 38. *Expenses:* (2006–07) $5435.

IVY TECH COMMUNITY COLLEGE–LAFAYETTE, LAFAYETTE

General Information State-supported, 2-year, coed college. Suburban setting. *Awards:* A. *Entrance level for U.S. students:* Noncompetitive. *Enrollment:* 5,970 total (51% women) including 0.1% international students. *Undergraduate faculty:* 325. *Library holdings:* 8,043 books, 200 current serial subscriptions, 2,234 audiovisual materials. *Total majors:* 42. *Expenses:* (2006–07) $5435.

IVY TECH COMMUNITY COLLEGE–NORTH CENTRAL, SOUTH BEND

General Information State-supported, 2-year, coed college. Suburban setting. *Awards:* A. *Entrance level for U.S. students:* Noncompetitive. *Enrollment:* 5,228 total (58% women) including 0.3% international students. *Undergraduate faculty:* 311. *Library holdings:* 6,246 books, 90 current serial subscriptions, 689 audiovisual materials. *Total majors:* 42. *Expenses:* (2006–07) $5435. *Financial aid:* Need-based financial aid available.

IVY TECH COMMUNITY COLLEGE–NORTHEAST, FORT WAYNE

General Information State-supported, 2-year, coed college. Urban setting. *Awards:* A. *Entrance level for U.S. students:* Noncompetitive. *Enrollment:* 6,082 total (61% women) including 0.1% international students. *Undergraduate faculty:* 435. *Library holdings:* 18,389 books, 110 current serial subscriptions, 3,397 audiovisual materials. *Total majors:* 39. *Expenses:* (2006–07) $5435.

IVY TECH COMMUNITY COLLEGE–NORTHWEST, GARY

General Information State-supported, primarily 2-year, coed college. Urban setting. *Awards:* A, B. *Entrance level for U.S. students:* Noncompetitive. *Enrollment:* 4,815 total (66% women) including 0.1% international students. *Undergraduate faculty:* 419. *Library holdings:* 13,805 books, 160 current serial subscriptions, 4,295 audiovisual materials. *Total majors:* 42. *Expenses:* (2006–07) $5435. *Financial aid:* Need-based financial aid available.

IVY TECH COMMUNITY COLLEGE–SOUTHEAST, MADISON

General Information State-supported, 2-year, coed college. Small town setting. *Awards:* A. *Entrance level for U.S. students:* Noncompetitive. *Enrollment:* 1,766 total (72% women) including 0.1% international students. *Undergraduate faculty:* 148. *Library holdings:* 9,027 books, 14,299 current serial subscriptions, 1,341 audiovisual materials. *Total majors:* 18. *Expenses:* (2006–07) $5435.

IVY TECH COMMUNITY COLLEGE–SOUTHWEST, EVANSVILLE

General Information State-supported, 2-year, coed college. Suburban setting. *Awards:* A. *Entrance level for U.S. students:* Noncompetitive. *Enrollment:* 4,858 total (54% women) including 0.05% international students. *Undergraduate faculty:* 308. *Library holdings:* 7,082 books, 107 current serial subscriptions, 1,755 audiovisual materials. *Total majors:* 42. *Expenses:* (2006–07) $5435.

IVY TECH COMMUNITY COLLEGE–WABASH VALLEY, TERRE HAUTE

General Information State-supported, 2-year, coed college. Suburban setting. *Awards:* A. *Entrance level for U.S. students:* Noncompetitive. *Enrollment:* 4,992 total (57% women) including 0.05% international students. *Undergraduate faculty:* 313. *Library holdings:* 4,403 books, 77 current serial subscriptions, 406 audiovisual materials. *Total majors:* 44. *Expenses:* (2006–07) $5435.

MANCHESTER COLLEGE, NORTH MANCHESTER

General Information Independent, 4-year, coed college, affiliated with Church of the Brethren. Small town setting. *Awards:* A, B, M. *Entrance level for U.S. students:* Moderately difficult. *Enrollment:* 1,056 total (51% women) including 4% international students from 26 foreign countries. *Faculty:* 90. *Total majors:* 59.

Information for International Students For fall 2006: 159 international students applied, 45 were accepted, 23 enrolled. Students can start in fall or spring. Transfers accepted from institutions abroad. *Admission tests:* Required: SAT, TOEFL (minimum score: iBT 79; paper-based 550; computer-based 213). TOEFL can be waived under certain conditions. *Application deadline:* 5/1. *Expenses:* (2007–08) $21,700; room and board, $7450 (on campus); room only, $4500 (on campus). *Financial aid:* Need-based college/university scholarships/grants from institutional funds, loans from institutional funds, on-campus employment. Non-need-based college/university scholarships/grants from institutional funds, on-campus employment. Forms required: CSS PROFILE. International transfer students are eligible to apply for aid. 63 international students on campus received college administered financial aid ($11,620 average). *Housing:* Guaranteed, also available during summer. *Services:* International student adviser on campus. ESL program at cooperating institution. ESL program available during the academic year. Internships and employment opportunities (on-campus) available. *Contact:* Executive Vice President, Manchester College, 604 East College Avenue, North Manchester, IN 46962. Telephone: 260-982-5055. Fax: 260-982-5239. E-mail: international@manchester.edu. URL: http://www.manchester.edu.

See In-Depth Description on page 119.

MARIAN COLLEGE, INDIANAPOLIS

General Information Independent Roman Catholic, coed institution. Suburban setting. *Awards:* A, B, M. *Entrance level for U.S. students:* Moderately difficult. *Enrollment:* 1,796 total; 1,779 undergraduates (70% women) including 0.1% international students from 9 foreign countries. *Faculty:* 138. *Library holdings:* 110,541 books, 221 current serial subscriptions, 2,167 audiovisual materials. *Total majors:* 36. *Expenses:* (2007–08) $20,800; room and board, $7100 (on campus). *Financial aid:* Need-based college/university scholarships/grants from institutional funds, athletic awards. Non-need financial aid available. Forms required: institution's own financial aid form. For fall 2005, 10 international students on campus received college administered financial aid ($2000 average).

OAKLAND CITY UNIVERSITY, OAKLAND CITY

General Information Independent General Baptist, coed institution. Rural setting. *Awards:* A, B, M, D, FP. *Entrance level for U.S. students:* Minimally difficult. *Enrollment:* 1,900 total; 1,566 undergraduates (54% women) including 2% international students from 18 foreign countries. *Faculty:* 183. *Library holdings:* 87,724 books, 222 current serial subscriptions, 2,570 audiovisual materials. *Total majors:* 60. *Expenses:* (2006–07) $14,220; room and board, $5400 (on campus); room only, $1760 (on campus). *Financial aid:* Non-need-based college/university scholarships/grants from institutional funds, athletic awards, on-campus employment. international students on campus received college administered aid averaging $6000.

PURDUE UNIVERSITY, WEST LAFAYETTE

General Information State-supported, coed university. Suburban setting. *Awards:* A, B, M, D, FP. *Entrance level for U.S. students:* Moderately difficult. *Enrollment:* 39,228 total; 31,290 undergraduates (41% women) including 6% international students. *Faculty:* 2,347. *Library holdings:* 2.5 million books, 20,829 current serial subscriptions. *Total majors:* 84.

Purdue University (continued)

Information for International Students For fall 2006: 2894 international students applied, 1888 were accepted, 591 enrolled. Students can start in fall, spring, or summer. Transfers accepted from institutions abroad. *Admission tests:* Required: TOEFL (minimum score: iBT 79; paper-based 550; computer-based 213). Recommended: SAT or ACT, SAT verbal score of 480 in lieu of TOEFL score meets English language requirement. *Application deadline:* 3/1. *Expenses:* (2006–07) $21,266; room and board, $7546 (on campus). *Financial aid:* Non-need-based college/university scholarships/grants from institutional funds, tuition waivers, athletic awards. For fall 2006 (estimated), 127 international students on campus received college administered financial aid ($1818 average). *Housing:* Available during summer. *Services:* International student adviser on campus. Internships and employment opportunities (on-campus and off-campus) available. *Contact:* Assistant Director, Purdue University, 475 Stadium Mall Drive, Schleman Hall of Student Services, Room 136, West Lafayette, IN 47907-2050. Telephone: 765-494-5770. Fax: 765-494-6340. E-mail: iss@purdue.edu. URL: http://www.purdue.edu.

PURDUE UNIVERSITY CALUMET, HAMMOND

General Information State-supported, coed institution. Urban setting. *Awards:* A, B, M. *Entrance level for U.S. students:* Moderately difficult. *Enrollment:* 9,303 total; 8,387 undergraduates (57% women) including 1% international students from 30 foreign countries. *Faculty:* 499. *Library holdings:* 269,648 books, 1,228 current serial subscriptions. *Total majors:* 62. *Expenses:* (2006–07) $12,160; room only, $4150 (on campus).

PURDUE UNIVERSITY NORTH CENTRAL, WESTVILLE

General Information State-supported, coed institution. Rural setting. *Awards:* A, B, M. *Entrance level for U.S. students:* Minimally difficult. *Enrollment:* 3,724 total; 3,635 undergraduates (58% women) including 0.2% international students from 6 foreign countries. *Faculty:* 260. *Library holdings:* 87,675 books, 403 current serial subscriptions. *Total majors:* 23. *Expenses:* (2006–07) $11,595.

ROSE-HULMAN INSTITUTE OF TECHNOLOGY, TERRE HAUTE

General Information Independent, coed, primarily men's institution. Suburban setting. *Awards:* B, M. *Entrance level for U.S. students:* Very difficult. *Enrollment:* 1,963 total; 1,862 undergraduates (19% women) including 2% international students from 21 foreign countries. *Faculty:* 161. *Library holdings:* 80,094 books, 20,934 current serial subscriptions, 429 audiovisual materials. *Total majors:* 16. *Expenses:* (2006–07) $28,995; room and board, $7869 (on campus); room only, $4491 (on campus). *Financial aid:* Non-need-based college/university scholarships/grants from institutional funds. For fall 2006 (estimated), 27 international students on campus received college administered financial aid ($5328 average).

SAINT JOSEPH'S COLLEGE, RENSSELAER

General Information Independent Roman Catholic, coed institution. Small town setting. *Awards:* A, B, M. *Entrance level for U.S. students:* Moderately difficult. *Enrollment:* 1,031 total; 1,030 undergraduates (59% women) including 1% international students from 6 foreign countries. *Faculty:* 89. *Library holdings:* 256,705 books, 399 current serial subscriptions, 23,637 audiovisual materials. *Total majors:* 33.

Information for International Students For fall 2006: 22 international students applied, 6 were accepted, 3 enrolled. Students can start in fall, winter, or summer. Transfers accepted from institutions abroad. *Admission tests:* Required: TOEFL (minimum score: paper-based 550; computer-based 213). TOEFL can be waived under certain conditions. *Application deadline:* Rolling. *Expenses:* (2006–07) $20,960; room and board, $6720 (on campus). *Financial aid:* Non-need-based college/university scholarships/grants from institutional funds, tuition waivers, athletic awards. International transfer students are eligible to apply for aid. For fall 2005, 6 international students on campus received college administered financial aid ($19,387 average). *Housing:* Guaranteed, also available during summer. Employment opportunities (on-campus) available. *Contact:* Director of Admissions, Saint Joseph's College, PO Box 890, Rensselaer, IN 47978. Telephone: 219-866-6170. Fax: 219-866-6122. E-mail: admissions@saintjoe.edu. URL: http://www.saintjoe.edu.

SAINT MARY-OF-THE-WOODS COLLEGE, SAINT MARY-OF-THE-WOODS

General Information Independent Roman Catholic, undergraduate: women only; graduate: coed institution. Rural setting. *Awards:* A, B, M (also offers external degree program with significant enrollment not reflected in profile). *Entrance level for U.S. students:* Moderately difficult. *Enrollment:* 1,668 total; 1,540 undergraduates (97% women) including 0.4% international students from 3 foreign countries. *Faculty:* 67. *Library holdings:* 155,771 books, 150 current serial subscriptions. *Total majors:* 61.

Information for International Students For fall 2006: 4 international students applied, 4 were accepted, 4 enrolled. Students can start in fall or winter. Transfers accepted from institutions abroad. *Admission tests:* Required: TOEFL (minimum score: paper-based 500; computer-based 173). Recommended: SAT, ACT. *Application deadline:* Rolling. *Expenses:* (2007–08) $20,180; room and board, $7380 (on campus); room only, $2880 (on campus). *Financial aid:* Need-based financial aid available. Forms required: institution's own financial aid form, International Student's Certification of Finances. *Housing:* Guaranteed. *Services:* International student adviser on campus. ESL program at cooperating institution. ESL program available during the academic year and the summer. Internships and employment opportunities (on-campus) available. *Contact:* Associate Director of Admissions, Saint Mary-of-the-Woods College, 115 Guerin Hall, Saint Mary-of-the-Woods, IN 47876. Telephone: 812-535-5229. Fax: 812-535-5010. E-mail: bmichel@smwc.edu. URL: http://www.smwc.edu.

SAINT MARY'S COLLEGE, NOTRE DAME

General Information Independent Roman Catholic, 4-year, women's college. Suburban setting. *Awards:* B. *Entrance level for U.S. students:* Moderately difficult. *Enrollment:* 1,527 total including 1% international students from 7 foreign countries. *Undergraduate faculty:* 205. *Library holdings:* 231,713 books, 679 current serial subscriptions. *Total majors:* 36.

Information for International Students For fall 2006: 42 international students applied, 18 were accepted, 2 enrolled. Students can start in fall or spring. Transfers accepted from institutions abroad. *Admission tests:* Required: SAT or ACT, TOEFL (minimum score: paper-based 550; computer-based 213). Recommended: SAT Subject Tests. TOEFL can be waived under certain conditions. *Application deadline:* Rolling. *Expenses:* (2007–08) $26,872; room and board, $8678 (on campus); room only, $5346 (on campus). *Financial aid:* Need-based and non-need-based financial aid available. Forms required: institution's own financial aid form. 3 international students on campus received college administered financial aid ($36,106 average). *Housing:* Guaranteed. *Services:* International student adviser on campus. Internships and employment opportunities (on-campus) available. *Contact:* Vice President for Enrollment Management, Office of Admissions, Saint Mary's College, Le Mans Hall, Admission Office, Notre Dame, IN 46556-5001. Telephone: 574-284-4755. Fax: 574-284-4841. E-mail: dmeyer@saintmarys.edu. URL: http://www.saintmarys.edu.

TAYLOR UNIVERSITY, UPLAND

General Information Independent interdenominational, coed institution. Rural setting. *Awards:* A, B, M. *Entrance level for U.S. students:* Very difficult. *Enrollment:* 1,854 total (55% women) including 2% international students from 23 foreign countries. *Faculty:* 192. *Library holdings:* 189,007 books, 12,625 current serial subscriptions. *Total majors:* 74.

Information for International Students For fall 2006: 37 international students applied, 23 were accepted, 11 enrolled. Students can start in fall or spring. Transfers accepted from institutions abroad. *Admission tests:* Required: TOEFL (minimum score: paper-based 550; computer-based 213). TOEFL can be waived under certain conditions. *Application deadline:* Rolling. *Expenses:* (2006–07) $22,028; room and board, $5867 (on campus); room only, $2868 (on campus). *Financial aid:* Non-need-based college/university scholarships/grants from institutional funds, athletic awards, loans from institutional funds, on-campus employment. Forms required: International Student's Certification of Finances. International transfer students are eligible to apply for aid. For fall 2006 (estimated), 26 international students on campus received college administered financial aid ($12,416 average). *Housing:* Guaranteed. *Services:* International student adviser on campus. Internships and employment opportunities (on-campus) available. *Contact:* International Student Recruiter, Taylor University, 236 West Reade Avenue, Admissions, Upland, IN 46989. Telephone: 765-998-5564. Fax: 765-998-4925. E-mail: intltu@taylor.edu. URL: http://www.taylor.edu.

TRI-STATE UNIVERSITY, ANGOLA

General Information Independent, coed institution. Small town setting. *Awards:* A, B, M. *Entrance level for U.S. students:* Moderately difficult. *Enrollment:* 1,210 total; 1,203 undergraduates (32% women) including 1% international students from 12 foreign countries. *Faculty:* 99. *Library holdings:* 73,859 books, 359 current serial subscriptions. *Total majors:* 42. *Expenses:* (2006–07) $21,210; room and board, $6240 (on campus). *Financial aid:* Need-based and non-need-based financial aid available. Forms required: International Student's Certification of Finances.

UNIVERSITY OF EVANSVILLE, EVANSVILLE

General Information Independent, coed institution, affiliated with United Methodist Church. Urban setting. *Awards:* A, B, M. *Entrance level for U.S. students:* Moderately difficult. *Enrollment:* 2,879 total; 2,813 undergraduates (60% women) including 6% international students from 46 foreign countries. *Faculty:* 239. *Library holdings:* 289,593 books, 970 current serial subscriptions, 11,534 audiovisual materials. *Total majors:* 88. *Expenses:* (2006–07) $22,980; room and board, $7120 (on campus); room only, $3540 (on campus). *Financial aid:* Need-based college/university scholarships/grants from institutional funds, athletic awards. Non-need-based college/university scholarships/grants from institutional funds, athletic awards, on-campus employment. Forms required: International Student's Financial Aid Application, International Student's Certification of Finances. For fall 2006 (estimated), 144 international students on campus received college administered financial aid ($9067 average).

UNIVERSITY OF INDIANAPOLIS, INDIANAPOLIS

General Information Independent, coed institution, affiliated with United Methodist Church. Urban setting. *Awards:* A, B, M, D. *Entrance level for U.S. students:* Moderately difficult. *Enrollment:* 4,389 total; 3,352 undergraduates (68% women) including 3% international students from 30 foreign countries. *Faculty:* 447. *Library holdings:* 173,363 books, 1,015 current serial subscriptions. *Total majors:* 69.

Information for International Students For fall 2006: 273 international students applied, 98 were accepted, 51 enrolled. Students can start in fall, winter, spring, or summer. Transfers accepted from institutions abroad. *Admission tests:* Required: SAT or ACT, TOEFL (minimum score: iBT 61; paper-based 500; computer-based 173). TOEFL can be waived under certain conditions. *Application deadline:* Rolling. *Expenses:* (2006–07) $18,850; room and board, $7380 (on campus); room only, $3490 (on campus). *Financial aid:* Need-based college/university scholarships/grants from institutional funds, loans from institutional funds, loans from outside sources, on-campus employment. Non-need-based college/university scholarships/grants from institutional funds, tuition waivers, athletic awards, loans from outside sources. International transfer students are eligible to apply for aid. 127 international students on campus received college administered financial aid ($1296 average). *Housing:* Guaranteed, also available during summer. *Services:* International student adviser on campus. Full-time and part-time ESL programs on campus. ESL program available during the academic year and the summer. Internships and employment opportunities (on-campus) available. *Contact:* Undergraduate International Admissions Coordinator, University of Indianapolis, 1400 East Hanna Avenue, Indianapolis, IN 46227. Telephone: 317-788-3600. Fax: 317-788-3300. E-mail: kgunyon@uindy.edu. URL: http://www.uindy.edu.

UNIVERSITY OF NOTRE DAME, NOTRE DAME

General Information Independent Roman Catholic, coed university. Suburban setting. *Awards:* B, M, D, FP. *Entrance level for U.S. students:* Most difficult. *Enrollment:* 11,603 total; 8,352 undergraduates (47% women) including 3% international students from 48 foreign countries. *Faculty:* 1,273. *Library holdings:* 2.9 million books, 10,553 current serial subscriptions, 21,095 audiovisual materials. *Total majors:* 55. *Expenses:* (2007–08) $35,187; room and board, $9290 (on campus). *Financial aid:* Need-based college/university scholarships/grants from institutional funds, loans from outside sources, on-campus employment. Non-need-based athletic awards, loans from outside sources, on-campus employment. Forms required: International Student's Financial Aid Application, International Student's Certification of Finances, additional documents as requested. For fall 2006 (estimated), 103 international students on campus received college administered financial aid ($24,723 average).

UNIVERSITY OF SAINT FRANCIS, FORT WAYNE

General Information Independent Roman Catholic, coed institution. Suburban setting. *Awards:* A, B, M. *Entrance level for U.S. students:* Moderately difficult. *Enrollment:* 2,039 total; 1,784 undergraduates (70% women). *Faculty:* 223. *Library holdings:* 50,186 books, 549 current serial subscriptions. *Total majors:* 52.

Information for International Students For fall 2006: 14 international students applied. Students can start in fall, winter, spring, or summer. Transfers accepted from institutions abroad. *Admission tests:* Required: TOEFL (minimum score: paper-based 550; computer-based 217; minimum score for ESL admission: paper-based 550; computer-based 217), must take ELS if TOEFL has not been taken. *Application deadline:* Rolling. *Expenses:*

(2006–07) $18,478; room and board, $5834 (on campus). *Financial aid:* Forms required: institution's own financial aid form. *Housing:* Guaranteed, also available during summer. *Contact:* Associate Director of Adult Admissions, University of Saint Francis, 2701 Spring Street, Fort Wayne, IN 46808-3994. Telephone: 260-434-7426. Fax: 260-434-7590. E-mail: jroth@sf.edu. URL: http://www.sf.edu.

UNIVERSITY OF SOUTHERN INDIANA, EVANSVILLE

General Information State-supported, coed institution. Suburban setting. *Awards:* A, B, M. *Entrance level for U.S. students:* Noncompetitive. *Enrollment:* 10,021 total; 9,298 undergraduates (60% women) including 1% international students from 26 foreign countries. *Faculty:* 629. *Library holdings:* 328,734 books, 15,153 current serial subscriptions, 5,587 audiovisual materials. *Total majors:* 55.

Information for International Students For fall 2006: 73 international students were accepted, 34 enrolled. Students can start in fall, spring, or summer. Transfers accepted from institutions abroad. *Admission tests:* Required: TOEFL (minimum score: paper-based 525; computer-based 197). Recommended: SAT or ACT. TOEFL can be waived under certain conditions. *Application deadline:* Rolling. *Expenses:* (2006–07) $10,691; room and board, $6492 (on campus); room only, $3234 (on campus). *Services:* International student adviser on campus. Full-time ESL program on campus. ESL program available during the academic year and the summer. Internships and employment opportunities (on-campus) available. *Contact:* Director, International Programs and Services, University of Southern Indiana, Evansville, IN 47712. Telephone: 812-465-1248. Fax: 812-465-1057. E-mail: intlprog@usi.edu. URL: http://www.usi.edu.

See In-Depth Description on page 225.

VALPARAISO UNIVERSITY, VALPARAISO

General Information Independent, coed institution, affiliated with Lutheran Church. Small town setting. *Awards:* A, B, M, FP. *Entrance level for U.S. students:* Moderately difficult. *Enrollment:* 3,868 total; 2,960 undergraduates (52% women) including 2% international students from 31 foreign countries. *Faculty:* 378. *Library holdings:* 471,645 books, 41,649 current serial subscriptions, 5,770 audiovisual materials. *Total majors:* 86.

Information for International Students For fall 2006: 194 international students applied, 75 were accepted, 34 enrolled. Students can start in fall, spring, or summer. Transfers accepted from institutions abroad. *Admission tests:* Recommended: SAT or ACT, TOEFL (minimum score: iBT 80; paper-based 550; computer-based 213; minimum score for ESL admission: iBT 80; paper-based 550; computer-based 213). TOEFL can be waived under certain conditions. *Application deadline:* Rolling. *Expenses:* (2006–07) $24,000; room and board, $6640 (on campus); room only, $4140 (on campus). *Financial aid:* Need-based college/university scholarships/grants from institutional funds, athletic awards. Non-need-based college/university scholarships/grants from institutional funds, athletic awards. Forms required: International Student's Certification of Finances. For fall 2006 (estimated), 24 international students on campus received college administered financial aid ($15,212 average). *Housing:* Guaranteed, also available during summer. *Services:* International student adviser on campus. Full-time and part-time ESL programs on campus. ESL program available during the academic year and the summer. Internships and employment opportunities (on-campus) available. *Contact:* Assistant Director of Admissions, Valparaiso University, Office of Admissions, 1700 Chapel Drive, Valparaiso, IN 46383. Telephone: 219-464-5011. Fax: 219-464-6868. E-mail: Jennifer.Smolnicky@valpo.edu. URL: http://www.valpo.edu.

VINCENNES UNIVERSITY, VINCENNES

General Information State-supported, 2-year, coed college. Small town setting. *Awards:* A. *Entrance level for U.S. students:* Noncompetitive. *Enrollment:* 5,175 total including 2% international students from 31 foreign countries. *Undergraduate faculty:* 812. *Library holdings:* 103,000 books, 557 current serial subscriptions, 5,260 audiovisual materials. *Total majors:* 155. *Financial aid:* Need-based college/university scholarships/grants from institutional funds, athletic awards. Non-need-based college/university scholarships/grants from institutional funds, athletic awards.

WABASH COLLEGE, CRAWFORDSVILLE

General Information Independent, 4-year, men's college. Small town setting. *Awards:* B. *Entrance level for U.S. students:* Moderately difficult. *Enrollment:* 874 total including 5% international students from 19 foreign countries. *Undergraduate faculty:* 88. *Library holdings:* 434,460 books, 5,530 current serial subscriptions. *Total majors:* 24.

Information for International Students For fall 2006: 148 international students applied, 21 were accepted, 15 enrolled.

Indiana

Wabash College (continued)

Students can start in fall. Transfers accepted from institutions abroad. *Admission tests:* Required: TOEFL (minimum score: paper-based 550; computer-based 213). Recommended: SAT or ACT. TOEFL can be waived under certain conditions. *Application deadline:* Rolling. *Expenses:* (2006–07) $24,792; room and board, $7064 (on campus); room only, $2877 (on campus). *Financial aid:* Need-based college/university scholarships/grants from institutional funds, loans from institutional funds, loans from outside sources, on-campus employment. Non-need-based college/university scholarships/grants from institutional funds, loans from institutional funds, loans from outside sources, on-campus employment. Forms required: International Student's Financial Aid Application, International Student's Certification of Finances. International transfer students are eligible to apply for aid. For fall 2006 (estimated), 40 international students on campus received college administered financial aid ($26,046 average). *Housing:* Guaranteed, also available during summer. *Services:* International student adviser on campus. Internships and employment opportunities (on-campus and off-campus) available. *Contact:* Dean of Admissions, Wabash College, PO Box 352, 301 West Wabash Avenue, Crawfordsville, IN 47933. Telephone: 765-361-6225. Fax: 765-361-6432. E-mail: kleins@wabash.edu. URL: http://www.wabash.edu.

IOWA

ASHFORD UNIVERSITY, CLINTON

General Information Proprietary, 4-year, coed college. Small town setting. *Awards:* B, M. *Entrance level for U.S. students:* Minimally difficult. *Enrollment:* 3,836 total; 3,485 undergraduates (77% women) including 0.3% international students. *Faculty:* 268. *Library holdings:* 98,974 books, 639 current serial subscriptions. *Total majors:* 32.

Information for International Students For fall 2006: 12 international students applied. Students can start in fall or spring. Transfers accepted from institutions abroad. *Admission tests:* Required: TOEFL (minimum score: iBT 79; paper-based 550; computer-based 213). Recommended: SAT or ACT, SAT Subject Tests. TOEFL can be waived under certain conditions. *Application deadline:* Rolling. *Expenses:* (2006–07) $15,340; room and board, $5800 (on campus); room only, $2500 (on campus). *Financial aid:* Need-based college/university scholarships/grants from institutional funds, athletic awards. Non-need-based college/university scholarships/grants from institutional funds, athletic awards, on-campus employment. Forms required: institution's own financial aid form, International Student's Certification of Finances. *Housing:* Guaranteed, also available during summer. *Services:* International student adviser on campus. Employment opportunities (on-campus) available. *Contact:* Director of Student Management, Ashford University, 400 North Bluff Boulevard, Clinton, IA 52733-2967. Telephone: 563-242-4023 Ext. 3401. Fax: 563-243-6102. E-mail: admissions@ashford.edu. URL: http://www.ashford.edu.

BRIAR CLIFF UNIVERSITY, SIOUX CITY

General Information Independent Roman Catholic, coed institution. Suburban setting. *Awards:* A, B, M. *Entrance level for U.S. students:* Moderately difficult. *Enrollment:* 1,146 total; 1,095 undergraduates (58% women) including 0.2% international students from 2 foreign countries. *Faculty:* 64. *Library holdings:* 84,540 books, 10,409 current serial subscriptions, 1,583 audiovisual materials. *Total majors:* 30. *Expenses:* (2006–07) $19,239; room and board, $5709 (on campus); room only, $2835 (on campus). *Financial aid:* Need-based and non-need-based financial aid available.

BUENA VISTA UNIVERSITY, STORM LAKE

General Information Independent, coed institution, affiliated with Presbyterian Church (U.S.A.). Small town setting. *Awards:* B, M. *Entrance level for U.S. students:* Moderately difficult. *Enrollment:* 1,229 total; 1,149 undergraduates (51% women) including 1% international students from 2 foreign countries. *Faculty:* 114. *Library holdings:* 144,000 books, 632 current serial subscriptions, 5,648 audiovisual materials. *Total majors:* 59. *Expenses:* (2006–07) $22,556; room and board, $6296 (on campus). *Financial aid:* Non-need-based college/university scholarships/grants from institutional funds, tuition waivers. 3 international students on campus received college administered financial aid ($19,324 average).

CENTRAL COLLEGE, PELLA

General Information Independent, 4-year, coed college, affiliated with Reformed Church in America. Small town setting. *Awards:* B.

Entrance level for U.S. students: Moderately difficult. *Enrollment:* 1,606 total (55% women) including 2% international students from 18 foreign countries. *Undergraduate faculty:* 141. *Library holdings:* 220,526 books, 1,161 current serial subscriptions. *Total majors:* 35. *Expenses:* (2006–07) $21,222; room and board, $7224 (on campus); room only, $3542 (on campus). *Financial aid:* Need-based college/university scholarships/grants from institutional funds, tuition waivers, loans from institutional funds, loans from outside sources, on-campus employment. Non-need-based college/university scholarships/grants from institutional funds, tuition waivers, loans from institutional funds, loans from outside sources, on-campus employment. Forms required: institution's own financial aid form. For fall 2006 (estimated), 21 international students on campus received college administered financial aid ($9163 average).

CLARKE COLLEGE, DUBUQUE

General Information Independent Roman Catholic, coed institution. Urban setting. *Awards:* A, B, M. *Entrance level for U.S. students:* Moderately difficult. *Enrollment:* 1,201 total; 1,006 undergraduates (71% women) including 1% international students from 8 foreign countries. *Faculty:* 135. *Library holdings:* 182,649 books, 508 current serial subscriptions, 1,262 audiovisual materials. *Total majors:* 42.

Information for International Students Students can start in fall or spring. Transfers accepted from institutions abroad. *Admission tests:* Required: TOEFL (minimum score: paper-based 550; computer-based 213). *Application deadline:* Rolling. *Expenses:* (2006–07) $20,297; room and board, $6574 (on campus); room only, $3198 (on campus). *Financial aid:* Need-based college/university scholarships/grants from institutional funds, tuition waivers, loans from institutional funds, loans from outside sources, on-campus employment. Non-need-based college/university scholarships/grants from institutional funds, tuition waivers, loans from outside sources, on-campus employment. Forms required: International Student's Certification of Finances. For fall 2006 (estimated), 1 international student on campus received college administered financial aid ($5500 average). *Housing:* Available during summer. *Services:* International student adviser on campus. ESL program at cooperating institution. ESL program available during the academic year and the summer. *Contact:* Director of Admissions, Clarke College, 1550 Clarke Drive, Dubuque, IA 52001-3198. Telephone: 563-588-6436. Fax: 563-588-6789. E-mail: andy.schroeder@clarke.edu. URL: http://www.clarke.edu.

CLINTON COMMUNITY COLLEGE, CLINTON

General Information State and locally supported, 2-year, coed college. Small town setting. *Awards:* A. *Entrance level for U.S. students:* Noncompetitive. *Enrollment:* 1,298 total (67% women) including 0.4% international students. *Undergraduate faculty:* 75. *Library holdings:* 18,701 books, 155 current serial subscriptions. *Total majors:* 14.

Information for International Students For fall 2006: 4 international students applied, 4 were accepted, 4 enrolled. Students can start in fall, spring, or summer. Transfers accepted from institutions abroad. *Admission tests:* Required: TOEFL (minimum score: paper-based 500; computer-based 173; minimum score for ESL admission: paper-based 500; computer-based 173). *Application deadline:* 6/28. *Services:* International student adviser on campus. ESL program at cooperating institution. ESL program available during the academic year. *Contact:* Assistant to the Executive Director/Admissions Coordinator, Clinton Community College, 1000 Lincoln Boulevard, Clinton, IA 52732-6299. Telephone: 563-244-7007. Fax: 563-244-7107. E-mail: scarmody@eicc.edu. URL: http://www.eicc.edu/ccc.

COE COLLEGE, CEDAR RAPIDS

General Information Independent, coed institution, affiliated with Presbyterian Church. Urban setting. *Awards:* B, M. *Entrance level for U.S. students:* Moderately difficult. *Enrollment:* 1,300 total; 1,275 undergraduates (54% women) including 4% international students from 18 foreign countries. *Faculty:* 142. *Library holdings:* 218,881 books, 1,576 current serial subscriptions. *Total majors:* 64.

Information for International Students For fall 2006: 98 international students applied, 33 were accepted, 11 enrolled. Students can start in fall or spring. Transfers accepted from institutions abroad. *Admission tests:* Required: SAT or ACT, TOEFL (minimum score: iBT 61; paper-based 500; computer-based 173; minimum score for ESL admission: paper-based 400; computer-based 97). TOEFL can be waived under certain conditions. *Application deadline:* 4/1. *Expenses:* (2007–08) $26,390; room and board, $6600 (on campus); room only, $2990 (on campus). *Financial aid:* Need-based college/university scholarships/grants from institutional funds. Non-need-based college/university scholarships/grants from institutional funds. Forms required: institution's own financial aid form. International transfer students are eligible to apply for aid. For fall 2006 (estimated), 36 international students on campus received college administered financial aid ($17,275 average). *Housing:* Guaranteed, also available during summer. *Services:* International student adviser on campus. Full-time ESL program on campus. ESL program available during the academic year and the summer. Internships and employment opportunities (on-campus) available. *Contact:* Associate Dean of Admission, Coe College, 1220 First Avenue, NE, Cedar Rapids, IA 52402. Telephone: 319-399-8500. Fax: 319-399-8816. E-mail: pcook@coe.edu. URL: http://www.coe.edu.

CORNELL COLLEGE, MOUNT VERNON

General Information Independent Methodist, 4-year, coed college. Small town setting. *Awards:* B. *Entrance level for U.S. students:* Moderately difficult. *Enrollment:* 1,121 total (53% women) including 3% international students from 21 foreign countries. *Undergraduate faculty:* 100. *Library holdings:* 194,131 books, 490 current serial subscriptions, 3,559 audiovisual materials. *Total majors:* 46.

Information for International Students For fall 2006: 131 international students applied, 31 were accepted, 14 enrolled. Students can start in fall. Transfers accepted from institutions abroad. *Admission tests:* Required: TOEFL (minimum score: iBT 79; paper-based 600; computer-based 250; minimum score for ESL admission: iBT 79; paper-based 600; computer-based 250), ELS. TOEFL can be waived under certain conditions. *Application deadline:* 3/1. *Expenses:* (2006–07) $24,800; room and board, $6660 (on campus); room only, $3100 (on campus). *Financial aid:* Need-based college/university scholarships/grants from institutional funds, on-campus employment. Non-need-based college/university scholarships/grants from institutional funds, on-campus employment. Forms required: institution's own financial aid form, International Student's Financial Aid Application, International Student's Certification of Finances. International transfer students are eligible to apply for aid. For fall 2006 (estimated), 28 international students on campus received college administered financial aid ($18,795 average). *Housing:* Guaranteed. *Services:* International student adviser on campus. Full-time ESL program on campus. ESL program available during the academic year. Internships and employment opportunities (on-campus) available. *Contact:* Assistant Director of Admission, Admission Office, Cornell College, 600 First Street, SW, Mount Vernon, IA 52314. Telephone: 319-895-4215. Fax: 319-895-4451. E-mail: international@cornellcollege.edu. URL: http://www.cornellcollege.edu.

DORDT COLLEGE, SIOUX CENTER

General Information Independent Christian Reformed, coed institution. Small town setting. *Awards:* A, B, M. *Entrance level for U.S. students:* Moderately difficult. *Enrollment:* 1,261 total; 1,259 undergraduates (53% women) including 15% international students from 14 foreign countries. *Faculty:* 98. *Library holdings:* 160,000 books, 6,597 current serial subscriptions. *Total majors:* 86.

Information for International Students Students can start in fall or spring. Transfers accepted from institutions abroad. *Admission tests:* Required: TOEFL (minimum score: paper-based 550; computer-based 213; minimum score for ESL admission: paper-based 550; computer-based 213), ELS. Recommended: SAT or ACT. *Application deadline:* 6/1. *Expenses:* (2006–07) $18,660; room and board, $5160 (on campus); room only, $2720 (on campus). *Financial aid:* Need-based college/university scholarships/grants from institutional funds, tuition waivers, athletic awards, loans from institutional funds, loans from outside sources, on-campus employment, Canadian exchange rate grant. Non-need-based college/university scholarships/grants from institutional funds, tuition waivers, athletic awards, loans from institutional funds, loans from outside sources, on-campus employment, Canadian exchange rate grant. Forms required: institution's own financial aid form, International Student's Financial Aid Application. For fall 2006 (estimated), 166 international students on campus received college administered financial aid ($14,200 average). *Housing:* Guaranteed, also available during summer. *Services:* International student adviser on campus. Full-time ESL program on campus. ESL program available during the academic year. *Contact:* Executive Director of Admissions, Dordt College, 498 4th Avenue, NE, Sioux Center, IA 51250. Telephone: 712-722-6080. Fax: 712-722-1198. E-mail: admissions@dordt.edu. URL: http://www.dordt.edu.

DRAKE UNIVERSITY, DES MOINES

General Information Independent, coed university. Suburban setting. *Awards:* B, M, D, FP. *Entrance level for U.S. students:* Moderately difficult. *Enrollment:* 5,366 total; 3,255 undergraduates (56% women) including 6% international students. *Faculty:* 391. *Library holdings:* 511,168 books, 31,500 current serial subscriptions, 2,163 audiovisual materials. *Total majors:* 66.

Information for International Students For fall 2006: 276 international students applied, 187 were accepted, 72 enrolled.

Students can start in fall or spring. Transfers accepted from institutions abroad. *Admission tests:* Required: TOEFL (minimum score: iBT 71; paper-based 530; computer-based 197). Recommended: SAT or ACT. TOEFL can be waived under certain conditions. *Application deadline:* Rolling. *Expenses:* (2006–07) $22,682; room and board, $6500 (on campus); room only, $3190 (on campus). *Financial aid:* Need-based college/university scholarships/grants from institutional funds. Non-need-based college/university scholarships/grants from institutional funds, athletic awards, loans from outside sources, on-campus employment. Forms required: institution's own financial aid form, International Student's Certification of Finances. International transfer students are eligible to apply for aid. For fall 2006 (estimated), 167 international students on campus received college administered financial aid ($12,684 average). *Housing:* Guaranteed, also available during summer. *Services:* International student adviser on campus. Full-time and part-time ESL programs on campus. ESL program available during the academic year and the summer. Internships and employment opportunities (on-campus) available. *Contact:* Associate Director for International and Graduate Admission, Drake University, Office of Admission, Des Moines, IA 50311. Telephone: 515-271-3181. Fax: 515-271-2831. E-mail: international@drake.edu. URL: http://www.drake.edu.

See In-Depth Description on page 69.

FAITH BAPTIST BIBLE COLLEGE AND THEOLOGICAL SEMINARY, ANKENY

General Information Independent, coed institution, affiliated with General Association of Regular Baptist Churches. Small town setting. *Awards:* A, B, M, FP. *Entrance level for U.S. students:* Minimally difficult. *Enrollment:* 404 total; 319 undergraduates (50% women) including 0.3% international students from 8 foreign countries. *Faculty:* 27. *Library holdings:* 63,840 books, 395 current serial subscriptions, 6,563 audiovisual materials. *Total majors:* 10. *Expenses:* (2006–07) $12,176; room and board, $4794 (on campus); room only, $2190 (on campus). *Financial aid:* Non-need financial aid available. Forms required: international scholarship application form.

GRACELAND UNIVERSITY, LAMONI

General Information Independent Community of Christ, coed institution. Rural setting. *Awards:* B, M. *Entrance level for U.S. students:* Moderately difficult. *Enrollment:* 2,116 total; 1,820 undergraduates (62% women) including 9% international students from 40 foreign countries. *Faculty:* 111. *Library holdings:* 193,172 books, 780 current serial subscriptions, 3,128 audiovisual materials. *Total majors:* 54. *Expenses:* (2007–08) $17,900; room and board, $6000 (on campus); room only, $2400 (on campus). *Financial aid:* Need-based college/university scholarships/grants from institutional funds, loans from institutional funds, on-campus employment. Non-need-based college/university scholarships/grants from institutional funds, tuition waivers, athletic awards, loans from institutional funds, loans from outside sources, on-campus employment. Forms required: International Student's Financial Aid Application, International Student's Certification of Finances. For fall 2006 (estimated), 216 international students on campus received college administered financial aid ($16,069 average).

GRAND VIEW COLLEGE, DES MOINES

General Information Independent, 4-year, coed college, affiliated with Evangelical Lutheran Church in America. Urban setting. *Awards:* A, B. *Entrance level for U.S. students:* Minimally difficult. *Enrollment:* 1,707 total (68% women) including 1% international students from 8 foreign countries. *Undergraduate faculty:* 174. *Library holdings:* 106,432 books, 13,068 current serial subscriptions, 4,686 audiovisual materials. *Total majors:* 29.

Information for International Students Students can start in fall, spring, or summer. Transfers accepted from institutions abroad. *Admission tests:* Required: ACT, TOEFL (minimum score: paper-based 550; computer-based 210). TOEFL can be waived under certain conditions. *Application deadline:* 6/1. *Expenses:* (2006–07) $16,940; room and board, $5596 (on campus). *Financial aid:* Need-based college/university scholarships/grants from institutional funds, athletic awards, loans from outside sources-if have US co-signer. Non-need-based college/university scholarships/grants from institutional funds, athletic awards, loans from outside sources-if have US co-signer. Forms required: institution's own financial aid form, International Student's Certification of Finances. International transfer students are eligible to apply for aid. 13 international students on campus received college administered financial aid ($12,014 average). *Housing:* Available during summer. *Services:* International student adviser on campus. ESL program at cooperating institution. Internships and employment opportunities (on-campus) available. *Contact:* Transfer Admissions Counselor, Grand View College, 1200 Grandview Avenue, Des Moines, IA

Grand View College (continued)

50316. Telephone: 515-263-2810. Fax: 515-263-2974.
E-mail: heaton@gvc.edu. URL: http://www.gvc.edu.

GRINNELL COLLEGE, GRINNELL

General Information Independent, 4-year, coed college. Small
town setting. *Awards:* B. *Entrance level for U.S. students:* Very
difficult. *Enrollment:* 1,589 total (54% women) including 10%
international students from 46 foreign countries. *Undergraduate
faculty:* 201. *Library holdings:* 1.1 million books, 20,186 current
serial subscriptions, 31,183 audiovisual materials. *Total majors:* 24.
Information for International Students For fall 2006: 1016
international students applied, 138 were accepted, 38 enrolled.
Students can start in fall or spring. Transfers accepted from
institutions abroad. *Admission tests:* Required: SAT or ACT, TOEFL
(minimum score: paper-based 550; computer-based 220). TOEFL
can be waived under certain conditions. *Application deadline:* 1/20.
Expenses: (2006–07) $29,030; room and board, $7700 (on campus);
room only, $3600 (on campus). *Financial aid:* Need-based
college/university scholarships/grants from institutional funds,
loans from institutional funds, on-campus employment.
Non-need-based college/university scholarships/grants from
institutional funds. Forms required: institution's own financial aid
form, International Student's Certification of Finances.
International transfer students are eligible to apply for aid. For fall
2006 (estimated), 145 international students on campus received
college administered financial aid ($24,955 average). *Housing:*
Guaranteed. *Services:* International student adviser on campus.
Internships and employment opportunities (on-campus) available.
Contact: Coordinator of International Admissions, Office of
Admission, Grinnell College, 1103 Park Street, Grinnell, IA 50112.
Telephone: 641-269-3600. Fax: 641-269-4800.
E-mail: askgrin@grinnell.edu. URL: http://www.grinnell.edu.

HAWKEYE COMMUNITY COLLEGE, WATERLOO

General Information State and locally supported, 2-year, coed
college. Rural setting. *Awards:* A. *Entrance level for U.S. students:*
Noncompetitive. *Enrollment:* 5,663 total (57% women) including
0.3% international students from 11 foreign countries.
Undergraduate faculty: 348. *Library holdings:* 42,327 books, 337
current serial subscriptions, 2,599 audiovisual materials.
Total majors: 55. *Expenses:* (2006–07) $6495.

IOWA LAKES COMMUNITY COLLEGE, ESTHERVILLE

General Information State and locally supported, 2-year, coed
college. Small town setting. *Awards:* A. *Entrance level for U.S.
students:* Noncompetitive. *Enrollment:* 3,052 total (55% women)
including 0.3% international students from 2 foreign countries.
Undergraduate faculty: 224. *Library holdings:* 36,881 books, 353
current serial subscriptions. *Total majors:* 195. *Expenses:* (2007–08)
$3616. *Financial aid:* Forms required: institution's own financial
aid form.

IOWA STATE UNIVERSITY OF SCIENCE AND TECHNOLOGY, AMES

General Information State-supported, coed university. Suburban
setting. *Awards:* B, M, D, FP. *Entrance level for U.S. students:*
Moderately difficult. *Enrollment:* 25,462 total; 20,440
undergraduates (44% women) including 3% international students
from 104 foreign countries. *Faculty:* 1,622. *Library holdings:* 2.5
million books, 52,533 current serial subscriptions. *Total majors:*
116.
Information for International Students For fall 2006: 709
international students applied, 492 were accepted, 146 enrolled.
Students can start in fall, spring, or summer. Transfers accepted
from institutions abroad. *Admission tests:* Recommended: SAT or
ACT, TOEFL (minimum score: iBT 68; paper-based 500;
computer-based 173), IELTS accepted in lieu of TOEFL. TOEFL can
be waived under certain conditions. *Application deadline:* 4/1.
Expenses: (2007–08) $16,919. *Financial aid:* Need-based
college/university scholarships/grants from institutional funds,
loans from institutional funds. Non-need-based college/university
scholarships/grants from institutional funds, athletic awards, loans
from outside sources, on-campus employment. Forms required:
institution's own financial aid form. International transfer students
are eligible to apply for aid. 148 international students on campus
received college administered financial aid ($3550 average).
Housing: Available during summer. *Services:* International student
adviser on campus. Full-time ESL program on campus. ESL
program available during the academic year and the summer.
Internships and employment opportunities (on-campus) available.
Contact: Assistant Director, International Admissions, Iowa State
University of Science and Technology, 100 Alumni Hall, Office of

Admissions, Ames, IA 50011-2011. Telephone: 515-294-5836.
Fax: 515-294-2592. E-mail: admissions@iastate.edu.
URL: http://www.iastate.edu.

IOWA WESTERN COMMUNITY COLLEGE, COUNCIL BLUFFS

General Information District-supported, 2-year, coed college.
Suburban setting. *Awards:* A. *Entrance level for U.S. students:*
Noncompetitive. *Enrollment:* 4,299 total including 2% international
students from 10 foreign countries. *Undergraduate faculty:* 222.
Library holdings: 59,200 books, 207 current serial subscriptions.
Total majors: 55.
Information for International Students For fall 2006: 250
international students applied, 250 were accepted, 173 enrolled.
Students can start in fall, winter, spring, or summer. Transfers
accepted from institutions abroad. *Admission tests:* Required:
COMPASS. Recommended: TOEFL (minimum score: iBT 61;
paper-based 500; computer-based 173). TOEFL can be waived under
certain conditions. *Application deadline:* 7/1. *Expenses:* (2006–07)
$5260; room and board, $4370 (on campus). *Financial aid:*
Need-based college/university scholarships/grants from institutional
funds, athletic awards, on-campus employment. Non-need-based
college/university scholarships/grants from institutional funds,
athletic awards, on-campus employment. Forms required:
International Student's Certification of Finances. *Housing:*
Guaranteed, also available during summer. *Services:* International
student adviser on campus. Full-time ESL program on campus.
ESL program available during the academic year and the summer.
Internships and employment opportunities (on-campus) available.
Contact: Director of International Programs, Iowa Western
Community College, 2700 College Road, Clark Hall, Council Bluffs,
IA 51503. Telephone: 712-325-3278. Fax: 712-388-6803.
E-mail: djensen@iwcc.edu. URL: http://www.iwcc.edu.

KIRKWOOD COMMUNITY COLLEGE, CEDAR RAPIDS

General Information State and locally supported, 2-year, coed
college. Suburban setting. *Awards:* A. *Entrance level for U.S.
students:* Noncompetitive. *Enrollment:* 15,064 total (54% women)
including 1% international students from 27 foreign countries.
Undergraduate faculty: 832. *Library holdings:* 60,622 books, 565
current serial subscriptions. *Total majors:* 108.
Information for International Students For fall 2006: 540
international students were accepted, 540 enrolled. Students can
start in fall, spring, or summer. Transfers accepted from
institutions abroad. *Admission tests:* Recommended: TOEFL
(minimum score: paper-based 500; computer-based 173). *Application
deadline:* Rolling. *Expenses:* (2007–08) $6180. *Services:*
International student adviser on campus. Full-time ESL program
on campus. ESL program available during the academic year and
the summer. Employment opportunities (on-campus) available.
Contact: International Student Advisor/International Admissions,
Kirkwood Community College, 6301 Kirkwood Boulevard, SW, PO
Box 2068, Cedar Rapids, IA 52406-2068. Telephone: 319-398-5579.
Fax: 319-398-1255. E-mail: gglick@kirkwood.edu.
URL: http://www.kirkwood.cc.ia.us.

LORAS COLLEGE, DUBUQUE

General Information Independent Roman Catholic, coed
institution. Suburban setting. *Awards:* A, B, M. *Entrance level for
U.S. students:* Moderately difficult. *Enrollment:* 1,673 total; 1,591
undergraduates (48% women) including 2% international students
from 9 foreign countries. *Faculty:* 162. *Library holdings:* 351,550
books, 554 current serial subscriptions. *Total majors:* 54. *Expenses:*
(2006–07) $22,053; room and board, $6305 (on campus); room only,
$3220 (on campus). *Financial aid:* Need-based college/university
scholarships/grants from institutional funds. Non-need-based
college/university scholarships/grants from institutional funds,
on-campus employment. Forms required: International Student's
Financial Aid Application, International Student's Certification of
Finances. For fall 2006 (estimated), 40 international students on
campus received college administered financial aid ($12,258
average).

LUTHER COLLEGE, DECORAH

General Information Independent, 4-year, coed college, affiliated
with Evangelical Lutheran Church in America. Small town setting.
Awards: B. *Entrance level for U.S. students:* Moderately difficult.
Enrollment: 2,504 total (59% women) including 3% international
students from 33 foreign countries. *Undergraduate faculty:* 246.
Library holdings: 334,814 books, 831 current serial subscriptions,
1,866 audiovisual materials. *Total majors:* 41.
Information for International Students For fall 2006: 215
international students applied, 72 were accepted, 28 enrolled.
Students can start in fall, winter, spring, or summer. Transfers
accepted from institutions abroad. *Admission tests:* Required:
TOEFL (minimum score: iBT 79; paper-based 550; computer-based

213). TOEFL can be waived under certain conditions. *Application deadline:* 5/1. *Expenses:* (2006–07) $26,380; room and board, $4290 (on campus); room only, $2100 (on campus). *Financial aid:* Need-based college/university scholarships/grants from institutional funds, loans from institutional funds, on-campus employment. Forms required: International Student's Financial Aid Application, International Student's Certification of Finances. International transfer students are eligible to apply for aid. For fall 2006 (estimated), 70 international students on campus received college administered financial aid ($22,024 average). *Housing:* Guaranteed, also available during summer. *Services:* International student adviser on campus. Internships and employment opportunities (on-campus) available. *Contact:* Executive Director of International Admissions, Luther College, 700 College Drive, Decorah, IA 52101. Telephone: 563-387-1062. Fax: 563-387-2159. E-mail: intladmissions@luther.edu. URL: http://www.luther.edu.

MAHARISHI UNIVERSITY OF MANAGEMENT, FAIRFIELD

General Information Independent, coed university. Small town setting. *Awards:* B, M, D. *Entrance level for U.S. students:* Moderately difficult. *Enrollment:* 931 total; 284 undergraduates (51% women) including 42% international students from 16 foreign countries. *Faculty:* 57. *Library holdings:* 137,775 books, 11,146 current serial subscriptions. *Total majors:* 10. *Expenses:* (2006–07) $24,430; room and board, $6000 (on campus). *Financial aid:* Need-based college/university scholarships/grants from institutional funds, tuition waivers, loans from institutional funds, on-campus employment. Non-need-based loans from outside sources. Forms required: institution's own financial aid form, International Student's Certification of Finances. For fall 2006 (estimated), 17 international students on campus received college administered financial aid ($15,925 average).

MORNINGSIDE COLLEGE, SIOUX CITY

General Information Independent, coed institution, affiliated with United Methodist Church. Suburban setting. *Awards:* B, M. *Entrance level for U.S. students:* Moderately difficult. *Enrollment:* 1,722 total; 1,232 undergraduates (54% women) including 1% international students from 7 foreign countries. *Faculty:* 152. *Library holdings:* 98,912 books, 485 current serial subscriptions, 2,701 audiovisual materials. *Total majors:* 43.

Information for International Students For fall 2006: 23 international students applied, 19 were accepted, 18 enrolled. Students can start in fall, winter, spring, or summer. Transfers accepted from institutions abroad. *Admission tests:* Required: TOEFL (minimum score: iBT 45; paper-based 450; computer-based 133; minimum score for ESL admission: iBT 45; paper-based 450; computer-based 133), ACT or SAT may be submitted in lieu of TOEFL. TOEFL can be waived under certain conditions. *Application deadline:* Rolling. *Expenses:* (2006–07) $19,902; room and board, $6227 (on campus); room only, $3213 (on campus). *Financial aid:* Non-need-based college/university scholarships/grants from institutional funds, athletic awards, loans from outside sources, on-campus employment. Forms required: International Student's Certification of Finances. For fall 2005, 26 international students on campus received college administered financial aid ($6852 average). *Housing:* Guaranteed, also available during summer. *Services:* International student adviser on campus. Full-time and part-time ESL programs on campus. ESL program available during the academic year. Internships and employment opportunities (on-campus) available. *Contact:* Vice President for Enrollment and Student Services, Morningside College, 1501 Morningside Avenue, Sioux City, IA 51106. Telephone: 712-274-5257. Fax: 712-274-5101. E-mail: curyte@morningside.edu. URL: http://www.morningside.edu.

MOUNT MERCY COLLEGE, CEDAR RAPIDS

General Information Independent Roman Catholic, 4-year, coed college. Suburban setting. *Awards:* B. *Entrance level for U.S. students:* Moderately difficult. *Enrollment:* 1,482 total (73% women) including 0.4% international students from 6 foreign countries. *Undergraduate faculty:* 153. *Library holdings:* 125,000 books, 10,900 current serial subscriptions, 5,437 audiovisual materials. *Total majors:* 35.

Information for International Students For fall 2006: 17 international students applied, 6 were accepted, 6 enrolled. Students can start in fall, winter, spring, or summer. Transfers accepted from institutions abroad. *Admission tests:* Required: TOEFL (minimum score: iBT 79; paper-based 550; computer-based 213). Recommended: STEP Eiken, IELTS. TOEFL can be waived under certain conditions. *Application deadline:* 6/1. *Expenses:* (2006–07) $18,930; room and board, $5970 (on campus). *Financial aid:* Need-based financial aid available. Non-need-based college/university scholarships/grants from institutional funds, on-campus employment. International transfer students are eligible

to apply for aid. For fall 2006 (estimated), 5 international students on campus received college administered financial aid ($6207 average). *Housing:* Guaranteed. *Services:* International student adviser on campus. ESL program at cooperating institution. ESL program available during the academic year. Employment opportunities (on-campus) available. *Contact:* Admission Representative, Mount Mercy College, 1330 Elmhurst Drive, NE, Cedar Rapids, IA 52402. Telephone: 319-368-6460. Fax: 319-363-5270. E-mail: jnewnum@mtmercy.edu. URL: http://www.mtmercy.edu.

NORTHEAST IOWA COMMUNITY COLLEGE, CALMAR

General Information State and locally supported, 2-year, coed college. Small town setting. *Awards:* A. *Entrance level for U.S. students:* Noncompetitive. *Enrollment:* 4,764 total (60% women) including 0.2% international students. *Undergraduate faculty:* 192. *Library holdings:* 21,337 books, 294 current serial subscriptions, 4,813 audiovisual materials. *Total majors:* 13. *Expenses:* (2007–08) $4352.

NORTH IOWA AREA COMMUNITY COLLEGE, MASON CITY

General Information State and locally supported, 2-year, coed college. Rural setting. *Awards:* A. *Entrance level for U.S. students:* Noncompetitive. *Enrollment:* 3,022 total (53% women) including 1% international students from 10 foreign countries. *Undergraduate faculty:* 160. *Library holdings:* 29,540 books, 413 current serial subscriptions, 7,773 audiovisual materials. *Total majors:* 29. *Expenses:* (2006–07) $4674; room and board, $4076 (on campus). *Financial aid:* Need-based college/university scholarships/grants from institutional funds, athletic awards, loans from outside sources, on-campus employment. Non-need-based college/university scholarships/grants from institutional funds, athletic awards, loans from outside sources, on-campus employment. Forms required: institution's own financial aid form.

ST. AMBROSE UNIVERSITY, DAVENPORT

General Information Independent Roman Catholic, coed institution. Urban setting. *Awards:* B, M, D. *Entrance level for U.S. students:* Moderately difficult. *Enrollment:* 3,780 total; 2,829 undergraduates (62% women) including 1% international students from 13 foreign countries. *Faculty:* 310. *Library holdings:* 150,328 books, 738 current serial subscriptions, 3,687 audiovisual materials. *Total majors:* 72.

Information for International Students For fall 2006: 40 international students applied, 12 were accepted, 11 enrolled. Students can start in fall, spring, or summer. Transfers accepted from institutions abroad. *Admission tests:* Required: TOEFL (minimum score: iBT 61; paper-based 500; computer-based 173). TOEFL can be waived under certain conditions. *Application deadline:* Rolling. *Financial aid:* Need-based college/university scholarships/grants from institutional funds, athletic awards, loans from outside sources, on-campus employment. Non-need-based athletic awards. Forms required: institution's own financial aid form. International transfer students are eligible to apply for aid. 24 international students on campus received college administered financial aid ($11,171 average). *Housing:* Guaranteed, also available during summer. *Services:* International student adviser on campus. ESL program at cooperating institution. Internships and employment opportunities (on-campus and off-campus) available. *Contact:* International Student Services, St. Ambrose University, 518 West Locust Street, Davenport, IA 52803. Telephone: 563-333-6309. Fax: 563-333-6256. E-mail: global@sau.edu. URL: http://www.sau.edu.

See In-Depth Description on page 164.

SCOTT COMMUNITY COLLEGE, BETTENDORF

General Information State and locally supported, 2-year, coed college. Urban setting. *Awards:* A. *Entrance level for U.S. students:* Noncompetitive. *Enrollment:* 4,697 total (61% women) including 1% international students. *Undergraduate faculty:* 322. *Library holdings:* 22,700 books, 183 current serial subscriptions. *Total majors:* 30.

Information for International Students For fall 2006: 45 international students applied, 45 were accepted, 43 enrolled. Students can start in fall, spring, or summer. Transfers accepted from institutions abroad. *Admission tests:* Required: TOEFL (minimum score: iBT 61; paper-based 500; computer-based 173). TOEFL can be waived under certain conditions. *Application deadline:* 8/7. *Expenses:* (2006–07) $4365. *Financial aid:* Need-based and non-need-based financial aid available. *Services:* International student adviser on campus. Full-time and part-time ESL programs on campus. ESL program available during the academic year and the summer. *Contact:* Academic Advisor/Coordinator International Students, Scott Community College, 500 Belmont Road, Bettendorf,

Scott Community College (continued)

IA 52722. Telephone: 563-441-4004. Fax: 563-441-4101.
E-mail: sbergren@eicc.edu. URL: http://www.eicc.edu/scc.

SIMPSON COLLEGE, INDIANOLA

General Information Independent United Methodist, 4-year, coed college. Small town setting. *Awards:* B. *Entrance level for U.S. students:* Moderately difficult. *Enrollment:* 2,060 total; 2,031 undergraduates (59% women) including 1% international students from 16 foreign countries. *Undergraduate faculty:* 181. *Library holdings:* 157,713 books, 558 current serial subscriptions. *Total majors:* 50.

Information for International Students For fall 2006: 61 international students applied, 25 were accepted, 4 enrolled. Students can start in fall. Transfers accepted from institutions abroad. *Admission tests:* Required: TOEFL (minimum score: iBT 80; paper-based 550; computer-based 213; minimum score for ESL admission: iBT 80; paper-based 550; computer-based 213). Recommended: SAT. *Application deadline:* Rolling. *Expenses:* (2007–08) $23,596; room and board, $6655 (on campus); room only, $3194 (on campus). *Financial aid:* Need-based college/university scholarships/grants from institutional funds, loans from outside sources, on-campus employment. Non-need-based college/university scholarships/grants from institutional funds, loans from outside sources, on-campus employment. Forms required: International Student's Financial Aid Application, International Student's Certification of Finances. International transfer students are eligible to apply for aid. For fall 2006 (estimated), 18 international students on campus received college administered financial aid ($18,351 average). *Housing:* Guaranteed, also available during summer. *Services:* International student adviser on campus. Part-time ESL program on campus. ESL program available during the summer. Internships and employment opportunities (on-campus) available. *Contact:* Director of Transfer and International Enrollment, Simpson College, 701 North C Street, Indianola, IA 50125. Telephone: 515-961-1624. Fax: 515-961-1870. E-mail: admiss@simpson.edu. URL: http://www.simpson.edu.

SOUTHWESTERN COMMUNITY COLLEGE, CRESTON

General Information State-supported, 2-year, coed college. Rural setting. *Awards:* A. *Entrance level for U.S. students:* Noncompetitive. *Enrollment:* 1,254 total (57% women) including 0.5% international students from 4 foreign countries. *Undergraduate faculty:* 96. *Library holdings:* 14,742 books, 170 current serial subscriptions, 1,174 audiovisual materials. *Total majors:* 16.

Information for International Students For fall 2006: 17 international students applied, 10 were accepted, 4 enrolled. Students can start in fall, winter, spring, or summer. *Admission tests:* Required: TOEFL (minimum score: paper-based 500; computer-based 173). Recommended: ACT, COMPASS. TOEFL can be waived under certain conditions. *Application deadline:* 7/1. *Expenses:* (2006–07) $4944; room and board, $3800 (on campus). *Financial aid:* Non-need-based college/university scholarships/grants from institutional funds, tuition waivers, athletic awards, on-campus employment. Forms required: International Student's Certification of Finances. *Housing:* Available during summer. *Services:* International student adviser on campus. Part-time ESL program on campus. ESL program available during the academic year. Employment opportunities (on-campus) available. *Contact:* Admissions Coordinator, Southwestern Community College, 1501 West Townline Street, Creston, IA 50801. Telephone: 641-782-7081 Ext. 453. Fax: 641-782-3312. E-mail: carstens@swcciowa.edu. URL: http://www.swcc.cc.ia.us.

UNIVERSITY OF DUBUQUE, DUBUQUE

General Information Independent Presbyterian, coed institution. Suburban setting. *Awards:* A, B, M, D, FP. *Entrance level for U.S. students:* Moderately difficult. *Enrollment:* 1,441 total; 1,179 undergraduates (38% women) including 1% international students from 2 foreign countries. *Faculty:* 158. *Library holdings:* 168,579 books, 484 current serial subscriptions, 1,169 audiovisual materials. *Total majors:* 32.

Information for International Students Students can start in fall or spring. Transfers accepted from institutions abroad. *Admission tests:* Required: TOEFL (minimum score: iBT 80; paper-based 500; computer-based 173). TOEFL can be waived under certain conditions. *Application deadline:* Rolling. *Expenses:* (2006–07) $17,470; room and board, $5950 (on campus); room only, $3100 (on campus). *Housing:* Guaranteed, also available during summer. *Services:* International student adviser on campus. Internships and employment opportunities (on-campus) available. *Contact:* Director, International Admission, University of Dubuque, 2000 University Avenue, Dubuque, IA 52001. Telephone: 319-589-3199. Fax: 319-589-3690. E-mail: bbroshou@dbq.edu. URL: http://www.dbq.edu.

THE UNIVERSITY OF IOWA, IOWA CITY

General Information State-supported, coed university. Small town setting. *Awards:* B, M, D, FP. *Entrance level for U.S. students:* Moderately difficult. *Enrollment:* 28,816 total; 20,738 undergraduates (53% women) including 2% international students from 57 foreign countries. *Faculty:* 1,673. *Library holdings:* 4 million books, 44,644 current serial subscriptions. *Total majors:* 144.

Information for International Students For fall 2006: 567 international students applied, 341 were accepted, 74 enrolled. Students can start in fall, winter, spring, or summer. Transfers accepted from institutions abroad. *Admission tests:* Required: TOEFL (minimum score: iBT 100; paper-based 600; computer-based 250; minimum score for ESL admission: iBT 100; paper-based 600; computer-based 250). Recommended: SAT or ACT. TOEFL can be waived under certain conditions. *Application deadline:* 4/1. *Expenses:* (2007–08) $19,465. *Housing:* Available during summer. *Services:* International student adviser on campus. Full-time ESL program on campus. ESL program available during the academic year and the summer. Internships and employment opportunities (on-campus) available. *Contact:* Program Assistant, International Admissions Office, The University of Iowa, 107 Calvin Hall, Iowa City, IA 52242-1396. Telephone: 319-335-1465. Fax: 319-335-1535. E-mail: admissions@uiowa.edu. URL: http://www.uiowa.edu.

UNIVERSITY OF NORTHERN IOWA, CEDAR FALLS

General Information State-supported, coed institution. Small town setting. *Awards:* B, M, D. *Entrance level for U.S. students:* Moderately difficult. *Enrollment:* 12,327 total; 10,727 undergraduates (57% women) including 2% international students from 74 foreign countries. *Faculty:* 810. *Library holdings:* 1.2 million books, 6,839 current serial subscriptions, 28,408 audiovisual materials. *Total majors:* 112.

Information for International Students For fall 2006: 140 international students applied, 97 were accepted, 63 enrolled. Students can start in fall, spring, or summer. Transfers accepted from institutions abroad. *Admission tests:* Required: TOEFL (minimum score: iBT 79; paper-based 550; computer-based 213). TOEFL can be waived under certain conditions. *Application deadline:* 5/1. *Expenses:* (2006–07) $14,028; room and board, $5740 (on campus); room only, $2695 (on campus). *Financial aid:* Non-need-based college/university scholarships/grants from institutional funds, athletic awards, loans from outside sources, on-campus employment. For fall 2006 (estimated), 82 international students on campus received college administered financial aid ($5630 average). *Housing:* Guaranteed, also available during summer. *Services:* International student adviser on campus. Full-time ESL program on campus. ESL program available during the academic year and the summer. Internships and employment opportunities (on-campus) available. *Contact:* International Admissions Assistant, University of Northern Iowa, 120 Gilchrist Hall, Cedar Falls, IA 50614-0018. Telephone: 319-273-2281. Fax: 319-273-2885. E-mail: rosty@uni.edu. URL: http://www.uni.edu.

See In-Depth Description on page 220.

UPPER IOWA UNIVERSITY, FAYETTE

General Information Independent, coed institution. Rural setting. *Awards:* A, B, M (also offers continuing education program with significant enrollment not reflected in profile). *Entrance level for U.S. students:* Moderately difficult. *Enrollment:* 696 total; 665 undergraduates (40% women). *Faculty:* 65. *Library holdings:* 64,043 books, 3,241 current serial subscriptions. *Total majors:* 39.

Information for International Students For fall 2006: 3 international students enrolled. Students can start in fall, spring, or summer. Transfers accepted from institutions abroad. *Admission tests:* Required: TOEFL (minimum score: iBT 61; paper-based 500; computer-based 173; minimum score for ESL admission: paper-based 500; computer-based 173). Recommended: SAT or ACT, SAT Subject Tests. TOEFL can be waived under certain conditions. *Application deadline:* 7/15. *Expenses:* (2007–08) $19,625; room and board, $6075 (on campus); room only, $2525 (on campus). *Financial aid:* Non-need financial aid available. International transfer students are eligible to apply for aid. *Housing:* Guaranteed, also available during summer. *Services:* International student adviser on campus. Full-time and part-time ESL programs on campus. ESL program available during the academic year. Internships available. *Contact:* International Admission Counselor, Upper Iowa University, 605 Washington Street, PO Box 1859, Fayette, IA 52142. Telephone: 563-425-5775. Fax: 563-425-5323. E-mail: moreb@uiu.edu. URL: http://www.uiu.edu.

WALDORF COLLEGE, FOREST CITY

General Information Independent Lutheran, 4-year, coed college. Rural setting. *Awards:* B. *Entrance level for U.S. students:* Moderately difficult. *Enrollment:* 670 total (50% women) including

5% international students from 14 foreign countries. *Undergraduate faculty:* 70. *Library holdings:* 33,422 books, 55,989 current serial subscriptions. *Total majors:* 31.

Information for International Students For fall 2006: 186 international students applied, 37 were accepted, 19 enrolled. Students can start in fall or winter. Transfers accepted from institutions abroad. *Admission tests:* Required: TOEFL (minimum score: iBT 61; paper-based 500; computer-based 173; minimum score for ESL admission: iBT 45; paper-based 450; computer-based 133). Recommended: SAT Subject Tests. TOEFL can be waived under certain conditions. *Application deadline:* 7/1. *Expenses:* (2006–07) $16,670; room and board, $5270 (on campus). *Financial aid:* Need-based financial aid available. Non-need-based college/university scholarships/grants from institutional funds, on-campus employment. Forms required: International Student's Certification of Finances. International transfer students are eligible to apply for aid. 33 international students on campus received college administered financial aid ($5000 average). *Housing:* Guaranteed, also available during summer. *Services:* International student adviser on campus. Full-time ESL program on campus. ESL program available during the summer. Internships and employment opportunities (on-campus) available. *Contact:* International Admission Coordinator, Waldorf College, 106 South Sixth Street, Forest City, IA 50436. Telephone: 641 585 8124. Fax: 641-585-8125. E-mail: hadleys@waldorf.edu. URL: http://www.waldorf.edu.

WARTBURG COLLEGE, WAVERLY

General Information Independent Lutheran, 4-year, coed college. Small town setting. *Awards:* B. *Entrance level for U.S. students:* Moderately difficult. *Enrollment:* 1,769 total (53% women) including 5% international students from 36 foreign countries. *Undergraduate faculty:* 164. *Total majors:* 52.

Information for International Students For fall 2006: 148 international students applied, 96 were accepted, 24 enrolled. Students can start in fall, winter, spring, or summer. Transfers accepted from institutions abroad. *Admission tests:* Required: TOEFL (minimum score: paper-based 480; computer-based 157; minimum score for ESL admission: paper-based 480; computer-based 157), ELS (minimum score: 112), IELTS, Eiken/STEP. *Application deadline:* Rolling. *Expenses:* (2006–07) $22,410; room and board, $6715 (on campus); room only, $3205 (on campus). *Financial aid:* Non-need-based college/university scholarships/grants from institutional funds, loans from outside sources, on-campus employment. Forms required: institution's own financial aid form. International transfer students are eligible to apply for aid. For fall 2005, 94 international students on campus received college administered financial aid ($11,237 average). *Housing:* Guaranteed, also available during summer. *Services:* International student adviser on campus. ESL program at cooperating institution. ESL program available during the academic year and the summer. Internships and employment opportunities (on-campus) available. *Contact:* Associate Director for International Admissions, Admissions Office, Wartburg College, 100 Wartburg Boulevard, Waverly, IA 50677-0903. Telephone: 319-352-8511. Fax: 319-352-8579. E-mail: david.fredrick@wartburg.edu. URL: http://www.wartburg.edu.

WESTERN IOWA TECH COMMUNITY COLLEGE, SIOUX CITY

General Information State-supported, 2-year, coed college. Urban setting. *Awards:* A. *Entrance level for U.S. students:* Noncompetitive. *Enrollment:* 5,334 total (56% women) including 0.1% international students. *Undergraduate faculty:* 306. *Library holdings:* 25,696 books, 1,886 current serial subscriptions, 3,456 audiovisual materials. *Total majors:* 26. *Expenses:* (2006–07) $4440; room only, $2160 (on campus).

KANSAS

ALLEN COUNTY COMMUNITY COLLEGE, IOLA

General Information State and locally supported, 2-year, coed college. Small town setting. *Awards:* A. *Entrance level for U.S. students:* Noncompetitive. *Enrollment:* 2,814 total including 1% international students from 16 foreign countries. *Undergraduate faculty:* 155. *Library holdings:* 49,416 books, 159 current serial subscriptions. *Total majors:* 69. *Expenses:* (2007–08) $2280.

BAKER UNIVERSITY, BALDWIN CITY

General Information Independent United Methodist, coed institution. Small town setting. *Awards:* B. *Entrance level for U.S. students:* Moderately difficult. *Enrollment:* 923 total (52% women) including 0.3% international students from 8 foreign countries.

Undergraduate faculty: 115. *Library holdings:* 132,325 books, 678 current serial subscriptions, 4,992 audiovisual materials. *Total majors:* 37.

Information for International Students For fall 2006: 22 international students applied, 2 were accepted, 2 enrolled. Students can start in fall, winter, spring, or summer. Transfers accepted from institutions abroad. *Admission tests:* Required: TOEFL (minimum score: paper-based 525; computer-based 195; minimum score for ESL admission: paper-based 390; computer-based 90). Recommended: SAT or ACT, ELS. TOEFL can be waived under certain conditions. *Application deadline:* Rolling. *Expenses:* (2006–07) $17,580; room and board, $5850 (on campus); room only, $2660 (on campus). *Financial aid:* Non-need-based college/university scholarships/grants from institutional funds, athletic awards, on-campus employment. Forms required: institution's own financial aid form. International transfer students are eligible to apply for aid. For fall 2006 (estimated), 8 international students on campus received college administered financial aid ($10,475 average). *Housing:* Guaranteed. *Services:* International student adviser on campus. Internships and employment opportunities (on-campus) available. *Contact:* Vice President for Enrollment Management and Financial Aid, Baker University, PO Box 65, Baldwin City, KS 66006. Telephone: 785 594 8420. Fax: 785 594 8420. E-mail: louise.cummings-simmons@bakeru.edu. URL: http://www.bakeru.edu.

BARTON COUNTY COMMUNITY COLLEGE, GREAT BEND

General Information State and locally supported, 2-year, coed college. Rural setting. *Awards:* A. *Entrance level for U.S. students:* Noncompetitive. *Enrollment:* 4,263 total (46% women) including 1% international students from 16 foreign countries. *Undergraduate faculty:* 190. *Library holdings:* 41,380 books, 66 current serial subscriptions, 1,325 audiovisual materials. *Total majors:* 84. *Expenses:* (2007–08) $2580; room and board, $3854 (on campus).

BENEDICTINE COLLEGE, ATCHISON

General Information Independent Roman Catholic, coed institution. Small town setting. *Awards:* A, B, M. *Entrance level for U.S. students:* Moderately difficult. *Enrollment:* 1,553 total; 1,468 undergraduates (53% women) including 3% international students from 21 foreign countries. *Faculty:* 112. *Library holdings:* 368,558 books, 504 current serial subscriptions. *Total majors:* 34. *Expenses:* (2006–07) $16,710; room and board, $6208 (on campus); room only, $2730 (on campus). *Financial aid:* Need-based college/university scholarships/grants from institutional funds, athletic awards, on-campus employment. Non-need-based college/university scholarships/grants from institutional funds, athletic awards, on-campus employment. Forms required: International Student's Certification of Finances, sponsor letter. For fall 2005, 33 international students on campus received college administered financial aid ($5122 average).

BETHANY COLLEGE, LINDSBORG

General Information Independent Lutheran, 4-year, coed college. Small town setting. *Awards:* B. *Entrance level for U.S. students:* Moderately difficult. *Enrollment:* 554 total (51% women) including 3% international students from 11 foreign countries. *Undergraduate faculty:* 81. *Library holdings:* 90,230 books, 709 current serial subscriptions, 1,232 audiovisual materials. *Total majors:* 41.

Information for International Students For fall 2006: 85 international students applied, 37 were accepted, 4 enrolled. Students can start in fall, winter, or spring. Transfers accepted from institutions abroad. *Admission tests:* Required: SAT or ACT, TOEFL (minimum score: paper-based 525; computer-based 195). TOEFL can be waived under certain conditions. *Application deadline:* 6/15. *Expenses:* (2007–08) $17,110; room and board, $5500 (on campus); room only, $3000 (on campus). *Financial aid:* Non-need-based tuition waivers. Forms required: International Student's Financial Aid Application, International Student's Certification of Finances. International transfer students are eligible to apply for aid. For fall 2006 (estimated), 14 international students on campus received college administered financial aid ($6614 average). *Housing:* Available during summer. *Services:* International student adviser on campus. ESL program at cooperating institution. Internships available. *Contact:* International Student Coordinator, Bethany College, 335 East Swensson Street, Lindsborg, KS 67456. Telephone: 785-227-3311 Ext. 8159. Fax: 785-227-2004. E-mail: bruces@bethanylb.edu. URL: http://www.bethanylb.edu.

BETHEL COLLEGE, NORTH NEWTON

General Information Independent, 4-year, coed college, affiliated with Mennonite Church USA. Small town setting. *Awards:* B. *Entrance level for U.S. students:* Moderately difficult. *Enrollment:*

Kansas

Bethel College (continued)

539 total (48% women) including 7% international students from 14 foreign countries. *Undergraduate faculty:* 65. *Library holdings:* 162,327 books, 38,356 current serial subscriptions, 3,665 audiovisual materials. *Total majors:* 27.

Information for International Students For fall 2006: 23 international students applied, 17 were accepted, 7 enrolled. Students can start in fall, winter, or spring. Transfers accepted from institutions abroad. *Admission tests:* Required: TOEFL (minimum score: paper-based 540; computer-based 207). Recommended: SAT or ACT. TOEFL can be waived under certain conditions. *Application deadline:* Rolling. *Expenses:* (2006–07) $16,700; room and board, $6100 (on campus); room only, $3200 (on campus). *Financial aid:* Need-based tuition waivers, on-campus employment. Non-need-based tuition waivers, on-campus employment. Forms required: institution's own financial aid form. International transfer students are eligible to apply for aid. For fall 2005, 7 international students on campus received college administered financial aid ($14,418 average). *Housing:* Guaranteed. Internships and employment opportunities (on-campus) available. *Contact:* Director of Admissions and Enrollment, Bethel College, 300 East 27th Street, North Newton, KS 67117. Telephone: 316-283-2500 Ext. 230. Fax: 316-284-5870. E-mail: admissions@bethelks.edu. URL: http://www.bethelks.edu.

BUTLER COMMUNITY COLLEGE, EL DORADO

General Information State and locally supported, 2-year, coed college. Small town setting. *Awards:* A. *Entrance level for U.S. students:* Noncompetitive. *Enrollment:* 8,863 total (60% women) including 3% international students from 21 foreign countries. *Undergraduate faculty:* 613. *Library holdings:* 38,000 books, 220 current serial subscriptions, 914 audiovisual materials. *Total majors:* 41. *Expenses:* (2006–07) $3710; room and board, $4420 (on campus). *Financial aid:* Non-need-based athletic awards, on-campus employment.

CENTRAL CHRISTIAN COLLEGE OF KANSAS, MCPHERSON

General Information Independent Free Methodist, 4-year, coed college. Small town setting. *Awards:* A, B. *Entrance level for U.S. students:* Moderately difficult. *Enrollment:* 349 total (48% women) including 3% international students from 3 foreign countries. *Undergraduate faculty:* 36. *Library holdings:* 45,357 books, 91 current serial subscriptions, 1,218 audiovisual materials. *Total majors:* 85.

Information for International Students For fall 2006: 8 international students applied, 5 were accepted, 3 enrolled. Students can start in fall, winter, or spring. Transfers accepted from institutions abroad. *Admission tests:* Required: TOEFL (minimum score: paper-based 500; computer-based 173; minimum score for ESL admission: paper-based 500; computer-based 173). Recommended: ACT, SAT Subject Tests, ELS. *Application deadline:* 6/1. *Expenses:* (2007–08) $15,300; room and board, $5200 (on campus); room only, $2400 (on campus). *Financial aid:* Non-need-based college/university scholarships/grants from institutional funds, athletic awards, loans from outside sources. Forms required: institution's own financial aid form. International transfer students are eligible to apply for aid. 4 international students on campus received college administered financial aid ($4656 average). *Housing:* Guaranteed. *Services:* International student adviser on campus. Internships and employment opportunities (on-campus) available. *Contact:* Dean of Admissions, Central Christian College of Kansas, 1200 South Main, PO Box 1403, McPherson, KS 67460. Telephone: 620-241-0723 Ext. 337. Fax: 620-241-6032. E-mail: colleenp@centralchristian.edu. URL: http://www.centralchristian.edu.

CLOUD COUNTY COMMUNITY COLLEGE, CONCORDIA

General Information State and locally supported, 2-year, coed college. Rural setting. *Awards:* A. *Entrance level for U.S. students:* Noncompetitive. *Enrollment:* 3,521 total including 0.4% international students from 5 foreign countries. *Undergraduate faculty:* 218. *Library holdings:* 18,010 books, 142 current serial subscriptions. *Total majors:* 29.

COFFEYVILLE COMMUNITY COLLEGE, COFFEYVILLE

General Information State and locally supported, 2-year, coed college. Small town setting. *Awards:* A. *Entrance level for U.S. students:* Noncompetitive. *Enrollment:* 1,766 total (54% women) including 1% international students from 4 foreign countries. *Undergraduate faculty:* 85. *Library holdings:* 27,482 books, 238 current serial subscriptions, 1,415 audiovisual materials. *Total majors:* 69.

Information for International Students For fall 2006: 35 international students applied, 35 were accepted, 35 enrolled.

Students can start in fall, spring, or summer. Transfers accepted from institutions abroad. *Admission tests:* Required: COMPASS. TOEFL can be waived under certain conditions. *Application deadline:* 8/1. *Housing:* Guaranteed, also available during summer. *Services:* International student adviser on campus. Full-time and part-time ESL programs on campus. ESL program available during the academic year and the summer. Employment opportunities (on-campus and off-campus) available. *Contact:* International Student Advisor, Coffeyville Community College, 400 West 11th, Coffeyville, KS 67337. Telephone: 620-251-7700 Ext. 2086. Fax: 620-252-7098. E-mail: marlal@coffeyville.edu. URL: http://www.coffeyville.edu.

COLBY COMMUNITY COLLEGE, COLBY

General Information State and locally supported, 2-year, coed college. Small town setting. *Awards:* A. *Entrance level for U.S. students:* Noncompetitive. *Enrollment:* 1,690 total (63% women) including international students from 5 foreign countries. *Undergraduate faculty:* 60. *Library holdings:* 32,000 books, 350 current serial subscriptions. *Total majors:* 58.

Information for International Students For fall 2006: 49 international students applied, 45 were accepted, 42 enrolled. Students can start in fall, spring, or summer. *Admission tests:* Required: TOEFL (minimum score: iBT 61; paper-based 475; computer-based 153; minimum score for ESL admission: paper-based 475; computer-based 153). Recommended: ELS. TOEFL can be waived under certain conditions. *Application deadline:* 7/15. *Expenses:* (2006–07) $3260; room and board, $3542 (on campus). *Housing:* Guaranteed, also available during summer. *Services:* International student adviser on campus. *Contact:* Admissions Counselor, Colby Community College, 1255 South Range Avenue, Colby, KS 67701. Telephone: 785-462-4690 Ext. 5498. Fax: 785-460-4691. E-mail: doug.johnson@colbycc.edu. URL: http://www.colbycc.edu.

COWLEY COUNTY COMMUNITY COLLEGE AND AREA VOCATIONAL–TECHNICAL SCHOOL, ARKANSAS CITY

General Information State and locally supported, 2-year, coed college. Small town setting. *Awards:* A. *Entrance level for U.S. students:* Noncompetitive. *Enrollment:* 4,679 total (59% women) including 1% international students from 12 foreign countries. *Undergraduate faculty:* 216. *Library holdings:* 26,000 books, 100 current serial subscriptions. *Total majors:* 42. *Expenses:* (2006–07) $3570; room and board, $3530 (on campus). *Financial aid:* Forms required: International Student's Certification of Finances.

EMPORIA STATE UNIVERSITY, EMPORIA

General Information State-supported, coed institution. Small town setting. *Awards:* B, M, D. *Entrance level for U.S. students:* Noncompetitive. *Enrollment:* 6,473 total; 4,458 undergraduates (61% women) including 6% international students from 30 foreign countries. *Faculty:* 284. *Library holdings:* 2.4 million books, 15,645 current serial subscriptions, 8,551 audiovisual materials. *Total majors:* 33.

Information for International Students For fall 2006: 210 international students applied, 185 were accepted, 130 enrolled. Students can start in fall, spring, or summer. Transfers accepted from institutions abroad. *Admission tests:* Required: TOEFL (minimum score: paper-based 525; computer-based 197; minimum score for ESL admission: paper-based 425; computer-based 113). Recommended: ACT. TOEFL can be waived under certain conditions. *Application deadline:* Rolling. *Expenses:* (2006–07) $10,938; room and board, $5170 (on campus); room only, $2552 (on campus). *Financial aid:* Need-based college/university scholarships/grants from institutional funds. Non-need-based college/university scholarships/grants from institutional funds. Forms required: institution's own financial aid form. International transfer students are eligible to apply for aid. For fall 2005, 17 international students on campus received college administered financial aid ($280 average). *Housing:* Guaranteed, also available during summer. *Services:* International student adviser on campus. Full-time and part-time ESL programs on campus. ESL program available during the academic year and the summer. Internships and employment opportunities (on-campus and off-campus) available. *Contact:* Administrative Specialist, Office of International Student Affairs, Emporia State University, 1200 Commercial, ESU Box 4041, Emporia, KS 66801-5087. Telephone: 620-341-5374. Fax: 620-341-5918. E-mail: oisa@emporia.edu. URL: http://www.emporia.edu.

See In-Depth Description on page 80.

FORT HAYS STATE UNIVERSITY, HAYS

General Information State-supported, coed institution. Small town setting. *Awards:* A, B, M. *Entrance level for U.S. students:* Noncompetitive. *Enrollment:* 7,403 total; 5,920 undergraduates (54% women) including 16% international students from 15 foreign countries. *Faculty:* 291. *Library holdings:* 624,637 books, 1,689 current serial subscriptions. *Total majors:* 55. *Expenses:* (2006–07) $10,032; room and board, $5553 (on campus); room only, $2823 (on campus). *Financial aid:* Need-based college/university scholarships/grants from institutional funds, tuition waivers, athletic awards, loans from outside sources, on-campus employment. Non-need-based college/university scholarships/grants from institutional funds, tuition waivers, athletic awards, loans from institutional funds, loans from outside sources, on-campus employment. international students on campus received college administered aid averaging $3543.

GARDEN CITY COMMUNITY COLLEGE, GARDEN CITY
General Information County supported, 2-year, coed college. Rural setting. *Awards:* A. *Entrance level for U.S. students:* Noncompetitive. *Enrollment:* 2,122 total (52% women) including 0.4% international students from 5 foreign countries. *Undergraduate faculty:* 171. *Library holdings:* 44,985 books, 93 current serial subscriptions, 415 audiovisual materials. *Total majors:* 64.
Information for International Students For fall 2006: 9 international students applied, 8 were accepted, 3 enrolled. Students can start in fall or spring. Transfers accepted from institutions abroad. *Admission tests:* Required: TOEFL (minimum score: iBT 61; paper-based 500; computer-based 173; minimum score for ESL admission: iBT 61; paper-based 500; computer-based 173). *Application deadline:* 7/1. *Expenses:* (2007–08) $2752; room and board, $4500 (on campus). *Financial aid:* Forms required: institutional scholarship application form. *Services:* International student adviser on campus. Employment opportunities (on-campus) available. *Contact:* Director of Admissions, Garden City Community College, 801 Campus Drive, Garden City, KS 67846. Telephone: 620-276-9531. Fax: 620-276-9650. E-mail: nikki.geier@gcccks.edu. URL: http://www.gcccks.edu.

HESSTON COLLEGE, HESSTON
General Information Independent Mennonite, 2-year, coed college. Small town setting. *Awards:* A. *Entrance level for U.S. students:* Noncompetitive. *Enrollment:* 462 total (55% women) including 9% international students from 14 foreign countries. *Undergraduate faculty:* 44. *Library holdings:* 35,000 books, 234 current serial subscriptions, 2,670 audiovisual materials. *Total majors:* 8.
Information for International Students For fall 2006: 200 international students applied, 50 were accepted, 23 enrolled. Students can start in fall or spring. Transfers accepted from institutions abroad. *Admission tests:* Required: TOEFL (minimum score: iBT 41; paper-based 440; computer-based 123; minimum score for ESL admission: iBT 41; paper-based 440; computer-based 123). TOEFL can be waived under certain conditions. *Application deadline:* Rolling. *Expenses:* (2007–08) $17,420; room and board, $6180 (on campus). *Financial aid:* Need-based college/university scholarships/grants from institutional funds, tuition waivers, athletic awards, loans from institutional funds, loans from outside sources, on-campus employment. Non-need-based college/university scholarships/grants from institutional funds, tuition waivers, athletic awards, loans from institutional funds, loans from outside sources, on-campus employment. International transfer students are eligible to apply for aid. *Housing:* Guaranteed. *Services:* International student adviser on campus. Full-time ESL program on campus. ESL program available during the academic year. Employment opportunities (on-campus) available. *Contact:* Director of International Student Admissions, Hesston College, PO Box 3000, Hesston, KS 67062. Telephone: 620-327-8133. Fax: 620-327-8246. E-mail: daveo@hesston.edu. URL: http://www.hesston.edu.

HUTCHINSON COMMUNITY COLLEGE AND AREA VOCATIONAL SCHOOL, HUTCHINSON
General Information State and locally supported, 2-year, coed college. Small town setting. *Awards:* A. *Entrance level for U.S. students:* Noncompetitive. *Enrollment:* 4,790 total (57% women) including 0.5% international students from 12 foreign countries. *Undergraduate faculty:* 332. *Library holdings:* 42,500 books, 245 current serial subscriptions, 3,150 audiovisual materials. *Total majors:* 40. *Expenses:* (2007–08) $3296; room and board, $4680 (on campus). *Financial aid:* Forms required: International Student's Certification of Finances.

INDEPENDENCE COMMUNITY COLLEGE, INDEPENDENCE
General Information State-supported, 2-year, coed college. Small town setting. *Awards:* A. *Entrance level for U.S. students:* Noncompetitive. *Enrollment:* 906 total (54% women) including 1% international students from 17 foreign countries. *Undergraduate faculty:* 94. *Library holdings:* 32,408 books, 166 current serial

subscriptions. *Total majors:* 40. *Expenses:* (2006–07) $2880; room and board, $4100 (on campus). *Financial aid:* Non-need financial aid available.

JOHNSON COUNTY COMMUNITY COLLEGE, OVERLAND PARK
General Information State and locally supported, 2-year, coed college. Suburban setting. *Awards:* A. *Entrance level for U.S. students:* Noncompetitive. *Enrollment:* 18,612 total (55% women) including 1% international students from 36 foreign countries. *Undergraduate faculty:* 837. *Library holdings:* 89,400 books, 708 current serial subscriptions, 4,770 audiovisual materials. *Total majors:* 36.
Information for International Students For fall 2006: 250 international students applied, 204 were accepted, 190 enrolled. Students can start in fall, winter, spring, or summer. Transfers accepted from institutions abroad. *Admission tests:* Required: TOEFL (minimum score: iBT 61; paper-based 500; computer-based 173; minimum score for ESL admission: paper-based 500; computer-based 173). TOEFL can be waived under certain conditions. *Application deadline:* 7/2. *Services:* International student adviser on campus. Full-time and part-time ESL programs on campus. ESL program available during the academic year and the summer. Internships and employment opportunities (on-campus and off-campus) available. *Contact:* Director of International Student Services/PDSO, Johnson County Community College, 12345 College Boulevard, Overland Park, KS 66210-1299. Telephone: 913-469-7680. Fax: 913-469-4474. E-mail: jjpitts@jccc.net. URL: http://www.johnco.cc.ks.us.

KANSAS CITY KANSAS COMMUNITY COLLEGE, KANSAS CITY
General Information State and locally supported, 2-year, coed college. Urban setting. *Awards:* A. *Entrance level for U.S. students:* Noncompetitive. *Enrollment:* 5,547 total (66% women) including 2% international students from 27 foreign countries. *Undergraduate faculty:* 407. *Library holdings:* 65,000 books, 200 current serial subscriptions, 7,000 audiovisual materials. *Total majors:* 22. *Expenses:* (2006–07) $4710.

KANSAS STATE UNIVERSITY, MANHATTAN
General Information State-supported, coed university. Suburban setting. *Awards:* A, B, M, D, FP. *Entrance level for U.S. students:* Noncompetitive. *Enrollment:* 23,141 total; 18,761 undergraduates (49% women) including 2% international students from 100 foreign countries. *Faculty:* 1,047. *Library holdings:* 1.6 million books, 1,365 current serial subscriptions. *Total majors:* 78.
Information for International Students For fall 2006: 1024 international students enrolled. Students can start in fall, winter, spring, or summer. Transfers accepted from institutions abroad. *Admission tests:* Required: TOEFL (minimum score: iBT 80; paper-based 550; computer-based 213). TOEFL can be waived under certain conditions. *Application deadline:* 6/1. *Expenses:* (2006–07) $14,520; room and board, $5912 (on campus). *Financial aid:* Forms required: institution's own financial aid form. *Housing:* Guaranteed, also available during summer. *Services:* International student adviser on campus. Full-time and part-time ESL programs on campus. ESL program available during the academic year and the summer. Internships and employment opportunities (on-campus) available. *Contact:* International Admissions Coordinator, Kansas State University, 304 Fairchild Hall, Manhattan, KS 66506. Telephone: 785-532-7277. Fax: 785-532-6550. E-mail: intlpreadmit@ksu.edu. URL: http://www.ksu.edu.

KANSAS WESLEYAN UNIVERSITY, SALINA
General Information Independent United Methodist, coed institution. Urban setting. *Awards:* A, B, M. *Entrance level for U.S. students:* Moderately difficult. *Enrollment:* 805 total; 768 undergraduates (59% women) including 0.4% international students from 4 foreign countries. *Faculty:* 59. *Library holdings:* 370 current serial subscriptions, 1,055 audiovisual materials. *Total majors:* 39.
Information for International Students For fall 2006: 20 international students applied, 15 were accepted, 12 enrolled. Students can start in fall or spring. Transfers accepted from institutions abroad. *Admission tests:* Required: SAT or ACT, TOEFL (minimum score: paper-based 500; computer-based 173; minimum score for ESL admission: paper-based 500; computer-based 173). Recommended: SAT Subject Tests. *Application deadline:* 6/1. *Expenses:* (2006–07) $16,600; room and board, $5800 (on campus); room only, $2400 (on campus). *Housing:* Guaranteed, also available during summer. *Services:* International student adviser on campus. Internships available. *Contact:* Director of Admissions, Kansas Wesleyan University, 100 East Claflin, Salina, KS 67401. Telephone: 785-827-5541 Ext. 1283. Fax: 785-827-0927. E-mail: jallen@kwu.edu. URL: http://www.kwu.edu.

MANHATTAN CHRISTIAN COLLEGE, MANHATTAN

General Information Independent, 4-year, coed college, affiliated with Christian Churches and Churches of Christ. Small town setting. *Awards:* A, B. *Entrance level for U.S. students:* Minimally difficult. *Enrollment:* 331 total (52% women) including 0.3% international students from 1 foreign country. *Undergraduate faculty:* 32. *Library holdings:* 3,300 books, 3,000 current serial subscriptions, 2,200 audiovisual materials. *Total majors:* 9. *Financial aid:* Need-based college/university scholarships/grants from institutional funds. Non-need-based college/university scholarships/grants from institutional funds.

MIDAMERICA NAZARENE UNIVERSITY, OLATHE

General Information Independent, coed institution, affiliated with Church of the Nazarene. Suburban setting. *Awards:* A, B, M. *Entrance level for U.S. students:* Minimally difficult. *Enrollment:* 1,779 total; 1,357 undergraduates (53% women) including 1% international students from 11 foreign countries. *Faculty:* 173. *Library holdings:* 132,991 books, 1,250 current serial subscriptions, 11,427 audiovisual materials. *Total majors:* 40.
Information for International Students For fall 2006: 7 international students enrolled. Students can start in fall, winter, spring, or summer. Transfers accepted from institutions abroad. *Admission tests:* Required: TOEFL (minimum score: paper-based 550; computer-based 214). *Application deadline:* Rolling. *Expenses:* (2006–07) $15,968; room and board, $5830 (on campus). *Financial aid:* Non-need-based college/university scholarships/grants from institutional funds, athletic awards, on-campus employment. For fall 2005, 19 international students on campus received college administered financial aid ($8897 average). *Services:* International student adviser on campus. Internships and employment opportunities (on-campus) available. *Contact:* International Student Advisor, MidAmerica Nazarene University, 2030 East College Way, Olathe, KS 66062. Telephone: 913-971-3765. Fax: 913-791-3481. E-mail: rorton@mnu.edu. URL: http://www.mnu.edu.

NEWMAN UNIVERSITY, WICHITA

General Information Independent Roman Catholic, coed institution. Urban setting. *Awards:* A, B, M. *Entrance level for U.S. students:* Minimally difficult. *Enrollment:* 2,104 total; 1,631 undergraduates (62% women) including 7% international students from 20 foreign countries. *Faculty:* 85. *Library holdings:* 108,735 books, 267 current serial subscriptions, 1,872 audiovisual materials. *Total majors:* 36. *Expenses:* (2006–07) $17,308; room and board, $5372 (on campus). *Financial aid:* Need-based and non-need-based financial aid available. Forms required: bank statement. For fall 2005, 173 international students on campus received college administered financial aid ($6658 average).

OTTAWA UNIVERSITY, OTTAWA

General Information Independent American Baptist Churches in the USA, coed institution. Small town setting. *Awards:* B (also offers master's, adult, international and on-line education programs with significant enrollment not reflected in profile). *Entrance level for U.S. students:* Moderately difficult. *Enrollment:* 382 total (47% women) including 2% international students from 6 foreign countries. *Undergraduate faculty:* 25. *Library holdings:* 75,401 books, 808 current serial subscriptions, 15 audiovisual materials. *Total majors:* 19.
Information for International Students For fall 2006: 23 international students applied, 10 were accepted, 2 enrolled. Students can start in fall, spring, or summer. Transfers accepted from institutions abroad. *Admission tests:* Required: TOEFL (minimum score: iBT 79; paper-based 550; computer-based 213). Recommended: ELS. TOEFL can be waived under certain conditions. *Application deadline:* Rolling. *Expenses:* (2007–08) $17,350; room and board, $5930 (on campus); room only, $2630 (on campus). *Financial aid:* Non-need financial aid available. Forms required: institution's own financial aid form. *Housing:* Guaranteed, also available during summer. *Services:* International student adviser on campus. Internships and employment opportunities (on-campus) available. *Contact:* Admissions Counselor and International Liaison, Ottawa University, 1001 South Cedar, #17, Ottawa, KS 66067-3399. Telephone: 785-242-5200 Ext. 5556. Fax: 785-229-1008. E-mail: elizabeth.mundhenke@ottawa.edu. URL: http://www.ottawa.edu.

PITTSBURG STATE UNIVERSITY, PITTSBURG

General Information State-supported, coed institution. Small town setting. *Awards:* B, M (associate, specialist in education). *Entrance level for U.S. students:* Noncompetitive. *Enrollment:* 6,859 total; 5,747 undergraduates (48% women) including 3% international students from 25 foreign countries. *Faculty:* 391. *Library holdings:* 705,267 books, 9,436 current serial subscriptions, 3,710 audiovisual materials. *Total majors:* 66.

Information for International Students Students can start in fall, winter, spring, or summer. Transfers accepted from institutions abroad. *Admission tests:* Required: TOEFL (minimum score: iBT 68; paper-based 520; computer-based 190), IELTS. TOEFL can be waived under certain conditions. *Application deadline:* 6/1. *Expenses:* (2006–07) $11,120; room and board, $4844 (on campus). *Housing:* Guaranteed, also available during summer. *Services:* International student adviser on campus. Full-time and part-time ESL programs on campus. ESL program available during the academic year and the summer. Internships and employment opportunities (on-campus) available. *Contact:* Director of International Affairs, Pittsburg State University, 1701 South Broadway, Pittsburg, KS 66762. Telephone: 620-235-4680. Fax: 620-235-4962. E-mail: colcese@pittstate.edu. URL: http://www.pittstate.edu.

PRATT COMMUNITY COLLEGE, PRATT

General Information State and locally supported, 2-year, coed college. Rural setting. *Awards:* A. *Entrance level for U.S. students:* Noncompetitive. *Enrollment:* 1,546 total (52% women) including 2% international students. *Undergraduate faculty:* 120. *Library holdings:* 33,000 books, 250 current serial subscriptions, 1,200 audiovisual materials. *Total majors:* 63. *Expenses:* (2006–07) $2272; room and board, $3768 (on campus). *Financial aid:* Need-based and non-need-based financial aid available. Forms required: institution's own financial aid form.

SOUTHWESTERN COLLEGE, WINFIELD

General Information Independent United Methodist, coed institution. Small town setting. *Awards:* B, M. *Entrance level for U.S. students:* Moderately difficult. *Enrollment:* 1,557 total; 1,373 undergraduates (49% women) including 1% international students from 8 foreign countries. *Faculty:* 180. *Library holdings:* 50,720 books, 19,999 current serial subscriptions, 5,456 audiovisual materials. *Total majors:* 37.
Information for International Students For fall 2006: 13 international students applied, 7 were accepted, 5 enrolled. Students can start in fall or spring. Transfers accepted from institutions abroad. *Admission tests:* Required: TOEFL (minimum score: paper-based 550; computer-based 213; minimum score for ESL admission: paper-based 550; computer-based 213). TOEFL can be waived under certain conditions. *Application deadline:* 7/1. *Expenses:* (2006–07) $16,900; room and board, $5438 (on campus); room only, $2428 (on campus). *Financial aid:* Need-based college/university scholarships/grants from institutional funds, athletic awards, loans from outside sources, on-campus employment. Non-need-based college/university scholarships/grants from institutional funds, athletic awards, loans from outside sources, on-campus employment. Forms required: institution's own financial aid form, International Student's Certification of Finances. International transfer students are eligible to apply for aid. 16 international students on campus received college administered financial aid ($9905 average). *Housing:* Guaranteed, also available during summer. *Services:* International student adviser on campus. ESL program at cooperating institution. ESL program available during the academic year and the summer. Internships and employment opportunities (on-campus) available. *Contact:* Director of Admission, Southwestern College, 100 College Street, Winfield, KS 67156. Telephone: 620-229-6236. Fax: 620-229-6344. E-mail: scadmit@sckans.edu. URL: http://www.sckans.edu.

TABOR COLLEGE, HILLSBORO

General Information Independent Mennonite Brethren, coed institution. Small town setting. *Awards:* A, B, M. *Entrance level for U.S. students:* Moderately difficult. *Enrollment:* 603 total; 599 undergraduates (47% women) including 1% international students from 6 foreign countries. *Faculty:* 57. *Library holdings:* 80,099 books, 265 current serial subscriptions, 1,109 audiovisual materials. *Total majors:* 53.
Information for International Students For fall 2006: 4 international students enrolled. Students can start in fall, winter, or spring. Transfers accepted from institutions abroad. *Admission tests:* Required: TOEFL (minimum score: paper-based 525; computer-based 195). Recommended: SAT or ACT. TOEFL can be waived under certain conditions. *Application deadline:* 6/15. *Expenses:* (2006–07) $16,734; room and board, $5900 (on campus); room only, $2300 (on campus). *Financial aid:* Need-based college/university scholarships/grants from institutional funds, athletic awards, on-campus employment. Non-need-based college/university scholarships/grants from institutional funds, athletic awards, on-campus employment. Forms required: International Student's Certification of Finances, admissions application. International transfer students are eligible to apply for aid. For fall 2005, 6 international students on campus received college administered financial aid ($11,738 average). *Housing:* Guaranteed. *Services:* International student adviser on campus.

ESL program at cooperating institution. ESL program available during the academic year. Internships and employment opportunities (on-campus) available. *Contact:* Admissions Counselor, Tabor College, 400 South Jefferson, Hillsboro, KS 67063-1799. Telephone: 620-947-3121 Ext. 1728. Fax: 620-947-6276. E-mail: ryank@tabor.edu. URL: http://www.tabor.edu.

UNIVERSITY OF KANSAS, LAWRENCE
General Information State-supported, coed university. Suburban setting. *Awards:* B, M, D, FP (University of Kansas is a single institution with academic programs and facilities at two primary locations: Lawrence and Kansas City.). *Entrance level for U.S. students:* Moderately difficult. *Enrollment:* 28,924 total; 21,353 undergraduates (50% women) including 3% international students from 111 foreign countries. *Faculty:* 1,283. *Library holdings:* 4.9 million books, 50,992 current serial subscriptions, 57,471 audiovisual materials. *Total majors:* 103.
Information for International Students For fall 2006: 567 international students applied, 382 were accepted, 176 enrolled. Students can start in fall, spring, or summer. Transfers accepted from institutions abroad. *Admission tests:* Recommended: SAT or ACT, TOEFL, IELTS if no TOEFL, on-site English test required before enrollment. TOEFL can be waived under certain conditions. *Application deadline:* 4/1. *Expenses:* (2006–07) $15,123; room and board, $5747 (on campus); room only, $2997 (on campus). *Financial aid:* Need-based college/university scholarships/grants from institutional funds. Non-need-based college/university scholarships/grants from institutional funds, loans from institutional funds. Forms required: institution's own financial aid form, International Student's Certification of Finances. International transfer students are eligible to apply for aid. For fall 2005, 80 international students on campus received college administered financial aid ($1463 average). *Housing:* Available during summer. *Services:* International student adviser on campus. Full-time and part-time ESL programs on campus. ESL program available during the academic year and the summer. Internships and employment opportunities (on-campus) available. *Contact:* Associate Director, International Student Services, Office of International Student Services, University of Kansas, 1450 Jayhawk Boulevard, Room 17, Strong Hall, ISSS, International Undergraduate Admissions, Lawrence, KS 66045-7535. Telephone: 785-864-2616. Fax: 785-864-3404. E-mail: issapps@ku.edu. URL: http://www.ku.edu.
See In-Depth Description on page 215.

UNIVERSITY OF SAINT MARY, LEAVENWORTH
General Information Independent Roman Catholic, coed institution. Small town setting. *Awards:* A, B, M. *Entrance level for U.S. students:* Moderately difficult. *Enrollment:* 837 total; 548 undergraduates (58% women) including 0.4% international students from 4 foreign countries. *Faculty:* 89. *Library holdings:* 118,195 books, 205 current serial subscriptions. *Total majors:* 28. *Expenses:* (2006–07) $16,410; room and board, $6100 (on campus); room only, $2600 (on campus).

WICHITA AREA TECHNICAL COLLEGE, WICHITA
General Information District-supported, 2-year, coed college. Urban setting. *Awards:* A. *Entrance level for U.S. students:* Minimally difficult. *Enrollment:* 693 total (50% women) including 0.2% international students. *Undergraduate faculty:* 58. *Library holdings:* 3,696 books, 57 current serial subscriptions, 1,611 audiovisual materials. *Total majors:* 4. *Expenses:* (2006–07) $11,946.

WICHITA STATE UNIVERSITY, WICHITA
General Information State-supported, coed university. Urban setting. *Awards:* A, B, M, D. *Entrance level for U.S. students:* Noncompetitive. *Enrollment:* 14,298 total; 11,203 undergraduates (56% women) including 5% international students from 91 foreign countries. *Faculty:* 524. *Library holdings:* 1.7 million books, 3,697 current serial subscriptions, 21,829 audiovisual materials. *Total majors:* 56.
Information for International Students For fall 2006: 2000 international students applied, 1000 were accepted, 500 enrolled. Students can start in fall, spring, or summer. Transfers accepted from institutions abroad. *Admission tests:* Required: TOEFL (minimum score: iBT 71; paper-based 530; computer-based 197). TOEFL can be waived under certain conditions. *Application deadline:* 7/1. *Expenses:* (2006–07) $11,828; room and board, $5276 (on campus). *Financial aid:* Non-need financial aid available. Forms required: scholarship application form. For fall 2005, international students on campus received college administered aid averaging $828. *Housing:* Guaranteed, also available during summer. *Services:* International student adviser on campus. Full-time and part-time ESL programs on campus. ESL program available during the academic year and the summer. Internships and employment opportunities (on-campus and off-campus) available. *Contact:*

Associate Director, Office of International Education, Wichita State University, Office of International Education, Wichita, KS 67260-0122. Telephone: 316-978-3232. Fax: 316-978-3777. E-mail: international@wichita.edu. URL: http://www.wichita.edu.
See In-Depth Description on page 248.

KENTUCKY

ALICE LLOYD COLLEGE, PIPPA PASSES
General Information Independent, 4-year, coed college. Rural setting. *Awards:* B. *Entrance level for U.S. students:* Moderately difficult. *Enrollment:* 613 total (52% women) including 0.2% international students from 1 foreign country. *Undergraduate faculty:* 41. *Library holdings:* 171,464 books, 112 current serial subscriptions, 4,061 audiovisual materials. *Total majors:* 14. *Expenses:* (2006–07) room and board, $3900 (on campus); room only, $1800 (on campus). *Financial aid:* Need-based on-campus employment. Non-need-based on-campus employment. Forms required: International Student's Certification of Finances.

ASBURY COLLEGE, WILMORE
General Information Independent nondenominational, coed institution. Small town setting. *Awards:* B, M. *Entrance level for U.S. students:* Moderately difficult. *Enrollment:* 1,220 total; 1,155 undergraduates (58% women) including 1% international students from 9 foreign countries. *Faculty:* 144. *Library holdings:* 146,708 books, 511 current serial subscriptions, 9,280 audiovisual materials. *Total majors:* 37. *Expenses:* (2007–08) $21,286; room and board, $5152 (on campus); room only, $3024 (on campus). *Financial aid:* Need-based college/university scholarships/grants from institutional funds, tuition waivers, loans from outside sources, on-campus employment. Non-need-based college/university scholarships/grants from institutional funds, tuition waivers, athletic awards, loans from outside sources, on-campus employment. Forms required: institution's own financial aid form, International Student's Certification of Finances. For fall 2006 (estimated), 5 international students on campus received college administered financial aid ($1970 average).

BELLARMINE UNIVERSITY, LOUISVILLE
General Information Independent Roman Catholic, coed institution. Suburban setting. *Awards:* B, M, D. *Entrance level for U.S. students:* Moderately difficult. *Enrollment:* 2,627 total; 2,006 undergraduates (66% women) including 2% international students from 24 foreign countries. *Faculty:* 300. *Library holdings:* 118,707 books, 19,687 current serial subscriptions, 3,172 audiovisual materials. *Total majors:* 54. *Expenses:* (2006–07) $24,150; room and board, $6880 (on campus); room only, $3860 (on campus). *Financial aid:* Need-based college/university scholarships/grants from institutional funds, athletic awards, on-campus employment. Non-need-based college/university scholarships/grants from institutional funds, athletic awards, on-campus employment. Forms required: International Student's Certification of Finances. For fall 2006 (estimated), 41 international students on campus received college administered financial aid ($19,385 average).

BEREA COLLEGE, BEREA
General Information Independent, 4-year, coed college. Small town setting. *Awards:* B. *Entrance level for U.S. students:* Very difficult. *Enrollment:* 1,576 total (60% women) including 8% international students from 64 foreign countries. *Undergraduate faculty:* 173. *Library holdings:* 366,926 books, 1,067 current serial subscriptions, 11,299 audiovisual materials. *Total majors:* 52.
Information for International Students For fall 2006: 700 international students applied, 30 were accepted, 30 enrolled. Students can start in fall. Transfers accepted from institutions abroad. *Admission tests:* Required: TOEFL (minimum score: iBT 61; paper-based 500; computer-based 172). TOEFL can be waived under certain conditions. *Application deadline:* 2/1. *Expenses:* (2006–07) room and board, $5230 (on campus). *Financial aid:* Need-based college/university scholarships/grants from institutional funds, loans from institutional funds, loans from outside sources, on-campus employment. Forms required: institution's own financial aid form. International transfer students are eligible to apply for aid. For fall 2006 (estimated), 110 international students on campus received college administered financial aid ($29,432 average). *Housing:* Guaranteed, also available during summer. *Services:* International student adviser on campus. Internships and employment opportunities (on-campus) available. *Contact:* Director of Admissions, Berea College, CPO Box 2220, Berea, KY 40404. Telephone: 859-985-3500. Fax: 859-985-3512. E-mail: admissions@berea.edu. URL: http://www.berea.edu.

BRESCIA UNIVERSITY, OWENSBORO

General Information Independent Roman Catholic, coed institution. Urban setting. *Awards:* A, B, M. *Entrance level for U.S. students:* Moderately difficult. *Enrollment:* 709 total; 669 undergraduates (57% women) including 13% international students. *Faculty:* 75. *Library holdings:* 2,466 current serial subscriptions, 6,717 audiovisual materials. *Total majors:* 33.

Information for International Students For fall 2006: 28 international students applied, 7 were accepted, 6 enrolled. Students can start in fall, spring, or summer. Transfers accepted from institutions abroad. *Admission tests:* Required: TOEFL (minimum score: iBT 79; paper-based 550; computer-based 213). Recommended: SAT or ACT. TOEFL can be waived under certain conditions. *Application deadline:* Rolling. *Expenses:* (2006–07) $13,620; room and board, $5800 (on campus). *Financial aid:* Non-need financial aid available. Forms required: institution's own financial aid form. *Housing:* Guaranteed. *Services:* International student adviser on campus. Full-time ESL program on campus. ESL program available during the academic year and the summer. *Contact:* Dean of Enrollment, Brescia University, 717 Frederica Street, Owensboro, KY 42301. Telephone: 270-686-4316. Fax: 270-686-4314. E-mail: chris.houk@brescia.edu. URL: http://www.brescia.edu.

CAMPBELLSVILLE UNIVERSITY, CAMPBELLSVILLE

General Information Independent, coed institution, affiliated with Kentucky Baptist Convention. Small town setting. *Awards:* A, B, M. *Entrance level for U.S. students:* Moderately difficult. *Enrollment:* 2,376 total; 1,988 undergraduates (58% women) including 5% international students from 29 foreign countries. *Faculty:* 223. *Library holdings:* 172,000 books, 12,777 current serial subscriptions. *Total majors:* 54. *Expenses:* (2007–08) $17,260; room and board, $6230 (on campus). *Financial aid:* Need-based college/university scholarships/grants from institutional funds, tuition waivers, athletic awards, on-campus employment. Non-need-based college/university scholarships/grants from institutional funds, tuition waivers, athletic awards, on-campus employment. Forms required: institution's own financial aid form. For fall 2005, 59 international students on campus received college administered financial aid ($10,640 average).

CENTRE COLLEGE, DANVILLE

General Information Independent, 4-year, coed college, affiliated with Presbyterian Church (U.S.A.). Small town setting. *Awards:* B. *Entrance level for U.S. students:* Very difficult. *Enrollment:* 1,147 total (53% women) including 2% international students from 16 foreign countries. *Undergraduate faculty:* 133. *Library holdings:* 217,751 books, 750 current serial subscriptions. *Total majors:* 28.

Information for International Students For fall 2006: 113 international students applied, 10 were accepted, 2 enrolled. Students can start in fall. Transfers accepted from institutions abroad. *Admission tests:* Required: TOEFL (minimum score: iBT 92; paper-based 580; computer-based 237). Recommended: SAT or ACT, SAT Subject Tests, ELS. *Application deadline:* 2/1. *Expenses:* (2006–07) $33,000. *Financial aid:* Need-based college/university scholarships/grants from institutional funds, on-campus employment. Non-need-based college/university scholarships/grants from institutional funds. Forms required: International Student's Financial Aid Application, International Student's Certification of Finances. International transfer students are eligible to apply for aid. For fall 2006 (estimated), 22 international students on campus received college administered financial aid ($22,760 average). *Housing:* Guaranteed, also available during summer. *Services:* International student adviser on campus. Internships and employment opportunities (on-campus) available. *Contact:* Associate Director of Admission, Centre College, 600 West Walnut Street, Danville, KY 40422. Telephone: 859-238-5350. Fax: 859-238-5373. E-mail: johnstns@centre.edu. URL: http://www.centre.edu.

EASTERN KENTUCKY UNIVERSITY, RICHMOND

General Information State-supported, coed institution. Small town setting. *Awards:* A, B, M. *Entrance level for U.S. students:* Noncompetitive. *Enrollment:* 15,763 total; 13,623 undergraduates (60% women) including 1% international students from 37 foreign countries. *Faculty:* 948. *Library holdings:* 799,496 books, 2,901 current serial subscriptions, 14,021 audiovisual materials. *Total majors:* 135. *Expenses:* (2006–07) $14,538; room and board, $5392 (on campus); room only, $2792 (on campus). *Financial aid:* Non-need-based college/university scholarships/grants from institutional funds, tuition waivers, athletic awards, loans from institutional funds, loans from outside sources, on-campus employment. Forms required: institution's own financial aid form. For fall 2006 (estimated), 73 international students on campus received college administered financial aid ($1571 average).

GEORGETOWN COLLEGE, GEORGETOWN

General Information Independent, coed institution, affiliated with Baptist Church. Suburban setting. *Awards:* B, M. *Entrance level for U.S. students:* Moderately difficult. *Enrollment:* 1,910 total; 1,407 undergraduates (57% women) including 1% international students from 11 foreign countries. *Faculty:* 160. *Library holdings:* 167,547 books, 526 current serial subscriptions, 6,047 audiovisual materials. *Total majors:* 32.

Information for International Students For fall 2006: 22 international students applied, 22 were accepted, 5 enrolled. Students can start in fall or spring. Transfers accepted from institutions abroad. *Admission tests:* Required: TOEFL (minimum score: iBT 68; paper-based 520; computer-based 190; minimum score for ESL admission: paper-based 520; computer-based 190). Recommended: SAT or ACT. *Application deadline:* 6/15. *Expenses:* (2007–08) $22,360; room and board, $6380 (on campus); room only, $3080 (on campus). *Financial aid:* Need-based college/university scholarships/grants from institutional funds, athletic awards, on-campus employment. Non-need-based college/university scholarships/grants from institutional funds, athletic awards, on-campus employment. Forms required: institution's own financial aid form, International Student's Certification of Finances. International transfer students are eligible to apply for aid. *Services:* International student adviser on campus. Internships and employment opportunities (on-campus and off-campus) available. *Contact:* Director of Admissions, Office of Admissions, Georgetown College, 400 East College Street, Georgetown, KY 40324-1696. Telephone: 502-863-8181. Fax: 502-868-7733. E-mail: admissions@georgetowncollege.edu. URL: http://www.georgetowncollege.edu.

HOPKINSVILLE COMMUNITY COLLEGE, HOPKINSVILLE

General Information State-supported, 2-year, coed college. Small town setting. *Awards:* A. *Entrance level for U.S. students:* Noncompetitive. *Enrollment:* 3,353 total (67% women) including international students from 2 foreign countries. *Undergraduate faculty:* 156. *Total majors:* 17.

Information for International Students For fall 2006: 1 international student applied, 1 was accepted, 1 enrolled. Students can start in fall, winter, or summer. Transfers accepted from institutions abroad. *Admission tests:* Required: TOEFL (minimum score: paper-based 500; computer-based 61). *Application deadline:* Rolling. *Expenses:* (2007–08) $4140. *Services:* International student adviser on campus. Employment opportunities (on-campus) available. *Contact:* Registrar, Hopkinsville Community College, PO Box 2100, Hopkinsville, KY 42241. Telephone: 270-707-3811 Ext. 6195. Fax: 270-886-0237. E-mail: ruthann.rettie@kctcs.edu. URL: http://www.hopcc.kctcs.edu.

JEFFERSON COMMUNITY AND TECHNICAL COLLEGE, LOUISVILLE

General Information State-supported, 2-year, coed college. Urban setting. *Awards:* A. *Entrance level for U.S. students:* Noncompetitive. *Enrollment:* 14,710 total (52% women) including 0.5% international students. *Undergraduate faculty:* 652. *Library holdings:* 76,578 books, 391 current serial subscriptions. *Total majors:* 18. *Expenses:* (2007–08) $10,425. *Financial aid:* Need-based college/university scholarships/grants from institutional funds. Non-need-based college/university scholarships/grants from institutional funds.

KENTUCKY CHRISTIAN UNIVERSITY, GRAYSON

General Information Independent, coed institution, affiliated with Christian Churches and Churches of Christ. Rural setting. *Awards:* A, B, M. *Entrance level for U.S. students:* Moderately difficult. *Enrollment:* 556 total; 538 undergraduates (57% women) including 2% international students from 6 foreign countries. *Faculty:* 47. *Library holdings:* 103,323 books, 395 current serial subscriptions. *Total majors:* 13. *Expenses:* (2006–07) $12,630; room and board, $4624 (on campus).

KENTUCKY WESLEYAN COLLEGE, OWENSBORO

General Information Independent Methodist, 4-year, coed college. Suburban setting. *Awards:* B. *Entrance level for U.S. students:* Moderately difficult. *Enrollment:* 968 total (45% women) including 1% international students from 5 foreign countries. *Undergraduate faculty:* 102. *Library holdings:* 108,266 books, 144 current serial subscriptions, 1,850 audiovisual materials. *Total majors:* 41.

Information for International Students For fall 2006: 29 international students applied, 6 were accepted, 4 enrolled. Students can start in fall or spring. Transfers accepted from institutions abroad. *Admission tests:* Required: TOEFL (minimum score: paper-based 500; computer-based 173; minimum score for ESL admission: paper-based 500; computer-based 173).

Recommended: SAT or ACT. TOEFL can be waived under certain conditions. *Application deadline:* Rolling. *Expenses:* (2006–07) $13,600; room and board, $5750 (on campus); room only, $2600 (on campus). *Financial aid:* Need-based college/university scholarships/grants from institutional funds, athletic awards. Non-need-based college/university scholarships/grants from institutional funds, athletic awards. Forms required: institution's own financial aid form. International transfer students are eligible to apply for aid. *Housing:* Guaranteed, also available during summer. *Services:* International student adviser on campus. *Contact:* Dean of Admission and Financial Aid, Kentucky Wesleyan College, 3000 Frederica Street, Administration Building, Owensboro, KY 42301. Telephone: 270-852-3120. Fax: 270-852-3133. E-mail: cbacon@kec.edu. URL: http://www.kwc.edu.

LINDSEY WILSON COLLEGE, COLUMBIA

General Information Independent United Methodist, coed institution. Rural setting. *Awards:* A, B, M. *Entrance level for U.S. students:* Minimally difficult. *Enrollment:* 1,832 total; 1,620 undergraduates (66% women) including 4% international students from 33 foreign countries. *Faculty:* 120. *Library holdings:* 80,000 books, 1,500 current serial subscriptions. *Total majors:* 36. *Expenses:* (2007–08) $15,806; room and board, $6540 (on campus). *Financial aid:* Need-based college/university scholarships/grants from institutional funds, athletic awards. Non-need-based college/university scholarships/grants from institutional funds, athletic awards.

MOREHEAD STATE UNIVERSITY, MOREHEAD

General Information State-supported, coed institution. Small town setting. *Awards:* A, B, M. *Entrance level for U.S. students:* Minimally difficult. *Enrollment:* 9,025 total; 7,512 undergraduates (62% women) including 0.3% international students from 17 foreign countries. *Faculty:* 528. *Library holdings:* 523,767 books, 26,817 current serial subscriptions, 21,458 audiovisual materials. *Total majors:* 49.

Information for International Students For fall 2006: 25 international students applied, 12 were accepted, 10 enrolled. Students can start in fall, spring, or summer. Transfers accepted from institutions abroad. *Admission tests:* Required: SAT or ACT, TOEFL (minimum score: paper-based 500; computer-based 173; minimum score for ESL admission: paper-based 500; computer-based 173). Recommended: ACT. TOEFL can be waived under certain conditions. *Application deadline:* Rolling. *Expenses:* (2006–07) $12,950; room and board, $5208 (on campus). *Financial aid:* Non-need-based college/university scholarships/grants from institutional funds. Forms required: Institution's application for admission for international students. For fall 2006 (estimated), 4 international students on campus received college administered financial aid ($5000 average). *Housing:* Guaranteed, also available during summer. *Services:* International student adviser on campus. Internships and employment opportunities (on-campus) available. *Contact:* International Admissions Specialist, Morehead State University, Office of Enrollment Services, Morehead State University, Morehead, KY 40351. Telephone: 606-783-2000. Fax: 606-783-5038. URL: http://www.moreheadstate.edu.

MURRAY STATE UNIVERSITY, MURRAY

General Information State-supported, coed institution. Small town setting. *Awards:* B, M. *Entrance level for U.S. students:* Moderately difficult. *Enrollment:* 10,298 total; 8,601 undergraduates (58% women) including 1% international students from 56 foreign countries. *Faculty:* 590. *Library holdings:* 518,450 books, 1,381 current serial subscriptions, 10,885 audiovisual materials. *Total majors:* 112. *Expenses:* (2007–08) $7496; room and board, $5670 (on campus); room only, $3036 (on campus). *Financial aid:* Need-based college/university scholarships/grants from institutional funds, tuition waivers, athletic awards, on-campus employment. Non-need-based college/university scholarships/grants from institutional funds, tuition waivers, athletic awards, loans from institutional funds, on-campus employment. Forms required: institution's own financial aid form, International Student's Certification of Finances, institutional scholarship application form. For fall 2006 (estimated), 267 international students on campus received college administered financial aid ($3490 average).

NORTHERN KENTUCKY UNIVERSITY, HIGHLAND HEIGHTS

General Information State-supported, coed institution. Suburban setting. *Awards:* A, B, M, FP. *Entrance level for U.S. students:* Noncompetitive. *Enrollment:* 14,617 total; 12,647 undergraduates (58% women) including 1% international students from 53 foreign countries. *Faculty:* 1,089. *Library holdings:* 667,064 books, 1,731 current serial subscriptions, 4,406 audiovisual materials. *Total majors:* 74.

Information for International Students Students can start in fall or spring. Transfers accepted from institutions abroad. *Admission tests:* Required: TOEFL (minimum score: iBT 61; paper-based 500; computer-based 173; minimum score for ESL admission: iBT 61; paper-based 500; computer-based 173). Recommended: SAT, ACT. TOEFL can be waived under certain conditions. *Application deadline:* 6/1. *Expenses:* (2006–07) $10,200; room and board, $5690 (on campus); room only, $3450 (on campus). *Financial aid:* Need-based college/university scholarships/grants from institutional funds, athletic awards, on-campus employment. Non-need-based college/university scholarships/grants from institutional funds, athletic awards, on-campus employment. International transfer students are eligible to apply for aid. *Housing:* Guaranteed, also available during summer. *Services:* International student adviser on campus. Internships and employment opportunities (on-campus and off-campus) available. *Contact:* International Student Affairs, International Student Affairs Office, Northern Kentucky University, University Center 366, Highland Heights, KY 41099. Telephone: 859-572-6517. Fax: 859-572-6178. E-mail: isa@nku.edu. URL: http://www.nku.edu.
See In-Depth Description on page 142.

PIKEVILLE COLLEGE, PIKEVILLE

General Information Independent, coed institution, affiliated with Presbyterian Church (U.S.A.). Small town setting. *Awards:* A, B, FP. *Entrance level for U.S. students:* Noncompetitive. *Enrollment:* 1,098 total; 795 undergraduates (53% women) including 1% international students from 4 foreign countries. *Faculty:* 69. *Library holdings:* 72,673 books, 219 current serial subscriptions. *Total majors:* 25. *Expenses:* (2006–07) $12,750; room and board, $5000 (on campus). *Financial aid:* Need-based college/university scholarships/grants from institutional funds, athletic awards, on-campus employment. Forms required: institution's own financial aid form, International Student's Financial Aid Application, International Student's Certification of Finances. 4 international students on campus received college administered financial aid ($15,948 average).

SOUTHEAST KENTUCKY COMMUNITY AND TECHNICAL COLLEGE, CUMBERLAND

General Information State-supported, 2-year, coed college. Small town setting. *Awards:* A. *Entrance level for U.S. students:* Noncompetitive. *Enrollment:* 4,578 total including 0.04% international students. *Undergraduate faculty:* 175. *Library holdings:* 25,921 books, 200 current serial subscriptions. *Total majors:* 14. *Expenses:* (2007–08) $8424. *Financial aid:* Forms required: CSS PROFILE.

SPALDING UNIVERSITY, LOUISVILLE

General Information Independent, coed institution, affiliated with Roman Catholic Church. Urban setting. *Awards:* A, B, M, D. *Entrance level for U.S. students:* Moderately difficult. *Enrollment:* 1,641 total; 900 undergraduates (80% women) including 2% international students from 27 foreign countries. *Faculty:* 174. *Library holdings:* 160,954 books, 655 current serial subscriptions, 30,140 audiovisual materials. *Total majors:* 23. *Expenses:* (2006–07) $15,900; room and board, $3672 (on campus); room only, $2100 (on campus). *Financial aid:* Non-need financial aid available. Forms required: institution's own financial aid form.

SULLIVAN UNIVERSITY, LOUISVILLE

General Information Proprietary, coed institution. Suburban setting. *Awards:* A, B, M. *Entrance level for U.S. students:* Minimally difficult. *Enrollment:* 4,505 total; 4,324 undergraduates (53% women) including 0.1% international students from 11 foreign countries. *Faculty:* 269. *Library holdings:* 22,500 books, 16,500 current serial subscriptions. *Total majors:* 13.

Information for International Students For fall 2006: 96 international students applied, 80 were accepted, 80 enrolled. Students can start in fall, winter, spring, or summer. Transfers accepted from institutions abroad. *Admission tests:* Required: TOEFL (minimum score: paper-based 500; computer-based 197). *Application deadline:* Rolling. *Expenses:* (2006–07) $14,265; room only, $4320 (on campus). *Financial aid:* Need-based financial aid available. Forms required: institution's own financial aid form. 2 international students on campus received college administered financial aid ($4000 average). Employment opportunities (off-campus) available. *Contact:* Director of Admissions, Sullivan University, 3101 Bardstown Road, Louisville, KY 40205. Telephone: 502-456-6505. Fax: 502-456-0040. URL: http://www.sullivan.edu.
See In-Depth Description on page 199.

THOMAS MORE COLLEGE, CRESTVIEW HILLS

General Information Independent Roman Catholic, coed institution. Suburban setting. *Awards:* A, B, M. *Entrance level for*

Thomas More College (continued)

U.S. students: Moderately difficult. *Enrollment:* 1,400 total; 1,325 undergraduates (53% women) including 0.2% international students from 5 foreign countries. *Faculty:* 129. *Library holdings:* 115,345 books, 498 current serial subscriptions, 2,292 audiovisual materials. *Total majors:* 42.

Information for International Students For fall 2006: 19 international students applied, 8 were accepted, 7 enrolled. Students can start in fall, spring, or summer. Transfers accepted from institutions abroad. *Admission tests:* Required: TOEFL (minimum score: iBT 66; paper-based 515; computer-based 187; minimum score for ESL admission: iBT 66; paper-based 515; computer-based 187). *Application deadline:* 8/15. *Expenses:* (2007–08) $21,220; room and board, $6250 (on campus); room only, $2900 (on campus). *Financial aid:* Need-based college/university scholarships/grants from institutional funds, on-campus employment. Non-need-based college/university scholarships/grants from institutional funds, on-campus employment. Forms required: institution's own financial aid form, the Brown Global Perspectives Endowment Fund application form. For fall 2005, 8 international students on campus received college administered financial aid ($19,176 average). *Housing:* Guaranteed, also available during summer. *Services:* International student adviser on campus. Employment opportunities (on-campus) available. *Contact:* Admissions Counselor for International Students, Thomas More College, 333 Thomas More Parkway, Crestview Hills, KY 41017-3495. Telephone: 859-344-3307. Fax: 859-344-3444. E-mail: jennifer.mason@thomasmore.edu. URL: http://www.thomasmore.edu.

UNION COLLEGE, BARBOURVILLE

General Information Independent United Methodist, coed institution. Small town setting. *Awards:* B, M. *Entrance level for U.S. students:* Moderately difficult. *Enrollment:* 1,389 total; 653 undergraduates (44% women) including 4% international students from 15 foreign countries. *Faculty:* 85. *Library holdings:* 209,013 books, 15,717 current serial subscriptions. *Total majors:* 21. *Expenses:* (2006–07) $15,650; room and board, $5000 (on campus); room only, $2000 (on campus). *Financial aid:* Need-based college/university scholarships/grants from institutional funds, tuition waivers, athletic awards. Non-need-based college/university scholarships/grants from institutional funds, tuition waivers, athletic awards. Forms required: International Student's Financial Aid Application, International Student's Certification of Finances. For fall 2006 (estimated), 20 international students on campus received college administered financial aid ($10,315 average).

UNIVERSITY OF KENTUCKY, LEXINGTON

General Information State-supported, coed university. Urban setting. *Awards:* B, M, D, FP. *Entrance level for U.S. students:* Moderately difficult. *Enrollment:* 26,382 total; 19,292 undergraduates (51% women) including 1% international students from 91 foreign countries. *Faculty:* 1,724. *Library holdings:* 3.1 million books, 29,633 current serial subscriptions, 86,690 audiovisual materials. *Total majors:* 80. *Expenses:* (2007–08) $14,896; room and board, $7970 (on campus); room only, $3785 (on campus). *Financial aid:* Non-need-based college/university scholarships/grants from institutional funds, tuition waivers, athletic awards, loans from institutional funds, loans from outside sources, on-campus employment. For fall 2005, 90 international students on campus received college administered financial aid ($9676 average).

UNIVERSITY OF LOUISVILLE, LOUISVILLE

General Information State-supported, coed university. Urban setting. *Awards:* A, B, M, D, FP. *Entrance level for U.S. students:* Moderately difficult. *Enrollment:* 20,804 total; 14,995 undergraduates (53% women) including 2% international students from 62 foreign countries. *Faculty:* 1,335. *Library holdings:* 2.1 million books, 37,931 current serial subscriptions, 32,093 audiovisual materials. *Total majors:* 50. *Expenses:* (2006–07) $16,072; room and board, $5096 (on campus); room only, $3396 (on campus).

UNIVERSITY OF THE CUMBERLANDS, WILLIAMSBURG

General Information Independent Kentucky Baptist, coed institution. Rural setting. *Awards:* A, B, M. *Entrance level for U.S. students:* Moderately difficult. *Enrollment:* 1,884 total; 1,525 undergraduates (53% women) including 2% international students from 23 foreign countries. *Faculty:* 126. *Library holdings:* 198,188 books, 24,787 current serial subscriptions, 2,526 audiovisual materials. *Total majors:* 34. *Expenses:* (2007–08) $13,658; room and board, $6626 (on campus). *Financial aid:* Need-based college/university scholarships/grants from institutional funds, athletic awards, on-campus employment. Non-need-based

college/university scholarships/grants from institutional funds, athletic awards, on-campus employment. For fall 2006 (estimated), 35 international students on campus received college administered financial aid ($12,642 average).

WESTERN KENTUCKY UNIVERSITY, BOWLING GREEN

General Information State-supported, coed institution. Suburban setting. *Awards:* A, B, M. *Entrance level for U.S. students:* Moderately difficult. *Enrollment:* 18,660 total; 16,063 undergraduates (58% women) including 2% international students from 45 foreign countries. *Faculty:* 1,109. *Library holdings:* 1.2 million books, 4,080 current serial subscriptions, 23,068 audiovisual materials. *Total majors:* 85.

Information for International Students For fall 2006: 558 international students applied, 558 were accepted, 558 enrolled. Students can start in fall, winter, spring, or summer. Transfers accepted from institutions abroad. *Admission tests:* Required: TOEFL (minimum score: paper-based 525; computer-based 197). TOEFL can be waived under certain conditions. *Application deadline:* 4/1. *Expenses:* (2006–07) $14,400; room and board, $5348 (on campus); room only, $2940 (on campus). *Financial aid:* Non-need-based college/university scholarships/grants from institutional funds, athletic awards, loans from outside sources, on-campus employment. 54 international students on campus received college administered financial aid ($6542 average). *Housing:* Guaranteed, also available during summer. *Services:* International student adviser on campus. Full-time and part-time ESL programs on campus. ESL program available during the academic year and the summer. Internships and employment opportunities (on-campus) available. *Contact:* Coordinator of International Admissions, Office of Admissions, Western Kentucky University, 1 Big Red Way, 1906 College Heights Boulevard, Bowling Green, KY 42101-3576. Telephone: 270-745-2551. Fax: 270-745-6133. E-mail: raza.tiwana@wku.edu. URL: http://www.wku.edu.

LOUISIANA

CENTENARY COLLEGE OF LOUISIANA, SHREVEPORT

General Information Independent United Methodist, coed institution. Suburban setting. *Awards:* B, M. *Entrance level for U.S. students:* Moderately difficult. *Enrollment:* 1,044 total; 904 undergraduates (62% women) including 2% international students from 14 foreign countries. *Faculty:* 122. *Library holdings:* 186,564 books, 59,899 current serial subscriptions, 5,945 audiovisual materials. *Total majors:* 66. *Expenses:* (2006–07) $18,900; room and board, $6780 (on campus); room only, $3310 (on campus). *Financial aid:* Non-need-based college/university scholarships/grants from institutional funds, athletic awards. Forms required: institution's own financial aid form, International Student's Certification of Finances. 17 international students on campus received college administered financial aid ($18,020 average).

DELGADO COMMUNITY COLLEGE, NEW ORLEANS

General Information State-supported, 2-year, coed college. Urban setting. *Awards:* A. *Entrance level for U.S. students:* Noncompetitive. *Enrollment:* 16,501 total (70% women) including international students from 3 foreign countries. *Undergraduate faculty:* 833. *Library holdings:* 110,000 books, 1,299 current serial subscriptions. *Total majors:* 44. *Expenses:* (2006–07) $4824.

GRAMBLING STATE UNIVERSITY, GRAMBLING

General Information State-supported, coed university. Small town setting. *Awards:* A, B, M, D. *Entrance level for U.S. students:* Noncompetitive. *Enrollment:* 5,065 total; 4,584 undergraduates (57% women) including 4% international students from 22 foreign countries. *Faculty:* 284. *Library holdings:* 275,048 books, 1,600 current serial subscriptions, 5,760 audiovisual materials. *Total majors:* 51.

Information for International Students For fall 2006: 300 international students applied, 168 were accepted, 168 enrolled. Students can start in fall, spring, or summer. Transfers accepted from institutions abroad. *Admission tests:* Required: SAT or ACT, TOEFL (minimum score: paper-based 500; computer-based 173). TOEFL can be waived under certain conditions. *Application deadline:* 6/1. *Expenses:* (2006–07) $8956; room and board, $4718 (on campus); room only, $2476 (on campus). *Financial aid:* Non-need-based college/university scholarships/grants from institutional funds, tuition waivers, athletic awards, on-campus employment. Forms required: scholarship application form. International transfer students are eligible to apply for aid. For fall 2005, 115 international students on campus received college administered financial aid ($5250 average). *Housing:* Guaranteed.

Services: International student adviser on campus. ESL program at cooperating institution. ESL program available during the academic year. Internships and employment opportunities (on-campus) available. *Contact:* Executive Associate Vice President for International Affairs and Programs, Grambling State University, 100 Founder Street, Grambling Hall, Suite 222, Grambling, LA 71245-0864. Telephone: 318-274-7798. Fax: 318-274-3256. URL: http://www.gram.edu.

LOUISIANA STATE UNIVERSITY AND AGRICULTURAL AND MECHANICAL COLLEGE, BATON ROUGE

General Information State-supported, coed university. Urban setting. *Awards:* B, M, D, FP. *Entrance level for U.S. students:* Moderately difficult. *Enrollment:* 29,925 total; 24,583 undergraduates (52% women) including 2% international students from 85 foreign countries. *Faculty:* 1,422. *Library holdings:* 1.4 million books, 58,918 current serial subscriptions. *Total majors:* 69. *Expenses:* (2006–07) $12,749; room and board, $6498 (on campus); room only, $3930 (on campus). *Financial aid:* Non-need-based tuition waivers, athletic awards, loans from outside sources, on-campus employment. Forms required: institution's own financial aid form. For fall 2005, 325 international students on campus received college administered financial aid ($6067 average).

LOUISIANA STATE UNIVERSITY AT ALEXANDRIA, ALEXANDRIA

General Information State-supported, primarily 2-year, coed college. Rural setting. *Awards:* A, B. *Entrance level for U.S. students:* Noncompetitive. *Enrollment:* 2,988 total (74% women) including 0.5% international students from 6 foreign countries. *Undergraduate faculty:* 180. *Library holdings:* 154,935 books, 354 current serial subscriptions, 5,949 audiovisual materials. *Total majors:* 20.

Information for International Students For fall 2006: 4 international students applied, 4 were accepted, 4 enrolled. Students can start in fall, spring, or summer. Transfers accepted from institutions abroad. *Admission tests:* Required: ACT, TOEFL (minimum score: iBT 61; paper-based 500; computer-based 173). *Application deadline:* 5/1. *Expenses:* (2006–07) $5570. *Financial aid:* Forms required: institution's own financial aid form, FAFSA. *Housing:* Available during summer. *Services:* International student adviser on campus. Internships and employment opportunities (on-campus) available. *Contact:* Admissions Counselor, Louisiana State University at Alexandria, 8100 Highway 71 South, Alexandria, LA 71302-9121. Telephone: 318-473-6508. Fax: 318-473-6418. E-mail: skieffer@lsua.edu. URL: http://www.lsua.edu.

LOUISIANA STATE UNIVERSITY IN SHREVEPORT, SHREVEPORT

General Information State-supported, coed institution. Urban setting. *Awards:* B, M. *Entrance level for U.S. students:* Noncompetitive. *Enrollment:* 4,023 total; 3,620 undergraduates (64% women) including 1% international students from 6 foreign countries. *Faculty:* 227. *Library holdings:* 279,821 books, 1,190 current serial subscriptions. *Total majors:* 40. *Expenses:* (2006–07) $7921.

LOYOLA UNIVERSITY NEW ORLEANS, NEW ORLEANS

General Information Independent Roman Catholic (Jesuit), coed institution. Urban setting. *Awards:* B, M, FP. *Entrance level for U.S. students:* Moderately difficult. *Enrollment:* 4,604 total; 2,991 undergraduates (59% women) including 2% international students from 38 foreign countries. *Faculty:* 396. *Library holdings:* 409,782 books, 37,520 current serial subscriptions, 14,057 audiovisual materials. *Total majors:* 49. *Expenses:* (2007–08) $26,508; room and board, $9150 (on campus); room only, $5488 (on campus). *Financial aid:* Non-need financial aid available. Forms required: International Student's Certification of Finances. For fall 2006 (estimated), 44 international students on campus received college administered financial aid ($10,115 average).

MCNEESE STATE UNIVERSITY, LAKE CHARLES

General Information State-supported, coed institution. Suburban setting. *Awards:* A, B, M. *Entrance level for U.S. students:* Moderately difficult. *Enrollment:* 8,343 total; 7,336 undergraduates (60% women) including 2% international students from 44 foreign countries. *Faculty:* 392. *Library holdings:* 332,521 books, 22,177 current serial subscriptions. *Total majors:* 69.

Information for International Students For fall 2006: 122 international students applied, 79 were accepted, 68 enrolled. Students can start in fall, spring, or summer. Transfers accepted from institutions abroad. *Admission tests:* Required: ACT, TOEFL (minimum score: iBT 61; paper-based 500; computer-based 173). Recommended: ELS, IELTS. TOEFL can be waived under certain conditions. *Application deadline:* 4/15. *Expenses:* (2006–07) $9327;

room and board, $4450 (on campus). *Financial aid:* Need-based and non-need-based financial aid available. Forms required: institution's own financial aid form, CSS PROFILE. *Housing:* Available during summer. *Services:* International student adviser on campus. Full-time and part-time ESL programs on campus. ESL program available during the academic year and the summer. Internships and employment opportunities (on-campus and off-campus) available. *Contact:* International Student Affairs Officer, McNeese State University, PO Box 92495, Office of the Registrar, Lake Charles, LA 70609. Telephone: 337-475-5243. Fax: 337-475-5151. E-mail: pgirard@mcneese.edu. URL: http://www.mcneese.edu.

See In-Depth Description on page 125.

NICHOLLS STATE UNIVERSITY, THIBODAUX

General Information State-supported, coed institution. Small town setting. *Awards:* A, B, M. *Entrance level for U.S. students:* Noncompetitive. *Enrollment:* 6,805 total; 6,130 undergraduates (62% women) including 1% international students from 32 foreign countries. *Faculty:* 283. *Total majors:* 52. *Expenses:* (2006–07) $8919; room and board, $4038 (on campus). *Financial aid:* Need-based on-campus employment. Non-need-based college/university scholarships/grants from institutional funds, loans from outside sources, on-campus employment. Forms required: institution's own financial aid form. For fall 2005, 21 international students on campus received college administered financial aid ($4926 average).

NORTHWESTERN STATE UNIVERSITY OF LOUISIANA, NATCHITOCHES

General Information State-supported, coed institution. Small town setting. *Awards:* A, B, M. *Entrance level for U.S. students:* Moderately difficult. *Enrollment:* 9,431 total; 8,248 undergraduates (68% women) including 0.4% international students from 26 foreign countries. *Faculty:* 607. *Library holdings:* 861,048 books, 1,403 current serial subscriptions, 1,456 audiovisual materials. *Total majors:* 52.

Information for International Students For fall 2006: 20 international students applied, 12 were accepted, 11 enrolled. Students can start in fall, spring, or summer. Transfers accepted from institutions abroad. *Admission tests:* Required: SAT or ACT, TOEFL (minimum score: iBT 61; paper-based 500; computer-based 173). Recommended: SAT, ACT, ELS. TOEFL can be waived under certain conditions. *Application deadline:* 6/1. *Expenses:* (2006–07) $9631; room and board, $4686 (on campus); room only, $2816 (on campus). *Financial aid:* Non-need-based college/university scholarships/grants from institutional funds, loans from outside sources, on-campus employment. Forms required: institution's own financial aid form. For fall 2005, 16 international students on campus received college administered financial aid ($5862 average). *Housing:* Available during summer. *Services:* International student adviser on campus. Internships and employment opportunities (on-campus) available. *Contact:* Director of Admissions, Northwestern State University of Louisiana, 200 Central Avenue, Roy Hall, Suite 209, Natchitoches, LA 71497. Telephone: 318-357-4078. Fax: 318-357-4660. E-mail: andrea@nsula.edu. URL: http://www.nsula.edu.

SOUTHEASTERN LOUISIANA UNIVERSITY, HAMMOND

General Information State-supported, coed institution. Small town setting. *Awards:* A, B, M. *Entrance level for U.S. students:* Moderately difficult. *Enrollment:* 15,118 total; 13,552 undergraduates (62% women) including 1% international students from 56 foreign countries. *Faculty:* 683. *Library holdings:* 623,746 books, 2,707 current serial subscriptions, 9,905 audiovisual materials. *Total majors:* 48. *Expenses:* (2006–07) $8751; room and board, $5750 (on campus); room only, $3600 (on campus). *Financial aid:* Non-need-based college/university scholarships/grants from institutional funds, tuition waivers, athletic awards, loans from institutional funds, loans from outside sources, on-campus employment. Forms required: International Student's Certification of Finances.

SOUTHERN UNIVERSITY AND AGRICULTURAL AND MECHANICAL COLLEGE, BATON ROUGE

General Information State-supported, coed institution. Suburban setting. *Awards:* A, B, M, D. *Entrance level for U.S. students:* Moderately difficult. *Enrollment:* 8,619 total; 7,331 undergraduates (62% women) including 2% international students from 29 foreign countries. *Faculty:* 546. *Library holdings:* 835,325 books, 2,921 current serial subscriptions, 22,938 audiovisual materials. *Total majors:* 66. *Expenses:* (2007–08) $9458; room and board, $5030 (on campus).

TULANE UNIVERSITY, NEW ORLEANS

General Information Independent, coed university. Urban setting. *Awards:* A, B, M, D, FP. *Entrance level for U.S. students:* Very

Tulane University (continued)

difficult. *Enrollment:* 10,606 total; 6,533 undergraduates (52% women) including 2% international students from 42 foreign countries. *Faculty:* 1,319. *Library holdings:* 2.5 million books, 12,607 current serial subscriptions, 1,764 audiovisual materials. *Total majors:* 85. *Expenses:* (2006–07) $34,896; room and board, $8397 (on campus); room only, $4987 (on campus). *Financial aid:* Need-based college/university scholarships/grants from institutional funds, loans from outside sources. Non-need-based college/university scholarships/grants from institutional funds, loans from outside sources. Forms required: International Student's Financial Aid Application, International Student's Certification of Finances. For fall 2005, 50 international students on campus received college administered financial aid ($15,135 average).

UNIVERSITY OF LOUISIANA AT LAFAYETTE, LAFAYETTE

General Information State-supported, coed university. Urban setting. *Awards:* B, M, D. *Entrance level for U.S. students:* Moderately difficult. *Enrollment:* 16,302 total; 14,923 undergraduates (58% women) including 1% international students from 69 foreign countries. *Faculty:* 695. *Library holdings:* 999,913 books, 2,851 current serial subscriptions, 10,807 audiovisual materials. *Total majors:* 89. *Expenses:* (2006–07) $9592; room and board, $3770 (on campus).

UNIVERSITY OF LOUISIANA AT MONROE, MONROE

General Information State-supported, coed university. Urban setting. *Awards:* A, B, M, D, FP. *Entrance level for U.S. students:* Noncompetitive. *Enrollment:* 8,571 total; 7,284 undergraduates (64% women) including 1% international students from 40 foreign countries. *Faculty:* 429. *Library holdings:* 645,612 books, 935 audiovisual materials. *Total majors:* 57.

UNIVERSITY OF NEW ORLEANS, NEW ORLEANS

General Information State-supported, coed university. Urban setting. *Awards:* B, M, D. *Entrance level for U.S. students:* Moderately difficult. *Enrollment:* 11,747 total; 9,156 undergraduates (54% women) including 3% international students from 74 foreign countries. *Faculty:* 654. *Library holdings:* 896,000 books, 4,950 current serial subscriptions, 22,775 audiovisual materials. *Total majors:* 50.

Information for International Students Students can start in fall, spring, or summer. Transfers accepted from institutions abroad. *Admission tests:* Required: TOEFL (minimum score: iBT 71; paper-based 525; computer-based 195). Recommended: SAT or ACT. TOEFL can be waived under certain conditions. *Application deadline:* 6/1. *Expenses:* (2007–08) $10,854; room and board, $4734 (on campus). *Financial aid:* Need-based college/university scholarships/grants from institutional funds, loans from outside sources. Non-need-based college/university scholarships/grants from institutional funds, tuition waivers, athletic awards, loans from outside sources. International transfer students are eligible to apply for aid. For fall 2006 (estimated), 140 international students on campus received college administered financial aid ($6680 average). *Housing:* Available during summer. *Services:* International student adviser on campus. Full-time ESL program on campus. ESL program available during the academic year and the summer. Internships and employment opportunities (on-campus and off-campus) available. *Contact:* Assistant Director of International Admissions, University of New Orleans, 2000 Lakeshore Drive, Administration Building, Room 103, New Orleans, LA 70148-2135. Telephone: 504-280-5494. Fax: 504-280-5522. E-mail: admissions@uno.edu. URL: http://www.uno.edu.

See In-Depth Description on page 219.

UNIVERSITY OF PHOENIX–LOUISIANA CAMPUS, METAIRIE

General Information Proprietary, coed institution. Urban setting. *Awards:* B, M. *Entrance level for U.S. students:* Noncompetitive. *Enrollment:* 2,747 total; 2,085 undergraduates (71% women) including 20% international students. *Faculty:* 304. *Library holdings:* 444 books, 666 current serial subscriptions. *Total majors:* 31. *Expenses:* (2006–07) $9090.

XAVIER UNIVERSITY OF LOUISIANA, NEW ORLEANS

General Information Independent Roman Catholic, coed institution. Urban setting. *Awards:* B, M, FP. *Entrance level for U.S. students:* Moderately difficult. *Enrollment:* 3,012 total; 2,272 undergraduates (71% women) including 2% international students from 8 foreign countries. *Faculty:* 181. *Library holdings:* 251,757 books, 1,816 current serial subscriptions, 6,457 audiovisual materials. *Total majors:* 54. *Expenses:* (2006–07) $13,900; room and board, $7200 (on campus).

MAINE

BATES COLLEGE, LEWISTON

General Information Independent, 4-year, coed college. Small town setting. *Awards:* B. *Entrance level for U.S. students:* Most difficult. *Enrollment:* 1,744 total (52% women) including 5% international students from 78 foreign countries. *Undergraduate faculty:* 193. *Library holdings:* 588,211 books, 25,674 current serial subscriptions. *Total majors:* 36.

Information for International Students For fall 2006: 868 international students applied, 108 were accepted, 28 enrolled. Students can start in fall or winter. Transfers accepted from institutions abroad. *Admission tests:* Required: TOEFL (minimum score: iBT 100; paper-based 600; computer-based 250). *Application deadline:* 1/1. *Expenses:* (2006–07) $44,350. *Financial aid:* Need-based college/university scholarships/grants from institutional funds, loans from outside sources, on-campus employment. Forms required: institution's own financial aid form, Canadian applicants must file the CSS PROFILE. International transfer students are eligible to apply for aid. For fall 2005, 70 international students on campus received college administered financial aid ($36,536 average). *Housing:* Guaranteed, also available during summer. *Services:* International student adviser on campus. Internships and employment opportunities (on-campus) available. *Contact:* Associate Dean of International Admissions, Bates College, 23 Campus Avenue, Lewiston, ME 04240. Telephone: 207-786-6000. Fax: 207-786-6025. E-mail: admissions@bates.edu. URL: http://www.bates.edu.

BOWDOIN COLLEGE, BRUNSWICK

General Information Independent, 4-year, coed college. Small town setting. *Awards:* B. *Entrance level for U.S. students:* Most difficult. *Enrollment:* 1,734 total (51% women) including 3% international students from 31 foreign countries. *Undergraduate faculty:* 193. *Library holdings:* 1 million books, 9,121 current serial subscriptions, 25,315 audiovisual materials. *Total majors:* 43.

Information for International Students For fall 2006: 502 international students applied, 41 were accepted, 20 enrolled. Students can start in fall. Transfers accepted from institutions abroad. *Admission tests:* Required: TOEFL (minimum score: iBT 100; paper-based 600; computer-based 250). *Application deadline:* 1/1. *Expenses:* (2006–07) $34,640; room and board, $9310 (on campus); room only, $4300 (on campus). *Financial aid:* Need-based college/university scholarships/grants from institutional funds, tuition waivers, loans from institutional funds, loans from outside sources, on-campus employment, grants/scholarships from outside sources. Non-need-based on-campus employment. Forms required: institution's own financial aid form, CSS PROFILE, International Student's Financial Aid Application. For fall 2006 (estimated), 31 international students on campus received college administered financial aid ($35,354 average). *Housing:* Guaranteed, also available during summer. *Services:* International student adviser on campus. Internships and employment opportunities (on-campus) available. *Contact:* Assistant Dean of Admissions, Bowdoin College, 5000 College Station, Brunswick, ME 04011-8441. Telephone: 207-725-3190. Fax: 207-725-3101. E-mail: ekrivick@bowdoin.edu. URL: http://www.bowdoin.edu.

COLBY COLLEGE, WATERVILLE

General Information Independent, 4-year, coed college. Small town setting. *Awards:* B. *Entrance level for U.S. students:* Most difficult. *Enrollment:* 1,865 total (54% women) including 7% international students from 69 foreign countries. *Undergraduate faculty:* 226. *Library holdings:* 350,000 books, 1,850 current serial subscriptions. *Total majors:* 41.

Information for International Students For fall 2006: 862 international students applied, 124 were accepted, 54 enrolled. Students can start in fall or spring. *Admission tests:* Required: SAT or ACT, TOEFL (minimum score: paper-based 600; computer-based 250; minimum score for ESL admission: paper-based 550; computer-based 213), SAT may be substituted for TOEFL, students whose current language of instruction is English are not required to submit a TOEFL result. TOEFL can be waived under certain conditions. *Application deadline:* 1/1. *Expenses:* (2006–07) $44,080. *Financial aid:* Need-based college/university scholarships/grants from institutional funds, loans from institutional funds, on-campus employment. Forms required: CSS PROFILE. International transfer students are eligible to apply for aid. For fall 2006 (estimated), 130 international students on campus received college administered financial aid ($40,500 average). *Housing:* Guaranteed, also available during summer. *Services:* International student adviser on campus. Part-time ESL program on campus. ESL program available during the academic year. Internships and employment opportunities (on-campus) available. *Contact:* Dean of Admissions and Financial Aid, Colby College, 4800 Mayflower Hill, Waterville, ME

04901-8848. Telephone: 207-859-4800. Fax: 207-859-4828.
E-mail: admissions@colby.edu. URL: http://www.colby.edu.

COLLEGE OF THE ATLANTIC, BAR HARBOR

General Information Independent, coed institution. Small town setting. *Awards:* B, M. *Entrance level for U.S. students:* Very difficult. *Enrollment:* 339 total; 335 undergraduates (67% women) including 16% international students from 36 foreign countries. *Faculty:* 39. *Library holdings:* 50,000 books, 3,000 current serial subscriptions. *Total majors:* 37.

Information for International Students For fall 2006: 56 international students applied, 24 were accepted, 10 enrolled. Students can start in fall. Transfers accepted from institutions abroad. *Admission tests:* Required: TOEFL (minimum score: paper based 550; computer based 213). TOEFL can be waived under certain conditions. *Application deadline:* 2/15. *Expenses:* (2006–07) $28,140; room and board, $7710 (on campus); room only, $4800 (on campus). *Financial aid:* Need-based college/university scholarships/grants from institutional funds, on-campus employment. Forms required: International Student's Financial Aid Application, International Student's Certification of Finances. 58 international students on campus received college administered financial aid ($37,455 average). *Housing:* Guaranteed. *Services:* International student adviser on campus. Internships and employment opportunities (on-campus) available. *Contact:* Director of Admission, College of the Atlantic, 105 Eden Street, Bar Harbor, ME 04609-1198. Telephone: 207-288-5015. Fax: 207-288-4126. E-mail: sbaker@coa.edu. URL: http://www.coa.edu.

HUSSON COLLEGE, BANGOR

General Information Independent, coed institution. Suburban setting. *Awards:* A, B, M. *Entrance level for U.S. students:* Moderately difficult. *Enrollment:* 2,242 total; 1,984 undergraduates (59% women) including 1% international students from 15 foreign countries. *Faculty:* 58. *Library holdings:* 39,020 books, 40 current serial subscriptions, 146 audiovisual materials. *Total majors:* 28. *Expenses:* (2006–07) $11,770; room and board, $6240 (on campus). *Financial aid:* Non-need-based college/university scholarships/grants from institutional funds, on-campus employment. Forms required: International Student's Certification of Finances. For fall 2006 (estimated), 1,998 international students on campus received college administered financial aid ($10,115 average).

MAINE COLLEGE OF ART, PORTLAND

General Information Independent, coed institution. Urban setting. *Awards:* B, M. *Entrance level for U.S. students:* Moderately difficult. *Enrollment:* 409 total; 381 undergraduates (65% women) including 1% international students. *Faculty:* 70. *Library holdings:* 24,609 books, 100 current serial subscriptions. *Total majors:* 9.

Information for International Students For fall 2006: 8 international students applied, 5 were accepted. Students can start in fall or spring. Transfers accepted from institutions abroad. *Admission tests:* Required: TOEFL (minimum score: iBT 79; paper-based 550; computer-based 213). TOEFL can be waived under certain conditions. *Application deadline:* Rolling. *Expenses:* (2007–08) $26,060; room and board, $9270 (on campus). *Financial aid:* Need-based college/university scholarships/grants from institutional funds, on-campus employment. Non-need-based college/university scholarships/grants from institutional funds, on-campus employment. Forms required: institution's own financial aid form. 5 international students on campus received college administered financial aid ($8155 average). *Services:* ESL program at cooperating institution. ESL program available during the academic year and the summer. Internships and employment opportunities (on-campus) available. *Contact:* Director of Admissions, Maine College of Art, 97 Spring Street, Portland, ME 04101. Telephone: 207-775-5157 Ext. 254. Fax: 207-772-5069. E-mail: ktownsend@meca.edu. URL: http://www.meca.edu.

MAINE MARITIME ACADEMY, CASTINE

General Information State-supported, coed, primarily men's institution. Small town setting. *Awards:* A, B, M. *Entrance level for U.S. students:* Moderately difficult. *Enrollment:* 858 total; 836 undergraduates (16% women) including 0.5% international students from 8 foreign countries. *Faculty:* 90. *Library holdings:* 427,532 books, 347 current serial subscriptions, 2,161 audiovisual materials. *Total majors:* 11. *Expenses:* (2006–07) $14,505; room and board, $7050 (on campus); room only, $2540 (on campus). *Financial aid:* Need-based college/university scholarships/grants from institutional funds, loans from institutional funds, loans from outside sources, on-campus employment. Non-need-based college/university scholarships/grants from institutional funds, loans from institutional funds, loans from outside sources, on-campus employment. Forms required: income tax form(s), verification worksheet.

NORTHERN MAINE COMMUNITY COLLEGE, PRESQUE ISLE

General Information State-related, 2-year, coed college. Small town setting. *Awards:* A. *Entrance level for U.S. students:* Minimally difficult. *Enrollment:* 901 total (52% women) including 3% international students from 7 foreign countries. *Undergraduate faculty:* 81. *Library holdings:* 14,600 books, 125 current serial subscriptions, 200 audiovisual materials. *Total majors:* 20. *Expenses:* (2007–08) $4188; room and board, $4930 (on campus); room only, $1900 (on campus). *Financial aid:* Need-based college/university scholarships/grants from institutional funds. Non-need-based college/university scholarships/grants from institutional funds. Forms required: institutional scholarship application.

SAINT JOSEPH'S COLLEGE OF MAINE, STANDISH

General Information Independent, coed institution, affiliated with Roman Catholic Church. Small town setting. *Awards:* B, M (profile does not include enrollment in distance learning master's program). *Entrance level for U.S. students:* Moderately difficult. *Enrollment:* 1,050 total (65% women) including international students from 1 foreign country. *Faculty:* 126. *Library holdings:* 113,453 books, 15,646 current serial subscriptions, 1,043 audiovisual materials. *Total majors:* 40. *Expenses:* (2006–07) $21,760; room and board, $9030 (on campus). *Financial aid:* Non-need-based college/university scholarships/grants from institutional funds. Forms required: International Student's Certification of Finances. For fall 2006 (estimated), 1 international student on campus received college administered financial aid ($2000 average).

UNITY COLLEGE, UNITY

General Information Independent, 4-year, coed college. Rural setting. *Awards:* A, B. *Entrance level for U.S. students:* Moderately difficult. *Enrollment:* 562 total (33% women) including 1% international students from 2 foreign countries. *Undergraduate faculty:* 44. *Library holdings:* 46,000 books, 650 current serial subscriptions. *Total majors:* 14. *Expenses:* (2007–08) $19,630. *Financial aid:* Non-need-based college/university scholarships/grants from institutional funds, on-campus employment. For fall 2006 (estimated), 1 international student on campus received college administered financial aid ($7000 average).

UNIVERSITY OF MAINE, ORONO

General Information State-supported, coed university. Small town setting. *Awards:* B, M, D. *Entrance level for U.S. students:* Moderately difficult. *Enrollment:* 11,435 total; 9,179 undergraduates (52% women) including 2% international students from 65 foreign countries. *Faculty:* 823. *Library holdings:* 1.1 million books, 13,041 current serial subscriptions, 26,647 audiovisual materials. *Total majors:* 108. *Expenses:* (2006–07) $18,414; room and board, $7125 (on campus); room only, $3593 (on campus). *Financial aid:* Need-based tuition waivers, on-campus employment, graduate assistantships. Non-need-based tuition waivers, on-campus employment, graduate assistantships. For fall 2006 (estimated), 11 international students on campus received college administered financial aid ($15,057 average).

UNIVERSITY OF MAINE AT FARMINGTON, FARMINGTON

General Information State-supported, 4-year, coed college. Small town setting. *Awards:* B. *Entrance level for U.S. students:* Moderately difficult. *Enrollment:* 2,424 total (67% women) including 0.2% international students from 7 foreign countries. *Undergraduate faculty:* 171. *Library holdings:* 98,248 books, 577 current serial subscriptions, 7,663 audiovisual materials. *Total majors:* 40.

Information for International Students For fall 2006: 30 international students applied, 5 were accepted, 1 enrolled. Students can start in fall or spring. Transfers accepted from institutions abroad. *Admission tests:* Required: TOEFL (minimum score: iBT 99; paper-based 550; computer-based 213). TOEFL can be waived under certain conditions. *Application deadline:* 6/1. *Expenses:* (2006–07) $14,120; room and board, $6312 (on campus); room only, $3360 (on campus). *Financial aid:* Need-based tuition waivers, on-campus employment. Non-need-based tuition waivers, loans from outside sources, on-campus employment. Forms required: International Student's Financial Aid Application, International Student's Certification of Finances. International transfer students are eligible to apply for aid. For fall 2006 (estimated), 11 international students on campus received college administered financial aid ($6570 average). *Housing:* Guaranteed, also available during summer. *Services:* International student adviser on campus. Internships and employment opportunities (on-campus) available. *Contact:* Associate Director of Admissions, Admissions Office, University of Maine at Farmington, Admissions

University of Maine at Farmington (continued)
Office, 246 Main Street, Farmington, ME 04938.
Telephone: 207-778-7050. Fax: 207-778-8182.
E-mail: ellrich@maine.edu. URL: http://www.umf.maine.edu.

UNIVERSITY OF MAINE AT FORT KENT, FORT KENT

General Information State-supported, 4-year, coed college. Rural
setting. *Awards:* A, B. *Entrance level for U.S. students:* Moderately
difficult. *Enrollment:* 1,076 total including 27% international
students from 12 foreign countries. *Undergraduate faculty:* 72.
Library holdings: 69,189 books, 335 current serial subscriptions,
4,254 audiovisual materials. *Total majors:* 25.
Information for International Students For fall 2006: 43
international students applied, 13 were accepted, 10 enrolled.
Students can start in fall or spring. Transfers accepted from
institutions abroad. *Admission tests:* Required: TOEFL (minimum
score: iBT 61; paper-based 500; computer-based 173). TOEFL can
be waived under certain conditions. *Application deadline:* Rolling.
Financial aid: Need-based college/university scholarships/grants
from institutional funds, tuition waivers. Non-need-based
college/university scholarships/grants from institutional funds,
tuition waivers. For fall 2006 (estimated), 22 international students
on campus received college administered financial aid ($9600
average). *Housing:* Guaranteed, also available during summer.
Internships and employment opportunities (on-campus) available.
Contact: Acting Director of Admissions, University of Maine at Fort
Kent, 23 University Drive, Fort Kent, ME 04743.
Telephone: 207-834-7602. Fax: 207-834-7609.
E-mail: jillb@maine.edu. URL: http://www.umfk.maine.edu.

UNIVERSITY OF MAINE AT PRESQUE ISLE, PRESQUE ISLE

General Information State-supported, 4-year, coed college. Small
town setting. *Awards:* A, B. *Entrance level for U.S. students:*
Minimally difficult. *Enrollment:* 1,548 total (66% women) including
9% international students from 4 foreign countries. *Undergraduate
faculty:* 116. *Library holdings:* 455,372 books, 2,500 current serial
subscriptions, 1,281 audiovisual materials. *Total majors:* 28.
Information for International Students For fall 2006: 300
international students applied, 250 were accepted, 220 enrolled.
Students can start in fall, spring, or summer. Transfers accepted
from institutions abroad. *Admission tests:* Required: TOEFL
(minimum score: paper-based 550; computer-based 215). TOEFL
can be waived under certain conditions. *Application deadline:*
Rolling. *Expenses:* (2006–07) $12,280; room and board, $5658 (on
campus); room only, $3240 (on campus). *Financial aid:* Non-need
financial aid available. Forms required: institution's own financial
aid form. International transfer students are eligible to apply for
aid. For fall 2005, 16 international students on campus received
college administered financial aid ($7199 average). *Services:*
International student adviser on campus. *Contact:* Senior
Admissions Associate, University of Maine at Presque Isle, 181
Main Street, Presque Isle, ME 04769. Telephone: 207-768-9534.
Fax: 207-764-9608. E-mail: sullivam@polaris.umpi.maine.edu.
URL: http://www.umpi.maine.edu.

UNIVERSITY OF NEW ENGLAND, BIDDEFORD

General Information Independent, coed institution. Small town
setting. *Awards:* A, B, M, FP. *Entrance level for U.S. students:*
Moderately difficult. *Enrollment:* 3,379 total; 1,856 undergraduates
(74% women) including 0.3% international students from 3 foreign
countries. *Faculty:* 279. *Library holdings:* 144,632 books, 27,285
current serial subscriptions, 10,690 audiovisual materials.
Total majors: 38. *Expenses:* (2006–07) $23,790; room and board,
$9255 (on campus). *Financial aid:* Non-need-based
college/university scholarships/grants from institutional funds. For
fall 2006 (estimated), 1 international student on campus received
college administered financial aid ($3000 average).

UNIVERSITY OF SOUTHERN MAINE, PORTLAND

General Information State-supported, coed institution. Suburban
setting. *Awards:* A, B, M, D, FP. *Entrance level for U.S. students:*
Moderately difficult. *Enrollment:* 10,478 total; 8,287
undergraduates (59% women) including 0.1% international
students. *Faculty:* 704. *Library holdings:* 545,246 books, 2,585
current serial subscriptions, 2,705 audiovisual materials.
Total majors: 46.
Information for International Students For fall 2006: 43
international students applied, 9 were accepted, 6 enrolled.
Students can start in fall or spring. Transfers accepted from
institutions abroad. *Admission tests:* Required: TOEFL (minimum
score: iBT 79; paper-based 550; computer-based 213; minimum
score for ESL admission: iBT 54; paper-based 480; computer-based
157). Recommended: SAT or ACT. TOEFL can be waived under
certain conditions. *Application deadline:* 5/1. *Expenses:* (2006–07)

$15,566; room and board, $7444 (on campus); room only, $3834 (on
campus). *Financial aid:* Non-need financial aid available. 13
international students on campus received college administered
financial aid ($6958 average). *Housing:* Guaranteed, also available
during summer. *Services:* International student adviser on campus.
Full-time and part-time ESL programs on campus. ESL program
available during the academic year and the summer. Internships
and employment opportunities (on-campus) available. *Contact:*
Associate Director of Undergraduate Admission, University of
Southern Maine, 37 College Avenue, Gorham, ME 04038.
Telephone: 207-780-5670. Fax: 207-780-5640.
E-mail: usmadm@usm.maine.edu. URL: http://www.usm.maine.edu.

See In-Depth Description on page 226.

YORK COUNTY COMMUNITY COLLEGE, WELLS

General Information State-supported, 2-year, coed college. Small
town setting. *Awards:* A. *Entrance level for U.S. students:*
Noncompetitive. *Enrollment:* 949 total including international
students from 2 foreign countries. *Undergraduate faculty:* 71.
Library holdings: 4,000 books, 75 current serial subscriptions.
Total majors: 11. *Expenses:* (2006–07) $6000.

MARYLAND

ALLEGANY COLLEGE OF MARYLAND, CUMBERLAND

General Information State and locally supported, 2-year, coed
college. Small town setting. *Awards:* A. *Entrance level for U.S.
students:* Noncompetitive. *Enrollment:* 3,538 total (65% women).
Undergraduate faculty: 236. *Library holdings:* 86,636 books, 313
current serial subscriptions. *Total majors:* 26. *Expenses:* (2006–07)
$6404; room only, $4720 (on campus).

BALTIMORE INTERNATIONAL COLLEGE, BALTIMORE

General Information Independent, primarily 2-year, coed college.
Urban setting. *Awards:* A, B, M. *Entrance level for U.S. students:*
Minimally difficult. *Enrollment:* 516 total (53% women) including
1% international students from 5 foreign countries. *Faculty:* 32.
Library holdings: 13,000 books, 200 current serial subscriptions,
1,000 audiovisual materials. *Total majors:* 4. *Expenses:* (2006–07)
$15,599; room and board, $5729 (on campus); room only, $3418 (on
campus). *Financial aid:* Non-need financial aid available. Forms
required: institution's own financial aid form, International
Student's Certification of Finances.

BOWIE STATE UNIVERSITY, BOWIE

General Information State-supported, coed institution. Small
town setting. *Awards:* B, M, D. *Entrance level for U.S. students:*
Minimally difficult. *Enrollment:* 5,291 total; 4,074 undergraduates
(64% women) including 6% international students. *Faculty:* 359.
Library holdings: 331,640 books, 3,152 current serial subscriptions.
Total majors: 29. *Expenses:* (2006–07) $15,248; room and board,
$5992 (on campus); room only, $3632 (on campus).

CARROLL COMMUNITY COLLEGE, WESTMINSTER

General Information State and locally supported, 2-year, coed
college. Suburban setting. *Awards:* A. *Entrance level for U.S.
students:* Noncompetitive. *Enrollment:* 3,216 total (64% women)
including 0.3% international students from 8 foreign countries.
Undergraduate faculty: 208. *Library holdings:* 39,187 books, 318
current serial subscriptions. *Total majors:* 15. *Expenses:* (2007–08)
$6788.

CECIL COMMUNITY COLLEGE, NORTH EAST

General Information County-supported, 2-year, coed college.
Small town setting. *Awards:* A. *Entrance level for U.S. students:*
Noncompetitive. *Enrollment:* 1,945 total (65% women) including
0.3% international students from 4 foreign countries.
Undergraduate faculty: 185. *Library holdings:* 37,354 books, 202
current serial subscriptions, 1,205 audiovisual materials.
Total majors: 34. *Expenses:* (2006–07) $6945. *Financial aid:*
Need-based and non-need-based financial aid available.

COLLEGE OF SOUTHERN MARYLAND, LA PLATA

General Information State and locally supported, 2-year, coed
college. Rural setting. *Awards:* A. *Entrance level for U.S. students:*
Noncompetitive. *Enrollment:* 7,546 total (66% women).
Undergraduate faculty: 433. *Library holdings:* 44,896 books, 166
current serial subscriptions, 14,013 audiovisual materials.
Total majors: 28.
Information for International Students For fall 2006: 20
international students applied, 20 were accepted, 12 enrolled.
Students can start in fall, spring, or summer. Transfers accepted
from institutions abroad. *Admission tests:* Required: TOEFL

(minimum score: iBT 61; paper-based 500; computer-based 173). TOEFL can be waived under certain conditions. *Application deadline:* 6/15. *Financial aid:* Forms required: institution's own financial aid form. Employment opportunities (on-campus) available. *Contact:* Director, Admissions, College of Southern Maryland, 8730 Mitchell Road, PO Box 910, La Plata, MD 20646-0910. Telephone: 301-934-2251 Ext. 7853. Fax: 301-934-7698. E-mail: JuliaP@csmd.edu. URL: http://www.csmd.edu.

COLUMBIA UNION COLLEGE, TAKOMA PARK

General Information Independent Seventh-day Adventist, coed institution. Suburban setting. *Awards:* A, B, M. *Entrance level for U.S. students:* Moderately difficult. *Enrollment:* 1,092 total; 1,033 undergraduates (64% women) including 4% international students from 37 foreign countries. *Faculty:* 53. *Library holdings:* 141,534 books, 9,000 current serial subscriptions. *Total majors:* 37.
Information for International Students For fall 2006: 53 international students applied, 21 were accepted, 18 enrolled. Students can start in fall or spring. Transfers accepted from institutions abroad. *Admission tests:* Required: TOEFL (minimum score: paper-based 550; computer-based 213; minimum score for ESL admission: paper-based 550; computer-based 213). Recommended: ACT, SAT Subject Tests. TOEFL can be waived under certain conditions. *Application deadline:* 4/15. *Expenses:* (2006–07) $18,439; room and board, $6247 (on campus). *Financial aid:* Need-based and non-need-based financial aid available. International transfer students are eligible to apply for aid. *Housing:* Guaranteed, also available during summer. *Services:* International student adviser on campus. ESL program at cooperating institution. ESL program available during the academic year and the summer. Internships and employment opportunities (on-campus) available. *Contact:* Assistant Director of Enrollment Services, Columbia Union College, 7600 Flower Avenue, Takoma Park, MD 20912. Telephone: 301-891-4080. Fax: 301-891-4167. E-mail: ealmeida@cuc.edu. URL: http://www.cuc.edu.

DEVRY UNIVERSITY, BETHESDA

General Information Proprietary, coed institution. *Awards:* B, M. *Entrance level for U.S. students:* Minimally difficult. *Enrollment:* 98 total; 41 undergraduates (41% women) including 7% international students. *Faculty:* 3. *Total majors:* 2. *Expenses:* (2007–08) $14,440.

FROSTBURG STATE UNIVERSITY, FROSTBURG

General Information State-supported, coed institution. Small town setting. *Awards:* B, M. *Entrance level for U.S. students:* Moderately difficult. *Enrollment:* 4,910 total; 4,252 undergraduates (48% women) including 1% international students from 27 foreign countries. *Faculty:* 352. *Library holdings:* 261,712 books, 2,430 current serial subscriptions. *Total majors:* 46.
Information for International Students For fall 2006: 57 international students applied, 34 were accepted, 24 enrolled. Students can start in fall, winter, spring, or summer. Transfers accepted from institutions abroad. *Admission tests:* Required: SAT or ACT, TOEFL (minimum score: iBT 79; paper-based 550; computer-based 213). *Application deadline:* 6/1. *Expenses:* (2007–08) $16,162; room and board, $6746 (on campus); room only, $3340 (on campus). *Housing:* Available during summer. *Services:* International student adviser on campus. Employment opportunities (on-campus) available. *Contact:* Interim Director, Center for International Education, Office of International Education, Frostburg State University, Center for International Education, 101 Braddock Road, Frostburg, MD 21532. Telephone: 301-687-3091. Fax: 301-687-3057. E-mail: hbullamore@frostburg.edu. URL: http://www.frostburg.edu.

GOUCHER COLLEGE, BALTIMORE

General Information Independent, coed institution. Suburban setting. *Awards:* B, M. *Entrance level for U.S. students:* Moderately difficult. *Enrollment:* 2,310 total; 1,446 undergraduates (66% women) including 0.4% international students from 6 foreign countries. *Faculty:* 226. *Library holdings:* 305,486 books, 27,416 current serial subscriptions, 5,511 audiovisual materials. *Total majors:* 31. *Expenses:* (2006–07) $29,325; room and board, $8925 (on campus); room only, $3125 (on campus). *Financial aid:* Need-based college/university scholarships/grants from institutional funds, loans from outside sources. Non-need-based college/university scholarships/grants from institutional funds, tuition waivers, loans from outside sources, on-campus employment. Forms required: CSS PROFILE, International Student's Certification of Finances. For fall 2005, 9 international students on campus received college administered financial aid ($15,197 average).

GRIGGS UNIVERSITY, SILVER SPRING

General Information Independent Seventh-day Adventist, 4-year, coed college. Suburban setting. *Awards:* A, B (offers only external degree programs). *Entrance level for U.S. students:* Minimally

difficult. *Enrollment:* 486 total including international students from 11 foreign countries. *Undergraduate faculty:* 38. *Total majors:* 4. *Expenses:* (2006–07) $7720.

HOOD COLLEGE, FREDERICK

General Information Independent, coed institution. Suburban setting. *Awards:* B, M (also offers adult program with significant enrollment not reflected in profile). *Entrance level for U.S. students:* Moderately difficult. *Enrollment:* 2,248 total; 1,274 undergraduates (71% women) including 2% international students from 23 foreign countries. *Faculty:* 238. *Library holdings:* 206,800 books, 28,377 current serial subscriptions, 5,899 audiovisual materials. *Total majors:* 29. *Expenses:* (2006–07) $23,655; room and board, $8135 (on campus); room only, $4250 (on campus). *Financial aid:* Need-based and non-need-based financial aid available. Forms required: institution's own financial aid form. For fall 2006 (estimated), 30 international students on campus received college administered financial aid ($17,235 average).

THE JOHNS HOPKINS UNIVERSITY, BALTIMORE

General Information Independent, coed university. Urban setting. *Awards:* B, M, D, FP. *Entrance level for U.S. students:* Most difficult. *Enrollment:* 6,124 total; 4,478 undergraduates (47% women) including 5% international students from 52 foreign countries. *Library holdings:* 3.5 million books, 30,023 current serial subscriptions. *Total majors:* 59.
Information for International Students For fall 2006: 1683 international students applied, 211 were accepted, 80 enrolled. Students can start in fall. Transfers accepted from institutions abroad. *Admission tests:* Required: SAT or ACT, TOEFL (minimum score: paper-based 600; computer-based 250). Recommended: SAT Subject Tests. TOEFL can be waived under certain conditions. *Application deadline:* 1/1. *Expenses:* (2006–07) $33,900; room and board, $10,622 (on campus); room only, $6096 (on campus). *Financial aid:* Need-based college/university scholarships/grants from institutional funds, loans from outside sources, on-campus employment. Non-need-based college/university scholarships/grants from institutional funds, loans from outside sources, on-campus employment. Forms required: institution's own financial aid form, International Student's Financial Aid Application, International Student's Certification of Finances, income documentation. For fall 2006 (estimated), 27 international students on campus received college administered financial aid ($20,181 average). *Services:* International student adviser on campus. ESL program available during the summer. Internships and employment opportunities (on-campus and off-campus) available. *Contact:* Director of Undergraduate Admissions, The Johns Hopkins University, 3400 North Charles Street, Garland Hall, Room 140, Baltimore, MD 21218. Telephone: 410-516-8171. Fax: 410-516-6025. E-mail: lattin1@jhu.edu. URL: http://www.jhu.edu.

LOYOLA COLLEGE IN MARYLAND, BALTIMORE

General Information Independent Roman Catholic (Jesuit), coed institution. Urban setting. *Awards:* B, M, D. *Entrance level for U.S. students:* Moderately difficult. *Enrollment:* 6,035 total; 3,502 undergraduates (60% women) including 1% international students from 26 foreign countries. *Faculty:* 552. *Library holdings:* 293,639 books, 2,126 current serial subscriptions. *Total majors:* 32. *Expenses:* (2006–07) $31,715; room and board, $9578 (on campus); room only, $7578 (on campus).

MARYLAND INSTITUTE COLLEGE OF ART, BALTIMORE

General Information Independent, coed institution. Urban setting. *Awards:* B, M. *Entrance level for U.S. students:* Very difficult. *Enrollment:* 1,866 total; 1,640 undergraduates (65% women) including 5% international students from 49 foreign countries. *Faculty:* 294. *Library holdings:* 76,500 books, 315 current serial subscriptions, 4,800 audiovisual materials. *Total majors:* 17. *Expenses:* (2006–07) $28,670; room and board, $7910 (on campus); room only, $5850 (on campus). *Financial aid:* Non-need financial aid available. Forms required: scholarship application form.

MCDANIEL COLLEGE, WESTMINSTER

General Information Independent, coed institution. Suburban setting. *Awards:* B, M. *Entrance level for U.S. students:* Moderately difficult. *Enrollment:* 3,671 total; 1,771 undergraduates (56% women) including 1% international students from 15 foreign countries. *Faculty:* 201. *Library holdings:* 422,055 books, 19,356 current serial subscriptions. *Total majors:* 28.
Information for International Students For fall 2006: 31 international students applied, 10 were accepted, 6 enrolled. Students can start in fall. *Admission tests:* Required: TOEFL (minimum score: iBT 80; paper-based 550; computer-based 213). Recommended: SAT or ACT. TOEFL can be waived under certain conditions. *Application deadline:* 2/1. *Expenses:* (2006–07) $27,280;

McDaniel College (continued)

room and board, $5900 (on campus); room only, $3200 (on campus). *Financial aid:* Non-need-based college/university scholarships/grants from institutional funds, loans from outside sources. Forms required: International Student's Certification of Finances. 18 international students on campus received college administered financial aid ($19,466 average). *Housing:* Guaranteed. *Services:* International student adviser on campus. Internships and employment opportunities (on-campus) available. *Contact:* Vice President for Enrollment Management and Dean of Admissions, McDaniel College, 2 College Hill, Westminster, MD 21157. Telephone: 410-857-2230. Fax: 410-857-2757. E-mail: admissions@mcdaniel.edu. URL: http://www.mcdaniel.edu.

MONTGOMERY COLLEGE, ROCKVILLE

General Information State and locally supported, 2-year, coed college. Suburban setting. *Awards:* A. *Entrance level for U.S. students:* Noncompetitive. *Enrollment:* 22,893 total (55% women) including 8% international students from 174 foreign countries. *Undergraduate faculty:* 1,347. *Total majors:* 31. *Expenses:* (2007–08) $9996.

MOUNT ST. MARY'S UNIVERSITY, EMMITSBURG

General Information Independent Roman Catholic, coed institution. Rural setting. *Awards:* B, M, FP. *Entrance level for U.S. students:* Moderately difficult. *Enrollment:* 2,186 total; 1,695 undergraduates (60% women) including 1% international students from 9 foreign countries. *Faculty:* 190. *Library holdings:* 211,201 books, 905 current serial subscriptions, 5,108 audiovisual materials. *Total majors:* 28. *Expenses:* (2007–08) $25,890; room and board, $9130 (on campus); room only, $4600 (on campus). *Financial aid:* Need-based college/university scholarships/grants from institutional funds, loans from outside sources, on-campus employment. Non-need-based college/university scholarships/grants from institutional funds, tuition waivers, athletic awards, loans from outside sources. Forms required: institution's own financial aid form. For fall 2006 (estimated), 10 international students on campus received college administered financial aid ($19,384 average).

PEABODY CONSERVATORY OF MUSIC OF THE JOHNS HOPKINS UNIVERSITY, BALTIMORE

General Information Independent, coed institution. Urban setting. *Awards:* B, M, D. *Entrance level for U.S. students:* Very difficult. *Enrollment:* 675 total; 335 undergraduates (48% women) including 19% international students from 15 foreign countries. *Faculty:* 165. *Library holdings:* 92,000 books, 225 current serial subscriptions. *Total majors:* 8. *Expenses:* (2006–07) $29,990; room and board, $9500 (on campus). *Financial aid:* Non-need-based college/university scholarships/grants from institutional funds, loans from outside sources, on-campus employment. Forms required: International Student's Certification of Finances. For fall 2005, international students on campus received college administered aid averaging $15,498.

ST. JOHN'S COLLEGE, ANNAPOLIS

General Information Independent, coed institution. Small town setting. *Awards:* B, M. *Entrance level for U.S. students:* Moderately difficult. *Enrollment:* 600 total; 510 undergraduates (45% women) including 1% international students from 8 foreign countries. *Faculty:* 77. *Library holdings:* 124,500 books, 123 current serial subscriptions, 4,200 audiovisual materials. *Total majors:* 3.
Information for International Students For fall 2006: 4 international students applied, 2 were accepted, 2 enrolled. Students can start in fall or spring. Transfers accepted from institutions abroad. *Admission tests:* Required: SAT, TOEFL (minimum score: paper-based 550; computer-based 213). TOEFL can be waived under certain conditions. *Application deadline:* Rolling. *Expenses:* (2006–07) $34,506; room and board, $8270 (on campus). *Financial aid:* Need-based college/university scholarships/grants from institutional funds, loans from institutional funds. Forms required: International Student's Financial Aid Application, International Student's Certification of Finances. International transfer students are eligible to apply for aid. For fall 2006 (estimated), 3 international students on campus received college administered financial aid ($25,567 average). *Housing:* Guaranteed. *Services:* International student adviser on campus. Internships and employment opportunities (on-campus) available. *Contact:* Director of Admissions, Admissions Office, St. John's College, PO Box 2800, Annapolis, MD 21404. Telephone: 410-626-2522. Fax: 410-269-7916. E-mail: admissions@sjca.edu. URL: http://www.stjohnscollege.edu.

ST. MARY'S COLLEGE OF MARYLAND, ST. MARY'S CITY

General Information State-supported, 4-year, coed college. Rural setting. *Awards:* B. *Entrance level for U.S. students:* Very difficult.

Enrollment: 1,957 total; 1,948 undergraduates (57% women) including 1% international students from 34 foreign countries. *Undergraduate faculty:* 210. *Library holdings:* 161,177 books, 1,170 current serial subscriptions, 16,740 audiovisual materials. *Total majors:* 23.
Information for International Students For fall 2006: 44 international students applied, 25 were accepted, 11 enrolled. Students can start in fall. Transfers accepted from institutions abroad. *Admission tests:* Required: SAT or ACT, TOEFL (minimum score: paper-based 550; computer-based 250). Recommended: ACT. TOEFL can be waived under certain conditions. *Application deadline:* 1/15. *Expenses:* (2007–08) $22,323; room and board, $8855 (on campus); room only, $5060 (on campus). *Financial aid:* Need-based college/university scholarships/grants from institutional funds. Non-need-based college/university scholarships/grants from institutional funds. Forms required: International Student's Financial Aid Application, International Student's Certification of Finances. *Housing:* Guaranteed, also available during summer. *Services:* International student adviser on campus. Internships and employment opportunities (on-campus and off-campus) available. *Contact:* Director of Admissions, Office of Admission, St. Mary's College of Maryland, Office of Admissions, St. Mary's City, MD 20686. Telephone: 240-895-5000. Fax: 240-895-5001. E-mail: rjedgar@smcm.edu. URL: http://www.smcm.edu.

SALISBURY UNIVERSITY, SALISBURY

General Information State-supported, coed institution. Small town setting. *Awards:* B, M. *Entrance level for U.S. students:* Moderately difficult. *Enrollment:* 7,383 total; 6,791 undergraduates (55% women) including 1% international students from 46 foreign countries. *Faculty:* 489. *Library holdings:* 269,550 books, 1,235 current serial subscriptions. *Total majors:* 42. *Expenses:* (2006–07) $14,306; room and board, $7058 (on campus); room only, $3732 (on campus). *Financial aid:* Non-need-based college/university scholarships/grants from institutional funds.

TOWSON UNIVERSITY, TOWSON

General Information State-supported, coed university. Suburban setting. *Awards:* B, M, D. *Entrance level for U.S. students:* Moderately difficult. *Enrollment:* 18,921 total; 15,374 undergraduates (60% women) including 3% international students from 106 foreign countries. *Faculty:* 1,289. *Library holdings:* 580,036 books, 4,154 current serial subscriptions, 16,761 audiovisual materials. *Total majors:* 50. *Expenses:* (2006–07) $16,522; room and board, $7506 (on campus); room only, $4500 (on campus). *Financial aid:* Non-need-based college/university scholarships/grants from institutional funds, athletic awards, on-campus employment. 148 international students on campus received college administered financial aid ($8169 average).

UNIVERSITY OF BALTIMORE, BALTIMORE

General Information State-supported, coed institution. Urban setting. *Awards:* B, M, D, FP. *Entrance level for U.S. students:* Noncompetitive. *Enrollment:* 4,948 total; 2,116 undergraduates (59% women) including 8% international students from 62 foreign countries. *Faculty:* 363. *Library holdings:* 258,747 books, 10,738 current serial subscriptions. *Total majors:* 29.
Information for International Students For fall 2006: 47 international students applied, 22 were accepted, 16 enrolled. Students can start in fall, spring, or summer. Transfers accepted from institutions abroad. *Admission tests:* Required: SAT or ACT, TOEFL (minimum score: iBT 79; paper-based 550; computer-based 213). Recommended: SAT/ACT not required for transfer applicants. *Application deadline:* 2/15. *Expenses:* (2006–07) $18,156. *Financial aid:* Non-need financial aid available. International transfer students are eligible to apply for aid. *Services:* International student adviser on campus. Internships and employment opportunities (on-campus and off-campus) available. *Contact:* International Student and Scholar Advisor, University of Baltimore, 1420 North Charles Street, Baltimore, MD 21201-5779. Telephone: 410-837-4756. Fax: 410-837-6676. E-mail: intladms@ubalt.edu. URL: http://www.ubalt.edu.

UNIVERSITY OF MARYLAND, BALTIMORE COUNTY, BALTIMORE

General Information State-supported, coed university. Suburban setting. *Awards:* B, M, D. *Entrance level for U.S. students:* Moderately difficult. *Enrollment:* 11,798 total; 9,416 undergraduates (46% women) including 4% international students from 90 foreign countries. *Faculty:* 762. *Library holdings:* 1.3 million books, 4,170 current serial subscriptions, 7,500 audiovisual materials. *Total majors:* 58.
Information for International Students For fall 2006: 193 international students applied, 122 were accepted, 63 enrolled. Students can start in fall, winter, spring, or summer. Transfers accepted from institutions abroad. *Admission tests:* Required:

TOEFL (minimum score: iBT 80; paper-based 550; computer-based 213; minimum score for ESL admission: iBT 48; paper-based 460; computer-based 140), IELTS is also accepted for English proficiency. TOEFL can be waived under certain conditions. *Application deadline:* 2/1. *Expenses:* (2006–07) $17,354; room and board, $8381 (on campus); room only, $5127 (on campus). *Financial aid:* Non-need-based college/university scholarships/grants from institutional funds, tuition waivers, athletic awards. For fall 2005, 110 international students on campus received college administered financial aid ($5053 average). *Housing:* Guaranteed, also available during summer. *Services:* International student adviser on campus. Full-time and part-time ESL programs on campus. ESL program available during the academic year and the summer. Internships and employment opportunities (on-campus and off-campus) available. *Contact:* Assistant Director of Admissions and Orientation, Undergraduate Admissions Office, University of Maryland, Baltimore County, 1000 Hilltop Circle, Baltimore, MD 21250. Telephone: 410-455-2292. Fax: 410-455-1094. E-mail: ljsmith@umbc.edu. URL: http://www.umbc.edu.

UNIVERSITY OF MARYLAND, COLLEGE PARK, COLLEGE PARK

General Information State-supported, coed university. Suburban setting. *Awards:* B, M, D, FP. *Entrance level for U.S. students:* Moderately difficult. *Enrollment:* 35,300 total; 25,373 undergraduates (49% women) including 2% international students from 159 foreign countries. *Faculty:* 2,070. *Library holdings:* 3 million books, 34,091 current serial subscriptions, 244,911 audiovisual materials. *Total majors:* 93.

Information for International Students For fall 2006: 525 international students applied, 136 were accepted, 45 enrolled. Students can start in fall or spring. Transfers accepted from institutions abroad. *Admission tests:* Required: SAT or ACT, TOEFL (minimum score: iBT 84; paper-based 575; computer-based 233), IELTS. TOEFL can be waived under certain conditions. *Application deadline:* 12/1. *Expenses:* (2006–07) $21,345; room and board, $8422 (on campus); room only, $4997 (on campus). *Services:* International student adviser on campus. Full-time and part-time ESL programs on campus. ESL program available during the academic year and the summer. Internships and employment opportunities (on-campus) available. *Contact:* Assistant Director of International Education Services, University of Maryland, College Park, 3117 Mitchell Building, College Park, MD 20742. Telephone: 301-314-7745. Fax: 301-314-9347. E-mail: bvarsa@deans.umd.edu. URL: http://www.maryland.edu.

UNIVERSITY OF MARYLAND UNIVERSITY COLLEGE, ADELPHI

General Information State-supported, coed institution. Suburban setting. *Awards:* A, B, M, D (offers primarily part-time evening and weekend degree programs at more than 30 off-campus locations in Maryland and the Washington, DC area, and more than 180 military communities in Europe and Asia with military enrollment not reflected in this profile; associate of arts program available to military students only). *Entrance level for U.S. students:* Noncompetitive. *Enrollment:* 33,096 total; 22,898 undergraduates (59% women) including 2% international students from 49 foreign countries. *Faculty:* 1,590. *Library holdings:* 192,154 current serial subscriptions, 25 audiovisual materials. *Total majors:* 19. *Expenses:* (2006–07) $10,656.

UNIVERSITY OF PHOENIX–MARYLAND CAMPUS, COLUMBIA

General Information Proprietary, coed institution. Urban setting. *Awards:* B, M. *Entrance level for U.S. students:* Noncompetitive. *Enrollment:* 1,823 total; 1,434 undergraduates (62% women) including 14% international students. *Faculty:* 436. *Library holdings:* 1,759 books, 692 current serial subscriptions. *Total majors:* 22. *Expenses:* (2006–07) $11,820.

WASHINGTON BIBLE COLLEGE, LANHAM

General Information Independent nondenominational, 4-year, coed college. Suburban setting. *Awards:* A, B. *Entrance level for U.S. students:* Moderately difficult. *Enrollment:* 331 total including 2% international students from 8 foreign countries. *Undergraduate faculty:* 14. *Library holdings:* 78,000 books, 525 current serial subscriptions. *Total majors:* 8.

Information for International Students Students can start in fall, winter, spring, or summer. Transfers accepted from institutions abroad. *Admission tests:* Required: TOEFL (minimum score: paper-based 550; computer-based 213). *Application deadline:* 7/31. *Financial aid:* Need-based financial aid available. Non-need-based college/university scholarships/grants from institutional funds, on-campus employment. Forms required: International Student's Certification of Finances. International transfer students are eligible to apply for aid. For fall 2005, 4 international students on

campus received college administered financial aid ($4083 average). *Housing:* Guaranteed. *Services:* International student adviser on campus. Full-time ESL program on campus. ESL program available during the academic year. *Contact:* Director of Admissions, Washington Bible College, 6511 Princess Garden Parkway, Lanham, MD 20706. Telephone: 301-552-1400 Ext. 1208. Fax: 301-552-2775. E-mail: mjohnson@bible.edu. URL: http://www.bible.edu.

WASHINGTON COLLEGE, CHESTERTOWN

General Information Independent, coed institution. Small town setting. *Awards:* B, M. *Entrance level for U.S. students:* Moderately difficult. *Enrollment:* 1,381 total; 1,307 undergraduates (60% women) including 3% international students from 28 foreign countries. *Faculty:* 146. *Library holdings:* 243,030 books, 4,667 current serial subscriptions. *Total majors:* 34.

Information for International Students For fall 2006: 33 international students applied, 24 were accepted, 7 enrolled. Students can start in fall or spring. Transfers accepted from institutions abroad. *Admission tests:* Required: TOEFL (minimum score: iBT 79; paper-based 550; computer-based 213). Recommended: SAT or ACT. TOEFL can be waived under certain conditions. *Application deadline:* 2/15. *Expenses:* (2006–07) $30,200; room and board, $6450 (on campus); room only, $3250 (on campus). *Financial aid:* Non-need-based college/university scholarships/grants from institutional funds. Forms required: International Student's Financial Aid Application, International Student's Certification of Finances. International transfer students are eligible to apply for aid. For fall 2005, 31 international students on campus received college administered financial aid ($9374 average). *Services:* International student adviser on campus. Internships and employment opportunities (on-campus) available. *Contact:* Associate Director of Admissions, Washington College, 300 Washington Avenue, Chestertown, MD 21620. Telephone: 410-778-7700. Fax: 410-778-7287. E-mail: tlittlefield2@washcoll.edu. URL: http://www.washcoll.edu.

See In-Depth Description on page 241.

MASSACHUSETTS

AMERICAN INTERNATIONAL COLLEGE, SPRINGFIELD

General Information Independent, coed institution. Urban setting. *Awards:* A, B, M, D. *Entrance level for U.S. students:* Moderately difficult. *Enrollment:* 1,815 total; 1,398 undergraduates (59% women) including 1% international students from 52 foreign countries. *Faculty:* 159. *Library holdings:* 118,000 books, 390 current serial subscriptions. *Total majors:* 45. *Expenses:* (2006–07) $20,990; room and board, $9270 (on campus). *Financial aid:* Need-based college/university scholarships/grants from institutional funds, athletic awards, loans from outside sources, on-campus employment. Non-need-based college/university scholarships/grants from institutional funds, athletic awards, loans from outside sources, on-campus employment. Forms required: International Student's Certification of Finances.

ANNA MARIA COLLEGE, PAXTON

General Information Independent Roman Catholic, coed institution. Rural setting. *Awards:* A, B, M. *Entrance level for U.S. students:* Moderately difficult. *Enrollment:* 1,200 total; 809 undergraduates (58% women) including 0.2% international students from 2 foreign countries. *Faculty:* 181. *Library holdings:* 79,039 books, 318 current serial subscriptions. *Total majors:* 28.

Information for International Students For fall 2006: 16 international students applied, 8 were accepted, 2 enrolled. Students can start in fall or spring. Transfers accepted from institutions abroad. *Admission tests:* Required: TOEFL (minimum score: paper-based 470; computer-based 150). Recommended: SAT, ACT. *Application deadline:* Rolling. *Expenses:* (2006–07) $23,234; room and board, $8410 (on campus). *Financial aid:* Non-need-based college/university scholarships/grants from institutional funds, tuition waivers, loans from institutional funds, loans from outside sources. For fall 2005, 1 international student on campus received college administered financial aid ($4000 average). *Services:* International student adviser on campus. Internships available. *Contact:* Director of Recruitment and Admissions, Anna Maria College, 50 Sunset Lane, Paxton, MA 01612. Telephone: 508-849-3360. Fax: 508-849-3362. E-mail: tdonahue@annamaria.edu. URL: http://www.annamaria.edu.

See In-Depth Description on page 34.

THE ART INSTITUTE OF BOSTON AT LESLEY UNIVERSITY, BOSTON

General Information Independent, coed institution. Urban setting. *Awards:* B, M. *Entrance level for U.S. students:* Moderately difficult. *Enrollment:* 6,539 total; 1,351 undergraduates (75% women) including 2% international students from 24 foreign countries. *Faculty:* 185. *Library holdings:* 100,000 books, 1,160 current serial subscriptions, 49,943 audiovisual materials. *Total majors:* 4.

Information for International Students For fall 2006: 72 international students applied, 42 were accepted, 13 enrolled. Students can start in fall, winter, spring, or summer. Transfers accepted from institutions abroad. *Admission tests:* Required: TOEFL or IELTS. Recommended: SAT. *Application deadline:* Rolling. *Expenses:* (2007–08) $23,450; room and board, $12,100 (on campus); room only, $6800 (on campus). *Financial aid:* International transfer students are eligible to apply for aid. *Services:* International student adviser on campus. ESL program at cooperating institution. Internships and employment opportunities (on-campus) available. *Contact:* International Admissions Advisor, The Art Institute of Boston at Lesley University, 700 Beacon Street, Boston, MA 02215. Telephone: 617-585-6700. Fax: 617-437-1226. E-mail: admissions@aiboston.edu. URL: http://www.aiboston.edu.

See In-Depth Description on page 35.

ASSUMPTION COLLEGE, WORCESTER

General Information Independent Roman Catholic, coed institution. Suburban setting. *Awards:* B, M. *Entrance level for U.S. students:* Moderately difficult. *Enrollment:* 2,498 total; 2,129 undergraduates (60% women) including 0.4% international students from 8 foreign countries. *Faculty:* 226. *Library holdings:* 133,030 books, 1,892 current serial subscriptions, 2,820 audiovisual materials. *Total majors:* 31.

Information for International Students For fall 2006: 43 international students applied, 13 were accepted, 2 enrolled. Students can start in fall or spring. Transfers accepted from institutions abroad. *Admission tests:* Required: SAT or ACT, TOEFL (minimum score: iBT 80; paper-based 550; computer-based 213). TOEFL can be waived under certain conditions. *Application deadline:* 3/1. *Expenses:* (2006–07) $26,060; room and board, $5775 (on campus); room only, $3395 (on campus). *Financial aid:* Non-need-based college/university scholarships/grants from institutional funds, tuition waivers, athletic awards. International transfer students are eligible to apply for aid. For fall 2006 (estimated), 2 international students on campus received college administered financial aid ($11,500 average). *Housing:* Guaranteed, also available during summer. *Services:* International student adviser on campus. Internships and employment opportunities (on-campus) available. *Contact:* Director of Admissions, Assumption College, 500 Salisbury Street, Worcester, MA 01609. Telephone: 508-767-7107. Fax: 508-799-4412. E-mail: silva@assumption.edu. URL: http://www.assumption.edu.

BABSON COLLEGE, WELLESLEY

General Information Independent, coed institution. Suburban setting. *Awards:* B, M. *Entrance level for U.S. students:* Very difficult. *Enrollment:* 3,359 total; 1,776 undergraduates (39% women) including 17% international students from 69 foreign countries. *Faculty:* 242. *Library holdings:* 131,436 books, 626 current serial subscriptions. *Total majors:* 24.

Information for International Students For fall 2006: 625 international students applied, 251 were accepted, 73 enrolled. Students can start in fall or spring. Transfers accepted from institutions abroad. *Admission tests:* Required: SAT or ACT, TOEFL (minimum score: iBT 100). Recommended: SAT Subject Tests. TOEFL can be waived under certain conditions. *Application deadline:* 1/15. *Expenses:* (2007–08) $34,112; room and board, $11,670 (on campus); room only, $7530 (on campus). *Financial aid:* Non-need-based college/university scholarships/grants from institutional funds. Forms required: International Student's Certification of Finances. For fall 2006 (estimated), 12 international students on campus received college administered financial aid ($17,922 average). *Housing:* Guaranteed, also available during summer. *Services:* International student adviser on campus. Internships and employment opportunities (on-campus and off-campus) available. *Contact:* Assistant Director of Undergraduate Admission, Babson College, 231 Forest Street, Lunder Undergraduate Admission Center at Mustard Hall, Babson Park, MA 02457. Telephone: 781-239-5522. Fax: 781-239-4135. E-mail: afowkes@babson.edu. URL: http://www.babson.edu.

BAY PATH COLLEGE, LONGMEADOW

General Information Independent, undergraduate: women only; graduate: coed institution. Suburban setting. *Awards:* A, B, M. *Entrance level for U.S. students:* Moderately difficult. *Enrollment:* 1,479 total; 1,321 undergraduates (100% women) including 1% international students from 6 foreign countries. *Faculty:* 128. *Library holdings:* 55,060 books, 132 current serial subscriptions. *Total majors:* 12.

Information for International Students Students can start in fall or spring. Transfers accepted from institutions abroad. *Admission tests:* Required: TOEFL (minimum score: paper-based 500; computer-based 187; minimum score for ESL admission: paper-based 450; computer-based 133). Recommended: SAT or ACT. TOEFL can be waived under certain conditions. *Application deadline:* Rolling. *Expenses:* (2007–08) $22,073; room and board, $9200 (on campus). *Financial aid:* Non-need financial aid available. Forms required: International Student's Certification of Finances. 11 international students on campus received college administered financial aid ($8685 average). *Housing:* Guaranteed. *Services:* International student adviser on campus. Full-time ESL program on campus. ESL program available during the academic year. Internships and employment opportunities (on-campus) available. *Contact:* Assistant Director and Coordinator of International Initiatives, Bay Path College, 588 Longmeadow Street, Longmeadow, MA 01106-2292. Telephone: 413-565-1000 Ext. 3139. Fax: 413-565-1105. E-mail: mhudgik@baypath.edu. URL: http://www.baypath.edu.

BAY STATE COLLEGE, BOSTON

General Information Independent, primarily 2-year, coed college. Urban setting. *Awards:* A, B. *Entrance level for U.S. students:* Minimally difficult. *Enrollment:* 757 total including 1% international students from 11 foreign countries. *Undergraduate faculty:* 66. *Library holdings:* 4,490 books, 262 current serial subscriptions, 471 audiovisual materials. *Total majors:* 18. *Expenses:* (2006–07) $16,250; room and board, $10,075 (on campus).

BENJAMIN FRANKLIN INSTITUTE OF TECHNOLOGY, BOSTON

General Information Independent, primarily 2-year, coed, primarily men's college. Urban setting. *Awards:* A, B. *Entrance level for U.S. students:* Minimally difficult. *Enrollment:* 386 total including 0.3% international students. *Undergraduate faculty:* 42. *Library holdings:* 10,000 books, 90 current serial subscriptions. *Total majors:* 11. *Expenses:* (2006–07) $12,750.

BENTLEY COLLEGE, WALTHAM

General Information Independent, coed institution. Suburban setting. *Awards:* A, B, M. *Entrance level for U.S. students:* Very difficult. *Enrollment:* 5,497 total; 4,241 undergraduates (41% women) including 8% international students from 74 foreign countries. *Faculty:* 473. *Library holdings:* 146,104 books, 30,800 current serial subscriptions, 7,002 audiovisual materials. *Total majors:* 14.

Information for International Students For fall 2006: 628 international students applied, 199 were accepted, 42 enrolled. Students can start in fall or spring. Transfers accepted from institutions abroad. *Admission tests:* Required: SAT or ACT, TOEFL (minimum score: paper-based 550; computer-based 213). TOEFL can be waived under certain conditions. *Application deadline:* 2/1. *Expenses:* (2006–07) $30,044; room and board, $10,530 (on campus); room only, $6280 (on campus). *Housing:* Guaranteed, also available during summer. *Services:* International student adviser on campus. Internships and employment opportunities (on-campus) available. *Contact:* Associate Director of International Admissions, Bentley College, 175 Forest Street, Waltham, MA 02452-4705. Telephone: 781-891-2244. Fax: 781-891-3414. E-mail: ugadmission@bentley.edu. URL: http://www.bentley.edu.

See In-Depth Description on page 41.

BERKSHIRE COMMUNITY COLLEGE, PITTSFIELD

General Information State-supported, 2-year, coed college. Suburban setting. *Awards:* A. *Entrance level for U.S. students:* Noncompetitive. *Enrollment:* 2,225 total (64% women) including 2% international students from 18 foreign countries. *Undergraduate faculty:* 176. *Library holdings:* 72,325 books, 319 current serial subscriptions, 13,304 audiovisual materials. *Total majors:* 28.

Information for International Students For fall 2006: 51 international students applied, 43 were accepted, 35 enrolled. Students can start in fall, spring, or summer. Transfers accepted from institutions abroad. *Admission tests:* Required: TOEFL (minimum score: paper-based 500; computer-based 173). TOEFL can be waived under certain conditions. *Application deadline:* Rolling. *Expenses:* (2007–08) $8556. *Services:* International student adviser on campus. Full-time ESL program on campus. ESL program available during the academic year. Internships and employment opportunities (on-campus) available. *Contact:* Acting Dean of Student Affairs and Enrollment, Berkshire Community College, 1350 West Street, Pittsfield, MA 01201.

Telephone: 413-236-1601. Fax: 413-496-9511.
E-mail: mbullock@berkshirecc.edu.
URL: http://www.berkshirecc.edu.

BOSTON COLLEGE, CHESTNUT HILL

General Information Independent Roman Catholic (Jesuit), coed university. Suburban setting. *Awards:* B, M, D, FP (also offers continuing education program with significant enrollment not reflected in profile). *Entrance level for U.S. students:* Very difficult. *Enrollment:* 13,652 total; 9,020 undergraduates (52% women) including 2% international students from 66 foreign countries. *Faculty:* 1,221. *Library holdings:* 2.1 million books, 52,338 current serial subscriptions, 171,099 audiovisual materials. *Total majors:* 45. *Expenses:* (2006–07) $33,506; room and board, $11,438 (on campus); room only, $7338 (on campus).

BOSTON UNIVERSITY, BOSTON

General Information Independent, coed university. Urban setting. *Awards:* B, M, D, FP. *Entrance level for U.S. students:* Very difficult. *Enrollment:* 31,574 total; 18,521 undergraduates (59% women) including 6% international students from 100 foreign countries. *Faculty:* 2,489. *Library holdings:* 2.4 million books, 33,983 current serial subscriptions. *Total majors:* 121.

Information for International Students For fall 2006: 2398 international students applied, 959 were accepted, 240 enrolled. Students can start in fall or spring. Transfers accepted from institutions abroad. *Admission tests:* Required: SAT or ACT, TOEFL (minimum score: paper-based 550; computer-based 213), two SAT Subject Tests. Recommended: SAT Subject Tests. *Application deadline:* 1/1. *Expenses:* (2006–07) $33,792; room and board, $10,480 (on campus); room only, $6760 (on campus). *Financial aid:* Need-based financial aid available. Non-need-based college/university scholarships/grants from institutional funds, athletic awards. Forms required: International Student's Certification of Finances. 147 international students on campus received college administered financial aid ($22,689 average). *Housing:* Guaranteed, also available during summer. *Services:* International student adviser on campus. Full-time and part-time ESL programs on campus. ESL program available during the academic year and the summer. Internships and employment opportunities (on-campus) available. *Contact:* Assistant Director of International Admissions, Boston University, 121 Bay State Road, Boston, MA 02215. Telephone: 617-353-4492. Fax: 617 353 5334. E-mail: intadmis@bu.edu. URL: http://www.bu.edu.

See In-Depth Description on page 43.

BRANDEIS UNIVERSITY, WALTHAM

General Information Independent, coed university. Suburban setting. *Awards:* B, M, D. *Entrance level for U.S. students:* Most difficult. *Enrollment:* 5,313 total; 3,304 undergraduates (56% women) including 7% international students. *Faculty:* 458. *Library holdings:* 1.2 million books, 38,717 audiovisual materials. *Total majors:* 46. *Expenses:* (2006–07) $34,035; room and board, $9463 (on campus); room only, $5315 (on campus). *Financial aid:* Need-based college/university scholarships/grants from institutional funds, tuition waivers, loans from institutional funds, loans from outside sources, on-campus employment. Non-need-based college/university scholarships/grants from institutional funds, tuition waivers, loans from outside sources. Forms required: institution's own financial aid form, CSS PROFILE, International Student's Financial Aid Application, International Student's Certification of Finances. For fall 2006 (estimated), 131 international students on campus received college administered financial aid ($27,908 average).

BRIDGEWATER STATE COLLEGE, BRIDGEWATER

General Information State-supported, coed institution. Suburban setting. *Awards:* B, M. *Entrance level for U.S. students:* Moderately difficult. *Enrollment:* 9,655 total; 7,825 undergraduates (58% women) including 1% international students from 22 foreign countries. *Faculty:* 567. *Library holdings:* 577,881 books, 31,617 current serial subscriptions. *Total majors:* 75. *Expenses:* (2006–07) $12,006; room and board, $6852 (on campus).

BRISTOL COMMUNITY COLLEGE, FALL RIVER

General Information State-supported, 2-year, coed college. Urban setting. *Awards:* A. *Entrance level for U.S. students:* Noncompetitive. *Enrollment:* 6,873 total (63% women) including 0.2% international students from 25 foreign countries. *Undergraduate faculty:* 792. *Library holdings:* 65,000 books, 380 current serial subscriptions. *Total majors:* 48. *Expenses:* (2006–07) $8064.

BUNKER HILL COMMUNITY COLLEGE, BOSTON

General Information State-supported, 2-year, coed college. Urban setting. *Awards:* A. *Entrance level for U.S. students:*

Noncompetitive. *Enrollment:* 7,837 total (60% women) including 6% international students from 93 foreign countries. *Undergraduate faculty:* 448. *Library holdings:* 65,953 books, 330 current serial subscriptions, 934 audiovisual materials. *Total majors:* 39.

Information for International Students For fall 2006: 750 international students applied, 650 were accepted, 614 enrolled. Students can start in fall, spring, or summer. Transfers accepted from institutions abroad. *Admission tests:* Required: TOEFL (minimum score: iBT 60; paper-based 500; computer-based 173; minimum score for ESL admission: iBT 38; paper-based 423; computer-based 113). TOEFL can be waived under certain conditions. *Application deadline:* 7/15. *Expenses:* (2006–07) $7344. *Services:* International student adviser on campus. Full-time ESL program on campus. ESL program available during the academic year and the summer. Internships and employment opportunities (on-campus) available. *Contact:* International Center, Bunker Hill Community College, 250 New Rutherford Avenue, Boston, MA 02129-2925. Telephone: 617-228-2460. Fax: 617-228-2442. E-mail: international@bhcc.mass.edu. URL: http://www.bhcc.mass.edu.

See In-Depth Description on page 47.

CAMBRIDGE COLLEGE, CAMBRIDGE

General Information Independent, coed institution. Urban setting. *Awards:* B, M, D. *Entrance level for U.S. students:* Minimally difficult. *Enrollment:* 4,670 total; 1,064 undergraduates (70% women) including 2% international students from 50 foreign countries. *Faculty:* 945. *Library holdings:* 30,000 books, 21 current serial subscriptions. *Total majors:* 4. *Expenses:* (2006–07) $8890.

CLARK UNIVERSITY, WORCESTER

General Information Independent, coed university. Urban setting. *Awards:* B, M, D. *Entrance level for U.S. students:* Moderately difficult. *Enrollment:* 3,071 total; 2,262 undergraduates (60% women) including 8% international students from 61 foreign countries. *Faculty:* 278. *Library holdings:* 289,658 books, 1,383 current serial subscriptions. *Total majors:* 49.

Information for International Students For fall 2006: 428 international students applied, 209 were accepted, 59 enrolled. Students can start in fall. Transfers accepted from institutions abroad. *Admission tests:* Required: TOEFL (minimum score: iBT 80; paper-based 550; computer-based 213; minimum score for ESL admission: iBT 60; paper-based 500; computer-based 173), SAT or ACT required for native English speakers (in place of TOEFL). Recommended: SAT or ACT. TOEFL can be waived under certain conditions. *Application deadline:* 1/15. *Expenses:* (2006–07) $31,465; room and board, $5900 (on campus); room only, $3550 (on campus). *Financial aid:* Non-need financial aid available. Forms required: institution's own financial aid form. International transfer students are eligible to apply for aid. For fall 2006 (estimated), 123 international students on campus received college administered financial aid ($20,733 average). *Housing:* Available during summer. *Services:* International student adviser on campus. Full-time and part-time ESL programs on campus. ESL program available during the academic year and the summer. Internships and employment opportunities (on-campus and off-campus) available. *Contact:* Senior Assistant Director of Admissions/Coordinator of International Recruitment, Clark University, 950 Main Street, Worcester, MA 01610-1477. Telephone: 508-793-7431. Fax: 508-793-8821. E-mail: intadmissions@clarku.edu. URL: http://www.clarku.edu.

COLLEGE OF THE HOLY CROSS, WORCESTER

General Information Independent Roman Catholic (Jesuit), 4-year, coed college. Suburban setting. *Awards:* B (standardized tests are optional for admission to the College of Holy Cross). *Entrance level for U.S. students:* Very difficult. *Enrollment:* 2,821 total (56% women) including 1% international students from 13 foreign countries. *Undergraduate faculty:* 299. *Library holdings:* 606,847 books, 1,570 current serial subscriptions, 28,126 audiovisual materials. *Total majors:* 33.

Information for International Students For fall 2006: 79 international students applied, 17 were accepted, 7 enrolled. Students can start in fall. Transfers accepted from institutions abroad. *Admission tests:* Required: TOEFL (minimum score: paper-based 550; computer-based 213; minimum score for ESL admission: paper-based 550; computer-based 213). TOEFL can be waived under certain conditions. *Application deadline:* 1/15. *Expenses:* (2006–07) $33,313; room and board, $9580 (on campus); room only, $4790 (on campus). *Housing:* Guaranteed. *Services:* International student adviser on campus. Internships and employment opportunities (on-campus) available. *Contact:* Director of Admissions, College of the Holy Cross, 1 College Street, Worcester, MA 01610-2395. Telephone: 508-793-2443. Fax: 508-793-3888. E-mail: admissions@holycross.edu. URL: http://www.holycross.edu.

Massachusetts

CURRY COLLEGE, MILTON

General Information Independent, coed institution. Suburban setting. *Awards:* B, M. *Entrance level for U.S. students:* Moderately difficult. *Enrollment:* 3,073 total; 2,765 undergraduates (57% women) including 1% international students from 12 foreign countries. *Faculty:* 372. *Library holdings:* 90,000 books, 675 current serial subscriptions. *Total majors:* 28. *Expenses:* (2006–07) $24,300; room and board, $9640 (on campus); room only, $5640 (on campus).

DEAN COLLEGE, FRANKLIN

General Information Independent, primarily 2-year, coed college. Small town setting. *Awards:* A, B. *Entrance level for U.S. students:* Minimally difficult. *Enrollment:* 1,106 total (48% women) including 9% international students from 131 foreign countries. *Undergraduate faculty:* 112. *Library holdings:* 45,565 books, 174 current serial subscriptions, 1,203 audiovisual materials. *Total majors:* 12.

Information for International Students For fall 2006: 148 international students applied, 117 were accepted, 63 enrolled. Students can start in fall or spring. Transfers accepted from institutions abroad. *Admission tests:* Required: TOEFL (minimum score: iBT 62; paper-based 500; computer-based 173; minimum score for ESL admission: iBT 32; paper-based 425; computer-based 110). Recommended: SAT or ACT. TOEFL can be waived under certain conditions. *Application deadline:* Rolling. *Expenses:* (2007–08) $25,420; room and board, $10,960 (on campus); room only, $6930 (on campus). *Financial aid:* Non-need financial aid available. *Housing:* Guaranteed, also available during summer. *Services:* International student adviser on campus. Full-time and part-time ESL programs on campus. ESL program available during the academic year and the summer. Employment opportunities (on-campus) available. *Contact:* Associate Director of Admissions, Dean College, 99 Main Street, Franklin, MA 02038. Telephone: 508-541-1512. Fax: 508-541-8726. E-mail: cwalker@dean.edu. URL: http://www.dean.edu.

EASTERN NAZARENE COLLEGE, QUINCY

General Information Independent, coed institution, affiliated with Church of the Nazarene. Suburban setting. *Awards:* A, B, M. *Entrance level for U.S. students:* Moderately difficult. *Enrollment:* 1,212 total; 1,069 undergraduates (61% women) including 1% international students from 18 foreign countries. *Faculty:* 48. *Library holdings:* 117,540 books, 466 current serial subscriptions. *Total majors:* 47. *Expenses:* (2007–08) $20,574; room and board, $7395 (on campus). *Financial aid:* Need-based and non-need-based financial aid available. Forms required: institution's own financial aid form, International Student's Financial Aid Application, International Student's Certification of Finances. 18 international students on campus received college administered financial aid ($7185 average).

ELMS COLLEGE, CHICOPEE

General Information Independent Roman Catholic, coed, primarily women's institution. Suburban setting. *Awards:* A, B, M. *Entrance level for U.S. students:* Moderately difficult. *Enrollment:* 1,234 total; 1,066 undergraduates (81% women) including 0.2% international students from 1 foreign country. *Faculty:* 146. *Library holdings:* 111,379 books, 529 current serial subscriptions, 2,948 audiovisual materials. *Total majors:* 42.

Information for International Students Students can start in fall. Transfers accepted from institutions abroad. *Admission tests:* Required: TOEFL (minimum score: paper-based 450; computer-based 133; minimum score for ESL admission: paper-based 450; computer-based 133). Recommended: SAT or ACT. *Application deadline:* 5/15. *Expenses:* (2006–07) $21,520; room and board, $8400 (on campus). *Financial aid:* Forms required: International Student's Financial Aid Application, International Student's Certification of Finances. *Housing:* Guaranteed. *Services:* International student adviser on campus. Full-time ESL program on campus. ESL program available during the academic year. *Contact:* Director of Admission, Elms College, 291 Springfield Street, Office of Admission, Chicopee, MA 01013. Telephone: 413-592-3189. Fax: 413-594-2781. E-mail: admissions@elms.edu. URL: http://www.elms.edu.

EMERSON COLLEGE, BOSTON

General Information Independent, coed institution. Urban setting. *Awards:* B, M, D. *Entrance level for U.S. students:* Very difficult. *Enrollment:* 4,324 total; 3,402 undergraduates (56% women) including 2% international students from 50 foreign countries. *Faculty:* 378. *Library holdings:* 165,000 books, 10,700 current serial subscriptions. *Total majors:* 29.

Information for International Students For fall 2006: 150 international students applied, 75 were accepted, 30 enrolled. Students can start in fall or spring. Transfers accepted from institutions abroad. *Admission tests:* Required: SAT or ACT, TOEFL (minimum score: iBT 100; paper-based 550; computer-based 213). *Application deadline:* 1/5. *Expenses:* (2006–07) $25,894; room and board, $10,870 (on campus). *Financial aid:* Need-based on-campus employment. Non-need-based college/university scholarships/grants from institutional funds, on-campus employment. Forms required: International Student's Certification of Finances. For fall 2005, 13 international students on campus received college administered financial aid ($9538 average). *Services:* International student adviser on campus. Internships and employment opportunities (on-campus) available. *Contact:* Assistant Director of Undergraduate Admission, Emerson College, 120 Boylston Street, Boston, MA 02116-4624. Telephone: 617-824-8600. Fax: 617-824-8609. E-mail: international@emerson.edu. URL: http://www.emerson.edu.

See In-Depth Description on page 79.

EMMANUEL COLLEGE, BOSTON

General Information Independent Roman Catholic, coed institution. Urban setting. *Awards:* B, M. *Entrance level for U.S. students:* Moderately difficult. *Enrollment:* 2,340 total; 2,156 undergraduates (75% women) including 2% international students from 45 foreign countries. *Faculty:* 271. *Total majors:* 35.

Information for International Students For fall 2006: 190 international students applied, 61 were accepted, 7 enrolled. Students can start in fall or spring. Transfers accepted from institutions abroad. *Admission tests:* Required: TOEFL (minimum score: iBT 80; paper-based 550; computer-based 213), ELS (minimum score: 112). Recommended: SAT or ACT. *Application deadline:* 3/1. *Expenses:* (2006–07) $24,200; room and board, $10,400 (on campus). *Financial aid:* Non-need-based college/university scholarships/grants from institutional funds, loans from outside sources, on-campus employment. Forms required: International Student's Certification of Finances. International transfer students are eligible to apply for aid. For fall 2006 (estimated), 12 international students on campus received college administered financial aid ($16,525 average). *Housing:* Guaranteed, also available during summer. *Services:* International student adviser on campus. Internships and employment opportunities (on-campus) available. *Contact:* Assistant Director/International Student Coordinator, Emmanuel College, Office of Admissions, 400 The Fenway, Boston, MA 02115. Telephone: 617-735-9715. Fax: 617-735-9801. E-mail: enroll@emmanuel.edu. URL: http://www.emmanuel.edu.

ENDICOTT COLLEGE, BEVERLY

General Information Independent, coed institution. Suburban setting. *Awards:* A, B, M. *Entrance level for U.S. students:* Moderately difficult. *Enrollment:* 3,810 university total (56% women) including 2% international students from 29 foreign countries. *Faculty:* 150. *Library holdings:* 121,000 books, 3,500 current serial subscriptions. *Total majors:* 22. *Expenses:* (2006–07) $21,374; room and board, $10,254 (on campus); room only, $7188 (on campus). *Financial aid:* Non-need-based college/university scholarships/grants from institutional funds. For fall 2006 (estimated), 18 international students on campus received college administered financial aid ($16,073 average).

FISHER COLLEGE, BOSTON

General Information Independent, primarily 2-year, coed college. Urban setting. *Awards:* A, B. *Entrance level for U.S. students:* Minimally difficult. *Enrollment:* 507 total (66% women) including 11% international students from 21 foreign countries. *Undergraduate faculty:* 48. *Library holdings:* 30,000 books, 160 current serial subscriptions. *Total majors:* 11. *Expenses:* (2007–08) $21,015; room and board, $11,550 (on campus). *Financial aid:* Non-need financial aid available.

FITCHBURG STATE COLLEGE, FITCHBURG

General Information State-supported, coed institution. Suburban setting. *Awards:* B, M. *Entrance level for U.S. students:* Moderately difficult. *Enrollment:* 5,508 total; 3,768 undergraduates (56% women) including 1% international students. *Faculty:* 259. *Library holdings:* 242,418 books, 2,208 current serial subscriptions, 1,845 audiovisual materials. *Total majors:* 58. *Expenses:* (2006–07) $11,622; room and board, $6486 (on campus).

FRAMINGHAM STATE COLLEGE, FRAMINGHAM

General Information State-supported, coed institution. Suburban setting. *Awards:* B, M. *Entrance level for U.S. students:* Moderately difficult. *Enrollment:* 5,861 total; 3,829 undergraduates (65% women) including 1% international students from 20 foreign countries. *Faculty:* 230. *Library holdings:* 165,219 books, 409 current serial subscriptions, 3,313 audiovisual materials. *Total majors:* 89. *Expenses:* (2006–07) $11,529; room and board, $6699 (on campus); room only, $4339 (on campus).

GORDON COLLEGE, WENHAM

General Information Independent nondenominational, coed institution. Suburban setting. *Awards:* B, M. *Entrance level for U.S. students:* Moderately difficult. *Enrollment:* 1,660 total; 1,528 undergraduates (64% women) including 2% international students from 26 foreign countries. *Faculty:* 145. *Library holdings:* 142,688 books, 8,555 current serial subscriptions. *Total majors:* 32. *Expenses:* (2006–07) $24,278; room and board, $6640 (on campus); room only, $4466 (on campus). *Financial aid:* Need-based college/university scholarships/grants from institutional funds, on-campus employment. Non-need-based college/university scholarships/grants from institutional funds, on-campus employment. Forms required: institution's own financial aid form, International Student's Certification of Finances.

GREENFIELD COMMUNITY COLLEGE, GREENFIELD

General Information State-supported, 2-year, coed college. Small town setting. *Awards:* A. *Entrance level for U.S. students:* Noncompetitive. *Enrollment:* 2,217 total (63% women) including international students from 7 foreign countries. *Undergraduate faculty:* 199. *Library holdings:* 52,690 books, 356 current serial subscriptions. *Total majors:* 29.

Information for International Students For fall 2006: 35 international students applied, 31 were accepted, 27 enrolled. Students can start in fall or spring. Transfers accepted from institutions abroad. *Admission tests:* Required: TOEFL (minimum score: paper-based 550; computer-based 213). TOEFL can be waived under certain conditions. *Application deadline:* Rolling. *Expenses:* (2006–07) $11,747. *Financial aid:* Need-based college/university scholarships/grants from institutional funds, tuition waivers, loans from institutional funds, on-campus employment. Non-need-based college/university scholarships/grants from institutional funds, athletic awards. *Services:* International student adviser on campus. Full-time and part-time ESL programs on campus. ESL program available during the academic year. Employment opportunities (on-campus) available. *Contact:* Assistant Director of Admission, Greenfield Community College, One College Drive, Greenfield, MA 01301. Telephone: 413-775-1840. Fax: 413-773-5129. E-mail: vlasenko@gcc.mass.edu. URL: http://www.gcc.mass.edu.

HAMPSHIRE COLLEGE, AMHERST

General Information Independent, 4-year, coed college. Small town setting. *Awards:* B. *Entrance level for U.S. students:* Moderately difficult. *Enrollment:* 1,448 total (59% women) including 3% international students from 32 foreign countries. *Undergraduate faculty:* 149. *Library holdings:* 129,350 books, 2,288 current serial subscriptions, 39,683 audiovisual materials. *Total majors:* 46.

Information for International Students For fall 2006: 154 international students applied, 32 were accepted, 9 enrolled. Students can start in fall or spring. Transfers accepted from institutions abroad. *Admission tests:* Required: TOEFL (minimum score: paper-based 577; computer-based 233). TOEFL can be waived under certain conditions. *Application deadline:* 1/15. *Expenses:* (2006–07) $34,605; room and board, $9030 (on campus); room only, $5759 (on campus). *Financial aid:* Need-based college/university scholarships/grants from institutional funds, on-campus employment. Non-need-based college/university scholarships/grants from institutional funds, on-campus employment. Forms required: International Student's Financial Aid Application, International Student's Certification of Finances. International transfer students are eligible to apply for aid. 41 international students on campus received college administered financial aid ($31,329 average). *Housing:* Guaranteed. *Services:* International student adviser on campus. Internships and employment opportunities (on-campus) available. *Contact:* Associate Director of Admissions, Admissions Office, Hampshire College, 893 West Street, Amherst, MA 01002. Telephone: 413-559-5471. Fax: 413-559-5631. E-mail: admissions@hampshire.edu. URL: http://www.hampshire.edu.

HARVARD UNIVERSITY, CAMBRIDGE

General Information Independent, coed university. Urban setting. *Awards:* B, M, D, FP. *Entrance level for U.S. students:* Most difficult. *Enrollment:* 19,538 total; 6,715 undergraduates (49% women) including 9% international students from 95 foreign countries. *Faculty:* 2,035. *Total majors:* 141.

Information for International Students For fall 2006: 3433 international students applied, 185 were accepted, 152 enrolled. Students can start in fall. Transfers accepted from institutions abroad. *Admission tests:* Required: SAT or ACT, SAT Subject Tests. *Application deadline:* 1/1. *Expenses:* (2006–07) $33,709; room and board, $9946 (on campus); room only, $5328 (on campus). *Financial aid:* Need-based college/university scholarships/grants from institutional funds, loans from institutional funds, on-campus employment. Forms required: institution's own financial aid form, income tax form(s), wage statements. International transfer students are eligible to apply for aid. For fall 2006 (estimated), 471 international students on campus received college administered financial aid ($40,500 average). *Housing:* Guaranteed, also available during summer. *Services:* International student adviser on campus. Internships and employment opportunities (on-campus) available. *Contact:* Harvard College Office of Admissions and Financial Aid, International Admissions, Harvard University, 86 Brattle Street, Cambridge, MA 02138. Telephone: 617-495-1551. Fax: 617-495-8821. E-mail: college@fas.harvard.edu. URL: http://www.harvard.edu.

HELLENIC COLLEGE, BROOKLINE

General Information Independent Greek Orthodox, 4-year, coed college. Suburban setting. *Awards:* B (also offers graduate degree programs through Holy Cross Greek Orthodox School of Theology). *Entrance level for U.S. students:* Minimally difficult. *Enrollment:* 191 total; 82 undergraduates (44% women) including 20% international students from 11 foreign countries. *Undergraduate faculty:* 29. *Library holdings:* 115,805 books, 721 current serial subscriptions. *Total majors:* 6.

Information for International Students For fall 2006: 13 international students applied, 10 were accepted, 5 enrolled. Students can start in fall or spring. Transfers accepted from institutions abroad. *Admission tests:* Required: TOEFL (minimum score: iBT 61; paper-based 500; computer-based 173; minimum score for ESL admission: iBT 61; paper-based 500; computer-based 173). Recommended: SAT or ACT from English speaking schools. *Application deadline:* 8/1. *Expenses:* (2006–07) $16,515; room and board, $10,370 (on campus). *Financial aid:* Need-based college/university scholarships/grants from institutional funds. Non-need financial aid available. Forms required: institution's own financial aid form, International Student's Financial Aid Application, International Student's Certification of Finances. For fall 2005, international students on campus received college administered aid averaging $14,125. *Housing:* Guaranteed, also available during summer. *Services:* International student adviser on campus. *Contact:* Director of Admissions, Hellenic College, 50 Goddard Avenue, Brookline, MA 02445. Telephone: 617-731-3500 Ext. 260. Fax: 617-850-1460. E-mail: sdaly@hchc.edu. URL: http://www.hchc.edu.

HOLYOKE COMMUNITY COLLEGE, HOLYOKE

General Information State-supported, 2-year, coed college. Small town setting. *Awards:* A. *Entrance level for U.S. students:* Noncompetitive. *Enrollment:* 6,297 total (64% women) including 1% international students. *Undergraduate faculty:* 446. *Library holdings:* 76,322 books, 284 current serial subscriptions, 6,583 audiovisual materials. *Total majors:* 42. *Expenses:* (2007–08) $7712.

LASELL COLLEGE, NEWTON

General Information Independent, coed institution. Suburban setting. *Awards:* B, M. *Entrance level for U.S. students:* Moderately difficult. *Enrollment:* 1,253 total; 1,216 undergraduates (69% women) including 3% international students from 15 foreign countries. *Faculty:* 162. *Library holdings:* 60,250 books, 474 current serial subscriptions, 9,844 audiovisual materials. *Total majors:* 28. *Expenses:* (2006–07) $20,900; room and board, $9200 (on campus). *Financial aid:* Need-based financial aid available. Non-need-based on-campus employment. Forms required: institution's own financial aid form. For fall 2005, 1 international student on campus received college administered financial aid ($5000 average).

LESLEY UNIVERSITY, CAMBRIDGE

General Information Independent, coed institution. Urban setting. *Awards:* A, B, M, D. *Entrance level for U.S. students:* Moderately difficult. *Enrollment:* 6,539 total; 1,351 undergraduates (75% women) including 2% international students from 24 foreign countries. *Faculty:* 212. *Library holdings:* 118,729 books, 1,150 current serial subscriptions, 49,943 audiovisual materials. *Total majors:* 22. *Expenses:* (2007–08) $25,850; room and board, $12,100 (on campus); room only, $6800 (on campus).

MASSACHUSETTS BAY COMMUNITY COLLEGE, WELLESLEY HILLS

General Information State-supported, 2-year, coed college. Suburban setting. *Awards:* A. *Entrance level for U.S. students:* Noncompetitive. *Enrollment:* 5,015 total (58% women) including 2% international students from 50 foreign countries. *Undergraduate faculty:* 336. *Library holdings:* 50,333 books, 291 current serial subscriptions, 4,650 audiovisual materials. *Total majors:* 30.

Massachusetts

Information for International Students For fall 2006: 120 international students applied, 117 were accepted, 58 enrolled. Students can start in fall, spring, or summer. Transfers accepted from institutions abroad. *Admission tests:* Required: TOEFL (minimum score: paper-based 500; computer-based 173), placement test. TOEFL can be waived under certain conditions. *Application deadline:* Rolling. *Expenses:* (2006–07) $9790. *Financial aid:* Non-need-based loans from outside sources. *Services:* International student adviser on campus. Full-time and part-time ESL programs on campus. ESL program available during the academic year. Internships and employment opportunities (on-campus) available. *Contact:* Director of Admissions, Massachusetts Bay Community College, 50 Oakland Street, Wellesley Hills, MA 02481. Telephone: 781-239-5001. Fax: 617-239-1047. E-mail: draposa@massbay.edu. URL: http://www.massbay.edu.

MASSACHUSETTS COLLEGE OF ART, BOSTON

General Information State-supported, coed institution. Urban setting. *Awards:* B, M. *Entrance level for U.S. students:* Very difficult. *Enrollment:* 2,286 total; 2,136 undergraduates (66% women) including 3% international students from 22 foreign countries. *Faculty:* 209. *Library holdings:* 231,586 books, 757 current serial subscriptions. *Total majors:* 17.

Information for International Students For fall 2006: 80 international students applied, 48 were accepted, 20 enrolled. Students can start in fall, spring, or summer. Transfers accepted from institutions abroad. *Admission tests:* Required: SAT or ACT, TOEFL (minimum score: iBT 85; paper-based 550; computer-based 213). *Application deadline:* 3/1. *Expenses:* (2006–07) $20,600; room and board, $11,090 (on campus). *Housing:* Available during summer. *Services:* International student adviser on campus. Internships and employment opportunities (on-campus) available. *Contact:* Interim Director of Admissions, Massachusetts College of Art, 621 Huntington Avenue, Boston, MA 02115. Telephone: 617-879-7222. Fax: 617-879-7250. E-mail: lpolanco@massart.edu. URL: http://www.massart.edu.

MASSACHUSETTS COLLEGE OF PHARMACY AND HEALTH SCIENCES, BOSTON

General Information Independent, coed university. Urban setting. *Awards:* B, M, D, FP. *Entrance level for U.S. students:* Moderately difficult. *Enrollment:* 3,298 total; 2,187 undergraduates (68% women) including 3% international students from 40 foreign countries. *Faculty:* 176. *Library holdings:* 32,000 books, 700 current serial subscriptions. *Total majors:* 12. *Expenses:* (2006–07) $21,880; room and board, $11,300 (on campus). *Financial aid:* Forms required: International Student's Certification of Finances.

MASSACHUSETTS INSTITUTE OF TECHNOLOGY, CAMBRIDGE

General Information Independent, coed university. Urban setting. *Awards:* B, M, D. *Entrance level for U.S. students:* Most difficult. *Enrollment:* 10,253 total; 4,127 undergraduates (44% women) including 8% international students from 86 foreign countries. *Faculty:* 1,613. *Library holdings:* 964,656 books, 22,991 current serial subscriptions, 33,005 audiovisual materials. *Total majors:* 33.

Information for International Students For fall 2006: 2712 international students applied, 112 were accepted, 83 enrolled. Students can start in fall. Transfers accepted from institutions abroad. *Admission tests:* Required: SAT or ACT, SAT Subject Tests. Recommended: TOEFL. TOEFL can be waived under certain conditions. *Application deadline:* 1/1. *Expenses:* (2006–07) $33,600; room and board, $9950 (on campus); room only, $5600 (on campus). *Financial aid:* Need-based college/university scholarships/grants from institutional funds, loans from institutional funds, on-campus employment. Non-need-based on-campus employment, outside scholarships. Forms required: equivalent of parents' complete federal income tax returns. International transfer students are eligible to apply for aid. For fall 2005, 235 international students on campus received college administered financial aid ($31,612 average). *Housing:* Guaranteed, also available during summer. *Services:* International student adviser on campus. ESL program available during the academic year. Internships and employment opportunities (on-campus and off-campus) available. *Contact:* Associate Director of Admissions, Massachusetts Institute of Technology, 77 Massachusetts Avenue, Room 3-108, Cambridge, MA 02139-4307. Telephone: 617-253-4791. Fax: 617-258-8304. E-mail: mitintl@mit.edu. URL: http://web.mit.edu.

MASSACHUSETTS MARITIME ACADEMY, BUZZARDS BAY

General Information State-supported, coed, primarily men's institution. Small town setting. *Awards:* B, M. *Entrance level for U.S. students:* Moderately difficult. *Enrollment:* 1,008 total; 969

undergraduates (12% women) including 1% international students from 4 foreign countries. *Faculty:* 70. *Library holdings:* 55,000 books, 253 current serial subscriptions, 200 audiovisual materials. *Total majors:* 8. *Expenses:* (2006–07) $16,595; room and board, $6935 (on campus); room only, $3569 (on campus). *Financial aid:* Need-based college/university scholarships/grants from institutional funds, tuition waivers, loans from outside sources, on-campus employment, Montgomery GI Bill Education Benefits. Non-need-based college/university scholarships/grants from institutional funds, tuition waivers, loans from outside sources, Montomgery GI Bill Education Benefits. Forms required: institution's own financial aid form, scholarship application form. For fall 2005, 5 international students on campus received college administered financial aid ($12,252 average).

MERRIMACK COLLEGE, NORTH ANDOVER

General Information Independent Roman Catholic, coed institution. Suburban setting. *Awards:* A, B, M. *Entrance level for U.S. students:* Moderately difficult. *Enrollment:* 2,251 total; 2,213 undergraduates (53% women) including 1% international students from 14 foreign countries. *Faculty:* 208. *Library holdings:* 120,836 books, 2,066 current serial subscriptions, 2,462 audiovisual materials. *Total majors:* 42. *Expenses:* (2006–07) $27,070; room and board, $10,705 (on campus); room only, $6050 (on campus). *Financial aid:* Need-based college/university scholarships/grants from institutional funds. Non-need-based athletic awards. Forms required: International Student's Financial Aid Application, International Student's Certification of Finances. For fall 2005, 2 international students on campus received college administered financial aid ($10,000 average).

MIDDLESEX COMMUNITY COLLEGE, BEDFORD

General Information State-supported, 2-year, coed college. Suburban setting. *Awards:* A. *Entrance level for U.S. students:* Noncompetitive. *Enrollment:* 8,016 total. *Undergraduate faculty:* 468. *Library holdings:* 52,960 books, 538 current serial subscriptions. *Total majors:* 39.

MOUNT HOLYOKE COLLEGE, SOUTH HADLEY

General Information Independent, women's institution. Small town setting. *Awards:* B, M. *Entrance level for U.S. students:* Very difficult. *Enrollment:* 2,153 total; 2,149 undergraduates including 17% international students from 71 foreign countries. *Faculty:* 242. *Total majors:* 48.

Information for International Students For fall 2006: 779 international students applied, 202 were accepted, 89 enrolled. Students can start in fall or spring. Transfers accepted from institutions abroad. *Admission tests:* TOEFL can be waived under certain conditions. *Application deadline:* 1/15. *Expenses:* (2006–07) $34,266; room and board, $10,040 (on campus); room only, $5130 (on campus). *Financial aid:* Need-based college/university scholarships/grants from institutional funds, loans from institutional funds, loans from outside sources, on-campus employment. Non-need-based college/university scholarships/grants from institutional funds, loans from outside sources, on-campus employment. Forms required: International Student's Financial Aid Application, International Student's Certification of Finances, parent income tax or income verification document. International transfer students are eligible to apply for aid. For fall 2006 (estimated), 300 international students on campus received college administered financial aid ($38,377 average). *Housing:* Guaranteed, also available during summer. *Services:* International student adviser on campus. ESL program at cooperating institution. ESL program available during the academic year. Internships and employment opportunities (on-campus) available. *Contact:* Assistant Director of Admission, Mount Holyoke College, Office of Admission, Newhall Center, 50 College Street, South Hadley, MA 01075. Telephone: 413-538-2769. Fax: 413-538-2409. E-mail: ontia@mtholyoke.edu. URL: http://www.mtholyoke.edu.

See In-Depth Description on page 133.

MOUNT IDA COLLEGE, NEWTON

General Information Independent, 4-year, coed college. Suburban setting. *Awards:* A, B. *Entrance level for U.S. students:* Moderately difficult. *Enrollment:* 1,367 total (69% women) including 5% international students from 25 foreign countries. *Undergraduate faculty:* 170. *Library holdings:* 94,464 books, 3,735 current serial subscriptions, 3,655 audiovisual materials. *Total majors:* 24.

Information for International Students For fall 2006: 84 international students applied, 62 were accepted, 22 enrolled. Students can start in fall or spring. Transfers accepted from institutions abroad. *Admission tests:* Required: SAT or ACT, TOEFL (minimum score: iBT 70; paper-based 525; computer-based 197; minimum score for ESL admission: iBT 52; paper-based 470; computer-based 150). Recommended: ACT. TOEFL can be waived under certain conditions. *Application deadline:* Rolling. *Expenses:*

(2007–08) $21,330; room and board, $10,635 (on campus). *Financial aid:* Need-based college/university scholarships/grants from institutional funds, loans from outside sources, on-campus employment. Non-need-based college/university scholarships/grants from institutional funds, tuition waivers, on-campus employment. For fall 2006 (estimated), 76 international students on campus received college administered financial aid ($1792 average). *Housing:* Guaranteed. *Services:* International student adviser on campus. Full-time ESL program on campus. ESL program available during the academic year. Internships and employment opportunities (on-campus) available. *Contact:* Associate Dean of Admissions, Mount Ida College, 777 Dedham Street, Newton, MA 02459. Telephone: 617-928-4500 Ext. 4508. Fax: 617-928-4507. E-mail: nrlemelman@mountida.edu. URL: http://www.mountida.edu.

See In-Depth Description on page 134.

MOUNT WACHUSETT COMMUNITY COLLEGE, GARDNER

General Information State-supported, 2-year, coed college. Small town setting. *Awards:* A. *Entrance level for U.S. students:* Noncompetitive. *Enrollment:* 3,937 total (67% women) including 1% international students from 14 foreign countries. *Undergraduate faculty:* 221. *Library holdings:* 54,084 books, 27,248 current serial subscriptions, 2,509 audiovisual materials. *Total majors:* 35. *Expenses:* (2007–08) $10,560. *Financial aid:* Need-based college/university scholarships/grants from institutional funds, tuition waivers, on-campus employment. Non-need-based college/university scholarships/grants from institutional funds, on-campus employment. Forms required: institution's own financial aid form.

THE NEW ENGLAND COLLEGE OF OPTOMETRY, BOSTON

General Information Independent, coed college. Urban setting. *Awards:* FP. *Entrance level for U.S. students:* Moderately difficult. *Library holdings:* 10,485 books, 275 current serial subscriptions. *Total majors:* 1.

Information for International Students Students can start in fall or summer. *Admission tests:* Required: TOEFL (minimum score: paper-based 550; computer-based 213; minimum score for ESL admission: paper-based 550; computer-based 213), OAT. *Application deadline:* 3/31. *Contact:* Director of Admissions, The New England College of Optometry, 424 Beacon Street, Boston, MA 02115. Telephone: 617-236-6210. Fax: 617-369-0162. E-mail: farrat@ne-optometry.edu. URL: http://www.neco.edu.

NEW ENGLAND CONSERVATORY OF MUSIC, BOSTON

General Information Independent, coed institution. Urban setting. *Awards:* B, M, D. *Entrance level for U.S. students:* Very difficult. *Enrollment:* 792 total; 379 undergraduates (45% women) including 6% international students from 20 foreign countries. *Faculty:* 214. *Library holdings:* 86,403 books, 300 current serial subscriptions, 55,939 audiovisual materials. *Total majors:* 8. *Expenses:* (2007–08) $30,975; room and board, $11,300 (on campus). *Financial aid:* Need-based college/university scholarships/grants from institutional funds, loans from outside sources, on-campus employment. Non-need-based college/university scholarships/grants from institutional funds, on-campus employment. Forms required: institution's own financial aid form. 53 international students on campus received college administered financial aid ($17,074 average).

NICHOLS COLLEGE, DUDLEY

General Information Independent, coed institution. Suburban setting. *Awards:* A, B, M. *Entrance level for U.S. students:* Moderately difficult. *Enrollment:* 1,470 total; 1,215 undergraduates (42% women) including 0.3% international students from 5 foreign countries. *Faculty:* 65. *Library holdings:* 70,046 books, 161 current serial subscriptions, 1,553 audiovisual materials. *Total majors:* 14.

Information for International Students For fall 2006: 8 international students applied, 7 were accepted, 2 enrolled. Students can start in fall or spring. Transfers accepted from institutions abroad. *Admission tests:* Required: TOEFL (minimum score: paper-based 550; computer-based 213). Recommended: SAT or ACT. *Application deadline:* Rolling. *Expenses:* (2006–07) $23,900; room and board, $8800 (on campus); room only, $4800 (on campus). *Financial aid:* Need-based financial aid available. Non-need-based college/university scholarships/grants from institutional funds, loans from outside sources. Forms required: International Student's Certification of Finances. For fall 2005, 3 international students on campus received college administered financial aid ($7833 average). *Housing:* Guaranteed. Internships and employment opportunities (on-campus) available. *Contact:* Admissions Counselor, Office of Admissions, Nichols College, Office of Admissions, PO Box 5000, Dudley, MA 01571. Telephone: 508-213-2371. Fax: 508-943-9885. E-mail: paul.brower@nichols.edu. URL: http://www.nichols.edu.

NORTHEASTERN UNIVERSITY, BOSTON

General Information Independent, coed university. Urban setting. *Awards:* B, M, D, FP. *Entrance level for U.S. students:* Very difficult. *Enrollment:* 20,605 total; 15,195 undergraduates (50% women) including 4% international students from 88 foreign countries. *Faculty:* 1,273. *Library holdings:* 994,122 books, 6,773 current serial subscriptions. *Total majors:* 83.

Information for International Students For fall 2006: 1128 international students applied, 669 were accepted, 103 enrolled. Students can start in fall or winter. *Admission tests:* Required: SAT or ACT, TOEFL (minimum score: paper-based 550; computer-based 213). *Application deadline:* 1/15. *Expenses:* (2006–07) $30,309; room and board, $10,970 (on campus); room only, $5840 (on campus). *Financial aid:* Non-need financial aid available. Forms required: International Student's Certification of Finances. For fall 2006 (estimated), 95 international students on campus received college administered financial aid ($21,240 average). *Contact:* International Admissions, Northeastern University, 150 Richards Hall, 360 Huntington Avenue, Boston, MA 02115. Telephone: 617-373-2200. Fax: 617-373-8780. E-mail: internationaladmissions@neu.edu. URL: http://www.northeastern.edu.

See In-Depth Description on page 141.

NORTHERN ESSEX COMMUNITY COLLEGE, HAVERHILL

General Information State-supported, 2-year, coed college. Suburban setting. *Awards:* A. *Entrance level for U.S. students:* Noncompetitive. *Enrollment:* 6,362 total including 1% international students. *Undergraduate faculty:* 497. *Library holdings:* 61,120 books, 598 current serial subscriptions. *Total majors:* 59. *Expenses:* (2006–07) $3660. *Financial aid:* Need-based loans from institutional funds.

NORTH SHORE COMMUNITY COLLEGE, DANVERS

General Information State-supported, 2-year, coed college. Suburban setting. *Awards:* A. *Entrance level for U.S. students:* Noncompetitive. *Enrollment:* 6,910 total (61% women) including 0.3% international students from 8 foreign countries. *Undergraduate faculty:* 412. *Library holdings:* 71,548 books, 403 current serial subscriptions, 7,058 audiovisual materials. *Total majors:* 43. *Expenses:* (2007–08) $8352. *Financial aid:* Need-based loans from outside sources. Non-need-based loans from outside sources.

PINE MANOR COLLEGE, CHESTNUT HILL

General Information Independent, 4-year, women's college. Suburban setting. *Awards:* A, B. *Entrance level for U.S. students:* Moderately difficult. *Enrollment:* 491 total including 6% international students from 22 foreign countries. *Undergraduate faculty:* 76. *Library holdings:* 65,632 books, 272 current serial subscriptions, 1,944 audiovisual materials. *Total majors:* 16. *Expenses:* (2007–08) $17,750; room and board, $10,570 (on campus). *Financial aid:* Need-based college/university scholarships/grants from institutional funds. Non-need financial aid available. 30 international students on campus received college administered financial aid ($6427 average).

QUINSIGAMOND COMMUNITY COLLEGE, WORCESTER

General Information State-supported, 2-year, coed college. Urban setting. *Awards:* A. *Entrance level for U.S. students:* Moderately difficult. *Enrollment:* 5,970 total (60% women) including 0.5% international students from 13 foreign countries. *Undergraduate faculty:* 398. *Library holdings:* 54,000 books, 310 current serial subscriptions, 230 audiovisual materials. *Total majors:* 27.

REGIS COLLEGE, WESTON

General Information Independent Roman Catholic, coed institution. Small town setting. *Awards:* A, B, M. *Entrance level for U.S. students:* Moderately difficult. *Enrollment:* 1,314 total; 859 undergraduates (98% women) including 1% international students from 8 foreign countries. *Faculty:* 109. *Library holdings:* 139,837 books, 787 current serial subscriptions, 6,204 audiovisual materials. *Total majors:* 23. *Expenses:* (2006–07) $23,680; room and board, $10,580 (on campus); room only, $5370 (on campus). *Financial aid:* Need-based college/university scholarships/grants from institutional funds. Non-need-based college/university scholarships/grants from institutional funds. Forms required: institution's own financial aid form. For fall 2006 (estimated), 3 international students on campus received college administered financial aid ($26,333 average).

SALEM STATE COLLEGE, SALEM

General Information State-supported, coed institution. Suburban setting. *Awards:* B, M. *Entrance level for U.S. students:* Minimally difficult. *Enrollment:* 10,230 total; 7,455 undergraduates (63%

Massachusetts

Salem State College (continued)

women) including 4% international students from 49 foreign
countries. *Faculty:* 717. *Library holdings:* 277,985 books, 1,914
current serial subscriptions, 3,811 audiovisual materials.
Total majors: 60. *Expenses:* (2006–07) $12,110; room only, $5380 (on
campus).

SCHOOL OF THE MUSEUM OF FINE ARTS, BOSTON, BOSTON
General Information Independent, coed institution. Urban
setting. *Awards:* B, M. *Entrance level for U.S. students:* Moderately
difficult. *Enrollment:* 733 total; 634 undergraduates (65% women)
including 6% international students from 28 foreign countries.
Faculty: 180. *Library holdings:* 1 million books, 523 current serial
subscriptions, 408 audiovisual materials. *Total majors:* 20.
Information for International Students For fall 2006: 128
international students applied, 89 were accepted, 73 enrolled.
Students can start in fall or spring. Transfers accepted from
institutions abroad. *Admission tests:* Required: TOEFL (minimum
score: iBT 80; paper-based 550; computer-based 213; minimum
score for ESL admission: iBT 80; paper-based 550; computer-based
213), ELS. Recommended: SAT or ACT. TOEFL can be waived
under certain conditions. *Application deadline:* 2/1. *Expenses:*
(2006–07) $26,244; room only, $11,380 (on campus). *Financial aid:*
Need-based college/university scholarships/grants from institutional
funds. Non-need-based college/university scholarships/grants from
institutional funds. Forms required: institution's own financial aid
form. International transfer students are eligible to apply for aid.
Housing: Available during summer. *Services:* International student
adviser on campus. ESL program at cooperating institution. ESL
program available during the academic year and the summer.
Internships and employment opportunities (on-campus) available.
Contact: Associate Dean of Admissions, School of the Museum of
Fine Arts, Boston, 230 The Fenway, Boston, MA 02115.
Telephone: 617-369-3626 Ext. 3133. Fax: 617-643-6078.
E-mail: admissions@smfa.edu. URL: http://www.smfa.edu.
See In-Depth Description on page 181.

SIMMONS COLLEGE, BOSTON
General Information Independent, undergraduate: women only;
graduate: coed university. Urban setting. *Awards:* B, M, D.
Entrance level for U.S. students: Moderately difficult. *Enrollment:*
4,849 total; 2,009 undergraduates (100% women) including 2%
international students from 61 foreign countries. *Faculty:* 374.
Library holdings: 243,161 books, 1,696 current serial subscriptions,
6,202 audiovisual materials. *Total majors:* 52.
Information for International Students For fall 2006: 111
international students applied, 48 were accepted, 20 enrolled.
Students can start in fall, spring, or summer. Transfers accepted
from institutions abroad. *Admission tests:* Required: TOEFL
(minimum score: iBT 83; paper-based 560; computer-based 220;
minimum score for ESL admission: iBT 83; paper-based 560;
computer-based 220), IELTS. Recommended: SAT or ACT. TOEFL
can be waived under certain conditions. *Application deadline:* 2/1.
Expenses: (2006–07) $26,705; room and board, $10,710 (on campus).
Financial aid: Non-need-based college/university
scholarships/grants from institutional funds, tuition waivers.
Housing: Guaranteed. *Services:* International student adviser on
campus. Internships and employment opportunities (on-campus)
available. *Contact:* Assistant Director of Admission and Coordinator
of International Recruitment, Admission Office, Simmons College,
300 The Fenway, Boston, MA 02115. Telephone: 617-521-2051.
Fax: 617-521-3190. E-mail: ugadm@simmons.edu.
URL: http://www.simmons.edu.
See In-Depth Description on page 186.

SMITH COLLEGE, NORTHAMPTON
General Information Independent, undergraduate: women only;
graduate: coed institution. Small town setting. *Awards:* B, M, D.
Entrance level for U.S. students: Very difficult. *Enrollment:* 3,092
total; 2,634 undergraduates (100% women) including 7%
international students from 56 foreign countries. *Faculty:* 313.
Library holdings: 1.4 million books, 8,741 current serial
subscriptions, 68,550 audiovisual materials. *Total majors:* 51.
Expenses: (2006–07) $32,558; room and board, $10,880 (on campus).
Financial aid: Need-based and non-need-based financial aid
available. Forms required: institution's own financial aid form,
International Student's Certification of Finances, foreign income tax
returns-translated to English. For fall 2006 (estimated), 110
international students on campus received college administered
financial aid ($38,450 average).

SPRINGFIELD COLLEGE, SPRINGFIELD
General Information Independent, coed institution. Suburban
setting. *Awards:* B, M, D. *Entrance level for U.S. students:*
Moderately difficult. *Enrollment:* 3,155 total; 2,217 undergraduates
(48% women) including 0.2% international students. *Faculty:* 342.
Library holdings: 125,000 books, 850 current serial subscriptions.
Total majors: 40. *Expenses:* (2006–07) $22,715; room and board,
$8130 (on campus); room only, $4400 (on campus).

SPRINGFIELD TECHNICAL COMMUNITY COLLEGE, SPRINGFIELD
General Information State-supported, 2-year, coed college. Urban
setting. *Awards:* A. *Entrance level for U.S. students:*
Noncompetitive. *Enrollment:* 5,992 total (59% women) including 1%
international students. *Undergraduate faculty:* 341. *Library
holdings:* 61,857 books, 266 current serial subscriptions, 16,810
audiovisual materials. *Total majors:* 57. *Expenses:* (2007–08) $9966.

STONEHILL COLLEGE, EASTON
General Information Independent Roman Catholic, coed
institution. Suburban setting. *Awards:* B, M. *Entrance level for U.S.
students:* Very difficult. *Enrollment:* 2,386 total; 2,371
undergraduates (60% women) including 0.3% international students
from 9 foreign countries. *Faculty:* 255. *Library holdings:* 205,400
books, 2,196 current serial subscriptions, 7,123 audiovisual
materials. *Total majors:* 32. *Expenses:* (2006–07) $26,345; room and
board, $11,040 (on campus); room only, $8990 (on campus).
Financial aid: Forms required: International Student's Certification
of Finances.

SUFFOLK UNIVERSITY, BOSTON
General Information Independent, coed institution. Urban
setting. *Awards:* A, B, M, D, FP (doctoral degree in law). *Entrance
level for U.S. students:* Moderately difficult. *Enrollment:* 8,863 total;
5,214 undergraduates (58% women) including 9% international
students from 99 foreign countries. *Faculty:* 980. *Library holdings:*
120,389 books, 24,598 current serial subscriptions, 558 audiovisual
materials. *Total majors:* 61.
Information for International Students Students can start in
fall or spring. Transfers accepted from institutions abroad.
Admission tests: Required: TOEFL (minimum score: paper-based
525; computer-based 197; minimum score for ESL admission:
paper-based 450; computer-based 110), SAT required for applicants
whose first language is English. TOEFL can be waived under
certain conditions. *Application deadline:* 6/30. *Expenses:* (2006–07)
$22,690; room and board, $12,756 (on campus); room only, $10,596
(on campus). *Financial aid:* Need-based college/university
scholarships/grants from institutional funds, loans from
institutional funds, loans from outside sources, on-campus
employment. Non-need-based college/university scholarships/grants
from institutional funds, loans from institutional funds, loans from
outside sources, on-campus employment. Forms required: aid is
merit based and is determined by GPA. International transfer
students are eligible to apply for aid. For fall 2006 (estimated), 118
international students on campus received college administered
financial aid ($6872 average). *Housing:* Available during summer.
Services: International student adviser on campus. Part-time ESL
program on campus. ESL program available during the academic
year and the summer. Internships and employment opportunities
(on-campus and off-campus) available. *Contact:* Director of
Undergraduate Admissions, Suffolk University, Boston, MA 02108.
Telephone: 617-573-8460. Fax: 617-557-1574.
E-mail: admission@suffolk.edu. URL: http://www.suffolk.edu.
See In-Depth Description on page 198.

TUFTS UNIVERSITY, MEDFORD
General Information Independent, coed university. Suburban
setting. *Awards:* B, M, D, FP. *Entrance level for U.S. students:* Most
difficult. *Enrollment:* 9,638 total; 4,995 undergraduates (51%
women) including 6% international students from 67 foreign
countries. *Faculty:* 1,056. *Library holdings:* 1.7 million books, 4,341
current serial subscriptions, 40,307 audiovisual materials.
Total majors: 64. *Expenses:* (2006–07) $34,730; room and board,
$9770 (on campus); room only, $5020 (on campus). *Financial aid:*
Need-based college/university scholarships/grants from institutional
funds, on-campus employment. Forms required: International
Student's Financial Aid Application, income and asset
documentation. For fall 2006 (estimated), 42 international students
on campus received college administered financial aid ($27,715
average).

UNIVERSITY OF MASSACHUSETTS AMHERST, AMHERST
General Information State-supported, coed university. Small
town setting. *Awards:* A, B, M, D. *Entrance level for U.S. students:*
Moderately difficult. *Enrollment:* 25,593 total; 19,823
undergraduates (49% women) including 1% international students
from 97 foreign countries. *Faculty:* 1,346. *Library holdings:* 3.2
million books, 40,749 current serial subscriptions, 24,180

audiovisual materials. *Total majors:* 85. *Expenses:* (2006–07) $17,818; room and board, $6989 (on campus); room only, $3905 (on campus).

UNIVERSITY OF MASSACHUSETTS BOSTON, BOSTON
General Information State-supported, coed university. Urban setting. *Awards:* B, M, D. *Entrance level for U.S. students:* Moderately difficult. *Enrollment:* 12,362 total; 9,246 undergraduates (57% women) including 3% international students from 133 foreign countries. *Faculty:* 815. *Library holdings:* 584,015 books, 25,575 current serial subscriptions. *Total majors:* 41. *Expenses:* (2006–07) $16,590.

UNIVERSITY OF MASSACHUSETTS DARTMOUTH, NORTH DARTMOUTH
General Information State-supported, coed university. Suburban setting. *Awards:* B, M, D. *Entrance level for U.S. students:* Moderately difficult. *Enrollment:* 8,756 total; 7,626 undergraduates (51% women) including 0.4% international students from 18 foreign countries. *Faculty:* 583. *Library holdings:* 468,266 books, 2,800 current serial subscriptions, 8,179 audiovisual materials. *Total majors:* 48. *Expenses:* (2006–07) $14,991; room and board, $8162 (on campus); room only, $5400 (on campus). *Financial aid:* Need-based college/university scholarships/grants from institutional funds, tuition waivers, loans from outside sources, on-campus employment. Non-need-based college/university scholarships/grants from institutional funds, tuition waivers, loans from outside sources, on-campus employment.

UNIVERSITY OF MASSACHUSETTS LOWELL, LOWELL
General Information State-supported, coed university. Urban setting. *Awards:* A, B, M, D. *Entrance level for U.S. students:* Moderately difficult. *Enrollment:* 11,208 total; 8,649 undergraduates (40% women) including 1% international students from 12 foreign countries. *Faculty:* 629. *Library holdings:* 517,960 books, 12,300 current serial subscriptions, 14,189 audiovisual materials. *Total majors:* 38. *Expenses:* (2006–07) $15,557; room and board, $6365 (on campus); room only, $3955 (on campus).

WELLESLEY COLLEGE, WELLESLEY
General Information Independent, 4-year, women's college. Suburban setting. *Awards:* B (double bachelor's degree with Massachusetts Institute of Technology). *Entrance level for U.S. students:* Most difficult. *Enrollment:* 2,318 total including 8% international students from 77 foreign countries. *Undergraduate faculty:* 320. *Library holdings:* 864,020 books, 18,180 current serial subscriptions, 31,155 audiovisual materials. *Total majors:* 54. *Expenses:* (2006–07) $33,072; room and board, $10,216 (on campus); room only, $5176 (on campus). *Financial aid:* Need-based college/university scholarships/grants from institutional funds, loans from institutional funds, on-campus employment. Forms required: institution's own financial aid form, International Student's Financial Aid Application, International Student's Certification of Finances, copy of most recent tax return from parents' native country or statement of earnings from. For fall 2006 (estimated), 121 international students on campus received college administered financial aid ($40,812 average).

WENTWORTH INSTITUTE OF TECHNOLOGY, BOSTON
General Information Independent, 4-year, coed college. Urban setting. *Awards:* A, B. *Entrance level for U.S. students:* Moderately difficult. *Enrollment:* 3,613 total (19% women) including 3% international students from 50 foreign countries. *Undergraduate faculty:* 269. *Library holdings:* 77,000 books, 500 current serial subscriptions. *Total majors:* 21.
Information for International Students For fall 2006: 126 international students applied, 93 were accepted, 35 enrolled. Students can start in fall or spring. Transfers accepted from institutions abroad. *Admission tests:* TOEFL can be waived under certain conditions. *Application deadline:* Rolling. *Expenses:* (2006–07) $19,300; room and board, $9300 (on campus). *Financial aid:* Non-need-based college/university scholarships/grants from institutional funds. For fall 2006 (estimated), international students on campus received college administered aid averaging $3000. *Services:* International student adviser on campus. Internships and employment opportunities (on-campus and off-campus) available. *Contact:* Admissions Office, Wentworth Institute of Technology, 550 Huntington Avenue, Boston, MA 02115. Telephone: 617-989-4000. Fax: 617-989-4010. E-mail: admissions@wit.edu. URL: http://www.wit.edu.

See In-Depth Description on page 243.

WESTERN NEW ENGLAND COLLEGE, SPRINGFIELD
General Information Independent, coed institution. Suburban setting. *Awards:* A, B, M, FP. *Entrance level for U.S. students:*
Moderately difficult. *Enrollment:* 3,753 total; 2,813 undergraduates (38% women) including 0.1% international students from 4 foreign countries. *Faculty:* 294. *Library holdings:* 100,010 books, 787 current serial subscriptions. *Total majors:* 35.
Information for International Students For fall 2006: 44 international students applied, 14 were accepted. Students can start in fall or spring. Transfers accepted from institutions abroad. *Admission tests:* Required: either SAT, ACT, or TOEFL is required. Recommended: TOEFL (minimum score: iBT 61; paper-based 500; computer-based 173; minimum score for ESL admission: iBT 61; paper-based 500; computer-based 173). TOEFL can be waived under certain conditions. *Application deadline:* Rolling. *Expenses:* (2007–08) $25,942; room and board, $9998 (on campus). *Financial aid:* Non-need financial aid available. International transfer students are eligible to apply for aid. *Housing:* Guaranteed. *Services:* International student adviser on campus. Internships and employment opportunities (on-campus) available. *Contact:* Assistant Director of Admissions, Western New England College, 1215 Wilbraham Road, Springfield, MA 01119-2654. Telephone: 413-782-1321. Fax: 413-782-1777. E-mail: ugradmis@wnec.edu. URL: http://www.wnec.edu.

See In-Depth Description on page 245.

WHEATON COLLEGE, NORTON
General Information Independent, 4-year, coed college. Small town setting. *Awards:* B. *Entrance level for U.S. students:* Very difficult. *Enrollment:* 1,561 total (62% women) including 2% international students from 34 foreign countries. *Undergraduate faculty:* 158. *Library holdings:* 397,883 books, 10,923 current serial subscriptions, 14,595 audiovisual materials. *Total majors:* 37. *Expenses:* (2006–07) $34,610; room and board, $8150 (on campus); room only, $4300 (on campus). *Financial aid:* Non-need-based college/university scholarships/grants from institutional funds, on-campus employment. Forms required: International Student's Certification of Finances. For fall 2006 (estimated), 21 international students on campus received college administered financial aid ($32,117 average).

WHEELOCK COLLEGE, BOSTON
General Information Independent, coed, primarily women's institution. Urban setting. *Awards:* A, B, M. *Entrance level for U.S. students:* Moderately difficult. *Enrollment:* 1,023 total; 728 undergraduates (96% women) including 1% international students. *Faculty:* 179. *Library holdings:* 83,267 books, 535 current serial subscriptions, 3,504 audiovisual materials. *Total majors:* 8. *Expenses:* (2006–07) $24,090; room and board, $9910 (on campus). *Financial aid:* Non-need-based college/university scholarships/grants from institutional funds. Forms required: International Student's Certification of Finances. 2 international students on campus received college administered financial aid ($7695 average).

WILLIAMS COLLEGE, WILLIAMSTOWN
General Information Independent, coed institution. Small town setting. *Awards:* B, M. *Entrance level for U.S. students:* Most difficult. *Enrollment:* 2,049 total; 2,003 undergraduates (51% women) including 6% international students from 63 foreign countries. *Faculty:* 313. *Library holdings:* 932,000 books, 12,063 current serial subscriptions, 38,076 audiovisual materials. *Total majors:* 33.
Information for International Students For fall 2006: 1034 international students applied, 98 were accepted, 41 enrolled. Students can start in fall. *Admission tests:* Required: SAT or ACT, SAT Subject Tests. Recommended: TOEFL should be submitted if SAT tests are not offered, ACT writing may be submitted in place of SAT. TOEFL can be waived under certain conditions. *Application deadline:* 1/1. *Expenses:* (2006–07) $33,700; room and board, $8950 (on campus); room only, $4540 (on campus). *Financial aid:* Need-based college/university scholarships/grants from institutional funds, loans from institutional funds, on-campus employment. Forms required: International Student's Financial Aid Application, International Student's Certification of Finances, certified income statement on employer's letterhead. For fall 2006 (estimated), 108 international students on campus received college administered financial aid ($42,041 average). *Housing:* Guaranteed. *Services:* International student adviser on campus. Employment opportunities (on-campus) available. *Contact:* Associate Director of Admission, Office of Admission, Williams College, 33 Stetson Court, Williamstown, MA 01267. Telephone: 413-597-2211. Fax: 413-597-4052. E-mail: kparkins@williams.edu. URL: http://www.williams.edu.

WORCESTER POLYTECHNIC INSTITUTE, WORCESTER
General Information Independent, coed university. Suburban setting. *Awards:* B, M, D. *Entrance level for U.S. students:* Very difficult. *Enrollment:* 3,918 total; 2,866 undergraduates (25%

Worcester Polytechnic Institute (continued)
women) including 7% international students from 81 foreign countries. *Faculty:* 314. *Library holdings:* 310,265 books, 23,591 current serial subscriptions, 1,989 audiovisual materials. *Total majors:* 48.
Information for International Students For fall 2006: 471 international students applied, 307 were accepted, 86 enrolled. Students can start in fall or spring. Transfers accepted from institutions abroad. *Admission tests:* Required: SAT or ACT, TOEFL (minimum score: iBT 79; paper-based 550; computer-based 213; minimum score for ESL admission: iBT 61; paper-based 500; computer-based 173), IELTS or MELAB accepted in place of TOEFL. Recommended: SAT Subject Tests. TOEFL can be waived under certain conditions. *Application deadline:* 2/1. *Expenses:* (2006–07) $33,318; room and board, $9950 (on campus); room only, $5840 (on campus). *Financial aid:* Need-based college/university scholarships/grants from institutional funds, loans from institutional funds. Non-need-based college/university scholarships/grants from institutional funds. Forms required: International Student's Financial Aid Application, International Student's Certification of Finances. For fall 2006 (estimated), 154 international students on campus received college administered financial aid ($20,577 average). *Housing:* Available during summer. *Services:* International student adviser on campus. Full-time and part-time ESL programs on campus. ESL program available during the academic year and the summer. Internships and employment opportunities (on-campus and off-campus) available. *Contact:* Coordinator of International Admissions, Office of Admissions, Worcester Polytechnic Institute, Bartlett Center, 100 Institute Road, Worcester, MA 01609. Telephone: 508-831-5286. Fax: 508-831-5875. E-mail: intl_admissions@wpi.edu. URL: http://www.wpi.edu.

See In-Depth Description on page 250.

WORCESTER STATE COLLEGE, WORCESTER

General Information State-supported, coed institution. Urban setting. *Awards:* B, M. *Entrance level for U.S. students:* Moderately difficult. *Enrollment:* 5,440 total; 4,626 undergraduates (60% women) including 2% international students from 26 foreign countries. *Faculty:* 385. *Library holdings:* 197,235 books, 568 current serial subscriptions, 3,326 audiovisual materials. *Total majors:* 23.
Information for International Students For fall 2006: 200 international students applied, 100 were accepted, 50 enrolled. Students can start in fall, spring, or summer. Transfers accepted from institutions abroad. *Admission tests:* Required: SAT, TOEFL (minimum score: paper-based 550; computer-based 200). Recommended: ELS. TOEFL can be waived under certain conditions. *Application deadline:* 5/1. *Expenses:* (2006–07) $11,619; room and board, $7738 (on campus); room only, $5238 (on campus). *Housing:* Guaranteed, also available during summer. *Services:* International student adviser on campus. Full-time and part-time ESL programs on campus. ESL program available during the academic year and the summer. Internships and employment opportunities (on-campus) available. *Contact:* Associate Director, Admission Office, Worcester State College, 486 Chandler Street, Worcester, MA 01602. Telephone: 508-929-8758. Fax: 508-929-8183. E-mail: bmcelroy@worcester.edu. URL: http://www.worcester.edu.

MICHIGAN

ADRIAN COLLEGE, ADRIAN

General Information Independent, 4-year, coed college, affiliated with United Methodist Church. Small town setting. *Awards:* A, B. *Entrance level for U.S. students:* Moderately difficult. *Enrollment:* 1,051 total (50% women) including 1% international students from 5 foreign countries. *Undergraduate faculty:* 139. *Library holdings:* 150,595 books, 571 current serial subscriptions, 1,597 audiovisual materials. *Total majors:* 45.
Information for International Students For fall 2006: 15 international students applied, 5 were accepted. Students can start in fall or spring. Transfers accepted from institutions abroad. *Admission tests:* Required: TOEFL (minimum score: paper-based 500; computer-based 173). Recommended: SAT or ACT. TOEFL can be waived under certain conditions. *Application deadline:* 5/15. *Expenses:* (2007–08) $19,900; room and board, $6780 (on campus); room only, $3000 (on campus). *Financial aid:* Need-based college/university scholarships/grants from institutional funds. Non-need-based college/university scholarships/grants from institutional funds. Forms required: institution's own financial aid form, International Student's Certification of Finances. International transfer students are eligible to apply for aid. For fall 2005, 13 international students on campus received college

administered financial aid ($10,206 average). *Housing:* Guaranteed, also available during summer. *Services:* International student adviser on campus. Part-time ESL program on campus. ESL program available during the academic year. Internships and employment opportunities (on-campus) available. *Contact:* International Admissions Counselor, Adrian College, 110 South Madison Street, Adrian, MI 49221-2575. Telephone: 517-264-3155. Fax: 517-264-3331. E-mail: admissions@adrian.edu. URL: http://www.adrian.edu.

See In-Depth Description on page 29.

ALBION COLLEGE, ALBION

General Information Independent Methodist, 4-year, coed college. Small town setting. *Awards:* B. *Entrance level for U.S. students:* Moderately difficult. *Enrollment:* 1,941 total (56% women) including 1% international students from 19 foreign countries. *Undergraduate faculty:* 170. *Library holdings:* 363,000 books, 2,016 current serial subscriptions, 6,540 audiovisual materials. *Total majors:* 37.
Information for International Students For fall 2006: 100 international students applied, 25 were accepted, 5 enrolled. Students can start in fall or spring. Transfers accepted from institutions abroad. *Admission tests:* Required: TOEFL (minimum score: paper-based 550; computer-based 270). Recommended: SAT or ACT. TOEFL can be waived under certain conditions. *Application deadline:* 4/1. *Expenses:* (2006–07) $26,122; room and board, $7406 (on campus); room only, $3622 (on campus). *Financial aid:* Need-based college/university scholarships/grants from institutional funds, on-campus employment. Non-need-based college/university scholarships/grants from institutional funds, on-campus employment. Forms required: institution's own financial aid form, International Student's Certification of Finances. International transfer students are eligible to apply for aid. For fall 2006 (estimated), 9 international students on campus received college administered financial aid ($16,861 average). *Housing:* Guaranteed, also available during summer. *Services:* International student adviser on campus. ESL program at cooperating institution. ESL program available during the academic year and the summer. Internships and employment opportunities (on-campus and off-campus) available. *Contact:* Vice President for Enrollment, Albion College, 611 East Porter Street, Albion, MI 49224. Telephone: 517-629-0756. Fax: 517-629-0569. E-mail: dhawsey@albion.edu. URL: http://www.albion.edu.

ALMA COLLEGE, ALMA

General Information Independent Presbyterian, 4-year, coed college. Small town setting. *Awards:* B. *Entrance level for U.S. students:* Moderately difficult. *Enrollment:* 1,215 total (59% women) including 1% international students from 7 foreign countries. *Undergraduate faculty:* 117. *Library holdings:* 271,614 books, 1,562 current serial subscriptions, 8,933 audiovisual materials. *Total majors:* 69. *Expenses:* (2006–07) $22,380; room and board, $7774 (on campus); room only, $3830 (on campus). *Financial aid:* Need-based college/university scholarships/grants from institutional funds. Non-need-based college/university scholarships/grants from institutional funds. Forms required: International Student's Financial Aid Application, International Student's Certification of Finances. For fall 2006 (estimated), 13 international students on campus received college administered financial aid ($8196 average).

ANDREWS UNIVERSITY, BERRIEN SPRINGS

General Information Independent Seventh-day Adventist, coed university. Small town setting. *Awards:* A, B, M, D, FP. *Entrance level for U.S. students:* Moderately difficult. *Enrollment:* 3,195 total; 1,733 undergraduates (55% women) including 13% international students from 50 foreign countries. *Faculty:* 266. *Library holdings:* 512,100 books, 3,032 current serial subscriptions. *Total majors:* 82. *Expenses:* (2007–08) $19,528; room and board, $6750 (on campus); room only, $3250 (on campus). *Financial aid:* Need-based financial aid available. Non-need-based college/university scholarships/grants from institutional funds, tuition waivers, on-campus employment. For fall 2005, 166 international students on campus received college administered financial aid ($10,771 average).

AQUINAS COLLEGE, GRAND RAPIDS

General Information Independent Roman Catholic, coed institution. Suburban setting. *Awards:* A, B, M. *Entrance level for U.S. students:* Moderately difficult. *Enrollment:* 2,098 total; 1,780 undergraduates (64% women) including 0.3% international students from 6 foreign countries. *Faculty:* 151. *Library holdings:* 112,458 books, 14,725 current serial subscriptions. *Total majors:* 63.
Information for International Students For fall 2006: 1 international student applied, 1 was accepted, 1 enrolled. Students can start in fall or spring. Transfers accepted from institutions abroad. *Admission tests:* Required: TOEFL (minimum score: iBT 79; paper-based 550; computer-based 213). Recommended: SAT, ACT, ELS. *Application deadline:* 5/1. *Expenses:* (2007–08) $20,048; room

and board, $6422 (on campus); room only, $2966 (on campus). *Financial aid:* Non-need financial aid available. Forms required: institution's own financial aid form. 9 international students on campus received college administered financial aid ($12,198 average). *Housing:* Guaranteed, also available during summer. *Services:* International student adviser on campus. ESL program at cooperating institution. ESL program available during the academic year and the summer. Employment opportunities (on-campus) available. *Contact:* Dean of Admissions, Aquinas College, 1607 Robinson Road, Grand Rapids, MI 49506. Telephone: 616-632-2900. Fax: 616-732-4469. E-mail: admissions@aquinas.edu. URL: http://www.aquinas.edu.

BAKER COLLEGE OF FLINT, FLINT

General Information Independent, 4-year, coed college. Urban setting. *Awards:* A, B. *Entrance level for U.S. students:* Noncompetitive. *Enrollment:* 5,776 total. *Undergraduate faculty:* 315. *Library holdings:* 168,700 books. *Total majors:* 55.
Information for International Students For fall 2006: 10 international students applied, 8 were accepted, 6 enrolled. Students can start in fall, winter, spring, or summer. Transfers accepted from institutions abroad. *Admission tests:* Required: TOEFL (minimum score: paper-based 500; computer-based 173; minimum score for ESL admission: paper-based 500; computer-based 173). TOEFL can be waived under certain conditions. *Application deadline:* 6/15. *Expenses:* (2007–08) $6660; room only, $2600 (on campus). *Housing:* Available during summer. *Services:* International student adviser on campus. ESL program at cooperating institution. ESL program available during the academic year. *Contact:* Admissions Officer, Baker College of Flint, 1050 West Bristol Road, Flint, MI 48507-5508. Telephone: 810-766-4000. Fax: 810-766-4049. E-mail: haellena.weems@baker.edu. URL: http://www.baker.edu.

CALVIN COLLEGE, GRAND RAPIDS

General Information Independent, coed institution, affiliated with Christian Reformed Church. Suburban setting. *Awards:* B, M. *Entrance level for U.S. students:* Moderately difficult. *Enrollment:* 4,187 total; 4,130 undergraduates (54% women) including 7% international students from 48 foreign countries. *Faculty:* 411. *Library holdings:* 824,806 books, 14,464 current serial subscriptions, 26,191 audiovisual materials. *Total majors:* 83.
Information for International Students For fall 2006: 164 international students applied, 145 were accepted, 81 enrolled. Students can start in fall, winter, spring, or summer. Transfers accepted from institutions abroad. *Admission tests:* Required: SAT or ACT, TOEFL (minimum score: paper-based 550; computer-based 213). TOEFL can be waived under certain conditions. *Application deadline:* Rolling. *Expenses:* (2006–07) $20,470; room and board, $7040 (on campus); room only, $3830 (on campus). *Financial aid:* Need-based college/university scholarships/grants from institutional funds, tuition waivers, loans from institutional funds, loans from outside sources, on-campus employment. Non-need-based college/university scholarships/grants from institutional funds, tuition waivers, loans from institutional funds, loans from outside sources, on-campus employment. Forms required: institution's own financial aid form, International Student's Certification of Finances. International transfer students are eligible to apply for aid. For fall 2006 (estimated), 300 international students on campus received college administered financial aid ($11,000 average). *Housing:* Guaranteed, also available during summer. *Services:* International student adviser on campus. Internships and employment opportunities (on-campus) available. *Contact:* Assistant Director of Admissions, Calvin College, 3201 Burton Street, SE, Grand Rapids, MI 49546. Telephone: 616-526-6106. Fax: 616-526-6777. E-mail: intladm@calvin.edu. URL: http://www.calvin.edu.

See In-Depth Description on page 50.

CENTRAL MICHIGAN UNIVERSITY, MOUNT PLEASANT

General Information State-supported, coed university. Small town setting. *Awards:* B, M, D. *Entrance level for U.S. students:* Moderately difficult. *Enrollment:* 26,710 total; 20,129 undergraduates (56% women) including 1% international students from 43 foreign countries. *Faculty:* 1,119. *Library holdings:* 1 million books, 7,392 current serial subscriptions. *Total majors:* 117.
Information for International Students For fall 2006: 198 international students applied, 108 were accepted, 48 enrolled. Students can start in fall, winter, spring, or summer. Transfers accepted from institutions abroad. *Admission tests:* Required: TOEFL (minimum score: iBT 61; paper-based 500; computer-based 173). TOEFL can be waived under certain conditions. *Application deadline:* 5/1. *Expenses:* (2006–07) $15,915; room and board, $6824 (on campus); room only, $3412 (on campus). *Financial aid:* Need-based college/university scholarships/grants from institutional funds, tuition waivers, athletic awards, loans from outside sources,

on-campus employment. Non-need-based college/university scholarships/grants from institutional funds, tuition waivers, athletic awards, loans from outside sources, on-campus employment. International transfer students are eligible to apply for aid. For fall 2006 (estimated), 62 international students on campus received college administered financial aid ($9783 average). *Housing:* Guaranteed, also available during summer. *Services:* International student adviser on campus. Full-time ESL program on campus. ESL program available during the academic year and the summer. Employment opportunities (on-campus) available. *Contact:* Director, Central Michigan University, Bovee UC 106, Mount Pleasant, MI 48859. Telephone: 989-774-4308. Fax: 989-774-3690. E-mail: intlapp@cmich.edu. URL: http://www.cmich.edu.

See In-Depth Description on page 53.

CLEARY UNIVERSITY, ANN ARBOR

General Information Independent, coed institution. Suburban setting. *Awards:* A, B, M. *Entrance level for U.S. students:* Moderately difficult. *Enrollment:* 691 total; 626 undergraduates including 0.3% international students from 2 foreign countries. *Faculty:* 127. *Library holdings:* 10,000 books, 330 audiovisual materials. *Total majors:* 10. *Expenses:* (2007–08) $14,160. *Financial aid:* Need-based college/university scholarships/grants from institutional funds, tuition waivers, loans from outside sources. Non-need-based college/university scholarships/grants from institutional funds, tuition waivers. Forms required: International Student's Certification of Finances.

CONCORDIA UNIVERSITY, ANN ARBOR

General Information Independent, coed institution, affiliated with Lutheran Church–Missouri Synod. Suburban setting. *Awards:* A, B, M. *Entrance level for U.S. students:* Moderately difficult. *Enrollment:* 736 total; 562 undergraduates (57% women) including 1% international students from 3 foreign countries. *Faculty:* 85. *Library holdings:* 117,000 books, 660 current serial subscriptions, 1,400 audiovisual materials. *Total majors:* 45. *Expenses:* (2006–07) $19,060; room and board, $7350 (on campus); room only, $5290 (on campus). *Financial aid:* Non-need-based college/university scholarships/grants from institutional funds, tuition waivers, athletic awards. Forms required: institution's own financial aid form. For fall 2005, 9 international students on campus received college administered financial aid ($11,503 average).

CORNERSTONE UNIVERSITY, GRAND RAPIDS

General Information Independent nondenominational, coed institution. Suburban setting. *Awards:* A, B, M, FP. *Entrance level for U.S. students:* Minimally difficult. *Enrollment:* 2,509 total; 1,981 undergraduates (61% women) including 1% international students from 3 foreign countries. *Faculty:* 136. *Library holdings:* 109,376 books, 1,073 current serial subscriptions. *Total majors:* 52. *Expenses:* (2006–07) $17,080; room and board, $5860 (on campus). *Financial aid:* Need-based college/university scholarships/grants from institutional funds, athletic awards, on-campus employment. Non-need-based college/university scholarships/grants from institutional funds, athletic awards, on-campus employment. Forms required: institution's own financial aid form. 12 international students on campus received college administered financial aid ($3614 average).

DAVENPORT UNIVERSITY, DEARBORN

General Information Independent, coed institution. Suburban setting. *Awards:* A, B, M. *Entrance level for U.S. students:* Minimally difficult. *Enrollment:* 12,617 total; 11,954 undergraduates (75% women) including 0.1% international students. *Faculty:* 1,157. *Library holdings:* 132,595 books, 434 current serial subscriptions, 10,256 audiovisual materials. *Total majors:* 28. *Expenses:* (2007–08) $9956; room and board, $4450 (on campus). *Financial aid:* Need-based loans from outside sources. Non-need-based college/university scholarships/grants from institutional funds, loans from outside sources. Forms required: International Student's Certification of Finances, scholarship app., if applicable. international students on campus received college administered aid averaging $435.

DAVENPORT UNIVERSITY, MIDLAND

General Information Independent, primarily 2-year, coed college. Urban setting. *Awards:* A, B. *Entrance level for U.S. students:* Noncompetitive. *Enrollment:* 13,124 university total. *Total majors:* 18.
Information for International Students For fall 2006: 450 international students applied, 349 were accepted, 325 enrolled. Students can start in fall, winter, or spring. Transfers accepted from institutions abroad. *Admission tests:* Required: TOEFL (minimum score: paper-based 500; computer-based 173). Recommended: SAT or ACT, SAT Subject Tests. *Application*

Davenport University (continued)

deadline: 8/1. *Financial aid:* Non-need financial aid available. Forms required: International Student's Certification of Finances, TOEFL score. 24 international students on campus received college administered financial aid ($896 average). *Services:* International student adviser on campus. Full-time ESL program on campus. ESL program available during the academic year and the summer. Employment opportunities (on-campus) available. *Contact:* Director of International Enrollment and Programs, Admissions Office, Davenport University, 6191 Kraft Avenue, SE, Grand Rapids, MI 49503. Telephone: 616-698-7111. Fax: 616-554-5213. E-mail: mike.zhang@davenport.edu. URL: http://www.davenport.edu.

DELTA COLLEGE, UNIVERSITY CENTER

General Information District-supported, 2-year, coed college. Rural setting. *Awards:* A. *Entrance level for U.S. students:* Noncompetitive. *Enrollment:* 10,210 total (56% women) including 1% international students from 22 foreign countries. *Undergraduate faculty:* 511. *Library holdings:* 93,167 books, 400 current serial subscriptions, 4,200 audiovisual materials. *Total majors:* 71.
Information for International Students For fall 2006: 26 international students applied, 11 were accepted, 11 enrolled. Students can start in fall, winter, spring, or summer. Transfers accepted from institutions abroad. *Admission tests:* Required: TOEFL (minimum score: paper-based 500; computer-based 173). TOEFL can be waived under certain conditions. *Application deadline:* 6/1. *Expenses:* (2006–07) $4104. *Financial aid:* Non-need-based loans from institutional funds, loans from outside sources. *Services:* International student adviser on campus. ESL program at cooperating institution. Employment opportunities (on-campus and off-campus) available. *Contact:* Assistant Director of Records, Delta College, 1961 Delta Road, University Center, MI 48710. Telephone: 989-686-9320. Fax: 989-667-2221. E-mail: danielsegura@delta.edu. URL: http://www.delta.edu.

EASTERN MICHIGAN UNIVERSITY, YPSILANTI

General Information State-supported, coed institution. Suburban setting. *Awards:* B, M, D. *Entrance level for U.S. students:* Moderately difficult. *Enrollment:* 22,821 total; 18,172 undergraduates (59% women) including 1% international students from 55 foreign countries. *Faculty:* 1,242. *Library holdings:* 658,648 books, 4,457 current serial subscriptions, 11,524 audiovisual materials. *Total majors:* 132. *Expenses:* (2006–07) $18,290; room and board, $6610 (on campus); room only, $3104 (on campus). *Financial aid:* Non-need-based college/university scholarships/grants from institutional funds, athletic awards, loans from outside sources, on-campus employment. Forms required: scholarship application. For fall 2005, 104 international students on campus received college administered financial aid ($15,634 average).

FERRIS STATE UNIVERSITY, BIG RAPIDS

General Information State-supported, coed institution. Small town setting. *Awards:* A, B, M, FP (Associate). *Entrance level for U.S. students:* Minimally difficult. *Enrollment:* 12,575 total; 11,409 undergraduates (47% women) including 1% international students from 39 foreign countries. *Faculty:* 864. *Library holdings:* 354,173 books, 1,049 current serial subscriptions. *Total majors:* 96.
Information for International Students For fall 2006: 519 international students applied, 126 were accepted, 49 enrolled. Students can start in fall, spring, or summer. Transfers accepted from institutions abroad. *Admission tests:* Required: TOEFL (minimum score: iBT 61; paper-based 500; computer-based 173), MELAB, IELTS. Recommended: SAT or ACT, SAT Subject Tests. TOEFL can be waived under certain conditions. *Application deadline:* 6/15. *Expenses:* (2006–07) $14,782; room and board, $7220 (on campus); room only, $3668 (on campus). *Housing:* Guaranteed, also available during summer. *Services:* International student adviser on campus. Internships and employment opportunities (on-campus) available. *Contact:* Coordinator of International Student Recruitment, Office of International Affairs, Ferris State University, CSS 201, 1201 South State Street, Big Rapids, MI 49307-2747. Telephone: 231-591-5444. Fax: 231-591-3944. E-mail: international@ferris.edu. URL: http://www.ferris.edu.

See In-Depth Description on page 82.

FINLANDIA UNIVERSITY, HANCOCK

General Information Independent, 4-year, coed college, affiliated with Evangelical Lutheran Church in America. Small town setting. *Awards:* A, B. *Entrance level for U.S. students:* Minimally difficult. *Enrollment:* 584 total (67% women) including 4% international students. *Undergraduate faculty:* 78. *Library holdings:* 68,803 books, 997 current serial subscriptions, 2,865 audiovisual materials. *Total majors:* 15. *Expenses:* (2006–07) $16,300; room and board,

$5524 (on campus). *Financial aid:* Need-based financial aid available. Non-need-based college/university scholarships/grants from institutional funds, tuition waivers. Forms required: International Student's Certification of Finances. 20 international students on campus received college administered financial aid ($2500 average).

GLEN OAKS COMMUNITY COLLEGE, CENTREVILLE

General Information State and locally supported, 2-year, coed college. Rural setting. *Awards:* A. *Entrance level for U.S. students:* Noncompetitive. *Enrollment:* 1,710 total (61% women) including 0.1% international students. *Undergraduate faculty:* 109. *Library holdings:* 37,087 books, 347 current serial subscriptions. *Total majors:* 5.
Information for International Students For fall 2006: 20 international students applied, 8 were accepted, 8 enrolled. Students can start in fall, winter, spring, or summer. Transfers accepted from institutions abroad. *Admission tests:* Required: TOEFL (minimum score: iBT 63; paper-based 500; computer-based 173). TOEFL can be waived under certain conditions. *Application deadline:* Rolling. *Financial aid:* Forms required: institution's own financial aid form. *Services:* International student adviser on campus. Internships and employment opportunities (on-campus and off-campus) available. *Contact:* PDSO/Counselor, Glen Oaks Community College, 62249 Shimmel Road, Centreville, MI 49032. Telephone: 269-467-9945 Ext. 244. Fax: 269-467-9068. E-mail: chayden@glenoaks.edu. URL: http://www.glenoaks.edu.

GRAND RAPIDS COMMUNITY COLLEGE, GRAND RAPIDS

General Information District-supported, 2-year, coed college. Urban setting. *Awards:* A. *Entrance level for U.S. students:* Noncompetitive. *Enrollment:* 15,224 total (52% women) including 1% international students from 6 foreign countries. *Undergraduate faculty:* 672. *Library holdings:* 163,225 books, 10,711 current serial subscriptions. *Total majors:* 30. *Expenses:* (2006–07) $6160. *Financial aid:* Non-need-based college/university scholarships/grants from institutional funds, on-campus employment.

GRAND VALLEY STATE UNIVERSITY, ALLENDALE

General Information State-supported, coed institution. Small town setting. *Awards:* B, M. *Entrance level for U.S. students:* Moderately difficult. *Enrollment:* 23,295 total; 19,578 undergraduates (61% women) including 1% international students from 51 foreign countries. *Faculty:* 1,414. *Library holdings:* 634,000 books, 5,000 current serial subscriptions. *Total majors:* 122.
Information for International Students For fall 2006: 471 international students applied, 160 were accepted. Students can start in fall or winter. Transfers accepted from institutions abroad. *Admission tests:* Required: TOEFL (minimum score: iBT 79; paper-based 550; computer-based 213). TOEFL can be waived under certain conditions. *Application deadline:* 5/1. *Expenses:* (2006–07) $12,510; room and board, $6600 (on campus); room only, $4700 (on campus). *Financial aid:* Need-based college/university scholarships/grants from institutional funds, athletic awards. Non-need-based college/university scholarships/grants from institutional funds, athletic awards. Forms required: International Student's Certification of Finances. International transfer students are eligible to apply for aid. For fall 2006 (estimated), 80 international students on campus received college administered financial aid ($5680 average). *Services:* International student adviser on campus. ESL program at cooperating institution. ESL program available during the academic year. Internships and employment opportunities (on-campus) available. *Contact:* Associate Director for International Recruitment, Grand Valley State University, 1 Campus Drive, Allendale, MI 49401-9403. Telephone: 616-331-2025. Fax: 616-331-2000. E-mail: global@gvsu.edu. URL: http://www.gvsu.edu.

See In-Depth Description on page 95.

GREAT LAKES CHRISTIAN COLLEGE, LANSING

General Information Independent, 4-year, coed college, affiliated with Christian Churches and Churches of Christ. Suburban setting. *Awards:* A, B. *Entrance level for U.S. students:* Moderately difficult. *Enrollment:* 207 total including 2% international students from 3 foreign countries. *Undergraduate faculty:* 30. *Library holdings:* 60,244 books, 8,942 current serial subscriptions. *Total majors:* 6.
Information for International Students For fall 2006: 2 international students applied, 2 were accepted, 2 enrolled. Students can start in fall or spring. *Admission tests:* Required: TOEFL (minimum score: iBT 79; paper-based 550; computer-based 210). Recommended: SAT or ACT, SAT Subject Tests. *Application deadline:* Rolling. *Expenses:* (2007–08) $10,458; room and board, $6200 (on campus). *Financial aid:* Need-based and non-need-based financial aid available. *Housing:* Guaranteed, also available during

summer. *Services:* International student adviser on campus. Employment opportunities (on-campus) available. *Contact:* Director of Admissions and College Relations, Great Lakes Christian College, 6211 West Willow Highway, Lansing, MI 48917-1299. Telephone: 517-321-0242 Ext. 230. Fax: 517-321-5902. E-mail: admissions@glcc.edu. URL: http://www.glcc.edu.

HENRY FORD COMMUNITY COLLEGE, DEARBORN

General Information District-supported, 2-year, coed college. Suburban setting. *Awards:* A. *Entrance level for U.S. students:* Noncompetitive. *Enrollment:* 13,000 total including 0.2% international students from 18 foreign countries. *Undergraduate faculty:* 770. *Library holdings:* 80,000 books, 650 current serial subscriptions. *Total majors:* 53.

Information for International Students Students can start in fall, winter, spring, or summer. Transfers accepted from institutions abroad. *Admission tests:* Required: TOEFL (minimum score: paper-based 550; computer-based 213; minimum score for ESL admission: paper-based 550; computer-based 213), ASSET, COMPASS. Recommended: ELS. *Application deadline:* 6/1. *Expenses:* (2007–08) $3264. *Services:* Full-time and part-time ESL programs on campus. ESL program available during the academic year and the summer. Employment opportunities (on-campus and off-campus) available. *Contact:* International Student Advisor, International Student Office, Henry Ford Community College, 5101 Evergreen, Dearborn, MI 48128-1495. Telephone: 313-317-6519. Fax: 313-845-6464. E-mail: bbibbs@hfcc.edu. URL: http://www.hfcc.edu.

HILLSDALE COLLEGE, HILLSDALE

General Information Independent, 4-year, coed college. Small town setting. *Awards:* B. *Entrance level for U.S. students:* Very difficult. *Enrollment:* 1,346 total (52% women) including international students from 13 foreign countries. *Undergraduate faculty:* 149. *Library holdings:* 240,000 books, 1,650 current serial subscriptions, 8,000 audiovisual materials. *Total majors:* 43.

Information for International Students For fall 2006: 40 international students applied, 20 were accepted, 6 enrolled. Students can start in fall, spring, or summer. Transfers accepted from institutions abroad. *Admission tests:* Required: TOEFL. Recommended: SAT or ACT. *Application deadline:* 2/15. *Expenses:* (2006–07) $18,260; room and board, $7030 (on campus); room only, $3530 (on campus). *Financial aid:* Non-need-based college/university scholarships/grants from institutional funds, athletic awards, on-campus employment. Forms required: International Student's Financial Aid Application, International Student's Certification of Finances. International transfer students are eligible to apply for aid. For fall 2006 (estimated), 10 international students on campus received college administered financial aid ($14,000 average). *Housing:* Guaranteed. *Services:* International student adviser on campus. Internships and employment opportunities (on-campus) available. *Contact:* Director of Admissions, Hillsdale College, Hillsdale, MI 49242. Telephone: 517-607-2327. Fax: 517-607-2223. E-mail: admissions@hillsdale.edu. URL: http://www.hillsdale.edu.

See In-Depth Description on page 98.

HOPE COLLEGE, HOLLAND

General Information Independent, 4-year, coed college, affiliated with Reformed Church in America. Suburban setting. *Awards:* B. *Entrance level for U.S. students:* Moderately difficult. *Enrollment:* 3,203 total (60% women) including 2% international students from 33 foreign countries. *Undergraduate faculty:* 322. *Library holdings:* 358,329 books, 2,878 current serial subscriptions, 13,263 audiovisual materials. *Total majors:* 84.

Information for International Students For fall 2006: 38 international students applied, 15 were accepted, 7 enrolled. Students can start in fall or spring. Transfers accepted from institutions abroad. *Admission tests:* Required: TOEFL (minimum score: paper-based 550; computer-based 213). Recommended: SAT. *Application deadline:* 2/15. *Expenses:* (2006–07) $22,570; room and board, $6982 (on campus). *Financial aid:* Need-based college/university scholarships/grants from institutional funds. Non-need-based college/university scholarships/grants from institutional funds. Forms required: International Student's Certification of Finances. International transfer students are eligible to apply for aid. For fall 2006 (estimated), 28 international students on campus received college administered financial aid ($19,719 average). *Housing:* Guaranteed, also available during summer. *Services:* International student adviser on campus. Internships and employment opportunities (on-campus) available. *Contact:* Associate Director of Admissions, Hope College, 69 East 10th Street, PO Box 9000, Holland, MI 49422-9000. Telephone: 616-395-7850. Fax: 616-395-7130. E-mail: camp@hope.edu. URL: http://www.hope.edu.

JACKSON COMMUNITY COLLEGE, JACKSON

General Information County-supported, 2-year, coed college. Suburban setting. *Awards:* A. *Entrance level for U.S. students:* Noncompetitive. *Enrollment:* 5,870 total (64% women) including 0.1% international students. *Undergraduate faculty:* 332. *Library holdings:* 67,000 books, 300 current serial subscriptions, 2,000 audiovisual materials. *Total majors:* 26. *Expenses:* (2006–07) $3768.

KELLOGG COMMUNITY COLLEGE, BATTLE CREEK

General Information State and locally supported, 2-year, coed college. Urban setting. *Awards:* A. *Entrance level for U.S. students:* Noncompetitive. *Enrollment:* 5,326 total (67% women) including 0.5% international students from 11 foreign countries. *Undergraduate faculty:* 380. *Library holdings:* 42,131 books, 172 current serial subscriptions. *Total majors:* 73. *Expenses:* (2007–08) $4980.

KETTERING UNIVERSITY, FLINT

General Information Independent, coed institution. Urban setting. *Awards:* B, M. *Entrance level for U.S. students:* Very difficult. *Enrollment:* 2,809 total; 2,290 undergraduates (15% women) including 2% international students from 17 foreign countries. *Faculty:* 146. *Library holdings:* 122,360 books, 525 current serial subscriptions, 1,280 audiovisual materials. *Total majors:* 22.

Information for International Students For fall 2006: 58 international students applied, 9 were accepted, 3 enrolled. Students can start in fall, winter, spring, or summer. Transfers accepted from institutions abroad. *Admission tests:* Required: TOEFL (minimum score: paper-based 550; computer-based 213; minimum score for ESL admission: paper-based 500; computer-based 173). Recommended: SAT or ACT. TOEFL can be waived under certain conditions. *Application deadline:* Rolling. *Expenses:* (2006–07) $24,908; room and board, $5690 (on campus); room only, $3600 (on campus). *Housing:* Guaranteed, also available during summer. *Services:* International student adviser on campus. ESL program at cooperating institution. Internships and employment opportunities (on-campus and off-campus) available. *Contact:* International Student Liaison, Kettering University, 1700 West 3rd Avenue, Flint, MI 48504. Telephone: 810-762-7865. Fax: 810-762-9837. E-mail: khafer@kettering.edu. URL: http://www.kettering.edu.

KIRTLAND COMMUNITY COLLEGE, ROSCOMMON

General Information District-supported, 2-year, coed college. Rural setting. *Awards:* A. *Entrance level for U.S. students:* Noncompetitive. *Enrollment:* 1,624 total (61% women) including 0.1% international students from 2 foreign countries. *Undergraduate faculty:* 82. *Library holdings:* 35,000 books, 317 current serial subscriptions. *Total majors:* 20. *Expenses:* (2007–08) $5283; room only, $2800 (on campus).

KUYPER COLLEGE, GRAND RAPIDS

General Information Independent religious, 4-year, coed college. Suburban setting. *Awards:* A, B. *Entrance level for U.S. students:* Moderately difficult. *Enrollment:* 290 total (52% women) including 8% international students from 8 foreign countries. *Undergraduate faculty:* 26. *Library holdings:* 56,177 books, 254 current serial subscriptions. *Total majors:* 21. *Expenses:* (2007–08) $12,725; room and board, $5700 (on campus). *Financial aid:* Need-based college/university scholarships/grants from institutional funds, on-campus employment. Non-need-based college/university scholarships/grants from institutional funds, on-campus employment. Forms required: International Student's Financial Aid Application. For fall 2006 (estimated), 12 international students on campus received college administered financial aid ($12,233 average).

LAKE MICHIGAN COLLEGE, BENTON HARBOR

General Information District-supported, 2-year, coed college. Small town setting. *Awards:* A. *Entrance level for U.S. students:* Noncompetitive. *Enrollment:* 4,043 total (60% women) including 1% international students. *Undergraduate faculty:* 227. *Library holdings:* 79,000 books, 280 current serial subscriptions. *Total majors:* 25. *Expenses:* (2006–07) $5010. *Financial aid:* Non-need-based college/university scholarships/grants from institutional funds, athletic awards, loans from outside sources, on-campus employment. Forms required: International Student's Certification of Finances.

LANSING COMMUNITY COLLEGE, LANSING

General Information State and locally supported, 2-year, coed college. Urban setting. *Awards:* A. *Entrance level for U.S. students:* Noncompetitive. *Enrollment:* 20,394 total (54% women) including

Lansing Community College (continued)

1% international students from 54 foreign countries. *Undergraduate faculty:* 1,444. *Library holdings:* 98,125 books, 600 current serial subscriptions. *Total majors:* 104.

Information for International Students For fall 2006: 217 international students applied, 167 were accepted, 167 enrolled. Students can start in fall, spring, or summer. Transfers accepted from institutions abroad. *Admission tests:* Required: TOEFL (minimum score: paper-based 500; computer-based 173), in-house assessment testing. TOEFL can be waived under certain conditions. *Application deadline:* 4/10. *Expenses:* (2007–08) $5450. *Services:* International student adviser on campus. Full-time and part-time ESL programs on campus. ESL program available during the academic year and the summer. Internships and employment opportunities (on-campus and off-campus) available. *Contact:* International Admissions Specialist, Lansing Community College, 1121 Admissions Office, PO Box 40010, Lansing, MI 48901-7210. Telephone: 517-483-1984. Fax: 517-483-1170. E-mail: greend@lcc.edu. URL: http://www.lcc.edu.

LAWRENCE TECHNOLOGICAL UNIVERSITY, SOUTHFIELD

General Information Independent, coed university. Suburban setting. *Awards:* A, B, M, D. *Entrance level for U.S. students:* Moderately difficult. *Enrollment:* 4,049 total; 2,680 undergraduates (23% women) including 1% international students from 25 foreign countries. *Faculty:* 375. *Library holdings:* 128,000 books, 750 current serial subscriptions, 136 audiovisual materials. *Total majors:* 34. *Expenses:* (2006–07) $19,443; room and board, $7266 (on campus); room only, $5286 (on campus). *Financial aid:* Need-based loans from outside sources. Non-need-based college/university scholarships/grants from institutional funds, loans from outside sources, on-campus employment. Forms required: institution's own financial aid form.

MACOMB COMMUNITY COLLEGE, WARREN

General Information District-supported, 2-year, coed college. Suburban setting. *Awards:* A. *Entrance level for U.S. students:* Noncompetitive. *Enrollment:* 21,131 total (52% women) including 4% international students. *Undergraduate faculty:* 1,016. *Library holdings:* 159,226 books, 4,240 current serial subscriptions. *Total majors:* 73. *Expenses:* (2006–07) $4225. *Financial aid:* Need-based college/university scholarships/grants from institutional funds, athletic awards, loans from outside sources, on-campus employment. Non-need-based college/university scholarships/grants from institutional funds, tuition waivers, athletic awards, loans from outside sources. Forms required: International Student's Certification of Finances.

MADONNA UNIVERSITY, LIVONIA

General Information Independent Roman Catholic, coed institution. Suburban setting. *Awards:* A, B, M. *Entrance level for U.S. students:* Moderately difficult. *Enrollment:* 4,156 total; 3,264 undergraduates (76% women) including 3% international students from 36 foreign countries. *Faculty:* 368. *Library holdings:* 199,144 books, 1,679 current serial subscriptions, 938 audiovisual materials. *Total majors:* 87. *Expenses:* (2006–07) $10,960; room and board, $5946 (on campus); room only, $2652 (on campus).

MARYGROVE COLLEGE, DETROIT

General Information Independent Roman Catholic, coed, primarily women's institution. Urban setting. *Awards:* A, B, M. *Entrance level for U.S. students:* Moderately difficult. *Enrollment:* 2,953 total; 780 undergraduates (79% women) including 2% international students from 9 foreign countries. *Faculty:* 64. *Library holdings:* 86,268 books, 72,048 current serial subscriptions. *Total majors:* 32. *Expenses:* (2006–07) $13,960; room and board, $6400 (on campus).

MICHIGAN STATE UNIVERSITY, EAST LANSING

General Information State-supported, coed university. Suburban setting. *Awards:* B, M, D, FP. *Entrance level for U.S. students:* Moderately difficult. *Enrollment:* 45,520 total; 35,821 undergraduates (54% women) including 3% international students from 100 foreign countries. *Faculty:* 2,910. *Library holdings:* 4.8 million books, 37,832 current serial subscriptions, 342,873 audiovisual materials. *Total majors:* 130. *Expenses:* (2006–07) $21,488; room and board, $6044 (on campus); room only, $2618 (on campus). *Financial aid:* Non-need-based college/university scholarships/grants from institutional funds, tuition waivers, athletic awards, loans from outside sources, on-campus employment. Forms required: International Student's Certification of Finances. For fall 2006 (estimated), 133 international students on campus received college administered financial aid ($4867 average).

MICHIGAN TECHNOLOGICAL UNIVERSITY, HOUGHTON

General Information State-supported, coed university. Small town setting. *Awards:* A, B, M, D. *Entrance level for U.S. students:* Moderately difficult. *Enrollment:* 6,550 total; 5,634 undergraduates (23% women) including 4% international students from 73 foreign countries. *Faculty:* 489. *Library holdings:* 799,775 books, 2,777 current serial subscriptions, 6,797 audiovisual materials. *Total majors:* 88.

Information for International Students For fall 2006: 299 international students applied, 142 were accepted, 39 enrolled. Students can start in fall, spring, or summer. Transfers accepted from institutions abroad. *Admission tests:* Required: SAT, ACT, or TOEFL (minimum score: iBT 61; paper-based 500; computer-based 173). Recommended: IELTS. TOEFL can be waived under certain conditions. *Application deadline:* Rolling. *Expenses:* (2006–07) $20,679; room and board, $6840 (on campus); room only, $3461 (on campus). *Financial aid:* Need-based college/university scholarships/grants from institutional funds, loans from outside sources, on-campus employment. Non-need-based college/university scholarships/grants from institutional funds, athletic awards, loans from outside sources, on-campus employment. Forms required: institution's own financial aid form. International transfer students are eligible to apply for aid. For fall 2006 (estimated), 126 international students on campus received college administered financial aid ($9774 average). *Housing:* Guaranteed, also available during summer. *Services:* International student adviser on campus. Full-time and part-time ESL programs on campus. ESL program available during the academic year and the summer. Internships and employment opportunities (on-campus and off-campus) available. *Contact:* International Admissions Coordinator, Michigan Technological University, 1400 Townsend Drive, Houghton, MI 49931. Telephone: 906-487-2160. Fax: 906-487-1891. E-mail: emmurrel@mtu.edu. URL: http://www.mtu.edu.

MID MICHIGAN COMMUNITY COLLEGE, HARRISON

General Information State and locally supported, 2-year, coed college. Rural setting. *Awards:* A. *Entrance level for U.S. students:* Noncompetitive. *Enrollment:* 3,232 total (63% women) including 0.3% international students. *Undergraduate faculty:* 256. *Library holdings:* 29,450 books, 200 current serial subscriptions. *Total majors:* 52. *Expenses:* (2006–07) $5380. *Financial aid:* Need-based financial aid available. Forms required: institution's own financial aid form.

MOTT COMMUNITY COLLEGE, FLINT

General Information District-supported, 2-year, coed college. Urban setting. *Awards:* A. *Entrance level for U.S. students:* Noncompetitive. *Enrollment:* 10,299 total (61% women) including 0.3% international students from 33 foreign countries. *Undergraduate faculty:* 509. *Library holdings:* 112,251 books, 325 current serial subscriptions. *Total majors:* 50.

Information for International Students For fall 2006: 200 international students applied, 100 were accepted, 75 enrolled. Students can start in fall, winter, spring, or summer. Transfers accepted from institutions abroad. *Admission tests:* Required: MELAB. Recommended: TOEFL (minimum score: paper-based 500; computer-based 173; minimum score for ESL admission: paper-based 500; computer-based 173). *Application deadline:* Rolling. *Expenses:* (2006–07) $4873. *Financial aid:* Forms required: International Student's Certification of Finances. *Services:* ESL program at cooperating institution. ESL program available during the academic year. Employment opportunities (on-campus) available. *Contact:* International Student Coordinator, Mott Community College, 1401 East Court Street, Prahl College Center, Office of Admission, Flint, MI 48503. Telephone: 810-762-0358. Fax: 810-232-9442. E-mail: rbroomfield@mcc.edu. URL: http://www.mcc.edu.

NORTHERN MICHIGAN UNIVERSITY, MARQUETTE

General Information State-supported, coed institution. Small town setting. *Awards:* A, B, M. *Entrance level for U.S. students:* Minimally difficult. *Enrollment:* 9,353 total; 8,702 undergraduates (53% women) including 1% international students from 17 foreign countries. *Faculty:* 471. *Library holdings:* 615,406 books, 4,573 current serial subscriptions, 8,251 audiovisual materials. *Total majors:* 110.

Information for International Students For fall 2006: 95 international students applied, 17 were accepted, 17 enrolled. Students can start in fall, winter, or summer. Transfers accepted from institutions abroad. *Admission tests:* Required: TOEFL (minimum score: paper-based 500; computer-based 173; minimum score for ESL admission: paper-based 500; computer-based 173), ELS. TOEFL can be waived under certain conditions. *Application deadline:* Rolling. *Expenses:* (2006–07) $10,077; room and board,

$6874 (on campus); room only, $3366 (on campus). *Financial aid:* Non-need-based college/university scholarships/grants from institutional funds, athletic awards, loans from outside sources. Forms required: International Student's Certification of Finances. International transfer students are eligible to apply for aid. *Housing:* Guaranteed, also available during summer. *Services:* International student adviser on campus. Full-time and part-time ESL programs on campus. ESL program available during the academic year and the summer. Internships and employment opportunities (on-campus and off-campus) available. *Contact:* Director of International Affairs, Northern Michigan University, 1401 Presque Isle Avenue, Marquette, MI 49855. Telephone: 906-227-2510. Fax: 906-227-2533. E-mail: iao@nmu.edu. URL: http://www.nmu.edu.

NORTHWESTERN MICHIGAN COLLEGE, TRAVERSE CITY

General Information State and locally supported, 2-year, coed college. Small town setting. *Awards:* A. *Entrance level for U.S. students:* Noncompetitive. *Enrollment:* 4,609 total (59% women). *Undergraduate faculty:* 307. *Library holdings:* 97,458 books, 9,820 current serial subscriptions, 3,000 audiovisual materials. *Total majors:* 44. *Expenses:* (2006–07) $5108; room and board, $6800 (on campus). *Financial aid:* Need-based college/university scholarships/grants from institutional funds, tuition waivers, loans from outside sources, on-campus employment. Non-need-based college/university scholarships/grants from institutional funds, tuition waivers, loans from outside sources, on-campus employment.

NORTHWOOD UNIVERSITY, MIDLAND

General Information Independent, coed institution. Small town setting. *Awards:* A, B, M. *Entrance level for U.S. students:* Moderately difficult. *Enrollment:* 4,125 total; 3,802 undergraduates (44% women) including 8% international students from 26 foreign countries. *Faculty:* 82. *Library holdings:* 40,063 books, 335 current serial subscriptions. *Total majors:* 15. *Expenses:* (2007–08) $16,455; room and board, $7194 (on campus); room only, $3474 (on campus). *Financial aid:* Non-need-based college/university scholarships/grants from institutional funds, athletic awards. Forms required: International Student's Certification of Finances. For fall 2006 (estimated), 225 international students on campus received college administered financial aid ($4085 average).

OAKLAND COMMUNITY COLLEGE, BLOOMFIELD HILLS

General Information State and locally supported, 2-year, coed college. Suburban setting. *Awards:* A. *Entrance level for U.S. students:* Noncompetitive. *Enrollment:* 24,123 total (58% women) including 8% international students from 375 foreign countries. *Undergraduate faculty:* 960. *Library holdings:* 251,482 books, 2,649 current serial subscriptions, 10,393 audiovisual materials. *Total majors:* 90. *Expenses:* (2006–07) $4115.

OAKLAND UNIVERSITY, ROCHESTER

General Information State-supported, coed university. Suburban setting. *Awards:* B, M, D. *Entrance level for U.S. students:* Moderately difficult. *Enrollment:* 17,737 total; 13,701 undergraduates (62% women) including 1% international students from 60 foreign countries. *Faculty:* 906. *Library holdings:* 2.1 million books, 11,896 current serial subscriptions, 18,767 audiovisual materials. *Total majors:* 58.

Information for International Students For fall 2006: 104 international students enrolled. Students can start in fall, winter, or spring. Transfers accepted from institutions abroad. *Admission tests:* Required: TOEFL (minimum score: iBT 77; paper-based 550; computer-based 213; minimum score for ESL admission: iBT 68; paper-based 520; computer-based 190). Recommended: ACT. TOEFL can be waived under certain conditions. *Application deadline:* 6/15. *Expenses:* (2006–07) $15,472; room and board, $6354 (on campus). *Financial aid:* Non-need financial aid available. *Housing:* Available during summer. *Services:* International student adviser on campus. Full-time and part-time ESL programs on campus. ESL program available during the academic year. Internships and employment opportunities (on-campus) available. *Contact:* International Admissions Advisor, Admissions Office, Oakland University, 101 North Foundation Hall, Rochester, MI 48309-4475. Telephone: 248-370-3360. Fax: 248-370-4462. E-mail: ouinfo@oakland.edu. URL: http://www.oakland.edu.

SAGINAW VALLEY STATE UNIVERSITY, UNIVERSITY CENTER

General Information State-supported, coed institution. Rural setting. *Awards:* B, M. *Entrance level for U.S. students:* Moderately difficult. *Enrollment:* 9,543 total; 7,933 undergraduates (60% women) including 3% international students from 46 foreign countries. *Faculty:* 570. *Library holdings:* 641,190 books, 11,770

current serial subscriptions, 6,380 audiovisual materials. *Total majors:* 50. *Expenses:* (2006–07) $12,540; room and board, $6380 (on campus); room only, $3830 (on campus). *Financial aid:* Non-need financial aid available. Forms required: International Student's Certification of Finances. 221 international students on campus received college administered financial aid ($866 average).

SCHOOLCRAFT COLLEGE, LIVONIA

General Information District-supported, 2-year, coed college. Suburban setting. *Awards:* A. *Entrance level for U.S. students:* Noncompetitive. *Enrollment:* 11,105 total (56% women) including 1% international students. *Undergraduate faculty:* 429. *Total majors:* 36. *Expenses:* (2007–08) $4810.

SOUTHWESTERN MICHIGAN COLLEGE, DOWAGIAC

General Information State and locally supported, 2-year, coed college. Rural setting. *Awards:* A. *Entrance level for U.S. students:* Noncompetitive. *Enrollment:* 2,500 total (65% women) including 4% international students from 27 foreign countries. *Undergraduate faculty:* 145. *Library holdings:* 36,877 books, 127 current serial subscriptions, 1,537 audiovisual materials. *Total majors:* 27. *Expenses:* (2007–08) $3991. *Financial aid:* Need-based college/university scholarships/grants from institutional funds, tuition waivers, loans from outside sources, on-campus employment. Non-need-based college/university scholarships/grants from institutional funds, tuition waivers, loans from institutional funds, loans from outside sources, on-campus employment. Forms required: institution's own financial aid form.

SPRING ARBOR UNIVERSITY, SPRING ARBOR

General Information Independent Free Methodist, coed institution. Small town setting. *Awards:* A, B, M. *Entrance level for U.S. students:* Moderately difficult. *Enrollment:* 3,714 total; 2,609 undergraduates (67% women) including 1% international students from 7 foreign countries. *Faculty:* 133. *Library holdings:* 111,736 books, 665 current serial subscriptions, 3,775 audiovisual materials. *Total majors:* 32.

Information for International Students For fall 2006: 4 international students enrolled. Students can start in fall, winter, or spring. Transfers accepted from institutions abroad. *Admission tests:* Required: TOEFL (minimum score: paper-based 525; computer-based 197). Recommended: SAT or ACT. *Application deadline:* 4/1. *Expenses:* (2006–07) $17,386; room and board, $6070 (on campus); room only, $2850 (on campus). *Financial aid:* Need-based financial aid available. Non-need-based college/university scholarships/grants from institutional funds, tuition waivers, athletic awards. Forms required: institution's own financial aid form, International Student's Certification of Finances. International transfer students are eligible to apply for aid. For fall 2006 (estimated), 29 international students on campus received college administered financial aid ($6429 average). *Housing:* Guaranteed, also available during summer. *Services:* International student adviser on campus. Part-time ESL program on campus. ESL program available during the academic year. Internships and employment opportunities (on-campus) available. *Contact:* Assistant to the Director of Admissions, Office of Admissions, Spring Arbor University, 106 East Main Street, Station #4, Spring Arbor, MI 49283-9984. Telephone: 517-750-6471. Fax: 517-750-6620. E-mail: admissions@admin.arbor.edu. URL: http://www.arbor.edu.

UNIVERSITY OF DETROIT MERCY, DETROIT

General Information Independent Roman Catholic (Jesuit), coed university. Urban setting. *Awards:* A, B, M, D, FP. *Entrance level for U.S. students:* Moderately difficult. *Enrollment:* 5,521 total; 3,311 undergraduates (67% women) including 3% international students from 19 foreign countries. *Faculty:* 708. *Library holdings:* 9,340 current serial subscriptions, 32,053 audiovisual materials. *Total majors:* 64.

Information for International Students For fall 2006: 104 international students applied, 75 were accepted, 43 enrolled. Students can start in fall, winter, spring, or summer. Transfers accepted from institutions abroad. *Application deadline:* 3/1. *Expenses:* (2006–07) $23,970; room and board, $7622 (on campus); room only, $4460 (on campus). *Financial aid:* Non-need financial aid available. *Housing:* Available during summer. *Services:* International student adviser on campus. Full-time and part-time ESL programs on campus. ESL program available during the academic year and the summer. Employment opportunities (on-campus and off-campus) available. *Contact:* International Admissions Counselor, University of Detroit Mercy, 4001 West McNichols Road, Detroit, MI 48221-3038. Telephone: 313-993-1045. Fax: 313-993-3326. E-mail: mcguirf@udmercy.edu. URL: http://www.udmercy.edu.

UNIVERSITY OF MICHIGAN, ANN ARBOR

General Information State-supported, coed university. Suburban setting. *Awards:* B, M, D, FP. *Entrance level for U.S. students:* Very difficult. *Enrollment:* 40,025 total; 25,555 undergraduates (50% women) including 5% international students from 84 foreign countries. *Faculty:* 2,987. *Library holdings:* 8 million books, 67,554 current serial subscriptions, 92,392 audiovisual materials. *Total majors:* 125. *Expenses:* (2006–07) $28,570; room and board, $7838 (on campus).

UNIVERSITY OF MICHIGAN–DEARBORN, DEARBORN

General Information State-supported, coed institution. Suburban setting. *Awards:* B, M. *Entrance level for U.S. students:* Moderately difficult. *Enrollment:* 8,566 total; 6,612 undergraduates (53% women) including 1% international students from 27 foreign countries. *Faculty:* 481. *Library holdings:* 340,897 books, 1,099 current serial subscriptions. *Total majors:* 53. *Expenses:* (2006–07) $16,187. *Financial aid:* Non-need-based college/university scholarships/grants from institutional funds, loans from outside sources. For fall 2006 (estimated), 20 international students on campus received college administered financial aid ($7668 average).

UNIVERSITY OF MICHIGAN–FLINT, FLINT

General Information State-supported, coed institution. Urban setting. *Awards:* B, M, FP. *Entrance level for U.S. students:* Moderately difficult. *Enrollment:* 6,527 total; 5,600 undergraduates (63% women) including 1% international students from 26 foreign countries. *Faculty:* 445. *Library holdings:* 259,260 books, 911 current serial subscriptions. *Total majors:* 77.
Information for International Students For fall 2006: 65 international students applied, 60 were accepted, 30 enrolled. Students can start in fall, winter, spring, or summer. Transfers accepted from institutions abroad. *Admission tests:* Required: TOEFL (minimum score: iBT 61; paper-based 500; computer-based 173; minimum score for ESL admission: paper-based 550; computer-based 213). TOEFL can be waived under certain conditions. *Application deadline:* Rolling. *Expenses:* (2006–07) $13,152. *Financial aid:* Need-based loans from outside sources. Non-need-based college/university scholarships/grants from institutional funds, loans from outside sources. Forms required: scholarship application. International transfer students are eligible to apply for aid. For fall 2005, 8 international students on campus received college administered financial aid ($1000 average). *Services:* International student adviser on campus. ESL program at cooperating institution. Internships and employment opportunities (on-campus) available. *Contact:* International Admissions Counselor, University of Michigan–Flint, 245 University Pavilion, 303 East Kearsley Street, Flint, MI 48502-1950. Telephone: 810-762-3300. Fax: 810-762-3272. E-mail: international@umflint.edu. URL: http://www.umflint.edu.

UNIVERSITY OF PHOENIX–METRO DETROIT CAMPUS, TROY

General Information Proprietary, coed institution. Urban setting. *Awards:* B, M. *Entrance level for U.S. students:* Noncompetitive. *Enrollment:* 3,918 total; 2,948 undergraduates (70% women) including 3% international students. *Faculty:* 772. *Library holdings:* 1,759 books, 692 current serial subscriptions. *Total majors:* 23. *Expenses:* (2006–07) $11,700.

UNIVERSITY OF PHOENIX–WEST MICHIGAN CAMPUS, WALKER

General Information Proprietary, coed institution. Urban setting. *Awards:* B, M. *Entrance level for U.S. students:* Noncompetitive. *Enrollment:* 1,004 total; 812 undergraduates (62% women) including 4% international students. *Faculty:* 370. *Library holdings:* 1,759 books, 692 current serial subscriptions. *Total majors:* 14. *Expenses:* (2006–07) $11,400.

WAYNE STATE UNIVERSITY, DETROIT

General Information State-supported, coed university. Urban setting. *Awards:* B, M, D, FP. *Entrance level for U.S. students:* Moderately difficult. *Enrollment:* 33,137 total; 20,737 undergraduates (59% women) including 4% international students from 57 foreign countries. *Faculty:* 1,917. *Library holdings:* 1.9 million books, 18,645 current serial subscriptions, 70,131 audiovisual materials. *Total majors:* 83. *Expenses:* (2006–07) $14,570; room and board, $6575 (on campus).

WESTERN MICHIGAN UNIVERSITY, KALAMAZOO

General Information State-supported, coed university. Urban setting. *Awards:* B, M, D (specialist). *Entrance level for U.S. students:* Moderately difficult. *Enrollment:* 24,841 total; 20,081 undergraduates (51% women) including 2% international students from 84 foreign countries. *Faculty:* 1,412. *Library holdings:* 4.5

million books, 10,074 current serial subscriptions, 27,891 audiovisual materials. *Total majors:* 149. *Expenses:* (2006–07) $16,806; room and board, $6877 (on campus); room only, $3638 (on campus). *Financial aid:* Non-need financial aid available. Forms required: International Student's Financial Aid Application, International Student's Certification of Finances. 200 international students on campus received college administered financial aid ($7500 average).

MINNESOTA

ACADEMY COLLEGE, MINNEAPOLIS

General Information Proprietary, primarily 2-year, coed college. Urban setting. *Awards:* A, B. *Entrance level for U.S. students:* Minimally difficult. *Enrollment:* 320 total. *Undergraduate faculty:* 54. *Library holdings:* 1,309 books, 22 current serial subscriptions, 88 audiovisual materials. *Total majors:* 25.
Information for International Students For fall 2006: 1 international student applied, 1 was accepted, 1 enrolled. Students can start in fall, winter, spring, or summer. Transfers accepted from institutions abroad. *Admission tests:* Required: orientation exam. Recommended: TOEFL. *Application deadline:* Rolling. *Expenses:* (2006–07) $18,239. *Financial aid:* Forms required: institution's own financial aid form. *Services:* International student adviser on campus. Part-time ESL program on campus. ESL program available during the academic year and the summer. Internships and employment opportunities (off-campus) available. *Contact:* Director of Finance, Academy College, 1101 East 78th Street, Bloomington, MN 55420. Telephone: 952-851-0066. Fax: 952-851-0094. E-mail: kmacleod@academycollege.edu. URL: http://www.academycollege.edu.

ANOKA-RAMSEY COMMUNITY COLLEGE, COON RAPIDS

General Information State-supported, 2-year, coed college. Suburban setting. *Awards:* A. *Entrance level for U.S. students:* Noncompetitive. *Enrollment:* 6,009 total including 0.5% international students. *Undergraduate faculty:* 247. *Library holdings:* 41,300 books, 235 current serial subscriptions, 800 audiovisual materials. *Total majors:* 16. *Expenses:* (2006–07) $7194. *Financial aid:* Forms required: institution's own financial aid form, FAFSA, institutional verification, worksheet, income tax return or source of foreign income.

AUGSBURG COLLEGE, MINNEAPOLIS

General Information Independent Lutheran, coed institution. Urban setting. *Awards:* B, M. *Entrance level for U.S. students:* Moderately difficult. *Enrollment:* 3,732 total; 2,921 undergraduates (57% women) including 1% international students from 24 foreign countries. *Faculty:* 355. *Library holdings:* 146,166 books, 754 current serial subscriptions. *Total majors:* 64. *Expenses:* (2006–07) $23,422; room and board, $6604 (on campus); room only, $3396 (on campus). *Financial aid:* Need-based college/university scholarships/grants from institutional funds, tuition waivers, loans from outside sources, on-campus employment. Non-need-based college/university scholarships/grants from institutional funds, tuition waivers, loans from outside sources, on-campus employment. Forms required: institution's own financial aid form, International Student's Financial Aid Application, International Student's Certification of Finances. For fall 2005, 54 international students on campus received college administered financial aid ($8369 average).

BEMIDJI STATE UNIVERSITY, BEMIDJI

General Information State-supported, coed institution. Small town setting. *Awards:* A, B, M. *Entrance level for U.S. students:* Moderately difficult. *Enrollment:* 4,918 total; 4,388 undergraduates (54% women) including 6% international students from 41 foreign countries. *Faculty:* 362. *Library holdings:* 554,087 books, 991 current serial subscriptions. *Total majors:* 72.
Information for International Students For fall 2006: 170 international students enrolled. Students can start in fall or spring. Transfers accepted from institutions abroad. *Admission tests:* Required: TOEFL (minimum score: iBT 61; paper-based 500; computer-based 173). TOEFL can be waived under certain conditions. *Application deadline:* Rolling. *Expenses:* (2006–07) $6690; room and board, $5860 (on campus); room only, $3628 (on campus). *Financial aid:* Need-based and non-need-based financial aid available. *Housing:* Guaranteed, also available during summer. *Services:* International student adviser on campus. Part-time ESL program on campus. ESL program available during the academic year. Employment opportunities (on-campus) available. *Contact:* Bemidji State University, 1500 Birchmont Drive, NE, Deputy Hall

103, Bemidji, MN 56601. Telephone: 218-755-4096.
Fax: 218-755-2074. E-mail: pjanssen@bemidjistate.edu.
URL: http://www.bemidjistate.edu.

BETHEL UNIVERSITY, ST. PAUL

General Information Independent, coed institution, affiliated with Baptist General Conference. Suburban setting. *Awards:* A, B, M. *Entrance level for U.S. students:* Moderately difficult. *Enrollment:* 5,185 total; 3,321 undergraduates (61% women) including 0.2% international students from 16 foreign countries. *Faculty:* 284. *Library holdings:* 184,000 books, 21,343 current serial subscriptions, 14,171 audiovisual materials. *Total majors:* 55.

Information for International Students For fall 2006: 13 international students applied, 6 were accepted, 2 enrolled. Students can start in fall or spring. Transfers accepted from institutions abroad. *Admission tests:* Required: TOEFL (minimum score: paper-based 525; computer-based 195). TOEFL can be waived under certain conditions. *Application deadline:* Rolling. *Expenses:* (2007–08) $24,510; room and board, $7380 (on campus); room only, $4400 (on campus). *Financial aid:* Need-based college/university scholarships/grants from institutional funds, on-campus employment. Non-need-based college/university scholarships/grants from institutional funds, on-campus employment. Forms required: institution's own financial aid form, International Student's Certification of Finances. International transfer students are eligible to apply for aid. For fall 2006 (estimated), 3 international students on campus received college administered financial aid ($18,655 average). *Housing:* Available during summer. *Services:* International student adviser on campus. Internships and employment opportunities (on-campus) available. *Contact:* Senior Admissions Counselor, Bethel University, 3900 Bethel Drive, St. Paul, MN 55112. Telephone: 651-638-6242. Fax: 651-635-1490. E-mail: d-yoshitani@bethel.edu. URL: http://www.bethel.edu.

CAPELLA UNIVERSITY, MINNEAPOLIS

General Information Proprietary, coed institution. Urban setting. *Awards:* B, M, D, FP (offers only distance learning degree programs). *Entrance level for U.S. students:* Minimally difficult. *Enrollment:* 17,203 total; 2,478 undergraduates (50% women) including 2% international students from 9 foreign countries. *Faculty:* 796. *Total majors:* 9. *Expenses:* (2007–08) $10,440.

CARLETON COLLEGE, NORTHFIELD

General Information Independent, 4-year, coed college. Small town setting. *Awards:* B. *Entrance level for U.S. students:* Very difficult. *Enrollment:* 1,980 total (53% women) including 5% international students from 30 foreign countries. *Undergraduate faculty:* 225. *Library holdings:* 1.1 million books, 10,964 current serial subscriptions. *Total majors:* 35.

Information for International Students For fall 2006: 1000 international students applied, 80 were accepted, 28 enrolled. Students can start in fall. Transfers accepted from institutions abroad. *Admission tests:* Required: SAT or ACT, TOEFL (minimum score: iBT 100; paper-based 600; computer-based 250). Recommended: Cambridge IELTS exam when TOEFL not available. *Application deadline:* 1/15. *Expenses:* (2006–07) $34,272; room and board, $8592 (on campus); room only, $4299 (on campus). *Financial aid:* Need-based college/university scholarships/grants from institutional funds, on-campus employment. Non-need-based college/university scholarships/grants from institutional funds, on-campus employment. Forms required: International Student's Financial Aid Application, International Student's Certification of Finances. International transfer students are eligible to apply for aid. For fall 2005, 70 international students on campus received college administered financial aid ($28,413 average). *Housing:* Guaranteed, also available during summer. *Services:* International student adviser on campus. Internships and employment opportunities (on-campus) available. *Contact:* Dean of Admissions, Carleton College, 100 South College Street, Northfield, MN 55057. Telephone: 507-646-4190. Fax: 507-646-4526. E-mail: admissions@carleton.edu. URL: http://www.carleton.edu.

CENTRAL LAKES COLLEGE, BRAINERD

General Information State-supported, 2-year, coed college. Small town setting. *Awards:* A. *Entrance level for U.S. students:* Noncompetitive. *Enrollment:* 2,831 total. *Undergraduate faculty:* 162. *Library holdings:* 16,052 books, 286 current serial subscriptions. *Total majors:* 10.

Information for International Students For fall 2006: 8 international students applied, 8 were accepted, 8 enrolled. Students can start in fall or spring. Transfers accepted from institutions abroad. *Admission tests:* Required: TOEFL (minimum score: iBT 79; paper-based 550; computer-based 213), ACCUPLACER. *Application deadline:* 7/1. *Expenses:* (2006–07) $4521. *Financial aid:* Need-based and non-need-based financial aid available. Forms required: institution's own financial aid form.

Services: International student adviser on campus. Employment opportunities (on-campus) available. *Contact:* Admissions Representative, Central Lakes College, 501 West College Drive, Brainerd, MN 56401. Telephone: 218-855-8263. Fax: 218-855-8230. E-mail: jjenkins@clcmn.edu. URL: http://www.clcmn.edu.

CENTURY COLLEGE, WHITE BEAR LAKE

General Information State-supported, 2-year, coed college. Suburban setting. *Awards:* A. *Entrance level for U.S. students:* Noncompetitive. *Enrollment:* 8,323 total (59% women) including 1% international students from 39 foreign countries. *Undergraduate faculty:* 323. *Library holdings:* 56,867 books, 486 current serial subscriptions, 3,569 audiovisual materials. *Total majors:* 36.

Information for International Students For fall 2006: 32 international students applied, 15 were accepted, 10 enrolled. Students can start in fall or spring. Transfers accepted from institutions abroad. *Admission tests:* Required: TOEFL (minimum score: iBT 61; paper-based 500; computer-based 173; minimum score for ESL admission: iBT 61; paper-based 500; computer-based 173), ELS (minimum score: 30). Recommended: MELAB. TOEFL can be waived under certain conditions. *Application deadline:* 5/1. *Expenses:* (2006–07) $8054. *Services:* International student adviser on campus. Full-time and part-time ESL programs on campus. ESL program available during the academic year and the summer. Internships and employment opportunities (on-campus) available. *Contact:* International Admissions, Admission Office, Century College, 700 East 7th Street, St. Paul, MN 55106. Telephone: 651-793-1222. Fax: 651-793-1546. E-mail: debbie.palm@metrostate.edu. URL: http://www.century.edu.

COLLEGE OF SAINT BENEDICT, SAINT JOSEPH

General Information Independent Roman Catholic, 4-year, coed, primarily women's college, coordinate with Saint John's University (MN). Small town setting. *Awards:* B. *Entrance level for U.S. students:* Moderately difficult. *Enrollment:* 2,059 total (100% women) including 4% international students from 20 foreign countries. *Undergraduate faculty:* 178. *Library holdings:* 481,338 books, 5,315 current serial subscriptions, 34,985 audiovisual materials. *Total majors:* 49.

Information for International Students For fall 2006: 87 international students applied, 54 were accepted, 27 enrolled. Students can start in fall or spring. Transfers accepted from institutions abroad. *Admission tests:* Required: TOEFL (minimum score: paper-based 500; computer-based 173; minimum score for ESL admission: paper-based 500; computer-based 173). Recommended: SAT or ACT. TOEFL can be waived under certain conditions. *Application deadline:* Rolling. *Expenses:* (2006–07) $24,924; room and board, $6898 (on campus); room only, $3546 (on campus). *Financial aid:* Need-based college/university scholarships/grants from institutional funds, on-campus employment. Non-need-based college/university scholarships/grants from institutional funds, on-campus employment. Forms required: International Student's Financial Aid Application, International Student's Certification of Finances. International transfer students are eligible to apply for aid. For fall 2005, 88 international students on campus received college administered financial aid ($14,588 average). *Housing:* Guaranteed, also available during summer. *Services:* International student adviser on campus. ESL program at cooperating institution. ESL program available during the academic year and the summer. Internships and employment opportunities (on-campus) available. *Contact:* Director of International Student Admission, College of Saint Benedict, Admissions Office, Collegeville, MN 56321. Telephone: 320-363-2190. Fax: 320-363-3206. E-mail: ryoung@csbsju.edu. URL: http://www.csbsju.edu.

COLLEGE OF ST. CATHERINE, ST. PAUL

General Information Independent Roman Catholic, undergraduate: women only; graduate: coed institution. Urban setting. *Awards:* A, B, M, D. *Entrance level for U.S. students:* Moderately difficult. *Enrollment:* 5,246 total; 3,831 undergraduates (96% women) including 2% international students from 16 foreign countries. *Faculty:* 483. *Library holdings:* 263,495 books, 1,141 current serial subscriptions. *Total majors:* 76.

Information for International Students For fall 2006: 81 international students applied, 34 were accepted, 21 enrolled. Students can start in fall or winter. Transfers accepted from institutions abroad. *Admission tests:* Required: TOEFL (minimum score: iBT 61; paper-based 500; computer-based 173). Recommended: SAT. TOEFL can be waived under certain conditions. *Application deadline:* 3/15. *Expenses:* (2006–07) $22,880; room and board, $6432 (on campus); room only, $3592 (on campus). *Financial aid:* Need-based and non-need-based financial aid available. Forms required: institution's own financial aid form, International Student's Financial Aid Application, International Student's Certification of Finances. International transfer students

College of St. Catherine (continued)
are eligible to apply for aid. For fall 2006 (estimated), 56
international students on campus received college administered
financial aid ($9547 average). *Housing:* Guaranteed, also available
during summer. *Services:* International student adviser on campus.
ESL program at cooperating institution. Internships and
employment opportunities (on-campus) available. *Contact:* Assistant
Director, International Admission, Office of International
Admission, F-29, College of St. Catherine, 2004 Randolph Avenue,
F-29, St. Paul, MN 55105. Telephone: 651-690-6029.
Fax: 651-690-8824. E-mail: international@stkate.edu.
URL: http://www.stkate.edu.

THE COLLEGE OF ST. SCHOLASTICA, DULUTH

General Information Independent, coed institution, affiliated
with Roman Catholic Church. Suburban setting. *Awards:* B, M, FP.
Entrance level for U.S. students: Moderately difficult. *Enrollment:*
3,304 total; 2,648 undergraduates (69% women) including 4%
international students from 22 foreign countries. *Faculty:* 260.
Library holdings: 130,353 books, 21,656 current serial
subscriptions, 5,418 audiovisual materials. *Total majors:* 33.
Expenses: (2006–07) $23,574; room and board, $6514 (on campus);
room only, $3708 (on campus). *Financial aid:* Need-based
college/university scholarships/grants from institutional funds,
loans from outside sources, on-campus employment.
Non-need-based college/university scholarships/grants from
institutional funds, loans from outside sources, on-campus
employment. Forms required: institution's own financial aid form,
International Student's Certification of Finances. For fall 2006
(estimated), 100 international students on campus received college
administered financial aid ($20,345 average).

CONCORDIA COLLEGE, MOORHEAD

General Information Independent, 4-year, coed college, affiliated
with Evangelical Lutheran Church in America. Suburban setting.
Awards: B, M. *Entrance level for U.S. students:* Moderately difficult.
Enrollment: 2,764 total; 2,759 undergraduates (63% women)
including 4% international students from 35 foreign countries.
Faculty: 238. *Library holdings:* 325,408 books, 3,528 current serial
subscriptions, 23,205 audiovisual materials. *Total majors:* 81.
Information for International Students For fall 2006: 131
international students applied, 92 were accepted, 53 enrolled.
Students can start in fall or spring. Transfers accepted from
institutions abroad. *Admission tests:* Required: TOEFL (minimum
score: iBT 73; paper-based 533; computer-based 200).
Recommended: SAT or ACT, IELTS is preferred test of English.
Application deadline: Rolling. *Expenses:* (2006–07) $20,980; room
and board, $5090 (on campus); room only, $2460 (on campus).
Financial aid: Need-based college/university scholarships/grants
from institutional funds, loans from outside sources, on-campus
employment. Non-need-based college/university scholarships/grants
from institutional funds, loans from outside sources, on-campus
employment. Forms required: International Student's Financial Aid
Application, International Student's Certification of Finances.
International transfer students are eligible to apply for aid. For fall
2006 (estimated), 100 international students on campus received
college administered financial aid ($13,077 average). *Housing:*
Guaranteed, also available during summer. *Services:* International
student adviser on campus. ESL program at cooperating institution.
ESL program available during the academic year and the summer.
Internships and employment opportunities (on-campus and
off-campus) available. *Contact:* Director of International Student
Recruiting and Support, Concordia College, 901 South 8th Street,
Moorhead, MN 56562. Telephone: 218-299-3004. Fax: 218-299-4720.
E-mail: admissions@cord.edu.
URL: http://www.concordiacollege.edu.

CONCORDIA UNIVERSITY, ST. PAUL, ST. PAUL

General Information Independent, coed institution, affiliated
with Lutheran Church–Missouri Synod. Urban setting. *Awards:* A,
B, M. *Entrance level for U.S. students:* Minimally difficult.
Enrollment: 2,046 total; 1,708 undergraduates (61% women)
including 0.3% international students from 4 foreign countries.
Faculty: 437. *Library holdings:* 113,256 books, 336 current serial
subscriptions, 3,171 audiovisual materials. *Total majors:* 43.
Expenses: (2007–08) $23,496; room and board, $6776 (on campus).
Financial aid: Non-need-based college/university
scholarships/grants from institutional funds, athletic awards, loans
from outside sources. Forms required: institution's own financial
aid form. For fall 2006 (estimated), 1 international student on
campus received college administered financial aid ($10,000
average).

CROWN COLLEGE, ST. BONIFACIUS

General Information Independent, coed institution, affiliated
with The Christian and Missionary Alliance. Suburban setting.

Awards: A, B, M. *Entrance level for U.S. students:* Minimally
difficult. *Enrollment:* 1,344 total; 1,231 undergraduates (59%
women) including 0.2% international students from 4 foreign
countries. *Faculty:* 155. *Library holdings:* 96,222 books, 19,179
current serial subscriptions, 1,523 audiovisual materials.
Total majors: 31. *Expenses:* (2007–08) $18,588; room and board,
$6922 (on campus); room only, $3834 (on campus). *Financial aid:*
Non-need-based college/university scholarships/grants from
institutional funds, loans from outside sources. Forms required:
institution's own financial aid form, International Student's
Certification of Finances. For fall 2006 (estimated), 2 international
students on campus received college administered financial aid
($7074 average).

DAKOTA COUNTY TECHNICAL COLLEGE, ROSEMOUNT

General Information State-supported, 2-year, coed college.
Suburban setting. *Awards:* A. *Entrance level for U.S. students:*
Noncompetitive. *Enrollment:* 6,069 total (42% women) including 1%
international students from 21 foreign countries. *Undergraduate
faculty:* 199. *Library holdings:* 15,693 books, 258 current serial
subscriptions, 1,164 audiovisual materials. *Total majors:* 59.
Information for International Students For fall 2006: 28
international students applied, 22 were accepted, 7 enrolled.
Students can start in fall or spring. Transfers accepted from
institutions abroad. *Admission tests:* Required: TOEFL (minimum
score: iBT 61; paper-based 500; computer-based 173; minimum
score for ESL admission: iBT 32; paper-based 400; computer-based
97), ACCUPLACER. TOEFL can be waived under certain
conditions. *Application deadline:* 6/1. *Expenses:* (2006–07) $9246.
Financial aid: Need-based college/university scholarships/grants
from institutional funds, on-campus employment. Non-need-based
college/university scholarships/grants from institutional funds,
loans from outside sources, on-campus employment. *Services:*
International student adviser on campus. Full-time ESL program
on campus. ESL program available during the academic year.
Internships available. *Contact:* Admissions Director, Dakota County
Technical College, 1300 145th Street East, Rosemount, MN 55068.
Telephone: 651-423-8399. Fax: 651-423-8775.
E-mail: patrick.lair@dctc.edu. URL: http://www.dctc.edu.

GUSTAVUS ADOLPHUS COLLEGE, ST. PETER

General Information Independent, 4-year, coed college, affiliated
with Evangelical Lutheran Church in America. Small town setting.
Awards: B. *Entrance level for U.S. students:* Very difficult.
Enrollment: 2,618 total (57% women) including 1% international
students from 14 foreign countries. *Undergraduate faculty:* 267.
Library holdings: 297,861 books, 17,078 current serial
subscriptions, 17,359 audiovisual materials. *Total majors:* 64.
Information for International Students For fall 2006: 71
international students applied, 13 were accepted, 6 enrolled.
Students can start in fall or spring. Transfers accepted from
institutions abroad. *Admission tests:* Required: TOEFL (minimum
score: iBT 80; paper-based 550; computer-based 213).
Recommended: SAT or ACT. *Application deadline:* 3/1. *Expenses:*
(2007–08) $28,515; room and board, $4275 (on campus); room only,
$2500 (on campus). *Financial aid:* Need-based college/university
scholarships/grants from institutional funds, loans from outside
sources, on-campus employment. Non-need-based college/university
scholarships/grants from institutional funds, loans from outside
sources, on-campus employment. Forms required: International
Student's Financial Aid Application, International Student's
Certification of Finances. International transfer students are
eligible to apply for aid. 30 international students on campus
received college administered financial aid ($18,000 average).
Housing: Guaranteed, also available during summer. *Services:*
International student adviser on campus. Internships and
employment opportunities (on-campus) available. *Contact:*
International Student Services Coordinator, Admission Office,
Gustavus Adolphus College, Office of International Education, 800
West College Avenue, Saint Peter, MN 56082.
Telephone: 507-933-7493. Fax: 507-933-7900.
E-mail: jeffa@gustavus.edu. URL: http://www.gustavus.edu.

HAMLINE UNIVERSITY, ST. PAUL

General Information Independent, coed institution, affiliated
with United Methodist Church. Urban setting. *Awards:* B, M, D,
FP. *Entrance level for U.S. students:* Moderately difficult.
Enrollment: 4,575 total; 2,012 undergraduates (59% women)
including 3% international students from 35 foreign countries.
Faculty: 481. *Library holdings:* 228,973 books, 1,681 current serial
subscriptions, 4,886 audiovisual materials. *Total majors:* 61.
Expenses: (2006–07) $25,040; room and board, $7280 (on campus);
room only, $3682 (on campus).

Minnesota

ITASCA COMMUNITY COLLEGE, GRAND RAPIDS
General Information State-supported, 2-year, coed college. Rural setting. *Awards:* A. *Entrance level for U.S. students:* Noncompetitive. *Enrollment:* 1,185 total including 2% international students from 2 foreign countries. *Undergraduate faculty:* 77. *Library holdings:* 28,790 books, 280 current serial subscriptions. *Total majors:* 30.
Information for International Students For fall 2006: 27 international students applied, 27 were accepted, 27 enrolled. Students can start in fall, spring, or summer. Transfers accepted from institutions abroad. *Admission tests:* Required: TOEFL (minimum score: paper-based 500; computer-based 173). TOEFL can be waived under certain conditions. *Application deadline:* Rolling. *Expenses:* (2006–07) $4906; room and board, $3850 (on campus); room only, $3000 (on campus). *Financial aid:* Need-based college/university scholarships/grants from institutional funds. Non-need-based college/university scholarships/grants from institutional funds, on-campus employment. Forms required: Institutional Scholarship application. *Housing:* Available during summer. *Services:* International student adviser on campus. Internships available. *Contact:* Director, Enrollment Services, Itasca Community College, 1851 East Highway 169, Grand Rapids, MN 55744. Telephone: 218-327-4464. Fax: 218-327-4350. E-mail: cperry@itascacc.edu. URL: http://www.itascacc.edu.

MCNALLY SMITH COLLEGE OF MUSIC, SAINT PAUL
General Information Proprietary, primarily 2-year, coed college. Urban setting. *Awards:* A, B. *Entrance level for U.S. students:* Noncompetitive. *Enrollment:* 474 total (15% women) including 2% international students from 6 foreign countries. *Undergraduate faculty:* 61. *Library holdings:* 4,500 books, 50 current serial subscriptions, 4,000 audiovisual materials. *Total majors:* 4.
Information for International Students For fall 2006: 12 international students applied, 10 were accepted, 10 enrolled. Students can start in fall, spring, or summer. Transfers accepted from institutions abroad. *Admission tests:* Required: TOEFL (minimum score: paper-based 500; computer-based 173), entrance exam. TOEFL can be waived under certain conditions. *Application deadline:* Rolling. *Expenses:* (2007–08) $19,575. *Services:* International student adviser on campus. Internships and employment opportunities (on-campus) available. *Contact:* Director of Admissions, McNally Smith College of Music, 19 Exchange Street East, St. Paul, MN 55101-2220. Telephone: 651-291-0177. Fax: 651-291-0366. E-mail: khawks@mcnallysmith.edu. URL: http://www.mcnallysmith.edu.

MESABI RANGE COMMUNITY AND TECHNICAL COLLEGE, VIRGINIA
General Information State-supported, 2-year, coed college. Small town setting. *Awards:* A. *Entrance level for U.S. students:* Noncompetitive. *Enrollment:* 1,467 total. *Undergraduate faculty:* 137. *Library holdings:* 23,000 books, 167 current serial subscriptions. *Total majors:* 16.
Information for International Students Students can start in fall, spring, or summer. Transfers accepted from institutions abroad. *Admission tests:* Required: TOEFL (minimum score: paper-based 500; computer-based 173; minimum score for ESL admission: paper-based 500; computer-based 173). *Application deadline:* Rolling. *Expenses:* (2006–07) $5,198; room only, $3352 (on campus). *Financial aid:* Non-need-based loans from outside sources. *Housing:* Available during summer. *Services:* International student adviser on campus. ESL program at cooperating institution. ESL program available during the academic year. *Contact:* Director of Enrollment Services, Mesabi Range Community and Technical College, 1001 Chestnut Street West, Virginia, MN 55792. Telephone: 218-749-0314. Fax: 218-749-0318. E-mail: b.kochevar@mr.mnscu.edu. URL: http://www.mr.mnscu.edu.

MINNEAPOLIS COLLEGE OF ART AND DESIGN, MINNEAPOLIS
General Information Independent, coed institution. Urban setting. *Awards:* B, M. *Entrance level for U.S. students:* Moderately difficult. *Enrollment:* 749 total; 702 undergraduates (52% women) including 2% international students. *Faculty:* 105. *Library holdings:* 47,166 books, 196 current serial subscriptions, 139,245 audiovisual materials. *Total majors:* 11. *Expenses:* (2007–08) $27,200; room only, $4160 (on campus). *Financial aid:* Non-need financial aid available. 3 international students on campus received college administered financial aid ($6000 average).

MINNEAPOLIS COMMUNITY AND TECHNICAL COLLEGE, MINNEAPOLIS
General Information State-supported, 2-year, coed college. Urban setting. *Awards:* A. *Entrance level for U.S. students:* Noncompetitive. *Enrollment:* 7,618 total (55% women) including 2%

international students. *Undergraduate faculty:* 487. *Library holdings:* 65,865 books, 600 current serial subscriptions. *Total majors:* 25. *Expenses:* (2006–07) $8207. *Financial aid:* Non-need-based on-campus employment. Forms required: FAFSA.

MINNESOTA STATE COLLEGE–SOUTHEAST TECHNICAL, WINONA
General Information State-supported, 2-year, coed college. Small town setting. *Awards:* A. *Entrance level for U.S. students:* Noncompetitive. *Enrollment:* 1,900 total (58% women) including 3% international students. *Undergraduate faculty:* 100. *Library holdings:* 8,000 books, 150 current serial subscriptions, 50 audiovisual materials. *Total majors:* 28.
Information for International Students For fall 2006: 18 international students applied, 18 were accepted, 18 enrolled. Students can start in fall, spring, or summer. Transfers accepted from institutions abroad. *Admission tests:* Required: TOEFL, ACCUPLACER. TOEFL can be waived under certain conditions. *Application deadline:* Rolling. *Expenses:* (2007–08) $8505. *Financial aid:* Forms required: institution's own financial aid form, International Student's Financial Aid Application. *Services:* International student adviser on campus. *Contact:* Counselor, Minnesota State College–Southeast Technical, 1250 Homer Road, PO Box 409, Winona, MN 55987. Telephone: 507-453-2731. Fax: 507-453-2715. E-mail: aducett@southeastmn.edu. URL: http://www.southeastmn.edu.

MINNESOTA STATE COMMUNITY AND TECHNICAL COLLEGE–FERGUS FALLS, FERGUS FALLS
General Information State-supported, 2-year, coed college. Rural setting. *Awards:* A. *Entrance level for U.S. students:* Noncompetitive. *Enrollment:* 6,093 total (58% women) including 0.05% international students from 2 foreign countries. *Undergraduate faculty:* 341. *Library holdings:* 30,000 books, 173 current serial subscriptions. *Total majors:* 41. *Expenses:* (2007–08) $4720; room only, $3100 (on campus). *Financial aid:* Forms required: International Student's Certification of Finances.

MINNESOTA STATE UNIVERSITY MANKATO, MANKATO
General Information State-supported, coed institution. Small town setting. *Awards:* A, B, M. *Entrance level for U.S. students:* Moderately difficult. *Enrollment:* 14,148 total; 12,534 undergraduates (53% women) including 3% international students from 68 foreign countries. *Faculty:* 717. *Library holdings:* 474,252 books, 3,400 current serial subscriptions. *Total majors:* 127.
Information for International Students For fall 2006: 193 international students applied, 111 were accepted, 70 enrolled. Students can start in fall or spring. Transfers accepted from institutions abroad. *Admission tests:* Required: TOEFL (minimum score: paper-based 500; computer-based 173), ELS (minimum score: 109). *Application deadline:* 4/1. *Expenses:* (2006–07) $11,668; room and board, $5099 (on campus). *Financial aid:* Need-based college/university scholarships/grants from institutional funds, tuition waivers, athletic awards, loans from outside sources, on-campus employment. Non-need-based college/university scholarships/grants from institutional funds, tuition waivers, athletic awards, loans from outside sources, on-campus employment. Forms required: International Student's Certification of Finances. For fall 2006 (estimated), 74 international students on campus received college administered financial aid ($5625 average). *Housing:* Available during summer. *Services:* International student adviser on campus. Internships and employment opportunities (on-campus) available. *Contact:* Associate Director, Minnesota State University Mankato, Admissions, TC 122, Mankato, MN 56001. Telephone: 507-389-1822. Fax: 507-389-1511. E-mail: diane.berge@mnsu.edu. URL: http://www.mnsu.edu.

MINNESOTA STATE UNIVERSITY MOORHEAD, MOORHEAD
General Information State-supported, coed institution. Urban setting. *Awards:* A, B, M. *Entrance level for U.S. students:* Moderately difficult. *Enrollment:* 7,652 total; 7,242 undergraduates (59% women) including 3% international students from 32 foreign countries. *Faculty:* 303. *Library holdings:* 367,334 books, 1,539 current serial subscriptions. *Total majors:* 93.
Information for International Students For fall 2006: 181 international students applied, 141 were accepted, 83 enrolled. Students can start in fall or spring. Transfers accepted from institutions abroad. *Admission tests:* Required: TOEFL (minimum score: iBT 61; paper-based 500; computer-based 173). Recommended: SAT or ACT. *Application deadline:* 6/1. *Expenses:* (2006–07) $5,721; room and board, $5420 (on campus); room only, $3348 (on campus). *Financial aid:* Non-need-based tuition waivers, athletic awards, loans from outside sources, on-campus employment. Forms required: International Student's Certification

Minnesota State University Moorhead (continued)
of Finances. 183 international students on campus received college administered financial aid ($4172 average). *Housing:* Available during summer. *Services:* International student adviser on campus. Internships and employment opportunities (on-campus and off-campus) available. *Contact:* Assistant Director of International Programs, Minnesota State University Moorhead, 1104 7th Avenue South, Moorhead, MN 56563. Telephone: 218-477-2940. Fax: 218-499-5928. E-mail: gillette@mnstate.edu. URL: http://www.mnstate.edu.

NORMANDALE COMMUNITY COLLEGE, BLOOMINGTON
General Information State-supported, 2-year, coed college. Suburban setting. *Awards:* A. *Entrance level for U.S. students:* Noncompetitive. *Enrollment:* 8,261 total including 1% international students. *Undergraduate faculty:* 230. *Library holdings:* 98,141 books, 623 current serial subscriptions, 43,561 audiovisual materials. *Total majors:* 29. *Expenses:* (2006–07) $8734. *Financial aid:* Need-based college/university scholarships/grants from institutional funds.

NORTH CENTRAL UNIVERSITY, MINNEAPOLIS
General Information Independent, 4-year, coed college, affiliated with Assemblies of God. Urban setting. *Awards:* A, B. *Entrance level for U.S. students:* Noncompetitive. *Enrollment:* 1,241 total (56% women) including 1% international students from 11 foreign countries. *Undergraduate faculty:* 80. *Library holdings:* 70,041 books, 384 current serial subscriptions. *Total majors:* 31.
Information for International Students For fall 2006: 3 international students applied, 1 was accepted. Students can start in fall or spring. Transfers accepted from institutions abroad. *Admission tests:* Required: SAT or ACT, TOEFL (minimum score: paper-based 500; computer-based 200). TOEFL can be waived under certain conditions. *Application deadline:* 6/1. *Expenses:* (2006–07) $12,946; room and board, $4612 (on campus); room only, $2110 (on campus). *Financial aid:* Non-need financial aid available. *Housing:* Guaranteed, also available during summer. *Services:* International student adviser on campus. Internships and employment opportunities (on-campus and off-campus) available. *Contact:* International Student Advisor, North Central University, 910 Elliot Avenue, Minneapolis, MN 55404. Telephone: 612-343-4460. Fax: 612-343-4146. E-mail: admissions@northcentral.edu. URL: http://www.northcentral.edu.

NORTH HENNEPIN COMMUNITY COLLEGE, BROOKLYN PARK
General Information State-supported, 2-year, coed college. Suburban setting. *Awards:* A. *Entrance level for U.S. students:* Noncompetitive. *Enrollment:* 6,292 total (60% women) including 1% international students from 62 foreign countries. *Undergraduate faculty:* 231. *Library holdings:* 70,776 books, 2,500 current serial subscriptions, 2,822 audiovisual materials. *Total majors:* 16. *Expenses:* (2007–08) $6,095.

NORTHLAND COMMUNITY AND TECHNICAL COLLEGE–THIEF RIVER FALLS, THIEF RIVER FALLS
General Information State-supported, 2-year, coed college. Rural setting. *Awards:* A. *Entrance level for U.S. students:* Noncompetitive. *Enrollment:* 4,120 total including 0.2% international students from 3 foreign countries. *Undergraduate faculty:* 250. *Total majors:* 46. *Expenses:* (2007–08) $5372. *Financial aid:* Need-based on-campus employment. Non-need-based on-campus employment.

RASMUSSEN COLLEGE MANKATO, MANKATO
General Information Proprietary, 2-year, coed, primarily women's college. Suburban setting. *Awards:* A. *Entrance level for U.S. students:* Minimally difficult. *Enrollment:* 463 total. *Undergraduate faculty:* 42. *Library holdings:* 1,000 books, 3 current serial subscriptions. *Total majors:* 36.
Information for International Students Students can start in fall, winter, spring, or summer. *Admission tests:* Required: TOEFL (minimum score: paper-based 500; computer-based 173; minimum score for ESL admission: paper-based 500; computer-based 173), STEP. *Application deadline:* Rolling. *Financial aid:* Need-based and non-need-based financial aid available. Forms required: institution's own financial aid form. *Services:* ESL program at cooperating institution. ESL program available during the academic year and the summer. Internships available. *Contact:* Admissions Representative, Rasmussen College Mankato, 501 Holly Lane, Mankato, MN 56001. Telephone: 507-625-6556. Fax: 507-625-6557. E-mail: lisac@rasmussen.edu. URL: http://www.rasmussen.edu.

RIDGEWATER COLLEGE, WILLMAR
General Information State-supported, 2-year, coed college. Small town setting. *Awards:* A. *Entrance level for U.S. students:* Noncompetitive. *Enrollment:* 3,918 total (57% women) including 0.03% international students. *Undergraduate faculty:* 224. *Library holdings:* 30,000 books, 401 current serial subscriptions. *Total majors:* 73.
Information for International Students For fall 2006: 7 international students enrolled. Students can start in fall, spring, or summer. Transfers accepted from institutions abroad. *Admission tests:* Required: TOEFL (minimum score: paper-based 500; computer-based 173). TOEFL can be waived under certain conditions. *Application deadline:* 8/1. *Expenses:* (2006–07) $4,645. *Financial aid:* Non-need-based loans from outside sources, on-campus employment. *Services:* International student adviser on campus. Part-time ESL program on campus. ESL program available during the academic year. *Contact:* Director of Admissions and Career Services, Ridgewater College, PO Box 1097, Willmar, MN 56201. Telephone: 320-222-7646. Fax: 320-222-8045. E-mail: sally.kerfeld@ridgewater.edu. URL: http://www.ridgewater.mnscu.edu.

ST. CLOUD STATE UNIVERSITY, ST. CLOUD
General Information State-supported, coed institution. Suburban setting. *Awards:* A, B, M. *Entrance level for U.S. students:* Moderately difficult. *Enrollment:* 15,964 total; 14,486 undergraduates (55% women) including 4% international students from 85 foreign countries. *Faculty:* 934. *Library holdings:* 897,973 books, 1,737 current serial subscriptions, 24,929 audiovisual materials. *Total majors:* 147. *Expenses:* (2006–07) $11,625; room and board, $5194 (on campus).

ST. CLOUD TECHNICAL COLLEGE, ST. CLOUD
General Information State-supported, 2-year, coed college. Urban setting. *Awards:* A. *Entrance level for U.S. students:* Noncompetitive. *Enrollment:* 3,405 total (52% women) including 0.2% international students from 6 foreign countries. *Undergraduate faculty:* 251. *Library holdings:* 10,000 books, 600 current serial subscriptions. *Total majors:* 52. *Expenses:* (2006–07) $7,658.

SAINT JOHN'S UNIVERSITY, COLLEGEVILLE
General Information Independent Roman Catholic, coed, primarily men's institution, coordinate with College of Saint Benedict. Rural setting. *Awards:* B, M, FP. *Entrance level for U.S. students:* Moderately difficult. *Enrollment:* 2,044 total; 1,919 undergraduates including 4% international students from 29 foreign countries. *Faculty:* 164. *Library holdings:* 481,338 books, 5,315 current serial subscriptions, 34,985 audiovisual materials. *Total majors:* 48.
Information for International Students For fall 2006: 56 international students applied, 27 were accepted, 18 enrolled. Students can start in fall or spring. Transfers accepted from institutions abroad. *Admission tests:* Required: TOEFL (minimum score: paper-based 500; computer-based 173; minimum score for ESL admission: paper-based 500; computer-based 173). Recommended: SAT or ACT. TOEFL can be waived under certain conditions. *Application deadline:* Rolling. *Expenses:* (2006–07) $24,924; room and board, $6496 (on campus); room only, $3262 (on campus). *Financial aid:* Need-based college/university scholarships/grants from institutional funds, loans from outside sources, on-campus employment. Non-need-based college/university scholarships/grants from institutional funds, loans from outside sources, on-campus employment. Forms required: institution's own financial aid form, International Student's Certification of Finances. International transfer students are eligible to apply for aid. For fall 2006 (estimated), 84 international students on campus received college administered financial aid ($19,509 average). *Housing:* Guaranteed, also available during summer. *Services:* International student adviser on campus. ESL program at cooperating institution. ESL program available during the academic year and the summer. Internships and employment opportunities (on-campus) available. *Contact:* Director of International Student Admission, Saint John's University, Admissions Office, Collegeville, MN 56321-7155. Telephone: 320-363-2190. Fax: 320-363-3206. E-mail: ryoung@csbsju.edu. URL: http://www.csbsju.edu.

SAINT MARY'S UNIVERSITY OF MINNESOTA, WINONA
General Information Independent Roman Catholic, coed institution. Small town setting. *Awards:* B, M, D. *Entrance level for U.S. students:* Moderately difficult. *Enrollment:* 5,566 total; 1,818 undergraduates (53% women) including 1% international students from 13 foreign countries. *Faculty:* 569. *Library holdings:* 222,153 books, 19,948 current serial subscriptions, 8,650 audiovisual materials. *Total majors:* 61.

Information for International Students For fall 2006: 22 international students applied, 17 were accepted, 11 enrolled. Students can start in fall or spring. Transfers accepted from institutions abroad. *Admission tests:* Required: TOEFL (minimum score: iBT 79; paper-based 550; computer-based 213). Recommended: SAT or ACT, SAT Subject Tests. *Application deadline:* 6/1. *Expenses:* (2007–08) $22,398; room and board, $6130 (on campus); room only, $3430 (on campus). *Financial aid:* Need-based college/university scholarships/grants from institutional funds. Non-need-based college/university scholarships/grants from institutional funds. Forms required: International Student's Financial Aid Application, International Student's Certification of Finances. International transfer students are eligible to apply for aid. For fall 2006 (estimated), 10 international students on campus received college administered financial aid ($25,391 average). *Housing:* Guaranteed, also available during summer. *Services:* International student adviser on campus. Full-time ESL program on campus. ESL program available during the academic year. Internships and employment opportunities (on-campus) available. *Contact:* Director for International and Diversity Admission, Saint Mary's University of Minnesota, 700 Terrace Heights, #34, Winona, MN 55987. Telephone: 507-457-1483. Fax: 507-457-6917. E-mail: mgarza@smumn.edu. URL: http://www.smumn.edu.

ST. OLAF COLLEGE, NORTHFIELD

General Information Independent Lutheran, 4-year, coed college. Small town setting. *Awards:* B. *Entrance level for U.S. students:* Very difficult. *Enrollment:* 3,041 total (56% women) including 1% international students from 18 foreign countries. *Undergraduate faculty:* 324. *Library holdings:* 1.1 million books, 2,319 current serial subscriptions, 24,205 audiovisual materials. *Total majors:* 50.

Information for International Students For fall 2006: 108 international students applied, 32 were accepted, 17 enrolled. Students can start in fall, winter, or spring. Transfers accepted from institutions abroad. *Admission tests:* Required: SAT or ACT, TOEFL (minimum score: paper-based 550; computer-based 213). TOEFL can be waived under certain conditions. *Application deadline:* Rolling. *Expenses:* (2007–08) $30,600; room and board, $7900 (on campus); room only, $3650 (on campus). *Financial aid:* Need-based college/university scholarships/grants from institutional funds, on-campus employment. Non-need-based college/university scholarships/grants from institutional funds. Forms required: International Student's Financial Aid Application, International Student's Certification of Finances. International transfer students are eligible to apply for aid. For fall 2006 (estimated), 20 international students on campus received college administered financial aid ($12,833 average). *Housing:* Guaranteed. *Services:* International student adviser on campus. Internships and employment opportunities (on-campus) available. *Contact:* Associate Director of Admissions, St. Olaf College, Office of Admissions, 1520 St. Olaf Avenue, Northfield, MN 55057. Telephone: 507-646-3995. Fax: 507-646-3832. E-mail: admissions@stolaf.edu. URL: http://www.stolaf.edu.

SAINT PAUL COLLEGE–A COMMUNITY & TECHNICAL COLLEGE, ST. PAUL

General Information State-related, 2-year, coed college. Urban setting. *Awards:* A. *Entrance level for U.S. students:* Noncompetitive. *Enrollment:* 5,259 total including 0.02% international students. *Undergraduate faculty:* 316. *Library holdings:* 12,000 books, 110 current serial subscriptions. *Total majors:* 13. *Expenses:* (2007–08) $8330.

SOUTHWEST MINNESOTA STATE UNIVERSITY, MARSHALL

General Information State-supported, coed institution. Small town setting. *Awards:* A, B, M. *Entrance level for U.S. students:* Minimally difficult. *Enrollment:* 6,126 total; 5,605 undergraduates (58% women) including 8% international students from 22 foreign countries. *Faculty:* 195. *Library holdings:* 197,057 books, 768 current serial subscriptions, 11,511 audiovisual materials. *Total majors:* 50.

Information for International Students For fall 2006: 263 international students applied, 211 were accepted, 81 enrolled. Students can start in fall or spring. Transfers accepted from institutions abroad. *Admission tests:* Required: TOEFL (minimum score: iBT 61; paper-based 500; computer-based 173), ELS (minimum score: 109). Recommended: SAT, ACT, SAT Subject Tests. TOEFL can be waived under certain conditions. *Application deadline:* 6/15. *Expenses:* (2006–07) room and board, $5360 (on campus); room only, $3360 (on campus). *Financial aid:* Non-need-based college/university scholarships/grants from institutional funds, tuition waivers, athletic awards, loans from outside sources, on-campus employment. Forms required: institution's own financial aid form, International Student's Certification of Finances. For fall 2006 (estimated), 16 international

students on campus received college administered financial aid ($2573 average). *Housing:* Available during summer. *Services:* International student adviser on campus. Internships and employment opportunities (on-campus) available. *Contact:* Assistant Director of International Student Services, Office of Admission, Southwest Minnesota State University, 1501 State Street, International Student Services Office, Marshall, MN 56258. Telephone: 507-537-6216. Fax: 507-537-7224. E-mail: wymer@southwestmsu.edu. URL: http://www.southwest.msus.edu.

UNIVERSITY OF MINNESOTA, CROOKSTON, CROOKSTON

General Information State-supported, 4-year, coed college. Rural setting. *Awards:* A, B. *Entrance level for U.S. students:* Moderately difficult. *Enrollment:* 2,414 total (52% women) including 4% international students from 13 foreign countries. *Undergraduate faculty:* 108. *Library holdings:* 54,887 books, 3,415 current serial subscriptions, 1,515 audiovisual materials. *Total majors:* 32.

Information for International Students For fall 2006: 40 international students applied, 35 were accepted, 29 enrolled. Students can start in fall or spring. Transfers accepted from institutions abroad. *Admission tests:* Recommended: TOEFL (minimum score: iBT 68; paper-based 520; computer-based 190; minimum score for ESL admission: iBT 32; paper-based 400; computer-based 97), MELAB or IELTS. TOEFL can be waived under certain conditions. *Application deadline:* Rolling. *Expenses:* (2007–08) $9065; room and board, $5750 (on campus); room only, $2725 (on campus). *Financial aid:* Non-need-based college/university scholarships/grants from institutional funds, tuition waivers, athletic awards, loans from outside sources, on-campus employment. Forms required: institution's own financial aid form, International Student's Certification of Finances. International transfer students are eligible to apply for aid. *Housing:* Guaranteed, also available during summer. *Services:* International student adviser on campus. Full-time ESL program on campus. ESL program available during the academic year. Internships and employment opportunities (on-campus) available. *Contact:* International Programs, University of Minnesota, Crookston, 240 Student Center, 2900 University Avenue, Crookston, MN 56716-5001. Telephone: 218-281-8339. Fax: 218-281-8588. E-mail: rhowe@umcrookston.edu. URL: http://www.crk.umn.edu.

UNIVERSITY OF MINNESOTA, DULUTH, DULUTH

General Information State-supported, coed institution. Suburban setting. *Awards:* B, M, FP. *Entrance level for U.S. students:* Moderately difficult. *Enrollment:* 11,090 total; 10,372 undergraduates (48% women) including 2% international students from 38 foreign countries. *Faculty:* 523. *Library holdings:* 608,579 books, 52,595 current serial subscriptions, 21,204 audiovisual materials. *Total majors:* 69. *Expenses:* (2006–07) $20,546; room and board, $5722 (on campus). *Financial aid:* Need-based and non-need-based financial aid available. Forms required: institution's own financial aid form, International Student's Certification of Finances. For fall 2005, 132 international students on campus received college administered financial aid ($8126 average).

UNIVERSITY OF MINNESOTA, MORRIS, MORRIS

General Information State-supported, 4-year, coed college. Small town setting. *Awards:* B. *Entrance level for U.S. students:* Moderately difficult. *Enrollment:* 1,740 total (58% women) including 2% international students from 11 foreign countries. *Undergraduate faculty:* 174. *Library holdings:* 191,469 books, 9,042 current serial subscriptions. *Total majors:* 42.

Information for International Students For fall 2006: 21 international students applied, 11 were accepted, 10 enrolled. Students can start in fall, spring, or summer. Transfers accepted from institutions abroad. *Admission tests:* Required: TOEFL (minimum score: paper-based 550; computer-based 213). TOEFL can be waived under certain conditions. *Application deadline:* 6/1. *Expenses:* (2007–08) $9112; room and board, $6260 (on campus); room only, $2980 (on campus). *Financial aid:* Need-based college/university scholarships/grants from institutional funds. Non-need financial aid available. Forms required: institution's own financial aid form, International Student's Certification of Finances. *Housing:* Guaranteed, also available during summer. *Services:* International student adviser on campus. Part-time ESL program on campus. ESL program available during the academic year and the summer. Internships and employment opportunities (on-campus) available. *Contact:* Associate Vice Chancellor for Enrollment, Office of Admissions and Financial Aid, University of Minnesota, Morris, 600 East 4th Street, 105 Behmler Hall, Morris, MN 56267. Telephone: 320-589-6035. Fax: 320-589-1673. E-mail: admissions@morris.umn.edu. URL: http://www.mrs.umn.edu.

UNIVERSITY OF MINNESOTA, TWIN CITIES CAMPUS, MINNEAPOLIS

General Information State-supported, coed university. Urban setting. *Awards:* B, M, D, FP. *Entrance level for U.S. students:* Moderately difficult. *Enrollment:* 50,402 total; 32,113 undergraduates (53% women) including 2% international students from 77 foreign countries. *Faculty:* 1,974. *Library holdings:* 5.7 million books, 45,000 current serial subscriptions, 1.2 million audiovisual materials. *Total majors:* 132. *Expenses:* (2006–07) $20,803; room and board, $6996 (on campus); room only, $4042 (on campus). *Financial aid:* Need-based and non-need-based financial aid available. Forms required: institution's own financial aid form.

UNIVERSITY OF ST. THOMAS, ST. PAUL

General Information Independent Roman Catholic, coed university. Urban setting. *Awards:* B, M, D, FP. *Entrance level for U.S. students:* Moderately difficult. *Enrollment:* 10,712 total; 5,807 undergraduates (50% women) including 1% international students from 7 foreign countries. *Faculty:* 776. *Library holdings:* 510,355 books, 2,743 current serial subscriptions, 7,824 audiovisual materials. *Total majors:* 85. *Expenses:* (2006–07) $24,808; room and board, $6882 (on campus); room only, $4042 (on campus). *Financial aid:* Need-based financial aid available. Non-need-based college/university scholarships/grants from institutional funds, loans from outside sources, on-campus employment. Forms required: International Student's Financial Aid Application, International Student's Certification of Finances. For fall 2006 (estimated), 31 international students on campus received college administered financial aid ($13,755 average).

WALDEN UNIVERSITY, MINNEAPOLIS

General Information Proprietary, coed institution. *Awards:* B, M, D. *Entrance level for U.S. students:* Difficulty N/R. *Enrollment:* 27,633 total; 1,690 undergraduates (56% women) including 36% international students from 12 foreign countries. *Faculty:* 1,254. *Total majors:* 5. *Expenses:* (2006–07) $8640.

WINONA STATE UNIVERSITY, WINONA

General Information State-supported, coed institution. Small town setting. *Awards:* A, B, M. *Entrance level for U.S. students:* Moderately difficult. *Enrollment:* 8,220 total; 7,608 undergraduates (62% women) including 4% international students from 48 foreign countries. *Faculty:* 456. *Library holdings:* 350,000 books, 1,000 current serial subscriptions, 8,000 audiovisual materials. *Total majors:* 104.

Information for International Students For fall 2006: 300 international students applied, 186 were accepted, 107 enrolled. Students can start in fall, spring, or summer. Transfers accepted from institutions abroad. *Admission tests:* Required: TOEFL (minimum score: iBT 68; paper-based 520; computer-based 190). Recommended: SAT or ACT. TOEFL can be waived under certain conditions. *Application deadline:* 7/16. *Expenses:* (2006–07) $11,400; room and board, $6300 (on campus). *Financial aid:* International transfer students are eligible to apply for aid. *Housing:* Available during summer. *Services:* International student adviser on campus. ESL program at cooperating institution. ESL program available during the academic year. Internships and employment opportunities (on-campus) available. *Contact:* Director of International Services, Winona State University, 128 Kryzsko Commons, Winona, MN 55987. Telephone: 507-457-5303. Fax: 507-457-2474. E-mail: intrec@winona.edu.

MISSISSIPPI

ALCORN STATE UNIVERSITY, ALCORN STATE

General Information State-supported, coed institution. Rural setting. *Awards:* A, B, M. *Entrance level for U.S. students:* Minimally difficult. *Enrollment:* 3,584 total; 3,015 undergraduates (64% women) including 2% international students from 13 foreign countries. *Faculty:* 203. *Library holdings:* 229,238 books, 1,046 current serial subscriptions, 8,878 audiovisual materials. *Total majors:* 37. *Expenses:* (2006–07) $9332; room and board, $4616 (on campus); room only, $2330 (on campus). *Financial aid:* Non-need financial aid available. Forms required: institution's own financial aid form.

BELHAVEN COLLEGE, JACKSON

General Information Independent Presbyterian, coed institution. Urban setting. *Awards:* A, B, M. *Entrance level for U.S. students:* Moderately difficult. *Enrollment:* 2,575 total; 2,215 undergraduates (66% women) including 1% international students from 18 foreign countries. *Faculty:* 287. *Library holdings:* 102,432 books, 457 current serial subscriptions, 2,110 audiovisual materials.

Total majors: 26. *Expenses:* (2007–08) $15,580; room and board, $6000 (on campus). *Financial aid:* Need-based college/university scholarships/grants from institutional funds, athletic awards, on-campus employment. Non-need-based college/university scholarships/grants from institutional funds, athletic awards, on-campus employment. Forms required: International Student's Certification of Finances. For fall 2005, 32 international students on campus received college administered financial aid ($5644 average).

BLUE MOUNTAIN COLLEGE, BLUE MOUNTAIN

General Information Independent Southern Baptist, 4-year, coed college. Rural setting. *Awards:* B. *Entrance level for U.S. students:* Minimally difficult. *Enrollment:* 365 total (77% women) including 0.3% international students from 2 foreign countries. *Undergraduate faculty:* 36. *Library holdings:* 59,431 books, 186 current serial subscriptions, 3,645 audiovisual materials. *Total majors:* 28.

Information for International Students Students can start in fall, spring, or summer. *Admission tests:* Required: TOEFL (minimum score: paper-based 500; computer-based 173). *Application deadline:* Rolling. *Expenses:* (2006–07) $7490; room and board, $3766 (on campus); room only, $1400 (on campus). *Financial aid:* Need-based and non-need-based financial aid available. Forms required: institution's own financial aid form, International Student's Financial Aid Application. *Contact:* Director of Admissions, Blue Mountain College, PO Box 160, 201 West Main Street, Blue Mountain, MS 38610. Telephone: 662-685-4161 Ext. 176. Fax: 662-685-4776. E-mail: mteel@bmc.edu. URL: http://www.bmc.edu.

JACKSON STATE UNIVERSITY, JACKSON

General Information State-supported, coed university. Urban setting. *Awards:* B, M, D. *Entrance level for U.S. students:* Minimally difficult. *Enrollment:* 8,256 total; 6,523 undergraduates (62% women) including 1% international students from 15 foreign countries. *Faculty:* 474. *Library holdings:* 236,933 books, 3,409 current serial subscriptions, 4,285 audiovisual materials. *Total majors:* 61. *Expenses:* (2006–07) $9540; room and board, $5212 (on campus); room only, $3116 (on campus).

MAGNOLIA BIBLE COLLEGE, KOSCIUSKO

General Information Independent, 4-year, coed, primarily men's college, affiliated with Church of Christ. Small town setting. *Awards:* B. *Entrance level for U.S. students:* Noncompetitive. *Enrollment:* 28 total (11% women). *Undergraduate faculty:* 7. *Library holdings:* 34,000 books, 150 current serial subscriptions, 400 audiovisual materials. *Total majors:* 1. *Expenses:* (2007–08) $6540; room only, $1500 (on campus). *Financial aid:* Need-based college/university scholarships/grants from institutional funds, tuition waivers. Non-need-based college/university scholarships/grants from institutional funds, tuition waivers. Forms required: institution's own financial aid form. 1 international student on campus received college administered financial aid ($3000 average).

MERIDIAN COMMUNITY COLLEGE, MERIDIAN

General Information State and locally supported, 2-year, coed college. Small town setting. *Awards:* A. *Entrance level for U.S. students:* Noncompetitive. *Enrollment:* 3,572 total including 0.1% international students. *Undergraduate faculty:* 256. *Library holdings:* 50,000 books, 600 current serial subscriptions. *Total majors:* 21. *Expenses:* (2007–08) $2896; room and board, $2600 (on campus). *Financial aid:* Need-based and non-need-based financial aid available. Forms required: International Student's Certification of Finances.

MILLSAPS COLLEGE, JACKSON

General Information Independent United Methodist, coed institution. Urban setting. *Awards:* B, M. *Entrance level for U.S. students:* Moderately difficult. *Enrollment:* 1,084 total; 1,003 undergraduates (51% women) including 1% international students from 7 foreign countries. *Faculty:* 99. *Library holdings:* 194,797 books, 16,221 current serial subscriptions, 8,554 audiovisual materials. *Total majors:* 27.

Information for International Students For fall 2006: 28 international students applied, 12 were accepted, 5 enrolled. Students can start in fall, spring, or summer. Transfers accepted from institutions abroad. *Admission tests:* Recommended: SAT or ACT, TOEFL (minimum score: iBT 80; paper-based 550; computer-based 220). TOEFL can be waived under certain conditions. *Application deadline:* Rolling. *Expenses:* (2007–08) $23,352; room and board, $8368 (on campus); room only, $4708 (on campus). *Financial aid:* Need-based college/university scholarships/grants from institutional funds. Non-need-based college/university scholarships/grants from institutional funds.

Forms required: institution's own financial aid form. International transfer students are eligible to apply for aid. For fall 2006 (estimated), 6 international students on campus received college administered financial aid ($15,338 average). *Housing:* Guaranteed, also available during summer. *Services:* International student adviser on campus. Internships and employment opportunities (on-campus) available. *Contact:* Dean of Admissions and Financial Aid, Millsaps College, 1701 North State Street, Jackson, MS 39210-0001. Telephone: 601-974-1050. Fax: 601-974-1059. E-mail: hendrag@millsaps.edu. URL: http://www.millsaps.edu.

MISSISSIPPI COLLEGE, CLINTON
General Information Independent Southern Baptist, coed institution. Suburban setting. *Awards:* B, M, FP. *Entrance level for U.S. students:* Moderately difficult. *Enrollment:* 4,039 total; 2,633 undergraduates (61% women) including 2% international students from 19 foreign countries. *Faculty:* 344. *Library holdings:* 370,404 books, 4,742 current serial subscriptions, 18,348 audiovisual materials. *Total majors:* 60. *Expenses:* (2007–08) $12,494; room and board, $5500 (on campus); room only, $3700 (on campus).

MISSISSIPPI STATE UNIVERSITY, MISSISSIPPI STATE
General Information State-supported, coed university. Small town setting. *Awards:* B, M, D, FP. *Entrance level for U.S. students:* Moderately difficult. *Enrollment:* 16,206 total; 12,630 undergraduates (48% women) including 1% international students from 38 foreign countries. *Faculty:* 1,032. *Library holdings:* 2.4 million books, 39,772 current serial subscriptions, 324,334 audiovisual materials. *Total majors:* 71. *Expenses:* (2006–07) $10,552; room and board, $6331 (on campus); room only, $3296 (on campus).

MISSISSIPPI UNIVERSITY FOR WOMEN, COLUMBUS
General Information State-supported, coed, primarily women's institution. Small town setting. *Awards:* A, B, M. *Entrance level for U.S. students:* Moderately difficult. *Enrollment:* 2,328 total; 2,166 undergraduates including 2% international students. *Faculty:* 214. *Library holdings:* 426,543 books, 1,629 current serial subscriptions, 164 audiovisual materials. *Total majors:* 39.
Information for International Students For fall 2006: 17 international students applied, 7 were accepted, 4 enrolled. Students can start in fall or spring. Transfers accepted from institutions abroad. *Admission tests:* Required: SAT or ACT, TOEFL (minimum score: paper-based 525; computer-based 197). TOEFL can be waived under certain conditions. *Application deadline:* Rolling. *Financial aid:* Non-need-based college/university scholarships/grants from institutional funds, on-campus employment. Forms required: International Student's Certification of Finances. 25 international students on campus received college administered financial aid ($3500 average). *Housing:* Guaranteed, also available during summer. *Services:* International student adviser on campus. Internships and employment opportunities (on-campus) available. *Contact:* Director of Admissions, Mississippi University for Women, 1100 College Street, MUW-1613, International Programs, Columbus, MS 39701. Telephone: 662-326-7105. Fax: 662-241-7481. E-mail: sbrady@muw.edu. URL: http://www.muw.edu.

UNIVERSITY OF MISSISSIPPI, OXFORD
General Information State-supported, coed university. Small town setting. *Awards:* B, M, D, FP. *Entrance level for U.S. students:* Moderately difficult. *Enrollment:* 15,220 total; 12,661 undergraduates (53% women) including 1% international students from 65 foreign countries. *Faculty:* 797. *Library holdings:* 1.3 million books, 11,523 current serial subscriptions. *Total majors:* 63. *Expenses:* (2006–07) $10,548; room and board, $5892 (on campus); room only, $3000 (on campus). *Financial aid:* Need-based tuition waivers, athletic awards, loans from institutional funds, loans from outside sources, on-campus employment. Non-need-based college/university scholarships/grants from institutional funds, tuition waivers, athletic awards, loans from institutional funds, loans from outside sources, on-campus employment. 70 international students on campus received college administered financial aid ($8151 average).

UNIVERSITY OF SOUTHERN MISSISSIPPI, HATTIESBURG
General Information State-supported, coed university. Suburban setting. *Awards:* B, M, D. *Entrance level for U.S. students:* Moderately difficult. *Enrollment:* 14,777 total; 12,122 undergraduates (61% women) including 1% international students from 43 foreign countries. *Faculty:* 860. *Library holdings:* 1.5 million books, 37,095 current serial subscriptions, 37,400 audiovisual materials. *Total majors:* 66. *Expenses:* (2006–07) $10,742; room and board, $5070 (on campus); room only, $3010 (on campus). *Financial aid:* Need-based college/university

scholarships/grants from institutional funds. Non-need-based college/university scholarships/grants from institutional funds, tuition waivers, athletic awards, loans from outside sources. For fall 2005, 99 international students on campus received college administered financial aid ($6536 average).

WESLEY COLLEGE, FLORENCE
General Information Independent Congregational Methodist, 4-year, coed college. Small town setting. *Awards:* B. *Entrance level for U.S. students:* Noncompetitive. *Enrollment:* 80 total (43% women) including 3% international students from 3 foreign countries. *Undergraduate faculty:* 18. *Library holdings:* 25,000 books, 96 current serial subscriptions. *Total majors:* 2. *Expenses:* (2006–07) $8040; room and board, $3640 (on campus). *Financial aid:* Non-need financial aid available.

WILLIAM CAREY COLLEGE, HATTIESBURG
General Information Independent Southern Baptist, coed institution. Small town setting. *Awards:* B, M. *Entrance level for U.S. students:* Moderately difficult. *Enrollment:* 2,493 total; 1,653 undergraduates (72% women) including 2% international students from 18 foreign countries. *Faculty:* 210. *Library holdings:* 92,290 books, 662 current serial subscriptions, 698 audiovisual materials. *Total majors:* 32. *Expenses:* (2006–07) $8715; room and board, $3615 (on campus); room only, $1305 (on campus). *Financial aid:* Need-based college/university scholarships/grants from institutional funds, athletic awards. Non-need-based college/university scholarships/grants from institutional funds, athletic awards, on-campus employment. Forms required: International Student's Certification of Finances. For fall 2006 (estimated), 39 international students on campus received college administered financial aid ($5000 average).

MISSOURI

AVILA UNIVERSITY, KANSAS CITY
General Information Independent Roman Catholic, coed institution. Suburban setting. *Awards:* B, M. *Entrance level for U.S. students:* Minimally difficult. *Enrollment:* 1,683 total; 1,130 undergraduates (67% women) including 4% international students from 30 foreign countries. *Faculty:* 203. *Library holdings:* 80,865 books, 7,179 current serial subscriptions. *Total majors:* 32. *Expenses:* (2007–08) $18,850; room and board, $5750 (on campus); room only, $2750 (on campus). *Financial aid:* Need-based college/university scholarships/grants from institutional funds, on-campus employment. Non-need-based athletic awards. Forms required: institution's own financial aid form. For fall 2005, 1,141 international students on campus received college administered financial aid ($13,943 average).

BARNES-JEWISH COLLEGE OF NURSING AND ALLIED HEALTH, ST. LOUIS
General Information Independent, coed, primarily women's institution. Urban setting. *Awards:* A, B, M. *Entrance level for U.S. students:* Moderately difficult. *Enrollment:* 665 total; 604 undergraduates (85% women) including 5% international students from 11 foreign countries. *Faculty:* 43. *Library holdings:* 3,765 books, 232 current serial subscriptions, 400 audiovisual materials. *Total majors:* 3.
Information for International Students Students can start in fall, spring, or summer. Transfers accepted from institutions abroad. *Admission tests:* Required: TOEFL (minimum score: iBT 85; paper-based 575; computer-based 240). Recommended: ELS. *Application deadline:* 5/15. *Financial aid:* Non-need financial aid available. Forms required: institution's own financial aid form. *Services:* International student adviser on campus. ESL program at cooperating institution. ESL program available during the academic year. Employment opportunities (on-campus) available. *Contact:* Student Services Coordinator, Barnes-Jewish College of Nursing and Allied Health, 306 South Kingshighway Boulevard, St Louis, MO 63110. Telephone: 314-454-8686. Fax: 314-454-5239. E-mail: mlj6257@bjc.org. URL: http://www.barnesjewishcollege.edu.

CENTRAL METHODIST UNIVERSITY, FAYETTE
General Information Independent Methodist, coed institution. Small town setting. *Awards:* A, B, M. *Entrance level for U.S. students:* Moderately difficult. *Enrollment:* 841 total (52% women) including 1% international students. *Faculty:* 83. *Library holdings:* 97,793 books, 316 current serial subscriptions, 379 audiovisual materials. *Total majors:* 47. *Expenses:* (2007–08) $17,160; room and board, $5720 (on campus). *Financial aid:* Non-need financial aid available. Forms required: institution's own financial aid form, International Student's Certification of Finances. For fall 2006

Central Methodist University (continued)

(estimated), 2 international students on campus received college administered financial aid ($10,250 average).

CLEVELAND CHIROPRACTIC COLLEGE-KANSAS CITY CAMPUS, KANSAS CITY

General Information Independent, coed institution. Urban setting. *Awards:* B, FP. *Entrance level for U.S. students:* Noncompetitive. *Enrollment:* 479 total; 86 undergraduates (30% women) including 1% international students from 1 foreign country. *Faculty:* 47. *Library holdings:* 15,000 books, 6,100 current serial subscriptions, 12,300 audiovisual materials. *Total majors:* 1. *Expenses:* (2006–07) $13,057.

COLLEGE OF THE OZARKS, POINT LOOKOUT

General Information Independent Presbyterian, 4-year, coed college. Small town setting. *Awards:* B. *Entrance level for U.S. students:* Moderately difficult. *Enrollment:* 1,345 total (54% women) including 1% international students from 13 foreign countries. *Undergraduate faculty:* 133. *Library holdings:* 119,276 books, 539 current serial subscriptions, 2,744 audiovisual materials. *Total majors:* 95.

Information for International Students For fall 2006: 108 international students applied, 3 were accepted, 3 enrolled. Students can start in fall or spring. Transfers accepted from institutions abroad. *Admission tests:* Required: SAT or ACT, TOEFL (minimum score: paper-based 550; computer-based 213). TOEFL can be waived under certain conditions. *Application deadline:* 2/15. *Financial aid:* Need-based financial aid available. Non-need-based college/university scholarships/grants from institutional funds, athletic awards, on-campus employment. Forms required: International Student's Certification of Finances. International transfer students are eligible to apply for aid. 16 international students on campus received college administered financial aid ($15,400 average). *Housing:* Guaranteed, also available during summer. *Services:* International student adviser on campus. Internships and employment opportunities (on-campus) available. *Contact:* Director of Admissions, Admission Office, College of the Ozarks, PO Box 17, Point Lookout, MO 65726. Telephone: 417-334-6411. Fax: 417-335-2618. E-mail: admiss4@cofo.edu. URL: http://www.cofo.edu.

COLUMBIA COLLEGE, COLUMBIA

General Information Independent, coed institution, affiliated with Christian Church (Disciples of Christ). Small town setting. *Awards:* A, B, M (offers continuing education program with significant enrollment not reflected in profile). *Entrance level for U.S. students:* Moderately difficult. *Enrollment:* 1,186 total; 1,036 undergraduates (60% women) including 6% international students from 27 foreign countries. *Faculty:* 89. *Library holdings:* 62,265 books, 382 current serial subscriptions. *Total majors:* 37.

Information for International Students For fall 2006: 85 international students applied, 40 were accepted, 25 enrolled. Students can start in fall, spring, or summer. Transfers accepted from institutions abroad. *Admission tests:* Required: TOEFL (minimum score: iBT 70; paper-based 500; computer-based 175). Recommended: SAT or ACT. TOEFL can be waived under certain conditions. *Application deadline:* Rolling. *Expenses:* (2006–07) $12,414; room and board, $5164 (on campus); room only, $3248 (on campus). *Financial aid:* Need-based college/university scholarships/grants from institutional funds, athletic awards, on-campus employment. Non-need-based college/university scholarships/grants from institutional funds, athletic awards, on-campus employment. Forms required: institution's own financial aid form. International transfer students are eligible to apply for aid. For fall 2006 (estimated), 43 international students on campus received college administered financial aid ($8084 average). *Services:* International student adviser on campus. Full-time ESL program on campus. ESL program available during the academic year. Internships and employment opportunities (on-campus) available. *Contact:* Director of Admissions, Columbia College, Columbia, MO 65216. Telephone: 573-875-7352. Fax: 573-875-7506. E-mail: international@ccis.edu. URL: http://www.ccis.edu.

See In-Depth Description on page 62.

COTTEY COLLEGE, NEVADA

General Information Independent, 2-year, women's college. Small town setting. *Awards:* A. *Entrance level for U.S. students:* Moderately difficult. *Enrollment:* 318 total including 8% international students from 15 foreign countries. *Library holdings:* 54,200 books, 246 current serial subscriptions. *Total majors:* 2. *Expenses:* (2007–08) $13,510; room and board, $5200 (on campus). *Financial aid:* Need-based college/university scholarships/grants from institutional funds, athletic awards, on-campus employment,

International Peace Scholarship. Non-need-based athletic awards. Forms required: institution's own financial aid form.

CROWDER COLLEGE, NEOSHO

General Information State and locally supported, 2-year, coed college. Rural setting. *Awards:* A. *Entrance level for U.S. students:* Noncompetitive. *Enrollment:* 2,930 total (63% women) including 1% international students from 16 foreign countries. *Undergraduate faculty:* 269. *Library holdings:* 37,452 books, 163 current serial subscriptions. *Total majors:* 35. *Expenses:* (2007–08) $3900; room and board, $3870 (on campus).

CULVER-STOCKTON COLLEGE, CANTON

General Information Independent, 4-year, coed college, affiliated with Christian Church (Disciples of Christ). Rural setting. *Awards:* B. *Entrance level for U.S. students:* Moderately difficult. *Enrollment:* 869 total (58% women) including 1% international students from 4 foreign countries. *Undergraduate faculty:* 52. *Library holdings:* 162,680 books, 16,233 current serial subscriptions, 3,688 audiovisual materials. *Total majors:* 29.

Information for International Students For fall 2006: 23 international students applied, 5 were accepted, 3 enrolled. Students can start in fall or spring. Transfers accepted from institutions abroad. *Admission tests:* Required: TOEFL (minimum score: iBT 61; paper-based 500; computer-based 173). Recommended: SAT or ACT. TOEFL can be waived under certain conditions. *Application deadline:* Rolling. *Expenses:* (2007–08) $16,600; room and board, $6850 (on campus); room only, $3100 (on campus). *Financial aid:* Need-based college/university scholarships/grants from institutional funds, athletic awards, loans from outside sources, on-campus employment. Non-need-based college/university scholarships/grants from institutional funds, athletic awards, loans from outside sources, on-campus employment. Forms required: institution's own financial aid form. International transfer students are eligible to apply for aid. For fall 2006 (estimated), 4 international students on campus received college administered financial aid ($7750 average). *Housing:* Guaranteed. *Services:* International student adviser on campus. Internships and employment opportunities (on-campus) available. *Contact:* Vice President for Enrollment and College Marketing, Culver-Stockton College, One College Hill, Henderson Hall, Canton, MO 63435. Telephone: 573-288-6423. Fax: 573-288-6618. E-mail: mkhoury@culver.edu. URL: http://www.culver.edu.

DEVRY UNIVERSITY, KANSAS CITY

General Information Proprietary, 4-year, coed college. Urban setting. *Awards:* A, B, M. *Entrance level for U.S. students:* Minimally difficult. *Enrollment:* 1,148 total; 1,013 undergraduates (29% women) including 0.4% international students. *Faculty:* 95. *Library holdings:* 15,000 books, 68 current serial subscriptions. *Total majors:* 9. *Expenses:* (2007–08) $13,220.

DRURY UNIVERSITY, SPRINGFIELD

General Information Independent, coed institution. Urban setting. *Awards:* B, M (also offers evening program with significant enrollment not reflected in profile). *Entrance level for U.S. students:* Moderately difficult. *Enrollment:* 2,053 total; 1,606 undergraduates (54% women) including 5% international students from 33 foreign countries. *Faculty:* 167. *Library holdings:* 168,600 books, 1,755 current serial subscriptions, 4,245 audiovisual materials. *Total majors:* 58.

Information for International Students For fall 2006: 85 international students applied, 34 were accepted, 34 enrolled. Students can start in fall, winter, spring, or summer. Transfers accepted from institutions abroad. *Admission tests:* Required: SAT or ACT, TOEFL (minimum score: iBT 71; paper-based 530; computer-based 197; minimum score for ESL admission: iBT 54; paper-based 480; computer-based 157), ELS (minimum score: 54). *Application deadline:* Rolling. *Expenses:* (2006–07) $15,512; room and board, $5790 (on campus). *Financial aid:* Non-need-based college/university scholarships/grants from institutional funds, athletic awards, loans from institutional funds, loans from outside sources, on-campus employment. Forms required: institution's own financial aid form. International transfer students are eligible to apply for aid. For fall 2006 (estimated), 29 international students on campus received college administered financial aid ($3000 average). *Housing:* Guaranteed, also available during summer. *Services:* International student adviser on campus. Full-time and part-time ESL programs on campus. ESL program available during the academic year. Internships and employment opportunities (on-campus) available. *Contact:* International Admission Coordinator, Drury University, 900 North Benton Avenue, Admissions Office, Springfield, MO 65802. Telephone: 417-873-7205. Fax: 417-866-3873. E-mail: druryad@drury.edu. URL: http://www.drury.edu.

EAST CENTRAL COLLEGE, UNION

General Information District-supported, 2-year, coed college. Rural setting. *Awards:* A. *Entrance level for U.S. students:* Noncompetitive. *Enrollment:* 3,474 total (61% women) including 0.2% international students. *Undergraduate faculty:* 187. *Total majors:* 53.

Information for International Students For fall 2006: 9 international students were accepted, 9 enrolled. Students can start in fall, spring, or summer. Transfers accepted from institutions abroad. *Admission tests:* Required: TOEFL (minimum score: iBT 79; paper-based 550; computer-based 213). Recommended: ACT. TOEFL can be waived under certain conditions. *Application deadline:* 7/15. *Expenses:* (2007–08) $3384. *Financial aid:* Need-based and non-need-based financial aid available. International transfer students are eligible to apply for aid. *Services:* International student adviser on campus. ESL program at cooperating institution. Employment opportunities (on-campus) available. *Contact:* International Student Advisor, East Central College, 1964 Prairie Dell Road, Union, MO 63084. Telephone: 636-583-5195 Ext. 2226. Fax: 636-583-1897. E-mail: weinhota@eastcentral.edu. URL: http://www.eastcentral.edu.

EVANGEL UNIVERSITY, SPRINGFIELD

General Information Independent, coed institution, affiliated with Assemblies of God. Urban setting. *Awards:* A, B, M. *Entrance level for U.S. students:* Moderately difficult. *Enrollment:* 1,721 total; 1,640 undergraduates (60% women) including 0.5% international students from 6 foreign countries. *Faculty:* 156. *Library holdings:* 100,691 books, 1,060 current serial subscriptions. *Total majors:* 56. *Expenses:* (2007–08) $14,300; room and board, $5120 (on campus); room only, $2580 (on campus).

FONTBONNE UNIVERSITY, ST. LOUIS

General Information Independent Roman Catholic, coed institution. Suburban setting. *Awards:* B, M. *Entrance level for U.S. students:* Moderately difficult. *Enrollment:* 2,924 total; 2,061 undergraduates (72% women) including 1% international students from 1 foreign country. *Faculty:* 339. *Library holdings:* 88,063 books, 19,532 current serial subscriptions, 3,084 audiovisual materials. *Total majors:* 41. *Expenses:* (2006–07) $17,440; room and board, $6357 (on campus). *Financial aid:* Non-need financial aid available. Forms required: institution's own financial aid form, International Student's Certification of Finances.

GLOBAL UNIVERSITY OF THE ASSEMBLIES OF GOD, SPRINGFIELD

General Information Independent, coed institution, affiliated with Assemblies of God. Small town setting. *Awards:* A, B, M, FP (offers only external degree programs). *Entrance level for U.S. students:* Noncompetitive. *Enrollment:* 5,033 total; 4,807 undergraduates including international students from 127 foreign countries. *Faculty:* 605. *Library holdings:* 180 current serial subscriptions. *Total majors:* 7. *Expenses:* (2006–07) $2376.

JEFFERSON COLLEGE, HILLSBORO

General Information State-supported, 2-year, coed college. Rural setting. *Awards:* A. *Entrance level for U.S. students:* Noncompetitive. *Enrollment:* 4,065 total (61% women) including 1% international students. *Undergraduate faculty:* 218. *Library holdings:* 70,402 books, 242 current serial subscriptions, 5,085 audiovisual materials. *Total majors:* 63. *Expenses:* (2006–07) $3810; room only, $2871 (on campus).

KANSAS CITY ART INSTITUTE, KANSAS CITY

General Information Independent, 4-year, coed college. Urban setting. *Awards:* B. *Entrance level for U.S. students:* Moderately difficult. *Enrollment:* 674 total (57% women) including 1% international students from 8 foreign countries. *Undergraduate faculty:* 112. *Library holdings:* 32,235 books, 133 current serial subscriptions. *Total majors:* 12.

Information for International Students Students can start in fall or spring. Transfers accepted from institutions abroad. *Admission tests:* Required: TOEFL (minimum score: iBT 79; paper-based 550; computer-based 213; minimum score for ESL admission: iBT 79; paper-based 550; computer-based 213). Recommended: SAT or ACT. TOEFL can be waived under certain conditions. *Application deadline:* 1/15. *Expenses:* (2007–08) $25,680; room and board, $7874 (on campus). *Financial aid:* Need-based college/university scholarships/grants from institutional funds, loans from outside sources, on-campus employment. Non-need-based college/university scholarships/grants from institutional funds, loans from outside sources, on-campus employment. Forms required: institution's own financial aid form, International Student's Certification of Finances. International transfer students are eligible to apply for aid. For fall 2005, 4

international students on campus received college administered financial aid ($11,000 average). *Services:* International student adviser on campus. ESL program available during the academic year. Internships and employment opportunities (on-campus) available. *Contact:* Vice President for Enrollment Management, Kansas City Art Institute, 4415 Warwick Boulevard, Kansas City, MO 64111. Telephone: 816-802-3300. Fax: 816-802-3309. E-mail: lstone@kcai.edu. URL: http://www.kcai.edu.

LINCOLN UNIVERSITY, JEFFERSON CITY

General Information State-supported, coed institution. Small town setting. *Awards:* A, B, M. *Entrance level for U.S. students:* Noncompetitive. *Enrollment:* 3,224 total; 2,927 undergraduates (59% women) including 5% international students from 21 foreign countries. *Faculty:* 199. *Library holdings:* 204,948 books, 368 current serial subscriptions, 5,497 audiovisual materials. *Total majors:* 41. *Expenses:* (2007–08) $8,952; room and board, $3990 (on campus); room only, $2050 (on campus). *Financial aid:* Need-based college/university scholarships/grants from institutional funds, tuition waivers, athletic awards, loans from outside sources, on-campus employment. Non-need-based college/university scholarships/grants from institutional funds, tuition waivers, athletic awards, loans from outside sources, on-campus employment. Forms required: institution's own financial aid form, International Student's Certification of Finances. For fall 2005, 117 international students on campus received college administered financial aid ($5600 average).

LINDENWOOD UNIVERSITY, ST. CHARLES

General Information Independent Presbyterian, coed institution. Suburban setting. *Awards:* B, M (education specialist). *Entrance level for U.S. students:* Moderately difficult. *Enrollment:* 9,525 total; 6,068 undergraduates (57% women) including 7% international students from 65 foreign countries. *Faculty:* 453. *Library holdings:* 122,358 books, 28,732 current serial subscriptions, 1,342 audiovisual materials. *Total majors:* 87. *Expenses:* (2007–08) $12,700; room and board, $6200 (on campus); room only, $3100 (on campus). *Financial aid:* Need-based college/university scholarships/grants from institutional funds, loans from outside sources, on-campus employment. Non-need-based college/university scholarships/grants from institutional funds, loans from outside sources, on-campus employment. Forms required: International Student's Certification of Finances.

LINN STATE TECHNICAL COLLEGE, LINN

General Information State-supported, 2-year, coed, primarily men's college. Rural setting. *Awards:* A. *Entrance level for U.S. students:* Moderately difficult. *Enrollment:* 877 total (9% women) including 0.2% international students from 1 foreign country. *Undergraduate faculty:* 88. *Library holdings:* 14,932 books, 144 current serial subscriptions, 1,707 audiovisual materials. *Total majors:* 16. *Expenses:* (2007–08) $9390; room and board, $1910 (on campus); room only, $1485 (on campus). *Financial aid:* Forms required: institution's own financial aid form, International Student's Certification of Finances.

LOGAN UNIVERSITY-COLLEGE OF CHIROPRACTIC, CHESTERFIELD

General Information Independent, coed institution. Suburban setting. *Awards:* B, FP. *Entrance level for U.S. students:* Moderately difficult. *Enrollment:* 1,098 total; 123 undergraduates including 2% international students from 2 foreign countries. *Faculty:* 85. *Library holdings:* 14,001 books, 163 current serial subscriptions, 2,366 audiovisual materials. *Total majors:* 1. *Expenses:* (2006–07) $3750. *Financial aid:* Forms required: International Student's Certification of Finances.

MARYVILLE UNIVERSITY OF SAINT LOUIS, ST. LOUIS

General Information Independent, coed institution. Suburban setting. *Awards:* B, M, D. *Entrance level for U.S. students:* Moderately difficult. *Enrollment:* 3,333 total; 2,748 undergraduates (77% women) including 1% international students from 14 foreign countries. *Faculty:* 355. *Library holdings:* 213,053 books, 14,110 current serial subscriptions. *Total majors:* 48.

Information for International Students For fall 2006: 29 international students applied, 7 were accepted, 1 enrolled. Students can start in fall, spring, or summer. Transfers accepted from institutions abroad. *Admission tests:* Required: TOEFL (minimum score: iBT 61; paper-based 500; computer-based 173). Recommended: SAT or ACT. *Application deadline:* Rolling. *Expenses:* (2006–07) $18,120; room and board, $7720 (on campus); room only, $6800 (on campus). *Financial aid:* Need-based financial aid available. Non-need-based college/university scholarships/grants from institutional funds, loans from outside sources, on-campus employment. Forms required: International Student's Certification of Finances. International transfer students are eligible to apply for

Maryville University of Saint Louis (continued)

aid. For fall 2006 (estimated), 4 international students on campus received college administered financial aid ($13,155 average). *Housing:* Available during summer. *Services:* International student adviser on campus. ESL program at cooperating institution. ESL program available during the academic year and the summer. Internships and employment opportunities (on-campus) available. *Contact:* Assistant Director of Admissions and Coordinator of International Recruitment, Maryville University of Saint Louis, 650 Maryville University Drive, St. Louis, MO 63141. Telephone: 314-529-9350. Fax: 314-529-9927. E-mail: admissions@maryville.edu. URL: http://www.maryville.edu.

METROPOLITAN COMMUNITY COLLEGE–LONGVIEW, LEE'S SUMMIT

General Information State and locally supported, 2-year, coed college. Suburban setting. *Awards:* A. *Entrance level for U.S. students:* Noncompetitive. *Enrollment:* 5,667 total (58% women) including 0.03% international students from 1 foreign country. *Undergraduate faculty:* 380. *Library holdings:* 56,266 books, 288 current serial subscriptions. *Total majors:* 25. *Expenses:* (2006–07) $5400.

METROPOLITAN COMMUNITY COLLEGE–PENN VALLEY, KANSAS CITY

General Information State and locally supported, 2-year, coed college. Urban setting. *Awards:* A. *Entrance level for U.S. students:* Noncompetitive. *Enrollment:* 4,627 total (72% women) including 0.03% international students from 1 foreign country. *Undergraduate faculty:* 437. *Library holdings:* 91,428 books, 89,242 current serial subscriptions. *Total majors:* 31. *Expenses:* (2006–07) $5400.

MISSOURI BAPTIST UNIVERSITY, ST. LOUIS

General Information Independent Southern Baptist, coed institution. Suburban setting. *Awards:* A, B, M. *Entrance level for U.S. students:* Moderately difficult. *Enrollment:* 4,511 total; 3,496 undergraduates (62% women) including 5% international students from 20 foreign countries. *Faculty:* 191. *Library holdings:* 71,634 books, 452 current serial subscriptions, 2,155 audiovisual materials. *Total majors:* 33.

Information for International Students For fall 2006: 100 international students applied, 50 were accepted, 25 enrolled. Students can start in fall or spring. Transfers accepted from institutions abroad. *Admission tests:* Required: TOEFL (minimum score: iBT 61; paper-based 500; computer-based 173). Recommended: SAT or ACT. TOEFL can be waived under certain conditions. *Application deadline:* Rolling. *Expenses:* (2006–07) $14,810; room and board, $5990 (on campus). *Financial aid:* Non-need financial aid available. Forms required: institution's own financial aid form. International transfer students are eligible to apply for aid. *Services:* International student adviser on campus. ESL program at cooperating institution. Employment opportunities (on-campus) available. *Contact:* Director, International Student Services, Missouri Baptist University, One College Park Drive, Saint Louis, MO 63141-8698. Telephone: 314-744-5301. Fax: 314-392-2292. E-mail: cruseye@mobap.edu. URL: http://www.mobap.edu.

MISSOURI SOUTHERN STATE UNIVERSITY, JOPLIN

General Information State-supported, 4-year, coed college. Small town setting. *Awards:* A, B, M. *Entrance level for U.S. students:* Moderately difficult. *Enrollment:* 5,675 total; 5,666 undergraduates (59% women) including 1% international students from 34 foreign countries. *Faculty:* 307. *Total majors:* 58. *Expenses:* (2007–08) $8326; room and board, $4720 (on campus). *Financial aid:* Need-based college/university scholarships/grants from institutional funds, tuition waivers, athletic awards. Non-need-based college/university scholarships/grants from institutional funds, tuition waivers, athletic awards. Forms required: International Student's Certification of Finances. 12 international students on campus received college administered financial aid ($1700 average).

MISSOURI STATE UNIVERSITY, SPRINGFIELD

General Information State-supported, coed institution. Suburban setting. *Awards:* B, M, D. *Entrance level for U.S. students:* Moderately difficult. *Enrollment:* 19,218 total; 16,234 undergraduates (56% women) including 2% international students from 81 foreign countries. *Faculty:* 1,027. *Library holdings:* 1.7 million books, 4,238 current serial subscriptions, 33,547 audiovisual materials. *Total majors:* 91. *Expenses:* (2007–08) $10,658; room and board, $5358 (on campus); room only, $3600 (on campus). *Financial aid:* Need-based college/university scholarships/grants from institutional funds, on-campus employment. Non-need-based college/university scholarships/grants from institutional funds, tuition waivers, athletic awards, loans from outside sources,

on-campus employment. Forms required: International Student's Financial Aid Application, International Student's Certification of Finances. For fall 2006 (estimated), 339 international students on campus received college administered financial aid ($7513 average).

MISSOURI STATE UNIVERSITY–WEST PLAINS, WEST PLAINS

General Information State-supported, 2-year, coed college. Small town setting. *Awards:* A. *Entrance level for U.S. students:* Noncompetitive. *Enrollment:* 1,592 total (65% women) including 1% international students from 6 foreign countries. *Undergraduate faculty:* 112. *Library holdings:* 21,210 books, 189 current serial subscriptions. *Total majors:* 18. *Expenses:* (2007–08) $6364; room and board, $4632 (on campus).

MISSOURI TECH, ST. LOUIS

General Information Proprietary, 4-year, coed, primarily men's college. Suburban setting. *Awards:* A, B. *Entrance level for U.S. students:* Moderately difficult. *Enrollment:* 201 total (11% women) including 3% international students. *Undergraduate faculty:* 11. *Total majors:* 7. *Expenses:* (2006–07) $14,630. *Financial aid:* Need-based and non-need-based financial aid available. Forms required: International Student's Financial Aid Application, International Student's Certification of Finances.

MISSOURI VALLEY COLLEGE, MARSHALL

General Information Independent, 4-year, coed college, affiliated with Presbyterian Church. Small town setting. *Awards:* A, B. *Entrance level for U.S. students:* Minimally difficult. *Enrollment:* 1,606 total (45% women) including 11% international students from 32 foreign countries. *Undergraduate faculty:* 119. *Library holdings:* 71,203 books, 338 current serial subscriptions, 2,456 audiovisual materials. *Total majors:* 40. *Expenses:* (2007–08) $15,450; room and board, $5850 (on campus); room only, $3000 (on campus). *Financial aid:* Need-based college/university scholarships/grants from institutional funds, tuition waivers, athletic awards. Non-need-based college/university scholarships/grants from institutional funds, tuition waivers, athletic awards. Forms required: International Student's Certification of Finances. For fall 2006 (estimated), 58 international students on campus received college administered financial aid ($9658 average).

MOBERLY AREA COMMUNITY COLLEGE, MOBERLY

General Information State and locally supported, 2-year, coed college. Small town setting. *Awards:* A. *Entrance level for U.S. students:* Noncompetitive. *Enrollment:* 3,710 total (61% women) including 0.1% international students. *Undergraduate faculty:* 246. *Library holdings:* 23,027 books, 88 current serial subscriptions. *Total majors:* 15. *Expenses:* (2007–08) $4380; room only, $2200 (on campus).

NORTH CENTRAL MISSOURI COLLEGE, TRENTON

General Information District-supported, 2-year, coed college. Small town setting. *Awards:* A. *Entrance level for U.S. students:* Noncompetitive. *Enrollment:* 1,458 total (70% women) including 0.3% international students. *Undergraduate faculty:* 117. *Library holdings:* 34,748 books, 6,122 current serial subscriptions, 1,326 audiovisual materials. *Total majors:* 21. *Expenses:* (2007–08) $4470; room and board, $4506 (on campus). *Financial aid:* Forms required: institution's own financial aid form.

NORTHWEST MISSOURI STATE UNIVERSITY, MARYVILLE

General Information State-supported, coed institution. Small town setting. *Awards:* B, M. *Entrance level for U.S. students:* Moderately difficult. *Enrollment:* 6,220 total; 5,280 undergraduates (56% women) including 2% international students from 6 foreign countries. *Faculty:* 284. *Library holdings:* 371,026 books, 24,054 current serial subscriptions, 6,253 audiovisual materials. *Total majors:* 116.

Information for International Students For fall 2006: 782 international students applied, 479 were accepted, 137 enrolled. Students can start in fall, spring, or summer. Transfers accepted from institutions abroad. *Admission tests:* Required: TOEFL (minimum score: iBT 61; paper-based 500; computer-based 173). Recommended: ACT, SAT Subject Tests. TOEFL can be waived under certain conditions. *Application deadline:* 7/1. *Expenses:* (2006–07) $8064. *Financial aid:* Non-need financial aid available. *Housing:* Guaranteed, also available during summer. *Services:* International student adviser on campus. Full-time ESL program on campus. ESL program available during the academic year and the summer. Employment opportunities (on-campus) available. *Contact:* International Admissions Specialist, Northwest Missouri State University, 800 University Drive, AD 245, Maryville, MO 64468. Telephone: 660-562-1149. Fax: 660-562-1821. E-mail: kbaud@nwmissouri.edu. URL: http://www.nwmissouri.edu.

PARK UNIVERSITY, PARKVILLE

General Information Independent, coed institution. Suburban setting. *Awards:* A, B, M. *Entrance level for U.S. students:* Moderately difficult. *Enrollment:* 13,182 total; 12,629 undergraduates (48% women) including 2% international students from 91 foreign countries. *Faculty:* 876. *Library holdings:* 150,503 books, 591 current serial subscriptions. *Total majors:* 52.
Information for International Students For fall 2006: 114 international students enrolled. Students can start in fall or spring. Transfers accepted from institutions abroad. *Admission tests:* TOEFL can be waived under certain conditions. *Application deadline:* 7/1. *Expenses:* (2007–08) $7340; room and board, $5406 (on campus); room only, $3180 (on campus). *Financial aid:* Non-need financial aid available. Forms required: institution's own financial aid form. *Housing:* Guaranteed, also available during summer. *Services:* International student adviser on campus. Full-time ESL program on campus. ESL program available during the academic year. Employment opportunities (on-campus) available. *Contact:* Assistant Director, Park University, 8700 North West River Park Drive, Box 3, Parkville, MO 64152-3795. Telephone: 816-584-6834. Fax: 816-505-5443. E-mail: Kimberly.Connelly@park.edu. URL: http://www.park.edu.

PATRICIA STEVENS COLLEGE, ST. LOUIS

General Information Proprietary, 2-year, coed, primarily women's college. Urban setting. *Awards:* A. *Entrance level for U.S. students:* Difficulty N/R. *Enrollment:* 212 total. *Undergraduate faculty:* 32. *Total majors:* 7.
Information for International Students Students can start in fall, winter, spring, or summer. Transfers accepted from institutions abroad. *Admission tests:* Recommended: TOEFL. *Application deadline:* Rolling. *Expenses:* (2006–07) $10,050. *Services:* ESL program at cooperating institution. *Contact:* President, Patricia Stevens College, 330 north 4th strret suite 306, St. Louis, MO 63102. Telephone: 314-421-0949 Ext. 23. Fax: 314-421-0304. E-mail: info@patriciastevenscollege.com. URL: http://www.patriciastevenscollege.edu.

RANKEN TECHNICAL COLLEGE, ST. LOUIS

General Information Independent, primarily 2-year, coed, primarily men's college. Urban setting. *Awards:* A, B. *Entrance level for U.S. students:* Moderately difficult. *Enrollment:* 1,423 total (4% women). *Undergraduate faculty:* 67. *Library holdings:* 11,000 books, 182 current serial subscriptions. *Total majors:* 11.

RESEARCH COLLEGE OF NURSING, KANSAS CITY

General Information Independent, coed, primarily women's institution. Urban setting. *Awards:* B, M (bachelor's degree offered jointly with Rockhurst College). *Entrance level for U.S. students:* Moderately difficult. *Enrollment:* 406 total; 339 undergraduates (91% women) including 1% international students. *Faculty:* 29. *Library holdings:* 150,000 books, 675 current serial subscriptions. *Total majors:* 1. *Expenses:* (2007–08) $22,000. *Financial aid:* Need-based financial aid available.

ROCKHURST UNIVERSITY, KANSAS CITY

General Information Independent Roman Catholic (Jesuit), coed institution. Urban setting. *Awards:* B, M, D. *Entrance level for U.S. students:* Moderately difficult. *Enrollment:* 3,066 total; 2,222 undergraduates (59% women) including 1% international students from 10 foreign countries. *Faculty:* 226. *Library holdings:* 450,000 books, 278,790 current serial subscriptions, 3,394 audiovisual materials. *Total majors:* 31. *Expenses:* (2007–08) $22,990; room and board, $6200 (on campus). *Financial aid:* Non-need-based college/university scholarships/grants from institutional funds, athletic awards, on-campus employment. Forms required: International Student's Certification of Finances. For fall 2006 (estimated), 10 international students on campus received college administered financial aid ($21,055 average).

SAINT CHARLES COMMUNITY COLLEGE, ST. PETERS

General Information State-supported, 2-year, coed college. Suburban setting. *Awards:* A. *Entrance level for U.S. students:* Noncompetitive. *Enrollment:* 6,844 total (60% women) including 0.5% international students from 31 foreign countries. *Undergraduate faculty:* 442. *Library holdings:* 89,165 books, 295 current serial subscriptions, 7,200 audiovisual materials. *Total majors:* 22.
Information for International Students For fall 2006: 37 international students applied, 33 were accepted, 33 enrolled. Students can start in fall, spring, or summer. Transfers accepted from institutions abroad. *Admission tests:* Required: TOEFL (minimum score: paper-based 500; computer-based 173). Recommended: SAT or ACT. TOEFL can be waived under certain conditions. *Application deadline:* 5/5. *Expenses:* (2007–08) $5250.

Services: International student adviser on campus. Part-time ESL program on campus. ESL program available during the academic year and the summer. Internships available. *Contact:* International Student Advisor, Saint Charles Community College, 4601 Mid Rivers Mall Drive, St. Peters, MO 63376-0975. Telephone: 636-922-8000. Fax: 636-922-8236. E-mail: mkilleen@stchas.edu. URL: http://www.stchas.edu.

ST. LOUIS COLLEGE OF PHARMACY, ST. LOUIS

General Information Independent, coed institution. Urban setting. *Awards:* M, FP. *Entrance level for U.S. students:* Moderately difficult. *Enrollment:* 1,126 total including 1% international students from 3 foreign countries. *Faculty:* 101. *Library holdings:* 73,411 books, 153 current serial subscriptions, 50 audiovisual materials. *Total majors:* 1. *Expenses:* (2007–08) $19,750; room and board, $7823 (on campus). *Financial aid:* Need-based and non-need-based financial aid available. Forms required: institution's own financial aid form, International Student's Certification of Finances.

ST. LOUIS COMMUNITY COLLEGE AT FLORISSANT VALLEY, ST. LOUIS

General Information District-supported, 2-year, coed college. Suburban setting. *Awards:* A. *Entrance level for U.S. students:* Noncompetitive. *Enrollment:* including international students from 31 foreign countries. *Library holdings:* 90,021 books, 655 current serial subscriptions. *Total majors:* 48.
Information for International Students For fall 2006: 23 international students applied, 4 were accepted, 2 enrolled. Students can start in fall, winter, spring, or summer. Transfers accepted from institutions abroad. *Admission tests:* Required: TOEFL (minimum score: iBT 61; paper-based 500; computer-based 173; minimum score for ESL admission: iBT 61; paper-based 500; computer-based 173). TOEFL can be waived under certain conditions. *Application deadline:* 7/22. *Services:* International student adviser on campus. ESL program at cooperating institution. ESL program available during the academic year. Employment opportunities (on-campus and off-campus) available. *Contact:* Admissions Assistant III, St. Louis Community College at Florissant Valley, 3400 Pershall Road, St. Louis, MO 63135. Telephone: 314-513-4245. Fax: 314-513-4724. E-mail: lsmith@stlcc.edu. URL: http://www.stlcc.edu.

SAINT LOUIS UNIVERSITY, ST. LOUIS

General Information Independent Roman Catholic (Jesuit), coed university. Urban setting. *Awards:* B, M, D, FP. *Entrance level for U.S. students:* Moderately difficult. *Enrollment:* 12,034 total; 7,479 undergraduates (58% women) including 2% international students from 50 foreign countries. *Faculty:* 1,004. *Library holdings:* 1.9 million books, 14,395 current serial subscriptions, 174,702 audiovisual materials. *Total majors:* 72.
Information for International Students For fall 2006: 654 international students applied, 209 were accepted, 51 enrolled. Students can start in fall, spring, or summer. Transfers accepted from institutions abroad. *Admission tests:* Required: TOEFL (minimum score: iBT 71; paper-based 527; computer-based 197; minimum score for ESL admission: iBT 48; paper-based 460; computer-based 140). Recommended: SAT or ACT, SAT Subject Tests, ELS. TOEFL can be waived under certain conditions. *Application deadline:* Rolling. *Expenses:* (2006–07) $26,648; room and board, $8230 (on campus); room only, $4700 (on campus). *Financial aid:* Need-based college/university scholarships/grants from institutional funds. Non-need-based college/university scholarships/grants from institutional funds, athletic awards. International transfer students are eligible to apply for aid. For fall 2005, 114 international students on campus received college administered financial aid ($11,370 average). *Services:* International student adviser on campus. Full-time and part-time ESL programs on campus. ESL program available during the academic year and the summer. Internships and employment opportunities (on-campus and off-campus) available. *Contact:* International Admission Counselor, Saint Louis University, International Center, DuBourg Hall, Room 150, 221 North Grand Boulevard, St. Louis, MO 63103. Telephone: 314-977-2490. Fax: 314-977-3412. E-mail: icadmit@slu.edu. URL: http://www.slu.edu.
See In-Depth Description on page 168.

SOUTHEAST MISSOURI HOSPITAL COLLEGE OF NURSING AND HEALTH SCIENCES, CAPE GIRARDEAU

General Information Independent, 2-year, coed college. Rural setting. *Awards:* A. *Entrance level for U.S. students:* Moderately difficult. *Enrollment:* 221 total (72% women) including 1% international students from 1 foreign country. *Total majors:* 2. *Expenses:* (2007–08) $10,464.

SOUTHEAST MISSOURI STATE UNIVERSITY, CAPE GIRARDEAU

General Information State-supported, coed institution. Small town setting. *Awards:* A, B, M. *Entrance level for U.S. students:* Moderately difficult. *Enrollment:* 10,477 total; 8,977 undergraduates (60% women) including 2% international students from 33 foreign countries. *Faculty:* 579. *Library holdings:* 429,108 books, 32,455 current serial subscriptions, 14,279 audiovisual materials. *Total majors:* 70.

Information for International Students For fall 2006: 33 international students applied, 25 were accepted, 20 enrolled. Students can start in fall, winter, spring, or summer. Transfers accepted from institutions abroad. *Admission tests:* Required: TOEFL (minimum score: iBT 61; paper-based 500; computer-based 173). TOEFL can be waived under certain conditions. *Application deadline:* 6/15. *Expenses:* (2006–07) $9630; room and board, $5647 (on campus); room only, $3363 (on campus). *Financial aid:* Need-based financial aid available. Non-need-based college/university scholarships/grants from institutional funds, athletic awards, on-campus employment. For fall 2005, 30 international students on campus received college administered financial aid ($7784 average). *Housing:* Guaranteed, also available during summer. *Services:* International student adviser on campus. Full-time ESL program on campus. ESL program available during the academic year and the summer. Internships and employment opportunities (on-campus) available. *Contact:* Assistant Director for International Admissions, Southeast Missouri State University, One University Plaza, Mail Stop 2000, Cape Girardeau, MO 63701-4799. Telephone: 573-986-6863. Fax: 573-986-6866. E-mail: intadmit@semo.edu. URL: http://www.semo.edu.

See In-Depth Description on page 190.

SOUTHWEST BAPTIST UNIVERSITY, BOLIVAR

General Information Independent Southern Baptist, coed institution. Small town setting. *Awards:* A, B, M, D. *Entrance level for U.S. students:* Moderately difficult. *Enrollment:* 3,503 total; 2,730 undergraduates (66% women) including 1% international students from 15 foreign countries. *Faculty:* 248. *Library holdings:* 180,115 books, 22,080 current serial subscriptions, 8,028 audiovisual materials. *Total majors:* 41. *Expenses:* (2006–07) $14,100; room and board, $4200 (on campus); room only, $2200 (on campus). *Financial aid:* Need-based college/university scholarships/grants from institutional funds, loans from outside sources. Non-need-based college/university scholarships/grants from institutional funds, athletic awards, loans from outside sources. Forms required: FAFSA. For fall 2006 (estimated), 16 international students on campus received college administered financial aid ($11,191 average).

STEPHENS COLLEGE, COLUMBIA

General Information Independent, undergraduate: women only; graduate: coed institution. Urban setting. *Awards:* B, M. *Entrance level for U.S. students:* Moderately difficult. *Enrollment:* 964 total; 845 undergraduates (97% women) including 0.5% international students from 3 foreign countries. *Faculty:* 91. *Library holdings:* 125,000 books, 7,393 current serial subscriptions, 850 audiovisual materials. *Total majors:* 35. *Expenses:* (2006–07) $20,500; room and board, $7975 (on campus); room only, $4760 (on campus).

THREE RIVERS COMMUNITY COLLEGE, POPLAR BLUFF

General Information State and locally supported, 2-year, coed college. Rural setting. *Awards:* A. *Entrance level for U.S. students:* Noncompetitive. *Enrollment:* 2,996 total (69% women). *Undergraduate faculty:* 171. *Library holdings:* 35,629 books, 185 current serial subscriptions, 1,095 audiovisual materials. *Total majors:* 24. *Expenses:* (2007–08) $4415; room only, $3114 (on campus). *Financial aid:* Forms required: institution's own financial aid form.

TRUMAN STATE UNIVERSITY, KIRKSVILLE

General Information State-supported, coed institution. Small town setting. *Awards:* B, M. *Entrance level for U.S. students:* Moderately difficult. *Enrollment:* 5,762 total; 5,524 undergraduates (58% women) including 3% international students from 42 foreign countries. *Faculty:* 363. *Library holdings:* 499,536 books, 3,340 current serial subscriptions, 24,802 audiovisual materials. *Total majors:* 57.

Information for International Students For fall 2006: 150 international students applied, 135 were accepted, 82 enrolled. Students can start in fall or spring. Transfers accepted from institutions abroad. *Admission tests:* Required: TOEFL (minimum score: iBT 79; paper-based 550; computer-based 213). Recommended: SAT. *Application deadline:* 6/1. *Expenses:* (2006–07) $10,772; room and board, $5570 (on campus). *Financial aid:* Non-need-based college/university scholarships/grants from institutional funds, athletic awards, loans from institutional funds, loans from outside sources, on-campus employment. Forms required: institution's own financial aid form, International Student's Certification of Finances. International transfer students are eligible to apply for aid. For fall 2005, 34 international students on campus received college administered financial aid ($3670 average). *Housing:* Guaranteed. *Services:* International student adviser on campus. Employment opportunities (on-campus) available. *Contact:* International Admissions Coordinator, Truman State University, KB 120, 100 East Normal, Kirksville, MO 63501-4221. Telephone: 660-785-4215. Fax: 660-785-5395. E-mail: intladmit@truman.edu. URL: http://www.truman.edu.

UNIVERSITY OF CENTRAL MISSOURI, WARRENSBURG

General Information State-supported, coed institution. Small town setting. *Awards:* A, B, M. *Entrance level for U.S. students:* Moderately difficult. *Enrollment:* 10,711 total; 8,970 undergraduates (56% women) including 2% international students from 53 foreign countries. *Faculty:* 596. *Library holdings:* 2.1 million books, 1,703 current serial subscriptions, 18,434 audiovisual materials. *Total majors:* 72.

Information for International Students For fall 2006: 335 international students applied, 294 were accepted, 116 enrolled. Students can start in fall, spring, or summer. Transfers accepted from institutions abroad. *Admission tests:* Required: TOEFL (minimum score: iBT 61; paper-based 500; computer-based 173). Recommended: SAT or ACT, SAT Subject Tests. TOEFL can be waived under certain conditions. *Application deadline:* 5/1. *Expenses:* (2006–07) $11,250; room and board, $5109 (on campus); room only, $4606 (on campus). *Financial aid:* Need-based financial aid available. Non-need-based college/university scholarships/grants from institutional funds, athletic awards, loans from outside sources, on-campus employment. Forms required: institution's own financial aid form. International transfer students are eligible to apply for aid. For fall 2005, international students on campus received college administered aid averaging $4500. *Housing:* Guaranteed, also available during summer. *Services:* International student adviser on campus. Full-time and part-time ESL programs on campus. ESL program available during the academic year and the summer. Internships and employment opportunities (on-campus and off-campus) available. *Contact:* Director of International Admissions, University of Central Missouri, Ward Edwards 1200, Warrensburg, MO 64093. Telephone: 660-543-4762. Fax: 660-543-4201. E-mail: intladmit@ucmo.edu. URL: http://www.cmsu.edu.

See In-Depth Description on page 208.

UNIVERSITY OF MISSOURI–COLUMBIA, COLUMBIA

General Information State-supported, coed university. Suburban setting. *Awards:* B, M, D, FP. *Entrance level for U.S. students:* Moderately difficult. *Enrollment:* 28,253 total; 21,551 undergraduates (51% women) including 1% international students from 92 foreign countries. *Faculty:* 1,126. *Library holdings:* 3.2 million books, 36,244 current serial subscriptions, 4,870 audiovisual materials. *Total majors:* 124.

Information for International Students Students can start in fall, spring, or summer. Transfers accepted from institutions abroad. *Admission tests:* Required: TOEFL (minimum score: iBT 61; paper-based 500; computer-based 173; minimum score for ESL admission: iBT 61; paper-based 500; computer-based 173). Recommended: SAT or ACT. TOEFL can be waived under certain conditions. *Application deadline:* Rolling. *Expenses:* (2006–07) $16,890; room and board, $6977 (on campus); room only, $3837 (on campus). *Financial aid:* Non-need financial aid available. Forms required: institution's own financial aid form, International Student's Certification of Finances. *Housing:* Available during summer. *Services:* International student adviser on campus. Full-time and part-time ESL programs on campus. ESL program available during the academic year and the summer. Internships and employment opportunities (on-campus) available. *Contact:* Assistant Director of Admissions, University of Missouri–Columbia, 230 Jesse Hall, Columbia, MO 65211-1300. Telephone: 573-882-3858. Fax: 573-882-7887. E-mail: inter@missouri.edu. URL: http://www.missouri.edu.

UNIVERSITY OF MISSOURI–KANSAS CITY, KANSAS CITY

General Information State-supported, coed university. Urban setting. *Awards:* B, M, D, FP. *Entrance level for U.S. students:* Moderately difficult. *Enrollment:* 14,213 total; 9,383 undergraduates (59% women) including 3% international students from 63 foreign countries. *Faculty:* 1,100. *Library holdings:* 1.3 million books, 25,022 current serial subscriptions, 421,713 audiovisual materials. *Total majors:* 50. *Expenses:* (2006–07)

$17,858; room and board, $6823 (on campus). *Financial aid:* Need-based non-resident scholarship. Non-need-based non-resident scholarship.

UNIVERSITY OF MISSOURI–ROLLA, ROLLA
General Information State-supported, coed university. Small town setting. *Awards:* B, M, D. *Entrance level for U.S. students:* Very difficult. *Enrollment:* 5,858 total; 4,515 undergraduates (23% women) including 3% international students from 25 foreign countries. *Faculty:* 418. *Library holdings:* 255,768 books, 1,495 current serial subscriptions, 6,353 audiovisual materials. *Total majors:* 40. *Expenses:* (2006–07) $18,155; room and board, $6185 (on campus). *Financial aid:* Non-need financial aid available. Forms required: institution's own financial aid form.

UNIVERSITY OF MISSOURI–ST. LOUIS, ST. LOUIS
General Information State-supported, coed university. Suburban setting. *Awards:* B, M, D, FP. *Entrance level for U.S. students:* Moderately difficult. *Enrollment:* 15,540 total; 12,470 undergraduates (60% women) including 2% international students from 58 foreign countries. *Faculty:* 811. *Library holdings:* 1.2 million books, 3,174 current serial subscriptions, 3,902 audiovisual materials. *Total majors:* 71.

Information for International Students For fall 2006: 319 international students applied, 194 were accepted, 115 enrolled. Students can start in fall, spring, or summer. Transfers accepted from institutions abroad. *Admission tests:* Required: TOEFL (minimum score: iBT 61; paper-based 500; computer-based 173; minimum score for ESL admission: iBT 48; paper-based 450; computer-based 133), ELS. Recommended: SAT or ACT, SAT Subject Tests, IELTS may be substituted for TOEFL. TOEFL can be waived under certain conditions. *Application deadline:* 5/1. *Expenses:* (2006–07) $18,234; room and board, $7178 (on campus); room only, $5298 (on campus). *Financial aid:* Non-need-based college/university scholarships/grants from institutional funds. Forms required: International Student's Certification of Finances. 150 international students on campus received college administered financial aid ($9871 average). *Housing:* Guaranteed, also available during summer. *Services:* International student adviser on campus. Full-time ESL program on campus. ESL program available during the academic year and the summer. Internships and employment opportunities (on-campus) available. *Contact:* International Admissions Officer, University of Missouri–St. Louis, One University Boulevard, #261 MSC, St. Louis, MO 63121. Telephone: 314-516-5229. Fax: 314-516-5636. E-mail: iss@umsl.edu. URL: http://www.umsl.edu.

See In-Depth Description on page 216.

UNIVERSITY OF PHOENIX–KANSAS CITY CAMPUS, KANSAS CITY
General Information Proprietary, coed institution. Urban setting. *Awards:* B, M. *Entrance level for U.S. students:* Noncompetitive. *Enrollment:* 1,201 total; 928 undergraduates (61% women) including 12% international students. *Faculty:* 241. *Library holdings:* 1,759 books, 692 current serial subscriptions. *Total majors:* 21. *Expenses:* (2006–07) $11,064.

UNIVERSITY OF PHOENIX–ST. LOUIS CAMPUS, ST. LOUIS
General Information Proprietary, coed institution. Urban setting. *Awards:* B, M. *Entrance level for U.S. students:* Noncompetitive. *Enrollment:* 964 total; 834 undergraduates (59% women) including 6% international students. *Faculty:* 203. *Library holdings:* 1,759 books, 692 current serial subscriptions. *Total majors:* 28. *Expenses:* (2006–07) $11,910.

UNIVERSITY OF PHOENIX–SPRINGFIELD CAMPUS, SPRINGFIELD
General Information Proprietary, coed institution. Urban setting. *Awards:* B, M. *Entrance level for U.S. students:* Noncompetitive. *Enrollment:* 305 total; 265 undergraduates (55% women) including 5% international students from 89 foreign countries. *Faculty:* 35. *Library holdings:* 1,759 books, 692 current serial subscriptions. *Total majors:* 27. *Expenses:* (2006–07) $9750.

WASHINGTON UNIVERSITY IN ST. LOUIS, ST. LOUIS
General Information Independent, coed university. Suburban setting. *Awards:* B, M, D, FP. *Entrance level for U.S. students:* Most difficult. *Enrollment:* 13,355 total; 7,386 undergraduates (52% women) including 4% international students from 59 foreign countries. *Faculty:* 1,076. *Library holdings:* 1.7 million books, 44,806 current serial subscriptions, 83,027 audiovisual materials. *Total majors:* 167.

Information for International Students For fall 2006: 54 international students enrolled. Students can start in fall. Transfers accepted from institutions abroad. *Admission tests:* Required: SAT or ACT, TOEFL (minimum score: iBT 79; paper-based 550; computer-based 213). *Application deadline:* 1/15. *Expenses:* (2007–08) $35,524; room and board, $11,252 (on campus); room only, $7102 (on campus). *Financial aid:* Need-based and non-need-based financial aid available. Forms required: Washington University International Student Application for Financial Assistance. *Housing:* Guaranteed, also available during summer. *Services:* International student adviser on campus. Part-time ESL program on campus. ESL program available during the academic year. Employment opportunities (on-campus) available. *Contact:* Director of International Recruitment, Washington University in St. Louis, Campus Box 1089, One Brookings Drive, St. Louis, MO 63130-4899. Telephone: 314-935-4893. Fax: 314-935-4290. E-mail: admissions@wustl.edu. URL: http://www.wustl.edu.

WEBSTER UNIVERSITY, ST. LOUIS
General Information Independent, coed institution. Suburban setting. *Awards:* B, M, D. *Entrance level for U.S. students:* Moderately difficult. *Enrollment:* 7,840 total; 3,567 undergraduates (59% women) including 3% international students from 38 foreign countries. *Faculty:* 749. *Library holdings:* 283,742 books, 2,429 current serial subscriptions. *Total majors:* 56. *Expenses:* (2006–07) $18,240; room and board, $7403 (on campus); room only, $3944 (on campus). *Financial aid:* Need-based college/university scholarships/grants from institutional funds, on-campus employment. Non-need-based college/university scholarships/grants from institutional funds, loans from outside sources, on-campus employment.

WENTWORTH MILITARY ACADEMY AND JUNIOR COLLEGE, LEXINGTON
General Information Independent, 2-year, coed college. Small town setting. *Awards:* A. *Entrance level for U.S. students:* Moderately difficult. *Enrollment:* 561 total (54% women) including 0.4% international students from 4 foreign countries. *Undergraduate faculty:* 63. *Library holdings:* 18,890 books, 49 current serial subscriptions, 919 audiovisual materials. *Total majors:* 1. *Expenses:* (2006–07) $3480. *Financial aid:* Forms required: institution's own financial aid form.

WILLIAM WOODS UNIVERSITY, FULTON
General Information Independent, coed institution, affiliated with Christian Church (Disciples of Christ). Small town setting. *Awards:* A, B, M. *Entrance level for U.S. students:* Moderately difficult. *Enrollment:* 2,893 total; 1,162 undergraduates (75% women) including 2% international students from 10 foreign countries. *Faculty:* 274. *Library holdings:* 139,986 books, 11,713 current serial subscriptions. *Total majors:* 46. *Expenses:* (2006–07) $15,570; room and board, $6100 (on campus). *Financial aid:* Non-need-based college/university scholarships/grants from institutional funds, athletic awards, on-campus employment. Forms required: institution's own financial aid form. For fall 2005, 2 international students on campus received college administered financial aid ($10,125 average).

MONTANA

CARROLL COLLEGE, HELENA
General Information Independent Roman Catholic, 4-year, coed college. Small town setting. *Awards:* A, B. *Entrance level for U.S. students:* Moderately difficult. *Enrollment:* 1,452 total (57% women) including 1% international students from 14 foreign countries. *Undergraduate faculty:* 134. *Library holdings:* 89,003 books, 2,721 current serial subscriptions, 3,890 audiovisual materials. *Total majors:* 56.

Information for International Students For fall 2006: 15 international students applied, 11 were accepted, 8 enrolled. Students can start in fall or spring. Transfers accepted from institutions abroad. *Admission tests:* Required: TOEFL (minimum score: iBT 80; paper-based 550; computer-based 213). Recommended: SAT or ACT. TOEFL can be waived under certain conditions. *Application deadline:* Rolling. *Expenses:* (2006–07) $18,410; room and board, $6350 (on campus). *Financial aid:* Need-based college/university scholarships/grants from institutional funds, athletic awards. Non-need-based college/university scholarships/grants from institutional funds, athletic awards. International transfer students are eligible to apply for aid. For fall 2005, 11 international students on campus received college administered financial aid ($5143 average). *Housing:* Guaranteed, also available during summer. *Services:* International student adviser on campus. Full-time ESL program on campus. ESL program available during the academic year. Internships and

Carroll College (continued)

employment opportunities (on-campus and off-campus) available. *Contact:* Director for International Programs, Carroll College, 1601 North Benton Avenue, Helena, MT 59625. Telephone: 406-447-5406. Fax: 406-447-5461. E-mail: mlewis@carroll.edu. URL: http://www.carroll.edu.

DAWSON COMMUNITY COLLEGE, GLENDIVE
General Information State and locally supported, 2-year, coed college. Rural setting. *Awards:* A. *Entrance level for U.S. students:* Noncompetitive. *Enrollment:* 539 total (55% women) including international students from 2 foreign countries. *Undergraduate faculty:* 49. *Library holdings:* 18,870 books, 1,112 audiovisual materials. *Total majors:* 10.

MONTANA STATE UNIVERSITY, BOZEMAN
General Information State-supported, coed university. Small town setting. *Awards:* B, M, D. *Entrance level for U.S. students:* Moderately difficult. *Enrollment:* 12,338 total; 10,832 undergraduates (46% women) including 1% international students from 69 foreign countries. *Faculty:* 805. *Library holdings:* 712,241 books, 8,757 current serial subscriptions, 9,346 audiovisual materials. *Total majors:* 55. *Expenses:* (2006–07) $15,522; room and board, $6450 (on campus). *Financial aid:* Need-based college/university scholarships/grants from institutional funds, tuition waivers, loans from institutional funds, loans from outside sources, on-campus employment. Non-need-based college/university scholarships/grants from institutional funds, tuition waivers, loans from institutional funds, loans from outside sources, on-campus employment. Forms required: International Student's Certification of Finances. For fall 2005, 67 international students on campus received college administered financial aid ($18,037 average).

MONTANA STATE UNIVERSITY–BILLINGS, BILLINGS
General Information State-supported, coed institution. Urban setting. *Awards:* A, B, M. *Entrance level for U.S. students:* Moderately difficult. *Enrollment:* 4,799 total; 4,312 undergraduates (63% women) including 1% international students from 18 foreign countries. *Faculty:* 286. *Library holdings:* 488,004 books, 3,276 current serial subscriptions. *Total majors:* 75. *Expenses:* (2006–07) $14,409; room and board, $4310 (on campus). *Financial aid:* Need-based college/university scholarships/grants from institutional funds, tuition waivers, loans from outside sources, on-campus employment. Non-need-based loans from outside sources. For fall 2005, 39 international students on campus received college administered financial aid ($6902 average).

MONTANA TECH OF THE UNIVERSITY OF MONTANA, BUTTE
General Information State-supported, coed institution. Small town setting. *Awards:* A, B, M. *Entrance level for U.S. students:* Moderately difficult. *Enrollment:* 2,951 total; 2,850 undergraduates (43% women) including international students from 18 foreign countries. *Faculty:* 149. *Library holdings:* 165,734 books, 20,233 current serial subscriptions. *Total majors:* 53.
Information for International Students For fall 2006: 28 international students applied, 28 were accepted, 28 enrolled. Students can start in fall, spring, or summer. Transfers accepted from institutions abroad. *Admission tests:* Required: TOEFL (minimum score: iBT 71; paper-based 525; computer-based 195). TOEFL can be waived under certain conditions. *Application deadline:* Rolling. *Expenses:* (2006–07) $14,766; room and board, $5594 (on campus); room only, $2410 (on campus). *Financial aid:* Need-based college/university scholarships/grants from institutional funds, on-campus employment. Non-need-based college/university scholarships/grants from institutional funds, tuition waivers, athletic awards, on-campus employment. International transfer students are eligible to apply for aid. *Housing:* Available during summer. *Services:* International student adviser on campus. ESL program at cooperating institution. ESL program available during the academic year and the summer. Internships and employment opportunities (on-campus and off-campus) available. *Contact:* Director of Admissions, Montana Tech of The University of Montana, 1300 West Park Street, Butte, MT 59701. Telephone: 406-496-4178. Fax: 406-496-4710. E-mail: tcampeau@mtech.edu. URL: http://www.mtech.edu.

ROCKY MOUNTAIN COLLEGE, BILLINGS
General Information Independent interdenominational, coed institution. Urban setting. *Awards:* A, B, M. *Entrance level for U.S. students:* Moderately difficult. *Enrollment:* 912 total; 863 undergraduates (55% women) including 5% international students from 15 foreign countries. *Faculty:* 112. *Library holdings:* 100,078 books, 378 current serial subscriptions, 1,359 audiovisual materials. *Total majors:* 50.

Information for International Students For fall 2006: 28 international students applied, 12 were accepted, 9 enrolled. Students can start in fall or spring. Transfers accepted from institutions abroad. *Admission tests:* Required: TOEFL (minimum score: iBT 72; paper-based 525; computer-based 197; minimum score for ESL admission: paper-based 525; computer-based 197). Recommended: SAT or ACT. TOEFL can be waived under certain conditions. *Application deadline:* Rolling. *Expenses:* (2006–07) $16,642; room and board, $5608 (on campus); room only, $2550 (on campus). *Financial aid:* Non-need financial aid available. Forms required: institution's own financial aid form, International Student's Certification of Finances. International transfer students are eligible to apply for aid. 38 international students on campus received college administered financial aid ($9752 average). *Housing:* Guaranteed, also available during summer. *Services:* International student adviser on campus. Part-time ESL program on campus. ESL program available during the academic year. Internships and employment opportunities (on-campus and off-campus) available. *Contact:* Director of International Programs, Rocky Mountain College, 1511 Poly Drive, Billings, MT 59102. Telephone: 406-657-1107. Fax: 406-259-9751. E-mail: briggsk@rocky.edu. URL: http://www.rocky.edu.

UNIVERSITY OF GREAT FALLS, GREAT FALLS
General Information Independent Roman Catholic, coed institution. Urban setting. *Awards:* A, B, M. *Entrance level for U.S. students:* Noncompetitive. *Enrollment:* 716 total; 632 undergraduates (69% women) including 1% international students from 3 foreign countries. *Faculty:* 103. *Library holdings:* 108,926 books, 457 current serial subscriptions, 1,620 audiovisual materials. *Total majors:* 76. *Expenses:* (2007–08) $16,350; room and board, $5800 (on campus); room only, $2700 (on campus). *Financial aid:* Need-based college/university scholarships/grants from institutional funds, tuition waivers, on-campus employment. Non-need-based college/university scholarships/grants from institutional funds, tuition waivers, athletic awards. Forms required: International Student's Certification of Finances. For fall 2006 (estimated), 13 international students on campus received college administered financial aid ($10,419 average).

THE UNIVERSITY OF MONTANA, MISSOULA
General Information State-supported, coed university. Urban setting. *Awards:* A, B, M, D, FP. *Entrance level for U.S. students:* Moderately difficult. *Enrollment:* 13,558 total; 11,431 undergraduates including 2% international students from 61 foreign countries. *Library holdings:* 1.4 million books, 7,279 current serial subscriptions, 56,866 audiovisual materials. *Total majors:* 119. *Expenses:* (2006–07) $14,484; room and board, $5860 (on campus); room only, $2660 (on campus). *Financial aid:* Need-based and non-need-based financial aid available. 61 international students on campus received college administered financial aid ($8501 average).

THE UNIVERSITY OF MONTANA–WESTERN, DILLON
General Information State-supported, 4-year, coed college. Small town setting. *Awards:* A, B. *Entrance level for U.S. students:* Minimally difficult. *Enrollment:* 1,176 total (57% women) including 1% international students from 4 foreign countries. *Undergraduate faculty:* 85. *Library holdings:* 137,258 books, 8,345 current serial subscriptions, 3,338 audiovisual materials. *Total majors:* 41. *Expenses:* (2007–08) $12,532; room and board, $5250 (on campus); room only, $2080 (on campus). *Financial aid:* Need-based tuition waivers, athletic awards, on-campus employment. Non-need-based tuition waivers, athletic awards, on-campus employment. Forms required: institution's own financial aid form. 4 international students on campus received college administered financial aid ($15,650 average).

NEBRASKA

BELLEVUE UNIVERSITY, BELLEVUE
General Information Independent, coed institution. Suburban setting. *Awards:* B, M. *Entrance level for U.S. students:* Noncompetitive. *Enrollment:* 6,808 total; 4,900 undergraduates (46% women) including 6% international students from 66 foreign countries. *Faculty:* 370. *Library holdings:* 100,904 books, 12,468 current serial subscriptions. *Total majors:* 14. *Expenses:* (2007–08) $5795. *Financial aid:* Non-need-based college/university scholarships/grants from institutional funds. Forms required: International Student's Certification of Finances.

CENTRAL COMMUNITY COLLEGE–COLUMBUS CAMPUS, COLUMBUS

General Information State and locally supported, 2-year, coed college. Small town setting. *Awards:* A. *Entrance level for U.S. students:* Noncompetitive. *Enrollment:* 2,091 total (63% women). *Undergraduate faculty:* 89. *Library holdings:* 22,000 books, 118 current serial subscriptions. *Total majors:* 22.

Information for International Students Students can start in fall, winter, spring, or summer. Transfers accepted from institutions abroad. *Admission tests:* Required: TOEFL (minimum score: paper-based 500; computer-based 173; minimum score for ESL admission: paper-based 500; computer-based 173). TOEFL can be waived under certain conditions. *Application deadline:* Rolling. *Expenses:* (2007–08) $2544; room and board, $3944 (on campus). *Housing:* Available during summer. *Services:* International student adviser on campus. ESL program at cooperating institution. ESL program available during the academic year and the summer. Employment opportunities (on-campus and off-campus) available. *Contact:* Recruiting and Admissions Coordinator, Central Community College–Columbus Campus, 4500 Sixty Third Street, PO Box 1027, Columbus, NE 68602-1027. Telephone: 402-564-7132. Fax: 402-562-1201. E-mail: myoung@cccneb.edu. URL: http://www.cccneb.edu.

CENTRAL COMMUNITY COLLEGE–GRAND ISLAND CAMPUS, GRAND ISLAND

General Information State and locally supported, 2-year, coed college. Small town setting. *Awards:* A. *Entrance level for U.S. students:* Noncompetitive. *Enrollment:* 2,890 total (67% women) including international students from 1 foreign country. *Undergraduate faculty:* 112. *Library holdings:* 5,700 books, 94 current serial subscriptions. *Total majors:* 22.

Information for International Students Students can start in fall, winter, spring, or summer. Transfers accepted from institutions abroad. *Admission tests:* Required: TOEFL (minimum score: paper-based 500; computer-based 173; minimum score for ESL admission: paper-based 500; computer-based 173). TOEFL can be waived under certain conditions. *Application deadline:* Rolling. *Expenses:* (2007–08) $2544; room and board, $3944 (on campus). *Financial aid:* Need-based college/university scholarships/grants from institutional funds, tuition waivers, loans from institutional funds, on-campus employment. Non-need-based college/university scholarships/grants from institutional funds, tuition waivers, loans from institutional funds, on-campus employment. Forms required: institution's own financial aid form. *Housing:* Available during summer. *Services:* International student adviser on campus. ESL program at cooperating institution. ESL program available during the academic year and the summer. Employment opportunities (on-campus and off-campus) available. *Contact:* Admissions Director, Central Community College–Grand Island Campus, 3134 West Highway 34, PO Box 4903, Grand Island, NE 68802-4903. Telephone: 308-398-7406. Fax: 308-399-4222. E-mail: ekohout@cccneb.edu. URL: http://www.cccneb.edu.

CENTRAL COMMUNITY COLLEGE–HASTINGS CAMPUS, HASTINGS

General Information State and locally supported, 2-year, coed college. Small town setting. *Awards:* A. *Entrance level for U.S. students:* Noncompetitive. *Enrollment:* 2,485 total (56% women) including 0.1% international students. *Undergraduate faculty:* 90. *Library holdings:* 4,025 books, 52 current serial subscriptions. *Total majors:* 36.

Information for International Students Students can start in fall, winter, spring, or summer. Transfers accepted from institutions abroad. *Admission tests:* Required: TOEFL (minimum score: paper-based 500; computer-based 173; minimum score for ESL admission: paper-based 500; computer-based 173). TOEFL can be waived under certain conditions. *Application deadline:* Rolling. *Expenses:* (2007–08) $2544; room and board, $3944 (on campus). *Housing:* Available during summer. *Services:* International student adviser on campus. ESL program at cooperating institution. ESL program available during the academic year and the summer. Employment opportunities (on-campus and off-campus) available. *Contact:* Admissions and Recruiting Director, Central Community College–Hastings Campus, East Highway 6, PO Box 1024, Hastings, NE 68902-1024. Telephone: 402-461-2503. Fax: 402-461-2454. E-mail: rglenn@cccneb.edu. URL: http://www.cccneb.edu.

CHADRON STATE COLLEGE, CHADRON

General Information State-supported, coed institution. Small town setting. *Awards:* B, M. *Entrance level for U.S. students:* Noncompetitive. *Enrollment:* 2,636 total; 2,316 undergraduates (58% women) including 1% international students from 5 foreign countries. *Faculty:* 110. *Library holdings:* 593,140 books, 619 current serial subscriptions, 5,596 audiovisual materials. *Total majors:* 46. *Financial aid:* Non-need financial aid available.

CONCORDIA UNIVERSITY, SEWARD

General Information Independent, coed institution, affiliated with Lutheran Church–Missouri Synod. Small town setting. *Awards:* B, M. *Entrance level for U.S. students:* Moderately difficult. *Enrollment:* 1,251 total; 1,107 undergraduates (54% women) including 1% international students from 8 foreign countries. *Faculty:* 133. *Library holdings:* 189,104 books, 15,981 current serial subscriptions, 9,756 audiovisual materials. *Total majors:* 73. *Expenses:* (2007–08) $19,790; room and board, $5070 (on campus); room only, $2170 (on campus). *Financial aid:* Need-based college/university scholarships/grants from institutional funds. Non-need-based college/university scholarships/grants from institutional funds, tuition waivers, athletic awards, loans from outside sources. Forms required: institution's own financial aid form. For fall 2006 (estimated), 6 international students on campus received college administered financial aid ($6409 average).

CREIGHTON UNIVERSITY, OMAHA

General Information Independent Roman Catholic (Jesuit), coed university. Urban setting. *Awards:* A, B, M, D, FP. *Entrance level for U.S. students:* Moderately difficult. *Enrollment:* 6,981 total; 4,075 undergraduates (60% women) including 1% international students from 33 foreign countries. *Faculty:* 654. *Library holdings:* 466,556 books, 27,144 current serial subscriptions, 9,502 audiovisual materials. *Total majors:* 46. *Expenses:* (2006–07) $25,126; room and board, $7842 (on campus); room only, $4420 (on campus). *Financial aid:* Non-need-based college/university scholarships/grants from institutional funds, athletic awards, loans from outside sources, on-campus employment. For fall 2006 (estimated), 11 international students on campus received college administered financial aid ($4772 average).

DANA COLLEGE, BLAIR

General Information Independent, 4-year, coed college, affiliated with Evangelical Lutheran Church in America. Small town setting. *Awards:* B. *Entrance level for U.S. students:* Moderately difficult. *Enrollment:* 601 total (47% women) including 1% international students from 3 foreign countries. *Undergraduate faculty:* 69. *Library holdings:* 177,500 books, 5,000 current serial subscriptions. *Total majors:* 41.

Information for International Students For fall 2006: 7 international students applied, 5 were accepted, 5 enrolled. Students can start in fall. Transfers accepted from institutions abroad. *Admission tests:* Required: TOEFL (minimum score: paper-based 500; computer-based 173). *Application deadline:* 5/31. *Expenses:* (2006–07) $18,650; room and board, $5390 (on campus); room only, $2160 (on campus). *Financial aid:* Need-based college/university scholarships/grants from institutional funds. Non-need financial aid available. Forms required: International Student's Financial Aid Application. International transfer students are eligible to apply for aid. For fall 2006 (estimated), 1 international student on campus received college administered financial aid ($12,500 average). *Housing:* Guaranteed, also available during summer. *Services:* International student adviser on campus. Internships and employment opportunities (on-campus) available. *Contact:* Associate Director of Admissions, Dana College, 2848 College Drive, Blair, NE 68008. Telephone: 402-426-7224. Fax: 402-426-7373. E-mail: dwork@dana.edu. URL: http://www.dana.edu.

DOANE COLLEGE, CRETE

General Information Independent, coed institution, affiliated with United Church of Christ. Small town setting. *Awards:* B, M (non-traditional undergraduate programs and graduate programs offered at Lincoln campus). *Entrance level for U.S. students:* Moderately difficult. *Enrollment:* 922 total (55% women) including 0.4% international students from 2 foreign countries. *Faculty:* 139. *Library holdings:* 351,653 books, 25,589 current serial subscriptions, 3,015 audiovisual materials. *Total majors:* 40. *Expenses:* (2007–08) $19,150; room and board, $5410 (on campus); room only, $1950 (on campus).

GRACE UNIVERSITY, OMAHA

General Information Independent interdenominational, coed institution. Urban setting. *Awards:* A, B, M. *Entrance level for U.S. students:* Moderately difficult. *Enrollment:* 513 total; 427 undergraduates (57% women) including international students from 4 foreign countries. *Faculty:* 50. *Library holdings:* 46,736 books, 3,721 current serial subscriptions, 3,882 audiovisual materials. *Total majors:* 39. *Expenses:* (2006–07) $13,970; room and board, $5350 (on campus); room only, $2450 (on campus). *Financial aid:* Need-based college/university scholarships/grants from institutional funds, on-campus employment. Non-need-based college/university

Grace University (continued)

scholarships/grants from institutional funds, on-campus employment. Forms required: institution's own financial aid form, International Student's Certification of Finances. For fall 2006 (estimated), 2 international students on campus received college administered financial aid ($1500 average).

HASTINGS COLLEGE, HASTINGS

General Information Independent Presbyterian, coed institution. Small town setting. *Awards:* B, M. *Entrance level for U.S. students:* Moderately difficult. *Enrollment:* 1,137 total; 1,093 undergraduates (49% women) including 1% international students from 4 foreign countries. *Faculty:* 128. *Library holdings:* 113,318 books, 636 current serial subscriptions. *Total majors:* 81. *Expenses:* (2006–07) $18,302; room and board, $5148 (on campus); room only, $2200 (on campus). *Financial aid:* Need-based college/university scholarships/grants from institutional funds, athletic awards, loans from outside sources, on-campus employment. Non-need-based college/university scholarships/grants from institutional funds, athletic awards, loans from outside sources, on-campus employment. Forms required: institution's own financial aid form.

METROPOLITAN COMMUNITY COLLEGE, OMAHA

General Information State and locally supported, 2-year, coed college. Urban setting. *Awards:* A. *Entrance level for U.S. students:* Noncompetitive. *Enrollment:* 14,098 total (56% women) including 0.1% international students. *Undergraduate faculty:* 877. *Library holdings:* 43,788 books, 453 current serial subscriptions, 8,008 audiovisual materials. *Total majors:* 33. *Expenses:* (2007–08) $2,992; room and board, $3555 (on campus).

NEBRASKA METHODIST COLLEGE, OMAHA

General Information Independent, coed, primarily women's institution, affiliated with United Methodist Church. Urban setting. *Awards:* A, B, M. *Entrance level for U.S. students:* Moderately difficult. *Enrollment:* 512 total; 446 undergraduates (89% women) including 0.2% international students from 1 foreign country. *Faculty:* 57. *Library holdings:* 8,656 books, 475 current serial subscriptions. *Total majors:* 6.
Information for International Students For fall 2006: 2 international students applied, 2 were accepted, 1 enrolled. Students can start in fall or spring. Transfers accepted from institutions abroad. *Admission tests:* Required: TOEFL (minimum score: iBT 80; paper-based 550; computer-based 213; minimum score for ESL admission: paper-based 550; computer-based 213). Recommended: ACT, ELS. *Application deadline:* 3/1. *Expenses:* (2007–08) $13,230; room only, $2384 (on campus). *Housing:* Available during summer. *Services:* ESL program at cooperating institution. ESL program available during the academic year and the summer. Employment opportunities (on-campus) available. *Contact:* Director of Admissions, Nebraska Methodist College, 720 North 87th Street, Omaha, NE 68114. Telephone: 402-354-7205. Fax: 402-354-7020. E-mail: Deann.Sterner@methodistcollege.edu. URL: http://www.methodistcollege.edu.

NEBRASKA WESLEYAN UNIVERSITY, LINCOLN

General Information Independent United Methodist, coed institution. Suburban setting. *Awards:* B, M. *Entrance level for U.S. students:* Moderately difficult. *Enrollment:* 2,068 total; 1,864 undergraduates (57% women) including 0.2% international students from 13 foreign countries. *Faculty:* 217. *Library holdings:* 178,531 books, 743 current serial subscriptions. *Total majors:* 50.
Information for International Students Students can start in fall or spring. Transfers accepted from institutions abroad. *Admission tests:* Required: TOEFL (minimum score: iBT 71; paper-based 525; computer-based 197). Recommended: STEP-Eiken or IELTS in lieu of TOEFL. *Application deadline:* 6/1. *Expenses:* (2006–07) $19,302; room and board, $5165 (on campus). *Financial aid:* Need-based college/university scholarships/grants from institutional funds, loans from outside sources, on-campus employment. Non-need financial aid available. Forms required: International Student's Certification of Finances. International transfer students are eligible to apply for aid. For fall 2006 (estimated), 2 international students on campus received college administered financial aid ($6881 average). *Housing:* Guaranteed, also available during summer. *Services:* International student adviser on campus. ESL program at cooperating institution. Internships and employment opportunities (on-campus) available. *Contact:* International Student Advisor, Nebraska Wesleyan University, 5000 St. Paul Avenue, Lincoln, NE 68504. Telephone: 402-465-2520. Fax: 402-465-2179. E-mail: yiwasaki@nebrwesleyan.edu. URL: http://www.nebrwesleyan.edu.

NORTHEAST COMMUNITY COLLEGE, NORFOLK

General Information State and locally supported, 2-year, coed college. Small town setting. *Awards:* A. *Entrance level for U.S. students:* Noncompetitive. *Enrollment:* 5,261 total (47% women). *Undergraduate faculty:* 376. *Library holdings:* 52,494 books, 11,140 current serial subscriptions, 1,805 audiovisual materials. *Total majors:* 76.
Information for International Students For fall 2006: 7 international students applied, 7 were accepted, 7 enrolled. Students can start in fall, spring, or summer. Transfers accepted from institutions abroad. *Admission tests:* Required: TOEFL (minimum score: paper-based 500; computer-based 173). Recommended: SAT or ACT, ASSET. TOEFL can be waived under certain conditions. *Application deadline:* 6/1. *Expenses:* (2007–08) $2832; room and board, $3908 (on campus). *Financial aid:* Need-based college/university scholarships/grants from institutional funds, loans from institutional funds, on-campus employment. Non-need-based college/university scholarships/grants from institutional funds, tuition waivers, athletic awards, on-campus employment. Forms required: International Student's Certification of Finances. *Housing:* Available during summer. *Services:* International student adviser on campus. Part-time ESL program on campus. ESL program available during the academic year and the summer. Employment opportunities (on-campus) available. *Contact:* Advisor/Recruiter, Northeast Community College, 801 East Benjamin Avenue, PO Box 469, Norfolk, NE 68702-0469. Telephone: 402-844-7282. Fax: 402-844-7396. E-mail: shelley@northeastcollege.com. URL: http://www.northeastcollege.com.

PERU STATE COLLEGE, PERU

General Information State-supported, coed institution. Rural setting. *Awards:* B, M. *Entrance level for U.S. students:* Noncompetitive. *Enrollment:* 1,677 total; 1,487 undergraduates (54% women) including 1% international students from 7 foreign countries. *Faculty:* 130. *Library holdings:* 177,373 books, 232 current serial subscriptions. *Total majors:* 41.
Information for International Students Students can start in fall or spring. Transfers accepted from institutions abroad. *Admission tests:* Required: TOEFL (minimum score: paper-based 550; computer-based 230). Recommended: SAT or ACT. *Application deadline:* 6/1. *Expenses:* (2006–07) $6,906; room and board, $4620 (on campus). *Financial aid:* Non-need-based tuition waivers, athletic awards. Forms required: scholarship application form. *Housing:* Guaranteed, also available during summer. *Services:* International student adviser on campus. Internships and employment opportunities (on-campus and off-campus) available. *Contact:* Director of Admissions and Retention, Peru State College, PO Box 10, Peru, NE 68421-0010. Telephone: 402-872-2221. Fax: 402-872-2296. E-mail: admissions@oakmail.peru.edu. URL: http://www.peru.edu.

UNION COLLEGE, LINCOLN

General Information Independent Seventh-day Adventist, coed institution. Suburban setting. *Awards:* A, B, M. *Entrance level for U.S. students:* Moderately difficult. *Enrollment:* 982 total; 912 undergraduates (54% women) including 9% international students from 29 foreign countries. *Faculty:* 102. *Library holdings:* 147,813 books, 1,357 current serial subscriptions. *Total majors:* 54. *Expenses:* (2006–07) $15,230; room and board, $4218 (on campus); room only, $2898 (on campus).

UNIVERSITY OF NEBRASKA AT KEARNEY, KEARNEY

General Information State-supported, coed institution. Small town setting. *Awards:* B, M. *Entrance level for U.S. students:* Moderately difficult. *Enrollment:* 6,468 total; 5,276 undergraduates (54% women) including 7% international students from 40 foreign countries. *Faculty:* 377. *Library holdings:* 320,915 books, 1,657 current serial subscriptions. *Total majors:* 41. *Expenses:* (2006–07) $8838; room and board, $5686 (on campus). *Financial aid:* Non-need financial aid available. For fall 2005, 131 international students on campus received college administered financial aid ($2387 average).

UNIVERSITY OF NEBRASKA AT OMAHA, OMAHA

General Information State-supported, coed university. Urban setting. *Awards:* B, M, D. *Entrance level for U.S. students:* Minimally difficult. *Enrollment:* 13,906 total; 11,156 undergraduates (52% women) including 2% international students from 75 foreign countries. *Faculty:* 865. *Library holdings:* 700,000 books, 37,000 current serial subscriptions. *Total majors:* 73. *Expenses:* (2006–07) $13,646; room and board, $6630 (on campus); room only, $4110 (on campus). *Financial aid:* Non-need-based college/university scholarships/grants from institutional funds, tuition waivers, loans from institutional funds. Forms required:

institution's own financial aid form. For fall 2005, 20 international students on campus received college administered financial aid ($2030 average).

UNIVERSITY OF NEBRASKA–LINCOLN, LINCOLN
General Information State-supported, coed university. Urban setting. *Awards:* A, B, M, D, FP. *Entrance level for U.S. students:* Moderately difficult. *Enrollment:* 22,106 total; 17,371 undergraduates (46% women) including 3% international students from 112 foreign countries. *Faculty:* 1,060. *Library holdings:* 3.4 million books, 50,817 current serial subscriptions, 7,079 audiovisual materials. *Total majors:* 128.
Information for International Students For fall 2006: 390 international students applied, 170 were accepted, 90 enrolled. Students can start in fall, winter, spring, or summer. Transfers accepted from institutions abroad. *Admission tests:* Required: TOEFL (minimum score: iBT 70; paper-based 523; computer-based 193). Recommended: SAT. *Application deadline:* 5/1. *Expenses:* (2006–07) $15,317; room and board, $6183 (on campus); room only, $3262 (on campus). *Financial aid:* Need-based financial aid available. Non-need-based college/university scholarships/grants from institutional funds, athletic awards. *Housing:* Guaranteed, also available during summer. *Services:* International student adviser on campus. Full-time and part-time ESL programs on campus. ESL program available during the academic year and the summer. Internships and employment opportunities (on-campus) available. *Contact:* Assistant Director of Admissions, University of Nebraska–Lincoln, Office of Admissions, 1410 Q Street, Lincoln, NE 68588-0417. Telephone: 402-472-2023 Ext. 0981. Fax: 402-472-0670. E-mail: carmenmcgee.admissions@unl.edu. URL: http://www.unl.edu.

See In-Depth Description on page 217.

UNIVERSITY OF NEBRASKA MEDICAL CENTER, OMAHA
General Information State-supported, coed institution. Urban setting. *Awards:* B, M, D, FP. *Entrance level for U.S. students:* Moderately difficult. *Enrollment:* 2,995 total; 851 undergraduates (90% women) including 1% international students from 6 foreign countries. *Faculty:* 1,007. *Library holdings:* 241,551 books, 4,280 current serial subscriptions. *Total majors:* 7. *Expenses:* (2006–07) $13,740.

WAYNE STATE COLLEGE, WAYNE
General Information State-supported, coed institution. Small town setting. *Awards:* B, M. *Entrance level for U.S. students:* Noncompetitive. *Enrollment:* 3,407 total; 2,748 undergraduates (56% women) including 1% international students from 12 foreign countries. *Faculty:* 204. *Library holdings:* 245,259 books, 14,975 current serial subscriptions, 6,622 audiovisual materials. *Total majors:* 75.
Information for International Students For fall 2006: 9 international students applied, 5 were accepted, 5 enrolled. Students can start in fall, spring, or summer. Transfers accepted from institutions abroad. *Admission tests:* Required: TOEFL (minimum score: iBT 80; paper-based 550; computer-based 213), IELTS may replace TOEFL. Recommended: SAT or ACT. TOEFL can be waived under certain conditions. *Application deadline:* Rolling. *Expenses:* (2006–07) $7088; room and board, $4470 (on campus); room only, $2170 (on campus). *Financial aid:* Need-based college/university scholarships/grants from institutional funds, loans from institutional funds, on-campus employment. Non-need-based college/university scholarships/grants from institutional funds, tuition waivers, athletic awards. *Housing:* Guaranteed, also available during summer. *Services:* International student adviser on campus. ESL program at cooperating institution. ESL program available during the academic year. Internships and employment opportunities (on-campus) available. *Contact:* Office Assistant II, Wayne State College, 1111 Main Street, Wayne, NE 68787. Telephone: 402-375-7539. Fax: 402-375-7180. E-mail: demorlo1@wsc.edu. URL: http://www.wsc.edu.

YORK COLLEGE, YORK
General Information Independent, 4-year, coed college, affiliated with Church of Christ. Small town setting. *Awards:* A, B. *Entrance level for U.S. students:* Moderately difficult. *Enrollment:* 440 total (51% women) including 2% international students from 9 foreign countries. *Undergraduate faculty:* 65. *Library holdings:* 134,738 books, 292 current serial subscriptions, 2,566 audiovisual materials. *Total majors:* 38.
Information for International Students For fall 2006: 15 international students applied, 9 were accepted, 8 enrolled. Students can start in fall, spring, or summer. Transfers accepted from institutions abroad. *Admission tests:* Required: SAT or ACT, TOEFL (minimum score: paper-based 500; computer-based 173). Recommended: SAT, ACT, SAT Subject Tests, ELS. TOEFL can be waived under certain conditions. *Application deadline:* 7/1. *Expenses:* (2006–07) $13,500; room and board, $4300 (on campus). *Financial aid:* Need-based on-campus employment. Non-need-based college/university scholarships/grants from institutional funds, athletic awards, loans from institutional funds, on-campus employment. International transfer students are eligible to apply for aid. 11 international students on campus received college administered financial aid ($7520 average). *Housing:* Guaranteed, also available during summer. *Services:* International student adviser on campus. Internships and employment opportunities (on-campus) available. *Contact:* Director of Admissions, York College, 1125 East 8th Street, York, NE 68467. Telephone: 402-363-5620. Fax: 402-363-5623. E-mail: clones@york.edu. URL: http://www.york.edu.

NEVADA

DEVRY UNIVERSITY, HENDERSON
General Information Proprietary, coed institution. *Awards:* A, B, M. *Entrance level for U.S. students:* Minimally difficult. *Enrollment:* 149 total; 97 undergraduates (41% women) including 2% international students. *Faculty:* 1. *Total majors:* 2. *Expenses:* (2007–08) $13,020.

SIERRA NEVADA COLLEGE, INCLINE VILLAGE
General Information Independent, coed institution. Small town setting. *Awards:* B, M. *Entrance level for U.S. students:* Moderately difficult. *Enrollment:* 492 total; 302 undergraduates (51% women) including 3% international students from 5 foreign countries. *Faculty:* 75. *Library holdings:* 35,000 books, 175 current serial subscriptions. *Total majors:* 11. *Financial aid:* Need-based college/university scholarships/grants from institutional funds, tuition waivers, athletic awards, loans from outside sources, on-campus employment. Non-need-based college/university scholarships/grants from institutional funds, tuition waivers, athletic awards, loans from outside sources. Forms required: institution's own financial aid form. 5 international students on campus received college administered financial aid ($8000 average).

UNIVERSITY OF NEVADA, LAS VEGAS, LAS VEGAS
General Information State-supported, coed university. Urban setting. *Awards:* B, M, D, FP. *Entrance level for U.S. students:* Moderately difficult. *Enrollment:* 27,933 total; 21,853 undergraduates (56% women) including 4% international students from 54 foreign countries. *Faculty:* 1,677. *Library holdings:* 1.3 million books, 18,568 current serial subscriptions, 14,235 audiovisual materials. *Total majors:* 86. *Expenses:* (2007–08) $14,976; room and board, $8857 (on campus); room only, $5600 (on campus). *Financial aid:* Need-based college/university scholarships/grants from institutional funds, tuition waivers, athletic awards, loans from institutional funds, on-campus employment. Non-need-based college/university scholarships/grants from institutional funds, tuition waivers, athletic awards, loans from institutional funds, on-campus employment. Forms required: institution's own financial aid form, International Student's Certification of Finances. For fall 2005, 55 international students on campus received college administered financial aid ($3000 average).

UNIVERSITY OF NEVADA, RENO, RENO
General Information State-supported, coed university. Urban setting. *Awards:* B, M, D, FP. *Entrance level for U.S. students:* Moderately difficult. *Enrollment:* 16,663 total; 13,134 undergraduates (54% women) including 3% international students from 48 foreign countries. *Faculty:* 988. *Library holdings:* 1.2 million books, 19,058 current serial subscriptions, 49,433 audiovisual materials. *Total majors:* 97.
Information for International Students For fall 2006: 133 international students applied, 94 were accepted, 57 enrolled. Students can start in fall or spring. Transfers accepted from institutions abroad. *Admission tests:* Required: TOEFL (minimum score: iBT 61; paper-based 500; computer-based 173), IELTS. TOEFL can be waived under certain conditions. *Application deadline:* Rolling. *Expenses:* (2006–07) $13,406; room and board, $8199 (on campus); room only, $4400 (on campus). *Financial aid:* Non-need-based college/university scholarships/grants from institutional funds, tuition waivers, athletic awards, loans from outside sources, on-campus employment. International transfer students are eligible to apply for aid. 76 international students on campus received college administered financial aid ($6319 average). *Housing:* Guaranteed, also available during summer. *Services:* International student adviser on campus. Full-time ESL program on campus. ESL program available during the academic year and the summer. Internships and employment opportunities (on-campus

University of Nevada, Reno (continued)

and off-campus) available. *Contact:* International Admissions and Recruitment Coordinator, University of Nevada, Reno, Office of International Students and Scholars, 120 Student Services Building, MS 074, Reno, NV 89557. Telephone: 775-784-6874. Fax: 775-327-5845. E-mail: iap@unr.nevada.edu. URL: http://www.unr.edu.

UNIVERSITY OF PHOENIX–NEVADA CAMPUS, LAS VEGAS

General Information Proprietary, coed institution. Urban setting. *Awards:* B, M. *Entrance level for U.S. students:* Noncompetitive. *Enrollment:* 3,484 total; 2,379 undergraduates (64% women) including 10% international students. *Faculty:* 668. *Library holdings:* 1,759 books, 692 current serial subscriptions. *Total majors:* 27. *Expenses:* (2006–07) $10,200.

WESTERN NEVADA COMMUNITY COLLEGE, CARSON CITY

General Information State-supported, 2-year, coed college. Small town setting. *Awards:* A. *Entrance level for U.S. students:* Noncompetitive. *Enrollment:* 5,531 total (58% women) including 0.02% international students from 3 foreign countries. *Undergraduate faculty:* 386. *Library holdings:* 50,612 books, 197 current serial subscriptions, 29,216 audiovisual materials. *Total majors:* 42. *Expenses:* (2007–08) $7,148; room and board, $8550 (on campus); room only, $6750 (on campus).

NEW HAMPSHIRE

COLBY-SAWYER COLLEGE, NEW LONDON

General Information Independent, 4-year, coed college. Small town setting. *Awards:* A, B. *Entrance level for U.S. students:* Moderately difficult. *Enrollment:* 909 total (66% women) including 1% international students from 8 foreign countries. *Undergraduate faculty:* 126. *Library holdings:* 93,696 books, 27,072 current serial subscriptions, 2,315 audiovisual materials. *Total majors:* 20. **Information for International Students** For fall 2006: 64 international students applied, 22 were accepted, 4 enrolled. Students can start in fall or spring. Transfers accepted from institutions abroad. *Admission tests:* Required: TOEFL (minimum score: paper-based 500; computer-based 173; minimum score for ESL admission: paper-based 500; computer-based 173). Recommended: SAT, ACT, ELS. TOEFL can be waived under certain conditions. *Application deadline:* Rolling. *Expenses:* (2007–08) $28,010; room and board, $9900 (on campus); room only, $5600 (on campus). *Financial aid:* Non-need-based college/university scholarships/grants from institutional funds, on-campus employment. Forms required: International Student's Certification of Finances. International transfer students are eligible to apply for aid. 5 international students on campus received college administered financial aid ($11,584 average). *Housing:* Guaranteed. *Services:* International student adviser on campus. Full-time ESL program on campus. ESL program available during the academic year. Internships and employment opportunities (on-campus) available. *Contact:* Assistant Director of International Admissions, Colby-Sawyer College, 541 Main Street, New London, NH 03257. Telephone: 603-526-3759. Fax: 603-526-3452. E-mail: csadmiss@colby-sawyer.edu. URL: http://www.colby-sawyer.edu.

See In-Depth Description on page 59.

DARTMOUTH COLLEGE, HANOVER

General Information Independent, coed university. Small town setting. *Awards:* B, M, D, FP. *Entrance level for U.S. students:* Most difficult. *Enrollment:* 5,753 total; 4,085 undergraduates (51% women) including 6% international students from 47 foreign countries. *Faculty:* 647. *Total majors:* 60. *Expenses:* (2007–08) $33,297; room and board, $9840 (on campus); room only, $5895 (on campus). *Financial aid:* Need-based college/university scholarships/grants from institutional funds, loans from institutional funds, on-campus employment. Forms required: institution's own financial aid form, International Student's Certification of Finances, parent's tax return from country of residence or statement from employer. 181 international students on campus received college administered financial aid ($34,607 average).

KEENE STATE COLLEGE, KEENE

General Information State-supported, coed institution. Small town setting. *Awards:* B, M. *Entrance level for U.S. students:* Moderately difficult. *Enrollment:* 4,940 total; 4,767 undergraduates (58% women) including 1% international students from 4 foreign

countries. *Faculty:* 405. *Library holdings:* 324,176 books, 1,486 current serial subscriptions, 8,160 audiovisual materials. *Total majors:* 91. *Expenses:* (2006–07) $15,092; room and board, $7026 (on campus); room only, $4700 (on campus). *Financial aid:* Non-need financial aid available. Forms required: International Student's Certification of Finances. For fall 2005, 11 international students on campus received college administered financial aid ($11,174 average).

MAGDALEN COLLEGE, WARNER

General Information Independent Roman Catholic, 4-year, coed college. Small town setting. *Awards:* A, B. *Entrance level for U.S. students:* Moderately difficult. *Enrollment:* 73 total (53% women) including 4% international students from 1 foreign country. *Undergraduate faculty:* 9. *Library holdings:* 26,000 books, 10 current serial subscriptions. *Total majors:* 1. *Financial aid:* Need-based college/university scholarships/grants from institutional funds, loans from outside sources. Forms required: institution's own financial aid form. For fall 2006 (estimated), 3 international students on campus received college administered financial aid ($2416 average).

MCINTOSH COLLEGE, DOVER

General Information Proprietary, 2-year, coed college. Small town setting. *Awards:* A. *Entrance level for U.S. students:* Noncompetitive. *Enrollment:* 750 total including 1% international students. *Undergraduate faculty:* 100. *Library holdings:* 11,000 books, 130 current serial subscriptions. *Total majors:* 12. *Financial aid:* Need-based and non-need-based financial aid available.

NEW ENGLAND COLLEGE, HENNIKER

General Information Independent, coed institution. Small town setting. *Awards:* A, B, M. *Entrance level for U.S. students:* Moderately difficult. *Enrollment:* 1,340 total; 1,065 undergraduates (49% women) including 3% international students from 20 foreign countries. *Faculty:* 107. *Library holdings:* 110,000 books, 160,000 current serial subscriptions. *Total majors:* 40. **Information for International Students** For fall 2006: 2021 international students applied, 1682 were accepted, 356 enrolled. Students can start in fall or spring. Transfers accepted from institutions abroad. *Admission tests:* Required: TOEFL (minimum score: iBT 79; paper-based 550; computer-based 213; minimum score for ESL admission: paper-based 450; computer-based 133), ELS. TOEFL can be waived under certain conditions. *Application deadline:* Rolling. *Financial aid:* Need-based college/university scholarships/grants from institutional funds, tuition waivers, on-campus employment. Non-need-based college/university scholarships/grants from institutional funds, tuition waivers, on-campus employment. Forms required: institution's own financial aid form, International Student's Certification of Finances. International transfer students are eligible to apply for aid. For fall 2006 (estimated), international students on campus received college administered aid averaging $15,128. *Housing:* Guaranteed, also available during summer. *Services:* International student adviser on campus. Full-time ESL program on campus. ESL program available during the academic year. Internships and employment opportunities (on-campus) available. *Contact:* Director of Admission, New England College, 180 Bridge Street, Henniker, NH 03242-3273. Telephone: 603-428-2223. Fax: 603-428-3155. E-mail: admission@nec.edu. URL: http://www.nec.edu.

See In-Depth Description on page 136.

NEW HAMPSHIRE COMMUNITY TECHNICAL COLLEGE, NASHUA/CLAREMONT, NASHUA

General Information State-supported, 2-year, coed college. Urban setting. *Awards:* A. *Entrance level for U.S. students:* Minimally difficult. *Enrollment:* 1,725 total. *Undergraduate faculty:* 108. *Library holdings:* 22,000 books, 250 current serial subscriptions. *Total majors:* 31. *Expenses:* (2006–07) $12,544.

PLYMOUTH STATE UNIVERSITY, PLYMOUTH

General Information State-supported, coed institution. Small town setting. *Awards:* B, M. *Entrance level for U.S. students:* Moderately difficult. *Enrollment:* 5,872 total; 4,297 undergraduates (48% women) including 1% international students from 12 foreign countries. *Faculty:* 367. *Library holdings:* 335,230 books, 2,213 current serial subscriptions. *Total majors:* 43. **Information for International Students** Students can start in fall or spring. Transfers accepted from institutions abroad. *Admission tests:* Required: TOEFL. Recommended: SAT or ACT, SAT Subject Tests. *Application deadline:* Rolling. *Expenses:* (2007–08) $15,366; room and board, $7893 (on campus). *Financial aid:* Non-need-based college/university scholarships/grants from institutional funds. Forms required: International Student's Certification of Finances. 3 international students on campus received college administered financial aid ($5750 average).

Housing: Guaranteed, also available during summer. *Services:* International student adviser on campus. *Contact:* Associate Director of Admission, Admissions Office, Plymouth State University, Plymouth, NH 03264. Telephone: 603-535-5000 Ext. 2438. Fax: 603-535-2714. E-mail: pscadmit@psc.plymouth.edu. URL: http://www.plymouth.edu.

RIVIER COLLEGE, NASHUA
General Information Independent Roman Catholic, coed institution. Suburban setting. *Awards:* A, B, M. *Entrance level for U.S. students:* Moderately difficult. *Enrollment:* 2,320 total; 1,462 undergraduates (79% women) including 0.1% international students from 7 foreign countries. *Faculty:* 178. *Library holdings:* 92,000 books, 500 current serial subscriptions, 4,000 audiovisual materials. *Total majors:* 41. *Expenses:* (2007–08) $21,695; room and board, $7942 (on campus). *Financial aid:* Non-need-based college/university scholarships/grants from institutional funds, loans from outside sources. For fall 2005, international students on campus received college administered aid averaging $3000.

SAINT ANSELM COLLEGE, MANCHESTER
General Information Independent Roman Catholic, 4-year, coed college. Suburban setting. *Awards:* B. *Entrance level for U.S. students:* Moderately difficult. *Enrollment:* 1,986 total (58% women) including 1% international students from 15 foreign countries. *Undergraduate faculty:* 177. *Library holdings:* 222,000 books, 1,900 current serial subscriptions, 8,000 audiovisual materials. *Total majors:* 30.
Information for International Students Students can start in fall or spring. Transfers accepted from institutions abroad. *Admission tests:* Required: TOEFL (minimum score: paper-based 550; computer-based 250). Recommended: SAT, ACT. *Application deadline:* 2/1. *Financial aid:* Need-based college/university scholarships/grants from institutional funds, on-campus employment. Non-need-based college/university scholarships/grants from institutional funds, athletic awards, on-campus employment. Forms required: International Student's Financial Aid Application, International Student's Certification of Finances. International transfer students are eligible to apply for aid. 10 international students on campus received college administered financial aid ($33,034 average). *Housing:* Guaranteed. *Services:* International student adviser on campus. Internships and employment opportunities (on-campus) available. *Contact:* Dean of Admission, Office of Admissions, Saint Anselm College, Manchester, NH 03102. Telephone: 603-641-7500. Fax: 603-641-7550. URL: http://www.anselm.edu.

See In-Depth Description on page 165.

SOUTHERN NEW HAMPSHIRE UNIVERSITY, MANCHESTER
General Information Independent, coed institution. Suburban setting. *Awards:* A, B, M, D. *Entrance level for U.S. students:* Moderately difficult. *Enrollment:* 3,490 total; 1,686 undergraduates (56% women) including 4% international students from 63 foreign countries. *Faculty:* 380. *Library holdings:* 89,338 books, 17,577 current serial subscriptions, 2,752 audiovisual materials. *Total majors:* 37.
Information for International Students Students can start in fall, winter, spring, or summer. Transfers accepted from institutions abroad. *Admission tests:* Required: TOEFL (minimum score: paper-based 500; computer-based 173; minimum score for ESL admission: paper-based 340; computer-based 60). TOEFL can be waived under certain conditions. *Application deadline:* Rolling. *Expenses:* (2007–08) $23,346; room and board, $8970 (on campus); room only, $6400 (on campus). *Financial aid:* Non-need-based college/university scholarships/grants from institutional funds, athletic awards, loans from outside sources, on-campus employment. International transfer students are eligible to apply for aid. For fall 2006 (estimated), 28 international students on campus received college administered financial aid ($13,964 average). *Housing:* Guaranteed, also available during summer. *Services:* International student adviser on campus. Full-time ESL program on campus. ESL program available during the academic year and the summer. Internships and employment opportunities (on-campus) available. *Contact:* Director of International Admissions, Southern New Hampshire University, 2500 North River Road, Manchester, NH 03106. Telephone: 603-645-9629. Fax: 603-645-9603. E-mail: s.harvey@snhu.edu. URL: http://www.snhu.edu.

UNIVERSITY OF NEW HAMPSHIRE, DURHAM
General Information State-supported, coed university. Small town setting. *Awards:* A, B, M, D. *Entrance level for U.S. students:* Moderately difficult. *Enrollment:* 14,848 total; 11,971 undergraduates (56% women) including 1% international students from 36 foreign countries. *Faculty:* 948. *Library holdings:* 1.8

million books, 36,313 current serial subscriptions, 39,508 audiovisual materials. *Total majors:* 142. *Expenses:* (2006–07) $22,851; room and board, $7584 (on campus); room only, $4606 (on campus). *Financial aid:* Need-based college/university scholarships/grants from institutional funds. Non-need-based college/university scholarships/grants from institutional funds, athletic awards. For fall 2005, 54 international students on campus received college administered financial aid ($22,805 average).

UNIVERSITY OF NEW HAMPSHIRE AT MANCHESTER, MANCHESTER
General Information State-supported, coed institution. Urban setting. *Awards:* A, B, M. *Entrance level for U.S. students:* Moderately difficult. *Enrollment:* 1,013 total (55% women) including 0.3% international students from 5 foreign countries. *Faculty:* 91. *Library holdings:* 31,147 books, 202 current serial subscriptions, 3,349 audiovisual materials. *Total majors:* 13. *Expenses:* (2006–07) $19,378. *Financial aid:* Need-based college/university scholarships/grants from institutional funds. Non-need-based college/university scholarships/grants from institutional funds.

NEW JERSEY

ASSUMPTION COLLEGE FOR SISTERS, MENDHAM
General Information Independent Roman Catholic, 2-year, women's college. Rural setting. *Awards:* A. *Entrance level for U.S. students:* Noncompetitive. *Enrollment:* 37 total including 84% international students from 5 foreign countries. *Undergraduate faculty:* 17. *Library holdings:* 25,000 books, 50 current serial subscriptions, 3,000 audiovisual materials. *Total majors:* 2. *Expenses:* (2006–07) $3350.

ATLANTIC CAPE COMMUNITY COLLEGE, MAYS LANDING
General Information County-supported, 2-year, coed college. Small town setting. *Awards:* A. *Entrance level for U.S. students:* Noncompetitive. *Enrollment:* 6,845 total (63% women) including 1% international students from 17 foreign countries. *Undergraduate faculty:* 378. *Library holdings:* 78,000 books, 300 current serial subscriptions, 1,000 audiovisual materials. *Total majors:* 31. *Expenses:* (2006–07) $10,030. *Financial aid:* Forms required: institution's own financial aid form.

BERGEN COMMUNITY COLLEGE, PARAMUS
General Information County-supported, 2-year, coed college. Suburban setting. *Awards:* A. *Entrance level for U.S. students:* Noncompetitive. *Enrollment:* 14,608 total including 8% international students from 120 foreign countries. *Undergraduate faculty:* 799. *Total majors:* 55. *Expenses:* (2007–08) $5736.

BERKELEY COLLEGE, WEST PATERSON
General Information Proprietary, primarily 2-year, coed college. Suburban setting. *Awards:* A, B. *Entrance level for U.S. students:* Minimally difficult. *Enrollment:* 2,729 total (72% women) including 1% international students from 25 foreign countries. *Undergraduate faculty:* 144. *Library holdings:* 49,584 books, 224 current serial subscriptions. *Total majors:* 11. *Expenses:* (2007–08) $18,150; room and board, $9000 (on campus). *Financial aid:* Forms required: institution's own financial aid form, International Student's Certification of Finances.

BURLINGTON COUNTY COLLEGE, PEMBERTON
General Information County-supported, 2-year, coed college. Suburban setting. *Awards:* A. *Entrance level for U.S. students:* Noncompetitive. *Enrollment:* 7,797 total (60% women). *Undergraduate faculty:* 471. *Library holdings:* 92,400 books, 1,750 current serial subscriptions. *Total majors:* 49. *Expenses:* (2007–08) $4994. *Financial aid:* Need-based loans from outside sources, on-campus employment. Non-need-based loans from outside sources, on-campus employment. Forms required: institution's own financial aid form, International Student's Financial Aid Application.

CALDWELL COLLEGE, CALDWELL
General Information Independent Roman Catholic, coed institution. Suburban setting. *Awards:* B, M. *Entrance level for U.S. students:* Moderately difficult. *Enrollment:* 2,291 total; 1,691 undergraduates (68% women) including 5% international students from 23 foreign countries. *Faculty:* 184. *Library holdings:* 146,353 books, 443 current serial subscriptions, 1,346 audiovisual materials. *Total majors:* 26.
Information for International Students For fall 2006: 65 international students applied, 27 were accepted, 15 enrolled.

Caldwell College (continued)

Students can start in fall or spring. Transfers accepted from institutions abroad. *Admission tests:* Required: SAT or ACT, TOEFL (minimum score: iBT 70; paper-based 570; computer-based 250; minimum score for ESL admission: paper-based 500; computer-based 200). TOEFL can be waived under certain conditions. *Application deadline:* Rolling. *Expenses:* (2007–08) $22,120; room and board, $9220 (on campus). *Financial aid:* Non-need-based college/university scholarships/grants from institutional funds, athletic awards, on-campus employment. Forms required: institution's own financial aid form. 27 international students on campus received college administered financial aid ($7000 average). *Housing:* Available during summer. *Services:* International student adviser on campus. Part-time ESL program on campus. ESL program available during the academic year. Internships and employment opportunities (on-campus) available. *Contact:* International Admissions Counselor, Caldwell College, 9 Ryerson Avenue, Caldwell, NJ 07006. Telephone: 973-618-3620. Fax: 973-618-3600. E-mail: ggiordano@caldwell.edu. URL: http://www.caldwell.edu.

CENTENARY COLLEGE, HACKETTSTOWN

General Information Independent, coed institution, affiliated with United Methodist Church. Suburban setting. *Awards:* A, B, M. *Entrance level for U.S. students:* Moderately difficult. *Enrollment:* 2,662 total; 1,952 undergraduates (66% women) including 2% international students from 14 foreign countries. *Faculty:* 323. *Library holdings:* 67,272 books, 211 current serial subscriptions. *Total majors:* 24.

Information for International Students For fall 2006: 81 international students applied, 68 were accepted, 33 enrolled. Students can start in fall, winter, spring, or summer. Transfers accepted from institutions abroad. *Admission tests:* Required: TOEFL (minimum score: paper-based 450; computer-based 133; minimum score for ESL admission: paper-based 450; computer-based 133). Recommended: TOEIC. TOEFL can be waived under certain conditions. *Application deadline:* Rolling. *Expenses:* (2006–07) $22,415; room and board, $8400 (on campus). *Financial aid:* Non-need-based college/university scholarships/grants from institutional funds, tuition waivers, loans from outside sources, on-campus employment. International transfer students are eligible to apply for aid. For fall 2006 (estimated), 17 international students on campus received college administered financial aid ($2692 average). *Housing:* Guaranteed, also available during summer. *Services:* International student adviser on campus. Full-time and part-time ESL programs on campus. ESL program available during the academic year and the summer. Internships and employment opportunities (on-campus and off-campus) available. *Contact:* International Liaison, Centenary College, 400 Jefferson Street, Hackettstown, NJ 07840. Telephone: 908-852-1400 Ext. 2221. Fax: 908-979-4351. E-mail: younga@centenarycollege.edu. URL: http://www.centenarycollege.edu.

THE COLLEGE OF NEW JERSEY, EWING

General Information State-supported, coed institution. Suburban setting. *Awards:* B, M. *Entrance level for U.S. students:* Very difficult. *Enrollment:* 6,934 total; 6,094 undergraduates (58% women) including 0.1% international students from 13 foreign countries. *Faculty:* 703. *Library holdings:* 662,152 books, 429,632 current serial subscriptions, 13,886 audiovisual materials. *Total majors:* 53. *Expenses:* (2006–07) $17,099; room and board, $8843 (on campus); room only, $6380 (on campus).

COLLEGE OF SAINT ELIZABETH, MORRISTOWN

General Information Independent Roman Catholic, undergraduate: women only; graduate: coed institution. Suburban setting. *Awards:* B, M (also offers coed adult undergraduate degree program and coed graduate programs). *Entrance level for U.S. students:* Moderately difficult. *Enrollment:* 1,982 total; 1,260 undergraduates (91% women) including 4% international students from 37 foreign countries. *Faculty:* 197. *Library holdings:* 109,352 books, 561 current serial subscriptions, 2,418 audiovisual materials. *Total majors:* 25. *Expenses:* (2006–07) $21,150; room and board, $9424 (on campus). *Financial aid:* Forms required: institution's own financial aid form. For fall 2006 (estimated), 10 international students on campus received college administered financial aid ($30,574 average).

COUNTY COLLEGE OF MORRIS, RANDOLPH

General Information County-supported, 2-year, coed college. Suburban setting. *Awards:* A. *Entrance level for U.S. students:* Noncompetitive. *Enrollment:* 8,496 total. *Undergraduate faculty:* 497. *Library holdings:* 102,550 books, 819 current serial subscriptions. *Total majors:* 28.

Information for International Students Students can start in fall or spring. Transfers accepted from institutions abroad.

Admission tests: Required: TOEFL (minimum score: iBT 97; minimum score for ESL admission: iBT 97). *Application deadline:* 7/1. *Financial aid:* Need-based loans from outside sources. Non-need-based athletic awards, loans from outside sources, on-campus employment. Forms required: institution's own financial aid form. *Services:* International student adviser on campus. Full-time and part-time ESL programs on campus. ESL program available during the academic year and the summer. Internships and employment opportunities (on-campus and off-campus) available. *Contact:* Associate Admissions Officer, County College of Morris. Telephone: 973-328-5097. Fax: 201-328-5199. E-mail: admiss@ccm.edu. URL: http://www.ccm.edu.

DEVRY UNIVERSITY, NORTH BRUNSWICK

General Information Proprietary, 4-year, coed college. Urban setting. *Awards:* A, B. *Entrance level for U.S. students:* Minimally difficult. *Enrollment:* 1,417 total (25% women) including 3% international students. *Undergraduate faculty:* 152. *Library holdings:* 32,109 books, 210 current serial subscriptions. *Total majors:* 8. *Expenses:* (2007–08) $13,220.

DREW UNIVERSITY, MADISON

General Information Independent, coed university, affiliated with United Methodist Church. Suburban setting. *Awards:* B, M, D, FP. *Entrance level for U.S. students:* Moderately difficult. *Enrollment:* 2,647 total; 1,656 undergraduates (60% women) including 1% international students from 16 foreign countries. *Faculty:* 241. *Library holdings:* 581,734 books, 2,597 audiovisual materials. *Total majors:* 30.

Information for International Students Students can start in fall or spring. Transfers accepted from institutions abroad. *Admission tests:* Required: SAT or ACT, TOEFL (minimum score: paper-based 550; computer-based 213). TOEFL can be waived under certain conditions. *Application deadline:* 2/15. *Expenses:* (2006–07) $33,068; room and board, $9000 (on campus); room only, $5818 (on campus). *Financial aid:* Need-based college/university scholarships/grants from institutional funds. Non-need-based college/university scholarships/grants from institutional funds. Forms required: institution's own financial aid form, International Student's Financial Aid Application. For fall 2005, 7 international students on campus received college administered financial aid ($13,936 average). *Housing:* Guaranteed. *Services:* International student adviser on campus. Internships and employment opportunities (on-campus and off-campus) available. *Contact:* Associate Dean and Director of College Admissions, Drew University, 36 Madison Avenue, Undergraduate Admissions, Madison, NJ 07940. Telephone: 973-408-3739. Fax: 973-408-3068. E-mail: cadm@drew.edu. URL: http://www.drew.edu.

ESSEX COUNTY COLLEGE, NEWARK

General Information County-supported, 2-year, coed college. Urban setting. *Awards:* A. *Entrance level for U.S. students:* Noncompetitive. *Enrollment:* 10,972 total (61% women) including 8% international students from 67 foreign countries. *Undergraduate faculty:* 654. *Library holdings:* 91,000 books, 639 current serial subscriptions. *Total majors:* 48. *Expenses:* (2007–08) $6165. *Financial aid:* Need-based tuition waivers.

FAIRLEIGH DICKINSON UNIVERSITY, COLLEGE AT FLORHAM, MADISON

General Information Independent, coed institution. Suburban setting. *Awards:* A, B, M. *Entrance level for U.S. students:* Moderately difficult. *Enrollment:* 3,562 total; 2,632 undergraduates (53% women) including 1% international students from 18 foreign countries. *Faculty:* 304. *Library holdings:* 227,700 books, 1,230 current serial subscriptions, 690 audiovisual materials. *Total majors:* 30.

Information for International Students Students can start in fall or spring. Transfers accepted from institutions abroad. *Admission tests:* Required: TOEFL (minimum score: iBT 79; paper-based 550; computer-based 213). Recommended: SAT or ACT. TOEFL can be waived under certain conditions. *Application deadline:* 7/1. *Expenses:* (2006–07) $26,518; room and board, $9472 (on campus); room only, $5730 (on campus). *Financial aid:* Non-need financial aid available. Forms required: institution's own financial aid form. International transfer students are eligible to apply for aid. 2 international students on campus received college administered financial aid ($9500 average). *Housing:* Available during summer. *Services:* International student adviser on campus. Full-time and part-time ESL programs on campus. ESL program available during the academic year and the summer. Internships and employment opportunities (on-campus and off-campus) available. *Contact:* Director of International Admissions, Fairleigh Dickinson University, College at Florham, 1000 River Road,

T-KB1-01, Teaneck, NJ 07666. Telephone: 201-692-2205.
Fax: 201-692-2560. E-mail: global@fdu.edu.
URL: http://www.fdu.edu.

See In-Depth Description on page 81.

FAIRLEIGH DICKINSON UNIVERSITY, METROPOLITAN CAMPUS, TEANECK

General Information Independent, coed institution. Suburban
setting. *Awards:* A, B, M, D. *Entrance level for U.S. students:*
Moderately difficult. *Enrollment:* 8,491 total; 5,903 undergraduates
(54% women) including 4% international students from 61 foreign
countries. *Faculty:* 625. *Library holdings:* 371,900 books, 1,690
current serial subscriptions, 3,100 audiovisual materials.
Total majors: 43.

Information for International Students For fall 2006: 532
international students applied, 209 were accepted, 61 enrolled.
Students can start in fall or spring. Transfers accepted from
institutions abroad. *Admission tests:* Required: TOEFL (minimum
score: iBT 79; paper-based 550; computer-based 213; minimum
score for ESL admission: iBT 79). Recommended: SAT. TOEFL can
be waived under certain conditions. *Application deadline:* 7/1.
Expenses: (2006–07) $24,644; room and board, $9974 (on campus);
room only, $6232 (on campus). *Financial aid:* Non-need financial
aid available. Forms required: institution's own financial aid form.
International transfer students are eligible to apply for aid. 2
international students on campus received college administered
financial aid ($2500 average). *Housing:* Available during summer.
Services: International student adviser on campus. Full-time and
part-time ESL programs on campus. ESL program available during
the academic year and the summer. Internships and employment
opportunities (on-campus and off-campus) available. *Contact:*
Director of International Admissions, Office of International
Admissions, Fairleigh Dickinson University, Metropolitan Campus,
1000 River Road, T-KB1-01, Teaneck, NJ 07666.
Telephone: 201-692-2205. Fax: 201-692-2560.
E-mail: global@fdu.edu. URL: http://www.fdu.edu.

See In-Depth Description on page 81.

GEORGIAN COURT UNIVERSITY, LAKEWOOD

General Information Independent Roman Catholic,
undergraduate: women only; graduate: coed institution. Suburban
setting. *Awards:* B, M. *Entrance level for U.S. students:* Moderately
difficult. *Enrollment:* 3,047 total; 1,968 undergraduates (91%
women) including 1% international students from 13 foreign
countries. *Faculty:* 294. *Library holdings:* 145,413 books, 1,123
current serial subscriptions. *Total majors:* 26. *Expenses:* (2006–07)
$20,632; room and board, $7800 (on campus). *Financial aid:*
Need-based college/university scholarships/grants from institutional
funds, loans from outside sources, on-campus employment.
Non-need-based on-campus employment. Forms required:
institution's own financial aid form. 14 international students on
campus received college administered financial aid ($15,228
average).

KEAN UNIVERSITY, UNION

General Information State-supported, coed institution. Suburban
setting. *Awards:* B, M. *Entrance level for U.S. students:* Moderately
difficult. *Enrollment:* 13,050 total; 9,990 undergraduates (63%
women) including 2% international students from 64 foreign
countries. *Faculty:* 1,222. *Library holdings:* 321,261 books, 2,790
current serial subscriptions, 6,651 audiovisual materials.
Total majors: 48.

Information for International Students For fall 2006: 42
international students applied, 41 were accepted, 35 enrolled.
Students can start in fall, spring, or summer. Transfers accepted
from institutions abroad. *Admission tests:* Required: placement test.
Application deadline: 5/31. *Expenses:* (2006–07) $10,863; room and
board, $8880 (on campus); room only, $6180 (on campus). *Financial
aid:* Non-need-based college/university scholarships/grants from
institutional funds, tuition waivers, loans from outside sources,
on-campus employment. Forms required: institution's own financial
aid form. For fall 2006 (estimated), 21 international students on
campus received college administered financial aid ($1506 average).
Housing: Guaranteed, also available during summer. *Services:*
International student adviser on campus. Full-time ESL program
on campus. ESL program available during the academic year.
Internships and employment opportunities (on-campus) available.
Contact: Associate Director of Admissions, Kean University, Office
of Admissions, 1000 Morris Avenue, Union, NJ 07083.
Telephone: 908-737-7100. Fax: 908-737-7105.
E-mail: pknox@kean.edu. URL: http://www.kean.edu.

MERCER COUNTY COMMUNITY COLLEGE, TRENTON

General Information State and locally supported, 2-year, coed
college. Suburban setting. *Awards:* A. *Entrance level for U.S.
students:* Noncompetitive. *Enrollment:* 8,928 total (57% women)

including 5% international students. *Undergraduate faculty:* 529.
Library holdings: 57,317 books, 8,934 audiovisual materials.
Total majors: 51. *Expenses:* (2006–07) $6540. *Financial aid:*
Need-based college/university scholarships/grants from institutional
funds. Non-need-based college/university scholarships/grants from
institutional funds, tuition waivers, athletic awards.

MIDDLESEX COUNTY COLLEGE, EDISON

General Information County-supported, 2-year, coed college.
Suburban setting. *Awards:* A. *Entrance level for U.S. students:*
Noncompetitive. *Enrollment:* 11,276 total. *Undergraduate faculty:*
552. *Library holdings:* 85,160 books, 599 current serial
subscriptions, 5,642 audiovisual materials. *Total majors:* 68.

MONMOUTH UNIVERSITY, WEST LONG BRANCH

General Information Independent, coed institution. Suburban
setting. *Awards:* A, B, M. *Entrance level for U.S. students:*
Moderately difficult. *Enrollment:* 6,399 total; 4,621 undergraduates
(58% women) including 1% international students from 16 foreign
countries. *Faculty:* 535. *Library holdings:* 280,000 books, 25,196
current serial subscriptions. *Total majors:* 28.

Information for International Students For fall 2006: 78
international students applied, 22 were accepted, 11 enrolled.
Students can start in fall or spring. Transfers accepted from
institutions abroad. *Admission tests:* Required: TOEFL (minimum
score: iBT 79; paper-based 550; computer-based 213), ELS
(minimum score: 112), IELTS, CAE, MELAB. Recommended: SAT.
TOEFL can be waived under certain conditions. *Application
deadline:* 6/1. *Expenses:* (2006–07) $21,868; room and board, $8472
(on campus); room only, $4754 (on campus). *Financial aid:*
Need-based college/university scholarships/grants from institutional
funds, tuition waivers, athletic awards, loans from institutional
funds, loans from outside sources, on-campus employment.
Non-need-based college/university scholarships/grants from
institutional funds, tuition waivers, athletic awards, loans from
institutional funds, loans from outside sources, on-campus
employment. For fall 2006 (estimated), 23 international students on
campus received college administered financial aid ($22,279
average). *Housing:* Available during summer. *Services:* International
student adviser on campus. Internships and employment
opportunities (on-campus) available. *Contact:* Assistant Director of
Undergraduate Admission, Monmouth University, 400 Cedar
Avenue, West Long Branch, NJ 07764-1898.
Telephone: 732-571-3456. Fax: 732-263-5166.
E-mail: admission@monmouth.edu.
URL: http://www.monmouth.edu.

See In-Depth Description on page 130.

MONTCLAIR STATE UNIVERSITY, MONTCLAIR

General Information State-supported, coed institution. Suburban
setting. *Awards:* B, M, D. *Entrance level for U.S. students:*
Moderately difficult. *Enrollment:* 16,076 total; 12,365
undergraduates (60% women) including 3% international students
from 87 foreign countries. *Faculty:* 1,197. *Library holdings:* 495,462
books, 3,094 current serial subscriptions, 14,184 audiovisual
materials. *Total majors:* 46.

Information for International Students Students can start in
fall, spring, or summer. Transfers accepted from institutions
abroad. *Admission tests:* Required: TOEFL (minimum score: iBT 80;
paper-based 500; computer-based 173). TOEFL can be waived under
certain conditions. *Application deadline:* 3/1. *Expenses:* (2006–07)
$13,758; room and board, $8988 (on campus); room only, $5998 (on
campus). *Financial aid:* Need-based financial aid available.
Non-need-based college/university scholarships/grants from
institutional funds, loans from outside sources, on-campus
employment. Forms required: International Student's Certification
of Finances. For fall 2006 (estimated), 180 international students
on campus received college administered financial aid ($2680
average). *Housing:* Guaranteed, also available during summer.
Services: International student adviser on campus. ESL program
available during the academic year and the summer. Internships
and employment opportunities (on-campus and off-campus)
available. *Contact:* Director of Admissions, Montclair State
University, Undergraduate Admissions, Russ Hall, 1 Normal
Avenue, Montclair, NJ 07043. Telephone: 973-655-5116.
Fax: 973-655-7700. E-mail: langdonj@mail.montclair.edu.
URL: http://www.montclair.edu.

See In-Depth Description on page 131.

NEW JERSEY CITY UNIVERSITY, JERSEY CITY

General Information State-supported, coed institution. Urban
setting. *Awards:* B, M. *Entrance level for U.S. students:* Moderately
difficult. *Enrollment:* 8,523 total; 6,158 undergraduates (63%
women) including 1% international students from 15 foreign
countries. *Faculty:* 627. *Library holdings:* 212,786 books, 1,260
current serial subscriptions, 2,234 audiovisual materials.

New Jersey City University (continued)

Total majors: 27. *Expenses:* (2006–07) $13,336; room and board, $7880 (on campus); room only, $5000 (on campus).

NEW JERSEY INSTITUTE OF TECHNOLOGY, NEWARK

General Information State-supported, coed university. Urban setting. *Awards:* B, M, D. *Entrance level for U.S. students:* Moderately difficult. *Enrollment:* 8,209 total; 5,380 undergraduates (20% women) including 6% international students from 99 foreign countries. *Faculty:* 646. *Library holdings:* 160,000 books, 1,100 current serial subscriptions. *Total majors:* 29. *Expenses:* (2006–07) $17,290; room and board, $8980 (on campus). *Financial aid:* Need-based college/university scholarships/grants from institutional funds, tuition waivers, loans from institutional funds, on-campus employment. Non-need financial aid available. Forms required: International Student's Certification of Finances, Albert Dorman Admission Application. 50 international students on campus received college administered financial aid ($12,819 average).

OCEAN COUNTY COLLEGE, TOMS RIVER

General Information County-supported, 2-year, coed college. Small town setting. *Awards:* A. *Entrance level for U.S. students:* Noncompetitive. *Enrollment:* 8,449 total (59% women) including 0.4% international students from 6 foreign countries. *Undergraduate faculty:* 410. *Library holdings:* 74,215 books, 428 current serial subscriptions. *Total majors:* 27. *Expenses:* (2006–07) $6240.

PRINCETON UNIVERSITY, PRINCETON

General Information Independent, coed university. Suburban setting. *Awards:* B, M, D. *Entrance level for U.S. students:* Most difficult. *Enrollment:* 7,242 total; 4,923 undergraduates (46% women) including 9% international students from 94 foreign countries. *Faculty:* 1,025. *Library holdings:* 6.5 million books, 63,987 current serial subscriptions, 91,857 audiovisual materials. *Total majors:* 35. *Expenses:* (2007–08) $33,000; room and board, $10,980 (on campus); room only, $5980 (on campus). *Financial aid:* Need-based college/university scholarships/grants from institutional funds, loans from institutional funds, on-campus employment. Forms required: institution's own financial aid form. For fall 2005, 316 international students on campus received college administered financial aid ($36,809 average).

RAMAPO COLLEGE OF NEW JERSEY, MAHWAH

General Information State-supported, coed institution. Suburban setting. *Awards:* B, M. *Entrance level for U.S. students:* Moderately difficult. *Enrollment:* 5,499 total; 5,188 undergraduates (60% women) including 3% international students from 48 foreign countries. *Faculty:* 430. *Library holdings:* 168,408 books, 453 current serial subscriptions, 5,038 audiovisual materials. *Total majors:* 39.

Information for International Students Students can start in fall or spring. Transfers accepted from institutions abroad. *Admission tests:* Required: TOEFL (minimum score: paper-based 500; computer-based 173; minimum score for ESL admission: paper-based 500; computer-based 173). Recommended: SAT. *Application deadline:* 2/15. *Expenses:* (2006–07) $14,807; room and board, $9924 (on campus); room only, $7220 (on campus). *Financial aid:* Need-based college/university scholarships/grants from institutional funds, loans from outside sources, on-campus employment. Non-need-based college/university scholarships/grants from institutional funds, loans from outside sources, on-campus employment. 73 international students on campus received college administered financial aid ($16,209 average). *Housing:* Guaranteed. *Services:* International student adviser on campus. Part-time ESL program on campus. ESL program available during the academic year. Internships and employment opportunities (on-campus and off-campus) available. *Contact:* Assistant Director of Admissions, Ramapo College of New Jersey, 505 Ramapo Valley Road, Mahwah, NJ 07430-1680. Telephone: 201-684-7300. Fax: 201-684-7964. E-mail: admis@ramapo.edu. URL: http://www.ramapo.edu.

RARITAN VALLEY COMMUNITY COLLEGE, SOMERVILLE

General Information County-supported, 2-year, coed college. Small town setting. *Awards:* A. *Entrance level for U.S. students:* Noncompetitive. *Enrollment:* 6,408 total (57% women) including 5% international students. *Undergraduate faculty:* 402. *Library holdings:* 82,975 books, 335 current serial subscriptions, 1,396 audiovisual materials. *Total majors:* 46.

Information for International Students For fall 2006: 26 international students applied, 22 were accepted, 18 enrolled. Students can start in fall or spring. Transfers accepted from institutions abroad. *Admission tests:* Required: TOEFL (minimum score: iBT 61; paper-based 500; computer-based 173; minimum

score for ESL admission: iBT 61; paper-based 500; computer-based 173), TOEFL or IELTS language testing. TOEFL can be waived under certain conditions. *Application deadline:* 6/1. *Expenses:* (2007–08) $3490. *Financial aid:* Need-based college/university scholarships/grants from institutional funds. Non-need-based college/university scholarships/grants from institutional funds. *Services:* International student adviser on campus. Part-time ESL program on campus. ESL program available during the academic year and the summer. Internships and employment opportunities (on-campus) available. *Contact:* International Student Advisor, Raritan Valley Community College, PO Box 3300, Somerville, NJ 08876-1265. Telephone: 908-526-1200 Ext. 8452. Fax: 908-704-3442. E-mail: esulliva@raritanval.edu. URL: http://www.raritanval.edu.

THE RICHARD STOCKTON COLLEGE OF NEW JERSEY, POMONA

General Information State-supported, coed institution. Suburban setting. *Awards:* B, M. *Entrance level for U.S. students:* Very difficult. *Enrollment:* 7,212 total; 6,726 undergraduates (58% women) including 0.5% international students from 16 foreign countries. *Faculty:* 440. *Library holdings:* 268,411 books, 24,364 current serial subscriptions, 14,834 audiovisual materials. *Total majors:* 31. *Expenses:* (2006–07) $13,350; room and board, $8446 (on campus); room only, $5,790 (on campus).

RIDER UNIVERSITY, LAWRENCEVILLE

General Information Independent, coed institution. Suburban setting. *Awards:* A, B, M. *Entrance level for U.S. students:* Moderately difficult. *Enrollment:* 5,790 total; 4,586 undergraduates (60% women) including 2% international students from 46 foreign countries. *Faculty:* 518. *Library holdings:* 430,197 books, 30,125 current serial subscriptions, 21,471 audiovisual materials. *Total majors:* 59.

Information for International Students For fall 2006: 160 international students applied, 104 were accepted, 55 enrolled. Students can start in fall or spring. Transfers accepted from institutions abroad. *Admission tests:* Required: TOEFL (minimum score: paper-based 550; computer-based 213). Recommended: SAT or ACT. *Application deadline:* 6/1. *Expenses:* (2006–07) $24,790; room and board, $9280 (on campus); room only, $5220 (on campus). *Financial aid:* Need-based loans from outside sources. Non-need-based loans from outside sources. Forms required: institution's own financial aid form. *Housing:* Guaranteed, also available during summer. *Services:* International student adviser on campus. Part-time ESL program on campus. ESL program available during the academic year. Internships and employment opportunities (on-campus) available. *Contact:* International Admissions Counselor, Office of Admissions, Rider University, Ciambelli Hall 205B, 2083 Lawrenceville Road, Lawrenceville, NJ 08648-3099. Telephone: 609-896-5194. Fax: 609-896-5177. E-mail: athomson@rider.edu. URL: http://www.rider.edu.

See In-Depth Description on page 158.

ROWAN UNIVERSITY, GLASSBORO

General Information State-supported, coed institution. Suburban setting. *Awards:* B, M, D. *Entrance level for U.S. students:* Moderately difficult. *Enrollment:* 9,578 total; 8,430 undergraduates (54% women) including international students from 35 foreign countries. *Faculty:* 1,063. *Library holdings:* 316,500 books, 1,858 current serial subscriptions, 52,834 audiovisual materials. *Total majors:* 38. *Expenses:* (2006–07) $16,130; room and board, $8742 (on campus). *Financial aid:* Need-based college/university scholarships/grants from institutional funds, tuition waivers. Non-need-based college/university scholarships/grants from institutional funds, tuition waivers.

RUTGERS, THE STATE UNIVERSITY OF NEW JERSEY, CAMDEN, CAMDEN

General Information State-supported, coed university. *Awards:* B, M, FP. *Entrance level for U.S. students:* Moderately difficult. *Enrollment:* 5,165 total; 3,694 undergraduates (57% women) including 0.5% international students. *Faculty:* 401. *Library holdings:* 714,447 books, 5,189 current serial subscriptions, 326 audiovisual materials. *Total majors:* 33. *Expenses:* (2006–07) $18,263; room and board, $8596 (on campus); room only, $6136 (on campus). *Financial aid:* Non-need financial aid available. Forms required: International Student's Certification of Finances. For fall 2006 (estimated), 2 international students on campus received college administered financial aid ($1188 average).

RUTGERS, THE STATE UNIVERSITY OF NEW JERSEY, NEWARK, NEWARK

General Information State-supported, coed university. Urban setting. *Awards:* B, M, D, FP. *Entrance level for U.S. students:* Moderately difficult. *Enrollment:* 10,203 total; 6,503 undergraduates (56% women) including 2% international students from 65 foreign countries. *Faculty:* 606. *Library holdings:* 941,103 books, 6,408 current serial subscriptions, 34,994 audiovisual materials. *Total majors:* 51. *Expenses:* (2006–07) $18,039; room and board, $9535 (on campus); room only, $6057 (on campus). *Financial aid:* Non-need financial aid available. Forms required: International Student's Financial Aid Application, International Student's Certification of Finances. For fall 2006 (estimated), 4 international students on campus received college administered financial aid ($1156 average).

RUTGERS, THE STATE UNIVERSITY OF NEW JERSEY, NEW BRUNSWICK, NEW BRUNSWICK

General Information State-supported, coed university. Urban setting. *Awards:* B, M, D, FP. *Entrance level for U.S. students:* Moderately difficult. *Enrollment:* 34,392 total; 26,691 undergraduates (50% women) including 2% international students from 112 foreign countries. *Faculty:* 2,212. *Library holdings:* 4.7 million books, 17,182 current serial subscriptions, 91,657 audiovisual materials. *Total majors:* 122. *Expenses:* (2006–07) $18,463; room and board, $9312 (on campus); room only, $5682 (on campus). *Financial aid:* Non-need financial aid available. Forms required: International Student's Certification of Finances. For fall 2006 (estimated), 1 international student on campus received college administered financial aid ($200 average).

SAINT PETER'S COLLEGE, JERSEY CITY

General Information Independent Roman Catholic (Jesuit), coed institution. Urban setting. *Awards:* A, B, M. *Entrance level for U.S. students:* Moderately difficult. *Enrollment:* 3,117 total; 2,398 undergraduates (54% women) including 3% international students from 24 foreign countries. *Faculty:* 271. *Library holdings:* 178,587 books, 1,741 current serial subscriptions, 330 audiovisual materials. *Total majors:* 46. *Expenses:* (2006–07) $22,650; room and board, $9260 (on campus); room only, $5930 (on campus). *Financial aid:* Need-based and non-need-based financial aid available. 72 international students on campus received college administered financial aid ($4025 average).

SALEM COMMUNITY COLLEGE, CARNEYS POINT

General Information County-supported, 2-year, coed college. Small town setting. *Awards:* A. *Entrance level for U.S. students:* Noncompetitive. *Enrollment:* 1,251 total (64% women) including 5% international students. *Undergraduate faculty:* 66. *Library holdings:* 28,951 books, 240 current serial subscriptions. *Total majors:* 30. *Expenses:* (2006–07) $3605. *Financial aid:* Need-based college/university scholarships/grants from institutional funds, tuition waivers, athletic awards, loans from outside sources, on-campus employment. Non-need-based college/university scholarships/grants from institutional funds, tuition waivers, athletic awards.

SETON HALL UNIVERSITY, SOUTH ORANGE

General Information Independent Roman Catholic, coed university. Suburban setting. *Awards:* B, M, D, FP. *Entrance level for U.S. students:* Moderately difficult. *Enrollment:* 9,637 total; 5,335 undergraduates (54% women) including 1% international students from 49 foreign countries. *Faculty:* 926. *Library holdings:* 506,042 books, 1,475 current serial subscriptions, 2,225 audiovisual materials. *Total majors:* 48.

Information for International Students Students can start in fall, spring, or summer. Transfers accepted from institutions abroad. *Admission tests:* Required: SAT or ACT, TOEFL (minimum score: paper-based 550; computer-based 173; minimum score for ESL admission: paper-based 450; computer-based 133). TOEFL can be waived under certain conditions. *Application deadline:* Rolling. *Expenses:* (2006–07) $24,720; room and board, $10,466 (on campus); room only, $6664 (on campus). *Financial aid:* Non-need financial aid available. International transfer students are eligible to apply for aid. 90 international students on campus received college administered financial aid ($14,279 average). *Housing:* Guaranteed, also available during summer. *Services:* International student adviser on campus. Full-time ESL program on campus. ESL program available during the academic year and the summer. Internships and employment opportunities (on-campus and off-campus) available. *Contact:* Director of Admissions, Seton Hall University, 400 South Orange Avenue, South Orange, NJ 07079. Telephone: 973-275-2576. Fax: 753-275-2040. E-mail: thehall@shu.edu. URL: http://www.shu.edu.

See In-Depth Description on page 183.

STEVENS INSTITUTE OF TECHNOLOGY, HOBOKEN

General Information Independent, coed university. Urban setting. *Awards:* B, M, D. *Entrance level for U.S. students:* Very difficult. *Enrollment:* 4,829 total; 1,853 undergraduates (24% women) including 5% international students from 27 foreign countries. *Faculty:* 329. *Library holdings:* 115,234 books, 134 current serial

subscriptions. *Total majors:* 26. *Expenses:* (2006–07) $33,115; room and board, $10,000 (on campus); room only, $4950 (on campus). *Financial aid:* Non-need-based college/university scholarships/grants from institutional funds, loans from outside sources. For fall 2005, 50 international students on campus received college administered financial aid ($4200 average).

SUSSEX COUNTY COMMUNITY COLLEGE, NEWTON

General Information State and locally supported, 2-year, coed college. Small town setting. *Awards:* A. *Entrance level for U.S. students:* Noncompetitive. *Enrollment:* 3,461 total (60% women) including 1% international students. *Undergraduate faculty:* 233. *Library holdings:* 34,346 books, 266 current serial subscriptions, 602 audiovisual materials. *Total majors:* 21.

Information for International Students For fall 2006: 10 international students applied, 10 were accepted, 6 enrolled. Students can start in fall or spring. Transfers accepted from institutions abroad. *Admission tests:* Required: ELS. *Application deadline:* 8/10. *Expenses:* (2006–07) $5130. *Financial aid:* Forms required: institution's own financial aid form, income documentation. *Services:* International student adviser on campus. Full-time and part-time ESL programs on campus. ESL program available during the academic year. *Contact:* International Student Advisor, Sussex County Community College, One College Hill, Newton, NJ 07860. Telephone: 973-300-2211. Fax: 973-579-5226. E-mail: bharford@sussex.edu. URL: http://www.sussex.edu.

THOMAS EDISON STATE COLLEGE, TRENTON

General Information State-supported, coed institution. Urban setting. *Awards:* A, B, M (offers only distance learning degree programs). *Entrance level for U.S. students:* Noncompetitive. *Enrollment:* 13,173 total; 12,729 undergraduates (39% women) including 2% international students from 69 foreign countries. *Total majors:* 99.

UNION COUNTY COLLEGE, CRANFORD

General Information State and locally supported, 2-year, coed college. Urban setting. *Awards:* A. *Entrance level for U.S. students:* Noncompetitive. *Enrollment:* 11,166 total (64% women) including 3% international students from 79 foreign countries. *Undergraduate faculty:* 436. *Library holdings:* 137,731 books, 20,938 current serial subscriptions, 3,610 audiovisual materials. *Total majors:* 35. *Expenses:* (2007–08) $5700.

WESTMINSTER CHOIR COLLEGE OF RIDER UNIVERSITY, PRINCETON

General Information Independent, coed institution. Small town setting. *Awards:* B, M. *Entrance level for U.S. students:* Moderately difficult. *Enrollment:* 452 total; 333 undergraduates (64% women) including 4% international students. *Faculty:* 101. *Library holdings:* 55,000 books, 160 current serial subscriptions. *Total majors:* 9.

Information for International Students For fall 2006: 7 international students applied, 4 were accepted, 2 enrolled. Students can start in fall or spring. Transfers accepted from institutions abroad. *Admission tests:* Required: TOEFL (minimum score: iBT 80; paper-based 550; computer-based 213). Recommended: SAT or ACT. *Application deadline:* 6/1. *Expenses:* (2006–07) $24,770; room and board, $9280 (on campus); room only, $5220 (on campus). *Housing:* Guaranteed, also available during summer. *Services:* International student adviser on campus. Internships and employment opportunities (on-campus) available. *Contact:* Associate Director, Westminster Choir College of Rider University, 101 Walnut Lane, Princeton, NJ 08540-3899. Telephone: 609-921-7100 Ext. 8210. Fax: 609-921-2538. E-mail: wccadmission@rider.edu. URL: http://westminster.rider.edu.

See In-Depth Description on page 247.

NEW MEXICO

CENTRAL NEW MEXICO COMMUNITY COLLEGE, ALBUQUERQUE

General Information State-supported, 2-year, coed college. Urban setting. *Awards:* A. *Entrance level for U.S. students:* Noncompetitive. *Enrollment:* 22,615 total (59% women) including 0.4% international students. *Undergraduate faculty:* 991. *Total majors:* 35. *Expenses:* (2006–07) $7,820. *Financial aid:* Need-based college/university scholarships/grants from institutional funds, tuition waivers, loans from institutional funds, loans from outside sources, on-campus employment. Non-need-based loans from outside sources, on-campus employment.

New Mexico

CLOVIS COMMUNITY COLLEGE, CLOVIS

General Information State-supported, 2-year, coed college. Small town setting. *Awards:* A. *Entrance level for U.S. students:* Noncompetitive. *Enrollment:* 3,522 total (67% women) including 0.05% international students from 2 foreign countries. *Undergraduate faculty:* 184. *Library holdings:* 52,000 books, 370 current serial subscriptions. *Total majors:* 36. *Expenses:* (2007–08) $1516.

COLLEGE OF SANTA FE, SANTA FE

General Information Independent, coed institution. Suburban setting. *Awards:* A, B, M. *Entrance level for U.S. students:* Moderately difficult. *Enrollment:* 2,004 total; 1,362 undergraduates (55% women) including 1% international students. *Faculty:* 267. *Total majors:* 43. *Expenses:* (2007–08) $26,072; room and board, $7585 (on campus); room only, $3692 (on campus). *Financial aid:* Non-need financial aid available. Forms required: International Student's Certification of Finances. For fall 2005, 3 international students on campus received college administered financial aid ($5500 average).

COLLEGE OF THE SOUTHWEST, HOBBS

General Information Independent, coed institution. Small town setting. *Awards:* B, M. *Entrance level for U.S. students:* Moderately difficult. *Enrollment:* 741 total; 608 undergraduates (62% women) including 4% international students from 11 foreign countries. *Faculty:* 90. *Library holdings:* 76,217 books, 287 current serial subscriptions. *Total majors:* 22. *Expenses:* (2006–07) $10,500; room and board, $5400 (on campus). *Financial aid:* Need-based on-campus employment. Non-need-based college/university scholarships/grants from institutional funds, athletic awards. Forms required: institution's own financial aid form, International Student's Certification of Finances. For fall 2006 (estimated), 13 international students on campus received college administered financial aid ($7399 average).

DOÑA ANA BRANCH COMMUNITY COLLEGE, LAS CRUCES

General Information State and locally supported, 2-year, coed college. Urban setting. *Awards:* A. *Entrance level for U.S. students:* Noncompetitive. *Enrollment:* 6,347 total (56% women) including 1% international students. *Undergraduate faculty:* 396. *Library holdings:* 17,140 books, 213 current serial subscriptions. *Total majors:* 22. *Expenses:* (2006–07) $3384; room and board, $5576 (on campus); room only, $3226 (on campus). *Financial aid:* Need-based and non-need-based financial aid available.

EASTERN NEW MEXICO UNIVERSITY, PORTALES

General Information State-supported, coed institution. Rural setting. *Awards:* A, B, M. *Entrance level for U.S. students:* Minimally difficult. *Enrollment:* 4,033 total; 3,291 undergraduates (56% women) including 1% international students from 16 foreign countries. *Faculty:* 263. *Library holdings:* 305,108 books, 7,621 current serial subscriptions. *Total majors:* 45. *Expenses:* (2006–07) $8520; room and board, $4568 (on campus); room only, $2178 (on campus). *Financial aid:* Non-need financial aid available. Forms required: institution's own financial aid form.

NEW MEXICO HIGHLANDS UNIVERSITY, LAS VEGAS

General Information State-supported, coed institution. Small town setting. *Awards:* A, B, M. *Entrance level for U.S. students:* Minimally difficult. *Enrollment:* 3,750 total; 1,986 undergraduates (62% women) including 0.4% international students from 3 foreign countries. *Faculty:* 109. *Library holdings:* 386,489 books, 740 current serial subscriptions. *Total majors:* 45.
Information for International Students Students can start in fall or spring. Transfers accepted from institutions abroad. *Admission tests:* Required: TOEFL (minimum score: iBT 61; paper-based 500; computer-based 173). Recommended: ACT. TOEFL can be waived under certain conditions. *Application deadline:* Rolling. *Expenses:* (2006–07) $3656; room and board, $4476 (on campus); room only, $2056 (on campus). *Financial aid:* Need-based financial aid available. Non-need-based college/university scholarships/grants from institutional funds, tuition waivers, athletic awards, on-campus employment. Forms required: I-20 Form. 11 international students on campus received college administered financial aid ($200 average). *Services:* International student adviser on campus. *Contact:* International Education Center Director, New Mexico Highlands University, NMHU International Education Center, Box 9000, Las Vegas, NM 87701. Telephone: 505-454-3058. Fax: 505-454-3511. E-mail: eclayton@nmhu.edu. URL: http://www.nmhu.edu.

NEW MEXICO INSTITUTE OF MINING AND TECHNOLOGY, SOCORRO

General Information State-supported, coed university. Small town setting. *Awards:* A, B, M, D. *Entrance level for U.S. students:* Moderately difficult. *Enrollment:* 1,846 total; 1,336 undergraduates (33% women) including 2% international students from 29 foreign countries. *Faculty:* 147. *Library holdings:* 321,829 books, 884 current serial subscriptions. *Total majors:* 24.
Information for International Students For fall 2006: 10 international students applied, 3 were accepted, 2 enrolled. Students can start in fall, spring, or summer. Transfers accepted from institutions abroad. *Admission tests:* Required: TOEFL (minimum score: paper-based 540; computer-based 207). Recommended: SAT or ACT. *Application deadline:* 7/1. *Expenses:* (2006–07) $11,405; room and board, $5090 (on campus); room only, $2290 (on campus). *Financial aid:* Non-need-based college/university scholarships/grants from institutional funds, loans from outside sources, on-campus employment. Forms required: International Student's Certification of Finances. 18 international students on campus received college administered financial aid ($6096 average). *Services:* International student adviser on campus. ESL program at cooperating institution. ESL program available during the academic year and the summer. Employment opportunities (on-campus) available. *Contact:* Director of Admission, New Mexico Institute of Mining and Technology, Admission Office, 801 Leroy Place, Socorro, NM 87801. Telephone: 505-835-5424. Fax: 505-835-5989. E-mail: admission@admin.nmt.edu. URL: http://www.nmt.edu.

NEW MEXICO MILITARY INSTITUTE, ROSWELL

General Information State-supported, 2-year, coed, primarily men's college. Small town setting. *Awards:* A. *Entrance level for U.S. students:* Moderately difficult. *Enrollment:* 480 total including 7% international students from 9 foreign countries. *Undergraduate faculty:* 65. *Library holdings:* 65,000 books, 200 current serial subscriptions. *Total majors:* 28.
Information for International Students Students can start in fall or spring. Transfers accepted from institutions abroad. *Admission tests:* Required: TOEFL (minimum score: paper-based 500; computer-based 173). Recommended: SAT, ACT. *Application deadline:* Rolling. *Expenses:* (2007–08) $6190; room and board, $3736 (on campus). *Financial aid:* Need-based college/university scholarships/grants from institutional funds, on-campus employment. Non-need-based college/university scholarships/grants from institutional funds, athletic awards, on-campus employment. *Housing:* Guaranteed. *Services:* International student adviser on campus. Part-time ESL program on campus. ESL program available during the summer. Employment opportunities (on-campus) available. *Contact:* Associate Director of Admissions, New Mexico Military Institute, 101 West College Boulevard, Roswell, NM 88201-5173. Telephone: 505-624-8050. Fax: 505-624-8058. E-mail: admissions@nmmi.edu. URL: http://www.nmmi.edu.

NEW MEXICO STATE UNIVERSITY, LAS CRUCES

General Information State-supported, coed university. Suburban setting. *Awards:* A, B, M, D. *Entrance level for U.S. students:* Moderately difficult. *Enrollment:* 16,415 total; 13,210 undergraduates (56% women) including 1% international students from 39 foreign countries. *Faculty:* 908. *Library holdings:* 1.7 million books, 2,890 current serial subscriptions, 4,332 audiovisual materials. *Total majors:* 82.
Information for International Students For fall 2006: 247 international students applied, 211 were accepted, 145 enrolled. Students can start in fall, spring, or summer. Transfers accepted from institutions abroad. *Admission tests:* Required: TOEFL (minimum score: iBT 61; paper-based 500; computer-based 173). *Application deadline:* Rolling. *Expenses:* (2006–07) $13,804; room and board, $5576 (on campus); room only, $3226 (on campus). *Financial aid:* Need-based college/university scholarships/grants from institutional funds, tuition waivers, athletic awards, loans from outside sources, on-campus employment. Non-need-based college/university scholarships/grants from institutional funds, tuition waivers, athletic awards, loans from outside sources, on-campus employment. For fall 2006 (estimated), 320 international students on campus received college administered financial aid ($4953 average). *Housing:* Available during summer. *Services:* International student adviser on campus. Full-time and part-time ESL programs on campus. ESL program available during the academic year and the summer. Internships and employment opportunities (on-campus and off-campus) available. *Contact:* Assistant Dean, New Mexico State University, International Programs, MSC 3567, Box 30001, Las Cruces, NM 88003. Telephone: 505-646-2017. Fax: 505-646-2558. E-mail: ias@nmsu.edu. URL: http://www.nmsu.edu.

NEW MEXICO STATE UNIVERSITY–ALAMOGORDO, ALAMOGORDO

General Information State-supported, 2-year, coed college. Small town setting. *Awards:* A. *Entrance level for U.S. students:* Noncompetitive. *Enrollment:* 1,897 total (65% women) including 1% international students from 3 foreign countries. *Undergraduate faculty:* 98. *Library holdings:* 39,000 books, 350 current serial subscriptions. *Total majors:* 16.

Information for International Students For fall 2006: 20 international students applied, 20 were accepted, 20 enrolled. Students can start in fall, spring, or summer. Transfers accepted from institutions abroad. *Admission tests:* Required: TOEFL (minimum score: iBT 61; paper-based 500; computer-based 173; minimum score for ESL admission: iBT 61; paper-based 500; computer-based 173), ELS. TOEFL can be waived under certain conditions. *Application deadline:* 3/15. *Expenses:* (2007–08) $4008. *Financial aid:* Forms required: institution's own financial aid form. *Services:* International student adviser on campus. ESL program at cooperating institution. *Contact:* Campus Student Services Officer, New Mexico State University–Alamogordo, 2400 North Scenic Drive, Alamogordo, NM 88310. Telephone: 505-439-3716. Fax: 505-439-3760. URL: http://alamo.nmsu.edu.

ST. JOHN'S COLLEGE, SANTA FE

General Information Independent, coed institution. Suburban setting. *Awards:* B, M. *Entrance level for U.S. students:* Very difficult. *Enrollment:* 520 total; 434 undergraduates (44% women) including 2% international students from 7 foreign countries. *Faculty:* 72. *Library holdings:* 65,000 books, 140 current serial subscriptions. *Total majors:* 22.

Information for International Students For fall 2006: 8 international students applied, 4 were accepted, 2 enrolled. Students can start in fall or spring. Transfers accepted from institutions abroad. *Admission tests:* Required: SAT or ACT, TOEFL (minimum score: paper-based 550; computer-based 213). TOEFL can be waived under certain conditions. *Application deadline:* 3/1. *Expenses:* (2007–08) $36,596; room and board, $8684 (on campus). *Financial aid:* Need-based financial aid available. Forms required: International Student's Financial Aid Application. International transfer students are eligible to apply for aid. For fall 2006 (estimated), 6 international students on campus received college administered financial aid ($39,834 average). *Housing:* Guaranteed, also available during summer. *Services:* International student adviser on campus. Employment opportunities (on-campus) available. *Contact:* Director of Admissions, St. John's College, Office of Admissions, 1160 Camino Cruz Blanca, Santa Fe, NM 87505. Telephone: 505-984-6060. Fax: 505-984-6162. E-mail: admissions@sjcsf.edu. URL: http://www.stjohnscollege.edu.

See In-Depth Description on page 166.

SAN JUAN COLLEGE, FARMINGTON

General Information State-supported, 2-year, coed college. Small town setting. *Awards:* A. *Entrance level for U.S. students:* Noncompetitive. *Enrollment:* 6,366 total (48% women) including 0.05% international students from 2 foreign countries. *Undergraduate faculty:* 374. *Library holdings:* 81,116 books, 6,677 current serial subscriptions. *Total majors:* 52. *Expenses:* (2006–07) $960.

SANTA FE COMMUNITY COLLEGE, SANTA FE

General Information State and locally supported, 2-year, coed college. Suburban setting. *Awards:* A. *Entrance level for U.S. students:* Noncompetitive. *Enrollment:* 5,412 total (63% women) including 0.2% international students from 6 foreign countries. *Undergraduate faculty:* 352. *Library holdings:* 38,226 books, 206 current serial subscriptions, 2,010 audiovisual materials. *Total majors:* 30.

Information for International Students For fall 2006: 5 international students applied, 4 were accepted, 4 enrolled. Students can start in fall, winter, spring, or summer. Transfers accepted from institutions abroad. *Admission tests:* Required: TOEFL (minimum score: iBT 66; paper-based 517; computer-based 187; minimum score for ESL admission: iBT 66; paper-based 517; computer-based 187), ELS. *Application deadline:* 6/8. *Expenses:* (2006–07) $2469. *Financial aid:* Need-based on-campus employment. Non-need-based on-campus employment. *Services:* International student adviser on campus. Full-time and part-time ESL programs on campus. ESL program available during the academic year. Internships and employment opportunities (on-campus) available. *Contact:* Primary Student Designated Officer (PDSO), Santa Fe Community College, 6401 Richard's Avenue, Santa Fe, NM 87508. Telephone: 505-428-1261. Fax: 505-428-1237. E-mail: atupler@sfccnm.edu. URL: http://www.sfccnm.edu.

UNIVERSITY OF NEW MEXICO, ALBUQUERQUE

General Information State-supported, coed university. Urban setting. *Awards:* A, B, M, D, FP. *Entrance level for U.S. students:* Moderately difficult. *Enrollment:* 26,172 total; 18,725 undergraduates (58% women) including 1% international students from 67 foreign countries. *Faculty:* 1,411. *Library holdings:* 2.7 million books, 592,243 current serial subscriptions. *Total majors:* 82.

Information for International Students Students can start in fall, spring, or summer. Transfers accepted from institutions abroad. *Admission tests:* Required: TOEFL (minimum score: iBT 68; paper-based 520; computer-based 190; minimum score for ESL admission: iBT 68; paper-based 520; computer-based 190). TOEFL can be waived under certain conditions. *Application deadline:* 3/1. *Expenses:* (2006–07) $14,177; room and board, $6680 (on campus); room only, $3900 (on campus). *Financial aid:* Non-need financial aid available. Forms required: institution's own financial aid form. International transfer students are eligible to apply for aid. 62 international students on campus received college administered financial aid ($11,499 average). *Housing:* Available during summer. *Services:* International student adviser on campus. Full-time and part-time ESL programs on campus. ESL program available during the academic year and the summer. Employment opportunities (on-campus) available. *Contact:* Associate Director of Admissions, Office of International Admissions, University of New Mexico, International Admissions, Student Services Building, Suite 140, Albuquerque, NM 87131-2046. Telephone: 505-277-5829. Fax: 505-277-6686. E-mail: goglobal@unm.edu. URL: http://www.unm.edu.

See In-Depth Description on page 218.

UNIVERSITY OF PHOENIX–NEW MEXICO CAMPUS, ALBUQUERQUE

General Information Proprietary, coed institution. Urban setting. *Awards:* B, M. *Entrance level for U.S. students:* Noncompetitive. *Enrollment:* 4,586 total; 3,537 undergraduates (63% women) including 11% international students. *Faculty:* 658. *Library holdings:* 1,759 books, 692 current serial subscriptions. *Total majors:* 13. *Expenses:* (2006–07) $9750.

WESTERN NEW MEXICO UNIVERSITY, SILVER CITY

General Information State-supported, coed institution. Rural setting. *Awards:* A, B, M. *Entrance level for U.S. students:* Noncompetitive. *Enrollment:* 3,074 total; 2,555 undergraduates including international students from 6 foreign countries. *Faculty:* 145. *Library holdings:* 245,146 books, 236 current serial subscriptions. *Total majors:* 53.

Information for International Students For fall 2006: 9 international students applied, 9 were accepted, 7 enrolled. Students can start in fall, spring, or summer. Transfers accepted from institutions abroad. *Admission tests:* Required: SAT or ACT, TOEFL (minimum score: paper-based 550; computer-based 213). TOEFL can be waived under certain conditions. *Application deadline:* 6/1. *Expenses:* (2006–07) $11,322; room and board, $4590 (on campus); room only, $1760 (on campus). *Financial aid:* Non-need-based on-campus employment. International transfer students are eligible to apply for aid. *Housing:* Guaranteed, also available during summer. *Services:* International student adviser on campus. Full-time ESL program on campus. ESL program available during the academic year and the summer. Internships and employment opportunities (on-campus) available. *Contact:* Director of Admissions, Western New Mexico University, 1000 West College Avenue, Silver City, NM 88061. Telephone: 505-538-6000. Fax: 505-538-6127. E-mail: tresslerd@wnmu.edu. URL: http://www.wnmu.edu.

NEW YORK

ADELPHI UNIVERSITY, GARDEN CITY

General Information Independent, coed university. Suburban setting. *Awards:* A, B, M, D. *Entrance level for U.S. students:* Moderately difficult. *Enrollment:* 8,053 total; 4,930 undergraduates (73% women) including 4% international students from 45 foreign countries. *Faculty:* 908. *Library holdings:* 667,293 books, 28,856 current serial subscriptions, 30,372 audiovisual materials. *Total majors:* 41.

Information for International Students For fall 2006: 740 international students applied, 355 were accepted. Students can start in fall or spring. *Admission tests:* Required: TOEFL (minimum score: iBT 80; paper-based 550; computer-based 250), SAT or ACT required for new freshman from English-speaking countries. *Application deadline:* 5/1. *Expenses:* (2006–07) $20,900; room and board, $9500 (on campus); room only, $6350 (on campus). *Financial aid:* Non-need-based college/university scholarships/grants from institutional funds, athletic awards, loans from outside sources, on-campus employment. Forms required: International Student's

Adelphi University (continued)

Certification of Finances. For fall 2005, 198 international students on campus received college administered financial aid ($8783 average). *Services:* International student adviser on campus. Full-time ESL program on campus. ESL program available during the academic year and the summer. Internships and employment opportunities (on-campus) available. *Contact:* Assistant Director of International Admissions, Adelphi University, Garden City, NY 11530. Telephone: 516-877-3050. Fax: 516-877-3039. E-mail: intladmissions@adelphi.edu. URL: http://www.adelphi.edu.

See In-Depth Description on page 28.

ALBANY COLLEGE OF PHARMACY OF UNION UNIVERSITY, ALBANY

General Information Independent, coed institution. Urban setting. *Awards:* B, FP. *Entrance level for U.S. students:* Moderately difficult. *Enrollment:* 1,230 total; 892 undergraduates (57% women) including 8% international students from 8 foreign countries. *Faculty:* 84. *Library holdings:* 16,124 books, 3,576 current serial subscriptions. *Total majors:* 4.

Information for International Students For fall 2006: 87 international students applied, 38 were accepted, 16 enrolled. Students can start in fall or summer. Transfers accepted from institutions abroad. *Admission tests:* Required: SAT or ACT, TOEFL (minimum score: iBT 100; paper-based 600; computer-based 250), TSE. TOEFL can be waived under certain conditions. *Application deadline:* 2/1. *Expenses:* (2006–07) $19,820; room and board, $6900 (on campus); room only, $5100 (on campus). *Financial aid:* Forms required: International Student's Certification of Finances. *Housing:* Available during summer. *Services:* International student adviser on campus. Internships and employment opportunities (on-campus) available. *Contact:* Assistant Registrar, Albany College of Pharmacy of Union University, 106 New Scotland Avenue, Albany, NY 12208-3425. Telephone: 518-694-7201. Fax: 518-694-7202. E-mail: tynanc@acp.edu. URL: http://www.acp.edu.

ALFRED UNIVERSITY, ALFRED

General Information Independent, coed university. Rural setting. *Awards:* B, M, D. *Entrance level for U.S. students:* Moderately difficult. *Enrollment:* 2,310 total; 1,991 undergraduates (52% women) including international students from 32 foreign countries. *Faculty:* 220. *Library holdings:* 288,667 books, 1,478 current serial subscriptions, 4,191 audiovisual materials. *Total majors:* 41. *Expenses:* (2007–08) $23,162; room and board, $10,384 (on campus); room only, $5384 (on campus). *Financial aid:* Non-need-based college/university scholarships/grants from institutional funds. Forms required: institution's own financial aid form, International Student's Financial Aid Application, International Student's Certification of Finances. For fall 2006 (estimated), 48 international students on campus received college administered financial aid ($8127 average).

AMERICAN ACADEMY OF DRAMATIC ARTS, NEW YORK

General Information Independent, 2-year, coed college. Urban setting. *Awards:* A. *Entrance level for U.S. students:* Moderately difficult. *Enrollment:* 248 total (65% women) including 19% international students from 17 foreign countries. *Undergraduate faculty:* 27. *Library holdings:* 7,467 books, 24 current serial subscriptions, 570 audiovisual materials. *Total majors:* 1.

Information for International Students Students can start in fall, winter, spring, or summer. *Admission tests:* Recommended: SAT or ACT. *Application deadline:* Rolling. *Expenses:* (2006–07) $17,400. *Financial aid:* Need-based college/university scholarships/grants from institutional funds, loans from outside sources, on-campus employment. Non-need-based college/university scholarships/grants from institutional funds, loans from outside sources, on-campus employment. *Housing:* Available during summer. *Services:* International student adviser on campus. *Contact:* Director of Admissions, American Academy of Dramatic Arts, 120 Madison Avenue, New York, NY 10016-7004. Telephone: 212-686-9244. Fax: 212-685-8093. E-mail: admissions-ny@aada.org. URL: http://www.aada.org.

See In-Depth Description on page 31.

ASA INSTITUTE, THE COLLEGE OF ADVANCED TECHNOLOGY, BROOKLYN

General Information Proprietary, 2-year, coed college. *Awards:* A. *Entrance level for U.S. students:* Difficulty N/R. *Enrollment:* 2,977 total. *Total majors:* 9. *Expenses:* (2006–07) $11,499.

BARD COLLEGE, ANNANDALE-ON-HUDSON

General Information Independent, coed institution. Rural setting. *Awards:* A, B, M, D. *Entrance level for U.S. students:* Very difficult.

Enrollment: 2,012 total; 1,735 undergraduates (56% women) including 9% international students from 47 foreign countries. *Faculty:* 237. *Library holdings:* 402,000 books, 15,450 current serial subscriptions, 4,725 audiovisual materials. *Total majors:* 88.

Information for International Students For fall 2006: 387 international students applied, 92 were accepted, 53 enrolled. Students can start in fall or spring. Transfers accepted from institutions abroad. *Admission tests:* Required: TOEFL (minimum score: paper-based 600; computer-based 250; minimum score for ESL admission: paper-based 600; computer-based 250). Recommended: SAT or ACT, SAT Subject Tests. TOEFL can be waived under certain conditions. *Application deadline:* 1/15. *Expenses:* (2006–07) $34,080; room and board, $9850 (on campus); room only, $4950 (on campus). *Financial aid:* Need-based college/university scholarships/grants from institutional funds, loans from institutional funds, on-campus employment. Non-need-based college/university scholarships/grants from institutional funds. Forms required: International Student's Financial Aid Application, International Student's Certification of Finances. International transfer students are eligible to apply for aid. For fall 2006 (estimated), 137 international students on campus received college administered financial aid ($29,172 average). *Housing:* Guaranteed. *Services:* International student adviser on campus. Internships and employment opportunities (on-campus) available. *Contact:* Director of International Recruitment, Bard College, PO Box 5000, Annandale-on-Hudson, NY 12504-5000. Telephone: 845-758-7472. Fax: 845-758-5208. E-mail: brien@bard.edu. URL: http://www.bard.edu.

BARNARD COLLEGE, NEW YORK

General Information Independent, 4-year, women's college. Urban setting. *Awards:* B. *Entrance level for U.S. students:* Most difficult. *Enrollment:* 2,350 total including 3% international students from 40 foreign countries. *Undergraduate faculty:* 324. *Library holdings:* 205,912 books, 463 current serial subscriptions. *Total majors:* 57.

Information for International Students For fall 2006: 268 international students applied, 41 were accepted, 17 enrolled. Students can start in fall. Transfers accepted from institutions abroad. *Admission tests:* Required: SAT or ACT, TOEFL (minimum score: iBT 100; paper-based 600; computer-based 250), ACT writing test (if submitting the ACT). TOEFL can be waived under certain conditions. *Application deadline:* 1/1. *Expenses:* (2006–07) $33,078; room and board, $11,392 (on campus); room only, $6900 (on campus). *Financial aid:* Need-based college/university scholarships/grants from institutional funds, loans from institutional funds, on-campus employment. Non-need-based loans from outside sources. Forms required: institution's own financial aid form, International Student's Financial Aid Application, International Student's Certification of Finances. For fall 2006 (estimated), 7 international students on campus received college administered financial aid ($30,722 average). *Housing:* Guaranteed. *Services:* International student adviser on campus. Internships and employment opportunities (on-campus) available. *Contact:* Senior Admissions Officer, Barnard College, 3009 Broadway, New York, NY 10027. Telephone: 212-854-2014. Fax: 212-854-6220. E-mail: lkaub@barnard.edu. URL: http://www.barnard.edu.

See In-Depth Description on page 37.

BERKELEY COLLEGE-NEW YORK CITY CAMPUS, NEW YORK

General Information Proprietary, primarily 2-year, coed college. Urban setting. *Awards:* A, B. *Entrance level for U.S. students:* Minimally difficult. *Enrollment:* 2,412 total (70% women) including 15% international students from 66 foreign countries. *Undergraduate faculty:* 140. *Library holdings:* 13,164 books, 138 current serial subscriptions. *Total majors:* 12.

Information for International Students For fall 2006: 850 international students applied, 800 were accepted, 550 enrolled. Students can start in fall, winter, spring, or summer. Transfers accepted from institutions abroad. *Admission tests:* Required: TOEFL (minimum score: iBT 61; paper-based 500; computer-based 173; minimum score for ESL admission: paper-based 450; computer-based 133). TOEFL can be waived under certain conditions. *Application deadline:* Rolling. *Expenses:* (2007–08) $18,150. *Financial aid:* Need-based and non-need-based financial aid available. Forms required: institution's own financial aid form, International Student's Certification of Finances. International transfer students are eligible to apply for aid. *Services:* International student adviser on campus. Full-time ESL program on campus. ESL program available during the academic year and the summer. Internships and employment opportunities (on-campus and off-campus) available. *Contact:* Vice President, International Enrollment Services, Berkeley College-New York City Campus, 12 East 41 Street, 14th Floor, New York, NY 10017. Telephone: 212-687-3730. Fax: 212-986-7827.

E-mail: international@berkeleycollege.edu.
URL: http://www.berkeleycollege.edu.

See In-Depth Description on page 42.

BERKELEY COLLEGE-WESTCHESTER CAMPUS, WHITE PLAINS

General Information Proprietary, primarily 2-year, coed college. Suburban setting. *Awards:* A, B. *Entrance level for U.S. students:* Minimally difficult. *Enrollment:* 640 total (70% women) including 7% international students from 28 foreign countries. *Undergraduate faculty:* 42. *Library holdings:* 9,526 books, 66 current serial subscriptions, 777 audiovisual materials. *Total majors:* 11.

Information for International Students For fall 2006: 150 international students applied, 120 were accepted, 80 enrolled. Students can start in fall, winter, spring, or summer. Transfers accepted from institutions abroad. *Admission tests:* Required: TOEFL (minimum score: iBT 61; paper-based 500; computer-based 173; minimum score for ESL admission: paper-based 500; computer-based 173), ELS (minimum score: 109). TOEFL can be waived under certain conditions. *Application deadline:* Rolling. *Expenses:* (2007–08) $18,150; room and board, $9000 (on campus). *Financial aid:* Forms required: institution's own financial aid form, International Student's Certification of Finances. International transfer students are eligible to apply for aid. *Housing:* Guaranteed, also available during summer. *Services:* International student adviser on campus. Full-time ESL program on campus. ESL program available during the academic year and the summer. Internships and employment opportunities (on-campus and off-campus) available. *Contact:* Vice President, International Enrollment Services, Berkeley College-Westchester Campus, 12 East 41 Street, 14th Floor, New York, NY 10017. Telephone: 212-687-3730. Fax: 212-986-7827. E-mail: international@berkeleycollege.edu. URL: http://www.berkeleycollege.edu.

BERNARD M. BARUCH COLLEGE OF THE CITY UNIVERSITY OF NEW YORK, NEW YORK

General Information State and locally supported, coed institution. Urban setting. *Awards:* B, M, D. *Entrance level for U.S. students:* Very difficult. *Enrollment:* 15,730 total; 12,796 undergraduates (53% women) including 13% international students from 166 foreign countries. *Faculty:* 1,021. *Library holdings:* 456,132 books, 35,000 current serial subscriptions. *Total majors:* 33. *Expenses:* (2006–07) $8960. *Financial aid:* Non-need financial aid available. For fall 2005, 300 international students on campus received college administered financial aid ($830 average).

BOROUGH OF MANHATTAN COMMUNITY COLLEGE OF THE CITY UNIVERSITY OF NEW YORK, NEW YORK

General Information State and locally supported, 2-year, coed college. Urban setting. *Awards:* A. *Entrance level for U.S. students:* Noncompetitive. *Enrollment:* 18,776 total (63% women) including 11% international students from 100 foreign countries. *Undergraduate faculty:* 1,075. *Library holdings:* 101,869 books, 8,594 current serial subscriptions, 1,343 audiovisual materials. *Total majors:* 17. *Expenses:* (2006–07) $5968.

BRIARCLIFFE COLLEGE, BETHPAGE

General Information Proprietary, 4-year, coed college. Suburban setting. *Awards:* A, B. *Entrance level for U.S. students:* Noncompetitive. *Enrollment:* 2,343 total (49% women) including 2% international students from 5 foreign countries. *Undergraduate faculty:* 247. *Total majors:* 11. *Expenses:* (2006–07) $15,892; room and board, $7938 (on campus).

BRONX COMMUNITY COLLEGE OF THE CITY UNIVERSITY OF NEW YORK, BRONX

General Information State and locally supported, 2-year, coed college. Urban setting. *Awards:* A. *Entrance level for U.S. students:* Noncompetitive. *Enrollment:* 8,470 total (64% women) including 11% international students from 100 foreign countries. *Undergraduate faculty:* 547. *Library holdings:* 75,000 books, 800 current serial subscriptions. *Total majors:* 27.

Information for International Students For fall 2006: 200 international students applied, 118 were accepted, 60 enrolled. Students can start in fall or spring. Transfers accepted from institutions abroad. *Admission tests:* Required: TOEFL (minimum score: paper-based 500; computer-based 173; minimum score for ESL admission: paper-based 500; computer-based 173). TOEFL can be waived under certain conditions. *Application deadline:* 8/15. *Expenses:* (2006–07) $4844. *Services:* International student adviser on campus. ESL program at cooperating institution. Internships and employment opportunities (on-campus and off-campus) available. *Contact:* Director of Admissions, Bronx Community College of the City University of New York, University Avenue and

West 181st Street, Loew Hall, Room 224, Bronx, NY 10453. Telephone: 718-289-5892. Fax: 718-289-6352. E-mail: internationalstudent@bcc.cuny.edu. URL: http://www.bcc.cuny.edu.

BROOME COMMUNITY COLLEGE, BINGHAMTON

General Information State and locally supported, 2-year, coed college. Suburban setting. *Awards:* A. *Entrance level for U.S. students:* Noncompetitive. *Enrollment:* 6,282 total (56% women) including 2% international students from 33 foreign countries. *Undergraduate faculty:* 406. *Total majors:* 35.

Information for International Students For fall 2006: 38 international students were accepted, 16 enrolled. Students can start in fall or spring. Transfers accepted from institutions abroad. *Admission tests:* Required: TOEFL or 4 years of English language study. Recommended: TOEFL (minimum score: iBT 70; paper-based 523; computer-based 193; minimum score for ESL admission: iBT 32; paper-based 400; computer-based 97). TOEFL can be waived under certain conditions. *Application deadline:* Rolling. *Expenses:* (2006–07) $6233. *Financial aid:* Forms required: International Student's Certification of Finances. *Services:* International student adviser on campus. Full-time ESL program on campus. ESL program available during the academic year. Internships and employment opportunities (on-campus) available. *Contact:* Assistant Director, Admissions, Admissions Office, Broome Community College, PO Box 1017, 907 Front Street, Binghamton, NY 13902. Telephone: 607-778-5001. Fax: 607-778-5442. E-mail: carra_m@sunybroome.edu. URL: http://www.sunybroome.edu.

BRYANT AND STRATTON COLLEGE, SYRACUSE

General Information Proprietary, 2-year, coed college. Urban setting. *Awards:* A. *Entrance level for U.S. students:* Minimally difficult. *Enrollment:* 636 total (77% women) including 1% international students from 2 foreign countries. *Undergraduate faculty:* 51. *Library holdings:* 1,325 books, 40 current serial subscriptions, 40 audiovisual materials. *Total majors:* 9. *Financial aid:* Forms required: International Student's Certification of Finances.

BUFFALO STATE COLLEGE, STATE UNIVERSITY OF NEW YORK, BUFFALO

General Information State-supported, coed institution. Urban setting. *Awards:* B, M. *Entrance level for U.S. students:* Moderately difficult. *Enrollment:* 11,220 total; 9,314 undergraduates (59% women) including 0.4% international students from 8 foreign countries. *Faculty:* 755. *Library holdings:* 489,069 books, 2,847 current serial subscriptions. *Total majors:* 80. *Expenses:* (2006–07) $11,545; room and board, $7482 (on campus); room only, $4570 (on campus).

CANISIUS COLLEGE, BUFFALO

General Information Independent Roman Catholic (Jesuit), coed institution. Urban setting. *Awards:* B, M. *Entrance level for U.S. students:* Moderately difficult. *Enrollment:* 4,850 total; 3,461 undergraduates (56% women) including 3% international students from 31 foreign countries. *Faculty:* 532. *Library holdings:* 379,498 books, 24,000 current serial subscriptions, 9,596 audiovisual materials. *Total majors:* 54. *Expenses:* (2006–07) $24,937; room and board, $9480 (on campus); room only, $5620 (on campus). *Financial aid:* Need-based college/university scholarships/grants from institutional funds, athletic awards, loans from outside sources, on-campus employment. Non-need-based college/university scholarships/grants from institutional funds. Forms required: institution's own financial aid form. For fall 2006 (estimated), 110 international students on campus received college administered financial aid ($17,952 average).

CAYUGA COUNTY COMMUNITY COLLEGE, AUBURN

General Information State and locally supported, 2-year, coed college. Small town setting. *Awards:* A. *Entrance level for U.S. students:* Noncompetitive. *Enrollment:* 3,896 total (60% women) including 0.5% international students from 3 foreign countries. *Undergraduate faculty:* 155. *Library holdings:* 82,205 books, 527 current serial subscriptions, 8,930 audiovisual materials. *Total majors:* 26.

CAZENOVIA COLLEGE, CAZENOVIA

General Information Independent, 4-year, coed college. Small town setting. *Awards:* A, B. *Entrance level for U.S. students:* Minimally difficult. *Enrollment:* 1,006 total (78% women) including 0.2% international students from 3 foreign countries. *Undergraduate faculty:* 141. *Library holdings:* 83,340 books, 61,278 current serial subscriptions, 4,160 audiovisual materials. *Total majors:* 21.

Cazenovia College (continued)

Information for International Students For fall 2006: 10 international students applied, 5 were accepted, 2 enrolled. Students can start in fall or spring. Transfers accepted from institutions abroad. *Admission tests:* Required: TOEFL (minimum score: paper-based 550; computer-based 213). Recommended: SAT or ACT. TOEFL can be waived under certain conditions. *Application deadline:* Rolling. *Expenses:* (2007–08) $21,490; room and board, $8940 (on campus). *Financial aid:* Need-based college/university scholarships/grants from institutional funds. Non-need-based college/university scholarships/grants from institutional funds. Forms required: International Student's Financial Aid Application, International Student's Certification of Finances. For fall 2006 (estimated), 1 international student on campus received college administered financial aid ($2500 average). *Housing:* Guaranteed, also available during summer. *Services:* International student adviser on campus. Internships available. *Contact:* Dean of Admissions and Financial Aid, Cazenovia College, 22 Sullivan Street, Cazenovia, NY 13035. Telephone: 315-655-7208. Fax: 315-655-4860. E-mail: rcroot@cazenovia.edu. URL: http://www.cazenovia.edu.

CITY COLLEGE OF THE CITY UNIVERSITY OF NEW YORK, NEW YORK

General Information State and locally supported, coed university. Urban setting. *Awards:* B, M, FP. *Entrance level for U.S. students:* Moderately difficult. *Enrollment:* 13,244 total; 10,314 undergraduates (50% women) including 15% international students from 130 foreign countries. *Faculty:* 1,012. *Library holdings:* 1.4 million books, 31,000 current serial subscriptions, 26,380 audiovisual materials. *Total majors:* 66.

Information for International Students Students can start in fall or spring. Transfers accepted from institutions abroad. *Admission tests:* Required: TOEFL (minimum score: paper-based 500; computer-based 173; minimum score for ESL admission: paper-based 500; computer-based 173). Recommended: SAT. *Application deadline:* 12/1. *Expenses:* (2006–07) $8,919; room only, $9135 (on campus). *Services:* International student adviser on campus. Full-time and part-time ESL programs on campus. ESL program available during the academic year and the summer. Internships and employment opportunities (on-campus) available. *Contact:* Director of Admissions, Office of Admissions, City College of the City University of New York, 160 Convent Avenue, Wille Administration Building, Room 101, New York, NY 10031. Telephone: 212-650 6977. Fax: 212-650-6417. E-mail: admissions@ccny.cuny.edu. URL: http://www.ccny.cuny.edu.

CLARKSON UNIVERSITY, POTSDAM

General Information Independent, coed university. Small town setting. *Awards:* B, M, D. *Entrance level for U.S. students:* Very difficult. *Enrollment:* 2,964 total; 2,545 undergraduates (26% women) including 3% international students from 22 foreign countries. *Faculty:* 198. *Library holdings:* 269,059 books, 1,778 current serial subscriptions, 2,128 audiovisual materials. *Total majors:* 60.

Information for International Students For fall 2006: 252 international students applied, 72 were accepted, 35 enrolled. Students can start in fall or spring. Transfers accepted from institutions abroad. *Admission tests:* Required: SAT or ACT, TOEFL (minimum score: iBT 80; paper-based 550; computer-based 213). TOEFL can be waived under certain conditions. *Application deadline:* 7/1. *Expenses:* (2006–07) $27,090; room and board, $9648 (on campus); room only, $5058 (on campus). *Financial aid:* Non-need-based college/university scholarships/grants from institutional funds, athletic awards, loans from outside sources. Forms required: International Student's Certification of Finances. International transfer students are eligible to apply for aid. For fall 2006 (estimated), 43 international students on campus received college administered financial aid ($7163 average). *Housing:* Guaranteed. *Services:* International student adviser on campus. Internships and employment opportunities (on-campus) available. *Contact:* Assistant Director of Undergraduate Admission and Coordinator of International Admission, Clarkson University, 8 Clarkson Avenue, Box 5610, Potsdam, NY 13699. Telephone: 315-268-2125. Fax: 315-268-7647. E-mail: pperrier@clarkson.edu. URL: http://www.clarkson.edu.

See In-Depth Description on page 58.

CLINTON COMMUNITY COLLEGE, PLATTSBURGH

General Information State and locally supported, 2-year, coed college. Small town setting. *Awards:* A. *Entrance level for U.S. students:* Noncompetitive. *Enrollment:* 2,192 total (57% women) including 2% international students from 9 foreign countries. *Undergraduate faculty:* 142. *Library holdings:* 33,862 books, 288

current serial subscriptions, 257 audiovisual materials. *Total majors:* 17. *Financial aid:* Need-based and non-need-based financial aid available.

COLGATE UNIVERSITY, HAMILTON

General Information Independent, coed institution. Rural setting. *Awards:* B, M. *Entrance level for U.S. students:* Most difficult. *Enrollment:* 2,788 total; 2,782 undergraduates (52% women) including 5% international students from 34 foreign countries. *Faculty:* 322. *Library holdings:* 1.2 million books, 29,632 current serial subscriptions, 16,184 audiovisual materials. *Total majors:* 52. *Expenses:* (2006–07) $35,030; room and board, $8530 (on campus); room only, $4120 (on campus). *Financial aid:* Need-based college/university scholarships/grants from institutional funds, athletic awards, on-campus employment. Non-need-based athletic awards, on-campus employment. Forms required: International Student's Financial Aid Application, International Student's Certification of Finances. For fall 2006 (estimated), 119 international students on campus received college administered financial aid ($38,211 average).

COLLEGE OF MOUNT SAINT VINCENT, RIVERDALE

General Information Independent, coed institution. Suburban setting. *Awards:* A, B, M. *Entrance level for U.S. students:* Moderately difficult. *Enrollment:* 1,812 total; 1,497 undergraduates (75% women) including 0.1% international students. *Faculty:* 156. *Library holdings:* 104,158 books. *Total majors:* 31. *Expenses:* (2007–08) $22,750; room and board, $8925 (on campus). *Financial aid:* Non-need financial aid available.

THE COLLEGE OF NEW ROCHELLE, NEW ROCHELLE

General Information Independent, coed, primarily women's institution. Suburban setting. *Awards:* B, M (also offers a non-traditional adult program with significant enrollment not reflected in profile). *Entrance level for U.S. students:* Moderately difficult. *Enrollment:* 2,341 total; 1,064 undergraduates (93% women) including 1% international students from 10 foreign countries. *Faculty:* 207. *Library holdings:* 220,000 books, 1,450 current serial subscriptions. *Total majors:* 36. *Expenses:* (2006–07) $21,910; room and board, $8200 (on campus). *Financial aid:* Non-need-based college/university scholarships/grants from institutional funds. Forms required: application for admissions. For fall 2005, 12 international students on campus received college administered financial aid ($12,475 average).

THE COLLEGE OF SAINT ROSE, ALBANY

General Information Independent, coed institution. Urban setting. *Awards:* B, M. *Entrance level for U.S. students:* Moderately difficult. *Enrollment:* 5,062 total; 3,116 undergraduates (72% women) including 0.1% international students from 2 foreign countries. *Faculty:* 464. *Library holdings:* 205,938 books, 925 current serial subscriptions, 1,513 audiovisual materials. *Total majors:* 42. *Expenses:* (2006–07) $19,258; room and board, $8116 (on campus); room only, $3868 (on campus). *Financial aid:* Non-need financial aid available. Forms required: institution's own financial aid form.

COLLEGE OF STATEN ISLAND OF THE CITY UNIVERSITY OF NEW YORK, STATEN ISLAND

General Information State and locally supported, coed institution. Urban setting. *Awards:* A, B, M. *Entrance level for U.S. students:* Moderately difficult. *Enrollment:* 12,313 total; 11,263 undergraduates (59% women) including 5% international students from 106 foreign countries. *Faculty:* 851. *Library holdings:* 229,000 books, 25,000 current serial subscriptions, 4,100 audiovisual materials. *Total majors:* 40. *Expenses:* (2006–07) $8968. *Financial aid:* Need-based college/university scholarships/grants from institutional funds, on-campus employment. Non-need-based college/university scholarships/grants from institutional funds. Forms required: International Student's Certification of Finances. For fall 2005, international students on campus received college administered aid averaging $1000.

COLUMBIA COLLEGE, NEW YORK

General Information Independent, 4-year, coed college. Urban setting. *Awards:* B. *Entrance level for U.S. students:* Most difficult. *Enrollment:* 4,184 total (52% women) including 6% international students from 72 foreign countries. *Undergraduate faculty:* 1,057. *Library holdings:* 7.2 million books, 66,000 current serial subscriptions. *Total majors:* 64. *Expenses:* (2006–07) $35,164; room and board, $9648 (on campus); room only, $5640 (on campus). *Financial aid:* Need-based college/university scholarships/grants from institutional funds. Forms required: institution's own financial aid form, International Student's Financial Aid Application. 102 international students on campus received college administered financial aid ($30,392 average).

COLUMBIA-GREENE COMMUNITY COLLEGE, HUDSON

General Information State and locally supported, 2-year, coed college. Rural setting. *Awards:* A. *Entrance level for U.S. students:* Noncompetitive. *Enrollment:* 1,771 total (60% women) including 0.3% international students from 5 foreign countries. *Undergraduate faculty:* 110. *Library holdings:* 62,694 books, 674 current serial subscriptions, 25 audiovisual materials. *Total majors:* 23. *Expenses:* (2006–07) $6232.

COLUMBIA UNIVERSITY, SCHOOL OF GENERAL STUDIES, NEW YORK

General Information Independent, 4-year, coed college. Urban setting. *Awards:* B. *Entrance level for U.S. students:* Most difficult. *Enrollment:* 1,260 total (51% women). *Undergraduate faculty:* 784. *Library holdings:* 5.6 million books, 59,400 current serial subscriptions. *Total majors:* 45.

Information for International Students For fall 2006: 155 international students applied, 61 were accepted, 29 enrolled. Students can start in fall or spring. Transfers accepted from institutions abroad. *Admission tests:* Required: TOEFL (minimum score: iBT 100; paper-based 600; computer-based 250). Recommended: SAT. *Application deadline:* 4/1. *Expenses:* (2006–07) $33,906; room and board, $8913 (on campus); room only, $5723 (on campus). *Financial aid:* Non-need-based college/university scholarships/grants from institutional funds, loans from outside sources, on-campus employment. Forms required: institution's own financial aid form. For fall 2006 (estimated), 93 international students on campus received college administered financial aid ($7868 average). *Housing:* Available during summer. *Services:* International student adviser on campus. Full-time and part-time ESL programs on campus. ESL program available during the academic year. Internships and employment opportunities (on-campus and off-campus) available. *Contact:* Dean of Admissions, Columbia University, School of General Studies, 408 Lewisohn Hall, MC 4101, 2970 Broadway, New York, NY 10027. Telephone: 212-854-2772. Fax: 212-854-6316. E-mail: gsadmit@columbia.edu. URL: http://www.gs.columbia.edu.

See In-Depth Description on page 63.

COLUMBIA UNIVERSITY, THE FU FOUNDATION SCHOOL OF ENGINEERING AND APPLIED SCIENCE, NEW YORK

General Information Independent, coed university. Urban setting. *Awards:* B, M, D. *Entrance level for U.S. students:* Most difficult. *Enrollment:* 1,409 total (29% women) including 13% international students from 59 foreign countries. *Faculty:* 137. *Library holdings:* 7.2 million books, 66,000 current serial subscriptions. *Total majors:* 15. *Expenses:* (2006–07) $35,164; room and board, $9648 (on campus); room only, $5640 (on campus). *Financial aid:* Need-based college/university scholarships/grants from institutional funds. Forms required: institution's own financial aid form, International Student's Financial Aid Application. 64 international students on campus received college administered financial aid ($24,070 average).

CONCORDIA COLLEGE, BRONXVILLE

General Information Independent Lutheran, 4-year, coed college. Suburban setting. *Awards:* A, B. *Entrance level for U.S. students:* Moderately difficult. *Enrollment:* 646 total (60% women) including international students from 35 foreign countries. *Undergraduate faculty:* 77. *Library holdings:* 71,500 books, 467 current serial subscriptions. *Total majors:* 23.

Information for International Students For fall 2006: 128 international students applied, 59 were accepted, 30 enrolled. Students can start in fall, spring, or summer. Transfers accepted from institutions abroad. *Admission tests:* Required: SAT, TOEFL (minimum score: iBT 80; paper-based 550; computer-based 213; minimum score for ESL admission: iBT 80; paper-based 550; computer-based 213). Recommended: ACT. TOEFL can be waived under certain conditions. *Application deadline:* Rolling. *Expenses:* (2006–07) $21,600; room and board, $8230 (on campus); room only, $4600 (on campus). *Financial aid:* Non-need financial aid available. Forms required: institution's own financial aid form, International Student's Certification of Finances. International transfer students are eligible to apply for aid. *Housing:* Guaranteed, also available during summer. *Services:* International student adviser on campus. Full-time and part-time ESL programs on campus. ESL program available during the academic year and the summer. Internships and employment opportunities (on-campus) available. *Contact:* Assistant Director of Admissions, Concordia College, 171 White Plains Road, Bronxville, NY 10708. Telephone: 914-337-9300 Ext. 2152. Fax: 914-395-4500. E-mail: admission@concordia-ny.edu. URL: http://www.concordia-ny.edu.

COOPER UNION FOR THE ADVANCEMENT OF SCIENCE AND ART, NEW YORK

General Information Independent, coed institution. Urban setting. *Awards:* B (also offers master's program primarily made up of currently-enrolled students). *Entrance level for U.S. students:* Most difficult. *Enrollment:* 968 total; 920 undergraduates (38% women) including 10% international students. *Undergraduate faculty:* 211. *Library holdings:* 103,289 books, 4,254 current serial subscriptions, 1,247 audiovisual materials. *Total majors:* 8.

Information for International Students For fall 2006: 21 international students enrolled. Students can start in fall. Transfers accepted from institutions abroad. *Admission tests:* Required: SAT or ACT, SAT Subject Tests, TOEFL (minimum score: iBT 100; paper-based 600; computer-based 250), home test and portfolio required for art and architecture applicants. TOEFL can be waived under certain conditions. *Application deadline:* 1/1. *Expenses:* (2007–08) room and board, $13,500 (on campus); room only, $9500 (on campus). *Financial aid:* Need-based financial aid available. Non-need-based college/university scholarships/grants from institutional funds. Forms required: CSS PROFILE, International Student's Certification of Finances. International transfer students are eligible to apply for aid. For fall 2005, 100 international students on campus received college administered financial aid ($27,500 average). *Services:* International student adviser on campus. Internships and employment opportunities (on-campus and off-campus) available. *Contact:* Associate Director of Admissions, Cooper Union for the Advancement of Science and Art, 30 Cooper Square, Office of Admissions and Records, New York, NY 10003. Telephone: 212-353-4120. Fax: 212-353-4342. E-mail: falls@cooper.edu. URL: http://www.cooper.edu.

CORNELL UNIVERSITY, ITHACA

General Information Independent, coed university. Small town setting. *Awards:* B, M, D, FP. *Entrance level for U.S. students:* Most difficult. *Enrollment:* 19,639 total; 13,562 undergraduates (49% women) including 8% international students from 109 foreign countries. *Faculty:* 1,869. *Library holdings:* 7.2 million books, 64,760 current serial subscriptions, 427,798 audiovisual materials. *Total majors:* 156. *Expenses:* (2006–07) $32,981; room and board, $10,776 (on campus); room only, $6390 (on campus). *Financial aid:* Need-based financial aid available. Forms required: institution's own financial aid form, International Student's Certification of Finances, alien registration card. For fall 2006 (estimated), 241 international students on campus received college administered financial aid ($21,715 average).

CORNING COMMUNITY COLLEGE, CORNING

General Information State and locally supported, 2-year, coed college. Rural setting. *Awards:* A. *Entrance level for U.S. students:* Noncompetitive. *Enrollment:* 5,310 total (57% women) including 0.1% international students. *Undergraduate faculty:* 258. *Library holdings:* 71,233 books, 2,500 current serial subscriptions, 4,290 audiovisual materials. *Total majors:* 44. *Expenses:* (2006–07) $6200.

DAEMEN COLLEGE, AMHERST

General Information Independent, coed institution. Suburban setting. *Awards:* B, M, FP. *Entrance level for U.S. students:* Moderately difficult. *Enrollment:* 2,414 total; 1,648 undergraduates (76% women) including 0.3% international students from 4 foreign countries. *Faculty:* 269. *Library holdings:* 127,232 books, 889 current serial subscriptions, 10,584 audiovisual materials. *Total majors:* 32.

Information for International Students For fall 2006: 28 international students applied, 15 were accepted, 1 enrolled. Students can start in fall or spring. Transfers accepted from institutions abroad. *Admission tests:* Recommended: SAT or ACT, SAT Subject Tests, TOEFL (minimum score: paper-based 500; computer-based 173), ELS. TOEFL can be waived under certain conditions. *Application deadline:* Rolling. *Expenses:* (2006–07) $17,690; room and board, $8190 (on campus). *Financial aid:* Non-need-based athletic awards, loans from outside sources. Forms required: International Student's Certification of Finances. International transfer students are eligible to apply for aid. For fall 2005, 4 international students on campus received college administered financial aid ($14,173 average). *Housing:* Available during summer. *Services:* International student adviser on campus. Part-time ESL program on campus. Internships and employment opportunities (on-campus and off-campus) available. *Contact:* Associate Director of Admissions, Daemen College, 4380 Main Street, Amherst, NY 14226. Telephone: 716-839-8225. Fax: 716-839-8229. E-mail: kshallow@daemen.edu. URL: http://www.daemen.edu.

DEVRY INSTITUTE OF TECHNOLOGY, LONG ISLAND CITY

General Information Proprietary, 4-year, coed college. Urban setting. *Awards:* A, B, M. *Entrance level for U.S. students:*

DeVry Institute of Technology (continued)
Minimally difficult. *Enrollment:* 1,254 total; 1,128 undergraduates (26% women) including 1% international students. *Faculty:* 110. *Library holdings:* 14,078 books, 62 current serial subscriptions. *Total majors:* 8. *Expenses:* (2007–08) $14,640.

DOWLING COLLEGE, OAKDALE
General Information Independent, coed institution. Suburban setting. *Awards:* B, M, D. *Entrance level for U.S. students:* Moderately difficult. *Enrollment:* 5,546 total; 3,052 undergraduates (60% women) including 5% international students from 53 foreign countries. *Faculty:* 407. *Library holdings:* 119,360 books, 3,131 current serial subscriptions. *Total majors:* 52. *Expenses:* (2006–07) $18,430; room and board, $8988 (on campus). *Financial aid:* Need-based college/university scholarships/grants from institutional funds, tuition waivers, athletic awards, loans from outside sources, on-campus employment, off-campus employment. Non-need-based college/university scholarships/grants from institutional funds, tuition waivers, athletic awards, loans from outside sources, on-campus employment. Forms required: institution's own financial aid form, International Student's Financial Aid Application, International Student's Certification of Finances. For fall 2006 (estimated), 104 international students on campus received college administered financial aid ($11,677 average).

D'YOUVILLE COLLEGE, BUFFALO
General Information Independent, coed institution. Urban setting. *Awards:* B, M, D, FP. *Entrance level for U.S. students:* Moderately difficult. *Enrollment:* 3,024 total; 1,620 undergraduates (75% women) including 11% international students from 34 foreign countries. *Library holdings:* 122,057 books, 665 current serial subscriptions. *Total majors:* 33.
Information for International Students For fall 2006: 168 international students applied, 79 were accepted, 49 enrolled. Students can start in fall, spring, or summer. Transfers accepted from institutions abroad. *Admission tests:* Required: SAT or ACT, TOEFL (minimum score: iBT 61; paper-based 500; computer-based 173). Recommended: SAT, ACT. TOEFL can be waived under certain conditions. *Application deadline:* Rolling. *Expenses:* (2006–07) $17,000; room and board, $8300 (on campus); room only, $6800 (on campus). *Financial aid:* Need-based loans from outside sources. Non-need-based college/university scholarships/grants from institutional funds, loans from outside sources. International transfer students are eligible to apply for aid. *Housing:* Guaranteed, also available during summer. *Services:* International student adviser on campus. ESL program at cooperating institution. ESL program available during the academic year and the summer. Internships and employment opportunities (on-campus) available. *Contact:* Director of Admissions and Financial Aid, D'Youville College, 320 Porter Avenue, Buffalo, NY 14201. Telephone: 716-829-7600. Fax: 716-829-7900. E-mail: admiss@dyc.edu. URL: http://www.dyc.edu.

ELMIRA COLLEGE, ELMIRA
General Information Independent, 4-year, coed college. Small town setting. *Awards:* B, M. *Entrance level for U.S. students:* Moderately difficult. *Enrollment:* 1,853 total; 1,484 undergraduates (71% women) including 4% international students from 23 foreign countries. *Faculty:* 99. *Library holdings:* 391,038 books, 859 current serial subscriptions, 4,428 audiovisual materials. *Total majors:* 67.
Information for International Students For fall 2006: 251 international students applied, 42 were accepted, 15 enrolled. Students can start in fall, winter, or summer. Transfers accepted from institutions abroad. *Admission tests:* Required: TOEFL (minimum score: iBT 61; paper-based 500; computer-based 173; minimum score for ESL admission: paper-based 450; computer-based 133). TOEFL can be waived under certain conditions. *Application deadline:* 4/1. *Expenses:* (2006–07) $30,050; room and board, $9100 (on campus). *Financial aid:* Need-based college/university scholarships/grants from institutional funds, loans from outside sources. Non-need-based college/university scholarships/grants from institutional funds, loans from outside sources, on-campus employment. Forms required: International Student's Financial Aid Application, International Student's Certification of Finances. International transfer students are eligible to apply for aid. For fall 2006 (estimated), 80 international students on campus received college administered financial aid ($21,851 average). *Housing:* Guaranteed, also available during summer. *Services:* International student adviser on campus. Full-time ESL program on campus. ESL program available during the academic year and the summer. Internships and employment opportunities (on-campus) available. *Contact:* Dean of Admissions, Elmira College, One Park Place, Elmira, NY 14901. Telephone: 607-735-1724. Fax: 607-735-1718. E-mail: admissions@elmira.edu. URL: http://www.elmira.edu.
See In-Depth Description on page 77.

ERIE COMMUNITY COLLEGE, BUFFALO
General Information State and locally supported, 2-year, coed college. Urban setting. *Awards:* A. *Entrance level for U.S. students:* Noncompetitive. *Enrollment:* 2,993 total (62% women) including 0.2% international students from 3 foreign countries. *Undergraduate faculty:* 318. *Library holdings:* 25,350 books, 168 current serial subscriptions, 1,800 audiovisual materials. *Total majors:* 19. *Expenses:* (2006–07) $6294.

ERIE COMMUNITY COLLEGE, NORTH CAMPUS, WILLIAMSVILLE
General Information State and locally supported, 2-year, coed college. Suburban setting. *Awards:* A. *Entrance level for U.S. students:* Noncompetitive. *Enrollment:* 5,859 total (50% women) including 1% international students from 20 foreign countries. *Undergraduate faculty:* 505. *Library holdings:* 52,961 books, 311 current serial subscriptions, 5,315 audiovisual materials. *Total majors:* 26. *Expenses:* (2006–07) $6294.

ERIE COMMUNITY COLLEGE, SOUTH CAMPUS, ORCHARD PARK
General Information State and locally supported, 2-year, coed college. Suburban setting. *Awards:* A. *Entrance level for U.S. students:* Noncompetitive. *Enrollment:* 4,160 total (44% women) including 0.2% international students from 4 foreign countries. *Undergraduate faculty:* 486. *Library holdings:* 63,844 books, 204 current serial subscriptions, 1,578 audiovisual materials. *Total majors:* 20. *Expenses:* (2006–07) $6294.

EXCELSIOR COLLEGE, ALBANY
General Information Independent, coed institution. Urban setting. *Awards:* A, B, M (offers only external degree programs). *Entrance level for U.S. students:* Noncompetitive. *Enrollment:* 30,680 total; 29,989 undergraduates (54% women) including 2% international students from 51 foreign countries. *Faculty:* 232. *Total majors:* 42.

FASHION INSTITUTE OF TECHNOLOGY, NEW YORK
General Information State and locally supported, coed, primarily women's institution. Urban setting. *Awards:* A, B, M. *Entrance level for U.S. students:* Moderately difficult. *Enrollment:* 10,010 total; 9,825 undergraduates (85% women) including 11% international students from 61 foreign countries. *Faculty:* 908. *Library holdings:* 240,712 books, 3,378 current serial subscriptions, 134,534 audiovisual materials. *Total majors:* 21. *Expenses:* (2007–08) $11,030; room and board, $11,213 (on campus); room only, $7823 (on campus).

FIORELLO H. LAGUARDIA COMMUNITY COLLEGE OF THE CITY UNIVERSITY OF NEW YORK, LONG ISLAND CITY
General Information State and locally supported, 2-year, coed college. Urban setting. *Awards:* A. *Entrance level for U.S. students:* Noncompetitive. *Enrollment:* 13,489 total (64% women) including 16% international students from 135 foreign countries. *Undergraduate faculty:* 773. *Library holdings:* 121,631 books, 760 current serial subscriptions, 5,529 audiovisual materials. *Total majors:* 33. *Expenses:* (2006–07) $4706.

FIVE TOWNS COLLEGE, DIX HILLS
General Information Independent, coed institution. Suburban setting. *Awards:* A, B, M, D. *Entrance level for U.S. students:* Moderately difficult. *Enrollment:* 1,254 total; 1,195 undergraduates (39% women) including international students from 4 foreign countries. *Faculty:* 128. *Library holdings:* 40,000 books, 565 current serial subscriptions. *Total majors:* 19.
Information for International Students For fall 2006: 8 international students applied, 8 were accepted, 8 enrolled. Students can start in fall or spring. Transfers accepted from institutions abroad. *Admission tests:* Required: TOEFL (minimum score: iBT 80; paper-based 550; computer-based 213). Recommended: SAT or ACT, ELS. TOEFL can be waived under certain conditions. *Application deadline:* Rolling. *Expenses:* (2007–08) $17,085; room and board, $16,800 (on campus). *Financial aid:* Need-based loans from outside sources. Non-need-based loans from outside sources. *Housing:* Available during summer. *Services:* International student adviser on campus. ESL program at cooperating institution. ESL program available during the academic year. Internships available. *Contact:* International Student Advisor, Five Towns College, 305 North Service Road, Dix Hills, NY 11746-5871. Telephone: 631-424-7000 Ext. 2131. Fax: 631-656-2172. E-mail: mmaltz@ftc.edu. URL: http://www.fivetowns.edu.

FORDHAM UNIVERSITY, NEW YORK

General Information Independent Roman Catholic (Jesuit), coed university. Urban setting. *Awards:* B, M, D, FP (branch locations at Rose Hill and Lincoln Center). *Entrance level for U.S. students:* Very difficult. *Enrollment:* 14,732 total; 7,701 undergraduates (58% women) including 2% international students from 48 foreign countries. *Library holdings:* 2.4 million books, 32,300 current serial subscriptions, 32,621 audiovisual materials. *Total majors:* 94.

Information for International Students Students can start in fall or spring. Transfers accepted from institutions abroad. *Admission tests:* Required: TOEFL (minimum score: iBT 90; paper-based 575; computer-based 231; minimum score for ESL admission: iBT 80; paper-based 550; computer-based 210). Recommended: SAT or ACT. *Application deadline:* 1/15. *Expenses:* (2006–07) $30,655; room and board, $11,630 (on campus); room only, $7260 (on campus). *Financial aid:* Non-need-based college/university scholarships/grants from institutional funds, athletic awards. Forms required: International Student's Financial Aid Application, International Student's Certification of Finances. 30 international students on campus received college administered financial aid ($18,526 average). *Services:* International student adviser on campus. Full-time and part-time ESL programs on campus. ESL program available during the academic year and the summer. Internships available. *Contact:* Associate Director for International Admission, Fordham University, 441 East Fordham Road, Bronx, NY 10458. Telephone: 718-817-5204. Fax: 718-817-2424. E-mail: esser@fordham.edu. URL: http://www.fordham.edu.

See In-Depth Description on page 87.

FULTON-MONTGOMERY COMMUNITY COLLEGE, JOHNSTOWN

General Information State and locally supported, 2-year, coed college. Rural setting. *Awards:* A. *Entrance level for U.S. students:* Noncompetitive. *Enrollment:* 2,157 total (58% women) including 6% international students from 18 foreign countries. *Undergraduate faculty:* 98. *Library holdings:* 51,642 books, 139 current serial subscriptions, 1,536 audiovisual materials. *Total majors:* 44.

Information for International Students For fall 2006: 200 international students applied, 171 were accepted, 63 enrolled. Students can start in fall, spring, or summer. Transfers accepted from institutions abroad. *Admission tests:* Recommended: TOEFL (minimum score: iBT 61; paper-based 500; computer-based 173). TOEFL can be waived under certain conditions. *Application deadline:* Rolling. *Expenses:* (2006–07) $6240. *Housing:* Guaranteed, also available during summer. *Services:* International student adviser on campus. Full-time ESL program on campus. ESL program available during the academic year and the summer. Internships and employment opportunities (on-campus) available. *Contact:* Director of International Student Programs, Fulton-Montgomery Community College, 2805 State Highway 67, Johnstown, NY 12095. Telephone: 518-762-4651 Ext. 4750. Fax: 518-762-7835. E-mail: intl@fmcc.suny.edu. URL: http://www.fmcc.suny.edu.

GENESEE COMMUNITY COLLEGE, BATAVIA

General Information State and locally supported, 2-year, coed college. Small town setting. *Awards:* A. *Entrance level for U.S. students:* Noncompetitive. *Enrollment:* 6,490 total (65% women) including 3% international students from 26 foreign countries. *Undergraduate faculty:* 312. *Library holdings:* 78,273 books, 332 current serial subscriptions, 4,729 audiovisual materials. *Total majors:* 37.

Information for International Students For fall 2006: 92 international students applied, 77 were accepted, 67 enrolled. Students can start in fall, spring, or summer. Transfers accepted from institutions abroad. *Admission tests:* TOEFL can be waived under certain conditions. *Application deadline:* Rolling. *Expenses:* (2006–07) $3890; room only, $4250 (on campus). *Financial aid:* Need-based college/university scholarships/grants from institutional funds, on-campus employment. Non-need-based college/university scholarships/grants from institutional funds, tuition waivers, athletic awards, on-campus employment. *Housing:* Available during summer. *Services:* International student adviser on campus. ESL program at cooperating institution. ESL program available during the academic year and the summer. Internships and employment opportunities (on-campus) available. *Contact:* International Admission Advisor, Genesee Community College, One College Road, Admissions Office, Batavia, NY 14020. Telephone: 585-345-6800. Fax: 585-345-6842. E-mail: mapentz@genesee.edu. URL: http://www.genesee.edu.

See In-Depth Description on page 89.

GLOBE INSTITUTE OF TECHNOLOGY, NEW YORK

General Information Proprietary, 4-year, coed college. Urban setting. *Awards:* A, B. *Entrance level for U.S. students:* Minimally

difficult. *Enrollment:* 1,671 total (64% women) including 0.4% international students. *Undergraduate faculty:* 113. *Library holdings:* 20,000 books, 1,237 current serial subscriptions. *Total majors:* 11.

Information for International Students For fall 2006: 150 international students applied, 150 were accepted, 100 enrolled. Students can start in fall, winter, spring, or summer. Transfers accepted from institutions abroad. *Application deadline:* 9/15. *Expenses:* (2006–07) $9086; room only, $3600 (on campus). *Housing:* Guaranteed, also available during summer. *Services:* International student adviser on campus. Full-time and part-time ESL programs on campus. ESL program available during the academic year and the summer. Internships and employment opportunities (on-campus and off-campus) available. *Contact:* Admissions Director, Globe Institute of Technology, 291 Broadway, New York, NY 10007. Telephone: 212-349-4330 Ext. 1624. Fax: 212-227-5920. E-mail: admissions@globe.edu. URL: http://www.globe.edu.

HAMILTON COLLEGE, CLINTON

General Information Independent, 4-year, coed college. Small town setting. *Awards:* B. *Entrance level for U.S. students:* Very difficult. *Enrollment:* 1,821 total (50% women) including 5% international students from 46 foreign countries. *Undergraduate faculty:* 213. *Library holdings:* 538,377 books, 3,585 current serial subscriptions. *Total majors:* 46.

Information for International Students For fall 2006: 643 international students applied, 72 were accepted, 31 enrolled. Students can start in fall. Transfers accepted from institutions abroad. *Admission tests:* Recommended: SAT or ACT, SAT Subject Tests, TOEFL (minimum score: iBT 95; paper-based 600; computer-based 250). TOEFL can be waived under certain conditions. *Application deadline:* 1/1. *Expenses:* (2006–07) $34,980; room and board, $8910 (on campus); room only, $4860 (on campus). *Financial aid:* Need-based and non-need-based financial aid available. Forms required: International Student's Financial Aid Application, International Student's Certification of Finances. For fall 2006 (estimated), 91 international students on campus received college administered financial aid ($33,486 average). *Housing:* Guaranteed, also available during summer. *Services:* International student adviser on campus. Full-time ESL program on campus. ESL program available during the academic year. Internships and employment opportunities (on-campus) available. *Contact:* Director of International Admission, Office of Admission, Hamilton College, 198 College Hill Road, Clinton, NY 13323. Telephone: 315-859-4421. Fax: 315-859-4457. E-mail: admissio@hamilton.edu. URL: http://www.hamilton.edu.

HARTWICK COLLEGE, ONEONTA

General Information Independent, 4-year, coed college. Small town setting. *Awards:* B. *Entrance level for U.S. students:* Moderately difficult. *Enrollment:* 1,519 total (57% women) including 3% international students from 34 foreign countries. *Undergraduate faculty:* 169. *Library holdings:* 311,063 books, 720 current serial subscriptions, 3,574 audiovisual materials. *Total majors:* 33.

Information for International Students For fall 2006: 161 international students applied, 35 were accepted, 3 enrolled. Students can start in fall, winter, or spring. Transfers accepted from institutions abroad. *Application deadline:* 2/15. *Expenses:* (2006–07) $28,030; room and board, $7910 (on campus); room only, $4080 (on campus). *Financial aid:* Need-based and non-need-based financial aid available. Forms required: institution's own financial aid form, International Student's Financial Aid Application, International Student's Certification of Finances. International transfer students are eligible to apply for aid. 49 international students on campus received college administered financial aid ($19,856 average). *Housing:* Guaranteed, also available during summer. *Services:* International student adviser on campus. Internships and employment opportunities (on-campus) available. *Contact:* Senior Associate Director of Admissions, Hartwick College, 1 Hartwick Drive, Oneonta, NY 13820. Telephone: 607-431-4150. Fax: 607-431-4154. E-mail: cabrerar@hartwick.edu. URL: http://www.hartwick.edu.

HILBERT COLLEGE, HAMBURG

General Information Independent, 4-year, coed college. Small town setting. *Awards:* A, B. *Entrance level for U.S. students:* Minimally difficult. *Enrollment:* 1,064 total (63% women) including 0.1% international students from 1 foreign country. *Undergraduate faculty:* 119. *Library holdings:* 41,322 books, 12,300 current serial subscriptions, 1,066 audiovisual materials. *Total majors:* 13.

Information for International Students For fall 2006: 5 international students applied, 5 were accepted. Students can start in fall, spring, or summer. Transfers accepted from institutions abroad. *Admission tests:* Required: TOEFL. *Application deadline:* Rolling. *Expenses:* (2006–07) $15,700; room and board, $5900 (on campus); room only, $2600 (on campus). *Financial aid:*

Hilbert College (continued)

Non-need-based college/university scholarships/grants from institutional funds. Forms required: institution's own financial aid form. For fall 2006 (estimated), 1 international student on campus received college administered financial aid ($3400 average). *Housing:* Guaranteed. *Contact:* Director of Admissions, Hilbert College, 5200 South Park Avenue, Hamburg, NY 14075. Telephone: 716-649-7900 Ext. 244. Fax: 716-649-0702. E-mail: tlee@hilbert.edu. URL: http://www.hilbert.edu.

HOFSTRA UNIVERSITY, HEMPSTEAD

General Information Independent, coed university. Suburban setting. *Awards:* B, M, D, FP. *Entrance level for U.S. students:* Moderately difficult. *Enrollment:* 12,550 total; 8,498 undergraduates (53% women) including 2% international students from 47 foreign countries. *Faculty:* 1,206. *Library holdings:* 1.2 million books, 9,950 current serial subscriptions, 14,730 audiovisual materials. *Total majors:* 129.

Information for International Students For fall 2006: 315 international students applied, 186 were accepted, 28 enrolled. Students can start in fall or spring. Transfers accepted from institutions abroad. *Admission tests:* Required: TOEFL (minimum score: paper-based 550; computer-based 213; minimum score for ESL admission: paper-based 550; computer-based 213). *Application deadline:* Rolling. *Expenses:* (2006–07) $24,830; room and board, $9800 (on campus); room only, $6500 (on campus). *Financial aid:* Non-need-based college/university scholarships/grants from institutional funds, tuition waivers, athletic awards, loans from outside sources, on-campus employment. Forms required: International Student's Certification of Finances. International transfer students are eligible to apply for aid. For fall 2005, 55 international students on campus received college administered financial aid ($20,485 average). *Housing:* Available during summer. *Services:* International student adviser on campus. Part-time ESL program on campus. ESL program available during the academic year. Internships and employment opportunities (on-campus) available. *Contact:* Dean of Admission and Financial Aid, International Students Office, Hofstra University, 100 Hofstra University, Hempstead, NY 11549-1000. Telephone: 516-463-6700. Fax: 516-463-5100. URL: http://www.hofstra.edu.

See In-Depth Description on page 99.

HOLY TRINITY ORTHODOX SEMINARY, JORDANVILLE

General Information Independent Russian Orthodox, 5-year, men's college. Rural setting. *Awards:* B. *Entrance level for U.S. students:* Noncompetitive. *Enrollment:* 28 total including 64% international students from 11 foreign countries. *Undergraduate faculty:* 15. *Library holdings:* 25,000 books, 200 current serial subscriptions. *Total majors:* 1. *Expenses:* (2006–07) $3025; room and board, $2500 (on campus).

HOUGHTON COLLEGE, HOUGHTON

General Information Independent Wesleyan, coed institution. Rural setting. *Awards:* A, B, M. *Entrance level for U.S. students:* Moderately difficult. *Enrollment:* 1,432 total; 1,418 undergraduates (65% women) including 3% international students from 13 foreign countries. *Faculty:* 126. *Library holdings:* 265,000 books, 11,000 current serial subscriptions, 7,500 audiovisual materials. *Total majors:* 52. *Expenses:* (2006–07) $20,400; room and board, $6680 (on campus); room only, $3500 (on campus). *Financial aid:* Need-based college/university scholarships/grants from institutional funds, athletic awards, loans from outside sources, on-campus employment. Non-need-based college/university scholarships/grants from institutional funds, athletic awards, loans from outside sources, on-campus employment. Forms required: International Student's Certification of Finances. For fall 2006 (estimated), 49 international students on campus received college administered financial aid ($10,621 average).

HUDSON VALLEY COMMUNITY COLLEGE, TROY

General Information State and locally supported, 2-year, coed college. Suburban setting. *Awards:* A. *Entrance level for U.S. students:* Minimally difficult. *Enrollment:* 12,205 total including 1% international students from 18 foreign countries. *Undergraduate faculty:* 574. *Library holdings:* 148,189 books, 691 current serial subscriptions. *Total majors:* 41.

Information for International Students Students can start in fall or spring. Transfers accepted from institutions abroad. *Admission tests:* Required: TOEFL (minimum score: iBT 61; paper-based 500; computer-based 173). TOEFL can be waived under certain conditions. *Application deadline:* Rolling. *Expenses:* (2006–07) $8580. *Services:* International student adviser on campus. ESL program at cooperating institution. ESL program available during the academic year and the summer. Internships and employment opportunities (on-campus and off-campus)

available. *Contact:* Coordinator for International Student Services, Hudson Valley Community College, 80 Vandenburgh Avenue, Troy, NY 12180-6096. Telephone: 518-629-7567. Fax: 518-629-7496. E-mail: deitcjay@hvcc.edu. URL: http://www.hvcc.edu.

HUNTER COLLEGE OF THE CITY UNIVERSITY OF NEW YORK, NEW YORK

General Information State and locally supported, coed institution. Urban setting. *Awards:* B, M. *Entrance level for U.S. students:* Moderately difficult. *Enrollment:* 20,899 total; 15,805 undergraduates (68% women) including 10% international students from 150 foreign countries. *Faculty:* 1,497. *Library holdings:* 789,718 books, 4,282 current serial subscriptions. *Total majors:* 65. *Expenses:* (2006–07) $11,149; room only, $5083 (on campus).

IONA COLLEGE, NEW ROCHELLE

General Information Independent, coed institution, affiliated with Roman Catholic Church. Suburban setting. *Awards:* B, M. *Entrance level for U.S. students:* Moderately difficult. *Enrollment:* 4,242 total; 3,451 undergraduates (55% women) including 2% international students from 43 foreign countries. *Faculty:* 382. *Library holdings:* 281,876 books, 752 current serial subscriptions, 3,379 audiovisual materials. *Total majors:* 58. *Expenses:* (2006–07) $23,218; room and board, $9998 (on campus). *Financial aid:* Need-based athletic awards. Non-need-based college/university scholarships/grants from institutional funds, athletic awards. Forms required: institution's own financial aid form. For fall 2006 (estimated), 65 international students on campus received college administered financial aid ($14,412 average).

ITHACA COLLEGE, ITHACA

General Information Independent, coed institution. Small town setting. *Awards:* B, M, D. *Entrance level for U.S. students:* Moderately difficult. *Enrollment:* 6,409 total; 6,028 undergraduates (55% women) including 2% international students from 60 foreign countries. *Faculty:* 670. *Library holdings:* 363,648 books, 44,327 current serial subscriptions, 29,734 audiovisual materials. *Total majors:* 105. *Expenses:* (2006–07) $26,832; room and board, $10,314 (on campus); room only, $5388 (on campus). *Financial aid:* Need-based college/university scholarships/grants from institutional funds, loans from outside sources. Non-need-based college/university scholarships/grants from institutional funds, loans from outside sources. Forms required: International Student's Financial Aid Application, International Student's Certification of Finances. For fall 2006 (estimated), 127 international students on campus received college administered financial aid ($20,434 average).

JEFFERSON COMMUNITY COLLEGE, WATERTOWN

General Information State and locally supported, 2-year, coed college. Small town setting. *Awards:* A. *Entrance level for U.S. students:* Minimally difficult. *Enrollment:* 3,545 total (59% women) including 0.2% international students from 3 foreign countries. *Undergraduate faculty:* 212. *Library holdings:* 68,664 books, 233 current serial subscriptions, 4,756 audiovisual materials. *Total majors:* 20. *Expenses:* (2006–07) $5950. *Financial aid:* Forms required: institution's own financial aid form.

JOHN JAY COLLEGE OF CRIMINAL JUSTICE OF THE CITY UNIVERSITY OF NEW YORK, NEW YORK

General Information State and locally supported, coed institution. Urban setting. *Awards:* A, B, M, D. *Entrance level for U.S. students:* Moderately difficult. *Enrollment:* 12,984 total; 11,515 undergraduates. *Faculty:* 913. *Library holdings:* 310,000 books, 1,325 current serial subscriptions. *Total majors:* 15.

Information for International Students For fall 2006: 31 international students were accepted, 25 enrolled. Students can start in fall or spring. Transfers accepted from institutions abroad. *Admission tests:* Required: TOEFL (minimum score: paper-based 500; computer-based 173; minimum score for ESL admission: paper-based 500; computer-based 173). *Application deadline:* 3/15. *Financial aid:* Need-based college/university scholarships/grants from institutional funds, loans from outside sources. *Services:* International student adviser on campus. Full-time and part-time ESL programs on campus. ESL program available during the academic year. Internships and employment opportunities (on-campus) available. *Contact:* Associate Director of Admissions, John Jay College of Criminal Justice of the City University of New York, 445 West 59 Street, Room 4205, New York, NY 10019-1013. Telephone: 212-237-8897. Fax: 212-237-8777. E-mail: sylopez@jjay.cuny.edu. URL: http://www.jjay.cuny.edu.

THE JUILLIARD SCHOOL, NEW YORK

General Information Independent, coed institution. Urban setting. *Awards:* B, M, D. *Entrance level for U.S. students:* Most difficult. *Enrollment:* 808 total; 481 undergraduates (48% women) including 20% international students from 29 foreign countries. *Faculty:* 266. *Library holdings:* 80,793 books, 220 current serial subscriptions, 21,867 audiovisual materials. *Total majors:* 4. **Information for International Students** For fall 2006: 933 international students applied, 110 were accepted, 87 enrolled. Students can start in fall. Transfers accepted from institutions abroad. *Admission tests:* Required: TOEFL (minimum score: paper-based 550; computer-based 213; minimum score for ESL admission: paper-based 550; computer-based 213). *Application deadline:* 12/1. *Expenses:* (2006–07) $25,610; room and board, $10,095 (on campus). *Financial aid:* Need-based and non-need-based financial aid available. Forms required: institution's own financial aid form, salary documentation. International transfer students are eligible to apply for aid. international students on campus received college administered aid averaging $17,456. *Services:* International student adviser on campus. Full-time and part-time ESL programs on campus. ESL program available during the academic year. Employment opportunities (on-campus) available. *Contact:* Director of Admissions, The Juilliard School, Admissions, 60 Lincoln Center Plaza, New York, NY 10023-6590. Telephone: 212-799-5000 Ext. 223. Fax: 212-724-0263. E-mail: admissions@juilliard.edu. URL: http://www.juilliard.edu.

KEUKA COLLEGE, KEUKA PARK

General Information Independent, coed institution, affiliated with American Baptist Churches in the U.S.A.Rural setting. *Awards:* B, M. *Entrance level for U.S. students:* Moderately difficult. *Enrollment:* 1,521 total; 1,373 undergraduates (70% women) including 0.3% international students from 4 foreign countries. *Faculty:* 91. *Library holdings:* 112,541 books, 384 current serial subscriptions, 3,551 audiovisual materials. *Total majors:* 34. *Expenses:* (2006–07) $19,120; room and board, $8210 (on campus); room only, $3900 (on campus). *Financial aid:* Need-based and non-need-based financial aid available. Forms required: institution's own financial aid form. For fall 2006 (estimated), 4 international students on campus received college administered financial aid ($12,375 average).

KINGSBOROUGH COMMUNITY COLLEGE OF THE CITY UNIVERSITY OF NEW YORK, BROOKLYN

General Information State and locally supported, 2-year, coed college. Urban setting. *Awards:* A. *Entrance level for U.S. students:* Noncompetitive. *Enrollment:* 14,687 total (58% women) including 11% international students. *Undergraduate faculty:* 799. *Library holdings:* 185,912 books, 458 current serial subscriptions. *Total majors:* 38. *Expenses:* (2006–07) $4880. *Financial aid:* Forms required: International Student's Certification of Finances.

THE KING'S COLLEGE, NEW YORK

General Information Independent religious, 4-year, coed college. Urban setting. *Awards:* B. *Entrance level for U.S. students:* Very difficult. *Enrollment:* 246 total (64% women) including 7% international students from 19 foreign countries. *Undergraduate faculty:* 24. *Library holdings:* 12,000 books, 75 current serial subscriptions, 2 audiovisual materials. *Total majors:* 5. **Information for International Students** For fall 2006: 16 international students applied, 12 were accepted, 4 enrolled. Students can start in fall or spring. Transfers accepted from institutions abroad. *Admission tests:* Required: TOEFL (minimum score: iBT 92; paper-based 580; computer-based 237). Recommended: SAT or ACT. TOEFL can be waived under certain conditions. *Application deadline:* 2/1. *Expenses:* (2007–08) $20,790; room only, $8400 (on campus). *Financial aid:* International transfer students are eligible to apply for aid. *Housing:* Available during summer. *Services:* International student adviser on campus. ESL program at cooperating institution. ESL program available during the academic year and the summer. Internships and employment opportunities (on-campus) available. *Contact:* Assistant Director of Admissions, The King's College, 350 Fifth Avenue, 15th Floor, New York, NY 10118. Telephone: 212-659-7200. Fax: 212-659-3611. E-mail: info@tkc.edu. URL: http://www.tkc.edu.

LABORATORY INSTITUTE OF MERCHANDISING, NEW YORK

General Information Proprietary, 4-year, coed, primarily women's college. Urban setting. *Awards:* A, B. *Entrance level for U.S. students:* Moderately difficult. *Enrollment:* 970 total (95% women) including 1% international students from 11 foreign countries. *Undergraduate faculty:* 119. *Library holdings:* 10,300 books, 100 current serial subscriptions. *Total majors:* 2. *Expenses:* (2006–07) $17,700; room and board, $13,000 (on campus). *Financial aid:* Need-based financial aid available. Non-need-based college/university scholarships/grants from institutional funds. For fall 2006 (estimated), 1 international student on campus received college administered financial aid ($3000 average).

LEHMAN COLLEGE OF THE CITY UNIVERSITY OF NEW YORK, BRONX

General Information State and locally supported, coed institution. Urban setting. *Awards:* B, M. *Entrance level for U.S. students:* Moderately difficult. *Enrollment:* 10,814 total; 8,747 undergraduates (72% women) including 5% international students from 78 foreign countries. *Faculty:* 881. *Library holdings:* 592,698 books, 5,950 current serial subscriptions. *Total majors:* 53. *Expenses:* (2006–07) $11,090. *Financial aid:* Need-based college/university scholarships/grants from institutional funds, loans from outside sources. Non-need-based college/university scholarships/grants from institutional funds, loans from outside sources. 23 international students on campus received college administered financial aid ($1800 average).

LE MOYNE COLLEGE, SYRACUSE

General Information Independent Roman Catholic (Jesuit), coed institution. Suburban setting. *Awards:* B, M. *Entrance level for U.S. students:* Moderately difficult. *Enrollment:* 3,536 total; 2,771 undergraduates (63% women) including 1% international students from 10 foreign countries. *Faculty:* 338. *Library holdings:* 280,245 books, 35,430 current serial subscriptions, 12,387 audiovisual materials. *Total majors:* 54. *Expenses:* (2006–07) $22,580; room and board, $8620 (on campus); room only, $5450 (on campus). *Financial aid:* Non-need-based college/university scholarships/grants from institutional funds, athletic awards. For fall 2005, 12 international students on campus received college administered financial aid ($21,355 average).

LONG ISLAND BUSINESS INSTITUTE, COMMACK

General Information Proprietary, 2-year, coed, primarily women's college. Urban setting. *Awards:* A. *Entrance level for U.S. students:* Noncompetitive. *Enrollment:* 880 total (75% women) including 8% international students. *Undergraduate faculty:* 88. *Library holdings:* 2,158 books, 83 current serial subscriptions, 645 audiovisual materials. *Total majors:* 4. *Expenses:* (2007–08) $10,150.

LONG ISLAND UNIVERSITY, BROOKLYN CAMPUS, BROOKLYN

General Information Independent, coed university. Urban setting. *Awards:* A, B, M, D, FP. *Entrance level for U.S. students:* Minimally difficult. *Enrollment:* 8,144 total; 5,331 undergraduates (72% women) including 2% international students. *Faculty:* 954. *Total majors:* 64. *Financial aid:* Need-based athletic awards, loans from outside sources, on-campus employment. Non-need-based college/university scholarships/grants from institutional funds, athletic awards, loans from outside sources, on-campus employment. Forms required: FAFSA. For fall 2005, 11 international students on campus received college administered financial aid ($886 average).

LONG ISLAND UNIVERSITY, C.W. POST CAMPUS, BROOKVILLE

General Information Independent, coed institution. Suburban setting. *Awards:* B, M, D. *Entrance level for U.S. students:* Moderately difficult. *Enrollment:* 8,494 total; 5,436 undergraduates (62% women) including 4% international students. *Faculty:* 834. *Total majors:* 83. **Information for International Students** For fall 2006: 129 international students applied, 77 were accepted, 33 enrolled. Students can start in fall or spring. Transfers accepted from institutions abroad. *Admission tests:* Required: TOEFL (minimum score: iBT 71; paper-based 527; computer-based 197; minimum score for ESL admission: paper-based 423; computer-based 113). Recommended: SAT. TOEFL can be waived under certain conditions. *Application deadline:* 7/1. *Expenses:* (2006–07) $25,770; room and board, $9430 (on campus); room only, $6020 (on campus). *Financial aid:* Non-need financial aid available. Forms required: CSS PROFILE, International Student's Certification of Finances. International transfer students are eligible to apply for aid. *Housing:* Available during summer. *Services:* International student adviser on campus. Full-time ESL program on campus. ESL program available during the academic year and the summer. Internships and employment opportunities (on-campus) available. *Contact:* Assistant Director for International Admissions, Office of Admissions, Long Island University, C.W. Post Campus, 720 Northern Boulevard, Brookville, NY 11548-1300. Telephone: 516-299-2900. Fax: 516-299-2148. E-mail: toni.vicari@liu.edu. URL: http://www.liu.edu.

See In-Depth Description on page 117.

MANHATTAN COLLEGE, RIVERDALE

General Information Independent, coed institution, affiliated with Roman Catholic Church. Urban setting. *Awards:* B, M. *Entrance level for U.S. students:* Moderately difficult. *Enrollment:*

Manhattan College (continued)

3,357 total; 3,021 undergraduates (50% women) including international students from 30 foreign countries. *Faculty:* 331. *Library holdings:* 211,376 books, 1,190 current serial subscriptions. *Total majors:* 41.

Information for International Students For fall 2006: 4 international students enrolled. Students can start in fall or spring. Transfers accepted from institutions abroad. *Admission tests:* Required: SAT or ACT, TOEFL (minimum score: paper-based 520; computer-based 190). TOEFL can be waived under certain conditions. *Application deadline:* 4/1. *Expenses:* (2006–07) $21,550; room and board, $9325 (on campus). *Housing:* Guaranteed, also available during summer. *Services:* International student adviser on campus. Internships and employment opportunities (on-campus and off-campus) available. *Contact:* Vice President for Enrollment Management, Manhattan College, Riverdale, NY 10471. Telephone: 718-862-7200. Fax: 718-862-8019. E-mail: admit@manhattan.edu. URL: http://www.manhattan.edu.

MANHATTAN SCHOOL OF MUSIC, NEW YORK

General Information Independent, coed institution. Urban setting. *Awards:* B, M, D. *Entrance level for U.S. students:* Very difficult. *Enrollment:* 823 total; 379 undergraduates (49% women) including 25% international students from 34 foreign countries. *Faculty:* 403. *Library holdings:* 129,654 books, 117 current serial subscriptions, 374 audiovisual materials. *Total majors:* 6.

Information for International Students For fall 2006: 824 international students applied, 293 were accepted, 122 enrolled. Students can start in fall. Transfers accepted from institutions abroad. *Admission tests:* Required: TOEFL (minimum score: iBT 80; paper-based 550; computer-based 213; minimum score for ESL admission: iBT 80; paper-based 550; computer-based 213), EPT administered by American Language Program at Columbia University during audition week. TOEFL can be waived under certain conditions. *Application deadline:* 12/1. *Expenses:* (2006–07) $29,960; room and board, $12,800 (on campus); room only, $8400 (on campus). *Financial aid:* Need-based college/university scholarships/grants from institutional funds, loans from outside sources, on-campus employment. Non-need-based college/university scholarships/grants from institutional funds, loans from outside sources, on-campus employment. Forms required: institution's own financial aid form, International Student's Certification of Finances. International transfer students are eligible to apply for aid. 40 international students on campus received college administered financial aid ($13,316 average). *Services:* International student adviser on campus. ESL program at cooperating institution. ESL program available during the academic year and the summer. Employment opportunities (on-campus) available. *Contact:* Associate Dean for Enrollment Management, Admissions Office, Manhattan School of Music, 120 Claremont Avenue, New York, NY 10027. Telephone: 917-493-4501. Fax: 212-749-3025. E-mail: aanderson@msmnyc.edu. URL: http://www.msmnyc.edu.

MANHATTANVILLE COLLEGE, PURCHASE

General Information Independent, coed institution. Suburban setting. *Awards:* B, M. *Entrance level for U.S. students:* Moderately difficult. *Enrollment:* 2,974 total; 1,830 undergraduates (66% women) including 8% international students from 59 foreign countries. *Faculty:* 288. *Library holdings:* 239,202 books, 27,838 current serial subscriptions. *Total majors:* 42.

Information for International Students For fall 2006: 258 international students applied, 119 enrolled. Students can start in fall, spring, or summer. Transfers accepted from institutions abroad. *Admission tests:* Required: SAT or ACT, TOEFL (minimum score: paper-based 550; computer-based 213). Recommended: SAT, SAT Subject Tests. TOEFL can be waived under certain conditions. *Application deadline:* 3/1. *Expenses:* (2007–08) $30,776; room and board, $12,240 (on campus); room only, $7270 (on campus). *Financial aid:* Non-need-based college/university scholarships/grants from institutional funds. International transfer students are eligible to apply for aid. *Housing:* Guaranteed, also available during summer. *Services:* International student adviser on campus. Full-time and part-time ESL programs on campus. ESL program available during the academic year and the summer. Internships and employment opportunities (on-campus) available. *Contact:* Vice President, Enrollment Management, Manhattanville College, Purchase, NY 10577. Telephone: 914-323-5464. Fax: 914-694-1732. E-mail: admissions@manhattanville.edu. URL: http://www.manhattanville.edu.

See In-Depth Description on page 120.

MANNES COLLEGE THE NEW SCHOOL FOR MUSIC, NEW YORK

General Information Independent, coed institution. Urban setting. *Awards:* B, M. *Entrance level for U.S. students:* Very

difficult. *Enrollment:* 385 total; 201 undergraduates (57% women) including 31% international students from 27 foreign countries. *Faculty:* 257. *Library holdings:* 4.1 million books, 22,150 current serial subscriptions, 48,379 audiovisual materials. *Total majors:* 7. *Expenses:* (2007–08) $28,210; room and board, $11,750 (on campus); room only, $8750 (on campus). *Financial aid:* Need-based financial aid available. Forms required: institution's own financial aid form. For fall 2006 (estimated), 24 international students on campus received college administered financial aid ($12,890 average).

MARIA COLLEGE, ALBANY

General Information Independent, 2-year, coed college. Urban setting. *Awards:* A. *Entrance level for U.S. students:* Minimally difficult. *Enrollment:* 788 total (87% women) including 1% international students from 4 foreign countries. *Undergraduate faculty:* 65. *Library holdings:* 56,746 books, 160 current serial subscriptions, 375 audiovisual materials. *Total majors:* 12. *Expenses:* (2006–07) $8000.

MARIST COLLEGE, POUGHKEEPSIE

General Information Independent, coed institution. Small town setting. *Awards:* B, M. *Entrance level for U.S. students:* Very difficult. *Enrollment:* 5,877 total; 5,023 undergraduates (57% women) including 0.3% international students from 11 foreign countries. *Faculty:* 610. *Library holdings:* 197,209 books, 22,755 current serial subscriptions, 5,488 audiovisual materials. *Total majors:* 50. *Expenses:* (2006–07) $22,576; room and board, $9790 (on campus); room only, $6260 (on campus). *Financial aid:* Non-need-based college/university scholarships/grants from institutional funds, athletic awards, on-campus employment. Forms required: institution's own financial aid form. For fall 2006 (estimated), 9 international students on campus received college administered financial aid ($18,478 average).

MARYMOUNT MANHATTAN COLLEGE, NEW YORK

General Information Independent, 4-year, coed college. Urban setting. *Awards:* B. *Entrance level for U.S. students:* Moderately difficult. *Enrollment:* 1,938 total (77% women) including 3% international students from 32 foreign countries. *Undergraduate faculty:* 308. *Library holdings:* 102,000 books, 600 current serial subscriptions, 4,000 audiovisual materials. *Total majors:* 20.

Information for International Students For fall 2006: 85 international students applied, 51 were accepted, 22 enrolled. Students can start in fall or spring. Transfers accepted from institutions abroad. *Admission tests:* Required: TOEFL (minimum score: iBT 79; paper-based 550; computer-based 213). Recommended: SAT or ACT. TOEFL can be waived under certain conditions. *Application deadline:* Rolling. *Expenses:* (2006–07) $19,638; room and board, $12,090 (on campus); room only, $10,090 (on campus). *Financial aid:* Non-need financial aid available. *Housing:* Guaranteed. *Services:* International student adviser on campus. Internships and employment opportunities (on-campus) available. *Contact:* Marymount Manhattan College. Telephone: 212-517-0400. URL: http://www.mmm.edu.

See In-Depth Description on page 123.

MEDAILLE COLLEGE, BUFFALO

General Information Independent, coed institution. Urban setting. *Awards:* A, B, M. *Entrance level for U.S. students:* Moderately difficult. *Enrollment:* 2,971 total; 1,707 undergraduates (59% women) including 1% international students from 2 foreign countries. *Faculty:* 411. *Library holdings:* 56,854 books, 238 current serial subscriptions. *Total majors:* 29. *Expenses:* (2006–07) $15,780; room and board, $8024 (on campus). *Financial aid:* Need-based financial aid available.

MERCY COLLEGE, DOBBS FERRY

General Information Independent, coed institution. Suburban setting. *Awards:* A, B, M. *Entrance level for U.S. students:* Difficulty N/R. *Enrollment:* 9,120 total; 5,311 undergraduates (71% women) including 2% international students from 40 foreign countries. *Faculty:* 800. *Library holdings:* 322,610 books, 1,765 current serial subscriptions. *Total majors:* 41.

Information for International Students Students can start in fall or spring. Transfers accepted from institutions abroad. *Admission tests:* Required: TOEFL (minimum score: iBT 79; paper-based 550; computer-based 213; minimum score for ESL admission: iBT 44; paper-based 449; computer-based 132), ELS. TOEFL can be waived under certain conditions. *Application deadline:* Rolling. *Expenses:* (2007–08) $14,170. *Financial aid:* Need-based college/university scholarships/grants from institutional funds, athletic awards. Non-need-based college/university scholarships/grants from institutional funds, athletic awards. *Housing:* Available during summer. *Services:* International student adviser on campus. Full-time ESL program on campus. ESL program available during the academic year. Internships and employment opportunities (on-campus) available. *Contact:* Admissions Department, Admissions Office, Mercy College, 555 Broadway, Dobbs Ferry, NY 10522. Telephone: 914-674-7600. Fax: 914-674-7382. E-mail: admissions@mercy.edu. URL: http://www.mercy.edu.

METROPOLITAN COLLEGE OF NEW YORK, NEW YORK

General Information Independent, coed, primarily women's institution. Urban setting. *Awards:* A, B, M. *Entrance level for U.S. students:* Moderately difficult. *Enrollment:* 1,238 total; 850 undergraduates including 2% international students. *Faculty:* 224. *Library holdings:* 31,766 books, 459 audiovisual materials. *Total majors:* 4. *Expenses:* (2006–07) $16,460.

MILDRED ELLEY, LATHAM

General Information Proprietary, 2-year. Suburban setting. *Awards:* A. *Entrance level for U.S. students:* Difficulty N/R. *Enrollment:* 394 total. *Undergraduate faculty:* 31. *Total majors:* 5.

MOHAWK VALLEY COMMUNITY COLLEGE, UTICA

General Information State and locally supported, 2-year, coed college. Urban setting. *Awards:* A. *Entrance level for U.S. students:* Noncompetitive. *Enrollment:* 5,895 total (54% women) including 1% international students from 11 foreign countries. *Undergraduate faculty:* 292. *Library holdings:* 94,200 books, 628 current serial subscriptions, 8,860 audiovisual materials. *Total majors:* 73. *Expenses:* (2006–07) $6584; room and board, $6530 (on campus); room only, $3710 (on campus).

MOLLOY COLLEGE, ROCKVILLE CENTRE

General Information Independent, coed institution. Suburban setting. *Awards:* A, B, M. *Entrance level for U.S. students:* Moderately difficult. *Enrollment:* 3,673 total; 2,834 undergraduates (78% women) including 0.3% international students from 9 foreign countries. *Faculty:* 403. *Library holdings:* 120,000 books, 680 current serial subscriptions, 3,860 audiovisual materials. *Total majors:* 44.
Information for International Students For fall 2006: 7 international students applied, 5 were accepted, 4 enrolled. Students can start in fall or spring. Transfers accepted from institutions abroad. *Admission tests:* Required: TOEFL (minimum score: paper-based 500; computer-based 173). TOEFL can be waived under certain conditions. *Application deadline:* Rolling. *Expenses:* (2006–07) $17,310. *Financial aid:* Need-based college/university scholarships/grants from institutional funds. Non-need-based college/university scholarships/grants from institutional funds, tuition waivers, athletic awards, loans from outside sources. Forms required: International Student Application for Admission. For fall 2006 (estimated), 8 international students on campus received college administered financial aid ($9863 average). *Services:* International student adviser on campus. Full-time and part-time ESL programs on campus. ESL program available during the academic year. Internships available. *Contact:* Director of Admissions, Molloy College, 1000 Hempstead Avenue, PO Box 5002, Rockville Centre, NY 11570. Telephone: 516-678-5000 Ext. 6230. Fax: 516-256-2286. E-mail: mlane@molloy.edu. URL: http://www.molloy.edu.

MONROE COLLEGE, BRONX

General Information Proprietary, coed institution. Urban setting. *Awards:* A, B, M. *Entrance level for U.S. students:* Moderately difficult. *Enrollment:* 4,361 total; 4,253 undergraduates (73% women) including 1% international students from 12 foreign countries. *Faculty:* 251. *Library holdings:* 28,000 books, 301 current serial subscriptions. *Total majors:* 8. *Expenses:* (2006–07) $10,200; room and board, $10,120 (on campus). *Financial aid:* Non-need-based athletic awards, loans from outside sources. Forms required: International Student's Certification of Finances.

MONROE COMMUNITY COLLEGE, ROCHESTER

General Information State and locally supported, 2-year, coed college. Suburban setting. *Awards:* A. *Entrance level for U.S. students:* Noncompetitive. *Enrollment:* 16,596 total (55% women) including 1% international students from 45 foreign countries. *Undergraduate faculty:* 1,192. *Library holdings:* 110,748 books, 745 current serial subscriptions, 4,100 audiovisual materials. *Total majors:* 67.

MOUNT SAINT MARY COLLEGE, NEWBURGH

General Information Independent, coed institution. Suburban setting. *Awards:* B, M. *Entrance level for U.S. students:* Moderately difficult. *Enrollment:* 2,601 total; 2,043 undergraduates (74% women). *Faculty:* 215. *Library holdings:* 118,207 books, 317 current

serial subscriptions, 5,963 audiovisual materials. *Total majors:* 35. *Expenses:* (2006–07) $18,290; room and board, $9040 (on campus); room only, $5050 (on campus).

NASSAU COMMUNITY COLLEGE, GARDEN CITY

General Information State and locally supported, 2-year, coed college. Suburban setting. *Awards:* A. *Entrance level for U.S. students:* Noncompetitive. *Enrollment:* 21,229 total (52% women) including 5% international students from 54 foreign countries. *Undergraduate faculty:* 1,278. *Library holdings:* 179,920 books, 421 current serial subscriptions, 20,253 audiovisual materials. *Total majors:* 55.
Information for International Students Students can start in fall or spring. Transfers accepted from institutions abroad. *Admission tests:* Required: in-house academic placement test. Recommended: SAT or ACT, TOEFL. *Application deadline:* Rolling. *Expenses:* (2007–08) $6844. *Services:* International student adviser on campus. Full-time ESL program on campus. ESL program available during the academic year and the summer. Internships and employment opportunities (on-campus and off-campus) available. *Contact:* Assistant Director of Admissions, Nassau Community College, 1 Education Drive, Garden City, NY 11530-6793. Telephone: 516-572-7053. Fax: 516-572-9743. E-mail: iglesil@ncc.edu. URL: http://www.ncc.edu.

NAZARETH COLLEGE OF ROCHESTER, ROCHESTER

General Information Independent, coed institution. Suburban setting. *Awards:* B, M, D. *Entrance level for U.S. students:* Moderately difficult. *Enrollment:* 3,179 total; 2,148 undergraduates (76% women) including 1% international students from 26 foreign countries. *Faculty:* 341. *Library holdings:* 283,248 books, 16,102 current serial subscriptions. *Total majors:* 72. *Expenses:* (2006–07) $21,640; room and board, $9080 (on campus); room only, $4960 (on campus). *Financial aid:* Need-based loans from outside sources. Non-need-based loans from outside sources.

THE NEW SCHOOL FOR GENERAL STUDIES, NEW YORK

General Information Independent, coed institution. Urban setting. *Awards:* B, M, D. *Entrance level for U.S. students:* Moderately difficult. *Enrollment:* 1,628 total; 690 undergraduates including 4% international students from 25 foreign countries. *Faculty:* 492. *Library holdings:* 368,890 books, 1,155 current serial subscriptions, 433,123 audiovisual materials. *Total majors:* 1. *Expenses:* (2006–07) $19,810; room and board, $11,750 (on campus); room only, $8750 (on campus). *Financial aid:* Need-based and non-need-based financial aid available. Forms required: International Student's Financial Aid Application. 10 international students on campus received college administered financial aid.

NEW YORK CITY COLLEGE OF TECHNOLOGY OF THE CITY UNIVERSITY OF NEW YORK, BROOKLYN

General Information State and locally supported, primarily 2-year, coed college. Urban setting. *Awards:* A, B. *Entrance level for U.S. students:* Noncompetitive. *Enrollment:* 13,368 total (50% women) including 10% international students from 59 foreign countries. *Undergraduate faculty:* 970. *Library holdings:* 183,000 books, 60,000 audiovisual materials. *Total majors:* 29. *Expenses:* (2006–07) $8909.

NEW YORK INSTITUTE OF TECHNOLOGY, OLD WESTBURY

General Information Independent, coed university. Suburban setting. *Awards:* A, B, M, D, FP. *Entrance level for U.S. students:* Moderately difficult. *Enrollment:* 11,404 total; 6,751 undergraduates (44% women) including 6% international students from 82 foreign countries. *Faculty:* 849. *Library holdings:* 272,227 books, 13,827 current serial subscriptions. *Total majors:* 70. *Expenses:* (2006–07) $20,358; room and board, $11,452 (on campus). *Financial aid:* Non-need financial aid available. Forms required: International Student's Financial Aid Application, International Student's Certification of Finances. For fall 2005, 264 international students on campus received college administered financial aid ($1467 average).

NEW YORK SCHOOL OF INTERIOR DESIGN, NEW YORK

General Information Independent, coed, primarily women's institution. Urban setting. *Awards:* A, B, M. *Entrance level for U.S. students:* Moderately difficult. *Enrollment:* 736 total; 718 undergraduates (91% women) including 8% international students from 24 foreign countries. *Faculty:* 79. *Library holdings:* 12,000 books, 110 current serial subscriptions, 50 audiovisual materials. *Total majors:* 1.

New York School of Interior Design (continued)

Information for International Students For fall 2006: 143
international students applied, 73 were accepted, 63 enrolled.
Students can start in fall, spring, or summer. Transfers accepted
from institutions abroad. *Admission tests:* Required: TOEFL
(minimum score: iBT 79; paper-based 550; computer-based 213).
TOEFL can be waived under certain conditions. *Application
deadline:* Rolling. *Expenses:* (2007–08) $20,750. *Services:*
International student adviser on campus. Internships and
employment opportunities (on-campus and off-campus) available.
Contact: International Student Advisor, New York School of Interior
Design, 170 East 70th Street, New York, NY 10021.
Telephone: 212-472-1500 Ext. 203. Fax: 212-472-1867.
E-mail: douglasd@nysid.edu. URL: http://www.nysid.edu.

See In-Depth Description on page 138.

NEW YORK UNIVERSITY, NEW YORK

General Information Independent, coed university. Urban setting.
Awards: A, B, M, D, FP. *Entrance level for U.S. students:* Most
difficult. *Enrollment:* 40,870 total; 20,965 undergraduates (62%
women) including 5% international students from 105 foreign
countries. *Faculty:* 4,380. *Library holdings:* 5.2 million books,
48,958 current serial subscriptions. *Total majors:* 116.
Information for International Students For fall 2006: 3500
international students applied, 1000 were accepted, 400 enrolled.
Students can start in fall or spring. Transfers accepted from
institutions abroad. *Admission tests:* Required: SAT or ACT, SAT
Subject Tests, TOEFL (minimum score: iBT 100; paper-based 600;
computer-based 250). Recommended: IELTS or TOEFL. TOEFL can
be waived under certain conditions. *Application deadline:* 1/15.
Expenses: (2006–07) $33,420; room and board, $11,780 (on campus).
Housing: Guaranteed, also available during summer. *Services:*
International student adviser on campus. Full-time and part-time
ESL programs on campus. ESL program available during the
academic year and the summer. Internships and employment
opportunities (on-campus and off-campus) available. *Contact:*
Director of International Admissions, Office of Undergraduate
Admissions, New York University, 22 Washington Square North,
New York, NY 10011. Telephone: 212-998-4530. Fax: 212-995-4902.
E-mail: vivian.cipolla@nyu.edu. URL: http://www.nyu.edu.

NIAGARA COUNTY COMMUNITY COLLEGE, SANBORN

General Information State and locally supported, 2-year, coed
college. Rural setting. *Awards:* A. *Entrance level for U.S. students:*
Noncompetitive. *Enrollment:* 5,944 total (60% women) including 1%
international students from 12 foreign countries. *Undergraduate
faculty:* 334. *Library holdings:* 93,055 books, 524 current serial
subscriptions. *Total majors:* 36. *Expenses:* (2006–07) $5054.
Financial aid: Need-based college/university scholarships/grants
from institutional funds, tuition waivers, athletic awards, loans
from institutional funds, loans from outside sources, on-campus
employment. Non-need-based college/university scholarships/grants
from institutional funds, tuition waivers, athletic awards, loans
from institutional funds, loans from outside sources, on-campus
employment. Forms required: FAFSA.

NIAGARA UNIVERSITY, NIAGARA FALLS

General Information Independent, coed institution, affiliated
with Roman Catholic Church. Suburban setting. *Awards:* A, B, M.
Entrance level for U.S. students: Moderately difficult. *Enrollment:*
3,881 total; 2,967 undergraduates (61% women) including 5%
international students from 12 foreign countries. *Faculty:* 335.
Library holdings: 273,753 books, 21,001 current serial
subscriptions. *Total majors:* 56.
Information for International Students For fall 2006: 127
international students applied, 77 were accepted, 44 enrolled.
Students can start in fall or spring. Transfers accepted from
institutions abroad. *Admission tests:* Required: TOEFL (minimum
score: iBT 79; paper-based 550; computer-based 227). TOEFL can
be waived under certain conditions. *Application deadline:* Rolling.
Expenses: (2006–07) $21,240; room and board, $8850 (on campus).
Housing: Guaranteed, also available during summer. *Services:*
International student adviser on campus. ESL program at
cooperating institution. Internships and employment opportunities
(on-campus) available. *Contact:* Associate Director of Admissions,
Niagara University, Bailo Hall, Niagara University, NY 14109.
Telephone: 716-286-8712. Fax: 716-286-8710.
E-mail: cds@niagara.edu. URL: http://www.niagara.edu.

NORTH COUNTRY COMMUNITY COLLEGE, SARANAC LAKE

General Information State and locally supported, 2-year, coed
college. Rural setting. *Awards:* A. *Entrance level for U.S. students:*
Minimally difficult. *Enrollment:* 1,636 total (66% women) including
1% international students from 6 foreign countries. *Undergraduate*

faculty: 151. *Library holdings:* 58,556 books, 177 current serial
subscriptions. *Total majors:* 14. *Expenses:* (2006–07) $7230; room
and board, $8150 (on campus).

NYACK COLLEGE, NYACK

General Information Independent, coed institution, affiliated
with The Christian and Missionary Alliance. Suburban setting.
Awards: A, B, M, FP. *Entrance level for U.S. students:* Moderately
difficult. *Enrollment:* 3,063 total; 1,970 undergraduates (59%
women) including 4% international students from 49 foreign
countries. *Total majors:* 28. *Expenses:* (2006–07) $15,400; room and
board, $7600 (on campus). *Financial aid:* Need-based loans from
outside sources, on-campus employment. Non-need-based
college/university scholarships/grants from institutional funds,
athletic awards, loans from outside sources, on-campus
employment. Forms required: institution's own financial aid form.
For fall 2005, 77 international students on campus received college
administered financial aid ($2518 average).

OHR SOMAYACH/JOSEPH TANENBAUM EDUCATIONAL CENTER, MONSEY

General Information Independent Jewish, 5-year, coed, primarily
men's college. Small town setting. *Awards:* B, FP. *Entrance level for
U.S. students:* Moderately difficult. *Enrollment:* 96 total; 88
undergraduates including 40% international students from 8
foreign countries. *Faculty:* 18. *Library holdings:* 2,300 books.
Total majors: 1. *Expenses:* (2007–08) $13,500.

ORANGE COUNTY COMMUNITY COLLEGE, MIDDLETOWN

General Information State and locally supported, 2-year, coed
college. Suburban setting. *Awards:* A. *Entrance level for U.S.
students:* Noncompetitive. *Enrollment:* 6,441 total (61% women)
including 0.05% international students from 20 foreign countries.
Undergraduate faculty: 382. *Library holdings:* 101,342 books, 345
current serial subscriptions, 1,408 audiovisual materials.
Total majors: 40. *Expenses:* (2006–07) $6350. *Financial aid:*
Need-based college/university scholarships/grants from institutional
funds, athletic awards, loans from institutional funds, loans from
outside sources, on-campus employment. Non-need-based
college/university scholarships/grants from institutional funds,
tuition waivers, athletic awards, loans from outside sources.

PACE UNIVERSITY, NEW YORK

General Information Independent, coed university. Urban setting.
Awards: A, B, M, D, FP. *Entrance level for U.S. students:*
Moderately difficult. *Enrollment:* 13,463 total; 8,030
undergraduates (61% women) including 3% international students
from 28 foreign countries. *Faculty:* 1,190. *Library holdings:* 824,533
books, 4,151 current serial subscriptions, 2,248 audiovisual
materials. *Total majors:* 75.
Information for International Students Students can start in
fall, spring, or summer. Transfers accepted from institutions
abroad. *Admission tests:* Required: TOEFL (minimum score: iBT 88;
paper-based 570; computer-based 230). TOEFL can be waived under
certain conditions. *Application deadline:* 4/30. *Expenses:* (2006–07)
$30,086; room and board, $9570 (on campus). *Financial aid:*
Non-need financial aid available. Forms required: International
Student's Certification of Finances. International transfer students
are eligible to apply for aid. 136 international students on campus
received college administered financial aid ($6122 average).
Services: International student adviser on campus. Full-time and
part-time ESL programs on campus. ESL program available during
the academic year and the summer. Internships and employment
opportunities (on-campus) available. *Contact:* Office of
Undergraduate Admission, Pace University, 1 Pace Plaza, New
York, NY 10038. Telephone: 212-346-1323. Fax: 212-346-1821.
URL: http://www.pace.edu.

See In-Depth Description on page 147.

PARSONS THE NEW SCHOOL FOR DESIGN, NEW YORK

General Information Independent, coed institution. Urban
setting. *Awards:* A, B, M. *Entrance level for U.S. students:* Very
difficult. *Enrollment:* 3,598 total; 3,180 undergraduates (79%
women) including 34% international students from 66 foreign
countries. *Faculty:* 941. *Library holdings:* 4.1 million books, 22,150
current serial subscriptions, 48,379 audiovisual materials.
Total majors: 12.
Information for International Students Students can start in
fall or spring. Transfers accepted from institutions abroad.
Admission tests: Required: SAT, TOEFL (minimum score:
paper-based 550; computer-based 213). TOEFL can be waived under
certain conditions. *Application deadline:* 3/1. *Expenses:* (2007–08)
$30,930; room and board, $11,750 (on campus); room only, $8750
(on campus). *Financial aid:* Need-based and non-need-based

financial aid available. Forms required: institution's own financial aid form. International transfer students are eligible to apply for aid. For fall 2006 (estimated), 682 international students on campus received college administered financial aid ($5104 average). *Housing:* Guaranteed, also available during summer. *Services:* International student adviser on campus. Full-time and part-time ESL programs on campus. ESL program available during the academic year and the summer. Internships and employment opportunities (on-campus) available. *Contact:* Parsons Admissions, Parsons The New School for Design, 2 West 13th Street, New York, NY 10011. Telephone: 212-229-8989. Fax: 212-229-5611. E-mail: parsadm@newschool.edu.
URL: http://www.parsons.newschool.edu.

See In-Depth Description on page 148.

PAUL SMITH'S COLLEGE OF ARTS AND SCIENCES, PAUL SMITHS

General Information Independent, 4-year, coed college. Rural setting. *Awards:* A, B. *Entrance level for U.S. students:* Minimally difficult. *Enrollment:* 870 total including international students from 3 foreign countries. *Undergraduate faculty:* 85. *Library holdings:* 56,000 books, 406 current serial subscriptions. *Total majors:* 13. *Expenses:* (2007–08) $19,500; room and board, $7800 (on campus). *Financial aid:* Need-based college/university scholarships/grants from institutional funds, loans from outside sources, on-campus employment. Non-need-based college/university scholarships/grants from institutional funds, loans from outside sources, on-campus employment. Forms required: institution's own financial aid form. For fall 2005, 2 international students on campus received college administered financial aid ($8533 average).

PHILLIPS BETH ISRAEL SCHOOL OF NURSING, NEW YORK

General Information Independent, 2-year, coed, primarily women's college. Urban setting. *Awards:* A. *Entrance level for U.S. students:* Moderately difficult. *Enrollment:* 200 total including 4% international students from 5 foreign countries. *Undergraduate faculty:* 18. *Library holdings:* 600 current serial subscriptions. *Total majors:* 2. *Expenses:* (2006–07) $16,560. *Financial aid:* Need-based college/university scholarships/grants from institutional funds. Non-need-based college/university scholarships/grants from institutional funds. Forms required: institution's own financial aid form.

POLYTECHNIC UNIVERSITY, BROOKLYN CAMPUS, BROOKLYN

General Information Independent, coed university. Urban setting. *Awards:* B, M, D. *Entrance level for U.S. students:* Very difficult. *Enrollment:* 2,919 total; 1,480 undergraduates (20% women) including 10% international students from 52 foreign countries. *Faculty:* 273. *Library holdings:* 150,000 books, 1,621 current serial subscriptions. *Total majors:* 15. *Expenses:* (2006–07) $29,789; room and board, $8500 (on campus); room only, $6500 (on campus). *Financial aid:* Need-based college/university scholarships/grants from institutional funds. Non-need-based college/university scholarships/grants from institutional funds. Forms required: institution's own financial aid form, International Student's Certification of Finances. 135 international students on campus received college administered financial aid ($16,124 average).

PRATT INSTITUTE, BROOKLYN

General Information Independent, coed institution. Urban setting. *Awards:* A, B, M, FP (Associate). *Entrance level for U.S. students:* Very difficult. *Enrollment:* 4,673 total; 3,067 undergraduates (59% women) including 9% international students from 36 foreign countries. *Faculty:* 960. *Library holdings:* 172,000 books, 540 current serial subscriptions. *Total majors:* 26.
Information for International Students For fall 2006: 631 international students applied, 299 were accepted, 93 enrolled. Students can start in fall or spring. Transfers accepted from institutions abroad. *Admission tests:* Required: TOEFL (minimum score: iBT 71; paper-based 530; computer-based 197; minimum score for ESL admission: iBT 61; paper-based 500; computer-based 173), IELTS or TOEFL. TOEFL can be waived under certain conditions. *Application deadline:* 2/1. *Expenses:* (2007–08) $31,080; room and board, $8918 (on campus); room only, $5718 (on campus). *Financial aid:* Non-need financial aid available. 23 international students on campus received college administered financial aid ($3765 average). *Housing:* Guaranteed, also available during summer. *Services:* International student adviser on campus. Full-time ESL program on campus. ESL program available during the academic year and the summer. Internships and employment opportunities (on-campus) available. *Contact:* Counselor for International Students, Pratt Institute, 200 Willoughby Avenue,

Brooklyn, NY 11205. Telephone: 718-636-3559. Fax: 718-636-3670. E-mail: aluhrsse@pratt.edu. URL: http://www.pratt.edu.

See In-Depth Description on page 152.

PURCHASE COLLEGE, STATE UNIVERSITY OF NEW YORK, PURCHASE

General Information State-supported, coed institution. Small town setting. *Awards:* B, M. *Entrance level for U.S. students:* Moderately difficult. *Enrollment:* 3,901 total; 3,754 undergraduates (54% women) including 2% international students from 21 foreign countries. *Faculty:* 362. *Library holdings:* 281,686 books, 1,990 current serial subscriptions. *Total majors:* 29. *Expenses:* (2006–07) $11,969; room and board, $9078 (on campus); room only, $5528 (on campus). *Financial aid:* Need-based college/university scholarships/grants from institutional funds, tuition waivers, loans from outside sources, on-campus employment. Non-need-based college/university scholarships/grants from institutional funds, tuition waivers, loans from outside sources, on-campus employment. Forms required: institution's own financial aid form, International Student's Certification of Finances, bank statement. For fall 2006 (estimated), 23 international students on campus received college administered financial aid ($3230 average).

QUEENS COLLEGE OF THE CITY UNIVERSITY OF NEW YORK, FLUSHING

General Information State and locally supported, coed institution. Urban setting. *Awards:* B, M. *Entrance level for U.S. students:* Very difficult. *Enrollment:* 18,107 total; 13,662 undergraduates (61% women) including 8% international students from 130 foreign countries. *Faculty:* 1,337. *Library holdings:* 1.1 million books, 2,689 current serial subscriptions, 35,721 audiovisual materials. *Total majors:* 64. *Expenses:* (2007–08) $11,177.

RENSSELAER POLYTECHNIC INSTITUTE, TROY

General Information Independent, coed university. Suburban setting. *Awards:* B, M, D. *Entrance level for U.S. students:* Very difficult. *Enrollment:* 7,433 total; 5,193 undergraduates (25% women) including 3% international students from 26 foreign countries. *Faculty:* 471. *Library holdings:* 309,171 books, 10,210 current serial subscriptions. *Total majors:* 51.
Information for International Students For fall 2006: 337 international students applied, 139 were accepted, 19 enrolled. Students can start in fall, spring, or summer. Transfers accepted from institutions abroad. *Admission tests:* Required: SAT or ACT, TOEFL (minimum score: iBT 88; paper-based 570; computer-based 230). Recommended: SAT Subject Tests. TOEFL can be waived under certain conditions. *Application deadline:* 1/15. *Expenses:* (2006–07) $33,496; room and board, $9915 (on campus); room only, $5568 (on campus). *Financial aid:* Non-need-based college/university scholarships/grants from institutional funds, athletic awards. For fall 2006 (estimated), 44 international students on campus received college administered financial aid ($27,235 average). *Housing:* Available during summer. *Services:* International student adviser on campus. ESL program at cooperating institution. ESL program available during the academic year and the summer. Internships and employment opportunities (on-campus and off-campus) available. *Contact:* Admissions Counselor, Rensselaer Polytechnic Institute, Troy, NY 12180-3590. Telephone: 518-276-6216. Fax: 518-276-4072. URL: http://www.rpi.edu.

See In-Depth Description on page 157.

ROBERTS WESLEYAN COLLEGE, ROCHESTER

General Information Independent, coed institution, affiliated with Free Methodist Church of North America. Suburban setting. *Awards:* A, B, M. *Entrance level for U.S. students:* Moderately difficult. *Enrollment:* 1,903 total; 1,346 undergraduates (68% women) including 2% international students from 22 foreign countries. *Faculty:* 246. *Library holdings:* 123,434 books, 1,057 current serial subscriptions, 3,895 audiovisual materials. *Total majors:* 55. *Expenses:* (2007–08) $21,656; room and board, $7774 (on campus); room only, $5388 (on campus). *Financial aid:* Need-based college/university scholarships/grants from institutional funds, athletic awards, on-campus employment. Non-need-based college/university scholarships/grants from institutional funds, athletic awards, on-campus employment. Forms required: International Student's Certification of Finances. For fall 2006 (estimated), 28 international students on campus received college administered financial aid ($13,769 average).

ROCHESTER INSTITUTE OF TECHNOLOGY, ROCHESTER

General Information Independent, coed institution. Suburban setting. *Awards:* A, B, M, D. *Entrance level for U.S. students:* Moderately difficult. *Enrollment:* 15,557 total; 13,140

Rochester Institute of Technology (continued)

undergraduates (31% women) including 11% international students from 90 foreign countries. *Faculty:* 1,203. *Library holdings:* 408,000 books, 2,800 current serial subscriptions. *Total majors:* 114. **Information for International Students** For fall 2006: 988 international students applied, 483 were accepted, 151 enrolled. Students can start in fall, winter, spring, or summer. Transfers accepted from institutions abroad. *Admission tests:* Required: TOEFL (minimum score: iBT 79; paper-based 550; computer-based 213; minimum score for ESL admission: iBT 61; paper-based 500; computer-based 173). Recommended: ACT. TOEFL can be waived under certain conditions. *Application deadline:* Rolling. *Expenses:* (2006–07) $25,011; room and board, $8748 (on campus); room only, $5034 (on campus). *Financial aid:* Need-based college/university scholarships/grants from institutional funds, loans from outside sources, on-campus employment. Non-need-based college/university scholarships/grants from institutional funds, loans from outside sources, on-campus employment. Forms required: International Student's Financial Aid Application, International Student's Certification of Finances. International transfer students are eligible to apply for aid. For fall 2005, 150 international students on campus received college administered financial aid ($5900 average). *Services:* International student adviser on campus. Full-time and part-time ESL programs on campus. ESL program available during the academic year and the summer. Internships and employment opportunities (on-campus and off-campus) available. *Contact:* Senior Associate Director and Director of Transfer, Admissions Office, Rochester Institute of Technology, Rochester, NY 14623-5604. Telephone: 585-475-6631. Fax: 585-475-7424. E-mail: admissions@rit.edu. URL: http://www.rit.edu.

See In-Depth Description on page 160.

SAGE COLLEGE OF ALBANY, ALBANY

General Information Independent, 4-year, coed college. Urban setting. *Awards:* A, B. *Entrance level for U.S. students:* Minimally difficult. *Enrollment:* 1,074 total (71% women) including 0.4% international students from 4 foreign countries. *Undergraduate faculty:* 87. *Library holdings:* 332,478 books, 42,506 current serial subscriptions, 33,013 audiovisual materials. *Total majors:* 23. **Information for International Students** For fall 2006: 4 international students applied, 4 were accepted, 1 enrolled. Students can start in fall or spring. Transfers accepted from institutions abroad. *Admission tests:* Required: TOEFL (minimum score: paper-based 500; computer-based 213; minimum score for ESL admission: paper-based 500; computer-based 213), ELS (minimum score: 109). Recommended: SAT or ACT. TOEFL can be waived under certain conditions. *Application deadline:* 8/1. *Expenses:* (2006–07) $17,670; room and board, $8520 (on campus); room only, $4430 (on campus). *Services:* International student adviser on campus. ESL program at cooperating institution. ESL program available during the academic year and the summer. Internships and employment opportunities (on-campus and off-campus) available. *Contact:* Director of Admission, Admissions Office, Sage College of Albany, 140 New Scotland Avenue, Albany, NY 12208. Telephone: 518-292-1926. Fax: 518-292-1910. E-mail: dworsa2@sage.edu. URL: http://www.sage.edu/sca/index.php.

ST. BONAVENTURE UNIVERSITY, ST. BONAVENTURE

General Information Independent, coed institution, affiliated with Roman Catholic Church. Small town setting. *Awards:* B, M. *Entrance level for U.S. students:* Moderately difficult. *Enrollment:* 2,614 total; 2,141 undergraduates (49% women) including 2% international students. *Faculty:* 207. *Library holdings:* 287,622 books, 1,584 current serial subscriptions, 8,891 audiovisual materials. *Total majors:* 59. *Expenses:* (2006–07) $22,515; room and board, $7760 (on campus); room only, $3960 (on campus). *Financial aid:* Non-need-based college/university scholarships/grants from institutional funds, athletic awards, loans from outside sources, on-campus employment.

ST. JOHN'S UNIVERSITY, QUEENS

General Information Independent, coed university, affiliated with Roman Catholic Church. Urban setting. *Awards:* A, B, M, D, FP. *Entrance level for U.S. students:* Moderately difficult. *Enrollment:* 20,069 total; 14,983 undergraduates (57% women) including 3% international students from 105 foreign countries. *Faculty:* 1,486. *Library holdings:* 1.2 million books, 27,423 current serial subscriptions, 20,556 audiovisual materials. *Total majors:* 105. *Expenses:* (2006–07) $24,970; room and board, $11,470 (on campus); room only, $7200 (on campus). *Financial aid:* Need-based financial aid available. Non-need-based college/university scholarships/grants from institutional funds. 148 international students on campus received college administered financial aid ($16,809 average).

ST. JOSEPH'S COLLEGE, NEW YORK, BROOKLYN

General Information Independent, coed institution. Urban setting. *Awards:* B, M. *Entrance level for U.S. students:* Moderately

difficult. *Enrollment:* 1,310 total; 1,087 undergraduates (78% women) including 1% international students from 10 foreign countries. *Faculty:* 137. *Library holdings:* 100,000 books, 432 current serial subscriptions. *Total majors:* 22. *Expenses:* (2006–07) $12,946. *Financial aid:* Non-need-based college/university scholarships/grants from institutional funds. Forms required: institution's own financial aid form. For fall 2006 (estimated), 3 international students on campus received college administered financial aid ($12,500 average).

ST. JOSEPH'S COLLEGE, SUFFOLK CAMPUS, PATCHOGUE

General Information Independent, coed institution. Small town setting. *Awards:* B, M. *Entrance level for U.S. students:* Moderately difficult. *Enrollment:* 3,833 total; 3,798 undergraduates (74% women) including international students from 6 foreign countries. *Faculty:* 380. *Library holdings:* 114,893 books, 638 current serial subscriptions. *Total majors:* 34. *Expenses:* (2006–07) $13,610. *Financial aid:* Need-based college/university scholarships/grants from institutional funds. Non-need-based college/university scholarships/grants from institutional funds. Forms required: institution's own financial aid form.

ST. LAWRENCE UNIVERSITY, CANTON

General Information Independent, coed institution. Small town setting. *Awards:* B, M. *Entrance level for U.S. students:* Very difficult. *Enrollment:* 2,303 total; 2,182 undergraduates (53% women) including 5% international students from 42 foreign countries. *Faculty:* 189. *Library holdings:* 576,086 books, 1,899 current serial subscriptions, 6,162 audiovisual materials. *Total majors:* 40. *Expenses:* (2006–07) $33,910; room and board, $8630 (on campus); room only, $4640 (on campus). *Financial aid:* Need-based college/university scholarships/grants from institutional funds, tuition waivers. Non-need-based college/university scholarships/grants from institutional funds, tuition waivers, athletic awards, loans from outside sources, on-campus employment. Forms required: International Student's Financial Aid Application, International Student's Certification of Finances. For fall 2006 (estimated), 109 international students on campus received college administered financial aid ($39,490 average).

ST. THOMAS AQUINAS COLLEGE, SPARKILL

General Information Independent, coed institution. Suburban setting. *Awards:* A, B, M. *Entrance level for U.S. students:* Moderately difficult. *Enrollment:* 2,232 total; 2,018 undergraduates (55% women) including 1% international students from 10 foreign countries. *Faculty:* 144. *Library holdings:* 94,913 books, 637 current serial subscriptions, 2,996 audiovisual materials. *Total majors:* 36. *Expenses:* (2007–08) $18,900; room and board, $9400 (on campus); room only, $5080 (on campus). *Financial aid:* Non-need financial aid available. Forms required: International Student's Financial Aid Application.

SARAH LAWRENCE COLLEGE, BRONXVILLE

General Information Independent, coed institution. Suburban setting. *Awards:* B, M. *Entrance level for U.S. students:* Very difficult. *Enrollment:* 1,709 total; 1,391 undergraduates (74% women) including 2% international students from 26 foreign countries. *Faculty:* 236. *Library holdings:* 298,611 books, 917 current serial subscriptions, 10,251 audiovisual materials. *Total majors:* 112. **Information for International Students** For fall 2006: 225 international students applied, 50 were accepted, 20 enrolled. Students can start in fall or spring. Transfers accepted from institutions abroad. *Admission tests:* Required: TOEFL (minimum score: paper-based 600; computer-based 250). TOEFL can be waived under certain conditions. *Application deadline:* 1/1. *Expenses:* (2006–07) $36,088; room and board, $12,152 (on campus); room only, $8056 (on campus). *Financial aid:* Need-based college/university scholarships/grants from institutional funds, on-campus employment. Forms required: CSS PROFILE, International Student's Financial Aid Application. International transfer students are eligible to apply for aid. For fall 2006 (estimated), 11 international students on campus received college administered financial aid ($31,128 average). *Housing:* Guaranteed. *Services:* International student adviser on campus. Internships and employment opportunities (on-campus) available. *Contact:* Director of International Admission, Sarah Lawrence College, Bronxville, NY 10708-5999. Telephone: 914-395-2505. Fax: 914-395-2515. E-mail: slcadmit@slc.edu. URL: http://www.sarahlawrence.edu.

See In-Depth Description on page 177.

SCHOOL OF VISUAL ARTS, NEW YORK

General Information Proprietary, coed institution. Urban setting. *Awards:* B, M. *Entrance level for U.S. students:* Moderately difficult. *Enrollment:* 3,715 total; 3,308 undergraduates (53% women)

New York

including 14% international students from 43 foreign countries. *Faculty:* 861. *Library holdings:* 71,490 books, 340 current serial subscriptions, 1,000 audiovisual materials. *Total majors:* 9.

Information for International Students For fall 2006: 228 international students applied, 119 were accepted, 30 enrolled. Students can start in fall or spring. Transfers accepted from institutions abroad. *Admission tests:* Required: TOEFL (minimum score: iBT 79; paper-based 550; computer-based 213; minimum score for ESL admission: iBT 61; paper-based 500; computer-based 173). TOEFL can be waived under certain conditions. *Application deadline:* 5/1. *Expenses:* (2006–07) $22,080; room and board, $12,300 (on campus); room only, $9800 (on campus). *Financial aid:* Non-need-based college/university scholarships/grants from institutional funds. Forms required: International Student's Certification of Finances. For fall 2006 (estimated), 175 international students on campus received college administered financial aid ($2971 average). *Housing:* Available during summer. *Services:* Full-time ESL program on campus. ESL program available during the academic year and the summer. Internships available. *Contact:* Director of Admissions, School of Visual Arts, 209 East 23rd Street, New York, NY 10010. Telephone: 212-592-2100. Fax: 212-592-2116. E-mail: admissions@sva.edu. URL: http://www.schoolofvisualarts.edu.

See In-Depth Description on page 182.

SIENA COLLEGE, LOUDONVILLE

General Information Independent Roman Catholic, 4-year, coed college. Suburban setting. *Awards:* B. *Entrance level for U.S. students:* Moderately difficult. *Enrollment:* 3,220 total (56% women) including 1% international students from 10 foreign countries. *Undergraduate faculty:* 307. *Library holdings:* 337,411 books, 6,470 current serial subscriptions, 6,080 audiovisual materials. *Total majors:* 27.

Information for International Students Students can start in fall or spring. Transfers accepted from institutions abroad. *Admission tests:* Required: SAT or ACT, TOEFL (minimum score: paper-based 550; computer-based 213). *Application deadline:* 3/1. *Expenses:* (2006–07) $21,460; room and board, $8475 (on campus); room only, $5280 (on campus). *Financial aid:* Non-need financial aid available. Forms required: institution's own financial aid form, International Student's Financial Aid Application, International Student's Certification of Finances. *Housing:* Available during summer. *Services:* International student adviser on campus. ESL program at cooperating institution. ESL program available during the academic year. Internships and employment opportunities (on-campus and off-campus) available. *Contact:* Assistant Director of Admissions, Siena College, 515 Loudon Road, Loudonville, NY 12211. Telephone: 518-783-2423. Fax: 518-786-2436. E-mail: jsloan@siena.edu. URL: http://www.siena.edu.

SKIDMORE COLLEGE, SARATOGA SPRINGS

General Information Independent, coed institution. Small town setting. *Awards:* B, M. *Entrance level for U.S. students:* Very difficult. *Enrollment:* 2,816 total; 2,759 undergraduates (60% women) including 2% international students from 31 foreign countries. *Faculty:* 338. *Library holdings:* 376,682 books, 959 current serial subscriptions, 11,078 audiovisual materials. *Total majors:* 42.

Information for International Students For fall 2006: 264 international students applied, 58 were accepted, 18 enrolled. Students can start in fall or spring. Transfers accepted from institutions abroad. *Admission tests:* Required: SAT or ACT, TOEFL (minimum score: iBT 96; paper-based 590; computer-based 243; minimum score for ESL admission: iBT 96; paper-based 590; computer-based 243). Recommended: SAT Subject Tests. *Application deadline:* 1/15. *Expenses:* (2006–07) $34,694; room and board, $9556 (on campus); room only, $5536 (on campus). *Financial aid:* Need-based college/university scholarships/grants from institutional funds, on-campus employment. Non-need-based on-campus employment. Forms required: International Student's Financial Aid Application, International Student's Certification of Finances. International transfer students are eligible to apply for aid. For fall 2005, 12 international students on campus received college administered financial aid ($44,271 average). *Housing:* Guaranteed, also available during summer. *Services:* International student adviser on campus. Internships and employment opportunities (on-campus) available. *Contact:* Dean of Admission and Student Aid, Skidmore College, 815 North Broadway, Saratoga Springs, NY 12866-1632. Telephone: 518-580-5570. Fax: 518-580-5584. E-mail: admissions@skidmore.edu. URL: http://www.skidmore.edu.

STATE UNIVERSITY OF NEW YORK AT BINGHAMTON, BINGHAMTON

General Information State-supported, coed university. Suburban setting. *Awards:* B, M, D. *Entrance level for U.S. students:* Very

difficult. *Enrollment:* 14,373 total; 11,523 undergraduates (48% women) including 7% international students from 65 foreign countries. *Faculty:* 889. *Library holdings:* 2.3 million books, 41,985 current serial subscriptions, 128,055 audiovisual materials. *Total majors:* 56. *Expenses:* (2006–07) $12,170; room and board, $8588 (on campus); room only, $5268 (on campus). *Financial aid:* Need-based financial aid available. Non-need-based college/university scholarships/grants from institutional funds, athletic awards, loans from outside sources, on-campus employment. Forms required: International Student's Certification of Finances. For fall 2006 (estimated), 43 international students on campus received college administered financial aid ($15,256 average).

STATE UNIVERSITY OF NEW YORK AT FREDONIA, FREDONIA

General Information State-supported, coed institution. Small town setting. *Awards:* B, M. *Entrance level for U.S. students:* Moderately difficult. *Enrollment:* 5,540 total; 5,046 undergraduates (56% women) including 0.1% international students from 9 foreign countries. *Faculty:* 444. *Library holdings:* 396,000 books, 2,270 current serial subscriptions. *Total majors:* 74. *Expenses:* (2006–07) $11,742; room and board, $8120 (on campus); room only, $4750 (on campus). *Financial aid:* Need-based college/university scholarships/grants from institutional funds. Non-need-based college/university scholarships/grants from institutional funds. Forms required: International Student's Certification of Finances. For fall 2006 (estimated), 4 international students on campus received college administered financial aid ($12,000 average).

STATE UNIVERSITY OF NEW YORK AT NEW PALTZ, NEW PALTZ

General Information State-supported, coed institution. Small town setting. *Awards:* B, M. *Entrance level for U.S. students:* Very difficult. *Enrollment:* 7,699 total; 6,263 undergraduates (68% women) including 3% international students from 36 foreign countries. *Faculty:* 703. *Library holdings:* 532,381 books, 1,515 current serial subscriptions, 1,614 audiovisual materials. *Total majors:* 73. *Expenses:* (2006–07) $11,600; room and board, $7630 (on campus); room only, $4840 (on campus).

STATE UNIVERSITY OF NEW YORK AT OSWEGO, OSWEGO

General Information State-supported, coed institution. Small town setting. *Awards:* B, M. *Entrance level for U.S. students:* Moderately difficult. *Enrollment:* 8,183 total; 7,096 undergraduates (53% women) including 1% international students from 19 foreign countries. *Faculty:* 507. *Library holdings:* 476,709 books, 2,654 current serial subscriptions, 32,359 audiovisual materials. *Total majors:* 64.

Information for International Students For fall 2006: 74 international students applied, 64 were accepted, 33 enrolled. Students can start in fall, winter, spring, or summer. Transfers accepted from institutions abroad. *Admission tests:* Required: TOEFL (minimum score: paper-based 550; computer-based 213; minimum score for ESL admission: paper-based 550; computer-based 213). TOEFL can be waived under certain conditions. *Application deadline:* Rolling. *Expenses:* (2006–07) $11,582; room and board, $8940 (on campus); room only, $5490 (on campus). *Financial aid:* Non-need-based college/university scholarships/grants from institutional funds. For fall 2005, 17 international students on campus received college administered financial aid ($4532 average). *Housing:* Guaranteed, also available during summer. *Services:* International student adviser on campus. Full-time ESL program on campus. ESL program available during the academic year and the summer. Internships and employment opportunities (on-campus) available. *Contact:* International Student Advisor and Recruiter, State University of New York at Oswego, 201B Culkin Hall, Oswego, NY 13126. Telephone: 315-312-5775. Fax: 315-312-2477. E-mail: oliver@oswego.edu. URL: http://www.oswego.edu.

STATE UNIVERSITY OF NEW YORK AT PLATTSBURGH, PLATTSBURGH

General Information State-supported, coed institution. Small town setting. *Awards:* B, M. *Entrance level for U.S. students:* Very difficult. *Enrollment:* 6,217 total; 5,567 undergraduates (57% women) including 6% international students from 45 foreign countries. *Faculty:* 487. *Library holdings:* 1.6 million books, 4,238 current serial subscriptions, 4,626 audiovisual materials. *Total majors:* 47.

Information for International Students For fall 2006: 394 international students applied, 254 were accepted, 126 enrolled. Students can start in fall or spring. Transfers accepted from institutions abroad. *Admission tests:* Recommended: SAT or ACT, TOEFL (minimum score: iBT 76; paper-based 540; computer-based

State University of New York at Plattsburgh (continued)

207; minimum score for ESL admission: iBT 45; paper-based 450; computer-based 133), IELTS accepted in place of TOEFL. TOEFL can be waived under certain conditions. *Application deadline:* 5/1. *Expenses:* (2006–07) $11,597; room and board, $7728 (on campus); room only, $4800 (on campus). *Financial aid:* Need-based college/university scholarships/grants from institutional funds, on-campus employment. Non-need-based college/university scholarships/grants from institutional funds, on-campus employment. Forms required: institution's own financial aid form, International Student's Certification of Finances. International transfer students are eligible to apply for aid. 300 international students on campus received college administered financial aid ($5500 average). *Housing:* Guaranteed, also available during summer. *Services:* International student adviser on campus. Full-time and part-time ESL programs on campus. ESL program available during the academic year and the summer. Internships and employment opportunities (on-campus and off-campus) available. *Contact:* Director, International Student Services, State University of New York at Plattsburgh, Kehoe Room 209, 101 Broad Street, Plattsburgh, NY 12901. Telephone: 518-564-3287. Fax: 518-564-3292. E-mail: iss@plattsburgh.edu. URL: http://www.plattsburgh.edu.

See In-Depth Description on page 195.

STATE UNIVERSITY OF NEW YORK COLLEGE AT BROCKPORT, BROCKPORT

General Information State-supported, coed institution. Small town setting. *Awards:* B, M. *Entrance level for U.S. students:* Moderately difficult. *Enrollment:* 8,312 total; 6,916 undergraduates (57% women) including 1% international students from 19 foreign countries. *Faculty:* 615. *Library holdings:* 995,618 books, 26,769 current serial subscriptions, 10,303 audiovisual materials. *Total majors:* 112. *Expenses:* (2006–07) $11,616; room and board, $7830 (on campus); room only, $5060 (on campus). *Financial aid:* Need-based college/university scholarships/grants from institutional funds, loans from outside sources. Non-need-based college/university scholarships/grants from institutional funds, loans from outside sources. 43 international students on campus received college administered financial aid ($12,573 average).

STATE UNIVERSITY OF NEW YORK COLLEGE AT CORTLAND, CORTLAND

General Information State-supported, coed institution. Small town setting. *Awards:* B, M. *Entrance level for U.S. students:* Moderately difficult. *Enrollment:* 6,995 total; 5,960 undergraduates (57% women) including 0.5% international students from 9 foreign countries. *Faculty:* 537. *Library holdings:* 82,257 books. *Total majors:* 57. *Expenses:* (2006–07) $10,610; room and board, $7850 (on campus); room only, $4460 (on campus).

STATE UNIVERSITY OF NEW YORK COLLEGE AT GENESEO, GENESEO

General Information State-supported, coed institution. Small town setting. *Awards:* B, M. *Entrance level for U.S. students:* Very difficult. *Enrollment:* 5,530 total; 5,358 undergraduates (59% women) including 3% international students from 31 foreign countries. *Faculty:* 329. *Library holdings:* 647,100 books, 25,822 current serial subscriptions, 28,134 audiovisual materials. *Total majors:* 45.

Information for International Students For fall 2006: 171 international students applied, 76 were accepted, 38 enrolled. Students can start in fall or spring. Transfers accepted from institutions abroad. *Admission tests:* Required: TOEFL (minimum score: iBT 71; paper-based 525; computer-based 197; minimum score for ESL admission: iBT 71; paper-based 525; computer-based 197), results of national exam taken in home country at the end of secondary study (if such exams are given). Recommended: SAT or ACT. *Application deadline:* 6/1. *Expenses:* (2006–07) $11,820; room and board, $7788 (on campus). *Financial aid:* Non-need-based college/university scholarships/grants from institutional funds. International transfer students are eligible to apply for aid. For fall 2006 (estimated), 104 international students on campus received college administered financial aid ($2944 average). *Housing:* Guaranteed, also available during summer. *Services:* International student adviser on campus. Part-time ESL program on campus. ESL program available during the academic year. Internships and employment opportunities (on-campus and off-campus) available. *Contact:* Director of International Student Services, State University of New York College at Geneseo, 1 College Circle, Blake C, Room 209, Geneseo, NY 14454. Telephone: 585-245-5404. Fax: 585-245-5405. E-mail: hope@geneseo.edu. URL: http://www.geneseo.edu.

See In-Depth Description on page 196.

STATE UNIVERSITY OF NEW YORK COLLEGE AT OLD WESTBURY, OLD WESTBURY

General Information State-supported, coed institution. Suburban setting. *Awards:* B, M. *Entrance level for U.S. students:* Moderately difficult. *Enrollment:* 3,450 total; 3,411 undergraduates (61% women) including 2% international students from 31 foreign countries. *Faculty:* 264. *Library holdings:* 246,811 books, 3,428 current serial subscriptions, 1,986 audiovisual materials. *Total majors:* 42. *Expenses:* (2006–07) $11,336; room and board, $8083 (on campus); room only, $5793 (on campus). *Financial aid:* Need-based college/university scholarships/grants from institutional funds, tuition waivers. Non-need-based college/university scholarships/grants from institutional funds, tuition waivers. Forms required: institution's own financial aid form.

STATE UNIVERSITY OF NEW YORK COLLEGE AT ONEONTA, ONEONTA

General Information State-supported, coed institution. Small town setting. *Awards:* B, M. *Entrance level for U.S. students:* Very difficult. *Enrollment:* 5,786 total; 5,596 undergraduates (58% women) including 2% international students from 19 foreign countries. *Faculty:* 475. *Library holdings:* 557,202 books, 21,346 current serial subscriptions, 11,307 audiovisual materials. *Total majors:* 71.

Information for International Students For fall 2006: 210 international students applied, 165 were accepted, 67 enrolled. Students can start in fall or spring. Transfers accepted from institutions abroad. *Admission tests:* Required: TOEFL (minimum score: iBT 70; paper-based 500; computer-based 173), school leaving exams. Recommended: SAT or ACT. TOEFL can be waived under certain conditions. *Application deadline:* Rolling. *Expenses:* (2006–07) $11,672; room and board, $7696 (on campus); room only, $4378 (on campus). *Housing:* Guaranteed, also available during summer. *Services:* International student adviser on campus. Employment opportunities (on-campus) available. *Contact:* Director of International Education, State University of New York College at Oneonta, 311 Netzer Administration Building, Oneonta, NY 13820. Telephone: 607-436-2076. Fax: 607-436-2475. E-mail: ahmedz@oneonta.edu. URL: http://www.oneonta.edu.

STATE UNIVERSITY OF NEW YORK COLLEGE AT POTSDAM, POTSDAM

General Information State-supported, coed institution. Small town setting. *Awards:* B, M. *Entrance level for U.S. students:* Moderately difficult. *Enrollment:* 4,332 total; 3,670 undergraduates (56% women) including 3% international students from 24 foreign countries. *Faculty:* 366. *Library holdings:* 322,591 books, 1,035 current serial subscriptions, 15,915 audiovisual materials. *Total majors:* 43. *Expenses:* (2006–07) $11,617; room and board, $8220 (on campus); room only, $4720 (on campus). *Financial aid:* Non-need-based college/university scholarships/grants from institutional funds, loans from outside sources. For fall 2006 (estimated), 99 international students on campus received college administered financial aid ($7873 average).

STATE UNIVERSITY OF NEW YORK COLLEGE OF AGRICULTURE AND TECHNOLOGY AT MORRISVILLE, MORRISVILLE

General Information State-supported, primarily 2-year, coed college. Rural setting. *Awards:* A, B. *Entrance level for U.S. students:* Minimally difficult. *Enrollment:* 3,288 total (41% women) including 3% international students from 8 foreign countries. *Undergraduate faculty:* 260. *Library holdings:* 100,000 books, 2,500 current serial subscriptions, 1,700 audiovisual materials. *Total majors:* 61. *Expenses:* (2006–07) $11,535; room and board, $7310 (on campus); room only, $3920 (on campus).

STATE UNIVERSITY OF NEW YORK COLLEGE OF ENVIRONMENTAL SCIENCE AND FORESTRY, SYRACUSE

General Information State-supported, coed university. Urban setting. *Awards:* A, B, M, D. *Entrance level for U.S. students:* Moderately difficult. *Enrollment:* 2,069 total; 1,544 undergraduates (38% women) including 1% international students from 8 foreign countries. *Faculty:* 159. *Library holdings:* 135,341 books, 2,000 current serial subscriptions, 150 audiovisual materials. *Total majors:* 48. *Expenses:* (2007–08) $11,329; room and board, $10,600 (on campus); room only, $5210 (on campus). *Financial aid:* Non-need-based college/university scholarships/grants from institutional funds. Forms required: State University of New York Foreign Student Financial Statement.

STATE UNIVERSITY OF NEW YORK COLLEGE OF TECHNOLOGY AT DELHI, DELHI

General Information State-supported, primarily 2-year, coed college. Rural setting. *Awards:* A, B. *Entrance level for U.S.

students: Moderately difficult. *Enrollment:* 2,557 total including 2% international students from 3 foreign countries. *Undergraduate faculty:* 130. *Library holdings:* 47,909 books, 384 current serial subscriptions. *Total majors:* 33. *Expenses:* (2006–07) $8458; room and board, $7880 (on campus). *Financial aid:* Non-need-based college/university scholarships/grants from institutional funds.

STATE UNIVERSITY OF NEW YORK DOWNSTATE MEDICAL CENTER, BROOKLYN

General Information State-supported, coed institution. Urban setting. *Awards:* B, M, D, FP. *Entrance level for U.S. students:* Moderately difficult. *Enrollment:* 1,609 total; 350 undergraduates (83% women) including 1% international students. *Faculty:* 981. *Library holdings:* 357,209 books, 2,104 current serial subscriptions. *Total majors:* 6. *Expenses:* (2006–07) $11,005; room and board, $12,260 (on campus).

STATE UNIVERSITY OF NEW YORK EMPIRE STATE COLLEGE, SARATOGA SPRINGS

General Information State-supported, coed institution. Small town setting. *Awards:* A, B, M (branch locations at 7 regional centers with 35 auxiliary units). *Entrance level for U.S. students:* Minimally difficult. *Enrollment:* 12,038 total; 11,429 undergraduates (62% women) including 6% international students from 4 foreign countries. *Faculty:* 1,118. *Library holdings:* 11,000 books, 10,000 current serial subscriptions. *Total majors:* 14. *Expenses:* (2007–08) $10,835.

STATE UNIVERSITY OF NEW YORK INSTITUTE OF TECHNOLOGY, UTICA

General Information State-supported, coed institution. Suburban setting. *Awards:* B, M. *Entrance level for U.S. students:* Difficulty N/R. *Enrollment:* 2,587 total; 2,069 undergraduates (50% women) including 1% international students from 13 foreign countries. *Faculty:* 167. *Library holdings:* 200,730 books, 372 current serial subscriptions, 11,762 audiovisual materials. *Total majors:* 19. *Expenses:* (2006–07) $11,577; room and board, $7600 (on campus).

STATE UNIVERSITY OF NEW YORK MARITIME COLLEGE, THROGGS NECK

General Information State-supported, coed, primarily men's institution. Suburban setting. *Awards:* A, B, M. *Entrance level for U.S. students:* Moderately difficult. *Enrollment:* 1,316 total; 1,181 undergraduates (11% women) including 6% international students from 20 foreign countries. *Faculty:* 107. *Library holdings:* 85,984 books, 774 audiovisual materials. *Total majors:* 12. *Expenses:* (2007–08) $12,810; room and board, $8919 (on campus); room only, $5570 (on campus).

STATE UNIVERSITY OF NEW YORK UPSTATE MEDICAL UNIVERSITY, SYRACUSE

General Information State-supported, coed institution. Urban setting. *Awards:* B, M, D, FP. *Entrance level for U.S. students:* Moderately difficult. *Enrollment:* 1,236 total; 255 undergraduates (71% women) including 2% international students from 4 foreign countries. *Faculty:* 685. *Library holdings:* 132,500 books, 1,800 current serial subscriptions. *Total majors:* 8. *Expenses:* (2007–08) $21,666; room only, $3930 (on campus).

STONY BROOK UNIVERSITY, STATE UNIVERSITY OF NEW YORK, STONY BROOK

General Information State-supported, coed university. Small town setting. *Awards:* B, M, D, FP. *Entrance level for U.S. students:* Very difficult. *Enrollment:* 22,522 total; 14,847 undergraduates (50% women) including 5% international students from 88 foreign countries. *Faculty:* 1,440. *Library holdings:* 1.9 million books, 29,275 current serial subscriptions, 42,764 audiovisual materials. *Total majors:* 58.
Information for International Students For fall 2006: 1052 international students applied, 321 were accepted, 130 enrolled. Students can start in fall or spring. Transfers accepted from institutions abroad. *Admission tests:* Required: TOEFL (minimum score: iBT 80; paper-based 550; computer-based 213; minimum score for ESL admission: iBT 80; paper-based 550; computer-based 213), ELS. Recommended: SAT or ACT, SAT Subject Tests. TOEFL can be waived under certain conditions. *Application deadline:* 4/1. *Expenses:* (2006–07) $11,891; room and board, $8394 (on campus). *Financial aid:* Non-need-based college/university scholarships/grants from institutional funds, athletic awards, loans from outside sources, on-campus employment. For fall 2005, 96 international students on campus received college administered financial aid ($8571 average). *Housing:* Guaranteed, also available during summer. *Services:* International student adviser on campus. Full-time and part-time ESL programs on campus. ESL program available during the academic year and the summer. Internships

and employment opportunities (on-campus) available. *Contact:* International Admissions Counselor, Stony Brook University, State University of New York, 118 Administration Building, Undergraduate Admissions, Stony Brook, NY 11794-1901. Telephone: 631-632-1214. Fax: 631-632-9898. E-mail: enrollintl@stonybrook.edu. URL: http://www.sunysb.edu.

See In-Depth Description on page 197.

SUFFOLK COUNTY COMMUNITY COLLEGE, SELDEN

General Information State and locally supported, 2-year, coed college. Small town setting. *Awards:* A. *Entrance level for U.S. students:* Noncompetitive. *Enrollment:* 20,280 total (59% women) including 1% international students. *Undergraduate faculty:* 1,162. *Library holdings:* 659 current serial subscriptions. *Total majors:* 60.
Information for International Students For fall 2006: 140 international students applied, 121 were accepted, 71 enrolled. Students can start in fall or spring. Transfers accepted from institutions abroad. *Application deadline:* 6/30. *Financial aid:* Forms required: International Student's Certification of Finances. *Services:* International student adviser on campus. Full-time and part-time ESL programs on campus. ESL program available during the academic year and the summer. Internships available. *Contact:* Executive Director of Admissions and Enrollment Management, Suffolk County Community College, 533 College Road, Selden, NY 11784. Telephone: 516-451-4000. Fax: 516-451-4415. E-mail: admissions@sunysuffolk.edu. URL: http://www.sunysuffolk.edu.

SULLIVAN COUNTY COMMUNITY COLLEGE, LOCH SHELDRAKE

General Information State and locally supported, 2-year, coed college. Rural setting. *Awards:* A. *Entrance level for U.S. students:* Noncompetitive. *Enrollment:* 1,684 total (60% women) including 1% international students from 9 foreign countries. *Undergraduate faculty:* 114. *Library holdings:* 65,699 books, 400 current serial subscriptions. *Total majors:* 31. *Expenses:* (2006–07) $6706; room and board, $6500 (on campus); room only, $4080 (on campus).

SYRACUSE UNIVERSITY, SYRACUSE

General Information Independent, coed university. Urban setting. *Awards:* B, M, D, FP. *Entrance level for U.S. students:* Very difficult. *Enrollment:* 17,492 total; 11,546 undergraduates (55% women) including 3% international students from 93 foreign countries. *Faculty:* 1,432. *Library holdings:* 3.2 million books, 20,637 current serial subscriptions, 430,826 audiovisual materials. *Total majors:* 147.
Information for International Students Students can start in fall or spring. Transfers accepted from institutions abroad. *Admission tests:* Required: SAT or ACT, TOEFL (minimum score: iBT 80; paper-based 550; computer-based 213), IELTS also accepted. TOEFL can be waived under certain conditions. *Application deadline:* 1/1. *Expenses:* (2006–07) $29,965; room and board, $10,420 (on campus); room only, $5390 (on campus). *Financial aid:* Non-need-based college/university scholarships/grants from institutional funds. International transfer students are eligible to apply for aid. *Housing:* Guaranteed. *Services:* International student adviser on campus. Full-time ESL program on campus. ESL program available during the academic year and the summer. Internships and employment opportunities (on-campus and off-campus) available. *Contact:* Associate Director of Admissions, Office of Admissions, Syracuse University, 100 Crouse Hinds Hall, 900 South Crouse Avenue, Syracuse, NY 13244-1100. Telephone: 315-443-3846. Fax: 315-443-4226. E-mail: sbokeefe@syr.edu. URL: http://www.syracuse.edu.

See In-Depth Description on page 200.

TOMPKINS CORTLAND COMMUNITY COLLEGE, DRYDEN

General Information State and locally supported, 2-year, coed college. Rural setting. *Awards:* A. *Entrance level for U.S. students:* Noncompetitive. *Enrollment:* 3,009 total (58% women) including 3% international students from 22 foreign countries. *Undergraduate faculty:* 275. *Library holdings:* 53,897 books, 537 current serial subscriptions, 9,115 audiovisual materials. *Total majors:* 45. *Expenses:* (2007–08) $7538; room only, $5200 (on campus).

UNION COLLEGE, SCHENECTADY

General Information Independent, 4-year, coed college. Urban setting. *Awards:* B. *Entrance level for U.S. students:* Very difficult. *Enrollment:* 2,212 total (47% women) including 2% international students from 20 foreign countries. *Undergraduate faculty:* 223. *Library holdings:* 604,412 books, 4,453 current serial subscriptions, 906 audiovisual materials. *Total majors:* 28.
Information for International Students For fall 2006: 280 international students applied, 51 were accepted, 16 enrolled.

Union College (continued)

Students can start in fall. Transfers accepted from institutions abroad. *Admission tests:* Recommended: SAT or ACT, SAT Subject Tests, TOEFL (minimum score: iBT 90; paper-based 600; computer-based 250), submission of standardized test is not required although SAT or ACT is highly recommended. TOEFL can be waived under certain conditions. *Application deadline:* 1/15. *Expenses:* (2006–07) $44,043. *Financial aid:* Need-based college/university scholarships/grants from institutional funds, loans from institutional funds, on-campus employment. Non-need-based college/university scholarships/grants from institutional funds. Forms required: International Student's Financial Aid Application, International Student's Certification of Finances. International transfer students are eligible to apply for aid. 33 international students on campus received college administered financial aid ($32,294 average). *Services:* International student adviser on campus. Internships and employment opportunities (on-campus and off-campus) available. *Contact:* Assistant Dean of Admissions, Union College, Grant Hall, Schenectady, NY 12308. Telephone: 518-388-6112. Fax: 518-388-6986. E-mail: admissions@union.edu. URL: http://www.union.edu.

UNIVERSITY AT ALBANY, STATE UNIVERSITY OF NEW YORK, ALBANY

General Information State-supported, coed university. Suburban setting. *Awards:* B, M, D. *Entrance level for U.S. students:* Moderately difficult. *Enrollment:* 17,434 total; 12,457 undergraduates (50% women) including 2% international students from 57 foreign countries. *Faculty:* 1,214. *Library holdings:* 2.2 million books, 42,829 current serial subscriptions, 15,936 audiovisual materials. *Total majors:* 69. *Expenses:* (2006–07) $12,199; room and board, $8605 (on campus); room only, $5269 (on campus). *Financial aid:* Forms required: International Student's Certification of Finances.

UNIVERSITY AT BUFFALO, THE STATE UNIVERSITY OF NEW YORK, BUFFALO

General Information State-supported, coed university. Suburban setting. *Awards:* B, M, D, FP. *Entrance level for U.S. students:* Moderately difficult. *Enrollment:* 27,220 total; 18,165 undergraduates (46% women) including 7% international students from 78 foreign countries. *Faculty:* 1,748. *Library holdings:* 3.4 million books, 34,126 current serial subscriptions, 188,300 audiovisual materials. *Total majors:* 81.
Information for International Students Students can start in fall or spring. Transfers accepted from institutions abroad. *Admission tests:* Required: TOEFL (minimum score: iBT 79; paper-based 550; computer-based 213). Recommended: SAT. TOEFL can be waived under certain conditions. *Application deadline:* Rolling. *Expenses:* (2006–07) $12,388; room and board, $8108 (on campus); room only, $5008 (on campus). *Financial aid:* Non-need-based college/university scholarships/grants from institutional funds, tuition waivers, athletic awards, loans from institutional funds, loans from outside sources, on-campus employment. For fall 2006 (estimated), 108 international students on campus received college administered financial aid ($2567 average). *Housing:* Guaranteed, also available during summer. *Services:* International student adviser on campus. Full-time ESL program on campus. ESL program available during the academic year and the summer. Internships and employment opportunities (on-campus) available. *Contact:* Director of International Enrollment Management, Office of International Enrollment Management, University at Buffalo, the State University of New York, 411 Capen Hall, Buffalo, NY 14260-1604. Telephone: 716-645-2368. Fax: 716-645-2528. E-mail: intiem@buffalo.edu. URL: http://www.buffalo.edu.

See In-Depth Description on page 206.

UNIVERSITY OF ROCHESTER, ROCHESTER

General Information Independent, coed university. Suburban setting. *Awards:* B, M, D, FP. *Entrance level for U.S. students:* Very difficult. *Enrollment:* 8,846 total; 4,904 undergraduates (51% women) including 5% international students from 39 foreign countries. *Faculty:* 763. *Library holdings:* 3 million books, 11,254 current serial subscriptions. *Total majors:* 50.
Information for International Students For fall 2006: 532 international students applied, 230 were accepted, 51 enrolled. Students can start in fall or spring. *Admission tests:* Required: SAT, TOEFL. *Application deadline:* 12/1. *Expenses:* (2007–08) $35,190; room and board, $10,640 (on campus); room only, $6200 (on campus). *Financial aid:* Need-based college/university scholarships/grants from institutional funds, loans from outside sources, on-campus employment. Non-need-based college/university scholarships/grants from institutional funds, loans from outside

sources, on-campus employment. Forms required: CSS PROFILE, International Student's Financial Aid Application, International Student's Certification of Finances. For fall 2006 (estimated), 33 international students on campus received college administered financial aid ($10,075 average). *Contact:* Director of International Admissions, University of Rochester, Rochester, NY 14627-0251. Telephone: 585-275-3221. Fax: 585-461-4595. E-mail: international@admissions.rochester.edu. URL: http://www.rochester.edu.

See In-Depth Description on page 222.

UTICA COLLEGE, UTICA

General Information Independent, coed institution. Suburban setting. *Awards:* B, M, FP. *Entrance level for U.S. students:* Moderately difficult. *Enrollment:* 2,952 total; 2,429 undergraduates (60% women) including 1% international students from 15 foreign countries. *Faculty:* 290. *Library holdings:* 184,918 books, 1,249 current serial subscriptions, 9,737 audiovisual materials. *Total majors:* 44.
Information for International Students For fall 2006: 91 international students applied, 45 were accepted, 20 enrolled. Students can start in fall, spring, or summer. Transfers accepted from institutions abroad. *Admission tests:* Required: TOEFL (minimum score: paper-based 525; computer-based 195; minimum score for ESL admission: paper-based 525; computer-based 195). Recommended: IELTS, APIEL, Kaplan, other tests of English proficiency. TOEFL can be waived under certain conditions. *Application deadline:* Rolling. *Expenses:* (2006–07) $23,440; room and board, $9510 (on campus). *Financial aid:* Need-based college/university scholarships/grants from institutional funds, tuition waivers, loans from outside sources, on-campus employment. Non-need-based college/university scholarships/grants from institutional funds, loans from outside sources, on-campus employment. Forms required: International Student's Certification of Finances. For fall 2005, 14 international students on campus received college administered financial aid ($8108 average). *Housing:* Guaranteed, also available during summer. *Services:* International student adviser on campus. ESL program at cooperating institution. ESL program available during the academic year and the summer. Internships and employment opportunities (on-campus) available. *Contact:* Director of International Admissions, Utica College, 1600 Burrstone Road, Utica, NY 13502-4892. Telephone: 315-792-3753. Fax: 315-223-2515. E-mail: ccominsky@utica.edu. URL: http://www.utica.edu.

See In-Depth Description on page 239.

VASSAR COLLEGE, POUGHKEEPSIE

General Information Independent, coed institution. Suburban setting. *Awards:* B, M. *Entrance level for U.S. students:* Very difficult. *Enrollment:* 2,424 total; 2,423 undergraduates (60% women) including 5% international students from 43 foreign countries. *Faculty:* 318. *Library holdings:* 886,097 books, 5,302 current serial subscriptions, 20,448 audiovisual materials. *Total majors:* 51. *Expenses:* (2006–07) $36,030; room and board, $8130 (on campus); room only, $4310 (on campus). *Financial aid:* Need-based college/university scholarships/grants from institutional funds, loans from outside sources, on-campus employment. Non-need-based loans from outside sources, on-campus employment. Forms required: International Student's Financial Aid Application, International Student's Certification of Finances. For fall 2006 (estimated), 122 international students on campus received college administered financial aid ($38,847 average).

VAUGHN COLLEGE OF AERONAUTICS AND TECHNOLOGY, FLUSHING

General Information Independent, 4-year, coed, primarily men's college. Urban setting. *Awards:* A, B. *Entrance level for U.S. students:* Minimally difficult. *Enrollment:* 1,097 total (13% women) including 3% international students from 15 foreign countries. *Undergraduate faculty:* 96. *Library holdings:* 62,000 books, 400 current serial subscriptions. *Total majors:* 9. *Expenses:* (2007–08) $14,280; room and board, $10,000 (on campus). *Financial aid:* Non-need financial aid available. For fall 2005, 20 international students on campus received college administered financial aid ($500 average).

WAGNER COLLEGE, STATEN ISLAND

General Information Independent, coed institution. Urban setting. *Awards:* B, M. *Entrance level for U.S. students:* Moderately difficult. *Enrollment:* 2,280 total; 1,941 undergraduates (64% women) including 1% international students from 14 foreign countries. *Faculty:* 231. *Library holdings:* 310,000 books, 1,000 current serial subscriptions, 1,616 audiovisual materials. *Total majors:* 35. *Expenses:* (2006–07) $27,400; room and board, $8400 (on campus). *Financial aid:* Non-need financial aid available. Forms required: institution's own financial aid form. For fall 2006 (estimated), 3 international students on campus received college administered financial aid ($4633 average).

WELLS COLLEGE, AURORA

General Information Independent, 4-year, coed, primarily women's college. Rural setting. *Awards:* B. *Entrance level for U.S. students:* Moderately difficult. *Enrollment:* 481 total (84% women) including 2% international students from 8 foreign countries. *Undergraduate faculty:* 78. *Library holdings:* 213,221 books, 380 current serial subscriptions, 979 audiovisual materials. *Total majors:* 40.

Information for International Students For fall 2006: 124 international students applied, 14 were accepted, 3 enrolled. Students can start in fall or spring. Transfers accepted from institutions abroad. *Admission tests:* Required: TOEFL (minimum score: iBT 80; paper-based 550; computer-based 213). Recommended: SAT or ACT. TOEFL can be waived under certain conditions. *Application deadline:* 3/1. *Expenses:* (2006–07) $16,680; room and board, $7500 (on campus); room only, $3750 (on campus). *Financial aid:* Non-need-based college/university scholarships/grants from institutional funds, on-campus employment. Forms required: International Student's Certification of Finances. International transfer students are eligible to apply for aid. For fall 2006 (estimated), 8 international students on campus received college administered financial aid ($5563 average). *Housing:* Guaranteed. *Services:* International student adviser on campus. ESL program at cooperating institution. ESL program available during the summer. Internships and employment opportunities (on-campus) available. *Contact:* Associate Director of Admissions, Wells College, 170 Main Street, Aurora, NY 13026. Telephone: 315-364-3264. Fax: 315-364-3227. E-mail: admissions@wells.edu. URL: http://www.wells.edu.

WESTCHESTER COMMUNITY COLLEGE, VALHALLA

General Information State and locally supported, 2-year, coed college. Suburban setting. *Awards:* A. *Entrance level for U.S. students:* Noncompetitive. *Enrollment:* 11,579 total (56% women) including 2% international students from 58 foreign countries. *Undergraduate faculty:* 497. *Library holdings:* 132,181 books, 318 current serial subscriptions, 9,434 audiovisual materials. *Total majors:* 52. *Expenses:* (2007–08) $8989. *Financial aid:* Non-need-based college/university scholarships/grants from institutional funds.

WOOD TOBE–COBURN SCHOOL, NEW YORK

General Information Proprietary, 2-year, coed, primarily women's college. Urban setting. *Awards:* A. *Entrance level for U.S. students:* Minimally difficult. *Enrollment:* 269 total (77% women) including 2% international students. *Undergraduate faculty:* 21. *Library holdings:* 698 books, 45 current serial subscriptions. *Total majors:* 9. *Expenses:* (2006–07) $14,400.

YORK COLLEGE OF THE CITY UNIVERSITY OF NEW YORK, JAMAICA

General Information State and locally supported, 4-year, coed college. Urban setting. *Awards:* B. *Entrance level for U.S. students:* Moderately difficult. *Enrollment:* 6,185 total (68% women) including international students from 119 foreign countries. *Undergraduate faculty:* 456. *Library holdings:* 182,141 books, 1,978 current serial subscriptions. *Total majors:* 36.

Information for International Students For fall 2006: 100 international students applied, 70 were accepted, 50 enrolled. Students can start in fall or spring. Transfers accepted from institutions abroad. *Admission tests:* Required: TOEFL (minimum score: paper-based 500; computer-based 150; minimum score for ESL admission: paper-based 500; computer-based 150). Recommended: SAT or ACT. *Application deadline:* Rolling. *Expenses:* (2007–08) $8820. *Financial aid:* Need-based and non-need-based financial aid available. *Services:* International student adviser on campus. Full-time ESL program on campus. ESL program available during the academic year. Internships and employment opportunities (on-campus) available. *Contact:* International Admissions Advisor, York College of the City University of New York, 94-20 Guy Brewer Boulevard, Room 1B07, Jamaica, NY 11451. Telephone: 718-262-2169. Fax: 718-262-2601. E-mail: jcontrer@york.cuny.edu. URL: http://www.york.cuny.edu.

NORTH CAROLINA

ALAMANCE COMMUNITY COLLEGE, GRAHAM

General Information State-supported, 2-year, coed college. Small town setting. *Awards:* A. *Entrance level for U.S. students:* Noncompetitive. *Enrollment:* 4,637 total (66% women) including 0.03% international students from 1 foreign country. *Undergraduate faculty:* 381. *Library holdings:* 22,114 books, 185 current serial subscriptions. *Total majors:* 33.

Information for International Students For fall 2006: 1 international student applied, 1 was accepted, 1 enrolled. Students can start in fall or spring. *Admission tests:* Required: TOEFL (minimum score: iBT 79; paper-based 550; computer-based 217). *Application deadline:* Rolling. *Expenses:* (2006–07) $7054. *Financial aid:* Need-based college/university scholarships/grants from institutional funds, loans from institutional funds, loans from outside sources, on-campus employment. Non-need-based on-campus employment. Forms required: institution's own financial aid form. *Services:* International student adviser on campus. *Contact:* Placement Coordinator, Alamance Community College, PO Box 8000, Graham, NC 27253. Telephone: 336-506-4140. Fax: 336-506-4264. E-mail: barretmc@alamancecc.edu. URL: http://www.alamance.cc.nc.us.

APPALACHIAN STATE UNIVERSITY, BOONE

General Information State-supported, coed institution. Small town setting. *Awards:* B, M, D. *Entrance level for U.S. students:* Moderately difficult. *Enrollment:* 15,117 total; 13,447 undergraduates (50% women) including 0.5% international students from 36 foreign countries. *Faculty:* 1,042. *Library holdings:* 906,756 books, 5,543 current serial subscriptions, 11,974 audiovisual materials. *Total majors:* 84. *Expenses:* (2006–07) $13,929; room and board, $5760 (on campus); room only, $3100 (on campus).

BELMONT ABBEY COLLEGE, BELMONT

General Information Independent Roman Catholic, 4-year, coed college. Small town setting. *Awards:* B. *Entrance level for U.S. students:* Moderately difficult. *Enrollment:* 1,110 total (57% women) including 4% international students from 17 foreign countries. *Undergraduate faculty:* 90. *Library holdings:* 118,827 books, 275 current serial subscriptions, 7,418 audiovisual materials. *Total majors:* 23. *Expenses:* (2006–07) $17,302; room and board, $9430 (on campus); room only, $5450 (on campus). *Financial aid:* Need-based athletic awards. Non-need-based college/university scholarships/grants from institutional funds, athletic awards. For fall 2006 (estimated), 46 international students on campus received college administered financial aid ($6800 average).

CALDWELL COMMUNITY COLLEGE AND TECHNICAL INSTITUTE, HUDSON

General Information State-supported, 2-year, coed college. Small town setting. *Awards:* A. *Entrance level for U.S. students:* Noncompetitive. *Enrollment:* 3,878 total (56% women) including international students from 15 foreign countries. *Undergraduate faculty:* 432. *Library holdings:* 50,770 books, 251 current serial subscriptions. *Total majors:* 25. *Expenses:* (2006–07) $6585.

CAMPBELL UNIVERSITY, BUIES CREEK

General Information Independent, coed university, affiliated with North Carolina Baptist State Convention. Rural setting. *Awards:* A, B, M, D, FP. *Entrance level for U.S. students:* Moderately difficult. *Enrollment:* 6,033 total; 4,384 undergraduates (52% women) including international students from 50 foreign countries. *Faculty:* 336. *Library holdings:* 231,298 books, 17,268 current serial subscriptions. *Total majors:* 98. *Expenses:* (2007–08) $18,598; room and board, $6160 (on campus).

CATAWBA COLLEGE, SALISBURY

General Information Independent, coed institution, affiliated with United Church of Christ. Small town setting. *Awards:* B, M. *Entrance level for U.S. students:* Moderately difficult. *Enrollment:* 1,269 total; 1,235 undergraduates (51% women) including 1% international students from 12 foreign countries. *Faculty:* 100. *Library holdings:* 112,447 books, 604 current serial subscriptions. *Total majors:* 42. *Expenses:* (2006–07) $19,690; room and board, $6570 (on campus). *Financial aid:* Non-need-based college/university scholarships/grants from institutional funds, athletic awards, on-campus employment. Forms required: International Student's Certification of Finances. For fall 2006 (estimated), 12 international students on campus received college administered financial aid ($17,502 average).

CATAWBA VALLEY COMMUNITY COLLEGE, HICKORY

General Information State and locally supported, 2-year, coed college. Small town setting. *Awards:* A. *Entrance level for U.S. students:* Noncompetitive. *Enrollment:* 4,869 total (60% women) including 0.2% international students from 5 foreign countries. *Undergraduate faculty:* 466. *Library holdings:* 25,000 books, 610 current serial subscriptions, 700 audiovisual materials. *Total majors:* 42. *Expenses:* (2006–07) $7048.

CENTRAL PIEDMONT COMMUNITY COLLEGE, CHARLOTTE

General Information State and locally supported, 2-year, coed college. Urban setting. *Awards:* A. *Entrance level for U.S. students:* Noncompetitive. *Enrollment:* 16,631 total (58% women) including 9% international students from 117 foreign countries. *Undergraduate faculty:* 2,034. *Library holdings:* 102,649 books, 750 current serial subscriptions, 17,802 audiovisual materials. *Total majors:* 69.

Information for International Students For fall 2006: 295 international students applied, 295 were accepted, 115 enrolled. Students can start in fall, spring, or summer. Transfers accepted from institutions abroad. *Admission tests:* Recommended: TOEFL (minimum score: iBT 66; paper-based 500; computer-based 173). TOEFL can be waived under certain conditions. *Application deadline:* Rolling. *Expenses:* (2006–07) $7194. *Financial aid:* Need-based college/university scholarships/grants from institutional funds, loans from institutional funds, loans from outside sources, on-campus employment. Non-need-based college/university scholarships/grants from institutional funds, loans from outside sources. *Services:* International student adviser on campus. Full-time ESL program on campus. ESL program available during the academic year and the summer. Internships and employment opportunities (on-campus) available. *Contact:* Coordinator, International Admissions, International Student Office, Central Piedmont Community College, PO Box 35009, Charlotte, NC 28235. Telephone: 704-330-6456. Fax: 704-330-6130. E-mail: dotty.holley@cpcc.edu. URL: http://www.cpcc.edu.

CHOWAN UNIVERSITY, MURFREESBORO

General Information Independent Baptist, 4-year, coed college. Rural setting. *Awards:* A, B. *Entrance level for U.S. students:* Minimally difficult. *Enrollment:* 800 total (44% women) including 10% international students from 3 foreign countries. *Undergraduate faculty:* 79. *Library holdings:* 93,676 books, 1,113 current serial subscriptions, 4,569 audiovisual materials. *Total majors:* 37. *Expenses:* (2006–07) $16,040; room and board, $6800 (on campus); room only, $3200 (on campus). *Financial aid:* Non-need-based college/university scholarships/grants from institutional funds, on-campus employment. Forms required: International Student's Certification of Finances. For fall 2005, 6 international students on campus received college administered financial aid ($2500 average).

COASTAL CAROLINA COMMUNITY COLLEGE, JACKSONVILLE

General Information State and locally supported, 2-year, coed college. Small town setting. *Awards:* A. *Entrance level for U.S. students:* Noncompetitive. *Enrollment:* 4,111 total (65% women) including 1% international students from 5 foreign countries. *Undergraduate faculty:* 261. *Library holdings:* 44,062 books, 266 current serial subscriptions. *Total majors:* 19. *Expenses:* (2007–08) $7054. *Financial aid:* Forms required: institution's own financial aid form.

DAVIDSON COLLEGE, DAVIDSON

General Information Independent Presbyterian, 4-year, coed college. Small town setting. *Awards:* B. *Entrance level for U.S. students:* Very difficult. *Enrollment:* 1,667 total (50% women) including 4% international students from 33 foreign countries. *Undergraduate faculty:* 172. *Library holdings:* 422,035 books, 2,767 current serial subscriptions. *Total majors:* 21.

Information for International Students For fall 2006: 300 international students applied, 30 were accepted, 16 enrolled. Students can start in fall. *Admission tests:* Required: SAT or ACT, TOEFL (minimum score: iBT 100; paper-based 600; computer-based 250). Recommended: SAT Subject Tests. TOEFL can be waived under certain conditions. *Application deadline:* 1/2. *Expenses:* (2006–07) $30,194; room and board, $8590 (on campus). *Financial aid:* Need-based college/university scholarships/grants from institutional funds, loans from outside sources, on-campus employment. Non-need-based college/university scholarships/grants from institutional funds, athletic awards, loans from outside sources. Forms required: International Student's Financial Aid Application, International Student's Certification of Finances. For fall 2005, 38 international students on campus received college administered financial aid ($29,707 average). *Housing:* Guaranteed. *Services:* International student adviser on campus. Employment opportunities (on-campus) available. *Contact:* Admissions Assistant, Davidson College, PO Box 7156, Davidson, NC 28035. Telephone: 704-894-2054. Fax: 704-892-2016. E-mail: caalexander@davidson.edu. URL: http://www.davidson.edu.

DEVRY UNIVERSITY, CHARLOTTE

General Information Proprietary, coed institution. *Awards:* B, M. *Entrance level for U.S. students:* Minimally difficult. *Enrollment:*

187 total; 82 undergraduates (55% women) including 2% international students. *Faculty:* 12. *Total majors:* 2. *Expenses:* (2007–08) $13,020.

DUKE UNIVERSITY, DURHAM

General Information Independent, coed university, affiliated with United Methodist Church. Suburban setting. *Awards:* B, M, D, FP. *Entrance level for U.S. students:* Most difficult. *Enrollment:* 13,373 total; 6,330 undergraduates (49% women) including 6% international students from 89 foreign countries. *Library holdings:* 5.6 million books, 31,892 current serial subscriptions, 59,547 audiovisual materials. *Total majors:* 45. *Expenses:* (2006–07) $33,963; room and board, $9152 (on campus); room only, $4950 (on campus). *Financial aid:* Need-based college/university scholarships/grants from institutional funds, athletic awards, loans from outside sources, on-campus employment. Non-need-based college/university scholarships/grants from institutional funds, athletic awards, loans from outside sources. Forms required: International Student's Financial Aid Application. For fall 2006 (estimated), 99 international students on campus received college administered financial aid ($35,508 average).

EAST CAROLINA UNIVERSITY, GREENVILLE

General Information State-supported, coed university. Urban setting. *Awards:* B, M, D, FP. *Entrance level for U.S. students:* Moderately difficult. *Enrollment:* 24,351 total; 18,587 undergraduates (59% women) including 0.3% international students. *Faculty:* 1,894. *Library holdings:* 2 million books, 252,699 current serial subscriptions. *Total majors:* 92.

Information for International Students For fall 2006: 88 international students applied, 57 were accepted, 34 enrolled. Students can start in fall, spring, or summer. Transfers accepted from institutions abroad. *Admission tests:* Required: TOEFL (minimum score: iBT 80; paper-based 550; computer-based 213). TOEFL can be waived under certain conditions. *Application deadline:* Rolling. *Expenses:* (2006–07) $14,517; room and board, $6940 (on campus); room only, $3790 (on campus). *Housing:* Guaranteed, also available during summer. *Services:* International student adviser on campus. Internships and employment opportunities (on-campus) available. *Contact:* Assistant Director for International Student Recruitment, East Carolina University, 306 East 9th Street, Greenville, NC 27858. Telephone: 252-328-6769. Fax: 252-328-4813. E-mail: intlprgm@ecu.edu. URL: http://www.ecu.edu.

See In-Depth Description on page 71.

ELON UNIVERSITY, ELON

General Information Independent, coed institution, affiliated with United Church of Christ. Suburban setting. *Awards:* B, M, D, FP. *Entrance level for U.S. students:* Moderately difficult. *Enrollment:* 5,230 total; 4,849 undergraduates (60% women) including 2% international students from 38 foreign countries. *Faculty:* 400. *Library holdings:* 250,119 books, 4,955 current serial subscriptions, 17,297 audiovisual materials. *Total majors:* 51.

Information for International Students For fall 2006: 183 international students applied, 95 were accepted, 27 enrolled. Students can start in fall or spring. Transfers accepted from institutions abroad. *Admission tests:* Required: SAT or ACT, TOEFL (minimum score: iBT 79; paper-based 550; computer-based 213; minimum score for ESL admission: iBT 79; paper-based 500; computer-based 213). TOEFL can be waived under certain conditions. *Application deadline:* 1/10. *Expenses:* (2006–07) $20,441; room and board, $6850 (on campus). *Financial aid:* Need-based college/university scholarships/grants from institutional funds, athletic awards. Non-need-based college/university scholarships/grants from institutional funds, athletic awards, on-campus employment. Forms required: International Student's Certification of Finances. *Housing:* Guaranteed, also available during summer. *Services:* International student adviser on campus. Internships and employment opportunities (on-campus) available. *Contact:* Director of International Admissions/Associate Director of Admissions, Elon University, 100 Campus Drive, 2700 Campus Box, Elon, NC 27244. Telephone: 336-278-3566. Fax: 336-278-7699. E-mail: admissions@elon.edu. URL: http://www.elon.edu.

FAYETTEVILLE STATE UNIVERSITY, FAYETTEVILLE

General Information State-supported, coed institution. Urban setting. *Awards:* B, M, D. *Entrance level for U.S. students:* Minimally difficult. *Enrollment:* 6,301 total; 5,399 undergraduates (69% women) including 0.3% international students from 3. foreign countries. *Faculty:* 331. *Library holdings:* 334,089 books, 2,735 current serial subscriptions, 17,458 audiovisual materials. *Total majors:* 34. *Expenses:* (2007–08) $13,564; room and board, $4870 (on campus); room only, $2870 (on campus).

FAYETTEVILLE TECHNICAL COMMUNITY COLLEGE, FAYETTEVILLE

General Information State-supported, 2-year, coed college. Suburban setting. *Awards:* A. *Entrance level for U.S. students:* Noncompetitive. *Enrollment:* 10,290 total (70% women) including 0.3% international students from 9 foreign countries. *Undergraduate faculty:* 842. *Library holdings:* 64,143 books, 319 current serial subscriptions, 7,797 audiovisual materials. *Total majors:* 53. *Expenses:* (2006–07) $7054. *Financial aid:* Forms required: institution's own financial aid form.

FORSYTH TECHNICAL COMMUNITY COLLEGE, WINSTON-SALEM

General Information State supported, 2-year, coed college. Suburban setting. *Awards:* A. *Entrance level for U.S. students:* Noncompetitive. *Enrollment:* 6,978 total (64% women) including 2% international students. *Undergraduate faculty:* 486. *Library holdings:* 41,606 books, 358 current serial subscriptions. *Total majors:* 38. *Expenses:* (2006–07) $5303. *Financial aid:* Forms required: FTCC International Student Scholarship Application.

GARDNER-WEBB UNIVERSITY, BOILING SPRINGS

General Information Independent Baptist, coed institution. Small town setting. *Awards:* A, B, M, D, FP. *Entrance level for U.S. students:* Moderately difficult. *Enrollment:* 3,840 total; 2,659 undergraduates (67% women) including international students from 31 foreign countries. *Faculty:* 339. *Library holdings:* 236,000 books, 15,000 current serial subscriptions, 10,400 audiovisual materials. *Total majors:* 53.
Information for International Students For fall 2006: 30 international students applied, 26 were accepted, 26 enrolled. Students can start in fall, spring, or summer. Transfers accepted from institutions abroad. *Admission tests:* Required: SAT or ACT, TOEFL (minimum score: paper-based 500; computer-based 175; minimum score for ESL admission: paper-based 500; computer-based 175). *Application deadline:* Rolling. *Expenses:* (2006–07) $17,590; room and board, $5740 (on campus); room only, $2950 (on campus). *Financial aid:* Non-need-based college/university scholarships/grants from institutional funds, athletic awards. Forms required: International Student's Certification of Finances. *Housing:* Guaranteed, also available during summer. *Services:* International student adviser on campus. Internships and employment opportunities (on-campus and off-campus) available. *Contact:* Assistant Director of Admissions, Gardner-Webb University, PO Box 817, Boiling Springs, NC 28017. Telephone: 704-434-4495. Fax: 704-434-4488. E-mail: cmckinney@gardner-webb.edu. URL: http://www.gardner-webb.edu.

GUILFORD COLLEGE, GREENSBORO

General Information Independent, 4-year, coed college, affiliated with Society of Friends. Suburban setting. *Awards:* B. *Entrance level for U.S. students:* Moderately difficult. *Enrollment:* 2,687 total (62% women) including 1% international students from 17 foreign countries. *Undergraduate faculty:* 210. *Library holdings:* 236,698 books, 28,790 current serial subscriptions, 4,068 audiovisual materials. *Total majors:* 37. *Expenses:* (2006–07) $23,020; room and board, $6690 (on campus). *Financial aid:* Need-based college/university scholarships/grants from institutional funds. Non-need-based college/university scholarships/grants from institutional funds, on-campus employment. Forms required: International Student's Financial Aid Application, International Student's Certification of Finances. For fall 2006 (estimated), 11 international students on campus received college administered financial aid ($18,091 average).

HIGH POINT UNIVERSITY, HIGH POINT

General Information Independent United Methodist, coed institution. Suburban setting. *Awards:* B, M. *Entrance level for U.S. students:* Moderately difficult. *Enrollment:* 2,811 total; 2,564 undergraduates (62% women) including 3% international students from 40 foreign countries. *Faculty:* 267. *Library holdings:* 204,141 books, 23,767 current serial subscriptions, 7,988 audiovisual materials. *Total majors:* 49. *Expenses:* (2007–08) $19,850; room and board, $7960 (on campus); room only, $3600 (on campus). *Financial aid:* Non-need financial aid available. Forms required: International Student's Certification of Finances. 10 international students on campus received college administered financial aid ($4000 average).

ISOTHERMAL COMMUNITY COLLEGE, SPINDALE

General Information State-supported, 2-year, coed college. Rural setting. *Awards:* A. *Entrance level for U.S. students:* Noncompetitive. *Enrollment:* 2,005 total (65% women) including 0.3% international students from 3 foreign countries. *Undergraduate faculty:* 114. *Library holdings:* 35,200 books, 289 current serial subscriptions. *Total majors:* 34.

Information for International Students For fall 2006: 31 international students applied, 11 enrolled. Students can start in fall, spring, or summer. Transfers accepted from institutions abroad. *Admission tests:* Required: TOEFL (minimum score: paper-based 500; computer-based 173), ASSET placement test. TOEFL can be waived under certain conditions. *Application deadline:* Rolling. *Expenses:* (2006–07) $6612. *Financial aid:* Need-based college/university scholarships/grants from institutional funds, on-campus employment. Non-need-based college/university scholarships/grants from institutional funds. *Services:* Full-time and part-time ESL programs on campus. ESL program available during the academic year and the summer. *Contact:* Director, Enrollment Management, Isothermal Community College, PO Box 804, Spindale, NC 28160. Telephone: 828-286-3636 Ext. 288. Fax: 828-286-8109. E-mail: mkilloran@isothermal.edu. URL: http://www.isothermal.edu.

LEES-MCRAE COLLEGE, BANNER ELK

General Information Independent, 4-year, coed college, affiliated with Presbyterian Church (U.S.A.). Rural setting. *Awards:* B. *Entrance level for U.S. students:* Minimally difficult. *Enrollment:* 882 total (56% women) including 1% international students from 20 foreign countries. *Undergraduate faculty:* 56. *Library holdings:* 88,756 books, 429 current serial subscriptions. *Total majors:* 29.
Information for International Students For fall 2006: 44 international students applied, 27 were accepted, 17 enrolled. Students can start in fall or spring. Transfers accepted from institutions abroad. *Admission tests:* Required: TOEFL (minimum score: paper-based 500; computer-based 173). TOEFL can be waived under certain conditions. *Application deadline:* Rolling. *Expenses:* (2007–08) $19,500; room and board, $6500 (on campus). *Financial aid:* Non-need financial aid available. International transfer students are eligible to apply for aid. 40 international students on campus received college administered financial aid ($11,539 average). *Housing:* Guaranteed. *Services:* International student adviser on campus. Part-time ESL program on campus. ESL program available during the academic year. Internships and employment opportunities (on-campus) available. *Contact:* Associate Director of Admissions, Lees-McRae College, PO Box 128, Banner Elk, NC 28604. Telephone: 828-898-8701. Fax: 828-898-8707. E-mail: hinshaw@lmc.edu. URL: http://www2.lmc.edu.

MEREDITH COLLEGE, RALEIGH

General Information Independent, undergraduate: women only; graduate: coed institution. Urban setting. *Awards:* B, M. *Entrance level for U.S. students:* Moderately difficult. *Enrollment:* 2,139 total; 1,990 undergraduates (99% women) including 1% international students from 13 foreign countries. *Faculty:* 281. *Library holdings:* 186,100 books, 669 current serial subscriptions. *Total majors:* 57. *Expenses:* (2006–07) $21,200; room and board, $5940 (on campus). *Financial aid:* Need-based and non-need-based financial aid available. Forms required: letter of financial circumstances. For fall 2006 (estimated), 6 international students on campus received college administered financial aid ($7512 average).

METHODIST UNIVERSITY, FAYETTEVILLE

General Information Independent United Methodist, coed institution. Suburban setting. *Awards:* A, B, M. *Entrance level for U.S. students:* Moderately difficult. *Enrollment:* 2,082 total; 1,996 undergraduates (46% women) including 4% international students from 31 foreign countries. *Faculty:* 212. *Library holdings:* 86,259 books, 571 current serial subscriptions. *Total majors:* 56. *Expenses:* (2007–08) $20,080; room and board, $7550 (on campus); room only, $3800 (on campus). *Financial aid:* Need-based college/university scholarships/grants from institutional funds, loans from outside sources, on-campus employment. Non-need-based college/university scholarships/grants from institutional funds, loans from outside sources, on-campus employment. For fall 2005, 61 international students on campus received college administered financial aid ($19,074 average).

MONTGOMERY COMMUNITY COLLEGE, TROY

General Information State-supported, 2-year, coed college. Rural setting. *Awards:* A. *Entrance level for U.S. students:* Noncompetitive. *Enrollment:* 850 total (69% women) including 0.2% international students. *Undergraduate faculty:* 73. *Library holdings:* 14,859 books, 99 current serial subscriptions, 500 audiovisual materials. *Total majors:* 11. *Financial aid:* Need-based college/university scholarships/grants from institutional funds. Non-need-based college/university scholarships/grants from institutional funds. Forms required: institution's own financial aid form.

MONTREAT COLLEGE, MONTREAT

General Information Independent, coed institution, affiliated with Presbyterian Church (U.S.A.). Small town setting. *Awards:* A,

Montreat College (continued)

B, M. *Entrance level for U.S. students:* Moderately difficult. *Enrollment:* 1,039 total; 959 undergraduates (61% women) including 2% international students from 10 foreign countries. *Faculty:* 86. *Library holdings:* 68,100 books, 426 current serial subscriptions. *Total majors:* 14. *Expenses:* (2006–07) $16,182; room and board, $5258 (on campus). *Financial aid:* Need-based college/university scholarships/grants from institutional funds, athletic awards, on-campus employment. Non-need-based college/university scholarships/grants from institutional funds, athletic awards, loans from outside sources. Forms required: institution's own financial aid form. For fall 2006 (estimated), 17 international students on campus received college administered financial aid ($7500 average).

NORTH CAROLINA AGRICULTURAL AND TECHNICAL STATE UNIVERSITY, GREENSBORO

General Information State-supported, coed university. Urban setting. *Awards:* B, M, D. *Entrance level for U.S. students:* Moderately difficult. *Enrollment:* 11,098 total; 9,687 undergraduates (53% women) including 0.4% international students. *Faculty:* 495. *Library holdings:* 597,093 books, 40,425 current serial subscriptions, 37,886 audiovisual materials. *Total majors:* 59. *Expenses:* (2006–07) $13,314; room and board, $6686 (on campus). *Financial aid:* Non-need financial aid available. For fall 2005, 30 international students on campus received college administered financial aid ($11,897 average).

NORTH CAROLINA CENTRAL UNIVERSITY, DURHAM

General Information State-supported, coed institution. Urban setting. *Awards:* B, M, FP. *Entrance level for U.S. students:* Minimally difficult. *Enrollment:* 8,675 total; 6,614 undergraduates (65% women) including 1% international students from 14 foreign countries. *Faculty:* 553. *Library holdings:* 573,199 books, 1,963 current serial subscriptions, 7,741 audiovisual materials. *Total majors:* 51. *Expenses:* (2006–07) $13,200; room and board, $4972 (on campus); room only, $2838 (on campus). *Financial aid:* Non-need financial aid available.

NORTH CAROLINA SCHOOL OF THE ARTS, WINSTON-SALEM

General Information State-supported, coed institution. Urban setting. *Awards:* B, M. *Entrance level for U.S. students:* Very difficult. *Enrollment:* 845 total; 727 undergraduates (42% women) including 1% international students from 9 foreign countries. *Faculty:* 178. *Library holdings:* 87,917 books, 490 current serial subscriptions. *Total majors:* 9. *Expenses:* (2006–07) $16,171; room and board, $6139 (on campus); room only, $3189 (on campus). *Financial aid:* Non-need-based college/university scholarships/grants from institutional funds, tuition waivers. Forms required: International Student's Certification of Finances. For fall 2005, 4 international students on campus received college administered financial aid ($8605 average).

NORTH CAROLINA STATE UNIVERSITY, RALEIGH

General Information State-supported, coed university. Urban setting. *Awards:* A, B, M, D, FP. *Entrance level for U.S. students:* Very difficult. *Enrollment:* 31,130 total; 23,730 undergraduates (43% women) including 1% international students from 54 foreign countries. *Faculty:* 1,845. *Library holdings:* 3.7 million books, 49,480 current serial subscriptions, 25,022 audiovisual materials. *Total majors:* 121.

Information for International Students For fall 2006: 366 international students applied, 85 were accepted, 45 enrolled. Students can start in fall or spring. Transfers accepted from institutions abroad. *Admission tests:* Required: SAT or ACT, TOEFL (minimum score: paper-based 550; computer-based 213). TOEFL can be waived under certain conditions. *Application deadline:* 2/1. *Expenses:* (2007–08) $17,315; room and board, $7373 (on campus); room only, $4460 (on campus). *Financial aid:* Non-need-based college/university scholarships/grants from institutional funds, athletic awards. Forms required: International Student's Certification of Finances, scholarship application form. For fall 2006 (estimated), 32 international students on campus received college administered financial aid ($2474 average). *Housing:* Guaranteed, also available during summer. *Services:* International student adviser on campus. ESL program at cooperating institution. Internships and employment opportunities (on-campus) available. *Contact:* Associate Director of Admissions, North Carolina State University, 203 Peele Hall, Box 7103, Raleigh, NC 27695-7103. Telephone: 919-515-2434. Fax: 919-515-5039. E-mail: vern_granger@ncsu.edu. URL: http://www.ncsu.edu.

PEACE COLLEGE, RALEIGH

General Information Independent, 4-year, women's college, affiliated with Presbyterian Church (U.S.A.). Urban setting. *Awards:* B. *Entrance level for U.S. students:* Moderately difficult. *Enrollment:* 651 total. *Undergraduate faculty:* 78. *Library holdings:* 51,118 books, 3,900 current serial subscriptions. *Total majors:* 13.

Information for International Students Students can start in fall, spring, or summer. Transfers accepted from institutions abroad. *Admission tests:* Required: TOEFL (minimum score: paper-based 550; computer-based 200). Recommended: SAT or ACT, ELS. TOEFL can be waived under certain conditions. *Application deadline:* 7/1. *Expenses:* (2006–07) $21,140; room and board, $7230 (on campus); room only, $5035 (on campus). *Financial aid:* Non-need-based college/university scholarships/grants from institutional funds. International transfer students are eligible to apply for aid. For fall 2005, 6 international students on campus received college administered financial aid ($6534 average). *Housing:* Guaranteed, also available during summer. *Services:* International student adviser on campus. Internships and employment opportunities (on-campus and off-campus) available. *Contact:* Dean of Admissions, Peace College, 15 East Peace Street, Raleigh, NC 27604-1149. Telephone: 919-508-2000 Ext. 2016. Fax: 919-508-2306. E-mail: mtgreen@peace.edu. URL: http://www.peace.edu.

PFEIFFER UNIVERSITY, MISENHEIMER

General Information Independent United Methodist, coed institution. Rural setting. *Awards:* B, M. *Entrance level for U.S. students:* Moderately difficult. *Enrollment:* 2,116 total; 1,133 undergraduates (59% women) including 3% international students from 11 foreign countries. *Faculty:* 162. *Library holdings:* 125,972 books, 288 current serial subscriptions, 3,702 audiovisual materials. *Total majors:* 45. *Expenses:* (2006–07) $16,450; room and board, $6650 (on campus); room only, $3910 (on campus). *Financial aid:* Need-based college/university scholarships/grants from institutional funds, athletic awards. Non-need-based college/university scholarships/grants from institutional funds, athletic awards. Forms required: institution's own financial aid form, International Student's Certification of Finances. For fall 2005, 26 international students on campus received college administered financial aid ($3519 average).

PIEDMONT COMMUNITY COLLEGE, ROXBORO

General Information State-supported, 2-year, coed college. Small town setting. *Awards:* A. *Entrance level for U.S. students:* Noncompetitive. *Enrollment:* 2,189 total (56% women) including 0.2% international students from 2 foreign countries. *Undergraduate faculty:* 157. *Library holdings:* 24,166 books, 278 current serial subscriptions. *Total majors:* 11.

Information for International Students Students can start in fall, winter, spring, or summer. Transfers accepted from institutions abroad. *Admission tests:* Required: TOEFL (minimum score: paper-based 550; computer-based 300), ASSET/COMPASS. Recommended: SAT or ACT. *Application deadline:* Rolling. *Financial aid:* Forms required: institution's own financial aid form. *Services:* International student adviser on campus. *Contact:* Dean of Student Affairs, Piedmont Community College, PO Box 1197, Roxboro, NC 27573. Telephone: 336-599-1181 Ext. 266. Fax: 336-598-9283. E-mail: moralen@piedmont.cc.edu. URL: http://www.piedmont.cc.nc.us.

QUEENS UNIVERSITY OF CHARLOTTE, CHARLOTTE

General Information Independent Presbyterian, coed institution. Suburban setting. *Awards:* A, B, M. *Entrance level for U.S. students:* Moderately difficult. *Enrollment:* 2,118 total; 1,668 undergraduates (78% women) including 5% international students from 20 foreign countries. *Faculty:* 116. *Library holdings:* 126,242 books, 592 current serial subscriptions. *Total majors:* 36. *Expenses:* (2006–07) $19,450; room and board, $6980 (on campus). *Financial aid:* Non-need financial aid available. 30 international students on campus received college administered financial aid ($9133 average).

RICHMOND COMMUNITY COLLEGE, HAMLET

General Information State-supported, 2-year, coed college. Rural setting. *Awards:* A. *Entrance level for U.S. students:* Noncompetitive. *Enrollment:* 1,472 total (73% women). *Undergraduate faculty:* 60. *Library holdings:* 26,381 books, 192 current serial subscriptions, 1,676 audiovisual materials. *Total majors:* 16.

Information for International Students For fall 2006: 4 international students applied. Students can start in fall, spring, or summer. Transfers accepted from institutions abroad. *Admission tests:* Required: TOEFL (minimum score: iBT 45; paper-based 450; computer-based 133). *Application deadline:* Rolling. *Expenses:* (2006–07) $7062. *Financial aid:* Need-based college/university scholarships/grants from institutional funds. Non-need-based college/university scholarships/grants from institutional funds. *Services:* Full-time and part-time ESL programs on campus. ESL program available during the academic year and the summer. *Contact:* Registrar, Richmond Community College, PO Box 1189,

Hamlet, NC 28345. Telephone: 910-410-1737. Fax: 910-582-7102.
E-mail: wandaw@richmond.cc.nc.us.
URL: http://www.richmondcc.edu.

ROANOKE BIBLE COLLEGE, ELIZABETH CITY
General Information Independent Christian, 4-year, coed college. Small town setting. *Awards:* A, B. *Entrance level for U.S. students:* Minimally difficult. *Enrollment:* 156 total (49% women) including international students from 3 foreign countries. *Undergraduate faculty:* 28. *Library holdings:* 28,164 books, 436 current serial subscriptions, 1,751 audiovisual materials. *Total majors:* 3.
Information for International Students For fall 2006: 4 international students applied, 1 was accepted, 1 enrolled. Students can start in fall or spring. Transfers accepted from institutions abroad. *Admission tests:* Required: TOEFL (minimum score: paper-based 500; computer-based 222). Recommended: SAT or ACT. TOEFL can be waived under certain conditions. *Application deadline:* 4/1. *Expenses:* (2007–08) $9915; room and board, $5720 (on campus); room only, $3120 (on campus). *Financial aid:* Need-based college/university scholarships/grants from institutional funds, loans from outside sources. Forms required: institution's own financial aid form. *Housing:* Available during summer. Employment opportunities (on-campus) available. *Contact:* Admissions Administrator, Roanoke Bible College, 715 North Poindexter Street, Elizabeth City, NC 27909. Telephone: 252-334-2028. Fax: 252-334-2064. E-mail: admissions@roanokebible.edu. URL: http://www.roanokebible.edu.

ROCKINGHAM COMMUNITY COLLEGE, WENTWORTH
General Information State-supported, 2-year, coed college. Rural setting. *Awards:* A. *Entrance level for U.S. students:* Noncompetitive. *Enrollment:* 2,036 total (66% women) including 0.4% international students from 1 foreign country. *Undergraduate faculty:* 111. *Library holdings:* 43,044 books, 374 current serial subscriptions, 3,990 audiovisual materials. *Total majors:* 32. *Expenses:* (2006–07) $7093. *Financial aid:* Non-need financial aid available.

SALEM COLLEGE, WINSTON-SALEM
General Information Independent Moravian, undergraduate: women only; graduate: coed institution. Urban setting. *Awards:* B, M (only students age 23 or over are eligible to enroll part-time; men may attend evening program only). *Entrance level for U.S. students:* Moderately difficult. *Enrollment:* 1,094 total; 860 undergraduates (96% women) including 11% international students from 17 foreign countries. *Faculty:* 103. *Library holdings:* 151,719 books, 679 current serial subscriptions, 14,187 audiovisual materials. *Total majors:* 29. *Expenses:* (2006–07) $17,949; room and board, $9551 (on campus). *Financial aid:* Need-based financial aid available. Forms required: institution's own financial aid form.

SHAW UNIVERSITY, RALEIGH
General Information Independent Baptist, coed institution. Urban setting. *Awards:* A, B, M, FP. *Entrance level for U.S. students:* Minimally difficult. *Enrollment:* 2,882 total; 2,669 undergraduates (64% women) including 2% international students from 19 foreign countries. *Faculty:* 284. *Library holdings:* 154,368 books, 15,500 current serial subscriptions. *Total majors:* 36. *Expenses:* (2006–07) $10,020; room and board, $6410 (on campus); room only, $3010 (on campus). *Financial aid:* Need-based and non-need-based financial aid available. Forms required: institution's own financial aid form. For fall 2005, 33 international students on campus received college administered financial aid ($3756 average).

SOUTHEASTERN COMMUNITY COLLEGE, WHITEVILLE
General Information State-supported, 2-year, coed college. Rural setting. *Awards:* A. *Entrance level for U.S. students:* Noncompetitive. *Enrollment:* 1,949 total including 0.1% international students from 2 foreign countries. *Undergraduate faculty:* 91. *Library holdings:* 50,297 books, 192 current serial subscriptions. *Total majors:* 21. *Expenses:* (2006–07) $7089.

SOUTHWESTERN COMMUNITY COLLEGE, SYLVA
General Information State-supported, 2-year, coed college. Small town setting. *Awards:* A. *Entrance level for U.S. students:* Noncompetitive. *Enrollment:* 2,065 total (64% women) including 1% international students from 1 foreign country. *Undergraduate faculty:* 260. *Library holdings:* 37,860 books, 166 current serial subscriptions, 1,603 audiovisual materials. *Total majors:* 32.
Information for International Students For fall 2006: 32 international students applied, 32 were accepted, 26 enrolled. Students can start in fall, spring, or summer. Transfers accepted from institutions abroad. *Admission tests:* Required: TOEFL (minimum score: iBT 61; paper-based 500; computer-based 173; minimum score for ESL admission: iBT 61; paper-based 500; computer-based 173), ELS, ACCUPLACER. Recommended: SAT or ACT. *Application deadline:* Rolling. *Expenses:* (2006–07) $6211. *Financial aid:* International transfer students are eligible to apply for aid. *Services:* International student adviser on campus. Part-time ESL program on campus. ESL program available during the academic year and the summer. Internships and employment opportunities (on-campus) available. *Contact:* Registrar and International Student Coordinator, Southwestern Community College, 447 College Drive, Sylva, NC 28779. Telephone: 828-586-4091 Ext. 406. Fax: 828-631-3381. E-mail: christyd@southwesterncc.edu. URL: http://www.southwest.cc.nc.us.

SURRY COMMUNITY COLLEGE, DOBSON
General Information State-supported, 2-year, coed college. Rural setting. *Awards:* A. *Entrance level for U.S. students:* Noncompetitive. *Enrollment:* 3,600 total including 0.2% international students. *Undergraduate faculty:* 450. *Library holdings:* 47,526 books, 362 current serial subscriptions. *Total majors:* 29. *Expenses:* (2006–07) $7093.

THE UNIVERSITY OF NORTH CAROLINA AT ASHEVILLE, ASHEVILLE
General Information State-supported, coed institution. Suburban setting. *Awards:* B, M. *Entrance level for U.S. students:* Moderately difficult. *Enrollment:* 3,635 total; 3,609 undergraduates (57% women) including 1% international students from 18 foreign countries. *Faculty:* 304. *Library holdings:* 264,248 books, 6,405 current serial subscriptions, 12,319 audiovisual materials. *Total majors:* 29.
Information for International Students For fall 2006: 66 international students applied, 45 were accepted, 21 enrolled. Students can start in fall or spring. Transfers accepted from institutions abroad. *Admission tests:* Required: TOEFL (minimum score: paper-based 550; computer-based 213), SAT or ACT may substitute for TOEFL. *Application deadline:* 4/1. *Expenses:* (2006–07) $14,007; room and board, $5880 (on campus); room only, $3200 (on campus). *Services:* International student adviser on campus. Employment opportunities (on-campus) available. *Contact:* International Admissions Officer, The University of North Carolina at Asheville, One University Heights, Asheville, NC 28804-8510. Telephone: 828-251-6481. Fax: 828-251-6841. E-mail: lmcbride@unca.edu. URL: http://www.unca.edu.

THE UNIVERSITY OF NORTH CAROLINA AT CHAPEL HILL, CHAPEL HILL
General Information State-supported, coed university. Suburban setting. *Awards:* B, M, D, FP. *Entrance level for U.S. students:* Very difficult. *Enrollment:* 27,717 total; 17,124 undergraduates (59% women) including 1% international students from 111 foreign countries. *Faculty:* 1,613. *Library holdings:* 5.7 million books, 53,444 current serial subscriptions, 316,829 audiovisual materials. *Total majors:* 61. *Expenses:* (2006–07) $19,681; room and board, $6846 (on campus); room only, $3960 (on campus). *Financial aid:* Forms required: International Student's Certification of Finances.

THE UNIVERSITY OF NORTH CAROLINA AT CHARLOTTE, CHARLOTTE
General Information State-supported, coed university. Suburban setting. *Awards:* B, M, D. *Entrance level for U.S. students:* Moderately difficult. *Enrollment:* 21,519 total; 17,032 undergraduates (53% women) including 2% international students from 89 foreign countries. *Faculty:* 1,245. *Library holdings:* 969,680 books, 32,486 current serial subscriptions, 164,103 audiovisual materials. *Total majors:* 72. *Expenses:* (2006–07) $14,307; room and board, $5790 (on campus); room only, $2940 (on campus).

THE UNIVERSITY OF NORTH CAROLINA AT GREENSBORO, GREENSBORO
General Information State-supported, coed university. Urban setting. *Awards:* B, M, D. *Entrance level for U.S. students:* Moderately difficult. *Enrollment:* 16,728 total; 12,921 undergraduates (68% women) including 1% international students from 20 foreign countries. *Faculty:* 1,001. *Library holdings:* 740,000 books, 4,000 current serial subscriptions. *Total majors:* 77. *Expenses:* (2007–08) $15,297; room and board, $6051 (on campus); room only, $3427 (on campus). *Financial aid:* Need-based college/university scholarships/grants from institutional funds, tuition waivers, loans from institutional funds. Non-need-based college/university scholarships/grants from institutional funds, tuition waivers, athletic awards, on-campus employment. Forms required: institution's own financial aid form, International Student's Financial Aid Application. For fall 2006 (estimated), 23 international students on campus received college administered financial aid ($14,542 average).

North Carolina

THE UNIVERSITY OF NORTH CAROLINA AT PEMBROKE, PEMBROKE

General Information State-supported, coed institution. Rural setting. *Awards:* B, M. *Entrance level for U.S. students:* Moderately difficult. *Enrollment:* 5,827 total; 5,158 undergraduates (64% women) including 1% international students from 20 foreign countries. *Faculty:* 416. *Library holdings:* 342,723 books, 113,823 current serial subscriptions, 3,577 audiovisual materials. *Total majors:* 42.

Information for International Students Students can start in fall, spring, or summer. Transfers accepted from institutions abroad. *Admission tests:* Required: TOEFL (minimum score: iBT 61; paper-based 500; computer-based 173). TOEFL can be waived under certain conditions. *Application deadline:* Rolling. *Expenses:* (2006–07) $14,640; room and board, $5517 (on campus). *Financial aid:* Non-need-based college/university scholarships/grants from institutional funds. For fall 2006 (estimated), 19 international students on campus received college administered financial aid ($13,157 average). *Housing:* Guaranteed, also available during summer. *Services:* International student adviser on campus. Full-time ESL program on campus. ESL program available during the academic year. *Contact:* Director of Admissions, Office of Admissions, The University of North Carolina at Pembroke, PO Box 1510, Office of Admissions, Pembroke, NC 28372. Telephone: 910-521-6262. Fax: 910-521-6497. E-mail: admissions@uncp.edu. URL: http://www.uncp.edu.

THE UNIVERSITY OF NORTH CAROLINA WILMINGTON, WILMINGTON

General Information State-supported, coed institution. Urban setting. *Awards:* B, M, D. *Entrance level for U.S. students:* Moderately difficult. *Enrollment:* 11,793 total; 10,759 undergraduates (58% women) including 0.2% international students from 17 foreign countries. *Faculty:* 784. *Library holdings:* 553,391 books, 22,218 current serial subscriptions. *Total majors:* 62. *Expenses:* (2006–07) $14,095; room and board, $6722 (on campus). *Financial aid:* Need-based financial aid available. Non-need-based college/university scholarships/grants from institutional funds, athletic awards, loans from outside sources. For fall 2005, 20 international students on campus received college administered financial aid ($14,019 average).

UNIVERSITY OF PHOENIX–RALEIGH CAMPUS, RALEIGH

General Information Proprietary, coed institution. Urban setting. *Awards:* B, M. *Entrance level for U.S. students:* Noncompetitive. *Enrollment:* 526 total; 326 undergraduates (60% women) including 3% international students. *Faculty:* 70. *Library holdings:* 1,759 books, 692 current serial subscriptions. *Total majors:* 8. *Expenses:* (2006–07) $10,770.

VANCE-GRANVILLE COMMUNITY COLLEGE, HENDERSON

General Information State-supported, 2-year, coed college. Rural setting. *Awards:* A. *Entrance level for U.S. students:* Noncompetitive. *Enrollment:* 4,057 total (66% women) including 1% international students from 15 foreign countries. *Undergraduate faculty:* 353. *Library holdings:* 38,720 books, 317 current serial subscriptions. *Total majors:* 30.

WAKE FOREST UNIVERSITY, WINSTON-SALEM

General Information Independent, coed university. Suburban setting. *Awards:* B, M, D, FP. *Entrance level for U.S. students:* Very difficult. *Enrollment:* 6,739 total; 4,332 undergraduates (51% women) including 1% international students from 25 foreign countries. *Faculty:* 600. *Library holdings:* 923,123 books, 16,448 current serial subscriptions. *Total majors:* 37.

Information for International Students Students can start in fall. Transfers accepted from institutions abroad. *Admission tests:* Required: SAT, TOEFL (minimum score: paper-based 600; computer-based 250). Recommended: SAT Subject Tests. TOEFL can be waived under certain conditions. *Application deadline:* 1/15. *Expenses:* (2007–08) $34,330; room and board, $9500 (on campus); room only, $6000 (on campus). *Financial aid:* Non-need-based college/university scholarships/grants from institutional funds, athletic awards. Forms required: International Student's Certification of Finances. For fall 2005, 30 international students on campus received college administered financial aid ($32,560 average). *Housing:* Available during summer. *Services:* International student adviser on campus. *Contact:* Associate Director of Admissions, Wake Forest University, Reynolda Station, PO Box 7305, Winston-Salem, NC 27109. Telephone: 336-758-5201. Fax: 336-758-4324. E-mail: marlowad@wfu.edu. URL: http://www.wfu.edu.

WARREN WILSON COLLEGE, SWANNANOA

General Information Independent, coed institution, affiliated with Presbyterian Church (U.S.A.). Small town setting. *Awards:* B, M. *Entrance level for U.S. students:* Moderately difficult. *Enrollment:* 908 total; 841 undergraduates (60% women) including 3% international students from 8 foreign countries. *Faculty:* 99. *Library holdings:* 106,837 books. *Total majors:* 27.

Information for International Students Students can start in fall or spring. Transfers accepted from institutions abroad. *Admission tests:* Required: TOEFL (minimum score: paper-based 550; computer-based 213). Recommended: SAT, ACT. *Application deadline:* 3/15. *Expenses:* (2007–08) $21,084; room and board, $6700 (on campus). *Financial aid:* Need-based college/university scholarships/grants from institutional funds, loans from outside sources, on-campus employment. Non-need-based college/university scholarships/grants from institutional funds, loans from outside sources, on-campus employment. Forms required: institution's own financial aid form. International transfer students are eligible to apply for aid. For fall 2006 (estimated), 21 international students on campus received college administered financial aid ($14,673 average). *Housing:* Guaranteed, also available during summer. *Services:* International student adviser on campus. Part-time ESL program on campus. ESL program available during the summer. Internships and employment opportunities (on-campus and off-campus) available. *Contact:* Dean of Admission, Admission Office, Warren Wilson College, Asheville, NC 28804. Telephone: 828-298-3325 Ext. 0240. Fax: 828-298-1440. E-mail: admit@warren-wilson.edu. URL: http://www.warren-wilson.edu.

WESTERN CAROLINA UNIVERSITY, CULLOWHEE

General Information State-supported, coed institution. Rural setting. *Awards:* B, M, D. *Entrance level for U.S. students:* Moderately difficult. *Enrollment:* 8,861 total; 7,146 undergraduates (52% women) including 1% international students from 43 foreign countries. *Faculty:* 701. *Library holdings:* 692,253 books, 33,950 current serial subscriptions, 12,734 audiovisual materials. *Total majors:* 66. *Expenses:* (2006–07) $14,124; room and board, $5210 (on campus); room only, $2660 (on campus).

WINGATE UNIVERSITY, WINGATE

General Information Independent Baptist, coed institution. Small town setting. *Awards:* B, M, FP. *Entrance level for U.S. students:* Moderately difficult. *Enrollment:* 1,809 total; 1,390 undergraduates (53% women) including 2% international students from 12 foreign countries. *Faculty:* 162. *Library holdings:* 107,187 books, 15,325 current serial subscriptions. *Total majors:* 39. *Expenses:* (2006–07) $17,650; room and board, $6750 (on campus); room only, $3375 (on campus).

WINSTON-SALEM STATE UNIVERSITY, WINSTON-SALEM

General Information State-supported, coed institution. Urban setting. *Awards:* B, M. *Entrance level for U.S. students:* Minimally difficult. *Enrollment:* 5,650 total; 5,329 undergraduates (70% women) including 0.04% international students from 8 foreign countries. *Faculty:* 400. *Library holdings:* 197,765 books, 1,010 current serial subscriptions. *Total majors:* 41. *Expenses:* (2006–07) $11,749; room and board, $5476 (on campus); room only, $3270 (on campus). *Financial aid:* Non-need-based alternative loans.

NORTH DAKOTA

LAKE REGION STATE COLLEGE, DEVILS LAKE

General Information State-supported, 2-year, coed college. Small town setting. *Awards:* A. *Entrance level for U.S. students:* Noncompetitive. *Enrollment:* 1,471 total (58% women) including 2% international students from 12 foreign countries. *Undergraduate faculty:* 106. *Library holdings:* 42,000 books, 200 current serial subscriptions, 2,000 audiovisual materials. *Total majors:* 37.

Information for International Students For fall 2006: 23 international students applied, 23 were accepted, 15 enrolled. Students can start in fall, spring, or summer. Transfers accepted from institutions abroad. *Admission tests:* Required: TOEFL (minimum score: paper-based 525; computer-based 190; minimum score for ESL admission: paper-based 450; computer-based 170). Recommended: SAT, ACT, COMPASS. TOEFL can be waived under certain conditions. *Application deadline:* Rolling. *Expenses:* (2006–07) $3563; room and board, $4030 (on campus). *Financial aid:* Need-based college/university scholarships/grants from institutional funds, tuition waivers, athletic awards, on-campus employment. Non-need-based college/university scholarships/grants from institutional funds, tuition waivers, athletic awards, loans from outside sources, on-campus employment. Forms required: International Student's Certification of Finances. *Housing:* Guaranteed, also available during summer. *Services:* International student adviser on campus. Part-time ESL program on campus. ESL program available during the academic year. Internships and employment opportunities (on-campus and off-campus) available. *Contact:* Vice President of Student Services, Lake Region State College, 1801 College Drive North, Devils Lake, ND 58301. Telephone: 701-662-1600 Ext. 513. Fax: 701-662-1581. E-mail: laurel.goulding@lrsc.nodak.edu. URL: http://www.lrsc.nodak.edu.

MAYVILLE STATE UNIVERSITY, MAYVILLE

General Information State-supported, 4-year, coed college. Rural setting. *Awards:* A, B. *Entrance level for U.S. students:* Noncompetitive. *Enrollment:* 832 total (50% women) including 4% international students from 5 foreign countries. *Undergraduate faculty:* 74. *Library holdings:* 93,684 books, 424 current serial subscriptions, 12,262 audiovisual materials. *Total majors:* 37. *Expenses:* (2006–07) $7064; room and board, $3884 (on campus); room only, $1576 (on campus). *Financial aid:* Need-based college/university scholarships/grants from institutional funds, tuition waivers, athletic awards. Non-need-based college/university scholarships/grants from institutional funds, tuition waivers, athletic awards. Forms required: International Student's Certification of Finances.

MINOT STATE UNIVERSITY, MINOT

General Information State-supported, coed institution. Small town setting. *Awards:* A, B, M. *Entrance level for U.S. students:* Minimally difficult. *Enrollment:* 3,712 total; 3,433 undergraduates (62% women) including 8% international students from 20 foreign countries. *Faculty:* 278. *Library holdings:* 428,407 books, 693 current serial subscriptions, 123,173 audiovisual materials. *Total majors:* 58.

Information for International Students For fall 2006: 166 international students applied, 112 were accepted, 81 enrolled. Students can start in fall, spring, or summer. Transfers accepted from institutions abroad. *Admission tests:* Required: TOEFL (minimum score: iBT 71; paper-based 525; computer-based 195). Recommended: ACT. TOEFL can be waived under certain conditions. *Application deadline:* Rolling. *Expenses:* (2006–07) $10,818; room and board, $5294 (on campus); room only, $2600 (on campus). *Financial aid:* Need-based tuition waivers, athletic awards. Non-need-based tuition waivers, athletic awards, on-campus employment. Forms required: institution's own financial aid form. International transfer students are eligible to apply for aid. 16 international students on campus received college administered financial aid ($3553 average). *Housing:* Guaranteed, also available during summer. *Services:* International student adviser on campus. Internships and employment opportunities (on-campus and off-campus) available. *Contact:* International Student Coordinator, Minot State University, 500 University Avenue West, International Student Office, Minot, ND 58707. Telephone: 701-858-3348. Fax: 701-858-3888. E-mail: ronnie.walker@minotstateu.edu. URL: http://www.minotstateu.edu.

MINOT STATE UNIVERSITY–BOTTINEAU CAMPUS, BOTTINEAU

General Information State-supported, 2-year, coed college. Rural setting. *Awards:* A. *Entrance level for U.S. students:* Noncompetitive. *Enrollment:* 605 total (58% women) including 3% international students from 5 foreign countries. *Undergraduate faculty:* 44. *Library holdings:* 45,000 books, 250 current serial subscriptions. *Total majors:* 36. *Expenses:* (2007–08) $4,789; room and board, $3890 (on campus); room only, $1523 (on campus).

NORTH DAKOTA STATE COLLEGE OF SCIENCE, WAHPETON

General Information State-supported, 2-year, coed college. Rural setting. *Awards:* A. *Entrance level for U.S. students:* Noncompetitive. *Enrollment:* 2,468 total (37% women) including 1% international students from 11 foreign countries. *Undergraduate faculty:* 140. *Library holdings:* 124,508 books, 852 current serial subscriptions, 4,178 audiovisual materials. *Total majors:* 31.

Information for International Students For fall 2006: 28 international students applied, 28 were accepted, 2 enrolled. Students can start in fall, spring, or summer. Transfers accepted from institutions abroad. *Admission tests:* Required: ELS (minimum score: 109). TOEFL can be waived under certain conditions. *Application deadline:* Rolling. *Expenses:* (2006–07) $9197; room and board, $4638 (on campus). *Financial aid:* Non-need financial aid available. Forms required: Tuition Waiver Application form. *Housing:* Guaranteed, also available during summer. *Services:* International student adviser on campus. Part-time ESL program

on campus. ESL program available during the academic year. Employment opportunities (on-campus) available. *Contact:* Director of Enrollment Services, Office of Admissions, North Dakota State College of Science, 800 6th Street North, Wahpeton, ND 58076-0002. Telephone: 701-671-2189. Fax: 701-671-2201. E-mail: Karen.Reilly@ndscs.nodak.edu. URL: http://www.ndscs.nodak.edu.

NORTH DAKOTA STATE UNIVERSITY, FARGO

General Information State-supported, coed university. Urban setting. *Awards:* B, M, D, FP. *Entrance level for U.S. students:* Moderately difficult. *Enrollment:* 12,258 total; 10,596 undergraduates (45% women) including 3% international students from 70 foreign countries. *Faculty:* 630. *Library holdings:* 303,274 books, 2,499 current serial subscriptions, 3,276 audiovisual materials. *Total majors:* 95.

Information for International Students For fall 2006: 283 international students applied, 183 were accepted, 146 enrolled. Students can start in fall or spring. Transfers accepted from institutions abroad. *Admission tests:* Required: TOEFL (minimum score: iBT 70; paper-based 525; computer-based 193; minimum score for ESL admission: iBT 41; paper-based 440; computer-based 123). Recommended: SAT or ACT. TOEFL can be waived under certain conditions. *Application deadline:* 5/1. *Expenses:* (2006–07) $13,695; room and board, $5477 (on campus); room only, $2277 (on campus). *Financial aid:* Need-based and non-need-based financial aid available. Forms required: institution's own financial aid form. International transfer students are eligible to apply for aid. *Housing:* Guaranteed, also available during summer. *Services:* International student adviser on campus. Full-time and part-time ESL programs on campus. ESL program available during the academic year and the summer. Internships and employment opportunities (on-campus and off-campus) available. *Contact:* International Student Advisor, North Dakota State University, PO Box 5582, Administration Avenue/Ceres Hall 338, Fargo, ND 58105-5582. Telephone: 701-231-7895. Fax: 701-231-1014. E-mail: ndsu.international@ndsu.edu. URL: http://www.ndsu.edu.

See In-Depth Description on page 140.

UNIVERSITY OF MARY, BISMARCK

General Information Independent Roman Catholic, coed institution. Suburban setting. *Awards:* A, B, M, D. *Entrance level for U.S. students:* Moderately difficult. *Enrollment:* 2,765 total; 2,106 undergraduates (60% women) including 1% international students from 14 foreign countries. *Faculty:* 313. *Library holdings:* 78,137 books, 567 current serial subscriptions, 7,866 audiovisual materials. *Total majors:* 37. *Expenses:* (2007–08) $11,780; room and board, $4260 (on campus); room only, $1840 (on campus). *Financial aid:* Need-based college/university scholarships/grants from institutional funds, tuition waivers, athletic awards. Non-need-based college/university scholarships/grants from institutional funds, tuition waivers, athletic awards. Forms required: International Student's Certification of Finances.

UNIVERSITY OF NORTH DAKOTA, GRAND FORKS

General Information State-supported, coed university. Urban setting. *Awards:* B, M, D, FP. *Entrance level for U.S. students:* Minimally difficult. *Enrollment:* 12,834 total; 10,376 undergraduates (46% women) including 2% international students from 27 foreign countries. *Faculty:* 627. *Library holdings:* 1.5 million books, 16,153 current serial subscriptions, 2,928 audiovisual materials. *Total majors:* 86. *Expenses:* (2006–07) $13,786; room and board, $5085 (on campus); room only, $2137 (on campus). *Financial aid:* Need-based tuition waivers, athletic awards, loans from outside sources, on-campus employment. Non-need-based tuition waivers, athletic awards, loans from outside sources, on-campus employment. Forms required: institution's own financial aid form. 31 international students on campus received college administered financial aid ($7624 average).

WILLISTON STATE COLLEGE, WILLISTON

General Information State-supported, 2-year, coed college. Small town setting. *Awards:* A. *Entrance level for U.S. students:* Noncompetitive. *Enrollment:* 947 total (73% women) including 3% international students from 3 foreign countries. *Undergraduate faculty:* 93. *Library holdings:* 16,218 books, 214 current serial subscriptions, 475 audiovisual materials. *Total majors:* 15.

Information for International Students For fall 2006: 26 international students enrolled. Students can start in fall or spring. Transfers accepted from institutions abroad. *Admission tests:* Required: TOEFL (minimum score: paper-based 525; computer-based 197). Recommended: ACT. TOEFL can be waived under certain conditions. *Application deadline:* Rolling. *Financial aid:* Need-based and non-need-based financial aid available. Forms required: International Student's Financial Aid Application. *Housing:* Available during summer. *Services:* International student

Williston State College (continued)

adviser on campus. Employment opportunities (on-campus) available. *Contact:* Director for Admission and Records, Williston State College, 1410 University Avenue, PO Box 1326, Williston, ND 58802-1326. Telephone: 701-774-4554. Fax: 701-774-4211. E-mail: jan.solem@wsc.nodak.edu. URL: http://www.wsc.nodak.edu.

OHIO

ANTIOCH COLLEGE, YELLOW SPRINGS

General Information Independent, 4-year, coed college. Small town setting. *Awards:* B. *Entrance level for U.S. students:* Moderately difficult. *Enrollment:* 341 total; 330 undergraduates (61% women) including international students from 2 foreign countries. *Undergraduate faculty:* 59. *Library holdings:* 300,000 books, 10,504 current serial subscriptions, 6,259 audiovisual materials. *Total majors:* 56.
Information for International Students For fall 2006: 60 international students applied, 14 were accepted, 4 enrolled. Students can start in fall. Transfers accepted from institutions abroad. *Admission tests:* Required: TOEFL (minimum score: paper-based 550, computer-based 195). TOEFL can be waived under certain conditions. *Application deadline:* 2/1. *Expenses:* (2007–08) $28,550; room and board, $7354 (on campus); room only, $3597 (on campus). *Financial aid:* Need-based college/university scholarships/grants from institutional funds, loans from outside sources, on-campus employment. Non-need-based college/university scholarships/grants from institutional funds, loans from outside sources. Forms required: institution's own financial aid form, International Student's Certification of Finances. International transfer students are eligible to apply for aid. For fall 2006 (estimated), 5 international students on campus received college administered financial aid ($25,343 average). *Housing:* Guaranteed. *Services:* International student adviser on campus. Internships and employment opportunities (on-campus and off-campus) available. *Contact:* Associate Director of Admissions and Financial Aid, Office of Admissions and Financial Aid, Antioch College, Office of Admissions, 795 Livermore Street, Yellow Springs, OH 45387. Telephone: 937-769-1110. Fax: 937-769-1133. E-mail: aglukhov@antioch-college.edu. URL: http://www.antioch-college.edu.

ART ACADEMY OF CINCINNATI, CINCINNATI

General Information Independent, coed institution. Urban setting. *Awards:* A, B, M. *Entrance level for U.S. students:* Moderately difficult. *Enrollment:* 164 total; 163 undergraduates (55% women) including 2% international students from 7 foreign countries. *Faculty:* 61. *Library holdings:* 66,404 books, 150 current serial subscriptions, 588 audiovisual materials. *Total majors:* 11. *Expenses:* (2006–07) $19,600. *Financial aid:* Need-based college/university scholarships/grants from institutional funds. Non-need-based college/university scholarships/grants from institutional funds. 3 international students on campus received college administered financial aid ($5050 average).

ASHLAND UNIVERSITY, ASHLAND

General Information Independent, coed institution, affiliated with Brethren Church. Small town setting. *Awards:* A, B, M, D, FP. *Entrance level for U.S. students:* Moderately difficult. *Enrollment:* 6,472 total; 2,791 undergraduates (59% women) including 1% international students from 23 foreign countries. *Faculty:* 593. *Library holdings:* 205,200 books, 1,625 current serial subscriptions, 3,550 audiovisual materials. *Total majors:* 70.
Information for International Students For fall 2006: 127 international students applied, 63 were accepted, 45 enrolled. Students can start in fall or spring. Transfers accepted from institutions abroad. *Admission tests:* Required: TOEFL (minimum score: iBT 65; paper-based 500; computer-based 173). Recommended: SAT or ACT. TOEFL can be waived under certain conditions. *Application deadline:* 7/1. *Expenses:* (2006–07) $21,430; room and board, $7790 (on campus); room only, $4184 (on campus). *Financial aid:* Need-based college/university scholarships/grants from institutional funds, tuition waivers, athletic awards. Non-need-based college/university scholarships/grants from institutional funds, tuition waivers, athletic awards. Forms required: institution's own financial aid form, International Student's Certification of Finances. International transfer students are eligible to apply for aid. For fall 2005, 43 international students on campus received college administered financial aid ($10,241 average). *Housing:* Guaranteed, also available during summer. *Services:* International student adviser on campus. Full-time ESL program on campus. ESL program available during the academic year and the summer. Employment opportunities (on-campus)

available. *Contact:* Associate Director, International Student Services, Ashland University, 401 College Avenue, Ashland, OH 44805-3799. Telephone: 419-289-5926. Fax: 419-289-5629. E-mail: iss@ashland.edu. URL: http://www.exploreashland.com.
See In-Depth Description on page 36.

BALDWIN-WALLACE COLLEGE, BEREA

General Information Independent Methodist, coed institution. Suburban setting. *Awards:* B, M. *Entrance level for U.S. students:* Moderately difficult. *Enrollment:* 4,365 total; 3,625 undergraduates (60% women) including 1% international students from 15 foreign countries. *Faculty:* 382. *Library holdings:* 200,000 books, 22,000 current serial subscriptions. *Total majors:* 62.
Information for International Students For fall 2006: 82 international students applied, 26 were accepted, 14 enrolled. Students can start in fall, spring, or summer. Transfers accepted from institutions abroad. *Admission tests:* Required: SAT or ACT, TOEFL (minimum score: iBT 69; paper-based 523; computer-based 193; minimum score for ESL admission: iBT 61; paper-based 500; computer-based 173). Recommended: IELTS, score of 5.5 or better. TOEFL can be waived under certain conditions. *Application deadline:* Rolling. *Expenses:* (2006–07) $21,236; room and board, $6974 (on campus); room only, $3406 (on campus). *Financial aid:* Need-based college/university scholarships/grants from institutional funds. Non-need-based college/university scholarships/grants from institutional funds. Forms required: International Student's Certification of Finances. International transfer students are eligible to apply for aid. For fall 2006 (estimated), 20 international students on campus received college administered financial aid ($7781 average). *Housing:* Guaranteed, also available during summer. *Services:* International student adviser on campus. Part-time ESL program on campus. ESL program available during the academic year and the summer. Internships and employment opportunities (on-campus) available. *Contact:* Assistant Director of Admission, Baldwin-Wallace College, 275 Eastland Road, Berea, OH 44017-2088. Telephone: 440-826-8009. Fax: 440-826-3830. E-mail: tcochran@bw.edu. URL: http://www.bw.edu.

BLUFFTON UNIVERSITY, BLUFFTON

General Information Independent Mennonite, coed institution. Small town setting. *Awards:* B, M. *Entrance level for U.S. students:* Moderately difficult. *Enrollment:* 1,155 total; 1,030 undergraduates (54% women) including 2% international students from 17 foreign countries. *Faculty:* 113. *Library holdings:* 168,888 books, 263 current serial subscriptions. *Total majors:* 39. *Expenses:* (2006–07) $20,570; room and board, $7082 (on campus); room only, $3260 (on campus). *Financial aid:* Need-based college/university scholarships/grants from institutional funds, on-campus employment. Non-need-based college/university scholarships/grants from institutional funds, on-campus employment. Forms required: International Student's Certification of Finances. For fall 2006 (estimated), 19 international students on campus received college administered financial aid ($12,265 average).

BOWLING GREEN STATE UNIVERSITY, BOWLING GREEN

General Information State-supported, coed university. Small town setting. *Awards:* B, M, D. *Entrance level for U.S. students:* Moderately difficult. *Enrollment:* 19,108 total; 16,085 undergraduates (55% women) including 1% international students from 47 foreign countries. *Faculty:* 1,032. *Total majors:* 132. *Expenses:* (2006–07) $16,368; room and board, $6684 (on campus); room only, $4084 (on campus). *Financial aid:* Non-need-based college/university scholarships/grants from institutional funds, athletic awards, on-campus employment.

BOWLING GREEN STATE UNIVERSITY–FIRELANDS COLLEGE, HURON

General Information State-supported, primarily 2-year, coed college. Rural setting. *Awards:* A, B (also offers some upper-level and graduate courses). *Entrance level for U.S. students:* Noncompetitive. *Enrollment:* 2,024 total (65% women). *Undergraduate faculty:* 121. *Library holdings:* 31,262 books, 223 current serial subscriptions. *Total majors:* 28.
Information for International Students Students can start in fall, spring, or summer. Transfers accepted from institutions abroad. *Admission tests:* Required: TOEFL (minimum score: iBT 61; paper-based 500; computer-based 173). TOEFL can be waived under certain conditions. *Application deadline:* 8/1. *Expenses:* (2006–07) $11,536; room and board, $6050 (on campus). *Services:* ESL program at cooperating institution. Internships and employment opportunities (on-campus) available. *Contact:* Student Services Counselor, Bowling Green State University–Firelands College, Bowling Green, OH 43403. Telephone: 419-372-4760. E-mail: PattonY@bgnet.bgsu.edu. URL: http://www.firelands.bgsu.edu.

BRYANT AND STRATTON COLLEGE, CLEVELAND

General Information Proprietary, 4-year, coed college. Urban setting. *Awards:* A, B. *Entrance level for U.S. students:* Minimally difficult. *Enrollment:* 524 total. *Undergraduate faculty:* 37. *Library holdings:* 4,466 books, 80 current serial subscriptions, 159 audiovisual materials. *Total majors:* 9.

CAPITAL UNIVERSITY, COLUMBUS

General Information Independent, coed institution, affiliated with Evangelical Lutheran Church in America. Suburban setting. *Awards:* B, M, FP. *Entrance level for U.S. students:* Moderately difficult. *Enrollment:* 3,825 total; 2,824 undergraduates (62% women) including 1% international students from 15 foreign countries. *Faculty:* 419 *Library holdings:* 196,000 books, 7,055 current serial subscriptions, 16,000 audiovisual materials. *Total majors:* 90.

Information for International Students For fall 2006: 9 international students were accepted, 2 enrolled. Students can start in fall, spring, or summer. Transfers accepted from institutions abroad. *Admission tests:* Required: TOEFL (minimum score: iBT 61; paper-based 500; computer-based 173). Recommended: SAT, ACT, SAT Subject Tests, NCLEX for nursing transfers. TOEFL can be waived under certain conditions. *Application deadline:* Rolling. *Expenses:* (2006–07) $25,100; room and board, $6552 (on campus). *Financial aid:* Need-based and non-need-based financial aid available. Forms required: International Student's Certification of Finances. International transfer students are eligible to apply for aid. 13 international students on campus received college administered financial aid ($7500 average). *Housing:* Available during summer. *Services:* International student adviser on campus. Full-time ESL program on campus. ESL program available during the academic year and the summer. Internships and employment opportunities (on-campus and off-campus) available. *Contact:* Director of International Education, Capital University, Office of International Education, 1 College and Main, Columbus, OH 43209-2394. Telephone: 614-236-6170. Fax: 614-236-6171. E-mail: international@capital.edu. URL: http://www.capital.edu.

CASE WESTERN RESERVE UNIVERSITY, CLEVELAND

General Information Independent, coed university. Urban setting. *Awards:* B, M, D, FP. *Entrance level for U.S. students:* Very difficult. *Enrollment:* 9,592 total; 4,080 undergraduates (42% women) including 4% international students from 28 foreign countries. *Faculty:* 863. *Library holdings:* 2.5 million books, 20,265 current serial subscriptions, 56,916 audiovisual materials. *Total majors:* 63. *Expenses:* (2006–07) $31,738; room and board, $9280 (on campus); room only, $5440 (on campus). *Financial aid:* Need-based tuition waivers, loans from outside sources, on-campus employment. Non-need-based tuition waivers, loans from outside sources, on-campus employment.

CEDARVILLE UNIVERSITY, CEDARVILLE

General Information Independent Baptist, coed institution. Rural setting. *Awards:* B, M. *Entrance level for U.S. students:* Moderately difficult. *Enrollment:* 3,112 total; 3,064 undergraduates (55% women) including 1% international students from 16 foreign countries. *Faculty:* 262. *Library holdings:* 170,561 books, 6,400 current serial subscriptions, 15,868 audiovisual materials. *Total majors:* 77. *Expenses:* (2006–07) $19,800; room and board, $5010 (on campus); room only, $2684 (on campus). *Financial aid:* Need-based college/university scholarships/grants from institutional funds, athletic awards, loans from institutional funds, loans from outside sources, on-campus employment. Non-need-based college/university scholarships/grants from institutional funds, athletic awards, loans from institutional funds, loans from outside sources, on-campus employment. Forms required: international student cost analysis. For fall 2006 (estimated), 10 international students on campus received college administered financial aid ($15,458 average).

CENTRAL STATE UNIVERSITY, WILBERFORCE

General Information State-supported, coed institution. Rural setting. *Awards:* B, M. *Entrance level for U.S. students:* Minimally difficult. *Enrollment:* 1,766 total; 1,747 undergraduates (50% women) including 1% international students from 8 foreign countries. *Faculty:* 179. *Library holdings:* 280,470 books, 26,066 current serial subscriptions. *Total majors:* 37. *Expenses:* (2006–07) $11,462; room and board, $7402 (on campus); room only, $3978 (on campus). *Financial aid:* Need-based college/university scholarships/grants from institutional funds, on-campus employment. Non-need-based college/university scholarships/grants from institutional funds, tuition waivers, athletic awards.

CINCINNATI CHRISTIAN UNIVERSITY, CINCINNATI

General Information Independent, coed institution, affiliated with Church of Christ. Urban setting. *Awards:* A, B, M, FP.

Entrance level for U.S. students: Minimally difficult. *Enrollment:* 1,125 total; 841 undergraduates (48% women) including 1% international students from 65 foreign countries. *Faculty:* 68. *Library holdings:* 9,400 books, 656 current serial subscriptions. *Total majors:* 12. *Expenses:* (2006–07) $11,420; room and board, $5960 (on campus). *Financial aid:* Need-based loans from outside sources, on-campus employment. Non-need-based college/university scholarships/grants from institutional funds, tuition waivers, loans from outside sources, on-campus employment. Forms required: institution's own financial aid form, International Student's Certification of Finances. 6 international students on campus received college administered financial aid ($7106 average).

CINCINNATI STATE TECHNICAL AND COMMUNITY COLLEGE, CINCINNATI

General Information State-supported, 2-year, coed college. Urban setting. *Awards:* A. *Entrance level for U.S. students:* Noncompetitive. *Enrollment:* 8,277 total (55% women) including 3% international students from 76 foreign countries. *Undergraduate faculty:* 570. *Library holdings:* 39,802 books, 309 current serial subscriptions, 3,570 audiovisual materials. *Total majors:* 65. *Expenses:* (2006–07) $9080. *Financial aid:* Need-based college/university scholarships/grants from institutional funds, tuition waivers, athletic awards, loans from outside sources, on-campus employment. Non-need-based college/university scholarships/grants from institutional funds, tuition waivers, athletic awards, loans from outside sources, on-campus employment.

THE CLEVELAND INSTITUTE OF ART, CLEVELAND

General Information Independent, coed institution. Urban setting. *Awards:* B, M. *Entrance level for U.S. students:* Moderately difficult. *Enrollment:* 610 total; 604 undergraduates (52% women) including 3% international students from 16 foreign countries. *Faculty:* 101. *Library holdings:* 42,000 books, 250 current serial subscriptions. *Total majors:* 17. *Financial aid:* Need-based college/university scholarships/grants from institutional funds, tuition waivers, loans from institutional funds, on-campus employment. Non-need-based college/university scholarships/grants from institutional funds, tuition waivers, loans from outside sources. Forms required: institution's own financial aid form. For fall 2006 (estimated), 5 international students on campus received college administered financial aid ($6800 average).

CLEVELAND INSTITUTE OF MUSIC, CLEVELAND

General Information Independent, coed institution. Urban setting. *Awards:* B, M, D. *Entrance level for U.S. students:* Very difficult. *Enrollment:* 426 total; 234 undergraduates (54% women) including 13% international students from 17 foreign countries. *Faculty:* 105. *Library holdings:* 50,924 books, 115 current serial subscriptions. *Total majors:* 6.

Information for International Students For fall 2006: 83 international students applied, 50 were accepted, 30 enrolled. Students can start in fall or spring. Transfers accepted from institutions abroad. *Admission tests:* Required: TOEFL (minimum score: iBT 80; paper-based 550; computer-based 213). *Application deadline:* 12/1. *Expenses:* (2006–07) $29,034; room and board, $9334 (on campus); room only, $5440 (on campus). *Financial aid:* Need-based college/university scholarships/grants from institutional funds, loans from institutional funds, loans from outside sources, on-campus employment. Non-need-based college/university scholarships/grants from institutional funds, loans from outside sources, on-campus employment. Forms required: institution's own financial aid form, International Student's Financial Aid Application, International Student's Certification of Finances. International transfer students are eligible to apply for aid. *Services:* International student adviser on campus. Employment opportunities (on-campus) available. *Contact:* Director of Admission, Cleveland Institute of Music, 11021 East Boulevard, Cleveland, OH 44106-1705. Telephone: 216-795-3107. Fax: 216-795-3161. E-mail: admission@cim.edu. URL: http://www.cim.edu.

CLEVELAND STATE UNIVERSITY, CLEVELAND

General Information State-supported, coed university. Urban setting. *Awards:* B, M, D, FP. *Entrance level for U.S. students:* Moderately difficult. *Enrollment:* 15,483 total; 9,878 undergraduates (56% women) including 2% international students from 75 foreign countries. *Faculty:* 963. *Library holdings:* 847,731 books, 7,826 current serial subscriptions, 143,894 audiovisual materials. *Total majors:* 83.

Information for International Students For fall 2006: 261 international students applied, 154 were accepted, 69 enrolled. Students can start in fall, spring, or summer. Transfers accepted from institutions abroad. *Admission tests:* Required: SAT or ACT, TOEFL (minimum score: paper-based 525; computer-based 197; minimum score for ESL admission: paper-based 525;

Cleveland State University (continued)

computer-based 197). *Application deadline:* 5/15. *Expenses:* (2006–07) $10,664; room and board, $7800 (on campus); room only, $5000 (on campus). *Financial aid:* Need-based loans from outside sources. Non-need-based college/university scholarships/grants from institutional funds, tuition waivers, athletic awards, on-campus employment. Forms required: International Student's Certification of Finances. For fall 2006 (estimated), 47 international students on campus received college administered financial aid ($12,605 average). *Housing:* Available during summer. *Services:* International student adviser on campus. Full-time and part-time ESL programs on campus. ESL program available during the academic year and the summer. Internships and employment opportunities (on-campus) available. *Contact:* Associate Director of International Admissions, Cleveland State University, 2121 Euclid Avenue, University Center, Room 302, Cleveland, OH 44115. Telephone: 216-687-3910. Fax: 216-687-3965. E-mail: apprequest@csuohio.edu. URL: http://www.csuohio.edu.

COLLEGE OF MOUNT ST. JOSEPH, CINCINNATI

General Information Independent Roman Catholic, coed institution. Suburban setting. *Awards:* A, B, M, D. *Entrance level for U.S. students:* Moderately difficult. *Enrollment:* 2,259 total; 1,916 undergraduates (68% women) including 0.3% international students from 7 foreign countries. *Faculty:* 238. *Library holdings:* 97,172 books, 9,000 current serial subscriptions, 1,818 audiovisual materials. *Total majors:* 39. *Expenses:* (2007–08) $20,050; room and board, $6300 (on campus); room only, $3100 (on campus). *Financial aid:* Non need-based college/university scholarships/grants from institutional funds. Forms required: FAFSA. For fall 2005, 3 international students on campus received college administered financial aid ($6300 average).

COLUMBUS COLLEGE OF ART & DESIGN, COLUMBUS

General Information Independent, 4-year, coed college. Urban setting. *Awards:* B. *Entrance level for U.S. students:* Moderately difficult. *Enrollment:* 1,581 total (57% women) including 6% international students from 37 foreign countries. *Undergraduate faculty:* 170. *Library holdings:* 50,920 books, 275 current serial subscriptions, 540 audiovisual materials. *Total majors:* 7. **Information for International Students** For fall 2006: 50 international students applied, 21 were accepted, 14 enrolled. Students can start in fall or spring. Transfers accepted from institutions abroad. *Admission tests:* Required: TOEFL (minimum score: iBT 61; paper-based 500; computer-based 173). TOEFL can be waived under certain conditions. *Application deadline:* 7/1. *Expenses:* (2006–07) $21,346; room and board, $6600 (on campus). *Financial aid:* Need-based college/university scholarships/grants from institutional funds. Non-need-based college/university scholarships/grants from institutional funds, tuition waivers, loans from institutional funds, on-campus employment. Forms required: institution's own financial aid form. International transfer students are eligible to apply for aid. For fall 2005, 32 international students on campus received college administered financial aid ($8058 average). *Services:* International student adviser on campus. Internships and employment opportunities (on-campus) available. *Contact:* International Student Advisor, Columbus College of Art & Design, 107 North Ninth Street, Columbus, OH 43215-1700. Telephone: 614-222-3265. Fax: 614-232-8344. E-mail: jneeley@ccad.edu. URL: http://www.ccad.edu.

COLUMBUS STATE COMMUNITY COLLEGE, COLUMBUS

General Information State-supported, 2-year, coed college. Urban setting. *Awards:* A. *Entrance level for U.S. students:* Noncompetitive. *Enrollment:* 21,872 total (59% women) including 1% international students from 127 foreign countries. *Undergraduate faculty:* 1,667. *Library holdings:* 38,192 books, 489 current serial subscriptions, 7,903 audiovisual materials. *Total majors:* 74. *Expenses:* (2006–07) $6300. *Financial aid:* Non-need financial aid available.

CUYAHOGA COMMUNITY COLLEGE, CLEVELAND

General Information State and locally supported, 2-year, coed college. Urban setting. *Awards:* A. *Entrance level for U.S. students:* Noncompetitive. *Enrollment:* 24,796 total (62% women) including 2% international students from 78 foreign countries. *Undergraduate faculty:* 1,440. *Library holdings:* 177,767 books, 1,135 current serial subscriptions. *Total majors:* 32. *Expenses:* (2006–07) $6541. *Financial aid:* Need-based college/university scholarships/grants from institutional funds, loans from outside sources, on-campus employment. Non-need-based college/university scholarships/grants from institutional funds, athletic awards, loans from outside sources, on-campus employment. Forms required: International Student's Certification of Finances.

DEFIANCE COLLEGE, DEFIANCE

General Information Independent, coed institution, affiliated with United Church of Christ. Small town setting. *Awards:* A, B, M. *Entrance level for U.S. students:* Moderately difficult. *Enrollment:* 930 total; 827 undergraduates (56% women) including international students from 4 foreign countries. *Faculty:* 88. *Library holdings:* 88,000 books, 424 current serial subscriptions, 25,000 audiovisual materials. *Total majors:* 38. **Information for International Students** Students can start in fall, winter, spring, or summer. Transfers accepted from institutions abroad. *Admission tests:* Required: TOEFL (minimum score: paper-based 550; computer-based 213). Recommended: SAT or ACT. TOEFL can be waived under certain conditions. *Application deadline:* 7/1. *Expenses:* (2006–07) $19,740; room and board, $6170 (on campus); room only, $3150 (on campus). *Financial aid:* Non-need-based college/university scholarships/grants from institutional funds, on-campus employment. Forms required: International Student's Certification of Finances. International transfer students are eligible to apply for aid. For fall 2005, 1 international student on campus received college administered financial aid ($9235 average). *Services:* International student adviser on campus. Employment opportunities (on-campus) available. *Contact:* Director of Admissions, Defiance College, 701 North Clinton Street, Defiance, OH 43512. Telephone: 419-783-2365. Fax: 419-783-2468. E-mail: bharsha@defiance.edu. URL: http://www.defiance.edu.

DENISON UNIVERSITY, GRANVILLE

General Information Independent, 4-year, coed college. Small town setting. *Awards:* B. *Entrance level for U.S. students:* Very difficult. *Enrollment:* 2,263 total (57% women) including 4% international students from 27 foreign countries. *Undergraduate faculty:* 207. *Library holdings:* 767,118 books, 6,616 current serial subscriptions, 32,745 audiovisual materials. *Total majors:* 39. **Information for International Students** For fall 2006: 290 international students applied, 72 were accepted, 25 enrolled. Students can start in fall or spring. Transfers accepted from institutions abroad. *Admission tests:* Required: SAT or ACT. Recommended: TOEFL (minimum score: paper-based 550; computer-based 213). TOEFL can be waived under certain conditions. *Application deadline:* 1/15. *Expenses:* (2006–07) $30,660; room and board, $8560 (on campus); room only, $4740 (on campus). *Financial aid:* Need-based college/university scholarships/grants from institutional funds. Non-need-based college/university scholarships/grants from institutional funds, on-campus employment. Forms required: institution's own financial aid form, International Student's Financial Aid Application, International Student's Certification of Finances. International transfer students are eligible to apply for aid. For fall 2006 (estimated), 88 international students on campus received college administered financial aid ($19,603 average). *Housing:* Guaranteed, also available during summer. *Services:* International student adviser on campus. Internships and employment opportunities (on-campus and off-campus) available. *Contact:* Senior Associate Director of Admissions, Denison University, Office of Admissions, Box 740, 100 Chapel Drive, Granville, OH 43023. Telephone: 740-587-6789. Fax: 740-587-6352. E-mail: leavell@denison.edu. URL: http://www.denison.edu.

DEVRY UNIVERSITY, COLUMBUS

General Information Proprietary, coed institution. Urban setting. *Awards:* A, B, M. *Entrance level for U.S. students:* Minimally difficult. *Enrollment:* 2,546 total; 2,328 undergraduates (35% women) including 0.3% international students. *Faculty:* 106. *Library holdings:* 30,000 books, 5,892 current serial subscriptions. *Total majors:* 9. *Expenses:* (2007–08) $13,220.

EDISON STATE COMMUNITY COLLEGE, PIQUA

General Information State-supported, 2-year, coed college. Small town setting. *Awards:* A. *Entrance level for U.S. students:* Noncompetitive. *Enrollment:* 3,000 total (64% women). *Undergraduate faculty:* 298. *Library holdings:* 29,851 books, 542 current serial subscriptions, 2,424 audiovisual materials. *Total majors:* 38. *Financial aid:* Forms required: CSS PROFILE.

FRANCISCAN UNIVERSITY OF STEUBENVILLE, STEUBENVILLE

General Information Independent Roman Catholic, coed institution. Suburban setting. *Awards:* A, B, M. *Entrance level for U.S. students:* Moderately difficult. *Enrollment:* 2,387 total; 1,982 undergraduates (60% women) including 1% international students from 11 foreign countries. *Faculty:* 189. *Library holdings:* 236,689 books, 392 current serial subscriptions, 1,260 audiovisual materials. *Total majors:* 31. *Expenses:* (2006–07) $18,250; room and board, $6300 (on campus); room only, $3600 (on campus). *Financial aid:* Need-based and non-need-based financial aid available. Forms required: International Student's Financial Aid Application. 18 international students on campus received college administered financial aid ($6007 average).

FRANKLIN UNIVERSITY, COLUMBUS

General Information Independent, coed institution. Urban setting. *Awards:* A, B, M. *Entrance level for U.S. students:* Noncompetitive. *Enrollment:* 6,823 total; 5,820 undergraduates (55% women) including 5% international students from 65 foreign countries. *Faculty:* 599. *Library holdings:* 27,547 books, 15,290 current serial subscriptions, 246 audiovisual materials. *Total majors:* 13. *Expenses:* (2006–07) $7620. *Financial aid:* Non-need financial aid available. 22 international students on campus received college administered financial aid ($2109 average).

HEIDELBERG COLLEGE, TIFFIN

General Information Independent, coed institution, affiliated with United Church of Christ. Small town setting. *Awards:* B, M. *Entrance level for U.S. students:* Moderately difficult. *Enrollment:* 1,569 total; 1,330 undergraduates (52% women) including 2% international students from 10 foreign countries. *Faculty:* 159. *Library holdings:* 268,702 books, 513 current serial subscriptions. *Total majors:* 46. *Expenses:* (2007–08) $18,618; room and board, $7902 (on campus); room only, $3740 (on campus). *Financial aid.* Need-based college/university scholarships/grants from institutional funds. Non-need-based college/university scholarships/grants from institutional funds. 23 international students on campus received college administered financial aid ($8478 average).

HIRAM COLLEGE, HIRAM

General Information Independent, 4-year, coed college, affiliated with Christian Church (Disciples of Christ). Rural setting. *Awards:* B, M. *Entrance level for U.S. students:* Moderately difficult. *Enrollment:* 1,239 total; 1,205 undergraduates (56% women) including 3% international students from 19 foreign countries. *Faculty:* 103. *Library holdings:* 187,451 books, 3,993 current serial subscriptions, 10,351 audiovisual materials. *Total majors:* 38. **Information for International Students** For fall 2006: 94 international students applied, 46 were accepted, 16 enrolled. Students can start in fall. Transfers accepted from institutions abroad. *Admission tests:* Required: SAT or ACT, TOEFL (minimum score: iBT 80; paper-based 550; computer-based 213; minimum score for ESL admission: iBT 57; paper-based 485; computer-based 163). Recommended: SAT, ELS Level 112 accepted in place of TOEFL 550. TOEFL can be waived under certain conditions. *Application deadline:* 2/1. *Expenses:* (2006–07) $24,885; room and board, $7781 (on campus); room only, $3801 (on campus). *Financial aid:* Non-need financial aid available. Forms required: institution's own financial aid form. International transfer students are eligible to apply for aid. 32 international students on campus received college administered financial aid ($8623 average). *Housing:* Guaranteed, also available during summer. *Services:* International student adviser on campus. Full-time ESL program on campus. ESL program available during the academic year. Internships and employment opportunities (on-campus) available. *Contact:* Director of International Admission, Hiram College, Admission Office, Teachout Price Hall, 6832 Hinsdale Street, PO Box 96, Hiram, OH 44234. Telephone: 330-569-5169. Fax: 330-569-5944. E-mail: interal@hiram.edu. URL: http://www.hiram.edu.

JAMES A. RHODES STATE COLLEGE, LIMA

General Information State-supported, 2-year, coed college. Rural setting. *Awards:* A. *Entrance level for U.S. students:* Noncompetitive. *Enrollment:* 2,842 total (69% women). *Undergraduate faculty:* 226. *Library holdings:* 80,000 books. *Total majors:* 33.
Information for International Students For fall 2006: 1 international student applied, 1 was accepted. Students can start in fall, winter, spring, or summer. Transfers accepted from institutions abroad. *Admission tests:* Required: TOEFL (minimum score: iBT 79; paper-based 550; computer-based 213), ELS. TOEFL can be waived under certain conditions. *Application deadline:* 9/1. *Financial aid:* Forms required: International Student's Certification of Finances. *Services:* International student adviser on campus. ESL program at cooperating institution. ESL program available during the academic year and the summer. Employment opportunities (on-campus) available. *Contact:* Coordinator, Territory Management, James A. Rhodes State College, 4240 Campus Drive, Lima, OH 45804-3597. Telephone: 419-995-8010. Fax: 419-995-8098. E-mail: teman.c@rhodesstate.edu. URL: http://www.rhodesstate.edu.

JOHN CARROLL UNIVERSITY, UNIVERSITY HEIGHTS

General Information Independent Roman Catholic (Jesuit), coed institution. Suburban setting. *Awards:* B, M. *Entrance level for U.S. students:* Moderately difficult. *Enrollment:* 4,101 total; 3,350 undergraduates (54% women). *Faculty:* 409. *Library holdings:* 620,000 books, 2,198 current serial subscriptions, 5,820 audiovisual materials. *Total majors:* 50.
Information for International Students For fall 2006: 19 international students applied, 5 were accepted, 4 enrolled. Students can start in fall or spring. Transfers accepted from institutions abroad. *Admission tests:* Required: TOEFL (minimum score: iBT 79; paper-based 550; computer-based 213). Recommended: SAT or ACT. TOEFL can be waived under certain conditions. *Application deadline:* 2/1. *Expenses:* (2006–07) $25,072; room and board, $7790 (on campus). *Housing:* Guaranteed, also available during summer. *Services:* International student adviser on campus. Internships and employment opportunities (on-campus) available. *Contact:* Director of Transfer and International Admission, Office of Admission, John Carroll University, 20700 North Park Boulevard, Cleveland, OH 44118. Telephone: 216-397-4294. Fax: 216-397-4981. E-mail: admission@jcu.edu. URL: http://www.jcu.edu.

KENT STATE UNIVERSITY, KENT

General Information State-supported, coed university. Suburban setting. *Awards:* A, B, M, D. *Entrance level for U.S. students:* Moderately difficult. *Enrollment:* 22,697 total; 18,136 undergraduates (59% women) including 1% international students from 68 foreign countries. *Faculty:* 1,449. *Library holdings:* 2.3 million books, 12,000 current serial subscriptions, 15,578 audiovisual materials. *Total majors:* 125.
Information for International Students For fall 2006: 370 international students applied, 306 were accepted, 237 enrolled. Students can start in fall, spring, or summer. Transfers accepted from institutions abroad. *Admission tests:* Required: TOEFL (minimum score: iBT 71; paper-based 525; computer-based 197), MELAB if no TOEFL. TOEFL can be waived under certain conditions. *Application deadline:* Rolling. *Expenses:* (2006–07) $15,862; room and board, $6880 (on campus); room only, $4200 (on campus). *Financial aid:* Forms required: International Student's Certification of Finances. International transfer students are eligible to apply for aid. For fall 2006 (estimated), 54 international students on campus received college administered financial aid ($14,615 average). *Housing:* Guaranteed, also available during summer. *Services:* International student adviser on campus. Full-time and part-time ESL programs on campus. ESL program available during the academic year and the summer. Internships and employment opportunities (on-campus) available. *Contact:* Director, International Recruitment and Admissions, Kent State University, Office of International Affairs, 106 Van Campen Hall, 21 Loop Road, Kent, OH 44242. Telephone: 330-672-2444. Fax: 330-672-2499. E-mail: tmckown@kent.edu. URL: http://www.kent.edu.

KENT STATE UNIVERSITY, ASHTABULA CAMPUS, ASHTABULA

General Information State-supported, primarily 2-year, coed college. Small town setting. *Awards:* A, B (also offers some upper-level and graduate courses). *Entrance level for U.S. students:* Noncompetitive. *Enrollment:* 1,396 total including 0.4% international students. *Undergraduate faculty:* 80. *Library holdings:* 51,884 books, 225 current serial subscriptions. *Total majors:* 20.
Information for International Students Students can start in fall, spring, or summer. Transfers accepted from institutions abroad. *Admission tests:* Required: TOEFL (minimum score: iBT 71; paper-based 525; computer-based 197), MELAB if no TOEFL. TOEFL can be waived under certain conditions. *Application deadline:* Rolling. *Financial aid:* Non-need financial aid available. Forms required: International Student's Certification of Finances. International transfer students are eligible to apply for aid. Internships and employment opportunities (on-campus) available. *Contact:* Director, International Recruitment, Admissions, and Advising, Office of Admissions, Kent State University, Ashtabula Campus, 106 Van Campen Hall, 21 Loop Road, Kent, OH 44242. Telephone: 330-672-7980. Fax: 330-672-4025. E-mail: tmckown@kent.edu. URL: http://www.ashtabula.kent.edu.

KENT STATE UNIVERSITY, EAST LIVERPOOL CAMPUS, EAST LIVERPOOL

General Information State-supported, 2-year, coed college. Small town setting. *Awards:* A (also offers some upper-level and graduate courses). *Entrance level for U.S. students:* Noncompetitive. *Enrollment:* 657 total. *Undergraduate faculty:* 75. *Library holdings:* 31,320 books, 135 current serial subscriptions. *Total majors:* 10.
Information for International Students Students can start in fall, spring, or summer. Transfers accepted from institutions abroad. *Admission tests:* Required: TOEFL (minimum score: paper-based 525; computer-based 197), MELAB if no TOEFL. TOEFL can be waived under certain conditions. *Application

Kent State University, East Liverpool Campus (continued)
deadline: Rolling. *Expenses:* (2006–07) $12,202. *Financial aid:*
Non-need financial aid available. Forms required: International
Student's Certification of Finances, University Scholarship
Application. International transfer students are eligible to apply for
aid. *Housing:* Guaranteed, also available during summer. *Services:*
International student adviser on campus. Full-time and part-time
ESL programs on campus. ESL program available during the
academic year and the summer. Internships and employment
opportunities (on-campus) available. *Contact:* Director,
International Recruitment, Admissions, and Advising, Office of
Admissions, Kent State University, East Liverpool Campus, 106
Van Campen Hall, 21 Loop Road, Kent, OH 44242.
Telephone: 330-672-7980. Fax: 330-672-4025.
E-mail: tmckown@kent.edu. URL: http://www.kenteliv.kent.edu.

KENT STATE UNIVERSITY, GEAUGA CAMPUS, BURTON

General Information State-supported, primarily 2-year, coed
college. Rural setting. *Awards:* A, B. *Entrance level for U.S.
students:* Noncompetitive. *Enrollment:* 1,062 total (58% women)
including 0.2% international students from 1 foreign country.
Undergraduate faculty: 87. *Library holdings:* 8,300 books, 6,600
current serial subscriptions. *Total majors:* 8.
Information for International Students Students can start in
fall, spring, or summer. Transfers accepted from institutions
abroad. *Admission tests:* Required: TOEFL (minimum score: iBT 71;
paper-based 525; computer-based 197), MELAB if no TOEFL.
TOEFL can be waived under certain conditions. *Application
deadline:* Rolling. *Expenses:* (2006–07) $12,202. *Financial aid:*
Forms required: International Student's Certification of Finances.
International transfer students are eligible to apply for aid.
Contact: Director, International Recruitment, Admissions, and
Advising, Office of Admissions, Kent State University, Geauga
Campus, 106 Van Campen Hall, 21 Loop Road, Kent, OH 44242.
Telephone: 330-672-7980. Fax: 330-672-4025.
E-mail: tmckown@kent.edu. URL: http://www.geauga.kent.edu.

KENT STATE UNIVERSITY, SALEM CAMPUS, SALEM

General Information State-supported, primarily 2-year, coed
college. Rural setting. *Awards:* A, B (also offers some upper-level
and graduate courses). *Entrance level for U.S. students:*
Noncompetitive. *Enrollment:* 1,332 total including international
students from 2 foreign countries. *Undergraduate faculty:* 106.
Library holdings: 19,000 books, 163 current serial subscriptions,
158 audiovisual materials. *Total majors:* 22.
Information for International Students Students can start in
fall, spring, or summer. Transfers accepted from institutions
abroad. *Admission tests:* Required: TOEFL (minimum score: iBT 71;
paper-based 525; computer-based 197), MELAB if no TOEFL.
TOEFL can be waived under certain conditions. *Application
deadline:* Rolling. *Financial aid:* Forms required: International
Student's Certification of Finances. International transfer students
are eligible to apply for aid. 1 international student on campus
received college administered financial aid ($6101 average).
Contact: Director, International Recruitment, Admissions, and
Advising, Office of Admissions, Kent State University, Salem
Campus, 106 Van Campen Hall, 21 Loop Road, Kent, OH
44242-0001. Telephone: 330-672-7980. Fax: 330-672-4025.
E-mail: tmckown@kent.edu. URL: http://www.salem.kent.edu.

KENT STATE UNIVERSITY, STARK CAMPUS, CANTON

General Information State-supported, primarily 2-year, coed
college. Suburban setting. *Awards:* A, B (also offers some graduate
courses). *Entrance level for U.S. students:* Noncompetitive.
Enrollment: 3,736 total. *Undergraduate faculty:* 200. *Library
holdings:* 72,807 books, 313 current serial subscriptions.
Total majors: 6.
Information for International Students Students can start in
fall, spring, or summer. Transfers accepted from institutions
abroad. *Admission tests:* Required: TOEFL (minimum score: iBT 71;
paper-based 525; computer-based 197), MELAB if no TOEFL.
TOEFL can be waived under certain conditions. *Application
deadline:* Rolling. *Financial aid:* Non-need financial aid available.
Forms required: International Student's Certification of Finances.
International transfer students are eligible to apply for aid. 4
international students on campus received college administered
financial aid ($2607 average). *Contact:* Director, International
Recruitment, Admissions, and Advising, Office of Admissions, Kent
State University, Stark Campus, 106 Van Campen Hall, 21 Loop
Road, Kent, OH 44242. Telephone: 330-672-7980.
Fax: 330-672-4025. E-mail: tmckown@kent.edu.
URL: http://www.stark.kent.edu.

KENT STATE UNIVERSITY, TRUMBULL CAMPUS, WARREN

General Information State-supported, primarily 2-year, coed
college. Suburban setting. *Awards:* A, B (also offers some
upper-level and graduate courses). *Entrance level for U.S. students:*
Noncompetitive. *Enrollment:* 2,015 total (64% women) including
0.2% international students from 3 foreign countries.
Undergraduate faculty: 123. *Library holdings:* 65,951 books, 759
current serial subscriptions. *Total majors:* 12.
Information for International Students Students can start in
fall, spring, or summer. Transfers accepted from institutions
abroad. *Admission tests:* Required: TOEFL (minimum score: iBT 71;
paper-based 525; computer-based 197), MELAB if no TOEFL.
TOEFL can be waived under certain conditions. *Application
deadline:* Rolling. *Expenses:* (2006–07) $12,018. *Financial aid:*
Forms required: International Student's Certification of Finances.
International transfer students are eligible to apply for aid. 1
international student on campus received college administered
financial aid ($4995 average). *Contact:* Director, International
Recruitment, Admissions, and Advising, Office of Admissions, Kent
State University, Trumbull Campus, 106 Van Campen Hall, 21 Loop
Road, Kent, OH 44242-0001. Telephone: 330-672-7980.
Fax: 330-672-4025. E-mail: tmckown@kent.edu.
URL: http://www.trumbull.kent.edu.

KENT STATE UNIVERSITY, TUSCARAWAS CAMPUS, NEW PHILADELPHIA

General Information State-supported, primarily 2-year, coed
college. Small town setting. *Awards:* A, B, M (also offers some
upper-level and graduate courses). *Entrance level for U.S. students:*
Noncompetitive. *Enrollment:* 2,021 total (60% women) including
0.2% international students. *Faculty:* 115. *Library holdings:* 63,880
books, 208 current serial subscriptions, 1,179 audiovisual materials.
Total majors: 16.
Information for International Students Students can start in
fall, spring, or summer. Transfers accepted from institutions
abroad. *Admission tests:* Required: TOEFL (minimum score: iBT 71;
paper-based 525; computer-based 197), MELAB if no TOEFL.
TOEFL can be waived under certain conditions. *Application
deadline:* Rolling. *Expenses:* (2006–07) $12,202. *Financial aid:*
Forms required: International Student's Certification of Finances.
International transfer students are eligible to apply for aid.
Contact: Director, International Recruitment, Admissions, and
Advising, Office of Admissions, Kent State University, Tuscarawas
Campus, 106 Van Campen Hall, 21 Loop Road, Kent, OH
44242-0001. Telephone: 330-672-7980. Fax: 330-672-4025.
E-mail: tmckown@kent.edu. URL: http://www.tusc.kent.edu.

KENYON COLLEGE, GAMBIER

General Information Independent, 4-year, coed college. Rural
setting. *Awards:* B. *Entrance level for U.S. students:* Very difficult.
Enrollment: 1,661 total (53% women) including 3% international
students from 28 foreign countries. *Undergraduate faculty:* 186.
Library holdings: 826,059 books, 8,574 current serial subscriptions.
Total majors: 54.
Information for International Students For fall 2006: 362
international students applied, 38 were accepted, 17 enrolled.
Students can start in fall. Transfers accepted from institutions
abroad. *Admission tests:* Required: TOEFL (minimum score: iBT 96;
paper-based 590; computer-based 243). Recommended: SAT or ACT.
Application deadline: 1/1. *Expenses:* (2006–07) $36,050; room and
board, $5900 (on campus); room only, $2780 (on campus). *Financial
aid:* Need-based college/university scholarships/grants from
institutional funds, loans from institutional funds, on-campus
employment. Non-need-based college/university scholarships/grants
from institutional funds, on-campus employment. Forms required:
International Student's Financial Aid Application, International
Student's Certification of Finances. International transfer students
are eligible to apply for aid. For fall 2006 (estimated), 43
international students on campus received college administered
financial aid ($39,566 average). *Housing:* Guaranteed. *Services:*
International student adviser on campus. Internships and
employment opportunities (on-campus) available. *Contact:* Associate
Dean of Admissions and Director of International Admissions,
Kenyon College, Ransom Hall, Gambier, OH 43022-9623.
Telephone: 740-427-5776. Fax: 740-427-5770.
E-mail: admissions@kenyon.edu. URL: http://www.kenyon.edu.

KETTERING COLLEGE OF MEDICAL ARTS, KETTERING

General Information Independent Seventh-day Adventist,
primarily 2-year, coed, primarily women's college. Suburban setting.
Awards: A, B. *Entrance level for U.S. students:* Moderately difficult.
Enrollment: 803 total (80% women) including 2% international
students from 10 foreign countries. *Undergraduate faculty:* 61.
Library holdings: 29,390 books, 266 current serial subscriptions.

Total majors: 7. *Expenses:* (2007–08) $7548; room and board, $5400 (on campus); room only, $2400 (on campus). *Financial aid:* Forms required: International Student's Certification of Finances.

LAKE ERIE COLLEGE, PAINESVILLE

General Information Independent, coed institution. Small town setting. *Awards:* B, M. *Entrance level for U.S. students:* Minimally difficult. *Enrollment:* 952 total; 682 undergraduates (73% women) including 0.4% international students from 5 foreign countries. *Faculty:* 93. *Library holdings:* 87,000 books, 6,050 current serial subscriptions, 2,000 audiovisual materials. *Total majors:* 29.

LAURA AND ALVIN SIEGAL COLLEGE OF JUDAIC STUDIES, BEACHWOOD

General Information Independent, coed institution. Suburban setting. *Awards:* B, M. *Entrance level for U.S. students:* Noncompetitive. *Enrollment:* 146 total; 11 undergraduates (73% women). *Faculty:* 42. *Library holdings:* 28,000 books, 100 current serial subscriptions. *Total majors:* 7. *Expenses:* (2006–07) $15,775. *Financial aid:* Need-based college/university scholarships/grants from institutional funds, on-campus employment. Non-need-based college/university scholarships/grants from institutional funds, on-campus employment. Forms required: institution's own financial aid form.

LOURDES COLLEGE, SYLVANIA

General Information Independent Roman Catholic, coed institution. Suburban setting. *Awards:* A, B, M. *Entrance level for U.S. students:* Difficulty N/R. *Enrollment:* 1,881 total; 1,733 undergraduates (84% women) including 0.2% international students. *Faculty:* 178. *Library holdings:* 62,222 books, 6,200 current serial subscriptions, 170 audiovisual materials. *Total majors:* 21. *Expenses:* (2006–07) $13,200. *Financial aid:* Non-need-based college/university scholarships/grants from institutional funds.

MALONE COLLEGE, CANTON

General Information Independent, coed institution, affiliated with Evangelical Friends Church–Eastern Region. Suburban setting. *Awards:* B, M. *Entrance level for U.S. students:* Moderately difficult. *Enrollment:* 2,296 total; 1,960 undergraduates (61% women) including 1% international students from 8 foreign countries. *Faculty:* 209. *Library holdings:* 245,530 books, 6,869 current serial subscriptions, 13,354 audiovisual materials. *Total majors:* 43. *Expenses:* (2006–07) $17,790; room and board, $6400 (on campus); room only, $3300 (on campus). *Financial aid:* Need-based college/university scholarships/grants from institutional funds, athletic awards. Non-need-based college/university scholarships/grants from institutional funds, athletic awards, on-campus employment. Forms required: FAFSA and verification documents if required. For fall 2006 (estimated), 26 international students on campus received college administered financial aid ($11,960 average).

MARIETTA COLLEGE, MARIETTA

General Information Independent, coed institution. Small town setting. *Awards:* A, B, M. *Entrance level for U.S. students:* Moderately difficult. *Enrollment:* 1,530 total; 1,412 undergraduates (51% women) including 5% international students from 14 foreign countries. *Faculty:* 139. *Library holdings:* 246,706 books, 28,188 current serial subscriptions, 6,147 audiovisual materials. *Total majors:* 40. *Expenses:* (2006–07) $23,815; room and board, $7030 (on campus); room only, $3900 (on campus). *Financial aid:* Non-need financial aid available. 26 international students on campus received college administered financial aid ($6598 average).

MIAMI UNIVERSITY, OXFORD

General Information State-related, coed university. Small town setting. *Awards:* A, B, M, D. *Entrance level for U.S. students:* Moderately difficult. *Enrollment:* 16,329 total; 14,551 undergraduates (54% women) including 1% international students from 32 foreign countries. *Faculty:* 1,272. *Library holdings:* 2.7 million books, 14,089 current serial subscriptions. *Total majors:* 111.
Information for International Students For fall 2006: 272 international students applied, 128 were accepted, 64 enrolled. Students can start in fall or spring. Transfers accepted from institutions abroad. *Admission tests:* Required: TOEFL (minimum score: iBT 72; paper-based 530; computer-based 200). Recommended: SAT or ACT. TOEFL can be waived under certain conditions. *Application deadline:* 3/1. *Expenses:* (2006–07) $23,017; room and board, $8140 (on campus); room only, $4160 (on campus). *Financial aid:* Non-need financial aid available. For fall 2006 (estimated), 195 international students on campus received college administered financial aid ($11,945 average). *Housing:* Guaranteed, also available during summer. *Services:* International student adviser on campus. ESL program at cooperating institution. ESL

program available during the academic year and the summer. Employment opportunities (on-campus) available. *Contact:* Associate Director, International Recruitment, Miami University, 301 South Campus Avenue, Office of Admission, Oxford, OH 45056. Telephone: 513-529-2288. Fax: 513-529-1550. E-mail: internationaladmission@muohio.edu. URL: http://www.muohio.edu.

MOUNT VERNON NAZARENE UNIVERSITY, MOUNT VERNON

General Information Independent Nazarene, coed institution. Small town setting. *Awards:* A, B, M. *Entrance level for U.S. students:* Moderately difficult. *Enrollment:* 2,670 total; 2,171 undergraduates (59% women) including 0.4% international students from 5 foreign countries. *Faculty:* 244. *Library holdings:* 99,914 books, 7,341 current serial subscriptions, 3,472 audiovisual materials. *Total majors:* 65. *Expenses:* (2007–08) $18,064; room and board, $5286 (on campus); room only, $2954 (on campus). *Financial aid:* Need-based college/university scholarships/grants from institutional funds, athletic awards, on-campus employment. Non-need-based college/university scholarships/grants from institutional funds, athletic awards. Forms required: institution's own financial aid form, International Student's Financial Aid Application, International Student's Certification of Finances. For fall 2006 (estimated), 9 international students on campus received college administered financial aid ($13,397 average).

MUSKINGUM COLLEGE, NEW CONCORD

General Information Independent, coed institution, affiliated with Presbyterian Church (U.S.A.). Small town setting. *Awards:* B, M. *Entrance level for U.S. students:* Moderately difficult. *Enrollment:* 2,396 total; 1,634 undergraduates (50% women) including 2% international students from 19 foreign countries. *Faculty:* 139. *Library holdings:* 233,000 books, 900 current serial subscriptions, 6,000 audiovisual materials. *Total majors:* 59.
Information for International Students For fall 2006: 30 international students applied, 26 were accepted, 6 enrolled. Students can start in fall or spring. Transfers accepted from institutions abroad. *Admission tests:* Required: TOEFL (minimum score: iBT 80; paper-based 550; computer-based 213; minimum score for ESL admission: iBT 64; paper-based 507; computer-based 180). Recommended: SAT or ACT, IELTS, Step EIKEN. TOEFL can be waived under certain conditions. *Application deadline:* 6/1. *Expenses:* (2006–07) $17,380; room and board, $6840 (on campus); room only, $3420 (on campus). *Financial aid:* Need-based college/university scholarships/grants from institutional funds, on-campus employment. Non-need-based college/university scholarships/grants from institutional funds, on-campus employment. Forms required: institution's own financial aid form. International transfer students are eligible to apply for aid. 31 international students on campus received college administered financial aid ($9937 average). *Housing:* Guaranteed. *Services:* International student adviser on campus. Part-time ESL program on campus. ESL program available during the academic year. Internships and employment opportunities (on-campus) available. *Contact:* Coordinator, International Enrollment, Muskingum College, 163 Stormont Street, New Concord, OH 43762. Telephone: 740-826-8127. Fax: 740-826-6113. E-mail: klasota@muskingum.edu. URL: http://www.muskingum.edu.

MYERS UNIVERSITY, CLEVELAND

General Information Independent, coed institution. Urban setting. *Awards:* A, B, M. *Entrance level for U.S. students:* Minimally difficult. *Enrollment:* 1,177 total; 1,096 undergraduates (71% women). *Faculty:* 165. *Library holdings:* 15,027 books, 140 current serial subscriptions, 377 audiovisual materials. *Total majors:* 14. *Financial aid:* Need-based college/university scholarships/grants from institutional funds. Non-need-based college/university scholarships/grants from institutional funds, athletic awards. Forms required: institution's own financial aid form.

NORTH CENTRAL STATE COLLEGE, MANSFIELD

General Information State-supported, 2-year, coed college. Suburban setting. *Awards:* A. *Entrance level for U.S. students:* Noncompetitive. *Enrollment:* 3,333 total. *Undergraduate faculty:* 199. *Library holdings:* 52,700 books, 410 current serial subscriptions. *Total majors:* 26. *Expenses:* (2006–07) $7,268.

NORTHWEST STATE COMMUNITY COLLEGE, ARCHBOLD

General Information State-supported, 2-year, coed college. Rural setting. *Awards:* A. *Entrance level for U.S. students:* Noncompetitive. *Enrollment:* 3,145 total (58% women) including 0.1% international students. *Undergraduate faculty:* 172. *Library

Northwest State Community College (continued)
holdings: 15,321 books, 1,680 current serial subscriptions, 1,913 audiovisual materials. *Total majors:* 32.

NOTRE DAME COLLEGE, SOUTH EUCLID

General Information Independent Roman Catholic, coed institution. Suburban setting. *Awards:* A, B, M. *Entrance level for U.S. students:* Moderately difficult. *Enrollment:* 1,393 total; 1,240 undergraduates (66% women) including 4% international students from 19 foreign countries. *Faculty:* 118. *Library holdings:* 9,983 audiovisual materials. *Total majors:* 33.

Information for International Students For fall 2006: 68 international students applied, 30 were accepted, 17 enrolled. Students can start in fall or spring. Transfers accepted from institutions abroad. *Admission tests:* Required: SAT, ACT, TOEFL (minimum score: paper-based 550; computer-based 213), ELS (minimum score: 112). *Application deadline:* Rolling. *Expenses:* (2006–07) $20,130; room and board, $6850 (on campus); room only, $3400 (on campus). *Financial aid:* Non-need financial aid available. Forms required: International Student's Financial Aid Application, International Student's Certification of Finances. International transfer students are eligible to apply for aid. 13 international students on campus received college administered financial aid ($10,000 average). *Housing:* Available during summer. *Services:* International student adviser on campus. ESL program at cooperating institution. ESL program available during the academic year and the summer. Internships and employment opportunities (on-campus) available. *Contact:* International Student Advisor and Recruiter, Notre Dame College, 4545 College Road, South Euclid, OH 44121. Telephone: 216-373-5384. Fax: 216-373-5278. E-mail: cnolan@ndc.edu. URL: http://www.notredamecollege.edu.

OBERLIN COLLEGE, OBERLIN

General Information Independent, coed institution. Small town setting. *Awards:* B, M. *Entrance level for U.S. students:* Very difficult. *Enrollment:* 2,841 total; 2,829 undergraduates (55% women) including 6% international students from 44 foreign countries. *Faculty:* 334. *Library holdings:* 1.5 million books, 4,560 current serial subscriptions. *Total majors:* 54. *Expenses:* (2006–07) $34,426; room and board, $8720 (on campus); room only, $4580 (on campus). *Financial aid:* Need-based college/university scholarships/grants from institutional funds, loans from institutional funds, on-campus employment. Non-need-based college/university scholarships/grants from institutional funds, loans from institutional funds, on-campus employment. Forms required: institution's own financial aid form, International Student's Financial Aid Application, International Student's Certification of Finances. For fall 2006 (estimated), 153 international students on campus received college administered financial aid ($32,070 average).

OHIO DOMINICAN UNIVERSITY, COLUMBUS

General Information Independent Roman Catholic, coed institution. Urban setting. *Awards:* A, B, M. *Entrance level for U.S. students:* Moderately difficult. *Enrollment:* 3,054 total; 2,518 undergraduates (62% women) including 0.4% international students from 10 foreign countries. *Faculty:* 217. *Library holdings:* 104,739 books, 511 current serial subscriptions, 3,470 audiovisual materials. *Total majors:* 48. *Expenses:* (2006–07) $20,570; room and board, $6800 (on campus). *Financial aid:* Non-need financial aid available. For fall 2006 (estimated), 23 international students on campus received college administered financial aid ($2000 average).

OHIO INSTITUTE OF PHOTOGRAPHY AND TECHNOLOGY, DAYTON

General Information Proprietary, 2-year, coed college. Urban setting. *Awards:* A. *Entrance level for U.S. students:* Moderately difficult. *Enrollment:* 740 total (78% women). *Undergraduate faculty:* 46. *Library holdings:* 640 books, 35 current serial subscriptions. *Total majors:* 4. *Expenses:* (2006–07) $18,889.

OHIO NORTHERN UNIVERSITY, ADA

General Information Independent, coed institution, affiliated with United Methodist Church. Small town setting. *Awards:* B, M, FP. *Entrance level for U.S. students:* Moderately difficult. *Enrollment:* 3,620 total; 2,612 undergraduates (47% women) including 1% international students from 15 foreign countries. *Faculty:* 307. *Total majors:* 111. *Expenses:* (2006–07) $28,260; room and board, $7080 (on campus); room only, $3540 (on campus). *Financial aid:* Non-need-based college/university scholarships/grants from institutional funds, loans from outside sources, on-campus employment. Forms required: institution's own financial aid form. For fall 2005, 9 international students on campus received college administered financial aid ($7281 average).

THE OHIO STATE UNIVERSITY, COLUMBUS

General Information State-supported, coed university. Urban setting. *Awards:* A, B, M, D, FP. *Entrance level for U.S. students:* Moderately difficult. *Enrollment:* 51,818 total; 38,479 undergraduates (47% women) including 2% international students from 74 foreign countries. *Faculty:* 4,031. *Library holdings:* 5.9 million books, 43,086 current serial subscriptions, 68,454 audiovisual materials. *Total majors:* 170. *Expenses:* (2006–07) $20,454; room and board, $6720 (on campus). *Financial aid:* Non-need-based college/university scholarships/grants from institutional funds, tuition waivers, athletic awards, loans from institutional funds, loans from outside sources, on-campus employment. Forms required: institution's own "Affidavit of Financial Support for International Students". For fall 2006 (estimated), 54 international students on campus received college administered financial aid ($4627 average).

THE OHIO STATE UNIVERSITY AGRICULTURAL TECHNICAL INSTITUTE, WOOSTER

General Information State-supported, 2-year, coed college. Small town setting. *Awards:* A. *Entrance level for U.S. students:* Noncompetitive. *Enrollment:* 747 total (35% women) including 0.4% international students from 2 foreign countries. *Undergraduate faculty:* 70. *Library holdings:* 19,009 books, 595 current serial subscriptions. *Total majors:* 36. *Expenses:* (2006–07) $17,792; room and board, $5748 (on campus); room only, $4803 (on campus).

THE OHIO STATE UNIVERSITY AT MARION, MARION

General Information State-supported, coed institution. Small town setting. *Awards:* A, B, M. *Entrance level for U.S. students:* Noncompetitive. *Enrollment:* 1,538 total; 1,432 undergraduates (56% women) including 0.2% international students from 3 foreign countries. *Faculty:* 112. *Library holdings:* 40,000 books, 400 current serial subscriptions, 3,800 audiovisual materials. *Total majors:* 6. *Expenses:* (2006–07) $18,153.

THE OHIO STATE UNIVERSITY–NEWARK CAMPUS, NEWARK

General Information State-supported, coed institution. Small town setting. *Awards:* A, B, M. *Entrance level for U.S. students:* Noncompetitive. *Enrollment:* 2,310 total; 2,240 undergraduates (54% women) including 0.1% international students from 12 foreign countries. *Faculty:* 135. *Library holdings:* 49,000 books, 423 current serial subscriptions, 2,680 audiovisual materials. *Total majors:* 6. *Expenses:* (2006–07) $18,153; room only, $4989 (on campus).

OHIO UNIVERSITY, ATHENS

General Information State-supported, coed university. Small town setting. *Awards:* A, B, M, D, FP. *Entrance level for U.S. students:* Moderately difficult. *Enrollment:* 20,593 total; 17,176 undergraduates (51% women) including 1% international students from 109 foreign countries. *Faculty:* 1,188. *Library holdings:* 2.7 million books, 27,606 current serial subscriptions, 93,337 audiovisual materials. *Total majors:* 173. *Expenses:* (2006–07) $17,811; room and board, $7839 (on campus); room only, $4008 (on campus).

OHIO WESLEYAN UNIVERSITY, DELAWARE

General Information Independent United Methodist, 4-year, coed college. Small town setting. *Awards:* B. *Entrance level for U.S. students:* Very difficult. *Enrollment:* 1,935 total (52% women) including 8% international students from 45 foreign countries. *Undergraduate faculty:* 182. *Library holdings:* 441,912 books, 1,073 current serial subscriptions. *Total majors:* 90.

Information for International Students For fall 2006: 567 international students applied, 209 were accepted, 48 enrolled. Students can start in fall or spring. Transfers accepted from institutions abroad. *Admission tests:* Required: SAT or ACT, TOEFL (minimum score: iBT 80; paper-based 550; computer-based 213). Recommended: SAT Subject Tests. TOEFL can be waived under certain conditions. *Application deadline:* 3/1. *Expenses:* (2006–07) $30,290; room and board, $7790 (on campus); room only, $3880 (on campus). *Financial aid:* Need-based college/university scholarships/grants from institutional funds, tuition waivers, loans from institutional funds, loans from outside sources, on-campus employment. Non-need-based college/university scholarships/grants from institutional funds, tuition waivers, loans from institutional funds, loans from outside sources, on-campus employment. Forms required: institution's own financial aid form, International Student's Financial Aid Application, International Student's Certification of Finances. International transfer students are eligible to apply for aid. 154 international students on campus received college administered financial aid ($18,373 average). *Housing:* Guaranteed, also available during summer. *Services:* International student adviser on campus. Internships and employment opportunities (on-campus and off-campus) available.

Contact: Associate Dean and Director of International Recruitment, Ohio Wesleyan University, 61 South Sandusky Street, Delaware, OH 43015. Telephone: 740-368-3029. Fax: 740-368-3066. E-mail: owuintl@cc.owu.edu. URL: http://www.owu.edu.

OTTERBEIN COLLEGE, WESTERVILLE
General Information Independent United Methodist, coed institution. Suburban setting. *Awards:* B, M. *Entrance level for U.S. students:* Moderately difficult. *Enrollment:* 3,176 total; 2,804 undergraduates (64% women) including international students from 12 foreign countries. *Faculty:* 275. *Library holdings:* 182,629 books, 1,012 current serial subscriptions. *Total majors:* 60.
Information for International Students For fall 2006: 30 international students applied, 6 were accepted, 2 enrolled. Students can start in fall, winter, or spring. Transfers accepted from institutions abroad. *Admission tests:* Required: TOEFL (minimum score: iBT 69; paper-based 523; computer-based 193). Recommended: SAT or ACT. TOEFL can be waived under certain conditions. *Application deadline:* Rolling. *Expenses:* (2006–07) $23,871; room and board, $6789 (on campus); room only, $3174 (on campus). *Financial aid:* Need-based and non-need-based financial aid available. *Housing:* Guaranteed, also available during summer. *Services:* International student adviser on campus. Internships and employment opportunities (on-campus and off-campus) available. *Contact:* Admission Counselor, Otterbein College, Office of Admission, One Otterbein College, Westerville, OH 43081. Telephone: 614-823-1500. Fax: 614-823-1200. E-mail: kcoffman@otterbein.edu. URL: http://www.otterbein.edu.
See In-Depth Description on page 146.

OWENS COMMUNITY COLLEGE, TOLEDO
General Information State-supported, 2-year, coed college. Suburban setting. *Awards:* A. *Entrance level for U.S. students:* Noncompetitive. *Enrollment:* 19,141 total (46% women) including 0.1% international students from 44 foreign countries. *Undergraduate faculty:* 1,302. *Library holdings:* 78,344 books, 6,230 current serial subscriptions. *Total majors:* 25.
Information for International Students For fall 2006: 105 international students applied, 105 were accepted, 105 enrolled. Students can start in fall, spring, or summer. Transfers accepted from institutions abroad. *Admission tests:* Required: TOEFL (minimum score: paper-based 500; computer-based 173), ELS. TOEFL can be waived under certain conditions. *Application deadline:* Rolling. *Expenses:* (2007–08) $5932. *Services:* International student adviser on campus. Full-time and part-time ESL programs on campus. ESL program available during the academic year. Internships and employment opportunities (on-campus) available. *Contact:* Administrator, Owens Community College, Box 10000, Toledo, OH 43699-1947. Telephone: 567-661-7510. Fax: 567-661-7734. E-mail: cesar_hernandez@owens.edu. URL: http://www.owens.edu.

PONTIFICAL COLLEGE JOSEPHINUM, COLUMBUS
General Information Independent Roman Catholic, coed, primarily men's institution. Suburban setting. *Awards:* B, M, FP. *Entrance level for U.S. students:* Minimally difficult. *Enrollment:* 153 total; 104 undergraduates including 8% international students from 1 foreign country. *Faculty:* 50. *Library holdings:* 137,883 books, 465 current serial subscriptions. *Total majors:* 6.
Information for International Students For fall 2006: 4 international students applied, 4 were accepted, 4 enrolled. Students can start in fall. *Admission tests:* Required: SAT, ACT, SAT Subject Tests, TOEFL (minimum score: paper-based 600; computer-based 250; minimum score for ESL admission: paper-based 600; computer-based 250). Recommended: SAT or ACT. *Application deadline:* Rolling. *Expenses:* (2007–08) $15,680; room and board, $7498 (on campus). *Financial aid:* Need-based financial aid available. Forms required: institution's own financial aid form. *Housing:* Guaranteed. *Services:* International student adviser on campus. Full-time ESL program on campus. ESL program available during the academic year. Employment opportunities (on-campus) available. *Contact:* Registrar, Pontifical College Josephinum, 7625 North High Street, Columbus, OH 43235. Telephone: 614-985-2226. Fax: 614-885-2307. E-mail: bcouts@pcj.edu. URL: http://www.pcj.edu.

SCHOOL OF ADVERTISING ART, KETTERING
General Information Proprietary, 2-year, coed college. Suburban setting. *Awards:* A. *Entrance level for U.S. students:* Minimally difficult. *Enrollment:* 146 total (51% women) including 1% international students. *Undergraduate faculty:* 20. *Total majors:* 1. *Expenses:* (2006–07) $17,985.

SINCLAIR COMMUNITY COLLEGE, DAYTON
General Information State and locally supported, 2-year, coed college. Urban setting. *Awards:* A. *Entrance level for U.S. students:*

Noncompetitive. *Enrollment:* 19,563 total (57% women) including 1% international students. *Undergraduate faculty:* 1,117. *Library holdings:* 147,613 books, 576 current serial subscriptions, 9,293 audiovisual materials. *Total majors:* 89. *Expenses:* (2006–07) $6525. *Financial aid:* Forms required: institution's own financial aid form.

SOUTHERN STATE COMMUNITY COLLEGE, HILLSBORO
General Information State-supported, 2-year, coed college. Rural setting. *Awards:* A. *Entrance level for U.S. students:* Noncompetitive. *Enrollment:* 2,363 total including 0.04% international students. *Undergraduate faculty:* 144. *Library holdings:* 48,500 books, 2,900 current serial subscriptions, 8,950 audiovisual materials. *Total majors:* 15. *Expenses:* (2006–07) $6528.

STARK STATE COLLEGE OF TECHNOLOGY, NORTH CANTON
General Information State and locally supported, 2-year, coed college. Suburban setting. *Awards:* A. *Entrance level for U.S. students:* Noncompetitive. *Enrollment:* 6,857 total (58% women) including 0.2% international students. *Undergraduate faculty:* 603. *Library holdings:* 70,000 books, 425 current serial subscriptions. *Total majors:* 49. *Expenses:* (2006–07) $5610. *Financial aid:* Need-based college/university scholarships/grants from institutional funds, on-campus employment. Non-need-based college/university scholarships/grants from institutional funds. Forms required: institution's own financial aid form, International Student's Certification of Finances.

TIFFIN UNIVERSITY, TIFFIN
General Information Independent, coed institution. Small town setting. *Awards:* A, B, M. *Entrance level for U.S. students:* Minimally difficult. *Enrollment:* 1,977 total; 1,437 undergraduates (53% women) including 4% international students from 16 foreign countries. *Faculty:* 137. *Library holdings:* 29,779 books, 250 current serial subscriptions, 536 audiovisual materials. *Total majors:* 21. *Expenses:* (2006–07) $15,870; room and board, $6775 (on campus); room only, $3525 (on campus). *Financial aid:* Need-based college/university scholarships/grants from institutional funds, loans from outside sources, on-campus employment, state and private scholarships, SEOG, PELL. Non-need financial aid available. Forms required: International Student's Certification of Finances. For fall 2006 (estimated), 57 international students on campus received college administered financial aid ($6436 average).

UNION INSTITUTE & UNIVERSITY, CINCINNATI
General Information Independent, coed university. Urban setting. *Awards:* B, M, D. *Entrance level for U.S. students:* Moderately difficult. *Enrollment:* 2,379 total; 1,122 undergraduates (68% women) including 0.1% international students from 6 foreign countries. *Faculty:* 169. *Library holdings:* 50,000 books, 300 audiovisual materials. *Total majors:* 12. *Financial aid:* Need-based and non-need-based financial aid available. Forms required: institution's own financial aid form.

THE UNIVERSITY OF AKRON, AKRON
General Information State-supported, coed university. Urban setting. *Awards:* B, M, D, FP (associate). *Entrance level for U.S. students:* Moderately difficult. *Enrollment:* 21,882 total; 18,016 undergraduates (52% women) including 1% international students from 47 foreign countries. *Faculty:* 1,497. *Library holdings:* 1.3 million books, 13,677 current serial subscriptions, 46,248 audiovisual materials. *Total majors:* 235. *Expenses:* (2006–07) $17,631; room and board, $7640 (on campus); room only, $4764 (on campus). *Financial aid:* Need-based on-campus employment. Non-need-based college/university scholarships/grants from institutional funds, athletic awards, on-campus employment. Forms required: International Student's Financial Aid Application, International Student's Certification of Finances. For fall 2005, 44 international students on campus received college administered financial aid ($2873 average).

UNIVERSITY OF CINCINNATI, CINCINNATI
General Information State-supported, coed university. Urban setting. *Awards:* A, B, M, D, FP. *Entrance level for U.S. students:* Moderately difficult. *Enrollment:* 27,932 total; 19,512 undergraduates (50% women) including 1% international students from 123 foreign countries. *Faculty:* 1,241. *Library holdings:* 3 million books, 16,560 current serial subscriptions. *Total majors:* 144.
Information for International Students Students can start in fall, winter, spring, or summer. *Admission tests:* Required: SAT, TOEFL, or IELTS. TOEFL can be waived under certain conditions. *Application deadline:* Rolling. *Expenses:* (2006–07) $23,922; room and board, $9246 (on campus); room only, $5874 (on campus). *Financial aid:* Need-based college/university scholarships/grants

University of Cincinnati (continued)

from institutional funds, tuition waivers, athletic awards, loans from institutional funds, loans from outside sources, on-campus employment. Non-need-based college/university scholarships/grants from institutional funds, tuition waivers, athletic awards, loans from institutional funds, loans from outside sources, on-campus employment. Forms required: FAFSA. For fall 2005, 61 international students on campus received college administered financial aid ($12,504 average). *Housing:* Available during summer. *Services:* International student adviser on campus. *Contact:* Associate Director, Admissions, Office of Admissions, University of Cincinnati, University Pavilion, Cincinnati, OH 45221. Telephone: 513-556-1073. E-mail: jonathan.weller@uc.edu. URL: http://www.uc.edu.

See In-Depth Description on page 210.

UNIVERSITY OF CINCINNATI RAYMOND WALTERS COLLEGE, CINCINNATI

General Information State-supported, 2-year, coed college. Suburban setting. *Awards:* A. *Entrance level for U.S. students:* Noncompetitive. *Enrollment:* 4,421 total (68% women) including 0.03% international students. *Undergraduate faculty:* 121. *Library holdings:* 48,226 books, 636 current serial subscriptions, 2,220 audiovisual materials. *Total majors:* 37.

Information for International Students Students can start in fall, winter, spring, or summer. Transfers accepted from institutions abroad. *Admission tests:* Required: TOEFL or college placement test. *Application deadline:* Rolling. *Financial aid:* Non-need financial aid available. Forms required: International Student's Certification of Finances. *Services:* ESL program at cooperating institution. Employment opportunities (on-campus) available. *Contact:* Director of Enrollment Services, Admissions Office, University of Cincinnati Raymond Walters College, 9555 Plainfield Road, Cincinnati, OH 45236-1096. Telephone: 513-745-5700. Fax: 513-745-5768. E-mail: colrel@ucrwcu.rwc.uc.edu. URL: http://www.rwc.uc.edu.

UNIVERSITY OF DAYTON, DAYTON

General Information Independent Roman Catholic, coed university. Suburban setting. *Awards:* B, M, D, FP. *Entrance level for U.S. students:* Moderately difficult. *Enrollment:* 10,503 total; 7,473 undergraduates (50% women) including 1% international students from 25 foreign countries. *Faculty:* 914. *Library holdings:* 973,842 books, 10,481 current serial subscriptions, 2,186 audiovisual materials. *Total majors:* 74.

Information for International Students For fall 2006: 388 international students applied, 44 were accepted, 15 enrolled. Students can start in fall, winter, or summer. Transfers accepted from institutions abroad. *Admission tests:* Required: TOEFL (minimum score: iBT 70; paper-based 523; computer-based 193). Recommended: SAT or ACT, ELPT (min. score of 956) or APIEL (min. score of 3) in lieu of TOEFL. TOEFL can be waived under certain conditions. *Application deadline:* 5/1. *Expenses:* (2006–07) $23,970; room and board, $7190 (on campus); room only, $4300 (on campus). *Financial aid:* Non-need-based college/university scholarships/grants from institutional funds. For fall 2005, 28 international students on campus received college administered financial aid ($4776 average). *Services:* International student adviser on campus. Full-time and part-time ESL programs on campus. ESL program available during the academic year and the summer. Internships and employment opportunities (on-campus and off-campus) available. *Contact:* Associate Director of International Recruitment, University of Dayton, 300 College Park, Dayton, OH 45469-1300. Telephone: 937-229-4411. Fax: 937-229-4729. E-mail: jhuart@udayton.edu. URL: http://www.udayton.edu.

See In-Depth Description on page 211.

THE UNIVERSITY OF FINDLAY, FINDLAY

General Information Independent, coed institution, affiliated with Church of God. Small town setting. *Awards:* A, B, M. *Entrance level for U.S. students:* Moderately difficult. *Enrollment:* 6,182 total; 4,926 undergraduates (61% women) including 6% international students from 34 foreign countries. *Faculty:* 299. *Library holdings:* 132,052 books, 23,128 current serial subscriptions. *Total majors:* 58.

Information for International Students Students can start in fall, spring, or summer. Transfers accepted from institutions abroad. *Admission tests:* Recommended: TOEFL (minimum score: iBT 61; paper-based 500; computer-based 173), IELTS. TOEFL can be waived under certain conditions. *Application deadline:* Rolling. *Expenses:* (2006–07) $22,796; room and board, $7792 (on campus); room only, $3906 (on campus). *Financial aid:* Non-need-based college/university scholarships/grants from institutional funds, loans from outside sources. Forms required: International Student's Certification of Finances. For fall 2006 (estimated), 150

international students on campus received college administered financial aid ($1019 average). *Housing:* Guaranteed, also available during summer. *Services:* International student adviser on campus. Full-time and part-time ESL programs on campus. ESL program available during the academic year and the summer. Internships and employment opportunities (on-campus) available. *Contact:* Director of International Admissions and Services, The University of Findlay, 1000 North Main Street, Findlay, OH 45840. Telephone: 419-434-4558. Fax: 419-434-5507. E-mail: international@findlay.edu. URL: http://www.findlay.edu.

UNIVERSITY OF NORTHWESTERN OHIO, LIMA

General Information Independent, primarily 2-year, coed college. Small town setting. *Awards:* A, B. *Entrance level for U.S. students:* Noncompetitive. *Enrollment:* 2,915 total (21% women). *Undergraduate faculty:* 107. *Library holdings:* 4,553 books, 95 current serial subscriptions. *Total majors:* 16.

UNIVERSITY OF PHOENIX–CLEVELAND CAMPUS, INDEPENDENCE

General Information Proprietary, coed institution. Urban setting. *Awards:* B, M. *Entrance level for U.S. students:* Noncompetitive. *Enrollment:* 865 total; 663 undergraduates (69% women) including 9% international students. *Faculty:* 201. *Library holdings:* 1,759 books, 692 current serial subscriptions. *Total majors:* 27. *Expenses:* (2006–07) $11,910.

UNIVERSITY OF RIO GRANDE, RIO GRANDE

General Information Independent, coed institution. Rural setting. *Awards:* A, B, M. *Entrance level for U.S. students:* Noncompetitive. *Enrollment:* 2,429 total; 2,107 undergraduates (59% women) including 0.3% international students from 7 foreign countries. *Faculty:* 308. *Library holdings:* 96,731 books, 850 current serial subscriptions. *Total majors:* 71. *Expenses:* (2006–07) $14,670; room and board, $6788 (on campus). *Financial aid:* Need-based financial aid available. Non-need-based college/university scholarships/grants from institutional funds, athletic awards, on-campus employment. 27 international students on campus received college administered financial aid.

THE UNIVERSITY OF TOLEDO, TOLEDO

General Information State-supported, coed university. Suburban setting. *Awards:* A, B, M, D, FP. *Entrance level for U.S. students:* Noncompetitive. *Enrollment:* 19,374 total; 16,067 undergraduates (49% women) including 2% international students from 88 foreign countries. *Faculty:* 1,145. *Library holdings:* 1.8 million books, 6,500 current serial subscriptions. *Total majors:* 173. *Expenses:* (2006–07) $16,738; room and board, $7894 (on campus); room only, $5044 (on campus). *Financial aid:* Need-based financial aid available. Non-need-based college/university scholarships/grants from institutional funds, athletic awards. Forms required: admissions application. For fall 2005, 14 international students on campus received college administered financial aid ($4424 average).

URBANA UNIVERSITY, URBANA

General Information Independent, coed institution, affiliated with Church of the New Jerusalem. Small town setting. *Awards:* A, B, M. *Entrance level for U.S. students:* Moderately difficult. *Enrollment:* 1,551 total; 1,461 undergraduates (53% women) including 1% international students. *Faculty:* 120. *Library holdings:* 61,600 books, 800 current serial subscriptions, 22,036 audiovisual materials. *Total majors:* 28. *Expenses:* (2006–07) $16,254; room and board, $6612 (on campus); room only, $2234 (on campus). *Financial aid:* Non-need-based college/university scholarships/grants from institutional funds, athletic awards. Forms required: institution's own financial aid form.

WALSH UNIVERSITY, NORTH CANTON

General Information Independent Roman Catholic, coed institution. Small town setting. *Awards:* A, B, M. *Entrance level for U.S. students:* Moderately difficult. *Enrollment:* 2,396 total; 2,078 undergraduates (64% women) including 1% international students from 13 foreign countries. *Faculty:* 217. *Library holdings:* 199,543 books, 5,586 current serial subscriptions, 2,369 audiovisual materials. *Total majors:* 37. *Expenses:* (2007–08) $18,900; room and board, $7430 (on campus); room only, $5100 (on campus). *Financial aid:* Non-need financial aid available. Forms required: institution's own financial aid form, FAFSA. 37 international students on campus received college administered financial aid ($7800 average).

WILMINGTON COLLEGE, WILMINGTON

General Information Independent Friends, coed institution. Small town setting. *Awards:* B, M. *Entrance level for U.S. students:* Moderately difficult. *Enrollment:* 1,704 total; 1,666 undergraduates (55% women) including 1% international students from 6 foreign countries. *Faculty:* 122. *Library holdings:* 103,706 books, 408 current serial subscriptions, 1,280 audiovisual materials. *Total majors:* 42.

Information for International Students For fall 2006: 9 international students applied, 9 were accepted, 8 enrolled. Students can start in fall or spring. Transfers accepted from institutions abroad. *Admission tests:* Required: TOEFL (minimum score: iBT 71; paper-based 500; computer-based 173). Recommended: SAT or ACT. TOEFL can be waived under certain conditions. *Application deadline:* 5/15. *Expenses:* (2006–07) $20,656; room and board, $7406 (on campus); room only, $3496 (on campus). *Financial aid:* Need-based financial aid available. Forms required: International Student's Financial Aid Application. International transfer students are eligible to apply for aid. 7 international students on campus received college administered financial aid ($9061 average). *Housing:* Guaranteed, also available during summer. *Services:* International student adviser on campus. ESL program at cooperating institution. Internships and employment opportunities (on-campus) available. *Contact:* Vice President for Enrollment Management, Wilmington College, Pyle Center, Box 1325, Wilmington, OH 45177. Telephone: 937-382-6661 Ext. 264. Fax: 937-383-8542. E-mail: mark_denniston@wilmington.edu. URL: http://www.wilmington.edu.

WITTENBERG UNIVERSITY, SPRINGFIELD
General Information Independent, coed institution, affiliated with Evangelical Lutheran Church. Suburban setting. *Awards:* B, M. *Entrance level for U.S. students:* Moderately difficult. *Enrollment:* 2,089 total; 2,059 undergraduates (55% women) including 2% international students from 23 foreign countries. *Faculty:* 195. *Library holdings:* 407,502 books, 958 current serial subscriptions. *Total majors:* 38. *Expenses:* (2007–08) $31,400; room and board, $7870 (on campus); room only, $4110 (on campus). *Financial aid:* Need-based college/university scholarships/grants from institutional funds. Non-need-based college/university scholarships/grants from institutional funds, tuition waivers, loans from institutional funds, loans from outside sources, on-campus employment. Forms required: International Student's Financial Aid Application, International Student's Certification of Finances. For fall 2005, 34 international students on campus received college administered financial aid ($17,500 average).

WRIGHT STATE UNIVERSITY, DAYTON
General Information State-supported, coed university. Suburban setting. *Awards:* A, B, M, D, FP. *Entrance level for U.S. students:* Minimally difficult. *Enrollment:* 16,207 total; 12,268 undergraduates (56% women) including 2% international students from 66 foreign countries. *Faculty:* 647. *Library holdings:* 703,000 books, 443,200 current serial subscriptions, 29,800 audiovisual materials. *Total majors:* 163. *Expenses:* (2006–07) $14,004; room and board, $7180 (on campus).

XAVIER UNIVERSITY, CINCINNATI
General Information Independent Roman Catholic, coed institution. Urban setting. *Awards:* A, B, M, D. *Entrance level for U.S. students:* Moderately difficult. *Enrollment:* 6,666 total; 3,910 undergraduates (57% women) including 1% international students from 45 foreign countries. *Faculty:* 601. *Library holdings:* 227,200 books, 21,650 current serial subscriptions, 5,870 audiovisual materials. *Total majors:* 56. *Expenses:* (2006–07) $23,880; room and board, $8640 (on campus); room only, $4710 (on campus). *Financial aid:* Need-based college/university scholarships/grants from institutional funds, loans from outside sources, on-campus employment. Non-need-based college/university scholarships/grants from institutional funds, athletic awards, loans from outside sources, on-campus employment. Forms required: contact Office of International Student Services. For fall 2006 (estimated), 27 international students on campus received college administered financial aid ($12,660 average).

YOUNGSTOWN STATE UNIVERSITY, YOUNGSTOWN
General Information State-supported, coed institution. Urban setting. *Awards:* A, B, M, D. *Entrance level for U.S. students:* Noncompetitive. *Enrollment:* 13,178 total; 11,987 undergraduates (55% women) including 0.5% international students from 55 foreign countries. *Faculty:* 969. *Library holdings:* 868,835 books, 22,277 current serial subscriptions, 21,119 audiovisual materials. *Total majors:* 121. *Expenses:* (2006–07) $12,205; room and board, $6490 (on campus).

OKLAHOMA

BACONE COLLEGE, MUSKOGEE
General Information Independent, 4-year, coed college, affiliated with American Baptist Churches in the U.S.A. Small town setting.

Awards: A, B. *Entrance level for U.S. students:* Minimally difficult. *Enrollment:* 914 total (54% women) including 3% international students from 10 foreign countries. *Undergraduate faculty:* 55. *Library holdings:* 34,564 books, 121 current serial subscriptions, 185 audiovisual materials. *Total majors:* 31. *Financial aid:* Forms required: International Student's Certification of Finances.

CAMERON UNIVERSITY, LAWTON
General Information State-supported, coed institution. Small town setting. *Awards:* B, M. *Entrance level for U.S. students:* Minimally difficult. *Enrollment:* 5,734 total; 5,327 undergraduates (62% women) including 2% international students from 44 foreign countries. *Faculty:* 313. *Library holdings:* 262,835 books, 4,272 current serial subscriptions, 2,868 audiovisual materials. *Total majors:* 39.

Information for International Students For fall 2006: 185 international students applied, 81 were accepted, 54 enrolled. Students can start in fall, spring, or summer. Transfers accepted from institutions abroad. *Admission tests:* Required: SAT or ACT, TOEFL (minimum score: iBT 61; paper-based 500; computer-based 173). TOEFL can be waived under certain conditions. *Application deadline:* 6/1. *Expenses:* (2006–07) $8298; room and board, $3282 (on campus). *Financial aid:* Non-need-based tuition waivers, on-campus employment. International transfer students are eligible to apply for aid. *Housing:* Guaranteed, also available during summer. *Services:* International student adviser on campus. Internships and employment opportunities (on-campus and off-campus) available. *Contact:* International Student Admissions Coordinator, Cameron University, International Office, 2800 West Gore Boulevard, Lawton, OK 73505. Telephone: 580-591-8019. Fax: 580-581-5416. E-mail: mgustafson@cameron.edu. URL: http://www.cameron.edu.

CARL ALBERT STATE COLLEGE, POTEAU
General Information State-supported, 2-year, coed college. Small town setting. *Awards:* A. *Entrance level for U.S. students:* Noncompetitive. *Enrollment:* 2,501 total (69% women) including 1% international students. *Undergraduate faculty:* 154. *Library holdings:* 27,200 books, 1,350 current serial subscriptions. *Total majors:* 28. *Expenses:* (2006–07) $4043; room and board, $2500 (on campus). *Financial aid:* Need-based college/university scholarships/grants from institutional funds, tuition waivers, on-campus employment, state grant. Non-need-based college/university scholarships/grants from institutional funds, tuition waivers, on-campus employment.

CONNORS STATE COLLEGE, WARNER
General Information State-supported, 2-year, coed college. Rural setting. *Awards:* A. *Entrance level for U.S. students:* Noncompetitive. *Enrollment:* 2,335 total including 1% international students from 4 foreign countries. *Undergraduate faculty:* 116. *Library holdings:* 63,728 books, 319 current serial subscriptions. *Total majors:* 21.

Information for International Students Students can start in fall, spring, or summer. Transfers accepted from institutions abroad. *Admission tests:* Required: SAT or ACT, TOEFL. *Application deadline:* 7/31. *Expenses:* (2006–07) $5199; room and board, $5,980 (on campus); room only, $3,646 (on campus). *Financial aid:* Forms required: institution's own financial aid form. *Services:* International student adviser on campus. ESL program at cooperating institution. Employment opportunities (on-campus) available. *Contact:* Registrar, Connors State College, Route One Box 1000, Warner, OK 74469, Uruguay. Telephone: 918-463-2931 Ext. 6233. Fax: 918-463-6227. E-mail: sbaker@connorsstate.edu. URL: http://www.connorsstate.edu.

EAST CENTRAL UNIVERSITY, ADA
General Information State-supported, coed institution. Small town setting. *Awards:* B, M. *Entrance level for U.S. students:* Minimally difficult. *Enrollment:* 4,506 total; 3,761 undergraduates (58% women) including 2% international students from 28 foreign countries. *Faculty:* 246. *Library holdings:* 182,126 books, 25,076 current serial subscriptions, 906 audiovisual materials. *Total majors:* 81. *Expenses:* (2006–07) $8,476; room and board, $3190 (on campus); room only, $1200 (on campus). *Financial aid:* Need-based college/university scholarships/grants from institutional funds, tuition waivers, athletic awards. Non-need-based college/university scholarships/grants from institutional funds, tuition waivers, athletic awards. 50 international students on campus received college administered financial aid ($4228 average).

HILLSDALE FREE WILL BAPTIST COLLEGE, MOORE
General Information Independent Free Will Baptist, coed institution. Suburban setting. *Awards:* A, B, M. *Entrance level for U.S. students:* Noncompetitive. *Enrollment:* 230 total; 207 undergraduates (43% women) including 5% international students

Oklahoma

Hillsdale Free Will Baptist College (continued)
from 4 foreign countries. *Faculty:* 42. *Library holdings:* 28,000 books, 200 current serial subscriptions, 541 audiovisual materials. *Total majors:* 16.

Information for International Students Students can start in fall or spring. Transfers accepted from institutions abroad. *Admission tests:* Required: TOEFL (minimum score: paper-based 500; computer-based 173). Recommended: ACT. TOEFL can be waived under certain conditions. *Application deadline:* 7/31. *Expenses:* (2007–08) $8070; room and board, $4458 (on campus). *Services:* International student adviser on campus. ESL program at cooperating institution. *Contact:* Director of International Students, Hillsdale Free Will Baptist College, PO Box 7208, Moore, OK 73153. Telephone: 405-912-9111. Fax: 405-912-9050. E-mail: tepps@hc.edu. URL: http://www.hc.edu.

LANGSTON UNIVERSITY, LANGSTON

General Information State-supported, coed institution. Rural setting. *Awards:* A, B, M. *Entrance level for U.S. students:* Minimally difficult. *Enrollment:* 2,526 undergraduates including international students from 8 foreign countries. *Library holdings:* 97,565 books, 1,235 current serial subscriptions, 4,974 audiovisual materials. *Total majors:* 56.

Information for International Students For fall 2006: 150 international students applied, 100 were accepted, 10 enrolled. Students can start in fall, spring, or summer. *Admission tests:* Required: ACT, TOEFL (minimum score: iBT 16; paper-based 500; computer-based 300; minimum score for ESL admission: iBT 16; paper-based 500; computer-based 300). TOEFL can be waived under certain conditions. *Application deadline:* 6/15. *Financial aid:* Need-based college/university scholarships/grants from institutional funds, tuition waivers, athletic awards, loans from outside sources. Non-need-based college/university scholarships/grants from institutional funds, tuition waivers, athletic awards, loans from outside sources. Forms required: institution's own financial aid form. 23 international students on campus received college administered financial aid ($789 average). *Housing:* Guaranteed, also available during summer. *Services:* ESL program at cooperating institution. ESL program available during the academic year. Internships and employment opportunities (on-campus and off-campus) available. *Contact:* International Student Counselor and Registrar, Registrars Office, Langston University, PO Box 728, Langston, OK 73050. Telephone: 405-466-3225. Fax: 405-466-3381. URL: http://www.lunet.edu.

NORTHEASTERN STATE UNIVERSITY, TAHLEQUAH

General Information State-supported, coed institution. Small town setting. *Awards:* B, M, FP. *Entrance level for U.S. students:* Moderately difficult. *Enrollment:* 9,540 total; 8,499 undergraduates (61% women) including 3% international students from 41 foreign countries. *Faculty:* 459. *Library holdings:* 466,526 books, 17,570 current serial subscriptions, 7,871 audiovisual materials. *Total majors:* 65. *Expenses:* (2006–07) $8589; room and board, $3600 (on campus). *Financial aid:* Need-based college/university scholarships/grants from institutional funds, tuition waivers, athletic awards. Non-need-based college/university scholarships/grants from institutional funds, tuition waivers, athletic awards. Forms required: institution's own financial aid form. For fall 2006 (estimated), 79 international students on campus received college administered financial aid ($6292 average).

NORTHWESTERN OKLAHOMA STATE UNIVERSITY, ALVA

General Information State-supported, coed institution. Small town setting. *Awards:* B, M. *Entrance level for U.S. students:* Moderately difficult. *Enrollment:* 2,024 total; 1,778 undergraduates (59% women) including 3% international students from 30 foreign countries. *Faculty:* 144. *Library holdings:* 344,640 books, 3,990 current serial subscriptions, 3,609 audiovisual materials. *Total majors:* 37. *Expenses:* (2006–07) $8550; room and board, $3310 (on campus); room only, $1250 (on campus). *Financial aid:* Non-need-based college/university scholarships/grants from institutional funds, athletic awards, on-campus employment. Forms required: institutional scholarship application form. For fall 2005, 31 international students on campus received college administered financial aid ($1498 average).

OKLAHOMA CITY COMMUNITY COLLEGE, OKLAHOMA CITY

General Information State-supported, 2-year, coed college. Urban setting. *Awards:* A. *Entrance level for U.S. students:* Noncompetitive. *Enrollment:* 12,516 total (57% women) including 5% international students from 58 foreign countries. *Undergraduate faculty:* 546. *Total majors:* 44. *Expenses:* (2006–07) $5836. *Financial aid:* Non-need-based alternative loans.

OKLAHOMA CITY UNIVERSITY, OKLAHOMA CITY

General Information Independent United Methodist, coed institution. Urban setting. *Awards:* B, M, FP. *Entrance level for U.S. students:* Moderately difficult. *Enrollment:* 3,713 total; 2,100 undergraduates (63% women) including 20% international students from 43 foreign countries. *Faculty:* 285. *Library holdings:* 520,953 books, 14,000 current serial subscriptions, 1,611 audiovisual materials. *Total majors:* 74. *Expenses:* (2006–07) $19,400; room and board, $6560 (on campus); room only, $3215 (on campus). *Financial aid:* Need-based college/university scholarships/grants from institutional funds, on-campus employment. international students on campus received college administered aid averaging $8603.

OKLAHOMA PANHANDLE STATE UNIVERSITY, GOODWELL

General Information State-supported, 4-year, coed college. Rural setting. *Awards:* A, B. *Entrance level for U.S. students:* Noncompetitive. *Enrollment:* 1,136 total (53% women) including 2% international students from 12 foreign countries. *Undergraduate faculty:* 92. *Total majors:* 32.

Information for International Students Students can start in fall or spring. Transfers accepted from institutions abroad. *Admission tests:* Required: TOEFL (minimum score: paper-based 500; computer-based 173; minimum score for ESL admission: paper-based 500; computer-based 173). TOEFL can be waived under certain conditions. *Application deadline:* 6/15. *Expenses:* (2006–07) $3521; room and board, $3200 (on campus); room only, $900 (on campus). *Financial aid:* Need-based college/university scholarships/grants from institutional funds, tuition waivers, athletic awards, loans from institutional funds, loans from outside sources, on-campus employment. Non-need-based college/university scholarships/grants from institutional funds, tuition waivers, athletic awards. Forms required: institution's own financial aid form. *Housing:* Guaranteed. *Services:* International student adviser on campus. Part-time ESL program on campus. ESL program available during the academic year. Employment opportunities (on-campus) available. *Contact:* Admissions Counselor, Oklahoma Panhandle State University, PO Box 430, Goodwell, OK 73939. Telephone: 580-349-2611. Fax: 580-349-2302. E-mail: jolie@opsu.edu. URL: http://www.opsu.edu.

OKLAHOMA STATE UNIVERSITY, STILLWATER

General Information State-supported, coed university. Small town setting. *Awards:* B, M, D, FP. *Entrance level for U.S. students:* Moderately difficult. *Enrollment:* 23,307 total; 18,737 undergraduates (49% women) including 3% international students from 82 foreign countries. *Faculty:* 1,245. *Library holdings:* 2.6 million books, 38,745 current serial subscriptions, 19,510 audiovisual materials. *Total majors:* 80.

Information for International Students For fall 2006: 416 international students applied, 156 were accepted, 154 enrolled. Students can start in fall, spring, or summer. Transfers accepted from institutions abroad. *Admission tests:* Required: TOEFL (minimum score: paper-based 500; computer-based 173). Recommended: SAT or ACT. TOEFL can be waived under certain conditions. *Application deadline:* 5/1. *Expenses:* (2006–07) $13,569; room and board, $6015 (on campus); room only, $3015 (on campus). *Financial aid:* Non-need-based college/university scholarships/grants from institutional funds, tuition waivers, athletic awards, on-campus employment. Forms required: admissions and scholarships applications. For fall 2006 (estimated), 2,300 international students on campus received college administered financial aid. *Housing:* Available during summer. *Services:* International student adviser on campus. Full-time and part-time ESL programs on campus. ESL program available during the academic year and the summer. Employment opportunities (on-campus) available. *Contact:* International Admissions Staff, Office of International Admissions, Oklahoma State University, Office of Undergraduate Admissions, 219 Student Union, Stillwater, OK 74078. Telephone: 405-744-7379. Fax: 405-744-7092. E-mail: admissions@okstate.edu. URL: http://osu.okstate.edu.

See In-Depth Description on page 144.

OKLAHOMA STATE UNIVERSITY, OKLAHOMA CITY, OKLAHOMA CITY

General Information State-supported, 2-year, coed college. Urban setting. *Awards:* A. *Entrance level for U.S. students:* Noncompetitive. *Enrollment:* 5,704 total (61% women) including 1% international students from 15 foreign countries. *Undergraduate faculty:* 250. *Library holdings:* 11,973 books, 244 current serial subscriptions. *Total majors:* 29. *Expenses:* (2007–08) $5300.

OKLAHOMA WESLEYAN UNIVERSITY, BARTLESVILLE

General Information Independent, coed institution, affiliated with Wesleyan Church. Small town setting. *Awards:* A, B, M.

Entrance level for U.S. students: Minimally difficult. *Enrollment:* 1,159 total; 1,113 undergraduates (64% women) including 1% international students from 12 foreign countries. *Faculty:* 35. *Library holdings:* 124,722 books, 300 current serial subscriptions. *Total majors:* 37.

Information for International Students For fall 2006: 4 international students applied, 4 were accepted, 3 enrolled. Students can start in fall, spring, or summer. Transfers accepted from institutions abroad. *Admission tests:* Recommended: TOEFL (minimum score: paper-based 500; computer-based 173), ELS. TOEFL can be waived under certain conditions. *Application deadline:* 7/15. *Expenses:* (2007–08) $15,500; room and board, $5800 (on campus); room only, $3050 (on campus). *Financial aid:* Need-based college/university scholarships/grants from institutional funds, athletic awards, activity scholarships (music, forensics, etc.). Non-need financial aid available. Forms required: institution's own financial aid form, International Student's Financial Aid Application, International Student's Certification of Finances. International transfer students are eligible to apply for aid. 12 international students on campus received college administered financial aid ($1500 average). *Housing:* Guaranteed. *Services:* International student adviser on campus. Full-time ESL program on campus. ESL program available during the academic year. Employment opportunities (on-campus) available. *Contact:* Enrollment Counselor, Oklahoma Wesleyan University, 2201 Silver Lake Road, Bartlesville, OK 74006. Telephone: 918-335-6219 Ext. 297. Fax: 918-335-6229. E-mail: admissions@okwu.edu. URL: http://www.okwu.edu.

ORAL ROBERTS UNIVERSITY, TULSA

General Information Independent interdenominational, coed institution. Urban setting. *Awards:* B, M, D, FP. *Entrance level for U.S. students:* Moderately difficult. *Enrollment:* 3,244 total; 2,758 undergraduates (59% women) including 5% international students from 41 foreign countries. *Faculty:* 291. *Library holdings:* 216,691 books, 600 current serial subscriptions. *Total majors:* 78. *Expenses:* (2007–08) $17,400; room and board, $7350 (on campus). *Financial aid:* Need-based and non-need-based financial aid available. Forms required: International Student's Financial Aid Application. For fall 2006 (estimated), 205 international students on campus received college administered financial aid ($7667 average).

REDLANDS COMMUNITY COLLEGE, EL RENO

General Information State-supported, 2-year, coed college. Suburban setting. *Awards:* A. *Entrance level for U.S. students:* Noncompetitive. *Enrollment:* 2,323 total (63% women) including 2% international students from 7 foreign countries. *Undergraduate faculty:* 125. *Library holdings:* 14,810 books, 292 current serial subscriptions, 19,075 audiovisual materials. *Total majors:* 32.

Information for International Students For fall 2006: 18 international students applied, 18 were accepted, 18 enrolled. Students can start in fall, winter, spring, or summer. Transfers accepted from institutions abroad. *Admission tests:* Required: TOEFL (minimum score: paper-based 500; computer-based 173), ASSET. Recommended: ACT, ELS. TOEFL can be waived under certain conditions. *Application deadline:* Rolling. *Financial aid:* Forms required: International Student's Certification of Finances. *Housing:* Available during summer. *Services:* International student adviser on campus. ESL program at cooperating institution. Employment opportunities (on-campus) available. *Contact:* International Student Advisor, Redlands Community College, 1300 South Country Club Road, Office of Admissions, El Reno, OK 73036. Telephone: 405-262-2552 Ext. 1427. Fax: 405-422-1239. E-mail: duel@redlandscc.edu. URL: http://www.redlandscc.edu.

ROSE STATE COLLEGE, MIDWEST CITY

General Information State and locally supported, 2-year, coed college. Suburban setting. *Awards:* A. *Entrance level for U.S. students:* Noncompetitive. *Enrollment:* 7,000 total including international students from 33 foreign countries. *Undergraduate faculty:* 412. *Library holdings:* 90,000 books, 443 current serial subscriptions, 9,620 audiovisual materials. *Total majors:* 49.

Information for International Students For fall 2006: 35 international students applied, 35 were accepted, 35 enrolled. Students can start in fall, spring, or summer. Transfers accepted from institutions abroad. *Admission tests:* Required: TOEFL (minimum score: iBT 61; paper-based 500; computer-based 173). Recommended: ACT. *Application deadline:* 6/1. *Expenses:* (2006–07) $6517. *Services:* International student adviser on campus. ESL program at cooperating institution. ESL program available during the academic year. Employment opportunities (on-campus) available. *Contact:* Admissions Specialist, Admissions Office, Rose State College, 6420 SE 15th, Midwest City, OK 73110. Telephone: 405-736-0203. Fax: 405-736-0309. E-mail: dsorrell@rose.edu. URL: http://www.rose.edu.

ST. GREGORY'S UNIVERSITY, SHAWNEE

General Information Independent Roman Catholic, 4-year, coed college. Small town setting. *Awards:* A, B. *Entrance level for U.S. students:* Minimally difficult. *Enrollment:* 860 total; 823 undergraduates (56% women) including 7% international students from 16 foreign countries. *Undergraduate faculty:* 46. *Library holdings:* 85,622 books, 2,060 current serial subscriptions, 1,009 audiovisual materials. *Total majors:* 46.

Information for International Students For fall 2006: 32 international students applied, 30 were accepted, 22 enrolled. Students can start in fall, spring, or summer. Transfers accepted from institutions abroad. *Admission tests:* Required: TOEFL (minimum score: iBT 61; paper-based 500; computer-based 173; minimum score for ESL admission: iBT 61; paper-based 500; computer-based 173). Recommended: ELS. TOEFL can be waived under certain conditions. *Application deadline:* Rolling. *Expenses:* (2006–07) $13,772; room and board, $5636 (on campus); room only, $3200 (on campus). *Financial aid:* Need-based college/university scholarships/grants from institutional funds, athletic awards, on-campus employment. Non-need-based college/university scholarships/grants from institutional funds, tuition waivers, athletic awards, loans from outside sources, on-campus employment. For fall 2005, 27 international students on campus received college administered financial aid ($4880 average). *Housing:* Guaranteed, also available during summer. *Services:* International student adviser on campus. Full-time ESL program on campus. ESL program available during the academic year and the summer. Internships and employment opportunities (on-campus) available. *Contact:* Director of International Office, St. Gregory's University, 1900 West MacArthur Drive, Shawnee, OK 74804. Telephone: 405-878-5177. Fax: 405-878-5198. E-mail: int-admissions@stgregorys.edu. URL: http://www.stgregorys.edu.

SEMINOLE STATE COLLEGE, SEMINOLE

General Information State-supported, 2-year, coed college. Small town setting. *Awards:* A. *Entrance level for U.S. students:* Noncompetitive. *Enrollment:* 2,534 total (69% women) including 1% international students from 5 foreign countries. *Undergraduate faculty:* 101. *Library holdings:* 27,507 books, 200 current serial subscriptions. *Total majors:* 18. *Expenses:* (2006–07) $4308; room and board, $4940 (on campus). *Financial aid:* Forms required: institution's own financial aid form, alien registration card.

SOUTHEASTERN OKLAHOMA STATE UNIVERSITY, DURANT

General Information State-supported, coed institution. Small town setting. *Awards:* B, M. *Entrance level for U.S. students:* Moderately difficult. *Enrollment:* 3,872 total; 3,533 undergraduates (56% women) including 1% international students from 27 foreign countries. *Faculty:* 229. *Library holdings:* 277,902 books, 930 current serial subscriptions, 5,082 audiovisual materials. *Total majors:* 54. *Expenses:* (2006–07) $8846; room and board, $5348 (on campus); room only, $2566 (on campus). *Financial aid:* Need-based tuition waivers, on-campus employment. Non-need-based college/university scholarships/grants from institutional funds, tuition waivers, athletic awards, loans from institutional funds, on-campus employment. Forms required: institution's own financial aid form. For fall 2005, 11 international students on campus received college administered financial aid ($5924 average).

SOUTHERN NAZARENE UNIVERSITY, BETHANY

General Information Independent Nazarene, coed institution. Suburban setting. *Awards:* A, B, M. *Entrance level for U.S. students:* Noncompetitive. *Enrollment:* 2,218 total; 1,793 undergraduates (51% women) including 0.1% international students. *Faculty:* 176. *Library holdings:* 95,535 books, 225 current serial subscriptions, 4,257 audiovisual materials. *Total majors:* 64. *Expenses:* (2006–07) $15,024; room and board, $5378 (on campus); room only, $2458 (on campus). *Financial aid:* Need-based college/university scholarships/grants from institutional funds, athletic awards. Non-need-based college/university scholarships/grants from institutional funds, athletic awards. Forms required: institution's own financial aid form.

SOUTHWESTERN OKLAHOMA STATE UNIVERSITY, WEATHERFORD

General Information State-supported, coed institution. Small town setting. *Awards:* B, M, FP. *Entrance level for U.S. students:* Minimally difficult. *Enrollment:* 5,164 total; 4,397 undergraduates (58% women) including 3% international students from 32 foreign countries. *Faculty:* 225. *Library holdings:* 217,051 books, 1,230 current serial subscriptions, 6,718 audiovisual materials. *Total majors:* 53. *Expenses:* (2006–07) $7950; room and board, $3330 (on campus); room only, $1450 (on campus).

SPARTAN COLLEGE OF AERONAUTICS AND TECHNOLOGY, TULSA

General Information Proprietary, primarily 2-year, coed, primarily men's college. Urban setting. *Awards:* A, B. *Entrance level for U.S. students:* Noncompetitive. *Enrollment:* 1,500 total including international students from 40 foreign countries. *Undergraduate faculty:* 150. *Library holdings:* 18,000 books, 160 current serial subscriptions. *Total majors:* 6. *Financial aid:* Need-based college/university scholarships/grants from institutional funds, loans from outside sources, on-campus employment. Non-need-based college/university scholarships/grants from institutional funds, loans from outside sources. Forms required: institution's own financial aid form.

UNIVERSITY OF CENTRAL OKLAHOMA, EDMOND

General Information State-supported, coed institution. Suburban setting. *Awards:* B, M. *Entrance level for U.S. students:* Minimally difficult. *Enrollment:* 15,723 total; 14,429 undergraduates (58% women) including 7% international students from 76 foreign countries. *Faculty:* 803. *Library holdings:* 582,547 books, 3,130 current serial subscriptions, 28,555 audiovisual materials. *Total majors:* 88. *Expenses:* (2006–07) $8924; room and board, $4763 (on campus); room only, $2383 (on campus).

UNIVERSITY OF OKLAHOMA, NORMAN

General Information State-supported, coed university. Suburban setting. *Awards:* B, M, D, FP. *Entrance level for U.S. students:* Moderately difficult. *Enrollment:* 26,002 total; 19,600 undergraduates (49% women) including 2% international students from 80 foreign countries. *Faculty:* 1,296. *Library holdings:* 4.6 million books, 58,399 current serial subscriptions, 6,703 audiovisual materials. *Total majors:* 104. *Expenses:* (2006–07) $13,399; room and board, $6863 (on campus); room only, $3753 (on campus). *Financial aid:* Non-need-based college/university scholarships/grants from institutional funds, tuition waivers, athletic awards, loans from institutional funds, loans from outside sources, on-campus employment. Forms required: Cleo Cross application. For fall 2005, 274 international students on campus received college administered financial aid ($789 average).

UNIVERSITY OF OKLAHOMA HEALTH SCIENCES CENTER, OKLAHOMA CITY

General Information State-supported, coed institution. Urban setting. *Awards:* B, M, D, FP. *Entrance level for U.S. students:* Difficulty N/R. *Enrollment:* 3,726 total; 992 undergraduates (87% women) including 1% international students from 1 foreign country. *Faculty:* 423. *Library holdings:* 300,260 books, 4,028 current serial subscriptions. *Total majors:* 10. *Expenses:* (2006–07) $12,717.

UNIVERSITY OF PHOENIX–OKLAHOMA CITY CAMPUS, OKLAHOMA CITY

General Information Proprietary, coed institution. Urban setting. *Awards:* B, M. *Entrance level for U.S. students:* Noncompetitive. *Enrollment:* 1,080 total; 915 undergraduates (63% women) including 5% international students. *Faculty:* 265. *Library holdings:* 1,759 books, 692 current serial subscriptions. *Total majors:* 16. *Expenses:* (2006–07) $9750.

UNIVERSITY OF PHOENIX–TULSA CAMPUS, TULSA

General Information Proprietary, coed institution. Urban setting. *Awards:* B, M. *Entrance level for U.S. students:* Noncompetitive. *Enrollment:* 1,169 total; 1,018 undergraduates (59% women) including 24% international students. *Faculty:* 309. *Library holdings:* 1,759 books, 692 current serial subscriptions. *Total majors:* 16. *Expenses:* (2006–07) $9750.

UNIVERSITY OF TULSA, TULSA

General Information Independent, coed university, affiliated with Presbyterian Church (U.S.A.). Urban setting. *Awards:* B, M, D, FP. *Entrance level for U.S. students:* Very difficult. *Enrollment:* 4,125 total; 2,882 undergraduates (50% women) including 9% international students from 48 foreign countries. *Faculty:* 376. *Library holdings:* 1.2 million books, 26,228 current serial subscriptions, 18,905 audiovisual materials. *Total majors:* 54. **Information for International Students** For fall 2006: 279 international students applied, 227 were accepted, 63 enrolled. Students can start in fall, spring, or summer. Transfers accepted from institutions abroad. *Admission tests:* Required: TOEFL (minimum score: iBT 61; paper-based 500; computer-based 173). TOEFL can be waived under certain conditions. *Application deadline:* 7/15. *Expenses:* (2007–08) $21,770; room and board, $7404 (on campus); room only, $4090 (on campus). *Housing:* Guaranteed, also available during summer. *Services:* International student adviser on campus. Full-time and part-time ESL programs on campus. ESL program available during the academic year and the summer. Internships and employment opportunities (on-campus and off-campus) available. *Contact:* Dean of International Students and Programs, University of Tulsa, 600 South College Avenue, Tulsa, OK 74104-3189. Telephone: 918-631-2329. Fax: 918-631-3322. E-mail: inst@utulsa.edu. URL: http://www.utulsa.edu.

See In-Depth Description on page 231.

OREGON

THE ART INSTITUTE OF PORTLAND, PORTLAND

General Information Proprietary, 4-year, coed college. Urban setting. *Awards:* A, B. *Entrance level for U.S. students:* Minimally difficult. *Enrollment:* 1,614 total (53% women) including international students from 14 foreign countries. *Undergraduate faculty:* 104. *Library holdings:* 26,078 books, 208 current serial subscriptions. *Total majors:* 7. *Expenses:* (2006–07) $18,630; room and board, $8250 (on campus); room only, $5550 (on campus). *Financial aid:* Non-need-based college/university scholarships/grants from institutional funds, tuition waivers, loans from outside sources, on-campus employment.

BLUE MOUNTAIN COMMUNITY COLLEGE, PENDLETON

General Information State and locally supported, 2-year, coed college. Rural setting. *Awards:* A. *Entrance level for U.S. students:* Noncompetitive. *Enrollment:* 1,878 total (61% women) including 1% international students from 6 foreign countries. *Undergraduate faculty:* 224. *Library holdings:* 39,026 books, 271 current serial subscriptions, 1,879 audiovisual materials. *Total majors:* 22. *Expenses:* (2006–07) $4450.

CHEMEKETA COMMUNITY COLLEGE, SALEM

General Information State and locally supported, 2-year, coed college. Urban setting. *Awards:* A. *Entrance level for U.S. students:* Noncompetitive. *Enrollment:* 15,000 total. *Library holdings:* 801 audiovisual materials. *Total majors:* 48.
Information for International Students For fall 2006: 60 international students applied, 58 were accepted, 51 enrolled. Students can start in fall, winter, spring, or summer. Transfers accepted from institutions abroad. *Admission tests:* Required: ASSET. Recommended: TOEFL (minimum score: iBT 45; paper-based 450; computer-based 133). TOEFL can be waived under certain conditions. *Application deadline:* 7/1. *Housing:* Available during summer. *Services:* International student adviser on campus. Full-time ESL program on campus. ESL program available during the academic year and the summer. Internships and employment opportunities (on-campus) available. *Contact:* International Admissions, PDSO, Chemeketa Community College, PO Box 14007, 4000 Lancaster Drive, NE, Salem, OR 97309-7070. Telephone: 503-399-2527. Fax: 503-399-3908. E-mail: ngodfrey@chemeketa.edu. URL: http://www.chemeketa.edu.

CLACKAMAS COMMUNITY COLLEGE, OREGON CITY

General Information District-supported, 2-year, coed college. Suburban setting. *Awards:* A. *Entrance level for U.S. students:* Noncompetitive. *Enrollment:* 5,976 total (52% women) including 0.1% international students from 3 foreign countries. *Undergraduate faculty:* 608. *Library holdings:* 41,263 books, 274 current serial subscriptions, 1,141 audiovisual materials. *Total majors:* 15. *Expenses:* (2007–08) $9135.

CLATSOP COMMUNITY COLLEGE, ASTORIA

General Information County-supported, 2-year, coed college. Small town setting. *Awards:* A. *Entrance level for U.S. students:* Noncompetitive. *Enrollment:* 3,002 total including 1% international students from 1 foreign country. *Undergraduate faculty:* 113. *Library holdings:* 48,517 books, 180 current serial subscriptions, 5,000 audiovisual materials. *Total majors:* 12.
Information for International Students Students can start in fall, winter, or spring. Transfers accepted from institutions abroad. *Admission tests:* Required: TOEFL (minimum score: paper-based 520; computer-based 190; minimum score for ESL admission: paper-based 520; computer-based 190). Recommended: ELS, COMPASS. *Application deadline:* 8/6. *Expenses:* (2007–08) $5670. *Services:* International student adviser on campus. Part-time ESL program on campus. ESL program available during the academic year and the summer. *Contact:* Admissions Coordinator, Clatsop Community College, 1653 Jerome Avenue, Astoria, OR 97103. Telephone: 503-338-2411. Fax: 503-325-5738. E-mail: admissions@clatsopcc.edu. URL: http://www.clatsopcc.edu.

CONCORDIA UNIVERSITY, PORTLAND

General Information Independent, coed institution, affiliated with Lutheran Church–Missouri Synod. Urban setting. *Awards:* A, B, M. *Entrance level for U.S. students:* Moderately difficult. *Enrollment:* 1,598 total; 1,083 undergraduates (65% women) including 1% international students from 12 foreign countries. *Faculty:* 114. *Library holdings:* 74,326 books, 22,150 current serial subscriptions, 2,430 audiovisual materials. *Total majors:* 32. *Expenses:* (2007–08) $21,090; room and board, $6270 (on campus); room only, $2980 (on campus).

EASTERN OREGON UNIVERSITY, LA GRANDE

General Information State-supported, coed institution. Rural setting. *Awards:* B, M. *Entrance level for U.S. students:* Moderately difficult. *Enrollment:* 3,425 total; 3,038 undergraduates (61% women) including 3% international students from 31 foreign countries. *Faculty:* 117. *Library holdings:* 329,942 books, 998 current serial subscriptions. *Total majors:* 35. *Expenses:* (2006–07) $5829; room and board, $7776 (on campus). *Financial aid:* Non-need financial aid available. Forms required: International Student's Certification of Finances, scholarship application form. 4 international students on campus received college administered financial aid ($500 average).

EUGENE BIBLE COLLEGE, EUGENE

General Information Independent, 4-year, coed college, affiliated with Open Bible Standard Churches. Suburban setting. *Awards:* B. *Entrance level for U.S. students:* Minimally difficult. *Enrollment:* 222 total (44% women) including 1% international students from 2 foreign countries. *Undergraduate faculty:* 24. *Library holdings:* 35,000 books, 251 current serial subscriptions. *Total majors:* 7.

Information for International Students Students can start in fall, winter, or spring. Transfers accepted from institutions abroad. *Admission tests:* Required: TOEFL (minimum score: paper-based 500; computer-based 213; minimum score for ESL admission: paper-based 500; computer-based 213). Recommended: SAT or ACT, SAT Subject Tests. *Application deadline:* 9/1. *Expenses:* (2006–07) $8720; room and board, $4805 (on campus). *Financial aid:* Need-based and non-need-based financial aid available. Forms required: institution's own financial aid form, International Student's Certification of Finances. *Housing:* Guaranteed, also available during summer. *Services:* International student adviser on campus. *Contact:* Student Recruitment Coordinator, Eugene Bible College, 2155 Bailey Hill Road, Eugene, OR 97405. Telephone: 541-485-1780 Ext. 3106. Fax: 541-343-5801. E-mail: scott@ebc.edu. URL: http://www.ebc.edu.

EVEREST COLLEGE, PORTLAND

General Information Proprietary, 2-year, coed college. *Awards:* A. *Entrance level for U.S. students:* Difficulty N/R. *Enrollment:* 827 total. *Total majors:* 1.

Information for International Students For fall 2006: 10 international students applied, 10 were accepted, 8 enrolled. Students can start in fall, winter, spring, or summer. Transfers accepted from institutions abroad. *Admission tests:* Required: TOEFL (minimum score: paper-based 465; computer-based 145), CPAt. TOEFL can be waived under certain conditions. *Application deadline:* Rolling. *Expenses:* (2006–07) $12,459. *Services:* International student adviser on campus. Full-time ESL program on campus. ESL program available during the academic year and the summer. Internships available. *Contact:* Foreign Admissions Support, Everest College, 425 SW Washington Street, Portland, OR 97204. Telephone: 503-222-3225. Fax: 503-228-6926. E-mail: mzea@cci.edu. URL: http://www.western-college.com.

GEORGE FOX UNIVERSITY, NEWBERG

General Information Independent Friends, coed university. Small town setting. *Awards:* B, M, D, FP. *Entrance level for U.S. students:* Moderately difficult. *Enrollment:* 3,252 total; 1,864 undergraduates (61% women) including 2% international students from 13 foreign countries. *Faculty:* 324. *Library holdings:* 208,048 books, 3,900 current serial subscriptions, 6,335 audiovisual materials. *Total majors:* 62.

Information for International Students For fall 2006: 45 international students applied, 29 were accepted, 13 enrolled. Students can start in fall or spring. Transfers accepted from institutions abroad. *Admission tests:* Recommended: TOEFL (minimum score: iBT 79; paper-based 550; computer-based 213). TOEFL can be waived under certain conditions. *Application deadline:* 6/1. *Expenses:* (2007–08) $23,790; room and board, $7600 (on campus); room only, $4280 (on campus). *Financial aid:* Non-need financial aid available. Forms required: International Student's Certification of Finances. 25 international students on campus received college administered financial aid ($11,889 average). *Housing:* Guaranteed. *Services:* International student adviser on campus. Full-time ESL program on campus. ESL

program available during the academic year. Internships available. *Contact:* Executive Director of Admissions, George Fox University, 414 North Meridian Street, #6089, Newberg, OR 97132. Telephone: 503-538-8383 Ext. 2240. Fax: 503-554-3110. E-mail: admissions@georgefox.edu. URL: http://www.georgefox.edu.

LANE COMMUNITY COLLEGE, EUGENE

General Information State and locally supported, 2-year, coed college. Suburban setting. *Awards:* A. *Entrance level for U.S. students:* Noncompetitive. *Enrollment:* 11,834 total including 2% international students from 27 foreign countries. *Undergraduate faculty:* 585. *Library holdings:* 67,051 books, 513 current serial subscriptions. *Total majors:* 36. *Financial aid:* Non-need-based college/university scholarships/grants from institutional funds.

LEWIS & CLARK COLLEGE, PORTLAND

General Information Independent, coed institution. Suburban setting. *Awards:* B, M, D, FP. *Entrance level for U.S. students:* Very difficult. *Enrollment:* 3,641 total; 1,985 undergraduates (61% women) including 4% international students from 44 foreign countries. *Faculty:* 376. *Library holdings:* 227,609 books, 7,477 current serial subscriptions, 11,586 audiovisual materials. *Total majors:* 29.

Information for International Students For fall 2006: 186 international students applied, 86 were accepted, 30 enrolled. Students can start in fall, spring, or summer. Transfers accepted from institutions abroad. *Admission tests:* Required: TOEFL (minimum score: iBT 91; paper-based 575; computer-based 233; minimum score for ESL admission: iBT 61; paper-based 500; computer-based 173), MELAB, IELTS, ECEP, ELPT and some Cambridge Certificates acceptable in place of TOEFL. TOEFL can be waived under certain conditions. *Application deadline:* Rolling. *Expenses:* (2006–07) $29,772; room and board, $8048 (on campus); room only, $4172 (on campus). *Financial aid:* Need-based college/university scholarships/grants from institutional funds, loans from outside sources, on-campus employment. Non-need-based college/university scholarships/grants from institutional funds, loans from outside sources, on-campus employment. Forms required: International Student's Certification of Finances. International transfer students are eligible to apply for aid. For fall 2006 (estimated), 51 international students on campus received college administered financial aid ($16,727 average). *Housing:* Guaranteed, also available during summer. *Services:* International student adviser on campus. Full-time and part-time ESL programs on campus. ESL program available during the academic year and the summer. Internships and employment opportunities (on-campus) available. *Contact:* Associate Dean of Students/Director of International Students, Lewis & Clark College, 0615 SW Palatine Hill Road, International Student Services, MSC 192, Portland, OR 97219-7899. Telephone: 503-768-7305. Fax: 503-768-7301. E-mail: iso@lclark.edu. URL: http://www.lclark.edu.

LINFIELD COLLEGE, MCMINNVILLE

General Information Independent American Baptist Churches in the USA, 4-year, coed college. Small town setting. *Awards:* B. *Entrance level for U.S. students:* Moderately difficult. *Enrollment:* 1,754 total (54% women) including 2% international students from 21 foreign countries. *Undergraduate faculty:* 181. *Library holdings:* 179,098 books, 1,268 current serial subscriptions, 33,203 audiovisual materials. *Total majors:* 34.

Information for International Students For fall 2006: 129 international students applied, 73 were accepted, 37 enrolled. Students can start in fall or spring. Transfers accepted from institutions abroad. *Admission tests:* Required: TOEFL (minimum score: iBT 79; paper-based 550; computer-based 213; minimum score for ESL admission: iBT 45; paper-based 450; computer-based 133). Recommended: SAT or ACT. TOEFL can be waived under certain conditions. *Application deadline:* 4/15. *Expenses:* (2006–07) $24,174; room and board, $7080 (on campus); room only, $3760 (on campus). *Financial aid:* Need-based college/university scholarships/grants from institutional funds, tuition waivers, loans from outside sources, on-campus employment. Non-need-based college/university scholarships/grants from institutional funds, tuition waivers, loans from outside sources, on-campus employment. Forms required: International Student's Certification of Finances. International transfer students are eligible to apply for aid. For fall 2006 (estimated), 35 international students on campus received college administered financial aid ($14,260 average). *Housing:* Guaranteed. *Services:* International student adviser on campus. Full-time ESL program on campus. ESL program available during the academic year. Internships and employment opportunities (on-campus) available. *Contact:* Assistant Director for International Admission, Linfield College, Office of Admission, 900 SE Baker

Linfield College (continued)

Street, McMinnville, OR 97128-6894. Telephone: 503-883-2213 Ext. 2473. Fax: 503-883-2472. E-mail: fschrock@linfield.edu. URL: http://www.linfield.edu.

LINN-BENTON COMMUNITY COLLEGE, ALBANY

General Information State and locally supported, 2-year, coed college. Small town setting. *Awards:* A. *Entrance level for U.S. students:* Noncompetitive. *Enrollment:* 4,983 total (53% women) including 0.1% international students. *Undergraduate faculty:* 483. *Library holdings:* 42,561 books, 91 current serial subscriptions, 8,758 audiovisual materials. *Total majors:* 61. *Expenses:* (2006–07) $7470.

MARYLHURST UNIVERSITY, MARYLHURST

General Information Independent Roman Catholic, coed institution. Suburban setting. *Awards:* B, M. *Entrance level for U.S. students:* Noncompetitive. *Enrollment:* 1,249 total; 855 undergraduates (73% women) including 1% international students from 27 foreign countries. *Faculty:* 228. *Total majors:* 22.

Information for International Students For fall 2006: 12 international students applied, 11 were accepted, 7 enrolled. Students can start in fall, winter, spring, or summer. Transfers accepted from institutions abroad. *Admission tests:* Required: Michigan Test of English (assessment given on campus). Recommended: TOEFL (minimum score: iBT 64; paper-based 520; computer-based 190; minimum score for ESL admission: iBT 57; paper-based 490; computer-based 163), ELS. TOEFL can be waived under certain conditions. *Application deadline:* Rolling. *Expenses:* (2006–07) $14,220. *Services:* International student adviser on campus. Full-time and part-time ESL programs on campus. ESL program available during the academic year and the summer. *Contact:* International Admissions Specialist, Enrollment Management, Marylhurst University, 17600 Pacific Highway 43, Marylhurst, OR 97036. Telephone: 503-699-6268. Fax: 503-635-6585. E-mail: admissions@marylhurst.edu. URL: http://www.marylhurst.edu.

MT. HOOD COMMUNITY COLLEGE, GRESHAM

General Information State and locally supported, 2-year, coed college. Suburban setting. *Awards:* A. *Entrance level for U.S. students:* Noncompetitive. *Enrollment:* 8,771 total (56% women) including international students from 6 foreign countries. *Undergraduate faculty:* 638. *Library holdings:* 64,000 books, 412 current serial subscriptions. *Total majors:* 40. *Financial aid:* Forms required: institution's own financial aid form, FAFSA.

MULTNOMAH BIBLE COLLEGE AND BIBLICAL SEMINARY, PORTLAND

General Information Independent interdenominational, coed institution. Urban setting. *Awards:* B, M, FP. *Entrance level for U.S. students:* Moderately difficult. *Enrollment:* 827 total; 593 undergraduates (45% women) including 1% international students from 4 foreign countries. *Faculty:* 62. *Library holdings:* 108,297 books, 378 current serial subscriptions, 1,662 audiovisual materials. *Total majors:* 13. *Expenses:* (2006–07) room and board, $5340 (on campus). *Financial aid:* Non-need-based tuition waivers. Forms required: institution's own financial aid form. 5 international students on campus received college administered financial aid ($2770 average).

OREGON COLLEGE OF ART & CRAFT, PORTLAND

General Information Independent, 4-year, coed college. Urban setting. *Awards:* B. *Entrance level for U.S. students:* Minimally difficult. *Enrollment:* 153 total (59% women) including international students from 2 foreign countries. *Undergraduate faculty:* 23. *Library holdings:* 9,000 books, 90 current serial subscriptions. *Total majors:* 2. *Expenses:* (2006–07) $17,900; room only, $3600 (on campus).

OREGON HEALTH & SCIENCE UNIVERSITY, PORTLAND

General Information State-related, coed institution. Urban setting. *Awards:* B, M, D, FP. *Entrance level for U.S. students:* Moderately difficult. *Enrollment:* 2,418 total; 597 undergraduates (85% women) including 1% international students from 3 foreign countries. *Faculty:* 836. *Library holdings:* 200,771 books, 2,110 current serial subscriptions. *Total majors:* 2. *Expenses:* (2006–07) $23,348. *Financial aid:* Need-based college/university scholarships/grants from institutional funds, tuition waivers, loans from institutional funds, loans from outside sources. Non-need-based college/university scholarships/grants from institutional funds, tuition waivers, loans from institutional funds, loans from outside sources.

OREGON STATE UNIVERSITY, CORVALLIS

General Information State-supported, coed university. Small town setting. *Awards:* B, M, D, FP. *Entrance level for U.S. students:* Moderately difficult. *Enrollment:* 19,362 total; 15,829 undergraduates (47% women) including 1% international students from 100 foreign countries. *Faculty:* 1,166. *Library holdings:* 689,119 books, 12,254 current serial subscriptions. *Total majors:* 113.

Information for International Students For fall 2006: 402 international students applied, 130 were accepted, 53 enrolled. Students can start in fall, winter, spring, or summer. Transfers accepted from institutions abroad. *Admission tests:* Required: TOEFL (minimum score: iBT 80; paper-based 550; computer-based 213; minimum score for ESL admission: iBT 45; paper-based 450; computer-based 133). TOEFL can be waived under certain conditions. *Application deadline:* 4/1. *Expenses:* (2006–07) $17,559; room and board, $7344 (on campus). *Financial aid:* Need-based college/university scholarships/grants from institutional funds, athletic awards, loans from institutional funds, loans from outside sources, on-campus employment. Non-need-based college/university scholarships/grants from institutional funds, tuition waivers, athletic awards, loans from institutional funds, loans from outside sources, on-campus employment. Forms required: institution's own financial aid form. International transfer students are eligible to apply for aid. For fall 2005, 64 international students on campus received college administered financial aid ($8700 average). *Housing:* Available during summer. *Services:* International student adviser on campus. Full-time and part-time ESL programs on campus. ESL program available during the academic year and the summer. Internships and employment opportunities (on-campus and off-campus) available. *Contact:* Assistant Director, International Admissions, Office of Admission and Orientation, Oregon State University, 104 Kerr Administration Building, Corvallis, OR 97331-2106. Telephone: 541-737-4411. Fax: 541-737-2482. E-mail: osuadmit@oregonstate.edu. URL: http://oregonstate.edu.

See In-Depth Description on page 145.

PACIFIC NORTHWEST COLLEGE OF ART, PORTLAND

General Information Independent, 4-year, coed college. Urban setting. *Awards:* B. *Entrance level for U.S. students:* Moderately difficult. *Enrollment:* 293 total including 1% international students from 4 foreign countries. *Undergraduate faculty:* 51. *Library holdings:* 14,650 books, 65 current serial subscriptions, 350 audiovisual materials. *Total majors:* 9.

Information for International Students For fall 2006: 2 international students applied, 2 were accepted. Students can start in fall or spring. Transfers accepted from institutions abroad. *Admission tests:* Required: TOEFL (minimum score: paper-based 550; computer-based 215), ELS. TOEFL can be waived under certain conditions. *Application deadline:* 7/15. *Expenses:* (2006–07) $18,208; room and board, $6300 (on campus). *Financial aid:* Need-based college/university scholarships/grants from institutional funds, loans from outside sources, on-campus employment. Non-need-based college/university scholarships/grants from institutional funds, loans from outside sources, on-campus employment. Forms required: International Student's Certification of Finances. For fall 2006 (estimated), 3 international students on campus received college administered financial aid ($8005 average). Internships and employment opportunities (on-campus) available. *Contact:* Director of Admissions, Pacific Northwest College of Art, 1241 NW Johnson Street, Portland, OR 97209. Telephone: 503-821-8926. Fax: 503-821-8978. E-mail: csweet@pnca.edu. URL: http://www.pnca.edu.

PACIFIC UNIVERSITY, FOREST GROVE

General Information Independent, coed institution. Small town setting. *Awards:* B, M, D, FP. *Entrance level for U.S. students:* Moderately difficult. *Enrollment:* 2,790 total; 1,347 undergraduates (61% women) including 0.1% international students from 16 foreign countries. *Faculty:* 119. *Library holdings:* 206,198 books, 20,908 current serial subscriptions, 8,580 audiovisual materials. *Total majors:* 50. *Expenses:* (2007–08) $26,670; room and board, $7170 (on campus); room only, $3720 (on campus). *Financial aid:* Need-based financial aid available. Non-need-based college/university scholarships/grants from institutional funds, on-campus employment. Forms required: International Student's Certification of Finances. For fall 2005, 7 international students on campus received college administered financial aid ($7150 average).

PIONEER PACIFIC COLLEGE, WILSONVILLE

General Information Proprietary, primarily 2-year, coed college. Suburban setting. *Awards:* A, B. *Entrance level for U.S. students:* Noncompetitive. *Enrollment:* 986 total (77% women). *Undergraduate faculty:* 119. *Library holdings:* 2,500 books. *Total majors:* 10.

Information for International Students For fall 2006: 2 international students applied, 2 were accepted, 2 enrolled. Students can start in fall, winter, spring, or summer. *Admission tests:* Required: TOEFL (minimum score: paper-based 500; computer-based 173; minimum score for ESL admission: paper-based 500; computer-based 173), ELS (minimum score: 107), CPAT. TOEFL can be waived under certain conditions. *Application deadline:* Rolling. *Expenses:* (2007–08) $10,150. *Financial aid:* Forms required: International Student's Certification of Finances. Employment opportunities (off-campus) available. *Contact:* Director of Admissions, Pioneer Pacific College, 27501 SW Parkway Avenue, Wilsonville, OR 97070. Telephone: 503-654-8000. Fax: 503-659-6107. E-mail: klynn@pioneerpacific.edu. URL: http://www.pioneerpacific.edu.

PORTLAND COMMUNITY COLLEGE, PORTLAND

General Information State and locally supported, 2-year, coed college. Urban setting. *Awards:* A. *Entrance level for U.S. students:* Noncompetitive. *Enrollment:* 96,764 total including 0.4% international students from 34 foreign countries. *Undergraduate faculty:* 1,745. *Library holdings:* 91,472 books, 820 current serial subscriptions, 247 audiovisual materials. *Total majors:* 53.

Information for International Students For fall 2006: 448 international students applied, 383 were accepted, 254 enrolled. Students can start in fall, winter, spring, or summer. *Application deadline:* Rolling. *Expenses:* (2006–07) $8820. *Services:* International student adviser on campus. Full-time and part-time ESL programs on campus. ESL program available during the academic year and the summer. Internships and employment opportunities (on-campus) available. *Contact:* Program Assistant, Office of International Education, Portland Community College, Office of International Education, PO Box 19000, Portland, OR 97280. Telephone: 503-614-7150. Fax: 503-614-7170. E-mail: international@pcc.edu. URL: http://www.pcc.edu.

PORTLAND STATE UNIVERSITY, PORTLAND

General Information State-supported, coed university. Urban setting. *Awards:* B, M, D. *Entrance level for U.S. students:* Moderately difficult. *Enrollment:* 24,254 total; 17,998 undergraduates (54% women) including 4% international students from 79 foreign countries. *Faculty:* 1,260. *Library holdings:* 1.8 million books, 10,308 current serial subscriptions. *Total majors:* 63.

Information for International Students For fall 2006: 232 international students applied, 172 were accepted, 86 enrolled. Students can start in fall, winter, spring, or summer. Transfers accepted from institutions abroad. *Admission tests:* Required: TOEFL (minimum score: iBT 71; paper-based 525; computer-based 197; minimum score for ESL admission: paper-based 310; computer-based 40). TOEFL can be waived under certain conditions. *Application deadline:* Rolling. *Expenses:* (2006–07) $17,435; room and board, $8940 (on campus); room only, $6300 (on campus). *Financial aid:* Need-based college/university scholarships/grants from institutional funds, athletic awards, loans from outside sources. Non-need-based college/university scholarships/grants from institutional funds, athletic awards, loans from outside sources. Forms required: International Student's Financial Aid Application, International Student's Certification of Finances. International transfer students are eligible to apply for aid. For fall 2006 (estimated), 13 international students on campus received college administered financial aid ($2197 average). *Services:* International student adviser on campus. Full-time and part-time ESL programs on campus. ESL program available during the academic year and the summer. Employment opportunities (on-campus) available. *Contact:* Associate Director of International Admissions, Office of Admissions and Records, Portland State University, PO Box 901, Portland, OR 97207-0901. Telephone: 503-725-3511. Fax: 503-725-5525. E-mail: intladm@pdx.edu. URL: http://www.pdx.edu.

REED COLLEGE, PORTLAND

General Information Independent, coed institution. Urban setting. *Awards:* B, M. *Entrance level for U.S. students:* Most difficult. *Enrollment:* 1,436 total; 1,407 undergraduates (55% women) including 5% international students from 39 foreign countries. *Faculty:* 132. *Library holdings:* 564,598 books, 23,290 current serial subscriptions, 21,538 audiovisual materials. *Total majors:* 29.

Information for International Students Students can start in fall. Transfers accepted from institutions abroad. *Admission tests:* Required: SAT or ACT, TOEFL (minimum score: paper-based 600; computer-based 250). *Application deadline:* 1/15. *Expenses:* (2006–07) $34,530; room and board, $9000 (on campus); room only, $4660 (on campus). *Financial aid:* Need-based college/university scholarships/grants from institutional funds, loans from institutional funds, on-campus employment. Forms required:

institution's own financial aid form, International Student's Financial Aid Application, International Student's Certification of Finances. International transfer students are eligible to apply for aid. For fall 2006 (estimated), 40 international students on campus received college administered financial aid ($39,463 average). *Housing:* Guaranteed, also available during summer. *Services:* International student adviser on campus. Internships and employment opportunities (on-campus) available. *Contact:* Associate Dean of Admission, Reed College, 3203 SE Woodstock Boulevard, Portland, OR 97202. Telephone: 503-777-7511. Fax: 503-777-7553. E-mail: admission@reed.edu. URL: http://www.reed.edu.

ROGUE COMMUNITY COLLEGE, GRANTS PASS

General Information State and locally supported, 2-year, coed college. Rural setting. *Awards:* A. *Entrance level for U.S. students:* Noncompetitive. *Enrollment:* 4,341 total including 0.1% international students from 1 foreign country. *Undergraduate faculty:* 486. *Library holdings:* 33,000 books, 275 current serial subscriptions. *Total majors:* 19. *Expenses:* (2007–08) $3174.

SOUTHERN OREGON UNIVERSITY, ASHLAND

General Information State-supported, coed institution. Small town setting. *Awards:* B, M. *Entrance level for U.S. students:* Moderately difficult. *Enrollment:* 4,675 total; 4,130 undergraduates (58% women) including 2% international students from 33 foreign countries. *Faculty:* 289. *Library holdings:* 315,000 books, 1,949 current serial subscriptions, 7,800 audiovisual materials. *Total majors:* 40.

Information for International Students For fall 2006: 150 international students enrolled. Students can start in fall, winter, spring, or summer. Transfers accepted from institutions abroad. *Admission tests:* Required: TOEFL (minimum score: paper-based 520; computer-based 190). *Application deadline:* Rolling. *Expenses:* (2006–07) $14,691; room and board, $6468 (on campus). *Financial aid:* Need-based college/university scholarships/grants from institutional funds, tuition waivers. Non-need-based college/university scholarships/grants from institutional funds, tuition waivers. Forms required: institution's own financial aid form, International Student's Financial Aid Application, International Student's Certification of Finances. For fall 2006 (estimated), 29 international students on campus received college administered financial aid ($9626 average). *Housing:* Guaranteed. *Services:* International student adviser on campus. ESL program at cooperating institution. Internships and employment opportunities (on-campus) available. *Contact:* Credential Evaluator, Office of Admissions, Southern Oregon University, 1250 Siskiyou Boulevard, Ashland, OR 97520-5005. Telephone: 541-552-6981. Fax: 541-552-6614. E-mail: royce@sou.edu. URL: http://www.sou.edu.

SOUTHWESTERN OREGON COMMUNITY COLLEGE, COOS BAY

General Information State and locally supported, 2-year, coed college. Small town setting. *Awards:* A. *Entrance level for U.S. students:* Noncompetitive. *Enrollment:* 1,980 total (58% women) including 1% international students from 4 foreign countries. *Undergraduate faculty:* 219. *Library holdings:* 40,505 books, 218 current serial subscriptions, 3,673 audiovisual materials. *Total majors:* 30. *Expenses:* (2006–07) $3660; room and board, $6160 (on campus). *Financial aid:* Need-based and non-need-based financial aid available.

TREASURE VALLEY COMMUNITY COLLEGE, ONTARIO

General Information State and locally supported, 2-year, coed college. Small town setting. *Awards:* A. *Entrance level for U.S. students:* Noncompetitive. *Enrollment:* 1,912 total (63% women) including 0.2% international students from 2 foreign countries. *Undergraduate faculty:* 140. *Library holdings:* 28,000 books, 150 current serial subscriptions. *Total majors:* 40. *Expenses:* (2007–08) $3780; room and board, $4470 (on campus); room only, $1680 (on campus).

UMPQUA COMMUNITY COLLEGE, ROSEBURG

General Information State and locally supported, 2-year, coed college. Rural setting. *Awards:* A. *Entrance level for U.S. students:* Noncompetitive. *Enrollment:* 2,190 total (58% women) including 1% international students from 3 foreign countries. *Undergraduate faculty:* 385. *Library holdings:* 41,000 books, 350 current serial subscriptions. *Total majors:* 53. *Financial aid:* Need-based college/university scholarships/grants from institutional funds, tuition waivers, athletic awards, loans from institutional funds, loans from outside sources, on-campus employment. Non-need-based college/university scholarships/grants from institutional funds, athletic awards.

UNIVERSITY OF OREGON, EUGENE

General Information State-supported, coed university. Urban setting. *Awards:* B, M, D, FP. *Entrance level for U.S. students:* Moderately difficult. *Enrollment:* 20,348 total; 16,529 undergraduates (53% women) including 5% international students from 87 foreign countries. *Faculty:* 1,129. *Library holdings:* 2.7 million books, 18,826 current serial subscriptions, 443,827 audiovisual materials. *Total majors:* 96.

Information for International Students Students can start in fall, winter, spring, or summer. Transfers accepted from institutions abroad. *Admission tests:* Required: TOEFL (minimum score: iBT 61; paper-based 500; computer-based 173; minimum score for ESL admission: iBT 59; paper-based 450; computer-based 133), IELTS. Recommended: SAT. *Application deadline:* 3/15. *Expenses:* (2006–07) $18,252; room and board, $7827 (on campus). *Financial aid:* Need-based college/university scholarships/grants from institutional funds, tuition waivers, athletic awards, loans from institutional funds, on-campus employment, endowed scholarships. Non-need-based tuition waivers, athletic awards, on-campus employment. Forms required: institution's own financial aid form. International transfer students are eligible to apply for aid. 78 international students on campus received college administered financial aid ($7293 average). *Housing:* Available during summer. *Services:* International student adviser on campus. Full-time and part-time ESL programs on campus. ESL program available during the academic year and the summer. Internships and employment opportunities (on-campus) available. *Contact:* Assistant Director of Admissions, Office of Admissions, University of Oregon, 240 Oregon Hall, Eugene, OR 97403-1217. Telephone: 541-346-3201. Fax: 541-346-5815. E-mail: kpinar@uoregon.edu. URL: http://www.uoregon.edu.

UNIVERSITY OF PHOENIX–OREGON CAMPUS, TIGARD

General Information Proprietary, coed institution. Urban setting. *Awards:* B, M. *Entrance level for U.S. students:* Noncompetitive. *Enrollment:* 1,836 total; 1,481 undergraduates (53% women) including 7% international students. *Faculty:* 495. *Library holdings:* 1,759 books, 692 current serial subscriptions. *Total majors:* 18. *Expenses:* (2006–07) $10,770.

UNIVERSITY OF PORTLAND, PORTLAND

General Information Independent Roman Catholic, coed institution. Urban setting. *Awards:* B, M. *Entrance level for U.S. students:* Moderately difficult. *Enrollment:* 3,478 total; 2,907 undergraduates (63% women) including 1% international students from 19 foreign countries. *Faculty:* 306. *Library holdings:* 350,000 books, 1,400 current serial subscriptions, 11,044 audiovisual materials. *Total majors:* 42. *Expenses:* (2006–07) $26,390; room and board, $7850 (on campus); room only, $3925 (on campus). *Financial aid:* Need-based financial aid available. Non-need-based college/university scholarships/grants from institutional funds, athletic awards, on-campus employment. For fall 2005, 27 international students on campus received college administered financial aid ($22,623 average).

WARNER PACIFIC COLLEGE, PORTLAND

General Information Independent, coed institution, affiliated with Church of God. Urban setting. *Awards:* A, B, M. *Entrance level for U.S. students:* Moderately difficult. *Enrollment:* 740 total; 720 undergraduates (65% women) including 1% international students from 6 foreign countries. *Faculty:* 35. *Library holdings:* 54,000 books, 400 current serial subscriptions. *Total majors:* 34. *Expenses:* (2006–07) $22,408; room and board, $5740 (on campus). *Financial aid:* Need-based financial aid available. Non-need-based college/university scholarships/grants from institutional funds, athletic awards, loans from outside sources. Forms required: International Student's Certification of Finances. For fall 2006 (estimated), 6 international students on campus received college administered financial aid ($11,125 average).

WESTERN OREGON UNIVERSITY, MONMOUTH

General Information State-supported, coed institution. Rural setting. *Awards:* A, B, M. *Entrance level for U.S. students:* Moderately difficult. *Enrollment:* 4,885 total; 4,183 undergraduates (59% women) including 2% international students from 12 foreign countries. *Faculty:* 312. *Library holdings:* 227,707 books, 2,158 current serial subscriptions, 8,010 audiovisual materials. *Total majors:* 35. *Expenses:* (2006–07) $14,823; room and board, $7030 (on campus). *Financial aid:* Need-based tuition waivers. Non-need-based tuition waivers. Forms required: International Cultural Service Program Application. For fall 2006 (estimated), 53 international students on campus received college administered financial aid ($3377 average).

WILLAMETTE UNIVERSITY, SALEM

General Information Independent United Methodist, coed institution. Urban setting. *Awards:* B, M, FP. *Entrance level for U.S. students:* Very difficult. *Enrollment:* 2,747 total; 2,055 undergraduates (56% women) including 1% international students from 18 foreign countries. *Faculty:* 312. *Library holdings:* 317,000 books, 1,400 current serial subscriptions. *Total majors:* 40. *Expenses:* (2006–07) $30,018; room and board, $7250 (on campus). *Financial aid:* Need-based college/university scholarships/grants from institutional funds, tuition waivers, on-campus employment. Non-need-based college/university scholarships/grants from institutional funds, tuition waivers, on-campus employment. Forms required: institution's own financial aid form, International Student's Financial Aid Application. For fall 2005, 6 international students on campus received college administered financial aid ($21,328 average).

PENNSYLVANIA

ACADEMY OF MEDICAL ARTS AND BUSINESS, HARRISBURG

General Information Proprietary, 2-year, coed, primarily women's college. Suburban setting. *Awards:* A. *Entrance level for U.S. students:* Noncompetitive. *Enrollment:* 491 total. *Undergraduate faculty:* 27. *Library holdings:* 1,620 books, 30 current serial subscriptions, 30 audiovisual materials. *Total majors:* 14. *Expenses:* (2006–07) $11,669. *Financial aid:* Non-need-based college/university scholarships/grants from institutional funds, on-campus employment.

ALBRIGHT COLLEGE, READING

General Information Independent, coed institution, affiliated with United Methodist Church. Suburban setting. *Awards:* B, M. *Entrance level for U.S. students:* Moderately difficult. *Enrollment:* 2,222 total; 2,150 undergraduates (59% women) including 4% international students from 24 foreign countries. *Faculty:* 156. *Library holdings:* 229,725 books, 14,126 current serial subscriptions, 2,733 audiovisual materials. *Total majors:* 45. *Expenses:* (2006–07) $27,420; room and board, $8158 (on campus); room only, $4644 (on campus). *Financial aid:* Need-based and non-need-based financial aid available. Forms required: CSS PROFILE, International Student's Certification of Finances. For fall 2005, 19 international students on campus received college administered financial aid ($11,105 average).

ALLEGHENY COLLEGE, MEADVILLE

General Information Independent, 4-year, coed college. Small town setting. *Awards:* B. *Entrance level for U.S. students:* Very difficult. *Enrollment:* 2,095 total (54% women) including 1% international students from 31 foreign countries. *Undergraduate faculty:* 167. *Library holdings:* 294,646 books, 4,542 current serial subscriptions, 7,790 audiovisual materials. *Total majors:* 47.

Information for International Students For fall 2006: 241 international students applied, 19 were accepted, 6 enrolled. Students can start in fall or spring. Transfers accepted from institutions abroad. *Admission tests:* Required: TOEFL (minimum score: iBT 80; paper-based 550; computer-based 213). Recommended: SAT or ACT. TOEFL can be waived under certain conditions. *Application deadline:* 2/15. *Expenses:* (2007–08) $30,000; room and board, $7500 (on campus); room only, $3900 (on campus). *Financial aid:* Need-based college/university scholarships/grants from institutional funds, tuition waivers, on-campus employment, private loans from commercial lenders. Non-need-based college/university scholarships/grants from institutional funds, tuition waivers, on-campus employment, private loans from commercial lenders. Forms required: International Student's Financial Aid Application, International Student's Certification of Finances. International transfer students are eligible to apply for aid. For fall 2006 (estimated), 17 international students on campus received college administered financial aid ($15,382 average). *Housing:* Guaranteed, also available during summer. *Services:* International student adviser on campus. Internships and employment opportunities (on-campus) available. *Contact:* Admissions Counselor, Allegheny College, 520 North Main Street, Box 5, Meadville, PA 16335. Telephone: 814-332-6234. Fax: 814-337-0431. E-mail: bob.baldwin@allegheny.edu. URL: http://www.allegheny.edu.

ALVERNIA COLLEGE, READING

General Information Independent Roman Catholic, coed institution. Suburban setting. *Awards:* A, B, M. *Entrance level for U.S. students:* Moderately difficult. *Enrollment:* 2,735 total; 1,996 undergraduates (69% women) including 0.2% international students from 4 foreign countries. *Faculty:* 235. *Library holdings:* 89,399 books, 378 current serial subscriptions, 7,766 audiovisual materials. *Total majors:* 40.

Information for International Students For fall 2006: 12 international students applied, 3 were accepted, 3 enrolled. Students can start in fall or spring. Transfers accepted from institutions abroad. *Admission tests:* Required: TOEFL (minimum score: paper-based 550; computer-based 213; minimum score for ESL admission: paper-based 550; computer-based 213). Recommended: SAT or ACT, ELS. TOEFL can be waived under certain conditions. *Application deadline:* Rolling. *Expenses:* (2006–07) $20,422; room and board, $8193 (on campus); room only, $4173 (on campus). *Financial aid:* Non-need financial aid available. Forms required: FAFSA. International transfer students are eligible to apply for aid. *Housing:* Available during summer. *Services:* International student adviser on campus. Full-time ESL program on campus. ESL program available during the academic year and the summer. Internships and employment opportunities (on-campus) available. *Contact:* Admissions Counselor, Alvernia College, 400 St. Bernardine Street, Reading, PA 19607. Telephone: 610-568-1480. Fax: 610-790-2873. E-mail: paul.sadaphal@alvernia.edu. URL: http://www.alvernia.edu.

ANTONELLI INSTITUTE, ERDENIIEIM

General Information Proprietary, 2-year, coed college. Suburban setting. *Awards:* A. *Entrance level for U.S. students:* Noncompetitive. *Enrollment:* 189 total (65% women). *Undergraduate faculty:* 16. *Library holdings:* 4,000 books, 70 current serial subscriptions, 50 audiovisual materials. *Total majors:* 2. *Expenses:* (2006–07) $16,325; room only, $6100 (on campus).

ARCADIA UNIVERSITY, GLENSIDE

General Information Independent, coed institution, affiliated with Presbyterian Church (U.S.A.). Suburban setting. *Awards:* B, M, D. *Entrance level for U.S. students:* Moderately difficult. *Enrollment:* 3,595 total; 2,119 undergraduates (73% women) including 1% international students from 15 foreign countries. *Faculty:* 396. *Library holdings:* 137,347 books, 932 current serial subscriptions, 2,580 audiovisual materials. *Total majors:* 52.

Information for International Students For fall 2006: 116 international students applied, 58 were accepted, 6 enrolled. Students can start in fall or spring. Transfers accepted from institutions abroad. *Admission tests:* Required: TOEFL (minimum score: iBT 68; paper-based 520; computer-based 190), scores on any comprehensive national exams. Recommended: SAT. TOEFL can be waived under certain conditions. *Application deadline:* Rolling. *Expenses:* (2006–07) $25,990; room and board, $9660 (on campus); room only, $6680 (on campus). *Financial aid:* Need-based loans from outside sources, on-campus employment. Non-need-based college/university scholarships/grants from institutional funds, tuition waivers, loans from outside sources, on-campus employment. Forms required: International Student's Certification of Finances. International transfer students are eligible to apply for aid. For fall 2006 (estimated), 30 international students on campus received college administered financial aid ($15,208 average). *Housing:* Guaranteed. *Services:* International student adviser on campus. Internships and employment opportunities (on-campus) available. *Contact:* Enrollment Management Counselor, Arcadia University, 450 South Easton Road, Glenside, PA 19038-3295. Telephone: 215-572-2910. Fax: 215-572-4049. E-mail: international@arcadia.edu. URL: http://www.arcadia.edu.

THE ART INSTITUTE OF PHILADELPHIA, PHILADELPHIA

General Information Proprietary, primarily 2-year, coed college. Urban setting. *Awards:* A, B. *Entrance level for U.S. students:* Moderately difficult. *Enrollment:* 3,600 total (57% women) including 0.4% international students from 18 foreign countries. *Undergraduate faculty:* 211. *Library holdings:* 25,000 books, 150 current serial subscriptions, 2,000 audiovisual materials. *Total majors:* 13.

Information for International Students For fall 2006: 39 international students applied, 21 were accepted, 12 enrolled. Students can start in fall, winter, spring, or summer. Transfers accepted from institutions abroad. *Admission tests:* Required: TOEFL (minimum score: iBT 61; paper-based 500; computer-based 173), placement tests for English and mathematics. Recommended: ELS. *Application deadline:* Rolling. *Housing:* Guaranteed, also available during summer. *Services:* International student adviser on campus. ESL program at cooperating institution. ESL program available during the academic year and the summer. Internships and employment opportunities (on-campus) available. *Contact:* Assistant Director of International Admissions, The Art Institute of Philadelphia, 1622 Chestnut Street, Philadelphia, PA 19103. Telephone: 215-405-6363. Fax: 215-405-6399. E-mail: apanu@aii.edu. URL: http://www.aiph.artinstitutes.edu.

BAPTIST BIBLE COLLEGE OF PENNSYLVANIA, CLARKS SUMMIT

General Information Independent Baptist, coed institution. Suburban setting. *Awards:* A, B, M, D, FP. *Entrance level for U.S. students:* Minimally difficult. *Enrollment:* 917 total; 699 undergraduates (58% women) including 2% international students from 4 foreign countries. *Faculty:* 32. *Library holdings:* 104,534 books, 502 current serial subscriptions, 27,088 audiovisual materials. *Total majors:* 14. *Expenses:* (2006–07) $13,980; room and board, $5600 (on campus); room only, $2500 (on campus). *Financial aid:* Need-based and non-need-based financial aid available. 1 international student on campus received college administered financial aid ($4500 average).

BLOOMSBURG UNIVERSITY OF PENNSYLVANIA, BLOOMSBURG

General Information State-supported, coed institution. Small town setting. *Awards:* A, B, M, D. *Entrance level for U.S. students:* Moderately difficult. *Enrollment:* 8,723 total; 7,877 undergraduates (60% women) including 1% international students from 27 foreign countries. *Faculty:* 410. *Library holdings:* 472,982 books, 1,747 current serial subscriptions, 13,125 audiovisual materials. *Total majors:* 51. *Expenses:* (2006–07) $13,972; room and board, $5616 (on campus); room only, $3282 (on campus). *Financial aid:* Need-based tuition waivers. Forms required: International Student's Financial Aid Application, International Student's Certification of Finances. For fall 2006 (estimated), 28 international students on campus received college administered financial aid ($10,495 average).

BRYN ATHYN COLLEGE OF THE NEW CHURCH, BRYN ATHYN

General Information Independent Swedenborgian, coed institution. Suburban setting. *Awards:* A, B, M, FP. *Entrance level for U.S. students:* Minimally difficult. *Enrollment:* 155 total; 136 undergraduates (54% women) including 13% international students from 10 foreign countries. *Faculty:* 49. *Library holdings:* 119,009 books, 527 current serial subscriptions, 1,769 audiovisual materials. *Total majors:* 7. *Expenses:* (2007–08) $10,474; room and board, $5574 (on campus). *Financial aid:* Need-based financial aid available. Forms required: institution's own financial aid form. 27 international students on campus received college administered financial aid ($9530 average).

BRYN MAWR COLLEGE, BRYN MAWR

General Information Independent, undergraduate: women only; graduate: coed university. Suburban setting. *Awards:* B, M, D. *Entrance level for U.S. students:* Most difficult. *Enrollment:* 1,799 total; 1,378 undergraduates (97% women) including 6% international students from 42 foreign countries. *Faculty:* 182. *Library holdings:* 1.1 million books, 4,400 current serial subscriptions. *Total majors:* 33.

Information for International Students For fall 2006: 364 international students applied, 45 were accepted, 21 enrolled. Students can start in fall. Transfers accepted from institutions abroad. *Admission tests:* Required: SAT or ACT. Recommended: SAT, ACT, SAT Subject Tests, TOEFL (minimum score: iBT 95; paper-based 600; computer-based 250). TOEFL can be waived under certain conditions. *Application deadline:* 1/15. *Expenses:* (2006–07) $33,010; room and board, $10,550 (on campus); room only, $6030 (on campus). *Financial aid:* Need-based college/university scholarships/grants from institutional funds. Forms required: International Student's Financial Aid Application, International Student's Certification of Finances, statement of earnings from parents employer. 60 international students on campus received college administered financial aid ($40,310 average). *Housing:* Guaranteed, also available during summer. *Services:* International student adviser on campus. Internships and employment opportunities (on-campus) available. *Contact:* Director of International Recruitment, Bryn Mawr College, 101 North Merion Avenue, Gateway Admissions Office, Bryn Mawr, PA 19010-2899. Telephone: 610-526-5152. Fax: 610-526-7471. E-mail: jrussell@brynmawr.edu. URL: http://www.brynmawr.edu.

See In-Depth Description on page 45.

BUCKNELL UNIVERSITY, LEWISBURG

General Information Independent, coed institution. Small town setting. *Awards:* B, M. *Entrance level for U.S. students:* Most difficult. *Enrollment:* 3,706 total; 3,550 undergraduates (51% women) including 3% international students from 41 foreign countries. *Faculty:* 321. *Library holdings:* 804,890 books, 20,527 audiovisual materials. *Total majors:* 54.

Information for International Students For fall 2006: 374 international students applied, 64 were accepted, 23 enrolled. Students can start in fall. Transfers accepted from institutions

Bucknell University (continued)

abroad. *Admission tests:* Required: TOEFL (minimum score: paper-based 550; computer-based 213). Recommended: ACT. TOEFL can be waived under certain conditions. *Application deadline:* 1/1. *Expenses:* (2007–08) $38,134; room and board, $8052 (on campus); room only, $4452 (on campus). *Financial aid:* Need-based college/university scholarships/grants from institutional funds, athletic awards, on-campus employment. Non-need-based college/university scholarships/grants from institutional funds, athletic awards, on-campus employment. Forms required: International Student's Financial Aid Application, International Student's Certification of Finances. For fall 2006 (estimated), 19 international students on campus received college administered financial aid ($30,849 average). *Housing:* Guaranteed, also available during summer. *Services:* International student adviser on campus. Internships and employment opportunities (on-campus and off-campus) available. *Contact:* Associate Director of Admissions, Bucknell University, Office of Admissions, Lewisburg, PA 17837. Telephone: 570-577-1101. Fax: 570-577-3538. E-mail: admissions@bucknell.edu. URL: http://www.bucknell.edu.

See In-Depth Description on page 46.

BUCKS COUNTY COMMUNITY COLLEGE, NEWTOWN
General Information County-supported, 2-year, coed college. Suburban setting. *Awards:* A. *Entrance level for U.S. students:* Noncompetitive. *Enrollment:* 9,572 total (58% women) including 6% international students from 27 foreign countries. *Undergraduate faculty:* 568. *Library holdings:* 155,779 books, 515 current serial subscriptions. *Total majors:* 55. *Expenses:* (2007–08) $9614.

BUTLER COUNTY COMMUNITY COLLEGE, BUTLER
General Information County-supported, 2-year, coed college. Rural setting. *Awards:* A. *Entrance level for U.S. students:* Noncompetitive. *Enrollment:* 3,809 total (60% women) including 0.03% international students from 1 foreign country. *Undergraduate faculty:* 305. *Library holdings:* 70,000 books, 305 current serial subscriptions. *Total majors:* 49. *Expenses:* (2006–07) $7110. *Financial aid:* Forms required: International Student's Certification of Finances.

CABRINI COLLEGE, RADNOR
General Information Independent Roman Catholic, coed institution. Suburban setting. *Awards:* B, M. *Entrance level for U.S. students:* Moderately difficult. *Enrollment:* 2,389 total; 1,814 undergraduates (67% women) including 1% international students from 11 foreign countries. *Faculty:* 224. *Library holdings:* 229,204 books, 21,695 current serial subscriptions, 1,067 audiovisual materials. *Total majors:* 38. *Expenses:* (2006–07) $25,950; room and board, $9900 (on campus). *Financial aid:* Need-based college/university scholarships/grants from institutional funds. Non-need-based college/university scholarships/grants from institutional funds. For fall 2006 (estimated), 2 international students on campus received college administered financial aid ($16,060 average).

CALIFORNIA UNIVERSITY OF PENNSYLVANIA, CALIFORNIA
General Information State-supported, coed institution. Small town setting. *Awards:* A, B, M. *Entrance level for U.S. students:* Moderately difficult. *Enrollment:* 7,720 total; 6,299 undergraduates (52% women) including 1% international students from 21 foreign countries. *Faculty:* 402. *Library holdings:* 437,160 books, 881 current serial subscriptions. *Total majors:* 41. *Expenses:* (2006–07) $9106; room and board, $8144 (on campus); room only, $5392 (on campus). *Financial aid:* Need-based college/university scholarships/grants from institutional funds. Non-need-based college/university scholarships/grants from institutional funds. Forms required: FAFSA. For fall 2006 (estimated), international students on campus received college administered aid averaging $11,268.

CARLOW UNIVERSITY, PITTSBURGH
General Information Independent Roman Catholic, coed, primarily women's institution. Urban setting. *Awards:* B, M. *Entrance level for U.S. students:* Moderately difficult. *Enrollment:* 2,154 total; 1,632 undergraduates (94% women) including 0.2% international students from 8 foreign countries. *Faculty:* 224. *Library holdings:* 128,699 books, 362 current serial subscriptions, 4,878 audiovisual materials. *Total majors:* 37. **Information for International Students** For fall 2006: 153 international students applied, 8 were accepted, 7 enrolled. Students can start in fall, spring, or summer. Transfers accepted from institutions abroad. *Admission tests:* Required: TOEFL (minimum score: iBT 61; paper-based 500; computer-based 173). Recommended: SAT or ACT. *Application deadline:* Rolling.

Expenses: (2007–08) $19,514; room and board, $7684 (on campus); room only, $3926 (on campus). *Financial aid:* Need-based and non-need-based financial aid available. Forms required: institution's own financial aid form. International transfer students are eligible to apply for aid. international students on campus received college administered aid averaging $7611. *Services:* International student adviser on campus. ESL program at cooperating institution. ESL program available during the academic year and the summer. Employment opportunities (on-campus) available. *Contact:* Director, International Student Center, Carlow University, 3333 Fifth Avenue, Pittsburgh, PA 15213. Telephone: 412-578-6010. Fax: 412-578-8722. E-mail: nesgodajl@carlow.edu. URL: http://www.carlow.edu.

CARNEGIE MELLON UNIVERSITY, PITTSBURGH
General Information Independent, coed university. Urban setting. *Awards:* B, M, D. *Entrance level for U.S. students:* Most difficult. *Enrollment:* 10,120 total; 5,669 undergraduates (39% women) including 13% international students from 49 foreign countries. *Faculty:* 1,028. *Library holdings:* 1.1 million books, 28,769 current serial subscriptions, 30,059 audiovisual materials. *Total majors:* 71. *Expenses:* (2006–07) $34,578; room and board, $9280 (on campus); room only, $5440 (on campus).

CEDAR CREST COLLEGE, ALLENTOWN
General Information Independent, women's institution, affiliated with United Church of Christ. Suburban setting. *Awards:* A, B, M. *Entrance level for U.S. students:* Moderately difficult. *Enrollment:* 1,943 total; 1,865 undergraduates including 0.1% international students from 20 foreign countries. *Faculty:* 173. *Library holdings:* 140,886 books, 1,298 current serial subscriptions, 18,255 audiovisual materials. *Total majors:* 53. *Expenses:* (2007–08) $25,340; room and board, $8624 (on campus). *Financial aid:* Need-based college/university scholarships/grants from institutional funds, loans from institutional funds, on-campus employment. Non-need-based college/university scholarships/grants from institutional funds, loans from institutional funds, on-campus employment. Forms required: institution's own financial aid form, International Student's Financial Aid Application, International Student's Certification of Finances.

CHATHAM UNIVERSITY, PITTSBURGH
General Information Independent, undergraduate: women only; graduate: coed institution. Urban setting. *Awards:* B, M, D. *Entrance level for U.S. students:* Moderately difficult. *Enrollment:* 1,590 total; 805 undergraduates (94% women) including 6% international students from 17 foreign countries. *Faculty:* 207. *Library holdings:* 87,907 books, 783 current serial subscriptions, 789 audiovisual materials. *Total majors:* 46. **Information for International Students** For fall 2006: 30 international students applied, 12 were accepted, 10 enrolled. Students can start in fall, spring, or summer. Transfers accepted from institutions abroad. *Admission tests:* Required: TOEFL (minimum score: iBT 79; paper-based 550; computer-based 213; minimum score for ESL admission: iBT 61; paper-based 500; computer-based 173). Recommended: SAT, ACT, ELS, IELTS. TOEFL can be waived under certain conditions. *Application deadline:* Rolling. *Expenses:* (2006–07) $24,808; room and board, $7586 (on campus); room only, $3880 (on campus). *Financial aid:* Need-based loans from outside sources only with a U.S.-based co-signer. Non-need-based on-campus employment. Forms required: International Student's Certification of Finances. For fall 2006 (estimated), 29 international students on campus received college administered financial aid ($11,770 average). *Housing:* Guaranteed, also available during summer. *Services:* International student adviser on campus. Part-time ESL program on campus. ESL program available during the academic year and the summer. Internships and employment opportunities (on-campus) available. *Contact:* Assistant Director of International Admissions, Chatham University, Berry Hall, Woodland Road, Pittsburgh, PA 15232. Telephone: 412-365-1289. Fax: 412-365-1609. E-mail: tviti@chatham.edu. URL: http://www.chatham.edu.

CHESTNUT HILL COLLEGE, PHILADELPHIA
General Information Independent Roman Catholic, coed, primarily women's institution. Suburban setting. *Awards:* A, B, M, D (profile includes figures from both traditional and accelerated (part-time) programs). *Entrance level for U.S. students:* Moderately difficult. *Enrollment:* 1,918 total; 1,154 undergraduates (70% women) including 1% international students from 9 foreign countries. *Faculty:* 265. *Library holdings:* 128,489 books, 484 current serial subscriptions. *Total majors:* 37. *Expenses:* (2006–07) $22,750; room and board, $7950 (on campus). *Financial aid:* Need-based and non-need-based financial aid available. Forms required: International Student's Certification of Finances. For fall

2006 (estimated), 2 international students on campus received college administered financial aid ($27,725 average).

CHEYNEY UNIVERSITY OF PENNSYLVANIA, CHEYNEY

General Information State-supported, coed institution. Suburban setting. *Awards:* A, B, M. *Entrance level for U.S. students:* Minimally difficult. *Enrollment:* 1,667 total; 1,494 undergraduates (55% women) including 0.5% international students from 6 foreign countries. *Faculty:* 113. *Library holdings:* 361,539 books, 414 current serial subscriptions. *Total majors:* 31. *Expenses:* (2006–07) $13,678; room and board, $6006 (on campus); room only, $3358 (on campus). *Financial aid:* Non-need financial aid available. Forms required: International Student's Financial Aid Application.

CLARION UNIVERSITY OF PENNSYLVANIA, CLARION

General Information State-supported, coed institution. Rural setting. *Awards:* A, B, M. *Entrance level for U.S. students:* Minimally difficult. *Enrollment:* 6,591 total; 5,927 undergraduates (61% women) including 1% international students from 27 foreign countries. *Faculty:* 286. *Library holdings:* 442,871 books, 20,264 current serial subscriptions, 7,122 audiovisual materials. *Total majors:* 55.

Information for International Students For fall 2006: 52 international students applied, 25 were accepted, 18 enrolled. Students can start in fall, spring, or summer. Transfers accepted from institutions abroad. *Admission tests:* Required: TOEFL (minimum score: iBT 61; paper-based 500; computer-based 173; minimum score for ESL admission: paper-based 500; computer-based 173). Recommended: IELTS. TOEFL can be waived under certain conditions. *Application deadline:* Rolling. *Expenses:* (2006–07) $11,656; room and board, $5546 (on campus); room only, $3814 (on campus). *Financial aid:* Non-need-based college/university scholarships/grants from institutional funds, tuition waivers. Forms required: International Student's Certification of Finances, FAFSA. International transfer students are eligible to apply for aid. For fall 2006 (estimated), 31 international students on campus received college administered financial aid ($1722 average). *Services:* International student adviser on campus. Internships and employment opportunities (on-campus) available. *Contact:* Clarion University of Pennsylvania, Clarion, PA 16214. Telephone: 814-393-2340. Fax: 814-393-2341. E-mail: intlprograms@clarion.edu. URL: http://www.clarion.edu.

See In-Depth Description on page 57.

COLLEGE MISERICORDIA, DALLAS

General Information Independent Roman Catholic, coed institution. Small town setting. *Awards:* B, M, D. *Entrance level for U.S. students:* Moderately difficult. *Enrollment:* 2,358 total; 2,068 undergraduates (72% women) including 1% international students from 2 foreign countries. *Faculty:* 257. *Library holdings:* 75,777 books, 995 current serial subscriptions, 3,322 audiovisual materials. *Total majors:* 26.

Information for International Students For fall 2006: 2 international students applied, 2 were accepted, 2 enrolled. Students can start in fall, spring, or summer. Transfers accepted from institutions abroad. *Admission tests:* Required: TOEFL (minimum score: paper-based 500; computer-based 173). Recommended: SAT. TOEFL can be waived under certain conditions. *Application deadline:* Rolling. *Expenses:* (2006–07) $20,860; room and board, $8640 (on campus); room only, $4960 (on campus). *Financial aid:* Non-need-based college/university scholarships/grants from institutional funds. Forms required: institution's own financial aid form. International transfer students are eligible to apply for aid. For fall 2006 (estimated), 2 international students on campus received college administered financial aid ($12,505 average). *Housing:* Guaranteed, also available during summer. Internships and employment opportunities (on-campus) available. *Contact:* Executive Director of Admission and Financial Aid, College Misericordia, 301 Lake Street, Dallas, PA 18612. Telephone: 570-674-6461. Fax: 570-675-2441. E-mail: admiss@misericordia.edu. URL: http://www.misericordia.edu.

COMMONWEALTH TECHNICAL INSTITUTE, JOHNSTOWN

General Information State-supported, 2-year, coed college. Suburban setting. *Awards:* A. *Entrance level for U.S. students:* Noncompetitive. *Enrollment:* 275 total (35% women). *Undergraduate faculty:* 32. *Library holdings:* 4,294 books, 62 current serial subscriptions, 470 audiovisual materials. *Total majors:* 7. *Expenses:* (2006–07) room and board, $14,274 (on campus).

COMMUNITY COLLEGE OF ALLEGHENY COUNTY, PITTSBURGH

General Information County-supported, 2-year, coed college. Urban setting. *Awards:* A. *Entrance level for U.S. students:*

Noncompetitive. *Enrollment:* 18,404 total (57% women) including 1% international students from 79 foreign countries. *Undergraduate faculty:* 1,631. *Library holdings:* 272,697 books, 933 current serial subscriptions, 13,165 audiovisual materials. *Total majors:* 116. *Expenses:* (2006–07) $7495.

DELAWARE COUNTY COMMUNITY COLLEGE, MEDIA

General Information State and locally supported, 2-year, coed college. Suburban setting. *Awards:* A. *Entrance level for U.S. students:* Noncompetitive. *Enrollment:* 10,608 total (56% women) including 1% international students from 46 foreign countries. *Undergraduate faculty:* 665. *Library holdings:* 58,692 books, 421 current serial subscriptions, 3,251 audiovisual materials. *Total majors:* 49. *Expenses:* (2006–07) $6768. *Financial aid:* Need-based college/university scholarships/grants from institutional funds, tuition waivers, on-campus employment. Non-need-based college/university scholarships/grants from institutional funds, tuition waivers, on-campus employment. Forms required: institution's own financial aid form, International Student's Certification of Finances.

DELAWARE VALLEY COLLEGE, DOYLESTOWN

General Information Independent, coed institution. Suburban setting. *Awards:* A, B, M. *Entrance level for U.S. students:* Moderately difficult. *Enrollment:* 2,035 total; 1,959 undergraduates (57% women) including 0.1% international students from 8 foreign countries. *Faculty:* 190. *Library holdings:* 56,347 books, 728 current serial subscriptions. *Total majors:* 28. *Expenses:* (2007–08) $23,110; room and board, $8965 (on campus); room only, $4064 (on campus). *Financial aid:* Non-need-based college/university scholarships/grants from institutional funds, loans from outside sources, on-campus employment. Forms required: International Student's Certification of Finances. For fall 2006 (estimated), 1 international student on campus received college administered financial aid ($7500 average).

DESALES UNIVERSITY, CENTER VALLEY

General Information Independent Roman Catholic, coed institution. Suburban setting. *Awards:* B, M. *Entrance level for U.S. students:* Moderately difficult. *Enrollment:* 2,936 total; 2,126 undergraduates (59% women) including international students from 11 foreign countries. *Faculty:* 172. *Library holdings:* 151,999 books, 12,000 current serial subscriptions, 4,926 audiovisual materials. *Total majors:* 38.

Information for International Students For fall 2006: 19 international students applied, 5 were accepted, 3 enrolled. Students can start in fall or spring. Transfers accepted from institutions abroad. *Admission tests:* Required: TOEFL (minimum score: paper-based 550; computer-based 213). Recommended: SAT or ACT, SAT Subject Tests. TOEFL can be waived under certain conditions. *Application deadline:* 4/1. *Expenses:* (2006–07) $22,000; room and board, $8250 (on campus). *Financial aid:* Need-based and non-need-based financial aid available. Forms required: institution's own financial aid form. For fall 2006 (estimated), 4 international students on campus received college administered financial aid ($7156 average). *Services:* International student adviser on campus. ESL program at cooperating institution. Internships and employment opportunities (off-campus) available. *Contact:* Director of Multicultural and International Affairs, DeSales University, 2755 Station Avenue, Center Valley, PA 18034-9568. Telephone: 610-282-1100 Ext. 1721. Fax: 610-282-2254. E-mail: kerry.sethi@desales.edu. URL: http://www.desales.edu.

DEVRY UNIVERSITY, FORT WASHINGTON

General Information Proprietary, coed institution. *Awards:* A, B, M. *Entrance level for U.S. students:* Minimally difficult. *Enrollment:* 935 total; 829 undergraduates (31% women) including 1% international students. *Faculty:* 130. *Library holdings:* 12,755 books, 69 current serial subscriptions, 427 audiovisual materials. *Total majors:* 8. *Expenses:* (2007–08) $14,640.

DICKINSON COLLEGE, CARLISLE

General Information Independent, 4-year, coed college. Suburban setting. *Awards:* B. *Entrance level for U.S. students:* Very difficult. *Enrollment:* 2,400 total (56% women) including 6% international students from 37 foreign countries. *Undergraduate faculty:* 208. *Library holdings:* 517,000 books, 1,300 current serial subscriptions, 16,000 audiovisual materials. *Total majors:* 46. *Expenses:* (2007–08) $35,784; room and board, $8980 (on campus); room only, $4630 (on campus). *Financial aid:* Need-based college/university scholarships/grants from institutional funds, loans from institutional funds, on-campus employment. Non-need-based college/university scholarships/grants from institutional funds. Forms required: International Student's Financial Aid Application, International Student's Certification of Finances. For fall 2006

Dickinson College (continued)

(estimated), 94 international students on campus received college administered financial aid ($38,394 average).

DREXEL UNIVERSITY, PHILADELPHIA

General Information Independent, coed university. Urban setting. *Awards:* A, B, M, D, FP. *Entrance level for U.S. students:* Moderately difficult. *Enrollment:* 19,882 total; 12,908 undergraduates including 6% international students from 53 foreign countries. *Library holdings:* 570,335 books, 8,321 current serial subscriptions, 10,322 audiovisual materials. *Total majors:* 55. *Expenses:* (2006–07) $33,650; room and board, $11,010 (on campus); room only, $6555 (on campus). *Financial aid:* Non-need financial aid available. For fall 2005, 608 international students on campus received college administered financial aid ($12,513 average).

DUQUESNE UNIVERSITY, PITTSBURGH

General Information Independent Roman Catholic, coed university. Urban setting. *Awards:* B, M, D, FP. *Entrance level for U.S. students:* Moderately difficult. *Enrollment:* 10,110 total; 5,678 undergraduates (58% women) including 2% international students from 51 foreign countries. *Faculty:* 880. *Library holdings:* 703,981 books, 20,020 current serial subscriptions, 3,196 audiovisual materials. *Total majors:* 74.

Information for International Students For fall 2006: 431 international students applied, 232 were accepted, 101 enrolled. Students can start in fall, spring, or summer. Transfers accepted from institutions abroad. *Admission tests:* Recommended: ACT, TOEFL. TOEFL can be waived under certain conditions. *Application deadline:* Rolling. *Expenses:* (2006–07) $22,665; room and board, $8296 (on campus); room only, $4526 (on campus). *Financial aid:* Need-based athletic awards. Non-need-based athletic awards. Forms required: institution's own financial aid form. International transfer students are eligible to apply for aid. For fall 2006 (estimated), 70 international students on campus received college administered financial aid ($16,767 average). *Services:* International student adviser on campus. Full-time and part-time ESL programs on campus. ESL program available during the academic year and the summer. Internships and employment opportunities (on-campus) available. *Contact:* Assistant Director, International Admissions, Office of International Affairs, Duquesne University, Pittsburgh, PA 15282-1660. Telephone: 412-396-6113. Fax: 412-396-5178. E-mail: oip@duq.edu. URL: http://www.duq.edu.

See In-Depth Description on page 70.

EASTERN UNIVERSITY, ST. DAVIDS

General Information Independent American Baptist Churches in the USA, coed institution. Small town setting. *Awards:* A, B, M. *Entrance level for U.S. students:* Moderately difficult. *Enrollment:* 3,918 total; 2,382 undergraduates (66% women) including 3% international students from 13 foreign countries. *Faculty:* 343. *Library holdings:* 143,815 books, 1,215 current serial subscriptions. *Total majors:* 36.

Information for International Students For fall 2006: 65 international students applied, 10 were accepted, 3 enrolled. Students can start in fall or spring. Transfers accepted from institutions abroad. *Admission tests:* Required: TOEFL (minimum score: iBT 79; paper-based 550; computer-based 213). *Application deadline:* Rolling. *Expenses:* (2007–08) $21,350; room and board, $8350 (on campus); room only, $4550 (on campus). *Financial aid:* Non-need financial aid available. International transfer students are eligible to apply for aid. *Housing:* Available during summer. *Services:* International student adviser on campus. Internships and employment opportunities (on-campus) available. *Contact:* Director of Admissions, Eastern University, 1300 Eagle Road, St. Davids, PA 19087-3696. Telephone: 610-341-1376. Fax: 610-341-1723. E-mail: mdziedzi@eastern.edu. URL: http://www.eastern.edu.

EAST STROUDSBURG UNIVERSITY OF PENNSYLVANIA, EAST STROUDSBURG

General Information State-supported, coed institution. Small town setting. *Awards:* A, B, M. *Entrance level for U.S. students:* Moderately difficult. *Enrollment:* 7,013 total; 5,890 undergraduates (58% women) including 0.4% international students from 12 foreign countries. *Faculty:* 332. *Library holdings:* 449,107 books, 1,175 current serial subscriptions. *Total majors:* 50. *Expenses:* (2006–07) $14,200; room and board, $5302 (on campus); room only, $3506 (on campus). *Financial aid:* Need-based tuition waivers. Non-need-based athletic awards, loans from outside sources, on-campus employment. Forms required: International Student's Financial Aid Application, International Student's Certification of Finances. 23 international students on campus received college administered financial aid ($7898 average).

EDINBORO UNIVERSITY OF PENNSYLVANIA, EDINBORO

General Information State-supported, coed institution. Small town setting. *Awards:* A, B, M. *Entrance level for U.S. students:* Moderately difficult. *Enrollment:* 7,579 total; 6,443 undergraduates (57% women) including 1% international students from 31 foreign countries. *Faculty:* 403. *Library holdings:* 493,114 books, 1,409 current serial subscriptions, 13,805 audiovisual materials. *Total majors:* 55.

Information for International Students For fall 2006: 89 international students enrolled. Students can start in fall or spring. Transfers accepted from institutions abroad. *Admission tests:* Required: TOEFL (minimum score: paper-based 500; computer-based 173). TOEFL can be waived under certain conditions. *Application deadline:* 5/1. *Expenses:* (2006–07) $9004; room and board, $5718 (on campus); room only, $3600 (on campus). *Financial aid:* Need-based financial aid available. Non-need-based college/university scholarships/grants from institutional funds, tuition waivers, athletic awards, loans from institutional funds, loans from outside sources, on-campus employment. International transfer students are eligible to apply for aid. 166 international students on campus received college administered financial aid ($2785 average). *Housing:* Guaranteed. *Services:* International student adviser on campus. ESL program at cooperating institution. Internships and employment opportunities (on-campus) available. *Contact:* Admissions Office, Edinboro University of Pennsylvania, Edinboro, PA 16444. Telephone: 814-732-2761. Fax: 814-732-2420. URL: http://www.edinboro.edu.

See In-Depth Description on page 74.

ELIZABETHTOWN COLLEGE, ELIZABETHTOWN

General Information Independent, coed institution, affiliated with Church of the Brethren. Small town setting. *Awards:* A, B, M. *Entrance level for U.S. students:* Moderately difficult. *Enrollment:* 2,366 total; 2,330 undergraduates (65% women) including 0.2% international students from 29 foreign countries. *Faculty:* 215. *Library holdings:* 200,073 books, 17,206 current serial subscriptions, 10,568 audiovisual materials. *Total majors:* 50.

Information for International Students For fall 2006: 213 international students applied, 76 were accepted, 31 enrolled. Students can start in fall or spring. Transfers accepted from institutions abroad. *Admission tests:* Required: TOEFL (minimum score: iBT 75; paper-based 525; computer-based 200). TOEFL can be waived under certain conditions. *Application deadline:* 5/1. *Expenses:* (2007–08) $29,000; room and board, $7600 (on campus); room only, $3800 (on campus). *Financial aid:* Need-based college/university scholarships/grants from institutional funds. Non-need-based college/university scholarships/grants from institutional funds, on-campus employment. Forms required: International Student's Financial Aid Application, International Student's Certification of Finances. International transfer students are eligible to apply for aid. For fall 2006 (estimated), 50 international students on campus received college administered financial aid ($15,756 average). *Housing:* Guaranteed, also available during summer. *Services:* International student adviser on campus. Internships and employment opportunities (on-campus) available. *Contact:* Coordinator of International Recruitment, Elizabethtown College, Office of Admissions, One Alpha Drive, Elizabethtown, PA 17022-2298. Telephone: 717-361-1161. Fax: 717-361-1365. E-mail: smithke@etown.edu. URL: http://www.etown.edu.

See In-Depth Description on page 76.

FRANKLIN & MARSHALL COLLEGE, LANCASTER

General Information Independent, 4-year, coed college. Suburban setting. *Awards:* B. *Entrance level for U.S. students:* Very difficult. *Enrollment:* 2,028 total (49% women) including 8% international students from 40 foreign countries. *Undergraduate faculty:* 228. *Library holdings:* 494,099 books, 2,088 current serial subscriptions, 14,234 audiovisual materials. *Total majors:* 38. *Expenses:* (2006–07) $34,450; room and board, $8540 (on campus); room only, $5560 (on campus). *Financial aid:* Need-based college/university scholarships/grants from institutional funds, loans from institutional funds, on-campus employment. Non-need financial aid available. Forms required: institution's own financial aid form, International Student's Financial Aid Application, International Student's Certification of Finances, Ability to Pay Form and Visa documents. For fall 2006 (estimated), 145 international students on campus received college administered financial aid ($32,741 average).

GANNON UNIVERSITY, ERIE

General Information Independent Roman Catholic, coed institution. Urban setting. *Awards:* B, M, D (associate). *Entrance level for U.S. students:* Moderately difficult. *Enrollment:* 3,815 total; 2,675 undergraduates (59% women) including 1% international students from 11 foreign countries. *Faculty:* 312. *Library holdings:*

270,590 books, 14,301 current serial subscriptions, 3,523 audiovisual materials. *Total majors:* 65.

Information for International Students For fall 2006: 75 international students applied, 29 were accepted, 8 enrolled. Students can start in fall or spring. Transfers accepted from institutions abroad. *Admission tests:* Required: SAT or ACT, TOEFL (minimum score: paper-based 500; computer-based 173). TOEFL can be waived under certain conditions. *Application deadline:* 6/1. *Expenses:* (2006–07) $19,996; room and board, $7880 (on campus); room only, $4310 (on campus). *Financial aid:* Non-need-based college/university scholarships/grants from institutional funds, athletic awards, on-campus employment. Forms required: institution's own financial aid form, International Student's Certification of Finances. International transfer students are eligible to apply for aid. For fall 2006 (estimated), 29 international students on campus received college administered financial aid ($17,329 average). *Services:* International student adviser on campus. Internships and employment opportunities (on-campus) available. *Contact:* International Admissions Coordinator, Office of Admissions, Gannon University, 109 University Square, Erie, PA 16541. Telephone: 814-871-7240. Fax: 814-871-5803. E-mail: admissions@gannon.edu. URL: http://www.gannon.edu.

GENEVA COLLEGE, BEAVER FALLS
General Information Independent, coed institution, affiliated with Reformed Presbyterian Church of North America. Small town setting. *Awards:* A, B, M. *Entrance level for U.S. students:* Moderately difficult. *Enrollment:* 1,952 total; 1,659 undergraduates (56% women) including 1% international students from 7 foreign countries. *Faculty:* 210. *Library holdings:* 164,802 books, 797 current serial subscriptions, 15,155 audiovisual materials. *Total majors:* 38. *Expenses:* (2007–08) $19,430; room and board, $7200 (on campus). *Financial aid:* Need-based college/university scholarships/grants from institutional funds, on-campus employment. Non-need-based college/university scholarships/grants from institutional funds, on-campus employment. For fall 2006 (estimated), 7 international students on campus received college administered financial aid ($5704 average).

GETTYSBURG COLLEGE, GETTYSBURG
General Information Independent, 4-year, coed college, affiliated with Evangelical Lutheran Church in America. Small town setting. *Awards:* B. *Entrance level for U.S. students:* Most difficult. *Enrollment:* 2,689 total (54% women) including 1% international students from 27 foreign countries. *Undergraduate faculty:* 284. *Library holdings:* 393,163 books, 4,778 current serial subscriptions, 27,078 audiovisual materials. *Total majors:* 83.
Information for International Students For fall 2006: 13 international students enrolled. Students can start in fall or spring. Transfers accepted from institutions abroad. *Admission tests:* Required: TOEFL (minimum score: iBT 89; paper-based 570; computer-based 230). Recommended: SAT or ACT. TOEFL can be waived under certain conditions. *Application deadline:* 2/15. *Expenses:* (2006–07) $34,050; room and board, $8260 (on campus); room only, $4380 (on campus). *Financial aid:* Need-based college/university scholarships/grants from institutional funds, loans from institutional funds, on-campus employment. Forms required: International Student's Financial Aid Application, International Student's Certification of Finances. International transfer students are eligible to apply for aid. For fall 2005, 30 international students on campus received college administered financial aid ($29,681 average). *Housing:* Guaranteed, also available during summer. *Services:* International student adviser on campus. Internships and employment opportunities (on-campus) available. *Contact:* Director of Admissions, Eisenhower House/Admissions Office, Gettysburg College, Eisenhower House, 300 North Washington Street, Gettysburg, PA 17325-1484. Telephone: 717-337-6100. Fax: 717-337-6145. E-mail: intladmiss@gettysburg.edu. URL: http://www.gettysburg.edu.

GRATZ COLLEGE, MELROSE PARK
General Information Independent Jewish, coed institution. Suburban setting. *Awards:* B, M. *Entrance level for U.S. students:* Moderately difficult. *Enrollment:* 703 total; 13 undergraduates (85% women). *Faculty:* 15. *Library holdings:* 100,000 books, 175 current serial subscriptions. *Total majors:* 1.
Information for International Students For fall 2006: 2 international students applied, 2 accepted, 2 enrolled. Students can start in fall, spring, or summer. Transfers accepted from institutions abroad. *Admission tests:* Required: TOEFL (minimum score: iBT 85; paper-based 550; computer-based 230). TOEFL can be waived under certain conditions. *Application deadline:* Rolling. *Expenses:* (2006–07) $11,000. *Financial aid:* Need-based financial aid available. 1 international student on campus received college administered financial aid ($1638 average).

Services: International student adviser on campus. ESL program at cooperating institution. Employment opportunities (on-campus) available. *Contact:* Dean of Students, Gratz College, 7605 Old York Road, Melrose Park, PA 19027. Telephone: 215-635-7300 Ext. 168. Fax: 215-635-7399. E-mail: rsandberg@gratz.edu. URL: http://www.gratzcollege.edu.

GROVE CITY COLLEGE, GROVE CITY
General Information Independent Presbyterian, 4-year, coed college. Small town setting. *Awards:* B. *Entrance level for U.S. students:* Most difficult. *Enrollment:* 2,489 total (49% women) including 1% international students from 11 foreign countries. *Undergraduate faculty:* 189. *Library holdings:* 139,000 books, 550 current serial subscriptions. *Total majors:* 45. *Expenses:* (2006–07) $10,962; room and board, $5766 (on campus). *Financial aid:* Need-based college/university scholarships/grants from institutional funds, on-campus employment. Non-need-based college/university scholarships/grants from institutional funds, on-campus employment. Forms required: International Student's Financial Aid Application, International Student's Certification of Finances. For fall 2005, 11 international students on campus received college administered financial aid ($5960 average).

GWYNEDD-MERCY COLLEGE, GWYNEDD VALLEY
General Information Independent Roman Catholic, coed institution. Suburban setting. *Awards:* A, B, M. *Entrance level for U.S. students:* Moderately difficult. *Enrollment:* 2,727 total; 2,135 undergraduates (76% women) including 1% international students from 28 foreign countries. *Faculty:* 259. *Library holdings:* 101,552 books, 667 current serial subscriptions, 11,107 audiovisual materials. *Total majors:* 36. *Expenses:* (2007–08) $21,000; room and board, $8600 (on campus).

HARRISBURG AREA COMMUNITY COLLEGE, HARRISBURG
General Information State and locally supported, 2-year, coed college. Urban setting. *Awards:* A. *Entrance level for U.S. students:* Noncompetitive. *Enrollment:* 18,082 total (66% women) including 1% international students from 65 foreign countries. *Undergraduate faculty:* 1,169. *Library holdings:* 163,613 books, 843 current serial subscriptions, 9,510 audiovisual materials. *Total majors:* 85.
Information for International Students For fall 2006: 167 international students applied, 119 were accepted, 59 enrolled. Students can start in fall, spring, or summer. Transfers accepted from institutions abroad. *Admission tests:* TOEFL can be waived under certain conditions. *Application deadline:* Rolling. *Expenses:* (2006–07) $8565. *Services:* International student adviser on campus. Full-time and part-time ESL programs on campus. ESL program available during the academic year. Internships and employment opportunities (on-campus) available. *Contact:* International Admissions Coordinator, Harrisburg Area Community College, One HACC Drive, Harrisburg, PA 17110-2999. Telephone: 717-780-2403. Fax: 717-231-7674. E-mail: jclandis@hacc.edu. URL: http://www.hacc.edu.

HAVERFORD COLLEGE, HAVERFORD
General Information Independent, 4-year, coed college. Suburban setting. *Awards:* B. *Entrance level for U.S. students:* Most difficult. *Enrollment:* 1,168 total (53% women) including 4% international students from 47 foreign countries. *Undergraduate faculty:* 128. *Library holdings:* 773,401 books. *Total majors:* 44.
Information for International Students For fall 2006: 253 international students applied, 31 were accepted, 8 enrolled. Students can start in fall. Transfers accepted from institutions abroad. *Admission tests:* Required: SAT or ACT, SAT Subject Tests, TOEFL (minimum score: iBT 100; paper-based 600; computer-based 250). TOEFL can be waived under certain conditions. *Application deadline:* 1/15. *Expenses:* (2006–07) $33,710; room and board, $10,390 (on campus); room only, $5870 (on campus). *Financial aid:* Need-based college/university scholarships/grants from institutional funds, loans from outside sources, on-campus employment. Forms required: International Student's Financial Aid Application, CSS/Financial Aid PROFILE (if parent resides in U. S.). For fall 2006 (estimated), 12 international students on campus received college administered financial aid ($37,412 average). *Housing:* Guaranteed. *Services:* International student adviser on campus. Internships and employment opportunities (on-campus) available. *Contact:* Associate Director of Admission, Haverford College, 370 Lancaster Avenue, Haverford, PA 19041-1392. Telephone: 610-896-1350. Fax: 610-896-1338. E-mail: admission@haverford.edu. URL: http://www.haverford.edu.

HOLY FAMILY UNIVERSITY, PHILADELPHIA
General Information Independent Roman Catholic, coed institution. Suburban setting. *Awards:* A, B, M. *Entrance level for U.S. students:* Moderately difficult. *Enrollment:* 2,670 total; 1,782

Holy Family University (continued)

undergraduates (74% women) including 0.3% international students from 3 foreign countries. *Faculty:* 258. *Library holdings:* 126,780 books, 742 current serial subscriptions, 1,875 audiovisual materials. *Total majors:* 46.

Information for International Students For fall 2006: 15 international students applied, 5 were accepted, 3 enrolled. Students can start in fall or spring. Transfers accepted from institutions abroad. *Admission tests:* Required: SAT or ACT, TOEFL (minimum score: iBT 79; paper-based 550; computer-based 213). TOEFL can be waived under certain conditions. *Application deadline:* 6/1. *Expenses:* (2006–07) $18,850; room and board, $8300 (on campus); room only, $4900 (on campus). *Services:* International student adviser on campus. Internships available. *Contact:* Assistant Director of Admissions, Holy Family University, 9801 Frankford Avenue, Philadelphia, PA 19114. Telephone: 215-637-3050. Fax: 215-281-1022. E-mail: admissions@holyfamily.edu. URL: http://www.holyfamily.edu.

IMMACULATA UNIVERSITY, IMMACULATA

General Information Independent Roman Catholic, coed, primarily women's institution. Suburban setting. *Awards:* A, B, M, D. *Entrance level for U.S. students:* Moderately difficult. *Enrollment:* 4,067 total; 2,944 undergraduates (76% women) including 1% international students from 12 foreign countries. *Faculty:* 397. *Library holdings:* 143,145 books, 604 current serial subscriptions, 3,422 audiovisual materials. *Total majors:* 47. *Expenses:* (2007–08) $22,650; room and board, $9800 (on campus); room only, $5260 (on campus). *Financial aid:* Need-based and non-need-based financial aid available. 10 international students on campus received college administered financial aid ($1000 average).

INDIANA UNIVERSITY OF PENNSYLVANIA, INDIANA

General Information State-supported, coed university. Small town setting. *Awards:* A, B, M, D. *Entrance level for U.S. students:* Moderately difficult. *Enrollment:* 14,248 total; 11,976 undergraduates (54% women) including 2% international students from 72 foreign countries. *Faculty:* 733. *Library holdings:* 852,531 books, 16,290 current serial subscriptions. *Total majors:* 74.

Information for International Students Students can start in fall, spring, or summer. Transfers accepted from institutions abroad. *Admission tests:* Required: TOEFL (minimum score: iBT 61; paper-based 500; computer-based 173). *Application deadline:* Rolling. *Expenses:* (2006–07) $13,950; room and board, $5162 (on campus); room only, $3150 (on campus). *Financial aid:* Non-need-based tuition waivers, athletic awards, loans from outside sources, on-campus employment. Forms required: International Student's Certification of Finances. For fall 2005, 242 international students on campus received college administered financial aid ($6551 average). *Housing:* Guaranteed, also available during summer. *Services:* International student adviser on campus. Full-time and part-time ESL programs on campus. ESL program available during the academic year and the summer. Internships and employment opportunities (on-campus and off-campus) available. *Contact:* Office of International Affairs, Indiana University of Pennsylvania, 875 Grant Street, Wallace Annex, Indiana, PA 15705. Telephone: 724-357-2295. Fax: 724-357-2514. E-mail: intl-affairs@iup.edu. URL: http://www.iup.edu.

JUNIATA COLLEGE, HUNTINGDON

General Information Independent, 4-year, coed college, affiliated with Church of the Brethren. Small town setting. *Awards:* B. *Entrance level for U.S. students:* Moderately difficult. *Enrollment:* 1,460 total (53% women) including 5% international students from 36 foreign countries. *Undergraduate faculty:* 130. *Library holdings:* 350,000 books, 1,000 current serial subscriptions, 2,000 audiovisual materials. *Total majors:* 87.

Information for International Students For fall 2006: 102 international students applied, 39 were accepted, 18 enrolled. Students can start in fall or spring. Transfers accepted from institutions abroad. *Admission tests:* Required: SAT may be required for some applicants. Recommended: TOEFL (minimum score: iBT 80; paper-based 550; computer-based 213; minimum score for ESL admission: paper-based 450; computer-based 133). TOEFL can be waived under certain conditions. *Application deadline:* 3/1. *Expenses:* (2007–08) $28,920; room and board, $8040 (on campus); room only, $4220 (on campus). *Financial aid:* Need-based college/university scholarships/grants from institutional funds, tuition waivers, loans from institutional funds, loans from outside sources, on-campus employment. Non-need-based college/university scholarships/grants from institutional funds, tuition waivers, loans from institutional funds, loans from outside sources, on-campus employment. Forms required: International Student's Financial Aid Application, International Student's Certification of Finances. International transfer students are eligible to apply for aid. For fall 2006 (estimated), 38 international students on campus received college administered financial aid ($14,995 average). *Housing:* Guaranteed, also available during summer. *Services:* International student adviser on campus. Full-time and part-time ESL programs on campus. ESL program available during the academic year and the summer. Internships and employment opportunities (on-campus) available. *Contact:* Director of International Admissions, Juniata College, 1700 Moore Street, Huntingdon, PA 16652. Telephone: 814-641-3427. Fax: 814-641-3100. E-mail: usastudy@juniata.edu. URL: http://www.juniata.edu.

See In-Depth Description on page 108.

KEYSTONE COLLEGE, LA PLUME

General Information Independent, primarily 2-year, coed college. Rural setting. *Awards:* A, B. *Entrance level for U.S. students:* Minimally difficult. *Enrollment:* 1,708 total (62% women) including 0.5% international students from 7 foreign countries. *Undergraduate faculty:* 234. *Library holdings:* 65,000 books, 309 current serial subscriptions. *Total majors:* 65.

Information for International Students For fall 2006: 17 international students applied, 12 were accepted, 5 enrolled. Students can start in fall, spring, or summer. Transfers accepted from institutions abroad. *Admission tests:* Required: TOEFL (minimum score: iBT 80; paper-based 550; computer-based 213; minimum score for ESL admission: iBT 61; paper-based 500; computer-based 173), ELS. Recommended: SAT or ACT. TOEFL can be waived under certain conditions. *Application deadline:* 6/1. *Expenses:* (2007–08) $17,040; room and board, $8400 (on campus). *Financial aid:* International transfer students are eligible to apply for aid. *Housing:* Guaranteed, also available during summer. *Services:* International student adviser on campus. Internships and employment opportunities (on-campus) available. *Contact:* Director of Admissions, International Student Admissions, Keystone College, 1 College Green, La Plume, PA 18440. Telephone: 570-945-8112. Fax: 570-945-7916. E-mail: admissions@keystone.edu. URL: http://www.keystone.edu.

See In-Depth Description on page 110.

KING'S COLLEGE, WILKES-BARRE

General Information Independent Roman Catholic, coed institution. Urban setting. *Awards:* A, B, M. *Entrance level for U.S. students:* Moderately difficult. *Enrollment:* 2,386 total; 2,127 undergraduates (48% women) including 0.3% international students from 5 foreign countries. *Faculty:* 197. *Library holdings:* 176,537 books, 15,808 current serial subscriptions, 2,835 audiovisual materials. *Total majors:* 40. *Expenses:* (2006–07) $22,280; room and board, $8590 (on campus); room only, $3980 (on campus). *Financial aid:* Need-based college/university scholarships/grants from institutional funds, on-campus employment. Non-need-based college/university scholarships/grants from institutional funds, loans from outside sources. Forms required: institution's own financial aid form, International Student's Financial Aid Application, International Student's Certification of Finances. For fall 2006 (estimated), 3 international students on campus received college administered financial aid ($7500 average).

KUTZTOWN UNIVERSITY OF PENNSYLVANIA, KUTZTOWN

General Information State-supported, coed institution. Rural setting. *Awards:* B, M. *Entrance level for U.S. students:* Moderately difficult. *Enrollment:* 10,193 total; 9,189 undergraduates (59% women) including 1% international students from 29 foreign countries. *Faculty:* 501. *Library holdings:* 500,484 books, 15,600 current serial subscriptions. *Total majors:* 62. *Expenses:* (2006–07) $14,179; room and board, $6208 (on campus); room only, $4144 (on campus). *Financial aid:* Non-need financial aid available. Forms required: institution's own financial aid form, International Student's Certification of Finances. For fall 2006 (estimated), 52 international students on campus received college administered financial aid ($8623 average).

LAFAYETTE COLLEGE, EASTON

General Information Independent, 4-year, coed college, affiliated with Presbyterian Church (U.S.A.). Suburban setting. *Awards:* B. *Entrance level for U.S. students:* Most difficult. *Enrollment:* 2,381 total (48% women) including 6% international students from 41 foreign countries. *Undergraduate faculty:* 236. *Library holdings:* 530,000 books, 3,500 current serial subscriptions. *Total majors:* 34.

Information for International Students For fall 2006: 794 international students applied, 123 were accepted, 41 enrolled. Students can start in fall. Transfers accepted from institutions abroad. *Admission tests:* Required: SAT or ACT, TOEFL (minimum score: iBT 80; paper-based 550; computer-based 213). Recommended: SAT Subject Tests. TOEFL can be waived under certain conditions. *Application deadline:* 1/1. *Expenses:* (2007–08)

$33,811; room and board, $10,377 (on campus); room only, $6155 (on campus). *Financial aid:* Need-based college/university scholarships/grants from institutional funds, loans from institutional funds, on-campus employment. Forms required: International Student's Financial Aid Application, International Student's Certification of Finances. 109 international students on campus received college administered financial aid ($32,705 average). *Housing:* Guaranteed, also available during summer. *Services:* International student adviser on campus. Internships and employment opportunities (on-campus) available. *Contact:* Associate Director of Admissions and Coordinator of International Admissions, Lafayette College, Office of Admissions, 118 Markle Hall, Easton, PA 18042. Telephone: 610-330-5100. Fax: 610-330-5355. E-mail: internatl@lafayette.edu. URL: http://www.lafayette.edu.

LANCASTER BIBLE COLLEGE, LANCASTER

General Information Independent nondenominational, coed institution. Suburban setting. *Awards:* A, B, M. *Entrance level for U.S. students:* Minimally difficult. *Enrollment:* 958 total; 786 undergraduates (51% women) including 1% international students from 4 foreign countries. *Faculty:* 86. *Library holdings:* 132,599 books, 6,852 current serial subscriptions. *Total majors:* 17.

Information for International Students For fall 2006: 4 international students applied, 4 were accepted, 4 enrolled. Students can start in fall or spring. Transfers accepted from institutions abroad. *Admission tests:* Required: TOEFL (minimum score: iBT 69; paper-based 523; computer-based 193; minimum score for ESL admission: iBT 69; paper-based 523; computer-based 193). *Application deadline:* 6/1. *Expenses:* (2006–07) $13,800; room and board, $5980 (on campus); room only, $2620 (on campus). *Financial aid:* Need-based college/university scholarships/grants from institutional funds, loans from outside sources, on-campus employment. Non-need-based college/university scholarships/grants from institutional funds, loans from outside sources, on-campus employment. Forms required: International Student's Certification of Finances. For fall 2006 (estimated), 11 international students on campus received college administered financial aid ($2964 average). *Housing:* Guaranteed, also available during summer. *Services:* International student adviser on campus. *Contact:* Admissions Counselor, Lancaster Bible College, 901 Eden Road, PO Box 83403, Lancaster, PA 17608-3403. Telephone: 717-560-8271. Fax: 717-560-8213. E-mail: admissions@lbc.edu. URL: http://www.lbc.edu.

LA ROCHE COLLEGE, PITTSBURGH

General Information Independent, coed institution, affiliated with Roman Catholic Church. Suburban setting. *Awards:* A, B, M. *Entrance level for U.S. students:* Minimally difficult. *Enrollment:* 1,533 total; 1,367 undergraduates (69% women) including 10% international students from 38 foreign countries. *Faculty:* 191. *Library holdings:* 108,432 books, 601 current serial subscriptions. *Total majors:* 34. *Expenses:* (2006–07) $18,220; room and board, $7564 (on campus); room only, $4738 (on campus). *Financial aid:* Need-based financial aid available. Non-need-based college/university scholarships/grants from institutional funds. For fall 2006 (estimated), international students on campus received college administered aid averaging $6900.

LA SALLE UNIVERSITY, PHILADELPHIA

General Information Independent Roman Catholic, coed institution. Urban setting. *Awards:* A, B, M, D. *Entrance level for U.S. students:* Moderately difficult. *Enrollment:* 6,191 total; 4,315 undergraduates (61% women) including 1% international students from 36 foreign countries. *Faculty:* 371. *Library holdings:* 400,000 books, 9,250 current serial subscriptions, 5,000 audiovisual materials. *Total majors:* 61. *Expenses:* (2006–07) $27,810; room and board, $10,300 (on campus); room only, $5120 (on campus). *Financial aid:* Non-need financial aid available. Forms required: International Student's Certification of Finances.

LAUREL BUSINESS INSTITUTE, UNIONTOWN

General Information Proprietary, 2-year, coed college. Small town setting. *Awards:* A. *Entrance level for U.S. students:* Minimally difficult. *Enrollment:* 305 total (77% women) including 0.3% international students from 1 foreign country. *Undergraduate faculty:* 25. *Library holdings:* 1,537 books, 41 current serial subscriptions. *Total majors:* 28.

Information for International Students Students can start in fall, spring, or summer. Transfers accepted from institutions abroad. *Admission tests:* Required: Wonderlic. *Application deadline:* 9/1. *Expenses:* (2007–08) $13,440. Internships available. *Contact:* Office Supervisor, Laurel Business Institute, 11-15 Penn Street, PO Box 877, Uniontown, PA 15401. Telephone: 724-439-4900 Ext. 130. Fax: 724-439-3607. E-mail: dyuras@laurel.edu. URL: http://www.laurel.edu.

LEBANON VALLEY COLLEGE, ANNVILLE

General Information Independent United Methodist, coed institution. Small town setting. *Awards:* A, B, M, FP. *Entrance level for U.S. students:* Moderately difficult. *Enrollment:* 1,961 total; 1,804 undergraduates (55% women) including 0.5% international students from 5 foreign countries. *Faculty:* 187. *Library holdings:* 187,289 books, 820 current serial subscriptions, 12,632 audiovisual materials. *Total majors:* 53. *Expenses:* (2006–07) $26,385; room and board, $7115 (on campus); room only, $3475 (on campus). *Financial aid:* Need-based on-campus employment. Non-need-based college/university scholarships/grants from institutional funds, on-campus employment. Forms required: International Student's Financial Aid Application, International Student's Certification of Finances. For fall 2006 (estimated), 8 international students on campus received college administered financial aid ($10,556 average).

LEHIGH CARBON COMMUNITY COLLEGE, SCHNECKSVILLE

General Information State and locally supported, 2-year, coed college. Suburban setting. *Awards:* A. *Entrance level for U.S. students:* Noncompetitive. *Enrollment:* 7,076 total (61% women) including 0.3% international students from 43 foreign countries. *Undergraduate faculty:* 531. *Library holdings:* 54,366 books, 482 current serial subscriptions, 6,078 audiovisual materials. *Total majors:* 71. *Expenses:* (2007–08) $8190.

LEHIGH UNIVERSITY, BETHLEHEM

General Information Independent, coed university. Suburban setting. *Awards:* B, M, D. *Entrance level for U.S. students:* Most difficult. *Enrollment:* 6,858 total; 4,743 undergraduates (42% women) including 3% international students from 49 foreign countries. *Faculty:* 614. *Library holdings:* 1.2 million books, 6,271 current serial subscriptions. *Total majors:* 78. *Expenses:* (2006–07) $33,770; room and board, $8920 (on campus); room only, $5100 (on campus). *Financial aid:* Need-based college/university scholarships/grants from institutional funds, loans from institutional funds, loans from outside sources, on-campus employment. Non-need-based college/university scholarships/grants from institutional funds, athletic awards, loans from outside sources. Forms required: International Student's Financial Aid Application, International Student's Certification of Finances. For fall 2006 (estimated), 41 international students on campus received college administered financial aid ($39,366 average).

LINCOLN UNIVERSITY, LINCOLN UNIVERSITY

General Information State-related, coed institution. Rural setting. *Awards:* B, M. *Entrance level for U.S. students:* Moderately difficult. *Enrollment:* 2,423 total; 1,860 undergraduates (61% women) including 4% international students from 33 foreign countries. *Faculty:* 193. *Library holdings:* 179,435 books, 540 current serial subscriptions, 700 audiovisual materials. *Total majors:* 46. *Expenses:* (2006–07) $11,696; room and board, $7142 (on campus); room only, $3822 (on campus). *Financial aid:* Need-based college/university scholarships/grants from institutional funds, loans from outside sources, on-campus employment. Non-need-based college/university scholarships/grants from institutional funds, loans from outside sources, on-campus employment. Forms required: institution's own financial aid form. For fall 2006 (estimated), 47 international students on campus received college administered financial aid ($8375 average).

LOCK HAVEN UNIVERSITY OF PENNSYLVANIA, LOCK HAVEN

General Information State-supported, coed institution. Rural setting. *Awards:* A, B, M. *Entrance level for U.S. students:* Moderately difficult. *Enrollment:* 5,175 total; 4,890 undergraduates (58% women) including 1% international students. *Faculty:* 256. *Total majors:* 56. *Expenses:* (2006–07) $12,005; room and board, $6060 (on campus); room only, $3328 (on campus). *Financial aid:* Need-based college/university scholarships/grants from institutional funds, on-campus employment. Non-need-based college/university scholarships/grants from institutional funds, tuition waivers, athletic awards, on-campus employment. Forms required: International Student's Certification of Finances. For fall 2006 (estimated), 25 international students on campus received college administered financial aid ($12,460 average).

LUZERNE COUNTY COMMUNITY COLLEGE, NANTICOKE

General Information County-supported, 2-year, coed college. Suburban setting. *Awards:* A. *Entrance level for U.S. students:* Noncompetitive. *Enrollment:* 6,170 total (58% women) including 0.1% international students from 1 foreign country. *Undergraduate*

Luzerne County Community College (continued)
faculty: 475. *Library holdings:* 60,000 books, 744 current serial subscriptions, 3,000 audiovisual materials. *Total majors:* 75. *Expenses:* (2006–07) $7410.

LYCOMING COLLEGE, WILLIAMSPORT

General Information Independent United Methodist, 4-year, coed college. Small town setting. *Awards:* B. *Entrance level for U.S. students:* Moderately difficult. *Enrollment:* 1,430 total (57% women) including 1% international students from 13 foreign countries. *Undergraduate faculty:* 131. *Library holdings:* 183,395 books, 1,821 current serial subscriptions, 24 audiovisual materials. *Total majors:* 49.

Information for International Students For fall 2006: 21 international students applied, 10 were accepted, 3 enrolled. Students can start in fall or spring. *Admission tests:* Required: TOEFL (minimum score: paper-based 500; computer-based 173). Recommended: SAT or ACT. TOEFL can be waived under certain conditions. *Application deadline:* 5/1. *Expenses:* (2006–07) $25,605; room and board, $6826 (on campus); room only, $3490 (on campus). *Financial aid:* Need-based financial aid available. Non-need-based college/university scholarships/grants from institutional funds, on-campus employment. Forms required: institution's own financial aid form. For fall 2006 (estimated), 10 international students on campus received college administered financial aid ($17,067 average). *Housing:* Guaranteed, also available during summer. *Services:* International student adviser on campus. Internships and employment opportunities (on-campus) available. *Contact:* Dean of Admissions and Financial Aid, Lycoming College, 700 College Place, Williamsport, PA 17701. Telephone: 570-321-4026. Fax: 570-321-4317. E-mail: admissions@lycoming.edu. URL: http://www.lycoming.edu.

MANSFIELD UNIVERSITY OF PENNSYLVANIA, MANSFIELD

General Information State-supported, coed institution. Small town setting. *Awards:* A, B, M. *Entrance level for U.S. students:* Moderately difficult. *Enrollment:* 3,360 total; 2,936 undergraduates (61% women) including 1% international students from 23 foreign countries. *Faculty:* 227. *Library holdings:* 246,141 books, 2,948 current serial subscriptions, 26,742 audiovisual materials. *Total majors:* 82. *Expenses:* (2006–07) $14,236; room and board, $5934 (on campus). *Financial aid:* Need-based and non-need-based financial aid available. Forms required: International Student's Financial Aid Application, International Student's Certification of Finances. For fall 2005, 19 international students on campus received college administered financial aid ($8304 average).

MARYWOOD UNIVERSITY, SCRANTON

General Information Independent Roman Catholic, coed institution. Suburban setting. *Awards:* A, B, M, D. *Entrance level for U.S. students:* Moderately difficult. *Enrollment:* 3,180 total; 1,896 undergraduates (72% women) including 1% international students from 18 foreign countries. *Faculty:* 307. *Library holdings:* 219,794 books, 14,656 current serial subscriptions, 48,096 audiovisual materials. *Total majors:* 86.

Information for International Students For fall 2006: 62 international students applied, 14 were accepted, 9 enrolled. Students can start in fall or spring. Transfers accepted from institutions abroad. *Admission tests:* Required: TOEFL (minimum score: iBT 62; paper-based 500; computer-based 173; minimum score for ESL admission: paper-based 500; computer-based 173). TOEFL can be waived under certain conditions. *Application deadline:* 3/31. *Expenses:* (2007–08) $24,090; room and board, $10,410 (on campus); room only, $5980 (on campus). *Financial aid:* Non-need financial aid available. Forms required: International Student's Certification of Finances. International transfer students are eligible to apply for aid. For fall 2006 (estimated), 19 international students on campus received college administered financial aid ($16,105 average). *Housing:* Guaranteed, also available during summer. *Services:* International student adviser on campus. Full-time and part-time ESL programs on campus. ESL program available during the academic year and the summer. Internships and employment opportunities (on-campus) available. *Contact:* Director of Admissions, Marywood University, 2300 Adams Avenue, Scranton, PA 18509. Telephone: 570-348-6234. Fax: 570-961-4763. E-mail: ugadm@marywood.edu. URL: http://www.marywood.edu.
See In-Depth Description on page 124.

MERCYHURST COLLEGE, ERIE

General Information Independent Roman Catholic, coed institution. Suburban setting. *Awards:* A, B, M. *Entrance level for U.S. students:* Moderately difficult. *Enrollment:* 4,155 total; 3,856 undergraduates (59% women) including 5% international students from 26 foreign countries. *Faculty:* 296. *Library holdings:* 179,680

books, 1,013 current serial subscriptions. *Total majors:* 107. *Expenses:* (2006–07) $20,364; room and board, $7458 (on campus); room only, $3750 (on campus). *Financial aid:* Need-based college/university scholarships/grants from institutional funds, athletic awards, on-campus employment. Non-need-based college/university scholarships/grants from institutional funds, athletic awards, on-campus employment. Forms required: institution's own financial aid form, International Student's Certification of Finances. For fall 2005, 159 international students on campus received college administered financial aid ($16,619 average).

MILLERSVILLE UNIVERSITY OF PENNSYLVANIA, MILLERSVILLE

General Information State-supported, coed institution. Small town setting. *Awards:* A, B, M. *Entrance level for U.S. students:* Moderately difficult. *Enrollment:* 8,194 total; 7,206 undergraduates (57% women) including 0.3% international students from 53 foreign countries. *Faculty:* 433. *Library holdings:* 515,381 books, 10,105 current serial subscriptions, 13,770 audiovisual materials. *Total majors:* 48.

Information for International Students For fall 2006: 43 international students applied, 27 were accepted, 8 enrolled. Students can start in fall, winter, spring, or summer. Transfers accepted from institutions abroad. *Admission tests:* Required: TOEFL (minimum score: iBT 65; paper-based 500; computer-based 183). TOEFL can be waived under certain conditions. *Application deadline:* Rolling. *Expenses:* (2006–07) $13,958; room and board, $6566 (on campus); room only, $4000 (on campus). *Financial aid:* Non-need-based tuition waivers, on-campus employment. Forms required: International Student's Certification of Finances. International transfer students are eligible to apply for aid. *Housing:* Available during summer. *Services:* International student adviser on campus. Internships and employment opportunities (on-campus) available. *Contact:* Coordinator of International Student Admissions, Millersville University of Pennsylvania, PO Box 1002, Millersville, PA 17551-0302. Telephone: 717-872-3371. Fax: 717-871-2147. E-mail: Susan.Kastner@millersville.edu. URL: http://www.millersville.edu.

MONTGOMERY COUNTY COMMUNITY COLLEGE, BLUE BELL

General Information County-supported, 2-year, coed college. Suburban setting. *Awards:* A. *Entrance level for U.S. students:* Noncompetitive. *Enrollment:* 11,174 total (59% women) including 1% international students from 73 foreign countries. *Undergraduate faculty:* 668. *Library holdings:* 201,174 books, 550 current serial subscriptions. *Total majors:* 53. *Expenses:* (2007–08) $8610.

MOORE COLLEGE OF ART & DESIGN, PHILADELPHIA

General Information Independent, 4-year, women's college. Urban setting. *Awards:* B. *Entrance level for U.S. students:* Moderately difficult. *Enrollment:* 542 total; 507 undergraduates including 2% international students from 7 foreign countries. *Undergraduate faculty:* 110. *Library holdings:* 40,000 books. *Total majors:* 10.

Information for International Students For fall 2006: 18 international students applied, 13 were accepted, 6 enrolled. Students can start in fall or spring. Transfers accepted from institutions abroad. *Admission tests:* Required: TOEFL (minimum score: iBT 71; paper-based 527; computer-based 197); IELTS may substitute for TOEFL. *Application deadline:* Rolling. *Expenses:* (2007–08) $26,154; room and board, $9906 (on campus); room only, $5964 (on campus). *Financial aid:* Non-need-based college/university scholarships/grants from institutional funds, loans from outside sources. International transfer students are eligible to apply for aid. For fall 2005, 3 international students on campus received college administered financial aid ($4000 average). *Housing:* Guaranteed. *Services:* International student adviser on campus. ESL program at cooperating institution. ESL program available during the academic year and the summer. Internships available. *Contact:* Associate Director of Admissions, Moore College of Art & Design, 20th Street and the Parkway, Philadelphia, PA 19103-1179. Telephone: 215-965-4014. Fax: 215-568-3547. E-mail: lhoffman@moore.edu. URL: http://www.moore.edu.
See In-Depth Description on page 132.

MORAVIAN COLLEGE, BETHLEHEM

General Information Independent, coed institution, affiliated with Moravian Church. Suburban setting. *Awards:* B, M, FP. *Entrance level for U.S. students:* Moderately difficult. *Enrollment:* 1,965 total; 1,764 undergraduates (60% women) including 1% international students from 9 foreign countries. *Faculty:* 196. *Library holdings:* 260,363 books, 3,274 current serial subscriptions, 4,740 audiovisual materials. *Total majors:* 61.

Information for International Students For fall 2006: 74 international students applied, 6 were accepted, 3 enrolled. Students can start in fall or spring. Transfers accepted from institutions abroad. *Admission tests:* Required: SAT or ACT, TOEFL (minimum score: iBT 79; paper-based 550; computer-based 213). TOEFL can be waived under certain conditions. *Application deadline:* 2/15. *Expenses:* (2006–07) $26,775; room and board, $7760 (on campus); room only, $4360 (on campus). *Financial aid:* Need-based college/university scholarships/grants from institutional funds, on-campus employment. Non-need-based college/university scholarships/grants from institutional funds, on-campus employment. Forms required: International Student's Financial Aid Application, International Student's Certification of Finances. International transfer students are eligible to apply for aid. For fall 2006 (estimated), 16 international students on campus received college administered financial aid ($22,300 average). *Housing:* Guaranteed, also available during summer. *Services:* International student adviser on campus. Internships and employment opportunities (on-campus) available. *Contact:* Director of Admission, Moravian College, 1200 Main Street, Bethlehem, PA 18018. Telephone: 610-861-1320. Fax: 610-625-7930. E-mail: mackinj@moravian.edu. URL: http://www.moravian.edu.

MOUNT ALOYSIUS COLLEGE, CRESSON

General Information Independent Roman Catholic, coed institution. Small town setting. *Awards:* A, B, M. *Entrance level for U.S. students:* Minimally difficult. *Enrollment:* 1,587 total; 1,520 undergraduates (74% women) including 1% international students from 12 foreign countries. *Faculty:* 168. *Library holdings:* 91,544 books, 275 current serial subscriptions, 2,981 audiovisual materials. *Total majors:* 34. *Expenses:* (2006–07) $15,350; room and board, $6470 (on campus); room only, $3270 (on campus). *Financial aid:* Non-need-based college/university scholarships/grants from institutional funds, loans from outside sources. Forms required: Financial Affadavit of Support. For fall 2005, 8 international students on campus received college administered financial aid ($5800 average).

MUHLENBERG COLLEGE, ALLENTOWN

General Information Independent, 4-year, coed college, affiliated with Lutheran Church. Suburban setting. *Awards:* B. *Entrance level for U.S. students:* Very difficult. *Enrollment:* 2,500 total (60% women) including 0.2% international students from 5 foreign countries. *Undergraduate faculty:* 267. *Library holdings:* 309,550 books, 18,363 current serial subscriptions, 8,523 audiovisual materials. *Total majors:* 32. *Expenses:* (2006–07) $30,715; room and board, $7525 (on campus); room only, $4265 (on campus). *Financial aid:* Non-need financial aid available. Forms required: International Student's Financial Aid Application, International Student's Certification of Finances.

NEUMANN COLLEGE, ASTON

General Information Independent Roman Catholic, coed institution. Suburban setting. *Awards:* A, B, M. *Entrance level for U.S. students:* Moderately difficult. *Enrollment:* 2,969 total; 2,418 undergraduates (66% women) including 2% international students from 8 foreign countries. *Faculty:* 263. *Library holdings:* 75,000 books, 400 current serial subscriptions, 2,000 audiovisual materials. *Total majors:* 18. *Expenses:* (2006–07) $18,632; room and board, $8418 (on campus); room only, $4998 (on campus). *Financial aid:* Need-based college/university scholarships/grants from institutional funds. Non-need-based college/university scholarships/grants from institutional funds. Forms required: International Student's Certification of Finances. 4 international students on campus received college administered financial aid ($17,000 average).

NORTHAMPTON COUNTY AREA COMMUNITY COLLEGE, BETHLEHEM

General Information State and locally supported, 2-year, coed college. Suburban setting. *Awards:* A. *Entrance level for U.S. students:* Noncompetitive. *Enrollment:* 9,488 total (62% women) including 1% international students from 44 foreign countries. *Undergraduate faculty:* 575. *Library holdings:* 69,805 books, 311 current serial subscriptions, 10,275 audiovisual materials. *Total majors:* 57.
Information for International Students For fall 2006: 97 international students applied, 70 were accepted, 32 enrolled. Students can start in fall or spring. Transfers accepted from institutions abroad. *Application deadline:* Rolling. *Expenses:* (2006–07) $7170; room and board, $6114 (on campus); room only, $3536 (on campus). *Housing:* Available during summer. *Services:* International student adviser on campus. Full-time and part-time ESL programs on campus. ESL program available during the academic year. Employment opportunities (on-campus) available. *Contact:* Assistant Director, Admissions/International Students, Northampton County Area Community College, 3835 Green Pond

Road, Bethlehem, PA 18020. Telephone: 610-861-5504. Fax: 610-861-4562. E-mail: pboulous@northampton.edu. URL: http://www.northampton.edu.

PEIRCE COLLEGE, PHILADELPHIA

General Information Independent, 4-year, coed college. Urban setting. *Awards:* A, B. *Entrance level for U.S. students:* Noncompetitive. *Enrollment:* 2,179 total (74% women) including 2% international students from 32 foreign countries. *Undergraduate faculty:* 167. *Library holdings:* 52,126 books, 68 current serial subscriptions, 478 audiovisual materials. *Total majors:* 19. *Expenses:* (2006–07) $13,240. *Financial aid:* Non-need financial aid available. For fall 2005, 2 international students on campus received college administered financial aid ($2000 average).

PENN FOSTER CAREER SCHOOL, SCRANTON

General Information Proprietary, 2-year, coed college. *Awards:* A (offers only external degree programs conducted through home study). *Entrance level for U.S. students:* Noncompetitive. *Enrollment:* 18,881 total including international students from 15 foreign countries. *Undergraduate faculty:* 43. *Total majors:* 14.

PENN STATE BEAVER, MONACA

General Information State-related, primarily 2-year, coed college. Small town setting. *Awards:* A, B. *Entrance level for U.S. students:* Moderately difficult. *Enrollment:* 730 total (40% women) including 0.3% international students. *Undergraduate faculty:* 58. *Library holdings:* 39,861 books, 222 current serial subscriptions. *Total majors:* 118. *Expenses:* (2006–07) $15,796; room and board, $6850 (on campus); room only, $3620 (on campus).

PENN STATE DELAWARE COUNTY, MEDIA

General Information State-related, primarily 2-year, coed college. Small town setting. *Awards:* A, B. *Entrance level for U.S. students:* Moderately difficult. *Enrollment:* 1,631 total (43% women) including 1% international students. *Undergraduate faculty:* 124. *Library holdings:* 59,930 books, 457 current serial subscriptions. *Total majors:* 120. *Expenses:* (2006–07) $15,796.

PENN STATE DUBOIS, DUBOIS

General Information State-related, primarily 2-year, coed college. Small town setting. *Awards:* A, B. *Entrance level for U.S. students:* Moderately difficult. *Enrollment:* 811 total (53% women) including 0.2% international students. *Undergraduate faculty:* 86. *Library holdings:* 43,710 books, 224 current serial subscriptions, 1,091 audiovisual materials. *Total majors:* 127. *Expenses:* (2006–07) $15,786.

PENN STATE ERIE, THE BEHREND COLLEGE, ERIE

General Information State-related, coed institution. Suburban setting. *Awards:* A, B, M. *Entrance level for U.S. students:* Very difficult. *Enrollment:* 3,839 total; 3,675 undergraduates (34% women) including 1% international students from 22 foreign countries. *Faculty:* 265. *Library holdings:* 5 million books, 68,445 current serial subscriptions, 163,643 audiovisual materials. *Total majors:* 131. *Expenses:* (2006–07) $16,506; room and board, $6850 (on campus); room only, $3620 (on campus).

PENN STATE HARRISBURG, MIDDLETOWN

General Information State-related, coed institution. Small town setting. *Awards:* A, B, M, D. *Entrance level for U.S. students:* Very difficult. *Enrollment:* 3,799 total; 2,259 undergraduates (47% women) including 2% international students from 19 foreign countries. *Faculty:* 293. *Library holdings:* 5 million books, 68,445 current serial subscriptions, 163,643 audiovisual materials. *Total majors:* 33. *Expenses:* (2006–07) $16,496; room and board, $8430 (on campus); room only, $5200 (on campus).

PENN STATE HAZLETON, HAZLETON

General Information State-related, primarily 2-year, coed college. Small town setting. *Awards:* A, B. *Entrance level for U.S. students:* Moderately difficult. *Enrollment:* 1,143 total (39% women) including 0.2% international students. *Undergraduate faculty:* 81. *Library holdings:* 83,266 books, 996 current serial subscriptions, 6,771 audiovisual materials. *Total majors:* 125. *Expenses:* (2006–07) $15,796; room and board, $6850 (on campus); room only, $3620 (on campus).

PENN STATE LEHIGH VALLEY, FOGELSVILLE

General Information State-related, primarily 2-year, coed college. Small town setting. *Awards:* A, B. *Entrance level for U.S. students:* Moderately difficult. *Enrollment:* 758 total (42% women) including 0.5% international students. *Undergraduate faculty:* 70. *Library holdings:* 36,641 books, 152 current serial subscriptions. *Total majors:* 119. *Expenses:* (2006–07) $15,796.

Pennsylvania

PENN STATE MCKEESPORT, MCKEESPORT

General Information State-related, primarily 2-year, coed college. Small town setting. *Awards:* A, B. *Entrance level for U.S. students:* Moderately difficult. *Enrollment:* 761 total (43% women) including 0.5% international students. *Undergraduate faculty:* 72. *Library holdings:* 40,851 books, 300 current serial subscriptions, 2,783 audiovisual materials. *Total majors:* 119. *Expenses:* (2006–07) $15,796; room and board, $6850 (on campus); room only, $3620 (on campus).

PENN STATE MONT ALTO, MONT ALTO

General Information State-related, primarily 2-year, coed college. Small town setting. *Awards:* A, B. *Entrance level for U.S. students:* Moderately difficult. *Enrollment:* 1,032 total (59% women) including 0.2% international students. *Undergraduate faculty:* 95. *Library holdings:* 38,962 books, 273 current serial subscriptions. *Total majors:* 120. *Expenses:* (2006–07) $15,796; room and board, $6850 (on campus); room only, $3620 (on campus).

PENN STATE SCHUYLKILL, SCHUYLKILL HAVEN

General Information State-related, primarily 2-year, coed college. Small town setting. *Awards:* A, B (bachelor's degree programs completed at the Harrisburg campus). *Entrance level for U.S. students:* Moderately difficult. *Enrollment:* 911 total (55% women) including 0.1% international students. *Undergraduate faculty:* 62. *Library holdings:* 39,289 books, 518 current serial subscriptions, 930 audiovisual materials. *Total majors:* 124. *Expenses:* (2006–07) $15,776; room only, $4336 (on campus).

PENN STATE UNIVERSITY PARK, STATE COLLEGE

General Information State-related, coed university. Small town setting. *Awards:* A, B, M, D. *Entrance level for U.S. students:* Very difficult. *Enrollment:* 42,914 total; 36,613 undergraduates (45% women) including 2% international students from 77 foreign countries. *Faculty:* 2,582. *Library holdings:* 5 million books, 68,445 current serial subscriptions, 163,643 audiovisual materials. *Total majors:* 123. *Expenses:* (2006–07) $22,712; room and board, $6850 (on campus); room only, $3620 (on campus).

PENN STATE WORTHINGTON SCRANTON, DUNMORE

General Information State-related, primarily 2-year, coed college. Small town setting. *Awards:* A, B. *Entrance level for U.S. students:* Moderately difficult. *Enrollment:* 1,294 total (51% women) including 0.3% international students. *Undergraduate faculty:* 105. *Library holdings:* 53,572 books, 102 current serial subscriptions. *Total majors:* 119. *Expenses:* (2006–07) $15,776.

PENN STATE YORK, YORK

General Information State-related, primarily 2-year, coed college. Suburban setting. *Awards:* A, B (also offers up to 2 years of most bachelor's degree programs offered at University Park campus). *Entrance level for U.S. students:* Moderately difficult. *Enrollment:* 1,672 total (45% women) including 0.4% international students. *Undergraduate faculty:* 119. *Library holdings:* 49,996 books, 243 current serial subscriptions. *Total majors:* 126. *Expenses:* (2006–07) $15,776.

PENNSYLVANIA COLLEGE OF ART & DESIGN, LANCASTER

General Information Independent, 4-year, coed college. Urban setting. *Awards:* B. *Entrance level for U.S. students:* Moderately difficult. *Enrollment:* 255 total (58% women). *Undergraduate faculty:* 46. *Library holdings:* 30,000 books, 75 current serial subscriptions, 451 audiovisual materials. *Total majors:* 4.
Information for International Students Students can start in fall or spring. Transfers accepted from institutions abroad. *Admission tests:* Required: TOEFL (minimum score: paper-based 550; computer-based 213; minimum score for ESL admission: iBT 79). *Application deadline:* Rolling. *Expenses:* (2006–07) $14,057. Internships available. *Contact:* Director of Enrollment Management and Marketing, Pennsylvania College of Art & Design, 204 North Prince Street, PO Box 59, Lancaster, PA 17608.
Telephone: 717-396-7833 Ext. 1017. Fax: 717-396-1339.
E-mail: smatson@pcad.edu. URL: http://www.pcad.edu.

PENNSYLVANIA INSTITUTE OF TECHNOLOGY, MEDIA

General Information Independent, 2-year, coed college. Small town setting. *Awards:* A. *Entrance level for U.S. students:* Noncompetitive. *Enrollment:* 384 total (51% women). *Undergraduate faculty:* 47. *Library holdings:* 16,500 books, 217 current serial subscriptions. *Total majors:* 10. *Expenses:* (2006–07) $9330. *Financial aid:* Need-based college/university scholarships/grants from institutional funds, loans from outside sources, on-campus employment. Non-need-based college/university scholarships/grants from institutional funds, loans from outside sources, on-campus employment. Forms required: institution's own financial aid form.

PHILADELPHIA BIBLICAL UNIVERSITY, LANGHORNE

General Information Independent nondenominational, coed institution. Suburban setting. *Awards:* B, M, FP. *Entrance level for U.S. students:* Moderately difficult. *Enrollment:* 1,389 total; 1,058 undergraduates (53% women) including 1% international students from 14 foreign countries. *Faculty:* 156. *Library holdings:* 109,085 books, 803 current serial subscriptions, 8,452 audiovisual materials. *Total majors:* 11.
Information for International Students For fall 2006: 13 international students applied, 2 were accepted. Students can start in fall, spring, or summer. Transfers accepted from institutions abroad. *Admission tests:* Required: TOEFL (minimum score: paper-based 550; computer-based 213). Recommended: SAT or ACT. TOEFL can be waived under certain conditions. *Application deadline:* Rolling. *Expenses:* (2006–07) $15,875; room and board, $6550 (on campus); room only, $3400 (on campus). *Financial aid:* Need-based college/university scholarships/grants from institutional funds. Non-need-based college/university scholarships/grants from institutional funds. Forms required: institution's own financial aid form. International transfer students are eligible to apply for aid. For fall 2006 (estimated), 10 international students on campus received college administered financial aid ($7655 average). *Housing:* Guaranteed, also available during summer. *Services:* International student adviser on campus. Internships and employment opportunities (on-campus) available. *Contact:* International Counselor, Philadelphia Biblical University, 200 Manor Avenue, Langhorne, PA 19047-2990.
Telephone: 215-702-4241. Fax: 215-702-4248.
E-mail: admissions@pbu.edu. URL: http://www.pbu.edu.

PHILADELPHIA UNIVERSITY, PHILADELPHIA

General Information Independent, coed institution. Suburban setting. *Awards:* A, B, M, D. *Entrance level for U.S. students:* Moderately difficult. *Enrollment:* 3,256 total; 2,747 undergraduates (70% women) including 2% international students from 26 foreign countries. *Faculty:* 412. *Library holdings:* 108,141 books, 991 current serial subscriptions, 47,818 audiovisual materials. *Total majors:* 32.
Information for International Students For fall 2006: 261 international students applied, 91 were accepted, 14 enrolled. Students can start in fall or spring. Transfers accepted from institutions abroad. *Admission tests:* Required: TOEFL (minimum score: iBT 59; paper-based 500; computer-based 170). TOEFL can be waived under certain conditions. *Application deadline:* Rolling. *Expenses:* (2006–07) $23,818; room and board, $8212 (on campus); room only, $4046 (on campus). *Financial aid:* Non-need-based college/university scholarships/grants from institutional funds, athletic awards, on-campus employment. For fall 2006 (estimated), 39 international students on campus received college administered financial aid ($4538 average). *Housing:* Available during summer. *Services:* International student adviser on campus. ESL program at cooperating institution. ESL program available during the academic year and the summer. Internships and employment opportunities (on-campus and off-campus) available. *Contact:* Assistant Director of Admissions, Philadelphia University, Philadelphia, PA 19144.
Telephone: 215-951-2800. Fax: 215-951-2907.
URL: http://www.philau.edu.

See In-Depth Description on page 150.

PITTSBURGH INSTITUTE OF MORTUARY SCIENCE, INCORPORATED, PITTSBURGH

General Information Independent, 2-year, coed college. Urban setting. *Awards:* A. *Entrance level for U.S. students:* Noncompetitive. *Enrollment:* 192 total (43% women). *Undergraduate faculty:* 16. *Library holdings:* 2,167 books, 48 current serial subscriptions. *Total majors:* 1. *Expenses:* (2006–07) $8170. *Financial aid:* Need-based college/university scholarships/grants from institutional funds, loans from outside sources. Non-need-based college/university scholarships/grants from institutional funds, loans from outside sources. Forms required: International Student's Certification of Finances.

POINT PARK UNIVERSITY, PITTSBURGH

General Information Independent, coed institution. Urban setting. *Awards:* A, B, M. *Entrance level for U.S. students:* Moderately difficult. *Enrollment:* 3,546 total; 3,072 undergraduates (59% women) including 1% international students from 18 foreign countries. *Faculty:* 431. *Library holdings:* 125,000 books, 230 current serial subscriptions. *Total majors:* 54. *Expenses:* (2006–07) $17,770; room and board, $7880 (on campus); room only, $3720 (on campus). *Financial aid:* Need-based college/university scholarships/grants from institutional funds, athletic awards, loans from outside sources. Non-need-based college/university scholarships/grants from institutional funds, athletic awards, loans from outside sources. 32 international students on campus received college administered financial aid ($6160 average).

READING AREA COMMUNITY COLLEGE, READING
General Information County-supported, 2-year, coed college. Urban setting. *Awards:* A. *Entrance level for U.S. students:* Noncompetitive. *Enrollment:* 4,158 total (67% women) including 1% international students from 10 foreign countries. *Undergraduate faculty:* 223. *Library holdings:* 25,541 books, 284 current serial subscriptions. *Total majors:* 54.

ROBERT MORRIS UNIVERSITY, MOON TOWNSHIP
General Information Independent, coed university. Suburban setting. *Awards:* B, M, D. *Entrance level for U.S. students:* Moderately difficult. *Enrollment:* 5,065 total; 3,945 undergraduates (46% women) including 2% international students from 27 foreign countries. *Faculty:* 364. *Library holdings:* 135,806 books, 580 current serial subscriptions, 2,852 audiovisual materials. *Total majors:* 37. *Expenses:* (2006–07) $16,290; room and board, $8410 (on campus); room only, $4890 (on campus). *Financial aid:* Need-based college/university scholarships/grants from institutional funds, tuition waivers, athletic awards, loans from outside sources, on-campus employment. Non-need-based college/university scholarships/grants from institutional funds, tuition waivers, athletic awards, loans from outside sources, on-campus employment. For fall 2006 (estimated), 47 international students on campus received college administered financial aid ($16,172 average).

ROSEMONT COLLEGE, ROSEMONT
General Information Independent Roman Catholic, undergraduate: women only; graduate: coed institution. Suburban setting. *Awards:* B, M. *Entrance level for U.S. students:* Moderately difficult. *Enrollment:* 995 total; 578 undergraduates (95% women) including 2% international students from 13 foreign countries. *Faculty:* 77. *Library holdings:* 164,388 books, 1,155 current serial subscriptions, 2,893 audiovisual materials. *Total majors:* 24. *Expenses:* (2007–08) $22,835; room and board, $9200 (on campus). *Financial aid:* Non-need-based college/university scholarships/grants from institutional funds, on-campus employment. For fall 2006 (estimated), 10 international students on campus received college administered financial aid ($16,514 average).

ST. CHARLES BORROMEO SEMINARY, OVERBROOK, WYNNEWOOD
General Information Independent Roman Catholic, undergraduate: men only; graduate: coed institution. Suburban setting. *Awards:* B, M, FP (also offers coed part-time programs). *Entrance level for U.S. students:* Moderately difficult. *Enrollment:* 293 total; 154 undergraduates (38% women) including 4% international students from 2 foreign countries. *Faculty:* 28. *Library holdings:* 113,761 books, 575 current serial subscriptions. *Total majors:* 1.
Information for International Students Students can start in fall, spring, or summer. Transfers accepted from institutions abroad. *Admission tests:* Required: TOEFL. Recommended: SAT or ACT. TOEFL can be waived under certain conditions. *Application deadline:* Rolling. *Expenses:* (2006–07) $11,734; room and board, $7875 (on campus). *Financial aid:* International transfer students are eligible to apply for aid. *Housing:* Guaranteed, also available during summer. *Services:* Part-time ESL program on campus. ESL program available during the academic year. Employment opportunities (on-campus) available. *Contact:* Vice Rector, St. Charles Borromeo Seminary, Overbrook, 100 East Wynnewood Road, Wynnewood, PA 19096. Telephone: 610-785-6271. Fax: 610-617-9267. E-mail: frmfitzg@adphila.org. URL: http://www.scs.edu.

SAINT FRANCIS UNIVERSITY, LORETTO
General Information Independent Roman Catholic, coed institution. Rural setting. *Awards:* A, B, M. *Entrance level for U.S. students:* Moderately difficult. *Enrollment:* 2,014 total; 1,410 undergraduates (61% women) including 0.3% international students from 9 foreign countries. *Faculty:* 187. *Library holdings:* 118,333 books, 7,202 current serial subscriptions. *Total majors:* 71.
Information for International Students For fall 2006: 15 international students applied, 10 were accepted, 6 enrolled. Students can start in fall, spring, or summer. Transfers accepted from institutions abroad. *Admission tests:* Required: SAT or ACT, TOEFL (minimum score: paper-based 500). *Application deadline:* Rolling. *Expenses:* (2006–07) $22,224; room and board, $7640 (on campus); room only, $3840 (on campus). *Financial aid:* Need-based college/university scholarships/grants

from institutional funds, tuition waivers, athletic awards, loans from outside sources, on-campus employment, FWS, Perkins, FSEOG, PELL. Non-need-based college/university scholarships/grants from institutional funds, tuition waivers, athletic awards, loans from outside sources, on-campus employment. Forms required: institution's own financial aid form, International Student's Certification of Finances. International transfer students are eligible to apply for aid. 10 international students on campus received college administered financial aid ($18,086 average). *Housing:* Guaranteed. *Services:* International student adviser on campus. Employment opportunities (on-campus) available. *Contact:* Dean of Enrollment Management, Saint Francis University, PO Box 600, Loretto, PA 15940-0600. Telephone: 814-472-3100. Fax: 814-472-3335. E-mail: admissions@francis.edu. URL: http://www.francis.edu.

SAINT JOSEPH'S UNIVERSITY, PHILADELPHIA
General Information Independent Roman Catholic (Jesuit), coed institution. Suburban setting. *Awards:* A, B, M, D. *Entrance level for U.S. students:* Very difficult. *Enrollment:* 7,535 total; 4,932 undergraduates (53% women) including 1% international students from 40 foreign countries. *Faculty:* 602. *Library holdings:* 366,300 books, 11,700 current serial subscriptions, 5,200 audiovisual materials. *Total majors:* 53. *Expenses:* (2006–07) $29,095; room and board, $10,170 (on campus); room only, $6480 (on campus). *Financial aid:* Non-need financial aid available. Forms required: International Student's Certification of Finances.

SAINT VINCENT COLLEGE, LATROBE
General Information Independent Roman Catholic, coed institution. Suburban setting. *Awards:* B, M. *Entrance level for U.S. students:* Moderately difficult. *Enrollment:* 1,818 total; 1,652 undergraduates (52% women) including 1% international students from 13 foreign countries. *Faculty:* 187. *Library holdings:* 276,145 books, 617 current serial subscriptions, 4,559 audiovisual materials. *Total majors:* 44.
Information for International Students For fall 2006: 29 international students applied, 3 were accepted, 2 enrolled. Students can start in fall or spring. Transfers accepted from institutions abroad. *Admission tests:* Required: SAT or ACT, TOEFL (minimum score: paper-based 550; computer-based 213). Recommended: SAT Subject Tests. TOEFL can be waived under certain conditions. *Application deadline:* Rolling. *Expenses:* (2006–07) $23,000; room and board, $7242 (on campus); room only, $3700 (on campus). *Financial aid:* Need-based college/university scholarships/grants from institutional funds, loans from outside sources, on-campus employment. Non-need-based college/university scholarships/grants from institutional funds, loans from outside sources, on-campus employment. Forms required: International Student's Financial Aid Application, International Student's Certification of Finances. International transfer students are eligible to apply for aid. For fall 2006 (estimated), 19 international students on campus received college administered financial aid ($18,109 average). *Housing:* Guaranteed. *Services:* International student adviser on campus. Internships and employment opportunities (on-campus and off-campus) available. *Contact:* International Admission Counselor, Saint Vincent College, 300 Fraser Purchase Road, Latrobe, PA 15650-2690. Telephone: 724-537-4540. Fax: 724-532-5069. E-mail: admission@stvincent.edu. URL: http://www.stvincent.edu.

SETON HILL UNIVERSITY, GREENSBURG
General Information Independent Roman Catholic, coed institution. Small town setting. *Awards:* B, M. *Entrance level for U.S. students:* Moderately difficult. *Enrollment:* 1,895 total; 1,549 undergraduates (62% women) including 2% international students from 14 foreign countries. *Faculty:* 192. *Library holdings:* 123,538 books, 423 current serial subscriptions, 6,684 audiovisual materials. *Total majors:* 91. *Expenses:* (2006–07) $23,380; room and board, $7230 (on campus). *Financial aid:* Need-based college/university scholarships/grants from institutional funds, on-campus employment. Non-need-based college/university scholarships/grants from institutional funds, on-campus employment. Forms required: institution's own financial aid form, International Student's Certification of Finances. For fall 2006 (estimated), 19 international students on campus received college administered financial aid ($20,764 average).

SHIPPENSBURG UNIVERSITY OF PENNSYLVANIA, SHIPPENSBURG
General Information State-supported, coed institution. Rural setting. *Awards:* B, M. *Entrance level for U.S. students:* Moderately difficult. *Enrollment:* 7,516 total; 6,423 undergraduates (52% women) including 0.2% international students from 15 foreign countries. *Faculty:* 378. *Library holdings:* 450,517 books, 1,243 current serial subscriptions, 78,144 audiovisual materials.

Shippensburg University of Pennsylvania (continued)

Total majors: 33. *Expenses:* (2006–07) $14,109; room and board, $5962 (on campus); room only, $3420 (on campus). *Financial aid:* Need-based tuition waivers. Non-need-based athletic awards, loans from outside sources, on-campus employment. Forms required: institution's own financial aid form. For fall 2006 (estimated), 11 international students on campus received college administered financial aid ($9198 average).

SLIPPERY ROCK UNIVERSITY OF PENNSYLVANIA, SLIPPERY ROCK

General Information State-supported, coed institution. Rural setting. *Awards:* B, M, D. *Entrance level for U.S. students:* Moderately difficult. *Enrollment:* 8,230 total; 7,545 undergraduates (56% women) including 1% international students from 39 foreign countries. *Faculty:* 361. *Library holdings:* 503,376 books, 599 current serial subscriptions. *Total majors:* 43.

Information for International Students For fall 2006: 197 international students applied, 96 were accepted, 61 enrolled. Students can start in fall or spring. Transfers accepted from institutions abroad. *Admission tests:* Recommended: IELTS or ELS in lieu of TOEFL. TOEFL can be waived under certain conditions. *Application deadline:* 4/1. *Expenses:* (2006–07) $8883; room and board, $4998 (on campus); room only, $2822 (on campus). *Financial aid:* Need-based college/university scholarships/grants from institutional funds, on-campus employment. Non-need-based college/university scholarships/grants from institutional funds, tuition waivers, athletic awards, loans from outside sources, on-campus employment. Forms required: institution's own financial aid form. International transfer students are eligible to apply for aid. For fall 2005, 91 international students on campus received college administered financial aid ($1980 average). *Housing:* Guaranteed, also available during summer. *Services:* International student adviser on campus. Internships and employment opportunities (on-campus) available. *Contact:* International Student Advisor, International Studies Office, Slippery Rock University of Pennsylvania, International Services Office, 1 Morrow Way, Slippery Rock, PA 16057. Telephone: 724-738-2603. Fax: 724-738-2289. E-mail: kelly.slogar@sru.edu. URL: http://www.sru.edu.

See In-Depth Description on page 188.

SUSQUEHANNA UNIVERSITY, SELINSGROVE

General Information Independent, 4-year, coed college, affiliated with Evangelical Lutheran Church in America. Suburban setting. *Awards:* B (also offers evening associate degree program limited to local adult students). *Entrance level for U.S. students:* Moderately difficult. *Enrollment:* 2,009 total (54% women) including 1% international students from 10 foreign countries. *Undergraduate faculty:* 189. *Library holdings:* 298,458 books, 15,989 current serial subscriptions, 7,856 audiovisual materials. *Total majors:* 54.

Information for International Students For fall 2006: 107 international students applied, 12 were accepted, 9 enrolled. Students can start in fall or spring. Transfers accepted from institutions abroad. *Admission tests:* Required: TOEFL (minimum score: paper-based 550; computer-based 213). Recommended: SAT or ACT, SAT Subject Tests. TOEFL can be waived under certain conditions. *Application deadline:* 3/1. *Expenses:* (2006–07) $27,620; room and board, $7600 (on campus); room only, $4000 (on campus). *Financial aid:* Need-based college/university scholarships/grants from institutional funds. Non-need-based college/university scholarships/grants from institutional funds. Forms required: International Student's Financial Aid Application, International Student's Certification of Finances. 13 international students on campus received college administered financial aid ($21,895 average). *Housing:* Guaranteed, also available during summer. *Services:* International student adviser on campus. Internships and employment opportunities (on-campus) available. *Contact:* Associate Director of Admissions, Office of Admission, Susquehanna University, 514 University Avenue, Selinsgrove, PA 17870-1040. Telephone: 570-372-4260. Fax: 570-372-2722. E-mail: moy@susqu.edu. URL: http://www.susqu.edu.

SWARTHMORE COLLEGE, SWARTHMORE

General Information Independent, 4-year, coed college. Suburban setting. *Awards:* B. *Entrance level for U.S. students:* Most difficult. *Enrollment:* 1,484 total (52% women) including 6% international students from 40 foreign countries. *Undergraduate faculty:* 202. *Library holdings:* 800,667 books, 8,190 current serial subscriptions, 22,862 audiovisual materials. *Total majors:* 44.

Information for International Students For fall 2006: 670 international students applied, 43 were accepted, 22 enrolled. Students can start in fall. Transfers accepted from institutions abroad. *Admission tests:* Required: SAT or ACT, SAT Subject Tests. Recommended: TOEFL. *Application deadline:* 1/1. *Expenses:*

(2006–07) $33,232; room and board, $10,300 (on campus); room only, $5280 (on campus). *Financial aid:* Need-based college/university scholarships/grants from institutional funds, loans from institutional funds, on-campus employment. Forms required: institution's own financial aid form, International Student's Certification of Finances, income statement from employer. For fall 2006 (estimated), 46 international students on campus received college administered financial aid ($38,560 average). *Housing:* Guaranteed. *Services:* International student adviser on campus. Internships and employment opportunities (on-campus) available. *Contact:* Director of International Recruitment, Swarthmore College, 500 College Avenue, Swarthmore, PA 19081. Telephone: 610-328-8300. Fax: 610-328-8580. E-mail: admissions@swarthmore.edu. URL: http://www.swarthmore.edu.

TALMUDICAL YESHIVA OF PHILADELPHIA, PHILADELPHIA

General Information Independent Jewish, 4-year, men's college. Urban setting. *Awards:* B (also offers some graduate courses). *Entrance level for U.S. students:* Moderately difficult. *Enrollment:* 85 total including 13% international students from 4 foreign countries. *Undergraduate faculty:* 5. *Library holdings:* 4,800 books, 300 current serial subscriptions. *Total majors:* 2. *Financial aid:* Need-based financial aid available.

TEMPLE UNIVERSITY, PHILADELPHIA

General Information State-related, coed university. Urban setting. *Awards:* A, B, M, D, FP. *Entrance level for U.S. students:* Moderately difficult. *Enrollment:* 33,865 total; 24,674 undergraduates (55% women) including 3% international students from 94 foreign countries. *Faculty:* 2,716. *Library holdings:* 3.3 million books, 20,980 current serial subscriptions. *Total majors:* 118. *Expenses:* (2006–07) $18,224; room and board, $8230 (on campus); room only, $5404 (on campus). *Financial aid:* Need-based college/university scholarships/grants from institutional funds. Non-need-based college/university scholarships/grants from institutional funds. Forms required: institution's own financial aid form. For fall 2005, 123 international students on campus received college administered financial aid ($13,032 average).

THIEL COLLEGE, GREENVILLE

General Information Independent, 4-year, coed college, affiliated with Evangelical Lutheran Church in America. Rural setting. *Awards:* A, B. *Entrance level for U.S. students:* Moderately difficult. *Enrollment:* 1,279 total (47% women) including 4% international students from 13 foreign countries. *Undergraduate faculty:* 113. *Library holdings:* 186,643 books, 454 current serial subscriptions, 498 audiovisual materials. *Total majors:* 40. *Expenses:* (2006–07) $18,720; room and board, $7574 (on campus); room only, $3900 (on campus). *Financial aid:* Non-need-based college/university scholarships/grants from institutional funds. Forms required: International Student's Financial Aid Application, International Student's Certification of Finances.

THOMAS JEFFERSON UNIVERSITY, PHILADELPHIA

General Information Independent, coed university. Urban setting. *Awards:* B, M, D. *Entrance level for U.S. students:* Moderately difficult. *Enrollment:* 2,867 total; 1,057 undergraduates (83% women) including 1% international students from 10 foreign countries. *Faculty:* 266. *Library holdings:* 170,000 books, 2,290 current serial subscriptions. *Total majors:* 8. *Expenses:* (2006–07) $22,884; room only, $3021 (on campus).

UNIVERSITY OF PENNSYLVANIA, PHILADELPHIA

General Information Independent, coed university. Urban setting. *Awards:* A, B, M, D, FP (also offers evening program with significant enrollment not reflected in profile). *Entrance level for U.S. students:* Most difficult. *Enrollment:* 18,809 total; 9,730 undergraduates (50% women) including 11% international students from 110 foreign countries. *Faculty:* 1,701. *Library holdings:* 5.9 million books, 47,787 current serial subscriptions. *Total majors:* 95. *Expenses:* (2006–07) $34,156; room and board, $9804 (on campus); room only, $6022 (on campus). *Financial aid:* Need-based financial aid available. Forms required: institution's own financial aid form, CSS PROFILE, International Student's Financial Aid Application, International Student's Certification of Finances, parent and student income tax forms. For fall 2005, 263 international students on campus received college administered financial aid ($33,092 average).

UNIVERSITY OF PHOENIX–PHILADELPHIA CAMPUS, WAYNE

General Information Proprietary, coed institution. Urban setting. *Awards:* B, M. *Entrance level for U.S. students:* Noncompetitive. *Enrollment:* 1,611 total; 1,270 undergraduates (65% women) including 6% international students. *Faculty:* 286. *Library holdings:* 1,759 books, 692 current serial subscriptions. *Total majors:* 25. *Expenses:* (2006–07) $13,050.

UNIVERSITY OF PHOENIX–PITTSBURGH CAMPUS, PITTSBURGH

General Information Proprietary, coed institution. Urban setting. *Awards:* B, M. *Entrance level for U.S. students:* Noncompetitive. *Enrollment:* 408 total; 301 undergraduates (57% women) including 5% international students. *Faculty:* 198. *Library holdings:* 1,759 books, 692 current serial subscriptions. *Total majors:* 24. *Expenses:* (2006–07) $13,050.

UNIVERSITY OF PITTSBURGH, PITTSBURGH

General Information State-related, coed university. Urban setting. *Awards:* B, M, D, FP. *Entrance level for U.S. students:* Moderately difficult. *Enrollment:* 26,860 total; 17,246 undergraduates (52% women) including 1% international students from 49 foreign countries. *Faculty:* 2,157. *Library holdings:* 4.6 million books, 3,767 current serial subscriptions. *Total majors:* 86.
Information for International Students For fall 2006: 326 international students applied, 90 were accepted, 41 enrolled. Students can start in fall, spring, or summer. Transfers accepted from institutions abroad. *Admission tests:* Required: TOEFL (minimum score: iBT 80; paper-based 550; computer-based 213), IELTS in lieu of TOEFL. Recommended: SAT, ACT. TOEFL can be waived under certain conditions. *Application deadline:* 2/1. *Expenses:* (2006–07) $21,456; room and board, $7800 (on campus); room only, $4790 (on campus). *Housing:* Guaranteed, also available during summer. *Services:* International student adviser on campus. Full-time ESL program on campus. ESL program available during the academic year and the summer. Internships and employment opportunities (on-campus and off-campus) available. *Contact:* Assistant Director for International Admissions, University of Pittsburgh, Office of International Services, 3959 Fifth Avenue, WPU 708, Pittsburgh, PA 15260. Telephone: 412-624-7129. Fax: 412-624-7105. E-mail: gfk1@pitt.edu. URL: http://www.pitt.edu.

UNIVERSITY OF PITTSBURGH AT BRADFORD, BRADFORD

General Information State-related, 4-year, coed college. Small town setting. *Awards:* A, B. *Entrance level for U.S. students:* Minimally difficult. *Enrollment:* 1,319 total (57% women) including international students from 9 foreign countries. *Undergraduate faculty:* 124. *Library holdings:* 95,271 books, 343 current serial subscriptions, 6,061 audiovisual materials. *Total majors:* 25.
Information for International Students For fall 2006: 10 international students applied, 8 were accepted, 2 enrolled. Students can start in fall or spring. Transfers accepted from institutions abroad. *Admission tests:* Required: TOEFL (minimum score: paper-based 550; computer-based 213). TOEFL can be waived under certain conditions. *Application deadline:* 2/1. *Expenses:* (2006–07) $20,486; room and board, $6650 (on campus). *Financial aid:* Non-need-based college/university scholarships/grants from institutional funds, loans from outside sources. Forms required: International Student's Certification of Finances. International transfer students are eligible to apply for aid. For fall 2006 (estimated), 1 international student on campus received college administered financial aid ($6500 average). *Housing:* Guaranteed. Internships available. *Contact:* Director of Admissions, Admissions Office, University of Pittsburgh at Bradford, 300 Campus Drive, Bradford, PA 16701. Telephone: 814-362-7555. Fax: 814-362-5150. E-mail: nazemetz@exchange.upb.pitt.edu. URL: http://www.upb.pitt.edu.

UNIVERSITY OF PITTSBURGH AT JOHNSTOWN, JOHNSTOWN

General Information State-related, 4-year, coed college. Suburban setting. *Awards:* A, B. *Entrance level for U.S. students:* Moderately difficult. *Enrollment:* 3,142 total (48% women) including international students from 1 foreign country. *Library holdings:* 145,507 books, 450 current serial subscriptions. *Total majors:* 50. *Expenses:* (2006–07) $20,468; room and board, $6200 (on campus); room only, $3800 (on campus).

THE UNIVERSITY OF SCRANTON, SCRANTON

General Information Independent Roman Catholic (Jesuit), coed institution. Urban setting. *Awards:* A, B, M, D. *Entrance level for U.S. students:* Moderately difficult. *Enrollment:* 5,353 total; 3,999 undergraduates (57% women) including 0.4% international students from 12 foreign countries. *Faculty:* 509. *Library holdings:* 481,542 books, 1,579 current serial subscriptions. *Total majors:* 56. *Expenses:* (2006–07) $25,938; room and board, $10,224 (on campus); room only, $6016 (on campus). *Financial aid:* Non-need-based college/university scholarships/grants from institutional funds,

on-campus employment. 11 international students on campus received college administered financial aid ($28,582 average).

THE UNIVERSITY OF THE ARTS, PHILADELPHIA

General Information Independent, coed institution. Urban setting. *Awards:* B, M. *Entrance level for U.S. students:* Moderately difficult. *Enrollment:* 2,315 total; 2,117 undergraduates (54% women) including 3% international students from 39 foreign countries. *Faculty:* 472. *Library holdings:* 123,175 books, 538 current serial subscriptions. *Total majors:* 23.
Information for International Students Students can start in fall or spring. Transfers accepted from institutions abroad. *Admission tests:* Required: TOEFL or IELTS. *Application deadline:* Rolling. *Expenses:* (2006–07) $25,680; room only, $6300 (on campus). *Financial aid:* Non-need financial aid available. International transfer students are eligible to apply for aid. *Contact:* Director of Admission, The University of the Arts, 320 South Broad Street, Philadelphia, PA 19102. Telephone: 215-717-6000. Fax: 215-717-6045. E-mail: admis@uarts.edu. URL: http://www.uarts.edu.

UNIVERSITY OF THE SCIENCES IN PHILADELPHIA, PHILADELPHIA

General Information Independent, coed university. Urban setting. *Awards:* B, M, D, FP. *Entrance level for U.S. students:* Moderately difficult. *Enrollment:* 2,857 total; 2,020 undergraduates (59% women) including 1% international students from 13 foreign countries. *Faculty:* 235. *Library holdings:* 87,125 books, 9,817 current serial subscriptions. *Total majors:* 16. *Expenses:* (2006–07) $25,392; room and board, $9936 (on campus); room only, $6070 (on campus).

URSINUS COLLEGE, COLLEGEVILLE

General Information Independent, 4-year, coed college. Suburban setting. *Awards:* B. *Entrance level for U.S. students:* Very difficult. *Enrollment:* 1,589 total (53% women) including 1% international students from 14 foreign countries. *Undergraduate faculty:* 155. *Library holdings:* 200,000 books, 900 current serial subscriptions. *Total majors:* 36. *Expenses:* (2006–07) $33,350; room and board, $7600 (on campus). *Financial aid:* Non-need-based college/university scholarships/grants from institutional funds, on-campus employment. Forms required: International Student's Financial Aid Application, International Student's Certification of Finances. For fall 2005, 25 international students on campus received college administered financial aid ($17,500 average).

VALLEY FORGE MILITARY COLLEGE, WAYNE

General Information Independent, 2-year, coed college. Suburban setting. *Awards:* A. *Entrance level for U.S. students:* Moderately difficult. *Enrollment:* 165 total including 2% international students from 6 foreign countries. *Undergraduate faculty:* 26. *Library holdings:* 75,830 books, 189 current serial subscriptions, 326 audiovisual materials. *Total majors:* 5. *Expenses:* (2006–07) $19,693; room and board, $11,284 (on campus).

VILLANOVA UNIVERSITY, VILLANOVA

General Information Independent Roman Catholic, coed institution. Suburban setting. *Awards:* A, B, M, D, FP. *Entrance level for U.S. students:* Very difficult. *Enrollment:* 10,456 total; 7,254 undergraduates (51% women) including 2% international students from 32 foreign countries. *Faculty:* 904. *Library holdings:* 712,000 books, 12,000 current serial subscriptions, 8,000 audiovisual materials. *Total majors:* 44.
Information for International Students For fall 2006: 285 international students applied, 138 were accepted, 33 enrolled. Students can start in fall. Transfers accepted from institutions abroad. *Admission tests:* Required: SAT or ACT. Recommended: SAT, ACT, TOEFL (minimum score: iBT 88; paper-based 550; computer-based 213). TOEFL can be waived under certain conditions. *Application deadline:* 1/7. *Expenses:* (2006–07) $31,135; room and board, $9560 (on campus); room only, $5060 (on campus). *Financial aid:* Need-based college/university scholarships/grants from institutional funds, on-campus employment. Non-need-based college/university scholarships/grants from institutional funds, athletic awards, on-campus employment. Forms required: International Student's Financial Aid Application, International Student's Certification of Finances, proof of income from employer (in English). For fall 2005, 20 international students on campus received college administered financial aid ($19,857 average). *Services:* International student adviser on campus. ESL program at cooperating institution. ESL program available during the academic year. Internships and employment opportunities (on-campus) available. *Contact:* Associate Director of International Admissions, Villanova University, 800 Lancaster Avenue, University Admissions,

Villanova University (continued)
Austin Hall, Villanova, PA 19085. Telephone: 610-519-4000.
Fax: 610-519-6450. E-mail: gotovu@villanova.edu.
URL: http://www.villanova.edu.

WASHINGTON & JEFFERSON COLLEGE, WASHINGTON

General Information Independent, 4-year, coed college. Small town setting. *Awards:* A, B. *Entrance level for U.S. students:* Very difficult. *Enrollment:* 1,515 total (46% women) including 0.2% international students from 2 foreign countries. *Undergraduate faculty:* 145. *Library holdings:* 195,059 books, 9,925 current serial subscriptions, 5,180 audiovisual materials. *Total majors:* 27.
Information for International Students For fall 2006: 129 international students applied, 13 were accepted. Students can start in fall, winter, or spring. *Admission tests:* Required: SAT or ACT, TOEFL (minimum score: paper-based 500; computer-based 267). TOEFL can be waived under certain conditions. *Application deadline:* 3/1. *Expenses:* (2006–07) $28,080; room and board, $7602 (on campus); room only, $4442 (on campus). *Financial aid:* Need-based college/university scholarships/grants from institutional funds. Non-need-based loans from outside sources, on-campus employment. Forms required: International Student's Certification of Finances. For fall 2006 (estimated), 1 international student on campus received college administered financial aid ($34,682 average). *Housing:* Guaranteed. *Contact:* Assistant Director of Admission, Washington & Jefferson College, 60 South Lincoln Street, Washington, PA 15301. Telephone: 724-223-6025. Fax: 724-223-6534. E-mail: radkins@washjeff.edu. URL: http://www.washjeff.edu.

WAYNESBURG COLLEGE, WAYNESBURG

General Information Independent, coed institution, affiliated with Presbyterian Church (U.S.A.). Small town setting. *Awards:* A, B, M. *Entrance level for U.S. students:* Moderately difficult. *Enrollment:* 2,159 total; 1,616 undergraduates (62% women) including international students from 4 foreign countries. *Faculty:* 135. *Library holdings:* 100,000 books, 1,189 current serial subscriptions. *Total majors:* 50.
Information for International Students For fall 2006: 3 international students applied, 3 were accepted, 3 enrolled. Students can start in fall, spring, or summer. Transfers accepted from institutions abroad. *Admission tests:* Required: TOEFL (minimum score: paper-based 550; computer-based 213). Recommended: SAT or ACT, ELS. *Application deadline:* Rolling. *Expenses:* (2006–07) $15,780; room and board, $6370 (on campus); room only, $3250 (on campus). *Housing:* Guaranteed. *Services:* International student adviser on campus. Full-time ESL program on campus. ESL program available during the summer. *Contact:* Vice President, Enrollment, Waynesburg College, 51 West College Street, Waynesburg, PA 15370. Telephone: 412-852-3333. Fax: 412-627-8124. E-mail: rlking@waynesburg.edu. URL: http://www.waynesburg.edu.

WEST CHESTER UNIVERSITY OF PENNSYLVANIA, WEST CHESTER

General Information State-supported, coed institution. Suburban setting. *Awards:* B, M. *Entrance level for U.S. students:* Moderately difficult. *Enrollment:* 12,882 total; 10,821 undergraduates (62% women) including 0.3% international students. *Faculty:* 806. *Library holdings:* 752,451 books, 7,755 current serial subscriptions, 76,530 audiovisual materials. *Total majors:* 76. *Expenses:* (2006–07) $13,853; room and board, $6342 (on campus); room only, $4220 (on campus). *Financial aid:* Non-need financial aid available. 26 international students on campus received college administered financial aid ($3044 average).

WIDENER UNIVERSITY, CHESTER

General Information Independent, coed institution. Suburban setting. *Awards:* A, B, M, D, FP. *Entrance level for U.S. students:* Moderately difficult. *Enrollment:* 6,460 total; 3,220 undergraduates (58% women) including 1% international students from 17 foreign countries. *Faculty:* 587. *Library holdings:* 223,827 books, 2,276 current serial subscriptions. *Total majors:* 72.
Information for International Students For fall 2006: 185 international students applied, 85 were accepted, 20 enrolled. Students can start in fall, spring, or summer. Transfers accepted from institutions abroad. *Admission tests:* Required: TOEFL (minimum score: iBT 60; paper-based 500; computer-based 173). Recommended: SAT or ACT, IELTS. TOEFL can be waived under certain conditions. *Application deadline:* Rolling. *Expenses:* (2006–07) $26,750; room and board, $9640 (on campus); room only, $4800 (on campus). *Financial aid:* Non-need-based college/university scholarships/grants from institutional funds. Forms required: International Student's Certification of Finances.

International transfer students are eligible to apply for aid. For fall 2006 (estimated), 2 international students on campus received college administered financial aid ($5150 average). *Housing:* Guaranteed, also available during summer. *Services:* International student adviser on campus. Full-time and part-time ESL programs on campus. ESL program available during the academic year and the summer. Internships and employment opportunities (on-campus and off-campus) available. *Contact:* Coordinator of International Admissions, Widener University, One University Place, Chester, PA 19013-5792. Telephone: 610-499-4595. Fax: 610-499-4676. E-mail: eshyde@widener.edu. URL: http://www.widener.edu.

See In-Depth Description on page 249.

WILKES UNIVERSITY, WILKES-BARRE

General Information Independent, coed institution. Urban setting. *Awards:* B, M, FP. *Entrance level for U.S. students:* Moderately difficult. *Enrollment:* 4,777 total; 2,245 undergraduates (52% women) including 1% international students from 9 foreign countries. *Faculty:* 345. *Total majors:* 37.
Information for International Students Students can start in fall, spring, or summer. Transfers accepted from institutions abroad. *Admission tests:* Required: TOEFL (minimum score: paper-based 500; computer-based 173). Recommended: SAT or ACT. *Application deadline:* 6/15. *Expenses:* (2006–07) $22,990; room and board, $9860 (on campus); room only, $5940 (on campus). *Financial aid:* Non-need financial aid available. Forms required: institution's own financial aid form. *Housing:* Guaranteed, also available during summer. *Services:* International student adviser on campus. Employment opportunities (on-campus) available. *Contact:* Associate Dean, Wilkes University, 84 West South Street, Wilkes-Barre, PA 18766. Telephone: 570-408-4107. Fax: 570-408-7811. E-mail: barbara.king@wilkes.edu. URL: http://www.wilkes.edu.

WILSON COLLEGE, CHAMBERSBURG

General Information Independent, 4-year, women's college, affiliated with Presbyterian Church (U.S.A.). Small town setting. *Awards:* A, B. *Entrance level for U.S. students:* Moderately difficult. *Enrollment:* 770 total; 765 undergraduates including 7% international students from 15 foreign countries. *Undergraduate faculty:* 77. *Library holdings:* 177,191 books, 312 current serial subscriptions. *Total majors:* 23.
Information for International Students For fall 2006: 83 international students applied, 63 were accepted, 26 enrolled. Students can start in fall, spring, or summer. Transfers accepted from institutions abroad. *Admission tests:* Required: TOEFL (minimum score: iBT 61; paper-based 500; computer-based 173; minimum score for ESL admission: iBT 61; paper-based 500; computer-based 173), IELTS. Recommended: SAT or ACT. TOEFL can be waived under certain conditions. *Application deadline:* 5/20. *Expenses:* (2006–07) $21,830; room and board, $7916 (on campus); room only, $4078 (on campus). *Financial aid:* Need-based college/university scholarships/grants from institutional funds, loans from outside sources, on-campus employment. Non-need-based college/university scholarships/grants from institutional funds. Forms required: International Student's Financial Aid Application, International Student's Certification of Finances. International transfer students are eligible to apply for aid. For fall 2006 (estimated), 18 international students on campus received college administered financial aid ($16,511 average). *Housing:* Guaranteed, also available during summer. *Services:* International student adviser on campus. Full-time and part-time ESL programs on campus. ESL program available during the academic year and the summer. Internships and employment opportunities (on-campus) available. *Contact:* Associate Dean of Enrollment, Office of Admissions, Wilson College, 1015 Philadelphia Avenue, Chambersburg, PA 17201. Telephone: 717-262-2002. Fax: 717-262-2546. E-mail: admissions@wilson.edu. URL: http://www.wilson.edu.

YORK COLLEGE OF PENNSYLVANIA, YORK

General Information Independent, coed institution. Suburban setting. *Awards:* A, B, M. *Entrance level for U.S. students:* Moderately difficult. *Enrollment:* 5,664 total; 5,367 undergraduates (57% women) including 0.3% international students. *Faculty:* 427. *Library holdings:* 300,000 books, 1,400 current serial subscriptions. *Total majors:* 59.
Information for International Students For fall 2006: 27 international students applied, 15 were accepted, 7 enrolled. Students can start in fall or spring. Transfers accepted from institutions abroad. *Admission tests:* Required: TOEFL (minimum score: iBT 72; paper-based 530; computer-based 200; minimum score for ESL admission: paper-based 530; computer-based 200). Recommended: SAT or ACT, IELTS. TOEFL can be waived under certain conditions. *Application deadline:* 5/1. *Expenses:* (2006–07) $11,160; room and board, $6950 (on campus); room only, $3900 (on

campus). *Financial aid:* Non-need-based college/university scholarships/grants from institutional funds. For fall 2006 (estimated), 5 international students on campus received college administered financial aid ($500 average). *Housing:* Guaranteed. *Services:* International student adviser on campus. Internships and employment opportunities (on-campus) available. *Contact:* Associate Director of Admissions, York College of Pennsylvania, Country Club Road, York, PA 17405-7199. Telephone: 717-815-1786. Fax: 717-849-1607. E-mail: iramirez@ycp.edu. URL: http://www.ycp.edu.

PUERTO RICO

CARLOS ALBIZU UNIVERSITY, SAN JUAN
General Information Independent, coed institution. *Awards:* B, M, D. *Entrance level for U.S. students:* Difficulty N/R. *Enrollment:* 857 total; 166 undergraduates.

COLEGIO UNIVERSITARIO DE SAN JUAN, SAN JUAN
General Information City-supported, primarily 2-year, coed college. Urban setting. *Awards:* A, B. *Entrance level for U.S. students:* Noncompetitive. *Enrollment:* 777 total (47% women). *Undergraduate faculty:* 70. *Library holdings:* 14,298 books, 39 current serial subscriptions, 199 audiovisual materials. *Total majors:* 7.
Information for International Students Students can start in fall or winter. *Application deadline:* 5/31. *Expenses:* (2006–07) $3280; room and board, $4850 (on campus); room only, $1500 (on campus). *Financial aid:* Forms required: institution's own financial aid form, FAFSA. Employment opportunities (on-campus and off-campus) available. *Contact:* Dean of Students Affairs, Colegio Universitario de San Juan, 180 Jose Oliver Street, San Juan, PR 00918, Puerto Rico. Telephone: 787-250-7375. Fax: 787-250-7395. E-mail: vpagan01@sanjuancapital.com. URL: http://www.cunisanjuan.edu.

UNIVERSIDAD ADVENTISTA DE LAS ANTILLAS, MAYAGÜEZ
General Information Independent Seventh-day Adventist, coed institution. Rural setting. *Awards:* A, B, M. *Entrance level for U.S. students:* Minimally difficult. *Enrollment:* 889 total; 818 undergraduates (60% women) including 6% international students from 20 foreign countries. *Faculty:* 59. *Library holdings:* 86,465 books, 452 current serial subscriptions. *Total majors:* 24. *Expenses:* (2006–07) $4910; room and board, $2600 (on campus); room only, $800 (on campus). *Financial aid:* Non-need financial aid available. Forms required: institution's own financial aid form. 42 international students on campus received college administered financial aid ($2000 average).

UNIVERSITY OF PHOENIX–PUERTO RICO CAMPUS, GUAYNABO
General Information Proprietary, coed institution. Urban setting. *Awards:* B, M (courses conducted at 121 campuses and learning centers in 25 states). *Entrance level for U.S. students:* Noncompetitive. *Enrollment:* 2,853 total; 1,113 undergraduates (52% women) including 2% international students. *Faculty:* 65. *Library holdings:* 1,756 books, 692 current serial subscriptions. *Total majors:* 2. *Expenses:* (2006–07) $5880.

UNIVERSITY OF PUERTO RICO AT PONCE, PONCE
General Information Commonwealth-supported, 4-year, coed college. Urban setting. *Awards:* A, B. *Entrance level for U.S. students:* Moderately difficult. *Enrollment:* 3,486 total (66% women). *Undergraduate faculty:* 182. *Library holdings:* 53,000 books, 1,643 current serial subscriptions. *Total majors:* 13. *Expenses:* (2006–07) $3304.

UNIVERSITY OF PUERTO RICO, MAYAGÜEZ CAMPUS, MAYAGÜEZ
General Information Commonwealth-supported, coed university. Urban setting. *Awards:* B, M, D. *Entrance level for U.S. students:* Moderately difficult. *Enrollment:* 12,380 total; 11,305 undergraduates (50% women) including 0.2% international students from 21 foreign countries. *Faculty:* 766. *Library holdings:* 921,392 books, 590,716 current serial subscriptions. *Total majors:* 62. *Expenses:* (2007–08) $3341. *Financial aid:* Non-need-based tuition waivers, athletic awards, on-campus employment.

UNIVERSITY OF PUERTO RICO, RÍO PIEDRAS, SAN JUAN
General Information Commonwealth-supported, coed university. Urban setting. *Awards:* B, M, D, FP. *Entrance level for U.S.

students:* Very difficult. *Enrollment:* 20,528 total; 16,445 undergraduates (67% women) including 0.02% international students from 9 foreign countries. *Faculty:* 1,431. *Library holdings:* 1.8 million books, 5,599 current serial subscriptions, 5,599 audiovisual materials. *Total majors:* 68. *Expenses:* (2007–08) $3336; room and board, $4940 (on campus).

RHODE ISLAND

BROWN UNIVERSITY, PROVIDENCE
General Information Independent, coed university. Urban setting. *Awards:* B, M, D, FP. *Entrance level for U.S. students:* Most difficult. *Enrollment:* 8,125 total; 6,010 undergraduates (52% women) including 6% international students from 72 foreign countries. *Faculty:* 824. *Library holdings:* 3 million books, 17,000 current serial subscriptions. *Total majors:* 76. *Expenses:* (2006–07) $34,620; room and board, $9134 (on campus); room only, $5690 (on campus). *Financial aid:* Need-based college/university scholarships/grants from institutional funds, on-campus employment. Forms required: International Student's Financial Aid Application, International Student's Certification of Finances. 110 international students on campus received college administered financial aid ($35,161 average).

BRYANT UNIVERSITY, SMITHFIELD
General Information Independent, coed institution. Suburban setting. *Awards:* B, M. *Entrance level for U.S. students:* Moderately difficult. *Enrollment:* 3,651 total; 3,268 undergraduates (42% women) including 2% international students from 32 foreign countries. *Faculty:* 283. *Library holdings:* 143,393 books, 26,451 current serial subscriptions, 1,208 audiovisual materials. *Total majors:* 16.
Information for International Students For fall 2006: 233 international students applied, 111 were accepted, 42 enrolled. Students can start in fall or spring. Transfers accepted from institutions abroad. *Admission tests:* Required: SAT, SAT or ACT. Recommended: TOEFL (minimum score: iBT 80; paper-based 550; computer-based 213; minimum score for ESL admission: iBT 65; paper-based 520; computer-based 203). TOEFL can be waived under certain conditions. *Application deadline:* 2/1. *Expenses:* (2007–08) $27,639; room and board, $10,715 (on campus); room only, $6414 (on campus). *Financial aid:* Non-need-based college/university scholarships/grants from institutional funds, athletic awards, loans from outside sources, on-campus employment. Forms required: financial aid forms not recorded; not applicable. For fall 2006 (estimated), 31 international students on campus received college administered financial aid ($12,713 average). *Housing:* Guaranteed, also available during summer. *Services:* International student adviser on campus. ESL program at cooperating institution. ESL program available during the academic year. Internships and employment opportunities (on-campus and off-campus) available. *Contact:* Associate Director for International Admission, Bryant University, 1150 Douglas Pike, Smithfield, RI 02917. Telephone: 401-232-6107. Fax: 401-232-6741. E-mail: jeriksen@bryant.edu. URL: http://www.bryant.edu.
See In-Depth Description on page 44.

JOHNSON & WALES UNIVERSITY, PROVIDENCE
General Information Independent, coed institution. Urban setting. *Awards:* A, B, M, D (branch locations in Charleston, SC; Denver, CO; North Miami, FL; Norfolk, VA; Gothenberg, Sweden). *Entrance level for U.S. students:* Minimally difficult. *Enrollment:* 10,310 total; 9,349 undergraduates (52% women) including 4% international students from 78 foreign countries. *Faculty:* 417. *Library holdings:* 104,327 books, 415 current serial subscriptions, 3,687 audiovisual materials. *Total majors:* 38.
Information for International Students For fall 2006: 3000 international students applied, 2000 were accepted, 400 enrolled. Students can start in fall, winter, spring, or summer. Transfers accepted from institutions abroad. *Admission tests:* Required: TOEFL (minimum score: paper-based 550; computer-based 210; minimum score for ESL admission: paper-based 550; computer-based 210). *Application deadline:* Rolling. *Expenses:* (2007–08) $21,462; room and board, $7650 (on campus). *Financial aid:* Non-need-based college/university scholarships/grants from institutional funds. Forms required: International Student's Certification of Finances. International transfer students are eligible to apply for aid. For fall 2005, 206 international students on campus received college administered financial aid ($2723 average). *Services:* International student adviser on campus. Full-time ESL program on campus. ESL program available during the academic year and the summer. Internships and employment opportunities (on-campus) available. *Contact:* Director of International

Johnson & Wales University (continued)

Operations, Johnson & Wales University, 8 Abbott Park Place, Providence, RI 02903. Telephone: 401-598-1074. Fax: 401-598-4773. E-mail: intladm@jwu.edu. URL: http://www.jwu.edu.

See In-Depth Description on page 107.

NEW ENGLAND INSTITUTE OF TECHNOLOGY, WARWICK

General Information Independent, primarily 2-year, coed college. Suburban setting. *Awards:* A, B. *Entrance level for U.S. students:* Noncompetitive. *Enrollment:* 2,839 total including 6% international students from 22 foreign countries. *Undergraduate faculty:* 223. *Library holdings:* 42,614 books, 3,961 current serial subscriptions. *Total majors:* 17.

Information for International Students For fall 2006: 95 international students applied, 95 were accepted, 81 enrolled. Students can start in fall, winter, spring, or summer. Transfers accepted from institutions abroad. *Admission tests:* Required: on-site ACCUPLACER Online. *Application deadline:* Rolling. *Expenses:* (2006–07) $16,375. *Financial aid:* Forms required: International Student's Certification of Finances. *Services:* International student adviser on campus. *Contact:* Director of International Admissions, New England Institute of Technology, 2500 Post Road, Warwick, RI 02886. Telephone: 401-739-5000 Ext. 3489. Fax: 401-738-7122. E-mail: mseltzer@neit.edu. URL: http://www.neit.edu.

See In-Depth Description on page 137.

PROVIDENCE COLLEGE, PROVIDENCE

General Information Independent Roman Catholic, coed institution. Suburban setting. *Awards:* A, B, M. *Entrance level for U.S. students:* Very difficult. *Enrollment:* 4,835 total; 3,998 undergraduates (56% women) including 1% international students from 16 foreign countries. *Faculty:* 379. *Library holdings:* 567,761 books, 26,766 current serial subscriptions. *Total majors:* 39. *Expenses:* (2006–07) $27,345; room and board, $9765 (on campus); room only, $5365 (on campus). *Financial aid:* Non-need-based college/university scholarships/grants from institutional funds, athletic awards. Forms required: International Student's Certification of Finances. 33 international students on campus received college administered financial aid ($32,600 average).

RHODE ISLAND COLLEGE, PROVIDENCE

General Information State-supported, coed institution. Suburban setting. *Awards:* B, M, D. *Entrance level for U.S. students:* Difficulty N/R. *Enrollment:* 8,939 total; 7,581 undergraduates (67% women) including 0.5% international students from 5 foreign countries. *Faculty:* 696. *Library holdings:* 664,667 books, 2,251 current serial subscriptions. *Total majors:* 67. *Expenses:* (2006–07) $12,888; room and board, $7560 (on campus); room only, $4000 (on campus).

RHODE ISLAND SCHOOL OF DESIGN, PROVIDENCE

General Information Independent, coed institution. Urban setting. *Awards:* B, M, FP. *Entrance level for U.S. students:* Very difficult. *Enrollment:* 2,259 total; 1,863 undergraduates (66% women) including 15% international students from 49 foreign countries. *Faculty:* 503. *Library holdings:* 130,000 books, 400 current serial subscriptions. *Total majors:* 16. *Expenses:* (2007–08) $33,118; room and board, $9860 (on campus); room only, $5630 (on campus).

ROGER WILLIAMS UNIVERSITY, BRISTOL

General Information Independent, coed institution. Small town setting. *Awards:* A, B, M, FP. *Entrance level for U.S. students:* Moderately difficult. *Enrollment:* 5,172 total; 4,348 undergraduates (49% women) including 2% international students from 39 foreign countries. *Faculty:* 464. *Library holdings:* 216,424 books, 1,332 current serial subscriptions, 2,728 audiovisual materials. *Total majors:* 47.

Information for International Students Students can start in fall or spring. Transfers accepted from institutions abroad. *Admission tests:* Recommended: SAT, TOEFL. TOEFL can be waived under certain conditions. *Application deadline:* Rolling. *Expenses:* (2007–08) $25,759; room and board, $10,943 (on campus); room only, $5819 (on campus). *Financial aid:* Non-need-based college/university scholarships/grants from institutional funds. Forms required: International Student's Certification of Finances. For fall 2005, 30 international students on campus received college administered financial aid ($10,058 average). *Services:* International student adviser on campus. Full-time ESL program on campus. ESL program available during the academic year and the summer. Internships and employment opportunities (on-campus) available. *Contact:* Director of International and Transfer Admission, Roger Williams University, Bristol, RI

02809-2921. Telephone: 401-254-3500. Fax: 401-254-3557. E-mail: intadmit@rwu.edu. URL: http://www.rwu.edu.

See In-Depth Description on page 161.

SALVE REGINA UNIVERSITY, NEWPORT

General Information Independent Roman Catholic, coed institution. Suburban setting. *Awards:* A, B, M, D. *Entrance level for U.S. students:* Moderately difficult. *Enrollment:* 2,589 total; 2,090 undergraduates (71% women) including 1% international students from 12 foreign countries. *Faculty:* 252. *Library holdings:* 139,161 books, 1,221 current serial subscriptions. *Total majors:* 47. *Expenses:* (2006–07) $25,175; room and board, $9800 (on campus). *Financial aid:* Non-need-based college/university scholarships/grants from institutional funds, on-campus employment. Forms required: International Student's Financial Aid Application, International Student's Certification of Finances. For fall 2006 (estimated), 3 international students on campus received college administered financial aid ($24,300 average).

UNIVERSITY OF RHODE ISLAND, KINGSTON

General Information State-supported, coed university. Small town setting. *Awards:* B, M, D, FP. *Entrance level for U.S. students:* Moderately difficult. *Enrollment:* 15,062 total; 11,875 undergraduates (56% women) including 0.3% international students. *Faculty:* 706. *Library holdings:* 1.2 million books, 7,926 current serial subscriptions, 11,671 audiovisual materials. *Total majors:* 76.

Information for International Students For fall 2006: 157 international students applied, 71 were accepted, 10 enrolled. Students can start in fall or spring. Transfers accepted from institutions abroad. *Admission tests:* Required: SAT or ACT, TOEFL (minimum score: iBT 79; paper-based 550; computer-based 213). *Application deadline:* 3/1. *Expenses:* (2006–07) $21,424; room and board, $8466 (on campus); room only, $4814 (on campus). *Housing:* Available during summer. *Services:* International student adviser on campus. Internships and employment opportunities (on-campus and off-campus) available. *Contact:* Admission Advisor, University of Rhode Island, 14 Upper College Road, Kingston, RI 02881. Telephone: 401-874-7113. Fax: 401-874-5523. E-mail: nancys@uri.edu. URL: http://www.uri.edu.

SOUTH CAROLINA

BENEDICT COLLEGE, COLUMBIA

General Information Independent Baptist, 4-year, coed college. Urban setting. *Awards:* B. *Entrance level for U.S. students:* Minimally difficult. *Enrollment:* 3,005 total (50% women). *Undergraduate faculty:* 168. *Library holdings:* 114,770 books, 320 current serial subscriptions, 5,954 audiovisual materials. *Total majors:* 33.

Information for International Students For fall 2006: 72 international students were accepted, 72 enrolled. Students can start in fall, spring, or summer. Transfers accepted from institutions abroad. *Admission tests:* Required: SAT or ACT, TOEFL (minimum score: iBT 30; paper-based 500; computer-based 300; minimum score for ESL admission: paper-based 500; computer-based 300). Recommended: ELS. *Application deadline:* Rolling. *Expenses:* (2006–07) $13,602; room and board, $6256 (on campus). *Services:* International student adviser on campus. ESL program at cooperating institution. ESL program available during the academic year. *Contact:* Vice President, Institutional Effectiveness, Office of Enrollment Management, Benedict College, 1600 Harden Street, Columbia, SC 29204. Telephone: 803-705-4559. Fax: 803-253-5215. E-mail: knightg@benedict.edu. URL: http://www.benedict.edu.

CENTRAL CAROLINA TECHNICAL COLLEGE, SUMTER

General Information State-supported, 2-year, coed college. Small town setting. *Awards:* A. *Entrance level for U.S. students:* Noncompetitive. *Enrollment:* 3,244 total (70% women) including 0.2% international students. *Undergraduate faculty:* 180. *Library holdings:* 20,356 books, 245 current serial subscriptions. *Total majors:* 17. *Expenses:* (2006–07) $5181. *Financial aid:* Forms required: institution's own financial aid form.

CHARLESTON SOUTHERN UNIVERSITY, CHARLESTON

General Information Independent Baptist, coed institution. Suburban setting. *Awards:* B, M. *Entrance level for U.S. students:* Moderately difficult. *Enrollment:* 3,224 total; 2,769 undergraduates (62% women) including 2% international students from 21 foreign countries. *Faculty:* 178. *Library holdings:* 192,600 books, 1,111 current serial subscriptions. *Total majors:* 73. *Expenses:* (2006–07) $16,780; room and board, $6450 (on campus). *Financial aid:* Non-need financial aid available.

CLAFLIN UNIVERSITY, ORANGEBURG
General Information Independent United Methodist, coed institution. Small town setting. *Awards:* B, M. *Entrance level for U.S. students:* Minimally difficult. *Enrollment:* 1,758 total; 1,674 undergraduates (68% women) including 4% international students from 13 foreign countries. *Faculty:* 148. *Library holdings:* 160,006 books, 461 current serial subscriptions, 1,619 audiovisual materials. *Total majors:* 31.

Information for International Students For fall 2006: 10 international students enrolled. Students can start in fall or spring. Transfers accepted from institutions abroad. *Admission tests:* Required: SAT or ACT, TOEFL (minimum score: paper-based 500; computer-based 213). Recommended: SAT. TOEFL can be waived under certain conditions. *Application deadline:* 4/1. *Expenses:* (2006–07) $11,764; room and board, $6322 (on campus); room only, $2816 (on campus). *Financial aid:* Non-need financial aid available. Forms required: institution's own financial aid form. *Housing:* Guaranteed, also available during summer. *Services:* International student adviser on campus. Internships and employment opportunities (on-campus) available. *Contact:* International/Transfer Admissions Counselor, Claflin University, 400 Magnolia Street, Orangeburg, SC 29115. Telephone: 803-535-5637. Fax: 803-535-5385. E-mail: msingleton@claflin.edu. URL: http://www.claflin.edu.

CLEMSON UNIVERSITY, CLEMSON
General Information State-supported, coed university. Small town setting. *Awards:* B, M, D. *Entrance level for U.S. students:* Moderately difficult. *Enrollment:* 17,165 total; 14,096 undergraduates (46% women) including 1% international students from 84 foreign countries. *Faculty:* 1,178. *Library holdings:* 1.2 million books, 5,587 current serial subscriptions. *Total majors:* 77. *Expenses:* (2006–07) $20,292; room and board, $5874 (on campus); room only, $3500 (on campus).

COASTAL CAROLINA UNIVERSITY, CONWAY
General Information State-supported, coed institution. Suburban setting. *Awards:* B, M. *Entrance level for U.S. students:* Moderately difficult. *Enrollment:* 8,049 total; 6,660 undergraduates (53% women) including 2% international students from 32 foreign countries. *Faculty:* 443. *Library holdings:* 149,990 books, 14,771 current serial subscriptions, 4,712 audiovisual materials. *Total majors:* 31.

Information for International Students For fall 2006: 63 international students applied, 48 were accepted, 33 enrolled. Students can start in fall or spring. Transfers accepted from institutions abroad. *Admission tests:* Required: TOEFL (minimum score: paper-based 500; computer-based 173). Recommended: SAT or ACT. TOEFL can be waived under certain conditions. *Application deadline:* 8/1. *Expenses:* (2006–07) $16,190; room and board, $6690 (on campus); room only, $4220 (on campus). *Financial aid:* Non-need-based college/university scholarships/grants from institutional funds, tuition waivers, athletic awards, loans from outside sources, institutional work study. Forms required: International Student's Certification of Finances. International transfer students are eligible to apply for aid. For fall 2005, 67 international students on campus received college administered financial aid ($13,522 average). *Housing:* Guaranteed, also available during summer. *Services:* International student adviser on campus. Employment opportunities (on-campus) available. *Contact:* Director, International Programs, Office of International Programs, Coastal Carolina University, PO Box 261954, Conway, SC 29528-6054. Telephone: 843-349-2054. Fax: 843-349-2252. E-mail: parsons@coastal.edu. URL: http://www.coastal.edu.

COLLEGE OF CHARLESTON, CHARLESTON
General Information State-supported, coed institution. Urban setting. *Awards:* B, M (also offers graduate degree programs through University of Charleston, South Carolina). *Entrance level for U.S. students:* Moderately difficult. *Enrollment:* 11,218 total; 9,820 undergraduates (64% women) including 2% international students from 74 foreign countries. *Faculty:* 895. *Library holdings:* 701,774 books, 4,099 current serial subscriptions, 6,938 audiovisual materials. *Total majors:* 43. *Expenses:* (2006–07) $16,800; room and board, $7596 (on campus); room only, $5216 (on campus).

COLUMBIA COLLEGE, COLUMBIA
General Information Independent United Methodist, undergraduate: women only; graduate: coed institution. Suburban setting. *Awards:* B, M. *Entrance level for U.S. students:* Moderately difficult. *Enrollment:* 1,446 total; 1,143 undergraduates (98% women) including 2% international students from 17 foreign

countries. *Faculty:* 165. *Library holdings:* 146,135 books, 28,391 current serial subscriptions, 7,804 audiovisual materials. *Total majors:* 39. *Expenses:* (2006–07) $20,302; room and board, $6022 (on campus); room only, $3140 (on campus). *Financial aid:* Non-need-based college/university scholarships/grants from institutional funds, on-campus employment. Forms required: International Student's Financial Aid Application. For fall 2005, 5 international students on campus received college administered financial aid ($7312 average).

COLUMBIA INTERNATIONAL UNIVERSITY, COLUMBIA
General Information Independent nondenominational, coed institution. Suburban setting. *Awards:* A, B, M, D, FP. *Entrance level for U.S. students:* Minimally difficult. *Enrollment:* 959 total; 471 undergraduates (56% women) including 2% international students from 5 foreign countries. *Faculty:* 39. *Library holdings:* 144,388 books, 47,758 current serial subscriptions, 18,983 audiovisual materials. *Total majors:* 15. *Expenses:* (2006–07) $14,400; room and board, $5712 (on campus). *Financial aid:* Need-based college/university scholarships/grants from institutional funds, on-campus employment. Non-need-based college/university scholarships/grants from institutional funds, on-campus employment. Forms required: institution's own financial aid form, International Student's Certification of Finances. 32 international students on campus received college administered financial aid ($2002 average).

CONVERSE COLLEGE, SPARTANBURG
General Information Independent, undergraduate: women only; graduate: coed institution. Urban setting. *Awards:* B, M. *Entrance level for U.S. students:* Moderately difficult. *Enrollment:* 1,977 total; 752 undergraduates (100% women) including 4% international students from 8 foreign countries. *Faculty:* 174. *Library holdings:* 150,817 books, 19,808 current serial subscriptions, 20,515 audiovisual materials. *Total majors:* 40. *Expenses:* (2006–07) $22,234; room and board, $6848 (on campus). *Financial aid:* Need-based college/university scholarships/grants from institutional funds, athletic awards. Non-need-based college/university scholarships/grants from institutional funds, athletic awards. Forms required: International Student's Financial Aid Application, International Student's Certification of Finances. For fall 2006 (estimated), 34 international students on campus received college administered financial aid ($17,403 average).

ERSKINE COLLEGE, DUE WEST
General Information Independent, 4-year, coed college, affiliated with Associate Reformed Presbyterian Church. Rural setting. *Awards:* B, M, D, FP. *Entrance level for U.S. students:* Moderately difficult. *Enrollment:* 925 total; 601 undergraduates (55% women) including 2% international students from 8 foreign countries. *Faculty:* 68. *Library holdings:* 264,053 books, 1,045 current serial subscriptions, 1,907 audiovisual materials. *Total majors:* 30. *Expenses:* (2006–07) $20,275; room and board, $6951 (on campus). *Financial aid:* Need-based and non-need-based financial aid available. Forms required: institution's own financial aid form, International Student's Certification of Finances.

FRANCIS MARION UNIVERSITY, FLORENCE
General Information State-supported, coed institution. Rural setting. *Awards:* B, M. *Entrance level for U.S. students:* Moderately difficult. *Enrollment:* 4,075 total; 3,514 undergraduates (67% women) including 1% international students from 13 foreign countries. *Faculty:* 272. *Library holdings:* 396,204 books, 1,504 current serial subscriptions, 9,297 audiovisual materials. *Total majors:* 30. *Expenses:* (2006–07) $12,839; room and board, $5430 (on campus); room only, $2960 (on campus). *Financial aid:* Non-need-based college/university scholarships/grants from institutional funds, tuition waivers, athletic awards, loans from outside sources, on-campus employment. Forms required: institution's own financial aid form. For fall 2005, 7 international students on campus received college administered financial aid.

FURMAN UNIVERSITY, GREENVILLE
General Information Independent, coed institution. Suburban setting. *Awards:* B, M. *Entrance level for U.S. students:* Very difficult. *Enrollment:* 3,010 total; 2,759 undergraduates (56% women) including 2% international students from 41 foreign countries. *Faculty:* 274. *Library holdings:* 453,211 books, 2,052 current serial subscriptions. *Total majors:* 48.

Information for International Students For fall 2006: 103 international students applied, 13 were accepted, 10 enrolled. Students can start in fall, winter, or spring. Transfers accepted from institutions abroad. *Admission tests:* Required: SAT or ACT, TOEFL (minimum score: paper-based 570; computer-based 230; minimum score for ESL admission: paper-based 570; computer-based 230). TOEFL can be waived under certain

Furman University (continued)

conditions. *Application deadline:* 1/15. *Expenses:* (2006–07) $28,840; room and board, $7552 (on campus); room only, $3968 (on campus). *Financial aid:* Need-based college/university scholarships/grants from institutional funds, athletic awards, on-campus employment. Non-need-based college/university scholarships/grants from institutional funds, athletic awards, on-campus employment. Forms required: institution's own financial aid form, International Student's Certification of Finances. International transfer students are eligible to apply for aid. For fall 2006 (estimated), 33 international students on campus received college administered financial aid ($31,408 average). *Housing:* Guaranteed, also available during summer. *Services:* International student adviser on campus. Internships and employment opportunities (on-campus and off-campus) available. *Contact:* Director of Admissions, Furman University, 3300 Poinsett Highway, Greenville, SC 29613. Telephone: 864-294-2034. Fax: 864-294-2018. E-mail: admissions@furman.edu. URL: http://www.furman.edu.

GREENVILLE TECHNICAL COLLEGE, GREENVILLE

General Information State-supported, 2-year, coed college. Urban setting. *Awards:* A. *Entrance level for U.S. students:* Noncompetitive. *Enrollment:* 13,000 total including international students from 6 foreign countries. *Undergraduate faculty:* 478. *Library holdings:* 49,500 books, 658 current serial subscriptions. *Total majors:* 33.

HORRY-GEORGETOWN TECHNICAL COLLEGE, CONWAY

General Information State and locally supported, 2-year, coed college. Small town setting. *Awards:* A. *Entrance level for U.S. students:* Difficulty N/R. *Enrollment:* 5,362 total (66% women) including 2% international students from 22 foreign countries. *Undergraduate faculty:* 404. *Total majors:* 25. *Expenses:* (2006–07) $4408.

LANDER UNIVERSITY, GREENWOOD

General Information State-supported, coed institution. Small town setting. *Awards:* B, M. *Entrance level for U.S. students:* Moderately difficult. *Enrollment:* 2,682 total; 2,642 undergraduates (66% women) including 2% international students from 20 foreign countries. *Faculty:* 190. *Library holdings:* 186,690 books, 657 current serial subscriptions. *Total majors:* 25.

Information for International Students For fall 2006: 53 international students enrolled. Students can start in fall, spring, or summer. Transfers accepted from institutions abroad. *Admission tests:* Required: SAT or ACT, TOEFL (minimum score: paper-based 550; computer-based 213). *Application deadline:* Rolling. *Expenses:* (2006–07) $13,848; room and board, $5554 (on campus); room only, $3940 (on campus). *Financial aid:* Non-need financial aid available. 23 international students on campus received college administered financial aid ($2340 average). *Housing:* Available during summer. *Services:* International student adviser on campus. Internships and employment opportunities (on-campus) available. *Contact:* Director of Admissions, Office of Admissions, Lander University, 320 Stanley Avenue, Greenwood, SC 29649. Telephone: 864-388-8307. Fax: 864-388-8125. E-mail: jreece@lander.edu. URL: http://www.lander.edu.

LIMESTONE COLLEGE, GAFFNEY

General Information Independent, 4-year, coed college. Suburban setting. *Awards:* A, B. *Entrance level for U.S. students:* Moderately difficult. *Enrollment:* 728 total (43% women) including 4% international students from 8 foreign countries. *Undergraduate faculty:* 65. *Library holdings:* 105,551 books, 253 current serial subscriptions, 1,284 audiovisual materials. *Total majors:* 45.

Information for International Students For fall 2006: 53 international students applied, 53 were accepted, 37 enrolled. Students can start in fall, spring, or summer. Transfers accepted from institutions abroad. *Admission tests:* Required: SAT or ACT, TOEFL (minimum score: paper-based 500; computer-based 173). TOEFL can be waived under certain conditions. *Application deadline:* Rolling. *Expenses:* (2007–08) $15,900; room and board, $6200 (on campus). *Financial aid:* Need-based college/university scholarships/grants from institutional funds, athletic awards, on-campus employment. Non-need-based college/university scholarships/grants from institutional funds, athletic awards. Forms required: International Student's Certification of Finances. International transfer students are eligible to apply for aid. For fall 2005, 14 international students on campus received college administered financial aid ($10,416 average). *Housing:* Available during summer. *Services:* International student adviser on campus. Employment opportunities (on-campus) available. *Contact:* Vice President for Enrollment Services, Limestone College, 1115 College

Drive, Gaffney, SC 29340-3799. Telephone: 864-488-4549. Fax: 864-487-8706. E-mail: cphenicie@limestone.edu. URL: http://www.limestone.edu.

MIDLANDS TECHNICAL COLLEGE, COLUMBIA

General Information State and locally supported, 2-year, coed college. Suburban setting. *Awards:* A. *Entrance level for U.S. students:* Minimally difficult. *Enrollment:* 10,849 total (64% women) including 0.2% international students. *Undergraduate faculty:* 692. *Library holdings:* 97,568 books, 423 current serial subscriptions. *Total majors:* 50. *Expenses:* (2007–08) $9100. *Financial aid:* Need-based financial aid available.

SOUTHERN METHODIST COLLEGE, ORANGEBURG

General Information Independent religious, 4-year, coed college. *Awards:* A, B. *Entrance level for U.S. students:* Minimally difficult. *Enrollment:* 77 total (65% women) including 1% international students from 1 foreign country. *Undergraduate faculty:* 24. *Library holdings:* 21,743 books, 60 current serial subscriptions, 171 audiovisual materials. *Total majors:* 2. *Expenses:* (2006–07) $5800; room and board, $4400 (on campus). *Financial aid:* Need-based college/university scholarships/grants from institutional funds, tuition waivers, on-campus employment, dorm supervisors receive free room and board. Forms required: institution's own financial aid form.

SOUTHERN WESLEYAN UNIVERSITY, CENTRAL

General Information Independent, coed institution, affiliated with Wesleyan Church. Small town setting. *Awards:* A, B, M. *Entrance level for U.S. students:* Minimally difficult. *Enrollment:* 2,557 total; 1,802 undergraduates (64% women) including 1% international students from 13 foreign countries. *Faculty:* 234. *Library holdings:* 109,050 books, 530 current serial subscriptions, 4,020 audiovisual materials. *Total majors:* 34. *Expenses:* (2006–07) $16,150; room and board, $5800 (on campus); room only, $2150 (on campus). *Financial aid:* Need-based college/university scholarships/grants from institutional funds, athletic awards, on-campus employment. Non-need-based college/university scholarships/grants from institutional funds, athletic awards, on-campus employment. Forms required: institution's own financial aid form. For fall 2006 (estimated), 9 international students on campus received college administered financial aid ($14,481 average).

SPARTANBURG METHODIST COLLEGE, SPARTANBURG

General Information Independent Methodist, 2-year, coed college. Urban setting. *Awards:* A. *Entrance level for U.S. students:* Moderately difficult. *Enrollment:* 779 total (51% women) including 2% international students from 6 foreign countries. *Undergraduate faculty:* 46. *Library holdings:* 75,000 books, 5,000 current serial subscriptions, 3,150 audiovisual materials. *Total majors:* 4.

Information for International Students For fall 2006: 13 international students applied, 9 were accepted, 5 enrolled. Students can start in fall or spring. *Admission tests:* Required: TOEFL (minimum score: paper-based 525; computer-based 195; minimum score for ESL admission: paper-based 450; computer-based 133). Recommended: SAT or ACT. *Application deadline:* 5/30. *Financial aid:* Need-based college/university scholarships/grants from institutional funds, athletic awards. Non-need-based college/university scholarships/grants from institutional funds, athletic awards. Forms required: International Student's Certification of Finances. International transfer students are eligible to apply for aid. *Housing:* Guaranteed, also available during summer. *Services:* International student adviser on campus. Full-time ESL program on campus. ESL program available during the academic year. *Contact:* Vice President for Enrollment Management, Spartanburg Methodist College, 1000 Powell Mill Road, Spartanburg, SC 29301-5899. Telephone: 864-587-4223. Fax: 864-587-4355. E-mail: philbed@smcsc.edu. URL: http://www.smcsc.edu.

SPARTANBURG TECHNICAL COLLEGE, SPARTANBURG

General Information State-supported, 2-year, coed college. Suburban setting. *Awards:* A. *Entrance level for U.S. students:* Noncompetitive. *Enrollment:* 4,409 total. *Library holdings:* 36,173 books, 295 current serial subscriptions, 3,534 audiovisual materials. *Total majors:* 24. *Expenses:* (2006–07) $5510. *Financial aid:* Need-based college/university scholarships/grants from institutional funds, tuition waivers, loans from outside sources, on-campus employment. Non-need-based college/university scholarships/grants from institutional funds, tuition waivers, loans from outside sources. Forms required: institution's own financial aid form.

TRIDENT TECHNICAL COLLEGE, CHARLESTON
General Information State and locally supported, 2-year, coed college. Urban setting. *Awards:* A. *Entrance level for U.S. students:* Noncompetitive. *Enrollment:* 11,808 total (63% women). *Undergraduate faculty:* 597. *Library holdings:* 68,462 books, 868 current serial subscriptions. *Total majors:* 40. *Expenses:* (2006–07) $5898. *Financial aid:* Need-based college/university scholarships/grants from institutional funds, loans from outside sources, on-campus employment. Non-need-based college/university scholarships/grants from institutional funds, tuition waivers, loans from outside sources, on-campus employment.

UNIVERSITY OF SOUTH CAROLINA, COLUMBIA
General Information State-supported, coed university. Urban setting. *Awards:* B, M, D, FT. *Entrance level for U.S. students:* Moderately difficult. *Enrollment:* 27,390 total; 18,648 undergraduates (55% women) including 1% international students from 63 foreign countries. *Faculty:* 1,673. *Library holdings:* 3.6 million books, 53,610 current serial subscriptions, 50,403 audiovisual materials. *Total majors:* 65.
Information for International Students For fall 2006: 318 international students applied, 173 were accepted, 75 enrolled. Students can start in fall, winter, spring, or summer. Transfers accepted from institutions abroad. *Admission tests:* Required: TOEFL (minimum score: iBT 77; paper-based 550; computer-based 210; minimum score for ESL admission: iBT 61; paper-based 500; computer-based 173). *Application deadline:* 12/1. *Expenses:* (2006–07) $20,236; room and board, $6520 (on campus); room only, $4003 (on campus). *Housing:* Available during summer. *Services:* International student adviser on campus. Full-time ESL program on campus. ESL program available during the academic year and the summer. Internships and employment opportunities (on-campus) available. *Contact:* Associate Director of Admissions, Office of Undergraduate Admissions, University of South Carolina, Office of Undergraduate Admissions, Columbia, SC 29208. Telephone: 803-777-7700. Fax: 803-777-0101. E-mail: scott@gwm.sc.edu. URL: http://www.sc.edu.

UNIVERSITY OF SOUTH CAROLINA AIKEN, AIKEN
General Information State-supported, coed institution. Suburban setting. *Awards:* B, M. *Entrance level for U.S. students:* Moderately difficult. *Enrollment:* 3,380 total; 3,241 undergraduates (67% women) including 2% international students from 24 foreign countries. *Faculty:* 265. *Library holdings:* 156,750 books, 700 current serial subscriptions. *Total majors:* 21. *Expenses:* (2006–07) $13,280; room and board, $6370 (on campus); room only, $3930 (on campus). *Financial aid:* Need-based financial aid available.

UNIVERSITY OF SOUTH CAROLINA SUMTER, SUMTER
General Information State-supported, 2-year, coed college. Urban setting. *Awards:* A. *Entrance level for U.S. students:* Moderately difficult. *Enrollment:* 1,020 total (61% women) including 0.1% international students from 4 foreign countries. *Undergraduate faculty:* 75. *Library holdings:* 81,114 books, 1,114 current serial subscriptions, 913 audiovisual materials. *Total majors:* 2. *Expenses:* (2006–07) $11,228. *Financial aid:* Non-need-based loans from institutional funds, loans from outside sources, on-campus employment. Forms required: institution's own financial aid form.

UNIVERSITY OF SOUTH CAROLINA UNION, UNION
General Information State-supported, 2-year, coed college. Small town setting. *Awards:* A. *Entrance level for U.S. students:* Minimally difficult. *Enrollment:* 321 total (69% women). *Undergraduate faculty:* 25. *Total majors:* 2.
Information for International Students Students can start in fall, winter, spring, or summer. Transfers accepted from institutions abroad. *Admission tests:* Required: SAT or ACT, TOEFL (minimum score: paper-based 550; computer-based 220; minimum score for ESL admission: paper-based 550; computer-based 220). *Application deadline:* Rolling. *Expenses:* (2006–07) $11,068. *Services:* ESL program at cooperating institution. *Contact:* Enrollment Manager, University of South Carolina Union, PO Drawer 729, Union, SC 29379-0729. Telephone: 864-429-8728. E-mail: tyoung@sc.edu. URL: http://uscunion.sc.edu.

UNIVERSITY OF SOUTH CAROLINA UPSTATE, SPARTANBURG
General Information State-supported, coed institution. Urban setting. *Awards:* A, B, M. *Entrance level for U.S. students:* Moderately difficult. *Enrollment:* 4,610 total; 4,574 undergraduates (66% women) including 2% international students from 34 foreign countries. *Faculty:* 374. *Library holdings:* 188,572 books, 31,460 current serial subscriptions, 6,198 audiovisual materials. *Total majors:* 20.

Information for International Students Students can start in fall, spring, or summer. Transfers accepted from institutions abroad. *Admission tests:* Required: SAT or ACT, TOEFL (minimum score: paper-based 500; computer-based 173; minimum score for ESL admission: paper-based 500; computer-based 173). *Application deadline:* 7/15. *Expenses:* (2006–07) $14,752; room and board, $5240 (on campus); room only, $3200 (on campus). *Financial aid:* Need-based loans from outside sources. Non-need-based college/university scholarships/grants from institutional funds, tuition waivers, athletic awards, loans from outside sources. International transfer students are eligible to apply for aid. For fall 2006 (estimated), 51 international students on campus received college administered financial aid ($11,011 average). *Services:* International student adviser on campus. Full-time ESL program on campus. ESL program available during the academic year. Internships and employment opportunities (on-campus) available. *Contact:* Office of Admissions, University of South Carolina Upstate, 800 University Way, Spartanburg, SC 29303. Telephone: 864-503-5280. Fax: 864-503-5727. E-mail: admissions@uscupstate.edu. URL: http://www.uscupstate.edu.
See In-Depth Description on page 224.

WINTHROP UNIVERSITY, ROCK HILL
General Information State-supported, coed institution. Suburban setting. *Awards:* B, M. *Entrance level for U.S. students:* Moderately difficult. *Enrollment:* 6,292 total; 5,111 undergraduates (69% women) including 2% international students from 51 foreign countries. *Faculty:* 543. *Library holdings:* 425,648 books, 1,545 current serial subscriptions, 1,778 audiovisual materials. *Total majors:* 32. *Expenses:* (2006–07) $17,564; room and board, $5570 (on campus); room only, $3560 (on campus). *Financial aid:* Non-need-based college/university scholarships/grants from institutional funds, tuition waivers, athletic awards, loans from outside sources. For fall 2006 (estimated), 93 international students on campus received college administered financial aid ($12,756 average).

WOFFORD COLLEGE, SPARTANBURG
General Information Independent, 4-year, coed college, affiliated with United Methodist Church. Urban setting. *Awards:* B. *Entrance level for U.S. students:* Very difficult. *Enrollment:* 1,240 total (48% women) including 1% international students from 10 foreign countries. *Undergraduate faculty:* 129. *Library holdings:* 208,361 books, 26,971 current serial subscriptions, 4,184 audiovisual materials. *Total majors:* 30. *Expenses:* (2006–07) $26,110; room and board, $7260 (on campus). *Financial aid:* Need-based financial aid available. Non-need-based college/university scholarships/grants from institutional funds, on-campus employment. Forms required: International Student's Certification of Finances. For fall 2005, 7 international students on campus received college administered financial aid ($25,582 average).

SOUTH DAKOTA

AUGUSTANA COLLEGE, SIOUX FALLS
General Information Independent, coed institution, affiliated with Evangelical Lutheran Church in America. Urban setting. *Awards:* B, M. *Entrance level for U.S. students:* Moderately difficult. *Enrollment:* 1,768 total; 1,747 undergraduates (63% women) including 2% international students from 7 foreign countries. *Faculty:* 186. *Library holdings:* 279,918 books, 595 current serial subscriptions. *Total majors:* 52. *Expenses:* (2006–07) $19,986; room and board, $5664 (on campus); room only, $2700 (on campus). *Financial aid:* Need-based college/university scholarships/grants from institutional funds, tuition waivers, athletic awards, loans from institutional funds, loans from outside sources, on-campus employment. Non-need-based college/university scholarships/grants from institutional funds, tuition waivers, athletic awards, loans from institutional funds, loans from outside sources, on-campus employment. Forms required: institution's own financial aid form, International Student's Certification of Finances. For fall 2006 (estimated), 24 international students on campus received college administered financial aid ($5564 average).

BLACK HILLS STATE UNIVERSITY, SPEARFISH
General Information State-supported, coed institution. Small town setting. *Awards:* A, B, M. *Entrance level for U.S. students:* Minimally difficult. *Enrollment:* 3,896 total; 3,733 undergraduates (64% women) including 1% international students from 7 foreign countries. *Faculty:* 190. *Library holdings:* 310,210 books, 485 current serial subscriptions. *Total majors:* 47.

Black Hills State University (continued)

Information for International Students For fall 2006: 17
international students applied, 14 were accepted, 5 enrolled.
Students can start in fall, spring, or summer. Transfers accepted
from institutions abroad. *Admission tests:* Required: TOEFL
(minimum score: paper-based 500; computer-based 173; minimum
score for ESL admission: paper-based 500; computer-based 173).
Application deadline: 7/1. *Expenses:* (2006–07) $10,868; room and
board, $3988 (on campus); room only, $2202 (on campus). *Housing:*
Available during summer. *Services:* International student adviser on
campus. Employment opportunities (on-campus) available. *Contact:*
Dean of the Enrollment Center, Black Hills State University, 1200
University Street, USB 9502, Spearfish, SD 57799-9502.
Telephone: 605-642-6093. Fax: 605-642-6022.
E-mail: kristipearce@bhsu.edu. URL: http://www.bhsu.edu.

DAKOTA STATE UNIVERSITY, MADISON

General Information State-supported, coed institution. Rural
setting. *Awards:* A, B, M. *Entrance level for U.S. students:*
Minimally difficult. *Enrollment:* 2,392 total; 2,144 undergraduates
(54% women) including 1% international students from 4 foreign
countries. *Faculty:* 105. *Library holdings:* 95,819 books, 350 current
serial subscriptions. *Total majors:* 30. *Expenses:* (2006–07) $6890;
room and board, $3927 (on campus); room only, $1924 (on campus).
Financial aid: Non-need-based college/university
scholarships/grants from institutional funds. Forms required:
institutional scholarship application form. For fall 2005, 2
international students on campus received college administered
financial aid ($1000 average).

DAKOTA WESLEYAN UNIVERSITY, MITCHELL

General Information Independent United Methodist, coed
institution. Small town setting. *Awards:* A, B, M. *Entrance level for
U.S. students:* Moderately difficult. *Enrollment:* 776 total; 735
undergraduates (57% women) including 1% international students
from 9 foreign countries. *Faculty:* 80. *Library holdings:* 76,997
books, 742 current serial subscriptions, 3,929 audiovisual materials.
Total majors: 43.
Information for International Students For fall 2006: 1
international student applied, 1 was accepted. Students can start in
fall or spring. Transfers accepted from institutions abroad.
Admission tests: Required: TOEFL (minimum score: paper-based
500; computer-based 200), ELS. Recommended: ACT. *Application
deadline:* 5/1. *Expenses:* (2007–08) $17,500; room and board, $5400
(on campus); room only, $2200 (on campus). *Financial aid:*
Non-need financial aid available. Forms required: International
Student's Certification of Finances. 4 international students on
campus received college administered financial aid ($9700 average).
Housing: Guaranteed. *Services:* International student adviser on
campus. Internships and employment opportunities (on-campus)
available. *Contact:* Vice President of Academic Affairs and Dean,
Enrollment Services, Dakota Wesleyan University, 1200 West
University Avenue, Mitchell, SD 57301-4398.
Telephone: 605-995-2646. Fax: 605-995-2609.
E-mail: dowatt@dwu.edu. URL: http://www.dwu.edu.

MITCHELL TECHNICAL INSTITUTE, MITCHELL

General Information District-supported, 2-year, coed college.
Rural setting. *Awards:* A. *Entrance level for U.S. students:*
Minimally difficult. *Enrollment:* 832 total including international
students from 2 foreign countries. *Undergraduate faculty:* 57.
Library holdings: 100 current serial subscriptions. *Total majors:* 38.
Information for International Students For fall 2006: 9
international students applied, 3 were accepted, 2 enrolled.
Students can start in fall. *Admission tests:* Required: TOEFL
(minimum score: paper-based 500; computer-based 175).
Recommended: ACT. TOEFL can be waived under certain
conditions. *Application deadline:* Rolling. *Financial aid:*
Non-need-based loans from outside sources. *Services:* ESL program
at cooperating institution. ESL program available during the
academic year and the summer. Internships available. *Contact:*
Director of Student Services, Mitchell Technical Institute, 821
North Capital Street, Mitchell, SD 57301. Telephone: 605-995-3025.
Fax: 605-996-3299. E-mail: tim.edwards@mitchelltech.edu.
URL: http://mti.tec.sd.us.

NATIONAL AMERICAN UNIVERSITY, RAPID CITY

General Information Proprietary, coed institution. Urban setting.
Awards: A, B, M. *Entrance level for U.S. students:* Noncompetitive.
Enrollment: 475 total; 447 undergraduates (64% women) including
5% international students from 5 foreign countries. *Faculty:* 47.
Library holdings: 31,018 books, 268 current serial subscriptions.
Total majors: 18. *Expenses:* (2006–07) $11,570; room and board,
$3853 (on campus); room only, $1938 (on campus).

NORTHERN STATE UNIVERSITY, ABERDEEN

General Information State-supported, coed institution. Small
town setting. *Awards:* A, B, M. *Entrance level for U.S. students:*
Minimally difficult. *Enrollment:* 2,407 total; 2,183 undergraduates
(59% women) including 5% international students from 13 foreign
countries. *Faculty:* 93. *Library holdings:* 192,007 books, 882 current
serial subscriptions. *Total majors:* 52.
Information for International Students For fall 2006: 124
international students enrolled. Students can start in fall, spring,
or summer. Transfers accepted from institutions abroad. *Admission
tests:* Required: TOEFL (minimum score: paper-based 500;
computer-based 173), ELS. Recommended: ACT. *Application
deadline:* 8/15. *Expenses:* (2006–07) $10,169; room and board, $4102
(on campus); room only, $2145 (on campus). *Financial aid:*
Non-need-based college/university scholarships/grants from
institutional funds, athletic awards, on-campus employment. For
fall 2006 (estimated), 12 international students on campus received
college administered financial aid ($1777 average). *Housing:*
Guaranteed, also available during summer. *Services:* International
student adviser on campus. ESL program at cooperating institution.
ESL program available during the academic year and the summer.
Internships and employment opportunities (on-campus and
off-campus) available. *Contact:* Administrator of Admissions,
Northern State University, 1200 South Jay Street, Aberdeen, SD
57401-7198. Telephone: 605-626-2544. Fax: 605-626-2587.
E-mail: admissions@northern.edu. URL: http://www.northern.edu.

PRESENTATION COLLEGE, ABERDEEN

General Information Independent Roman Catholic, 4-year, coed
college. Small town setting. *Awards:* A, B. *Entrance level for U.S.
students:* Noncompetitive. *Enrollment:* 786 total (83% women)
including 1% international students from 3 foreign countries.
Undergraduate faculty: 97. *Library holdings:* 40,000 books, 430
current serial subscriptions. *Total majors:* 15.
Information for International Students For fall 2006: 10
international students applied, 5 were accepted, 1 enrolled.
Students can start in fall, spring, or summer. Transfers accepted
from institutions abroad. *Admission tests:* Required: TOEFL
(minimum score: paper-based 500; computer-based 173), ACT
residual if no ACT available. Recommended: ACT. TOEFL can be
waived under certain conditions. *Application deadline:* 6/1.
Expenses: (2006–07) $12,300; room and board, $4775 (on campus);
room only, $3975 (on campus). *Financial aid:* Need-based
college/university scholarships/grants from institutional funds,
tuition waivers, on-campus employment. Non-need-based
college/university scholarships/grants from institutional funds,
tuition waivers, on-campus employment. International transfer
students are eligible to apply for aid. For fall 2005, 6 international
students on campus received college administered financial aid
($3886 average). *Housing:* Available during summer. Internships
available. *Contact:* Dean of Admissions, Presentation College, 1500
North Main Street, Aberdeen, SD 57401. Telephone: 605-229-8492.
Fax: 605-229-8425. E-mail: lindnerjo@presentation.edu.
URL: http://www.presentation.edu.

SOUTH DAKOTA SCHOOL OF MINES AND TECHNOLOGY, RAPID CITY

General Information State-supported, coed university. Suburban
setting. *Awards:* A, B, M, D. *Entrance level for U.S. students:*
Moderately difficult. *Enrollment:* 2,124 total; 1,870 undergraduates
(31% women) including 1% international students from 11 foreign
countries. *Faculty:* 137. *Library holdings:* 273,243 books, 13,633
current serial subscriptions, 2,190 audiovisual materials.
Total majors: 18. *Expenses:* (2006–07) $6520; room and board,
$4410 (on campus); room only, $2240 (on campus). *Financial aid:*
Non-need financial aid available. Forms required: International
Student's Certification of Finances. 21 international students on
campus received college administered financial aid ($1325 average).

SOUTH DAKOTA STATE UNIVERSITY, BROOKINGS

General Information State-supported, coed university. Small
town setting. *Awards:* A, B, M, D, FP. *Entrance level for U.S.
students:* Minimally difficult. *Enrollment:* 11,303 total; 9,897
undergraduates (52% women) including 0.4% international students
from 26 foreign countries. *Faculty:* 598. *Library holdings:* 1 million
books, 29,255 current serial subscriptions, 13,123 audiovisual
materials. *Total majors:* 80.
Information for International Students For fall 2006: 61
international students applied, 36 were accepted, 23 enrolled.
Students can start in fall or spring. Transfers accepted from
institutions abroad. *Admission tests:* Required: TOEFL (minimum
score: iBT 61; paper-based 500; computer-based 173; minimum
score for ESL admission: paper-based 500; computer-based 173).
TOEFL can be waived under certain conditions. *Application
deadline:* 5/1. *Expenses:* (2006–07) $6243; room and board, $5029
(on campus); room only, $2240 (on campus). *Financial aid:*

Non-need-based athletic awards, loans from outside sources, on-campus employment. Forms required: scholarship application form. 8 international students on campus received college administered financial aid ($1326 average). *Housing:* Available during summer. *Services:* International student adviser on campus. ESL program at cooperating institution. ESL program available during the academic year and the summer. Employment opportunities (on-campus and off-campus) available. *Contact:* International Student Advisor, South Dakota State University, Administration Building 101/2201, Brookings, SD 57007. Telephone: 605-688-4122. Fax: 605-688-6540. E-mail: donna.raetzman@sdstate.edu. URL: http://www.sdstate.edu.

See In-Depth Description on page 189.

UNIVERSITY OF SIOUX FALLS, SIOUX FALLS

General Information Independent American Baptist Churches in the USA, coed institution. Suburban setting. *Awards:* A, B, M, D. *Entrance level for U.S. students:* Moderately difficult. *Enrollment:* 1,675 total; 1,270 undergraduates (55% women) including 0.2% international students from 3 foreign countries. *Faculty:* 140. *Library holdings:* 85,713 books, 378 current serial subscriptions. *Total majors:* 57.

Information for International Students For fall 2006: 37 international students applied, 11 were accepted, 3 enrolled. Students can start in fall, spring, or summer. Transfers accepted from institutions abroad. *Admission tests:* Required: TOEFL (minimum score: paper-based 500; computer-based 173). Recommended: SAT or ACT. *Application deadline:* Rolling. *Expenses:* (2007–08) $17,940; room and board, $5400 (on campus); room only, $2450 (on campus). *Financial aid:* Need-based college/university scholarships/grants from institutional funds, athletic awards. Non-need-based college/university scholarships/grants from institutional funds, athletic awards. Forms required: International Student's Certification of Finances. International transfer students are eligible to apply for aid. *Housing:* Guaranteed. *Services:* ESL program at cooperating institution. Internships and employment opportunities (on-campus) available. *Contact:* Admissions Counselor, University of Sioux Falls, 1101 West 22nd Street, Sioux Falls, SD 57105-1699. Telephone: 605-331-6601. Fax: 605-331-6615. E-mail: ashley.brown@usiouxfalls.edu. URL: http://www.usiouxfalls.edu.

THE UNIVERSITY OF SOUTH DAKOTA, VERMILLION

General Information State-supported, coed university. Small town setting. *Awards:* A, B, M, D, FP. *Entrance level for U.S. students:* Moderately difficult. *Enrollment:* 8,746 total; 6,468 undergraduates (62% women) including 1% international students from 31 foreign countries. *Faculty:* 335. *Library holdings:* 645,672 books, 2,647 current serial subscriptions. *Total majors:* 61. *Expenses:* (2006–07) $10,258; room and board, $4,964 (on campus); room only, $2,389 (on campus). *Financial aid:* Need-based and non-need-based financial aid available. Forms required: FAFSA.

TENNESSEE

AUSTIN PEAY STATE UNIVERSITY, CLARKSVILLE

General Information State-supported, coed institution. Suburban setting. *Awards:* A, B, M. *Entrance level for U.S. students:* Moderately difficult. *Enrollment:* 9,207 total; 8,467 undergraduates (63% women) including 0.5% international students from 17 foreign countries. *Faculty:* 494. *Library holdings:* 400,000 books, 1,754 current serial subscriptions. *Total majors:* 34.

Information for International Students For fall 2006: 45 international students enrolled. Students can start in fall, spring, or summer. Transfers accepted from institutions abroad. *Admission tests:* Required: TOEFL (minimum score: paper-based 500; computer-based 173). TOEFL can be waived under certain conditions. *Application deadline:* 7/1. *Expenses:* (2006–07) $14,531; room and board, $5190 (on campus); room only, $3200 (on campus). *Financial aid:* Non-need-based tuition waivers, athletic awards, loans from outside sources, on-campus employment. *Housing:* Available during summer. *Services:* International student adviser on campus. Full-time and part-time ESL programs on campus. ESL program available during the academic year and the summer. Employment opportunities (on-campus) available. *Contact:* Admissions Office Supervisor, Austin Peay State University, PO Box 4548, Clarksville, TN 37044. Telephone: 931-221-1023. Fax: 931-221-6168. E-mail: wadiak@apsu.edu. URL: http://www.apsu.edu.

BELMONT UNIVERSITY, NASHVILLE

General Information Independent Baptist, coed institution. Urban setting. *Awards:* B, M, D. *Entrance level for U.S. students:* Moderately difficult. *Enrollment:* 4,481 total; 3,774 undergraduates (60% women) including 1% international students from 27 foreign countries. *Faculty:* 466. *Library holdings:* 200,630 books, 1,415 current serial subscriptions, 29,312 audiovisual materials. *Total majors:* 67.

Information for International Students For fall 2006: 12 international students enrolled. Students can start in fall, spring, or summer. Transfers accepted from institutions abroad. *Admission tests:* Required: TOEFL (minimum score: paper-based 550; computer-based 213). *Application deadline:* Rolling. *Expenses:* (2007–08) $19,780; room and board, $9529 (on campus); room only, $6000 (on campus). *Financial aid:* Need-based college/university scholarships/grants from institutional funds, athletic awards. Non-need-based athletic awards. Forms required: institution's own financial aid form, International Student's Certification of Finances. For fall 2005, 6 international students on campus received college administered financial aid ($15,667 average). *Housing:* Guaranteed, also available during summer. *Services:* International student adviser on campus. Full-time and part-time ESL programs on campus. ESL program available during the academic year and the summer. Internships and employment opportunities (on-campus) available. *Contact:* Director of International Education, Belmont University, 1900 Belmont Boulevard, Rasmussen Center for International Education, Nashville, TN 37212. Telephone: 615-460-5500. Fax: 615-460-5539. E-mail: skinnerk@mail.belmont.edu. URL: http://www.belmont.edu.

See In-Depth Description on page 39.

CARSON-NEWMAN COLLEGE, JEFFERSON CITY

General Information Independent Southern Baptist, coed institution. Small town setting. *Awards:* A, B, M. *Entrance level for U.S. students:* Moderately difficult. *Enrollment:* 1,949 total; 1,799 undergraduates (57% women) including 3% international students from 22 foreign countries. *Faculty:* 189. *Library holdings:* 218,371 books, 3,966 current serial subscriptions. *Total majors:* 68.

Information for International Students For fall 2006: 48 international students applied, 23 were accepted, 18 enrolled. Students can start in fall, spring, or summer. Transfers accepted from institutions abroad. *Admission tests:* Required: SAT or ACT, TOEFL (minimum score: iBT 79; paper-based 550; computer-based 213). TOEFL can be waived under certain conditions. *Application deadline:* 6/1. *Expenses:* (2006–07) $16,060; room and board, $5200 (on campus); room only, $2250 (on campus). *Financial aid:* Need-based college/university scholarships/grants from institutional funds, athletic awards, loans from outside sources, on-campus employment. Non-need-based college/university scholarships/grants from institutional funds, athletic awards, loans from outside sources, on-campus employment. International transfer students are eligible to apply for aid. For fall 2006 (estimated), 51 international students on campus received college administered financial aid ($9496 average). *Housing:* Guaranteed, also available during summer. *Services:* International student adviser on campus. Full-time and part-time ESL programs on campus. ESL program available during the academic year and the summer. Internships and employment opportunities (on-campus) available. *Contact:* Coordinator of International Enrollment, Carson-Newman College, 1646 Russell Avenue, Jefferson City, TN 37760. Telephone: 865-471-4826. Fax: 865-471-4817. E-mail: rlane@cn.edu. URL: http://www.cn.edu.

CHATTANOOGA STATE TECHNICAL COMMUNITY COLLEGE, CHATTANOOGA

General Information State-supported, 2-year, coed college. Urban setting. *Awards:* A. *Entrance level for U.S. students:* Noncompetitive. *Enrollment:* 8,060 total (62% women) including 0.4% international students from 24 foreign countries. *Undergraduate faculty:* 602. *Library holdings:* 73,334 books, 803 current serial subscriptions. *Total majors:* 63.

Information for International Students For fall 2006: 30 international students applied, 30 were accepted, 30 enrolled. Students can start in fall or spring. Transfers accepted from institutions abroad. *Admission tests:* Required: SAT or ACT, TOEFL (minimum score: paper-based 500; computer-based 173; minimum score for ESL admission: paper-based 500; computer-based 173). Recommended: COMPASS. TOEFL can be waived under certain conditions. *Application deadline:* Rolling. *Expenses:* (2006–07) $8906. *Financial aid:* Forms required: International Student's Certification of Finances, Foundation Scholarship Application. *Services:* International student adviser on campus. ESL program at cooperating institution. Employment opportunities (on-campus) available. *Contact:* Admission and Records Office Supervisor, Chattanooga State Technical Community College, 4501 Amnicola Highway, Chattanooga, TN 37406-1018. Telephone: 423-697-2475.

Chattanooga State Technical Community College (continued)
Fax: 423-697-4709. E-mail: byrena.leeseberg@chattanoogastate.edu.
URL: http://www.chattanoogastate.edu.

CHRISTIAN BROTHERS UNIVERSITY, MEMPHIS

General Information Independent Roman Catholic, coed
institution. Urban setting. *Awards:* B, M. *Entrance level for U.S.
students:* Moderately difficult. *Enrollment:* 1,776 total; 1,451
undergraduates (55% women) including 2% international students
from 14 foreign countries. *Faculty:* 144. *Library holdings:* 107,000
books, 437 current serial subscriptions. *Total majors:* 27. *Expenses:*
(2006–07) $20,080; room and board, $5650 (on campus); room only,
$2540 (on campus). *Financial aid:* Need-based college/university
scholarships/grants from institutional funds, athletic awards, loans
from institutional funds, on-campus employment. Non-need-based
college/university scholarships/grants from institutional funds,
athletic awards, loans from institutional funds, on-campus
employment. For fall 2006 (estimated), 22 international students on
campus received college administered financial aid ($12,583
average).

CUMBERLAND UNIVERSITY, LEBANON

General Information Independent, coed institution. Small town
setting. *Awards:* A, B, M. *Entrance level for U.S. students:*
Moderately difficult. *Enrollment:* 1,345 total; 1,037 undergraduates
(55% women) including 4% international students from 28 foreign
countries. *Faculty:* 90. *Library holdings:* 50,000 books, 130 current
serial subscriptions. *Total majors:* 37.
Information for International Students For fall 2006: 36
international students applied, 15 were accepted, 14 enrolled.
Students can start in fall, winter, spring, or summer. Transfers
accepted from institutions abroad. *Admission tests:* Required: SAT
or ACT, TOEFL (minimum score: iBT 60; paper-based 500;
computer-based 173). *Application deadline:* Rolling. *Expenses:*
(2007–08) $15,510; room and board, $5313 (on campus); room only,
$2174 (on campus). *Financial aid:* Need-based financial aid
available. Non-need-based college/university scholarships/grants
from institutional funds, athletic awards, on-campus employment.
For fall 2006 (estimated), international students on campus
received college administered aid averaging $13,957. *Housing:*
Guaranteed, also available during summer. *Services:* International
student adviser on campus. ESL program at cooperating institution.
ESL program available during the academic year and the summer.
Internships and employment opportunities (on-campus and
off-campus) available. *Contact:* International Student Advisor/DSO,
Cumberland University, One Cumberland Square, Lebanon, TN
37087-3554. Telephone: 615-444-2562 Ext. 1224. Fax: 615-444-2569.
E-mail: ppope@cumberland.edu. URL: http://www.cumberland.edu.

EAST TENNESSEE STATE UNIVERSITY, JOHNSON CITY

General Information State-supported, coed university. Small
town setting. *Awards:* A, B, M, D, FP. *Entrance level for U.S.
students:* Moderately difficult. *Enrollment:* 12,390 total; 10,204
undergraduates (58% women) including 1% international students
from 42 foreign countries. *Faculty:* 784. *Library holdings:* 1.1
million books, 3,714 current serial subscriptions. *Total majors:* 38.
Information for International Students For fall 2006: 51
international students applied, 40 were accepted, 25 enrolled.
Students can start in fall, spring, or summer. Transfers accepted
from institutions abroad. *Admission tests:* Required: SAT or ACT,
TOEFL (minimum score: paper-based 500; computer-based 173).
TOEFL can be waived under certain conditions. *Application
deadline:* 7/1. *Expenses:* (2006–07) $14,331; room and board, $5024
(on campus); room only, $2426 (on campus). *Financial aid:*
Need-based tuition waivers, athletic awards, loans from
institutional funds. Non-need-based tuition waivers, athletic
awards, loans from institutional funds. *Housing:* Guaranteed, also
available during summer. *Services:* International student adviser on
campus. ESL program at cooperating institution. Internships and
employment opportunities (on-campus) available. *Contact:*
Coordinator of International Student Admissions, Admissions
Office, East Tennessee State University, PO Box 70731, Johnson
City, TN 37614. Telephone: 423-439-4213. Fax: 423-439-4630.
E-mail: wilkinson@etsu.edu. URL: http://www.etsu.edu.

FISK UNIVERSITY, NASHVILLE

General Information Independent, coed institution, affiliated
with United Church of Christ. Urban setting. *Awards:* B, M.
Entrance level for U.S. students: Moderately difficult. *Enrollment:*
890 total; 834 undergraduates (68% women) including 4%
international students from 7 foreign countries. *Faculty:* 91. *Library
holdings:* 127,070 books, 221 current serial subscriptions, 3,880
audiovisual materials. *Total majors:* 25. *Expenses:* (2006–07)
$13,970; room and board, $7010 (on campus); room only, $4050 (on

campus). *Financial aid:* Non-need financial aid available. 20
international students on campus received college administered
financial aid ($3500 average).

FREED-HARDEMAN UNIVERSITY, HENDERSON

General Information Independent, coed institution, affiliated
with Church of Christ. Small town setting. *Awards:* B, M. *Entrance
level for U.S. students:* Moderately difficult. *Enrollment:* 1,969 total;
1,473 undergraduates (54% women) including 3% international
students from 18 foreign countries. *Faculty:* 148. *Library holdings:*
154,689 books, 1,715 current serial subscriptions, 42,735
audiovisual materials. *Total majors:* 53. *Expenses:* (2006–07)
$13,192; room and board, $6560 (on campus); room only, $3700 (on
campus). *Financial aid:* Need-based college/university
scholarships/grants from institutional funds, athletic awards,
on-campus employment. Non-need-based college/university
scholarships/grants from institutional funds, athletic awards,
on-campus employment. For fall 2006 (estimated), 34 international
students on campus received college administered financial aid
($14,253 average).

HUNTINGTON COLLEGE OF HEALTH SCIENCES, KNOXVILLE

General Information Proprietary, coed institution. Suburban
setting. *Awards:* A, B, M (offers only external degree programs
conducted through home study). *Entrance level for U.S. students:*
Noncompetitive. *Enrollment:* 241 total including international
students from 15 foreign countries. *Faculty:* 6. *Total majors:* 2.
Information for International Students For fall 2006: 23
international students applied, 23 were accepted, 23 enrolled.
Students can start in fall, winter, spring, or summer. *Admission
tests:* Recommended: ELS. *Application deadline:* Rolling. *Services:*
International student adviser on campus. *Contact:*
Director/Registrar, Huntington College of Health Sciences, 1204
Kenesaw Avenue, Knoxville, TN 37919. Telephone: 800-290-4226.
Fax: 865-524-8339. E-mail: cfreeman@hchs.edu.
URL: http://www.hchs.edu.

JACKSON STATE COMMUNITY COLLEGE, JACKSON

General Information State-supported, 2-year, coed college.
Suburban setting. *Awards:* A. *Entrance level for U.S. students:*
Noncompetitive. *Enrollment:* 4,106 total (68% women) including
0.2% international students from 5 foreign countries.
Undergraduate faculty: 235. *Library holdings:* 62,500 books, 178
current serial subscriptions, 2,594 audiovisual materials.
Total majors: 15. *Expenses:* (2007–08) $9412. *Financial aid:*
Need-based college/university scholarships/grants from institutional
funds, loans from institutional funds, loans from outside sources,
on-campus employment. Non-need-based college/university
scholarships/grants from institutional funds, tuition waivers,
athletic awards, loans from institutional funds, loans from outside
sources, on-campus employment.

KING COLLEGE, BRISTOL

General Information Independent, coed institution, affiliated
with Presbyterian Church (U.S.A.). Suburban setting. *Awards:* B,
M. *Entrance level for U.S. students:* Moderately difficult.
Enrollment: 1,271 total; 1,122 undergraduates (64% women)
including 3% international students from 20 foreign countries.
Faculty: 122. *Library holdings:* 113,933 books, 468 current serial
subscriptions, 5,803 audiovisual materials. *Total majors:* 57.
Expenses: (2006–07) $19,262; room and board, $6508 (on campus);
room only, $3200 (on campus). *Financial aid:* Need-based tuition
waivers, athletic awards, loans from outside sources, on-campus
employment. Non-need-based college/university scholarships/grants
from institutional funds, tuition waivers, athletic awards, loans
from outside sources, on-campus employment. Forms required:
institution's own financial aid form, International Student's
Financial Aid Application, International Student's Certification of
Finances, bank statements. For fall 2006 (estimated), 34
international students on campus received college administered
financial aid ($14,799 average).

LEE UNIVERSITY, CLEVELAND

General Information Independent, coed institution, affiliated
with Church of God. Small town setting. *Awards:* B, M. *Entrance
level for U.S. students:* Minimally difficult. *Enrollment:* 4,012 total;
3,724 undergraduates (56% women) including 5% international
students from 51 foreign countries. *Faculty:* 320. *Library holdings:*
151,905 books, 10,000 current serial subscriptions, 5,448
audiovisual materials. *Total majors:* 33. *Expenses:* (2006–07)
$10,258; room and board, $5024 (on campus); room only, $2434 (on
campus). *Financial aid:* Need-based college/university
scholarships/grants from institutional funds, athletic awards,
on-campus employment. Non-need-based college/university
scholarships/grants from institutional funds, athletic awards, loans

from outside sources, on-campus employment. Forms required: institution's own financial aid form. For fall 2006 (estimated), 107 international students on campus received college administered financial aid ($6601 average).

LEMOYNE-OWEN COLLEGE, MEMPHIS
General Information Independent, 4-year, coed college, affiliated with United Church of Christ. Urban setting. *Awards:* B. *Entrance level for U.S. students:* Minimally difficult. *Enrollment:* 714 total (65% women) including 2% international students from 4 foreign countries. *Undergraduate faculty:* 72. *Library holdings:* 90,000 current serial subscriptions. *Total majors:* 20.
Information for International Students For fall 2006: 6 international students applied, 2 were accepted, 1 enrolled. Students can start in fall, spring, or summer. Transfers accepted from institutions abroad. *Admission tests:* Required: TOEFL (minimum score: paper-based 475; computer-based 150). *Application deadline:* Rolling. *Expenses:* (2006–07) $10,318; room and board, $4568 (on campus); room only, $2258 (on campus). *Financial aid:* Non-need-based college/university scholarships/grants from institutional funds, athletic awards. Forms required: institution's own financial aid form. International transfer students are eligible to apply for aid. *Housing:* Available during summer. *Services:* International student adviser on campus. Internships and employment opportunities (on campus) available. *Contact:* Counselor of Student Support Services, LeMoyne-Owen College, 807 Walker Avenue, Memphis, TN 38126. Telephone: 901-942-6228. Fax: 901-942-6246. E-mail: marieme_thiam@qm.lemoyne-owen.edu. URL: http://www.loc.edu.

LINCOLN MEMORIAL UNIVERSITY, HARROGATE
General Information Independent, coed institution. Small town setting. *Awards:* A, B, M. *Entrance level for U.S. students:* Moderately difficult. *Enrollment:* 2,981 total; 1,394 undergraduates (71% women) including 4% international students from 15 foreign countries. *Faculty:* 162. *Library holdings:* 174,737 books, 20,982 current serial subscriptions, 2,402 audiovisual materials. *Total majors:* 43. *Expenses:* (2007–08) $14,400. *Financial aid:* Non-need financial aid available. Forms required: scholarship application form. 18 international students on campus received college administered financial aid ($9000 average).

LIPSCOMB UNIVERSITY, NASHVILLE
General Information Independent, coed institution, affiliated with Church of Christ. Suburban setting. *Awards:* B, M, FP. *Entrance level for U.S. students:* Moderately difficult. *Enrollment:* 2,563 total; 2,289 undergraduates (57% women) including 1% international students from 21 foreign countries. *Faculty:* 260. *Library holdings:* 253,398 books, 850 current serial subscriptions. *Total majors:* 58.
Information for International Students For fall 2006: 48 international students applied, 13 were accepted, 8 enrolled. Students can start in fall, spring, or summer. Transfers accepted from institutions abroad. *Admission tests:* Required: TOEFL (minimum score: paper-based 554; computer-based 213; minimum score for ESL admission: paper-based 550; computer-based 213). Recommended: SAT. TOEFL can be waived under certain conditions. *Application deadline:* Rolling. *Expenses:* (2006–07) $15,566; room and board, $6730 (on campus). *Financial aid:* Need-based college/university scholarships/grants from institutional funds, athletic awards, on-campus employment. Non-need-based college/university scholarships/grants from institutional funds, athletic awards, on-campus employment. Forms required: International Student's Certification of Finances. *Housing:* Guaranteed, also available during summer. *Services:* International student adviser on campus. ESL program at cooperating institution. Internships and employment opportunities (on-campus) available. *Contact:* Senior Director of Enrollment, Lipscomb University, 3901 Granny White Pike, Nashville, TN 37204-3951. Telephone: 615-966-7064. Fax: 615-966-1804. E-mail: corey.patterson@lipscomb.edu. URL: http://www.lipscomb.edu.

MARYVILLE COLLEGE, MARYVILLE
General Information Independent Presbyterian, 4-year, coed college. Suburban setting. *Awards:* B. *Entrance level for U.S. students:* Moderately difficult. *Enrollment:* 1,155 total (56% women) including 5% international students from 25 foreign countries. *Undergraduate faculty:* 113. *Library holdings:* 131,838 books, 14,531 current serial subscriptions. *Total majors:* 50.
Information for International Students For fall 2006: 35 international students applied, 22 were accepted, 13 enrolled. Students can start in fall or spring. Transfers accepted from institutions abroad. *Admission tests:* Required: Michigan Test upon arrival. Recommended: TOEFL (minimum score: iBT 74; paper-based 525; computer-based 200). TOEFL can be waived under

certain conditions. *Application deadline:* Rolling. *Expenses:* (2006–07) $23,800; room and board, $7400 (on campus); room only, $3700 (on campus). *Financial aid:* Need-based college/university scholarships/grants from institutional funds, on-campus employment. Non-need-based college/university scholarships/grants from institutional funds, on-campus employment. Forms required: institution's own financial aid form, International Student's Certification of Finances. International transfer students are eligible to apply for aid. For fall 2005, 35 international students on campus received college administered financial aid ($11,009 average). *Housing:* Available during summer. *Services:* International student adviser on campus. Full-time and part-time ESL programs on campus. ESL program available during the academic year and the summer. Internships and employment opportunities (on-campus) available. *Contact:* Director of International Services, Maryville College, International House, 502 E.L. Alexander, Maryville, TN 37804. Telephone: 865-981-8183. Fax: 865-981-8010. E-mail: kelly.franklin@maryvillecollege.edu. URL: http://www.maryvillecollege.edu.

MEMPHIS COLLEGE OF ART, MEMPHIS
General Information Independent, coed institution. Urban setting. *Awards:* B, M. *Entrance level for U.S. students:* Moderately difficult. *Enrollment:* 308 total; 289 undergraduates (50% women) including 2% international students from 5 foreign countries. *Faculty:* 45. *Library holdings:* 14,500 books, 108 current serial subscriptions, 175 audiovisual materials. *Total majors:* 20. *Expenses:* (2007–08) $20,660; room only, $5760 (on campus). *Financial aid:* Non-need-based college/university scholarships/grants from institutional funds, on-campus employment. For fall 2006 (estimated), 4 international students on campus received college administered financial aid ($9550 average).

MIDDLE TENNESSEE STATE UNIVERSITY, MURFREESBORO
General Information State-supported, coed university. Urban setting. *Awards:* B, M, D. *Entrance level for U.S. students:* Moderately difficult. *Enrollment:* 22,863 total; 20,643 undergraduates (52% women). *Library holdings:* 748,888 books, 4,144 current serial subscriptions. *Total majors:* 61.
Information for International Students For fall 2006: 75 international students applied, 49 were accepted, 18 enrolled. Students can start in fall or spring. Transfers accepted from institutions abroad. *Admission tests:* Required: SAT or ACT, TOEFL (minimum score: iBT 61; paper-based 500; computer-based 173). TOEFL can be waived under certain conditions. *Application deadline:* 7/1. *Expenses:* (2006–07) $13,982; room and board, $5626 (on campus); room only, $3478 (on campus). *Housing:* Guaranteed. *Services:* International student adviser on campus. ESL program at cooperating institution. Internships and employment opportunities (on-campus) available. *Contact:* Director, International Programs and Services, Middle Tennessee State University, 1301 East Main Street, PO Box 100, Keathley University Center 124, Murfreesboro, TN 37132. Telephone: 615-898-2238. Fax: 615-898-5178. E-mail: twubnch@mtsu.edu. URL: http://www.mtsu.edu.

MILLIGAN COLLEGE, MILLIGAN COLLEGE
General Information Independent Christian, coed institution. Suburban setting. *Awards:* B, M. *Entrance level for U.S. students:* Moderately difficult. *Enrollment:* 951 total; 746 undergraduates (62% women) including 3% international students from 11 foreign countries. *Faculty:* 100. *Library holdings:* 179,619 books, 10,861 current serial subscriptions, 1,865 audiovisual materials. *Total majors:* 26.
Information for International Students For fall 2006: 32 international students applied, 16 were accepted, 7 enrolled. Students can start in fall, spring, or summer. Transfers accepted from institutions abroad. *Admission tests:* Required: TOEFL (minimum score: iBT 79; paper-based 550; computer-based 213). Recommended: SAT, ACT. TOEFL can be waived under certain conditions. *Application deadline:* 6/1. *Expenses:* (2006–07) $18,320; room and board, $5030 (on campus); room only, $2550 (on campus). *Financial aid:* Need-based college/university scholarships/grants from institutional funds, athletic awards, loans from outside sources. Non-need-based college/university scholarships/grants from institutional funds, athletic awards, loans from outside sources, on-campus employment. Forms required: INS-I-59 Form. International transfer students are eligible to apply for aid. For fall 2005, 17 international students on campus received college administered financial aid ($14,137 average). *Housing:* Guaranteed, also available during summer. *Services:* International student adviser on campus. ESL program at cooperating institution. ESL program available during the academic year. Internships and employment opportunities (on-campus) available. *Contact:* Director of Undergraduate Admissions, Milligan College, PO Box 210,

Milligan College (continued)

Milligan College, TN 37682. Telephone: 423-461-8730.
Fax: 423-461-8982. E-mail: tnbrinn@milligan.edu.
URL: http://www.milligan.edu.

MOTLOW STATE COMMUNITY COLLEGE, TULLAHOMA

General Information State-supported, 2-year, coed college. Rural setting. *Awards:* A. *Entrance level for U.S. students:* Noncompetitive. *Enrollment:* 3,833 total (65% women) including 0.2% international students from 5 foreign countries. *Undergraduate faculty:* 217. *Library holdings:* 116,049 books, 211 current serial subscriptions, 4,111 audiovisual materials. *Total majors:* 4.

Information for International Students For fall 2006: 18 international students enrolled. Students can start in fall, spring, or summer. Transfers accepted from institutions abroad. *Admission tests:* Required: ACT, TOEFL (minimum score: paper-based 500; computer-based 173). Recommended: ELS. *Application deadline:* Rolling. *Expenses:* (2006–07) $6661. *Financial aid:* Non-need-based college/university scholarships/grants from institutional funds, tuition waivers, athletic awards, loans from outside sources, on-campus employment. Forms required: institution's own financial aid form. *Contact:* Director of Admissions and Records, Motlow State Community College, PO Box 8500, Lynchburg, TN 37352. Telephone: 931-393-1500 Ext. 1530. Fax: 931-393-1681. E-mail: galsup@mscc.edu. URL: http://www.mscc.cc.tn.us.

NASHVILLE AUTO DIESEL COLLEGE, NASHVILLE

General Information Proprietary, 2-year, coed, primarily men's college. Urban setting. *Awards:* A. *Entrance level for U.S. students:* Minimally difficult. *Enrollment:* 1,306 total (0.4% women). *Undergraduate faculty:* 77. *Library holdings:* 1,309 books, 69 current serial subscriptions. *Total majors:* 3.

NATIONAL COLLEGE, BRISTOL

General Information Proprietary, 2-year, coed college. Small town setting. *Awards:* A. *Entrance level for U.S. students:* Noncompetitive. *Enrollment:* 319 total. *Undergraduate faculty:* 30. *Total majors:* 5. *Financial aid:* Forms required: institution's own financial aid form.

NORTH CENTRAL INSTITUTE, CLARKSVILLE

General Information Proprietary, 2-year, coed, primarily men's college. Suburban setting. *Awards:* A. *Entrance level for U.S. students:* Noncompetitive. *Enrollment:* 130 total (11% women). *Undergraduate faculty:* 17. *Library holdings:* 200 books, 12 current serial subscriptions, 20 audiovisual materials. *Total majors:* 2. *Expenses:* (2006–07) $15,600. *Financial aid:* Forms required: institution's own financial aid form.

NORTHEAST STATE TECHNICAL COMMUNITY COLLEGE, BLOUNTVILLE

General Information State-supported, 2-year, coed college. Small town setting. *Awards:* A. *Entrance level for U.S. students:* Noncompetitive. *Enrollment:* 5,154 total (54% women). *Undergraduate faculty:* 243. *Library holdings:* 49,684 books, 427 current serial subscriptions, 9,061 audiovisual materials. *Total majors:* 25.

Information for International Students For fall 2006: 3 international students applied, 3 were accepted, 2 enrolled. Students can start in fall, spring, or summer. Transfers accepted from institutions abroad. *Admission tests:* Required: ACT, TOEFL (minimum score: iBT 61; paper-based 500; computer-based 173; minimum score for ESL admission: iBT 61; paper-based 500; computer-based 173). *Application deadline:* Rolling. *Expenses:* (2006–07) $9166. *Services:* International student adviser on campus. ESL program at cooperating institution. ESL program available during the academic year. *Contact:* Registrar, Northeast State Technical Community College, PO Box 246, Blountville, TN 37617. Telephone: 423-323-0253. Fax: 423-323-0215. E-mail: bcbenton@northeaststate.edu. URL: http://www.northeaststate.edu.

O'MORE COLLEGE OF DESIGN, FRANKLIN

General Information Independent, 4-year, coed, primarily women's college. Small town setting. *Awards:* B. *Entrance level for U.S. students:* Moderately difficult. *Enrollment:* 194 total (88% women). *Undergraduate faculty:* 50. *Library holdings:* 4,000 books, 60 current serial subscriptions. *Total majors:* 4. *Expenses:* (2006–07) $7077.

PELLISSIPPI STATE TECHNICAL COMMUNITY COLLEGE, KNOXVILLE

General Information State-supported, 2-year, coed college. Suburban setting. *Awards:* A. *Entrance level for U.S. students:*

Noncompetitive. *Enrollment:* 7,686 total (54% women) including 1% international students. *Undergraduate faculty:* 412. *Library holdings:* 43,000 books, 527 current serial subscriptions. *Total majors:* 39.

Information for International Students For fall 2006: 18 international students applied, 18 were accepted, 13 enrolled. Students can start in fall or spring. Transfers accepted from institutions abroad. *Admission tests:* Required: TOEFL (minimum score: paper-based 450; computer-based 133; minimum score for ESL admission: paper-based 450; computer-based 133), placement test. TOEFL can be waived under certain conditions. *Application deadline:* 8/1. *Services:* International student adviser on campus. Full-time and part-time ESL programs on campus. ESL program available during the academic year. Internships and employment opportunities (on-campus and off-campus) available. *Contact:* Director of Enrollment Management and Community Relations, Admissions Office, Pellissippi State Technical Community College, 10915 Hardin Valley Road, PO Box 22990, Knoxville, TN 37933-0990. Telephone: 865-539-7013. Fax: 865-539-7217. E-mail: latouzeau@pstcc.edu. URL: http://www.pstcc.edu.

RHODES COLLEGE, MEMPHIS

General Information Independent Presbyterian, coed institution. Suburban setting. *Awards:* B, M (master's degree in accounting only). *Entrance level for U.S. students:* Very difficult. *Enrollment:* 1,696 total; 1,687 undergraduates (59% women) including 0.1% international students from 11 foreign countries. *Faculty:* 180. *Library holdings:* 274,886 books, 1,183 current serial subscriptions, 10,755 audiovisual materials. *Total majors:* 33.

Information for International Students Students can start in fall or spring. Transfers accepted from institutions abroad. *Admission tests:* Required: SAT or ACT, TOEFL (minimum score: paper-based 550; computer-based 213). TOEFL can be waived under certain conditions. *Application deadline:* 1/15. *Expenses:* (2006–07) $29,112; room and board, $7180 (on campus). *Financial aid:* Need-based and non-need-based financial aid available. Forms required: International Student's Financial Aid Application, International Student's Certification of Finances. International transfer students are eligible to apply for aid. For fall 2006 (estimated), 1 international student on campus received college administered financial aid ($12,548 average). *Housing:* Available during summer. *Services:* International student adviser on campus. Internships and employment opportunities (on-campus) available. *Contact:* Associate Director of Admissions, Office of Admissions, Rhodes College, 2000 North Parkway, Memphis, TN 38112. Telephone: 901-843-3700. Fax: 901-843-3631. E-mail: adminfo@rhodes.edu. URL: http://www.rhodes.edu.

ROANE STATE COMMUNITY COLLEGE, HARRIMAN

General Information State-supported, 2-year, coed college. Small town setting. *Awards:* A. *Entrance level for U.S. students:* Noncompetitive. *Enrollment:* 5,353 total (67% women) including 0.3% international students from 15 foreign countries. *Undergraduate faculty:* 359. *Library holdings:* 103,404 books. *Total majors:* 42. *Expenses:* (2007–08) $8821. *Financial aid:* Need-based college/university scholarships/grants from institutional funds, loans from outside sources, on-campus employment. Non-need-based college/university scholarships/grants from institutional funds, tuition waivers, athletic awards, loans from institutional funds. Forms required: all students must complete an online financial aid orientation.

SEWANEE: THE UNIVERSITY OF THE SOUTH, SEWANEE

General Information Independent Episcopal, coed institution. Small town setting. *Awards:* B, M, D, FP. *Entrance level for U.S. students:* Very difficult. *Enrollment:* 1,611 total; 1,518 undergraduates (52% women) including 2% international students from 22 foreign countries. *Faculty:* 174. *Library holdings:* 648,459 books, 3,444 current serial subscriptions. *Total majors:* 41. *Expenses:* (2007–08) $30,660; room and board, $8780 (on campus); room only, $4560 (on campus). *Financial aid:* Need-based college/university scholarships/grants from institutional funds, tuition waivers, athletic awards, loans from institutional funds, loans from outside sources, on-campus employment. Non-need-based college/university scholarships/grants from institutional funds, tuition waivers, athletic awards, loans from outside sources. Forms required: institution's own financial aid form, International Student's Financial Aid Application. For fall 2006 (estimated), 25 international students on campus received college administered financial aid ($34,378 average).

SOUTHERN ADVENTIST UNIVERSITY, COLLEGEDALE

General Information Independent Seventh-day Adventist, coed institution. Small town setting. *Awards:* A, B, M. *Entrance level for U.S. students:* Moderately difficult. *Enrollment:* 2,593 total; 2,451 undergraduates (55% women) including 6% international students. *Faculty:* 221. *Library holdings:* 154,987 books, 21,123 current serial subscriptions, 6,410 audiovisual materials. *Total majors:* 62. *Expenses:* (2007–08) $15,596; room and board, $4734 (on campus); room only, $2734 (on campus). *Financial aid:* Need-based college/university scholarships/grants from institutional funds, loans from institutional funds, loans from outside sources. Non-need-based college/university scholarships/grants from institutional funds, tuition waivers, loans from outside sources, on-campus employment. Forms required: International Student's Certification of Finances.

SOUTHWEST TENNESSEE COMMUNITY COLLEGE, MEMPHIS

General Information State-supported, 2-year, coed college. Urban setting. *Awards:* A. *Entrance level for U.S. students:* Noncompetitive. *Enrollment:* 11,556 total (65% women) including 1% international students. *Undergraduate faculty:* 566. *Library holdings:* 87,280 books, 522 current serial subscriptions, 10,588 audiovisual materials. *Total majors:* 32. *Financial aid:* Forms required: institution's own financial aid form, International Student's Certification of Finances.

TENNESSEE STATE UNIVERSITY, NASHVILLE

General Information State-supported, coed institution. Urban setting. *Awards:* A, B, M, D. *Entrance level for U.S. students:* Minimally difficult. *Enrollment:* 9,038 total; 7,112 undergraduates (65% women) including 1% international students from 33 foreign countries. *Faculty:* 637. *Library holdings:* 580,650 books. *Total majors:* 59. *Expenses:* (2006–07) $14,258; room and board, $5000 (on campus); room only, $2840 (on campus).

TENNESSEE TECHNOLOGICAL UNIVERSITY, COOKEVILLE

General Information State-supported, coed university. Small town setting. *Awards:* B, M, D. *Entrance level for U.S. students:* Moderately difficult. *Enrollment:* 9,733 total; 7,569 undergraduates (46% women) including 1% international students from 54 foreign countries. *Faculty:* 560. *Library holdings:* 640,056 books, 4,847 current serial subscriptions. *Total majors:* 69.
Information for International Students For fall 2006: 75 international students applied, 40 were accepted, 32 enrolled. Students can start in fall, spring, or summer. Transfers accepted from institutions abroad. *Admission tests:* Required: TOEFL (minimum score: iBT 58; paper-based 500; computer-based 173). Recommended: SAT or ACT, IELTS or TOEIC in lieu of TOEFL, computer-based or paper-based are accepted. *Application deadline:* 5/1. *Expenses:* (2006–07) $14,284; room and board, $5964 (on campus); room only, $3020 (on campus). *Financial aid:* Non-need-based athletic awards, loans from institutional funds, loans from outside sources, on-campus employment. *Housing:* Guaranteed. *Services:* International student adviser on campus. Part-time ESL program on campus. ESL program available during the summer. Internships and employment opportunities (on-campus and off-campus) available. *Contact:* Director of International Student Affairs, Tennessee Technological University, 1 William L. Jones Drive, Box 5093, Derryberry Hall 103, Cookeville, TN 38505. Telephone: 931-372-3634. Fax: 931-372-3674. E-mail: ttunewintl@yahoo.com. URL: http://www.tntech.edu.
See In-Depth Description on page 201.

TREVECCA NAZARENE UNIVERSITY, NASHVILLE

General Information Independent Nazarene, coed institution. Urban setting. *Awards:* A, B, M, D. *Entrance level for U.S. students:* Moderately difficult. *Enrollment:* 2,217 total; 1,247 undergraduates (56% women) including 2% international students from 12 foreign countries. *Faculty:* 219. *Library holdings:* 110,277 books, 485 current serial subscriptions, 3,758 audiovisual materials. *Total majors:* 36.
Information for International Students For fall 2006: 35 international students applied, 6 were accepted, 6 enrolled. Students can start in fall or spring. Transfers accepted from institutions abroad. *Admission tests:* Required: SAT or ACT, TOEFL (minimum score: iBT 61; paper-based 500; computer-based 173). *Application deadline:* 7/1. *Expenses:* (2006–07) $14,774; room and board, $6470 (on campus); room only, $2920 (on campus). *Financial aid:* Forms required: International Student's Certification of Finances. *Housing:* Available during summer. *Services:* International student adviser on campus. Internships and employment opportunities (on-campus) available. *Contact:* Director of Enrollment Systems, Trevecca Nazarene University, Office of Admissions, 333 Murfreesboro Road, Nashville, TN 37210. Telephone: 615-248-1320. Fax: 615-248-7406. E-mail: admissions_und@trevecca.edu. URL: http://www.trevecca.edu.

TUSCULUM COLLEGE, GREENEVILLE

General Information Independent Presbyterian, coed institution. Small town setting. *Awards:* B, M. *Entrance level for U.S. students:* Moderately difficult. *Enrollment:* 2,923 total; 2,600 undergraduates (60% women) including 2% international students from 19 foreign countries. *Faculty:* 150. *Library holdings:* 49,905 books, 1,000 current serial subscriptions. *Total majors:* 27.
Information for International Students For fall 2006: 67 international students applied, 57 were accepted, 27 enrolled. Students can start in fall or spring. Transfers accepted from institutions abroad. *Admission tests:* Required: SAT or ACT, TOEFL (minimum score: paper-based 550; computer-based 213; minimum score for ESL admission: paper-based 550; computer-based 213). *Application deadline:* Rolling. *Expenses:* (2006–07) $16,215; room and board, $6500 (on campus). *Financial aid:* Need-based financial aid available. Non-need-based college/university scholarships/grants from institutional funds, athletic awards, loans from outside sources, on-campus employment. Forms required: institution's own financial aid form. International transfer students are eligible to apply for aid. For fall 2005, 31 international students on campus received college administered financial aid ($6090 average). *Housing:* Guaranteed. *Services:* International student adviser on campus. Internships and employment opportunities (on-campus and off-campus) available. *Contact:* Director of Operations–Admissions, Tusculum College, PO Box 5051, Greeneville, TN 37743. Telephone: 423-636-7374. Fax: 423-798-1622. E-mail: mripley@tusculum.edu. URL: http://www.tusculum.edu.

UNION UNIVERSITY, JACKSON

General Information Independent Southern Baptist, coed institution. Small town setting. *Awards:* A, B, M, D. *Entrance level for U.S. students:* Moderately difficult. *Enrollment:* 2,934 total; 2,096 undergraduates (58% women) including 2% international students from 36 foreign countries. *Faculty:* 290. *Library holdings:* 149,255 books, 19,919 current serial subscriptions, 14,131 audiovisual materials. *Total majors:* 66. *Expenses:* (2007–08) $17,900. *Financial aid:* Non-need-based college/university scholarships/grants from institutional funds, athletic awards, on-campus employment. Forms required: institution's own financial aid form. 5 international students on campus received college administered financial aid ($4000 average).

UNIVERSITY OF MEMPHIS, MEMPHIS

General Information State-supported, coed university. Urban setting. *Awards:* B, M, D, FP. *Entrance level for U.S. students:* Moderately difficult. *Enrollment:* 20,562 total; 15,984 undergraduates (61% women) including 2% international students from 77 foreign countries. *Faculty:* 1,279. *Library holdings:* 1.3 million books, 9,393 current serial subscriptions, 27,391 audiovisual materials. *Total majors:* 66. *Expenses:* (2006–07) $15,472; room and board, $4720 (on campus); room only, $3120 (on campus). *Financial aid:* Need-based college/university scholarships/grants from institutional funds, athletic awards. Non-need-based college/university scholarships/grants from institutional funds, athletic awards, on-campus employment. 27 international students on campus received college administered financial aid ($3864 average).

THE UNIVERSITY OF TENNESSEE, KNOXVILLE

General Information State-supported, coed university. Urban setting. *Awards:* B, M, D, FP. *Entrance level for U.S. students:* Moderately difficult. *Enrollment:* 28,901 total; 20,619 undergraduates (51% women) including 1% international students from 70 foreign countries. *Faculty:* 1,625. *Library holdings:* 24.4 million books, 17,628 current serial subscriptions. *Total majors:* 92. *Expenses:* (2007–08) $17,430; room and board, $6358 (on campus); room only, $3348 (on campus). *Financial aid:* Need-based financial aid available. international students on campus received college administered aid averaging $13,247.

THE UNIVERSITY OF TENNESSEE AT CHATTANOOGA, CHATTANOOGA

General Information State-supported, coed institution. Urban setting. *Awards:* B, M, D, FP. *Entrance level for U.S. students:* Moderately difficult. *Enrollment:* 8,923 total; 7,544 undergraduates (57% women) including 1% international students from 37 foreign countries. *Faculty:* 733. *Library holdings:* 491,179 books, 1,847 current serial subscriptions. *Total majors:* 44. *Expenses:* (2006–07) $15,024; room and board, $6500 (on campus); room only, $4000 (on campus). *Financial aid:* Non-need-based college/university scholarships/grants from institutional funds, athletic awards. Forms required: scholarship application form. 40 international students on campus received college administered financial aid ($4500 average).

THE UNIVERSITY OF TENNESSEE AT MARTIN, MARTIN

General Information State-supported, coed institution. Small town setting. *Awards:* B, M. *Entrance level for U.S. students:* Moderately difficult. *Enrollment:* 6,893 total; 6,320 undergraduates (57% women) including 2% international students from 21 foreign countries. *Faculty:* 446. *Library holdings:* 488,807 books, 2,016 current serial subscriptions, 12,554 audiovisual materials. *Total majors:* 104.

Information for International Students Students can start in fall, winter, spring, or summer. Transfers accepted from institutions abroad. *Admission tests:* Required: TOEFL (minimum score: iBT 61; paper-based 500; computer-based 173). *Application deadline:* Rolling. *Expenses:* (2006–07) $14,137; room and board, $4410 (on campus); room only, $2100 (on campus). *Financial aid:* Need-based college/university scholarships/grants from institutional funds, loans from institutional funds, on-campus employment. Non-need-based college/university scholarships/grants from institutional funds, tuition waivers, athletic awards, loans from outside sources. *Housing:* Guaranteed, also available during summer. *Services:* International student adviser on campus. Full-time ESL program on campus. ESL program available during the academic year and the summer. Employment opportunities (on-campus) available. *Contact:* Assistant Director of Recruiting/Admissions, Office of International Programs/Admission, The University of Tennessee at Martin, International Programs/Admissions, 144 Gooch Hall, Martin, TN 38238-1000. Telephone: 901-587-7340. Fax: 901-587-7322. E-mail: vachikl@utm.edu. URL: http://www.utm.edu.

VANDERBILT UNIVERSITY, NASHVILLE

General Information Independent, coed university. Urban setting. *Awards:* B, M, D, FP. *Entrance level for U.S. students:* Very difficult. *Enrollment:* 11,607 total; 6,378 undergraduates (52% women) including 2% international students from 36 foreign countries. *Library holdings:* 1.8 million books, 26,885 current serial subscriptions, 153,450 audiovisual materials. *Total majors:* 56.

Information for International Students For fall 2006: 407 international students applied, 57 were accepted, 18 enrolled. Students can start in fall. Transfers accepted from institutions abroad. *Admission tests:* Required: SAT or ACT, TOEFL (minimum score: iBT 85; paper-based 570; computer-based 230). Recommended: SAT Subject Tests. TOEFL can be waived under certain conditions. *Application deadline:* 1/3. *Expenses:* (2006–07) $33,440; room and board, $10,890 (on campus); room only, $7100 (on campus). *Financial aid:* Need-based and non-need-based financial aid available. For fall 2006 (estimated), 13 international students on campus received college administered financial aid ($22,585 average). *Housing:* Guaranteed. *Services:* International student adviser on campus. Full-time ESL program on campus. ESL program available during the academic year and the summer. Internships and employment opportunities (on-campus) available. *Contact:* Associate Provost for Enrollment/Dean of Admissions, Vanderbilt University, 2305 West End Avenue, Nashville, TN 37203. Telephone: 615-322-2561. Fax: 615-343-7765. E-mail: admissions@vanderbilt.edu. URL: http://www.vanderbilt.edu.

VOLUNTEER STATE COMMUNITY COLLEGE, GALLATIN

General Information State-supported, 2-year, coed college. Small town setting. *Awards:* A. *Entrance level for U.S. students:* Noncompetitive. *Enrollment:* 7,370 total (64% women) including 0.4% international students from 29 foreign countries. *Undergraduate faculty:* 375. *Library holdings:* 53,000 books, 275 current serial subscriptions. *Total majors:* 11. *Expenses:* (2007–08) $9325.

WALTERS STATE COMMUNITY COLLEGE, MORRISTOWN

General Information State-supported, 2-year, coed college. Small town setting. *Awards:* A. *Entrance level for U.S. students:* Noncompetitive. *Enrollment:* 5,964 total (65% women) including 0.1% international students from 6 foreign countries. *Undergraduate faculty:* 288. *Library holdings:* 47,559 books, 189 current serial subscriptions, 22,677 audiovisual materials. *Total majors:* 20. *Expenses:* (2006–07) $9145.

TEXAS

ABILENE CHRISTIAN UNIVERSITY, ABILENE

General Information Independent, coed institution, affiliated with Church of Christ. Urban setting. *Awards:* A, B, M, D, FP. *Entrance level for U.S. students:* Moderately difficult. *Enrollment:* 4,777 total; 4,145 undergraduates (55% women) including 5% international students from 57 foreign countries. *Faculty:* 378. *Library holdings:* 503,707 books, 2,771 current serial subscriptions, 65,246 audiovisual materials. *Total majors:* 78. *Expenses:* (2007–08) $17,410; room and board, $6350 (on campus); room only, $2950 (on campus). *Financial aid:* Need-based college/university scholarships/grants from institutional funds, athletic awards, on-campus employment. Non-need-based college/university scholarships/grants from institutional funds, athletic awards, on-campus employment. Forms required: institution's own financial aid form. For fall 2006 (estimated), 174 international students on campus received college administered financial aid ($9807 average).

ALVIN COMMUNITY COLLEGE, ALVIN

General Information State and locally supported, 2-year, coed college. Small town setting. *Awards:* A. *Entrance level for U.S. students:* Noncompetitive. *Enrollment:* 3,932 total (56% women) including 0.3% international students from 5 foreign countries. *Undergraduate faculty:* 275. *Library holdings:* 28,361 books, 146 current serial subscriptions, 5 audiovisual materials. *Total majors:* 33.

Information for International Students For fall 2006: 25 international students applied, 8 were accepted, 3 enrolled. Students can start in fall, spring, or summer. Transfers accepted from institutions abroad. *Admission tests:* Required: TOEFL (minimum score: iBT 61; paper-based 500; computer-based 173), THEA or approved alternate test. TOEFL can be waived under certain conditions. *Application deadline:* Rolling. *Services:* International student adviser on campus. ESL program at cooperating institution. Employment opportunities (on-campus) available. *Contact:* International Advisor, Alvin Community College, 3110 Mustang Road, Alvin, TX 77511. Telephone: 281-756-3531. Fax: 281-756-3843. E-mail: gburgess@alvincollege.edu. URL: http://www.alvincollege.edu.

AMARILLO COLLEGE, AMARILLO

General Information State and locally supported, 2-year, coed college. Urban setting. *Awards:* A. *Entrance level for U.S. students:* Noncompetitive. *Enrollment:* 10,354 total including 0.02% international students. *Undergraduate faculty:* 234. *Library holdings:* 80,000 books, 110 current serial subscriptions. *Total majors:* 83. *Expenses:* (2006–07) $2382; room only, $2000 (on campus). *Financial aid:* Forms required: institution's own financial aid form.

ANGELO STATE UNIVERSITY, SAN ANGELO

General Information State-supported, coed institution. Urban setting. *Awards:* A, B, M. *Entrance level for U.S. students:* Moderately difficult. *Enrollment:* 6,265 total; 5,805 undergraduates (54% women) including 1% international students from 20 foreign countries. *Faculty:* 344. *Library holdings:* 50,963 books, 22,004 current serial subscriptions, 27,149 audiovisual materials. *Total majors:* 40. *Expenses:* (2006–07) $10,404; room and board, $5314 (on campus); room only, $3147 (on campus). *Financial aid:* Non-need financial aid available. Forms required: institution's own financial aid form.

THE ART INSTITUTE OF HOUSTON, HOUSTON

General Information Proprietary, 4-year, coed college. Urban setting. *Awards:* A, B. *Entrance level for U.S. students:* Moderately difficult. *Enrollment:* 1,619 total (53% women) including international students from 19 foreign countries. *Undergraduate faculty:* 86. *Library holdings:* 10,000 books, 188 current serial subscriptions. *Total majors:* 7.

Information for International Students For fall 2006: 18 international students applied, 17 were accepted, 12 enrolled. Students can start in fall, winter, spring, or summer. Transfers accepted from institutions abroad. *Admission tests:* Required: ELS, ACCUPLACER. Recommended: ACT, SAT Subject Tests, TOEFL (minimum score: iBT 61; paper-based 500; computer-based 173). TOEFL can be waived under certain conditions. *Application deadline:* Rolling. *Expenses:* (2007–08) $25,400; room only, $6996 (on campus). *Financial aid:* Forms required: International Student's Certification of Finances. *Housing:* Guaranteed, also available during summer. *Services:* International student adviser on campus. ESL program at cooperating institution. ESL program available during the academic year and the summer. Internships available. *Contact:* Director of International Admissions, The Art Institute of Houston, 1900 Yorktown, Houston, TX 77056. Telephone: 713-623-2040. Fax: 713-966-2797. E-mail: aihadm@www.aih.aii.edu. URL: http://www.aih.artinstitutes.edu.

AUSTIN COLLEGE, SHERMAN

General Information Independent Presbyterian, coed institution. Suburban setting. *Awards:* B, M. *Entrance level for U.S. students:* Very difficult. *Enrollment:* 1,354 total; 1,321 undergraduates (54% women) including 1% international students from 25 foreign countries. *Faculty:* 134. *Library holdings:* 240,944 books, 2,181 current serial subscriptions. *Total majors:* 31. *Expenses:* (2007–08) $24,945; room and board, $8234 (on campus). *Financial aid:* Need-based college/university scholarships/grants from institutional funds, loans from outside sources. Non-need-based college/university scholarships/grants from institutional funds, loans from outside sources. Forms required: institution's own financial aid form, International Student's Financial Aid Application, International Student's Certification of Finances. For fall 2006 (estimated), 19 international students on campus received college administered financial aid ($6049 average).

AUSTIN COMMUNITY COLLEGE, AUSTIN

General Information District-supported, 2-year, coed college. Urban setting. *Awards:* A. *Entrance level for U.S. students:* Noncompetitive. *Enrollment:* 31,908 total (57% women) including 2% international students from 93 foreign countries. *Undergraduate faculty:* 1,601. *Library holdings:* 115,567 books, 1,974 current serial subscriptions, 14,044 audiovisual materials. *Total majors:* 75. *Expenses:* (2006–07) $7968. *Financial aid:* Forms required: institution's own financial aid form.

BAPTIST UNIVERSITY OF THE AMERICAS, SAN ANTONIO

General Information Independent Baptist, 4-year, coed college. *Awards:* B (associate degree in Cross-Cultural Studies). *Entrance level for U.S. students:* Difficulty N/R. *Enrollment:* 171 total (34% women) including 30% international students. *Undergraduate faculty:* 16. *Total majors:* 2.

Information for International Students For fall 2006: 25 international students applied, 25 were accepted, 10 enrolled. Students can start in fall or spring. *Admission tests:* Required: TOEFL (minimum score: paper-based 550; computer-based 200), ELS. *Application deadline:* 7/15. *Expenses:* (2006–07) $3750; room and board, $1537 (on campus); room only, $500 (on campus). *Services:* International student adviser on campus. Full-time ESL program on campus. ESL program available during the academic year. Employment opportunities (on-campus) available. *Contact:* Director of Admissions and Campus Relations, Baptist University of the Americas, 8019 South Pan Am Expressway, San Antonio, TX 78224. Telephone: 210-924-4338 Ext. 202. Fax: 210-924-2701. E-mail: mranjel@bua.edu. URL: http://www.bua.edu.

BAYLOR UNIVERSITY, WACO

General Information Independent Baptist, coed university. Urban setting. *Awards:* B, M, D, FP. *Entrance level for U.S. students:* Moderately difficult. *Enrollment:* 14,040 total; 11,831 undergraduates (59% women) including 2% international students from 90 foreign countries. *Faculty:* 928. *Library holdings:* 2.3 million books, 8,429 current serial subscriptions. *Total majors:* 132. *Expenses:* (2007–08) $24,490; room and board, $7526 (on campus); room only, $3774 (on campus).

BRAZOSPORT COLLEGE, LAKE JACKSON

General Information State and locally supported, 2-year, coed college. Small town setting. *Awards:* A. *Entrance level for U.S. students:* Noncompetitive. *Enrollment:* 3,503 total (55% women) including 1% international students from 11 foreign countries. *Undergraduate faculty:* 166. *Library holdings:* 85,425 books, 339 current serial subscriptions, 397 audiovisual materials. *Total majors:* 75. *Expenses:* (2006–07) $3330.

BROOKHAVEN COLLEGE, FARMERS BRANCH

General Information County-supported, 2-year, coed college. Suburban setting. *Awards:* A. *Entrance level for U.S. students:* Noncompetitive. *Enrollment:* 10,269 total (58% women) including 2% international students from 68 foreign countries. *Undergraduate faculty:* 702. *Library holdings:* 58,225 books, 117 current serial subscriptions, 12,400 audiovisual materials. *Total majors:* 10. *Expenses:* (2007–08) $2760.

CEDAR VALLEY COLLEGE, LANCASTER

General Information State-supported, 2-year, coed college. Suburban setting. *Awards:* A. *Entrance level for U.S. students:* Noncompetitive. *Enrollment:* 4,504 total including 0.2% international students from 5 foreign countries. *Undergraduate faculty:* 174. *Library holdings:* 43,788 books, 217 current serial subscriptions. *Total majors:* 16. *Expenses:* (2006–07) $2880. *Financial aid:* Forms required: FAFSA.

CENTRAL TEXAS COLLEGE, KILLEEN

General Information State and locally supported, 2-year, coed college. Suburban setting. *Awards:* A. *Entrance level for U.S. students:* Noncompetitive. *Enrollment:* 17,726 total (48% women) including 1% international students from 19 foreign countries. *Undergraduate faculty:* 1,970. *Library holdings:* 80,381 books, 467 current serial subscriptions. *Total majors:* 48. *Expenses:* (2006–07) $4290; room and board, $4550 (on campus).

CLARENDON COLLEGE, CLARENDON

General Information State and locally supported, 2-year, coed college. Rural setting. *Awards:* A. *Entrance level for U.S. students:* Noncompetitive. *Enrollment:* 1,102 total (47% women) including 1% international students from 6 foreign countries. *Undergraduate faculty:* 76. *Library holdings:* 22,000 books, 89 current serial subscriptions. *Total majors:* 42.

Information for International Students For fall 2006: 18 international students applied, 16 were accepted, 15 enrolled. Students can start in fall or spring. Transfers accepted from institutions abroad. *Admission tests:* Required: TOEFL (minimum score: paper-based 525; computer-based 195), THEA. *Application deadline:* 6/1. *Expenses:* (2006–07) $2820; room and board, $3250 (on campus); room only, $1190 (on campus). *Financial aid:* Forms required: institution's own financial aid form. *Housing:* Guaranteed. *Services:* International student adviser on campus. Full-time and part-time ESL programs on campus. ESL program available during the academic year. Employment opportunities (on-campus) available. *Contact:* Director of Admissions/Registrar, Clarendon College, PO Box 968, Clarendon, TX 79226-0968. Telephone: 806-874-3571 Ext. 107. Fax: 806-874-3201. E-mail: sharon.hannon@clarendoncollege.edu. URL: http://www.clarendoncollege.edu.

COASTAL BEND COLLEGE, BEEVILLE

General Information County-supported, 2-year, coed college. Rural setting. *Awards:* A. *Entrance level for U.S. students:* Noncompetitive. *Enrollment:* 3,267 total (62% women) including 1% international students from 3 foreign countries. *Undergraduate faculty:* 165. *Library holdings:* 43,004 books, 1,341 current serial subscriptions, 2,179 audiovisual materials. *Total majors:* 67. *Expenses:* (2007–08) $3176; room only, $1560 (on campus).

COLLEGE OF THE MAINLAND, TEXAS CITY

General Information State and locally supported, 2-year, coed college. Suburban setting. *Awards:* A. *Entrance level for U.S. students:* Noncompetitive. *Enrollment:* 3,999 total (59% women) including 0.1% international students. *Undergraduate faculty:* 213. *Library holdings:* 84,128 books, 19,000 current serial subscriptions, 492 audiovisual materials. *Total majors:* 25. *Expenses:* (2006–07) $2423. *Financial aid:* Need-based college/university scholarships/grants from institutional funds. Non-need-based college/university scholarships/grants from institutional funds, on-campus employment. Forms required: institution's own financial aid form, TASFA State Application.

COLLIN COUNTY COMMUNITY COLLEGE DISTRICT, PLANO

General Information State and locally supported, 2-year, coed college. Suburban setting. *Awards:* A. *Entrance level for U.S. students:* Noncompetitive. *Enrollment:* 19,332 total (56% women) including 2% international students from 86 foreign countries. *Undergraduate faculty:* 1,102. *Library holdings:* 259,627 books, 909 current serial subscriptions, 24,981 audiovisual materials. *Total majors:* 31. *Expenses:* (2006–07) $2856. *Financial aid:* Forms required: institution's own financial aid form.

COMMONWEALTH INSTITUTE OF FUNERAL SERVICE, HOUSTON

General Information Independent, 2-year, coed college. Urban setting. *Awards:* A. *Entrance level for U.S. students:* Moderately difficult. *Enrollment:* 164 total (53% women). *Undergraduate faculty:* 13. *Library holdings:* 1,500 books, 12 current serial subscriptions. *Total majors:* 1. *Expenses:* (2006–07) $9500.

CONCORDIA UNIVERSITY AT AUSTIN, AUSTIN

General Information Independent, coed institution, affiliated with Lutheran Church–Missouri Synod. Urban setting. *Awards:* A, B, M. *Entrance level for U.S. students:* Moderately difficult. *Enrollment:* 1,254 total; 1,164 undergraduates (58% women) including 0.2% international students. *Faculty:* 172. *Library holdings:* 50,756 books, 814 current serial subscriptions, 3,859 audiovisual materials. *Total majors:* 21. *Expenses:* (2007–08) $18,910; room and board, $7300 (on campus); room only, $4600 (on campus). *Financial aid:* Non-need-based college/university

Concordia University at Austin (continued)
scholarships/grants from institutional funds, loans from outside sources. Forms required: institution's own financial aid form.

THE CRISWELL COLLEGE, DALLAS

General Information Independent, coed institution, affiliated with Southern Baptist Convention. Urban setting. *Awards:* A, B, M, FP. *Entrance level for U.S. students:* Minimally difficult. *Enrollment:* 451 total; 336 undergraduates. *Faculty:* 29. *Library holdings:* 95,000 books, 500 current serial subscriptions. *Total majors:* 5. *Financial aid:* Need-based and non-need-based financial aid available. Forms required: institution's own financial aid form. 13 international students on campus received college administered financial aid ($800 average).

DALLAS BAPTIST UNIVERSITY, DALLAS

General Information Independent, coed institution, affiliated with Baptist General Convention of Texas. Urban setting. *Awards:* A, B, M. *Entrance level for U.S. students:* Moderately difficult. *Enrollment:* 5,153 total; 3,610 undergraduates (60% women) including 7% international students from 42 foreign countries. *Faculty:* 488. *Library holdings:* 266,502 books, 402 current serial subscriptions, 4,099 audiovisual materials. *Total majors:* 45. *Expenses:* (2006–07) $13,650; room and board, $4959 (on campus); room only, $1990 (on campus). *Financial aid:* Need-based loans from outside sources, on-campus employment. Non-need-based college/university scholarships/grants from institutional funds, tuition waivers, athletic awards, loans from outside sources, on-campus employment. Forms required: institution's own financial aid form. For fall 2006 (estimated), 148 international students on campus received college administered financial aid ($3691 average).

DALLAS INSTITUTE OF FUNERAL SERVICE, DALLAS

General Information Independent, 2-year, coed college. Urban setting. *Awards:* A. *Entrance level for U.S. students:* Noncompetitive. *Enrollment:* 247 total (48% women). *Undergraduate faculty:* 10. *Total majors:* 1. *Expenses:* (2006–07) $10,050.

DEL MAR COLLEGE, CORPUS CHRISTI

General Information State and locally supported, 2-year, coed college. Urban setting. *Awards:* A. *Entrance level for U.S. students:* Noncompetitive. *Enrollment:* 11,338 total including 1% international students from 57 foreign countries. *Undergraduate faculty:* 697. *Library holdings:* 127,717 books, 739 current serial subscriptions. *Total majors:* 102.
Information for International Students For fall 2006: 75 international students applied, 75 were accepted, 60 enrolled. Students can start in fall, spring, or summer. Transfers accepted from institutions abroad. *Admission tests:* Required: THEA. Recommended: TOEFL, ELS. *Application deadline:* 7/1. *Expenses:* (2006–07) $4192. *Services:* Full-time ESL program on campus. ESL program available during the academic year and the summer. Employment opportunities (on-campus) available. *Contact:* Assistant Director of Admissions and Assistant Registrar, Del Mar College, 101 Baldwin Boulevard, Corpus Christi, TX 78404-3897. Telephone: 361-698-1248. Fax: 361-698-1595. E-mail: bthomps@delmar.edu. URL: http://www.delmar.edu.

DEVRY UNIVERSITY, HOUSTON

General Information Proprietary, coed institution. *Awards:* A, B, M. *Entrance level for U.S. students:* Difficulty N/R. *Enrollment:* 832 total; 723 undergraduates (40% women) including 1% international students. *Faculty:* 67. *Total majors:* 8. *Expenses:* (2007–08) $13,220.

DEVRY UNIVERSITY, IRVING

General Information Proprietary, coed institution. Suburban setting. *Awards:* A, B, M. *Entrance level for U.S. students:* Minimally difficult. *Enrollment:* 1,717 total; 1,474 undergraduates (31% women) including 0.5% international students. *Faculty:* 103. *Library holdings:* 21,500 books, 6,365 current serial subscriptions. *Total majors:* 10. *Expenses:* (2007–08) $13,220.

EASTFIELD COLLEGE, MESQUITE

General Information State and locally supported, 2-year, coed college. Suburban setting. *Awards:* A. *Entrance level for U.S. students:* Noncompetitive. *Enrollment:* 12,111 total (59% women) including 1% international students. *Undergraduate faculty:* 496. *Library holdings:* 66,988 books, 415 current serial subscriptions, 2,620 audiovisual materials. *Total majors:* 29. *Expenses:* (2006–07) $3450.

EAST TEXAS BAPTIST UNIVERSITY, MARSHALL

General Information Independent Baptist, 4-year, coed college. Small town setting. *Awards:* A, B. *Entrance level for U.S. students:* Moderately difficult. *Enrollment:* 1,365 total (54% women) including 1% international students from 12 foreign countries. *Undergraduate faculty:* 102. *Library holdings:* 182,701 books, 15,000 current serial subscriptions, 3,363 audiovisual materials. *Total majors:* 44.
Information for International Students For fall 2006: 38 international students applied, 17 were accepted, 12 enrolled. Students can start in fall, winter, spring, or summer. Transfers accepted from institutions abroad. *Admission tests:* Required: TOEFL (minimum score: paper-based 500; computer-based 173). Recommended: SAT or ACT. TOEFL can be waived under certain conditions. *Application deadline:* Rolling. *Expenses:* (2006–07) $13,700; room and board, $4190 (on campus). *Financial aid:* Need-based college/university scholarships/grants from institutional funds, loans from outside sources, on-campus employment. Non-need-based college/university scholarships/grants from institutional funds, loans from outside sources, on-campus employment. Forms required: institution's own financial aid form. International transfer students are eligible to apply for aid. For fall 2006 (estimated), 6 international students on campus received college administered financial aid ($1282 average). *Housing:* Guaranteed, also available during summer. *Services:* International student adviser on campus. Employment opportunities (on-campus) available. *Contact:* Director of International Education, East Texas Baptist University, Office of International Education, 1209 North Grove, Marshall, TX 75670. Telephone: 903-923-2172. Fax: 903-927-4448. E-mail: ahuesing@etbu.edu. URL: http://www.etbu.edu.

EL CENTRO COLLEGE, DALLAS

General Information County-supported, 2-year, coed college. Urban setting. *Awards:* A. *Entrance level for U.S. students:* Noncompetitive. *Enrollment:* 6,281 total (70% women) including 2% international students from 62 foreign countries. *Undergraduate faculty:* 446. *Library holdings:* 77,902 books, 224 current serial subscriptions, 585 audiovisual materials. *Total majors:* 46. *Expenses:* (2006–07) $2544. *Financial aid:* Non-need financial aid available.

GALVESTON COLLEGE, GALVESTON

General Information State and locally supported, 2-year, coed college. Urban setting. *Awards:* A. *Entrance level for U.S. students:* Noncompetitive. *Enrollment:* 2,230 total (65% women) including 1% international students from 19 foreign countries. *Undergraduate faculty:* 141. *Library holdings:* 45,193 books, 4,000 current serial subscriptions, 1,500 audiovisual materials. *Total majors:* 32. *Expenses:* (2006–07) $2230. *Financial aid:* Non-need financial aid available.

HALLMARK INSTITUTE OF AERONAUTICS, SAN ANTONIO

General Information Private, 2-year, coed college. *Awards:* A. *Entrance level for U.S. students:* Difficulty N/R. *Total majors:* 2. *Financial aid:* Need-based loans from outside sources. Non-need-based loans from outside sources. Forms required: International Student's Certification of Finances.

HARDIN-SIMMONS UNIVERSITY, ABILENE

General Information Independent Baptist, coed institution. Urban setting. *Awards:* B, M, D, FP. *Entrance level for U.S. students:* Moderately difficult. *Enrollment:* 2,372 total; 1,942 undergraduates (56% women) including 0.5% international students from 12 foreign countries. *Faculty:* 184. *Library holdings:* 245,587 books, 36,225 current serial subscriptions, 10,767 audiovisual materials. *Total majors:* 74.
Information for International Students For fall 2006: 17 international students applied, 6 were accepted, 6 enrolled. Students can start in fall, spring, or summer. Transfers accepted from institutions abroad. *Admission tests:* Required: TOEFL (minimum score: paper-based 550; computer-based 213). Recommended: SAT or ACT. TOEFL can be waived under certain conditions. *Application deadline:* 6/1. *Expenses:* (2007–08) $16,946; room and board, $4950 (on campus); room only, $2602 (on campus). *Financial aid:* Non-need-based college/university scholarships/grants from institutional funds, on-campus employment. Forms required: International Student's Financial Aid Application, International Student's Certification of Finances. International transfer students are eligible to apply for aid. For fall 2006 (estimated), 5 international students on campus received college administered financial aid ($6636 average). *Housing:* Guaranteed, also available during summer. *Services:* International student adviser on campus. ESL program at cooperating institution. ESL program available during the academic year. Employment opportunities (on-campus) available. *Contact:* Coordinator of Graduate Admissions, Office of Enrollment Services, Hardin-Simmons University, 2200 Hickory Street, Box 16210,

Abilene, TX 79698. Telephone: 325-670-1299. Fax: 325-671-2115. E-mail: maim@hsutx.edu. URL: http://www.hsutx.edu.

HILL COLLEGE OF THE HILL JUNIOR COLLEGE DISTRICT, HILLSBORO

General Information District-supported, 2-year, coed college. Small town setting. *Awards:* A. *Entrance level for U.S. students:* Noncompetitive. *Enrollment:* 3,236 total (60% women) including 2% international students from 28 foreign countries. *Undergraduate faculty:* 243. *Library holdings:* 40,000 books, 300 current serial subscriptions, 500 audiovisual materials. *Total majors:* 86.
Information for International Students For fall 2006: 32 international students applied, 16 were accepted, 11 enrolled. Students can start in fall or spring. Transfers accepted from institutions abroad. *Admission tests:* Required: TOEFL (minimum score: iBT 61; paper-based 500; computer-based 173), TSI. TOEFL can be waived under certain conditions. *Application deadline:* Rolling. *Expenses:* (2006–07) $2350; room and board, $1400 (on campus); room only, $350 (on campus). *Financial aid:* Forms required: institution's own financial aid form. *Housing:* Guaranteed, also available during summer. *Services:* International student adviser on campus. Part-time ESL program on campus. ESL program available during the academic year. *Contact:* International Student Coordinator, Hill College of the Hill Junior College District, PO Box 619, Hillsboro, TX 76645. Telephone: 254-582-2555 Ext. 202. Fax: 254-582-7591. E-mail: tnors@hillcollege.edu. URL: http://www.hillcollege.edu.

HOUSTON BAPTIST UNIVERSITY, HOUSTON

General Information Independent Baptist, coed institution. Urban setting. *Awards:* A, B, M. *Entrance level for U.S. students:* Moderately difficult. *Enrollment:* 2,143 total; 1,815 undergraduates (67% women) including 7% international students from 30 foreign countries. *Faculty:* 177. *Library holdings:* 209,366 books, 21,000 current serial subscriptions, 9,255 audiovisual materials. *Total majors:* 65. *Expenses:* (2007–08) $17,716; room and board, $4995 (on campus); room only, $2460 (on campus). *Financial aid:* Non-need financial aid available. Forms required: International Student's Certification of Finances.

HOUSTON COMMUNITY COLLEGE SYSTEM, HOUSTON

General Information State and locally supported, 2-year, coed college. Urban setting. *Awards:* A. *Entrance level for U.S. students:* Noncompetitive. *Enrollment:* 42,526 total (59% women) including 10% international students. *Undergraduate faculty:* 3,323. *Library holdings:* 140,674 books, 2,012 current serial subscriptions, 16,334 audiovisual materials. *Total majors:* 65.
Information for International Students For fall 2006: 3284 international students applied, 3284 were accepted, 3284 enrolled. Students can start in fall, spring, or summer. Transfers accepted from institutions abroad. *Admission tests:* Required: CELSA, THEA, COMPASS, or ASSET. Recommended: SAT or ACT, TOEFL (minimum score: iBT 79; paper-based 550; computer-based 213; minimum score for ESL admission: paper-based 550; computer-based 213). TOEFL can be waived under certain conditions. *Application deadline:* 7/1. *Expenses:* (2007–08) $3090. *Financial aid:* Forms required: institution's own financial aid form. *Services:* International student adviser on campus. Full-time ESL program on campus. ESL program available during the academic year. Employment opportunities (on-campus) available. *Contact:* Director of International/Veteran Student Services, Houston Community College System, PO Box 667517, 3100 Main Street, Houston, TX 77266-7517. Telephone: 713-718-8519. Fax: 713-718-2112. E-mail: emmett.pugh@hccs.edu. URL: http://www.hccs.edu.

HOWARD COLLEGE, BIG SPRING

General Information State and locally supported, 2-year, coed college. Small town setting. *Awards:* A. *Entrance level for U.S. students:* Noncompetitive. *Enrollment:* 2,725 total (62% women) including 0.2% international students from 2 foreign countries. *Undergraduate faculty:* 188. *Library holdings:* 30,921 books, 16,006 current serial subscriptions, 1,710 audiovisual materials. *Total majors:* 31.
Information for International Students For fall 2006: 12 international students applied, 12 were accepted, 12 enrolled. Students can start in fall, spring, or summer. Transfers accepted from institutions abroad. *Admission tests:* Required: TOEFL (minimum score: paper-based 500; computer-based 173), THEA, unless qualified for exemption by state rules. Recommended: SAT, ACT. TOEFL can be waived under certain conditions. *Application deadline:* 5/15. *Financial aid:* Forms required: institution's own financial aid form, FAFSA. *Housing:* Available during summer. *Services:* International student adviser on campus. Full-time and part-time ESL programs on campus. ESL program available during the academic year and the summer. Internships and employment opportunities (on-campus) available. *Contact:* International Student

Admissions Advisor/PDSO, Howard College, 1001 Birdwell Lane, Big Spring, TX 79720. Telephone: 432-264-5000 Ext. 5114. Fax: 432-264-5634. E-mail: lcurrie@howardcollege.edu. URL: http://www.howardcollege.edu.

HOWARD PAYNE UNIVERSITY, BROWNWOOD

General Information Independent, 4-year, coed college, affiliated with Baptist General Convention of Texas. Small town setting. *Awards:* A, B. *Entrance level for U.S. students:* Moderately difficult. *Enrollment:* 1,328 total; 1,317 undergraduates (49% women) including 0.2% international students from 2 foreign countries. *Undergraduate faculty:* 146. *Library holdings:* 75,055 books, 411 current serial subscriptions, 1,351 audiovisual materials. *Total majors:* 77.
Information for International Students For fall 2006: 5 international students applied, 1 was accepted, 1 enrolled. Students can start in fall, spring, or summer. Transfers accepted from institutions abroad. *Admission tests:* Required: TOEFL (minimum score: paper-based 550; computer-based 213), ELS. Recommended: SAT, ACT. TOEFL can be waived under certain conditions. *Application deadline:* 8/14. *Expenses:* (2007–08) $15,515; room and board, $2256 (on campus); room only, $1010 (on campus). *Financial aid:* Non-need financial aid available. Forms required: International Student's Certification of Finances. 2 international students on campus received college administered financial aid ($12,538 average). *Housing:* Guaranteed, also available during summer. *Services:* International student adviser on campus. Internships and employment opportunities (on-campus) available. *Contact:* Coordinator of International and Extended Education, Howard Payne University, 1000 Fisk Avenue, Brownwood, TX 76801. Telephone: 325-649-8406. Fax: 325-649-8927. E-mail: btaylor@hputx.edu. URL: http://www.hputx.edu.

JACKSONVILLE COLLEGE, JACKSONVILLE

General Information Independent Baptist, 2-year, coed college. Small town setting. *Awards:* A. *Entrance level for U.S. students:* Noncompetitive. *Enrollment:* 300 total (60% women) including 3% international students from 15 foreign countries. *Undergraduate faculty:* 24. *Library holdings:* 22,000 books, 170 current serial subscriptions. *Total majors:* 2. *Expenses:* (2006–07) $3107; room and board, $1373 (on campus). *Financial aid:* Forms required: institution's own financial aid form.

KILGORE COLLEGE, KILGORE

General Information State and locally supported, 2-year, coed college. Small town setting. *Awards:* A. *Entrance level for U.S. students:* Noncompetitive. *Enrollment:* 4,957 total (62% women) including 2% international students from 36 foreign countries. *Undergraduate faculty:* 247. *Library holdings:* 65,000 books, 6,679 current serial subscriptions, 13,351 audiovisual materials. *Total majors:* 65.
Information for International Students For fall 2006: 200 international students applied, 140 enrolled. Students can start in fall or spring. Transfers accepted from institutions abroad. *Application deadline:* Rolling. *Expenses:* (2006–07) $3472; room and board, $3580 (on campus); room only, $1580 (on campus). *Financial aid:* Forms required: institution's own financial aid form, income verification. *Services:* International student adviser on campus. Full-time and part-time ESL programs on campus. ESL program available during the academic year. *Contact:* Director, International Student Programs, Kilgore College, 1100 Broadway, Kilgore, TX 75662. Telephone: 903-983-8204. Fax: 903-983-8607. E-mail: bthornhill@kilgore.edu. URL: http://www.kilgore.edu.
See In-Depth Description on page 111.

KINGWOOD COLLEGE, KINGWOOD

General Information State and locally supported, 2-year, coed college. Suburban setting. *Awards:* A. *Entrance level for U.S. students:* Noncompetitive. *Enrollment:* 6,842 total (63% women) including 2% international students from 44 foreign countries. *Undergraduate faculty:* 387. *Library holdings:* 38,000 books, 262 current serial subscriptions, 3,177 audiovisual materials. *Total majors:* 17.
Information for International Students For fall 2006: 165 international students applied, 165 were accepted, 165 enrolled. Students can start in fall, spring, or summer. Transfers accepted from institutions abroad. *Admission tests:* Required: SAT or ACT, TOEFL. Recommended: ACT, CELT. TOEFL can be waived under certain conditions. *Application deadline:* Rolling. *Expenses:* (2006–07) $2304. *Financial aid:* Need-based college/university scholarships/grants from institutional funds, loans from institutional funds, on-campus employment. Non-need-based TPEG funds. Forms required: institution's own financial aid form, TASFAA (Texas Application for Student Financial Aid Assistance). *Services:* International student adviser on campus. Full-time ESL program on campus. ESL program available during the academic

Kingwood College (continued)

year and the summer. Internships and employment opportunities (on-campus) available. *Contact:* Kingwood College, 20000 Kingwood Drive, Kingwood, TX 77339-3801. Telephone: 281-312-1536. Fax: 281-312-1477. E-mail: Ursula.Sledge@nhmccd.edu. URL: http://kcweb.nhmccd.edu.

LAMAR STATE COLLEGE–PORT ARTHUR, PORT ARTHUR

General Information State-supported, 2-year, coed college. Suburban setting. *Awards:* A. *Entrance level for U.S. students:* Noncompetitive. *Enrollment:* 2,530 total (64% women) including 0.3% international students. *Undergraduate faculty:* 125. *Library holdings:* 43,726 books, 3,400 current serial subscriptions, 1,493 audiovisual materials. *Total majors:* 24.

Information for International Students Students can start in fall, spring, or summer. Transfers accepted from institutions abroad. *Admission tests:* Required: TOEFL (minimum score: paper-based 500; computer-based 173; minimum score for ESL admission: paper-based 500; computer-based 173), THEA, COMPASS or ASSET. TOEFL can be waived under certain conditions. *Application deadline:* 6/15. *Expenses:* (2006–07) $11,414. *Financial aid:* Need-based financial aid available. *Services:* International student adviser on campus. ESL program at cooperating institution. ESL program available during the academic year and the summer. *Contact:* Graduation Coordinator and Records Clerk, Lamar State College–Port Arthur, PO Box 310, 1500 Procter Street, Port Arthur, TX 77641-0310. Telephone: 409-984 6176. Fax: 409-984-6025. E-mail: Marie.Graham@lamarpa.edu. URL: http://www.lamarpa.edu.

LAMAR UNIVERSITY, BEAUMONT

General Information State-supported, coed university. Suburban setting. *Awards:* A, B, M, D. *Entrance level for U.S. students:* Minimally difficult. *Enrollment:* 10,595 total; 9,684 undergraduates (60% women) including 1% international students from 27 foreign countries. *Faculty:* 542. *Library holdings:* 698,285 books, 2,900 current serial subscriptions, 6,572 audiovisual materials. *Total majors:* 102. *Expenses:* (2006–07) $10,704; room and board, $5888 (on campus); room only, $3990 (on campus). *Financial aid:* Need-based college/university scholarships/grants from institutional funds. Forms required: institution's own financial aid form, FAFSA info, tax returns, W-2s, verification worksheet. For fall 2006 (estimated), international students on campus received college administered aid averaging $1500.

LAREDO COMMUNITY COLLEGE, LAREDO

General Information State and locally supported, 2-year, coed college. Urban setting. *Awards:* A. *Entrance level for U.S. students:* Noncompetitive. *Enrollment:* 8,152 total (58% women) including 3% international students from 5 foreign countries. *Undergraduate faculty:* 343. *Library holdings:* 88,006 books, 555 current serial subscriptions. *Total majors:* 29. *Expenses:* (2006–07) $3060; room and board, $4229 (on campus); room only, $2600 (on campus). *Financial aid:* Forms required: institution's own financial aid form.

LEE COLLEGE, BAYTOWN

General Information District-supported, 2-year, coed college. Suburban setting. *Awards:* A. *Entrance level for U.S. students:* Noncompetitive. *Enrollment:* 5,347 total (53% women) including 2% international students from 44 foreign countries. *Undergraduate faculty:* 399. *Library holdings:* 100,000 books, 660 current serial subscriptions. *Total majors:* 60. *Expenses:* (2006–07) $2277. *Financial aid:* Forms required: FAFSA.

LETOURNEAU UNIVERSITY, LONGVIEW

General Information Independent nondenominational, coed institution. Suburban setting. *Awards:* A, B, M. *Entrance level for U.S. students:* Difficulty N/R. *Enrollment:* 3,975 total; 3,635 undergraduates (58% women) including 1% international students from 27 foreign countries. *Faculty:* 352. *Library holdings:* 84,779 books, 383 current serial subscriptions, 3,144 audiovisual materials. *Total majors:* 41. *Expenses:* (2006–07) $16,920; room and board, $6570 (on campus). *Financial aid:* Non-need financial aid available. For fall 2005, 22 international students on campus received college administered financial aid ($3630 average).

LUBBOCK CHRISTIAN UNIVERSITY, LUBBOCK

General Information Independent, coed institution, affiliated with Church of Christ. Suburban setting. *Awards:* B, M, FP. *Entrance level for U.S. students:* Moderately difficult. *Enrollment:* 2,076 total; 1,832 undergraduates (57% women) including 1% international students from 13 foreign countries. *Faculty:* 154. *Library holdings:* 113,556 books, 545 current serial subscriptions.

Total majors: 44. *Expenses:* (2007–08) $14,290; room and board, $4750 (on campus). *Financial aid:* Non-need-based college/university scholarships/grants from institutional funds. Forms required: institution's own financial aid form. For fall 2006 (estimated), 8 international students on campus received college administered financial aid ($1313 average).

MCLENNAN COMMUNITY COLLEGE, WACO

General Information County-supported, 2-year, coed college. Urban setting. *Awards:* A. *Entrance level for U.S. students:* Noncompetitive. *Enrollment:* 7,794 total (67% women) including 0.4% international students. *Undergraduate faculty:* 389. *Library holdings:* 93,000 books, 400 current serial subscriptions. *Total majors:* 26. *Expenses:* (2007–08) $3000. *Financial aid:* Need-based college/university scholarships/grants from institutional funds, tuition waivers, athletic awards. Non-need-based college/university scholarships/grants from institutional funds, tuition waivers, athletic awards. Forms required: Institutional Application.

MCMURRY UNIVERSITY, ABILENE

General Information Independent United Methodist, 4-year, coed college. Urban setting. *Awards:* B. *Entrance level for U.S. students:* Moderately difficult. *Enrollment:* 1,385 total (50% women) including 1% international students from 9 foreign countries. *Undergraduate faculty:* 132. *Library holdings:* 156,550 books, 680 current serial subscriptions, 1,928 audiovisual materials. *Total majors:* 46.

Information for International Students For fall 2006: 41 international students applied, 9 were accepted, 4 enrolled. Students can start in fall, spring, or summer. Transfers accepted from institutions abroad. *Admission tests:* Required: TOEFL (minimum score: iBT 80; paper-based 550; computer-based 213). Recommended: SAT or ACT. TOEFL can be waived under certain conditions. *Application deadline:* Rolling. *Expenses:* (2007–08) $16,300; room and board, $6425 (on campus); room only, $3128 (on campus). *Financial aid:* Need-based college/university scholarships/grants from institutional funds, loans from outside sources, on-campus employment. Non-need-based college/university scholarships/grants from institutional funds, loans from outside sources, on-campus employment. For fall 2006 (estimated), 12 international students on campus received college administered financial aid ($12,060 average). *Housing:* Guaranteed, also available during summer. *Services:* International student adviser on campus. Internships and employment opportunities (on-campus) available. *Contact:* Director of Admission, McMurry University, McMurry Station Box 278, Abilene, TX 79697. Telephone: 325-793-4700. Fax: 325-793-4701. E-mail: admissions@mcm.edu. URL: http://www.mcm.edu.

MIDLAND COLLEGE, MIDLAND

General Information State and locally supported, primarily 2-year, coed college. Suburban setting. *Awards:* A, B. *Entrance level for U.S. students:* Noncompetitive. *Enrollment:* 5,531 total (57% women) including 1% international students from 31 foreign countries. *Undergraduate faculty:* 269. *Library holdings:* 65,760 books, 285 current serial subscriptions, 359 audiovisual materials. *Total majors:* 59.

Information for International Students For fall 2006: 30 international students applied, 15 were accepted, 10 enrolled. Students can start in fall, winter, spring, or summer. Transfers accepted from institutions abroad. *Admission tests:* Required: TOEFL (minimum score: paper-based 525; computer-based 193). *Application deadline:* 7/15. *Expenses:* (2006–07) $2702; room and board, $3600 (on campus). *Services:* International student adviser on campus. Part-time ESL program on campus. ESL program available during the academic year. *Contact:* Director of Counseling, Midland College, 3600 North Garfield, Midland, TX 79705. Telephone: 432-685-4505. Fax: 432-685-4623. E-mail: sgrinnan@midland.edu. URL: http://www.midland.edu.

MIDWESTERN STATE UNIVERSITY, WICHITA FALLS

General Information State-supported, coed institution. Urban setting. *Awards:* A, B, M. *Entrance level for U.S. students:* Minimally difficult. *Enrollment:* 6,042 total; 5,367 undergraduates (58% women) including 5% international students from 30 foreign countries. *Faculty:* 314. *Library holdings:* 441,251 books, 1,246 current serial subscriptions, 27,363 audiovisual materials. *Total majors:* 58.

Information for International Students For fall 2006: 350 international students applied, 150 were accepted, 80 enrolled. Students can start in fall, winter, spring, or summer. Transfers accepted from institutions abroad. *Admission tests:* Required: SAT or ACT, TOEFL (minimum score: iBT 79; paper-based 550; computer-based 213; minimum score for ESL admission: iBT 79; paper-based 550; computer-based 213). TOEFL can be waived under certain conditions. *Application deadline:* 4/1. *Expenses:* (2007–08)

$5616; room and board, $5220 (on campus); room only, $2660 (on campus). *Financial aid:* Need-based college/university scholarships/grants from institutional funds, tuition waivers, loans from outside sources, on-campus employment. Non-need-based college/university scholarships/grants from institutional funds, tuition waivers, athletic awards, loans from outside sources, on-campus employment, outside grants. Forms required: institution's own financial aid form. For fall 2006 (estimated), 220 international students on campus received college administered financial aid ($1479 average). *Housing:* Guaranteed, also available during summer. *Services:* International student adviser on campus. Full-time and part-time ESL programs on campus. ESL program available during the academic year. Employment opportunities (on-campus) available. *Contact:* Associate Director, Midwestern State University, Office of International Services, 3410 Taft Boulevard, Wichita Falls, TX 76308. Telephone: 940-397 4344. Fax: 940-397-4087. E-mail: kerrie.cale@nexus.mwsu.edu. URL: http://www.mwsu.edu.

MONTGOMERY COLLEGE, CONROE

General Information State and locally supported, 2-year, coed college. Suburban setting. *Awards:* A. *Entrance level for U.S. students:* Noncompetitive. *Enrollment:* 8,306 total (61% women) including 1% international students. *Undergraduate faculty:* 466. *Library holdings:* 4,000 books, 375 current serial subscriptions. *Total majors:* 18. *Expenses:* (2006–07) $2324. *Financial aid:* Need-based financial aid available. Forms required: institution's own financial aid form.

MOUNTAIN VIEW COLLEGE, DALLAS

General Information State and locally supported, 2-year, coed college. Urban setting. *Awards:* A. *Entrance level for U.S. students:* Noncompetitive. *Enrollment:* 6,496 total including 1% international students from 36 foreign countries. *Undergraduate faculty:* 310. *Total majors:* 16. *Expenses:* (2006–07) $2968.

NORTH LAKE COLLEGE, IRVING

General Information County-supported, 2-year, coed college. Suburban setting. *Awards:* A. *Entrance level for U.S. students:* Noncompetitive. *Enrollment:* 9,397 total (53% women) including 10% international students from 21 foreign countries. *Undergraduate faculty:* 537. *Library holdings:* 34,000 books, 400 current serial subscriptions. *Total majors:* 15.
Information for International Students For fall 2006: 175 international students applied, 150 were accepted, 140 enrolled. Students can start in fall, spring, or summer. Transfers accepted from institutions abroad. *Admission tests:* Required: TOEFL (minimum score: paper-based 530; computer-based 197). *Application deadline:* 6/1. *Expenses:* (2006–07) $3430. *Services:* International student adviser on campus. Full-time and part-time ESL programs on campus. ESL program available during the academic year. Internships and employment opportunities (on-campus) available. *Contact:* Director, ESOL/International Student Services, North Lake College, 5001 North MacArthur Boulevard, Irving, TX 75038-3899. Telephone: 972-273-3154. Fax: 972-273-3138. E-mail: sspence@dccccd.cdu. URL: http://www.northlakecollege.edu.

NORTHWEST VISTA COLLEGE, SAN ANTONIO

General Information State and locally supported, 2-year, coed college. Urban setting. *Awards:* A. *Entrance level for U.S. students:* Noncompetitive. *Enrollment:* 8,519 total including 0.2% international students. *Undergraduate faculty:* 497. *Total majors:* 16.
Information for International Students For fall 2006: 17 international students applied, 17 were accepted, 17 enrolled. Students can start in fall, spring, or summer. Transfers accepted from institutions abroad. *Admission tests:* Required: TOEFL (minimum score: iBT 45; paper-based 450; computer-based 133; minimum score for ESL admission: iBT 45; paper-based 450; computer-based 133), Michigan Exam. TOEFL can be waived under certain conditions. *Application deadline:* 8/1. *Expenses:* (2007–08) $4542. *Financial aid:* International transfer students are eligible to apply for aid. *Services:* International student adviser on campus. Full-time and part-time ESL programs on campus. ESL program available during the academic year and the summer. Internships and employment opportunities (on-campus) available. *Contact:* Student Success Professional, Northwest Vista College, 3535 North Ellison Drive, San Antonio, TX 78251. Telephone: 210-348-2334. Fax: 210-348-2024. E-mail: rgardner@accd.edu. URL: http://www.accd.edu/nvc.

NORTHWOOD UNIVERSITY, TEXAS CAMPUS, CEDAR HILL

General Information Independent, 4-year, coed college. Small town setting. *Awards:* A, B. *Entrance level for U.S. students:* Moderately difficult. *Enrollment:* 979 total (59% women) including

4% international students from 15 foreign countries. *Undergraduate faculty:* 32. *Library holdings:* 1,000 books, 140 current serial subscriptions, 427 audiovisual materials. *Total majors:* 13. *Expenses:* (2007–08) $16,455; room and board, $6888 (on campus); room only, $3720 (on campus). *Financial aid:* Non-need-based college/university scholarships/grants from institutional funds, tuition waivers, athletic awards, loans from outside sources. Forms required: International Student's Certification of Finances. For fall 2006 (estimated), 19 international students on campus received college administered financial aid ($8750 average).

OUR LADY OF THE LAKE UNIVERSITY OF SAN ANTONIO, SAN ANTONIO

General Information Independent Roman Catholic, coed institution. Urban setting. *Awards:* B, M, D. *Entrance level for U.S. students:* Moderately difficult. *Enrollment:* 2,783 total; 1,710 undergraduates (76% women) including 1% international students from 10 foreign countries. *Faculty:* 240. *Library holdings:* 162,154 books, 38,900 current serial subscriptions. *Total majors:* 31. *Expenses:* (2006–07) $18,400; room and board, $5767 (on campus); room only, $3388 (on campus). *Financial aid:* Non-need financial aid available. Forms required: International Student's Certification of Finances. 20 international students on campus received college administered financial aid ($6548 average).

PALO ALTO COLLEGE, SAN ANTONIO

General Information State and locally supported, 2-year, coed college. Urban setting. *Awards:* A. *Entrance level for U.S. students:* Noncompetitive. *Enrollment:* 8,038 total including 0.4% international students. *Undergraduate faculty:* 402. *Total majors:* 38. *Expenses:* (2007–08) $5736.

PANOLA COLLEGE, CARTHAGE

General Information State and locally supported, 2-year, coed college. Small town setting. *Awards:* A. *Entrance level for U.S. students:* Noncompetitive. *Enrollment:* 1,871 total (67% women) including 1% international students from 7 foreign countries. *Undergraduate faculty:* 63. *Library holdings:* 104,086 books, 347 current serial subscriptions, 300 audiovisual materials. *Total majors:* 5. *Expenses:* (2006–07) $2256; room and board, $3300 (on campus). *Financial aid:* Need-based college/university scholarships/grants from institutional funds, on-campus employment. Non-need-based college/university scholarships/grants from institutional funds, tuition waivers, athletic awards. Forms required: institution's own financial aid form.

PARIS JUNIOR COLLEGE, PARIS

General Information State and locally supported, 2-year, coed college. Rural setting. *Awards:* A. *Entrance level for U.S. students:* Noncompetitive. *Enrollment:* 4,118 total (64% women) including 0.2% international students. *Undergraduate faculty:* 209. *Library holdings:* 38,150 books, 404 current serial subscriptions. *Total majors:* 23. *Expenses:* (2006–07) $2748; room and board, $1882 (on campus); room only, $690 (on campus).

PRAIRIE VIEW A&M UNIVERSITY, PRAIRIE VIEW

General Information State-supported, coed institution. Small town setting. *Awards:* B, M, D. *Entrance level for U.S. students:* Moderately difficult. *Enrollment:* 8,023 total; 5,813 undergraduates (57% women) including 2% international students from 34 foreign countries. *Faculty:* 484. *Library holdings:* 1.1 million books, 39,724 current serial subscriptions, 2,986 audiovisual materials. *Total majors:* 41. *Expenses:* (2007–08) $17,671; room and board, $7226 (on campus); room only, $6342 (on campus). *Financial aid:* Non-need financial aid available. Forms required: institution's own financial aid form. 10 international students on campus received college administered financial aid ($7000 average).

RICE UNIVERSITY, HOUSTON

General Information Independent, coed university. Urban setting. *Awards:* B, M, D. *Entrance level for U.S. students:* Most difficult. *Enrollment:* 5,119 total; 3,049 undergraduates (49% women) including 4% international students from 44 foreign countries. *Faculty:* 701. *Library holdings:* 2.5 million books, 13,486 current serial subscriptions, 57,728 audiovisual materials. *Total majors:* 59. *Expenses:* (2007–08) $28,900; room and board, $10,250 (on campus); room only, $6750 (on campus). *Financial aid:* Non-need-based college/university scholarships/grants from institutional funds, athletic awards. Forms required: International Student's Certification of Finances. For fall 2006 (estimated), 43 international students on campus received college administered financial aid ($22,287 average).

ST. EDWARD'S UNIVERSITY, AUSTIN

General Information Independent Roman Catholic, coed institution. Urban setting. *Awards:* B, M. *Entrance level for U.S.*

Texas

St. Edward's University (continued)

students: Moderately difficult. *Enrollment:* 5,224 total; 4,229 undergraduates (60% women) including 2% international students from 36 foreign countries. *Faculty:* 472. *Library holdings:* 188,256 books, 464 current serial subscriptions, 3,177 audiovisual materials. *Total majors:* 49. *Expenses:* (2007–08) $20,400; room and board, $7460 (on campus); room only, $4310 (on campus).

ST. MARY'S UNIVERSITY OF SAN ANTONIO, SAN ANTONIO

General Information Independent Roman Catholic, coed institution. Urban setting. *Awards:* B, M, D, FP. *Entrance level for U.S. students:* Moderately difficult. *Enrollment:* 3,904 total; 2,400 undergraduates (60% women) including 4% international students from 31 foreign countries. *Faculty:* 333. *Library holdings:* 481,137 books, 1,213 current serial subscriptions. *Total majors:* 46.

Information for International Students For fall 2006: 197 international students applied, 25 were accepted, 16 enrolled. Students can start in fall, spring, or summer. Transfers accepted from institutions abroad. *Admission tests:* Required: TOEFL (minimum score: iBT 79; paper-based 550; computer-based 213; minimum score for ESL admission: iBT 45; paper-based 450; computer-based 133). *Application deadline:* Rolling. *Expenses:* (2006–07) $19,934; room and board, $6780 (on campus); room only, $3900 (on campus). *Financial aid:* Need-based financial aid available. Non-need-based college/university scholarships/grants from institutional funds, athletic awards, on-campus employment. Forms required: International Student's Certification of Finances. International transfer students are eligible to apply for aid. 104 international students on campus received college administered financial aid ($12,998 average). *Housing:* Guaranteed, also available during summer. *Services:* International student adviser on campus. Full-time ESL program on campus. ESL program available during the summer. Internships and employment opportunities (on-campus and off-campus) available. *Contact:* Director of Admissions, Admissions Office, St. Mary's University of San Antonio, One Camino Santa Maria, San Antonio, TX 78228. Telephone: 210-431-2266. Fax: 210-431-6742. E-mail: cbirdwell@stmarytx.edu. URL: http://www.stmarytx.edu.

See In-Depth Description on page 170.

ST. PHILIP'S COLLEGE, SAN ANTONIO

General Information District-supported, 2-year, coed college. Urban setting. *Awards:* A. *Entrance level for U.S. students:* Noncompetitive. *Enrollment:* 9,264 total (58% women) including 0.2% international students from 9 foreign countries. *Undergraduate faculty:* 581. *Library holdings:* 121,173 books, 623 current serial subscriptions, 11,577 audiovisual materials. *Total majors:* 73. *Expenses:* (2007–08) $5612.

SAM HOUSTON STATE UNIVERSITY, HUNTSVILLE

General Information State-supported, coed university. Small town setting. *Awards:* B, M, D. *Entrance level for U.S. students:* Moderately difficult. *Enrollment:* 15,935 total; 13,761 undergraduates (57% women) including 1% international students from 40 foreign countries. *Faculty:* 681. *Library holdings:* 1.2 million books, 4,521 current serial subscriptions. *Total majors:* 96.

Information for International Students For fall 2006: 235 international students applied, 124 were accepted, 47 enrolled. Students can start in fall, winter, spring, or summer. Transfers accepted from institutions abroad. *Admission tests:* Required: SAT or ACT, TOEFL (minimum score: paper-based 550; computer-based 213). TOEFL can be waived under certain conditions. *Application deadline:* Rolling. *Expenses:* (2006–07) $13,146; room and board, $5880 (on campus); room only, $3640 (on campus). *Financial aid:* Need-based college/university scholarships/grants from institutional funds, tuition waivers, athletic awards, loans from outside sources. Non-need-based college/university scholarships/grants from institutional funds, tuition waivers, athletic awards, loans from outside sources. Forms required: institution's own financial aid form. For fall 2005, 45 international students on campus received college administered financial aid ($2042 average). *Housing:* Available during summer. *Services:* International student adviser on campus. Full-time ESL program on campus. ESL program available during the academic year and the summer. Employment opportunities (on-campus) available. *Contact:* Undergraduate Admissions, Sam Houston State University, Box 2418, Huntsville, TX 77341-2418. Telephone: 936-294-1584. Fax: 936-294-3758. E-mail: admissions@shsu.edu. URL: http://www.shsu.edu.

See In-Depth Description on page 172.

SAN ANTONIO COLLEGE, SAN ANTONIO

General Information State and locally supported, 2-year, coed college. Urban setting. *Awards:* A. *Entrance level for U.S. students:* Noncompetitive. *Enrollment:* 21,800 total (60% women) including

2% international students from 112 foreign countries. *Undergraduate faculty:* 1,000. *Library holdings:* 233,714 books, 1,498 current serial subscriptions. *Total majors:* 44. *Expenses:* (2007–08) $4690.

SAN JACINTO COLLEGE CENTRAL CAMPUS, PASADENA

General Information State and locally supported, 2-year, coed college. Suburban setting. *Awards:* A. *Entrance level for U.S. students:* Noncompetitive. *Enrollment:* 11,370 total (55% women) including international students from 99 foreign countries. *Undergraduate faculty:* 530. *Library holdings:* 138,781 books, 465 current serial subscriptions, 771 audiovisual materials. *Total majors:* 84.

Information for International Students Students can start in fall, winter, spring, or summer. *Admission tests:* Required: TOEFL (minimum score: iBT 69; paper-based 525; computer-based 193; minimum score for ESL admission: iBT 16; paper-based 330; computer-based 53). Recommended: CELSA. TOEFL can be waived under certain conditions. *Application deadline:* Rolling. *Financial aid:* Forms required: International Student's Financial Aid Application, International Student's Certification of Finances. *Services:* International student adviser on campus. Full-time ESL program on campus. ESL program available during the academic year and the summer. Employment opportunities (on-campus) available. *Contact:* International Counselor, San Jacinto College Central Campus, 8060 Spencer Highway, Pasadena, TX 77505. Telephone: 281-998-6150 Ext. 1014. Fax: 281-478-2793. E-mail: monique.smith@sjcd.edu. URL: http://www.sjcd.edu.

SAN JACINTO COLLEGE NORTH CAMPUS, HOUSTON

General Information State and locally supported, 2-year, coed college. Suburban setting. *Awards:* A. *Entrance level for U.S. students:* Noncompetitive. *Enrollment:* 5,070 total (61% women) including international students from 61 foreign countries. *Undergraduate faculty:* 311. *Library holdings:* 53,007 books, 420 current serial subscriptions. *Total majors:* 64.

Information for International Students Students can start in fall, winter, spring, or summer. *Admission tests:* Required: TOEFL (minimum score: iBT 69; paper-based 525; computer-based 193; minimum score for ESL admission: iBT 16; paper-based 330; computer-based 53). Recommended: CELSA. TOEFL can be waived under certain conditions. *Application deadline:* Rolling. *Services:* International student adviser on campus. Full-time ESL program on campus. ESL program available during the academic year and the summer. Employment opportunities (on-campus) available. *Contact:* International Counselor, San Jacinto College North Campus, 5800 Uvalde Road, Houston, TX 77049. Telephone: 281-998-6150 Ext. 2317. Fax: 281-459-7149. E-mail: laronda.ashford@sjcd.edu. URL: http://www.sjcd.edu.

SAN JACINTO COLLEGE SOUTH CAMPUS, HOUSTON

General Information State and locally supported, 2-year, coed college. Suburban setting. *Awards:* A. *Entrance level for U.S. students:* Noncompetitive. *Enrollment:* 7,308 total (56% women) including international students from 110 foreign countries. *Undergraduate faculty:* 339. *Library holdings:* 63,000 books, 320 current serial subscriptions. *Total majors:* 38.

Information for International Students Students can start in fall, winter, spring, or summer. *Admission tests:* Required: TOEFL (minimum score: iBT 69; paper-based 525; computer-based 193; minimum score for ESL admission: iBT 16; paper-based 330; computer-based 53). Recommended: CELSA. TOEFL can be waived under certain conditions. *Application deadline:* Rolling. *Services:* International student adviser on campus. Full-time ESL program on campus. ESL program available during the academic year and the summer. Employment opportunities (on-campus) available. *Contact:* International Counselor, San Jacinto College South Campus, 13735 Beamer Road, Houston, TX 77089. Telephone: 281-929-6636. Fax: 281-929-4656. E-mail: nancy.hashemi@sjcd.edu. URL: http://www.sjcd.edu.

SCHREINER UNIVERSITY, KERRVILLE

General Information Independent Presbyterian, coed institution. Small town setting. *Awards:* A, B, M. *Entrance level for U.S. students:* Moderately difficult. *Enrollment:* 842 total; 793 undergraduates (60% women) including 1% international students from 2 foreign countries. *Faculty:* 82. *Library holdings:* 69,873 books, 225 current serial subscriptions, 477 audiovisual materials. *Total majors:* 33.

Information for International Students For fall 2006: 19 international students applied, 8 were accepted, 7 enrolled. Students can start in fall or spring. Transfers accepted from institutions abroad. *Admission tests:* Required: SAT or ACT, TOEFL (minimum score: iBT 79; paper-based 550; computer-based 213). Recommended: ELS. TOEFL can be waived under certain conditions. *Application deadline:* 4/1. *Expenses:* (2006–07) $15,879; room and board, $7566 (on campus); room only, $4134 (on campus). *Financial aid:* Need-based college/university scholarships/grants from institutional funds, loans from outside sources, on-campus employment. Non-need-based college/university scholarships/grants from institutional funds, loans from outside sources, on-campus employment. Forms required: institution's own financial aid form, International Student's Certification of Finances. 7 international students on campus received college administered financial aid ($6980 average). *Housing:* Guaranteed. *Services:* International student adviser on campus. Internships and employment opportunities (on-campus and off-campus) available. *Contact:* Admission Counselor, Office of Admission, Schreiner University, 2100 Memorial Boulevard, Kerrville, TX 78028. Telephone: 830-896-5411 Ext. 0224. Fax: 830-792-7226. E-mail: admissions@schreiner.edu. URL: http://www.schreiner.edu.

SOUTHERN METHODIST UNIVERSITY, DALLAS
General Information Independent, coed university, affiliated with United Methodist Church. Suburban setting. *Awards:* B, M, D, FP. *Entrance level for U.S. students:* Moderately difficult. *Enrollment:* 10,941 total; 6,296 undergraduates (55% women) including 5% international students from 66 foreign countries. *Faculty:* 924. *Library holdings:* 2.8 million books, 11,701 current serial subscriptions, 45,168 audiovisual materials. *Total majors:* 78. *Expenses:* (2007–08) $30,880; room and board, $10,825 (on campus); room only, $6730 (on campus). *Financial aid:* Non-need-based college/university scholarships/grants from institutional funds, athletic awards, loans from outside sources, on-campus employment. For fall 2006 (estimated), 126 international students on campus received college administered financial aid ($17,890 average).

SOUTH PLAINS COLLEGE, LEVELLAND
General Information State and locally supported, 2-year, coed college. Small town setting. *Awards:* A. *Entrance level for U.S. students:* Noncompetitive. *Enrollment:* 9,045 total (53% women) including 1% international students from 8 foreign countries. *Undergraduate faculty:* 454. *Library holdings:* 70,000 books, 310 current serial subscriptions. *Total majors:* 59. *Expenses:* (2007–08) $2396; room and board, $3300 (on campus).

SOUTH TEXAS COLLEGE, MCALLEN
General Information District-supported, primarily 2-year, coed college. Suburban setting. *Awards:* A, B. *Entrance level for U.S. students:* Noncompetitive. *Enrollment:* 18,460 total (59% women) including 0.4% international students. *Undergraduate faculty:* 598. *Library holdings:* 15,811 books, 192 current serial subscriptions. *Total majors:* 26. *Expenses:* (2006–07) $6410.

SOUTHWESTERN CHRISTIAN COLLEGE, TERRELL
General Information Independent, 4-year, coed college, affiliated with Church of Christ. Small town setting. *Awards:* A, B. *Entrance level for U.S. students:* Noncompetitive. *Enrollment:* 186 total including international students from 5 foreign countries. *Undergraduate faculty:* 26. *Library holdings:* 25,687 books, 158 current serial subscriptions. *Total majors:* 12. *Expenses:* (2006–07) $5887; room and board, $3631 (on campus); room only, $1600 (on campus).

STEPHEN F. AUSTIN STATE UNIVERSITY, NACOGDOCHES
General Information State-supported, coed institution. Small town setting. *Awards:* B, M, D. *Entrance level for U.S. students:* Moderately difficult. *Enrollment:* 11,756 total; 10,158 undergraduates (60% women) including 1% international students from 36 foreign countries. *Faculty:* 627. *Library holdings:* 722,251 books, 1,757 current serial subscriptions, 23,458 audiovisual materials. *Total majors:* 73. *Expenses:* (2006–07) $13,482; room and board, $6544 (on campus). *Financial aid:* Need-based college/university scholarships/grants from institutional funds. Forms required: institution's own financial aid form, hand calculated FAFSA form. For fall 2005, 114 international students on campus received college administered financial aid ($877 average).

TARLETON STATE UNIVERSITY, STEPHENVILLE
General Information State-supported, coed institution. Small town setting. *Awards:* A, B, M, D. *Entrance level for U.S. students:* Moderately difficult. *Enrollment:* 9,464 total; 7,864 undergraduates (56% women) including 1% international students from 9 foreign countries. *Faculty:* 528. *Library holdings:* 349,979 books, 19,844 current serial subscriptions, 9,394 audiovisual materials. *Total majors:* 77. *Expenses:* (2006–07) $10,126; room and board, $5802 (on campus); room only, $3106 (on campus).

TARRANT COUNTY COLLEGE DISTRICT, FORT WORTH
General Information County-supported, 2-year, coed college. Urban setting. *Awards:* A. *Entrance level for U.S. students:* Noncompetitive. *Enrollment:* 34,892 total (58% women) including 1% international students. *Undergraduate faculty:* 2,076. *Library holdings:* 197,352 books, 1,649 current serial subscriptions, 18,833 audiovisual materials. *Total majors:* 43. *Expenses:* (2006–07) $3600.

TEMPLE COLLEGE, TEMPLE
General Information District-supported, 2-year, coed college. Suburban setting. *Awards:* A. *Entrance level for U.S. students:* Noncompetitive. *Enrollment:* 4,279 total (65% women) including 0.2% international students from 7 foreign countries. *Undergraduate faculty:* 229. *Library holdings:* 55,536 books, 391 current serial subscriptions. *Total majors:* 20. *Expenses:* (2007–08) $5352; room and board, $6300 (on campus).

TEXAS A&M INTERNATIONAL UNIVERSITY, LAREDO
General Information State-supported, coed institution. Urban setting. *Awards:* B, M, D. *Entrance level for U.S. students:* Moderately difficult. *Enrollment:* 4,917 total; 3,892 undergraduates (61% women) including 3% international students from 36 foreign countries. *Faculty:* 298. *Library holdings:* 237,705 books, 5,459 current serial subscriptions, 2,959 audiovisual materials. *Total majors:* 34. *Expenses:* (2006–07) $12,988; room and board, $6500 (on campus); room only, $4610 (on campus). *Financial aid:* Need-based financial aid available. Forms required: institution's own financial aid form. 47 international students on campus received college administered financial aid ($4140 average).

TEXAS A&M UNIVERSITY, COLLEGE STATION
General Information State-supported, coed university. Suburban setting. *Awards:* B, M, D, FP. *Entrance level for U.S. students:* Moderately difficult. *Enrollment:* 45,380 total; 36,580 undergraduates (48% women) including 1% international students from 128 foreign countries. *Faculty:* 2,446. *Library holdings:* 3.6 million books, 43,949 current serial subscriptions, 44,088 audiovisual materials. *Total majors:* 107. *Expenses:* (2006–07) $15,216; room and board, $7660 (on campus); room only, $3804 (on campus). *Financial aid:* Need-based college/university scholarships/grants from institutional funds, tuition waivers, athletic awards, loans from institutional funds, loans from outside sources, on-campus employment. Non-need-based college/university scholarships/grants from institutional funds, tuition waivers, athletic awards, loans from institutional funds, loans from outside sources, on-campus employment. Forms required: institution's own financial aid form. For fall 2005, 243 international students on campus received college administered financial aid ($11,103 average).

TEXAS A&M UNIVERSITY AT GALVESTON, GALVESTON
General Information State-supported, coed institution. Suburban setting. *Awards:* B, M. *Entrance level for U.S. students:* Moderately difficult. *Enrollment:* 1,553 total; 1,520 undergraduates (42% women) including 1% international students from 9 foreign countries. *Faculty:* 170. *Library holdings:* 56,589 books, 640 current serial subscriptions. *Total majors:* 12.
Information for International Students For fall 2006: 13 international students applied, 8 were accepted, 6 enrolled. Students can start in fall, spring, or summer. Transfers accepted from institutions abroad. *Admission tests:* Required: SAT or ACT, TOEFL (minimum score: paper-based 550; computer-based 213; minimum score for ESL admission: paper-based 550; computer-based 213). *Application deadline:* 3/1. *Expenses:* (2006–07) $13,023; room and board, $4870 (on campus); room only, $1958 (on campus). *Housing:* Available during summer. *Services:* International student adviser on campus. ESL program at cooperating institution. Internships and employment opportunities (on-campus) available. *Contact:* Director of Admissions, Texas A&M University at Galveston, PO Box 1675, Galveston, TX 77553-1675. Telephone: 409-740-4448. Fax: 409-470-4731. E-mail: wilsons@tamug.tamu.edu. URL: http://www.tamug.edu.

TEXAS A&M UNIVERSITY–COMMERCE, COMMERCE
General Information State-supported, coed university. Small town setting. *Awards:* B, M, D. *Entrance level for U.S. students:* Moderately difficult. *Enrollment:* 8,556 total; 5,263 undergraduates including 1% international students. *Faculty:* 849. *Library holdings:* 1.1 million books, 15,952 current serial subscriptions, 9,938 audiovisual materials. *Total majors:* 67. *Expenses:* (2006–07) $13,522; room and board, $5740 (on campus); room only, $2600 (on campus).

TEXAS A&M UNIVERSITY–CORPUS CHRISTI, CORPUS CHRISTI

General Information State-supported, coed institution. Suburban setting. *Awards:* B, M, D. *Entrance level for U.S. students:* Moderately difficult. *Enrollment:* 8,585 total; 6,903 undergraduates (60% women) including 1% international students from 27 foreign countries. *Faculty:* 496. *Library holdings:* 731,586 books, 1,901 current serial subscriptions, 6,012 audiovisual materials. *Total majors:* 62.

Information for International Students For fall 2006: 91 international students applied, 87 were accepted, 52 enrolled. Students can start in fall, spring, or summer. Transfers accepted from institutions abroad. *Admission tests:* Required: SAT or ACT, TOEFL (minimum score: iBT 80; paper-based 550; computer-based 213). Recommended: SAT, ACT. TOEFL can be waived under certain conditions. *Application deadline:* 5/1. *Expenses:* (2006–07) $11,820. *Financial aid:* Non-need-based college/university scholarships/grants from institutional funds, tuition waivers, athletic awards, loans from outside sources, on-campus employment. For fall 2006 (estimated), 44 international students on campus received college administered financial aid ($7175 average). *Housing:* Available during summer. *Services:* International student adviser on campus. Full-time ESL program on campus. ESL program available during the academic year and the summer. Internships and employment opportunities (on-campus) available. *Contact:* Transfer Counselor and International Advisor, Texas A&M University–Corpus Christi, 6300 Ocean Drive, Admissions Office, Corpus Christi, TX 78412. Telephone: 512-825-2258. Fax: 512-825-5887. E-mail: Karin.Griffith@tamucc.edu. URL: http://www.tamucc.edu.

TEXAS A&M UNIVERSITY–KINGSVILLE, KINGSVILLE

General Information State-supported, coed university. Small town setting. *Awards:* B, M, D. *Entrance level for U.S. students:* Moderately difficult. *Enrollment:* 7,126 total; 5,645 undergraduates (52% women) including 1% international students from 61 foreign countries. *Faculty:* 438. *Library holdings:* 358,466 books, 2,304 current serial subscriptions, 3,224 audiovisual materials. *Total majors:* 72.

Information for International Students For fall 2006: 105 international students applied, 68 were accepted, 38 enrolled. Students can start in fall, winter, spring, or summer. Transfers accepted from institutions abroad. *Admission tests:* Required: TOEFL (minimum score: iBT 61; paper-based 500; computer-based 173). TOEFL can be waived under certain conditions. *Application deadline:* 6/1. *Housing:* Guaranteed, also available during summer. *Services:* International student adviser on campus. Full-time and part-time ESL programs on campus. ESL program available during the academic year and the summer. Internships and employment opportunities (on-campus) available. *Contact:* Administrative Clerk, Texas A&M University–Kingsville, MSC 128-Office of Admissions, 700 University Blvd., Kingsville, TX 78363. Telephone: 361-593-4994. Fax: 361-593-5509. E-mail: international.inquiries@tamuk.edu. URL: http://www.tamuk.edu.

TEXAS A&M UNIVERSITY–TEXARKANA, TEXARKANA

General Information State-supported, coed institution. Small town setting. *Awards:* B, M. *Entrance level for U.S. students:* Noncompetitive. *Enrollment:* 1,670 total; 1,006 undergraduates (73% women) including 0.2% international students from 2 foreign countries. *Faculty:* 108. *Library holdings:* 132,065 books, 6,561 current serial subscriptions, 360 audiovisual materials. *Total majors:* 19.

Information for International Students Transfers accepted from institutions abroad. *Admission tests:* Required: TOEFL (minimum score: iBT 79; paper-based 550; computer-based 213). *Application deadline:* 6/15. *Expenses:* (2006–07) $9244. *Contact:* Director of Student Services, Texas A&M University–Texarkana, PO Box 5518, 2600 North Robison Road, Texarkana, TX 75505. Telephone: 903-223-3062. Fax: 903-832-8890. E-mail: carl.greig@tamut.edu. URL: http://www.tamut.edu.

TEXAS CHRISTIAN UNIVERSITY, FORT WORTH

General Information Independent, coed university, affiliated with Christian Church (Disciples of Christ). Suburban setting. *Awards:* B, M, D, FP. *Entrance level for U.S. students:* Moderately difficult. *Enrollment:* 8,865 total; 7,267 undergraduates (59% women) including 4% international students from 75 foreign countries. *Faculty:* 803. *Library holdings:* 1.4 million books, 32,017 current serial subscriptions. *Total majors:* 86.

Information for International Students For fall 2006: 299 international students applied, 152 were accepted, 77 enrolled. Students can start in fall or spring. Transfers accepted from institutions abroad. *Admission tests:* Required: TOEFL (minimum score: iBT 80; paper-based 550; computer-based 213).

Recommended: SAT or ACT, IELTS, score of 6.5 or better. TOEFL can be waived under certain conditions. *Application deadline:* 3/1. *Expenses:* (2006–07) $23,020; room and board, $7520 (on campus); room only, $4320 (on campus). *Financial aid:* Need-based college/university scholarships/grants from institutional funds, athletic awards, loans from outside sources. Non-need-based college/university scholarships/grants from institutional funds, athletic awards, loans from outside sources, on-campus employment. Forms required: International Student's Financial Aid Application. International transfer students are eligible to apply for aid. For fall 2005, 196 international students on campus received college administered financial aid ($18,345 average). *Housing:* Available during summer. *Services:* International student adviser on campus. Full-time ESL program on campus. ESL program available during the academic year and the summer. Internships and employment opportunities (on-campus) available. *Contact:* Director of International Admissions, Texas Christian University, International Admissions, Box 297013, Fort Worth, TX 76129. Telephone: 817-257-7871. Fax: 817-257-5256. E-mail: k.scott@tcu.edu. URL: http://www.tcu.edu.

See In-Depth Description on page 202.

TEXAS LUTHERAN UNIVERSITY, SEGUIN

General Information Independent, 4-year, coed college, affiliated with Evangelical Lutheran Church. Suburban setting. *Awards:* B. *Entrance level for U.S. students:* Moderately difficult. *Enrollment:* 1,429 total (53% women) including 1% international students from 6 foreign countries. *Undergraduate faculty:* 143. *Library holdings:* 172,375 books, 565 current serial subscriptions, 4,302 audiovisual materials. *Total majors:* 42. *Expenses:* (2006–07) $18,840; room and board, $5600 (on campus); room only, $2600 (on campus). *Financial aid:* Need-based college/university scholarships/grants from institutional funds, tuition waivers. Non-need-based college/university scholarships/grants from institutional funds, tuition waivers. Forms required: institution's own financial aid form, International Student's Financial Aid Application. For fall 2005, 7 international students on campus received college administered financial aid ($5826 average).

TEXAS SOUTHERN UNIVERSITY, HOUSTON

General Information State-supported, coed university. Urban setting. *Awards:* B, M, D, FP. *Entrance level for U.S. students:* Noncompetitive. *Enrollment:* 11,224 total; 9,053 undergraduates (58% women) including 3% international students from 45 foreign countries. *Faculty:* 576. *Library holdings:* 264,254 books, 1,750 current serial subscriptions. *Total majors:* 106. *Expenses:* (2006–07) $10,795; room and board, $6402 (on campus). *Financial aid:* Need-based financial aid available.

TEXAS STATE TECHNICAL COLLEGE HARLINGEN, HARLINGEN

General Information State-supported, 2-year, coed college. Small town setting. *Awards:* A. *Entrance level for U.S. students:* Noncompetitive. *Enrollment:* 4,028 total (51% women) including 4% international students. *Undergraduate faculty:* 179. *Library holdings:* 25,000 books, 413 current serial subscriptions. *Total majors:* 44. *Expenses:* (2006–07) $5832; room only, $2085 (on campus). *Financial aid:* Forms required: FAFSA.

TEXAS STATE TECHNICAL COLLEGE WACO, WACO

General Information State-supported, 2-year, coed college. Suburban setting. *Awards:* A. *Entrance level for U.S. students:* Noncompetitive. *Enrollment:* 4,452 total (23% women) including 2% international students from 5 foreign countries. *Undergraduate faculty:* 278. *Library holdings:* 60,000 books, 400 current serial subscriptions, 2,324 audiovisual materials. *Total majors:* 45.

Information for International Students For fall 2006: 30 international students applied, 20 were accepted, 13 enrolled. Students can start in fall, winter, spring, or summer. *Admission tests:* Required: TOEFL (minimum score: paper-based 550; computer-based 213; minimum score for ESL admission: paper-based 550; computer-based 213). Recommended: ELS. TOEFL can be waived under certain conditions. *Application deadline:* 6/1. *Expenses:* (2006–07) $7460; room and board, $4100 (on campus); room only, $1860 (on campus). *Financial aid:* Need-based and non-need-based financial aid available. Forms required: institution's own financial aid form. *Housing:* Available during summer. *Services:* International student adviser on campus. Internships and employment opportunities (on-campus) available. *Contact:* Director of Admissions and Records, Texas State Technical College Waco, 3801 Campus Drive, Waco, TX 76705. Telephone: 254-867-2366. Fax: 254-867-2250. E-mail: dawn.khoury@tstc.edu. URL: http://waco.tstc.edu.

TEXAS STATE TECHNICAL COLLEGE WEST TEXAS, SWEETWATER

General Information State-supported, 2-year, coed college. Small town setting. *Awards:* A. *Entrance level for U.S. students:* Noncompetitive. *Enrollment:* 1,537 total (50% women) including 0.2% international students from 1 foreign country. *Undergraduate faculty:* 142. *Library holdings:* 59,711 books, 212,050 current serial subscriptions, 681 audiovisual materials. *Total majors:* 13.

Information for International Students Students can start in fall, spring, or summer. *Admission tests:* Required: TOEFL (minimum score: paper-based 550; computer-based 213; minimum score for ESL admission: paper-based 550; computer-based 213), TASP, approved alternate test, or in-house placement test. *Application deadline:* Rolling. *Expenses:* (2007–08) room and board, $6150 (on campus). *Financial aid:* Forms required: institution's own financial aid form. *Services:* International student adviser on campus. *Contact:* Assistant Director of Registration, Texas State Technical College West Texas, 300 Homer K. Taylor Drive, Sweetwater, TX 79556. Telephone: 325-235-7377. Fax: 325-235-7443. E-mail: oretha.pack@sweetwater.tstc.edu. URL: http://www.sweetwater.tstc.edu.

TEXAS STATE UNIVERSITY-SAN MARCOS, SAN MARCOS

General Information State-supported, coed university. Suburban setting. *Awards:* B, M, D. *Entrance level for U.S. students:* Moderately difficult. *Enrollment:* 27,485 total; 23,568 undergraduates (55% women) including 1% international students from 42 foreign countries. *Faculty:* 1,671. *Library holdings:* 1.4 million books, 8,330 current serial subscriptions, 277,806 audiovisual materials. *Total majors:* 94.

Information for International Students For fall 2006: 160 international students applied, 76 were accepted, 62 enrolled. Students can start in fall, winter, spring, or summer. Transfers accepted from institutions abroad. *Admission tests:* Required: TOEFL (minimum score: iBT 78; paper-based 550; computer-based 213), IELTS with overall band of 6.5 or higher. *Application deadline:* 6/1. *Expenses:* (2006–07) $13,902; room and board, $5878 (on campus); room only, $3730 (on campus). *Financial aid:* Need-based and non-need-based financial aid available. For fall 2006 (estimated), 246 international students on campus received college administered financial aid ($4919 average). *Services:* International student adviser on campus. Full-time and part-time ESL programs on campus. ESL program available during the academic year and the summer. Employment opportunities (on-campus) available. *Contact:* Head Processor for Undergraduate International Students, Office of Admission, Texas State University-San Marcos, Undergraduate Admissions, San Marcos, TX 78666. Telephone: 512-245-2759. Fax: 512-245-9020. E-mail: dr05@txstate.edu. URL: http://www.txstate.edu.

See In-Depth Description on page 203.

TEXAS TECH UNIVERSITY, LUBBOCK

General Information State-supported, coed university. Urban setting. *Awards:* B, M, D, FP. *Entrance level for U.S. students:* Moderately difficult. *Enrollment:* 27,996 total; 22,851 undergraduates (45% women) including 1% international students from 90 foreign countries. *Faculty:* 1,154. *Library holdings:* 2.4 million books, 30,823 current serial subscriptions. *Total majors:* 110. *Expenses:* (2006–07) $14,709; room and board, $7288 (on campus); room only, $3883 (on campus). *Financial aid:* Need-based college/university scholarships/grants from institutional funds, tuition waivers, loans from institutional funds, loans from outside sources, on-campus employment. Non-need-based college/university scholarships/grants from institutional funds, tuition waivers, loans from institutional funds, loans from outside sources, on-campus employment. Forms required: institution's own financial aid form, FAFSA with proper documentation of alien status.

TEXAS WESLEYAN UNIVERSITY, FORT WORTH

General Information Independent United Methodist, coed institution. Urban setting. *Awards:* B, M, FP. *Entrance level for U.S. students:* Moderately difficult. *Enrollment:* 2,930 total; 1,528 undergraduates (67% women). *Faculty:* 258. *Library holdings:* 192,044 books, 632 current serial subscriptions. *Total majors:* 70.

Information for International Students For fall 2006: 44 international students applied, 27 were accepted, 22 enrolled. Students can start in fall or spring. Transfers accepted from institutions abroad. *Admission tests:* Required: TOEFL (minimum score: iBT 68; paper-based 520; computer-based 190), IELTS also accepted. *Application deadline:* Rolling. *Expenses:* (2007–08) $15,715; room and board, $5500 (on campus); room only, $2750 (on campus). *Financial aid:* Need-based and non-need-based financial aid available. Forms required: institution's own financial aid form. International transfer students are eligible to apply for aid. *Housing:* Guaranteed, also available during summer. *Services:* International student adviser on campus. Employment opportunities (on-campus) available. *Contact:* International Student Advisor, Office of International Programs, Texas Wesleyan University, 1201 Wesleyan Street, Fort Worth, TX 76105-1536. Telephone: 817-531-4934. Fax: 817-531-4288. E-mail: aaustin@txwes.edu. URL: http://www.txwesleyan.edu.

See In-Depth Description on page 204.

TEXAS WOMAN'S UNIVERSITY, DENTON

General Information State-supported, coed, primarily women's university. Suburban setting. *Awards:* B, M, D. *Entrance level for U.S. students:* Minimally difficult. *Enrollment:* 11,832 total; 6,675 undergraduates (93% women) including 3% international students from 46 foreign countries. *Faculty:* 654. *Library holdings:* 572,500 books, 2,537 current serial subscriptions. *Total majors:* 37. *Expenses:* (2007–08) $14,082; room and board, $5846 (on campus); room only, $3825 (on campus). *Financial aid:* Need-based college/university scholarships/grants from institutional funds, tuition waivers, athletic awards, loans from institutional funds, loans from outside sources, on-campus employment. Non-need-based college/university scholarships/grants from institutional funds, tuition waivers, athletic awards, loans from institutional funds, loans from outside sources, on-campus employment. Forms required: institution's own financial aid form, International Student's Certification of Finances. For fall 2006 (estimated), 191 international students on campus received college administered financial aid ($7813 average).

TOMBALL COLLEGE, TOMBALL

General Information State and locally supported, 2-year, coed college. Suburban setting. *Awards:* A. *Entrance level for U.S. students:* Noncompetitive. *Enrollment:* 7,787 total (61% women) including 3% international students. *Undergraduate faculty:* 357. *Library holdings:* 24,063 books, 385 current serial subscriptions. *Total majors:* 10. *Expenses:* (2007–08) $2400. *Financial aid:* Need-based college/university scholarships/grants from institutional funds. Non-need-based college/university scholarships/grants from institutional funds. Forms required: institution's own financial aid form.

TRINITY UNIVERSITY, SAN ANTONIO

General Information Independent, coed institution, affiliated with Presbyterian Church. Urban setting. *Awards:* B, M. *Entrance level for U.S. students:* Very difficult. *Enrollment:* 2,693 total; 2,467 undergraduates (54% women) including 4% international students from 38 foreign countries. *Faculty:* 293. *Library holdings:* 937,261 books, 2,118 current serial subscriptions, 27,653 audiovisual materials. *Total majors:* 49.

Information for International Students For fall 2006: 150 international students applied, 30 were accepted, 21 enrolled. Students can start in fall or spring. Transfers accepted from institutions abroad. *Admission tests:* Required: SAT or ACT, TOEFL (minimum score: paper-based 600; computer-based 250). TOEFL can be waived under certain conditions. *Application deadline:* 2/1. *Expenses:* (2007–08) $25,022; room and board, $8270 (on campus); room only, $5380 (on campus). *Financial aid:* Non-need financial aid available. Forms required: admissions application. 27 international students on campus received college administered financial aid ($13,548 average). *Housing:* Guaranteed. *Services:* International student adviser on campus. Internships and employment opportunities (on-campus and off-campus) available. *Contact:* Director of International Admissions, Trinity University, One Trinity Place, Office of Admissions, San Antonio, TX 78212. Telephone: 210-999-7207. Fax: 210-999-8164. E-mail: admissions@trinity.edu. URL: http://www.trinity.edu.

TRINITY VALLEY COMMUNITY COLLEGE, ATHENS

General Information State and locally supported, 2-year, coed college. Small town setting. *Awards:* A. *Entrance level for U.S. students:* Noncompetitive. *Enrollment:* 5,821 total (56% women) including 1% international students. *Undergraduate faculty:* 273. *Library holdings:* 54,940 books, 257 current serial subscriptions, 1,954 audiovisual materials. *Total majors:* 54. *Expenses:* (2006–07) $4800; room and board, $3470 (on campus). *Financial aid:* Forms required: institution's own financial aid form.

UNIVERSITY OF DALLAS, IRVING

General Information Independent Roman Catholic, coed university. Suburban setting. *Awards:* B, M, D. *Entrance level for U.S. students:* Moderately difficult. *Enrollment:* 2,941 total; 1,188 undergraduates (56% women) including 1% international students from 12 foreign countries. *Faculty:* 233. *Library holdings:* 223,350 books, 691 current serial subscriptions. *Total majors:* 32. *Expenses:* (2007–08) $23,267; room and board, $7615 (on campus); room only, $4240 (on campus).

UNIVERSITY OF HOUSTON, HOUSTON

General Information State-supported, coed university. Urban setting. *Awards:* B, M, D, FP. *Entrance level for U.S. students:* Moderately difficult. *Enrollment:* 34,334 total; 27,400 undergraduates (52% women) including 4% international students from 140 foreign countries. *Faculty:* 1,823. *Library holdings:* 2.3 million books, 21,845 current serial subscriptions. *Total majors:* 99. *Expenses:* (2006–07) $15,159; room and board, $6418 (on campus); room only, $3632 (on campus). *Financial aid:* Need-based and non-need-based financial aid available. Forms required: institution's own financial aid form.

UNIVERSITY OF HOUSTON–CLEAR LAKE, HOUSTON

General Information State-supported, coed institution. Suburban setting. *Awards:* B, M. *Entrance level for U.S. students:* Minimally difficult. *Enrollment:* 7,853 total; 4,151 undergraduates (68% women) including 1% international students from 84 foreign countries. *Faculty:* 524. *Library holdings:* 650,000 books, 984 current serial subscriptions, 795 audiovisual materials. *Total majors:* 49. *Expenses:* (2006–07) $13,595. *Financial aid:* Need-based financial aid available. Forms required: institution's own financial aid form. international students on campus received college administered aid averaging $2000.

UNIVERSITY OF HOUSTON–DOWNTOWN, HOUSTON

General Information State-supported, coed institution. Urban setting. *Awards:* B, M. *Entrance level for U.S. students:* Noncompetitive. *Enrollment:* 11,449 total; 11,344 undergraduates (59% women) including 3% international students from 73 foreign countries. *Faculty:* 565. *Library holdings:* 296,000 books, 1,700 current serial subscriptions, 1,900 audiovisual materials. *Total majors:* 28. *Expenses:* (2006–07) $10,256. *Financial aid:* Need-based college/university scholarships/grants from institutional funds, tuition waivers, loans from outside sources. Non-need-based college/university scholarships/grants from institutional funds, tuition waivers, loans from outside sources. Forms required: institution's own financial aid form. 58 international students on campus received college administered financial aid ($2500 average).

UNIVERSITY OF HOUSTON–VICTORIA, VICTORIA

General Information State-supported, coed institution. Small town setting. *Awards:* B, M. *Entrance level for U.S. students:* Minimally difficult. *Enrollment:* 2,652 total; 1,315 undergraduates (74% women) including 1% international students from 7 foreign countries. *Faculty:* 137. *Library holdings:* 50,000 books, 70,000 current serial subscriptions, 12,773 audiovisual materials. *Total majors:* 10. *Expenses:* (2006–07) $12,930. *Financial aid:* Need-based loans from outside sources. Non-need-based college/university scholarships/grants from institutional funds, tuition waivers, loans from outside sources. Forms required: institution's own financial aid form.

UNIVERSITY OF MARY HARDIN-BAYLOR, BELTON

General Information Independent Southern Baptist, coed institution. Small town setting. *Awards:* B, M. *Entrance level for U.S. students:* Moderately difficult. *Enrollment:* 2,738 total; 2,600 undergraduates (64% women) including 0.3% international students from 11 foreign countries. *Faculty:* 227. *Library holdings:* 172,855 books, 990 current serial subscriptions, 8,133 audiovisual materials. *Total majors:* 53.
Information for International Students For fall 2006: 4 international students applied, 4 were accepted, 3 enrolled. Students can start in fall or spring. Transfers accepted from institutions abroad. *Admission tests:* Required: university administered test of language skills. Recommended: TOEFL (minimum score: iBT 80; paper-based 550; computer-based 220), ELS. TOEFL can be waived under certain conditions. *Application deadline:* Rolling. *Expenses:* (2006–07) $15,660; room and board, $5728 (on campus). *Financial aid:* Non-need-based college/university scholarships/grants from institutional funds, on-campus employment. Forms required: institution's own financial aid form. International transfer students are eligible to apply for aid. For fall 2005, 5 international students on campus received college administered financial aid ($2376 average). *Housing:* Guaranteed, also available during summer. *Services:* International student adviser on campus. Full-time ESL program on campus. ESL program available during the academic year and the summer. Internships and employment opportunities (on-campus) available. *Contact:* Director of International Student Services, University of Mary Hardin-Baylor, 900 College Street, Box 8367, Belton, TX 76513. Telephone: 254-295-4949. Fax: 817-295-4535. E-mail: etanaka@umhb.edu. URL: http://www.umhb.edu.

UNIVERSITY OF NORTH TEXAS, DENTON

General Information State-supported, coed university. Suburban setting. *Awards:* B, M, D. *Entrance level for U.S. students:* Moderately difficult. *Enrollment:* 33,443 total; 26,598 undergraduates (55% women) including 2% international students from 134 foreign countries. *Faculty:* 1,546. *Library holdings:* 2.1 million books, 30,391 current serial subscriptions, 141,822 audiovisual materials. *Total majors:* 103.
Information for International Students Students can start in fall, winter, spring, or summer. Transfers accepted from institutions abroad. *Admission tests:* TOEFL can be waived under certain conditions. *Application deadline:* 3/1. *Expenses:* (2006–07) $14,362; room and board, $5625 (on campus). *Financial aid:* Non-need-based college/university scholarships/grants from institutional funds, athletic awards, loans from institutional funds, on-campus employment. 75 international students on campus received college administered financial aid ($946 average). *Services:* International student adviser on campus. Full-time ESL program on campus. ESL program available during the academic year and the summer. Internships and employment opportunities (on-campus and off-campus) available. *Contact:* International Admissions Advisor, University of North Texas, PO Box 311067, Denton, TX 76203. Telephone: 940-565-2442. Fax: 940-565-4822. E-mail: international@unt.edu. URL: http://www.unt.edu.

See In-Depth Description on page 221.

UNIVERSITY OF PHOENIX–DALLAS CAMPUS, DALLAS

General Information Proprietary, coed institution. Urban setting. *Awards:* B, M. *Entrance level for U.S. students:* Noncompetitive. *Enrollment:* 2,539 total; 1,975 undergraduates (63% women) including 17% international students. *Faculty:* 450. *Library holdings:* 1,759 books, 692 current serial subscriptions. *Total majors:* 22. *Expenses:* (2006–07) $11,190.

UNIVERSITY OF PHOENIX–HOUSTON CAMPUS, HOUSTON

General Information Proprietary, coed institution. Urban setting. *Awards:* B, M. *Entrance level for U.S. students:* Noncompetitive. *Enrollment:* 4,532 total; 3,702 undergraduates (69% women) including 13% international students. *Faculty:* 772. *Library holdings:* 1,759 books, 692 current serial subscriptions. *Total majors:* 27. *Expenses:* (2006–07) $11,190.

UNIVERSITY OF ST. THOMAS, HOUSTON

General Information Independent Roman Catholic, coed institution. Urban setting. *Awards:* B, M, D, FP. *Entrance level for U.S. students:* Moderately difficult. *Enrollment:* 3,607 total; 1,805 undergraduates (61% women) including 3% international students from 40 foreign countries. *Faculty:* 275. *Library holdings:* 223,898 books, 19,351 current serial subscriptions, 1,474 audiovisual materials. *Total majors:* 36. *Expenses:* (2006–07) $17,868; room and board, $6700 (on campus); room only, $4000 (on campus). *Financial aid:* Non-need-based college/university scholarships/grants from institutional funds, on-campus employment. Forms required: International Student's Certification of Finances. For fall 2006 (estimated), 10 international students on campus received college administered financial aid ($4792 average).

THE UNIVERSITY OF TEXAS AT ARLINGTON, ARLINGTON

General Information State-supported, coed university. Urban setting. *Awards:* B, M, D. *Entrance level for U.S. students:* Moderately difficult. *Enrollment:* 24,825 total; 19,205 undergraduates (53% women) including 7% international students from 80 foreign countries. *Faculty:* 1,100. *Library holdings:* 1.2 million books, 40,965 current serial subscriptions, 9,200 audiovisual materials. *Total majors:* 61. *Expenses:* (2006–07) $14,650; room and board, $5553 (on campus); room only, $3046 (on campus). *Financial aid:* Need-based financial aid available. Non-need-based college/university scholarships/grants from institutional funds, tuition waivers, athletic awards, loans from institutional funds, loans from outside sources, on-campus employment. Forms required: institution's own financial aid form. For fall 2005, 360 international students on campus received college administered financial aid ($2788 average).

THE UNIVERSITY OF TEXAS AT AUSTIN, AUSTIN

General Information State-supported, coed university. Urban setting. *Awards:* B, M, D, FP. *Entrance level for U.S. students:* Very difficult. *Enrollment:* 49,697 total; 37,037 undergraduates (52% women) including 4% international students from 127 foreign countries. *Faculty:* 2,814. *Total majors:* 104. *Expenses:* (2006–07) $20,364; room and board, $8176 (on campus). *Financial aid:* Need-based college/university scholarships/grants from institutional funds, tuition waivers, loans from institutional funds, loans from outside sources, on-campus employment. Non-need-based college/university scholarships/grants from institutional funds, tuition waivers, loans from institutional funds, loans from outside sources, on-campus employment. Forms required: institution's own financial aid form, International Student's Certification of Finances, certain students have to submit paper FAFSA documents. For fall 2006 (estimated), 760 international students on campus received college administered financial aid ($6100 average).

THE UNIVERSITY OF TEXAS AT BROWNSVILLE, BROWNSVILLE

General Information State-supported, coed institution. Urban setting. *Awards:* A, B, M. *Entrance level for U.S. students:* Noncompetitive. *Enrollment:* 15,688 total; 14,867 undergraduates (59% women) including 4% international students from 16 foreign countries. *Faculty:* 693. *Library holdings:* 174,660 books, 4,447 current serial subscriptions. *Total majors:* 35. *Expenses:* (2006–07) $10,257; room only, $2300 (on campus). *Financial aid:* Need-based college/university scholarships/grants from institutional funds, tuition waivers. Forms required: institution's own financial aid form.

THE UNIVERSITY OF TEXAS AT DALLAS, RICHARDSON

General Information State-supported, coed university. Suburban setting. *Awards:* B, M, D. *Entrance level for U.S. students:* Very difficult. *Enrollment:* 14,523 total; 9,375 undergraduates (45% women) including 4% international students from 103 foreign countries. *Faculty:* 697. *Library holdings:* 1.5 million books, 197,047 current serial subscriptions, 6,117 audiovisual materials. *Total majors:* 35. *Expenses:* (2006–07) $15,820; room and board, $6540 (on campus). *Financial aid:* Need-based college/university scholarships/grants from institutional funds, loans from institutional funds, loans from outside sources, on-campus employment. Non-need-based college/university scholarships/grants from institutional funds, loans from institutional funds, loans from outside sources, on-campus employment. For fall 2006 (estimated), 119 international students on campus received college administered financial aid ($6193 average).

THE UNIVERSITY OF TEXAS AT EL PASO, EL PASO

General Information State-supported, coed university. Urban setting. *Awards:* B, M, D. *Entrance level for U.S. students:* Minimally difficult. *Enrollment:* 19,842 total; 16,793 undergraduates (55% women) including 10% international students from 67 foreign countries. *Faculty:* 1,083. *Library holdings:* 961,247 books, 3,005 current serial subscriptions. *Total majors:* 61. *Expenses:* (2006–07) $13,512; room only, $4185 (on campus). *Financial aid:* Need-based college/university scholarships/grants from institutional funds, athletic awards, loans from outside sources, on-campus employment. Non-need-based college/university scholarships/grants from institutional funds, loans from outside sources, on-campus employment. Forms required: institution's own financial aid form. For fall 2005, 317 international students on campus received college administered financial aid ($5717 average).

THE UNIVERSITY OF TEXAS AT SAN ANTONIO, SAN ANTONIO

General Information State-supported, coed university. Suburban setting. *Awards:* B, M, D. *Entrance level for U.S. students:* Moderately difficult. *Enrollment:* 28,380 total; 24,399 undergraduates (53% women) including 2% international students from 75 foreign countries. *Faculty:* 1,138. *Library holdings:* 730,678 books, 24,042 current serial subscriptions, 47,499 audiovisual materials. *Total majors:* 56.

Information for International Students For fall 2006: 509 international students applied, 352 were accepted, 156 enrolled. Students can start in fall, spring, or summer. Transfers accepted from institutions abroad. *Admission tests:* Required: TOEFL (minimum score: iBT 61; paper-based 500; computer-based 173; minimum score for ESL admission: iBT 32; paper-based 400; computer-based 97), IELTS accepted in lieu of TOEFL. Recommended: SAT or ACT. TOEFL can be waived under certain conditions. *Application deadline:* 6/1. *Expenses:* (2007–08) $14,949; room and board, $8169 (on campus); room only, $5616 (on campus). *Financial aid:* Need-based college/university scholarships/grants from institutional funds, tuition waivers, athletic awards, loans from outside sources. Non-need financial aid available. Forms required: institution's own financial aid form, International Student's Financial Aid Application. International transfer students are eligible to apply for aid. For fall 2005, 66 international students on campus received college administered financial aid ($1318 average). *Housing:* Available during summer. *Services:* International student adviser on campus. Full-time ESL program on campus. ESL program available during the academic year and the summer. *Contact:* Assistant Director of Admissions, Office of Admissions and Registrar, The University of Texas at San Antonio, Office of Admissions, Attention International Admissions, One UTSA Circle,

San Antonio, TX 78249-0616. Telephone: 210-458-4546. Fax: 210-458-7564. E-mail: IntlAdmissions@utsa.edu. URL: http://www.utsa.edu.

See In-Depth Description on page 229.

THE UNIVERSITY OF TEXAS AT TYLER, TYLER

General Information State-supported, coed institution. Urban setting. *Awards:* B, M. *Entrance level for U.S. students:* Moderately difficult. *Enrollment:* 5,926 total; 4,764 undergraduates (60% women) including 1% international students from 41 foreign countries. *Faculty:* 378. *Library holdings:* 486,895 books, 525 current serial subscriptions, 5,522 audiovisual materials. *Total majors:* 39. *Expenses:* (2007–08) $11,148. *Financial aid:* Need-based college/university scholarships/grants from institutional funds, tuition waivers, loans from institutional funds, loans from outside sources, on-campus employment. Non-need-based college/university scholarships/grants from institutional funds, tuition waivers, loans from institutional funds, loans from outside sources, on-campus employment. Forms required: institution's own financial aid form. For fall 2006 (estimated), 52 international students on campus received college administered financial aid ($1457 average).

THE UNIVERSITY OF TEXAS HEALTH SCIENCE CENTER AT HOUSTON, HOUSTON

General Information State-supported, coed institution. Urban setting. *Awards:* B, M, D, FP. *Entrance level for U.S. students:* Moderately difficult. *Enrollment:* 3,399 total; 381 undergraduates including 2% international students. *Faculty:* 1,247. *Library holdings:* 339,062 books, 5,581 current serial subscriptions, 885 audiovisual materials. *Total majors:* 2. *Financial aid:* Need-based financial aid available.

THE UNIVERSITY OF TEXAS MEDICAL BRANCH, GALVESTON

General Information State-supported, coed institution. Small town setting. *Awards:* B, M, D, FP. *Entrance level for U.S. students:* Very difficult. *Enrollment:* 2,255 total; 494 undergraduates (78% women) including 2% international students. *Total majors:* 3. *Expenses:* (2006–07) $12,552; room only, $3060 (on campus). *Financial aid:* Non-need-based loans from outside sources.

THE UNIVERSITY OF TEXAS–PAN AMERICAN, EDINBURG

General Information State-supported, coed institution. Small town setting. *Awards:* B, M, D. *Entrance level for U.S. students:* Noncompetitive. *Enrollment:* 17,337 total; 15,076 undergraduates (58% women) including 5% international students from 25 foreign countries. *Faculty:* 830. *Library holdings:* 598,008 books, 35,004 current serial subscriptions. *Total majors:* 58. *Expenses:* (2006–07) $12,147; room and board, $5095 (on campus); room only, $3140 (on campus). *Financial aid:* Need-based college/university scholarships/grants from institutional funds, loans from outside sources, on-campus employment. Non-need-based college/university scholarships/grants from institutional funds, tuition waivers, athletic awards, loans from institutional funds, loans from outside sources. Forms required: institution's own financial aid form. For fall 2005, 524 international students on campus received college administered financial aid ($5903 average).

THE UNIVERSITY OF TEXAS SOUTHWESTERN MEDICAL CENTER AT DALLAS, DALLAS

General Information State-supported, coed institution. Urban setting. *Awards:* B, M, D, FP. *Entrance level for U.S. students:* Moderately difficult. *Enrollment:* 2,434 total; 113 undergraduates (73% women) including 7% international students from 11 foreign countries. *Faculty:* 103. *Library holdings:* 257,782 books, 2,865 current serial subscriptions. *Total majors:* 4.

Information for International Students For fall 2006: 32 international students applied, 9 were accepted, 7 enrolled. Students can start in fall, winter, spring, or summer. Transfers accepted from institutions abroad. *Admission tests:* Required: TOEFL (minimum score: paper-based 633; computer-based 267). *Application deadline:* Rolling. *Expenses:* (2007–08) $12,445. *Services:* International student adviser on campus. ESL program at cooperating institution. *Contact:* Associate Director of Admissions, The University of Texas Southwestern Medical Center at Dallas, 5323 Harry Hines Boulevard, Dallas, TX 75235. Telephone: 214-648-3606. Fax: 214-648-3289. E-mail: mary.sayre@email.swmed.edu. URL: http://www.utsouthwestern.edu.

UNIVERSITY OF THE INCARNATE WORD, SAN ANTONIO

General Information Independent Roman Catholic, coed institution. Urban setting. *Awards:* A, B, M, D, FP. *Entrance level for U.S. students:* Moderately difficult. *Enrollment:* 5,619 total; 4,666 undergraduates (68% women) including 3% international students from 31 foreign countries. *Faculty:* 445. *Library holdings:* 335,298 books, 23,551 current serial subscriptions, 14,469 audiovisual materials. *Total majors:* 69.

Information for International Students For fall 2006: 129 international students applied, 97 were accepted. Students can start in fall, spring, or summer. Transfers accepted from institutions abroad. *Admission tests:* Required: TOEFL (minimum score: paper-based 550; computer-based 213; minimum score for ESL admission: paper-based 550; computer-based 213). Recommended: SAT or ACT. *Application deadline:* Rolling. *Expenses:* (2007–08) $19,060; room and board, $6994 (on campus); room only, $4080 (on campus). *Financial aid:* Need-based college/university scholarships/grants from institutional funds, tuition waivers, athletic awards, loans from outside sources. Non-need-based college/university scholarships/grants from institutional funds, tuition waivers, athletic awards, loans from outside sources. Forms required: institution's own financial aid form. For fall 2006 (estimated), 52 international students on campus received college administered financial aid ($5813 average). *Services:* International student adviser on campus. Full-time and part-time ESL programs on campus. ESL program available during the academic year and the summer. Internships and employment opportunities (on-campus) available. *Contact:* Office of Admissions, University of the Incarnate Word, 4301 Broadway, Box 283, San Antonio, TX 78209. Telephone: 210-829-6005. Fax: 210-829-3921. E-mail: admis@uiwtx.edu. URL: http://www.uiw.edu.

See In-Depth Description on page 230.

WAYLAND BAPTIST UNIVERSITY, PLAINVIEW

General Information Independent Baptist, coed institution. Small town setting. *Awards:* A, B, M (branch locations in Anchorage, AK; Amarillo, TX; Luke Airforce Base, AZ; Glorieta, NM; Aiea, HI; Lubbock, TX; San Antonio, TX; Wichita Falls, TX). *Entrance level for U.S. students:* Minimally difficult. *Enrollment:* 1,072 total; 962 undergraduates (57% women) including 2% international students from 15 foreign countries. *Faculty:* 93. *Library holdings:* 124,336 books, 527 current serial subscriptions, 12,247 audiovisual materials. *Total majors:* 27. *Expenses:* (2006–07) $10,800; room and board, $3584 (on campus); room only, $1276 (on campus). *Financial aid:* Need-based college/university scholarships/grants from institutional funds, athletic awards, on-campus employment. Non-need-based college/university scholarships/grants from institutional funds, athletic awards, on-campus employment. Forms required: institution's own financial aid form, International Student's Certification of Finances. For fall 2006 (estimated), 17 international students on campus received college administered financial aid ($8647 average).

WEATHERFORD COLLEGE, WEATHERFORD

General Information State and locally supported, 2-year, coed college. Small town setting. *Awards:* A. *Entrance level for U.S. students:* Noncompetitive. *Enrollment:* 4,552 total including 1% international students. *Undergraduate faculty:* 220. *Library holdings:* 59,499 books, 362 current serial subscriptions. *Total majors:* 15.

Information for International Students For fall 2006: 60 international students applied, 12 were accepted. Students can start in fall, spring, or summer. Transfers accepted from institutions abroad. *Admission tests:* Required: TOEFL (minimum score: iBT 68; paper-based 520; computer-based 190; minimum score for ESL admission: iBT 61; paper-based 500; computer-based 173), ELS (minimum score: 10), THEA/COMPASS. TOEFL can be waived under certain conditions. *Application deadline:* 6/1. *Expenses:* (2006–07) $3164; room and board, $6500 (on campus). *Housing:* Available during summer. *Services:* International student adviser on campus. Part-time ESL program on campus. ESL program available during the academic year and the summer. Employment opportunities (on-campus) available. *Contact:* Director of Admissions, Weatherford College, 225 College Park Drive, Weatherford, TX 76086. Telephone: 817-598-6248. Fax: 817-598-6205. E-mail: willingham@wc.edu. URL: http://www.wc.edu.

WEST TEXAS A&M UNIVERSITY, CANYON

General Information State-supported, coed institution. Small town setting. *Awards:* B, M, D. *Entrance level for U.S. students:* Moderately difficult. *Enrollment:* 7,412 total; 5,895 undergraduates (57% women) including 1% international students from 25 foreign countries. *Faculty:* 312. *Library holdings:* 1.1 million books, 19,022 current serial subscriptions, 4,924 audiovisual materials. *Total majors:* 59.

Information for International Students For fall 2006: 89 international students applied, 54 were accepted, 31 enrolled. Students can start in fall or spring. Transfers accepted from institutions abroad. *Admission tests:* Required: ACT, SAT Subject Tests, TOEFL (minimum score: iBT 71; paper-based 525; computer-based 197). TOEFL can be waived under certain conditions. *Application deadline:* 5/1. *Expenses:* (2007–08) $13,260; room and board, $5440 (on campus); room only, $2750 (on campus). *Financial aid:* Non-need-based college/university scholarships/grants from institutional funds, athletic awards. Forms required: scholarship application form. 56 international students on campus received college administered financial aid ($3290 average). *Housing:* Guaranteed, also available during summer. *Services:* International student adviser on campus. Full-time ESL program on campus. ESL program available during the academic year and the summer. Internships and employment opportunities (on-campus) available. *Contact:* Director, International Student Office, West Texas A&M University, WTAMU Box 60745, Canyon, TX 79016. Telephone: 806-651-2074. Fax: 806-651-2071. E-mail: kcombs@wtamu.edu. URL: http://www.wtamu.edu.

WESTWOOD COLLEGE–DALLAS, DALLAS

General Information Proprietary, 2-year, coed college. Urban setting. *Awards:* A. *Entrance level for U.S. students:* Difficulty N/R. *Enrollment:* 404 total (34% women) including 0.2% international students. *Undergraduate faculty:* 31. *Total majors:* 3.

WHARTON COUNTY JUNIOR COLLEGE, WHARTON

General Information State and locally supported, 2-year, coed college. Rural setting. *Awards:* A. *Entrance level for U.S. students:* Noncompetitive. *Enrollment:* 6,029 total including 4% international students from 5 foreign countries. *Undergraduate faculty:* 257. *Library holdings:* 51,478 books, 536 current serial subscriptions. *Total majors:* 29. *Expenses:* (2006–07) $2928; room and board, $2500 (on campus); room only, $600 (on campus). *Financial aid:* Forms required: institution's own financial aid form.

UTAH

BRIGHAM YOUNG UNIVERSITY, PROVO

General Information Independent, coed university, affiliated with The Church of Jesus Christ of Latter-day Saints. Suburban setting. *Awards:* B, M, D, FP. *Entrance level for U.S. students:* Moderately difficult. *Enrollment:* 34,185 total; 30,480 undergraduates (49% women) including 2% international students from 125 foreign countries. *Faculty:* 1,759. *Library holdings:* 3.5 million books, 27,161 current serial subscriptions. *Total majors:* 210. *Expenses:* (2007–08) $7680; room and board, $6460 (on campus). *Financial aid:* Need-based college/university scholarships/grants from institutional funds. Non-need-based college/university scholarships/grants from institutional funds. Forms required: International Student's Certification of Finances. For fall 2005, 621 international students on campus received college administered financial aid ($2771 average).

COLLEGE OF EASTERN UTAH, PRICE

General Information State-supported, 2-year, coed college. Small town setting. *Awards:* A. *Entrance level for U.S. students:* Noncompetitive. *Enrollment:* 2,294 total (55% women) including 1% international students. *Undergraduate faculty:* 189. *Library holdings:* 44,490 books, 1,464 audiovisual materials. *Total majors:* 15.

Information for International Students For fall 2006: 45 international students applied, 34 were accepted, 28 enrolled. Students can start in fall or spring. Transfers accepted from institutions abroad. *Admission tests:* Recommended: TOEFL (minimum score: iBT 61; paper-based 500; computer-based 173; minimum score for ESL admission: iBT 36; paper-based 420; computer-based 110). TOEFL can be waived under certain conditions. *Application deadline:* Rolling. *Expenses:* (2006–07) $7670; room and board, $3820 (on campus). *Financial aid:* Forms required: institution's own financial aid form. *Housing:* Guaranteed, also available during summer. *Services:* International student adviser on campus. Full-time ESL program on campus. ESL program available during the academic year. Employment opportunities (on-campus) available. *Contact:* Director, International Student Services, College of Eastern Utah, 451 East 400 North, Price, UT 84501. Telephone: 435-613-5333. Fax: 435-613-5814. E-mail: jane.johnson@ceu.edu. URL: http://www.ceu.edu.

DIXIE STATE COLLEGE OF UTAH, ST. GEORGE
General Information State-supported, primarily 2-year, coed college. Small town setting. *Awards:* A, B. *Entrance level for U.S. students:* Noncompetitive. *Enrollment:* 5,704 total (54% women) including 1% international students from 14 foreign countries. *Undergraduate faculty:* 337. *Library holdings:* 94,747 books, 263 current serial subscriptions. *Total majors:* 79. *Expenses:* (2007–08) $9466.

LDS BUSINESS COLLEGE, SALT LAKE CITY
General Information Independent, 2-year, coed college, affiliated with The Church of Jesus Christ of Latter-day Saints. Urban setting. *Awards:* A. *Entrance level for U.S. students:* Noncompetitive. *Enrollment:* 1,317 total (54% women) including 22% international students from 50 foreign countries. *Undergraduate faculty:* 102. *Library holdings:* 24,000 books, 130 current serial subscriptions. *Total majors:* 20.
Information for International Students For fall 2006: 219 international students applied, 110 were accepted, 89 enrolled. Students can start in fall or winter. Transfers accepted from institutions abroad. *Admission tests:* Required: TOEFL (minimum score: paper-based 500; computer-based 173). *Application deadline:* 7/31. *Expenses:* (2007–08) $2600; room and board, $4580 (on campus). *Financial aid:* Need-based college/university scholarships/grants from institutional funds, loans from outside sources. Non-need-based college/university scholarships/grants from institutional funds, loans from institutional funds, on-campus employment. *Services:* International student adviser on campus. Employment opportunities (on-campus and off-campus) available. *Contact:* Assistant Director of Admissions, LDS Business College, 95 North 300 West, Salt Lake City, UT 84101-3500. Telephone: 801-524-8145. Fax: 801-524-1900. E-mail: admissions@ldsbc.edu. URL: http://www.ldsbc.edu.

SALT LAKE COMMUNITY COLLEGE, SALT LAKE CITY
General Information State-supported, 2-year, coed college. Urban setting. *Awards:* A. *Entrance level for U.S. students:* Noncompetitive. *Enrollment:* 24,241 total (49% women) including 1% international students. *Undergraduate faculty:* 1,407. *Library holdings:* 96,470 books, 781 current serial subscriptions, 29,810 audiovisual materials. *Total majors:* 63. *Expenses:* (2006–07) $7,518.

SNOW COLLEGE, EPHRAIM
General Information State-supported, 2-year, coed college. Rural setting. *Awards:* A. *Entrance level for U.S. students:* Noncompetitive. *Enrollment:* 3,333 total (53% women) including 2% international students from 15 foreign countries. *Undergraduate faculty:* 253. *Library holdings:* 31,911 books, 1,870 audiovisual materials. *Total majors:* 66. *Expenses:* (2006–07) $7498; room and board, $4500 (on campus); room only, $900 (on campus). *Financial aid:* Need-based college/university scholarships/grants from institutional funds, loans from outside sources, on-campus employment, state grants/Loans (UHEA). Non-need-based college/university scholarships/grants from institutional funds, tuition waivers, athletic awards, loans from outside sources, on-campus employment. Forms required: institution's own financial aid form, International Student's Certification of Finances.

SOUTHERN UTAH UNIVERSITY, CEDAR CITY
General Information State-supported, coed institution. Small town setting. *Awards:* A, B, M. *Entrance level for U.S. students:* Moderately difficult. *Enrollment:* 7,029 total; 6,601 undergraduates (58% women) including 1% international students from 14 foreign countries. *Faculty:* 285. *Library holdings:* 180,424 books, 6,165 current serial subscriptions, 13,352 audiovisual materials. *Total majors:* 49.
Information for International Students Students can start in fall, spring, or summer. Transfers accepted from institutions abroad. *Admission tests:* Required: TOEFL (minimum score: iBT 61; paper-based 500; computer-based 173; minimum score for ESL admission: paper-based 500; computer-based 173), IELTS. Recommended: SAT or ACT. *Application deadline:* Rolling. *Expenses:* (2006–07) $11,107; room and board, $4154 (on campus). *Financial aid:* Need-based financial aid available. Forms required: institution's own financial aid form, sworn affidavit that student is making effort to achieve residency. For fall 2005, 3 international students on campus received college administered financial aid ($6520 average). *Housing:* Available during summer. *Services:* International student adviser on campus. Full-time ESL program on campus. ESL program available during the academic year. Internships and employment opportunities (on-campus) available. *Contact:* International Admissions, Southern Utah University, 351 West University Boulevard, Cedar City, UT 84720. Telephone: 435-586-7740. Fax: 435-865-8223. E-mail: international@suu.edu. URL: http://www.suu.edu.
See In-Depth Description on page 193.

UNIVERSITY OF PHOENIX–UTAH CAMPUS, SALT LAKE CITY
General Information Proprietary, coed institution. Urban setting. *Awards:* B, M. *Entrance level for U.S. students:* Noncompetitive. *Enrollment:* 3,986 total; 2,559 undergraduates (45% women) including 2% international students. *Faculty:* 761. *Library holdings:* 1,759 books, 692 current serial subscriptions. *Total majors:* 17. *Expenses:* (2006–07) $10,200.

UNIVERSITY OF UTAH, SALT LAKE CITY
General Information State-supported, coed university. Urban setting. *Awards:* B, M, D, FP. *Entrance level for U.S. students:* Moderately difficult. *Enrollment:* 28,619 total; 22,155 undergraduates (45% women) including 3% international students from 104 foreign countries. *Faculty:* 1,758. *Library holdings:* 6.2 million books, 33,517 current serial subscriptions, 74,731 audiovisual materials. *Total majors:* 129.
Information for International Students For fall 2006: 400 international students applied, 250 were accepted, 200 enrolled. Students can start in fall, spring, or summer. Transfers accepted from institutions abroad. *Admission tests:* Required: TOEFL (minimum score: paper-based 500; computer-based 173; minimum score for ESL admission: paper-based 450; computer-based 133). TOEFL can be waived under certain conditions. *Application deadline:* 4/1. *Expenses:* (2006–07) $14,593; room and board, $5828 (on campus); room only, $3016 (on campus). *Financial aid:* Need-based college/university scholarships/grants from institutional funds. Non-need financial aid available. Forms required: scholarship application. For fall 2005, 10 international students on campus received college administered financial aid ($3388 average). *Services:* International student adviser on campus. Full-time and part-time ESL programs on campus. ESL program available during the academic year and the summer. Internships and employment opportunities (on-campus and off-campus) available. *Contact:* Supervisor, International Admissions, Office of International Admissions, University of Utah, 201 South 1460 East, Room 250S, Salt Lake City, UT 84112-9057. Telephone: 801-581-3091. Fax: 801-585-7864. E-mail: cdyson@sa.utah.edu. URL: http://www.utah.edu.

UTAH STATE UNIVERSITY, LOGAN
General Information State-supported, coed university. Urban setting. *Awards:* A, B, M, D. *Entrance level for U.S. students:* Moderately difficult. *Enrollment:* 14,444 total; 12,779 undergraduates (48% women) including 3% international students from 52 foreign countries. *Faculty:* 739. *Library holdings:* 1.5 million books, 12,369 current serial subscriptions, 16,504 audiovisual materials. *Total majors:* 121.
Information for International Students Students can start in fall, spring, or summer. Transfers accepted from institutions abroad. *Admission tests:* Required: TOEFL (minimum score: iBT 61; paper-based 500; computer-based 173), ELS. TOEFL can be waived under certain conditions. *Application deadline:* Rolling. *Expenses:* (2006–07) $11,449; room and board, $4400 (on campus); room only, $1550 (on campus). *Financial aid:* International transfer students are eligible to apply for aid. *Housing:* Guaranteed, also available during summer. *Services:* International student adviser on campus. Full-time ESL program on campus. ESL program available during the academic year. Internships and employment opportunities (on-campus and off-campus) available. *Contact:* Director, Office of International Students and Scholars, Utah State University, 0140 Old Main Hill, TSC 313, Logan, UT 84322-0140. Telephone: 435-797-1843. Fax: 435-797-3522. E-mail: jpacheco@cc.usu.edu. URL: http://www.usu.edu.

UTAH VALLEY STATE COLLEGE, OREM
General Information State-supported, 4-year, coed college. Suburban setting. *Awards:* A, B. *Entrance level for U.S. students:* Noncompetitive. *Enrollment:* 23,305 total (43% women) including 0.4% international students from 78 foreign countries. *Undergraduate faculty:* 1,256. *Library holdings:* 173,000 books, 6,000 current serial subscriptions. *Total majors:* 77.
Information for International Students For fall 2006: 112 international students applied, 112 were accepted, 63 enrolled. Students can start in fall, spring, or summer. *Admission tests:* Required: TOEFL (minimum score: paper-based 500; computer-based 173). *Application deadline:* 6/22. *Expenses:* (2006–07) $10,338. *Services:* International student adviser on campus. Full-time and part-time ESL programs on campus. ESL program available during the academic year. Employment opportunities (on-campus and off-campus) available. *Contact:* International Admissions Specialist, Utah Valley State College, 800 West University Parkway, Orem, UT 84058-0001. Telephone: 801-863-8475. Fax: 801-225-4677. E-mail: whaleyco@uvsc.edu. URL: http://www.uvsc.edu.

WEBER STATE UNIVERSITY, OGDEN
General Information State-supported, coed institution. Urban setting. *Awards:* A, B, M. *Entrance level for U.S. students:* Noncompetitive. *Enrollment:* 18,303 total; 17,849 undergraduates (51% women) including 1% international students from 37 foreign countries. *Faculty:* 909. *Library holdings:* 734,487 books, 19,881 audiovisual materials. *Total majors:* 106. *Expenses:* (2006–07) $10,416; room and board, $5328 (on campus); room only, $2142 (on campus).

WESTMINSTER COLLEGE, SALT LAKE CITY
General Information Independent, coed institution. Suburban setting. *Awards:* B, M. *Entrance level for U.S. students:* Moderately difficult. *Enrollment:* 2,479 total; 1,959 undergraduates (58% women) including 1% international students from 29 foreign countries. *Faculty:* 246. *Library holdings:* 154,069 books, 695 current serial subscriptions, 7,350 audiovisual materials. *Total majors:* 33. *Expenses:* (2006–07) $21,030; room and board, $6140 (on campus). *Financial aid:* Need-based college/university scholarships/grants from institutional funds, tuition waivers, loans from institutional funds, loans from outside sources, on-campus employment. Non-need-based college/university scholarships/grants from institutional funds, athletic awards, loans from outside sources, on-campus employment. Forms required: International Student's Certification of Finances. For fall 2005, 20 international students on campus received college administered financial aid ($7000 average).

VERMONT

BENNINGTON COLLEGE, BENNINGTON
General Information Independent, coed institution. Small town setting. *Awards:* B, M. *Entrance level for U.S. students:* Very difficult. *Enrollment:* 657 total; 523 undergraduates (66% women) including 3% international students from 13 foreign countries. *Faculty:* 89. *Library holdings:* 121,500 books, 13,500 current serial subscriptions. *Total majors:* 85.
Information for International Students For fall 2006: 51 international students applied, 8 were accepted, 4 enrolled. Students can start in fall or spring. Transfers accepted from institutions abroad. *Admission tests:* Required: TOEFL (minimum score: iBT 90; paper-based 577; computer-based 233). Recommended: SAT or ACT. *Application deadline:* 1/3. *Expenses:* (2007–08) $36,800; room and board, $9380 (on campus); room only, $5030 (on campus). *Financial aid:* Need-based college/university scholarships/grants from institutional funds, loans from institutional funds, on-campus employment. Non-need-based on-campus employment. Forms required: International Student's Financial Aid Application, International Student's Certification of Finances, statement of parent earnings. International transfer students are eligible to apply for aid. For fall 2006 (estimated), 12 international students on campus received college administered financial aid ($31,023 average). *Housing:* Guaranteed, also available during summer. *Services:* International student adviser on campus. Internships and employment opportunities (on-campus) available. *Contact:* Dean of Admissions, Bennington College, One College Drive, Bennington, VT 05201. Telephone: 802-440-4312. Fax: 802-440-4320. E-mail: admissions@bennington.edu. URL: http://www.bennington.edu.

See In-Depth Description on page 40.

CASTLETON STATE COLLEGE, CASTLETON
General Information State-supported, coed institution. Rural setting. *Awards:* A, B, M. *Entrance level for U.S. students:* Moderately difficult. *Enrollment:* 2,130 total; 1,942 undergraduates (55% women) including 0.4% international students from 1 foreign country. *Faculty:* 202. *Library holdings:* 166,011 books, 739 current serial subscriptions. *Total majors:* 42. *Expenses:* (2007–08) $15,428; room and board, $7220 (on campus). *Financial aid:* Need-based college/university scholarships/grants from institutional funds, on-campus employment. Non-need-based college/university scholarships/grants from institutional funds, on-campus employment. Forms required: International Student's Financial Aid Application. 1 international student on campus received college administered financial aid ($13,626 average).

CHAMPLAIN COLLEGE, BURLINGTON
General Information Independent, coed institution. Suburban setting. *Awards:* A, B, M. *Entrance level for U.S. students:* Moderately difficult. *Enrollment:* 2,741 total; 2,657 undergraduates (51% women) including 0.2% international students from 26 foreign countries. *Faculty:* 256. *Library holdings:* 80,880 books, 21,150 current serial subscriptions, 1,154 audiovisual materials.

Total majors: 57. *Expenses:* (2007–08) $22,550; room and board, $10,910 (on campus); room only, $6510 (on campus). *Financial aid:* Need-based college/university scholarships/grants from institutional funds. Forms required: institution's own financial aid form. 8 international students on campus received college administered financial aid ($5000 average).

COLLEGE OF ST. JOSEPH, RUTLAND
General Information Independent Roman Catholic, coed institution. Small town setting. *Awards:* A, B, M. *Entrance level for U.S. students:* Minimally difficult. *Enrollment:* 509 total; 284 undergraduates (58% women) including 0.4% international students. *Faculty:* 68. *Library holdings:* 75,000 books, 3,000 current serial subscriptions. *Total majors:* 20. *Expenses:* (2006–07) $14,900; room and board, $7150 (on campus).

GREEN MOUNTAIN COLLEGE, POULTNEY
General Information Independent, coed institution. Small town setting. *Awards:* B, M. *Entrance level for U.S. students:* Moderately difficult. *Enrollment:* 759 total; 729 undergraduates (50% women) including 0.4% international students from 7 foreign countries. *Faculty:* 65. *Library holdings:* 95,140 books, 296 current serial subscriptions, 672 audiovisual materials. *Total majors:* 24.
Information for International Students For fall 2006: 101 international students applied, 30 were accepted, 2 enrolled. Students can start in fall or spring. Transfers accepted from institutions abroad. *Admission tests:* Required: TOEFL (minimum score: paper-based 500; computer-based 173; minimum score for ESL admission: paper-based 500; computer-based 173). Recommended: SAT or ACT. *Application deadline:* 6/1. *Expenses:* (2006–07) $23,329; room and board, $8426 (on campus); room only, $5076 (on campus). *Financial aid:* Need-based college/university scholarships/grants from institutional funds, loans from outside sources, on-campus employment. Non-need-based college/university scholarships/grants from institutional funds, loans from outside sources, on-campus employment. Forms required: institution's own financial aid form, International Student's Certification of Finances. International transfer students are eligible to apply for aid. For fall 2006 (estimated), 8 international students on campus received college administered financial aid ($22,373 average). *Housing:* Guaranteed. *Services:* International student adviser on campus. Internships and employment opportunities (on-campus) available. *Contact:* Dean of Enrollment, Green Mountain College, Office of Admissions, 1 College Circle, Poultney, VT 05764-1199. Telephone: 802-287-8000. Fax: 802-287-8099. E-mail: admiss@greenmtn.edu. URL: http://www.greenmtn.edu.

JOHNSON STATE COLLEGE, JOHNSON
General Information State-supported, coed institution. Rural setting. *Awards:* A, B, M. *Entrance level for U.S. students:* Moderately difficult. *Enrollment:* 1,866 total; 1,566 undergraduates (61% women) including 0.2% international students from 2 foreign countries. *Faculty:* 143. *Library holdings:* 100,053 books, 522 current serial subscriptions. *Total majors:* 58.
Information for International Students For fall 2006: 2 international students applied, 2 were accepted, 1 enrolled. Students can start in fall or spring. Transfers accepted from institutions abroad. *Admission tests:* Required: TOEFL (minimum score: paper-based 500; computer-based 173). TOEFL can be waived under certain conditions. *Application deadline:* Rolling. *Expenses:* (2007–08) $15,693; room and board, $7745 (on campus); room only, $4300 (on campus). *Financial aid:* Need-based and non-need-based financial aid available. Forms required: International Student's Certification of Finances. *Housing:* Guaranteed. *Services:* Part-time ESL program on campus. ESL program available during the academic year. Internships and employment opportunities (on-campus) available. *Contact:* Admissions Counselor/International Admissions Coordinator, Admissions Office, Johnson State College, 337 College Hill Road, Johnson, VT 05656-9898. Telephone: 802-635-1219. Fax: 802-635-1230. E-mail: elga.gruner@jsc.vsc.edu. URL: http://www.johnsonstatecollege.edu.

LANDMARK COLLEGE, PUTNEY
General Information Independent, 2-year, coed college. Rural setting. *Awards:* A. *Entrance level for U.S. students:* Moderately difficult. *Enrollment:* 460 total (27% women) including 3% international students from 7 foreign countries. *Undergraduate faculty:* 98. *Library holdings:* 31,371 books, 174 current serial subscriptions, 1,880 audiovisual materials. *Total majors:* 1. *Expenses:* (2007–08) $41,360; room and board, $7500 (on campus); room only, $3750 (on campus). *Financial aid:* Need-based college/university scholarships/grants from institutional funds. Non-need-based college/university scholarships/grants from institutional funds, loans from outside sources, on-campus

employment. Forms required: institution's own financial aid form, International Student's Certification of Finances.

LYNDON STATE COLLEGE, LYNDONVILLE

General Information State-supported, coed institution. Rural setting. *Awards:* A, B, M. *Entrance level for U.S. students:* Moderately difficult. *Enrollment:* 1,412 total; 1,342 undergraduates (47% women) including 0.1% international students from 15 foreign countries. *Faculty:* 162. *Library holdings:* 109,629 books, 16,468 current serial subscriptions. *Total majors:* 31.

Information for International Students For fall 2006: 4 international students applied, 2 were accepted. Students can start in fall or spring. Transfers accepted from institutions abroad. *Admission tests:* Required: TOEFL (minimum score: paper-based 500; computer-based 173). Recommended: SAT. TOEFL can be waived under certain conditions. *Application deadline:* 5/1. *Expenses:* (2006–07) $14,556; room and board, $6942 (on campus); room only, $4134 (on campus). *Services:* International student adviser on campus. Internships and employment opportunities (on-campus) available. *Contact:* Associate Director of Admissions, Lyndon State College, 1001 College Road, PO Box 919, Lyndonville, VT 05851. Telephone: 802-626-6413. Fax: 802-626-6335. E-mail: admissions@lyndonstate.edu. URL: http://www.lyndonstate.edu.

MARLBORO COLLEGE, MARLBORO

General Information Independent, coed institution. Rural setting. *Awards:* B, M, FP. *Entrance level for U.S. students:* Moderately difficult. *Enrollment:* 400 total; 329 undergraduates (53% women) including 0.3% international students from 3 foreign countries. *Faculty:* 57. *Library holdings:* 71,000 books, 275 current serial subscriptions. *Total majors:* 77.

Information for International Students For fall 2006: 28 international students applied, 11 were accepted, 2 enrolled. Students can start in fall or spring. Transfers accepted from institutions abroad. *Admission tests:* Required: TOEFL (minimum score: iBT 75; paper-based 550; computer-based 215). Recommended: SAT or ACT. TOEFL can be waived under certain conditions. *Application deadline:* 2/15. *Expenses:* (2007–08) $30,680; room and board, $8860 (on campus); room only, $4880 (on campus). *Financial aid:* Non-need-based college/university scholarships/grants from institutional funds. Forms required: International Student's Financial Aid Application, International Student's Certification of Finances. International transfer students are eligible to apply for aid. For fall 2005, 3 international students on campus received college administered financial aid ($10,000 average). *Housing:* Guaranteed. *Services:* International student adviser on campus. Internships and employment opportunities (on-campus) available. *Contact:* Associate Director of Admission, Office of Admissions, Marlboro College, Office of Admission, 2582 South Road, Marlboro, VT 05344. Telephone: 802-257-9230. Fax: 802-451-7555. E-mail: avantassel@marlboro.edu. URL: http://www.marlboro.edu.

MIDDLEBURY COLLEGE, MIDDLEBURY

General Information Independent, coed institution. Small town setting. *Awards:* B, M, D. *Entrance level for U.S. students:* Most difficult. *Enrollment:* 2,406 total (52% women) including 11% international students from 70 foreign countries. *Faculty:* 307. *Library holdings:* 853,000 books, 2,908 current serial subscriptions, 45,024 audiovisual materials. *Total majors:* 44.

Information for International Students For fall 2006: 912 international students applied, 175 were accepted, 73 enrolled. Students can start in fall or spring. Transfers accepted from institutions abroad. *Application deadline:* 1/1. *Expenses:* (2006–07) $44,330. *Financial aid:* Need-based college/university scholarships/grants from institutional funds, loans from institutional funds, on-campus employment. Forms required: institution's own financial aid form. International transfer students are eligible to apply for aid. For fall 2005, 193 international students on campus received college administered financial aid ($21,875 average). *Housing:* Guaranteed, also available during summer. *Services:* International student adviser on campus. Internships and employment opportunities (on-campus) available. *Contact:* Associate Director of International Admissions, Middlebury College, Middlebury, VT 05753. Telephone: 802-443-3000. Fax: 802-443-2056. E-mail: admissions@middlebury.edu. URL: http://www.middlebury.edu.

NEW ENGLAND CULINARY INSTITUTE, MONTPELIER

General Information Proprietary, primarily 2-year, coed college. Small town setting. *Awards:* A, B. *Entrance level for U.S. students:* Moderately difficult. *Enrollment:* 569 total (38% women). *Undergraduate faculty:* 85. *Library holdings:* 2,400 books, 30

current serial subscriptions, 35 audiovisual materials. *Total majors:* 4. *Expenses:* (2007–08) $25,452; room and board, $6565 (on campus).

SAINT MICHAEL'S COLLEGE, COLCHESTER

General Information Independent Roman Catholic, coed institution. Suburban setting. *Awards:* B, M. *Entrance level for U.S. students:* Moderately difficult. *Enrollment:* 2,437 total; 1,992 undergraduates (55% women) including 1% international students from 11 foreign countries. *Faculty:* 220. *Library holdings:* 241,574 books, 2,337 current serial subscriptions, 7,616 audiovisual materials. *Total majors:* 36.

Information for International Students For fall 2006: 41 international students applied, 21 were accepted, 4 enrolled. Students can start in fall, spring, or summer. Transfers accepted from institutions abroad. *Admission tests:* Required: TOEFL (minimum score: iBT 80; paper-based 550; computer-based 213). Recommended: SAT. *Application deadline:* 2/1. *Expenses:* (2006–07) $28,515; room and board, $6990 (on campus). *Financial aid:* Need-based college/university scholarships/grants from institutional funds, loans from outside sources, on-campus employment. Non-need-based college/university scholarships/grants from institutional funds, athletic awards, loans from outside sources. Forms required: institution's own financial aid form, International Student's Financial Aid Application. International transfer students are eligible to apply for aid. For fall 2006 (estimated), 20 international students on campus received college administered financial aid ($13,387 average). *Housing:* Guaranteed, also available during summer. *Services:* International student adviser on campus. Full-time ESL program on campus. ESL program available during the academic year and the summer. Internships and employment opportunities (on-campus) available. *Contact:* Assistant Director of Admission, Saint Michael's College, One Winooski Park, Colchester, VT 05439. Telephone: 802-654-3000. Fax: 802-654-2591. E-mail: mpreston@smcvt.edu. URL: http://www.smcvt.edu.

STERLING COLLEGE, CRAFTSBURY COMMON

General Information Independent, 4-year, coed college. Rural setting. *Awards:* A, B. *Entrance level for U.S. students:* Moderately difficult. *Enrollment:* 105 total (47% women). *Undergraduate faculty:* 40. *Library holdings:* 14,000 books, 500 audiovisual materials. *Total majors:* 85. *Expenses:* (2006–07) $17,780; room and board, $6520 (on campus); room only, $2970 (on campus). *Financial aid:* Need-based college/university scholarships/grants from institutional funds, on-campus employment. Non-need-based college/university scholarships/grants from institutional funds, on-campus employment. Forms required: institution's own financial aid form, International Student's Certification of Finances.

UNIVERSITY OF VERMONT, BURLINGTON

General Information State-supported, coed university. Suburban setting. *Awards:* B, M, D, FP. *Entrance level for U.S. students:* Moderately difficult. *Enrollment:* 11,870 total; 10,082 undergraduates (56% women) including 1% international students from 30 foreign countries. *Faculty:* 767. *Library holdings:* 2.4 million books, 20,216 current serial subscriptions. *Total majors:* 99. *Expenses:* (2006–07) $26,308; room and board, $7642 (on campus); room only, $5150 (on campus). *Financial aid:* Need-based athletic awards. Non-need-based college/university scholarships/grants from institutional funds, athletic awards. Forms required: International Student's Certification of Finances.

VERMONT TECHNICAL COLLEGE, RANDOLPH CENTER

General Information State-supported, 4-year, coed college. Rural setting. *Awards:* A, B. *Entrance level for U.S. students:* Minimally difficult. *Enrollment:* 1,454 total (41% women) including 0.1% international students from 1 foreign country. *Undergraduate faculty:* 139. *Library holdings:* 58,547 books, 314 current serial subscriptions, 4,267 audiovisual materials. *Total majors:* 20.

Information for International Students For fall 2006: 2 international students applied, 1 was accepted, 1 enrolled. Students can start in fall or spring. Transfers accepted from institutions abroad. *Admission tests:* Required: SAT or ACT, TOEFL (minimum score: paper-based 500; computer-based 173; minimum score for ESL admission: paper-based 500; computer-based 173). *Application deadline:* Rolling. *Expenses:* (2006–07) $16,120; room and board, $6942 (on campus); room only, $4134 (on campus). *Financial aid:* Need-based and non-need-based financial aid available. *Housing:* Guaranteed. *Services:* International student adviser on campus. Internships and employment opportunities (on-campus) available. *Contact:* Associate Director of Admissions, Admissions Office, Vermont Technical College, PO Box 500, Randolph Center, VT 05061. Telephone: 802-728-1297. Fax: 802-728-1321. E-mail: dmellar@vtc.edu. URL: http://www.vtc.edu.

WOODBURY COLLEGE, MONTPELIER
General Information Independent, 4-year, coed college. Small town setting. *Awards:* A, B. *Entrance level for U.S. students:* Noncompetitive. *Enrollment:* 132 total; 105 undergraduates (90% women). *Undergraduate faculty:* 32. *Library holdings:* 2,782 books. *Total majors:* 4. *Expenses:* (2006–07) $15,900. *Financial aid:* Need-based loans from outside sources. Non-need-based loans from outside sources. Forms required: institution's own financial aid form.

VIRGIN ISLANDS

UNIVERSITY OF THE VIRGIN ISLANDS, SAINT THOMAS
General Information Territory-supported, coed institution. Small town setting. *Awards:* A, B, M. *Entrance level for U.S. students:* Minimally difficult. *Enrollment:* 2,487 total; 2,272 undergraduates (76% women) including 6% international students from 11 foreign countries. *Faculty:* 260. *Library holdings:* 106,361 books, 113,623 current serial subscriptions, 3,000 audiovisual materials. *Total majors:* 23. *Expenses:* (2006–07) $10,326; room and board, $7550 (on campus); room only, $1100 (on campus).

VIRGINIA

AVERETT UNIVERSITY, DANVILLE
General Information Independent, coed institution, affiliated with Baptist General Association of Virginia. Small town setting. *Awards:* A, B, M. *Entrance level for U.S. students:* Moderately difficult. *Enrollment:* 883 total; 784 undergraduates (48% women) including 2% international students from 10 foreign countries. *Faculty:* 96. *Library holdings:* 109,414 books, 19,495 current serial subscriptions, 312 audiovisual materials. *Total majors:* 64.
Information for International Students For fall 2006: 20 international students applied, 17 were accepted, 3 enrolled. Students can start in fall, spring, or summer. Transfers accepted from institutions abroad. *Admission tests:* Required: TOEFL (minimum score: paper-based 500; computer-based 173). Recommended: SAT or ACT. TOEFL can be waived under certain conditions. *Application deadline:* Rolling. *Expenses:* (2007–08) $20,512; room and board, $7100 (on campus); room only, $4700 (on campus). *Financial aid:* Need-based college/university scholarships/grants from institutional funds, on-campus employment. Non-need-based college/university scholarships/grants from institutional funds. International transfer students are eligible to apply for aid. For fall 2006 (estimated), 18 international students on campus received college administered financial aid ($11,846 average). *Housing:* Guaranteed, also available during summer. *Services:* International student adviser on campus. ESL program at cooperating institution. ESL program available during the academic year. Internships and employment opportunities (on-campus and off-campus) available. *Contact:* Associate Director of Admissions, Averett University, 420 West Main Street, Danville, VA 24541. Telephone: 434-791-5666. Fax: 434-797-2784. E-mail: admit@averett.edu. URL: http://www.averett.edu.

CHRISTENDOM COLLEGE, FRONT ROYAL
General Information Independent Roman Catholic, coed institution. Rural setting. *Awards:* A, B, M. *Entrance level for U.S. students:* Very difficult. *Enrollment:* 451 total; 397 undergraduates (55% women) including 3% international students from 2 foreign countries. *Faculty:* 42. *Library holdings:* 64,265 books, 262 current serial subscriptions. *Total majors:* 8.
Information for International Students Students can start in fall or spring. Transfers accepted from institutions abroad. *Admission tests:* Required: SAT or ACT, TOEFL (minimum score: paper-based 500; computer-based 200). *Application deadline:* 4/1. *Expenses:* (2006–07) $16,740; room and board, $6066 (on campus). *Financial aid:* Non-need financial aid available. Forms required: institution's own financial aid form. 3 international students on campus received college administered financial aid ($4620 average). *Housing:* Guaranteed. Employment opportunities (on-campus) available. *Contact:* Director of Admissions, Christendom College, 134 Christendom Drive, Front Royal, VA 22630. Telephone: 540-636-2900 Ext. 0292. Fax: 540-636-1655. E-mail: admissions@christendom.edu. URL: http://www.christendom.edu.

THE COLLEGE OF WILLIAM AND MARY, WILLIAMSBURG
General Information State-supported, coed university. Small town setting. *Awards:* B, M, D, FP. *Entrance level for U.S. students:* Very difficult. *Enrollment:* 7,709 total; 5,734 undergraduates (54% women) including 2% international students from 52 foreign countries. *Faculty:* 758. *Library holdings:* 2.1 million books, 36,877 current serial subscriptions, 33,708 audiovisual materials. *Total majors:* 44. *Expenses:* (2006–07) $24,910; room and board, $6932 (on campus); room only, $4210 (on campus). *Financial aid:* Need-based and non-need-based financial aid available.

DEVRY UNIVERSITY, ARLINGTON
General Information Proprietary, coed institution. *Awards:* A, B, M. *Entrance level for U.S. students:* Minimally difficult. *Enrollment:* 615 total; 486 undergraduates (31% women) including 1% international students. *Faculty:* 56. *Library holdings:* 7,800 books, 6,500 current serial subscriptions. *Total majors:* 10. *Expenses:* (2007–08) $14,640.

EASTERN MENNONITE UNIVERSITY, HARRISONBURG
General Information Independent Mennonite, coed institution. Small town setting. *Awards:* A, B, M, FP. *Entrance level for U.S. students:* Moderately difficult. *Enrollment:* 1,324 total; 1,006 undergraduates (62% women) including 4% international students from 19 foreign countries. *Faculty:* 163. *Library holdings:* 169,785 books, 1,033 current serial subscriptions. *Total majors:* 58.
Information for International Students Students can start in fall, winter, or spring. Transfers accepted from institutions abroad. *Admission tests:* Required: TOEFL (minimum score: iBT 79; paper-based 550; computer-based 213; minimum score for ESL admission: iBT 61; paper-based 500; computer-based 173). Recommended: SAT or ACT. TOEFL can be waived under certain conditions. *Application deadline:* Rolling. *Expenses:* (2006–07) $20,712; room and board, $6550 (on campus); room only, $3550 (on campus). *Financial aid:* Need-based and non-need-based financial aid available. Forms required: International Student's Financial Aid Application, International Student's Certification of Finances. International transfer students are eligible to apply for aid. 45 international students on campus received college administered financial aid ($5507 average). *Services:* International student adviser on campus. Full-time and part-time ESL programs on campus. ESL program available during the academic year and the summer. Employment opportunities (on-campus) available. *Contact:* Director of International Student Services, Eastern Mennonite University, 1200 Park Road, Harrisonburg, VA 22802-2462. Telephone: 540-432-4118. Fax: 540-432-4444. E-mail: iss@emu.edu. URL: http://www.emu.edu.

ECPI COLLEGE OF TECHNOLOGY, VIRGINIA BEACH
General Information Proprietary, primarily 2-year, coed college. Suburban setting. *Awards:* A, B. *Entrance level for U.S. students:* Moderately difficult. *Enrollment:* 4,391 total (47% women). *Undergraduate faculty:* 130. *Total majors:* 20. *Expenses:* (2006–07) $9750. *Financial aid:* Need-based college/university scholarships/grants from institutional funds, loans from institutional funds, loans from outside sources, on-campus employment. Non-need-based college/university scholarships/grants from institutional funds, loans from institutional funds, loans from outside sources, on-campus employment. Forms required: institution's own financial aid form.

EMORY & HENRY COLLEGE, EMORY
General Information Independent United Methodist, coed institution. Rural setting. *Awards:* B, M. *Entrance level for U.S. students:* Moderately difficult. *Enrollment:* 1,051 total; 996 undergraduates (51% women) including 1% international students from 10 foreign countries. *Faculty:* 120. *Library holdings:* 343,443 books, 9,959 current serial subscriptions, 7,164 audiovisual materials. *Total majors:* 37. *Expenses:* (2006–07) $20,860; room and board, $7360 (on campus); room only, $3640 (on campus). *Financial aid:* Need-based college/university scholarships/grants from institutional funds, loans from institutional funds, loans from outside sources, on-campus employment. Non-need-based college/university scholarships/grants from institutional funds, loans from institutional funds, loans from outside sources, on-campus employment. Forms required: International Student's Certification of Finances, bank statement. 7 international students on campus received college administered financial aid ($15,686 average).

GEORGE MASON UNIVERSITY, FAIRFAX
General Information State-supported, coed university. Suburban setting. *Awards:* B, M, D, FP. *Entrance level for U.S. students:* Moderately difficult. *Enrollment:* 29,889 total; 18,221 undergraduates (54% women) including 4% international students

from 129 foreign countries. *Faculty:* 2,038. *Library holdings:* 1.5 million books, 27,708 current serial subscriptions, 27,344 audiovisual materials. *Total majors:* 47. *Expenses:* (2006–07) $18,552; room and board, $6750 (on campus); room only, $3850 (on campus).

HAMPDEN-SYDNEY COLLEGE, HAMPDEN-SYDNEY

General Information Independent, 4-year, men's college, affiliated with Presbyterian Church (U.S.A.). Rural setting. *Awards:* B. *Entrance level for U.S. students:* Moderately difficult. *Enrollment:* 1,106 total including 1% international students from 17 foreign countries. *Undergraduate faculty:* 112. *Library holdings:* 248,245 books, 18,315 current serial subscriptions. *Total majors:* 28.
Information for International Students For fall 2006: 20 international students applied, 10 were accepted, 5 enrolled. Students can start in fall. Transfers accepted from institutions abroad. *Admission tests:* Required: SAT or ACT, TOEFL (minimum score: paper-based 570; computer-based 230). Recommended: SAT Subject Tests. *Application deadline:* 3/1. *Expenses:* (2007–08) $27,732; room and board, $8671 (on campus); room only, $3608 (on campus). *Financial aid:* Need-based college/university scholarships/grants from institutional funds. Non-need-based college/university scholarships/grants from institutional funds. Forms required: CSS PROFILE, International Student's Financial Aid Application. For fall 2006 (estimated), 23 international students on campus received college administered financial aid ($17,080 average). *Housing:* Guaranteed. *Services:* International student adviser on campus. Internships and employment opportunities (on-campus) available. *Contact:* Associate Dean of Admissions, Hampden-Sydney College, Post Office Box 667, Graham Hall, Hampden-Sydney, VA 23943. Telephone: 434-223-6120. Fax: 434-223-6346. E-mail: admissions@hsc.edu. URL: http://www.hsc.edu.

HOLLINS UNIVERSITY, ROANOKE

General Information Independent, undergraduate: women only; graduate: coed institution. Suburban setting. *Awards:* B, M. *Entrance level for U.S. students:* Moderately difficult. *Enrollment:* 1,061 total; 799 undergraduates (99% women) including 3% international students from 9 foreign countries. *Faculty:* 101. *Library holdings:* 232,507 books, 43,004 current serial subscriptions, 7,493 audiovisual materials. *Total majors:* 30. *Expenses:* (2006–07) $24,325; room and board, $8650 (on campus); room only, $5170 (on campus). *Financial aid:* Need-based college/university scholarships/grants from institutional funds, on-campus employment. Non-need-based college/university scholarships/grants from institutional funds, on-campus employment. Forms required: International Student's Financial Aid Application, International Student's Certification of Finances. For fall 2005, 11 international students on campus received college administered financial aid ($13,602 average).

JAMES MADISON UNIVERSITY, HARRISONBURG

General Information State-supported, coed institution. Small town setting. *Awards:* B, M, D (also offers specialist in education degree). *Entrance level for U.S. students:* Very difficult. *Enrollment:* 17,393 total; 16,013 undergraduates (61% women) including 1% international students from 42 foreign countries. *Faculty:* 1,131. *Library holdings:* 659,136 books, 15,909 current serial subscriptions, 37,198 audiovisual materials. *Total majors:* 46.
Information for International Students For fall 2006: 175 international students applied, 102 were accepted, 55 enrolled. Students can start in fall, spring, or summer. Transfers accepted from institutions abroad. *Admission tests:* Required: TOEFL (minimum score: paper-based 570; computer-based 230). Recommended: SAT or ACT, O-level exams will substitute for SAT. TOEFL can be waived under certain conditions. *Application deadline:* 2/1. *Expenses:* (2006–07) $16,236; room and board, $6756 (on campus); room only, $3508 (on campus). *Financial aid:* Need-based college/university scholarships/grants from institutional funds, tuition waivers, athletic awards, loans from outside sources, on-campus employment. Non-need-based college/university scholarships/grants from institutional funds, tuition waivers, athletic awards, loans from outside sources, on-campus employment. For fall 2006 (estimated), 54 international students on campus received college administered financial aid ($13,983 average). *Housing:* Available during summer. *Services:* International student adviser on campus. ESL program at cooperating institution. ESL program available during the academic year and the summer. Internships and employment opportunities (on-campus) available. *Contact:* International Admissions Counselor, James Madison University, 800 South Main Street, Office of Admissions, MSC 0101, Harrisonburg, VA 22807. Telephone: 540-568-5681. Fax: 540-568-3332. E-mail: international@jmu.edu. URL: http://www.jmu.edu.

JOHN TYLER COMMUNITY COLLEGE, CHESTER

General Information State-supported, 2-year, coed college. Suburban setting. *Awards:* A. *Entrance level for U.S. students:* Noncompetitive. *Enrollment:* 7,165 total (62% women) including 0.2% international students from 2 foreign countries. *Undergraduate faculty:* 311. *Library holdings:* 49,393 books, 179 current serial subscriptions. *Total majors:* 14. *Expenses:* (2007–08) $7709.

LIBERTY UNIVERSITY, LYNCHBURG

General Information Independent nondenominational, coed institution. Suburban setting. *Awards:* A, B, M, D, FP (also offers external degree program with significant enrollment not reflected in profile). *Entrance level for U.S. students:* Minimally difficult. *Enrollment:* 17,606 total; 13,426 undergraduates (52% women) including 4% international students from 72 foreign countries. *Faculty:* 701. *Library holdings:* 260,295 books, 46,176 current serial subscriptions, 6,455 audiovisual materials. *Total majors:* 51.
Information for International Students For fall 2006: 9558 international students enrolled. Students can start in fall or spring. Transfers accepted from institutions abroad. *Admission tests:* Required: TOEFL (minimum score: iBT 61; paper-based 500; computer-based 173). Recommended: SAT or ACT, SAT Subject Tests, ELS. *Application deadline:* Rolling. *Expenses:* (2007–08) $15,800; room and board, $5400 (on campus). *Financial aid:* Need-based college/university scholarships/grants from institutional funds, loans from outside sources, on-campus employment. Non-need-based college/university scholarships/grants from institutional funds, athletic awards, loans from outside sources. Forms required: International Student's Certification of Finances. International transfer students are eligible to apply for aid. 301 international students on campus received college administered financial aid ($3640 average). *Housing:* Guaranteed, also available during summer. *Services:* International student adviser on campus. Full-time and part-time ESL programs on campus. ESL program available during the academic year and the summer. Internships and employment opportunities (on-campus) available. *Contact:* Director of International Student Services, Liberty University, 1971 University Boulevard, Lynchburg, VA 24502. Telephone: 434-592-4118. Fax: 434-522-0430. E-mail: international@liberty.edu. URL: http://www.liberty.edu.

LONGWOOD UNIVERSITY, FARMVILLE

General Information State-supported, coed institution. Small town setting. *Awards:* B, M. *Entrance level for U.S. students:* Moderately difficult. *Enrollment:* 4,479 total; 3,787 undergraduates (65% women) including 1% international students from 11 foreign countries. *Faculty:* 242. *Library holdings:* 325,290 books, 5,018 current serial subscriptions. *Total majors:* 74.
Information for International Students For fall 2006: 5 international students enrolled. Students can start in fall, spring, or summer. Transfers accepted from institutions abroad. *Admission tests:* Required: SAT or ACT, TOEFL (minimum score: paper-based 550; computer-based 213). *Application deadline:* 3/1. *Expenses:* (2006–07) $15,209; room and board, $6058 (on campus); room only, $3622 (on campus). *Financial aid:* Need-based college/university scholarships/grants from institutional funds, athletic awards, loans from institutional funds, loans from outside sources, on-campus employment. Non-need-based college/university scholarships/grants from institutional funds, athletic awards, loans from institutional funds, loans from outside sources, on-campus employment. Forms required: FAFSA. For fall 2006 (estimated), 28 international students on campus received college administered financial aid ($14,831 average). *Housing:* Available during summer. *Services:* International student adviser on campus. Part-time ESL program on campus. ESL program available during the summer. Internships and employment opportunities (on-campus) available. *Contact:* Senior Assistant Director of Admissions, Admissions Office, Longwood University, 201 High Street, Admissions Office, Farmville, VA 23909. Telephone: 434-395-2060. Fax: 434-395-2060. E-mail: admissions@longwood.edu. URL: http://www.longwood.edu.

LYNCHBURG COLLEGE, LYNCHBURG

General Information Independent, coed institution, affiliated with Christian Church (Disciples of Christ). Suburban setting. *Awards:* B, M. *Entrance level for U.S. students:* Moderately difficult. *Enrollment:* 2,398 total; 2,053 undergraduates (59% women) including 1% international students from 6 foreign countries. *Faculty:* 229. *Library holdings:* 225,000 books, 518 current serial subscriptions, 6,212 audiovisual materials. *Total majors:* 47.
Information for International Students For fall 2006: 30 international students applied, 19 were accepted, 10 enrolled. Students can start in fall or spring. Transfers accepted from institutions abroad. *Admission tests:* Required: SAT or ACT, TOEFL (minimum score: paper-based 525; computer-based 197). TOEFL can be waived under certain conditions. *Application deadline:*

Lynchburg College (continued)

Rolling. *Expenses:* (2006–07) $25,265; room and board, $7000 (on campus); room only, $3500 (on campus). *Financial aid:* Non-need-based college/university scholarships/grants from institutional funds. Forms required: International Student's Certification of Finances. International transfer students are eligible to apply for aid. For fall 2005, 8 international students on campus received college administered financial aid ($7813 average). *Housing:* Guaranteed. *Services:* International student adviser on campus. ESL program at cooperating institution. ESL program available during the summer. Internships and employment opportunities (on-campus) available. *Contact:* Director of Admissions, Lynchburg College, 1501 Lakeside Drive, Lynchburg, VA 24501-3199. Telephone: 804-544-8300. Fax: 804-544-8653. E-mail: waltersbower@lynchburg.edu. URL: http://www.lynchburg.edu.

MARY BALDWIN COLLEGE, STAUNTON

General Information Independent, coed, primarily women's institution. Small town setting. *Awards:* B, M. *Entrance level for U.S. students:* Moderately difficult. *Enrollment:* 1,755 total; 1,563 undergraduates (92% women) including 1% international students from 3 foreign countries. *Faculty:* 137. *Library holdings:* 152,862 books, 17,715 current serial subscriptions, 6,991 audiovisual materials. *Total majors:* 30.

Information for International Students For fall 2006: 20 international students applied, 15 were accepted, 8 enrolled. Students can start in fall or spring. Transfers accepted from institutions abroad. *Admission tests:* Required: TOEFL (minimum score: iBT 61; paper-based 500; computer-based 173). Recommended: SAT. TOEFL can be waived under certain conditions. *Application deadline:* Rolling. *Expenses:* (2006–07) $21,450; room and board, $6100 (on campus); room only, $3890 (on campus). *Financial aid:* Need-based college/university scholarships/grants from institutional funds, loans from outside sources, on-campus employment. Non-need-based college/university scholarships/grants from institutional funds, loans from outside sources, on-campus employment. Forms required: International Student's Certification of Finances. For fall 2006 (estimated), 20 international students on campus received college administered financial aid ($3946 average). *Housing:* Guaranteed. *Services:* International student adviser on campus. Employment opportunities (on-campus) available. *Contact:* Director of International Student Services, Mary Baldwin College, PO Box 1500, Staunton, VA 24402. Telephone: 540-887-7394. Fax: 540-887-7227. E-mail: lwells@mbc.edu. URL: http://www.mbc.edu.

MARYMOUNT UNIVERSITY, ARLINGTON

General Information Independent, coed institution, affiliated with Roman Catholic Church. Suburban setting. *Awards:* B, M, D (Associate). *Entrance level for U.S. students:* Moderately difficult. *Enrollment:* 3,604 total; 2,300 undergraduates (74% women) including 7% international students from 63 foreign countries. *Faculty:* 350. *Library holdings:* 187,097 books, 1,048 current serial subscriptions. *Total majors:* 37. *Expenses:* (2006–07) $19,199; room and board, $8212 (on campus). *Financial aid:* Non-need-based college/university scholarships/grants from institutional funds, loans from outside sources. Forms required: scholarship application form. For fall 2006 (estimated), 39 international students on campus received college administered financial aid ($10,912 average).

NEW RIVER COMMUNITY COLLEGE, DUBLIN

General Information State-supported, 2-year, coed college. Rural setting. *Awards:* A. *Entrance level for U.S. students:* Noncompetitive. *Enrollment:* 4,345 total (53% women) including international students from 21 foreign countries. *Undergraduate faculty:* 206. *Library holdings:* 33,993 books, 258 current serial subscriptions. *Total majors:* 30.

Information for International Students Students can start in fall, spring, or summer. Transfers accepted from institutions abroad. *Admission tests:* Required: TOEFL (minimum score: iBT 61; paper-based 500; computer-based 173; minimum score for ESL admission: iBT 61; paper-based 500; computer-based 173), math and English placement upon campus arrival. *Application deadline:* Rolling. *Expenses:* (2006–07) $7,216. *Services:* International student adviser on campus. ESL program at cooperating institution. ESL program available during the academic year and the summer. *Contact:* International Student Advisor, New River Community College, PO Box 1127, Dublin, VA 24084. Telephone: 540-674-3600 Ext. 4206. Fax: 540-674-3644. E-mail: nrwinna@nr.edu. URL: http://www.nr.cc.va.us.

NORFOLK STATE UNIVERSITY, NORFOLK

General Information State-supported, coed institution. Urban setting. *Entrance level for U.S. students:* Difficulty N/R. *Financial aid:* Non-need-based college/university scholarships/grants from institutional funds.

OLD DOMINION UNIVERSITY, NORFOLK

General Information State-supported, coed university. Urban setting. *Awards:* B, M, D. *Entrance level for U.S. students:* Difficulty N/R. *Enrollment:* 21,625 total; 15,464 undergraduates (58% women) including 2% international students from 86 foreign countries. *Faculty:* 1,017. *Library holdings:* 968,921 books, 16,371 current serial subscriptions, 52,071 audiovisual materials. *Total majors:* 85.

Information for International Students Students can start in fall, spring, or summer. Transfers accepted from institutions abroad. *Admission tests:* Required: TOEFL (minimum score: iBT 79; paper-based 550; computer-based 213; minimum score for ESL admission: paper-based 310; computer-based 40). TOEFL can be waived under certain conditions. *Application deadline:* 4/15. *Expenses:* (2006–07) $16,667; room and board, $6640 (on campus); room only, $3640 (on campus). *Financial aid:* Need-based and non-need-based financial aid available. Forms required: International Student's Certification of Finances. International transfer students are eligible to apply for aid. 49 international students on campus received college administered financial aid ($7137 average). *Housing:* Available during summer. *Services:* International student adviser on campus. Full-time and part-time ESL programs on campus. ESL program available during the academic year and the summer. Internships and employment opportunities (on-campus and off-campus) available. *Contact:* Director of International and Graduate Admissions, Old Dominion University, Office of International Admissions, 220 Rollins Hall, Norfolk, VA 23529-0093. Telephone: 757-683-3701. Fax: 757-683-3651. E-mail: intladm@odu.edu. URL: http://www.odu.edu.

PAUL D. CAMP COMMUNITY COLLEGE, FRANKLIN

General Information State-supported, 2-year, coed college. Small town setting. *Awards:* A. *Entrance level for U.S. students:* Noncompetitive. *Enrollment:* 1,636 total (66% women) including 0.1% international students from 2 foreign countries. *Undergraduate faculty:* 74. *Library holdings:* 22,000 books, 200 current serial subscriptions. *Total majors:* 6.

Information for International Students Students can start in fall, spring, or summer. Transfers accepted from institutions abroad. *Admission tests:* Required: TOEFL (minimum score: paper-based 450; computer-based 133). *Application deadline:* 8/15. *Services:* International student adviser on campus. *Contact:* Director of Assessment and Student Services, Paul D. Camp Community College, 100 North College Drive, PO Box 737, Franklin, VA 23851-0737. Telephone: 757-569-6725. Fax: 757-569-6795. E-mail: jstandahl@pc.vccs.edu. URL: http://www.pc.vccs.edu.

PIEDMONT VIRGINIA COMMUNITY COLLEGE, CHARLOTTESVILLE

General Information State-supported, 2-year, coed college. Suburban setting. *Awards:* A. *Entrance level for U.S. students:* Noncompetitive. *Enrollment:* 4,451 total (60% women) including 1% international students. *Undergraduate faculty:* 216. *Library holdings:* 39,117 books, 163 current serial subscriptions, 1,718 audiovisual materials. *Total majors:* 30. *Expenses:* (2007–08) $7984.

RADFORD UNIVERSITY, RADFORD

General Information State-supported, coed institution. Small town setting. *Awards:* B, M. *Entrance level for U.S. students:* Moderately difficult. *Enrollment:* 9,220 total; 8,155 undergraduates (58% women) including 1% international students from 51 foreign countries. *Faculty:* 580. *Library holdings:* 377,110 books, 4,801 current serial subscriptions, 16,388 audiovisual materials. *Total majors:* 42.

Information for International Students For fall 2006: 90 international students applied, 65 were accepted, 22 enrolled. Students can start in fall, spring, or summer. Transfers accepted from institutions abroad. *Admission tests:* Required: TOEFL (minimum score: iBT 68; paper-based 520; computer-based 190; minimum score for ESL admission: iBT 68; paper-based 500; computer-based 173). Recommended: SAT, ELS. TOEFL can be waived under certain conditions. *Application deadline:* 4/1. *Expenses:* (2006–07) $13,494; room and board, $6218 (on campus). *Financial aid:* Non-need-based loans from outside sources, on-campus employment. For fall 2006 (estimated), 9 international students on campus received college administered financial aid ($1498 average). *Housing:* Guaranteed, also available during summer. *Services:* International student adviser on campus. ESL program at cooperating institution. Internships and employment opportunities (on-campus) available. *Contact:* Associate Director of Admissions, Radford University, PO Box 6903, Radford, VA 24142. Telephone: 540-831-5371. Fax: 540-831-5038. E-mail: awjarich@radford.edu. URL: http://www.radford.edu.

See In-Depth Description on page 155.

RANDOLPH COLLEGE, LYNCHBURG

General Information Independent Methodist, 4-year, coed college. Suburban setting. *Awards:* B. *Entrance level for U.S. students:* Moderately difficult. *Enrollment:* 715 total; 706 undergraduates (99% women) including 11% international students from 40 foreign countries. *Undergraduate faculty:* 93. *Library holdings:* 197,332 books, 618 current serial subscriptions, 3,600 audiovisual materials. *Total majors:* 37.

Information for International Students For fall 2006: 138 international students applied, 80 were accepted, 27 enrolled. Students can start in fall or spring. Transfers accepted from institutions abroad. *Admission tests:* Recommended: SAT or ACT, TOEFL (minimum score: iBT 79; paper-based 550; computer-based 213), IELTS. TOEFL can be waived under certain conditions. *Application deadline:* Rolling. *Expenses:* (2006–07) $24,410; room and board, $8800 (on campus). *Financial aid:* Need-based college/university scholarships/grants from institutional funds, on-campus employment. Non-need-based college/university scholarships/grants from institutional funds. Forms required: International Student's Financial Aid Application, International Student's Certification of Finances. International transfer students are eligible to apply for aid. For fall 2006 (estimated), 72 international students on campus received college administered financial aid ($19,597 average). *Housing:* Guaranteed. *Services:* International student adviser on campus. Internships and employment opportunities (on-campus) available. *Contact:* Associate Director of Admissions for International Students, Randolph College, 2500 Rivermont Avenue, Lynchburg, VA 24503. Telephone: 434-947-8100. Fax: 434-947-8996. E-mail: jmcgrath@randolphcollege.edu. URL: http://www.randolphcollege.edu.

See In-Depth Description on page 156.

RANDOLPH-MACON COLLEGE, ASHLAND

General Information Independent United Methodist, 4-year, coed college. Suburban setting. *Awards:* B. *Entrance level for U.S. students:* Moderately difficult. *Enrollment:* 1,146 total (54% women) including 2% international students from 15 foreign countries. *Undergraduate faculty:* 152. *Library holdings:* 185,000 books, 17,000 current serial subscriptions, 5,000 audiovisual materials. *Total majors:* 30.

Information for International Students For fall 2006: 64 international students applied, 17 were accepted, 4 enrolled. Students can start in fall or spring. Transfers accepted from institutions abroad. *Admission tests:* Required: English proficiency determined by TOEFL or SAT. Recommended: SAT or ACT, TOEFL (minimum score: paper-based 550; computer-based 213). TOEFL can be waived under certain conditions. *Application deadline:* 3/1. *Expenses:* (2006–07) $25,345; room and board, $7695 (on campus); room only, $4190 (on campus). *Financial aid:* Non-need-based college/university scholarships/grants from institutional funds, loans from outside sources, on-campus employment. Forms required: International Student's Certification of Finances. International transfer students are eligible to apply for aid. For fall 2005, 13 international students on campus received college administered financial aid ($17,679 average). *Housing:* Guaranteed. *Services:* International student adviser on campus. Internships and employment opportunities (on-campus) available. *Contact:* Dean of Admissions and Financial Aid, Randolph-Macon College, PO Box 5005, Ashland, VA 23005-5505. Telephone: 804-752-7305. Fax: 804-752-4707. E-mail: admissions@rmc.edu. URL: http://www.rmc.edu.

REGENT UNIVERSITY, VIRGINIA BEACH

General Information Independent, coed institution. Suburban setting. *Awards:* B, M, D, FP. *Entrance level for U.S. students:* Minimally difficult. *Enrollment:* 4,266 total; 1,046 undergraduates (70% women) including 1% international students from 4 foreign countries. *Faculty:* 165. *Library holdings:* 769,590 books, 1,335 current serial subscriptions, 18,438 audiovisual materials. *Total majors:* 7. *Expenses:* (2006–07) $12,000.

RICHARD BLAND COLLEGE OF THE COLLEGE OF WILLIAM AND MARY, PETERSBURG

General Information State-supported, 2-year, coed college. Rural setting. *Awards:* A. *Entrance level for U.S. students:* Noncompetitive. *Enrollment:* 1,437 total (66% women). *Undergraduate faculty:* 66. *Library holdings:* 91,000 books, 9,000 current serial subscriptions, 2,400 audiovisual materials. *Total majors:* 1. *Expenses:* (2006–07) $10,240.

SHENANDOAH UNIVERSITY, WINCHESTER

General Information Independent United Methodist, coed institution. Small town setting. *Awards:* A, B, M, D, FP. *Entrance level for U.S. students:* Moderately difficult. *Enrollment:* 3,105 total; 1,522 undergraduates (59% women) including 4% international students from 27 foreign countries. *Faculty:* 340. *Library holdings:* 131,174 books, 19,479 current serial subscriptions, 31,143 audiovisual materials. *Total majors:* 36.

Information for International Students For fall 2006: 55 international students applied, 46 were accepted, 33 enrolled. Students can start in fall, spring, or summer. Transfers accepted from institutions abroad. *Admission tests:* Required: TOEFL (minimum score: iBT 71; paper-based 527; computer-based 179). Recommended: SAT or ACT. TOEFL can be waived under certain conditions. *Application deadline:* Rolling. *Expenses:* (2006–07) $21,240; room and board, $7650 (on campus). *Financial aid:* Need-based college/university scholarships/grants from institutional funds, loans from outside sources. Non-need-based college/university scholarships/grants from institutional funds, loans from outside sources, on-campus employment. International transfer students are eligible to apply for aid. 38 international students on campus received college administered financial aid ($9500 average). *Housing:* Guaranteed, also available during summer. *Services:* International student adviser on campus. Full-time ESL program on campus. ESL program available during the academic year and the summer. Internships and employment opportunities (on-campus and off-campus) available. *Contact:* International Admissions Coordinator, Shenandoah University, 1460 University Drive, Winchester, VA 22601. Telephone: 540-665-4520. Fax: 540-665-4627. E-mail: bgalipea@su.edu. URL: http://www.su.edu.

SOUTHSIDE VIRGINIA COMMUNITY COLLEGE, ALBERTA

General Information State-supported, 2-year, coed college. Rural setting. *Awards:* A. *Entrance level for U.S. students:* Noncompetitive. *Enrollment:* 4,686 total (65% women) including 0.04% international students from 2 foreign countries. *Undergraduate faculty:* 295. *Library holdings:* 27,691 books, 164 current serial subscriptions, 1,307 audiovisual materials. *Total majors:* 14. *Expenses:* (2006–07) $7,216. *Financial aid:* Forms required: institution's own financial aid form, FAFSA.

SOUTHWEST VIRGINIA COMMUNITY COLLEGE, RICHLANDS

General Information State-supported, 2-year, coed college. Rural setting. *Awards:* A. *Entrance level for U.S. students:* Noncompetitive. *Enrollment:* 3,580 total (56% women) including 0.03% international students from 1 foreign country. *Undergraduate faculty:* 226. *Library holdings:* 58,000 books, 225 current serial subscriptions. *Total majors:* 18. *Expenses:* (2006–07) $6720.

STRATFORD UNIVERSITY, FALLS CHURCH

General Information Proprietary, coed institution. Suburban setting. *Awards:* A, B, M. *Entrance level for U.S. students:* Minimally difficult. *Enrollment:* 486 total; 445 undergraduates (48% women) including 4% international students. *Faculty:* 61. *Library holdings:* 1,800 books, 75 current serial subscriptions, 283 audiovisual materials. *Total majors:* 8. *Expenses:* (2006–07) $12,098.

SWEET BRIAR COLLEGE, SWEET BRIAR

General Information Independent, women's institution. Rural setting. *Awards:* B, M. *Entrance level for U.S. students:* Moderately difficult. *Enrollment:* 751 total; 739 undergraduates including 1% international students from 12 foreign countries. *Faculty:* 97. *Library holdings:* 263,066 books, 18,676 current serial subscriptions, 12,175 audiovisual materials. *Total majors:* 35. *Expenses:* (2007–08) $25,015; room and board, $10,040 (on campus); room only, $4030 (on campus). *Financial aid:* Need-based financial aid available. Non-need-based college/university scholarships/grants from institutional funds, on-campus employment. For fall 2006 (estimated), 5 international students on campus received college administered financial aid ($13,830 average).

THOMAS NELSON COMMUNITY COLLEGE, HAMPTON

General Information State-supported, 2-year, coed college. Suburban setting. *Awards:* A. *Entrance level for U.S. students:* Noncompetitive. *Enrollment:* 8,595 total (59% women) including 0.05% international students. *Undergraduate faculty:* 433. *Library holdings:* 66,281 books, 467 current serial subscriptions. *Total majors:* 22. *Expenses:* (2006–07) $7177.

UNIVERSITY OF MARY WASHINGTON, FREDERICKSBURG

General Information State-supported, coed institution. Small town setting. *Awards:* B, M. *Entrance level for U.S. students:* Very difficult. *Enrollment:* 4,862 total; 4,183 undergraduates (66% women) including 1% international students from 15 foreign countries. *Faculty:* 354. *Library holdings:* 355,478 books, 2,419 current serial subscriptions. *Total majors:* 40.

Information for International Students Students can start in fall. Transfers accepted from institutions abroad. *Admission tests:* Required: SAT or ACT, TOEFL (minimum score: paper-based 570; computer-based 230). Recommended: SAT, SAT Subject Tests. TOEFL can be waived under certain conditions. *Application deadline:* 2/1. *Expenses:* (2006–07) $15,964; room and board, $6244 (on campus); room only, $3624 (on campus). *Financial aid:* International transfer students are eligible to apply for aid. *Services:* International student adviser on campus. Internships and employment opportunities (on-campus) available. *Contact:* Assistant Dean of Admissions, University of Mary Washington, 1301 College Avenue, Fredericksburg, VA 22401. Telephone: 540-654-2000. Fax: 540-654-1857. E-mail: admit@umw.edu. URL: http://www.umw.edu.

UNIVERSITY OF PHOENIX–NORTHERN VIRGINIA CAMPUS, RESTON

General Information Proprietary, coed institution. Urban setting. *Awards:* B, M. *Entrance level for U.S. students:* Noncompetitive. *Enrollment:* 938 total; 717 undergraduates (47% women) including 10% international students. *Faculty:* 287. *Library holdings:* 1,759 books, 692 current serial subscriptions. *Total majors:* 15. *Expenses:* (2006–07) $11,820.

UNIVERSITY OF PHOENIX–RICHMOND CAMPUS, RICHMOND

General Information Proprietary, coed institution. Urban setting. *Awards:* B, M. *Entrance level for U.S. students:* Noncompetitive. *Enrollment:* 351 total; 227 undergraduates (68% women) including 8% international students. *Faculty:* 129. *Library holdings:* 1,759 books, 692 current serial subscriptions. *Total majors:* 20. *Expenses:* (2006–07) $11,820.

UNIVERSITY OF RICHMOND, RICHMOND

General Information Independent, coed institution. Suburban setting. *Awards:* A, B, M, FP. *Entrance level for U.S. students:* Very difficult. *Enrollment:* 3,554 total; 2,857 undergraduates (51% women) including 6% international students from 32 foreign countries. *Faculty:* 343. *Library holdings:* 1.1 million books, 43,747 current serial subscriptions. *Total majors:* 53. *Expenses:* (2007–08) $37,610; room and board, $7200 (on campus); room only, $3230 (on campus). *Financial aid:* Need-based college/university scholarships/grants from institutional funds. Non-need-based college/university scholarships/grants from institutional funds, athletic awards, on-campus employment. Forms required: International Student's Financial Aid Application, International Student's Certification of Finances. For fall 2006 (estimated), 97 international students on campus received college administered financial aid ($35,600 average).

UNIVERSITY OF VIRGINIA, CHARLOTTESVILLE

General Information State-supported, coed university. Suburban setting. *Awards:* B, M, D, FP. *Entrance level for U.S. students:* Very difficult. *Enrollment:* 24,068 total; 14,676 undergraduates (55% women) including 5% international students from 73 foreign countries. *Faculty:* 1,295. *Library holdings:* 5.4 million books, 71,832 current serial subscriptions, 99,127 audiovisual materials. *Total majors:* 52.

Information for International Students For fall 2006: 1108 international students applied, 517 were accepted, 191 enrolled. Students can start in fall or spring. Transfers accepted from institutions abroad. *Admission tests:* Required: SAT or ACT, TOEFL (minimum score: paper-based 550; computer-based 213), IELTS. Recommended: SAT Subject Tests. TOEFL can be waived under certain conditions. *Application deadline:* 1/2. *Expenses:* (2006–07) $25,945; room and board, $6909 (on campus); room only, $3639 (on campus). *Housing:* Guaranteed, also available during summer. *Services:* International student adviser on campus. Full-time and part-time ESL programs on campus. ESL program available during the academic year and the summer. Internships and employment opportunities (on-campus) available. *Contact:* Director of International Admission, University of Virginia, Charlottesville, VA 22903. Telephone: 434-982-3200. Fax: 434-924-3587. E-mail: ppm@virginia.edu. URL: http://www.virginia.edu.

THE UNIVERSITY OF VIRGINIA'S COLLEGE AT WISE, WISE

General Information State-supported, 4-year, coed college. Small town setting. *Awards:* B. *Entrance level for U.S. students:* Moderately difficult. *Enrollment:* 1,911 total (55% women) including 0.5% international students from 8 foreign countries. *Undergraduate faculty:* 149. *Library holdings:* 143,930 books, 6,617 current serial subscriptions, 4,806 audiovisual materials. *Total majors:* 24. *Expenses:* (2007–08) $17,815; room and board, $6984 (on campus); room only, $3725 (on campus). *Financial aid:* Need-based college/university scholarships/grants from institutional funds, tuition waivers. Non-need-based college/university scholarships/grants from institutional funds, tuition waivers, athletic awards. Forms required: International Student's Certification of Finances. 9 international students on campus received college administered financial aid ($10,229 average).

VIRGINIA COMMONWEALTH UNIVERSITY, RICHMOND

General Information State-supported, coed university. Urban setting. *Awards:* B, M, D, FP. *Entrance level for U.S. students:* Difficulty N/R. *Enrollment:* 30,381 total; 21,260 undergraduates (59% women) including 3% international students from 79 foreign countries. *Faculty:* 2,813. *Library holdings:* 1.9 million books, 18,000 current serial subscriptions. *Total majors:* 55.

Information for International Students Students can start in fall, spring, or summer. Transfers accepted from institutions abroad. *Admission tests:* Required: TOEFL (minimum score: paper-based 550; computer-based 213). Recommended: SAT. *Application deadline:* Rolling. *Expenses:* (2006–07) $15,904; room and board, $7473 (on campus); room only, $4273 (on campus). *Financial aid:* Non-need-based college/university scholarships/grants from institutional funds, athletic awards, loans from outside sources. For fall 2005, 269 international students on campus received college administered financial aid ($11,347 average). *Housing:* Available during summer. *Services:* International student adviser on campus. Full-time and part-time ESL programs on campus. ESL program available during the academic year and the summer. Employment opportunities (on-campus) available. *Contact:* Executive Director, Virginia Commonwealth University, Office of International Education, 916 West Franklin Street, Room 203, Richmond, VA 23284. Telephone: 804-828-8471. Fax: 804-828-2552. E-mail: vcuia@vcu.edu. URL: http://www.vcu.edu.

See In-Depth Description on page 240.

VIRGINIA INTERMONT COLLEGE, BRISTOL

General Information Independent, 4-year, coed college, affiliated with Baptist Church. Small town setting. *Awards:* A, B. *Entrance level for U.S. students:* Minimally difficult. *Enrollment:* 916 total (69% women) including 8% international students from 28 foreign countries. *Undergraduate faculty:* 84. *Library holdings:* 109,773 books, 75 current serial subscriptions, 2,275 audiovisual materials. *Total majors:* 41. *Expenses:* (2006–07) $17,845; room and board, $6095 (on campus); room only, $2900 (on campus). *Financial aid:* Non-need-based college/university scholarships/grants from institutional funds, athletic awards, loans from outside sources, on-campus employment. Forms required: institution's own financial aid form. For fall 2005, 78 international students on campus received college administered financial aid ($12,065 average).

VIRGINIA POLYTECHNIC INSTITUTE AND STATE UNIVERSITY, BLACKSBURG

General Information State-supported, coed university. Small town setting. *Awards:* A, B, M, D, FP. *Entrance level for U.S. students:* Moderately difficult. *Enrollment:* 28,470 total; 21,997 undergraduates (42% women) including 2% international students from 76 foreign countries. *Faculty:* 1,586. *Library holdings:* 2.3 million books, 33,874 current serial subscriptions, 26,253 audiovisual materials. *Total majors:* 66.

Information for International Students For fall 2006: 530 international students applied, 293 were accepted, 82 enrolled. Students can start in fall, spring, or summer. Transfers accepted from institutions abroad. *Admission tests:* Required: SAT or ACT, TOEFL (minimum score: iBT 80; paper-based 550; computer-based 207). TOEFL can be waived under certain conditions. *Application deadline:* 1/15. *Expenses:* (2006–07) $18,929; room and board, $4700 (on campus); room only, $2578 (on campus). *Housing:* Available during summer. *Services:* International student adviser on campus. Full-time and part-time ESL programs on campus. ESL program available during the academic year and the summer. Internships and employment opportunities (on-campus) available. *Contact:* Assistant Director of Admissions, Virginia Polytechnic Institute and State University, 104 Burruss Hall, Blacksburg, VA 24061. Telephone: 540-231-6267. Fax: 540-231-3242. E-mail: smilley@vt.edu. URL: http://www.vt.edu.

VIRGINIA STATE UNIVERSITY, PETERSBURG

General Information State-supported, coed institution. Suburban setting. *Awards:* A, B, M, D. *Entrance level for U.S. students:* Minimally difficult. *Enrollment:* 4,872 total; 4,306 undergraduates

(60% women) including 0.3% international students from 35 foreign countries. *Faculty:* 336. *Library holdings:* 284,213 books, 2,381 current serial subscriptions, 26,492 audiovisual materials. *Total majors:* 33. *Expenses:* (2006–07) $12,512; room and board, $6884 (on campus); room only, $4047 (on campus). *Financial aid:* Non-need financial aid available. Forms required: institution's own financial aid form, FAFSA.

VIRGINIA UNIVERSITY OF LYNCHBURG, LYNCHBURG
General Information Independent religious, coed institution. Urban setting. *Entrance level for U.S. students:* Noncompetitive. *Enrollment:* 241 total; 155 undergraduates (47% women) including 1% international students from 1 foreign country. *Undergraduate faculty:* 82. *Library holdings:* 25,000 books, 96 current serial subscriptions. *Expenses:* (2007–08) $5300; room and board, $3600 (on campus).

VIRGINIA WESTERN COMMUNITY COLLEGE, ROANOKE
General Information State-supported, 2-year, coed college. Suburban setting. *Awards:* A. *Entrance level for U.S. students:* Noncompetitive. *Enrollment:* 8,362 total. *Undergraduate faculty:* 406. *Library holdings:* 67,129 books, 402 current serial subscriptions. *Total majors:* 25.

WASHINGTON AND LEE UNIVERSITY, LEXINGTON
General Information Independent, coed institution. Small town setting. *Awards:* B, M, FP. *Entrance level for U.S. students:* Most difficult. *Enrollment:* 2,148 total; 1,752 undergraduates (49% women) including 4% international students from 42 foreign countries. *Faculty:* 214. *Library holdings:* 936,448 books, 8,621 current serial subscriptions, 17,224 audiovisual materials. *Total majors:* 39. *Expenses:* (2006–07) $31,875; room and board, $8920 (on campus); room only, $4690 (on campus). *Financial aid:* Need-based college/university scholarships/grants from institutional funds, loans from institutional funds, loans from outside sources, on-campus employment. Non-need-based college/university scholarships/grants from institutional funds, loans from institutional funds, loans from outside sources, on-campus employment. Forms required: institution's own financial aid form, International Student's Financial Aid Application. For fall 2006 (estimated), 57 international students on campus received college administered financial aid ($37,305 average).

WYTHEVILLE COMMUNITY COLLEGE, WYTHEVILLE
General Information State-supported, 2-year, coed college. Rural setting. *Awards:* A. *Entrance level for U.S. students:* Noncompetitive. *Enrollment:* 2,450 total including international students from 1 foreign country. *Library holdings:* 29,000 books, 261 current serial subscriptions. *Total majors:* 22.
Information for International Students For fall 2006: 2 international students applied, 2 were accepted, 2 enrolled. Students can start in fall, spring, or summer. *Admission tests:* Recommended: TOEFL. TOEFL can be waived under certain conditions. *Application deadline:* 5/15. *Financial aid:* Forms required: institution's own financial aid form. *Contact:* Wytheville Community College. Telephone: 276-223-4700. Fax: 276-223-4860. URL: http://www.wcc.vccs.edu.

WASHINGTON

BASTYR UNIVERSITY, KENMORE
General Information Independent, coed institution. Suburban setting. *Awards:* B, M, FP. *Entrance level for U.S. students:* Difficulty N/R. *Enrollment:* 1,126 total; 263 undergraduates (81% women) including 4% international students from 8 foreign countries. *Faculty:* 151. *Library holdings:* 14,000 books, 265 current serial subscriptions. *Total majors:* 6.
Information for International Students For fall 2006: 9 international students applied, 6 were accepted, 6 enrolled. Students can start in fall. Transfers accepted from institutions abroad. *Admission tests:* Required: TOEFL (minimum score: iBT 79; paper-based 550; computer-based 213), Test of Spoken English, IELTS. Recommended: ELS. TOEFL can be waived under certain conditions. *Application deadline:* 3/15. *Expenses:* (2007–08) $16,365; room only, $3650 (on campus). *Financial aid:* Need-based and non-need-based financial aid available. *Housing:* Available during summer. *Services:* International student adviser on campus. Employment opportunities (on-campus) available. *Contact:* Assistant Director, Admissions Office, Bastyr University, 14500 Juanita Drive, NE, Kenmore, WA 98028. Telephone: 425-602-3330. Fax: 425-602-3090. E-mail: nshappart@bastyr.edu. URL: http://www.bastyr.edu.

BELLEVUE COMMUNITY COLLEGE, BELLEVUE
General Information State-supported, 2-year, coed college. Suburban setting. *Awards:* A. *Entrance level for U.S. students:* Noncompetitive. *Enrollment:* 13,716 undergraduates including 2% international students from 64 foreign countries. *Undergraduate faculty:* 516. *Library holdings:* 42,000 books, 485 current serial subscriptions. *Total majors:* 19. *Expenses:* (2006–07) $8109. *Financial aid:* Need-based college/university scholarships/grants from institutional funds, on-campus employment. Non-need-based college/university scholarships/grants from institutional funds, athletic awards, loans from outside sources. Forms required: institution's own financial aid form.

BIG BEND COMMUNITY COLLEGE, MOSES LAKE
General Information State-supported, 2-year, coed college. Small town setting. *Awards:* A. *Entrance level for U.S. students:* Noncompetitive. *Enrollment:* 2,697 total including international students from 2 foreign countries. *Undergraduate faculty:* 132. *Library holdings:* 41,900 books, 3,700 current serial subscriptions, 3,150 audiovisual materials. *Total majors:* 14. *Expenses:* (2007–08) $3166.

CASCADIA COMMUNITY COLLEGE, BOTHELL
General Information State-supported, 2-year, coed college. Suburban setting. *Awards:* A. *Entrance level for U.S. students:* Noncompetitive. *Enrollment:* 1,950 total (49% women) including 1% international students from 7 foreign countries. *Undergraduate faculty:* 94. *Library holdings:* 73,749 books, 850 current serial subscriptions, 6,100 audiovisual materials. *Total majors:* 3. *Expenses:* (2006–07) $7815.

CENTRALIA COLLEGE, CENTRALIA
General Information State-supported, 2-year, coed college. Small town setting. *Awards:* A. *Entrance level for U.S. students:* Noncompetitive. *Enrollment:* 3,808 total including 1% international students from 12 foreign countries. *Undergraduate faculty:* 240. *Library holdings:* 38,000 books, 225 current serial subscriptions, 5,000 audiovisual materials. *Total majors:* 66.
Information for International Students For fall 2006: 103 international students applied, 93 were accepted, 29 enrolled. Students can start in fall, winter, spring, or summer. Transfers accepted from institutions abroad. *Admission tests:* Recommended: TOEFL (minimum score: iBT 61; paper-based 500; computer-based 173). TOEFL can be waived under certain conditions. *Application deadline:* Rolling. *Expenses:* (2006–07) $3336. *Housing:* Available during summer. *Services:* International student adviser on campus. Full-time and part-time ESL programs on campus. ESL program available during the academic year and the summer. Employment opportunities (on-campus) available. *Contact:* Director, International Programs, Centralia College, 600 Centralia College Boulevard, Centralia, WA 98531-4099. Telephone: 360-736-9391 Ext. 492. Fax: 360-330-7503. E-mail: lnankani@centralia.edu. URL: http://www.centralia.edu.

See In-Depth Description on page 52.

CENTRAL WASHINGTON UNIVERSITY, ELLENSBURG
General Information State-supported, coed institution. Small town setting. *Awards:* B, M. *Entrance level for U.S. students:* Moderately difficult. *Enrollment:* 10,688 total; 10,145 undergraduates (53% women) including 2% international students from 46 foreign countries. *Faculty:* 579. *Library holdings:* 434,424 books, 1,469 current serial subscriptions. *Total majors:* 72. *Expenses:* (2006–07) $14,193; room and board, $7140 (on campus). *Financial aid:* Need-based loans from outside sources. Non-need-based tuition waivers. Forms required: International Student's Financial Aid Application. For fall 2005, 23 international students on campus received college administered financial aid ($2130 average).

CITY UNIVERSITY, BELLEVUE
General Information Independent, coed institution. Suburban setting. *Awards:* A, B, M. *Entrance level for U.S. students:* Noncompetitive. *Enrollment:* 4,020 total; 1,794 undergraduates (56% women) including 6% international students from 33 foreign countries. *Faculty:* 1,241. *Library holdings:* 32,329 books, 1,518 current serial subscriptions, 5,184 audiovisual materials. *Total majors:* 10.
Information for International Students For fall 2006: 87 international students applied, 66 were accepted, 48 enrolled. Students can start in fall, winter, spring, or summer. Transfers accepted from institutions abroad. *Admission tests:* Required: TOEFL (minimum score: iBT 76; paper-based 540; computer-based 207). TOEFL can be waived under certain conditions. *Application deadline:* Rolling. *Expenses:* (2006–07) $8160. *Services:* International student adviser on campus. Full-time and part-time

City University (continued)

ESL programs on campus. ESL program available during the academic year and the summer. Employment opportunities (on-campus) available. *Contact:* Director, International Admissions, City University, 11900 NE 1st Street, Bellevue, WA 98055. Telephone: 425-709-5315. Fax: 425-709-5319. E-mail: internatladmissions@cityu.edu. URL: http://www.cityu.edu.

See In-Depth Description on page 56.

CLARK COLLEGE, VANCOUVER

General Information State-supported, 2-year, coed college. Urban setting. *Awards:* A. *Entrance level for U.S. students:* Noncompetitive. *Enrollment:* 9,906 total (60% women) including 1% international students from 19 foreign countries. *Undergraduate faculty:* 591. *Library holdings:* 72,883 books, 390 current serial subscriptions, 2,246 audiovisual materials. *Total majors:* 35. *Expenses:* (2006–07) $2327; room and board, $5202 (on campus).

DEVRY UNIVERSITY, FEDERAL WAY

General Information Proprietary, coed institution. Suburban setting. *Awards:* A, B, M. *Entrance level for U.S. students:* Minimally difficult. *Enrollment:* 812 total; 730 undergraduates (27% women) including 1% international students. *Faculty:* 62. *Library holdings:* 6,021 books, 6,807 current serial subscriptions. *Total majors:* 11. *Expenses:* (2007–08) $14,640.

DIGIPEN INSTITUTE OF TECHNOLOGY, REDMOND

General Information Proprietary, coed institution. Suburban setting. *Awards:* A, B, M. *Entrance level for U.S. students:* Moderately difficult. *Enrollment:* 783 total; 745 undergraduates (8% women) including international students from 22 foreign countries. *Faculty:* 56. *Library holdings:* 2,117 books, 52 current serial subscriptions, 277 audiovisual materials. *Total majors:* 2. **Information for International Students** For fall 2006: 46 international students applied, 15 were accepted, 7 enrolled. Students can start in fall. Transfers accepted from institutions abroad. *Admission tests:* Required: TOEFL (minimum score: iBT 80; paper-based 550; computer-based 213). TOEFL can be waived under certain conditions. *Application deadline:* Rolling. *Expenses:* (2007–08) $16,880. *Services:* International student adviser on campus. Internships and employment opportunities (on-campus) available. *Contact:* Admissions Manager, DigiPen Institute of Technology, 5001 150th Avenue, NE, Redmond, WA 98052. Telephone: 425-895-4438. Fax: 425-558-0378. E-mail: akugler@digipen.edu. URL: http://www.digipen.edu.

EASTERN WASHINGTON UNIVERSITY, CHENEY

General Information State-supported, coed institution. Small town setting. *Awards:* B, M, D. *Entrance level for U.S. students:* Moderately difficult. *Enrollment:* 11,161 undergraduates including 1% international students from 34 foreign countries. *Library holdings:* 852,186 books, 6,429 current serial subscriptions, 31,832 audiovisual materials. *Total majors:* 109. *Expenses:* (2006–07) $13,622; room and board, $6182 (on campus).

EDMONDS COMMUNITY COLLEGE, LYNNWOOD

General Information State and locally supported, 2-year, coed college. Suburban setting. *Awards:* A. *Entrance level for U.S. students:* Noncompetitive. *Enrollment:* 7,581 total (57% women) including 11% international students from 55 foreign countries. *Undergraduate faculty:* 428. *Library holdings:* 47,947 books, 312 current serial subscriptions, 7,735 audiovisual materials. *Total majors:* 51. **Information for International Students** For fall 2006: 426 international students applied, 418 were accepted, 235 enrolled. Students can start in fall, winter, spring, or summer. Transfers accepted from institutions abroad. *Admission tests:* Required: English Placement Test upon arrival. *Application deadline:* Rolling. *Expenses:* (2006–07) $7939; room only, $4500 (on campus). *Financial aid:* Need-based and non-need-based financial aid available. Forms required: institution's own financial aid form. *Housing:* Guaranteed, also available during summer. *Services:* International student adviser on campus. Full-time and part-time ESL programs on campus. ESL program available during the academic year and the summer. Internships and employment opportunities (on-campus and off-campus) available. *Contact:* Office of Admissions, Edmonds Community College, 20000 68th Avenue West, Lynnwood, WA 98036-5444. Telephone: 425-640-1518. Fax: 425-774-0455. E-mail: issadmissions@edcc.ctc.edu. URL: http://www.edcc.edu.

THE EVERGREEN STATE COLLEGE, OLYMPIA

General Information State-supported, coed institution. Rural setting. *Awards:* B, M. *Entrance level for U.S. students:* Moderately difficult. *Enrollment:* 4,416 total; 4,124 undergraduates (55% women) including 0.4% international students from 7 foreign countries. *Faculty:* 232. *Library holdings:* 471,406 books, 12,579 current serial subscriptions, 89,195 audiovisual materials. *Total majors:* 23.

Information for International Students For fall 2006: 13 international students applied, 12 were accepted, 9 enrolled. Students can start in fall, winter, spring, or summer. Transfers accepted from institutions abroad. *Admission tests:* Required: TOEFL (minimum score: iBT 79; paper-based 550; computer-based 213). Recommended: SAT or ACT. TOEFL can be waived under certain conditions. *Application deadline:* Rolling. *Expenses:* (2006–07) $15,052; room and board, $7140 (on campus); room only, $4620 (on campus). *Financial aid:* Non-need-based college/university scholarships/grants from institutional funds, tuition waivers, athletic awards. 6 international students on campus received college administered financial aid ($10,891 average). *Housing:* Available during summer. *Services:* International student adviser on campus. ESL program at cooperating institution. ESL program available during the academic year. Internships and employment opportunities (on-campus and off-campus) available. *Contact:* Director of Admissions, The Evergreen State College, 2700 Evergreen Parkway, NW, MS Admissions, Olympia, WA 98505. Telephone: 360-867-6170. Fax: 360-867-6576. E-mail: admissions@evergreen.edu. URL: http://www.evergreen.edu.

GONZAGA UNIVERSITY, SPOKANE

General Information Independent Roman Catholic, coed institution. Urban setting. *Awards:* B, M, D, FP. *Entrance level for U.S. students:* Moderately difficult. *Enrollment:* 6,610 total; 4,275 undergraduates (54% women) including 1% international students from 36 foreign countries. *Faculty:* 639. *Library holdings:* 305,517 books, 32,106 current serial subscriptions. *Total majors:* 51. **Information for International Students** For fall 2006: 143 international students applied, 85 were accepted, 46 enrolled. Students can start in fall, winter, spring, or summer. Transfers accepted from institutions abroad. *Admission tests:* Required: TOEFL (minimum score: iBT 80; paper-based 550; computer-based 213). TOEFL can be waived under certain conditions. *Application deadline:* 8/1. *Expenses:* (2006–07) $25,012; room and board, $7220 (on campus); room only, $3560 (on campus). *Financial aid:* Non-need-based college/university scholarships/grants from institutional funds, tuition waivers, athletic awards, loans from outside sources, on-campus employment. International transfer students are eligible to apply for aid. *Housing:* Available during summer. *Services:* International student adviser on campus. Full-time ESL program on campus. ESL program available during the academic year and the summer. Internships and employment opportunities (on-campus) available. *Contact:* International Student Advisor, Gonzaga University, 502 East Boone Avenue, International Student Programs, Spokane, WA 99258-0088. Telephone: 509-323-6561. Fax: 509-323-5814. E-mail: terhark@gonzaga.edu. URL: http://www.gonzaga.edu.

GRAYS HARBOR COLLEGE, ABERDEEN

General Information State-supported, 2-year, coed college. Small town setting. *Awards:* A. *Entrance level for U.S. students:* Noncompetitive. *Enrollment:* 2,156 total (57% women) including 0.2% international students. *Undergraduate faculty:* 146. *Library holdings:* 39,220 books, 2,309 audiovisual materials. *Total majors:* 19.

Information for International Students For fall 2006: 3 international students enrolled. Students can start in fall, winter, spring, or summer. Transfers accepted from institutions abroad. *Admission tests:* Required: TOEFL (minimum score: paper-based 500; computer-based 173). TOEFL can be waived under certain conditions. *Application deadline:* Rolling. *Services:* International student adviser on campus. Full-time ESL program on campus. ESL program available during the academic year. Employment opportunities (on-campus) available. *Contact:* Associate Dean for Student Services, Grays Harbor College, 1620 Edward P. Smith Drive, Aberdeen, WA 98520. Telephone: 360-538-4030. Fax: 360-538-4293. E-mail: ndeverse@ghc.edu. URL: http://www.ghc.ctc.edu.

HIGHLINE COMMUNITY COLLEGE, DES MOINES

General Information State-supported, 2-year, coed college. Suburban setting. *Awards:* A. *Entrance level for U.S. students:* Noncompetitive. *Enrollment:* 6,372 total (64% women) including 0.2% international students. *Undergraduate faculty:* 356. *Library holdings:* 57,678 books, 585 current serial subscriptions. *Total majors:* 48.

LOWER COLUMBIA COLLEGE, LONGVIEW

General Information State-supported, 2-year, coed college. Small town setting. *Awards:* A. *Entrance level for U.S. students:* Noncompetitive. *Enrollment:* 3,268 total (65% women) including

0.1% international students from 5 foreign countries. *Undergraduate faculty:* 182. *Library holdings:* 41,991 books, 217 current serial subscriptions. *Total majors:* 79. *Expenses:* (2006–07) $3495. *Financial aid:* Need-based college/university scholarships/grants from institutional funds, tuition waivers, loans from outside sources, on-campus employment. Non-need-based college/university scholarships/grants from institutional funds, tuition waivers, athletic awards, loans from outside sources, on-campus employment. Forms required: institution's own financial aid form, income documentation.

NORTH SEATTLE COMMUNITY COLLEGE, SEATTLE
General Information State-supported, 2-year, coed college. Urban setting. *Awards:* A. *Entrance level for U.S. students:* Noncompetitive. *Enrollment:* 6,210 total (62% women). *Undergraduate faculty:* 280. *Library holdings:* 52,496 books, 594 current serial subscriptions. *Total majors:* 27. *Expenses:* (2006–07) $11,286. *Financial aid:* Forms required: institution's own financial aid form.

NORTHWEST COLLEGE OF ART, POULSBO
General Information Proprietary, 4-year, coed college. Small town setting. *Awards:* B. *Entrance level for U.S. students:* Moderately difficult. *Total majors:* 2. *Financial aid:* Non-need financial aid available.

NORTHWEST SCHOOL OF WOODEN BOATBUILDING, PORT TOWNSEND
General Information Independent, 2-year, coed college. *Awards:* A. *Entrance level for U.S. students:* Difficulty N/R. *Total majors:* 1.
Information for International Students For fall 2006: 2 international students applied, 2 were accepted, 2 enrolled. Students can start in fall, winter, spring, or summer. *Application deadline:* 7/15. *Services:* International student adviser on campus. *Contact:* Student Services Administrator, Northwest School of Wooden Boatbuilding, 42 North Water Street, Port Hadlock, WA 98339. Telephone: 360-385-4948. Fax: 360-385-5089. E-mail: Info@nwboatschool.org. URL: http://www.nwboatschool.org.

NORTHWEST UNIVERSITY, KIRKLAND
General Information Independent, coed institution, affiliated with Assemblies of God. Suburban setting. *Awards:* A, B, M. *Entrance level for U.S. students:* Moderately difficult. *Enrollment:* 1,265 total; 1,141 undergraduates (61% women) including 2% international students from 13 foreign countries. *Faculty:* 97. *Library holdings:* 120,226 books, 11,454 current serial subscriptions, 4,216 audiovisual materials. *Total majors:* 36.
Information for International Students For fall 2006: 9 international students applied, 7 were accepted, 5 enrolled. Students can start in fall, spring, or summer. Transfers accepted from institutions abroad. *Admission tests:* Required: TOEFL (minimum score: iBT 61; paper-based 500; computer-based 173; minimum score for ESL admission: iBT 31; paper-based 400; computer-based 97). Recommended: SAT or ACT. *Application deadline:* 7/1. *Expenses:* (2007–08) $19,762; room and board, $6578 (on campus). *Financial aid:* Need-based college/university scholarships/grants from institutional funds, on-campus employment. Non-need-based college/university scholarships/grants from institutional funds, athletic awards, on-campus employment. Forms required: International Student's Financial Aid Application, Institutional Affidavit of Financial Support. International transfer students are eligible to apply for aid. For fall 2006 (estimated), 15 international students on campus received college administered financial aid ($8702 average). *Housing:* Guaranteed, also available during summer. *Services:* International student adviser on campus. Full-time ESL program on campus. ESL program available during the academic year and the summer. Employment opportunities (on-campus) available. *Contact:* Director of Traditional Admissions, Northwest University, PO Box 579, Kirkland, WA 98083-0579. Telephone: 425-889-5212. Fax: 425-889-5224. E-mail: ben.thomas@northwestu.edu. URL: http://www.northwestu.edu.

OLYMPIC COLLEGE, BREMERTON
General Information State-supported, 2-year, coed college. Suburban setting. *Awards:* A. *Entrance level for U.S. students:* Noncompetitive. *Enrollment:* 6,765 total (56% women) including 0.3% international students from 4 foreign countries. *Undergraduate faculty:* 509. *Library holdings:* 60,000 books, 541 current serial subscriptions. *Total majors:* 46. *Expenses:* (2007–08) $4158.

PACIFIC LUTHERAN UNIVERSITY, TACOMA
General Information Independent, coed institution, affiliated with Evangelical Lutheran Church in America. Suburban setting.

Awards: B, M. *Entrance level for U.S. students:* Moderately difficult. *Enrollment:* 3,640 total; 3,340 undergraduates (64% women) including 5% international students from 25 foreign countries. *Faculty:* 266. *Library holdings:* 350,750 books, 3,433 current serial subscriptions, 12,954 audiovisual materials. *Total majors:* 60. *Expenses:* (2006–07) $23,450; room and board, $7140 (on campus); room only, $3510 (on campus). *Financial aid:* Non-need-based college/university scholarships/grants from institutional funds, on-campus employment. For fall 2006 (estimated), 158 international students on campus received college administered financial aid ($6043 average).

PENINSULA COLLEGE, PORT ANGELES
General Information State-supported, 2-year, coed college. Small town setting. *Awards:* A. *Entrance level for U.S. students:* Noncompetitive. *Enrollment:* 3,948 total including 1% international students from 11 foreign countries. *Undergraduate faculty:* 191. *Library holdings:* 33,736 books, 383 current serial subscriptions. *Total majors:* 19.
Information for International Students For fall 2006: 75 international students applied, 75 were accepted, 65 enrolled. Students can start in fall, winter, spring, or summer. Transfers accepted from institutions abroad. *Admission tests:* Recommended: TOEFL (minimum score: paper-based 500; computer-based 173), ELS. TOEFL can be waived under certain conditions. *Application deadline:* Rolling. *Expenses:* (2007–08) $3334. *Services:* International student adviser on campus. Full-time and part-time ESL programs on campus. ESL program available during the academic year. Employment opportunities (on-campus) available. *Contact:* Director of International Programs, Peninsula College, 1502 East Lauridsen Boulevard, Port Angeles, WA 98362. Telephone: 360-417-6491. Fax: 360-417-6482. E-mail: gliu@ctc.edu. URL: http://www.pc.ctc.edu.

See In-Depth Description on page 149.

PIERCE COLLEGE, PUYALLUP
General Information State-supported, 2-year, coed college. Suburban setting. *Awards:* A. *Entrance level for U.S. students:* Noncompetitive. *Enrollment:* 13,294 total including international students from 12 foreign countries. *Undergraduate faculty:* 590. *Library holdings:* 55,000 books, 425 current serial subscriptions. *Total majors:* 20.
Information for International Students For fall 2006: 190 international students applied, 180 were accepted, 150 enrolled. Students can start in fall, winter, spring, or summer. Transfers accepted from institutions abroad. *Admission tests:* Required: college assessment of English required upon arrival if TOEFL score not submitted. Recommended: TOEFL (minimum score: iBT 61; paper-based 500; computer-based 173). TOEFL can be waived under certain conditions. *Application deadline:* Rolling. *Services:* International student adviser on campus. Full-time and part-time ESL programs on campus. ESL program available during the academic year and the summer. Internships and employment opportunities (on-campus) available. *Contact:* Manager of International Student Services, Pierce College, 9401 Farwest Drive, SW, Lakewood, WA 98498-1999. Telephone: 253-964-6725. Fax: 253-964-6256. E-mail: mmeulblok@pierce.ctc.edu. URL: http://www.pierce.ctc.edu.

See In-Depth Description on page 151.

RENTON TECHNICAL COLLEGE, RENTON
General Information State-supported, 2-year, coed college. Suburban setting. *Awards:* A. *Entrance level for U.S. students:* Noncompetitive. *Enrollment:* 9,301 total including 0.4% international students from 13 foreign countries. *Undergraduate faculty:* 282. *Library holdings:* 12,876 books, 2,316 current serial subscriptions, 321 audiovisual materials. *Total majors:* 19.
Information for International Students For fall 2006: 20 international students applied, 17 were accepted, 15 enrolled. Students can start in fall, winter, or spring. Transfers accepted from institutions abroad. *Admission tests:* Required: COMPASS upon arrival. Recommended: TOEFL (minimum score: paper-based 500; computer-based 173), ELS. TOEFL can be waived under certain conditions. *Application deadline:* Rolling. *Financial aid:* Forms required: institution's own financial aid form. *Services:* International student adviser on campus. Full-time ESL program on campus. ESL program available during the academic year and the summer. *Contact:* Counselor, Renton Technical College, 3000 NE 4th Street, Renton, WA 98056-4195. Telephone: 425-235-5840. Fax: 425-235-7832. E-mail: bbennedsen@rtc.edu. URL: http://www.rtc.edu.

SAINT MARTIN'S UNIVERSITY, LACEY
General Information Independent Roman Catholic, coed institution. Suburban setting. *Awards:* B, M. *Entrance level for U.S. students:* Moderately difficult. *Enrollment:* 1,463 total; 1,180

Saint Martin's University (continued)

undergraduates (57% women) including 7% international students from 11 foreign countries. *Faculty:* 162. *Library holdings:* 86,461 books, 824 current serial subscriptions, 1,487 audiovisual materials. *Total majors:* 31. *Expenses:* (2006–07) $20,965; room and board, $6400 (on campus); room only, $3000 (on campus). *Financial aid:* Need-based college/university scholarships/grants from institutional funds, tuition waivers, athletic awards, on-campus employment. Non-need-based college/university scholarships/grants from institutional funds, tuition waivers, athletic awards, on-campus employment. Forms required: International Student's Certification of Finances. For fall 2005, 2 international students on campus received college administered financial aid ($16,360 average).

SEATTLE CENTRAL COMMUNITY COLLEGE, SEATTLE

General Information State-supported, 2-year, coed college. Urban setting. *Awards:* A. *Entrance level for U.S. students:* Noncompetitive. *Enrollment:* 9,418 total including 6% international students. *Undergraduate faculty:* 438. *Library holdings:* 56,338 books, 425 current serial subscriptions. *Total majors:* 25.

Information for International Students For fall 2006: 149 international students applied, 140 were accepted, 111 enrolled. Students can start in fall, winter, spring, or summer. Transfers accepted from institutions abroad. *Admission tests:* Recommended: TOEFL (minimum score: iBT 61; paper-based 470; computer-based 150). TOEFL can be waived under certain conditions. *Application deadline:* 7/30. *Services:* International student adviser on campus. Full-time and part-time ESL programs on campus. ESL program available during the academic year and the summer. Internships and employment opportunities (on-campus and off-campus) available. *Contact:* Manager, International Admissions and Services, Seattle Central Community College, International Education Programs, 1701 Broadway, Seattle, WA 98122. Telephone: 206-587-3893. Fax: 206-587-3868. E-mail: iepsccc@sccd.ctc.edu. URL: http://www.seattlecentral.edu.

SEATTLE PACIFIC UNIVERSITY, SEATTLE

General Information Independent Free Methodist, coed institution. Urban setting. *Awards:* B, M, D. *Entrance level for U.S. students:* Moderately difficult. *Enrollment:* 3,830 total; 2,979 undergraduates (67% women) including 1% international students from 24 foreign countries. *Faculty:* 364. *Library holdings:* 191,807 books, 1,230 current serial subscriptions, 4,408 audiovisual materials. *Total majors:* 54. *Expenses:* (2006–07) $23,391; room and board, $7818 (on campus); room only, $4212 (on campus). *Financial aid:* Non-need-based college/university scholarships/grants from institutional funds, loans from outside sources, on-campus employment. Forms required: International Student's Financial Aid Application. For fall 2006 (estimated), 6 international students on campus received college administered financial aid ($7083 average).

SEATTLE UNIVERSITY, SEATTLE

General Information Independent Roman Catholic, coed institution. Urban setting. *Awards:* B, M, D, FP. *Entrance level for U.S. students:* Moderately difficult. *Enrollment:* 7,226 total; 4,160 undergraduates (61% women) including 6% international students from 76 foreign countries. *Faculty:* 594. *Library holdings:* 141,478 books, 2,701 current serial subscriptions, 5,649 audiovisual materials. *Total majors:* 56.

Information for International Students For fall 2006: 195 international students were accepted, 70 enrolled. Students can start in fall, winter, spring, or summer. Transfers accepted from institutions abroad. *Admission tests:* Required: TOEFL (minimum score: iBT 68; paper-based 520; computer-based 190). TOEFL can be waived under certain conditions. *Application deadline:* 2/1. *Expenses:* (2006–07) $24,615; room and board, $7503 (on campus); room only, $4818 (on campus). *Financial aid:* International transfer students are eligible to apply for aid. *Housing:* Guaranteed, also available during summer. *Services:* International student adviser on campus. Internships and employment opportunities (on-campus) available. *Contact:* International Admissions Evaluator, Admissions Office, Seattle University, 901 12th Avenue, PO Box 22000, Seattle, WA 98122-1090. Telephone: 206-296.2000. Fax: 206-296.5656. E-mail: admissions@seattleu.edu. URL: http://www.seattleu.edu.

SHORELINE COMMUNITY COLLEGE, SHORELINE

General Information State-supported, 2-year, coed college. Suburban setting. *Awards:* A. *Entrance level for U.S. students:* Noncompetitive. *Enrollment:* 8,591 total. *Undergraduate faculty:* 415. *Library holdings:* 79,554 books, 1,735 current serial subscriptions. *Total majors:* 42. *Financial aid:* Forms required: institution's own financial aid form.

SKAGIT VALLEY COLLEGE, MOUNT VERNON

General Information State-supported, 2-year, coed college. Small town setting. *Awards:* A. *Entrance level for U.S. students:*

Noncompetitive. *Enrollment:* 6,858 total including international students from 23 foreign countries. *Undergraduate faculty:* 301. *Library holdings:* 78,631 books, 359 current serial subscriptions, 2,599 audiovisual materials. *Total majors:* 65.

Information for International Students For fall 2006: 170 international students applied, 140 were accepted, 98 enrolled. Students can start in fall, winter, spring, or summer. Transfers accepted from institutions abroad. *Admission tests:* Required: TOEFL (minimum score: iBT 45; paper-based 450; computer-based 133). TOEFL can be waived under certain conditions. *Application deadline:* Rolling. *Services:* International student adviser on campus. Full-time ESL program on campus. ESL program available during the academic year and the summer. Employment opportunities (on-campus) available. *Contact:* Director of International Programs, Skagit Valley College, Mount Vernon, WA 98273. Telephone: 360-416-7734. Fax: 360-416-7868. E-mail: internationaladmissions@skagit.edu. URL: http://www.skagit.edu.

See In-Depth Description on page 187.

SOUTH PUGET SOUND COMMUNITY COLLEGE, OLYMPIA

General Information State-supported, 2-year, coed college. Suburban setting. *Awards:* A. *Entrance level for U.S. students:* Noncompetitive. *Enrollment:* 6,351 total including international students from 19 foreign countries. *Undergraduate faculty:* 201. *Library holdings:* 30,000 books, 340 current serial subscriptions. *Total majors:* 30.

Information for International Students For fall 2006: 67 international students applied, 40 were accepted, 35 enrolled. Students can start in fall, winter, spring, or summer. Transfers accepted from institutions abroad. *Admission tests:* Required: placement test upon arrival. Recommended: TOEFL (minimum score: paper-based 500; computer-based 167). TOEFL can be waived under certain conditions. *Application deadline:* Rolling. *Housing:* Guaranteed, also available during summer. *Services:* International student adviser on campus. Full-time ESL program on campus. ESL program available during the academic year and the summer. Internships and employment opportunities (on-campus) available. *Contact:* Director of International Student Services, South Puget Sound Community College, 2011 Mottman Road, SW, Olympia, WA 98512-6292. Telephone: 360-596-5247. Fax: 360-596-5708. E-mail: mcavendish@spscc.ctc.edu. URL: http://www.spscc.ctc.edu.

See In-Depth Description on page 194.

SOUTH SEATTLE COMMUNITY COLLEGE, SEATTLE

General Information State-supported, 2-year, coed college. Urban setting. *Awards:* A. *Entrance level for U.S. students:* Noncompetitive. *Enrollment:* including international students from 24 foreign countries. *Undergraduate faculty:* 285. *Library holdings:* 34,000 books, 350 current serial subscriptions. *Total majors:* 28.

SPOKANE COMMUNITY COLLEGE, SPOKANE

General Information State-supported, 2-year, coed college. Urban setting. *Awards:* A. *Entrance level for U.S. students:* Noncompetitive. *Enrollment:* 5,874 total (58% women). *Undergraduate faculty:* 509. *Library holdings:* 38,967 books, 466 current serial subscriptions. *Total majors:* 53.

Information for International Students For fall 2006: 100 international students applied, 100 were accepted, 50 enrolled. Students can start in fall, winter, spring, or summer. Transfers accepted from institutions abroad. *Admission tests:* Recommended: TOEFL (minimum score: iBT 52; paper-based 470; computer-based 150). TOEFL can be waived under certain conditions. *Application deadline:* Rolling. *Expenses:* (2006–07) $3625. *Financial aid:* Need-based and non-need-based financial aid available. *Services:* International student adviser on campus. Full-time ESL program on campus. ESL program available during the academic year and the summer. Internships and employment opportunities (on-campus) available. *Contact:* Manager, International Marketing, Spokane Community College, International Programs Office, 1810 North Greene Street, Spokane, WA 99217. Telephone: 509-533-8885. Fax: 509-533-8683. E-mail: RobertR@SpokaneFalls.edu. URL: http://www.scc.spokane.edu.

SPOKANE FALLS COMMUNITY COLLEGE, SPOKANE

General Information State-supported, 2-year, coed college. Urban setting. *Awards:* A. *Entrance level for U.S. students:* Noncompetitive. *Enrollment:* 5,445 total (57% women) including 1% international students. *Undergraduate faculty:* 545. *Library holdings:* 58,000 books, 705 current serial subscriptions. *Total majors:* 31.

Information for International Students For fall 2006: 440 international students applied, 425 were accepted, 303 enrolled. Students can start in fall, winter, spring, or summer. Transfers accepted from institutions abroad. *Admission tests:* TOEFL can be waived under certain conditions. *Application deadline:* Rolling. *Expenses:* (2006–07) $3625. *Financial aid:* Forms required: institution's own financial aid form. *Services:* International student adviser on campus. Full-time ESL program on campus. ESL program available during the academic year and the summer. Internships and employment opportunities (on-campus) available. *Contact:* Manager of International Marketing, Spokane Falls Community College, 3410 West Fort George Wright Drive, MS 3011, Spokane, WA 99224-5288. Telephone: 509-533-4113. Fax: 509-533-4163. E-mail: RobertR@SpokaneFalls.edu. URL: http://www.spokanefalls.edu.

TACOMA COMMUNITY COLLEGE, TACOMA

General Information State-supported, 2-year, coed college. Urban setting. *Awards:* A. *Entrance level for U.S. students:* Noncompetitive. *Enrollment:* 6,056 total including 3% international students from 20 foreign countries. *Undergraduate faculty:* 334. *Library holdings:* 90,192 books, 269 current serial subscriptions, 5,281 audiovisual materials. *Total majors:* 75.

UNIVERSITY OF PHOENIX–WASHINGTON CAMPUS, SEATTLE

General Information Proprietary, coed institution. Urban setting. *Awards:* B, M. *Entrance level for U.S. students:* Noncompetitive. *Enrollment:* 1,758 total; 1,430 undergraduates (57% women) including 4% international students. *Faculty:* 258. *Library holdings:* 1,759 books, 692 current serial subscriptions. *Total majors:* 24. *Expenses:* (2006–07) $11,190.

UNIVERSITY OF PUGET SOUND, TACOMA

General Information Independent, coed institution. Suburban setting. *Awards:* B, M, FP. *Entrance level for U.S. students:* Moderately difficult. *Enrollment:* 2,819 total; 2,539 undergraduates (58% women) including 0.4% international students from 13 foreign countries. *Faculty:* 274. *Library holdings:* 364,662 books, 20,008 current serial subscriptions, 16,868 audiovisual materials. *Total majors:* 40.

Information for International Students For fall 2006: 169 international students applied, 14 were accepted, 3 enrolled. Students can start in fall or spring. Transfers accepted from institutions abroad. *Admission tests:* Required: SAT or ACT, TOEFL (minimum score: iBT 80; paper-based 550; computer-based 213). TOEFL can be waived under certain conditions. *Application deadline:* 3/1. *Expenses:* (2006–07) $30,060; room and board, $7670 (on campus); room only, $4190 (on campus). *Financial aid:* Non-need-based college/university scholarships/grants from institutional funds. Forms required: International Student's Financial Aid Application, International Student's Certification of Finances. International transfer students are eligible to apply for aid. For fall 2006 (estimated), 5 international students on campus received college administered financial aid ($12,200 average). *Housing:* Guaranteed. *Services:* International student adviser on campus. Internships and employment opportunities (on-campus and off-campus) available. *Contact:* International Admission Counselor, Office of Admission, University of Puget Sound, 1500 North Warner Street, Tacoma, WA 98416. Telephone: 253-756-3211. Fax: 253-756-3500. E-mail: admission@ups.edu. URL: http://www.ups.edu.

UNIVERSITY OF WASHINGTON, SEATTLE

General Information State-supported, coed university. Urban setting. *Awards:* B, M, D, FP. *Entrance level for U.S. students:* Moderately difficult. *Enrollment:* 39,524 total; 27,836 undergraduates (52% women) including 4% international students from 59 foreign countries. *Faculty:* 3,617. *Library holdings:* 5.8 million books, 50,245 current serial subscriptions. *Total majors:* 155.

Information for International Students For fall 2006: 1050 international students applied, 485 were accepted, 140 enrolled. Students can start in fall or summer. Transfers accepted from institutions abroad. *Admission tests:* Required: TOEFL (minimum score: paper-based 540; computer-based 207). Recommended: SAT or ACT. TOEFL can be waived under certain conditions. *Application deadline:* 1/15. *Expenses:* (2006–07) $21,286; room and board, $6561 (on campus). *Financial aid:* Need-based college/university scholarships/grants from institutional funds, tuition waivers, athletic awards, loans from outside sources, on-campus employment. Non-need-based loans from institutional funds, loans from outside sources, on-campus employment. *Housing:* Available during summer. *Services:* International student adviser on campus. Full-time and part-time ESL programs on campus. ESL program available during the academic year and the summer. Internships and employment opportunities (on-campus) available. *Contact:* International Undergraduate Admissions, University of Washington, 1410 NE Campus Parkway, 320 Schmitz Hall, Box

355852, Seattle, WA 98195-5852. Telephone: 206-543-9686. Fax: 206-685-3655. E-mail: intladm@u.washington.edu. URL: http://www.washington.edu.

UNIVERSITY OF WASHINGTON, BOTHELL, BOTHELL

General Information State-supported, coed institution. Suburban setting. *Awards:* B, M. *Entrance level for U.S. students:* Moderately difficult. *Enrollment:* 1,683 total; 1,441 undergraduates (55% women) including 1% international students from 5 foreign countries. *Faculty:* 103. *Library holdings:* 73,749 books, 720 current serial subscriptions, 6,100 audiovisual materials. *Total majors:* 5. *Expenses:* (2006–07) $21,157.

UNIVERSITY OF WASHINGTON, TACOMA, TACOMA

General Information State-supported, coed institution. Urban setting. *Awards:* B, M, FP. *Entrance level for U.S. students:* Difficulty N/R. *Enrollment:* 2,292 total; 1,856 undergraduates (60% women) including 1% international students from 4 foreign countries. *Faculty:* 142. *Library holdings:* 6.4 million books, 44,608 current serial subscriptions, 107,408 audiovisual materials. *Total majors:* 8. *Expenses:* (2007–08) $21,627.

WALLA WALLA COLLEGE, COLLEGE PLACE

General Information Independent Seventh-day Adventist, coed institution. Small town setting. *Awards:* A, B, M. *Entrance level for U.S. students:* Moderately difficult. *Enrollment:* 1,876 total; 1,635 undergraduates (48% women) including 1% international students from 19 foreign countries. *Faculty:* 181. *Library holdings:* 178,450 books, 1,105 current serial subscriptions. *Total majors:* 64. *Expenses:* (2006–07) $21,014; room and board, $4710 (on campus); room only, $2547 (on campus). *Financial aid:* Need-based college/university scholarships/grants from institutional funds, loans from institutional funds, loans from outside sources, on-campus employment. Non-need-based college/university scholarships/grants from institutional funds, loans from outside sources, on-campus employment. Forms required: International Student's Financial Aid Application. 54 international students on campus received college administered financial aid ($7341 average).

WASHINGTON STATE UNIVERSITY, PULLMAN

General Information State-supported, coed university. Rural setting. *Awards:* B, M, D, FP. *Entrance level for U.S. students:* Moderately difficult. *Enrollment:* 23,655 total; 19,554 undergraduates (52% women) including 2% international students from 51 foreign countries. *Faculty:* 1,501. *Library holdings:* 2.2 million books, 31,590 current serial subscriptions, 417,538 audiovisual materials. *Total majors:* 131.

Information for International Students For fall 2006: 766 international students applied, 442 were accepted, 202 enrolled. Students can start in fall, spring, or summer. Transfers accepted from institutions abroad. *Admission tests:* Required: TOEFL (minimum score: iBT 68; paper-based 520; computer-based 190). TOEFL can be waived under certain conditions. *Application deadline:* 1/31. *Expenses:* (2006–07) $16,087; room and board, $6890 (on campus); room only, $3390 (on campus). *Financial aid:* Need-based college/university scholarships/grants from institutional funds, tuition waivers, athletic awards. Non-need-based college/university scholarships/grants from institutional funds, tuition waivers, athletic awards, on-campus employment. Forms required: International Student's Certification of Finances. International transfer students are eligible to apply for aid. *Housing:* Guaranteed, also available during summer. *Services:* International student adviser on campus. Full-time ESL program on campus. ESL program available during the academic year and the summer. Employment opportunities (on-campus) available. *Contact:* International Enrollment Manager, Admissions Office, Washington State University, PO Box 645110, Pullman, WA 99164-5110. Telephone: 509-335-4508. Fax: 509-335-2373. E-mail: international@wsu.edu. URL: http://www.wsu.edu.

WESTERN WASHINGTON UNIVERSITY, BELLINGHAM

General Information State-supported, coed institution. Small town setting. *Awards:* B, M. *Entrance level for U.S. students:* Moderately difficult. *Enrollment:* 14,035 total; 12,838 undergraduates (55% women) including 0.2% international students from 29 foreign countries. *Faculty:* 651. *Library holdings:* 1.3 million books, 5,236 current serial subscriptions. *Total majors:* 99.

Information for International Students For fall 2006: 107 international students applied, 59 were accepted, 11 enrolled. Students can start in fall, winter, spring, or summer. Transfers accepted from institutions abroad. *Admission tests:* Required: TOEFL (minimum score: iBT 80; paper-based 550; computer-based 213; minimum score for ESL admission: iBT 71; paper-based 520; computer-based 190). Recommended: SAT or ACT. *Application deadline:* 3/1. *Expenses:* (2006–07) $15,550; room and board, $6785 (on campus); room only, $4409 (on campus). *Financial aid:*

Western Washington University (continued)
Non-need-based college/university scholarships/grants from
institutional funds, tuition waivers, loans from institutional funds,
on-campus employment. For fall 2006 (estimated), 5 international
students on campus received college administered financial aid
($2145 average). *Housing:* Available during summer. *Services:*
International student adviser on campus. Full-time and part-time
ESL programs on campus. ESL program available during the
academic year and the summer. Internships and employment
opportunities (on-campus) available. *Contact:* Program Manager,
Office of Admissions, Western Washington University, 516 High
Street, Bellingham, WA 98225-9009. Telephone: 360-650-7430.
Fax: 360-650-7369. E-mail: chris.mckenzie@wwu.edu.
URL: http://www.wwu.edu.

WHATCOM COMMUNITY COLLEGE, BELLINGHAM
General Information State-supported, 2-year, coed college. Small
town setting. *Awards:* A. *Entrance level for U.S. students:*
Noncompetitive. *Enrollment:* 4,173 total. *Undergraduate faculty:*
223. *Library holdings:* 14,680 books, 193 current serial
subscriptions, 3,653 audiovisual materials. *Total majors:* 14.
Information for International Students For fall 2006: 135
international students applied, 128 were accepted, 128 enrolled.
Students can start in fall, winter, spring, or summer. Transfers
accepted from institutions abroad. *Application deadline:* 8/20.
Services: International student adviser on campus. Full-time and
part-time ESL programs on campus. ESL program available during
the academic year and the summer. Internships and employment
opportunities (on-campus) available. *Contact:* International
Admissions Coordinator, Whatcom Community College, 237 West
Kellogg Road, International Admissions, Bellingham, WA 98226.
Telephone: 360-676-2170 Ext. 3294. Fax: 360-752-6767.
E-mail: ied@whatcom.ctc.edu. URL: http://www.whatcom.ctc.edu.

WHITWORTH COLLEGE, SPOKANE
General Information Independent Presbyterian, coed institution.
Suburban setting. *Awards:* B, M. *Entrance level for U.S. students:*
Very difficult. *Enrollment:* 2,504 total; 2,256 undergraduates (61%
women) including 1% international students from 25 foreign
countries. *Faculty:* 291. *Library holdings:* 17,982 books, 773 current
serial subscriptions. *Total majors:* 43. *Expenses:* (2007–08) $25,692;
room and board, $7294 (on campus). *Financial aid:* Need-based
college/university scholarships/grants from institutional funds,
on-campus employment. Non-need-based college/university
scholarships/grants from institutional funds. Forms required:
institution's own financial aid form. For fall 2006 (estimated), 9
international students on campus received college administered
financial aid ($16,449 average).

YAKIMA VALLEY COMMUNITY COLLEGE, YAKIMA
General Information State-supported, 2-year, coed college. Small
town setting. *Awards:* A. *Entrance level for U.S. students:*
Noncompetitive. *Enrollment:* 6,225 total including international
students from 10 foreign countries. *Undergraduate faculty:* 299.
Library holdings: 31,716 books, 860 current serial subscriptions.
Total majors: 38.

WEST VIRGINIA

ALDERSON-BROADDUS COLLEGE, PHILIPPI
General Information Independent, coed institution, affiliated
with American Baptist Churches in the U.S.A.Rural setting.
Awards: A, B, M. *Entrance level for U.S. students:* Moderately
difficult. *Enrollment:* 747 total; 623 undergraduates (69% women)
including 1% international students from 6 foreign countries.
Faculty: 86. *Library holdings:* 100,000 books, 11,000 current serial
subscriptions, 1,500 audiovisual materials. *Total majors:* 43.
Information for International Students For fall 2006: 3
international students applied, 3 were accepted, 2 enrolled.
Students can start in fall or spring. Transfers accepted from
institutions abroad. *Admission tests:* Required: ACT, TOEFL
(minimum score: paper-based 500; computer-based 173; minimum
score for ESL admission: paper-based 500; computer-based 173).
Recommended: SAT. *Application deadline:* 8/1. *Expenses:* (2006–07)
$19,090; room and board, $6160 (on campus); room only, $3000 (on
campus). *Financial aid:* Non-need-based college/university
scholarships/grants from institutional funds, athletic awards,
on-campus employment. Forms required: institution's own financial
aid form, International Student's Certification of Finances. For fall
2005, 11 international students on campus received college
administered financial aid ($5000 average). *Housing:* Guaranteed,
also available during summer. *Services:* International student
adviser on campus. Internships and employment opportunities

(on-campus) available. *Contact:* International Student Admissions
Counselor, Alderson-Broaddus College, Campus Box 2003, Philippi,
WV 26416-9980. Telephone: 304-457-6326. Fax: 304-457-6239.
E-mail: admissions@ab.edu. URL: http://www.ab.edu.

APPALACHIAN BIBLE COLLEGE, BRADLEY
General Information Independent nondenominational, 4-year,
coed college. Small town setting. *Awards:* A, B. *Entrance level for
U.S. students:* Minimally difficult. *Enrollment:* 274 total (50%
women) including international students from 8 foreign countries.
Undergraduate faculty: 18. *Library holdings:* 44,944 books, 347
current serial subscriptions. *Total majors:* 2. *Expenses:* (2007–08)
$9270; room and board, $4920 (on campus). *Financial aid:*
Need-based college/university scholarships/grants from institutional
funds, on-campus employment. Non-need financial aid available.
Forms required: institution's own financial aid form, International
Student's Certification of Finances. 9 international students on
campus received college administered financial aid ($2200 average).

BLUEFIELD STATE COLLEGE, BLUEFIELD
General Information State-supported, 4-year, coed college. Small
town setting. *Awards:* A, B. *Entrance level for U.S. students:*
Noncompetitive. *Enrollment:* 1,788 total (59% women) including 1%
international students from 16 foreign countries. *Undergraduate
faculty:* 124. *Library holdings:* 79,182 books, 89 current serial
subscriptions. *Total majors:* 28.
Information for International Students For fall 2006: 15
international students applied, 10 were accepted, 5 enrolled.
Students can start in fall, spring, or summer. Transfers accepted
from institutions abroad. *Admission tests:* Recommended: TOEFL
(minimum score: paper-based 500; computer-based 173). TOEFL
can be waived under certain conditions. *Application deadline:*
Rolling. *Expenses:* (2006–07) $7760. *Financial aid:* Non-need-based
college/university scholarships/grants from institutional funds,
tuition waivers, athletic awards, loans from outside sources,
on-campus employment. Forms required: International Student's
Certification of Finances. *Services:* International student adviser on
campus. Internships and employment opportunities (on-campus and
off-campus) available. *Contact:* Director of Enrollment Management,
Bluefield State College, 219 Rock Street, Bluefield, WV 24701.
Telephone: 304-327-4065. Fax: 304-325-7747.
E-mail: dscadmit@bluefieldwvnet.edu.
URL: http://www.bluefieldstate.edu.

BLUE RIDGE COMMUNITY AND TECHNICAL COLLEGE, MARTINSBURG
General Information County-supported, 2-year, coed college.
Awards: A. *Entrance level for U.S. students:* Noncompetitive.
Enrollment: 1,711 total (60% women) including 0.2% international
students. *Undergraduate faculty:* 70. *Total majors:* 15. *Expenses:*
(2006–07) $8542.

DAVIS & ELKINS COLLEGE, ELKINS
General Information Independent Presbyterian, 4-year, coed
college. Small town setting. *Awards:* A, B. *Entrance level for U.S.
students:* Moderately difficult. *Enrollment:* 636 total (66% women)
including 4% international students from 15 foreign countries.
Undergraduate faculty: 70. *Library holdings:* 226,705 books, 1,422
current serial subscriptions, 6,190 audiovisual materials.
Total majors: 48. *Expenses:* (2006–07) $17,730; room and board,
$6300 (on campus). *Financial aid:* Need-based college/university
scholarships/grants from institutional funds, athletic awards.
Non-need-based college/university scholarships/grants from
institutional funds, athletic awards. Forms required: International
Student's Financial Aid Application, International Student's
Certification of Finances. For fall 2005, 23 international students
on campus received college administered financial aid ($9020
average).

FAIRMONT STATE UNIVERSITY, FAIRMONT
General Information State-supported, coed institution. Small
town setting. *Awards:* A, B, M. *Entrance level for U.S. students:*
Minimally difficult. *Enrollment:* 7,417 total; 7,067 undergraduates
(57% women) including 1% international students from 19 foreign
countries. *Faculty:* 666. *Library holdings:* 280,000 books, 895
current serial subscriptions. *Total majors:* 60. *Expenses:* (2006–07)
$9128; room and board, $6052 (on campus); room only, $3192 (on
campus). *Financial aid:* Non-need-based college/university
scholarships/grants from institutional funds, tuition waivers. Forms
required: International Student's Certification of Finances, letter
requesting consideration for tuition waiver. 12 international
students on campus received college administered financial aid
($4710 average).

MARSHALL COMMUNITY AND TECHNICAL COLLEGE, HUNTINGTON

General Information County-supported, 2-year, coed college. Urban setting. *Awards:* A. *Entrance level for U.S. students:* Noncompetitive. *Enrollment:* 2,579 total (39% women) including 0.2% international students from 4 foreign countries. *Undergraduate faculty:* 126. *Library holdings:* 1.6 million books, 22,591 current serial subscriptions, 209,391 audiovisual materials. *Total majors:* 23. *Expenses:* (2006–07) $8142; room and board, $6492 (on campus); room only, $3618 (on campus).

MARSHALL UNIVERSITY, HUNTINGTON

General Information State-supported, coed university. Urban setting. *Awards:* A, B, M, D, FP. *Entrance level for U.S. students:* Moderately difficult. *Enrollment:* 13,936 total; 9,723 undergraduates (56% women) including 1% international students from 29 foreign countries. *Faculty:* 749. *Library holdings:* 1.6 million books, 22,591 current serial subscriptions, 209,391 audiovisual materials. *Total majors:* 46.

Information for International Students For fall 2006: 359 international students applied, 168 were accepted, 146 enrolled. Students can start in fall, spring, or summer. Transfers accepted from institutions abroad. *Admission tests:* Required: SAT or ACT, TOEFL (minimum score: iBT 61; paper-based 500; computer-based 173), ELS (minimum score: 109). TOEFL can be waived under certain conditions. *Application deadline:* 6/15. *Expenses:* (2006–07) $11,054; room and board, $6492 (on campus); room only, $3618 (on campus). *Housing:* Guaranteed, also available during summer. *Services:* International student adviser on campus. Full-time and part-time ESL programs on campus. ESL program available during the academic year and the summer. Internships and employment opportunities (on-campus and off-campus) available. *Contact:* Coordinator, International Educational Services, Marshall University, Center for International Programs, One John Marshall Drive, Huntington, WV 25755. Telephone: 304-696-7250. Fax: 304-696-6353. E-mail: carnes2@marshall.edu. URL: http://www.marshall.edu.

See In-Depth Description on page 122.

MOUNTAIN STATE UNIVERSITY, BECKLEY

General Information Independent, coed institution. Small town setting. *Awards:* A, B, M. *Entrance level for U.S. students:* Noncompetitive. *Enrollment:* 4,420 total; 3,921 undergraduates (66% women) including 2% international students from 49 foreign countries. *Faculty:* 368. *Library holdings:* 113,361 books, 155 current serial subscriptions, 4,877 audiovisual materials. *Total majors:* 61.

Information for International Students For fall 2006: 217 international students applied, 217 were accepted, 173 enrolled. Students can start in fall, spring, or summer. Transfers accepted from institutions abroad. *Admission tests:* TOEFL can be waived under certain conditions. *Application deadline:* Rolling. *Expenses:* (2006–07) $7800; room and board, $5636 (on campus); room only, $2810 (on campus). *Financial aid:* Need-based athletic awards, loans from outside sources, on-campus employment. Non-need-based athletic awards, loans from outside sources, on-campus employment. Forms required: International Student's Certification of Finances. *Housing:* Available during summer. *Services:* International student adviser on campus. Full-time ESL program on campus. ESL program available during the academic year and the summer. Internships and employment opportunities (on-campus and off-campus) available. *Contact:* Coordinator for International Student Services, Mountain State University, 609 South Kanawha Street, PO Box 9003, Beckley, WV 25802-9003. Telephone: 304-929-1551. Fax: 304-252-2896. E-mail: dheaster@mountainstate.edu. URL: http://www.mountainstate.edu.

SALEM INTERNATIONAL UNIVERSITY, SALEM

General Information Independent, coed institution. Rural setting. *Awards:* A, B, M. *Entrance level for U.S. students:* Minimally difficult. *Enrollment:* 786 total; 420 undergraduates (39% women) including 59% international students from 30 foreign countries. *Faculty:* 89. *Library holdings:* 106,991 books, 43 current serial subscriptions, 1,173 audiovisual materials. *Total majors:* 27. *Expenses:* (2006–07) $12,660; room and board, $5360 (on campus); room only, $1990 (on campus). *Financial aid:* Non-need-based college/university scholarships/grants from institutional funds, tuition waivers, athletic awards, loans from outside sources, on-campus employment. Forms required: International Student's Certification of Finances. For fall 2005, 293 international students on campus received college administered financial aid ($7376 average).

SHEPHERD UNIVERSITY, SHEPHERDSTOWN

General Information State-supported, coed institution. Small town setting. *Awards:* B, M. *Entrance level for U.S. students:* Moderately difficult. *Enrollment:* 4,091 total; 3,970 undergraduates (57% women) including 1% international students from 18 foreign countries. *Faculty:* 288. *Library holdings:* 190,586 books, 13,376 current serial subscriptions, 7,924 audiovisual materials. *Total majors:* 22.

Information for International Students For fall 2006: 21 international students applied, 10 were accepted, 7 enrolled. Students can start in fall, spring, or summer. Transfers accepted from institutions abroad. *Admission tests:* Required: SAT, ACT, TOEFL (minimum score: iBT 79; paper-based 550; computer-based 213). TOEFL can be waived under certain conditions. *Application deadline:* Rolling. *Expenses:* (2006–07) $11,464; room and board, $6456 (on campus). *Financial aid:* Need-based college/university scholarships/grants from institutional funds, tuition waivers, athletic awards, loans from outside sources, on-campus employment. Non-need-based college/university scholarships/grants from institutional funds, tuition waivers, athletic awards, loans from outside sources, on-campus employment. For fall 2006 (estimated), 7 international students on campus received college administered financial aid ($8400 average). *Housing:* Guaranteed, also available during summer. *Services:* International student adviser on campus. Internships and employment opportunities (on-campus) available. *Contact:* Admissions Counselor, Office of Admissions, Shepherd University, PO Box 3210, Shepherdstown, WV 25443-3210. Telephone: 304-876-5514. Fax: 304-876-5165. E-mail: wweaver@shepherd.edu. URL: http://www.shepherd.edu.

UNIVERSITY OF CHARLESTON, CHARLESTON

General Information Independent, coed institution. Urban setting. *Awards:* A, B, M. *Entrance level for U.S. students:* Moderately difficult. *Enrollment:* 1,202 total; 1,074 undergraduates (59% women) including 7% international students from 15 foreign countries. *Faculty:* 90. *Library holdings:* 164,457 books, 14,192 current serial subscriptions, 3,759 audiovisual materials. *Total majors:* 27.

Information for International Students Students can start in fall, winter, spring, or summer. Transfers accepted from institutions abroad. *Admission tests:* Required: SAT or ACT, TOEFL (minimum score: paper-based 550; computer-based 173). *Application deadline:* 7/15. *Expenses:* (2006–07) $21,000; room and board, $7600 (on campus); room only, $4175 (on campus). *Financial aid:* Need-based financial aid available. Non-need-based college/university scholarships/grants from institutional funds, athletic awards, loans from outside sources, on-campus employment. Forms required: International Student's Certification of Finances. International transfer students are eligible to apply for aid. For fall 2006 (estimated), 65 international students on campus received college administered financial aid ($19,202 average). *Housing:* Guaranteed, also available during summer. *Services:* International student adviser on campus. Part-time ESL program on campus. ESL program available during the academic year. Internships and employment opportunities (on-campus) available. *Contact:* Office of Admissions, University of Charleston, 2300 MacCorkle Avenue, SE, Charleston, WV 25304. Telephone: 304-357-4750. Fax: 307-357-4781. E-mail: admissions@ucwv.edu. URL: http://www.ucwv.edu.

See In-Depth Description on page 209.

WEST VIRGINIA NORTHERN COMMUNITY COLLEGE, WHEELING

General Information State-supported, 2-year, coed college. Small town setting. *Awards:* A. *Entrance level for U.S. students:* Noncompetitive. *Enrollment:* 2,842 total (69% women) including 0.1% international students. *Undergraduate faculty:* 150. *Library holdings:* 36,650 books, 188 current serial subscriptions, 3,495 audiovisual materials. *Total majors:* 18. *Expenses:* (2006–07) $5808.

WEST VIRGINIA UNIVERSITY, MORGANTOWN

General Information State-supported, coed university. Small town setting. *Awards:* B, M, D, FP. *Entrance level for U.S. students:* Moderately difficult. *Enrollment:* 27,115 total; 20,590 undergraduates (46% women) including 2% international students from 70 foreign countries. *Faculty:* 1,135. *Library holdings:* 1.7 million books, 9,107 current serial subscriptions, 233,301 audiovisual materials. *Total majors:* 75. *Expenses:* (2006–07) $13,840; room and board, $6630 (on campus); room only, $3500 (on campus).

WEST VIRGINIA WESLEYAN COLLEGE, BUCKHANNON

General Information Independent, coed institution, affiliated with United Methodist Church. Small town setting. *Awards:* B, M. *Entrance level for U.S. students:* Moderately difficult. *Enrollment:* 1,222 total; 1,176 undergraduates (55% women) including 3% international students from 13 foreign countries. *Faculty:* 137. *Library holdings:* 91,061 books, 2,462 current serial subscriptions. *Total majors:* 64. *Expenses:* (2007–08) $20,980; room and board,

West Virginia Wesleyan College (continued)
$6160 (on campus). *Financial aid:* Need-based athletic awards. Non-need-based college/university scholarships/grants from institutional funds, athletic awards.

WHEELING JESUIT UNIVERSITY, WHEELING

General Information Independent Roman Catholic (Jesuit), coed institution. Suburban setting. *Awards:* B, M, D. *Entrance level for U.S. students:* Moderately difficult. *Enrollment:* 1,402 total; 1,203 undergraduates (62% women) including 2% international students from 15 foreign countries. *Faculty:* 77. *Library holdings:* 144,242 books, 456 current serial subscriptions. *Total majors:* 54. *Expenses:* (2007–08) $23,490; room and board, $7230 (on campus); room only, $3350 (on campus). *Financial aid:* Non-need-based college/university scholarships/grants from institutional funds, athletic awards, on-campus employment. Forms required: institution's own financial aid form. For fall 2006 (estimated), 28 international students on campus received college administered financial aid ($16,341 average).

WISCONSIN

ALVERNO COLLEGE, MILWAUKEE

General Information Independent Roman Catholic, undergraduate: women only; graduate: coed institution. Suburban setting. *Awards:* A, B, M (also offers weekend program with significant enrollment not reflected in profile). *Entrance level for U.S. students:* Moderately difficult. *Enrollment:* 2,480 total; 2,245 undergraduates (99% women) including 1% international students. *Faculty:* 226. *Library holdings:* 95,622 books, 3,932 current serial subscriptions, 4,191 audiovisual materials. *Total majors:* 42.
Information for International Students For fall 2006: 8 international students were accepted, 8 enrolled. Students can start in fall or spring. Transfers accepted from institutions abroad. *Admission tests:* Required: TOEFL (minimum score: paper-based 520; computer-based 190; minimum score for ESL admission: iBT 72). TOEFL can be waived under certain conditions. *Application deadline:* Rolling. *Expenses:* (2007–08) $17,296; room and board, $6106 (on campus). *Financial aid:* Need-based loans from outside sources, on-campus employment. Non-need-based college/university scholarships/grants from institutional funds, loans from outside sources, on-campus employment. Forms required: institution's own financial aid form, International Student's Certification of Finances. International transfer students are eligible to apply for aid. *Housing:* Guaranteed, also available during summer. *Services:* International student adviser on campus. ESL program at cooperating institution. ESL program available during the academic year and the summer. Internships and employment opportunities (on-campus and off-campus) available. *Contact:* Assistant Director of International Center, Alverno College, 3400 South 43rd Street, PO Box 343922, Milwaukee, WI 53234-3922. Telephone: 414-382-6099. Fax: 414-382-6354. E-mail: international@alverno.edu. URL: http://www.alverno.edu.

See In-Depth Description on page 30.

BELOIT COLLEGE, BELOIT

General Information Independent, 4-year, coed college. Small town setting. *Awards:* B. *Entrance level for U.S. students:* Very difficult. *Enrollment:* 1,432 total (59% women) including 6% international students from 43 foreign countries. *Undergraduate faculty:* 136. *Library holdings:* 183,736 books, 946 current serial subscriptions. *Total majors:* 56.
Information for International Students For fall 2006: 302 international students applied, 117 were accepted, 44 enrolled. Students can start in fall or spring. Transfers accepted from institutions abroad. *Admission tests:* Required: TOEFL (minimum score: paper-based 525; computer-based 197). Recommended: SAT or ACT. TOEFL can be waived under certain conditions. *Application deadline:* Rolling. *Expenses:* (2006–07) $28,350; room and board, $6162 (on campus); room only, $3006 (on campus). *Financial aid:* Need-based college/university scholarships/grants from institutional funds, loans from institutional funds, on-campus employment. Non-need-based college/university scholarships/grants from institutional funds, loans from institutional funds, on-campus employment. Forms required: institution's own financial aid form, International Student's Certification of Finances. International transfer students are eligible to apply for aid. For fall 2006 (estimated), 66 international students on campus received college administered financial aid ($18,457 average). *Housing:* Guaranteed, also available during summer. *Services:* International student adviser on campus. Full-time ESL program on campus. Internships and employment opportunities (on-campus) available. *Contact:* Admission Counselor for International Students, Beloit College, 700

College Street, Beloit, WI 53511. Telephone: 608-363-2174. Fax: 608-363-2075. E-mail: priester@beloit.edu. URL: http://www.beloit.edu.

CARDINAL STRITCH UNIVERSITY, MILWAUKEE

General Information Independent Roman Catholic, coed institution. Suburban setting. *Awards:* A, B, M, D. *Entrance level for U.S. students:* Moderately difficult. *Enrollment:* 6,000 total; 3,237 undergraduates (69% women) including 2% international students from 17 foreign countries. *Faculty:* 449. *Library holdings:* 124,897 books, 667 current serial subscriptions. *Total majors:* 42.
Information for International Students For fall 2006: 150 international students applied, 20 were accepted, 13 enrolled. Students can start in fall or spring. Transfers accepted from institutions abroad. *Admission tests:* Required: TOEFL (minimum score: iBT 79; paper-based 550; computer-based 213). Recommended: SAT or ACT. TOEFL can be waived under certain conditions. *Application deadline:* 4/1. *Expenses:* (2006–07) $18,000; room and board, $5590 (on campus). *Financial aid:* Need-based and non-need-based financial aid available. Forms required: institution's own financial aid form, International Student's Certification of Finances. International transfer students are eligible to apply for aid. 63 international students on campus received college administered financial aid ($11,111 average). *Housing:* Guaranteed, also available during summer. *Services:* International student adviser on campus. Internships and employment opportunities (on-campus) available. *Contact:* Assistant Director of Admissions, Cardinal Stritch University, 6801 North Yates Road, Milwaukee, WI 53217-3985. Telephone: 414-410-4055. Fax: 414-410-4058. E-mail: naspaeth@stritch.edu. URL: http://www.stritch.edu.

CARROLL COLLEGE, WAUKESHA

General Information Independent Presbyterian, coed institution. Suburban setting. *Awards:* B, M. *Entrance level for U.S. students:* Moderately difficult. *Enrollment:* 3,292 total; 3,017 undergraduates (67% women) including 2% international students from 32 foreign countries. *Faculty:* 283. *Library holdings:* 150,000 books, 18,000 current serial subscriptions, 1,025 audiovisual materials. *Total majors:* 76.
Information for International Students For fall 2006: 54 international students applied, 33 were accepted, 19 enrolled. Students can start in fall or spring. Transfers accepted from institutions abroad. *Admission tests:* Required: TOEFL (minimum score: iBT 73; paper-based 550; computer-based 213). TOEFL can be waived under certain conditions. *Application deadline:* 7/1. *Expenses:* (2007–08) $20,830; room and board, $6350 (on campus); room only, $3450 (on campus). *Financial aid:* Need-based financial aid available. Non-need-based college/university scholarships/grants from institutional funds, loans from institutional funds, on-campus employment. Forms required: institution's own financial aid form, International Student's Certification of Finances. International transfer students are eligible to apply for aid. For fall 2006 (estimated), 33 international students on campus received college administered financial aid ($12,935 average). *Housing:* Guaranteed, also available during summer. *Services:* International student adviser on campus. Internships and employment opportunities (on-campus) available. *Contact:* Director of Caroll College Outreach Programs/Director of International Student Programming, Carroll College, 100 North East Avenue, Waukesha, WI 53186. Telephone: 262-524-7634. Fax: 262-524-7139. E-mail: morris@cc.edu. URL: http://www.cc.cdu.

CARTHAGE COLLEGE, KENOSHA

General Information Independent, coed institution, affiliated with Evangelical Lutheran Church in America. Suburban setting. *Awards:* B, M. *Entrance level for U.S. students:* Moderately difficult. *Enrollment:* 2,699 total; 2,594 undergraduates (59% women) including 1% international students from 11 foreign countries. *Faculty:* 210. *Library holdings:* 128,551 books, 425 current serial subscriptions, 4,361 audiovisual materials. *Total majors:* 48.
Information for International Students For fall 2006: 21 international students applied, 15 were accepted, 8 enrolled. Students can start in fall, winter, spring, or summer. Transfers accepted from institutions abroad. *Admission tests:* Required: TOEFL (minimum score: iBT 76; paper-based 500; computer-based 173; minimum score for ESL admission: paper-based 500; computer-based 173). Recommended: SAT or ACT, ELS. TOEFL can be waived under certain conditions. *Application deadline:* Rolling. *Expenses:* (2006–07) $23,650; room and board, $6800 (on campus). *Financial aid:* Non-need-based college/university scholarships/grants from institutional funds. Forms required: International Student's Certification of Finances. International transfer students are eligible to apply for aid. For fall 2006 (estimated), 12 international students on campus received college administered financial aid ($22,870 average). *Housing:* Guaranteed, also available during summer. *Services:* International student

adviser on campus. Internships and employment opportunities (on-campus) available. *Contact:* Transfer and International Student Recruiter, Carthage College, 2001 Alford Park Drive, Kenosha, WI 53140. Telephone: 262-551-6000 Ext. 5390. Fax: 262-551-5762. E-mail: mhamilton@carthage.edu. URL: http://www.carthage.edu.

CONCORDIA UNIVERSITY WISCONSIN, MEQUON

General Information Independent, coed institution, affiliated with Lutheran Church–Missouri Synod. Suburban setting. *Awards:* A, B, M, D. *Entrance level for U.S. students:* Moderately difficult. *Enrollment:* 5,574 total; 3,782 undergraduates (62% women) including 1% international students from 23 foreign countries. *Faculty:* 204. *Library holdings:* 79,341 books, 4,440 current serial subscriptions, 4,352 audiovisual materials. *Total majors:* 62. *Expenses:* (2006–07) $18,140; room and board, $6860 (on campus). *Financial aid:* Need-based college/university scholarships/grants from institutional funds. Non-need-based college/university scholarships/grants from institutional funds. Forms required: International Student's Financial Aid Application. For fall 2006 (estimated), 9 international students on campus received college administered financial aid ($5122 average).

EDGEWOOD COLLEGE, MADISON

General Information Independent Roman Catholic, coed institution. Urban setting. *Awards:* A, B, M, D. *Entrance level for U.S. students:* Moderately difficult. *Enrollment:* 2,565 total; 1,989 undergraduates (72% women) including 1% international students from 22 foreign countries. *Faculty:* 270. *Library holdings:* 90,253 books, 447 current serial subscriptions, 4,359 audiovisual materials. *Total majors:* 41.

Information for International Students For fall 2006: 15 international students were accepted, 11 enrolled. Students can start in fall or spring. Transfers accepted from institutions abroad. *Admission tests:* Required: TOEFL (minimum score: iBT 72; paper-based 525; computer-based 197). TOEFL can be waived under certain conditions. *Application deadline:* 7/1. *Expenses:* (2007–08) $19,080; room and board, $6535 (on campus); room only, $3335 (on campus). *Financial aid:* Non-need-based college/university scholarships/grants from institutional funds, loans from outside sources, on-campus employment. Forms required: institution's own financial aid form. *Housing:* Available during summer. *Services:* International student adviser on campus. ESL program at cooperating institution. ESL program available during the academic year and the summer. Internships and employment opportunities (on-campus) available. *Contact:* Director of Undergraduate Admissions, Edgewood College, 1000 Edgewood College Drive, Madison, WI 53711-1997. Telephone: 608-663-2294. Fax: 608-663-2214. E-mail: admissions@edgewood.edu. URL: http://www.edgewood.edu.

See In-Depth Description on page 73.

FOX VALLEY TECHNICAL COLLEGE, APPLETON

General Information State and locally supported, 2-year, coed college. Suburban setting. *Awards:* A. *Entrance level for U.S. students:* Noncompetitive. *Enrollment:* 7,462 total (51% women) including 0.1% international students. *Undergraduate faculty:* 1,059. *Library holdings:* 46,084 books, 212 current serial subscriptions, 8,526 audiovisual materials. *Total majors:* 35.

Information for International Students For fall 2006: 70 international students applied, 70 were accepted, 55 enrolled. Students can start in fall, winter, spring, or summer. Transfers accepted from institutions abroad. *Admission tests:* Required: TOEFL (minimum score: paper-based 500; computer-based 173), ACCUPLACER. TOEFL can be waived under certain conditions. *Application deadline:* Rolling. *Expenses:* (2007–08) $15,716. *Services:* International student adviser on campus. Full-time and part-time ESL programs on campus. ESL program available during the academic year. Internships and employment opportunities (on-campus and off-campus) available. *Contact:* Coordinator, Global Education and Services, Fox Valley Technical College, 1825 North Bluemound Drive, PO Box 2277, Appleton, WI 54912. Telephone: 920-735-4817. Fax: 920-735-4847. E-mail: lutzow@fvtc.edu. URL: http://www.fvtc.edu.

HERZING COLLEGE, MADISON

General Information Proprietary, primarily 2-year, coed, primarily men's college. Suburban setting. *Awards:* A, B. *Entrance level for U.S. students:* Moderately difficult. *Enrollment:* 650 total including international students from 2 foreign countries. *Undergraduate faculty:* 46. *Library holdings:* 1,500 books, 15 current serial subscriptions. *Total majors:* 5. *Expenses:* (2006–07) $10,768.

LAKELAND COLLEGE, SHEBOYGAN

General Information Independent, coed institution, affiliated with United Church of Christ. Rural setting. *Awards:* B, M. *Entrance level for U.S. students:* Minimally difficult. *Enrollment:* 4,047 total; 3,298 undergraduates (62% women) including 4% international students from 30 foreign countries. *Faculty:* 71. *Library holdings:* 64,970 books, 317 current serial subscriptions. *Total majors:* 29.

Information for International Students For fall 2006: 100 international students enrolled. Students can start in fall, spring, or summer. Transfers accepted from institutions abroad. *Admission tests:* Required: TOEFL (minimum score: iBT 65; paper-based 500; computer-based 173). Recommended: SAT or ACT. TOEFL can be waived under certain conditions. *Application deadline:* Rolling. *Expenses:* (2007–08) $17,595; room and board, $6145 (on campus). *Financial aid:* Need-based college/university scholarships/grants from institutional funds, on-campus employment. Non-need-based college/university scholarships/grants from institutional funds, on-campus employment. Forms required: International Student's Financial Aid Application, International Student's Certification of Finances. International transfer students are eligible to apply for aid. For fall 2006 (estimated), 141 international students on campus received college administered financial aid ($8353 average). *Housing:* Guaranteed, also available during summer. *Services:* International student adviser on campus. Full-time and part-time ESL programs on campus. ESL program available during the academic year and the summer. Internships and employment opportunities (on-campus and off-campus) available. *Contact:* Director of International Admissions, The International Student Office, Lakeland College, PO Box 359, Sheboygan, WI 53082-0359. Telephone: 920-565-1337. Fax: 920-565-1556. E-mail: liup@lakeland.edu. URL: http://www.lakeland.edu.

See In-Depth Description on page 112.

LAWRENCE UNIVERSITY, APPLETON

General Information Independent, 4-year, coed college. Small town setting. *Awards:* B. *Entrance level for U.S. students:* Very difficult. *Enrollment:* 1,480 total (55% women) including 7% international students from 42 foreign countries. *Undergraduate faculty:* 182. *Library holdings:* 395,000 books, 2,816 current serial subscriptions, 20,500 audiovisual materials. *Total majors:* 58.

Information for International Students For fall 2006: 317 international students applied, 103 were accepted, 47 enrolled. Students can start in fall. Transfers accepted from institutions abroad. *Admission tests:* Recommended: SAT or ACT, TOEFL (minimum score: iBT 90; paper-based 575; computer-based 233), IELTS. TOEFL can be waived under certain conditions. *Application deadline:* 1/15. *Expenses:* (2006–07) $29,598; room and board, $6882 (on campus); room only, $2934 (on campus). *Financial aid:* Need-based college/university scholarships/grants from institutional funds, loans from outside sources, on-campus employment. Non-need-based college/university scholarships/grants from institutional funds, loans from outside sources, on-campus employment. Forms required: International Student's Financial Aid Application, International Student's Certification of Finances. International transfer students are eligible to apply for aid. For fall 2006 (estimated), 99 international students on campus received college administered financial aid ($22,022 average). *Housing:* Guaranteed, also available during summer. *Services:* International student adviser on campus. Internships and employment opportunities (on-campus) available. *Contact:* Associate Director of Admissions, Lawrence University, PO Box 599, Appleton, WI 54912. Telephone: 920-832-7067. Fax: 920-832-6782. E-mail: excel.international@lawrence.edu. URL: http://www.lawrence.edu.

See In-Depth Description on page 114.

MARANATHA BAPTIST BIBLE COLLEGE, WATERTOWN

General Information Independent Baptist, coed institution. Small town setting. *Awards:* A, B, M. *Entrance level for U.S. students:* Noncompetitive. *Enrollment:* 876 total; 811 undergraduates (54% women) including 0.1% international students from 4 foreign countries. *Faculty:* 72. *Library holdings:* 122,251 books, 502 current serial subscriptions. *Total majors:* 19. *Expenses:* (2006–07) $9030; room and board, $5150 (on campus). *Financial aid:* Need-based on-campus employment. Non-need-based on-campus employment. Forms required: institution's own financial aid form.

MARIAN COLLEGE OF FOND DU LAC, FOND DU LAC

General Information Independent Roman Catholic, coed institution. Small town setting. *Awards:* B, M, D. *Entrance level for U.S. students:* Moderately difficult. *Enrollment:* 3,040 total; 2,126 undergraduates (73% women) including 1% international students from 5 foreign countries. *Faculty:* 278. *Library holdings:* 94,217 books, 952 current serial subscriptions, 1,320 audiovisual materials. *Total majors:* 50.

Information for International Students For fall 2006: 5 international students applied, 5 were accepted, 4 enrolled. Students can start in fall or spring. Transfers accepted from

Marian College of Fond du Lac (continued)

institutions abroad. *Admission tests:* Required: TOEFL (minimum score: paper-based 525; computer-based 193). TOEFL can be waived under certain conditions. *Application deadline:* 5/1. *Expenses:* (2006–07) $17,625; room and board, $5200 (on campus); room only, $3420 (on campus). *Financial aid:* Need-based college/university scholarships/grants from institutional funds. Non-need-based college/university scholarships/grants from institutional funds. Forms required: institution's own financial aid form, FAFSA. International transfer students are eligible to apply for aid. For fall 2006 (estimated), 12 international students on campus received college administered financial aid ($9480 average). *Housing:* Guaranteed. *Services:* International student adviser on campus. Internships and employment opportunities (on-campus) available. *Contact:* Director of Transfer and International Enrollment, Marian College of Fond du Lac, 45 South National Avenue, Fond du Lac, WI 54935-4699. Telephone: 920-923-8117. Fax: 920-923-8755. E-mail: jhartzell@mariancollege.edu. URL: http://www.mariancollege.edu.

MARQUETTE UNIVERSITY, MILWAUKEE

General Information Independent Roman Catholic (Jesuit), coed university. Urban setting. *Awards:* A, B, M, D, FP. *Entrance level for U.S. students:* Moderately difficult. *Enrollment:* 11,548 total; 8,048 undergraduates (54% women) including 2% international students from 48 foreign countries. *Faculty:* 1,054. *Library holdings:* 1.5 million books, 23,039 current serial subscriptions. *Total majors:* 85.

Information for International Students For fall 2006: 341 international students applied, 200 were accepted, 38 enrolled. Students can start in fall or spring. Transfers accepted from institutions abroad. *Admission tests:* Required: TOEFL (minimum score: iBT 76; paper-based 533; computer-based 200). Recommended: SAT or ACT, other tests/evidence are accepted in place of TOEFL. *Application deadline:* Rolling. *Expenses:* (2006–07) $25,074; room and board, $8120 (on campus); room only, $5278 (on campus). *Financial aid:* Non-need-based college/university scholarships/grants from institutional funds, loans from outside sources. Forms required: institution's own financial sponsorship form. International transfer students are eligible to apply for aid. For fall 2006 (estimated), 53 international students on campus received college administered financial aid ($10,961 average). *Housing:* Guaranteed, also available during summer. *Services:* International student adviser on campus. Part-time ESL program on campus. ESL program available during the academic year. Internships and employment opportunities (on-campus) available. *Contact:* Associate Director, Office of International Education, Marquette University, PO Box 1881, Office of International Education, AMU-425-S, Milwaukee, WI 53201-1881. Telephone: 414-288-7289. Fax: 414-288-3701. E-mail: welcome27@ask.mu.edu. URL: http://www.marquette.edu.
See In-Depth Description on page 121.

MILWAUKEE SCHOOL OF ENGINEERING, MILWAUKEE

General Information Independent, coed institution. Urban setting. *Awards:* B, M. *Entrance level for U.S. students:* Moderately difficult. *Enrollment:* 2,427 total; 2,203 undergraduates (18% women) including 2% international students from 19 foreign countries. *Faculty:* 224. *Library holdings:* 72,192 books, 376 current serial subscriptions, 1,421 audiovisual materials. *Total majors:* 14. *Expenses:* (2007–08) $25,980; room and board, $6501 (on campus); room only, $4170 (on campus). *Financial aid:* Non-need-based college/university scholarships/grants from institutional funds. Forms required: International Student's Certification of Finances. For fall 2005, 10 international students on campus received college administered financial aid ($5522 average).

MOUNT MARY COLLEGE, MILWAUKEE

General Information Independent Roman Catholic, undergraduate: women only; graduate: coed institution. Urban setting. *Awards:* B, M. *Entrance level for U.S. students:* Moderately difficult. *Enrollment:* 1,732 total; 1,459 undergraduates (97% women) including 1% international students from 9 foreign countries. *Faculty:* 213. *Library holdings:* 103,450 books, 22,210 current serial subscriptions, 8,104 audiovisual materials. *Total majors:* 53. *Expenses:* (2007–08) $19,204; room and board, $6195 (on campus). *Financial aid:* Need-based college/university scholarships/grants from institutional funds. Non-need-based college/university scholarships/grants from institutional funds, on-campus employment. Forms required: International Student's Certification of Finances. 9 international students on campus received college administered financial aid ($3100 average).

NORTHLAND COLLEGE, ASHLAND

General Information Independent, 4-year, coed college, affiliated with United Church of Christ. Small town setting. *Awards:* B.

Entrance level for U.S. students: Moderately difficult. *Enrollment:* 692 total (57% women) including 1% international students from 4 foreign countries. *Undergraduate faculty:* 73. *Library holdings:* 75,000 books, 260 current serial subscriptions. *Total majors:* 54.

Information for International Students For fall 2006: 46 international students applied, 6 were accepted, 4 enrolled. Students can start in fall or winter. Transfers accepted from institutions abroad. *Admission tests:* Required: TOEFL (minimum score: paper-based 525; computer-based 195). Recommended: SAT or ACT, ELS. TOEFL can be waived under certain conditions. *Application deadline:* Rolling. *Expenses:* (2007–08) $21,901; room and board, $6160 (on campus); room only, $2490 (on campus). *Financial aid:* Need-based college/university scholarships/grants from institutional funds. Non-need-based college/university scholarships/grants from institutional funds, loans from outside sources, on-campus employment. International transfer students are eligible to apply for aid. For fall 2006 (estimated), 10 international students on campus received college administered financial aid ($7354 average). *Housing:* Guaranteed, also available during summer. *Services:* International student adviser on campus. Employment opportunities (on-campus) available. *Contact:* Assistant Director of Admissions, Northland College, 1411 Ellis Avenue, Ashland, WI 54806. Telephone: 715-682-1224. Fax: 715-682-1258. E-mail: agregerson@northland.edu. URL: http://www.northland.edu.

ST. NORBERT COLLEGE, DE PERE

General Information Independent Roman Catholic, coed institution. Suburban setting. *Awards:* B, M. *Entrance level for U.S. students:* Moderately difficult. *Enrollment:* 2,072 total; 2,015 undergraduates (56% women) including 2% international students from 27 foreign countries. *Faculty:* 179. *Library holdings:* 223,096 books, 580 current serial subscriptions, 6,640 audiovisual materials. *Total majors:* 31. *Expenses:* (2006–07) $23,497; room and board, $6319 (on campus); room only, $3349 (on campus). *Financial aid:* Need-based college/university scholarships/grants from institutional funds, tuition waivers, on-campus employment. Non-need-based college/university scholarships/grants from institutional funds, tuition waivers, on-campus employment. Forms required: institution's own financial aid form, income tax form(s). For fall 2006 (estimated), 54 international students on campus received college administered financial aid ($13,384 average).

SILVER LAKE COLLEGE, MANITOWOC

General Information Independent Roman Catholic, coed institution. Rural setting. *Awards:* A, B, M. *Entrance level for U.S. students:* Minimally difficult. *Enrollment:* 939 total; 628 undergraduates (73% women) including 1% international students from 3 foreign countries. *Faculty:* 278. *Library holdings:* 61,574 books, 277 current serial subscriptions, 8,631 audiovisual materials. *Total majors:* 24. *Expenses:* (2007–08) $18,288; room only, $4650 (on campus). *Financial aid:* Non-need-based college/university scholarships/grants from institutional funds, athletic awards. Forms required: International Student's Certification of Finances. For fall 2006 (estimated), 1 international student on campus received college administered financial aid ($16,800 average).

UNIVERSITY OF PHOENIX–WISCONSIN CAMPUS, BROOKFIELD

General Information Proprietary, coed institution. Urban setting. *Awards:* B, M. *Entrance level for U.S. students:* Noncompetitive. *Enrollment:* 1,132 total; 883 undergraduates (59% women) including 4% international students. *Faculty:* 238. *Library holdings:* 1,959 books, 692 current serial subscriptions. *Total majors:* 11. *Expenses:* (2006–07) $11,010.

UNIVERSITY OF WISCONSIN–EAU CLAIRE, EAU CLAIRE

General Information State-supported, coed institution. Urban setting. *Awards:* A, B, M. *Entrance level for U.S. students:* Moderately difficult. *Enrollment:* 10,505 total; 10,031 undergraduates (59% women) including 1% international students from 40 foreign countries. *Faculty:* 518. *Library holdings:* 764,275 books, 2,448 current serial subscriptions. *Total majors:* 48.

Information for International Students For fall 2006: 140 international students enrolled. Students can start in fall or spring. Transfers accepted from institutions abroad. *Admission tests:* Required: TOEFL (minimum score: paper-based 525; computer-based 197; minimum score for ESL admission: paper-based 475; computer-based 153). *Application deadline:* 7/1. *Expenses:* (2006–07) $12,977; room and board, $4936 (on campus); room only, $2640 (on campus). *Financial aid:* Need-based college/university scholarships/grants from institutional funds, tuition waivers. Non-need-based loans from outside sources. Forms required: institution's own financial aid form, International Student's Certification of Finances. 57 international students on campus received college administered financial aid ($6154 average). *Housing:* Guaranteed. *Services:* International student adviser on campus. Full-time and part-time ESL programs on campus. ESL program available during the academic year. Internships available. *Contact:* International Student Advisor, Office of Admissions, University of Wisconsin–Eau Claire, 105 Garfield Avenue, Eau Claire, WI 54702-4004. Telephone: 715-836-4411. Fax: 715-836-4948. E-mail: huelsbpj@uwec.edu. URL: http://www.uwec.edu.

See In-Depth Description on page 232.

UNIVERSITY OF WISCONSIN–GREEN BAY, GREEN BAY

General Information State-supported, coed institution. Suburban setting. *Awards:* A, B, M. *Entrance level for U.S. students:* Moderately difficult. *Enrollment:* 5,803 total; 5,661 undergraduates (65% women) including 1% international students from 24 foreign countries. *Faculty:* 285. *Library holdings:* 333,482 books, 5,512 current serial subscriptions. *Total majors:* 35. *Expenses:* (2006–07) $13,190; room and board, $4700 (on campus); room only, $3000 (on campus). *Financial aid:* Need-based college/university scholarships/grants from institutional funds, tuition waivers, athletic awards, on-campus employment. Non-need-based college/university scholarships/grants from institutional funds, athletic awards, on-campus employment. Forms required: International Student's Certification of Finances. 28 international students on campus received college administered financial aid ($10,059 average).

UNIVERSITY OF WISCONSIN–LA CROSSE, LA CROSSE

General Information State-supported, coed institution. Suburban setting. *Awards:* A, B, M. *Entrance level for U.S. students:* Moderately difficult. *Enrollment:* 9,818 total; 8,306 undergraduates (59% women) including 1% international students from 42 foreign countries. *Faculty:* 443. *Library holdings:* 687,207 books, 1,181 current serial subscriptions. *Total majors:* 42.
Information for International Students For fall 2006: 216 international students applied, 188 were accepted, 160 enrolled. Students can start in fall, spring, or summer. Transfers accepted from institutions abroad. *Admission tests:* Recommended: TOEFL. TOEFL can be waived under certain conditions. *Application deadline:* 5/1. *Expenses:* (2006–07) $12,873; room and board, $4970 (on campus); room only, $2840 (on campus). *Financial aid:* Need-based college/university scholarships/grants from institutional funds, tuition waivers. Non-need-based college/university scholarships/grants from institutional funds. Forms required: institution's own financial aid form. For fall 2005, 85 international students on campus received college administered financial aid ($11,500 average). *Housing:* Available during summer. *Services:* International student adviser on campus. Full-time and part-time ESL programs on campus. ESL program available during the academic year and the summer. Internships and employment opportunities (on-campus) available. *Contact:* International Admissions Specialist, University of Wisconsin–La Crosse, Office of International Education, La Crosse, WI 54601. Telephone: 608-785-8016. Fax: 608-785-8923. E-mail: uwlworld@uwlax.edu. URL: http://www.uwlax.edu.

See In-Depth Description on page 233.

UNIVERSITY OF WISCONSIN–MADISON, MADISON

General Information State-supported, coed university. Urban setting. *Awards:* B, M, D, FP. *Entrance level for U.S. students:* Very difficult. *Enrollment:* 41,466 total; 30,055 undergraduates (53% women) including 4% international students from 110 foreign countries. *Faculty:* 2,975. *Total majors:* 136. *Expenses:* (2006–07) $20,726; room and board, $6920 (on campus).

UNIVERSITY OF WISCONSIN–MANITOWOC, MANITOWOC

General Information State-supported, 2-year, coed college. Small town setting. *Awards:* A. *Entrance level for U.S. students:* Minimally difficult. *Enrollment:* 588 total (53% women) including 0.2% international students. *Undergraduate faculty:* 40. *Library holdings:* 25,750 books, 150 current serial subscriptions. *Total majors:* 1.
Information for International Students Students can start in fall or spring. *Admission tests:* Required: TOEFL (minimum score: paper-based 500; computer-based 173). *Application deadline:* 7/1. *Expenses:* (2006–07) $13,099. *Financial aid:* Need-based tuition waivers. Non-need-based college/university scholarships/grants from institutional funds. *Contact:* Assistant Dean for Student Services, University of Wisconsin–Manitowoc, 705 Viebahn Road, Manitowoc, WI 54220. Telephone: 920-683-4707. Fax: 920-683-4776. E-mail: christopher.lewis@uwc.edu. URL: http://www.manitowoc.uwc.edu.

UNIVERSITY OF WISCONSIN–MARSHFIELD/WOOD COUNTY, MARSHFIELD

General Information State-supported, 2-year, coed college. Small town setting. *Awards:* A. *Entrance level for U.S. students:* Moderately difficult. *Enrollment:* 643 total including 0.2% international students from 1 foreign country. *Undergraduate faculty:* 36. *Library holdings:* 35,000 books, 185 current serial subscriptions. *Total majors:* 1.
Information for International Students For fall 2006: 1 international student applied, 1 was accepted, 1 enrolled. Students can start in fall, spring, or summer. *Admission tests:* Required: TOEFL (minimum score: paper-based 500; computer-based 173). TOEFL can be waived under certain conditions. *Application deadline:* 5/1. *Expenses:* (2006–07) $11,491. *Financial aid:* Need-based tuition waivers. Non-need-based college/university scholarships/grants from institutional funds. *Contact:* Admission, University of Wisconsin–Marshfield/Wood County, 2000 West 5th Street, Marshfield, WI 54449. Telephone: 715-389-6500. Fax: 715-389-1718. E-mail: juliene.krahn@uwc.edu. URL: http://marshfield.uwc.edu.

UNIVERSITY OF WISCONSIN–MILWAUKEE, MILWAUKEE

General Information State-supported, coed university. Urban setting. *Awards:* B, M, D. *Entrance level for U.S. students:* Moderately difficult. *Enrollment:* 28,309 total; 23,595 undergraduates (53% women) including 1% international students from 40 foreign countries. *Faculty:* 1,444. *Library holdings:* 1.4 million books, 8,240 current serial subscriptions. *Total majors:* 105. *Expenses:* (2006–07) $16,994; room and board, $5314 (on campus); room only, $3304 (on campus).

UNIVERSITY OF WISCONSIN–OSHKOSH, OSHKOSH

General Information State-supported, coed institution. Suburban setting. *Awards:* A, B, M. *Entrance level for U.S. students:* Moderately difficult. *Enrollment:* 11,080 total; 9,780 undergraduates (59% women) including 1% international students from 32 foreign countries. *Faculty:* 560. *Library holdings:* 446,774 books, 5,219 current serial subscriptions. *Total majors:* 56.
Information for International Students For fall 2006: 51 international students applied, 27 were accepted, 15 enrolled. Students can start in fall, spring, or summer. Transfers accepted from institutions abroad. *Admission tests:* Required: TOEFL (minimum score: paper-based 523; computer-based 193). *Application deadline:* Rolling. *Expenses:* (2006–07) $12,838; room and board, $5164 (on campus); room only, $3034 (on campus). *Financial aid:* International transfer students are eligible to apply for aid. *Housing:* Guaranteed, also available during summer. *Services:* International student adviser on campus. Internships and employment opportunities (on-campus and off-campus) available. *Contact:* International Student Services, Undergraduate Admissions Office, University of Wisconsin–Oshkosh, 800 Algoma Boulevard, Dempsey 146, Oshkosh, WI 54901. Telephone: 920-424-0775. Fax: 920-424-0185. E-mail: mylreab@uwosh.edu. URL: http://www.uwosh.edu.

UNIVERSITY OF WISCONSIN–PARKSIDE, KENOSHA

General Information State-supported, coed institution. Suburban setting. *Awards:* B, M. *Entrance level for U.S. students:* Moderately difficult. *Enrollment:* 4,914 total; 4,802 undergraduates (56% women) including 1% international students from 12 foreign countries. *Faculty:* 271. *Library holdings:* 400,000 books, 1,590 current serial subscriptions. *Total majors:* 37. *Expenses:* (2006–07) $12,860; room and board, $5277 (on campus); room only, $3217 (on campus). *Financial aid:* Need-based college/university scholarships/grants from institutional funds, tuition waivers, athletic awards, on-campus employment. Non-need-based college/university scholarships/grants from institutional funds, tuition waivers, athletic awards, on-campus employment.

UNIVERSITY OF WISCONSIN–PLATTEVILLE, PLATTEVILLE

General Information State-supported, coed institution. Small town setting. *Awards:* A, B, M. *Entrance level for U.S. students:* Moderately difficult. *Enrollment:* 6,732 total; 6,084 undergraduates (36% women) including 0.4% international students from 13 foreign countries. *Faculty:* 356. *Library holdings:* 362,247 books, 2,116 current serial subscriptions. *Total majors:* 50. *Expenses:* (2006–07) $12,924; room and board, $4880 (on campus); room only, $2624 (on campus). *Financial aid:* Forms required: International Student's Financial Aid Application.

UNIVERSITY OF WISCONSIN–RICHLAND, RICHLAND CENTER

General Information State-supported, 2-year, coed college. Rural setting. *Awards:* A. *Entrance level for U.S. students:* Moderately

University of Wisconsin–Richland (continued)

difficult. *Enrollment:* 464 total (58% women) including 4% international students from 15 foreign countries. *Undergraduate faculty:* 26. *Library holdings:* 45,000 books, 200 current serial subscriptions. *Total majors:* 2. *Expenses:* (2006–07) $11,658; room and board, $4730 (on campus); room only, $2990 (on campus). *Financial aid:* Need-based tuition waivers. Non-need-based college/university scholarships/grants from institutional funds.

UNIVERSITY OF WISCONSIN–RIVER FALLS, RIVER FALLS

General Information State-supported, coed institution. Suburban setting. *Awards:* B, M. *Entrance level for U.S. students:* Moderately difficult. *Enrollment:* 5,862 total; 5,275 undergraduates (60% women) including 0.3% international students from 18 foreign countries. *Faculty:* 330. *Library holdings:* 448,088 books, 1,660 current serial subscriptions, 7,500 audiovisual materials. *Total majors:* 80. *Expenses:* (2006–07) $13,202; room and board, $4586 (on campus); room only, $2716 (on campus).

UNIVERSITY OF WISCONSIN–STEVENS POINT, STEVENS POINT

General Information State-supported, coed institution. Small town setting. *Awards:* A, B, M. *Entrance level for U.S. students:* Moderately difficult. *Enrollment:* 8,842 total; 8,612 undergraduates (54% women) including 2% international students from 32 foreign countries. *Faculty:* 439. *Library holdings:* 1.1 million books, 18,428 current serial subscriptions, 8,850 audiovisual materials. *Total majors:* 55.

Information for International Students Students can start in fall, spring, or summer. Transfers accepted from institutions abroad. *Admission tests:* Required: TOEFL (minimum score: iBT 70; paper-based 523; computer-based 193). TOEFL can be waived under certain conditions. *Application deadline:* 7/1. *Expenses:* (2006–07) $12,933; room and board, $4542 (on campus); room only, $2726 (on campus). *Financial aid:* Need-based financial aid available. Non-need-based college/university scholarships/grants from institutional funds, tuition waivers, loans from outside sources, on-campus employment. Forms required: International Student's Certification of Finances. For fall 2005, 97 international students on campus received college administered financial aid ($5657 average). *Services:* International student adviser on campus. Full-time and part-time ESL programs on campus. ESL program available during the academic year and the summer. Employment opportunities (on-campus) available. *Contact:* Foreign Student Office, University of Wisconsin–Stevens Point, 1108 Fremont Street, #020 SSC, Stevens Point, WI 54481-3897. Telephone: 715-346-3849. Fax: 715-346-3819. E-mail: fso@uwsp.edu. URL: http://www.uwsp.edu.

See In-Depth Description on page 234.

UNIVERSITY OF WISCONSIN–STOUT, MENOMONIE

General Information State-supported, coed institution. Small town setting. *Awards:* B, M. *Entrance level for U.S. students:* Moderately difficult. *Enrollment:* 8,327 total; 7,492 undergraduates (49% women) including 1% international students. *Faculty:* 390. *Library holdings:* 229,986 books, 1,784 current serial subscriptions, 16,142 audiovisual materials. *Total majors:* 30.

Information for International Students For fall 2006: 105 international students applied, 100 were accepted, 97 enrolled. Students can start in fall, winter, spring, or summer. Transfers accepted from institutions abroad. *Admission tests:* Required: TOEFL (minimum score: iBT 61; paper-based 500; computer-based 173; minimum score for ESL admission: iBT 61; paper-based 500; computer-based 173). TOEFL can be waived under certain conditions. *Application deadline:* Rolling. *Expenses:* (2007–08) $14,613; room and board, $4884 (on campus); room only, $2990 (on campus). *Financial aid:* Non-need-based college/university scholarships/grants from institutional funds, tuition waivers, loans from outside sources, on-campus employment. Forms required: institution's own financial aid form, International Student's Certification of Finances. International transfer students are eligible to apply for aid. For fall 2006 (estimated), 70 international students on campus received college administered financial aid ($5138 average). *Housing:* Guaranteed, also available during summer. *Services:* International student adviser on campus. ESL program at cooperating institution. ESL program available during the academic year and the summer. Internships and employment opportunities (on-campus and off-campus) available. *Contact:* Associate Director, University of Wisconsin–Stout, Office of International Education, Menomonie, WI 54751. Telephone: 715-232-2132. Fax: 715-232-2500. E-mail: kuesterv@uwstout.edu. URL: http://www.uwstout.edu.

See In-Depth Description on page 235.

UNIVERSITY OF WISCONSIN–SUPERIOR, SUPERIOR

General Information State-supported, coed institution. Suburban setting. *Awards:* B, M (associate, educational specialist). *Entrance level for U.S. students:* Moderately difficult. *Enrollment:* 2,924 total; 2,626 undergraduates (58% women) including 4% international students from 30 foreign countries. *Faculty:* 173. *Library holdings:* 467,700 books, 753 current serial subscriptions. *Total majors:* 65.

Information for International Students For fall 2006: 78 international students applied, 54 were accepted, 31 enrolled. Students can start in fall or spring. Transfers accepted from institutions abroad. *Admission tests:* Required: TOEFL (minimum score: iBT 61; paper-based 500; computer-based 173). Recommended: SAT or ACT. TOEFL can be waived under certain conditions. *Application deadline:* 7/1. *Expenses:* (2006–07) $13,052; room and board, $4576 (on campus); room only, $2668 (on campus). *Financial aid:* Need-based and non-need-based financial aid available. Forms required: institution's own financial aid form. International transfer students are eligible to apply for aid. 162 international students on campus received college administered financial aid ($8676 average). *Housing:* Guaranteed, also available during summer. *Services:* International student adviser on campus. Full-time and part-time ESL programs on campus. ESL program available during the academic year. Internships and employment opportunities (on-campus and off-campus) available. *Contact:* International Student Services Specialist, University of Wisconsin–Superior, Main 337, Belknap & Catlin Avenues, Superior, WI 54880-4500. Telephone: 715-394-8052. Fax: 715-394-8363. E-mail: international@uwsuper.edu. URL: http://www.uwsuper.edu.

See In-Depth Description on page 236.

UNIVERSITY OF WISCONSIN–WHITEWATER, WHITEWATER

General Information State-supported, coed institution. Small town setting. *Awards:* A, B, M. *Entrance level for U.S. students:* Moderately difficult. *Enrollment:* 10,502 total; 9,210 undergraduates (51% women) including 1% international students from 25 foreign countries. *Faculty:* 502. *Library holdings:* 701,086 books, 4,589 current serial subscriptions, 19,427 audiovisual materials. *Total majors:* 56.

Information for International Students For fall 2006: 20 international students applied, 20 were accepted, 12 enrolled. Students can start in fall or spring. Transfers accepted from institutions abroad. *Admission tests:* Required: TOEFL (minimum score: paper-based 500; computer-based 173). TOEFL can be waived under certain conditions. *Application deadline:* 4/15. *Expenses:* (2006–07) $13,881; room and board, $4190 (on campus); room only, $2440 (on campus). *Financial aid:* Need-based tuition waivers. Non-need-based college/university scholarships/grants from institutional funds, tuition waivers, loans from outside sources, on-campus employment. Forms required: institution's own financial aid form, International Student's Certification of Finances, letter of appeal. International transfer students are eligible to apply for aid. *Housing:* Guaranteed, also available during summer. *Services:* International student adviser on campus. ESL program at cooperating institution. ESL program available during the academic year and the summer. Internships and employment opportunities (on-campus) available. *Contact:* Director, Office of Admissions, University of Wisconsin–Whitewater, Admissions Office, 800 West Main Street, Whitewater, WI 53190. Telephone: 262-472-1440. Fax: 262-472-1515. E-mail: uwwadmit@uww.edu. URL: http://www.uww.edu.

See In-Depth Description on page 237.

VITERBO UNIVERSITY, LA CROSSE

General Information Independent Roman Catholic, coed institution. Suburban setting. *Awards:* B, M. *Entrance level for U.S. students:* Moderately difficult. *Enrollment:* 2,991 total; 1,980 undergraduates (72% women) including 1% international students from 15 foreign countries. *Faculty:* 205. *Library holdings:* 92,036 books, 466 current serial subscriptions, 6,531 audiovisual materials. *Total majors:* 53.

Information for International Students For fall 2006: 35 international students applied, 19 were accepted, 9 enrolled. Students can start in fall. Transfers accepted from institutions abroad. *Admission tests:* Required: TOEFL (minimum score: iBT 79; paper-based 550; computer-based 213). TOEFL can be waived under certain conditions. *Application deadline:* 4/1. *Expenses:* (2007–08) $18,590; room and board, $6140 (on campus); room only, $3340 (on campus). *Financial aid:* Non-need financial aid available. Forms required: institution's own financial aid form, International Student's Certification of Finances. International transfer students are eligible to apply for aid. 11 international students on campus received college administered financial aid ($11,006 average). *Housing:* Guaranteed, also available during summer. *Services:* International student adviser on campus. ESL program at cooperating institution. ESL program available during the academic year and the summer. Internships and employment opportunities (on-campus) available. *Contact:* International Admissions Coordinator, Viterbo University, 900 Viterbo Drive, La Crosse, WI 54601. Telephone: 608-796-3172. Fax: 608-796-3050. E-mail: globaled@viterbo.edu. URL: http://www.viterbo.edu.

WYOMING

CASPER COLLEGE, CASPER

General Information District-supported, 2-year, coed college. Small town setting. *Awards:* A. *Entrance level for U.S. students:* Noncompetitive. *Enrollment:* 4,285 total (60% women) including 1% international students from 15 foreign countries. *Undergraduate faculty:* 252. *Library holdings:* 118,000 books, 500 current serial subscriptions. *Total majors:* 73. *Expenses:* (2006–07) $4440; room and board, $3590 (on campus). *Financial aid:* Need-based financial aid available. Non-need-based college/university scholarships/grants from institutional funds, athletic awards.

CENTRAL WYOMING COLLEGE, RIVERTON

General Information State and locally supported, 2-year, coed college. Small town setting. *Awards:* A. *Entrance level for U.S. students:* Noncompetitive. *Enrollment:* 1,711 total (66% women) including 2% international students from 8 foreign countries. *Undergraduate faculty:* 169. *Library holdings:* 78,167 books, 183 current serial subscriptions. *Total majors:* 41.

Information for International Students For fall 2006: 15 international students applied, 15 were accepted, 12 enrolled. Students can start in fall, spring, or summer. Transfers accepted from institutions abroad. *Admission tests:* Required: TOEFL (minimum score: paper-based 500; computer-based 175; minimum score for ESL admission: paper-based 425; computer-based 150). Recommended: ELS. TOEFL can be waived under certain conditions. *Application deadline:* Rolling. *Expenses:* (2007–08) $4968; room and board, $3280 (on campus); room only, $1600 (on campus). *Financial aid:* Non-need-based college/university scholarships/grants from institutional funds, on-campus employment. Forms required: International Student's Certification of Finances, Scholarship Application. International transfer students are eligible to apply for aid. *Housing:* Available during summer. *Services:* International student adviser on campus. Full-time and part-time ESL programs on campus. ESL program available during the summer. Employment opportunities (on-campus and off-campus) available. *Contact:* International Student Advisor, Central Wyoming College, 2660 Peck Avenue, Riverton, WY 82501. Telephone: 307-855-2270. Fax: 307-855-2093. E-mail: jharris@cwc.edu. URL: http://www.cwc.edu.

EASTERN WYOMING COLLEGE, TORRINGTON

General Information State and locally supported, 2-year, coed college. Rural setting. *Awards:* A. *Entrance level for U.S. students:* Noncompetitive. *Enrollment:* 1,346 total (67% women) including 1% international students from 3 foreign countries. *Undergraduate faculty:* 105. *Total majors:* 45.

Information for International Students For fall 2006: 12 international students applied, 6 were accepted, 4 enrolled. Students can start in fall or spring. *Admission tests:* Required: TOEFL (minimum score: paper-based 500; computer-based 173; minimum score for ESL admission: paper-based 500; computer-based 173). Recommended: ACT. TOEFL can be waived under certain conditions. *Application deadline:* 5/1. *Expenses:* (2006–07) $4656; room and board, $3220 (on campus); room only, $1364 (on campus). *Financial aid:* Need-based college/university scholarships/grants from institutional funds, loans from outside sources, on-campus employment. Non-need-based college/university scholarships/grants from institutional funds, tuition waivers, athletic awards, loans from outside sources, on-campus employment. Forms required: International Student's Certification of Finances. International transfer students are eligible to apply for aid. *Services:* International student adviser on campus. Internships and employment opportunities (on-campus) available. *Contact:* Dean of Students, Eastern Wyoming College, 3200 West C Street, Torrington, WY 82240. Telephone: 307-532-8257. Fax: 307-532-8222. E-mail: mcotant@ewc.wy.edu. URL: http://www.ewc.wy.edu.

LARAMIE COUNTY COMMUNITY COLLEGE, CHEYENNE

General Information State-supported, 2-year, coed college. Small town setting. *Awards:* A. *Entrance level for U.S. students:* Noncompetitive. *Enrollment:* 4,584 total (60% women) including 0.5% international students from 16 foreign countries.

Undergraduate faculty: 279. *Library holdings:* 54,396 books, 243 current serial subscriptions, 31,988 audiovisual materials. *Total majors:* 78.

Information for International Students For fall 2006: 35 international students applied, 30 were accepted, 25 enrolled. Students can start in fall, spring, or summer. Transfers accepted from institutions abroad. *Admission tests:* Recommended: TOEFL (minimum score: iBT 71; paper-based 500; computer-based 173). TOEFL can be waived under certain conditions. *Application deadline:* Rolling. *Expenses:* (2007–08) $5264; room and board, $5690 (on campus). *Housing:* Available during summer. *Services:* International student adviser on campus. Full-time and part-time ESL programs on campus. ESL program available during the academic year and the summer. Employment opportunities (on-campus) available. *Contact:* International Student Advisor, Laramie County Community College, Cheyenne, WY 82007-3299. Telephone: 307-778-1221. Fax: 307-778-1282. E-mail: diversity@lccc.wy.edu. URL: http://www.lccc.wy.edu.

See In-Depth Description on page 113.

NORTHWEST COLLEGE, POWELL

General Information State and locally supported, 2-year, coed college. Rural setting. *Awards:* A. *Entrance level for U.S. students:* Noncompetitive. *Enrollment:* 1,711 total (61% women) including 0.4% international students. *Undergraduate faculty:* 154. *Library holdings:* 55,330 books, 1,738 current serial subscriptions, 741 audiovisual materials. *Total majors:* 70.

Information for International Students For fall 2006: 17 international students applied, 17 were accepted, 17 enrolled. Students can start in fall or spring. Transfers accepted from institutions abroad. *Admission tests:* Required: TOEFL (minimum score: iBT 53; paper-based 477; computer-based 153). Recommended: ELS, COMPASS if no ACT or SAT, IELTS, or STEP. TOEFL can be waived under certain conditions. *Application deadline:* Rolling. *Housing:* Guaranteed, also available during summer. *Services:* International student adviser on campus. ESL program at cooperating institution. Internships and employment opportunities (on-campus) available. *Contact:* Multicultural Coordinator/International Admissions, Northwest College, 231 West 6th Street, Powell, WY 82435. Telephone: 307-754-6000 Ext. 6138. Fax: 307-754-6157. E-mail: mary.baumann@northwestcollege.edu. URL: http://www.northwestcollege.edu.

SHERIDAN COLLEGE–SHERIDAN AND GILLETTE, SHERIDAN

General Information State and locally supported, 2-year, coed college. Small town setting. *Awards:* A. *Entrance level for U.S. students:* Noncompetitive. *Enrollment:* 3,136 total (54% women) including 1% international students from 9 foreign countries. *Undergraduate faculty:* 164. *Library holdings:* 65,221 books, 581 current serial subscriptions. *Total majors:* 42.

Information for International Students For fall 2006: 15 international students applied, 15 were accepted, 15 enrolled. Students can start in fall, spring, or summer. Transfers accepted from institutions abroad. *Admission tests:* Required: TOEFL (minimum score: paper-based 500; computer-based 173). Recommended: SAT, ACT, SAT or ACT, SAT Subject Tests. TOEFL can be waived under certain conditions. *Application deadline:* 6/1. *Expenses:* (2007–08) $4992; room and board, $3920 (on campus). *Financial aid:* Non-need-based college/university scholarships/grants from institutional funds, tuition waivers, athletic awards, on-campus employment. *Housing:* Guaranteed, also available during summer. *Services:* International student adviser on campus. ESL program at cooperating institution. ESL program available during the academic year. Internships and employment opportunities (on-campus) available. *Contact:* International Student Coordinator, Sheridan College–Sheridan and Gillette, PO Box 1500, Sheridan, WY 82801. Telephone: 307-674-6446 Ext. 2002. Fax: 307-674-7205. E-mail: ckaiser@sheridan.edu. URL: http://www.sheridan.edu.

UNIVERSITY OF WYOMING, LARAMIE

General Information State-supported, coed university. Small town setting. *Awards:* B, M, D, FP. *Entrance level for U.S. students:* Moderately difficult. *Enrollment:* 13,203 total; 9,468 undergraduates (52% women) including 2% international students from 57 foreign countries. *Faculty:* 720. *Library holdings:* 2.4 million books, 11,668 current serial subscriptions, 9,961 audiovisual materials. *Total majors:* 78.

Information for International Students For fall 2006: 121 international students applied, 100 were accepted, 58 enrolled. Students can start in fall, spring, or summer. Transfers accepted from institutions abroad. *Admission tests:* Required: SAT or ACT, TOEFL (minimum score: paper-based 525; computer-based 197). TOEFL can be waived under certain conditions. *Application deadline:* 6/1. *Expenses:* (2007–08) $10,394; room and board, $7274

University of Wyoming (continued)

(on campus); room only, $3158 (on campus). *Financial aid:* Need-based financial aid available. Non-need-based college/university scholarships/grants from institutional funds, tuition waivers, athletic awards, loans from outside sources. International transfer students are eligible to apply for aid. For fall 2005, 107 international students on campus received college administered financial aid ($9570 average). *Housing:* Available during summer. *Services:* International student adviser on campus. Full-time ESL program on campus. ESL program available during the academic year and the summer. Internships and employment opportunities (on-campus and off-campus) available. *Contact:* Office Associate Senior, University of Wyoming, Admissions Office, Department 3435, 1000 East University Avenue, Laramie, WY 82071. Telephone: 307-766-5160. Fax: 307-766-4042. E-mail: why-wyo@uwyo.edu. URL: http://www.uwyo.edu.

See In-Depth Description on page 238.

WESTERN WYOMING COMMUNITY COLLEGE, ROCK SPRINGS

General Information State and locally supported, 2-year, coed college. Small town setting. *Awards:* A. *Entrance level for U.S. students:* Noncompetitive. *Enrollment:* 2,698 total (57% women) including 3% international students from 24 foreign countries.

Undergraduate faculty: 218. *Library holdings:* 107,669 books, 178 current serial subscriptions, 3,596 audiovisual materials. *Total majors:* 86.

Information for International Students For fall 2006: 60 international students applied, 60 were accepted, 30 enrolled. Students can start in fall or spring. Transfers accepted from institutions abroad. *Admission tests:* Recommended: SAT or ACT, TOEFL (minimum score: iBT 61; paper-based 500; computer-based 173; minimum score for ESL admission: iBT 32; paper-based 400; computer-based 97). TOEFL can be waived under certain conditions. *Application deadline:* 6/15. *Expenses:* (2007–08) $4804; room and board, $3394 (on campus); room only, $1768 (on campus). *Financial aid:* Forms required: institution's own financial aid form. International transfer students are eligible to apply for aid. *Housing:* Guaranteed, also available during summer. *Services:* International student adviser on campus. Full-time ESL program on campus. ESL program available during the academic year. Internships and employment opportunities (on-campus) available. *Contact:* Director of Admissions, Western Wyoming Community College, 2500 College Drive, Rock Springs, WY 82901. Telephone: 307-382-1633. Fax: 307-382-1636. E-mail: admissions@wwcc.wy.edu. URL: http://www.wwcc.wy.edu.

See In-Depth Description on page 246.

Appendixes

Glossary

Academic adviser—A faculty or staff member who assists students in their selection of academic courses and programs, often providing general counseling as well, although the role is occasionally filled by upperclass students. (See also *International student adviser.*)

Academic calendar—The period that makes up the school year, usually divided into two terms (semesters), three terms (trimesters), or four terms (quarters).

Accreditation—The "seal of approval" indicating that an academic institution has been recognized as providing at least an adequate education. There are general regional accrediting agencies and specific academic-area accrediting agencies. It is very important to be sure that the colleges you are interested in are accredited by the appropriate agencies. Regional accreditation guarantees a minimum of adequacy in terms of academic facilities and programs, not necessarily excellence. In most countries, government agencies concerned with the evaluation of credentials and degrees specify the type of accreditation required to recognize a course of study completed at an international institution. It would be wise to confirm such requirements with your appropriate home agency before leaving to study in the United States.

ACT—A standardized test offered by American College Testing, Inc., required for admission to some American colleges. (See also *SAT.*)

Advanced standing—At many colleges this may be achieved by scoring well on the Advanced Placement tests offered by the College Board or by receiving credit for academic work that is beyond the U.S. secondary school standard. Many international students are able to enter colleges in the United States with advanced standing because most non-U.S. secondary school curricula are at a somewhat higher level. However, U.S. colleges are not uniform in giving credit for academic work in other countries. International students applying for advanced credit can receive a wide variety of responses from U.S. colleges. There is generally no appeal on such divergent responses, which reflect the independent authority of U.S. colleges and universities.

American College Testing, Inc.—An organization that conducts standardized testing (ACT) and financial aid need analysis.

Application fee—Fees charged to cover the cost of processing your application. The fees vary from school to school but average $30–$40 for each application. Some colleges may waive this requirement if applicants provide financial documentation establishing that their resources do not permit payment of the fee.

Articulation agreement—An agreement between two schools that allows students to complete an associate degree program at one school and transfer to a related bachelor's degree program at another school with a minimum loss of credit and duplication of course work.

Associate degree—The degree awarded for successful completion of a two-year program, either terminal (occupational) or transfer (the first two years of a four-year program).

Automatic transfer—A plan in which a two-year branch of a larger educational system allows students in good standing to go on automatically to a bachelor's degree program on another campus of the system.

Bachelor's degree—The degree awarded upon successful completion of three to five years of study in the liberal arts and sciences or in professional or preprofessional areas.

Barrier-free campus—A campus that provides access for the disabled to all buildings and facilities.

Bursar—College or university treasurer and accountant.

Candidate notification date—The date by which an institution will announce its decision on a student's application.

Candidate's reply date—The date (May 1) established by the College Board, and accepted by many colleges, by which students must notify participating colleges that have accepted them whether or not they plan to attend in the fall. Not all colleges subscribe to this agreement, but most colleges set a date or an amount of time after notification by which the student must respond.

Catalog—Also known as bulletins and calendars, catalogs generally provide descriptions of all the courses an institution offers, its policies and philosophy, and a statement of all requirements for being admitted and earning a degree. Often catalogs must be purchased, since they are quite lengthy. For more general information, a college viewbook or prospectus (usually free) is quite helpful. (See also *College viewbook or prospectus.*) Catalogs of many colleges and universities are available at EducationUSA advising centers, Fulbright Commission offices, and American libraries in many countries.

Class rank—Students' standing in the secondary school class relative to their peers. Rank in class is one of several criteria used by admission officers to determine how well individuals have performed in their secondary school studies relative to their peers. It is reported as a raw number (such as third out of a class of 30) or in a rougher percentile (top third, top 10 percent, etc.).

College—A postsecondary institution that awards either the associate degree or the bachelor's degree. College-level work in America is the same as first-degree work at a university abroad. Colleges, unlike universities, tend to be small and to emphasize teaching and undergraduate education over research, since graduate (postbachelor's) programs are not usually offered. Colleges, in another sense, can also be educational divisions of a larger university, such as a college of arts and sciences.

College Board—A membership organization consisting of representatives from college admission and financial aid offices and secondary school guidance personnel. The Board contracts with Educational Testing Service to create and administer its Admissions Testing Program (SAT, SAT Subject Tests, Advanced Placement tests as well as reports to students indicating their performance on the tests).

College viewbook or prospectus—A pictorial brochure produced by colleges and universities to publicize themselves to prospective students. A viewbook or prospectus usually provides succinct information on entrance requirements, campus life, courses of study, costs, etc., and is a useful guide to an institution's image of itself.

Competitiveness—The degree of difficulty in gaining admission to a college or university. The highly competitive colleges are the most difficult; there can be as many as 10 candidates for every available place. The term may also be used to describe the atmosphere or environment of a campus; the more competitive it is, the more intense the academic pressures are.

Conditional admission—This is offered by some colleges to students who are lacking certain skills, often English language proficiency. A student matriculates at a given school, completes the requirements for conditional admission, such as reaching a higher level of English language ability, and then goes on to earn his or her degree. Sometimes conditional students are allowed to take courses outside of the area requiring special attention.

Cooperative education plan—A program offered by many colleges that enables a student to combine work and study, often in order to gain degree-related experience. A cooperative program may be alternating (work and study in alternating terms) or parallel (work and study scheduled within the same term). In most such programs it takes five years to earn a bachelor's degree. Because of U.S. immigration regulations, institutions offering cooperative education plans often find it difficult to place international students in work off campus. The institution will advise you if it believes it can do so. If an international student is placed in off-campus work, he or she will be using a portion of the practical-training eligibility allowed during the course of degree work by the U.S. Citizenship and Immigration Services (USCIS). This practical-training eligibility is not to be confused with the six, twelve, or eighteen months (depending on visa type) allowed following the taking of a degree.

Core course—Such courses are also known as distribution requirements and, as their name implies, constitute the core, or center, of a degree program. A few colleges have no required core courses, while others may require several terms of such courses. Usually, core courses represent a sampling of work in the arts, humanities, natural sciences, and social sciences (also known as the liberal arts and sciences).

Course load—The number of courses taken in a given term. Colleges usually specify a range for the number of courses or credits to be taken by full-time students. Current U.S. Citizenship and Immigration Services regulations require that an international student pursue a full-time course of study. While the academic institution is allowed to determine what constitutes a full course load, it generally means a minimum of 12 credit hours, or four courses, during each term.

Credit—The unit of measurement of academic work successfully completed. There are several different credit systems. Under one system, a course might be worth 1 credit, while in another system the same course would be worth 3 "credit hours" or "hours," indicating the amount of time spent each week in class. Sometimes courses that are more advanced—or that meet for more hours—offer greater credit.

Deadline—The time by which something must be done or submitted. There are deadlines by which you must file your application for admission (often nine or more months prior to the term you wish to enter), file for financial assistance (usually at the same time you apply for admission), and submit your response to the admission decision (you generally have two to three weeks to confirm your intention to attend). If you anticipate a delay in your mail response reaching an American college, you may be able to use a telex, fax, or cable as a means of communication. Look for a telex, fax, or cable identification on the letterhead or in the literature of the colleges to which you will be responding.

Dean/Director of Admission—The person in charge of the admission office. In some cases there will be a dean and a director in the same office. Usually the director will have responsibility for office procedures, and the dean will have broader policymaking responsibilities. Deans and directors often have little to do with the actual processing of students' applications but will chair the committee that makes the final decisions.

Early admission—A program in which a college accepts students to begin college work before they graduate from secondary school. Admission standards are more stringent for early admission candidates.

Early decision—A plan in which students apply in November or December and learn of the decision on their application during December or January. Accepted early decision students must withdraw their applications to other colleges and agree to matriculate at the college that accepts them.

Elective—A course in the curriculum that you select that is optional but needed as part of the total number of credits required for graduation.

English as a second language (ESL) or English as a foreign language (EFL) program—A program offered by some colleges or proprietary schools for students whose English proficiency is not up to standard.

English language test—Generally required of all applicants for whom English is not the native language. These tests are designed to measure proficiency in written and spoken English and are essential to the admission process. Each college has its own requirement for level of achievement on the test, usually the Test of English as a Foreign Language (TOEFL).

Enrollment deposit—A nonrefundable deposit of funds required of accepted students at many colleges to reserve a space in the incoming class.

Faculty—The professors and instructors at colleges and universities.

Financial aid—Money provided to help you meet the costs of attending college. It may come from your government, private agencies, colleges, and banks. There is merit-based financial aid (such as scholarships that reward superior academic or athletic achievement) and need-based financial aid (where the amount of money you get will be based upon your family's financial need). If you receive financial aid from a college, it usually comes in a "package" consisting of (1) a grant or scholarship, which you do not have to repay; (2) a loan, rarely given to international students but which must be repaid; and (3) a campus job, to allow you to earn money during the school year. Financial aid policies differ widely from school to school. Financial aid to international students is limited at most institutions, especially at the undergraduate level. As a

result of recent tax legislation in the United States, a grant or scholarship that provides funds for school expenses beyond tuition costs may be liable to U.S. federal and state taxes, as is income from paid employment on or off campus.

Foreign student adviser—See *International student adviser.*

Grade—The indication of the quality of students' academic work. When you complete a course or take a test, you are evaluated and given a grade. A very common grading system in the United States is a scale of A to F, where A is the highest possible grade and F stands for failure. A grade of B+ would be between an A and a B.

Grade point average (GPA)—A system of scoring student achievement used by many colleges and universities. A student's GPA is computed by multiplying the numerical grade received in each course by the number of credits offered for each course, then dividing by the total number of credit hours studied. Most institutions use the following grade conversion scale: A = 4, B = 3, C = 2, D = 1, and F = 0.

Graduation—The completion of one's studies, also referred to as commencement. Although graduation normally occurs four years after entry into a bachelor's program, some students complete the requirements early by obtaining advanced-standing credit or attending summer school. Some students take more than four years to graduate from a bachelor's program. Students enrolled in an associate degree program generally graduate after two years of study.

Grant—"Gift money," also known as a scholarship, provided by some schools to help students meet costs. Grant funds for expenses other than tuition and fees are currently subject to both U.S. federal and state taxes.

High school—The American term for secondary school, which usually must be completed before beginning undergraduate studies.

Honors program—An unusually challenging program for superior students with high grade achievement.

Independent study—An option that allows students to pursue independent research or undertake a creative project, usually with minimal faculty supervision. When offered, such study is usually assigned in the third or fourth year of study.

Insurance—This is often required to protect students against emergency health-care or hospitalization expenses. The cost of medical care in the United States is now so high that no student from abroad should be without such insurance. Generally, each college provides information regarding insurance policies at the time of admission. Information may also be obtained from NAFSA: Association of International Educators, 1307 New York Avenue, NW, Eighth Floor, Washington, D.C. 20005-4701, U.S.A.

International student adviser—A professional staff member employed by most colleges to assist international students. International (or foreign) student advisers provide advice on a wide variety of academic and personal matters. They counsel on legal matters such as visas and employment and provide information on housing as well as on- and off-campus activities.

Liberal arts—Also known as the liberal arts and sciences, this term refers to academic work in the humanities (languages, music, art, etc.), social sciences (economics, history, sociology, etc.), and natural sciences (mathematics, chemistry, physics, etc.), as opposed to technical or professional subjects. Many colleges have requirements that ensure students' exposure to a wide variety of liberal arts courses.

Loan—A supplementary source of funding that, for non-U.S. citizens, usually comes from the college itself, since bank loans are generally not available to students who are not U.S. citizens or permanent residents. Loans are generally awarded as part of a financial aid package and range from about $100 to $2500. Some colleges offer emergency loans, of small amounts, to meet unexpected expenses. International students should never count on receiving a loan, however, and must convince consular officers that all college and personal funding needs can be met before these officials will grant their visas.

Major—The academic area in which a student chooses to concentrate. Generally, major course requirements take up one quarter to one half of the student's undergraduate studies and are combined with other general education requirements.

Matriculation—Enrollment at a college or university to begin work toward an academic degree.

Midterm—Halfway point in a semester or trimester.

Minor—An academic subject area in which a student may take the second-greatest concentration of courses. While a major may require as many as sixteen courses for a degree, a minor may require only four or five courses.

Orientation—A period of time prior to matriculation, ranging from two days to a week, set aside for new students to come to campus to participate in an organized program designed to hasten academic and social acclimatization. Orientation programs include academic and personal counseling, social occasions, tours, and time for independent activity. These programs are generally required for international students.

Pass/fail grading system—An alternative to traditional letter or numerical grading systems; course credit is indicated simply by a pass or fail (or credit/no credit) notation.

Placement test—An examination offered to students after they have arrived on campus. Policies regarding placement tests vary, but many institutions recognize that international students will have pursued studies more advanced than those of their American peers and thus will allow students to accelerate their studies based on their scores on departmental examinations.

Prerequisite—A particular requirement that must be met as a condition for advancement. Fluency in English is usually a prerequisite for admission, and entry to upper-level courses usually requires successful completion of lower-level courses, known as prerequisites.

Quarter—A unit measuring the academic year. Under this system there are four quarters, or terms, each year: three composing the academic year and one in the summer. International students are generally required to attend classes during three quarters, but they have the option of attending all four if they wish to accelerate their academic program.

Reference—A letter of support and evaluation, also known as a recommendation, that is usually required for admission to an American college. References from teachers and headmasters are particularly helpful in international admission because the letter writer can help place an individual applicant's candidacy in the clearest context for evaluation. Often these letters must be submitted directly to the college by the individual writing the reference and are not included with the admission application.

Registrar—The college or university official who keeps records of enrollment and academic standing.

Residence hall—Also known as a dormitory, this is on-campus housing, which forms an integral part of the American college experience at most schools. Much informal interchange occurs in residence halls, where students have the opportunity to meet people with differing interests and backgrounds. Some residence halls have faculty members living in them, some do not. International houses or residences are enjoying a revival on many U.S. campuses, and they generally provide a balance of U.S. and international students. In on-campus residential life at most colleges, students have a great deal of freedom in arranging their eating, sleeping, and study schedules and are not closely regulated by faculty and administration officers. Some campuses, especially at two-year colleges, do not have on-campus residence halls for students. It is important to determine this in advance.

Resident—Usually American citizens who are natives of the state in which a college is located. The term "permanent resident" refers to individuals who have been granted such status by the U.S. Citizenship and Immigration Services (USCIS). Such persons are eligible for in-state or resident tuition at publicly supported colleges and universities in that state. Residents are also, in another use of the term, students who live on campus.

Rolling admission—A program adopted by many colleges through which admission applications are evaluated upon receipt and applicants are notified of the decision as soon as the application is processed.

SAT—A standardized test, offered by the College Board through Educational Testing Service, required for admission to many American colleges. (See also *ACT*.)

SAT Subject Tests—These tests are offered by Educational Testing Service for the College Board. They are designed to measure a candidate's proficiency in a specific subject, such as biology, chemistry, or psychology.

Scholarship—A form of financial assistance, also known as a grant or as gift aid, that students are not required to repay. Scholarships are based on merit, a special characteristic, or need. Scholarships are offered to students with excellent achievement in an area such as academics, athletics, or debating. If a family has the financial resources to be able to meet expenses at an American college, the student should probably not apply for a scholarship, lest he or she run the risk of not being admitted. Competition for scholarship money is very strong. Although funds are awarded primarily to students with financial need, most colleges and universities provide limited funds or no funds at all to international students. Some colleges provide funds only after the first year or in emergency circumstances (e.g., currency devaluation, death of a parent, etc.). International student applicants who emphasize that they must have financial aid run a greater risk of being denied admission than an American in the same situation.

Semester—A unit of the academic year. Under the semester system there are two terms in each nine-month academic year.

Social Security number—Identification number assigned to U.S. citizens by the government. Since these numbers are used by many colleges as identification numbers, the admission office often assigns a similar nine-digit number to noncitizens. This number helps distinguish between students with similar—or the same—names.

Standardized tests—These include the SAT, SAT Subject Tests, ACT, and Test of English as a Foreign Language (TOEFL). All of these tests are used, to some degree, in college admission. They measure aptitude and achievement and are used in combination with a student's secondary school record to help evaluate potential for academic success. Each

institution has its own policies and procedures regarding the use of these tests, and all candidates should plan on taking all of the required examinations.

Studio—A class, usually in the arts, where students are instructed or have practice in a "hands-on" fashion. Photography, painting, and dance are courses that are taught with some component of studio experience.

Summer school—Study during the summer months of June, July, and August, when colleges traditionally are closed or offer a limited number of courses. Some students take advantage of the summer sessions to pursue independent research, to accelerate the process of course completion in order to enter graduate study earlier, or to study English before regular matriculation in September.

Syllabus—Outline of a course.

Teaching assistant (TA)—A student, usually a graduate student, who helps professors with their teaching and advising roles. Students will most often encounter a TA, as they are known, in the laboratory or seminar section of a large lecture course at a large university. An increasing number of teaching assistants in American universities are international graduate students, particularly in engineering and other technical fields.

Test of English as a Foreign Language (TOEFL)—This is the test most often taken by students for whom English is not their native language. In cases in which students have been educated in a school where English is the language of instruction, they are sometimes exempted from this requirement. However, some colleges and universities even require the TOEFL for students from countries where English is the official language.

Transcript—The records of your academic work. You will always be required to submit an official, translated copy of your secondary school transcript when you apply for admission.

Transfer—The option of applying as an "upperclass" candidate at the same level from one American college to another. To be eligible for transfer admission, a student must usually meet the same requirements as a freshman candidate and must also have completed one or two years of college studies. If a student completes the first two years of a bachelor's program at one college and applies to, is admitted to, and enters the second as a third-year student, he or she should be able to finish the typical four-year program on time. The term "transfer" is also used to describe the process of a student moving from one American college to another.

Trimester—A unit of the academic year. Under the trimester system the nine-month academic year is divided into three 3-month terms.

Tuition—The fees that cover academic expenses. Other expenses, such as those for room and board (lodging and meals), health insurance, activities, and transportation, are not included in tuition figures. Each college will provide tuition and general expense estimates in its admission information.

Undergraduate—An associate or bachelor's degree candidate or a description of such a candidate's courses. Once students have earned a bachelor's degree, they are eligible for entry into graduate programs at the master's and doctoral levels.

University—A large educational institution comprising a number of divisions, including graduate and professional schools. Because universities usually have research as an important part of their mission, they may place less emphasis on undergraduate teaching. Academic offerings are usually more comprehensive than at smaller colleges. Occasionally a "university" will have no professional schools or offer no doctoral programs, while some "colleges" offer master's programs.

Waiting list—A list of students who were not initially accepted by an institution but who will be accepted at a later date if space becomes available. In many cases waiting list candidates are not notified of the final decision until late in the summer.

Work-study—Employment, usually on campus, awarded to eligible students as part of a financial aid package through the U.S. government's Federal Work-Study Program. While international students are not eligible for work-study jobs under this program, most are legally eligible to accept part-time employment on campus, with permission from the international (foreign) student adviser.

ZIP codes—Mailing codes used by the U.S. Postal Service.

Map of the United States

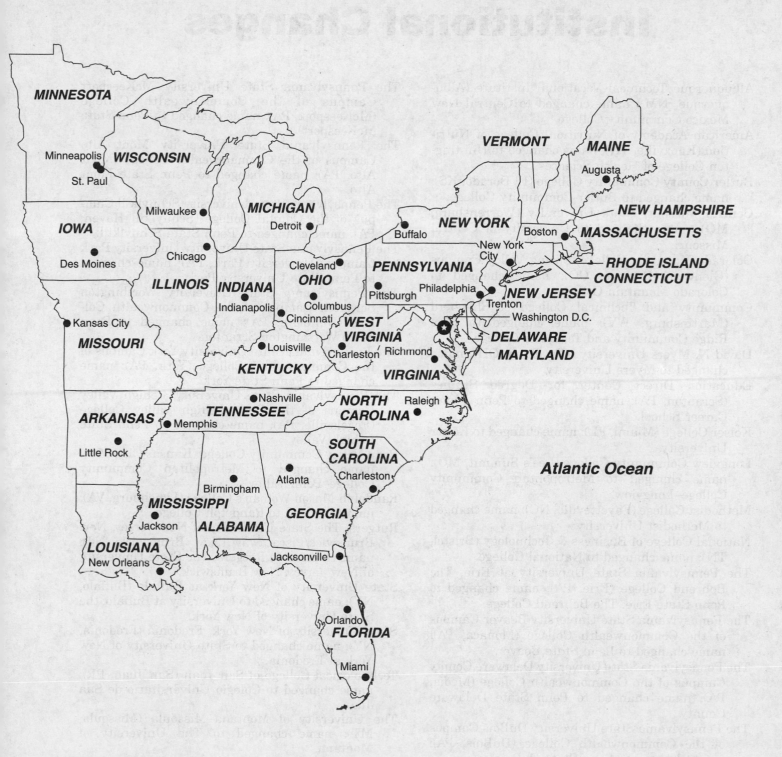

MINNESOTA

Minneapolis

St. Paul

WISCONSIN

Milwaukee

IOWA

Des Moines

Chicago

ILLINOIS

Kansas City

MISSOURI

MICHIGAN

Detroit

INDIANA

Indianapolis

Cleveland

OHIO

Columbus

Cincinnati

Louisville

KENTUCKY

WEST VIRGINIA

Charleston

Pittsburgh

Buffalo

PENNSYLVANIA

Philadelphia

VERMONT

MAINE

Augusta

NEW YORK

Boston

New York City

NEW HAMPSHIRE

MASSACHUSETTS

RHODE ISLAND

CONNECTICUT

NEW JERSEY

Trenton

Washington D.C.

DELAWARE

MARYLAND

Richmond

VIRGINIA

ARKANSAS

Little Rock

TENNESSEE

Nashville

Memphis

NORTH CAROLINA

Raleigh

SOUTH CAROLINA

Charleston

Atlantic Ocean

MISSISSIPPI

Jackson

Birmingham

ALABAMA

Atlanta

GEORGIA

LOUISIANA

New Orleans

Jacksonville

Orlando

FLORIDA

Miami

Institutional Changes

Albuquerque Technical Vocational Institute (Albuquerque, NM): name changed to Central New Mexico Community College.

American Academy of Nutrition, College of Nutrition (Knoxville, TN): name changed to Huntington College of Health Sciences.

Butler County Community College (El Dorado, KS): name changed to Butler Community College.

Central Missouri State University (Warrensburg, MO): name changed to University of Central Missouri.

Colorado Mountain College, Spring Valley Campus (Glenwood Springs, CO): name changed to Colorado Mountain College.

Community and Technical College of Shepherd (Martinsburg, WV): name changed to Blue Ridge Community and Technical College.

David N. Myers University (Cleveland, OH): name changed to Myers University.

Education Direct Center for Degree Studies (Scranton, PA): name changed to Penn Foster Career School.

Keiser College (Miami, FL): name changed to Keiser University.

Longview Community College (Lee's Summit, MO): name changed to Metropolitan Community College–Longview.

Methodist College (Fayetteville, NC): name changed to Methodist University.

National College of Business & Technology (Bristol, TN): name changed to National College.

The Pennsylvania State University at Erie, The Behrend College (Erie, PA): name changed to Penn State Erie, The Behrend College.

The Pennsylvania State University Beaver Campus of the Commonwealth College (Monaca, PA): name changed to Penn State Beaver.

The Pennsylvania State University Delaware County Campus of the Commonwealth College (Media, PA): name changed to Penn State Delaware County.

The Pennsylvania State University DuBois Campus of the Commonwealth College (DuBois, PA): name changed to Penn State DuBois.

The Pennsylvania State University Harrisburg Campus (Middletown, PA): name changed to Penn State Harrisburg.

The Pennsylvania State University Hazleton Campus of the Commonwealth College (Hazleton, PA): name changed to Penn State Hazleton.

The Pennsylvania State University McKeesport Campus of the Commonwealth College (McKeesport, PA): name changed to Penn State McKeesport.

The Pennsylvania State University Mont Alto Campus of the Commonwealth College (Mont Alto, PA): name changed to Penn State Mont Alto.

The Pennsylvania State University Schuylkill Campus of the Capital College (Schuylkill Haven, PA): name changed to Penn State Schuylkill.

The Pennsylvania State University University Park Campus (University Park, PA): name changed to Penn State University Park.

The Pennsylvania State University Worthington Scranton Campus of the Commonwealth College (Dunmore, PA): name changed to Penn State Worthington Scranton.

The Pennsylvania State University York Campus of the Commonwealth College (York, PA): name changed to Penn State York.

The Pennsylvania State University, Lehigh Valley Campus of the Berks-Lehigh Valley College (Fogelsville, PA): name changed to Penn State Lehigh Valley.

Penn Valley Community College (Kansas City, MO): name changed to Metropolitan Community College–Penn Valley.

Randolph-Macon Woman's College (Lynchburg, VA): name changed to Randolph College.

Rutgers, The State University of New Jersey, New Brunswick/Piscataway (New Brunswick, NJ): name changed to Rutgers, The State University of New Jersey, New Brunswick.

State University of New York at Buffalo (Buffalo, NY): name changed to University at Buffalo, the State University of New York.

State University of New York, Fredonia (Fredonia, NY): name changed to State University of New York at Fredonia.

Technological College of San Juan (San Juan, PR): name changed to Colegio Universitario de San Juan.

The University of Montana–Missoula (Missoula, MT): name changed to The University of Montana.

Western Business College (Portland, OR): name changed to Everest College.

Westwood College–Long Beach (Long Beach, CA): name changed to Westwood College–South Bay Campus.

William Rainey Harper College (Palatine, IL): name changed to Harper College.

Indexes

Colleges with ESL Programs

ALABAMA

Troy University
The University of Alabama
The University of Alabama in Huntsville
University of North Alabama

ARIZONA

Arizona State University
Cochise College, Sierra Vista
Glendale Community College
Mesa Community College

ARKANSAS

NorthWest Arkansas Community College
University of Arkansas

CALIFORNIA

California Polytechnic State University, San
  Luis Obispo
California State Polytechnic University, Pomona
California State University, Long Beach
California State University, Sacramento
Cañada College
Chaffey College
Chapman University
City College of San Francisco
College of the Canyons
College of the Desert
Cosumnes River College, Sacramento
Dominican University of California
East Los Angeles College
El Camino College
FIDM/The Fashion Institute of Design &
  Merchandising, Los Angeles Campus
Fresno Pacific University
Glendale Community College
Golden Gate University
Golden West College
Hope International University
Laney College
Las Positas College
Lincoln University
Long Beach City College
Los Angeles Harbor College
Los Angeles Mission College
Marymount College, Palos Verdes, California
Merritt College
Mills College
MiraCosta College
Modesto Junior College
Monterey Peninsula College
Northwestern Polytechnic University
Otis College of Art and Design
Palomar College
Sacramento City College
San Bernardino Valley College
San Diego State University
San Francisco Art Institute
San Francisco State University
Santa Barbara City College
Santa Monica College
Sierra College
University of La Verne
University of San Diego
University of San Francisco
West Valley College

COLORADO

Aims Community College
Colorado State University
Pikes Peak Community College
University of Colorado at Boulder
University of Denver

CONNECTICUT

Holy Apostles College and Seminary
Middlesex Community College
Mitchell College
Norwalk Community College
Sacred Heart University
University of Hartford

DELAWARE

Delaware Technical & Community College, Jack
  F. Owens Campus

DISTRICT OF COLUMBIA

American University
The Catholic University of America

FLORIDA

Barry University
Central Florida Community College
Eckerd College
Edison College
Embry-Riddle Aeronautical University
Florida Atlantic University
Florida Institute of Technology
Florida International University
Florida Keys Community College
Florida State University
Gulf Coast Community College
Miami Dade College
Nova Southeastern University
Saint Leo University
St. Petersburg College
St. Thomas University
Schiller International University
University of Central Florida
University of Miami
University of South Florida
University of West Florida
Webber International University

GEORGIA

Georgia Southern University
Georgia State University
Savannah College of Art and Design

GUAM

University of Guam

HAWAII

Hawaii Community College
Hawai'i Pacific University
Hawaii Tokai International College
Kapiolani Community College
Leeward Community College
Maui Community College
University of Hawaii at Manoa

IDAHO

Boise State University
Idaho State University
Lewis-Clark State College

ILLINOIS

City Colleges of Chicago, Harold Washington
  College
College of DuPage
College of Lake County
DePaul University
Harper College
Kankakee Community College
Lake Land College
Loyola University Chicago
North Central College
Roosevelt University
Sauk Valley Community College
School of the Art Institute of Chicago
Southern Illinois University Carbondale
University of Illinois at Springfield
Western Illinois University

INDIANA

Ball State University
Indiana University Bloomington
University of Indianapolis
University of Southern Indiana
Valparaiso University

IOWA

Coe College
Cornell College
Dordt College
Drake University
Iowa State University of Science and Technology
Iowa Western Community College
Kirkwood Community College
Morningside College
Scott Community College
Simpson College
Southwestern Community College
The University of Iowa
University of Northern Iowa
Upper Iowa University
Waldorf College

KANSAS

Coffeyville Community College
Emporia State University
Hesston College
Johnson County Community College
Kansas State University
Pittsburg State University
University of Kansas
Wichita State University

KENTUCKY

Brescia University
Western Kentucky University

LOUISIANA

McNeese State University
University of New Orleans

MAINE

Colby College
University of Southern Maine

MARYLAND

The Johns Hopkins University
University of Maryland, Baltimore County
University of Maryland, College Park
Washington Bible College

MASSACHUSETTS

Bay Path College
Berkshire Community College
Boston University
Bunker Hill Community College
Clark University
Dean College
Elms College
Greenfield Community College
Massachusetts Bay Community College
Massachusetts Institute of Technology
Mount Ida College
Suffolk University
Worcester Polytechnic Institute
Worcester State College

MICHIGAN

Adrian College
Central Michigan University
Davenport University, Midland
Henry Ford Community College
Lansing Community College
Michigan Technological University
Northern Michigan University
Oakland University
Spring Arbor University
University of Detroit Mercy

MINNESOTA
Academy College
Bemidji State University
Century College
Dakota County Technical College
Ridgewater College
Saint Mary's University of Minnesota
University of Minnesota, Crookston
University of Minnesota, Morris

MISSOURI
Columbia College
Drury University
Kansas City Art Institute
Northwest Missouri State University
Park University
Saint Charles Community College
Saint Louis University
Southeast Missouri State University
University of Central Missouri
University of Missouri–Columbia
University of Missouri–St. Louis
Washington University in St. Louis

MONTANA
Carroll College
Rocky Mountain College

NEBRASKA
Northeast Community College
University of Nebraska–Lincoln

NEVADA
University of Nevada, Reno

NEW HAMPSHIRE
Colby-Sawyer College
New England College
Southern New Hampshire University

NEW JERSEY
Caldwell College
Centenary College
County College of Morris
Fairleigh Dickinson University, College at Florham
Fairleigh Dickinson University, Metropolitan Campus
Kean University
Ramapo College of New Jersey
Raritan Valley Community College
Rider University
Seton Hall University
Sussex County Community College

NEW MEXICO
New Mexico Military Institute
New Mexico State University
Santa Fe Community College
University of New Mexico
Western New Mexico University

NEW YORK
Adelphi University
Berkeley College-New York City Campus
Berkeley College-Westchester Campus
Broome Community College
City College of the City University of New York
Columbia University, School of General Studies
Concordia College
Daemen College
Elmira College
Fordham University
Fulton-Montgomery Community College
Globe Institute of Technology
Hamilton College
Hofstra University
John Jay College of Criminal Justice of the City University of New York
The Juilliard School
Long Island University, C.W. Post Campus
Manhattanville College
Mercy College
Molloy College
Nassau Community College
New York University
Pace University
Parsons The New School for Design
Pratt Institute

Rochester Institute of Technology
School of Visual Arts
State University of New York at Oswego
State University of New York at Plattsburgh
State University of New York College at Geneseo
Stony Brook University, State University of New York
Suffolk County Community College
Syracuse University
University at Buffalo, the State University of New York
York College of the City University of New York

NORTH CAROLINA
Central Piedmont Community College
Isothermal Community College
Lees-McRae College
Richmond Community College
Southwestern Community College
The University of North Carolina at Pembroke
Warren Wilson College

NORTH DAKOTA
Lake Region State College
North Dakota State College of Science
North Dakota State University

OHIO
Ashland University
Baldwin-Wallace College
Capital University
Cleveland State University
Hiram College
Kent State University
Kent State University, East Liverpool Campus
Kent State University, Salem Campus
Muskingum College
Owens Community College, Toledo
Pontifical College Josephinum
University of Dayton
The University of Findlay

OKLAHOMA
Oklahoma Panhandle State University
Oklahoma State University
Oklahoma Wesleyan University
St. Gregory's University
University of Tulsa

OREGON
Chemeketa Community College
Clatsop Community College
Everest College
George Fox University
Lewis & Clark College
Linfield College
Marylhurst University
Oregon State University
Portland Community College
Portland State University
University of Oregon

PENNSYLVANIA
Alvernia College
Chatham University
Duquesne University
Harrisburg Area Community College
Indiana University of Pennsylvania
Juniata College
Marywood University
Northampton County Area Community College
St. Charles Borromeo Seminary, Overbrook
University of Pittsburgh
Waynesburg College
Widener University
Wilkes University
Wilson College

RHODE ISLAND
Johnson & Wales University
Roger Williams University

SOUTH CAROLINA
Spartanburg Methodist College
University of South Carolina
University of South Carolina Upstate

TENNESSEE
Austin Peay State University
Belmont University
Carson-Newman College
Maryville College
Pellissippi State Technical Community College
Tennessee Technological University
The University of Tennessee at Martin
Vanderbilt University

TEXAS
Baptist University of the Americas
Clarendon College
Del Mar College
Hill College of the Hill Junior College District
Houston Community College System
Howard College
Kilgore College
Kingwood College
Midland College
Midwestern State University
North Lake College
Northwest Vista College
St. Mary's University of San Antonio
Sam Houston State University
San Jacinto College Central Campus
San Jacinto College North Campus
San Jacinto College South Campus
Texas A&M University–Corpus Christi
Texas A&M University–Kingsville
Texas Christian University
Texas State University-San Marcos
University of Mary Hardin-Baylor
University of North Texas
The University of Texas at San Antonio
University of the Incarnate Word
Weatherford College
West Texas A&M University

UTAH
College of Eastern Utah
Southern Utah University
University of Utah
Utah State University
Utah Valley State College

VERMONT
Johnson State College
Saint Michael's College

VIRGINIA
Eastern Mennonite University
Liberty University
Longwood University
Old Dominion University
Shenandoah University
University of Virginia
Virginia Commonwealth University
Virginia Polytechnic Institute and State University

WASHINGTON
Centralia College
City University
Edmonds Community College
Gonzaga University
Grays Harbor College
Northwest University
Peninsula College
Pierce College
Renton Technical College
Seattle Central Community College
Skagit Valley College
South Puget Sound Community College
Spokane Community College
Spokane Falls Community College
University of Washington
Washington State University
Western Washington University
Whatcom Community College

WEST VIRGINIA
Marshall University
Mountain State University
University of Charleston

WISCONSIN
Beloit College
Fox Valley Technical College
Lakeland College
Marquette University

University of Wisconsin–Eau Claire
University of Wisconsin–La Crosse
University of Wisconsin–Stevens Point
University of Wisconsin–Superior

WYOMING
Central Wyoming College
Laramie County Community College
University of Wyoming
Western Wyoming Community College

Colleges with Articulation Agreements

ALABAMA
Calhoun Community College

ARIZONA
Cochise College, Sierra Vista
Glendale Community College
Mesa Community College

ARKANSAS
NorthWest Arkansas Community College
Southern Arkansas University Tech

CALIFORNIA
Cañada College
Cerro Coso Community College
Chabot College
Chaffey College
City College of San Francisco
College of the Canyons
College of the Desert
De Anza College
Diablo Valley College
East Los Angeles College
El Camino College
Foothill College
Fresno City College
Fullerton College
Glendale Community College
Golden West College
Las Positas College
Long Beach City College
Los Angeles Harbor College
Los Angeles Mission College
Los Angeles Pierce College
Los Angeles Southwest College
Marymount College, Palos Verdes, California
MiraCosta College
Modesto Junior College
Palomar College
Riverside Community College District
Sacramento City College
San Bernardino Valley College
San Diego City College
Santa Barbara City College
Santa Monica College
Santa Rosa Junior College
Sierra College
West Valley College

COLORADO
Aims Community College
Pikes Peak Community College

CONNECTICUT
Briarwood College
Middlesex Community College
Norwalk Community College

DELAWARE
Delaware Technical & Community College, Jack F. Owens Campus

FLORIDA
Central Florida Community College
Edison College
Florida Keys Community College
Gulf Coast Community College
Manatee Community College
Miami Dade College
St. Petersburg College

GEORGIA
Coastal Georgia Community College

Georgia Highlands College
South Georgia College

HAWAII
Hawaii Community College
Hawaii Tokai International College
Leeward Community College

ILLINOIS
City Colleges of Chicago, Harold Washington College
City Colleges of Chicago, Kennedy-King College
College of DuPage
College of Lake County
Joliet Junior College
Kankakee Community College
Lake Land College
Sauk Valley Community College

INDIANA
Ancilla College

IOWA
Clinton Community College
Iowa Western Community College
Kirkwood Community College
Scott Community College
Southwestern Community College

KANSAS
Coffeyville Community College
Colby Community College
Garden City Community College
Hesston College

KENTUCKY
Hopkinsville Community College

MARYLAND
College of Southern Maryland

MASSACHUSETTS
Berkshire Community College
Bunker Hill Community College
Dean College
Greenfield Community College
Massachusetts Bay Community College

MICHIGAN
Delta College
Glen Oaks Community College
Henry Ford Community College
Lansing Community College
Mott Community College

MINNESOTA
Central Lakes College
Century College
Dakota County Technical College
Itasca Community College
Minnesota State College–Southeast Technical
Rasmussen College Mankato
Ridgewater College

MISSOURI
East Central College
Patricia Stevens College
St. Louis Community College at Florissant Valley

NEBRASKA
Central Community College–Columbus Campus

Central Community College–Grand Island Campus
Central Community College–Hastings Campus
Northeast Community College

NEW JERSEY
County College of Morris
Raritan Valley Community College
Sussex County Community College

NEW MEXICO
New Mexico State University–Alamogordo
Santa Fe Community College

NEW YORK
American Academy of Dramatic Arts
Berkeley College-New York City Campus
Berkeley College-Westchester Campus
Bronx Community College of the City University of New York
Broome Community College
Fulton-Montgomery Community College
Genesee Community College
Hudson Valley Community College
Nassau Community College
Suffolk County Community College

NORTH CAROLINA
Alamance Community College
Central Piedmont Community College
Southwestern Community College

NORTH DAKOTA
Lake Region State College
Williston State College

OHIO
Bowling Green State University–Firelands College
James A. Rhodes State College
Owens Community College, Toledo
University of Cincinnati Raymond Walters College

OKLAHOMA
Connors State College
Redlands Community College

OREGON
Chemeketa Community College
Clatsop Community College
Pioneer Pacific College
Portland Community College

PENNSYLVANIA
Harrisburg Area Community College
Keystone College
Laurel Business Institute
Northampton County Area Community College

SOUTH CAROLINA
Spartanburg Methodist College

SOUTH DAKOTA
Mitchell Technical Institute

TENNESSEE
Chattanooga State Technical Community College
Motlow State Community College
Northeast State Technical Community College
Pellissippi State Technical Community College

TEXAS
Alvin Community College
Clarendon College
Del Mar College
Hill College of the Hill Junior College District
Houston Community College System
Howard College
Kilgore College
Kingwood College
Lamar State College–Port Arthur
Midland College
North Lake College
Northwest Vista College
San Jacinto College Central Campus
San Jacinto College North Campus
San Jacinto College South Campus
Texas State Technical College West Texas

Weatherford College

UTAH
College of Eastern Utah
LDS Business College

VIRGINIA
New River Community College
Wytheville Community College

WASHINGTON
Centralia College
Peninsula College
Pierce College
Renton Technical College
Seattle Central Community College
Skagit Valley College

South Puget Sound Community College
Spokane Community College
Spokane Falls Community College
Whatcom Community College

WISCONSIN
Fox Valley Technical College
University of Wisconsin–Manitowoc
University of Wisconsin–Marshfield/Wood County

WYOMING
Central Wyoming College
Eastern Wyoming College
Laramie County Community College
Northwest College
Sheridan College–Sheridan and Gillette
Western Wyoming Community College

Majors

Agriculture and Natural Resources Studies

Aims Comm Coll, CO	A
Alamance Comm Coll, NC	A
Alaska Pacific U, AK	B
Averett U, VA	B
Ball State U, IN	B
Berea Coll, KY	B
Berkshire Comm Coll, MA	A
Bronx Comm Coll of the City U of New York, NY	A
California Polytechnic State U, San Luis Obispo, CA	B
California State Polytechnic U, Pomona, CA	B
California State U, Sacramento, CA	B
Cameron U, OK	B
Capital U, OH	B
Carroll Coll, WI	B
Cazenovia Coll, NY	A
Centenary Coll, NJ	A,B
Central Christian Coll of Kansas, KS	A
Central Comm Coll–Columbus Campus, NE	A
Central Comm Coll–Hastings Campus, NE	A
Central Florida Comm Coll, FL	A
Central Michigan U, MI	B
Central Wyoming Coll, WY	A
Cerro Coso Comm Coll, CA	A
Chabot Coll, CA	A
Chattanooga State Tech Comm Coll, TN	A
Chemeketa Comm Coll, OR	A
City Coll of San Francisco, CA	A
Clarendon Coll, TX	A
Clark U, MA	B
Coastal Georgia Comm Coll, GA	A
Coffeyville Comm Coll, KS	A
Colby Comm Coll, KS	A
Coll of DuPage, IL	A
Coll of Lake County, IL	A
Coll of Saint Benedict, MN	B
Coll of Southern Maryland, MD	A
Coll of the Desert, CA	A
Coll of the Ozarks, MO	B
Colorado State U, CO	B
Cosumnes River Coll, Sacramento, CA	A
County Coll of Morris, NJ	A
Dakota County Tech Coll, MN	A
Dakota Wesleyan U, SD	A
Delaware Tech & Comm Coll, Jack F. Owens Campus, DE	A
Dordt Coll, IA	A,B
East Central Coll, MO	A
Eastern Mennonite U, VA	B
Eastern Wyoming Coll, WY	A
Edmonds Comm Coll, WA	A
El Camino Coll, CA	A
Ferris State U, MI	A
Foothill Coll, CA	A
Fort Lewis Coll, CO	B
Fox Valley Tech Coll, WI	A
Frostburg State U, MD	B
Fullerton Coll, CA	A
Fulton-Montgomery Comm Coll, NY	A
Garden City Comm Coll, KS	A
Georgia Coll & State U, GA	B
Georgia Highlands Coll, GA	A
Glendale Comm Coll, AZ	A
Golden West Coll, CA	A
Grand Valley State U, MI	B
Grays Harbor Coll, WA	A
Greenfield Comm Coll, MA	A
Green Mountain Coll, VT	B
Hardin-Simmons U, TX	B
Harper Coll, IL	A
Harrisburg Area Comm Coll, PA	A
Harvard U, MA	B
Hill Coll of the Hill Jr Coll District, TX	A
Howard Coll, TX	A
Huntington U, IN	B
Idaho State U, ID	A,B
Iowa State U of Science and Technology, IA	B
Iowa Western Comm Coll, IA	A
Itasca Comm Coll, MN	A
Johnson & Wales U, RI	A,B
Johnson State Coll, VT	B
Joliet Jr Coll, IL	A
Kansas State U, KS	B
Kent State U, OH	B
Kent State U, Geauga Campus, OH	A
Kent State U, Salem Campus, OH	A
Keystone Coll, PA	A
Kilgore Coll, TX	A
Kirkwood Comm Coll, IA	A
Lake Land Coll, IL	A
Lake Region State Coll, ND	A
Laney Coll, CA	A
Langston U, OK	B
Laramie County Comm Coll, WY	A
Lincoln Land Comm Coll, IL	A
Long Beach City Coll, CA	A
Los Angeles Pierce Coll, CA	A
Marlboro Coll, VT	B
Maui Comm Coll, HI	A
McNeese State U, LA	B
Merritt Coll, CA	A
Mesa Comm Coll, AZ	A
Miami Dade Coll, FL	A
Miami U, OH	B
Michigan Technological U, MI	B
Middle Tennessee State U, TN	B
MiraCosta Coll, CA	A
Mitchell Tech Inst, SD	A
Modesto Jr Coll, CA	A
Monterey Peninsula Coll, CA	A
Morehead State U, KY	A
Mountain State U, WV	B
Mount Ida Coll, MA	B
Muskingum Coll, OH	B
New Mexico Highlands U, NM	B
New Mexico State U, NM	B
North Carolina State U, NC	A,B
North Dakota State Coll of Science, ND	A
North Dakota State U, ND	B
Northeast Comm Coll, NE	A
Northern Arizona U, AZ	B
Northern Michigan U, MI	B
Northland Coll, WI	B
Northwest Coll, WY	A
Northwest Missouri State U, MO	B
Oklahoma Panhandle State U, OK	A
Oklahoma State U, OK	B
Orange Coast Coll, CA	A
Oregon State U, OR	B
Otterbein Coll, OH	B
Owens Comm Coll, Toledo, OH	A
Peninsula Coll, WA	A
Peru State Coll, NE	B
Pikes Peak Comm Coll, CO	A
Pittsburg State U, KS	B
Prescott Coll, AZ	A
Purdue U, IN	B
Redlands Comm Coll, OK	A
Ridgewater Coll, MN	A
Rochester Inst of Technology, NY	B
Rocky Mountain Coll, MT	B
Sacramento City Coll, CA	A
Saint John's U, MN	B
Saint Mary-of-the-Woods Coll, IN	A,B
Sam Houston State U, TX	B
San Diego State U, CA	B
Santa Barbara City Coll, CA	A
Santa Rosa Jr Coll, CA	A
Scott Comm Coll, IA	A
Sheridan Coll–Sheridan and Gillette, WY	A
Sierra Coll, CA	A
Skagit Valley Coll, WA	A
Slippery Rock U of Pennsylvania, PA	A
South Dakota State U, SD	B
Southeast Missouri State U, MO	B
Southern Arkansas U–Magnolia, AR	B
Southern Illinois U Carbondale, IL	A
South Georgia Coll, GA	A
South Puget Sound Comm Coll, WA	A
Southwestern Comm Coll, IA	A
Southwest Minnesota State U, MN	A,B
Spokane Comm Coll, WA	A
Tabor Coll, KS	B
Tennessee Technological U, TN	B
Texas A&M U at Galveston, TX	B
Texas A&M U–Kingsville, TX	B
Texas State Tech Coll Waco, TX	A
Texas State U-San Marcos, TX	B
Truman State U, MO	B
U of Arkansas, AR	B
U of Arkansas at Pine Bluff, AR	B
U of Central Missouri, MO	B
The U of Findlay, OH	A,B
U of Hawaii at Manoa, HI	B
U of La Verne, CA	B
U of Maine at Fort Kent, ME	B
U of Maryland, Coll Park, MD	B
U of Miami, FL	B
U of Michigan–Flint, MI	B
U of Minnesota, Crookston, MN	A,B
U of Missouri–Columbia, MO	B
U of Nebraska–Lincoln, NE	B
U of Nevada, Reno, NV	B
The U of North Carolina at Pembroke, NC	B
U of Rhode Island, RI	B
The U of Tennessee at Martin, TN	B
U of Washington, WA	B
U of Wisconsin–Stevens Point, WI	B
U of Wyoming, WY	B
Upper Iowa U, IA	B
Utah State U, UT	A,B
Vermont Tech Coll, VT	A
Virginia Polytechnic Inst and State U, VA	B
Washington State U, WA	B
Washington U in St. Louis, MO	B
Wayne State Coll, NE	B
Western Kentucky U, KY	A
Western New Mexico U, NM	B
Western Wyoming Comm Coll, WY	A
West Texas A&M U, TX	B
Wilmington Coll, OH	B
Wilson Coll, PA	B
Winona State U, MN	A,B
Yavapai Coll, AZ	A

Architecture and Related Programs

Arizona State U, AZ	B
Art Center Coll of Design, CA	B
Ball State U, IN	B
Barnard Coll, NY	B
Bennington Coll, VT	B
California Coll of the Arts, CA	B
California Polytechnic State U, San Luis Obispo, CA	B
California State Polytechnic U, Pomona, CA	B
The Catholic U of America, DC	B
Central Christian Coll of Kansas, KS	A
Central Michigan U, MI	B
Chatham U, PA	B
City Coll of San Francisco, CA	A
City Coll of the City U of New York, NY	B
Clarendon Coll, TX	A
Coe Coll, IA	B
Coll of the Atlantic, ME	B
Colorado State U, CO	B
Columbia U, School of General Studies, NY	B
Connecticut Coll, CT	B
Cooper Union for the Advancement of Science and Art, NY	B
Cornell U, IA	B
Cosumnes River Coll, Sacramento, CA	A
DePaul U, IL	B
Drury U, MO	B
East Carolina U, NC	B
Florida Atlantic U, FL	B
Florida International U, FL	B
Foothill Coll, CA	A
Frostburg State U, MD	B
Hampshire Coll, MA	B
Harper Coll, IL	A
Harrisburg Area Comm Coll, PA	A
Harvard U, MA	B
Hope Coll, MI	B
Illinois Inst of Technology, IL	B
Indiana U Bloomington, IN	B
Indiana U of Pennsylvania, PA	B
Iowa State U of Science and Technology, IA	B
Judson Coll, IL	B
Kansas State U, KS	B
Kent State U, OH	B
Keystone Coll, PA	A
Kirkwood Comm Coll, IA	A
Lansing Comm Coll, MI	A
Los Angeles Pierce Coll, CA	A
Massachusetts Coll of Art, MA	B
Massachusetts Inst of Technology, MA	B
Merritt Coll, CA	A
Miami U, OH	B
Minnesota State U Mankato, MN	B
Modesto Jr Coll, CA	A
New Mexico State U, NM	B
New York U, NY	B
North Carolina State U, NC	B
North Dakota State U, ND	B
Northeastern U, MA	B
Northwest Missouri State U, MO	B
Oklahoma State U, OK	B
Otis Coll of Art and Design, CA	B
Parsons The New School for Design, NY	B
Philadelphia U, PA	B
Plymouth State U, NH	B
Portland Comm Coll, OR	A
Portland State U, OR	B
Pratt Inst, NY	B
Prescott Coll, AZ	B
Purdue U, IN	B

A=Associate; B=Bachelor's Degree

College	Degree
Rensselaer Polytechnic Inst, NY	B
Roger Williams U, RI	B
Saint Louis U, MO	B
Santa Rosa Jr Coll, CA	A
Sauk Valley Comm Coll, IL	A
Savannah Coll of Art and Design, GA	B
School of the Art Inst of Chicago, IL	B
Southern California Inst of Architecture, CA	B
Southern Illinois U Carbondale, IL	B
Syracuse U, NY	B
Texas State U-San Marcos, TX	B
U at Buffalo, the State U of New York, NY	B
U of Arkansas, AR	B
U of Central Missouri, MO	B
U of Cincinnati, OH	B
U of Colorado at Boulder, CO	B
U of Detroit Mercy, MI	B
U of Hawaii at Manoa, HI	B
U of Kansas, KS	B
U of Maryland, Coll Park, MD	B
U of Miami, FL	B
U of Missouri–Columbia, MO	B
U of Nebraska–Lincoln, NE	B
U of New Mexico, NM	B
U of North Texas, TX	B
U of Oregon, OR	B
U of Rhode Island, RI	B
U of San Francisco, CA	B
The U of Texas at San Antonio, TX	B
U of Utah, UT	B
U of Virginia, VA	B
U of Washington, WA	B
Utah State U, UT	B
Virginia Polytechnic Inst and State U, VA	B
Washington State U, WA	B
Washington U in St. Louis, MO	B
Wentworth Inst of Technology, MA	B
West Valley Coll, CA	A
Woodbury U, CA	B

Area, Ethnic, and Cultural Studies

College	Degree
Adelphi U, NY	B
Albion Coll, MI	B
American U, DC	B
Antioch Coll, OH	B
Arizona State U, AZ	B
Ashland U, OH	B
Assumption Coll, MA	B
Ball State U, IN	B
Baptist U of the Americas, TX	A
Bard Coll, NY	B
Barnard Coll, NY	B
Bates Coll, ME	B
Beloit Coll, WI	B
Bemidji State U, MN	B
Bennington Coll, VT	B
Black Hills State U, SD	B
Boise State U, ID	B
Boston U, MA	B
Bowdoin Coll, ME	B
Bronx Comm Coll of the City U of New York, NY	A
Bryn Mawr Coll, PA	B
Bucknell U, PA	B
California State Polytechnic U, Pomona, CA	B
California State U, Long Beach, CA	B
California State U, Sacramento, CA	B
Calvin Coll, MI	B
Carleton Coll, MN	B
Central Michigan U, MI	B
Central Wyoming Coll, WY	A
City Coll of San Francisco, CA	A
City Coll of the City U of New York, NY	B
Claflin U, SC	B
Clark U, MA	B
Coe Coll, IA	B
Colby Coll, ME	B
Coll of the Holy Cross, MA	B
The Colorado Coll, CO	B
Colorado State U, CO	B
Columbia U, School of General Studies, NY	B
Concordia Coll, MN	B
Connecticut Coll, CT	B
Cornell Coll, IA	B
Cosumnes River Coll, Sacramento, CA	A
Cumberland U, TN	B
De Anza Coll, CA	A
Denison U, OH	B
DePaul U, IL	B
DePauw U, IN	B
Drew U, NJ	B
East Los Angeles Coll, CA	A
Eckerd Coll, FL	B
Edinboro U of Pennsylvania, PA	B
El Camino Coll, CA	A
Elmira Coll, NY	B
Emmanuel Coll, MA	B
Emory U, GA	B
The Evergreen State Coll, WA	B
Fairfield U, CT	B
Flagler Coll, FL	B
Florida International U, FL	B
Florida State U, FL	B
Foothill Coll, CA	A
Fordham U, NY	B
Fort Lewis Coll, CO	B
Fresno City Coll, CA	A
Fullerton Coll, CA	A
Furman U, SC	B
Georgetown Coll, KY	B
Georgia State U, GA	B
Gettysburg Coll, PA	B
Gonzaga U, WA	B
Grand Valley State U, MI	B
Greenfield Comm Coll, MA	A
Gustavus Adolphus Coll, MN	B
Hamilton Coll, NY	B
Hampshire Coll, MA	B
Harding U, AR	B
Harvard U, MA	B
Haverford Coll, PA	B
Hawai'i Pacific U, HI	B
Hillsdale Coll, MI	B
Hofstra U, NY	B
Hope Coll, MI	B
Howard Payne U, TX	B
Huntingdon Coll, AL	B
Idaho State U, ID	B
Illinois Wesleyan U, IL	B
Indiana U Bloomington, IN	B
Indiana Wesleyan U, IN	A,B
Iowa State U of Science and Technology, IA	B
Itasca Comm Coll, MN	A
John Carroll U, OH	B
The Johns Hopkins U, MD	B
Kennesaw State U, GA	B
Kent State U, OH	B
Kenyon Coll, OH	B
Knox Coll, IL	B
Lafayette Coll, PA	B
Laney Coll, CA	A
Lawrence U, WI	B
Lewis & Clark Coll, OR	B
Lipscomb U, TN	B
Long Island U, C.W. Post Campus, NY	B
Los Angeles Southwest Coll, CA	A
Luther Coll, IA	B
Lycoming Coll, PA	B
Manatee Comm Coll, FL	A
Manhattanville Coll, NY	B
Marlboro Coll, VT	B
Marquette U, WI	B
Mary Baldwin Coll, VA	B
Merritt Coll, CA	A
Miami Dade Coll, FL	A
Miami U, OH	B
Middlebury Coll, VT	B
Millersville U of Pennsylvania, PA	B
Millsaps Coll, MS	B
Mills Coll, CA	B
Minnesota State U Mankato, MN	B
Minnesota State U Moorhead, MN	B
MiraCosta Coll, CA	A
Monterey Peninsula Coll, CA	A
Mount Holyoke Coll, MA	B
Mount Ida Coll, MA	B
Muskingum Coll, OH	B
Nassau Comm Coll, NY	A
New Coll of California, CA	B
New York U, NY	B
North Central Coll, IL	B
Northeastern U, MA	B
Northern Arizona U, AZ	B
Northland Coll, WI	B
Northwest Coll, WY	A
Northwestern U, IL	B
Nova Southeastern U, FL	B
Oakland U, MI	B
Ohio Wesleyan U, OH	B
Oklahoma State U, OK	B
Old Dominion U, VA	B
Orange Coast Coll, CA	A
Oregon State U, OR	B
Pitzer Coll, CA	B
Pontifical Coll Josephinum, OH	B
Portland State U, OR	B
Prescott Coll, AZ	B
Purdue U, IN	B
Ramapo Coll of New Jersey, NJ	B
Randolph Coll, VA	B
Reed Coll, OR	B
Rhodes Coll, TN	B
Rider U, NJ	B
Roger Williams U, RI	B
Roosevelt U, IL	B
Sacramento City Coll, CA	A
Sacred Heart U, CT	A
Saint Francis U, PA	B
Saint Louis U, MO	B
Saint Mary-of-the-Woods Coll, IN	B
Saint Mary's Coll of California, CA	B
Saint Michael's Coll, VT	B
St. Olaf Coll, MN	B
San Diego City Coll, CA	A
San Diego State U, CA	B
San Francisco State U, CA	B
Santa Barbara City Coll, CA	A
Santa Fe Comm Coll, NM	A
Santa Monica Coll, CA	A
Santa Rosa Jr Coll, CA	A
Sarah Lawrence Coll, NY	B
Savannah State U, GA	B
Scripps Coll, CA	B
Seattle U, WA	B
Seton Hall U, NJ	B
Shenandoah U, VA	B
Siena Coll, NY	B
Simmons Coll, MA	B
Skagit Valley Coll, WA	A
Skidmore Coll, NY	B
Southeast Missouri State U, MO	B
Stanford U, CA	B
State U of New York at Oswego, NY	B
State U of New York at Plattsburgh, NY	B
State U of New York Coll at Geneseo, NY	B
State U of New York Coll at Oneonta, NY	B
Stony Brook U, State U of New York, NY	B
Suffolk U, MA	B
Swarthmore Coll, PA	B
Syracuse U, NY	B
Texas Christian U, TX	B
Texas State U-San Marcos, TX	B
Trinity Coll, CT	B
Trinity U, TX	B
Union Coll, NY	B
U at Buffalo, the State U of New York, NY	B
The U of Alabama, AL	B
U of Arkansas, AR	B
U of California, Santa Cruz, CA	B
U of Cincinnati, OH	B
U of Colorado at Boulder, CO	B
U of Dayton, OH	B
U of Denver, CO	B
U of Guam, GU	B
U of Hawaii at Manoa, HI	B
The U of Iowa, IA	B
U of Kansas, KS	B
U of Maryland, Baltimore County, MD	B
U of Maryland, Coll Park, MD	B
U of Mary Washington, VA	B
U of Miami, FL	B
U of Michigan–Flint, MI	B
U of Minnesota, Morris, MN	B
U of Missouri–Columbia, MO	B
U of Nebraska–Lincoln, NE	B
U of New Mexico, NM	B
The U of North Carolina at Pembroke, NC	B
U of Northern Iowa, IA	B
U of Oregon, OR	B
U of Pittsburgh, PA	B
U of Puget Sound, WA	B
U of Rhode Island, RI	B
U of Rochester, NY	B
U of San Diego, CA	B
U of San Francisco, CA	B
U of South Carolina, SC	B
U of Southern Maine, ME	B
U of South Florida, FL	B
The U of Texas at San Antonio, TX	B
U of the Incarnate Word, TX	B
U of Utah, UT	B
U of Virginia, VA	B
U of Washington, WA	B
U of Wisconsin–Eau Claire, WI	B
U of Wyoming, WY	B
Utah State U, UT	B
Valparaiso U, IN	B
Vanderbilt U, TN	B
Virginia Commonwealth U, VA	B
Warren Wilson Coll, NC	B
Washington Coll, MD	B
Washington State U, WA	B
Washington U in St. Louis, MO	B
Wells Coll, NY	B
Wesleyan U, CT	B
Western Illinois U, IL	B
Western New Mexico U, NM	B
Western Washington U, WA	B
Williams Coll, MA	B
York Coll of the City U of New York, NY	B

Art and Art-Related Fields

College	Degree
Academy Coll, MN	A
Adelphi U, NY	B
Adrian Coll, MI	A,B
Agnes Scott Coll, GA	B
Aims Comm Coll, CO	A
Alamance Comm Coll, NC	A
Albertus Magnus Coll, CT	B
Albion Coll, MI	B
Alderson-Broaddus Coll, WV	B
Allegheny Coll, PA	B
Alverno Coll, WI	B
Alvin Comm Coll, TX	A
American InterContinental U, CA	A,B
American InterContinental U, Atlanta, GA	A,B
American U, DC	B
Ancilla Coll, IN	A
Anna Maria Coll, MA	B
Antioch Coll, OH	B
Aquinas Coll, MI	B
Arcadia U, PA	B
Arizona State U, AZ	B
Art Center Coll of Design, CA	B
The Art Inst of Boston at Lesley U, MA	B
The Art Inst of Colorado, CO	A,B
The Art Inst of Houston, TX	B
The Art Inst of Philadelphia, PA	A,B
Ashford U, IA	B
Ashland U, OH	A,B
Assumption Coll, MA	B
Austin Peay State U, TN	B
Averett U, VA	B
Baker Coll of Flint, MI	A,B
Baker U, KS	B
Baldwin-Wallace Coll, OH	B
Ball State U, IN	B
Bard Coll, NY	B
Barnard Coll, NY	B

A=Associate; B=Bachelor's Degree

College	Code
Bates Coll, ME	B
Belmont U, TN	B
Beloit Coll, WI	B
Bemidji State U, MN	B
Benedict Coll, SC	B
Bennington Coll, VT	B
Berea Coll, KY	B
Berkshire Comm Coll, MA	A
Bethany Coll, KS	B
Bethel Coll, KS	B
Bethel U, MN	B
Black Hills State U, SD	B
Boise State U, ID	B
Boston U, MA	B
Bowdoin Coll, ME	B
Bowling Green State U–Firelands Coll, OH	B
Brescia U, KY	B
Bronx Comm Coll of the City U of New York, NY	A
Bryn Mawr Coll, PA	B
Bucknell U, PA	B
Bunker Hill Comm Coll, MA	A
Butler U, IN	B
Caldwell Coll, NJ	B
Calhoun Comm Coll, AL	A
California Coll of the Arts, CA	B
California Inst of the Arts, CA	B
California Lutheran U, CA	B
California Polytechnic State U, San Luis Obispo, CA	B
California State Polytechnic U, Pomona, CA	B
California State U, Long Beach, CA	B
California State U, Sacramento, CA	B
California State U, Stanislaus, CA	B
Calvin Coll, MI	B
Cameron U, OK	B
Cañada Coll, CA	A
Capital U, OH	B
Cardinal Stritch U, WI	B
Carleton Coll, MN	B
Carlow U, PA	B
Carroll Coll, MT	B
Carroll Coll, WI	A
Carson-Newman Coll, TN	B
Carthage Coll, WI	B
The Catholic U of America, DC	B
Cazenovia Coll, NY	B
Centenary Coll, NJ	B
Central Christian Coll of Kansas, KS	A
Central Comm Coll–Columbus Campus, NE	A
Central Comm Coll–Hastings Campus, NE	A
Centralia Coll, WA	A
Central Michigan U, MI	B
Central Piedmont Comm Coll, NC	A
Central Wyoming Coll, WY	A
Centre Coll, KY	B
Century Coll, MN	A
Cerro Coso Comm Coll, CA	A
Chabot Coll, CA	A
Chaffey Coll, CA	A
Chapman U, CA	B
Chatham U, PA	B
Chattanooga State Tech Comm Coll, TN	A
City Coll of San Francisco, CA	A
City Coll of the City U of New York, NY	B
City Colls of Chicago, Harold Washington Coll, IL	A
City Colls of Chicago, Kennedy-King Coll, IL	A
Claflin U, SC	B
Clarendon Coll, TX	A
Clarion U of Pennsylvania, PA	B
Clarke Coll, IA	B
Clark U, MA	B
Cleveland State U, OH	B
Coastal Carolina U, SC	B
Coastal Georgia Comm Coll, GA	A
Cochise Coll, Sierra Vista, AZ	A
Coe Coll, IA	B
Coffeyville Comm Coll, KS	A
Colby Coll, ME	B
Colby Comm Coll, KS	A

College	Code
Colby-Sawyer Coll, NH	B
Coll of DuPage, IL	A
Coll of Lake County, IL	A
Coll of Saint Benedict, MN	B
Coll of St. Catherine, MN	B
Coll of Southern Maryland, MD	A
Coll of the Atlantic, ME	B
Coll of the Canyons, CA	A
Coll of the Desert, CA	A
Coll of the Holy Cross, MA	B
Coll of the Ozarks, MO	B
The Colorado Coll, CO	B
Colorado State U, CO	B
Columbia Coll, MO	B
Columbia Coll Chicago, IL	B
Columbia U, School of General Studies, NY	B
Columbus Coll of Art & Design, OH	B
Concordia Coll, MN	B
Concordia Coll, NY	B
Concordia U, IL	B
Connecticut Coll, CT	B
Cooper Union for the Advancement of Science and Art, NY	B
Corcoran Coll of Art and Design, DC	A,B
Cornell Coll, IA	B
Cosumnes River Coll, Sacramento, CA	A
County Coll of Morris, NJ	A
Culver-Stockton Coll, MO	B
Cumberland U, TN	B
Daemen Coll, NY	B
Dakota County Tech Coll, MN	A
Dakota Wesleyan U, SD	B
Dana Coll, NE	B
Davidson Coll, NC	B
De Anza Coll, CA	A
Defiance Coll, OH	A,B
Del Mar Coll, TX	A
Delta Coll, MI	A
Denison U, OH	B
DePaul U, IL	B
DePauw U, IN	B
DigiPen Inst of Technology, WA	A,B
Dominican U of California, CA	B
Dordt Coll, IA	B
Drake U, IA	B
Drew U, NJ	B
Drury U, MO	B
Duquesne U, PA	B
East Carolina U, NC	B
East Central Coll, MO	A
Eastern Connecticut State U, CT	B
Eastern Mennonite U, VA	B
Eastern U, PA	B
Eastern Wyoming Coll, WY	A
East Los Angeles Coll, CA	A
East Tennessee State U, TN	B
Eckerd Coll, FL	B
Edgewood Coll, WI	B
Edinboro U of Pennsylvania, PA	B
Edison Coll, FL	A
El Camino Coll, CA	A
Elizabethtown Coll, PA	B
Elmira Coll, NY	B
Elms Coll, MA	B
Elon U, NC	B
Emerson Coll, MA	B
Emmanuel Coll, MA	B
Emory U, GA	B
Emporia State U, KS	B
The Evergreen State Coll, WA	B
Fairfield U, CT	B
Fairleigh Dickinson U, Coll at Florham, NJ	B
Fairleigh Dickinson U, Metropolitan Campus, NJ	B
Fashion Careers Coll, CA	A
Ferris State U, MI	A
FIDM/The Fashion Inst of Design & Merchandising, Los Angeles Campus, CA	A
Flagler Coll, FL	B
Florida Atlantic U, FL	B
Florida International U, FL	B
Florida Keys Comm Coll, FL	A
Florida State U, FL	B
Foothill Coll, CA	A
Fordham U, NY	B

College	Code
Fort Lewis Coll, CO	B
Fox Valley Tech Coll, WI	A
Fresno City Coll, CA	A
Frostburg State U, MD	B
Fullerton Coll, CA	A
Fulton-Montgomery Comm Coll, NY	A
Furman U, SC	B
Gannon U, PA	B
Garden City Comm Coll, KS	A
Gardner-Webb U, NC	B
Genesee Comm Coll, NY	A
George Fox U, OR	B
Georgetown Coll, KY	D
Georgia Coll & State U, GA	B
Georgia Highlands Coll, GA	A
Georgia Southern U, GA	B
Georgia State U, GA	B
Gettysburg Coll, PA	B
Glendale Comm Coll, AZ	A
Glendale Comm Coll, CA	A
Golden West Coll, CA	A
Gonzaga U, WA	B
Goshen Coll, IN	B
Grambling State U, LA	B
Grand Valley State U, MI	B
Grand View Coll, IA	B
Greenfield Comm Coll, MA	A
Green Mountain Coll, VT	B
Greenville Coll, IL	B
Grinnell Coll, IA	B
Gulf Coast Comm Coll, FL	A
Gustavus Adolphus Coll, MN	B
Hamilton Coll, NY	B
Hampden-Sydney Coll, VA	B
Hampshire Coll, MA	B
Harding U, AR	B
Hardin-Simmons U, TX	B
Harper Coll, IL	A
Harrington Coll of Design, IL	A,B
Harrisburg Area Comm Coll, PA	A
Hartwick Coll, NY	B
Harvard U, MA	B
Haverford Coll, PA	B
Henry Ford Comm Coll, MI	A
Hill Coll of the Hill Jr Coll District, TX	A
Hillsdale Coll, MI	B
Hiram Coll, OH	B
Hofstra U, NY	B
Holy Family U, PA	B
Hope Coll, MI	B
Houston Comm Coll System, TX	A
Howard Coll, TX	A
Howard Payne U, TX	B
Hudson Valley Comm Coll, NY	A
Huntingdon Coll, AL	B
Huntington U, IN	B
Idaho State U, ID	A,B
Illinois Coll, IL	B
The Illinois Inst of Art–Chicago, IL	A,B
Illinois Inst of Technology, IL	B
Illinois Wesleyan U, IL	B
Indiana U Bloomington, IN	A,B
Indiana U of Pennsylvania, PA	B
Indiana U South Bend, IN	B
Indiana U Southeast, IN	B
Indiana Wesleyan U, IN	A,B
Iowa State U of Science and Technology, IA	B
Iowa Western Comm Coll, IA	A
Isothermal Comm Coll, NC	A
Jacksonville State U, AL	B
Jacksonville U, FL	B
James Madison U, VA	B
John Carroll U, OH	B
The Johns Hopkins U, MD	B
Johnson County Comm Coll, KS	A
Johnson State Coll, VT	B
Joliet Jr Coll, IL	A
Judson Coll, IL	B
Juniata Coll, PA	B
Kankakee Comm Coll, IL	A
Kansas City Art Inst, MO	B
Kansas State U, KS	B
Kansas Wesleyan U, KS	B
Kean U, NJ	B
Kennesaw State U, GA	B
Kent State U, OH	B

College	Code
Kent State U, Stark Campus, OH	A
Kenyon Coll, OH	B
Keystone Coll, PA	A,B
Kilgore Coll, TX	A
Kingwood Coll, TX	A
Kirkwood Comm Coll, IA	A
Knox Coll, IL	B
Lafayette Coll, PA	B
Lakeland Coll, WI	B
Lander U, SC	B
Laney Coll, CA	A
Langston U, OK	B
Lansing Comm Coll, MI	A
Laramie County Comm Coll, WY	A
Las Positas Coll, CA	A
Lawrence U, WI	B
LDS Business Coll, UT	A
Leeward Comm Coll, HI	A
LeMoyne-Owen Coll, TN	B
Lewis & Clark Coll, OR	B
Limestone Coll, SC	B
Lincoln Land Comm Coll, IL	A
Linfield Coll, OR	B
Lipscomb U, TN	B
Long Beach City Coll, CA	A
Long Island U, C.W. Post Campus, NY	B
Longwood U, VA	B
Los Angeles Pierce Coll, CA	A
Luther Coll, IA	B
Lycoming Coll, PA	B
Lynchburg Coll, VA	B
Lyndon State Coll, VT	B
Maine Coll of Art, ME	B
Manatee Comm Coll, FL	A
Manchester Coll, IN	A,B
Manhattanville Coll, NY	B
Marian Coll of Fond du Lac, WI	B
Marlboro Coll, VT	B
Marshall U, WV	B
Mary Baldwin Coll, VA	B
Marylhurst U, OR	B
Marymount Manhattan Coll, NY	B
Maryville Coll, TN	B
Maryville U of Saint Louis, MO	B
Marywood U, PA	B
Massachusetts Coll of Art, MA	B
Maui Comm Coll, HI	A
McDaniel Coll, MD	B
McMurry U, TX	B
McNeese State U, LA	B
Mercy Coll, NY	A,B
Mesa Comm Coll, AZ	A
Mesa State Coll, CO	A,B
Miami Dade Coll, FL	A
Miami U, OH	B
Middlebury Coll, VT	B
Middlesex Comm Coll, CT	A
Middle Tennessee State U, TN	B
Midland Coll, TX	A
Midwestern State U, TX	B
Millersville U of Pennsylvania, PA	B
Milligan Coll, TN	B
Millsaps Coll, MS	B
Mills Coll, CA	B
Minnesota State U Mankato, MN	B
Minnesota State U Moorhead, MN	B
Minot State U, ND	B
MiraCosta Coll, CA	A
Mississippi U for Women, MS	B
Mitchell Coll, CT	A
Modesto Jr Coll, CA	A
Molloy Coll, NY	B
Monmouth U, NJ	B
Montclair State U, NJ	B
Monterey Peninsula Coll, CA	A
Moore Coll of Art & Design, PA	B
Moravian Coll, PA	B
Morehead State U, KY	B
Morningside Coll, IA	B
Mount Holyoke Coll, MA	B
Mount Ida Coll, MA	A,B
Mount Mercy Coll, IA	B
Muskingum Coll, OH	B
Nassau Comm Coll, NY	A
Nebraska Wesleyan U, NE	B
New Coll of Florida, FL	B
New England Coll, NH	B

New England Inst of
  Technology, RI A
New Mexico Highlands U, NM B
New Mexico Military Inst, NM A
New Mexico State U, NM B
New Mexico State
  U–Alamogordo, NM A
New York School of Interior
  Design, NY A,B
New York U, NY B
Northampton County Area
  Comm Coll, PA A
North Carolina State U, NC B
North Central Coll, IL B
North Dakota State U, ND B
Northeast Comm Coll, NE A
Northeastern U, MA B
Northern Arizona U, AZ B
Northern Kentucky U, KY B
Northern Michigan U, MI A,B
Northern State U, SD B
Northland Coll, WI B
Northwest Coll, WY A
Northwestern State U of
  Louisiana, LA B
Northwestern U, IL B
Northwest Missouri State U,
  MO B
Norwalk Comm Coll, CT A
Notre Dame Coll, OH B
Notre Dame de Namur U, CA B
Oakland U, MI B
Ohio Wesleyan U, OH B
Oklahoma State U, OK B
Old Dominion U, VA B
Orange Coast Coll, CA A
Oregon State U, OR B
Otis Coll of Art and Design, CA B
Ottawa U, KS B
Otterbein Coll, OH B
Owens Comm Coll, Toledo, OH B
Pace U, NY A
Pacific Northwest Coll of Art,
  OR B
Paier Coll of Art, Inc., CT A
Palomar Coll, CA A
Park U, MO B
Parsons The New School for
  Design, NY A,B
Patricia Stevens Coll, MO A
Peace Coll, NC B
Pellissippi State Tech Comm
  Coll, TN A
Pennsylvania Coll of Art &
  Design, PA B
Peru State Coll, NE B
Philadelphia U, PA B
Pikes Peak Comm Coll, CO A
Pittsburg State U, KS B
Pitzer Coll, CA B
Platt Coll San Diego, CA B
Plymouth State U, NH B
Portland Comm Coll, OR A
Portland State U, OR B
Pratt Inst, NY A,B
Prescott Coll, AZ B
Principia Coll, IL B
Purdue U, IN B
Quincy U, IL B
Radford U, VA B
Ramapo Coll of New Jersey, NJ B
Randolph Coll, VA B
Randolph-Macon Coll, VA B
Raritan Valley Comm Coll, NJ A
Redlands Comm Coll, OK B
Reed Coll, OR B
Rhodes Coll, TN B
Rider U, NJ B
Ridgewater Coll, MN A
Rochester Inst of Technology,
  NY A,B
Rocky Mountain Coll, MT B
Roger Williams U, RI B
Roosevelt U, IL B
Rose State Coll, OK A
Sacramento City Coll, CA A
Sacred Heart U, CT A,B
Sage Coll of Albany, NY A,B
St. Ambrose U, IA B
Saint Anselm Coll, NH B
Saint Charles Comm Coll, MO A
St. Gregory's U, OK A,B

Saint John's U, MN B
Saint Joseph's Coll, IN B
St. Louis Comm Coll at
  Florissant Valley, MO A
Saint Louis U, MO B
Saint Mary-of-the-Woods Coll,
  IN B
Saint Mary's Coll, IN B
Saint Mary's Coll of California,
  CA B
St. Mary's Coll of Maryland,
  MD B
Saint Mary's U of Minnesota,
  MN B
Saint Michael's Coll, VT B
St. Olaf Coll, MN B
St. Petersburg Coll, FL A
Saint Vincent Coll, PA B
Sam Houston State U, TX B
San Bernardino Valley Coll, CA A
San Diego City Coll, CA A
San Diego State U, CA B
San Francisco Art Inst, CA B
San Francisco State U, CA B
San Jacinto Coll Central
  Campus, TX A
San Jacinto Coll North
  Campus, TX A
San Jacinto Coll South
  Campus, TX A
Santa Barbara City Coll, CA A
Santa Fe Comm Coll, NM A
Santa Monica Coll, CA A
Santa Rosa Jr Coll, CA A
Sarah Lawrence Coll, NY B
Sauk Valley Comm Coll, IL A
Savannah Coll of Art and
  Design, GA B
Savannah State U, GA B
School of the Art Inst of
  Chicago, IL B
School of the Museum of Fine
  Arts, Boston, MA B
School of Visual Arts, NY B
Scott Comm Coll, IA A
Scripps Coll, CA B
Seattle Central Comm Coll, WA A
Seattle U, WA B
Seton Hall U, NJ B
Shenandoah U, VA B
Shepherd U, WV B
Sheridan Coll–Sheridan and
  Gillette, WY A
Shorter Coll, GA B
Siena Coll, NY B
Sierra Coll, CA A
Simmons Coll, MA B
Simpson Coll, IA B
Skagit Valley Coll, WA A
Skidmore Coll, NY B
Slippery Rock U of
  Pennsylvania, PA B
South Dakota State U, SD B
Southeast Missouri State U,
  MO B
Southern Arkansas
  U–Magnolia, AR B
Southern Illinois U Carbondale,
  IL B
Southern Illinois U
  Edwardsville, IL B
Southern Oregon U, OR B
Southern Utah U, UT A
Southwestern Comm Coll, NC A
Southwest Minnesota State U,
  MN B
Spokane Falls Comm Coll, WA A
Spring Arbor U, MI B
Stanford U, CA B
State U of New York at
  Oswego, NY B
State U of New York at
  Plattsburgh, NY B
State U of New York Coll at
  Geneseo, NY B
State U of New York Coll at
  Oneonta, NY B
Stony Brook U, State U of New
  York, NY B
Suffolk County Comm Coll, NY A
Suffolk U, MA A,B
Susquehanna U, PA B

Sussex County Comm Coll, NJ A
Swarthmore Coll, PA B
Syracuse U, NY B
Taylor U, IN B
Tennessee Technological U, TN B
Texas A&M U–Corpus Christi,
  TX B
Texas A&M U–Kingsville, TX B
Texas Christian U, TX B
Texas State Tech Coll Waco, TX A
Texas State U-San Marcos, TX B
Texas Wesleyan U, TX B
Thomas More Coll, KY B
Trinity Coll, CT B
Trinity U, TX B
Trinity (Washington) U, DC B
Troy U, AL B
Truman State U, MO B
Tusculum Coll, TN B
Union Coll, NY B
U at Buffalo, the State U of
  New York, NY B
The U of Alabama, AL B
The U of Alabama in
  Huntsville, AL B
U of Arkansas, AR B
U of Arkansas at Fort Smith,
  AR A
U of Arkansas at Pine Bluff,
  AR B
U of California, Santa Cruz, CA B
U of Central Florida, FL B
U of Central Missouri, MO B
U of Charleston, WV B
U of Cincinnati, OH B
U of Cincinnati Raymond
  Walters Coll, OH A
U of Colorado at Boulder, CO B
U of Colorado at Colorado
  Springs, CO B
U of Dayton, OH B
U of Denver, CO B
The U of Findlay, OH B
U of Guam, GU B
U of Hartford, CT B
U of Hawaii at Manoa, HI B
U of Indianapolis, IN B
The U of Iowa, IA B
U of Kansas, KS B
U of La Verne, CA B
U of Maine at Farmington, ME B
U of Maine at Presque Isle, ME A
U of Mary Hardin-Baylor, TX B
U of Maryland, Baltimore
  County, MD B
U of Maryland, Coll Park, MD B
U of Mary Washington, VA B
U of Miami, FL B
U of Michigan–Flint, MI B
U of Minnesota, Morris, MN B
U of Missouri–Columbia, MO B
U of Missouri–St. Louis, MO B
U of Nebraska–Lincoln, NE B
U of Nevada, Reno, NV B
U of New Mexico, NM B
U of New Orleans, LA B
U of North Alabama, AL B
The U of North Carolina at
  Asheville, NC B
The U of North Carolina at
  Pembroke, NC B
U of Northern Iowa, IA B
U of North Texas, TX B
U of Oregon, OR B
U of Pittsburgh, PA B
U of Puget Sound, WA B
U of Rhode Island, RI B
U of Rochester, NY B
U of Saint Francis, IN A,B
U of San Diego, CA B
U of San Francisco, CA B
U of Sioux Falls, SD B
U of South Carolina, SC B
U of Southern Indiana, IN B
U of Southern Maine, ME B
U of South Florida, FL B
The U of Tampa, FL B
The U of Tennessee at Martin,
  TN B
The U of Texas at San Antonio,
  TX B
The U of the Arts, PA B

U of the Incarnate Word, TX A,B
U of Tulsa, OK B
U of Utah, UT B
U of Virginia, VA B
U of Washington, WA B
U of West Florida, FL B
U of Wisconsin–Eau Claire, WI B
U of Wisconsin–La Crosse, WI B
U of Wisconsin–Oshkosh, WI B
U of Wisconsin–Stevens Point,
  WI B
U of Wisconsin–Superior, WI B
U of Wisconsin–Whitewater, WI B
U of Wyoming, WY B
Upper Iowa U, IA B
Utah State U, UT B
Utah Valley State Coll, UT A
Valparaiso U, IN B
Vanderbilt U, TN B
Villanova U, PA B
Virginia Commonwealth U, VA B
Virginia Polytechnic Inst and
  State U, VA B
Viterbo U, WI B
Wabash Coll, IN B
Wake Forest U, NC B
Warren Wilson Coll, NC B
Wartburg Coll, IA B
Washington & Jefferson Coll,
  PA B
Washington Coll, MD B
Washington State U, WA B
Washington U in St. Louis, MO B
Waynesburg Coll, PA B
Wayne State Coll, NE B
Wells Coll, NY B
Wentworth Inst of Technology,
  MA A,B
Wesleyan U, CT B
Western Illinois U, IL B
Western Kentucky U, KY B
Western New Mexico U, NM B
Western Washington U, WA B
Western Wyoming Comm Coll,
  WY A
Westmont Coll, CA B
West Texas A&M U, TX B
West Valley Coll, CA A
Whatcom Comm Coll, WA A
Wichita State U, KS B
Williams Coll, MA B
Wilson Coll, PA B
Winona State U, MN B
Woodbury U, CA B
Yavapai Coll, AZ A
York Coll of the City U of New
  York, NY B
Young Harris Coll, GA A

Biological Sciences
Adelphi U, NY B
Adrian Coll, MI A,B
Agnes Scott Coll, GA B
Albertus Magnus Coll, CT B
Albion Coll, MI B
Alderson-Broaddus Coll, WV B
Allegheny Coll, PA B
Alvernia Coll, PA B
Alverno Coll, WI B
Alvin Comm Coll, TX A
American U, DC B
Ancilla Coll, IN A
Anna Maria Coll, MA B
Antioch Coll, OH B
Aquinas Coll, MI B
Arcadia U, PA B
Arizona State U, AZ B
Ashford U, IA B
Ashland U, OH B
Assumption Coll, MA B
Austin Peay State U, TN B
Averett U, VA B
Baker U, KS B
Baldwin-Wallace Coll, OH B
Ball State U, IN B
Bard Coll, NY B
Barnard Coll, NY B
Barry U, FL B
Bates Coll, ME B
Bay Path Coll, MA B
Belmont U, TN B
Beloit Coll, WI B

A=Associate; B=Bachelor's Degree

Bemidji State U, MN	B
Benedict Coll, SC	B
Bennington Coll, VT	B
Berea Coll, KY	B
Berkshire Comm Coll, MA	A
Bethany Coll, KS	B
Bethel Coll, KS	B
Bethel U, MN	B
Black Hills State U, SD	B
Blue Mountain Coll, MS	B
Boise State U, ID	B
Boston U, MA	B
Bowdoin Coll, ME	B
Brescia U, KY	B
Bronx Comm Coll of the City U of New York, NY	A
Bryn Mawr Coll, PA	B
Bucknell U, PA	B
Butler U, IN	B
Caldwell Coll, NJ	B
Calhoun Comm Coll, AL	A
California Lutheran U, CA	B
California Polytechnic State U, San Luis Obispo, CA	B
California State Polytechnic U, Pomona, CA	B
California State U, Long Beach, CA	B
California State U, Sacramento, CA	B
California State U, Stanislaus, CA	B
Calvin Coll, MI	B
Cameron U, OK	B
Cañada Coll, CA	A
Capital U, OH	B
Cardinal Stritch U, WI	B
Carleton Coll, MN	B
Carlow U, PA	B
Carroll Coll, MT	B
Carroll Coll, WI	B
Carson-Newman Coll, TN	B
Carthage Coll, WI	B
The Catholic U of America, DC	B
Centenary Coll, NJ	B
Central Christian Coll of Kansas, KS	A
Centralia Coll, WA	A
Central Michigan U, MI	B
Central Piedmont Comm Coll, NC	A
Central Wyoming Coll, WY	A
Centre Coll, KY	B
Chabot Coll, CA	A
Chaffey Coll, CA	A
Chapman U, CA	B
Chatham U, PA	B
Chattanooga State Tech Comm Coll, TN	A
City Coll of San Francisco, CA	A
City Coll of the City U of New York, NY	B
City Colls of Chicago, Harold Washington Coll, IL	A
City Colls of Chicago, Kennedy-King Coll, IL	A
Claflin U, SC	B
Clarendon Coll, TX	A
Clarion U of Pennsylvania, PA	B
Clarke Coll, IA	B
Clarkson U, NY	B
Clark U, MA	B
Clearwater Christian Coll, FL	B
Cleveland State U, OH	B
Coastal Carolina U, SC	B
Coastal Georgia Comm Coll, GA	A
Cochise Coll, Sierra Vista, AZ	A
Coe Coll, IA	B
Coffeyville Comm Coll, KS	A
Colby Coll, ME	B
Colby Comm Coll, KS	A
Colby-Sawyer Coll, NH	B
Coll Misericordia, PA	B
Coll of Saint Benedict, MN	B
Coll of St. Catherine, MN	B
Coll of Southern Maryland, MD	A
Coll of the Atlantic, ME	B
Coll of the Canyons, CA	A
Coll of the Desert, CA	A
Coll of the Holy Cross, MA	B
Coll of the Ozarks, MO	B
The Colorado Coll, CO	B
Colorado State U, CO	B
Columbia Coll, MO	B
Columbia Union Coll, MD	B
Columbia U, School of General Studies, NY	B
Concordia Coll, MN	B
Concordia Coll, NY	B
Concordia U, IL	B
Connecticut Coll, CT	B
Connors State Coll, OK	A
Cornell Coll, IA	B
Cosumnes River Coll, Sacramento, CA	A
Culver-Stockton Coll, MO	B
Cumberland U, TN	A,B
Daemen Coll, NY	B
Dakota Wesleyan U, SD	B
Dana Coll, NE	B
Davidson Coll, NC	B
De Anza Coll, CA	A
Defiance Coll, OH	B
Del Mar Coll, TX	A
Denison U, OH	B
DePaul U, IL	B
DePauw U, IN	B
DeSales U, PA	B
Dominican U of California, CA	B
Dordt Coll, IA	B
Drake U, IA	B
Drew U, NJ	B
Drury U, MO	B
Duquesne U, PA	B
D'Youville Coll, NY	B
East Carolina U, NC	B
East Central Coll, MO	A
Eastern Connecticut State U, CT	B
Eastern Mennonite U, VA	B
Eastern U, PA	B
Eastern Wyoming Coll, WY	A
East Los Angeles Coll, CA	A
East Tennessee State U, TN	B
East Texas Baptist U, TX	B
Eckerd Coll, FL	B
Edgewood Coll, WI	B
Edinboro U of Pennsylvania, PA	B
El Camino Coll, CA	A
Elizabethtown Coll, PA	B
Elmira Coll, NY	B
Elms Coll, MA	B
Elon U, NC	B
Emmanuel Coll, MA	B
Emory U, GA	B
Emporia State U, KS	B
The Evergreen State Coll, WA	B
Fairfield U, CT	B
Fairleigh Dickinson U, Coll at Florham, NJ	B
Fairleigh Dickinson U, Metropolitan Campus, NJ	B
Ferris State U, MI	B
Florida Atlantic U, FL	B
Florida Inst of Technology, FL	B
Florida International U, FL	B
Florida State U, FL	B
Foothill Coll, CA	A
Fordham U, NY	B
Fort Lewis Coll, CO	B
Fresno Pacific U, CA	A,B
Frostburg State U, MD	B
Fullerton Coll, CA	A
Fulton-Montgomery Comm Coll, NY	A
Furman U, SC	B
Gannon U, PA	B
Gardner-Webb U, NC	B
George Fox U, OR	B
Georgetown Coll, KY	B
Georgia Coll & State U, GA	B
Georgia Southern U, GA	B
Georgia State U, GA	B
Gettysburg Coll, PA	B
Golden West Coll, CA	A
Gonzaga U, WA	B
Goshen Coll, IN	B
Grambling State U, LA	B
Grand Valley State U, MI	B
Grand View Coll, IA	B
Greenfield Comm Coll, MA	A
Green Mountain Coll, VT	B
Greenville Coll, IL	B
Grinnell Coll, IA	B
Gulf Coast Comm Coll, FL	A
Gustavus Adolphus Coll, MN	B
Hamilton Coll, NY	B
Hampden-Sydney Coll, VA	B
Hampshire Coll, MA	B
Harding U, AR	B
Hardin-Simmons U, TX	B
Harper Coll, IL	A
Harrisburg Area Comm Coll, PA	A
Hartwick Coll, NY	B
Harvard U, MA	B
Harvey Mudd Coll, CA	B
Haverford Coll, PA	B
Hawai'i Pacific U, HI	B
Hill Coll of the Hill Jr Coll District, TX	A
Hillsdale Coll, MI	B
Hiram Coll, OH	B
Hofstra U, NY	B
Holy Family U, PA	B
Hope Coll, MI	B
Howard Coll, TX	B
Howard Payne U, TX	B
Huntingdon Coll, AL	B
Huntington U, IN	B
Idaho State U, ID	A,B
Illinois Coll, IL	B
Illinois Inst of Technology, IL	B
Illinois Wesleyan U, IL	B
Indiana U Bloomington, IN	B
Indiana U of Pennsylvania, PA	B
Indiana U South Bend, IN	A,B
Indiana U Southeast, IN	B
Indiana Wesleyan U, IN	A,B
Iowa State U of Science and Technology, IA	B
Jacksonville State U, AL	B
Jacksonville U, FL	B
James Madison U, VA	B
John Carroll U, OH	B
The Johns Hopkins U, MD	B
Johnson State Coll, VT	B
Joliet Jr Coll, IL	A
Judson Coll, IL	B
Juniata Coll, PA	B
Kansas State U, KS	B
Kansas Wesleyan U, KS	B
Kean U, NJ	B
Kennesaw State U, GA	B
Kent State U, OH	B
Kentucky Wesleyan Coll, KY	B
Kenyon Coll, OH	B
Kettering U, MI	B
Keystone Coll, PA	A,B
Kingwood Coll, TX	A
Kirkwood Comm Coll, IA	A
Knox Coll, IL	B
Lafayette Coll, PA	B
Lakeland Coll, WI	B
Lander U, SC	B
Langston U, OK	B
Lansing Comm Coll, MI	A
Laramie County Comm Coll, WY	A
Lawrence U, WI	B
Lees-McRae Coll, NC	B
LeMoyne-Owen Coll, TN	B
Lewis & Clark Coll, OR	B
Lewis-Clark State Coll, ID	B
Liberty U, VA	B
Limestone Coll, SC	B
Linfield Coll, OR	B
Lipscomb U, TN	B
Long Beach City Coll, CA	A
Long Island U, C.W. Post Campus, NY	B
Longwood U, VA	B
Los Angeles Harbor Coll, CA	A
Los Angeles Mission Coll, CA	A
Los Angeles Southwest Coll, CA	A
Louisiana State U at Alexandria, LA	A,B
Loyola U Chicago, IL	B
Luther Coll, IA	B
Lycoming Coll, PA	B
Lynchburg Coll, VA	B
Lynn U, FL	B
Manatee Comm Coll, FL	A
Manchester Coll, IN	B
Manhattan Coll, NY	B
Manhattanville Coll, NY	B
Marian Coll of Fond du Lac, WI	B
Marlboro Coll, VT	B
Marquette U, WI	B
Marshall U, WV	B
Mary Baldwin Coll, VA	B
Marymount Manhattan Coll, NY	B
Maryville Coll, TN	B
Maryville U of Saint Louis, MO	B
Marywood U, PA	B
Massachusetts Inst of Technology, MA	B
McDaniel Coll, MD	B
McMurry U, TX	B
McNeese State U, LA	B
Mercy Coll, NY	B
Mesa Comm Coll, AZ	A
Mesa State Coll, CO	A,B
Miami Dade Coll, FL	A
Miami U, OH	B
Michigan Technological U, MI	B
MidAmerica Nazarene U, KS	B
Middlebury Coll, VT	B
Middle Tennessee State U, TN	B
Midland Coll, TX	A
Midwestern State U, TX	B
Millersville U of Pennsylvania, PA	B
Milligan Coll, TN	B
Millsaps Coll, MS	B
Mills Coll, CA	B
Minnesota State U Mankato, MN	B
Minnesota State U Moorhead, MN	B
Minot State U, ND	B
MiraCosta Coll, CA	A
Mississippi U for Women, MS	B
Missouri Baptist U, MO	B
Modesto Jr Coll, CA	A
Molloy Coll, NY	B
Monmouth U, NJ	B
Montana Tech of The U of Montana, MT	A,B
Montclair State U, NJ	B
Monterey Peninsula Coll, CA	A
Moravian Coll, PA	B
Morehead State U, KY	B
Morningside Coll, IA	B
Mount Holyoke Coll, MA	B
Mount Mercy Coll, IA	B
Muskingum Coll, OH	B
Nebraska Wesleyan U, NE	B
New Coll of Florida, FL	B
New England Coll, NH	B
New Mexico Highlands U, NM	B
New Mexico Inst of Mining and Technology, NM	B
New Mexico Military Inst, NM	A
New Mexico State U, NM	B
New York U, NY	B
Niagara U, NY	B
Northampton County Area Comm Coll, PA	A
North Carolina State U, NC	B
North Central Coll, IL	B
North Dakota State U, ND	B
Northeast Comm Coll, NE	A
Northeastern U, MA	B
Northern Arizona U, AZ	B
Northern Kentucky U, KY	B
Northern Michigan U, MI	B
Northern State U, SD	B
Northland Coll, WI	B
Northwest Coll, WY	A
Northwestern State U of Louisiana, LA	B
Northwestern U, IL	B
Northwest Missouri State U, MO	B
Notre Dame Coll, OH	B
Notre Dame de Namur U, CA	B
Nova Southeastern U, FL	B
Oakland U, MI	B
Ohio Wesleyan U, OH	B
Oklahoma Panhandle State U, OK	B
Oklahoma State U, OK	B
Oklahoma Wesleyan U, OK	A,B
Old Dominion U, VA	B
Orange Coast Coll, CA	A
Oregon State U, OR	B
Ottawa U, KS	B
Otterbein Coll, OH	B
Pace U, NY	B
Palomar Coll, CA	A
Park U, MO	B
Peace Coll, NC	B

College	Degree
Peru State Coll, NE	B
Philadelphia U, PA	B
Pittsburg State U, KS	B
Pitzer Coll, CA	B
Plymouth State U, NH	B
Portland State U, OR	B
Prescott Coll, AZ	B
Presentation Coll, SD	A,B
Principia Coll, IL	B
Purdue U, IN	B
Quincy U, IL	B
Quinnipiac U, CT	B
Radford U, VA	B
Ramapo Coll of New Jersey, NJ	B
Randolph Coll, VA	B
Randolph-Macon Coll, VA	B
Raritan Valley Comm Coll, NJ	A
Redlands Comm Coll, OK	A
Reed Coll, OR	B
Rensselaer Polytechnic Inst, NY	B
Rhodes Coll, TN	B
Rider U, NJ	B
Rochester Inst of Technology, NY	A,B
Rocky Mountain Coll, MT	B
Roger Williams U, RI	B
Roosevelt U, IL	B
Rose State Coll, OK	A
Sacred Heart U, CT	A,B
St. Ambrose U, IA	B
Saint Anselm Coll, NH	B
Saint Francis U, PA	B
St. Gregory's U, OK	B
Saint John's U, MN	B
Saint Joseph's Coll, IN	A,B
Saint Leo U, FL	B
Saint Louis U, MO	B
Saint Mary-of-the-Woods Coll, IN	B
Saint Mary's Coll, IN	B
Saint Mary's Coll of California, CA	B
St. Mary's Coll of Maryland, MD	B
Saint Mary's U of Minnesota, MN	B
St. Mary's U of San Antonio, TX	B
Saint Michael's Coll, VT	B
St. Olaf Coll, MN	B
St. Thomas U, FL	B
Saint Vincent Coll, PA	B
Sam Houston State U, TX	B
San Bernardino Valley Coll, CA	A
San Diego City Coll, CA	A
San Diego State U, CA	B
San Francisco State U, CA	B
San Jacinto Coll Central Campus, TX	A
San Jacinto Coll North Campus, TX	A
San Jacinto Coll South Campus, TX	A
Santa Barbara City Coll, CA	A
Santa Fe Comm Coll, NM	A
Santa Monica Coll, CA	A
Santa Rosa Jr Coll, CA	A
Sarah Lawrence Coll, NY	B
Sauk Valley Comm Coll, IL	A
Savannah State U, GA	B
Schreiner U, TX	B
Scripps Coll, CA	B
Seattle U, WA	B
Seton Hall U, NJ	B
Shenandoah U, VA	B
Shepherd U, WV	B
Sheridan Coll–Sheridan and Gillette, WY	A
Shorter Coll, GA	B
Siena Coll, NY	B
Sierra Coll, CA	A
Simmons Coll, MA	B
Simpson Coll, IA	B
Skagit Valley Coll, WA	A
Skidmore Coll, NY	B
Slippery Rock U of Pennsylvania, PA	B
South Dakota State U, SD	B
Southeast Missouri State U, MO	B

College	Degree
Southern Arkansas U–Magnolia, AR	B
Southern Illinois U Carbondale, IL	B
Southern Illinois U Edwardsville, IL	B
Southern Oregon U, OR	B
Southern Utah U, UT	B
South Georgia Coll, GA	A
Southwestern Coll, KS	B
Southwest Minnesota State U, MN	B
Spring Arbor U, MI	B
Stanford U, CA	B
State U of New York at Oswego, NY	B
State U of New York at Plattsburgh, NY	B
State U of New York Coll at Geneseo, NY	B
State U of New York Coll at Oneonta, NY	B
Stony Brook U, State U of New York, NY	B
Suffolk County Comm Coll, NY	A
Suffolk U, MA	B
Susquehanna U, PA	B
Swarthmore Coll, PA	B
Syracuse U, NY	B
Tabor Coll, KS	B
Taylor U, IN	B
Tennessee Technological U, TN	B
Texas A&M U–Corpus Christi, TX	B
Texas A&M U–Kingsville, TX	B
Texas A&M U–Texarkana, TX	B
Texas Christian U, TX	B
Texas State U-San Marcos, TX	B
Texas Wesleyan U, TX	B
Thomas More Coll, KY	A,B
Trevecca Nazarene U, TN	B
Trinity Coll, CT	B
Trinity U, TX	B
Trinity (Washington) U, DC	B
Troy U, AL	B
Truman State U, MO	B
Tusculum Coll, TN	B
Union Coll, NY	B
U at Buffalo, the State U of New York, NY	B
The U of Alabama, AL	B
The U of Alabama in Huntsville, AL	B
U of Arkansas, AR	B
U of Arkansas at Pine Bluff, AR	B
U of California, Santa Cruz, CA	B
U of Central Florida, FL	B
U of Central Missouri, MO	B
U of Charleston, WV	B
U of Cincinnati, OH	B
U of Cincinnati Raymond Walters Coll, OH	A
U of Colorado at Boulder, CO	B
U of Colorado at Colorado Springs, CO	B
U of Dayton, OH	B
U of Denver, CO	B
U of Detroit Mercy, MI	B
U of Dubuque, IA	A,B
The U of Findlay, OH	B
U of Guam, GU	B
U of Hartford, CT	B
U of Hawaii at Manoa, HI	B
U of Illinois at Springfield, IL	B
U of Indianapolis, IN	B
The U of Iowa, IA	B
U of Kansas, KS	B
U of La Verne, CA	B
U of Maine at Farmington, ME	B
U of Maine at Fort Kent, ME	B
U of Maine at Presque Isle, ME	B
U of Mary Hardin-Baylor, TX	B
U of Maryland, Baltimore County, MD	B
U of Maryland, Coll Park, MD	B
U of Mary Washington, VA	B
U of Miami, FL	B
U of Michigan–Flint, MI	B
U of Minnesota, Morris, MN	B
U of Missouri–Columbia, MO	B
U of Missouri–St. Louis, MO	B

College	Degree
U of Nebraska–Lincoln, NE	B
U of Nevada, Reno, NV	B
U of New Mexico, NM	B
U of New Orleans, LA	B
U of North Alabama, AL	B
The U of North Carolina at Asheville, NC	B
The U of North Carolina at Pembroke, NC	B
U of Northern Iowa, IA	B
U of North Texas, TX	B
U of Oregon, OR	B
U of Pittsburgh, PA	B
U of Pittsburgh at Bradford, PA	B
U of Puget Sound, WA	B
U of Rhode Island, RI	B
U of Rochester, NY	B
U of Saint Francis, IN	B
U of San Diego, CA	B
U of San Francisco, CA	B
U of Sioux Falls, SD	B
U of South Carolina, SC	B
U of South Carolina Upstate, SC	B
U of Southern Indiana, IN	B
U of Southern Maine, ME	B
U of South Florida, FL	B
The U of Tampa, FL	A,B
The U of Tennessee at Martin, TN	B
The U of Texas at San Antonio, TX	B
U of the Incarnate Word, TX	B
U of Tulsa, OK	B
U of Utah, UT	B
U of Virginia, VA	B
U of Washington, WA	B
U of West Florida, FL	B
U of Wisconsin–La Crosse, WI	B
U of Wisconsin–Oshkosh, WI	B
U of Wisconsin–Stevens Point, WI	B
U of Wisconsin–Superior, WI	B
U of Wisconsin–Whitewater, WI	B
U of Wyoming, WY	B
Upper Iowa U, IA	B
Utah State U, UT	B
Utah Valley State Coll, UT	A,B
Utica Coll, NY	B
Valparaiso U, IN	B
Vanderbilt U, TN	B
Vanguard U of Southern California, CA	B
Villanova U, PA	B
Virginia Commonwealth U, VA	B
Virginia Polytechnic Inst and State U, VA	B
Viterbo U, WI	B
Wabash Coll, IN	B
Wake Forest U, NC	B
Warren Wilson Coll, NC	B
Wartburg Coll, IA	B
Washington & Jefferson Coll, PA	B
Washington Coll, MD	B
Washington State U, WA	B
Washington U in St. Louis, MO	B
Waynesburg Coll, PA	B
Wayne State Coll, NE	B
Wells Coll, NY	B
Wesleyan U, CT	B
Western Illinois U, IL	B
Western Kentucky U, KY	B
Western New England Coll, MA	B
Western New Mexico U, NM	B
Western Washington U, WA	B
Western Wyoming Comm Coll, WY	A
Westmont Coll, CA	B
West Texas A&M U, TX	B
West Valley Coll, CA	A
Wichita State U, KS	B
Widener U, PA	B
Wilkes U, PA	B
Williams Coll, MA	B
Wilmington Coll, OH	B
Wilson Coll, PA	B
Winona State U, MN	B
Worcester Polytechnic Inst, MA	B
Worcester State Coll, MA	B
York Coll, NE	B
York Coll of Pennsylvania, PA	A,B

College	Degree
York Coll of the City U of New York, NY	B
Young Harris Coll, GA	A

Business

College	Degree
Academy Coll, MN	A,B
Adelphi U, NY	B
Adrian Coll, MI	A,B
Aims Comm Coll, CO	A
Alamance Comm Coll, NC	A
Alaska Pacific U, AK	A,B
Albertus Magnus Coll, CT	B
Albion Coll, MI	B
Alderson-Broaddus Coll, WV	A,B
Allegheny Coll, PA	B
Alvernia Coll, PA	A,B
Alverno Coll, WI	B
Alvin Comm Coll, TX	A
American InterContinental U, CA	A,B
American InterContinental U, Atlanta, GA	B
American U, DC	B
Ancilla Coll, IN	A
Anna Maria Coll, MA	A,B
Antioch Coll, OH	B
Aquinas Coll, MI	B
Arcadia U, PA	B
Arizona State U, AZ	B
Ashford U, IA	B
Ashland U, OH	B
Assumption Coll, MA	B
Austin Peay State U, TN	A,B
Averett U, VA	A,B
Babson Coll, MA	B
Baker Coll of Flint, MI	A,B
Baker U, KS	B
Baldwin-Wallace Coll, OH	B
Ball State U, IN	A,B
Barry U, FL	B
Bay Path Coll, MA	B
Beacon U, GA	B
Belmont U, TN	B
Beloit Coll, WI	B
Bemidji State U, MN	B
Benedict Coll, SC	B
Bentley Coll, MA	A,B
Berea Coll, KY	B
Berkeley Coll-New York City Campus, NY	A,B
Berkeley Coll-Westchester Campus, NY	A,B
Berkshire Comm Coll, MA	A
Bethany Coll, KS	B
Bethel Coll, KS	B
Bethel U, MN	B
Black Hills State U, SD	A
Bluefield State Coll, WV	A,B
Blue Mountain Coll, MS	B
Boise State U, ID	A,B
Boston U, MA	B
Bowling Green State U–Firelands Coll, OH	A
Brescia U, KY	A,B
Briarwood Coll, CT	A
Bronx Comm Coll of the City U of New York, NY	A
Broome Comm Coll, NY	A
Bryant U, RI	B
Bucknell U, PA	B
Bunker Hill Comm Coll, MA	A
Butler U, IN	B
Caldwell Coll, NJ	B
Calhoun Comm Coll, AL	A
California Lutheran U, CA	B
California Polytechnic State U, San Luis Obispo, CA	B
California State Polytechnic U, Pomona, CA	B
California State U, Long Beach, CA	B
California State U, Sacramento, CA	B
California State U, Stanislaus, CA	B
Calvin Coll, MI	B
Cameron U, OK	A,B
Cañada Coll, CA	A
Capital U, OH	B
Cardinal Stritch U, WI	A,B
Carlow U, PA	A,B
Carroll Coll, MT	A,B

A=Associate; B=Bachelor's Degree

College	Code
Carroll Coll, WI	B
Carson-Newman Coll, TN	B
Carthage Coll, WI	B
The Catholic U of America, DC	B
Cazenovia Coll, NY	A,B
Centenary Coll, NJ	B
Central Christian Coll of Kansas, KS	A,B
Central Comm Coll–Columbus Campus, NE	A
Central Comm Coll–Grand Island Campus, NE	A
Central Comm Coll–Hastings Campus, NE	A
Central Florida Comm Coll, FL	A
Centralia Coll, WA	A
Central Lakes Coll, MN	A
Central Michigan U, MI	B
Central Piedmont Comm Coll, NC	A
Central Wyoming Coll, WY	A
Century Coll, MN	A
Cerro Coso Comm Coll, CA	A
Chabot Coll, CA	A
Chaffey Coll, CA	A
Chapman U, CA	B
Chatham U, PA	B
Chattahoochee Tech Coll, GA	A
Chattanooga State Tech Comm Coll, TN	A
Chemeketa Comm Coll, OR	A
City Coll of San Francisco, CA	A
City Coll of the City U of New York, NY	B
City Colls of Chicago, Harold Washington Coll, IL	A
City Colls of Chicago, Kennedy-King Coll, IL	A
City U, WA	B
Claflin U, SC	B
Clarendon Coll, TX	A
Clarion U of Pennsylvania, PA	A,B
Clarke Coll, IA	B
Clarkson U, NY	B
Clark U, MA	B
Clatsop Comm Coll, OR	A
Clearwater Christian Coll, FL	A,B
Cleveland State U, OH	B
Clinton Comm Coll, IA	A
Coastal Carolina U, SC	B
Coastal Georgia Comm Coll, GA	A
Cochise Coll, Sierra Vista, AZ	B
Coe Coll, IA	B
Coffeyville Comm Coll, KS	A
Colby Comm Coll, KS	A
Colby-Sawyer Coll, NH	B
Colegio Universitario de San Juan, PR	A
Coll Misericordia, PA	B
Coll of DuPage, IL	A
Coll of Eastern Utah, UT	A
Coll of Lake County, IL	A
Coll of Saint Benedict, MN	B
Coll of St. Catherine, MN	B
Coll of Southern Maryland, MD	A
Coll of the Canyons, CA	A
Coll of the Desert, CA	A
Coll of the Holy Cross, MA	B
Coll of the Ozarks, MO	B
Colorado State U, CO	B
Columbia Coll, MO	A,B
Columbia Coll Chicago, IL	B
Columbia Union Coll, MD	A,B
Concordia Coll, AL	B
Concordia Coll, MN	B
Concordia Coll, NY	A,B
Concordia U, IL	B
Connors State Coll, OK	A
Cornell Coll, IA	B
Cosumnes River Coll, Sacramento, CA	A
County Coll of Morris, NJ	A
Culver-Stockton Coll, MO	B
Cumberland U, TN	A,B
Daemen Coll, NY	B
Dakota County Tech Coll, MN	A
Dakota Wesleyan U, SD	A,B
Dana Coll, NE	B
Davenport U, Midland, MI	A
Dean Coll, MA	A
De Anza Coll, CA	A
Defiance Coll, OH	A,B
DeKalb Tech Coll, GA	A
Delaware Tech & Comm Coll, Jack F. Owens Campus, DE	A
Del Mar Coll, TX	A
Delta Coll, MI	A
Denison U, OH	B
DePaul U, IL	B
DeSales U, PA	B
Dominican U of California, CA	B
Dordt Coll, IA	B
Drake U, IA	B
Drury U, MO	B
Duquesne U, PA	B
D'Youville Coll, NY	B
East Carolina U, NC	B
East Central Coll, MO	A
Eastern Connecticut State U, CT	B
Eastern Mennonite U, VA	B
Eastern U, PA	B
Eastern Wyoming Coll, WY	A
East Los Angeles Coll, CA	A
East Tennessee State U, TN	B
East Texas Baptist U, TX	B
Eckerd Coll, FL	B
Edgewood Coll, WI	B
Edinboro U of Pennsylvania, PA	A,B
Edison Coll, FL	A
Edmonds Comm Coll, WA	A
El Camino Coll, CA	A
Elizabethtown Coll, PA	B
Elmira Coll, NY	B
Elms Coll, MA	B
Elon U, NC	B
Emerson Coll, MA	B
Emmanuel Coll, MA	B
Emory U, GA	B
Emporia State U, KS	B
Everest Coll, OR	A
The Evergreen State Coll, WA	B
Fairfield U, CT	B
Fairleigh Dickinson U, Coll at Florham, NJ	B
Fairleigh Dickinson U, Metropolitan Campus, NJ	B
Ferris State U, MI	A,B
FIDM/The Fashion Inst of Design & Merchandising, Los Angeles Campus, CA	B
Five Towns Coll, NY	A,B
Flagler Coll, FL	B
Florida Atlantic U, FL	B
Florida Gulf Coast U, FL	B
Florida Inst of Technology, FL	B
Florida International U, FL	B
Florida Keys Comm Coll, FL	A
Florida State U, FL	B
Foothill Coll, CA	A
Fordham U, NY	B
Fort Lewis Coll, CO	B
Fox Valley Tech Coll, WI	A
Fresno City Coll, CA	A
Fresno Pacific U, CA	A,B
Frostburg State U, MD	B
Fullerton Coll, CA	A
Fulton-Montgomery Comm Coll, NY	A
Furman U, SC	B
Gannon U, PA	B
Garden City Comm Coll, KS	A
Gardner-Webb U, NC	B
GateWay Comm Coll, AZ	A
Genesee Comm Coll, NY	A
George Fox U, OR	B
Georgetown Coll, KY	B
Georgia Coll & State U, GA	B
Georgia Highlands Coll, GA	A
Georgia Southern U, GA	B
Georgia State U, GA	B
Gettysburg Coll, PA	B
Glendale Comm Coll, AZ	A
Glendale Comm Coll, CA	A
Glen Oaks Comm Coll, MI	A
Globe Inst of Technology, NY	A,B
Golden Gate U, CA	B
Golden West Coll, CA	A
Goldey-Beacom Coll, DE	A,B
Gonzaga U, WA	B
Goshen Coll, IN	B
Grambling State U, LA	B
Grand Valley State U, MI	B
Grand View Coll, IA	B
Grays Harbor Coll, WA	A
Greenfield Comm Coll, MA	A
Green Mountain Coll, VT	B
Greenville Coll, IL	B
Gulf Coast Comm Coll, FL	A
Gustavus Adolphus Coll, MN	B
Hampden-Sydney Coll, VA	B
Harding U, AR	B
Hardin-Simmons U, TX	B
Harper Coll, IL	A
Harrisburg Area Comm Coll, PA	A
Hartwick Coll, NY	B
Hawaii Comm Coll, HI	A
Hawai'i Pacific U, HI	A,B
Hellenic Coll, MA	B
Henry Ford Comm Coll, MI	A
Hesston Coll, KS	A
Hilbert Coll, NY	A,B
Hill Coll of the Hill Jr Coll District, TX	A
Hillsdale Coll, MI	B
Hillsdale Free Will Baptist Coll, OK	A,B
Hiram Coll, OH	B
Hofstra U, NY	B
Holy Family U, PA	B
Hope Coll, MI	B
Hope International U, CA	B
Hopkinsville Comm Coll, KY	A
Houston Comm Coll System, TX	A
Howard Coll, TX	A
Howard Payne U, TX	B
Hudson Valley Comm Coll, NY	A
Huntingdon Coll, AL	B
Huntington U, IN	B
Idaho State U, ID	A,B
Illinois Coll, IL	B
Illinois Inst of Technology, IL	B
Illinois Wesleyan U, IL	B
Indiana Tech, IN	A,B
Indiana U Bloomington, IN	A,B
Indiana U of Pennsylvania, PA	A,B
Indiana U South Bend, IN	A,B
Indiana U Southeast, IN	A,B
Indiana Wesleyan U, IN	A,B
Iowa State U of Science and Technology, IA	B
Iowa Western Comm Coll, IA	A
Isothermal Comm Coll, NC	A
Itasca Comm Coll, MN	A
Jacksonville State U, AL	B
Jacksonville U, FL	B
James A. Rhodes State Coll, OH	A
James Madison U, VA	B
John Carroll U, OH	B
John F. Kennedy U, CA	B
The Johns Hopkins U, MD	B
Johnson & Wales U, FL	A,B
Johnson & Wales U, RI	A,B
Johnson County Comm Coll, KS	A
Johnson State Coll, VT	A,B
Joliet Jr Coll, IL	A
Jones Coll, Jacksonville, FL	A,B
Judson Coll, IL	B
Juniata Coll, PA	B
Kankakee Comm Coll, IL	A
Kansas State U, KS	B
Kansas Wesleyan U, KS	A,B
Kapiolani Comm Coll, HI	A
Kean U, NJ	B
Kennesaw State U, GA	B
Kent State U, OH	A,B
Kent State U, Ashtabula Campus, OH	A
Kent State U, East Liverpool Campus, OH	A
Kent State U, Geauga Campus, OH	A,B
Kent State U, Salem Campus, OH	A,B
Kent State U, Stark Campus, OH	A
Kent State U, Trumbull Campus, OH	A,B
Kent State U, Tuscarawas Campus, OH	A,B
Kentucky Wesleyan Coll, KY	B
Kettering U, MI	B
Keystone Coll, PA	A,B
Kilgore Coll, TX	A
The King's Coll, NY	B
Kingwood Coll, TX	A
Kirkwood Comm Coll, IA	A
Lafayette Coll, PA	B
Lake Land Coll, IL	A
Lakeland Coll, WI	B
Lake Region State Coll, ND	A
Lamar State Coll–Port Arthur, TX	A
Lancaster Bible Coll, PA	A
Lander U, SC	B
Laney Coll, CA	A
Langston U, OK	B
Lansing Comm Coll, MI	A
Laramie County Comm Coll, WY	A
Las Positas Coll, CA	A
Laurel Business Inst, PA	A
LDS Business Coll, UT	A
Lees-McRae Coll, NC	B
Leeward Comm Coll, HI	A
LeMoyne-Owen Coll, TN	B
Lewis-Clark State Coll, ID	A,B
Liberty U, VA	B
Limestone Coll, SC	A,B
Lincoln Land Comm Coll, IL	A
Lincoln U, CA	B
Linfield Coll, OR	B
Lipscomb U, TN	B
Long Beach City Coll, CA	A
Long Island U, C.W. Post Campus, NY	B
Longwood U, VA	B
Los Angeles Harbor Coll, CA	A
Los Angeles Mission Coll, CA	A
Los Angeles Pierce Coll, CA	A
Los Angeles Southwest Coll, CA	A
Louisiana State U at Alexandria, LA	A,B
Loyola U Chicago, IL	B
Luther Coll, IA	B
Lycoming Coll, PA	B
Lynchburg Coll, VA	B
Lyndon State Coll, VT	A,B
Lynn U, FL	B
Manatee Comm Coll, FL	A
Manchester Coll, IN	A,B
Manhattan Coll, NY	B
Manhattanville Coll, NY	B
Marian Coll of Fond du Lac, WI	B
Marquette U, WI	B
Marshall U, WV	B
Mary Baldwin Coll, VA	B
Marylhurst U, OR	B
Marymount Manhattan Coll, NY	B
Maryville Coll, TN	B
Maryville U of Saint Louis, MO	B
Marywood U, PA	B
Massachusetts Bay Comm Coll, MA	A
Massachusetts Inst of Technology, MA	B
Maui Comm Coll, HI	A
McDaniel Coll, MD	B
McMurry U, TX	B
McNeese State U, LA	B
Menlo Coll, CA	B
Mercy Coll, NY	A,B
Merritt Coll, CA	A
Mesabi Range Comm and Tech Coll, MN	A
Mesa Comm Coll, AZ	A
Mesa State Coll, CO	A,B
Miami Dade Coll, FL	A
Miami U, OH	B
Michigan Technological U, MI	B
MidAmerica Nazarene U, KS	A,B
Middlesex Comm Coll, CT	A
Middle Tennessee State U, TN	B
Midland Coll, TX	A
Midstate Coll, IL	A,B
Midwestern State U, TX	B
Millersville U of Pennsylvania, PA	B
Milligan Coll, TN	B
Millsaps Coll, MS	B
Mills Coll, CA	B
Minnesota State Coll–Southeast Tech, MN	A
Minnesota State U Mankato, MN	B
Minnesota State U Moorhead, MN	B
Minot State U, ND	B
MiraCosta Coll, CA	A

College	Degree
Mississippi U for Women, MS	B
Missouri Baptist U, MO	A,B
Mitchell Coll, CT	A,B
Mitchell Tech Inst, SD	A
Modesto Jr Coll, CA	A
Molloy Coll, NY	B
Monmouth U, NJ	B
Montana Tech of The U of Montana, MT	A
Montclair State U, NJ	B
Monterey Peninsula Coll, CA	A
Moravian Coll, PA	B
Morehead State U, KY	B
Morningside Coll, IA	B
Motlow State Comm Coll, TN	A
Mott Comm Coll, MI	A
Mountain State U, WV	A,B
Mount Ida Coll, MA	A,B
Mount Mercy Coll, IA	B
Muskingum Coll, OH	B
Nassau Comm Coll, NY	A
Nebraska Wesleyan U, NE	B
New England Coll, NH	B
New England Inst of Technology, RI	A,B
New Mexico Highlands U, NM	B
New Mexico Inst of Mining and Technology, NM	A,B
New Mexico Military Inst, NM	A
New Mexico State U, NM	A,B
New Mexico State U–Alamogordo, NM	A
New River Comm Coll, VA	A
New York U, NY	B
Niagara U, NY	A,B
Nichols Coll, MA	A,B
Northampton County Area Comm Coll, PA	A
North Carolina State U, NC	B
North Central Coll, IL	B
North Central U, MN	A,B
North Dakota State Coll of Science, ND	A
North Dakota State U, ND	B
Northeast Comm Coll, NE	A
Northeastern U, MA	B
Northeast State Tech Comm Coll, TN	A
Northern Arizona U, AZ	B
Northern Kentucky U, KY	A,B
Northern Michigan U, MI	A,B
Northern State U, SD	A,B
North Lake Coll, TX	A
Northland Coll, WI	B
NorthWest Arkansas Comm Coll, AR	A
Northwest Coll, WY	A
Northwestern Polytechnic U, CA	B
Northwestern State U of Louisiana, LA	A,B
Northwestern U, IL	B
Northwest Missouri State U, MO	B
Northwest U, WA	B
Norwalk Comm Coll, CT	A
Notre Dame Coll, OH	A,B
Notre Dame de Namur U, CA	B
Nova Southeastern U, FL	B
Oakland U, MI	B
Ohio Wesleyan U, OH	B
Oklahoma Panhandle State U, OK	A,B
Oklahoma State U, OK	B
Oklahoma Wesleyan U, OK	A,B
Old Dominion U, VA	B
Orange Coast Coll, CA	A
Oregon State U, OR	B
Ottawa U, KS	B
Otterbein Coll, OH	B
Owens Comm Coll, Toledo, OH	A
Pace U, NY	B
Palomar Coll, CA	A
Park U, MO	A,B
Patricia Stevens Coll, MO	A
Paul D. Camp Comm Coll, VA	A
Peace Coll, NC	B
Pellissippi State Tech Comm Coll, TN	A
Peninsula Coll, WA	A
Peru State Coll, NE	B
Philadelphia Biblical U, PA	A
Philadelphia U, PA	B
Piedmont Comm Coll, NC	A
Pierce Coll, WA	A
Pikes Peak Comm Coll, CO	A
Pioneer Pacific Coll, OR	A,B
Pittsburg State U, KS	B
Pitzer Coll, CA	B
Plymouth State U, NH	B
Portland Comm Coll, OR	A
Portland State U, OR	B
Prescott Coll, AZ	B
Presentation Coll, SD	A,B
Principia Coll, IL	B
Purdue U, IN	A,B
Quincy U, IL	B
Quinnipiac U, CT	B
Radford U, VA	B
Ramapo Coll of New Jersey, NJ	B
Randolph-Macon Coll, VA	B
Raritan Valley Comm Coll, NJ	A
Rasmussen Coll Mankato, MN	A
Redlands Comm Coll, OK	A
Rensselaer Polytechnic Inst, NY	B
Renton Tech Coll, WA	A
Rhodes Coll, TN	B
Richmond Comm Coll, NC	A
Rider U, NJ	A,B
Ridgewater Coll, MN	A
Riverside Comm Coll District, CA	A
Rochester Inst of Technology, NY	A,B
Rocky Mountain Coll, MT	B
Roger Williams U, RI	A,B
Roosevelt U, IL	B
Rose State Coll, OK	A
Sacramento City Coll, CA	A
Sacred Heart U, CT	A,B
Sage Coll of Albany, NY	A,B
St. Ambrose U, IA	B
Saint Anselm Coll, NH	B
Saint Charles Comm Coll, MO	A
Saint Francis U, PA	A,B
St. Gregory's U, OK	A,B
Saint John's U, MN	B
Saint Joseph's Coll, IN	B
Saint Leo U, FL	B
St. Louis Comm Coll at Florissant Valley, MO	A
Saint Louis U, MO	B
Saint Mary-of-the-Woods Coll, IN	B
Saint Mary's Coll, IN	B
Saint Mary's Coll of California, CA	B
Saint Mary's U of Minnesota, MN	B
St. Mary's U of San Antonio, TX	B
Saint Michael's Coll, VT	B
St. Petersburg Coll, FL	A
St. Thomas U, FL	B
Saint Vincent Coll, PA	B
Sam Houston State U, TX	B
San Bernardino Valley Coll, CA	A
San Diego City Coll, CA	A
San Diego State U, CA	B
San Francisco State U, CA	B
San Jacinto Coll Central Campus, TX	A
San Jacinto Coll North Campus, TX	A
San Jacinto Coll South Campus, TX	A
Santa Barbara City Coll, CA	A
Santa Fe Comm Coll, NM	A
Santa Monica Coll, CA	A
Santa Rosa Jr Coll, CA	A
Sauk Valley Comm Coll, IL	A
Savannah State U, GA	B
Schiller International U, FL	A,B
Schreiner U, TX	B
Scott Comm Coll, IA	A
Scripps Coll, CA	B
Seattle Central Comm Coll, WA	A
Seattle U, WA	B
Seton Hall U, NJ	B
Shenandoah U, VA	B
Shepherd U, WV	B
Sheridan Coll–Sheridan and Gillette, WY	A
Shorter Coll, GA	B
Siena Coll, NY	B
Sierra Coll, CA	A
Simmons Coll, MA	B
Simpson Coll, IA	B
Skagit Valley Coll, WA	A
Skidmore Coll, NY	B
Slippery Rock U of Pennsylvania, PA	B
Southeast Missouri State U, MO	B
Southern Arkansas U–Magnolia, AR	A
Southern Arkansas U Tech, AR	A
Southern Illinois U Carbondale, IL	B
Southern Illinois U Edwardsville, IL	B
Southern New Hampshire U, NH	A,B
Southern Oregon U, OR	B
Southern Utah U, UT	B
South Georgia Coll, GA	A
South Puget Sound Comm Coll, WA	A
Southwestern Coll, KS	B
Southwestern Comm Coll, IA	B
Southwestern Comm Coll, NC	A
Southwest Minnesota State U, MN	A,B
Spartanburg Methodist Coll, SC	A
Spokane Comm Coll, WA	A
Spokane Falls Comm Coll, WA	A
Spring Arbor U, MI	B
State U of New York at Oswego, NY	B
State U of New York at Plattsburgh, NY	B
State U of New York Coll at Geneseo, NY	B
State U of New York Coll at Oneonta, NY	B
Stony Brook U, State U of New York, NY	B
Suffolk County Comm Coll, NY	A
Suffolk U, MA	B
Sullivan U, KY	A,B
Susquehanna U, PA	B
Sussex County Comm Coll, NJ	A
Syracuse U, NY	B
Tabor Coll, KS	A,B
Taylor U, IN	B
Tennessee Technological U, TN	B
Texas A&M U at Galveston, TX	B
Texas A&M U–Corpus Christi, TX	B
Texas A&M U–Kingsville, TX	B
Texas A&M U–Texarkana, TX	B
Texas Christian U, TX	B
Texas State U-San Marcos, TX	B
Texas Wesleyan U, TX	B
Thomas More Coll, KY	A,B
Trevecca Nazarene U, TN	B
Trinity Coll of Florida, FL	B
Trinity U, TX	B
Trinity (Washington) U, DC	B
Troy U, AL	A,B
Truman State U, MO	B
Tusculum Coll, TN	B
U at Buffalo, the State U of New York, NY	B
The U of Alabama, AL	B
The U of Alabama in Huntsville, AL	B
U of Arkansas, AR	B
U of Arkansas at Fort Smith, AR	A,B
U of Arkansas at Pine Bluff, AR	B
U of Baltimore, MD	B
U of California, Santa Cruz, CA	B
U of Central Florida, FL	B
U of Central Missouri, MO	A
U of Charleston, WV	A,B
U of Cincinnati, OH	A,B
U of Cincinnati Raymond Walters Coll, OH	A
U of Colorado at Boulder, CO	B
U of Colorado at Colorado Springs, CO	B
U of Dayton, OH	B
U of Denver, CO	B
U of Detroit Mercy, MI	B
U of Dubuque, IA	A,B
The U of Findlay, OH	A,B
U of Guam, GU	B
U of Hartford, CT	B
U of Hawaii at Manoa, HI	B
U of Illinois at Springfield, IL	B
U of Indianapolis, IN	A,B
The U of Iowa, IA	B
U of Kansas, KS	B
U of La Verne, CA	B
U of Maine at Farmington, ME	B
U of Maine at Fort Kent, ME	A,B
U of Maine at Presque Isle, ME	B
U of Mary Hardin-Baylor, TX	B
U of Maryland, Baltimore County, MD	B
U of Maryland, Coll Park, MD	B
U of Mary Washington, VA	B
U of Miami, FL	B
U of Michigan–Flint, MI	B
U of Minnesota, Crookston, MN	A,B
U of Minnesota, Morris, MN	B
U of Missouri–Columbia, MO	B
U of Missouri–St. Louis, MO	B
U of Nebraska–Lincoln, NE	B
U of Nevada, Reno, NV	B
U of New Mexico, NM	B
U of New Orleans, LA	B
U of North Alabama, AL	B
The U of North Carolina at Asheville, NC	B
The U of North Carolina at Pembroke, NC	B
U of Northern Iowa, IA	B
U of North Texas, TX	B
U of Oregon, OR	B
U of Pittsburgh, PA	B
U of Pittsburgh at Bradford, PA	B
U of Puget Sound, WA	B
U of Rhode Island, RI	B
U of Saint Francis, IN	A,B
U of San Diego, CA	B
U of San Francisco, CA	B
U of Sioux Falls, SD	A,B
U of South Carolina, SC	B
U of South Carolina Upstate, SC	B
U of Southern Indiana, IN	B
U of Southern Maine, ME	B
U of South Florida, FL	B
The U of Tampa, FL	B
The U of Tennessee at Martin, TN	B
The U of Texas at San Antonio, TX	B
U of the Incarnate Word, TX	B
U of Tulsa, OK	B
U of Utah, UT	B
U of Virginia, VA	B
U of Washington, WA	B
U of West Florida, FL	B
U of Wisconsin–Eau Claire, WI	B
U of Wisconsin–La Crosse, WI	B
U of Wisconsin–Oshkosh, WI	B
U of Wisconsin–Stevens Point, WI	B
U of Wisconsin–Stout, WI	B
U of Wisconsin–Superior, WI	B
U of Wisconsin–Whitewater, WI	B
U of Wyoming, WY	B
Upper Iowa U, IA	A,B
Utah State U, UT	A,B
Utah Valley State Coll, UT	A,B
Utica Coll, NY	B
Valparaiso U, IN	B
Vanderbilt U, TN	B
Vanguard U of Southern California, CA	B
Vermont Tech Coll, VT	A,B
Villanova U, PA	B
Virginia Commonwealth U, VA	B
Virginia Polytechnic Inst and State U, VA	B
Viterbo U, WI	B
Wake Forest U, NC	B
Waldorf Coll, IA	B
Warren Wilson Coll, NC	B
Wartburg Coll, IA	B
Washington & Jefferson Coll, PA	B

A=Associate; B=Bachelor's Degree

Institution	Degree
Washington Coll, MD	B
Washington State U, WA	B
Washington U in St. Louis, MO	B
Waynesburg Coll, PA	A,B
Wayne State Coll, NE	B
Weatherford Coll, TX	B
Webber International U, FL	A,B
Wells Coll, NY	B
Wentworth Inst of Technology, MA	A,B
Western Illinois U, IL	B
Western Kentucky U, KY	B
Western New England Coll, MA	B
Western New Mexico U, NM	A
Western Washington U, WA	B
Western Wyoming Comm Coll, WY	A
Westmont Coll, CA	B
West Texas A&M U, TX	B
West Valley Coll, CA	A
Whatcom Comm Coll, WA	A
Wichita State U, KS	B
Widener U, PA	B
Wilkes U, PA	B
Williston State Coll, ND	A
Wilmington Coll, OH	B
Wilson Coll, PA	A,B
Winona State U, MN	B
Woodbury U, CA	B
Worcester Polytechnic Inst, MA	B
Worcester State Coll, MA	B
Wytheville Comm Coll, VA	A
Yavapai Coll, AZ	A
York Coll, NE	B
York Coll of Pennsylvania, PA	A,B
York Coll of the City U of New York, NY	B
Young Harris Coll, GA	A

Communications, Journalism, Speech, and Mass Communications

Institution	Degree
Adrian Coll, MI	B
Allegheny Coll, PA	B
Alvernia Coll, PA	B
Alverno Coll, WI	B
Alvin Comm Coll, TX	A
American U, DC	B
Antioch Coll, OH	B
Aquinas Coll, MI	B
Arizona State U, AZ	B
Ashford U, IA	B
Ashland U, OH	A,B
Averett U, VA	B
Baker U, KS	B
Baldwin-Wallace Coll, OH	B
Ball State U, IN	A,B
Barry U, FL	B
Bates Coll, ME	B
Belmont U, TN	B
Bemidji State U, MN	B
Benedict Coll, SC	B
Bennington Coll, VT	B
Bethany Coll, KS	B
Bethel U, MN	B
Black Hills State U, SD	B
Boston U, MA	B
Briarwood Coll, CT	A
Broome Comm Coll, NY	A
Bryant U, RI	B
Bunker Hill Comm Coll, MA	A
Butler U, IN	B
Caldwell Coll, NJ	B
California Lutheran U, CA	B
California Polytechnic State U, San Luis Obispo, CA	B
California State Polytechnic U, Pomona, CA	B
California State U, Long Beach, CA	B
California State U, Sacramento, CA	B
California State U, Stanislaus, CA	B
Calvin Coll, MI	B
Cameron U, OK	A,B
Cañada Coll, CA	A
Capital U, OH	B
Cardinal Stritch U, WI	B
Carlow U, PA	B
Carroll Coll, MT	B
Carroll Coll, WI	B
Carson-Newman Coll, TN	B
Carthage Coll, WI	B
The Catholic U of America, DC	B
Central Christian Coll of Kansas, KS	A,B
Centralia Coll, WA	A
Central Michigan U, MI	B
Chabot Coll, CA	A
Chaffey Coll, CA	A
Chapman U, CA	B
Chatham U, PA	B
Chattanooga State Tech Comm Coll, TN	A
City Coll of San Francisco, CA	A
City Colls of Chicago, Harold Washington Coll, IL	A
City Colls of Chicago, Kennedy-King Coll, IL	A
Clarendon Coll, TX	A
Clarion U of Pennsylvania, PA	B
Clarkson U, NY	B
Clearwater Christian Coll, FL	B
Cleveland State U, OH	B
Cochise Coll, Sierra Vista, AZ	A
Coe Coll, IA	B
Coffeyville Comm Coll, KS	A
Colby Comm Coll, KS	A
Coll Misericordia, PA	B
Coll of Saint Benedict, MN	B
Coll of St. Catherine, MN	B
Coll of Southern Maryland, MD	A
Coll of the Canyons, CA	A
Coll of the Desert, CA	A
Coll of the Ozarks, MO	B
Colorado State U, CO	B
Columbia Coll Chicago, IL	B
Columbia Union Coll, MD	B
Concordia Coll, MN	B
Concordia U, IL	B
Connors State Coll, OK	B
Cornell Coll, IA	B
Cosumnes River Coll, Sacramento, CA	A
Dana Coll, NE	B
Dean Coll, MA	A
De Anza Coll, CA	A
Delaware Tech & Comm Coll, Jack F. Owens Campus, DE	A
Del Mar Coll, TX	A
Denison U, OH	B
DePaul U, IL	B
Dominican U of California, CA	B
Dordt Coll, IA	B
Drake U, IA	B
Drury U, MO	B
Duquesne U, PA	B
East Carolina U, NC	B
East Central Coll, MO	A
Eastern Connecticut State U, CT	B
Eastern Mennonite U, VA	B
Eastern U, PA	B
Eastern Wyoming Coll, WY	A
East Los Angeles Coll, CA	A
East Tennessee State U, TN	B
East Texas Baptist U, TX	B
Eckerd Coll, FL	B
Edinboro U of Pennsylvania, PA	B
El Camino Coll, CA	A
Elizabethtown Coll, PA	B
Elon U, NC	B
Embry-Riddle Aeronautical U, FL	B
Emerson Coll, MA	B
Emmanuel Coll, MA	B
Emory U, GA	B
Emporia State U, KS	B
Fairleigh Dickinson U, Coll at Florham, NJ	B
Fairleigh Dickinson U, Metropolitan Campus, NJ	B
Ferris State U, MI	B
Five Towns Coll, NY	A
Florida Atlantic U, FL	B
Florida Inst of Technology, FL	B
Florida International U, FL	B
Florida State U, FL	B
Foothill Coll, CA	A
Fordham U, NY	B
Fresno City Coll, CA	A
Frostburg State U, MD	B
Fullerton Coll, CA	A
Furman U, SC	B
Gannon U, PA	B
Garden City Comm Coll, KS	A
Gardner-Webb U, NC	B
George Fox U, OR	B
Georgia Coll & State U, GA	B
Georgia Highlands Coll, GA	A
Georgia Southern U, GA	B
Georgia State U, GA	B
Gettysburg Coll, PA	B
Glendale Comm Coll, CA	A
Golden West Coll, CA	A
Gonzaga U, WA	B
Goshen Coll, IN	B
Grand Valley State U, MI	B
Grand View Coll, IA	B
Green Mountain Coll, VT	B
Greenville Coll, IL	B
Gulf Coast Comm Coll, FL	A
Gustavus Adolphus Coll, MN	B
Harding U, AR	B
Hardin-Simmons U, TX	B
Harper Coll, IL	A
Harrisburg Area Comm Coll, PA	A
Hawai'i Pacific U, HI	B
Hill Coll of the Hill Jr Coll District, TX	A
Hillsdale Coll, MI	B
Hofstra U, NY	B
Holy Family U, PA	B
Hope Coll, MI	B
Howard Coll, TX	A
Howard Payne U, TX	B
Huntingdon Coll, AL	B
Huntington U, IN	B
Idaho State U, ID	A,B
Illinois Coll, IL	B
Indiana U Bloomington, IN	B
Indiana U of Pennsylvania, PA	B
Indiana U South Bend, IN	B
Indiana U Southeast, IN	A
Indiana Wesleyan U, IN	A,B
Iowa State U of Science and Technology, IA	B
Iowa Western Comm Coll, IA	A
Isothermal Comm Coll, NC	A
Jacksonville State U, AL	B
Jacksonville U, FL	B
James Madison U, VA	B
Johnson State Coll, VT	B
Judson Coll, IL	B
Juniata Coll, PA	B
Kansas State U, KS	B
Kansas Wesleyan U, KS	B
Kean U, NJ	B
Kennesaw State U, GA	B
Kent State U, OH	B
Kentucky Wesleyan Coll, KY	B
Keystone Coll, PA	A,B
Kilgore Coll, TX	A
Kirkwood Comm Coll, IA	A
Lake Land Coll, IL	A
Laney Coll, CA	A
Langston U, OK	B
Lansing Comm Coll, MI	A
Laramie County Comm Coll, WY	A
Lewis & Clark Coll, OR	B
Lewis-Clark State Coll, ID	B
Liberty U, VA	B
Linfield Coll, OR	B
Lipscomb U, TN	B
Long Beach City Coll, CA	A
Long Island U, C.W. Post Campus, NY	B
Longwood U, VA	B
Los Angeles Mission Coll, CA	A
Los Angeles Pierce Coll, CA	A
Los Angeles Southwest Coll, CA	A
Louisiana State U at Alexandria, LA	B
Loyola U Chicago, IL	B
Lynchburg Coll, VA	B
Lyndon State Coll, VT	A
Manatee Comm Coll, FL	A
Manchester Coll, IN	B
Marian Coll of Fond du Lac, WI	B
Marquette U, WI	B
Marshall U, WV	B
Mary Baldwin Coll, VA	B
Marylhurst U, OR	B
Marywood U, PA	B
Massachusetts Bay Comm Coll, MA	A
McDaniel Coll, MD	B
McMurry U, TX	B
McNeese State U, LA	B
Mesa State Coll, CO	B
Miami Dade Coll, FL	A
Miami U, OH	B
Michigan Technological U, MI	B
Middlesex Comm Coll, CT	A
Midland Coll, TX	A
Millersville U of Pennsylvania, PA	B
Minnesota State U Mankato, MN	B
Minnesota State U Moorhead, MN	B
Minot State U, ND	B
MiraCosta Coll, CA	A
Mississippi U for Women, MS	B
Missouri Baptist U, MO	B
Modesto Jr Coll, CA	A
Molloy Coll, NY	B
Monmouth U, NJ	B
Montana Tech of The U of Montana, MT	B
Montclair State U, NJ	B
Morehead State U, KY	B
Mount Mercy Coll, IA	B
Muskingum Coll, OH	B
Nassau Comm Coll, NY	A
Nebraska Wesleyan U, NE	B
New England Coll, NH	B
New Mexico Highlands U, NM	B
New Mexico State U, NM	B
New York U, NY	B
Northampton County Area Comm Coll, PA	A
North Carolina State U, NC	B
North Central Coll, IL	B
North Central U, MN	A,B
North Dakota State U, ND	B
Northeast Comm Coll, NE	A
Northeastern U, MA	B
Northern Arizona U, AZ	B
Northern Kentucky U, KY	B
Northern Michigan U, MI	B
Northern State U, SD	B
Northwest Coll, WY	A
Northwestern State U of Louisiana, LA	B
Northwestern U, IL	B
Northwest Missouri State U, MO	B
Notre Dame Coll, OH	B
Notre Dame de Namur U, CA	B
Oakland U, MI	B
Ohio Wesleyan U, OH	B
Oklahoma State U, OK	B
Old Dominion U, VA	B
Orange Coast Coll, CA	A
Oregon State U, OR	B
Otterbein Coll, OH	B
Pace U, NY	B
Palomar Coll, CA	A
Park U, MO	B
Peace Coll, NC	B
Pittsburg State U, KS	B
Plymouth State U, NH	B
Portland State U, OR	B
Prescott Coll, AZ	B
Presentation Coll, SD	A,B
Purdue U, IN	B
Quincy U, IL	B
Quinnipiac U, CT	B
Ramapo Coll of New Jersey, NJ	B
Randolph Coll, VA	B
Rensselaer Polytechnic Inst, NY	B
Rider U, NJ	B
Ridgewater Coll, MN	A
Rocky Mountain Coll, MT	B
Roosevelt U, IL	B
Rose State Coll, OK	A
Sacramento City Coll, CA	A
Sacred Heart U, CT	B
St. Ambrose U, IA	B
Saint Francis U, PA	B
St. Gregory's U, OK	B
Saint John's U, MN	B
Saint Leo U, FL	B
St. Louis Comm Coll at Florissant Valley, MO	A
Saint Louis U, MO	B
Saint Mary-of-the-Woods Coll, IN	B
Saint Mary's Coll, IN	B

College	Degree
Saint Mary's Coll of California, CA	B
St. Mary's U of San Antonio, TX	B
Saint Michael's Coll, VT	B
Saint Vincent Coll, PA	B
Sam Houston State U, TX	B
San Bernardino Valley Coll, CA	A
San Diego City Coll, CA	A
San Diego State U, CA	B
San Francisco State U, CA	B
San Jacinto Coll Central Campus, TX	A
San Jacinto Coll North Campus, TX	A
Santa Barbara City Coll, CA	A
Santa Monica Coll, CA	A
Santa Rosa Jr Coll, CA	A
Sauk Valley Comm Coll, IL	A
Seattle U, WA	B
Seton Hall U, NJ	B
Shenandoah U, VA	B
Shepherd U, WV	B
Sierra Coll, CA	A
Simpson Coll, IA	B
Skagit Valley Coll, WA	A
Slippery Rock U of Pennsylvania, PA	B
South Dakota State U, SD	B
Southeast Missouri State U, MO	B
Southern Arkansas U–Magnolia, AR	B
Southern Illinois U Carbondale, IL	B
Southern Illinois U Edwardsville, IL	B
Southern Oregon U, OR	B
Southern Utah U, UT	B
South Georgia Coll, GA	A
Southwest Minnesota State U, MN	B
Spring Arbor U, MI	B
Stanford U, CA	B
State U of New York at Oswego, NY	B
State U of New York at Plattsburgh, NY	B
State U of New York Coll at Geneseo, NY	B
State U of New York Coll at Oneonta, NY	B
Suffolk County Comm Coll, NY	A
Suffolk U, MA	B
Susquehanna U, PA	B
Sussex County Comm Coll, NJ	A
Syracuse U, NY	B
Tabor Coll, KS	B
Taylor U, IN	B
Tennessee Technological U, TN	B
Texas A&M U–Corpus Christi, TX	B
Texas A&M U–Kingsville, TX	B
Texas Christian U, TX	B
Texas State U-San Marcos, TX	B
Texas Wesleyan U, TX	B
Thomas More Coll, KY	A,B
Trevecca Nazarene U, TN	B
Trinity U, TX	B
Troy U, AL	B
Truman State U, MO	B
U at Buffalo, the State U of New York, NY	B
The U of Alabama, AL	B
The U of Alabama in Huntsville, AL	B
U of Arkansas, AR	B
U of Arkansas at Pine Bluff, AR	B
U of Baltimore, MD	B
U of Central Florida, FL	B
U of Central Missouri, MO	B
U of Cincinnati, OH	B
U of Colorado at Boulder, CO	B
U of Colorado at Colorado Springs, CO	B
U of Dayton, OH	B
U of Denver, CO	B
U of Detroit Mercy, MI	B
U of Dubuque, IA	B
The U of Findlay, OH	B
U of Hartford, CT	B
U of Hawaii at Manoa, HI	B
U of Indianapolis, IN	B
The U of Iowa, IA	B
U of Kansas, KS	B
U of La Verne, CA	B
U of Mary Hardin-Baylor, TX	B
U of Maryland, Coll Park, MD	B
U of Miami, FL	B
U of Michigan–Flint, MI	B
U of Minnesota, Morris, MN	B
U of Missouri–Columbia, MO	B
U of Missouri–St. Louis, MO	B
U of Nebraska–Lincoln, NE	B
U of Nevada, Reno, NV	B
U of New Mexico, NM	B
U of New Orleans, LA	B
U of North Alabama, AL	B
The U of North Carolina at Pembroke, NC	B
U of Northern Iowa, IA	B
U of North Texas, TX	B
U of Oregon, OR	B
U of Pittsburgh, PA	B
U of Puget Sound, WA	B
U of Rhode Island, RI	B
U of Saint Francis, IN	B
U of San Francisco, CA	B
U of Sioux Falls, SD	B
U of South Carolina, SC	B
U of South Carolina Upstate, SC	B
U of Southern Indiana, IN	B
U of Southern Maine, ME	B
U of South Florida, FL	B
The U of Tennessee at Martin, TN	B
The U of Texas at San Antonio, TX	B
The U of the Arts, PA	B
U of the Incarnate Word, TX	B
U of Tulsa, OK	B
U of Utah, UT	B
U of Virginia, VA	B
U of Washington, WA	B
U of West Florida, FL	B
U of Wisconsin–Eau Claire, WI	B
U of Wisconsin–La Crosse, WI	B
U of Wisconsin–Oshkosh, WI	B
U of Wisconsin–Stevens Point, WI	B
U of Wisconsin–Superior, WI	B
U of Wisconsin–Whitewater, WI	B
U of Wyoming, WY	B
Utah State U, UT	B
Utah Valley State Coll, UT	A
Utica Coll, NY	B
Valparaiso U, IN	B
Vanguard U of Southern California, CA	B
Virginia Polytechnic Inst and State U, VA	B
Wabash Coll, IN	B
Wake Forest U, NC	B
Waldorf Coll, IA	B
Wartburg Coll, IA	B
Washington State U, WA	B
Washington U in St. Louis, MO	B
Waynesburg Coll, PA	B
Wayne State Coll, NE	B
Western Illinois U, IL	B
Western Kentucky U, KY	B
Western New England Coll, MA	B
Western Washington U, WA	B
Western Wyoming Comm Coll, WY	A
Westmont Coll, CA	B
West Texas A&M U, TX	B
West Valley Coll, CA	A
Wichita State U, KS	B
Wilkes U, PA	B
Winona State U, MN	B
Woodbury U, CA	B
York Coll of Pennsylvania, PA	A,B
York Coll of the City U of New York, NY	B
Young Harris Coll, GA	A

Computer and Information Sciences

College	Degree
Academy Coll, MN	A
Adelphi U, NY	B
Aims Comm Coll, CO	A
Alamance Comm Coll, NC	A
Albertus Magnus Coll, CT	A,B
Albion Coll, MI	B
Alderson-Broaddus Coll, WV	A,B
Allegheny Coll, PA	B
Alvernia Coll, PA	A,B
Alverno Coll, WI	B
Alvin Comm Coll, TX	A
American InterContinental U, CA	B
American U, DC	B
Ancilla Coll, IN	A
Antioch Coll, OH	B
Aquinas Coll, MI	B
Arcadia U, PA	B
Arizona State U, AZ	B
Ashford U, IA	B
Ashland U, OH	B
Assumption Coll, MA	B
Austin Peay State U, TN	A
Averett U, VA	B
Babson Coll, MA	B
Baker Coll of Flint, MI	A,B
Baker U, KS	B
Baldwin-Wallace Coll, OH	B
Ball State U, IN	A,B
Bard Coll, NY	B
Barnard Coll, NY	B
Barry U, FL	B
Belmont U, TN	B
Beloit Coll, WI	B
Bemidji State U, MN	B
Benedict Coll, SC	B
Bennington Coll, VT	B
Bentley Coll, MA	B
Berkshire Comm Coll, MA	A
Bethel Coll, KS	B
Bethel U, MN	B
Black Hills State U, SD	A
Bluefield State Coll, WV	A,B
Boise State U, ID	B
Boston U, MA	B
Bowdoin Coll, ME	B
Bowling Green State U–Firelands Coll, OH	A
Bronx Comm Coll of the City U of New York, NY	A
Broome Comm Coll, NY	A
Bryant U, RI	B
Bucknell U, PA	B
Bunker Hill Comm Coll, MA	A
Butler U, IN	B
Caldwell Coll, NJ	B
Calhoun Comm Coll, AL	A
California Lutheran U, CA	B
California Polytechnic State U, San Luis Obispo, CA	B
California State Polytechnic U, Pomona, CA	B
California State U, Long Beach, CA	B
California State U, Sacramento, CA	B
California State U, Stanislaus, CA	B
Calvin Coll, MI	B
Cameron U, OK	A
Cañada Coll, CA	A
Capital U, OH	B
Cardinal Stritch U, WI	B
Carleton Coll, MN	B
Carlow U, PA	B
Carroll Coll, MT	A,B
Carroll Coll, WI	B
Carson-Newman Coll, TN	B
Carthage Coll, WI	B
The Catholic U of America, DC	B
Centenary Coll, NJ	B
Central Christian Coll of Kansas, KS	A
Central Comm Coll–Columbus Campus, NE	A
Central Comm Coll–Grand Island Campus, NE	A
Central Comm Coll–Hastings Campus, NE	A
Central Michigan U, MI	B
Central Piedmont Comm Coll, NC	A
Central Wyoming Coll, WY	A
Centre Coll, KY	B
Century Coll, MN	A
Cerro Coso Comm Coll, CA	A
Chabot Coll, CA	A
Chaffey Coll, CA	A
Chapman U, CA	B
Chatham U, PA	B
Chattahoochee Tech Coll, GA	A
Chattanooga State Tech Comm Coll, TN	A
Chemeketa Comm Coll, OR	A
City Coll of San Francisco, CA	A
City Coll of the City U of New York, NY	B
City Colls of Chicago, Harold Washington Coll, IL	A
City Colls of Chicago, Kennedy-King Coll, IL	A
City U, WA	B
Claflin U, SC	B
Clarendon Coll, TX	A
Clarion U of Pennsylvania, PA	B
Clarke Coll, IA	B
Clarkson U, NY	B
Clark U, MA	B
Cleveland State U, OH	B
Coastal Carolina U, SC	B
Coastal Georgia Comm Coll, GA	A
Cochise Coll, Sierra Vista, AZ	A
Coe Coll, IA	A
Coffeyville Comm Coll, KS	A
Colby Coll, ME	B
Colby Comm Coll, KS	A
Colegio Universitario de San Juan, PR	A
Coll Misericordia, PA	B
Coll of DuPage, IL	A
Coll of Lake County, IL	A
Coll of Saint Benedict, MN	B
Coll of St. Catherine, MN	B
Coll of Southern Maryland, MD	A
Coll of the Canyons, CA	A
Coll of the Desert, CA	A
Coll of the Holy Cross, MA	B
Coll of the Ozarks, MO	B
Colorado State U, CO	B
Columbia Coll, MO	A,B
Columbia Union Coll, MD	A,B
Columbia U, School of General Studies, NY	B
Concordia Coll, MN	B
Concordia U, IL	B
Connecticut Coll, CT	B
Connors State Coll, OK	A
Cornell Coll, IA	B
Cosumnes River Coll, Sacramento, CA	A
County Coll of Morris, NJ	A
Culver-Stockton Coll, MO	B
Dana Coll, NE	B
Davenport U, Midland, MI	A
De Anza Coll, CA	A
Defiance Coll, OH	A,B
DeKalb Tech Coll, GA	A
Delaware Tech & Comm Coll, Jack F. Owens Campus, DE	A
Del Mar Coll, TX	A
Delta Coll, MI	A
Denison U, OH	B
DePaul U, IL	B
DePauw U, IN	B
DeSales U, PA	B
Dordt Coll, IA	B
Drake U, IA	B
Drew U, NJ	B
Drury U, MO	B
Duquesne U, PA	B
East Carolina U, NC	B
Eastern Connecticut State U, CT	B
Eastern Mennonite U, VA	B
Eastern U, PA	B
Eastern Wyoming Coll, WY	A
East Los Angeles Coll, CA	A
East Tennessee State U, TN	B
East Texas Baptist U, TX	B
Eckerd Coll, FL	B
Edgewood Coll, WI	B
Edinboro U of Pennsylvania, PA	A,B
Edison Coll, FL	A
Edmonds Comm Coll, WA	A
El Camino Coll, CA	A

A=Associate; B=Bachelor's Degree

Institution	Degree
Elizabethtown Coll, PA	B
Elmira Coll, NY	B
Elms Coll, MA	B
Elon U, NC	B
Emory U, GA	B
Emporia State U, KS	B
The Evergreen State Coll, WA	B
Fairfield U, CT	B
Fairleigh Dickinson U, Coll at Florham, NJ	B
Fairleigh Dickinson U, Metropolitan Campus, NJ	B
Ferris State U, MI	B
Five Towns Coll, NY	A
Florida Atlantic U, FL	B
Florida Gulf Coast U, FL	B
Florida Inst of Technology, FL	B
Florida International U, FL	B
Florida Keys Comm Coll, FL	A
Florida State U, FL	B
Fordham U, NY	B
Fort Lewis Coll, CO	B
Fox Valley Tech Coll, WI	A
Fresno City Coll, CA	A
Fresno Pacific U, CA	B
Frostburg State U, MD	B
Fullerton Coll, CA	A
Fulton-Montgomery Comm Coll, NY	A
Furman U, SC	B
Gannon U, PA	B
Garden City Comm Coll, KS	A
Gardner-Webb U, NC	B
GateWay Comm Coll, AZ	A
Genesee Comm Coll, NY	A
George Fox U, OR	B
Georgetown Coll, KY	B
Georgia Coll & State U, GA	B
Georgia Highlands Coll, GA	A
Georgia Southern U, GA	B
Georgia State U, GA	B
Gettysburg Coll, PA	B
Glendale Comm Coll, AZ	A
Glendale Comm Coll, CA	A
Globe Inst of Technology, NY	A,B
Goldey-Beacom Coll, DE	A,B
Gonzaga U, WA	B
Goshen Coll, IN	B
Grambling State U, LA	B
Grand Valley State U, MI	B
Grand View Coll, IA	B
Grays Harbor Coll, WA	A
Greenfield Comm Coll, MA	A
Greenville Coll, IL	B
Grinnell Coll, IA	B
Gulf Coast Comm Coll, FL	A
Gustavus Adolphus Coll, MN	B
Hamilton Coll, NY	B
Hampden-Sydney Coll, VA	B
Hampshire Coll, MA	B
Harding U, AR	B
Hardin-Simmons U, TX	B
Harper Coll, IL	A
Harrisburg Area Comm Coll, PA	A
Hartwick Coll, NY	B
Harvard U, MA	B
Harvey Mudd Coll, CA	B
Haverford Coll, PA	B
Hawai'i Pacific U, HI	A
Henry Ford Comm Coll, MI	A
Hilbert Coll, NY	A
Hill Coll of the Hill Jr Coll District, TX	A
Hillsdale Coll, MI	B
Hiram Coll, OH	B
Hofstra U, NY	B
Holy Family U, PA	B
Hope Coll, MI	B
Hopkinsville Comm Coll, KY	A
Houston Comm Coll System, TX	A
Howard Coll, TX	A
Howard Payne U, TX	B
Huntingdon Coll, AL	B
Huntington U, IN	B
Idaho State U, ID	B
Illinois Coll, IL	B
Illinois Inst of Technology, IL	B
Illinois Wesleyan U, IL	B
Indiana Tech, IN	A,B
Indiana U Bloomington, IN	B
Indiana U of Pennsylvania, PA	B
Indiana U South Bend, IN	A,B
Indiana U Southeast, IN	A,B
Indiana Wesleyan U, IN	A,B
Iowa State U of Science and Technology, IA	B
Iowa Western Comm Coll, IA	A
Isothermal Comm Coll, NC	A
Jacksonville State U, AL	B
Jacksonville U, FL	B
James A. Rhodes State Coll, OH	A
James Madison U, VA	B
John Carroll U, OH	B
John Jay Coll of Criminal Justice of the City U of New York, NY	B
The Johns Hopkins U, MD	B
Johnson & Wales U, RI	A
Johnson State Coll, VT	B
Joliet Jr Coll, IL	A
Jones Coll, Jacksonville, FL	A,B
Judson Coll, IL	B
Juniata Coll, PA	B
Kankakee Comm Coll, IL	A
Kansas State U, KS	B
Kansas Wesleyan U, KS	A,B
Kapiolani Comm Coll, HI	A
Kean U, NJ	B
Kennesaw State U, GA	B
Kent State U, OH	A,B
Kent State U, Salem Campus, OH	A
Kentucky Wesleyan Coll, KY	B
Kettering U, MI	B
Keystone Coll, PA	A
Kilgore Coll, TX	A
Kingwood Coll, TX	A
Kirkwood Comm Coll, IA	A
Knox Coll, IL	B
Lafayette Coll, PA	B
Lakeland Coll, WI	B
Lake Region State Coll, ND	A
Lamar State Coll–Port Arthur, TX	A
Lancaster Bible Coll, PA	B
Lander U, SC	B
Laney Coll, CA	A
Langston U, OK	B
Lansing Comm Coll, MI	A
Laramie County Comm Coll, WY	A
Las Positas Coll, CA	A
Laurel Business Inst, PA	A
Lawrence U, WI	B
Lees-McRae Coll, NC	B
Leeward Comm Coll, HI	A
LeMoyne-Owen Coll, TN	B
Lewis & Clark Coll, OR	B
Lewis-Clark State Coll, ID	A,B
Liberty U, VA	B
Limestone Coll, SC	A,B
Lincoln U, CA	B
Linfield Coll, OR	B
Lipscomb U, TN	B
Long Beach City Coll, CA	A
Long Island U, C.W. Post Campus, NY	B
Longwood U, VA	B
Los Angeles Harbor Coll, CA	A
Los Angeles Mission Coll, CA	A
Los Angeles Pierce Coll, CA	A
Los Angeles Southwest Coll, CA	A
Loyola U Chicago, IL	B
Luther Coll, IA	B
Lycoming Coll, PA	B
Lynchburg Coll, VA	B
Lyndon State Coll, VT	A,B
Manatee Comm Coll, FL	A
Manchester Coll, IN	A,B
Manhattan Coll, NY	B
Manhattanville Coll, NY	B
Marlboro Coll, VT	B
Marquette U, WI	B
Marshall U, WV	B
Mary Baldwin Coll, VA	B
Maryville Coll, TN	B
Maryville U of Saint Louis, MO	B
Marywood U, PA	B
Massachusetts Bay Comm Coll, MA	A
Massachusetts Inst of Technology, MA	B
McDaniel Coll, MD	B
McMurry U, TX	B
Mercy Coll, NY	B
Merritt Coll, CA	A
Mesa Comm Coll, AZ	A
Mesa State Coll, CO	A,B
Miami Dade Coll, FL	A
Miami U, OH	B
Michigan Technological U, MI	B
MidAmerica Nazarene U, KS	B
Middlebury Coll, VT	B
Middlesex Comm Coll, CT	A
Middle Tennessee State U, TN	B
Midland Coll, TX	B
Midstate Coll, IL	A
Midwestern State U, TX	B
Millersville U of Pennsylvania, PA	A,B
Milligan Coll, TN	B
Millsaps Coll, MS	B
Mills Coll, CA	B
Minnesota State Coll–Southeast Tech, MN	A
Minnesota State U Mankato, MN	B
Minnesota State U Moorhead, MN	B
Minot State U, ND	B
MiraCosta Coll, CA	A
Mississippi U for Women, MS	B
Missouri Baptist U, MO	B
Mitchell Tech Inst, SD	A
Modesto Jr Coll, CA	A
Molloy Coll, NY	B
Monmouth U, NJ	B
Montana Tech of The U of Montana, MT	A,B
Montclair State U, NJ	B
Monterey Peninsula Coll, CA	A
Moravian Coll, PA	B
Morehead State U, KY	A,B
Morningside Coll, IA	B
Mott Comm Coll, MI	A
Mountain State U, WV	A,B
Mount Holyoke Coll, MA	B
Mount Mercy Coll, IA	B
Muskingum Coll, OH	B
Nassau Comm Coll, NY	A
Nebraska Wesleyan U, NE	B
New England Coll, NH	B
New England Inst of Technology, RI	A,B
New Mexico Highlands U, NM	B
New Mexico Inst of Mining and Technology, NM	B
New Mexico Military Inst, NM	A
New Mexico State U, NM	B
New Mexico State U–Alamogordo, NM	A
New River Comm Coll, VA	A
New York U, NY	A
Niagara U, NY	B
Nichols Coll, MA	B
Northampton County Area Comm Coll, PA	A
North Carolina State U, NC	B
North Central Coll, IL	B
North Dakota State U, ND	B
Northeast Comm Coll, NE	A
Northeastern U, MA	B
Northeast State Tech Comm Coll, TN	A
Northern Arizona U, AZ	B
Northern Kentucky U, KY	B
Northern Michigan U, MI	A,B
Northern State U, SD	B
North Lake Coll, TX	A
Northland Coll, WI	B
NorthWest Arkansas Comm Coll, AR	A
Northwest Coll, WY	A
Northwestern Polytechnic U, CA	B
Northwestern State U of Louisiana, LA	B
Northwestern U, IL	B
Northwest Missouri State U, MO	B
Northwest Vista Coll, TX	A
Norwalk Comm Coll, CT	A
Notre Dame Coll, OH	B
Notre Dame de Namur U, CA	B
Nova Southeastern U, FL	B
Oakland U, MI	B
Ohio Wesleyan U, OH	B
Oklahoma Panhandle State U, OK	A,B
Oklahoma State U, OK	B
Oklahoma Wesleyan U, OK	A,B
Old Dominion U, VA	B
Orange Coast Coll, CA	A
Oregon State U, OR	B
Ottawa U, KS	B
Otterbein Coll, OH	B
Owens Comm Coll, Toledo, OH	B
Pace U, NY	B
Palomar Coll, CA	A
Park U, MO	A,B
Paul D. Camp Comm Coll, VA	A
Pellissippi State Tech Comm Coll, TN	A
Peru State Coll, NE	B
Philadelphia U, PA	B
Pierce Coll, WA	A
Pikes Peak Comm Coll, CO	A
Pioneer Pacific Coll, OR	A
Pittsburg State U, KS	B
Plymouth State U, NH	B
Portland Comm Coll, OR	A
Portland State U, OR	B
Prescott Coll, AZ	B
Principia Coll, IL	B
Purdue U, IN	B
Quincy U, IL	B
Quinnipiac U, CT	B
Radford U, VA	B
Ramapo Coll of New Jersey, NJ	B
Randolph-Macon Coll, VA	B
Raritan Valley Comm Coll, NJ	A
Rasmussen Coll Mankato, MN	A
Redlands Comm Coll, OK	A
Rensselaer Polytechnic Inst, NY	B
Renton Tech Coll, WA	A
Rhodes Coll, TN	B
Richmond Comm Coll, NC	A
Rider U, NJ	B
Ridgewater Coll, MN	A
Riverside Comm Coll District, CA	A
Rochester Inst of Technology, NY	A,B
Rocky Mountain Coll, MT	B
Roger Williams U, RI	B
Roosevelt U, IL	B
Rose State Coll, OK	A
Sacramento City Coll, CA	A
Sacred Heart U, CT	A,B
Sage Coll of Albany, NY	A,B
St. Ambrose U, IA	B
Saint Anselm Coll, NH	B
Saint Charles Comm Coll, MO	A
Saint Francis U, PA	A,B
St. Gregory's U, OK	B
Saint John's U, MN	B
Saint Joseph's Coll, IN	A,B
Saint Leo U, FL	B
St. Louis Comm Coll at Florissant Valley, MO	A
Saint Louis U, MO	B
Saint Mary-of-the-Woods Coll, IN	B
Saint Mary's Coll, IN	B
St. Mary's Coll of Maryland, MD	B
Saint Mary's U of Minnesota, MN	B
St. Mary's U of San Antonio, TX	B
Saint Michael's Coll, VT	B
St. Olaf Coll, MN	B
St. Thomas U, FL	B
Saint Vincent Coll, PA	B
Sam Houston State U, TX	B
San Bernardino Valley Coll, CA	A
San Diego City Coll, CA	A
San Diego State U, CA	B
San Francisco State U, CA	B
San Jacinto Coll Central Campus, TX	A
San Jacinto Coll North Campus, TX	A
San Jacinto Coll South Campus, TX	A
Santa Barbara City Coll, CA	A
Santa Fe Comm Coll, NM	A
Santa Monica Coll, CA	A
Santa Rosa Jr Coll, CA	A
Sarah Lawrence Coll, NY	B
Savannah State U, GA	B
Schreiner U, TX	B

College	Degree
Scott Comm Coll, IA	A
Scripps Coll, CA	B
Seattle U, WA	B
Seton Hall U, NJ	B
Shepherd U, WV	B
Sheridan Coll–Sheridan and Gillette, WY	A
Shorter Coll, GA	B
Siena Coll, NY	B
Sierra Coll, CA	A
Simmons Coll, MA	B
Simpson Coll, IA	B
Skagit Valley Coll, WA	A
Skidmore Coll, NY	B
Slippery Rock U of Pennsylvania, PA	B
South Dakota State U, SD	B
Southeast Missouri State U, MO	B
Southern Arkansas U–Magnolia, AR	B
Southern Arkansas U Tech, AR	A
Southern Illinois U Carbondale, IL	B
Southern Illinois U Edwardsville, IL	B
Southern Oregon U, OR	B
Southern Utah U, UT	A
South Georgia Coll, GA	A
South Puget Sound Comm Coll, WA	A
Southwestern Coll, KS	B
Southwestern Comm Coll, IA	A
Southwestern Comm Coll, NC	A
Southwest Minnesota State U, MN	B
Spokane Comm Coll, WA	A
Spokane Falls Comm Coll, WA	A
Spring Arbor U, MI	B
Stanford U, CA	B
State U of New York at Oswego, NY	B
State U of New York at Plattsburgh, NY	B
State U of New York Coll at Geneseo, NY	B
State U of New York Coll at Oneonta, NY	B
Stony Brook U, State U of New York, NY	B
Suffolk County Comm Coll, NY	A
Suffolk U, MA	B
Sullivan U, KY	A,B
Susquehanna U, PA	B
Sussex County Comm Coll, NJ	A
Swarthmore Coll, PA	B
Syracuse U, NY	B
Tabor Coll, KS	A,B
Taylor U, IN	A
Tennessee Technological U, TN	B
Texas A&M U–Corpus Christi, TX	B
Texas A&M U–Kingsville, TX	B
Texas A&M U–Texarkana, TX	B
Texas Christian U, TX	B
Texas State Tech Coll Waco, TX	A
Texas State Tech Coll West Texas, TX	A
Texas State U-San Marcos, TX	B
Texas Wesleyan U, TX	B
Thomas More Coll, KY	A,B
Trevecca Nazarene U, TN	A,B
Trinity Coll, CT	B
Trinity U, TX	B
Troy U, AL	A,B
Truman State U, MO	B
Tusculum Coll, TN	B
Union Coll, NY	B
U at Buffalo, the State U of New York, NY	B
The U of Alabama, AL	B
The U of Alabama in Huntsville, AL	B
U of Arkansas, AR	B
U of Arkansas at Fort Smith, AR	B
U of Arkansas at Pine Bluff, AR	B
U of Baltimore, MD	B
U of California, Santa Cruz, CA	B
U of Central Florida, FL	B
U of Central Missouri, MO	B
U of Charleston, WV	A,B
U of Cincinnati, OH	A,B
U of Cincinnati Raymond Walters Coll, OH	A
U of Colorado at Boulder, CO	B
U of Colorado at Colorado Springs, CO	B
U of Dayton, OH	B
U of Denver, CO	B
U of Detroit Mercy, MI	B
U of Dubuque, IA	A,B
The U of Findlay, OH	A,B
U of Guam, GU	B
U of Hartford, CT	B
U of Hawaii at Manoa, HI	B
U of Illinois at Springfield, IL	B
The U of Iowa, IA	B
U of Kansas, KS	B
U of La Verne, CA	B
U of Maine at Farmington, ME	B
U of Maine at Fort Kent, ME	A,B
U of Mary Hardin-Baylor, TX	B
U of Maryland, Baltimore County, MD	B
U of Maryland, Coll Park, MD	B
U of Mary Washington, VA	B
U of Miami, FL	B
U of Michigan–Flint, MI	B
U of Minnesota, Crookston, MN	A,B
U of Minnesota, Morris, MN	B
U of Missouri–Columbia, MO	B
U of Missouri–St. Louis, MO	B
U of Nebraska–Lincoln, NE	B
U of Nevada, Reno, NV	B
U of New Mexico, NM	B
U of New Orleans, LA	B
U of North Alabama, AL	B
The U of North Carolina at Asheville, NC	B
The U of North Carolina at Pembroke, NC	B
U of Northern Iowa, IA	B
U of North Texas, TX	B
U of Oregon, OR	B
U of Pittsburgh, PA	B
U of Pittsburgh at Bradford, PA	A
U of Puget Sound, WA	B
U of Rhode Island, RI	B
U of Rochester, NY	B
U of San Diego, CA	B
U of San Francisco, CA	B
U of Sioux Falls, SD	B
U of South Carolina, SC	B
U of South Carolina Upstate, SC	B
U of Southern Indiana, IN	B
U of Southern Maine, ME	B
U of South Florida, FL	B
The U of Tampa, FL	A,B
The U of Tennessee at Martin, TN	B
The U of Texas at San Antonio, TX	B
U of the Incarnate Word, TX	B
U of Tulsa, OK	B
U of Utah, UT	B
U of Virginia, VA	B
U of Washington, WA	B
U of West Florida, FL	B
U of Wisconsin–Eau Claire, WI	B
U of Wisconsin–La Crosse, WI	B
U of Wisconsin–Oshkosh, WI	B
U of Wisconsin–Stevens Point, WI	B
U of Wisconsin–Superior, WI	B
U of Wisconsin–Whitewater, WI	B
U of Wyoming, WY	B
Upper Iowa U, IA	B
Utah State U, UT	B
Utah Valley State Coll, UT	A,B
Utica Coll, NY	B
Valparaiso U, IN	B
Vanderbilt U, TN	B
Villanova U, PA	B
Virginia Commonwealth U, VA	B
Virginia Polytechnic Inst and State U, VA	B
Viterbo U, WI	B
Wake Forest U, NC	B
Waldorf Coll, IA	B
Wartburg Coll, IA	B
Washington Coll, MD	B
Washington State U, WA	B
Washington U in St. Louis, MO	B
Waynesburg Coll, PA	B
Wayne State Coll, NE	B
Weatherford Coll, TX	B
Webber International U, FL	B
Wells Coll, NY	B
Wentworth Inst of Technology, MA	A,B
Wesleyan U, CT	B
Western Illinois U, IL	B
Western Kentucky U, KY	A
Western New England Coll, MA	B
Western New Mexico U, NM	B
Western Washington U, WA	B
Western Wyoming Comm Coll, WY	A
Westmont Coll, CA	B
West Texas A&M U, TX	B
West Valley Coll, CA	A
Whatcom Comm Coll, WA	A
Wichita State U, KS	B
Widener U, PA	B
Wilkes U, PA	B
Williams Coll, MA	B
Williston State Coll, ND	A
Wilmington Coll, OH	B
Wilson Coll, PA	A
Winona State U, MN	B
Woodbury U, CA	B
Worcester Polytechnic Inst, MA	B
Worcester State Coll, MA	B
Wytheville Comm Coll, VA	A
Yavapai Coll, AZ	A
York Coll of Pennsylvania, PA	B
York Coll of the City U of New York, NY	B
Young Harris Coll, GA	A

Dance

College	Degree
Adelphi U, NY	B
Antioch Coll, OH	B
Arizona State U, AZ	B
Ball State U, IN	B
Bard Coll, NY	B
Barnard Coll, NY	B
Bennington Coll, VT	B
Butler U, IN	B
California Inst of the Arts, CA	B
California State U, Long Beach, CA	B
California State U, Sacramento, CA	B
Cañada Coll, CA	A
Central Piedmont Comm Coll, NC	A
Chaffey Coll, CA	A
Chapman U, CA	B
Cleveland State U, OH	B
The Colorado Coll, CO	B
Colorado State U, CO	B
Columbia Coll Chicago, IL	B
Columbia U, School of General Studies, NY	B
Connecticut Coll, CT	B
Dean Coll, MA	A,B
Denison U, OH	B
DeSales U, PA	B
East Carolina U, NC	B
Elon U, NC	B
Emory U, GA	B
Florida International U, FL	B
Florida State U, FL	B
Fordham U, NY	B
Frostburg State U, MD	B
Fullerton Coll, CA	A
Glendale Comm Coll, CA	A
Gustavus Adolphus Coll, MN	B
Hamilton Coll, NY	B
Hampshire Coll, MA	B
Henry Ford Comm Coll, MI	A
Hofstra U, NY	B
Hope Coll, MI	B
Indiana U Bloomington, IN	B
Jacksonville U, FL	B
Johnson State Coll, VT	B
The Juilliard School, NY	B
Kent State U, OH	B
Kenyon Coll, OH	B
Kilgore Coll, TX	A
Laney Coll, CA	A
Lansing Comm Coll, MI	A
Long Beach City Coll, CA	A
Long Island U, C.W. Post Campus, NY	B
Luther Coll, IA	B
Manhattanville Coll, NY	B
Marlboro Coll, VT	B
Marymount Manhattan Coll, NY	B
Miami Dade Coll, FL	A
Middlebury Coll, VT	B
Mills Coll, CA	B
MiraCosta Coll, CA	A
Montclair State U, NJ	B
Monterey Peninsula Coll, CA	A
Mount Holyoke Coll, MA	B
Nassau Comm Coll, NY	A
New Mexico State U, NM	B
New York U, NY	B
Northwestern U, IL	B
Oakland U, MI	B
Old Dominion U, VA	B
Orange Coast Coll, CA	A
Palomar Coll, CA	A
Pitzer Coll, CA	B
Prescott Coll, AZ	B
Radford U, VA	B
Randolph Coll, VA	B
Reed Coll, OR	B
Roger Williams U, RI	B
St. Gregory's U, OK	B
Saint Mary's Coll of California, CA	B
St. Olaf Coll, MN	B
Sam Houston State U, TX	B
San Diego State U, CA	B
San Francisco State U, CA	B
Santa Monica Coll, CA	A
Santa Rosa Jr Coll, CA	A
Sarah Lawrence Coll, NY	B
Scripps Coll, CA	B
Shenandoah U, VA	B
Skidmore Coll, NY	B
Slippery Rock U of Pennsylvania, PA	B
Southern Utah U, UT	B
Swarthmore Coll, PA	B
Texas State U-San Marcos, TX	B
Trinity Coll, CT	B
U at Buffalo, the State U of New York, NY	B
The U of Alabama, AL	B
U of California, Santa Cruz, CA	B
U of Cincinnati, OH	B
U of Colorado at Boulder, CO	B
U of Hartford, CT	B
U of Hawaii at Manoa, HI	B
The U of Iowa, IA	B
U of Kansas, KS	B
U of Maryland, Baltimore County, MD	B
U of Maryland, Coll Park, MD	B
U of Miami, FL	B
U of Nebraska–Lincoln, NE	B
U of New Mexico, NM	B
U of North Texas, TX	B
U of Oregon, OR	B
U of South Florida, FL	B
The U of Tennessee at Martin, TN	B
The U of the Arts, PA	B
U of Utah, UT	B
U of Washington, WA	B
U of Wisconsin–Stevens Point, WI	B
Utah State U, UT	B
Utah Valley State Coll, UT	A
Virginia Commonwealth U, VA	B
Washington U in St. Louis, MO	B
Wells Coll, NY	B
Wesleyan U, CT	B
Western Wyoming Comm Coll, WY	A
Westmont Coll, CA	B
West Texas A&M U, TX	B

Education and Child Care

College	Degree
Adelphi U, NY	B
Adrian Coll, MI	A,B
Alamance Comm Coll, NC	A
Alaska Pacific U, AK	A,B
Albertus Magnus Coll, CT	B

A=Associate; B=Bachelor's Degree

Albion Coll, MI	B	Clark U, MA	B	Gardner-Webb U, NC	B
Alderson-Broaddus Coll, WV	B	Clearwater Christian Coll, FL	B	GateWay Comm Coll, AZ	A
Allegheny Coll, PA	B	Cleveland State U, OH	B	Genesee Comm Coll, NY	A
Alvernia Coll, PA	B	Coastal Carolina U, SC	B	George Fox U, OR	B
Alverno Coll, WI	A	Coastal Georgia Comm Coll, GA	A	Georgetown Coll, KY	B
Alvin Comm Coll, TX	A	Cochise Coll, Sierra Vista, AZ	A	Georgia Coll & State U, GA	B
American U, DC	B	Coe Coll, IA	B	Georgia Highlands Coll, GA	A
Ancilla Coll, IN	A	Coffeyville Comm Coll, KS	A	Georgia Southern U, GA	B
Anna Maria Coll, MA	B	Colby Comm Coll, KS	A	Georgia State U, GA	B
Antioch Coll, OH	B	Colby-Sawyer Coll, NH	B	Gettysburg Coll, PA	B
Aquinas Coll, MI	B	Coll Misericordia, PA	B	Glendale Comm Coll, CA	A
Arcadia U, PA	B	Coll of Lake County, IL	A	Gonzaga U, WA	B
Arizona State U, AZ	B	Coll of Saint Benedict, MN	B	Goshen Coll, IN	B
Ashford U, IA	B	Coll of St. Catherine, MN	B	Grambling State U, LA	B
Ashland U, OH	B	Coll of Southern Maryland, MD	B	Grand Valley State U, MI	B
Assumption Coll, MA	B	Coll of the Atlantic, ME	B	Grand View Coll, IA	B
Austin Peay State U, TN	B	Coll of the Canyons, CA	A	Great Lakes Christian Coll, MI	B
Averett U, VA	B	Coll of the Desert, CA	A	Greenfield Comm Coll, MA	A
Baker Coll of Flint, MI	A	Coll of the Ozarks, MO	B	Green Mountain Coll, VT	B
Baker U, KS	B	Colorado State U, CO	B	Greenville Coll, IL	B
Baldwin-Wallace Coll, OH	B	Columbia Coll, MO	B	Gulf Coast Comm Coll, FL	A
Ball State U, IN	B	Columbia Union Coll, MD	B	Gustavus Adolphus Coll, MN	B
Barnard Coll, NY	B	Concordia Coll, AL	B	Hampshire Coll, MA	B
Barry U, FL	B	Concordia Coll, MN	B	Harding U, AR	B
Bay Path Coll, MA	B	Concordia Coll, NY	B	Hardin-Simmons U, TX	B
Belmont U, TN	B	Concordia U, IL	B	Harper Coll, IL	A
Beloit Coll, WI	B	Connecticut Coll, CT	B	Harrisburg Area Comm Coll, PA	A
Bemidji State U, MN	B	Connors State Coll, OK	A	Hartwick Coll, NY	B
Benedict Coll, SC	B	Cornell Coll, IA	B	Haverford Coll, PA	B
Bennington Coll, VT	B	County Coll of Morris, NJ	A	Hawai'i Pacific U, HI	B
Berea Coll, KY	B	Culver-Stockton Coll, MO	B	Hellenic Coll, MA	B
Bethany Coll, KS	B	Cumberland U, TN	A,B	Hill Coll of the Hill Jr Coll District, TX	A
Bethel Coll, KS	B	Daemen Coll, NY	B	Hiram Coll, OH	B
Bethel U, MN	B	Dakota Wesleyan U, SD	B	Hofstra U, NY	B
Black Hills State U, SD	B	Dana Coll, NE	B	Holy Family U, PA	B
Bluefield State Coll, WV	B	Dean Coll, MA	A	Hope Coll, MI	B
Blue Mountain Coll, MS	B	Defiance Coll, OH	B	Hope International U, CA	B
Boise State U, ID	A	De Anza Coll, CA	A	Howard Coll, TX	A
Boston U, MA	B	Del Mar Coll, TX	A	Howard Payne U, TX	B
Bowling Green State U– Firelands Coll, OH	A	Denison U, OH	B	Huntingdon Coll, AL	B
Brescia U, KY	B	DePaul U, IL	B	Huntington U, IN	B
Bronx Comm Coll of the City U of New York, NY	A	DePauw U, IN	B	Idaho State U, ID	B
Bucknell U, PA	B	DeSales U, PA	B	Illinois Coll, IL	B
Bunker Hill Comm Coll, MA	A	Dordt Coll, IA	B	Illinois Wesleyan U, IL	B
Butler U, IN	B	Drake U, IA	B	Indiana U Bloomington, IN	B
Caldwell Coll, NJ	B	Drury U, MO	B	Indiana U of Pennsylvania, PA	B
Calhoun Comm Coll, AL	A	Duquesne U, PA	B	Indiana U South Bend, IN	B
California Lutheran U, CA	B	D'Youville Coll, NY	B	Indiana U Southeast, IN	B
California Polytechnic State U, San Luis Obispo, CA		East Carolina U, NC	B	Indiana Wesleyan U, IN	B
California State Polytechnic U, Pomona, CA	B	East Central Coll, MO	B	Iowa State U of Science and Technology, IA	B
California State U, Long Beach, CA		Eastern Connecticut State U, CT	B	Iowa Western Comm Coll, IA	A
California State U, Stanislaus, CA		Eastern Mennonite U, VA	B	Isothermal Comm Coll, NC	A
Calvin Coll, MI	B	Eastern U, PA	B	Itasca Comm Coll, MN	A
Cameron U, OK	B	Eastern Wyoming Coll, WY	A	Jacksonville State U, AL	B
Cañada Coll, CA	A	East Los Angeles Coll, CA	A	Jacksonville U, FL	B
Capital U, OH	B	East Tennessee State U, TN	B	James Madison U, VA	B
Cardinal Stritch U, WI	B	East Texas Baptist U, TX	B	John Carroll U, OH	B
Carlow U, PA	B	Edgewood Coll, WI	B	Johnson County Comm Coll, KS	A
Carroll Coll, MT	B	Edinboro U of Pennsylvania, PA	A,B	Johnson State Coll, VT	B
Carroll Coll, WI	B	El Camino Coll, CA	A	Joliet Jr Coll, IL	A
Carson-Newman Coll, TN	B	Elizabethtown Coll, PA	B	Judson Coll, IL	B
Carthage Coll, WI	B	Elmira Coll, NY	B	Juniata Coll, PA	B
The Catholic U of America, DC	B	Elms Coll, MA	B	Kankakee Comm Coll, IL	A
Centenary Coll, NJ	B	Elon U, NC	B	Kansas State U, KS	B
Central Christian Coll of Kansas, KS	A	Emerson Coll, MA	B	Kansas Wesleyan U, KS	B
Centralia Coll, WA	A	Emmanuel Coll, MA	B	Kean U, NJ	B
Central Michigan U, MI	B	Emory U, GA	B	Kennesaw State U, GA	B
Central Wyoming Coll, WY	A	Emporia State U, KS	B	Kent State U, OH	A,B
Centre Coll, KY	B	Fairfield U, CT	B	Kent State U, Salem Campus, OH	A,B
Century Coll, MN	A	Fairleigh Dickinson U, Metropolitan Campus, NJ	B	Kent State U, Stark Campus, OH	A
Chabot Coll, CA	A	Ferris State U, MI	B	Kentucky Wesleyan Coll, KY	B
Chaffey Coll, CA	A	Five Towns Coll, NY	B	Keystone Coll, PA	A,B
Chapman U, CA	B	Flagler Coll, FL	B	Kilgore Coll, TX	A
Chatham U, PA	B	Florida Atlantic U, FL	B	The King's Coll, NY	B
Chemeketa Comm Coll, OR	A	Florida Gulf Coast U, FL	B	Kingwood Coll, TX	A
City Coll of San Francisco, CA	A	Florida Inst of Technology, FL	B	Kirkwood Comm Coll, IA	A
City Coll of the City U of New York, NY	B	Florida International U, FL	B	Knox Coll, IL	B
City Colls of Chicago, Harold Washington Coll, IL	A	Florida State U, FL	B	Lakeland Coll, WI	B
City Colls of Chicago, Kennedy-King Coll, IL	A	Foothill Coll, CA	A	Lake Region State Coll, ND	A
City U, WA	B	Fordham U, NY	B	Lancaster Bible Coll, PA	B
Claflin U, SC	B	Fort Lewis Coll, CO	B	Lander U, SC	B
Clarendon Coll, TX	A	Fresno City Coll, CA	A	Laney Coll, CA	A
Clarion U of Pennsylvania, PA	B	Fresno Pacific U, CA	A,B	Langston U, OK	B
Clarke Coll, IA	B	Frostburg State U, MD	B	Lansing Comm Coll, MI	A
		Fullerton Coll, CA	A		
		Fulton-Montgomery Comm Coll, NY	A		
		Furman U, SC	B		
		Gannon U, PA	B		
		Garden City Comm Coll, KS	A		

Laramie County Comm Coll, WY	A
Las Positas Coll, CA	A
Lawrence U, WI	B
Lees-McRae Coll, NC	B
LeMoyne-Owen Coll, TN	B
Lewis-Clark State Coll, ID	B
Liberty U, VA	B
Limestone Coll, SC	B
Linfield Coll, OR	B
Lipscomb U, TN	B
Long Beach City Coll, CA	A
Long Island U, C.W. Post Campus, NY	B
Longwood U, VA	B
Los Angeles Mission Coll, CA	A
Los Angeles Southwest Coll, CA	A
Louisiana State U at Alexandria, LA	B
Loyola U Chicago, IL	B
Luther Coll, IA	B
Lycoming Coll, PA	B
Lynchburg Coll, VA	B
Lyndon State Coll, VT	A
Lynn U, FL	B
Manatee Comm Coll, FL	A
Manchester Coll, IN	B
Manhattan Coll, NY	B
Manhattanville Coll, NY	B
Marian Coll of Fond du Lac, WI	B
Marquette U, WI	B
Marshall U, WV	B
Maryville Coll, TN	B
Maryville U of Saint Louis, MO	B
Marywood U, PA	B
Massachusetts Coll of Art, MA	B
McDaniel Coll, MD	B
McMurry U, TX	B
McNeese State U, LA	B
Mercy Coll, NY	B
Merritt Coll, CA	A
Mesa Comm Coll, AZ	A
Mesa State Coll, CO	B
Miami Dade Coll, FL	A
Miami U, OH	B
Michigan Technological U, MI	B
MidAmerica Nazarene U, KS	B
Middle Tennessee State U, TN	B
Midland Coll, TX	A
Midwestern State U, TX	B
Millersville U of Pennsylvania, PA	B
Milligan Coll, TN	B
Millsaps Coll, MS	B
Minnesota State U Mankato, MN	B
Minnesota State U Moorhead, MN	B
Minot State U, ND	B
MiraCosta Coll, CA	A
Mississippi U for Women, MS	B
Missouri Baptist U, MO	B
Mitchell Coll, CT	A
Modesto Jr Coll, CA	A
Molloy Coll, NY	B
Monmouth U, NJ	B
Montclair State U, NJ	B
Monterey Peninsula Coll, CA	A
Moore Coll of Art & Design, PA	B
Moravian Coll, PA	B
Morehead State U, KY	B
Morningside Coll, IA	B
Mott Comm Coll, MI	A
Mountain State U, WV	B
Mount Holyoke Coll, MA	B
Mount Ida Coll, MA	A
Mount Mercy Coll, IA	B
Muskingum Coll, OH	B
Nebraska Wesleyan U, NE	B
New Coll of California, CA	B
New England Coll, NH	B
New Mexico Highlands U, NM	A,B
New Mexico Military Inst, NM	A
New Mexico State U, NM	B
New Mexico State U–Alamogordo, NM	A
New River Comm Coll, VA	A
New York U, NY	B
Niagara U, NY	B
Nichols Coll, MA	B
Northampton County Area Comm Coll, PA	A
North Carolina State U, NC	B
North Central Coll, IL	B

College	Degree
North Central U, MN	B
North Dakota State Coll of Science, ND	A
North Dakota State U, ND	B
Northeast Comm Coll, NE	A
Northeastern U, MA	B
Northern Arizona U, AZ	B
Northern Kentucky U, KY	A
Northern Michigan U, MI	B
Northern State U, SD	B
Northland Coll, WI	B
NorthWest Arkansas Comm Coll, AR	A
Northwest Coll, WY	A
Northwestern State U of Louisiana, LA	B
Northwestern U, IL	B
Northwest Missouri State U, MO	B
Northwest U, WA	B
Notre Dame Coll, OH	B
Notre Dame de Namur U, CA	B
Nova Southeastern U, FL	B
Oakland U, MI	B
Ohio Wesleyan U, OH	B
Oklahoma Panhandle State U, OK	B
Oklahoma State U, OK	B
Oklahoma Wesleyan U, OK	B
Old Dominion U, VA	B
Orange Coast Coll, CA	A
Oregon State U, OR	B
Ottawa U, KS	B
Otterbein Coll, OH	B
Pace U, NY	B
Palomar Coll, CA	A
Park U, MO	B
Parsons The New School for Design, NY	B
Paul D. Camp Comm Coll, VA	A
Peru State Coll, NE	B
Philadelphia Biblical U, PA	B
Pittsburg State U, KS	B
Plymouth State U, NH	B
Portland Comm Coll, OR	A
Portland State U, OR	B
Pratt Inst, NY	B
Prescott Coll, AZ	B
Principia Coll, IL	B
Purdue U, IN	A
Quincy U, IL	B
Quinnipiac U, CT	B
Radford U, VA	B
Randolph Coll, VA	B
Raritan Valley Comm Coll, NJ	A
Redlands Comm Coll, OK	A
Renton Tech Coll, WA	A
Rider U, NJ	B
Ridgewater Coll, MN	A
Rocky Mountain Coll, MT	B
Roger Williams U, RI	B
Roosevelt U, IL	B
Rose State Coll, OK	A
Sacramento City Coll, CA	A
Sacred Heart U, CT	B
St. Ambrose U, IA	B
Saint Anselm Coll, NH	B
Saint Francis U, PA	A,B
St. Gregory's U, OK	B
Saint John's U, MN	B
Saint Joseph's Coll, IN	B
Saint Leo U, FL	B
St. Louis Comm Coll at Florissant Valley, MO	A
Saint Louis U, MO	B
Saint Mary-of-the-Woods Coll, IN	B
Saint Mary's Coll, IN	B
Saint Mary's U of Minnesota, MN	B
St. Mary's U of San Antonio, TX	B
Saint Michael's Coll, VT	B
St. Olaf Coll, MN	B
St. Petersburg Coll, FL	B
St. Thomas U, FL	B
Saint Vincent Coll, PA	B
Sam Houston State U, TX	B
San Bernardino Valley Coll, CA	A
San Diego City Coll, CA	A
San Diego State U, CA	B
San Francisco State U, CA	B

College	Degree
San Jacinto Coll North Campus, TX	A
San Jacinto Coll South Campus, TX	A
Santa Barbara City Coll, CA	A
Santa Fe Comm Coll, NM	A
Santa Monica Coll, CA	A
Santa Rosa Jr Coll, CA	A
Sarah Lawrence Coll, NY	B
Sauk Valley Comm Coll, IL	A
School of the Art Inst of Chicago, IL	B
School of the Museum of Fine Arts, Boston, MA	B
Schreiner U, TX	B
Seton Hall U, NJ	B
Shenandoah U, VA	B
Shepherd U, WV	B
Sheridan Coll–Sheridan and Gillette, WY	A
Shorter Coll, GA	B
Siena Coll, NY	B
Sierra Coll, CA	A
Simmons Coll, MA	B
Simpson Coll, IA	B
Skagit Valley Coll, WA	A
Skidmore Coll, NY	B
Slippery Rock U of Pennsylvania, PA	B
South Dakota State U, SD	B
Southeast Missouri State U, MO	B
Southern Arkansas U–Magnolia, AR	B
Southern Illinois U Carbondale, IL	B
Southern Illinois U Edwardsville, IL	B
Southern New Hampshire U, NH	B
Southern Oregon U, OR	B
Southern Utah U, UT	B
South Georgia Coll, GA	A
Southwestern Coll, KS	B
Southwestern Comm Coll, NC	A
Southwest Minnesota State U, MN	B
Spring Arbor U, MI	B
State U of New York at Oswego, NY	B
State U of New York at Plattsburgh, NY	B
State U of New York Coll at Geneseo, NY	B
State U of New York Coll at Oneonta, NY	B
Suffolk U, MA	B
Susquehanna U, PA	B
Syracuse U, NY	B
Tabor Coll, KS	B
Taylor U, IN	B
Tennessee Technological U, TN	B
Texas A&M U–Corpus Christi, TX	B
Texas A&M U–Kingsville, TX	B
Texas Christian U, TX	B
Texas State Tech Coll Waco, TX	A
Texas Wesleyan U, TX	B
Thomas More Coll, KY	B
Trevecca Nazarene U, TN	B
Trinity Coll, CT	B
Trinity Coll of Florida, FL	B
Trinity (Washington) U, DC	B
Troy U, AL	B
Tusculum Coll, TN	B
The U of Alabama, AL	B
The U of Alabama in Huntsville, AL	B
U of Arkansas, AR	B
U of Arkansas at Fort Smith, AR	A,B
U of Arkansas at Pine Bluff, AR	B
U of California, Santa Cruz, CA	B
U of Central Florida, FL	B
U of Central Missouri, MO	B
U of Charleston, WV	B
U of Cincinnati, OH	A
U of Cincinnati Raymond Walters Coll, OH	A
U of Colorado at Boulder, CO	B
U of Dayton, OH	B

College	Degree
U of Denver, CO	B
U of Detroit Mercy, MI	B
The U of Findlay, OH	B
U of Guam, GU	B
U of Hartford, CT	B
U of Hawaii at Manoa, HI	B
U of Indianapolis, IN	B
The U of Iowa, IA	B
U of Kansas, KS	B
U of La Verne, CA	B
U of Maine at Farmington, ME	B
U of Maine at Fort Kent, ME	B
U of Maine at Presque Isle, ME	B
U of Mary Hardin-Baylor, TX	B
U of Maryland, Coll Park, MD	B
U of Mary Washington, VA	B
U of Miami, FL	B
U of Michigan–Flint, MI	B
U of Minnesota, Crookston, MN	B
U of Minnesota, Morris, MN	B
U of Missouri–Columbia, MO	B
U of Missouri–St. Louis, MO	B
U of Nebraska–Lincoln, NE	B
U of Nevada, Reno, NV	B
U of New Mexico, NM	A
U of New Orleans, LA	B
U of North Alabama, AL	B
The U of North Carolina at Pembroke, NC	B
U of Northern Iowa, IA	B
U of North Texas, TX	B
U of Oregon, OR	B
U of Pittsburgh, PA	B
U of Puget Sound, WA	B
U of Rhode Island, RI	B
U of Rochester, NY	B
U of Saint Francis, IN	B
U of San Francisco, CA	B
U of Sioux Falls, SD	B
U of South Carolina, SC	B
U of South Carolina Upstate, SC	B
U of Southern Indiana, IN	A
U of Southern Maine, ME	B
U of South Florida, FL	B
The U of Tampa, FL	B
The U of Tennessee at Martin, TN	B
The U of the Arts, PA	B
U of the Incarnate Word, TX	B
U of Tulsa, OK	B
U of Utah, UT	B
U of Virginia, VA	B
U of Washington, WA	B
U of West Florida, FL	B
U of Wisconsin–Eau Claire, WI	B
U of Wisconsin–La Crosse, WI	B
U of Wisconsin–Oshkosh, WI	B
U of Wisconsin–Stevens Point, WI	B
U of Wisconsin–Stout, WI	B
U of Wisconsin–Superior, WI	B
U of Wisconsin–Whitewater, WI	B
U of Wyoming, WY	B
Upper Iowa U, IA	B
Utah State U, UT	B
Utah Valley State Coll, UT	B
Utica Coll, NY	B
Valparaiso U, IN	B
Vanderbilt U, TN	B
VanderCook Coll of Music, IL	B
Vanguard U of Southern California, CA	B
Villanova U, PA	B
Virginia Commonwealth U, VA	B
Virginia Polytechnic Inst and State U, VA	B
Viterbo U, WI	B
Wake Forest U, NC	B
Waldorf Coll, IA	B
Warren Wilson Coll, NC	B
Wartburg Coll, IA	B
Washington & Jefferson Coll, PA	B
Washington Bible Coll, MD	B
Washington State U, WA	B
Washington U in St. Louis, MO	B
Waynesburg Coll, PA	B
Wayne State Coll, NE	B
Wells Coll, NY	B
Western Illinois U, IL	B

College	Degree
Western Kentucky U, KY	A
Western New England Coll, MA	B
Western New Mexico U, NM	B
Western Washington U, WA	B
Western Wyoming Comm Coll, WY	A
Westminster Choir Coll of Rider U, NJ	B
Westmont Coll, CA	B
West Valley Coll, CA	A
Wichita State U, KS	B
Widener U, PA	B
Wilkes U, PA	B
Wilmington Coll, OH	B
Wilson Coll, PA	A,B
Winona State U, MN	B
Worcester State Coll, MA	B
Wytheville Comm Coll, VA	B
York Coll, NE	B
York Coll of Pennsylvania, PA	B
York Coll of the City U of New York, NY	B
Young Harris Coll, GA	A

Engineering and Technology

College	Degree
Aims Comm Coll, CO	A
Alamance Comm Coll, NC	A
Alvernia Coll, PA	B
Alvin Comm Coll, TX	A
American U, DC	B
Arizona State U, AZ	B
Austin Peay State U, TN	B
Baker Coll of Flint, MI	A
Baldwin-Wallace Coll, OH	B
Ball State U, IN	A
Barry U, FL	B
Bates Coll, ME	B
Belmont U, TN	B
Beloit Coll, WI	B
Bemidji State U, MN	B
Berkshire Comm Coll, MA	A
Bethel U, MN	B
Bluefield State Coll, WV	A,B
Boise State U, ID	A,B
Boston U, MA	B
Bowling Green State U–Firelands Coll, OH	A
Brescia U, KY	A
Bronx Comm Coll of the City U of New York, NY	A
Broome Comm Coll, NY	A
Bucknell U, PA	B
Calhoun Comm Coll, AL	A
California Lutheran U, CA	B
California Polytechnic State U, San Luis Obispo, CA	B
California State Polytechnic U, Pomona, CA	B
California State U, Long Beach, CA	B
California State U, Sacramento, CA	B
Calvin Coll, MI	B
Cameron U, OK	A,B
Cañada Coll, CA	A
Capital U, OH	B
Carlow U, PA	B
Carroll Coll, MT	B
Carthage Coll, WI	B
The Catholic U of America, DC	B
Central Christian Coll of Kansas, KS	A
Central Comm Coll–Columbus Campus, NE	A
Central Comm Coll–Grand Island Campus, NE	A
Central Comm Coll–Hastings Campus, NE	A
Centralia Coll, WA	A
Central Michigan U, MI	B
Central Piedmont Comm Coll, NC	A
Century Coll, MN	A
Cerro Coso Comm Coll, CA	A
Chabot Coll, CA	A
Chaffey Coll, CA	A
Chatham U, PA	B
Chattahoochee Tech Coll, GA	A
Chattanooga State Tech Comm Coll, TN	A
Chemeketa Comm Coll, OR	A
City Coll of San Francisco, CA	A

A=Associate; B=Bachelor's Degree

City Coll of the City U of New York, NY	B
City Colls of Chicago, Harold Washington Coll, IL	A
City Colls of Chicago, Kennedy-King Coll, IL	A
Clarendon Coll, TX	A
Clarkson U, NY	B
Clark U, MA	B
Cleveland Inst of Music, OH	B
Cleveland State U, OH	B
Clinton Comm Coll, IA	A
Coastal Georgia Comm Coll, GA	A
Cochise Coll, Sierra Vista, AZ	A
Coffeyville Comm Coll, KS	A
Colby Comm Coll, KS	A
Colegio Universitario de San Juan, PR	A
Coll of DuPage, IL	A
Coll of Eastern Utah, UT	A
Coll of Lake County, IL	A
Coll of Southern Maryland, MD	A
Coll of the Canyons, CA	A
Coll of the Desert, CA	A
Coll of the Ozarks, MO	B
Colorado State U, CO	B
Columbia Coll, MO	A
Columbia Union Coll, MD	A
Connecticut Coll, CT	B
Connors State Coll, OK	A
Cooper Union for the Advancement of Science and Art, NY	B
Cosumnes River Coll, Sacramento, CA	A
County Coll of Morris, NJ	A
Dakota County Tech Coll, MN	A
Davenport U, Midland, MI	A
De Anza Coll, CA	A
DeKalb Tech Coll, GA	A
Delaware Tech & Comm Coll, Jack F. Owens Campus, DE	A
Del Mar Coll, TX	A
Delta Coll, MI	A
Dordt Coll, IA	B
Drake U, IA	B
Drury U, MO	B
East Carolina U, NC	B
East Central Coll, MO	A
East Los Angeles Coll, CA	A
East Tennessee State U, TN	B
Edgewood Coll, WI	A
Edinboro U of Pennsylvania, PA	B
Edison Coll, FL	A
Edmonds Comm Coll, WA	A
El Camino Coll, CA	A
Elizabethtown Coll, PA	B
Elon U, NC	B
Embry-Riddle Aeronautical U, FL	B
Fairfield U, CT	A,B
Fairleigh Dickinson U, Metropolitan Campus, NJ	B
Ferris State U, MI	A,B
Five Towns Coll, NY	A,B
Florida Atlantic U, FL	B
Florida Inst of Technology, FL	B
Florida International U, FL	B
Florida Keys Comm Coll, FL	A
Florida State U, FL	B
Foothill Coll, CA	A
Fort Lewis Coll, CO	B
Fox Valley Tech Coll, WI	A
Fresno City Coll, CA	A
Frostburg State U, MD	B
Fullerton Coll, CA	A
Fulton-Montgomery Comm Coll, NY	A
Gannon U, PA	B
Garden City Comm Coll, KS	A
GateWay Comm Coll, AZ	A
Genesee Comm Coll, NY	A
George Fox U, OR	B
Georgia Highlands Coll, GA	A
Georgia Southern U, GA	B
Glendale Comm Coll, AZ	A
Glendale Comm Coll, CA	A
Golden West Coll, CA	A
Gonzaga U, WA	B
Grambling State U, LA	B
Grand Valley State U, MI	B
Greenfield Comm Coll, MA	A

Gulf Coast Comm Coll, FL	A
Harding U, AR	B
Harper Coll, IL	A
Harrisburg Area Comm Coll, PA	A
Harvard U, MA	B
Harvey Mudd Coll, CA	B
Hawaii Comm Coll, HI	A
Henry Ford Comm Coll, MI	A
Hill Coll of the Hill Jr Coll District, TX	A
Hofstra U, NY	B
Hope Coll, MI	B
Hopkinsville Comm Coll, KY	A
Houston Comm Coll System, TX	A
Hudson Valley Comm Coll, NY	A
Idaho State U, ID	B
Illinois Inst of Technology, IL	B
Indiana Tech, IN	B
Indiana U Bloomington, IN	A
Indiana U of Pennsylvania, PA	B
Iowa State U of Science and Technology, IA	B
Iowa Western Comm Coll, IA	A
Isothermal Comm Coll, NC	A
Itasca Comm Coll, MN	A
Jacksonville State U, AL	B
Jacksonville U, FL	B
James A. Rhodes State Coll, OH	A
John Carroll U, OH	B
The Johns Hopkins U, MD	B
Johnson & Wales U, RI	A,B
Johnson County Comm Coll, KS	A
Joliet Jr Coll, IL	A
Juniata Coll, PA	B
Kankakee Comm Coll, IL	A
Kansas State U, KS	B
Kansas Wesleyan U, KS	B
Kapiolani Comm Coll, HI	A
Kent State U, Ashtabula Campus, OH	A
Kent State U, Trumbull Campus, OH	A
Kent State U, Tuscarawas Campus, OH	A
Kettering U, MI	B
Kilgore Coll, TX	A
Kirkwood Comm Coll, IA	A
Lafayette Coll, PA	B
Lake Land Coll, IL	A
Lake Region State Coll, ND	A
Lamar State Coll–Port Arthur, TX	A
Laney Coll, CA	A
Langston U, OK	B
Lansing Comm Coll, MI	A
Laramie County Comm Coll, WY	A
Las Positas Coll, CA	A
Lewis & Clark Coll, OR	B
Lincoln Land Comm Coll, IL	A
Lipscomb U, TN	B
Long Beach City Coll, CA	A
Los Angeles Harbor Coll, CA	A
Los Angeles Pierce Coll, CA	A
Los Angeles Southwest Coll, CA	A
Manatee Comm Coll, FL	A
Manchester Coll, IN	B
Manhattan Coll, NY	B
Marquette U, WI	B
Marshall U, WV	B
Maryville Coll, TN	B
Marywood U, PA	B
Massachusetts Bay Comm Coll, MA	A
Massachusetts Inst of Technology, MA	B
Maui Comm Coll, HI	A
McNeese State U, LA	A,B
Merritt Coll, CA	A
Mesabi Range Comm and Tech Coll, MN	A
Mesa Comm Coll, AZ	A
Mesa State Coll, CO	A
Miami Dade Coll, FL	A
Miami U, OH	B
Michigan Technological U, MI	A,B
Middlesex Comm Coll, CT	A
Middle Tennessee State U, TN	B
Midland Coll, TX	A
Midwestern State U, TX	B

Millersville U of Pennsylvania, PA	A
Mills Coll, CA	A
Minnesota State Coll–Southeast Tech, MN	A
Minnesota State U Mankato, MN	A
Minnesota State U Moorhead, MN	B
MiraCosta Coll, CA	A
Mitchell Coll, CT	A
Mitchell Tech Inst, SD	A
Modesto Jr Coll, CA	A
Montana Tech of The U of Montana, MT	A,B
Monterey Peninsula Coll, CA	A
Morningside Coll, IA	B
Mott Comm Coll, MI	A
Mountain State U, WV	A
Muskingum Coll, OH	B
Nassau Comm Coll, NY	A
New England Inst of Technology, RI	A,B
New Mexico Highlands U, NM	B
New Mexico Inst of Mining and Technology, NM	B
New Mexico Military Inst, NM	A
New Mexico State U, NM	B
New Mexico State U–Alamogordo, NM	A
New River Comm Coll, VA	A
Niagara U, NY	B
Northampton County Area Comm Coll, PA	A
North Carolina State U, NC	B
North Dakota State Coll of Science, ND	A
North Dakota State U, ND	B
Northeast Comm Coll, NE	A
Northeastern U, MA	B
Northeast State Tech Comm Coll, TN	A
Northern Arizona U, AZ	B
Northern Kentucky U, KY	B
Northern Michigan U, MI	A,B
Northern State U, SD	A,B
North Lake Coll, TX	A
NorthWest Arkansas Comm Coll, AR	A
Northwest Coll, WY	A
Northwestern Polytechnic U, CA	B
Northwestern State U of Louisiana, LA	A,B
Northwestern U, IL	B
Northwest Missouri State U, MO	B
Northwest Vista Coll, TX	A
Norwalk Comm Coll, CT	A
Oakland U, MI	B
Ohio Wesleyan U, OH	B
Oklahoma State U, OK	B
Old Dominion U, VA	B
Orange Coast Coll, CA	A
Oregon State U, OR	B
Owens Comm Coll, Toledo, OH	A
Palomar Coll, CA	A
Pellissippi State Tech Comm Coll, TN	A
Peninsula Coll, WA	A
Philadelphia U, PA	B
Piedmont Comm Coll, NC	A
Pierce Coll, WA	A
Pikes Peak Comm Coll, CO	A
Pittsburg State U, KS	A,B
Pitzer Coll, CA	B
Portland Comm Coll, OR	A
Portland State U, OR	B
Purdue U, IN	A,B
Randolph Coll, VA	B
Raritan Valley Comm Coll, NJ	A
Redlands Comm Coll, OK	A
Rensselaer Polytechnic Inst, NY	B
Renton Tech Coll, WA	A
Richmond Comm Coll, NC	A
Ridgewater Coll, MN	A
Riverside Comm Coll District, CA	A
Rochester Inst of Technology, NY	A,B
Roosevelt U, IL	B
Rose State Coll, OK	A
Sacramento City Coll, CA	A

St. Ambrose U, IA	B
Saint Anselm Coll, NH	B
Saint Charles Comm Coll, MO	A
Saint Francis U, PA	B
St. Gregory's U, OK	A
St. Louis Comm Coll at Florissant Valley, MO	A
Saint Louis U, MO	B
Saint Mary's Coll of California, CA	B
Saint Mary's U of Minnesota, MN	B
St. Mary's U of San Antonio, TX	B
St. Petersburg Coll, FL	A
Saint Vincent Coll, PA	B
Sam Houston State U, TX	B
San Bernardino Valley Coll, CA	A
San Diego City Coll, CA	A
San Diego State U, CA	B
San Francisco State U, CA	B
San Jacinto Coll Central Campus, TX	A
San Jacinto Coll North Campus, TX	A
San Jacinto Coll South Campus, TX	A
Santa Barbara City Coll, CA	A
Santa Fe Comm Coll, NM	A
Santa Monica Coll, CA	A
Santa Rosa Jr Coll, CA	A
Sauk Valley Comm Coll, IL	A
Savannah State U, GA	B
Schreiner U, TX	A
Scott Comm Coll, IA	A
Seattle Central Comm Coll, WA	A
Seattle U, WA	B
Sheridan Coll–Sheridan and Gillette, WY	A
Sierra Coll, CA	A
Skagit Valley Coll, WA	A
Slippery Rock U of Pennsylvania, PA	B
South Dakota State U, SD	B
Southeast Missouri State U, MO	B
Southern Arkansas U–Magnolia, AR	B
Southern Arkansas U Tech, AR	A
Southern Illinois U Carbondale, IL	B
Southern Illinois U Edwardsville, IL	B
Southern Utah U, UT	A,B
South Georgia Coll, GA	A
South Puget Sound Comm Coll, WA	A
Southwestern Coll, KS	A
Southwestern Comm Coll, IA	A
Southwestern Comm Coll, NC	A
Spokane Comm Coll, WA	A
Stanford U, CA	B
State U of New York Coll at Oneonta, NY	B
Stony Brook U, State U of New York, NY	B
Suffolk County Comm Coll, NY	A
Suffolk U, MA	B
Sussex County Comm Coll, NJ	A
Swarthmore Coll, PA	B
Syracuse U, NY	B
Taylor U, IN	B
Tennessee Technological U, TN	B
Texas A&M U at Galveston, TX	B
Texas A&M U–Corpus Christi, TX	B
Texas A&M U–Kingsville, TX	B
Texas Christian U, TX	B
Texas State Tech Coll Waco, TX	A
Texas State Tech Coll West Texas, TX	A
Texas State U-San Marcos, TX	B
Trinity Coll, CT	B
Trinity U, TX	B
Trinity (Washington) U, DC	B
Troy U, AL	B
Union Coll, NY	B
U at Buffalo, the State U of New York, NY	B
The U of Alabama, AL	B
The U of Alabama in Huntsville, AL	B
U of Arkansas, AR	B
U of California, Santa Cruz, CA	B

U of Central Florida, FL — B
U of Central Missouri, MO — B
U of Cincinnati, OH — A,B
U of Cincinnati Raymond Walters Coll, OH — A
U of Colorado at Boulder, CO — B
U of Colorado at Colorado Springs, CO — B
U of Dayton, OH — B
U of Denver, CO — B
U of Detroit Mercy, MI — B
U of Hartford, CT — A,B
U of Hawaii at Manoa, HI — B
U of Indianapolis, IN — B
The U of Iowa, IA — B
U of Kansas, KS — B
U of La Verne, CA — B
U of Maryland, Baltimore County, MD — B
U of Maryland, Coll Park, MD — B
U of Miami, FL — B
U of Michigan–Flint, MI — B
U of Missouri–Columbia, MO — B
U of Missouri–St. Louis, MO — B
U of Nebraska–Lincoln, NE — B
U of Nevada, Reno, NV — B
U of New Mexico, NM — B
U of New Orleans, LA — B
U of Northern Iowa, IA — B
U of North Texas, TX — B
U of Pittsburgh, PA — B
U of Rhode Island, RI — B
U of Rochester, NY — B
U of San Diego, CA — B
U of Sioux Falls, SD — A
U of South Carolina, SC — B
U of Southern Indiana, IN — B
U of Southern Maine, ME — B
U of South Florida, FL — B
The U of Tennessee at Martin, TN — B
The U of Texas at San Antonio, TX — B
U of Tulsa, OK — B
U of Utah, UT — B
U of Virginia, VA — B
U of Washington, WA — B
U of West Florida, FL — B
U of Wisconsin–Stout, WI — B
U of Wisconsin–Whitewater, WI — B
U of Wyoming, WY — B
Utah State U, UT — B
Utah Valley State Coll, UT — A
Valparaiso U, IN — B
Vanderbilt U, TN — B
Vermont Tech Coll, VT — A,B
Villanova U, PA — B
Virginia Commonwealth U, VA — B
Virginia Polytechnic Inst and State U, VA — B
Wake Forest U, NC — B
Waldorf Coll, IA — B
Wartburg Coll, IA — B
Washington State U, WA — B
Washington U in St. Louis, MO — B
Waynesburg Coll, PA — B
Wells Coll, NY — B
Wentworth Inst of Technology, MA — A,B
Western Kentucky U, KY — B
Western New England Coll, MA — B
Western New Mexico U, NM — A
Western Washington U, WA — B
Western Wyoming Comm Coll, WY — A
Westmont Coll, CA — B
West Texas A&M U, TX — B
Wichita State U, KS — B
Widener U, PA — A
Wilkes U, PA — B
Winona State U, MN — B
Worcester Polytechnic Inst, MA — B
Wytheville Comm Coll, VA — B
Yavapai Coll, AZ — A
York Coll of Pennsylvania, PA — B
York Coll of the City U of New York, NY — B
Young Harris Coll, GA — A

Film and Theater Arts

Adelphi U, NY — B
Adrian Coll, MI — A,B

Agnes Scott Coll, GA — B
Albertus Magnus Coll, CT — B
Albion Coll, MI — B
Alderson-Broaddus Coll, WV — B
Allegheny Coll, PA — B
Alvin Comm Coll, TX — A
American Academy of Dramatic Arts, NY — A
American InterContinental U, CA — B
American InterContinental U, Atlanta, GA — A,B
American U, DC — B
Antioch Coll, OH — B
Aquinas Coll, MI — B
Arcadia U, PA — B
Arizona State U, AZ — B
Art Center Coll of Design, CA — B
The Art Inst of Boston at Lesley U, MA — B
The Art Inst of Colorado, CO — A
The Art Inst of Philadelphia, PA — A,B
Ashland U, OH — B
Averett U, VA — B
Baker U, KS — B
Baldwin-Wallace Coll, OH — B
Ball State U, IN — B
Bard Coll, NY — B
Barnard Coll, NY — B
Barry U, FL — B
Bates Coll, ME — B
Belmont U, TN — B
Beloit Coll, WI — B
Bemidji State U, MN — B
Bennington Coll, VT — B
Berea Coll, KY — B
Berkshire Comm Coll, MA — A
Bethel Coll, KS — B
Bethel U, MN — B
Boise State U, ID — B
Boston U, MA — B
Bucknell U, PA — B
Bunker Hill Comm Coll, MA — A
Butler U, IN — B
Calhoun Comm Coll, AL — A
California Coll of the Arts, CA — B
California Inst of the Arts, CA — B
California Lutheran U, CA — B
California State Polytechnic U, Pomona, CA — B
California State U, Long Beach, CA — B
California State U, Sacramento, CA — B
California State U, Stanislaus, CA — B
Calvin Coll, MI — B
Cañada Coll, CA — A
Capital U, OH — B
Cardinal Stritch U, WI — B
Carroll Coll, MT — B
Carroll Coll, WI — B
Carson-Newman Coll, TN — B
Carthage Coll, WI — B
The Catholic U of America, DC — B
Cazenovia Coll, NY — B
Centenary Coll, NJ — B
Central Christian Coll of Kansas, KS — A
Centralia Coll, WA — A
Central Michigan U, MI — B
Central Wyoming Coll, WY — A
Centre Coll, KY — B
Chabot Coll, CA — A
Chaffey Coll, CA — A
Chapman U, CA — B
Chatham U, PA — B
City Coll of San Francisco, CA — A
City Coll of the City U of New York, NY — B
City Colls of Chicago, Harold Washington Coll, IL — A
Clarendon Coll, TX — A
Clarion U of Pennsylvania, PA — B
Clarke Coll, IA — B
Clark U, MA — B
Cleveland State U, OH — B
Coastal Carolina U, SC — B
Cochise Coll, Sierra Vista, AZ — A
Coe Coll, IA — B
Coffeyville Comm Coll, KS — A

Colby Coll, ME — B
Colby Comm Coll, KS — A
Coll of DuPage, IL — A
Coll of Saint Benedict, MN — B
Coll of St. Catherine, MN — B
Coll of Southern Maryland, MD — A
Coll of the Canyons, CA — A
Coll of the Desert, CA — A
Coll of the Holy Cross, MA — B
Coll of the Ozarks, MO — B
The Colorado Coll, CO — B
Colorado State U, CO — B
Columbia Coll, MO — B
Columbia Coll Chicago, IL — B
Columbia U, School of General Studies, NY — B
Columbus Coll of Art & Design, OH — B
Concordia Coll, MN — B
Concordia U, IL — B
Connecticut Coll, CT — B
Corcoran Coll of Art and Design, DC — A,B
Cornell Coll, IA — B
Cosumnes River Coll, Sacramento, CA — A
Culver-Stockton Coll, MO — B
Cumberland U, TN — B
Dakota County Tech Coll, MN — A
Dakota Wesleyan U, SD — B
Davidson Coll, NC — B
Dean Coll, MA — A
De Anza Coll, CA — A
Del Mar Coll, TX — A
Denison U, OH — B
DePaul U, IL — B
DePauw U, IN — B
DeSales U, PA — B
Dordt Coll, IA — B
Drake U, IA — B
Drew U, NJ — B
Drury U, MO — B
Duquesne U, PA — B
East Carolina U, NC — B
Eastern Mennonite U, VA — B
East Los Angeles Coll, CA — A
East Texas Baptist U, TX — B
Eckerd Coll, FL — B
Edgewood Coll, WI — B
Edinboro U of Pennsylvania, PA — B
El Camino Coll, CA — A
Elizabethtown Coll, PA — B
Elmira Coll, NY — B
Elon U, NC — B
Emerson Coll, MA — B
Emory U, GA — B
Emporia State U, KS — B
The Evergreen State Coll, WA — B
Fairleigh Dickinson U, Coll at Florham, NJ — B
Fairleigh Dickinson U, Metropolitan Campus, NJ — B
Five Towns Coll, NY — A,B
Flagler Coll, FL — B
Florida Atlantic U, FL — B
Florida International U, FL — B
Florida State U, FL — B
Foothill Coll, CA — A
Fordham U, NY — B
Fort Lewis Coll, CO — B
Fresno City Coll, CA — A
Frostburg State U, MD — B
Fullerton Coll, CA — A
Fulton-Montgomery Comm Coll, NY — A
Furman U, SC — B
Gannon U, PA — B
Garden City Comm Coll, KS — A
Gardner-Webb U, NC — B
Genesee Comm Coll, NY — A
George Fox U, OR — B
Georgetown Coll, KY — B
Georgia Coll & State U, GA — B
Georgia Southern U, GA — B
Georgia State U, GA — B
Gettysburg Coll, PA — B
Glendale Comm Coll, AZ — A
Glendale Comm Coll, CA — A
Gonzaga U, WA — B
Goshen Coll, IN — B
Grambling State U, LA — B

Grand Valley State U, MI — B
Grand View Coll, IA — B
Greenfield Comm Coll, MA — A
Greenville Coll, IL — B
Grinnell Coll, IA — B
Gustavus Adolphus Coll, MN — B
Hamilton Coll, NY — B
Hampshire Coll, MA — B
Harding U, AR — B
Hardin-Simmons U, TX — B
Harrisburg Area Comm Coll, PA — A
Hartwick Coll, NY — B
Harvard U, MA — B
Henry Ford Comm Coll, MI — A
Hill Coll of the Hill Jr Coll District, TX — A
Hillsdale Coll, MI — B
Hiram Coll, OH — B
Hofstra U, NY — B
Hope Coll, MI — B
Houston Comm Coll System, TX — A
Howard Coll, TX — A
Howard Payne U, TX — B
Huntingdon Coll, AL — B
Huntington U, IN — B
Idaho State U, ID — B
Illinois Coll, IL — B
The Illinois Inst of Art– Chicago, IL — B
Illinois Wesleyan U, IL — B
Indiana U Bloomington, IN — A,B
Indiana U of Pennsylvania, PA — B
Indiana U South Bend, IN — A
Indiana Wesleyan U, IN — B
Iowa State U of Science and Technology, IA — B
Jacksonville State U, AL — B
Jacksonville U, FL — B
James Madison U, VA — B
The Johns Hopkins U, MD — B
Johnson State Coll, VT — A
Judson Coll, IL — B
The Juilliard School, NY — B
Kansas City Art Inst, MO — B
Kansas State U, KS — B
Kansas Wesleyan U, KS — B
Kean U, NJ — B
Kennesaw State U, GA — B
Kent State U, OH — B
Kenyon Coll, OH — B
Keystone Coll, PA — A
Kilgore Coll, TX — A
Kirkwood Comm Coll, IA — A
Knox Coll, IL — B
Laney Coll, CA — A
Langston U, OK — B
Lansing Comm Coll, MI — A
Laramie County Comm Coll, WY — A
Lawrence U, WI — B
Lees-McRae Coll, NC — B
Lewis & Clark Coll, OR — B
Limestone Coll, SC — B
Linfield Coll, OR — B
Long Beach City Coll, CA — A
Long Island U, C.W. Post Campus, NY — B
Longwood U, VA — B
Los Angeles Mission Coll, CA — A
Los Angeles Pierce Coll, CA — A
Los Angeles Southwest Coll, CA — A
Loyola U Chicago, IL — B
Luther Coll, IA — B
Lycoming Coll, PA — B
Lynchburg Coll, VA — B
Maine Coll of Art, ME — B
Manatee Comm Coll, FL — A
Manchester Coll, IN — B
Marlboro Coll, VT — B
Marquette U, WI — B
Mary Baldwin Coll, VA — B
Marymount Manhattan Coll, NY — B
Maryville Coll, TN — B
Marywood U, PA — B
Massachusetts Coll of Art, MA — B
McDaniel Coll, MD — B
McMurry U, TX — B
McNeese State U, LA — B
Mesa State Coll, CO — A,B

A=Associate; B=Bachelor's Degree

Miami Dade Coll, FL — A
Miami U, OH — B
Michigan Technological U, MI — B
Middlebury Coll, VT — B
Middle Tennessee State U, TN — B
Midwestern State U, TX — B
Millsaps Coll, MS — B
Minnesota State U Mankato, MN — B
Minnesota State U Moorhead, MN — B
MiraCosta Coll, CA — A
Mississippi U for Women, MS — R
Modesto Jr Coll, CA — A
Montclair State U, NJ — B
Monterey Peninsula Coll, CA — A
Moore Coll of Art & Design, PA — B
Moravian Coll, PA — B
Morehead State U, KY — B
Morningside Coll, IA — B
Mott Comm Coll, MI — A
Mount Holyoke Coll, MA — B
Mount Mercy Coll, IA — B
Muskingum Coll, OH — B
Nassau Comm Coll, NY — A
Nebraska Wesleyan U, NE — B
New England Coll, NH — B
New Mexico State U, NM — B
New York U, NY — B
Niagara U, NY — B
North Carolina State U, NC — B
North Central Coll, IL — B
North Central U, MN — A,B
North Dakota State U, ND — B
Northeast Comm Coll, NE — A
Northeastern U, MA — B
Northern Arizona U, AZ — B
Northern Kentucky U, KY — B
Northern Michigan U, MI — B
Northern State U, SD — B
Northwest Coll, WY — A
Northwestern State U of Louisiana, LA — B
Northwestern U, IL — B
Northwest Missouri State U, MO — B
Northwest U, WA — B
Notre Dame de Namur U, CA — B
Nova Southeastern U, FL — R
Ohio Wesleyan U, OH — B
Oklahoma State U, OK — B
Old Dominion U, VA — B
Orange Coast Coll, CA — A
Otis Coll of Art and Design, CA — B
Ottawa U, KS — B
Otterbein Coll, OH — B
Pace U, NY — B
Pacific Northwest Coll of Art, OR — B
Paier Coll of Art, Inc., CT — B
Palomar Coll, CA — A
Park U, MO — B
Parsons The New School for Design, NY — B
Pellissippi State Tech Comm Coll, TN — A
Pennsylvania Coll of Art & Design, PA — B
Piedmont Comm Coll, NC — A
Pitzer Coll, CA — B
Plymouth State U, NH — B
Portland State U, OR — B
Pratt Inst, NY — B
Prescott Coll, AZ — B
Principia Coll, IL — B
Purdue U, IN — B
Quinnipiac U, CT — B
Radford U, VA — B
Randolph Coll, VA — B
Randolph-Macon Coll, VA — B
Raritan Valley Comm Coll, NJ — A
Reed Coll, OR — B
Rhodes Coll, TN — B
Ridgewater Coll, MN — A
Riverside Comm Coll District, CA — A
Rochester Inst of Technology, NY — A,B
Rocky Mountain Coll, MT — B
Roger Williams U, RI — B
Roosevelt U, IL — B
Rose State Coll, OK — A
Sacramento City Coll, CA — A
Sacred Heart U, CT — B

Sage Coll of Albany, NY — A
St. Ambrose U, IA — B
Saint John's U, MN — B
Saint Joseph's Coll, IN — B
St. Louis Comm Coll at Florissant Valley, MO — A
Saint Louis U, MO — B
Saint Mary-of-the-Woods Coll, IN — B
Saint Mary's Coll, IN — B
Saint Mary's Coll of California, CA — B
St. Mary's Coll of Maryland, MD — B
Saint Mary's U of Minnesota, MN — B
Saint Michael's Coll, VT — B
St. Olaf Coll, MN — B
Saint Vincent Coll, PA — B
Sam Houston State U, TX — B
San Bernardino Valley Coll, CA — A
San Diego City Coll, CA — A
San Diego State U, CA — B
San Francisco Art Inst, CA — B
San Francisco State U, CA — B
San Jacinto Coll Central Campus, TX — A
San Jacinto Coll North Campus, TX — A
Santa Barbara City Coll, CA — A
Santa Monica Coll, CA — A
Santa Rosa Jr Coll, CA — A
Sarah Lawrence Coll, NY — B
Sauk Valley Comm Coll, IL — A
Savannah Coll of Art and Design, GA — B
School of the Art Inst of Chicago, IL — B
School of the Museum of Fine Arts, Boston, MA — B
School of Visual Arts, NY — B
Schreiner U, TX — B
Scripps Coll, CA — B
Seattle Central Comm Coll, WA — A
Seattle U, WA — B
Shenandoah U, VA — B
Shorter Coll, GA — B
Sierra Coll, CA — A
Simpson Coll, IA — B
Skidmore Coll, NY — B
Slippery Rock U of Pennsylvania, PA — B
South Dakota State U, SD — B
Southeast Missouri State U, MO — B
Southern Arkansas U–Magnolia, AR — B
Southern Illinois U Carbondale, IL — B
Southern Illinois U Edwardsville, IL — B
Southern Oregon U, OR — B
Southern Utah U, UT — B
South Georgia Coll, GA — A
Southwest Minnesota State U, MN — B
Stanford U, CA — B
State U of New York at Oswego, NY — B
State U of New York at Plattsburgh, NY — B
State U of New York Coll at Geneseo, NY — B
State U of New York Coll at Oneonta, NY — B
Stony Brook U, State U of New York, NY — B
Suffolk County Comm Coll, NY — A
Suffolk U, MA — B
Susquehanna U, PA — B
Swarthmore Coll, PA — B
Syracuse U, NY — B
Taylor U, IN — B
Texas A&M U–Corpus Christi, TX — B
Texas A&M U–Kingsville, TX — B
Texas Christian U, TX — B
Texas State U-San Marcos, TX — B
Texas Wesleyan U, TX — B
Thomas More Coll, KY — A,B
Trevecca Nazarene U, TN — B
Trinity Coll, CT — B
Trinity U, TX — B
Troy U, AL — B

Truman State U, MO — B
U at Buffalo, the State U of New York, NY — B
The U of Alabama, AL — B
U of Arkansas, AR — B
U of Arkansas at Pine Bluff, AR — B
U of California, Santa Cruz, CA — B
U of Central Florida, FL — B
U of Central Missouri, MO — B
U of Cincinnati, OH — B
U of Colorado at Boulder, CO — B
U of Dayton, OH — B
U of Denver, CO — B
U of Detroit Mercy, MI — B
The U of Findlay, OH — B
U of Hartford, CT — B
U of Hawaii at Manoa, HI — B
U of Indianapolis, IN — B
The U of Iowa, IA — B
U of Kansas, KS — B
U of La Verne, CA — B
U of Maine at Farmington, ME — B
U of Mary Hardin-Baylor, TX — B
U of Maryland, Baltimore County, MD — B
U of Maryland, Coll Park, MD — B
U of Mary Washington, VA — B
U of Miami, FL — B
U of Michigan–Flint, MI — B
U of Minnesota, Morris, MN — B
U of Missouri–Columbia, MO — B
U of Missouri–St. Louis, MO — B
U of Nebraska–Lincoln, NE — B
U of Nevada, Reno, NV — B
U of New Mexico, NM — B
The U of North Carolina at Asheville, NC — B
The U of North Carolina at Pembroke, NC — B
U of Northern Iowa, IA — B
U of North Texas, TX — B
U of Oregon, OR — B
U of Pittsburgh, PA — B
U of Puget Sound, WA — B
U of Rochester, NY — B
U of San Diego, CA — B
U of Sioux Falls, SD — A,B
U of South Carolina, SC — B
U of Southern Indiana, IN — B
U of Southern Maine, ME — B
U of South Florida, FL — B
The U of Tampa, FL — B
The U of Tennessee at Martin, TN — B
The U of the Arts, PA — B
U of the Incarnate Word, TX — B
U of Tulsa, OK — B
U of Utah, UT — B
U of Virginia, VA — B
U of Washington, WA — B
U of West Florida, FL — B
U of Wisconsin–Eau Claire, WI — B
U of Wisconsin–La Crosse, WI — B
U of Wisconsin–Oshkosh, WI — B
U of Wisconsin–Stevens Point, WI — B
U of Wisconsin–Superior, WI — B
U of Wisconsin–Whitewater, WI — B
U of Wyoming, WY — B
Utah State U, UT — B
Utah Valley State Coll, UT — A
Valparaiso U, IN — B
Vanderbilt U, TN — B
Vanguard U of Southern California, CA — B
Virginia Commonwealth U, VA — B
Virginia Polytechnic Inst and State U, VA — B
Viterbo U, WI — B
Wabash Coll, IN — B
Wake Forest U, NC — B
Waldorf Coll, IA — B
Washington & Jefferson Coll, PA — B
Washington Coll, MD — B
Washington State U, WA — B
Washington U in St. Louis, MO — B
Wayne State Coll, NE — B
Wells Coll, NY — B
Wesleyan U, CT — B
Western Illinois U, IL — B
Western Kentucky U, KY — B
Western Washington U, WA — B

Western Wyoming Comm Coll, WY — A
Westmont Coll, CA — B
West Texas A&M U, TX — B
West Valley Coll, CA — A
Wichita State U, KS — B
Wilkes U, PA — B
Williams Coll, MA — B
Wilmington Coll, OH — B
Winona State U, MN — B
Yavapai Coll, AZ — A
York Coll of the City U of New York, NY — B
Young Harris Coll, GA — A

Health-Care Services and Sciences

Adelphi U, NY — B
Alamance Comm Coll, NC — A
Alaska Pacific U, AK — B
Albany Coll of Pharmacy of Union U, NY — B
Albertus Magnus Coll, CT — B
Alderson-Broaddus Coll, WV — B
Alvernia Coll, PA — A,B
Alverno Coll, WI — B
Alvin Comm Coll, TX — A
American U, DC — B
Ancilla Coll, IN — A
Anna Maria Coll, MA — B
Aquinas Coll, MI — B
Arcadia U, PA — B
Arizona State U, AZ — B
Ashford U, IA — B
Ashland U, OH — B
Austin Peay State U, TN — B
Averett U, VA — B
Baker Coll of Flint, MI — A,B
Baker U, KS — B
Baldwin-Wallace Coll, OH — B
Ball State U, IN — A,B
Barnes-Jewish Coll of Nursing and Allied Health, MO — A,B
Barry U, FL — B
Bastyr U, WA — B
Bay Path Coll, MA — B
Belmont U, TN — B
Bemidji State U, MN — B
Benedict Coll, SC — B
Berea Coll, KY — B
Berkshire Comm Coll, MA — A
Bethel Coll, KS — B
Bethel U, MN — B
Black Hills State U, SD — B
Bluefield State Coll, WV — A
Blue Mountain Coll, MS — B
Boise State U, ID — A,B
Boston U, MA — B
Bowling Green State U–Firelands Coll, OH — A
Brescia U, KY — B
Briarwood Coll, CT — A
Bronx Comm Coll of the City U of New York, NY — A
Broome Comm Coll, NY — A
Bunker Hill Comm Coll, MA — A
Butler U, IN — B
Caldwell Coll, NJ — B
Calhoun Comm Coll, AL — A
California State U, Long Beach, CA — B
California State U, Sacramento, CA — B
California State U, Stanislaus, CA — B
Calvin Coll, MI — B
Cameron U, OK — A
Cañada Coll, CA — A
Capital U, OH — B
Cardinal Stritch U, WI — A,B
Carlow U, PA — B
Carroll Coll, MT — B
Carroll Coll, WI — B
Carson-Newman Coll, TN — B
Carthage Coll, WI — B
The Catholic U of America, DC — B
Central Christian Coll of Kansas, KS — A
Central Comm Coll–Columbus Campus, NE — A
Central Comm Coll–Grand Island Campus, NE — A

College	
Central Comm Coll–Hastings Campus, NE	A
Central Florida Comm Coll, FL	A
Centralia Coll, WA	A
Central Lakes Coll, MN	A
Central Michigan U, MI	B
Central Piedmont Comm Coll, NC	A
Central Wyoming Coll, WY	A
Century Coll, MN	A
Cerro Coso Comm Coll, CA	A
Chabot Coll, CA	A
Chaffey Coll, CA	A
Chapman U, CA	B
Chatham U, PA	B
Chattahoochee Tech Coll, GA	A
Chattanooga State Tech Comm Coll, TN	A
Chemeketa Comm Coll, OR	A
City Coll of San Francisco, CA	A
City Colls of Chicago, Harold Washington Coll, IL	A
City Colls of Chicago, Kennedy-King Coll, IL	A
Clarendon Coll, TX	A
Clarion U of Pennsylvania, PA	A,B
Clarke Coll, IA	B
Clarkson U, NY	B
Clatsop Comm Coll, OR	A
Cleveland State U, OH	B
Clinton Comm Coll, IA	A
Coastal Carolina U, SC	B
Coastal Georgia Comm Coll, GA	A
Cochise Coll, Sierra Vista, AZ	A
Coe Coll, IA	B
Coffeyville Comm Coll, KS	A
Colby Comm Coll, KS	A
Colby-Sawyer Coll, NH	B
Colegio Universitario de San Juan, PR	A
Coll Misericordia, PA	B
Coll of DuPage, IL	A
Coll of Eastern Utah, UT	A
Coll of Lake County, IL	A
Coll of Saint Benedict, MN	B
Coll of St. Catherine, MN	A
Coll of Southern Maryland, MD	A
Coll of the Canyons, CA	A
Coll of the Desert, CA	A
Coll of the Ozarks, MO	A
Colorado State U, CO	B
Columbia Coll, MO	A
Columbia Coll Chicago, IL	B
Columbia Union Coll, MD	A,B
Concordia Coll, MN	B
Concordia U, IL	B
Connors State Coll, OK	A
Cosumnes River Coll, Sacramento, CA	A
County Coll of Morris, NJ	A
Culver-Stockton Coll, MO	B
Cumberland U, TN	B
Daemen Coll, NY	B
Dakota County Tech Coll, MN	A
Dakota Wesleyan U, SD	A
Davenport U, Midland, MI	A
De Anza Coll, CA	A
Defiance Coll, OH	B
DeKalb Tech Coll, GA	A
Delaware Tech & Comm Coll, Jack F. Owens Campus, DE	A
Del Mar Coll, TX	A
Delta Coll, MI	A
DePaul U, IL	B
DeSales U, PA	B
Dominican U of California, CA	B
Dordt Coll, IA	B
Drake U, IA	B
Drury U, MO	B
Duquesne U, PA	B
D'Youville Coll, NY	B
East Carolina U, NC	B
East Central Coll, MO	A
Eastern Mennonite U, VA	B
Eastern U, PA	B
Eastern Wyoming Coll, WY	A
East Los Angeles Coll, CA	A
East Tennessee State U, TN	B
East Texas Baptist U, TX	B
Edgewood Coll, WI	B

College	
Edinboro U of Pennsylvania, PA	B
Edison Coll, FL	A
Edmonds Comm Coll, WA	A
El Camino Coll, CA	A
Elizabethtown Coll, PA	B
Elmira Coll, NY	B
Elms Coll, MA	A
Elon U, NC	B
Emerson Coll, MA	B
Emmanuel Coll, MA	B
Emory U, GA	B
Emporia State U, KS	B
Fairfield U, CT	B
Fairleigh Dickinson U, Coll at Florham, NJ	A,B
Fairleigh Dickinson U, Metropolitan Campus, NJ	A,B
Ferris State U, MI	A,B
Florida Atlantic U, FL	B
Florida Gulf Coast U, FL	B
Florida International U, FL	B
Florida Keys Comm Coll, FL	A
Florida State U, FL	B
Foothill Coll, CA	A
Fox Valley Tech Coll, WI	A
Fresno City Coll, CA	A
Fulton-Montgomery Comm Coll, NY	A
Gannon U, PA	A,B
Garden City Comm Coll, KS	A
Gardner-Webb U, NC	A,B
GateWay Comm Coll, AZ	A
Genesee Comm Coll, NY	A
George Fox U, OR	B
Georgia Coll & State U, GA	B
Georgia Highlands Coll, GA	A
Georgia Southern U, GA	B
Georgia State U, GA	B
Gettysburg Coll, PA	B
Glendale Comm Coll, AZ	A
Glendale Comm Coll, CA	A
Glen Oaks Comm Coll, MI	A
Globe Inst of Technology, NY	A
Golden West Coll, CA	A
Gonzaga U, WA	B
Goshen Coll, IN	B
Grambling State U, LA	B
Grand Valley State U, MI	B
Grand View Coll, IA	B
Grays Harbor Coll, WA	A
Greenfield Comm Coll, MA	A
Gulf Coast Comm Coll, FL	A
Gustavus Adolphus Coll, MN	B
Hampshire Coll, MA	B
Harding U, AR	B
Hardin-Simmons U, TX	B
Harper Coll, IL	A
Harrisburg Area Comm Coll, PA	A
Hartwick Coll, NY	B
Hawaii Comm Coll, HI	A
Hawai'i Pacific U, HI	B
Henry Ford Comm Coll, MI	A
Hesston Coll, KS	A
Hill Coll of the Hill Jr Coll District, TX	A
Hillsdale Free Will Baptist Coll, OK	A
Hiram Coll, OH	B
Hofstra U, NY	B
Holy Family U, PA	A
Hope Coll, MI	B
Hope International U, CA	B
Hopkinsville Comm Coll, KY	A
Houston Comm Coll System, TX	A
Howard Coll, TX	A
Howard Payne U, TX	B
Hudson Valley Comm Coll, NY	A
Huntingdon Coll, AL	B
Idaho State U, ID	A,B
Illinois Coll, IL	B
Illinois Wesleyan U, IL	B
Indiana Tech, IN	A,B
Indiana U Bloomington, IN	B
Indiana U of Pennsylvania, PA	B
Indiana U South Bend, IN	A,B
Indiana U Southeast, IN	A,B
Indiana Wesleyan U, IN	A,B
Iowa Western Comm Coll, IA	A
Isothermal Comm Coll, NC	A

College	
Itasca Comm Coll, MN	A
Jacksonville State U, AL	B
Jacksonville U, FL	B
James A. Rhodes State Coll, OH	A
James Madison U, VA	B
The Johns Hopkins U, MD	B
Johnson County Comm Coll, KS	A
Johnson State Coll, VT	B
Joliet Jr Coll, IL	A
Jones Coll, Jacksonville, FL	A,B
Judson Coll, IL	B
Kankakee Comm Coll, IL	A
Kansas State U, KS	B
Kansas Wesleyan U, KS	A,B
Kapiolani Comm Coll, HI	A
Kean U, NJ	B
Kennesaw State U, GA	B
Kent State U, OH	A,B
Kent State U, Ashtabula Campus, OH	A
Kent State U, East Liverpool Campus, OH	A
Kent State U, Geauga Campus, OH	A
Kent State U, Salem Campus, OH	A,B
Kent State U, Trumbull Campus, OH	B
Kent State U, Tuscarawas Campus, OH	A,B
Kentucky Wesleyan Coll, KY	B
Keystone Coll, PA	A
Kilgore Coll, TX	A
Kingwood Coll, TX	A
Kirkwood Comm Coll, IA	A
Lake Land Coll, IL	A
Lake Region State Coll, ND	A
Lamar State Coll–Port Arthur, TX	A
Lander U, SC	B
Langston U, OK	B
Lansing Comm Coll, MI	A
Laramie County Comm Coll, WY	A
Laurel Business Inst, PA	A
LDS Business Coll, UT	A
Lewis-Clark State Coll, ID	A
Liberty U, VA	B
Lincoln Land Comm Coll, IL	A
Lipscomb U, TN	B
Long Beach City Coll, CA	A
Long Island U, C.W. Post Campus, NY	B
Longwood U, VA	B
Los Angeles Harbor Coll, CA	A
Los Angeles Pierce Coll, CA	A
Los Angeles Southwest Coll, CA	A
Louisiana State U at Alexandria, LA	A
Loyola U Chicago, IL	B
Luther Coll, IA	B
Lycoming Coll, PA	B
Lynchburg Coll, VA	B
Manatee Comm Coll, FL	A
Manchester Coll, IN	B
Manhattan Coll, NY	B
Marian Coll of Fond du Lac, WI	B
Marquette U, WI	B
Marshall U, WV	A,B
Mary Baldwin Coll, VA	B
Marymount Manhattan Coll, NY	B
Maryville Coll, TN	B
Maryville U of Saint Louis, MO	B
Marywood U, PA	B
Massachusetts Bay Comm Coll, MA	A
Maui Comm Coll, HI	A
McMurry U, TX	B
McNeese State U, LA	A,B
Mercy Coll, NY	A
Merritt Coll, CA	A
Mesabi Range Comm and Tech Coll, MN	A
Mesa Comm Coll, AZ	A
Mesa State Coll, CO	A,B
Miami Dade Coll, FL	A
Miami U, OH	B
Michigan Technological U, MI	B
MidAmerica Nazarene U, KS	B

College	
Middlesex Comm Coll, CT	A
Middle Tennessee State U, TN	B
Midland Coll, TX	A
Midstate Coll, IL	A
Midwestern State U, TX	B
Millersville U of Pennsylvania, PA	B
Milligan Coll, TN	B
Minnesota State Coll–Southeast Tech, MN	A
Minnesota State U Mankato, MN	A,B
Minnesota State U Moorhead, MN	B
Minot State U, ND	B
MiraCosta Coll, CA	A
Mississippi U for Women, MS	A,B
Missouri Baptist U, MO	B
Mitchell Coll, CT	A
Mitchell Tech Inst, SD	A
Modesto Jr Coll, CA	A
Molloy Coll, NY	B
Monmouth U, NJ	B
Montana Tech of The U of Montana, MT	A
Montclair State U, NJ	B
Monterey Peninsula Coll, CA	A
Moravian Coll, PA	B
Morehead State U, KY	A,B
Morningside Coll, IA	B
Motlow State Comm Coll, TN	A
Mott Comm Coll, MI	A
Mountain State U, WV	A,B
Mount Ida Coll, MA	A,B
Mount Mercy Coll, IA	B
Muskingum Coll, OH	B
Nassau Comm Coll, NY	A
Nebraska Methodist Coll, NE	A,B
Nebraska Wesleyan U, NE	B
The New England Coll of Optometry, MA	B
New England Inst of Technology, RI	A
New Mexico Highlands U, NM	B
New Mexico State U, NM	B
New Mexico State U–Alamogordo, NM	A
New River Comm Coll, VA	A
New York U, NY	A,B
Northampton County Area Comm Coll, PA	A
North Central Coll, IL	B
North Central U, MN	A
North Dakota State Coll of Science, ND	A
North Dakota State U, ND	B
Northeast Comm Coll, NE	A
Northeastern U, MA	B
Northeast State Tech Comm Coll, TN	A
Northern Arizona U, AZ	B
Northern Kentucky U, KY	A,B
Northern Michigan U, MI	B
Northern State U, SD	B
Northland Coll, WI	B
NorthWest Arkansas Comm Coll, AR	A
Northwest Coll, WY	A
Northwestern State U of Louisiana, LA	A,B
Northwestern U, IL	B
Northwest Missouri State U, MO	B
Northwest U, WA	A
Norwalk Comm Coll, CT	A
Nova Southeastern U, FL	B
Oakland U, MI	B
Ohio Wesleyan U, OH	B
Oklahoma Panhandle State U, OK	A,B
Oklahoma State U, OK	B
Oklahoma Wesleyan U, OK	B
Old Dominion U, VA	B
Orange Coast Coll, CA	A
Oregon State U, OR	B
Otterbein Coll, OH	B
Owens Comm Coll, Toledo, OH	A
Pace U, NY	B
Palomar Coll, CA	A
Park U, MO	B
Patricia Stevens Coll, MO	A
Peninsula Coll, WA	A

A=Associate; B=Bachelor's Degree

Peru State Coll, NE	B
Piedmont Comm Coll, NC	A
Pierce Coll, WA	A
Pikes Peak Comm Coll, CO	A
Pioneer Pacific Coll, OR	A,B
Pittsburg State U, KS	B
Plymouth State U, NH	B
Portland Comm Coll, OR	A
Prescott Coll, AZ	B
Presentation Coll, SD	A,B
Purdue U, IN	A,B
Quincy U, IL	B
Quinnipiac U, CT	B
Radford U, VA	B
Ramapo Coll of New Jersey, NJ	B
Raritan Valley Comm Coll, NJ	A
Rasmussen Coll Mankato, MN	A
Redlands Comm Coll, OK	A
Renton Tech Coll, WA	A
Richmond Comm Coll, NC	A
Rider U, NJ	A
Ridgewater Coll, MN	A
Riverside Comm Coll District, CA	A
Rochester Inst of Technology, NY	A
Roger Williams U, RI	B
Roosevelt U, IL	B
Rose State Coll, OK	A
Sacramento City Coll, CA	A
Sacred Heart U, CT	B
Sage Coll of Albany, NY	B
St. Ambrose U, IA	B
Saint Charles Comm Coll, MO	A
Saint Francis U, PA	B
Saint John's U, MN	B
Saint Joseph's Coll, IN	B
Saint Leo U, FL	B
St. Louis Comm Coll at Florissant Valley, MO	A
Saint Louis U, MO	B
Saint Mary-of-the-Woods Coll, IN	B
Saint Mary's Coll, IN	B
Saint Mary's Coll of California, CA	B
Saint Mary's U of Minnesota, MN	B
St. Olaf Coll, MN	B
St. Petersburg Coll, FL	A,B
Saint Vincent Coll, PA	B
Sam Houston State U, TX	B
San Bernardino Valley Coll, CA	A
San Diego City Coll, CA	A
San Diego State U, CA	B
San Francisco State U, CA	B
San Jacinto Coll Central Campus, TX	A
San Jacinto Coll North Campus, TX	A
San Jacinto Coll South Campus, TX	A
Santa Barbara City Coll, CA	A
Santa Fe Comm Coll, NM	A
Santa Monica Coll, CA	A
Santa Rosa Jr Coll, CA	A
Sauk Valley Comm Coll, IL	A
Scott Comm Coll, IA	A
Seattle Central Comm Coll, WA	A
Seattle U, WA	B
Seton Hall U, NJ	B
Shenandoah U, VA	A,B
Sheridan Coll–Sheridan and Gillette, WY	A
Shorter Coll, GA	B
Sierra Coll, CA	A
Simmons Coll, MA	B
Simpson Coll, IA	B
Skagit Valley Coll, WA	A
Slippery Rock U of Pennsylvania, PA	B
South Dakota State U, SD	B
Southeast Missouri State U, MO	B
Southern Arkansas U–Magnolia, AR	A
Southern Arkansas U Tech, AR	A
Southern Illinois U Carbondale, IL	A
Southern Illinois U Edwardsville, IL	B
Southern Oregon U, OR	B
South Georgia Coll, GA	A

South Puget Sound Comm Coll, WA	A
Southwestern Coll, KS	B
Southwestern Comm Coll, IA	A
Southwestern Comm Coll, NC	A
Spokane Comm Coll, WA	A
Spokane Falls Comm Coll, WA	A
Spring Arbor U, MI	B
State U of New York at Plattsburgh, NY	B
State U of New York Coll at Geneseo, NY	B
State U of New York Coll at Oneonta, NY	B
Stony Brook U, State U of New York, NY	B
Suffolk County Comm Coll, NY	A
Suffolk U, MA	B
Sussex County Comm Coll, NJ	A
Syracuse U, NY	B
Tabor Coll, KS	B
Taylor U, IN	B
Tennessee Technological U, TN	B
Texas A&M U–Corpus Christi, TX	B
Texas A&M U–Kingsville, TX	B
Texas A&M U–Texarkana, TX	B
Texas Christian U, TX	B
Texas State Tech Coll Waco, TX	A
Texas State Tech Coll West Texas, TX	A
Texas State U-San Marcos, TX	B
Thomas More Coll, KY	B
Trevecca Nazarene U, TN	B
Troy U, AL	A,B
Truman State U, MO	B
Tusculum Coll, TN	B
U at Buffalo, the State U of New York, NY	B
The U of Alabama, AL	B
The U of Alabama in Huntsville, AL	B
U of Arkansas, AR	B
U of Arkansas at Fort Smith, AR	A,B
U of Arkansas at Pine Bluff, AR	B
U of Central Florida, FL	B
U of Central Missouri, MO	B
U of Charleston, WV	A,B
U of Cincinnati, OH	A,B
U of Cincinnati Raymond Walters Coll, OH	A
U of Colorado at Colorado Springs, CO	B
U of Dayton, OH	B
U of Detroit Mercy, MI	B
U of Dubuque, IA	B
The U of Findlay, OH	A,B
U of Guam, GU	B
U of Hartford, CT	A,B
U of Hawaii at Manoa, HI	B
U of Indianapolis, IN	A,B
The U of Iowa, IA	B
U of Kansas, KS	B
U of La Verne, CA	B
U of Maine at Farmington, ME	B
U of Maine at Fort Kent, ME	B
U of Maine at Presque Isle, ME	B
U of Mary Hardin-Baylor, TX	B
U of Maryland, Baltimore County, MD	B
U of Maryland, Coll Park, MD	B
U of Miami, FL	B
U of Michigan–Flint, MI	B
U of Minnesota, Crookston, MN	B
U of Minnesota, Morris, MN	B
U of Missouri–Columbia, MO	B
U of Missouri–St. Louis, MO	B
U of Nebraska–Lincoln, NE	B
U of Nevada, Reno, NV	B
U of New Mexico, NM	A,B
U of New Orleans, LA	B
U of North Alabama, AL	B
The U of North Carolina at Pembroke, NC	B
U of Northern Iowa, IA	B
U of North Texas, TX	B
U of Oregon, OR	B
U of Pittsburgh, PA	B
U of Pittsburgh at Bradford, PA	A,B
U of Rhode Island, RI	B
U of Rochester, NY	B

U of Saint Francis, IN	A,B
U of San Francisco, CA	B
U of Sioux Falls, SD	B
U of South Carolina, SC	B
U of South Carolina Upstate, SC	A,B
U of Southern Indiana, IN	A,B
U of Southern Maine, ME	A,B
U of South Florida, FL	B
The U of Tampa, FL	B
The U of Tennessee at Martin, TN	B
The U of Texas at San Antonio, TX	B
The U of Texas Southwestern Medical Center at Dallas, TX	B
U of the Incarnate Word, TX	B
U of Tulsa, OK	B
U of Utah, UT	B
U of Virginia, VA	B
U of Washington, WA	B
U of West Florida, FL	B
U of Wisconsin–Eau Claire, WI	B
U of Wisconsin–La Crosse, WI	B
U of Wisconsin–Oshkosh, WI	B
U of Wisconsin–Stevens Point, WI	B
U of Wisconsin–Stout, WI	B
U of Wisconsin–Superior, WI	B
U of Wisconsin–Whitewater, WI	B
U of Wyoming, WY	B
Upper Iowa U, IA	B
Utah State U, UT	B
Utah Valley State Coll, UT	A,B
Utica Coll, NY	B
Valparaiso U, IN	B
Vanguard U of Southern California, CA	B
Vermont Tech Coll, VT	A
Villanova U, PA	B
Virginia Commonwealth U, VA	B
Viterbo U, WI	B
Wake Forest U, NC	B
Waldorf Coll, IA	B
Wartburg Coll, IA	B
Washington State U, WA	B
Waynesburg Coll, PA	B
Wayne State Coll, NE	B
Weatherford Coll, TX	A
Western Illinois U, IL	B
Western Kentucky U, KY	A,B
Western New Mexico U, NM	A
Western Washington U, WA	B
Western Wyoming Comm Coll, WY	A
West Texas A&M U, TX	B
West Valley Coll, CA	A
Whatcom Comm Coll, WA	A
Wichita State U, KS	A,B
Widener U, PA	B
Wilkes U, PA	B
Williston State Coll, ND	A
Wilson Coll, PA	B
Winona State U, MN	B
Worcester State Coll, MA	B
Wytheville Comm Coll, VA	A
Yavapai Coll, AZ	A
York Coll of Pennsylvania, PA	A,B
York Coll of the City U of New York, NY	B
Young Harris Coll, GA	A

Home Economics and Nutrition Studies

Adrian Coll, MI	A,B
Aims Comm Coll, CO	A
Albertus Magnus Coll, CT	B
Albion Coll, MI	B
Alderson-Broaddus Coll, WV	B
Alvin Comm Coll, TX	A
Antioch Coll, OH	B
Arcadia U, PA	B
Arizona State U, AZ	B
Ashford U, IA	B
Ashland U, OH	B
Baker Coll of Flint, MI	A
Ball State U, IN	B
Bastyr U, WA	B
Benedict Coll, SC	B
Berea Coll, KY	B
Black Hills State U, SD	B
Boise State U, ID	A

Bowling Green State U–Firelands Coll, OH	A
Briarwood Coll, CT	A
Bronx Comm Coll of the City U of New York, NY	A
Calhoun Comm Coll, AL	A
California Polytechnic State U, San Luis Obispo, CA	B
California State Polytechnic U, Pomona, CA	B
California State U, Long Beach, CA	B
Camcron U, OK	B
Carson-Newman Coll, TN	B
Cazenovia Coll, NY	A,B
Central Comm Coll–Columbus Campus, NE	A
Central Comm Coll–Grand Island Campus, NE	A
Central Comm Coll–Hastings Campus, NE	A
Centralia Coll, WA	A
Central Michigan U, MI	B
Central Piedmont Comm Coll, NC	A
Chabot Coll, CA	A
Chaffey Coll, CA	A
Chattahoochee Tech Coll, GA	A
Chattanooga State Tech Comm Coll, TN	A
Chemeketa Comm Coll, OR	A
City Colls of Chicago, Harold Washington Coll, IL	A
City Colls of Chicago, Kennedy-King Coll, IL	A
Coffeyville Comm Coll, KS	A
Colby Comm Coll, KS	A
Coll of DuPage, IL	A
Coll of Eastern Utah, UT	A
Coll of Saint Benedict, MN	B
Coll of St. Catherine, MN	B
Coll of Southern Maryland, MD	A
Coll of the Canyons, CA	A
Coll of the Ozarks, MO	B
Colorado State U, CO	B
Concordia Coll, MN	B
Connors State Coll, OK	A
Cosumnes River Coll, Sacramento, CA	A
Dakota County Tech Coll, MN	A
Dakota Wesleyan U, SD	A
De Anza Coll, CA	A
Delaware Tech & Comm Coll, Jack F. Owens Campus, DE	A
Del Mar Coll, TX	A
Delta Coll, MI	A
East Carolina U, NC	B
East Los Angeles Coll, CA	A
East Tennessee State U, TN	B
Eckerd Coll, FL	B
Edison Coll, FL	A
El Camino Coll, CA	A
Elmira Coll, NY	B
Elon U, NC	B
FIDM/The Fashion Inst of Design & Merchandising, Los Angeles Campus, CA	A
Florida State U, FL	B
Foothill Coll, CA	A
Fox Valley Tech Coll, WI	A
Fresno City Coll, CA	A
Fullerton Coll, CA	A
Fulton-Montgomery Comm Coll, NY	A
Garden City Comm Coll, KS	A
Genesee Comm Coll, NY	A
George Fox U, OR	B
Georgia Highlands Coll, GA	A
Georgia Southern U, GA	B
Georgia State U, GA	B
Glendale Comm Coll, AZ	A
Glendale Comm Coll, CA	A
Goshen Coll, IN	B
Grambling State U, LA	B
Grays Harbor Coll, WA	A
Greenfield Comm Coll, MA	A
Harding U, AR	B
Harper Coll, IL	A
Harrisburg Area Comm Coll, PA	A
Harvard U, MA	B
Hawaii Comm Coll, HI	A
Hawai'i Pacific U, HI	B
Hellenic Coll, MA	B

College	Degree
Henry Ford Comm Coll, MI	A
Hilbert Coll, NY	A,B
Hill Coll of the Hill Jr Coll District, TX	A
Hope Coll, MI	B
Hope International U, CA	A
Houston Comm Coll System, TX	A
Howard Coll, TX	A
Hudson Valley Comm Coll, NY	A
Huntington Coll of Health Sciences, TN	A
Idaho State U, ID	B
The Illinois Inst of Art–Chicago, IL	
Indiana Tech, IN	B
Indiana U Bloomington, IN	B
Indiana U of Pennsylvania, PA	B
Iowa State U of Science and Technology, IA	B
Iowa Western Comm Coll, IA	A
Itasca Comm Coll, MN	A
Jacksonville State U, AL	B
James A. Rhodes State Coll, OH	A
James Madison U, VA	B
Johnson & Wales U, RI	B
Judson Coll, IL	B
Kankakee Comm Coll, IL	A
Kansas State U, KS	B
Kent State U, OH	B
Kent State U, Ashtabula Campus, OH	A
Kent State U, Salem Campus, OH	A,B
Kentucky Wesleyan Coll, KY	B
Kirkwood Comm Coll, IA	A
Lake Land Coll, IL	A
Lamar State Coll–Port Arthur, TX	A
Langston U, OK	B
Lansing Comm Coll, MI	A
Leeward Comm Coll, HI	A
Lewis-Clark State Coll, ID	A,B
Liberty U, VA	B
Lipscomb U, TN	B
Long Beach City Coll, CA	A
Los Angeles Southwest Coll, CA	A
Loyola U Chicago, IL	B
Lynn U, FL	B
Marshall U, WV	B
Marywood U, PA	B
Massachusetts Bay Comm Coll, MA	A
Maui Comm Coll, HI	A
McNeese State U, LA	B
Mercy Coll, NY	B
Merritt Coll, CA	A
Mesabi Range Comm and Tech Coll, MN	A
Mesa Comm Coll, AZ	A
Mesa State Coll, CO	B
Miami Dade Coll, FL	A
Miami U, OH	B
Middlesex Comm Coll, CT	A
Middle Tennessee State U, TN	B
Minnesota State Coll–Southeast Tech, MN	A
Minnesota State U Mankato, MN	B
Mississippi U for Women, MS	B
Missouri Baptist U, MO	B
Mitchell Coll, CT	A,B
Modesto Jr Coll, CA	A
Monterey Peninsula Coll, CA	A
Mount Ida Coll, MA	A
New Mexico State U, NM	B
New River Comm Coll, VA	A
New York U, NY	A
North Dakota State U, ND	B
Northeastern U, MA	B
Northern Kentucky U, KY	A,B
Northern Michigan U, MI	A,B
Northwestern State U of Louisiana, LA	B
Northwest Missouri State U, MO	B
Norwalk Comm Coll, CT	A
Notre Dame de Namur U, CA	B
Oklahoma State U, OK	B
Orange Coast Coll, CA	A
Oregon State U, OR	B
Ottawa U, KS	B
Owens Comm Coll, Toledo, OH	A
Palomar Coll, CA	A
Park U, MO	B
Peninsula Coll, WA	A
Pikes Peak Comm Coll, CO	A
Pittsburg State U, KS	B
Portland Comm Coll, OR	A
Portland State U, OR	B
Prescott Coll, AZ	B
Purdue U, IN	B
Quinnipiac U, CT	B
Raritan Valley Comm Coll, NJ	A
Rasmussen Coll Mankato, MN	A
Redlands Comm Coll, OK	A
Richmond Comm Coll, NC	A
Ridgewater Coll, MN	A
Roosevelt U, IL	B
Rose State Coll, OK	A
Sacramento City Coll, CA	A
Saint Charles Comm Coll, MO	A
Saint John's U, MN	B
Saint Leo U, FL	B
St. Louis Comm Coll at Florissant Valley, MO	A
Saint Louis U, MO	B
Saint Mary-of-the-Woods Coll, IN	B
St. Olaf Coll, MN	B
St. Petersburg Coll, FL	A
Sam Houston State U, TX	B
San Bernardino Valley Coll, CA	A
San Diego State U, CA	B
San Francisco State U, CA	B
San Jacinto Coll Central Campus, TX	A
San Jacinto Coll North Campus, TX	A
Santa Monica Coll, CA	A
Santa Rosa Jr Coll, CA	A
Sarah Lawrence Coll, NY	B
Sauk Valley Comm Coll, IL	A
Seattle Central Comm Coll, WA	A
Shepherd U, WV	B
Sierra Coll, CA	A
Simmons Coll, MA	B
Skagit Valley Coll, WA	A
South Dakota State U, SD	B
Southeast Missouri State U, MO	B
Southern Illinois U Carbondale, IL	B
Southern New Hampshire U, NH	B
Southern Utah U, UT	A
South Puget Sound Comm Coll, WA	A
Southwestern Comm Coll, NC	A
Spokane Comm Coll, WA	A
Spring Arbor U, MI	B
State U of New York at Oswego, NY	B
State U of New York at Plattsburgh, NY	B
State U of New York Coll at Oneonta, NY	B
Suffolk County Comm Coll, NY	A
Suffolk U, MA	B
Sussex County Comm Coll, NJ	A
Syracuse U, NY	B
Tennessee Technological U, TN	B
Texas A&M U–Kingsville, TX	B
Texas State Tech Coll Waco, TX	A
Texas State U-San Marcos, TX	B
Trevecca Nazarene U, TN	B
Trinity (Washington) U, DC	B
The U of Alabama, AL	B
U of Arkansas, AR	B
U of Arkansas at Fort Smith, AR	A
U of Arkansas at Pine Bluff, AR	B
U of Central Missouri, MO	B
U of Cincinnati, OH	B
U of Dayton, OH	B
U of Detroit Mercy, MI	B
U of Hawaii at Manoa, HI	B
U of La Verne, CA	B
U of Maine at Fort Kent, ME	A
U of Maine at Presque Isle, ME	A
U of Maryland, Coll Park, MD	B
U of Minnesota, Morris, MN	B
U of Missouri–Columbia, MO	B
U of Nebraska–Lincoln, NE	B
U of Nevada, Reno, NV	B
U of New Mexico, NM	B
U of North Alabama, AL	B
U of Northern Iowa, IA	B
U of North Texas, TX	B
U of Oregon, OR	B
U of Pittsburgh, PA	B
U of Rhode Island, RI	B
U of Saint Francis, IN	A
The U of Tennessee at Martin, TN	B
U of the Incarnate Word, TX	B
U of Utah, UT	B
U of Wisconsin–Oshkosh, WI	B
U of Wisconsin–Stout, WI	B
U of Wyoming, WY	B
Upper Iowa U, IA	B
Utah State U, UT	B
Vanderbilt U, TN	B
Villanova U, PA	B
Virginia Polytechnic Inst and State U, VA	B
Washington State U, WA	B
Wayne State Coll, NE	B
Western Illinois U, IL	B
Western Kentucky U, KY	B
Western Washington U, WA	B

Hospitality and Recreation Careers

College	Degree
Alamance Comm Coll, NC	A
Alaska Pacific U, AK	B
Arizona State U, AZ	B
The Art Inst of Colorado, CO	A,B
The Art Inst of Houston, TX	A
The Art Inst of Philadelphia, PA	A
Ashland U, OH	B
Baker Coll of Flint, MI	A
Ball State U, IN	B
Belmont U, TN	B
Bemidji State U, MN	B
Benedict Coll, SC	B
Berkshire Comm Coll, MA	A
Bethany Coll, KS	B
Black Hills State U, SD	A,B
Boise State U, ID	A
Boston U, MA	B
Briarwood Coll, CT	A
Bunker Hill Comm Coll, MA	A
California Polytechnic State U, San Luis Obispo, CA	B
California State U, Long Beach, CA	B
California State U, Sacramento, CA	B
Calvin Coll, MI	B
Cañada Coll, CA	A
Carson-Newman Coll, TN	B
Central Christian Coll of Kansas, KS	A,B
Central Comm Coll–Hastings Campus, NE	A
Central Florida Comm Coll, FL	A
Centralia Coll, WA	A
Central Michigan U, MI	B
Central Piedmont Comm Coll, NC	A
Cerro Coso Comm Coll, CA	A
Chabot Coll, CA	A
Chattahoochee Tech Coll, GA	A
Chemeketa Comm Coll, OR	A
City Coll of San Francisco, CA	A
City Colls of Chicago, Harold Washington Coll, IL	A
City Colls of Chicago, Kennedy-King Coll, IL	A
Coastal Georgia Comm Coll, GA	A
Coll of DuPage, IL	A
Coll of Lake County, IL	A
Coll of the Desert, CA	A
Coll of the Ozarks, MO	B
Colorado State U, CO	B
County Coll of Morris, NJ	A
Cumberland U, TN	B
Dakota County Tech Coll, MN	A
Davenport U, Midland, MI	A
Delaware Tech & Comm Coll, Jack F. Owens Campus, DE	A
Del Mar Coll, TX	A
Dordt Coll, IA	B
East Carolina U, NC	B
East Central Coll, MO	A
Edison Coll, FL	A
Edmonds Comm Coll, WA	A
El Camino Coll, CA	A
Elon U, NC	B
Emporia State U, KS	B
Ferris State U, MI	A
Florida Atlantic U, FL	B
Florida International U, FL	B
Florida Keys Comm Coll, FL	A
Florida State U, FL	B
Foothill Coll, CA	A
Fort Lewis Coll, CO	B
Fox Valley Tech Coll, WI	A
Fresno City Coll, CA	A
Frostburg State U, MD	B
Fullerton Coll, CA	A
Genesee Comm Coll, NY	A
Georgia Coll & State U, GA	B
Georgia Southern U, GA	B
Glendale Comm Coll, CA	A
Globe Inst of Technology, NY	A
Grand Valley State U, MI	B
Greenfield Comm Coll, MA	A
Green Mountain Coll, VT	B
Greenville Coll, IL	B
Gulf Coast Comm Coll, FL	A
Harper Coll, IL	A
Harrisburg Area Comm Coll, PA	A
Hawai'i Pacific U, HI	B
Henry Ford Comm Coll, MI	A
Houston Comm Coll System, TX	A
Howard Payne U, TX	B
Huntingdon Coll, AL	B
Huntington U, IN	B
Idaho State U, ID	A
The Illinois Inst of Art–Chicago, IL	A
Indiana Tech, IN	A,B
Indiana U Bloomington, IN	B
Indiana U Southeast, IN	B
Indiana Wesleyan U, IN	B
International Coll of Hospitality Management, CT	A
Iowa Western Comm Coll, IA	A
Jacksonville State U, AL	B
James Madison U, VA	B
Johnson & Wales U, FL	A,B
Johnson & Wales U, RI	A,B
Johnson County Comm Coll, KS	A
Johnson State Coll, VT	A
Joliet Jr Coll, IL	A
Kansas State U, KS	B
Kapiolani Comm Coll, HI	A
Kean U, NJ	B
Kent State U, OH	B
Keystone Coll, PA	A,B
Kirkwood Comm Coll, IA	A
Laney Coll, CA	A
Lansing Comm Coll, MI	A
Leeward Comm Coll, HI	A
Lewis-Clark State Coll, ID	A,B
Long Beach City Coll, CA	A
Los Angeles Mission Coll, CA	A
Lyndon State Coll, VT	B
Marshall U, WV	B
Maryville Coll, TN	B
Marywood U, PA	B
Massachusetts Bay Comm Coll, MA	A
Merritt Coll, CA	A
Mesa State Coll, CO	A
Miami Dade Coll, FL	A
Middle Tennessee State U, TN	B
Midstate Coll, IL	A
Minnesota State U Mankato, MN	B
MiraCosta Coll, CA	A
Mississippi U for Women, MS	A
Mitchell Coll, CT	A
Mitchell Tech Inst, SD	A
Modesto Jr Coll, CA	A
Montclair State U, NJ	B
Monterey Peninsula Coll, CA	A
Mott Comm Coll, MI	A

A=Associate; B=Bachelor's Degree

Mountain State U, WV	A,B
New England Coll, NH	B
New Mexico Highlands U, NM	B
New Mexico State U, NM	B
New York U, NY	B
Niagara U, NY	B
North Carolina State U, NC	B
North Dakota State U, ND	B
Northern Arizona U, AZ	B
Northern Michigan U, MI	B
Northland Coll, WI	B
Northwest Coll, WY	A
Northwestern State U of Louisiana, LA	B
Northwest Missouri State U, MO	B
Norwalk Comm Coll, CT	A
Oklahoma Panhandle State U, OK	A,B
Old Dominion U, VA	B
Orange Coast Coll, CA	A
Oregon State U, OR	B
Palomar Coll, CA	A
Patricia Stevens Coll, MO	A
Pellissippi State Tech Comm Coll, TN	A
Prescott Coll, AZ	B
Quality Coll of Culinary Careers, CA	A
Radford U, VA	B
Raritan Valley Comm Coll, NJ	A
Rasmussen Coll Mankato, MN	A
Renton Tech Coll, WA	A
Ridgewater Coll, MN	A
Riverside Comm Coll District, CA	A
Rochester Inst of Technology, NY	A,B
Roosevelt U, IL	B
Rose State Coll, OK	A
Saint Francis U, PA	A
Saint Leo U, FL	B
St. Petersburg Coll, FL	A
St. Thomas U, FL	B
San Bernardino Valley Coll, CA	A
San Diego City Coll, CA	A
San Diego State U, CA	B
San Francisco State U, CA	B
San Jacinto Coll North Campus, TX	A
Santa Barbara City Coll, CA	A
Santa Fe Comm Coll, NM	A
Santa Monica Coll, CA	A
Santa Rosa Jr Coll, CA	A
Savannah State U, GA	B
Schiller International U, FL	A,B
Scott Comm Coll, IA	A
Seattle Central Comm Coll, WA	A
Shepherd U, WV	B
Sheridan Coll–Sheridan and Gillette, WY	A
Shorter Coll, GA	B
Skagit Valley Coll, WA	A
Slippery Rock U of Pennsylvania, PA	B
South Dakota State U, SD	B
Southeast Missouri State U, MO	B
Southern Illinois U Carbondale, IL	B
Southern New Hampshire U, NH	A
South Georgia Coll, GA	A
South Puget Sound Comm Coll, WA	A
Southwestern Comm Coll, NC	A
Spokane Comm Coll, WA	A
Suffolk County Comm Coll, NY	A
Sullivan U, KY	A,B
Syracuse U, NY	B
Texas State Tech Coll Waco, TX	A
Texas State U-San Marcos, TX	B
Troy U, AL	B
U of Arkansas at Pine Bluff, AR	B
U of Central Florida, FL	B
U of Central Missouri, MO	B
U of Denver, CO	B
U of Dubuque, IA	B
U of Hawaii at Manoa, HI	B
The U of Iowa, IA	B
U of Maine at Presque Isle, ME	A,B
U of Mary Hardin-Baylor, TX	B
U of Miami, FL	B

U of Minnesota, Crookston, MN	A
U of Missouri–Columbia, MO	B
U of Nevada, Reno, NV	B
U of New Mexico, NM	B
U of New Orleans, LA	B
The U of North Carolina at Pembroke, NC	B
U of Northern Iowa, IA	B
U of North Texas, TX	B
U of South Carolina, SC	B
U of South Florida, FL	B
The U of Tennessee at Martin, TN	B
The U of Texas at San Antonio, TX	B
U of Utah, UT	B
U of West Florida, FL	B
U of Wisconsin–La Crosse, WI	B
U of Wisconsin–Stout, WI	B
U of Wyoming, WY	B
Upper Iowa U, IA	B
Utah State U, UT	B
Utah Valley State Coll, UT	A,B
Virginia Commonwealth U, VA	B
Washington State U, WA	B
Webber International U, FL	A,B
Western Illinois U, IL	B
Western Kentucky U, KY	B
Western Washington U, WA	B
West Valley Coll, CA	A
Winona State U, MN	B
York Coll of Pennsylvania, PA	B
Young Harris Coll, GA	A

Humanities

Adelphi U, NY	B
Adrian Coll, MI	A,B
Agnes Scott Coll, GA	B
Albertus Magnus Coll, CT	B
Albion Coll, MI	B
Alderson-Broaddus Coll, WV	B
Allegheny Coll, PA	B
Alvernia Coll, PA	B
Alverno Coll, WI	B
American U, DC	B
Ancilla Coll, IN	A
Anna Maria Coll, MA	B
Antioch Coll, OH	B
Aquinas Coll, MI	B
Arcadia U, PA	B
Arizona State U, AZ	B
Ashford U, IA	B
Ashland U, OH	B
Assumption Coll, MA	B
Austin Peay State U, TN	B
Averett U, VA	B
Baker U, KS	B
Baldwin-Wallace Coll, OH	B
Ball State U, IN	B
Bard Coll, NY	B
Barnard Coll, NY	B
Barry U, FL	B
Bates Coll, ME	B
Belmont U, TN	B
Beloit Coll, WI	B
Bemidji State U, MN	B
Benedict Coll, SC	B
Bennington Coll, VT	B
Bentley Coll, MA	B
Berea Coll, KY	B
Bethany Coll, KS	B
Bethel Coll, KS	B
Bethel U, MN	B
Black Hills State U, SD	B
Blue Mountain Coll, MS	B
Boise State U, ID	B
Boston U, MA	B
Bowdoin Coll, ME	B
Brescia U, KY	A,B
Bryant U, RI	B
Bryn Mawr Coll, PA	B
Bucknell U, PA	B
Bunker Hill Comm Coll, MA	A
Butler U, IN	B
Caldwell Coll, NJ	B
Calhoun Comm Coll, AL	A
California Lutheran U, CA	B
California Polytechnic State U, San Luis Obispo, CA	B
California State Polytechnic U, Pomona, CA	B
California State U, Long Beach, CA	B

California State U, Sacramento, CA	B
California State U, Stanislaus, CA	B
Calvin Coll, MI	B
Cameron U, OK	B
Cañada Coll, CA	A
Capital U, OH	B
Cardinal Stritch U, WI	B
Carleton Coll, MN	B
Carlow U, PA	B
Carroll Coll, MT	A,B
Carroll Coll, WI	B
Carson-Newman Coll, TN	B
Carthage Coll, WI	B
The Catholic U of America, DC	B
Cazenovia Coll, NY	B
Centenary Coll, NJ	B
Central Christian Coll of Kansas, KS	A,B
Centralia Coll, WA	A
Central Michigan U, MI	B
Central Wyoming Coll, WY	A
Centre Coll, KY	B
Chabot Coll, CA	A
Chaffey Coll, CA	A
Chapman U, CA	B
Chatham U, PA	B
Chemeketa Comm Coll, OR	A
Christendom Coll, VA	B
City Coll of San Francisco, CA	A
City Coll of the City U of New York, NY	B
City Colls of Chicago, Harold Washington Coll, IL	A
Claflin U, SC	B
Clarendon Coll, TX	A
Clarion U of Pennsylvania, PA	B
Clarke Coll, IA	B
Clarkson U, NY	B
Clark U, MA	B
Clearwater Christian Coll, FL	B
Cleveland State U, OH	B
Coastal Carolina U, SC	B
Coastal Georgia Comm Coll, GA	A
Cochise Coll, Sierra Vista, AZ	A
Coe Coll, IA	B
Coffeyville Comm Coll, KS	A
Colby Coll, ME	B
Colby Comm Coll, KS	B
Colby-Sawyer Coll, NH	B
Coll Misericordia, PA	B
Coll of Lake County, IL	A
Coll of Saint Benedict, MN	B
Coll of St. Catherine, MN	B
Coll of Southern Maryland, MD	A
Coll of the Atlantic, ME	B
Coll of the Canyons, CA	A
Coll of the Desert, CA	A
Coll of the Holy Cross, MA	B
Coll of the Ozarks, MO	B
The Colorado Coll, CO	B
Colorado State U, CO	B
Columbia Coll, MO	B
Columbia Coll Chicago, IL	B
Columbia Union Coll, MD	B
Columbia U, School of General Studies, NY	B
Concordia Coll, MN	B
Concordia Coll, NY	B
Concordia U, IL	B
Connecticut Coll, CT	B
Cornell Coll, IA	B
Culver-Stockton Coll, MO	B
Cumberland U, TN	B
Daemen Coll, NY	B
Dakota Wesleyan U, SD	B
Dana Coll, NE	B
Davidson Coll, NC	B
De Anza Coll, CA	A
Defiance Coll, OH	B
Del Mar Coll, TX	A
Denison U, OH	B
DePaul U, IL	B
DePauw U, IN	B
DeSales U, PA	B
Dominican School of Philosophy and Theology, CA	B
Dominican U of California, CA	B
Dordt Coll, IA	B
Drake U, IA	B
Drew U, NJ	B
Drury U, MO	B

Duquesne U, PA	B
D'Youville Coll, NY	B
East Carolina U, NC	B
East Central Coll, MO	A
Eastern Connecticut State U, CT	B
Eastern Mennonite U, VA	B
Eastern U, PA	B
Eastern Wyoming Coll, WY	A
East Los Angeles Coll, CA	A
East Tennessee State U, TN	B
East Texas Baptist U, TX	B
Eckerd Coll, FL	B
Edgewood Coll, WI	B
Edinboro U of Pennsylvania, PA	B
El Camino Coll, CA	A
Elizabethtown Coll, PA	B
Elmira Coll, NY	B
Elms Coll, MA	B
Elon U, NC	B
Emerson Coll, MA	B
Emmanuel Coll, MA	B
Emory U, GA	B
Emporia State U, KS	B
Fairfield U, CT	B
Fairleigh Dickinson U, Coll at Florham, NJ	B
Fairleigh Dickinson U, Metropolitan Campus, NJ	B
Ferris State U, MI	A,B
Flagler Coll, FL	B
Florida Atlantic U, FL	B
Florida International U, FL	B
Florida State U, FL	B
Foothill Coll, CA	A
Fordham U, NY	B
Fort Lewis Coll, CO	B
Fresno City Coll, CA	A
Fresno Pacific U, CA	A,B
Frostburg State U, MD	B
Fullerton Coll, CA	A
Fulton-Montgomery Comm Coll, NY	A
Furman U, SC	B
Gannon U, PA	B
Garden City Comm Coll, KS	A
Gardner-Webb U, NC	B
George Fox U, OR	B
Georgetown Coll, KY	B
Georgia Coll & State U, GA	B
Georgia Highlands Coll, GA	A
Georgia Southern U, GA	B
Georgia State U, GA	B
Gettysburg Coll, PA	B
Glendale Comm Coll, CA	A
Golden West Coll, CA	A
Gonzaga U, WA	B
Goshen Coll, IN	B
Grambling State U, LA	B
Grand Valley State U, MI	B
Grand View Coll, IA	B
Green Mountain Coll, VT	B
Greenville Coll, IL	B
Grinnell Coll, IA	B
Gulf Coast Comm Coll, FL	A
Gustavus Adolphus Coll, MN	B
Hamilton Coll, NY	B
Hampden-Sydney Coll, VA	B
Hampshire Coll, MA	B
Harding U, AR	B
Hardin-Simmons U, TX	B
Hartwick Coll, NY	B
Harvard U, MA	B
Haverford Coll, PA	B
Hawai'i Pacific U, HI	B
Hawaii Tokai International Coll, HI	A
Hellenic Coll, MA	B
Hilbert Coll, NY	B
Hill Coll of the Hill Jr Coll District, TX	A
Hillsdale Coll, MI	B
Hillsdale Free Will Baptist Coll, OK	A
Hiram Coll, OH	B
Hofstra U, NY	B
Holy Apostles Coll and Seminary, CT	A,B
Holy Family U, PA	B
Hope Coll, MI	B
Houston Comm Coll System, TX	A
Howard Coll, TX	A

Howard Payne U, TX — A,B
Huntingdon Coll, AL — B
Huntington U, IN — B
Idaho State U, ID — A,B
Illinois Coll, IL — B
Illinois Inst of Technology, IL — B
Illinois Wesleyan U, IL — B
Indiana U Bloomington, IN — B
Indiana U of Pennsylvania, PA — B
Indiana U South Bend, IN — B
Indiana U Southeast, IN — B
Indiana Wesleyan U, IN — A,B
Iowa State U of Science and Technology, IA — B
Jacksonville State U, AL — B
Jacksonville U, FL — B
James Madison U, VA — B
John Carroll U, OH — B
The Johns Hopkins U, MD — B
Johnson State Coll, VT — B
Judson Coll, IL — B
Juniata Coll, PA — B
Kansas City Art Inst, MO — B
Kansas State U, KS — B
Kansas Wesleyan U, KS — B
Kean U, NJ — B
Kennesaw State U, GA — B
Kent State U, OH — B
Kent State U, Trumbull Campus, OH — B
Kentucky Wesleyan Coll, KY — B
Kenyon Coll, OH — B
Kilgore Coll, TX — A
Kingwood Coll, TX — A
Kirkwood Comm Coll, IA — A
Knox Coll, IL — B
Lafayette Coll, PA — B
Lakeland Coll, WI — B
Lander U, SC — B
Langston U, OK — B
Lansing Comm Coll, MI — A
Laramie County Comm Coll, WY — A
Lawrence U, WI — B
Lees-McRae Coll, NC — B
LeMoyne-Owen Coll, TN — B
Lewis & Clark Coll, OR — B
Lewis-Clark State Coll, ID — B
Liberty U, VA — A,B
Limestone Coll, SC — B
Lincoln Land Comm Coll, IL — A
Linfield Coll, OR — B
Lipscomb U, TN — B
Long Beach City Coll, CA — A
Long Island U, C.W. Post Campus, NY — B
Longwood U, VA — B
Los Angeles Mission Coll, CA — A
Los Angeles Southwest Coll, CA — A
Louisiana State U at Alexandria, LA — B
Loyola U Chicago, IL — B
Luther Coll, IA — B
Lycoming Coll, PA — B
Lynchburg Coll, VA — B
Lyndon State Coll, VT — B
Lynn U, FL — B
Manatee Comm Coll, FL — A
Manchester Coll, IN — A,B
Manhattan Coll, NY — B
Manhattanville Coll, NY — B
Marian Coll of Fond du Lac, WI — B
Marlboro Coll, VT — B
Marquette U, WI — B
Marshall U, WV — B
Mary Baldwin Coll, VA — B
Marylhurst U, OR — B
Marymount Manhattan Coll, NY — B
Maryville Coll, TN — B
Maryville U of Saint Louis, MO — B
Marywood U, PA — B
Massachusetts Inst of Technology, MA — B
McDaniel Coll, MD — B
McMurry U, TX — B
McNeese State U, LA — B
Mercy Coll, NY — B
Merritt Coll, CA — A
Mesa State Coll, CO — A,B
Miami Dade Coll, FL — A
Miami U, OH — B

Michigan Technological U, MI — B
MidAmerica Nazarene U, KS — B
Middlebury Coll, VT — B
Middle Tennessee State U, TN — B
Midland Coll, TX — A
Midwestern State U, TX — B
Millersville U of Pennsylvania, PA — B
Milligan Coll, TN — B
Millsaps Coll, MS — B
Mills Coll, CA — B
Minnesota State U Mankato, MN — B
Minnesota State U Moorhead, MN — B
Minot State U, ND — B
MiraCosta Coll, CA — A
Mississippi U for Women, MS — B
Missouri Baptist U, MO — A,B
Modesto Jr Coll, CA — A
Molloy Coll, NY — B
Monmouth U, NJ — B
Montana Tech of The U of Montana, MT — B
Montclair State U, NJ — B
Monterey Peninsula Coll, CA — B
Moravian Coll, PA — B
Morehead State U, KY — B
Morningside Coll, IA — B
Mountain State U, WV — B
Mount Holyoke Coll, MA — B
Mount Mercy Coll, IA — B
Muskingum Coll, OH — B
Nebraska Wesleyan U, NE — B
New Coll of California, CA — B
New Coll of Florida, FL — B
New England Coll, NH — B
New Mexico Highlands U, NM — B
New Mexico Inst of Mining and Technology, NM — B
New Mexico Military Inst, NM — A
New Mexico State U, NM — B
New York U, NY — B
Niagara U, NY — B
Nichols Coll, MA — B
North Carolina State U, NC — B
North Central Coll, IL — B
North Central U, MN — A
North Dakota State U, ND — B
Northeast Comm Coll, NE — A
Northeastern U, MA — B
Northern Arizona U, AZ — B
Northern Kentucky U, KY — B
Northern Michigan U, MI — B
Northern State U, SD — B
Northland Coll, WI — B
Northwest Coll, WY — A
Northwestern State U of Louisiana, LA — B
Northwestern U, IL — B
Northwest Missouri State U, MO — B
Northwest U, WA — B
Notre Dame Coll, OH — B
Notre Dame de Namur U, CA — B
Nova Southeastern U, FL — B
Oakland U, MI — B
Ohio Wesleyan U, OH — B
Oklahoma Panhandle State U, OK — B
Oklahoma State U, OK — B
Oklahoma Wesleyan U, OK — A,B
Old Dominion U, VA — B
Orange Coast Coll, CA — A
Oregon State U, OR — B
Ottawa U, KS — B
Otterbein Coll, OH — B
Pace U, NY — B
Park U, MO — B
Peace Coll, NC — B
Peru State Coll, NE — B
Philadelphia Biblical U, PA — B
Pittsburg State U, KS — B
Pitzer Coll, CA — B
Plymouth State U, NH — B
Pontifical Coll Josephinum, OH — B
Portland State U, OR — B
Pratt Inst, NY — B
Prescott Coll, AZ — B
Presentation Coll, SD — A
Principia Coll, IL — B
Purdue U, IN — B

Quincy U, IL — B
Quinnipiac U, CT — B
Radford U, VA — B
Ramapo Coll of New Jersey, NJ — B
Randolph Coll, VA — B
Randolph-Macon Coll, VA — B
Redlands Comm Coll, OK — A
Reed Coll, OR — B
Rensselaer Polytechnic Inst, NY — B
Rhodes Coll, TN — B
Rider U, NJ — B
Roanoke Bible Coll, NC — B
Rocky Mountain Coll, MT — B
Roger Williams U, RI — B
Roosevelt U, IL — B
Rose State Coll, OK — A
Sacramento City Coll, CA — A
Sacred Heart U, CT — A,B
St. Ambrose U, IA — B
Saint Anselm Coll, NH — B
St. Charles Borromeo Seminary, Overbrook, PA — B
Saint Francis U, PA — B
St. Gregory's U, OK — B
St. John's Coll, NM — B
Saint John's U, MN — B
Saint Joseph's Coll, IN — B
Saint Leo U, FL — B
Saint Louis U, MO — B
Saint Mary-of-the-Woods Coll, IN — B
Saint Mary's Coll, IN — B
Saint Mary's Coll of California, CA — B
St. Mary's Coll of Maryland, MD — B
Saint Mary's U of Minnesota, MN — B
St. Mary's U of San Antonio, TX — B
Saint Michael's Coll, VT — B
St. Olaf Coll, MN — B
St. Thomas U, FL — B
Saint Vincent Coll, PA — B
Sam Houston State U, TX — B
San Bernardino Valley Coll, CA — A
San Diego City Coll, CA — A
San Diego State U, CA — B
San Francisco State U, CA — B
San Jacinto Coll Central Campus, TX — A
San Jacinto Coll North Campus, TX — A
San Jacinto Coll South Campus, TX — A
Santa Barbara City Coll, CA — A
Santa Fe Comm Coll, NM — A
Santa Monica Coll, CA — A
Santa Rosa Jr Coll, CA — A
Sarah Lawrence Coll, NY — B
Sauk Valley Comm Coll, IL — A
Savannah State U, GA — B
School of the Art Inst of Chicago, IL — B
Schreiner U, TX — B
Scripps Coll, CA — B
Seattle U, WA — B
Seton Hall U, NJ — B
Shenandoah U, VA — B
Shepherd U, WV — B
Sheridan Coll–Sheridan and Gillette, WY — A
Shorter Coll, GA — B
Siena Coll, NY — B
Simmons Coll, MA — B
Simpson Coll, IA — B
Skagit Valley Coll, WA — A
Skidmore Coll, NY — B
Slippery Rock U of Pennsylvania, PA — B
South Dakota State U, SD — B
Southeast Missouri State U, MO — B
Southern Arkansas U–Magnolia, AR — B
Southern Illinois U Carbondale, IL — B
Southern Illinois U Edwardsville, IL — B
Southern New Hampshire U, NH — B

Southern Oregon U, OR — B
Southern Utah U, UT — B
South Georgia Coll, GA — A
Southwestern Coll, KS — B
Southwest Minnesota State U, MN —
Spring Arbor U, MI — B
Stanford U, CA — B
State U of New York at Oswego, NY — B
State U of New York at Plattsburgh, NY — B
State U of New York Coll at Geneseo, NY — B
State U of New York Coll at Oneonta, NY — B
Stony Brook U, State U of New York, NY — B
Suffolk County Comm Coll, NY — A
Suffolk U, MA — B
Susquehanna U, PA — B
Sussex County Comm Coll, NJ — A
Swarthmore Coll, PA — B
Syracuse U, NY — B
Tabor Coll, KS — A,B
Taylor U, IN — B
Tennessee Technological U, TN — B
Texas A&M U–Corpus Christi, TX — B
Texas A&M U–Kingsville, TX — B
Texas A&M U–Texarkana, TX — B
Texas Christian U, TX — B
Texas State U-San Marcos, TX — B
Texas Wesleyan U, TX — B
Thomas More Coll, KY — A,B
Trevecca Nazarene U, TN — B
Trinity Coll, CT — B
Trinity U, TX — B
Trinity (Washington) U, DC — B
Troy U, AL — B
Truman State U, MO — B
Tusculum Coll, TN — B
Union Coll, NY — B
U at Buffalo, the State U of New York, NY — B
The U of Alabama, AL — B
The U of Alabama in Huntsville, AL — B
U of Arkansas, AR — B
U of Arkansas at Fort Smith, AR — B
U of Arkansas at Pine Bluff, AR — B
U of Baltimore, MD — B
U of California, Santa Cruz, CA — B
U of Central Florida, FL — B
U of Central Missouri, MO — B
U of Cincinnati, OH — B
U of Colorado at Boulder, CO — B
U of Colorado at Colorado Springs, CO — B
U of Dayton, OH — B
U of Denver, CO — B
U of Detroit Mercy, MI — B
U of Dubuque, IA — A,B
The U of Findlay, OH — A,B
U of Guam, GU — B
U of Hartford, CT — B
U of Hawaii at Manoa, HI — B
U of Illinois at Springfield, IL — B
U of Indianapolis, IN — B
The U of Iowa, IA — B
U of Kansas, KS — B
U of La Verne, CA — B
U of Maine at Farmington, ME — B
U of Maine at Fort Kent, ME — B
U of Maine at Presque Isle, ME — A
U of Mary Hardin-Baylor, TX — B
U of Maryland, Baltimore County, MD — B
U of Maryland, Coll Park, MD — B
U of Mary Washington, VA — B
U of Miami, FL — B
U of Michigan–Flint, MI — B
U of Minnesota, Morris, MN — B
U of Missouri–Columbia, MO — B
U of Missouri–St. Louis, MO — B
U of Nebraska–Lincoln, NE — B
U of Nevada, Reno, NV — B
U of New Mexico, NM — B
U of New Orleans, LA — B
U of North Alabama, AL — B

A=Associate; B=Bachelor's Degree

The U of North Carolina at Asheville, NC — B
The U of North Carolina at Pembroke, NC — B
U of Northern Iowa, IA — B
U of North Texas, TX — B
U of Oregon, OR — B
U of Pittsburgh, PA — B
U of Pittsburgh at Bradford, PA — B
U of Puget Sound, WA — B
U of Rhode Island, RI — B
U of Rochester, NY — B
U of Saint Francis, IN — B
U of San Diego, CA — B
U of San Francisco, CA — B
U of Sioux Falls, SD — A,B
U of South Carolina, SC — B
U of South Carolina Upstate, SC — B
U of Southern Indiana, IN — B
U of Southern Maine, ME — B
U of South Florida, FL — B
The U of Tampa, FL — A,B
The U of Tennessee at Martin, TN — B
The U of Texas at San Antonio, TX — B
U of the Incarnate Word, TX — B
U of Tulsa, OK — B
U of Utah, UT — B
U of Virginia, VA — B
U of Washington, WA — B
U of West Florida, FL — B
U of Wisconsin–Eau Claire, WI — B
U of Wisconsin–La Crosse, WI — B
U of Wisconsin–Oshkosh, WI — B
U of Wisconsin–Stevens Point, WI — B
U of Wisconsin–Stout, WI — B
U of Wisconsin–Superior, WI — B
U of Wisconsin–Whitewater, WI — B
U of Wyoming, WY — B
Upper Iowa U, IA — B
Utah State U, UT — B
Utah Valley State Coll, UT — A,B
Utica Coll, NY — B
Valparaiso U, IN — B
Vanderbilt U, TN — B
Vanguard U of Southern California, CA — B
Villanova U, PA — B
Virginia Commonwealth U, VA — B
Virginia Polytechnic Inst and State U, VA — B
Viterbo U, WI — B
Wabash Coll, IN — B
Wake Forest U, NC — B
Waldorf Coll, IA — B
Warren Wilson Coll, NC — B
Wartburg Coll, IA — B
Washington & Jefferson Coll, PA — B
Washington Bible Coll, MD — A,B
Washington Coll, MD — B
Washington State U, WA — B
Washington U in St. Louis, MO — B
Waynesburg Coll, PA — B
Wayne State Coll, NE — B
Wells Coll, NY — B
Wesleyan U, CT — B
Western Illinois U, IL — B
Western Kentucky U, KY — B
Western New England Coll, MA — B
Western New Mexico U, NM — B
Western Washington U, WA — B
Western Wyoming Comm Coll, WY — A
Westmont Coll, CA — B
West Texas A&M U, TX — B
West Valley Coll, CA — A
Wichita State U, KS — B
Widener U, PA — B
Wilkes U, PA — B
Williams Coll, MA — B
Wilmington Coll, OH — B
Wilson Coll, PA — B
Winona State U, MN — B
Worcester Polytechnic Inst, MA — B
Worcester State Coll, MA — B
York Coll, NE — B
York Coll of Pennsylvania, PA — A,B
York Coll of the City U of New York, NY — B
Young Harris Coll, GA — A

Mathematics

Adelphi U, NY — B
Adrian Coll, MI — B
Agnes Scott Coll, GA — B
Albertus Magnus Coll, CT — B
Albion Coll, MI — B
Alderson-Broaddus Coll, WV — B
Allegheny Coll, PA — B
Alvernia Coll, PA — B
Alverno Coll, WI — B
Alvin Comm Coll, TX — A
American U, DC — B
Ancilla Coll, IN — A
Antioch Coll, OH — B
Aquinas Coll, MI — B
Arcadia U, PA — B
Arizona State U, AZ — B
Ashland U, OH — B
Assumption Coll, MA — B
Austin Peay State U, TN — B
Averett U, VA — B
Baker U, KS — B
Baldwin-Wallace Coll, OH — B
Ball State U, IN — B
Bard Coll, NY — B
Barnard Coll, NY — B
Barry U, FL — B
Bates Coll, ME — B
Belmont U, TN — B
Beloit Coll, WI — B
Bemidji State U, MN — B
Benedict Coll, SC — B
Bennington Coll, VT — B
Bentley Coll, MA — B
Berea Coll, KY — B
Bethany Coll, KS — B
Bethel Coll, KS — B
Bethel U, MN — B
Black Hills State U, SD — B
Blue Mountain Coll, MS — B
Boise State U, ID — B
Boston U, MA — B
Bowdoin Coll, ME — B
Brescia U, KY — B
Bronx Comm Coll of the City U of New York, NY — A
Bryn Mawr Coll, PA — B
Bucknell U, PA — B
Bunker Hill Comm Coll, MA — A
Butler U, IN — B
Caldwell Coll, NJ — B
Calhoun Comm Coll, AL — A
California Lutheran U, CA — B
California Polytechnic State U, San Luis Obispo, CA — B
California State Polytechnic U, Pomona, CA — B
California State U, Long Beach, CA — B
California State U, Sacramento, CA — B
California State U, Stanislaus, CA — B
Calvin Coll, MI — B
Cameron U, OK — B
Cañada Coll, CA — A
Capital U, OH — B
Cardinal Stritch U, WI — B
Carleton Coll, MN — B
Carlow U, PA — B
Carroll Coll, MT — B
Carroll Coll, WI — B
Carson-Newman Coll, TN — B
Carthage Coll, WI — B
The Catholic U of America, DC — B
Centenary Coll, NJ — B
Central Christian Coll of Kansas, KS — A
Centralia Coll, WA — A
Central Michigan U, MI — B
Centre Coll, KY — B
Chabot Coll, CA — A
Chaffey Coll, CA — A
Chapman U, CA — B
Chatham U, PA — B
Chemeketa Comm Coll, OR — A
City Coll of San Francisco, CA — A
City Coll of the City U of New York, NY — B
City Colls of Chicago, Harold Washington Coll, IL — A
City Colls of Chicago, Kennedy-King Coll, IL — A

Claflin U, SC — B
Clarendon Coll, TX — A
Clarion U of Pennsylvania, PA — B
Clarke Coll, IA — B
Clarkson U, NY — B
Clark U, MA — B
Clearwater Christian Coll, FL — B
Cleveland State U, OH — B
Coastal Carolina U, SC — B
Coastal Georgia Comm Coll, GA — A
Coe Coll, IA — B
Coffeyville Comm Coll, KS — A
Colby Coll, ME — B
Colby Comm Coll, KS — A
Coll Misericordia, PA — B
Coll of Saint Benedict, MN — B
Coll of St. Catherine, MN — B
Coll of the Canyons, CA — A
Coll of the Desert, CA — A
Coll of the Holy Cross, MA — B
Coll of the Ozarks, MO — B
The Colorado Coll, CO — B
Colorado State U, CO — B
Columbia Coll, MO — B
Columbia Union Coll, MD — B
Columbia U, School of General Studies, NY — B
Concordia Coll, MN — B
Concordia Coll, NY — B
Concordia U, IL — B
Connecticut Coll, CT — B
Connors State Coll, OK — A
Cornell Coll, IA — B
Cosumnes River Coll, Sacramento, CA — A
Culver-Stockton Coll, MO — B
Cumberland U, TN — B
Daemen Coll, NY — B
Dakota Wesleyan U, SD — B
Dana Coll, NE — B
Davidson Coll, NC — B
De Anza Coll, CA — A
Defiance Coll, OH — B
Del Mar Coll, TX — A
Denison U, OH — B
DePaul U, IL — B
DePauw U, IN — B
DeSales U, PA — B
Dordt Coll, IA — B
Drake U, IA — B
Drew U, NJ — B
Drury U, MO — B
Duquesne U, PA — B
East Carolina U, NC — B
Eastern Connecticut State U, CT — B
Eastern Mennonite U, VA — B
Eastern U, PA — B
Eastern Wyoming Coll, WY — A
East Los Angeles Coll, CA — A
East Tennessee State U, TN — B
East Texas Baptist U, TX — B
Eckerd Coll, FL — B
Edgewood Coll, WI — B
Edinboro U of Pennsylvania, PA — B
El Camino Coll, CA — A
Elizabethtown Coll, PA — B
Elmira Coll, NY — B
Elms Coll, MA — B
Elon U, NC — B
Emmanuel Coll, MA — B
Emory U, GA — B
Emporia State U, KS — B
Fairfield U, CT — B
Fairleigh Dickinson U, Coll at Florham, NJ — B
Fairleigh Dickinson U, Metropolitan Campus, NJ — B
Ferris State U, MI — B
Florida Atlantic U, FL — B
Florida Inst of Technology, FL — B
Florida International U, FL — B
Florida State U, FL — B
Foothill Coll, CA — A
Fordham U, NY — B
Fort Lewis Coll, CO — B
Fresno Pacific U, CA — A,B
Frostburg State U, MD — B
Fullerton Coll, CA — A
Fulton-Montgomery Comm Coll, NY — A
Furman U, SC — B

Gannon U, PA — B
Garden City Comm Coll, KS — A
Gardner-Webb U, NC — B
Genesee Comm Coll, NY — A
George Fox U, OR — B
Georgetown Coll, KY — B
Georgia Coll & State U, GA — B
Georgia Southern U, GA — B
Georgia State U, GA — B
Gettysburg Coll, PA — B
Glendale Comm Coll, CA — A
Golden West Coll, CA — A
Gonzaga U, WA — B
Goshen Coll, IN — B
Grambling State U, LA — B
Grand Valley State U, MI — B
Grand View Coll, IA — B
Greenfield Comm Coll, MA — A
Greenville Coll, IL — B
Grinnell Coll, IA — B
Gulf Coast Comm Coll, FL — A
Gustavus Adolphus Coll, MN — B
Hamilton Coll, NY — B
Hampden-Sydney Coll, VA — B
Hampshire Coll, MA — B
Harding U, AR — B
Hardin-Simmons U, TX — B
Harper Coll, IL — A
Harrisburg Area Comm Coll, PA — A
Hartwick Coll, NY — B
Harvard U, MA — B
Harvey Mudd Coll, CA — B
Haverford Coll, PA — B
Hawai'i Pacific U, HI — A,B
Hill Coll of the Hill Jr Coll District, TX — A
Hillsdale Coll, MI — B
Hillsdale Free Will Baptist Coll, OK — A
Hiram Coll, OH — B
Hofstra U, NY — B
Holy Family U, PA — B
Hope Coll, MI — B
Howard Coll, TX — A
Howard Payne U, TX — B
Huntingdon Coll, AL — B
Huntington U, IN — B
Idaho State U, ID — A,B
Illinois Coll, IL — B
Illinois Inst of Technology, IL — B
Illinois Wesleyan U, IL — B
Indiana U Bloomington, IN — B
Indiana U of Pennsylvania, PA — B
Indiana U South Bend, IN — B
Indiana U Southeast, IN — B
Indiana Wesleyan U, IN — A,B
Iowa State U of Science and Technology, IA — B
Jacksonville State U, AL — B
Jacksonville U, FL — B
James Madison U, VA — B
John Carroll U, OH — B
The Johns Hopkins U, MD — B
Johnson State Coll, VT — B
Joliet Jr Coll, IL — A
Judson Coll, IL — B
Juniata Coll, PA — B
Kansas State U, KS — B
Kansas Wesleyan U, KS — B
Kean U, NJ — B
Kennesaw State U, GA — B
Kent State U, OH — B
Kentucky Wesleyan Coll, KY — B
Kenyon Coll, OH — B
Kettering U, MI — B
Kilgore Coll, TX — A
Kingwood Coll, TX — A
Kirkwood Comm Coll, IA — A
Knox Coll, IL — B
Lafayette Coll, PA — B
Lakeland Coll, WI — B
Lander U, SC — B
Laney Coll, CA — A
Langston U, OK — B
Lansing Comm Coll, MI — A
Laramie County Comm Coll, WY — A
Lawrence U, WI — B
Lees-McRae Coll, NC — B
LeMoyne-Owen Coll, TN — B
Lewis & Clark Coll, OR — B
Lewis-Clark State Coll, ID — B
Liberty U, VA — B

College	Degree
Limestone Coll, SC	B
Linfield Coll, OR	B
Lipscomb U, TN	B
Long Beach City Coll, CA	A
Long Island U, C.W. Post Campus, NY	B
Longwood U, VA	B
Los Angeles Mission Coll, CA	A
Louisiana State U at Alexandria, LA	A,B
Loyola U Chicago, IL	B
Luther Coll, IA	B
Lycoming Coll, PA	B
Lynchburg Coll, VA	B
Lyndon State Coll, VT	B
Manatee Comm Coll, FL	A
Manchester Coll, IN	B
Manhattan Coll, NY	B
Manhattanville Coll, NY	B
Marian Coll of Fond du Lac, WI	B
Marlboro Coll, VT	B
Marquette U, WI	B
Marshall U, WV	B
Mary Baldwin Coll, VA	B
Maryville Coll, TN	B
Maryville U of Saint Louis, MO	B
Marywood U, PA	B
Massachusetts Inst of Technology, MA	B
McDaniel Coll, MD	B
McMurry U, TX	B
McNeese State U, LA	B
Mercy Coll, NY	B
Merritt Coll, CA	A
Mesa Comm Coll, AZ	A
Mesa State Coll, CO	A,B
Miami Dade Coll, FL	A
Miami U, OH	B
Michigan Technological U, MI	B
MidAmerica Nazarene U, KS	B
Middlebury Coll, VT	B
Middle Tennessee State U, TN	B
Midland Coll, TX	A
Midwestern State U, TX	B
Millersville U of Pennsylvania, PA	B
Milligan Coll, TN	B
Millsaps Coll, MS	B
Mills Coll, CA	B
Minnesota State U Mankato, MN	B
Minnesota State U Moorhead, MN	B
Minot State U, ND	B
MiraCosta Coll, CA	A
Mississippi U for Women, MS	B
Missouri Baptist U, MO	B
Modesto Jr Coll, CA	A
Molloy Coll, NY	B
Monmouth U, NJ	B
Montana Tech of The U of Montana, MT	B
Montclair State U, NJ	B
Monterey Peninsula Coll, CA	A
Moravian Coll, PA	B
Morehead State U, KY	B
Morningside Coll, IA	B
Mount Holyoke Coll, MA	B
Mount Mercy Coll, IA	B
Muskingum Coll, OH	B
Nassau Comm Coll, NY	A
Nebraska Wesleyan U, NE	B
New Coll of Florida, FL	B
New Mexico Highlands U, NM	B
New Mexico Inst of Mining and Technology, NM	B
New Mexico Military Inst, NM	A
New Mexico State U, NM	B
New York U, NY	B
Niagara U, NY	B
Nichols Coll, MA	B
Northampton County Area Comm Coll, PA	A
North Carolina State U, NC	B
North Central Coll, IL	B
North Dakota State U, ND	B
Northeast Comm Coll, NE	A
Northeastern U, MA	B
Northern Arizona U, AZ	B
Northern Kentucky U, KY	B
Northern Michigan U, MI	B
Northern State U, SD	B
Northland Coll, WI	B
Northwest Coll, WY	A
Northwestern State U of Louisiana, LA	B
Northwestern U, IL	B
Northwest Missouri State U, MO	B
Notre Dame Coll, OH	B
Oakland U, MI	B
Ohio Wesleyan U, OH	B
Oklahoma Panhandle State U, OK	B
Oklahoma State U, OK	B
Oklahoma Wesleyan U, OK	B
Old Dominion U, VA	B
Orange Coast Coll, CA	A
Oregon State U, OR	B
Ottawa U, KS	B
Otterbein Coll, OH	B
Pace U, NY	B
Palomar Coll, CA	A
Park U, MO	B
Peru State Coll, NE	B
Pittsburg State U, KS	B
Pitzer Coll, CA	B
Plymouth State U, NH	B
Portland State U, OR	B
Principia Coll, IL	B
Purdue U, IN	B
Quinnipiac U, CT	B
Radford U, VA	B
Ramapo Coll of New Jersey, NJ	B
Randolph Coll, VA	B
Randolph-Macon Coll, VA	B
Raritan Valley Comm Coll, NJ	A
Redlands Comm Coll, OK	A
Reed Coll, OR	B
Rensselaer Polytechnic Inst, NY	B
Rhodes Coll, TN	B
Rider U, NJ	B
Ridgewater Coll, MN	A
Rochester Inst of Technology, NY	A,B
Rocky Mountain Coll, MT	B
Roger Williams U, RI	B
Roosevelt U, IL	B
Rose State Coll, OK	A
Sacramento City Coll, CA	A
Sacred Heart U, CT	A,B
St. Ambrose U, IA	B
Saint Anselm Coll, NH	B
Saint Francis U, PA	B
St. Gregory's U, OK	B
St. John's Coll, NM	B
Saint John's U, MN	B
Saint Joseph's Coll, IN	B
Saint Leo U, FL	B
St. Louis Comm Coll at Florissant Valley, MO	A
Saint Louis U, MO	B
Saint Mary-of-the-Woods Coll, IN	B
Saint Mary's Coll, IN	B
Saint Mary's Coll of California, CA	B
St. Mary's Coll of Maryland, MD	B
Saint Mary's U of Minnesota, MN	B
St. Mary's U of San Antonio, TX	B
Saint Michael's Coll, VT	B
St. Olaf Coll, MN	B
Saint Vincent Coll, PA	B
Sam Houston State U, TX	B
San Bernardino Valley Coll, CA	A
San Diego City Coll, CA	A
San Diego State U, CA	B
San Francisco State U, CA	B
San Jacinto Coll Central Campus, TX	A
San Jacinto Coll North Campus, TX	A
San Jacinto Coll South Campus, TX	A
Santa Barbara City Coll, CA	A
Santa Monica Coll, CA	A
Santa Rosa Jr Coll, CA	A
Sarah Lawrence Coll, NY	B
Sauk Valley Comm Coll, IL	A
Savannah State U, GA	B
Schreiner U, TX	B
Scripps Coll, CA	B
Seattle U, WA	B
Seton Hall U, NJ	B
Shenandoah U, VA	B
Shepherd U, WV	B
Sheridan Coll–Sheridan and Gillette, WY	A
Shorter Coll, GA	B
Siena Coll, NY	B
Simmons Coll, MA	B
Simpson Coll, IA	B
Skagit Valley Coll, WA	A
Skidmore Coll, NY	B
Slippery Rock U of Pennsylvania, PA	B
South Dakota State U, SD	B
Southeast Missouri State U, MO	B
Southern Arkansas U–Magnolia, AR	B
Southern Illinois U Carbondale, IL	B
Southern Illinois U Edwardsville, IL	B
Southern Oregon U, OR	B
Southern Utah U, UT	B
South Georgia Coll, GA	A
Southwestern Coll, KS	B
Southwest Minnesota State U, MN	B
Spring Arbor U, MI	B
Stanford U, CA	B
State U of New York at Oswego, NY	B
State U of New York at Plattsburgh, NY	B
State U of New York Coll at Geneseo, NY	B
State U of New York Coll at Oneonta, NY	B
Stony Brook U, State U of New York, NY	B
Suffolk County Comm Coll, NY	A
Suffolk U, MA	B
Susquehanna U, PA	B
Swarthmore Coll, PA	B
Syracuse U, NY	B
Tabor Coll, KS	B
Taylor U, IN	B
Tennessee Technological U, TN	B
Texas A&M U–Corpus Christi, TX	B
Texas A&M U–Kingsville, TX	B
Texas A&M U–Texarkana, TX	B
Texas Christian U, TX	B
Texas State U-San Marcos, TX	B
Texas Wesleyan U, TX	B
Thomas More Coll, KY	A,B
Trevecca Nazarene U, TN	B
Trinity Coll, CT	B
Trinity U, TX	B
Trinity (Washington) U, DC	B
Troy U, AL	B
Truman State U, MO	B
Tusculum Coll, TN	B
Union Coll, NY	B
U at Buffalo, the State U of New York, NY	B
The U of Alabama, AL	B
The U of Alabama in Huntsville, AL	B
U of Arkansas, AR	B
U of Arkansas at Fort Smith, AR	B
U of Arkansas at Pine Bluff, AR	B
U of California, Santa Cruz, CA	B
U of Central Florida, FL	B
U of Central Missouri, MO	B
U of Cincinnati, OH	B
U of Colorado at Boulder, CO	B
U of Colorado at Colorado Springs, CO	B
U of Dayton, OH	B
U of Denver, CO	B
U of Detroit Mercy, MI	B
The U of Findlay, OH	B
U of Guam, GU	B
U of Hartford, CT	B
U of Hawaii at Manoa, HI	B
U of Illinois at Springfield, IL	B
U of Indianapolis, IN	B
The U of Iowa, IA	B
U of Kansas, KS	B
U of La Verne, CA	B
U of Maine at Farmington, ME	B
U of Mary Hardin-Baylor, TX	B
U of Maryland, Baltimore County, MD	B
U of Maryland, Coll Park, MD	B
U of Mary Washington, VA	B
U of Miami, FL	B
U of Michigan–Flint, MI	B
U of Minnesota, Morris, MN	B
U of Missouri–Columbia, MO	B
U of Missouri–St. Louis, MO	B
U of Nebraska–Lincoln, NE	B
U of Nevada, Reno, NV	B
U of New Mexico, NM	B
U of New Orleans, LA	B
U of North Alabama, AL	B
The U of North Carolina at Asheville, NC	B
The U of North Carolina at Pembroke, NC	B
U of Northern Iowa, IA	B
U of North Texas, TX	B
U of Oregon, OR	B
U of Pittsburgh, PA	B
U of Pittsburgh at Bradford, PA	B
U of Puget Sound, WA	B
U of Rhode Island, RI	B
U of Rochester, NY	B
U of Saint Francis, IN	B
U of San Diego, CA	B
U of San Francisco, CA	B
U of Sioux Falls, SD	B
U of South Carolina, SC	B
U of South Carolina Upstate, SC	B
U of Southern Indiana, IN	B
U of Southern Maine, ME	B
U of South Florida, FL	B
The U of Tampa, FL	A,B
The U of Tennessee at Martin, TN	B
The U of Texas at San Antonio, TX	B
U of the Incarnate Word, TX	B
U of Tulsa, OK	B
U of Utah, UT	B
U of Virginia, VA	B
U of Washington, WA	B
U of West Florida, FL	B
U of Wisconsin–Eau Claire, WI	B
U of Wisconsin–La Crosse, WI	B
U of Wisconsin–Oshkosh, WI	B
U of Wisconsin–Stevens Point, WI	B
U of Wisconsin–Stout, WI	B
U of Wisconsin–Superior, WI	B
U of Wisconsin–Whitewater, WI	B
U of Wyoming, WY	B
Upper Iowa U, IA	B
Utah State U, UT	B
Utah Valley State Coll, UT	A,B
Utica Coll, NY	B
Valparaiso U, IN	B
Vanderbilt U, TN	B
Vanguard U of Southern California, CA	B
Villanova U, PA	B
Virginia Commonwealth U, VA	B
Virginia Polytechnic Inst and State U, VA	B
Viterbo U, WI	B
Wabash Coll, IN	B
Wake Forest U, NC	B
Warren Wilson Coll, NC	B
Wartburg Coll, IA	B
Washington & Jefferson Coll, PA	B
Washington Coll, MD	B
Washington State U, WA	B
Washington U in St. Louis, MO	B
Waynesburg Coll, PA	B
Wayne State Coll, NE	B
Wells Coll, NY	B
Wesleyan U, CT	B
Western Illinois U, IL	B
Western Kentucky U, KY	B
Western New England Coll, MA	B
Western New Mexico U, NM	B

A=Associate; B=Bachelor's Degree

Institution	Degree
Western Washington U, WA	B
Western Wyoming Comm Coll, WY	A
Westmont Coll, CA	B
West Texas A&M U, TX	B
West Valley Coll, CA	A
Wichita State U, KS	B
Widener U, PA	B
Wilkes U, PA	B
Williams Coll, MA	B
Wilmington Coll, OH	B
Wilson Coll, PA	B
Winona State U, MN	B
Worcester Polytechnic Inst, MA	B
Worcester State Coll, MA	B
York Coll of Pennsylvania, PA	A,B
York Coll of the City U of New York, NY	B
Young Harris Coll, GA	A

Music

Institution	Degree
Adelphi U, NY	B
Adrian Coll, MI	B
Agnes Scott Coll, GA	B
Albion Coll, MI	B
Alderson-Broaddus Coll, WV	B
Allegheny Coll, PA	B
Alverno Coll, WI	A,B
Alvin Comm Coll, TX	A
American U, DC	B
Ancilla Coll, IN	A
Anna Maria Coll, MA	B
Antioch Coll, OH	B
Aquinas Coll, MI	A,B
Arizona State U, AZ	B
Ashford U, IA	B
Ashland U, OH	B
Austin Peay State U, TN	B
Averett U, VA	B
Baker U, KS	B
Baldwin-Wallace Coll, OH	B
Ball State U, IN	B
Bard Coll, NY	B
Barnard Coll, NY	B
Barry U, FL	B
Bates Coll, ME	B
Belmont U, TN	B
Beloit Coll, WI	B
Bemidji State U, MN	B
Benedict Coll, SC	B
Bennington Coll, VT	B
Berea Coll, KY	B
Berkshire Comm Coll, MA	B
Bethany Coll, KS	B
Bethel U, MN	B
Black Hills State U, SD	B
Blue Mountain Coll, MS	B
Boise State U, ID	B
Boston U, MA	B
Bowdoin Coll, ME	B
Bronx Comm Coll of the City U of New York, NY	A
Bryn Mawr Coll, PA	B
Bucknell U, PA	B
Butler U, IN	B
Caldwell Coll, NJ	B
Calhoun Comm Coll, AL	A
California Inst of the Arts, CA	B
California Lutheran U, CA	B
California Polytechnic State U, San Luis Obispo, CA	B
California State Polytechnic U, Pomona, CA	B
California State U, Long Beach, CA	B
California State U, Sacramento, CA	B
California State U, Stanislaus, CA	B
Calvin Coll, MI	B
Cameron U, OK	B
Cañada Coll, CA	A
Capital U, OH	B
Cardinal Stritch U, WI	B
Carleton Coll, MN	B
Carroll Coll, WI	B
Carson-Newman Coll, TN	B
Carthage Coll, WI	B
The Catholic U of America, DC	B
Central Christian Coll of Kansas, KS	A
Centralia Coll, WA	A
Central Michigan U, MI	B
Central Piedmont Comm Coll, NC	A
Central Wyoming Coll, WY	A
Centre Coll, KY	B
Century Coll, MN	A
Chabot Coll, CA	A
Chaffey Coll, CA	A
Chapman U, CA	B
Chatham U, PA	B
City Coll of San Francisco, CA	A
City Coll of the City U of New York, NY	B
City Colls of Chicago, Harold Washington Coll, IL	A
Claflin U, SC	B
Clarendon Coll, TX	A
Clarion U of Pennsylvania, PA	B
Clarke Coll, IA	B
Clark U, MA	B
Clearwater Christian Coll, FL	B
Cleveland Inst of Music, OH	B
Cleveland State U, OH	B
Coastal Carolina U, SC	B
Coe Coll, IA	B
Coffeyville Comm Coll, KS	A
Colby Coll, ME	B
Colby Comm Coll, KS	A
Coll of Lake County, IA	A
Coll of Saint Benedict, MN	B
Coll of St. Catherine, MN	B
Coll of Southern Maryland, MD	A
Coll of the Atlantic, ME	B
Coll of the Desert, CA	A
Coll of the Holy Cross, MA	B
Coll of the Ozarks, MO	B
The Colorado Coll, CO	B
Colorado State U, CO	B
Columbia Coll Chicago, IL	B
Columbia Union Coll, MD	B
Columbia U, School of General Studies, NY	B
Concordia Coll, MN	B
Concordia Coll, NY	B
Concordia U, IL	B
Connecticut Coll, CT	B
Cornell Coll, IA	B
Cosumnes River Coll, Sacramento, CA	A
Culver-Stockton Coll, MO	B
Cumberland U, TN	B
Dakota Wesleyan U, SD	B
Dana Coll, NE	B
Davidson Coll, NC	B
De Anza Coll, CA	A
Del Mar Coll, TX	A
Denison U, OH	B
DePaul U, IL	B
DePauw U, IN	B
Dominican U of California, CA	B
Dordt Coll, IA	B
Drake U, IA	B
Drew U, NJ	B
Drury U, MO	B
Duquesne U, PA	B
East Carolina U, NC	B
Eastern Mennonite U, VA	B
Eastern U, PA	B
Eastern Wyoming Coll, WY	A
East Los Angeles Coll, CA	A
East Tennessee State U, TN	B
East Texas Baptist U, TX	B
Eckerd Coll, FL	B
Edgewood Coll, WI	B
Edinboro U of Pennsylvania, PA	B
Edison Coll, FL	A
El Camino Coll, CA	A
Elizabethtown Coll, PA	B
Elmira Coll, NY	B
Elon U, NC	B
Emory U, GA	B
Emporia State U, KS	B
Eugene Bible Coll, OR	B
Fairfield U, CT	B
Ferris State U, MI	B
Five Towns Coll, NY	A,B
Florida Atlantic U, FL	B
Florida International U, FL	B
Florida State U, FL	B
Foothill Coll, CA	A
Fordham U, NY	B
Fort Lewis Coll, CO	B
Fresno City Coll, CA	A
Fresno Pacific U, CA	A,B
Frostburg State U, MD	B
Fullerton Coll, CA	A
Furman U, SC	B
Garden City Comm Coll, KS	A
Gardner-Webb U, NC	B
George Fox U, OR	B
Georgetown Coll, KY	B
Georgia Coll & State U, GA	B
Georgia Southern U, GA	B
Georgia State U, GA	B
Gettysburg Coll, PA	B
Glendale Comm Coll, CA	A
Golden West Coll, CA	A
Gonzaga U, WA	B
Goshen Coll, IN	B
Grambling State U, LA	B
Grand Valley State U, MI	B
Grand View Coll, IA	B
Great Lakes Christian Coll, MI	B
Greenville Coll, IL	B
Grinnell Coll, IA	B
Gulf Coast Comm Coll, FL	A
Gustavus Adolphus Coll, MN	B
Hamilton Coll, NY	B
Hampshire Coll, MA	B
Harding U, AR	B
Hardin-Simmons U, TX	B
Harper Coll, IL	A
Harrisburg Area Comm Coll, PA	A
Hartwick Coll, NY	B
Harvard U, MA	B
Haverford Coll, PA	B
Hill Coll of the Hill Jr Coll District, TX	A
Hillsdale Coll, MI	B
Hillsdale Free Will Baptist Coll, OK	A,B
Hiram Coll, OH	B
Hofstra U, NY	B
Hope Coll, MI	B
Hope International U, CA	B
Houston Comm Coll System, TX	A
Howard Payne U, TX	B
Huntingdon Coll, AL	B
Huntington U, IN	B
Idaho State U, ID	B
Illinois Coll, IL	B
Illinois Wesleyan U, IL	B
Indiana U Bloomington, IN	B
Indiana U of Pennsylvania, PA	B
Indiana U South Bend, IN	B
Indiana U Southeast, IN	B
Indiana Wesleyan U, IN	A,B
Iowa State U of Science and Technology, IA	B
Isothermal Comm Coll, NC	A
Jacksonville State U, AL	B
Jacksonville U, FL	B
James Madison U, VA	B
The Johns Hopkins U, MD	B
Johnson State Coll, VT	B
Judson Coll, IL	B
The Juilliard School, NY	B
Kansas State U, KS	B
Kean U, NJ	B
Kennesaw State U, GA	B
Kent State U, OH	B
Kenyon Coll, OH	B
Kilgore Coll, TX	A
Kirkwood Comm Coll, IA	A
Knox Coll, IL	B
Lafayette Coll, PA	B
Lakeland Coll, WI	B
Lancaster Bible Coll, PA	B
Lander U, SC	B
Laney Coll, CA	A
Langston U, OK	B
Lansing Comm Coll, MI	A
Laramie County Comm Coll, WY	A
Lawrence U, WI	B
Lewis & Clark Coll, OR	B
Liberty U, VA	B
Limestone Coll, SC	B
Lincoln Land Comm Coll, IL	A
Linfield Coll, OR	B
Lipscomb U, TN	B
Long Beach City Coll, CA	A
Long Island U, C.W. Post Campus, NY	B
Longwood U, VA	B
Los Angeles Mission Coll, CA	A
Los Angeles Pierce Coll, CA	A
Los Angeles Southwest Coll, CA	A
Loyola U Chicago, IL	B
Luther Coll, IA	B
Lycoming Coll, PA	B
Lynchburg Coll, VA	B
Lynn U, FL	B
Manatee Comm Coll, FL	A
Manchester Coll, IN	B
Manhattan School of Music, NY	B
Manhattanville Coll, NY	B
Marian Coll of Fond du Lac, WI	B
Marlboro Coll, VT	B
Mary Baldwin Coll, VA	B
Marylhurst U, OR	B
Maryville Coll, TN	B
Marywood U, PA	B
Massachusetts Inst of Technology, MA	B
McDaniel Coll, MD	B
McMurry U, TX	B
McNally Smith Coll of Music, MN	A,B
McNeese State U, LA	B
Mercy Coll, NY	B
Mesa Comm Coll, AZ	A
Mesa State Coll, CO	A,B
Miami Dade Coll, FL	A
Miami U, OH	B
MidAmerica Nazarene U, KS	A,B
Middlebury Coll, VT	B
Middle Tennessee State U, TN	B
Midland Coll, TX	A
Midwestern State U, TX	B
Millersville U of Pennsylvania, PA	B
Milligan Coll, TN	B
Millsaps Coll, MS	B
Mills Coll, CA	B
Minnesota State U Mankato, MN	B
Minnesota State U Moorhead, MN	B
Minot State U, ND	B
MiraCosta Coll, CA	A
Mississippi U for Women, MS	B
Missouri Baptist U, MO	B
Modesto Jr Coll, CA	A
Molloy Coll, NY	B
Monmouth U, NJ	B
Montclair State U, NJ	B
Monterey Peninsula Coll, CA	A
Moravian Coll, PA	B
Morehead State U, KY	B
Morningside Coll, IA	B
Mount Holyoke Coll, MA	B
Mount Mercy Coll, IA	B
Muskingum Coll, OH	B
Nassau Comm Coll, NY	A
Nebraska Wesleyan U, NE	B
New Coll of Florida, FL	B
New Mexico Highlands U, NM	B
New Mexico State U, NM	B
New York U, NY	B
North Central Coll, IL	B
North Central U, MN	A,B
North Dakota State U, ND	B
Northeast Comm Coll, NE	A
Northeastern U, MA	B
Northern Arizona U, AZ	B
Northern Kentucky U, KY	B
Northern Michigan U, MI	B
Northern State U, SD	B
Northland Coll, WI	B
Northwest Coll, WY	A
Northwestern State U of Louisiana, LA	B
Northwestern U, IL	B
Northwest Missouri State U, MO	B
Northwest U, WA	B
Notre Dame de Namur U, CA	B
Oakland U, MI	B
Ohio Wesleyan U, OH	B
Oklahoma State U, OK	B
Oklahoma Wesleyan U, OK	B
Old Dominion U, VA	B
Orange Coast Coll, CA	A
Oregon State U, OR	B
Ottawa U, KS	B
Otterbein Coll, OH	B
Palomar Coll, CA	A
Park U, MO	B
Peace Coll, NC	A

College	Degree
Peru State Coll, NE	B
Philadelphia Biblical U, PA	B
Pittsburg State U, KS	B
Pitzer Coll, CA	B
Plymouth State U, NH	B
Portland State U, OR	B
Principia Coll, IL	B
Quincy U, IL	B
Radford U, VA	B
Ramapo Coll of New Jersey, NJ	B
Randolph Coll, VA	B
Randolph-Macon Coll, VA	B
Raritan Valley Comm Coll, NJ	A
Reed Coll, OR	B
Rhodes Coll, TN	B
Rider U, NJ	B
Ridgewater Coll, MN	A
Rocky Mountain Coll, MT	B
Roosevelt U, IL	B
Rose State Coll, OK	A
Sacramento City Coll, CA	A
Sacred Heart U, CT	B
St. Ambrose U, IA	B
Saint John's U, MN	B
Saint Joseph's Coll, IN	B
St. Louis Comm Coll at Florissant Valley, MO	A
Saint Louis U, MO	B
Saint Mary-of-the-Woods Coll, IN	B
Saint Mary's Coll, IN	B
Saint Mary's Coll of California, CA	B
St. Mary's Coll of Maryland, MD	B
Saint Mary's U of Minnesota, MN	B
St. Mary's U of San Antonio, TX	B
Saint Michael's Coll, VT	B
St. Olaf Coll, MN	B
Saint Vincent Coll, PA	B
Sam Houston State U, TX	B
San Bernardino Valley Coll, CA	A
San Diego City Coll, CA	A
San Francisco State U, CA	B
San Jacinto Coll Central Campus, TX	B
San Jacinto Coll North Campus, TX	A
San Jacinto Coll South Campus, TX	A
Santa Barbara City Coll, CA	A
Santa Monica Coll, CA	A
Santa Rosa Jr Coll, CA	A
Sarah Lawrence Coll, NY	B
Sauk Valley Comm Coll, IL	A
Savannah State U, GA	B
Schreiner U, TX	B
Scripps Coll, CA	B
Seton Hall U, NJ	B
Shenandoah U, VA	B
Shepherd U, WV	B
Sheridan Coll–Sheridan and Gillette, WY	A
Shorter Coll, GA	B
Simmons Coll, MA	B
Simpson Coll, IA	B
Skagit Valley Coll, WA	A
Skidmore Coll, NY	B
Slippery Rock U of Pennsylvania, PA	B
South Dakota State U, SD	B
Southeast Missouri State U, MO	B
Southern Illinois U Carbondale, IL	B
Southern Illinois U Edwardsville, IL	B
Southern Oregon U, OR	B
Southern Utah U, UT	B
Southwestern Coll, KS	B
Southwestern Comm Coll, IA	A
Southwest Minnesota State U, MN	B
Spokane Falls Comm Coll, WA	A
Spring Arbor U, MI	B
Stanford U, CA	B
State U of New York at Oswego, NY	B
State U of New York at Plattsburgh, NY	B
State U of New York Coll at Geneseo, NY	B
State U of New York Coll at Oneonta, NY	B
Stony Brook U, State U of New York, NY	B
Suffolk County Comm Coll, NY	A
Susquehanna U, PA	B
Swarthmore Coll, PA	B
Syracuse U, NY	B
Tabor Coll, KS	B
Taylor U, IN	B
Tennessee Technological U, TN	B
Texas A&M U–Corpus Christi, TX	B
Texas A&M U–Kingsville, TX	B
Texas Christian U, TX	B
Texas State U-San Marcos, TX	B
Texas Wesleyan U, TX	B
Thomas More Coll, KY	A
Trevecca Nazarene U, TN	B
Trinity Coll, CT	B
Trinity U, TX	B
Truman State U, MO	B
U at Buffalo, the State U of New York, NY	B
The U of Alabama, AL	B
The U of Alabama in Huntsville, AL	B
U of Arkansas, AR	B
U of Arkansas at Fort Smith, AR	
U of Arkansas at Pine Bluff, AR	B
U of California, Santa Cruz, CA	B
U of Central Florida, FL	B
U of Central Missouri, MO	B
U of Cincinnati, OH	B
U of Colorado at Boulder, CO	B
U of Dayton, OH	B
U of Denver, CO	B
U of Hartford, CT	B
U of Hawaii at Manoa, HI	B
U of Indianapolis, IN	B
The U of Iowa, IA	B
U of Kansas, KS	B
U of La Verne, CA	B
U of Maine at Farmington, ME	B
U of Mary Hardin-Baylor, TX	B
U of Maryland, Baltimore County, MD	B
U of Maryland, Coll Park, MD	B
U of Mary Washington, VA	B
U of Miami, FL	B
U of Michigan–Flint, MI	B
U of Minnesota, Morris, MN	B
U of Missouri–Columbia, MO	B
U of Missouri–St. Louis, MO	B
U of Nebraska–Lincoln, NE	B
U of Nevada, Reno, NV	B
U of New Mexico, NM	B
U of New Orleans, LA	B
U of North Alabama, AL	B
The U of North Carolina at Asheville, NC	B
The U of North Carolina at Pembroke, NC	B
U of Northern Iowa, IA	B
U of North Texas, TX	B
U of Oregon, OR	B
U of Pittsburgh, PA	B
U of Puget Sound, WA	B
U of Rhode Island, RI	B
U of Rochester, NY	B
U of San Diego, CA	B
U of Sioux Falls, SD	B
U of South Carolina, SC	B
U of Southern Maine, ME	B
U of South Florida, FL	B
The U of Tampa, FL	A,B
The U of Tennessee at Martin, TN	B
The U of Texas at San Antonio, TX	B
The U of the Arts, PA	B
U of the Incarnate Word, TX	B
U of Tulsa, OK	B
U of Utah, UT	B
U of Virginia, VA	B
U of Washington, WA	B
U of West Florida, FL	B
U of Wisconsin–Eau Claire, WI	B
U of Wisconsin–La Crosse, WI	B
U of Wisconsin–Oshkosh, WI	B
U of Wisconsin–Stevens Point, WI	B
U of Wisconsin–Superior, WI	B
U of Wisconsin–Whitewater, WI	B
U of Wyoming, WY	B
Utah State U, UT	B
Utah Valley State Coll, UT	A
Valparaiso U, IN	B
Vanderbilt U, TN	B
Vanguard U of Southern California, CA	B
Virginia Commonwealth U, VA	B
Virginia Polytechnic Inst and State U, VA	B
Viterbo U, WI	B
Wabash Coll, IN	B
Wake Forest U, NC	B
Waldorf Coll, IA	B
Wartburg Coll, IA	B
Washington & Jefferson Coll, PA	B
Washington Bible Coll, MD	B
Washington Coll, MD	B
Washington State U, WA	B
Washington U in St. Louis, MO	B
Wayne State Coll, NE	B
Wells Coll, NY	B
Wesleyan U, CT	B
Western Illinois U, IL	B
Western Kentucky U, KY	B
Western New Mexico U, NM	B
Western Washington U, WA	B
Western Wyoming Comm Coll, WY	A
Westminster Choir Coll of Rider U, NJ	B
Westmont Coll, CA	B
West Texas A&M U, TX	B
West Valley Coll, CA	A
Wichita State U, KS	B
Wilkes U, PA	B
Williams Coll, MA	B
Winona State U, MN	B
Worcester Polytechnic Inst, MA	B
York Coll, NE	B
York Coll of Pennsylvania, PA	A,B
York Coll of the City U of New York, NY	B
Young Harris Coll, GA	A

Physical Sciences

College	Degree
Adelphi U, NY	B
Adrian Coll, MI	A,B
Agnes Scott Coll, GA	B
Albertus Magnus Coll, CT	B
Albion Coll, MI	B
Allegheny Coll, PA	B
Alvernia Coll, PA	B
Alverno Coll, WI	B
Alvin Comm Coll, TX	A
American U, DC	B
Ancilla Coll, IN	A
Antioch Coll, OH	B
Aquinas Coll, MI	B
Arcadia U, PA	B
Arizona State U, AZ	B
Ashland U, OH	B
Assumption Coll, MA	B
Austin Peay State U, TN	B
Averett U, VA	B
Baker U, KS	B
Baldwin-Wallace Coll, OH	B
Ball State U, IN	B
Bard Coll, NY	B
Barnard Coll, NY	B
Barry U, FL	B
Bates Coll, ME	B
Belmont U, TN	B
Beloit Coll, WI	B
Bemidji State U, MN	B
Benedict Coll, SC	B
Bennington Coll, VT	B
Berea Coll, KY	B
Bethany Coll, KS	B
Bethel Coll, KS	B
Bethel U, MN	B
Black Hills State U, SD	B
Blue Mountain Coll, MS	B
Boise State U, ID	B
Boston U, MA	B
Bowdoin Coll, ME	B
Brescia U, KY	B
Bronx Comm Coll of the City U of New York, NY	A
Bryn Mawr Coll, PA	B
Bucknell U, PA	B
Bunker Hill Comm Coll, MA	A
Butler U, IN	B
Caldwell Coll, NJ	B
California Lutheran U, CA	B
California Polytechnic State U, San Luis Obispo, CA	
California State Polytechnic U, Pomona, CA	B
California State U, Long Beach, CA	B
California State U, Sacramento, CA	B
California State U, Stanislaus, CA	B
Calvin Coll, MI	B
Cameron U, OK	B
Cañada Coll, CA	A
Capital U, OH	B
Cardinal Stritch U, WI	B
Carleton Coll, MN	B
Carlow U, PA	B
Carroll Coll, MT	B
Carroll Coll, WI	B
Carson-Newman Coll, TN	B
Carthage Coll, WI	B
The Catholic U of America, DC	B
Centralia Coll, WA	A
Central Michigan U, MI	B
Central Wyoming Coll, WY	A
Centre Coll, KY	B
Cerro Coso Comm Coll, CA	A
Chabot Coll, CA	A
Chaffey Coll, CA	A
Chapman U, CA	B
Chatham U, PA	B
Chattanooga State Tech Comm Coll, TN	A
City Coll of San Francisco, CA	A
City Coll of the City U of New York, NY	B
City Colls of Chicago, Harold Washington Coll, IL	A
City Colls of Chicago, Kennedy-King Coll, IL	A
Claflin U, SC	B
Clarendon Coll, TX	A
Clarion U of Pennsylvania, PA	B
Clarke Coll, IA	B
Clarkson U, NY	B
Clark U, MA	B
Cleveland State U, OH	B
Coastal Carolina U, SC	B
Coastal Georgia Comm Coll, GA	A
Cochise Coll, Sierra Vista, AZ	A
Coe Coll, IA	B
Coffeyville Comm Coll, KS	A
Colby Coll, ME	B
Colby Comm Coll, KS	A
Coll Misericordia, PA	B
Coll of Saint Benedict, MN	B
Coll of St. Catherine, MN	B
Coll of the Atlantic, ME	B
Coll of the Canyons, CA	A
Coll of the Desert, CA	A
Coll of the Holy Cross, MA	B
Coll of the Ozarks, MO	B
The Colorado Coll, CO	B
Colorado State U, CO	B
Columbia Coll, MO	B
Columbia Union Coll, MD	B
Columbia U, School of General Studies, NY	B
Concordia Coll, MN	B
Concordia U, IL	B
Connecticut Coll, CT	B
Connors State Coll, OK	A
Cornell Coll, IA	B
Cosumnes River Coll, Sacramento, CA	A
Dana Coll, NE	B
Davidson Coll, NC	B
De Anza Coll, CA	A
Defiance Coll, OH	B
Del Mar Coll, TX	A
Denison U, OH	B

A=Associate; B=Bachelor's Degree

DePaul U, IL — B
DePauw U, IN — B
DeSales U, PA — B
Dordt Coll, IA — B
Drake U, IA — B
Drew U, NJ — B
Drury U, MO — B
Duquesne U, PA — B
East Carolina U, NC — B
East Central Coll, MO — A
Eastern Mennonite U, VA — B
Eastern U, PA — B
East Los Angeles Coll, CA — A
East Tennessee State U, TN — B
East Texas Baptist U, TX — B
Eckerd Coll, FL — B
Edgewood Coll, WI — B
Edinboro U of Pennsylvania, PA — B
El Camino Coll, CA — A
Elizabethtown Coll, PA — B
Elmira Coll, NY — B
Elms Coll, MA — B
Elon U, NC — B
Embry-Riddle Aeronautical U, FL — B
Emmanuel Coll, MA — B
Emory U, GA — B
Emporia State U, KS — B
The Evergreen State Coll, WA — B
Fairfield U, CT — B
Fairleigh Dickinson U, Coll at Florham, NJ — B
Fairleigh Dickinson U, Metropolitan Campus, NJ — B
Ferris State U, MI — B
Florida Atlantic U, FL — B
Florida Inst of Technology, FL — B
Florida International U, FL — B
Florida State U, FL — B
Foothill Coll, CA — A
Fordham U, NY — B
Fort Lewis Coll, CO — B
Fresno City Coll, CA — A
Fresno Pacific U, CA — B
Frostburg State U, MD — B
Fullerton Coll, CA — A
Fulton-Montgomery Comm Coll, NY — A
Furman U, SC — B
Gannon U, PA — B
Gardner-Webb U, NC — B
George Fox U, OR — B
Georgetown Coll, KY — B
Georgia Coll & State U, GA — B
Georgia Highlands Coll, GA — A
Georgia Southern U, GA — B
Georgia State U, GA — B
Gettysburg Coll, PA — B
Golden West Coll, CA — A
Gonzaga U, WA — B
Goshen Coll, IN — B
Grambling State U, LA — B
Grand Valley State U, MI — B
Grand View Coll, IA — B
Greenville Coll, IL — B
Grinnell Coll, IA — B
Gustavus Adolphus Coll, MN — B
Hamilton Coll, NY — B
Hampden-Sydney Coll, VA — B
Hampshire Coll, MA — B
Harding U, AR — B
Hardin-Simmons U, TX — B
Harper Coll, IL — A
Harrisburg Area Comm Coll, PA — A
Hartwick Coll, NY — B
Harvard U, MA — B
Harvey Mudd Coll, CA — B
Haverford Coll, PA — B
Hill Coll of the Hill Jr Coll District, TX — A
Hillsdale Coll, MI — B
Hiram Coll, OH — B
Hofstra U, NY — B
Holy Family U, PA — B
Hope Coll, MI — B
Howard Coll, TX — A
Howard Payne U, TX — B
Huntingdon Coll, AL — B
Huntington U, IN — B
Idaho State U, ID — A,B
Illinois Coll, IL — B
Illinois Inst of Technology, IL — B

Illinois Wesleyan U, IL — B
Indiana U Bloomington, IN — B
Indiana U of Pennsylvania, PA — B
Indiana U South Bend, IN — A,B
Indiana U Southeast, IN — B
Indiana Wesleyan U, IN — A,B
Iowa State U of Science and Technology, IA — B
Jacksonville State U, AL — B
Jacksonville U, FL — B
James Madison U, VA — B
John Carroll U, OH — B
The Johns Hopkins U, MD — B
Joliet Jr Coll, IL — A
Judson Coll, IL — B
Juniata Coll, PA — B
Kansas State U, KS — B
Kansas Wesleyan U, KS — B
Kean U, NJ — B
Kennesaw State U, GA — B
Kent State U, OH — B
Kentucky Wesleyan Coll, KY — B
Kenyon Coll, OH — B
Kettering U, MI — B
Kilgore Coll, TX — A
Knox Coll, IL — B
Lafayette Coll, PA — B
Lakeland Coll, WI — B
Lander U, SC — B
Langston U, OK — B
Lansing Comm Coll, MI — A
Laramie County Comm Coll, WY — A
Lawrence U, WI — B
LeMoyne-Owen Coll, TN — B
Lewis & Clark Coll, OR — B
Lewis-Clark State Coll, ID — B
Limestone Coll, SC — B
Linfield Coll, OR — B
Lipscomb U, TN — B
Long Beach City Coll, CA — A
Long Island U, C.W. Post Campus, NY — B
Longwood U, VA — B
Los Angeles Harbor Coll, CA — A
Los Angeles Mission Coll, CA — A
Loyola U Chicago, IL — B
Luther Coll, IA — B
Lycoming Coll, PA — B
Lynchburg Coll, VA — B
Lyndon State Coll, VT — B
Manatee Comm Coll, FL — A
Manchester Coll, IN — B
Manhattan Coll, NY — B
Manhattanville Coll, NY — B
Marian Coll of Fond du Lac, WI — B
Marlboro Coll, VT — B
Marquette U, WI — B
Marshall U, WV — B
Mary Baldwin Coll, VA — B
Maryville Coll, TN — B
Maryville U of Saint Louis, MO — B
Massachusetts Inst of Technology, MA — B
McDaniel Coll, MD — B
McMurry U, TX — B
McNeese State U, LA — B
Mesa State Coll, CO — A,B
Miami Dade Coll, FL — B
Miami U, OH — B
Michigan Technological U, MI — B
MidAmerica Nazarene U, KS — B
Middlebury Coll, VT — B
Middle Tennessee State U, TN — B
Midland Coll, TX — A
Midwestern State U, TX — B
Millersville U of Pennsylvania, PA — B
Milligan Coll, TN — B
Millsaps Coll, MS — B
Mills Coll, CA — B
Minnesota State U Mankato, MN — B
Minnesota State U Moorhead, MN — B
Minot State U, ND — B
MiraCosta Coll, CA — A
Mississippi U for Women, MS — B
Missouri Baptist U, MO — B
Mitchell Coll, CT — A
Monmouth U, NJ — B
Montana Tech of The U of Montana, MT — B
Montclair State U, NJ — B

Monterey Peninsula Coll, CA — A
Moravian Coll, PA — B
Morehead State U, KY — B
Morningside Coll, IA — B
Mountain State U, WV — B
Mount Holyoke Coll, MA — B
Muskingum Coll, OH — B
Nebraska Wesleyan U, NE — B
New Coll of Florida, FL — B
New Mexico Highlands U, NM — B
New Mexico Inst of Mining and Technology, NM — B
New Mexico Military Inst, NM — A
New Mexico State U, NM — B
New York U, NY — B
Niagara U, NY — B
Northampton County Area Comm Coll, PA — A
North Carolina State U, NC — B
North Central Coll, IL — B
North Dakota State U, ND — B
Northeast Comm Coll, NE — A
Northeastern U, MA — B
Northeast State Tech Comm Coll, TN — A
Northern Arizona U, AZ — B
Northern Kentucky U, KY — B
Northern Michigan U, MI — B
Northern State U, SD — B
Northland Coll, WI — B
Northwest Coll, WY — A
Northwestern State U of Louisiana, LA — B
Northwestern U, IL — B
Northwest Missouri State U, MO — B
Notre Dame Coll, OH — B
Oakland U, MI — B
Ohio Wesleyan U, OH — B
Oklahoma Panhandle State U, OK — B
Oklahoma State U, OK — B
Oklahoma Wesleyan U, OK — A,B
Old Dominion U, VA — B
Orange Coast Coll, CA — A
Oregon State U, OR — B
Otterbein Coll, OH — B
Pace U, NY — B
Palomar Coll, CA — A
Park U, MO — B
Peru State Coll, NE — B
Philadelphia U, PA — B
Pittsburg State U, KS — B
Pitzer Coll, CA — B
Plymouth State U, NH — B
Portland Comm Coll, OR — A
Portland State U, OR — B
Presentation Coll, SD — A
Principia Coll, IL — B
Purdue U, IN — B
Quincy U, IL — B
Quinnipiac U, CT — B
Radford U, VA — B
Ramapo Coll of New Jersey, NJ — B
Randolph Coll, VA — B
Randolph-Macon Coll, VA — B
Raritan Valley Comm Coll, NJ — A
Redlands Comm Coll, OK — A
Reed Coll, OR — B
Rensselaer Polytechnic Inst, NY — B
Rhodes Coll, TN — B
Rider U, NJ — B
Ridgewater Coll, MN — A
Rochester Inst of Technology, NY — A,B
Rocky Mountain Coll, MT — B
Roger Williams U, RI — B
Roosevelt U, IL — B
Rose State Coll, OK — A
Sacramento City Coll, CA — A
Sacred Heart U, CT — A,B
St. Ambrose U, IA — B
Saint Francis U, PA — B
St. Gregory's U, OK — B
St. John's Coll, NM — B
Saint John's U, MN — B
Saint Joseph's Coll, IN — B
Saint Louis U, MO — B
Saint Mary's Coll, IN — B
Saint Mary's Coll of California, CA — B
St. Mary's Coll of Maryland, MD — B

Saint Mary's U of Minnesota, MN — B
St. Mary's U of San Antonio, TX — B
Saint Michael's Coll, VT — B
St. Olaf Coll, MN — B
St. Thomas U, FL — B
Saint Vincent Coll, PA — B
Sam Houston State U, TX — B
San Bernardino Valley Coll, CA — A
San Diego City Coll, CA — A
San Diego State U, CA — B
San Francisco State U, CA — B
San Jacinto Coll Central Campus, TX — A
San Jacinto Coll North Campus, TX — A
San Jacinto Coll South Campus, TX — A
Santa Barbara City Coll, CA — A
Santa Fe Comm Coll, NM — A
Santa Monica Coll, CA — A
Santa Rosa Jr Coll, CA — A
Sarah Lawrence Coll, NY — B
Sauk Valley Comm Coll, IL — A
Savannah State U, GA — B
Schreiner U, TX — B
Scripps Coll, CA — B
Seattle U, WA — B
Seton Hall U, NJ — B
Shenandoah U, VA — B
Shepherd U, WV — B
Shorter Coll, GA — B
Siena Coll, NY — B
Sierra Coll, CA — A
Simmons Coll, MA — B
Simpson Coll, IA — B
Skagit Valley Coll, WA — A
Skidmore Coll, NY — B
Slippery Rock U of Pennsylvania, PA — B
South Dakota State U, SD — B
Southeast Missouri State U, MO — B
Southern Arkansas U–Magnolia, AR — B
Southern Illinois U Carbondale, IL — B
Southern Illinois U Edwardsville, IL — B
Southern Oregon U, OR — B
Southern Utah U, UT — B
South Georgia Coll, GA — A
Southwestern Coll, KS — B
Southwest Minnesota State U, MN — B
Spring Arbor U, MI — B
Stanford U, CA — B
State U of New York at Oswego, NY — B
State U of New York at Plattsburgh, NY — B
State U of New York Coll at Geneseo, NY — B
State U of New York Coll at Oneonta, NY — B
Stony Brook U, State U of New York, NY — B
Suffolk County Comm Coll, NY — A
Suffolk U, MA — B
Susquehanna U, PA — B
Swarthmore Coll, PA — B
Syracuse U, NY — B
Tabor Coll, KS — B
Taylor U, IN — B
Tennessee Technological U, TN — B
Texas A&M U–Corpus Christi, TX — B
Texas A&M U–Kingsville, TX — B
Texas Christian U, TX — B
Texas State U-San Marcos, TX — B
Texas Wesleyan U, TX — B
Thomas More Coll, KY — A,B
Trevecca Nazarene U, TN — B
Trinity Coll, CT — B
Trinity U, TX — B
Trinity (Washington) U, DC — B
Troy U, AL — B
Truman State U, MO — B
Union Coll, NY — B
U at Buffalo, the State U of New York, NY — B
The U of Alabama, AL — B

The U of Alabama in Huntsville, AL	B
U of Arkansas, AR	B
U of Arkansas at Pine Bluff, AR	B
U of California, Santa Cruz, CA	B
U of Central Florida, FL	B
U of Central Missouri, MO	B
U of Charleston, WV	B
U of Cincinnati, OH	B
U of Cincinnati Raymond Walters Coll, OH	A
U of Colorado at Boulder, CO	B
U of Colorado at Colorado Springs, CO	B
U of Dayton, OH	B
U of Denver, CO	B
U of Detroit Mercy, MI	B
U of Guam, GU	B
U of Hartford, CT	B
U of Hawaii at Manoa, HI	B
U of Illinois at Springfield, IL	B
U of Indianapolis, IN	A,B
The U of Iowa, IA	B
U of Kansas, KS	B
U of La Verne, CA	B
U of Maine at Farmington, ME	B
U of Maine at Presque Isle, ME	B
U of Mary Hardin-Baylor, TX	B
U of Maryland, Baltimore County, MD	B
U of Maryland, Coll Park, MD	B
U of Mary Washington, VA	B
U of Miami, FL	B
U of Michigan–Flint, MI	B
U of Minnesota, Morris, MN	B
U of Missouri–Columbia, MO	B
U of Missouri–St. Louis, MO	B
U of Nebraska–Lincoln, NE	B
U of Nevada, Reno, NV	B
U of New Mexico, NM	B
U of New Orleans, LA	B
U of North Alabama, AL	B
The U of North Carolina at Asheville, NC	B
The U of North Carolina at Pembroke, NC	B
U of Northern Iowa, IA	B
U of North Texas, TX	B
U of Oregon, OR	B
U of Pittsburgh, PA	B
U of Pittsburgh at Bradford, PA	B
U of Puget Sound, WA	B
U of Rhode Island, RI	B
U of Rochester, NY	B
U of Saint Francis, IN	B
U of San Diego, CA	B
U of San Francisco, CA	B
U of Sioux Falls, SD	B
U of South Carolina, SC	B
U of South Carolina Upstate, SC	B
U of Southern Indiana, IN	B
U of Southern Maine, ME	B
U of South Florida, FL	B
The U of Tampa, FL	A,B
The U of Tennessee at Martin, TN	B
The U of Texas at San Antonio, TX	B
U of the Incarnate Word, TX	B
U of Tulsa, OK	B
U of Utah, UT	B
U of Virginia, VA	B
U of Washington, WA	B
U of West Florida, FL	B
U of Wisconsin–Eau Claire, WI	B
U of Wisconsin–La Crosse, WI	B
U of Wisconsin–Oshkosh, WI	B
U of Wisconsin–Stevens Point, WI	B
U of Wisconsin–Superior, WI	B
U of Wisconsin–Whitewater, WI	B
U of Wyoming, WY	B
Upper Iowa U, IA	B
Utah State U, UT	B
Utah Valley State Coll, UT	A,B
Utica Coll, NY	B
Valparaiso U, IN	B
Vanderbilt U, TN	B
Vanguard U of Southern California, CA	B

Villanova U, PA	B
Virginia Commonwealth U, VA	B
Virginia Polytechnic Inst and State U, VA	B
Viterbo U, WI	B
Wabash Coll, IN	B
Wake Forest U, NC	B
Warren Wilson Coll, NC	B
Wartburg Coll, IA	B
Washington & Jefferson Coll, PA	B
Washington Coll, MD	B
Washington State U, WA	B
Washington U in St. Louis, MO	B
Waynesburg Coll, PA	B
Wayne State Coll, NE	B
Wells Coll, NY	B
Wesleyan U, CT	B
Western Illinois U, IL	B
Western Kentucky U, KY	B
Western New England Coll, MA	B
Western New Mexico U, NM	B
Western Washington U, WA	B
Western Wyoming Comm Coll, WY	A
Westmont Coll, CA	B
West Texas A&M U, TX	B
West Valley Coll, CA	A
Wichita State U, KS	B
Widener U, PA	B
Wilkes U, PA	B
Williams Coll, MA	B
Wilmington Coll, OH	B
Wilson Coll, PA	B
Winona State U, MN	B
Worcester Polytechnic Inst, MA	B
Worcester State Coll, MA	B
York Coll of Pennsylvania, PA	A,B
York Coll of the City U of New York, NY	B
Young Harris Coll, GA	A

Pre-Professional Studies

Adrian Coll, MI	B
Albertus Magnus Coll, CT	B
Albion Coll, MI	B
Alderson-Broaddus Coll, WV	B
Allegheny Coll, PA	B
Alvernia Coll, PA	B
Alvin Comm Coll, TX	A
American U, DC	B
Antioch Coll, OH	B
Arcadia U, PA	B
Ashford U, IA	B
Ashland U, OH	B
Averett U, VA	B
Ball State U, IN	B
Bard Coll, NY	B
Barnard Coll, NY	B
Barry U, FL	B
Beloit Coll, WI	B
Bemidji State U, MN	B
Benedict Coll, SC	B
Bennington Coll, VT	B
Berea Coll, KY	B
Berkeley Coll-New York City Campus, NY	A
Berkeley Coll-Westchester Campus, NY	A
Blue Mountain Coll, MS	B
Boise State U, ID	B
Boston U, MA	B
Bowdoin Coll, ME	B
Calhoun Comm Coll, AL	A
California Polytechnic State U, San Luis Obispo, CA	B
California State Polytechnic U, Pomona, CA	B
Calvin Coll, MI	B
Capital U, OH	B
Cardinal Stritch U, WI	B
Carroll Coll, MT	B
Carroll Coll, WI	B
Carthage Coll, WI	B
Central Christian Coll of Kansas, KS	B
Centralia Coll, WA	A
City Coll of the City U of New York, NY	B
City Colls of Chicago, Harold Washington Coll, IL	A

City Colls of Chicago, Kennedy-King Coll, IL	A
Clarendon Coll, TX	A
Clarkson U, NY	B
Clark U, MA	B
Clearwater Christian Coll, FL	B
Coastal Georgia Comm Coll, GA	A
Coe Coll, IA	B
Colby Comm Coll, KS	A
Coll of Saint Benedict, MN	B
Coll of St. Catherine, MN	B
Coll of the Atlantic, ME	B
Coll of the Holy Cross, MA	B
Coll of the Ozarks, MO	B
Colorado State U, CO	B
Columbia Coll, MO	B
Columbia Union Coll, MD	B
Concordia Coll, MN	B
Concordia U, IL	B
Cumberland U, TN	B
Defiance Coll, OH	B
DeKalb Tech Coll, GA	A
Del Mar Coll, TX	A
DeSales U, PA	B
Dordt Coll, IA	B
Drake U, IA	B
Drury U, MO	B
D'Youville Coll, NY	B
Eastern Mennonite U, VA	B
Eastern Wyoming Coll, WY	A
Edgewood Coll, WI	B
Edison Coll, FL	A
Elizabethtown Coll, PA	B
Elmira Coll, NY	B
Elms Coll, MA	A,B
Elon U, NC	B
Ferris State U, MI	B
Florida State U, FL	B
Foothill Coll, CA	A
Fordham U, NY	B
Fresno Pacific U, CA	B
Furman U, SC	B
Gannon U, PA	B
Gardner-Webb U, NC	B
Gettysburg Coll, PA	B
Goshen Coll, IN	B
Grand Valley State U, MI	B
Gustavus Adolphus Coll, MN	B
Harding U, AR	B
Hardin-Simmons U, TX	B
Hartwick Coll, NY	B
Harvard U, MA	B
Haverford Coll, PA	B
Hawai'i Pacific U, HI	B
Hilbert Coll, NY	A,B
Hillsdale Coll, MI	B
Hiram Coll, OH	B
Hofstra U, NY	B
Holy Family U, PA	B
Howard Payne U, TX	B
Huntington U, IN	B
Illinois Coll, IL	B
Indiana U Bloomington, IN	B
Indiana Wesleyan U, IN	B
Iowa State U of Science and Technology, IA	B
Isothermal Comm Coll, NC	A
Jacksonville U, FL	B
John Carroll U, OH	B
Johnson State Coll, VT	B
Judson Coll, IL	B
Juniata Coll, PA	B
Kansas State U, KS	B
Kansas Wesleyan U, KS	B
Kent State U, OH	B
Kentucky Wesleyan Coll, KY	B
Kenyon Coll, OH	B
Kilgore Coll, TX	A
Kirkwood Comm Coll, IA	A
Langston U, OK	B
Laramie County Comm Coll, WY	A
Lawrence U, WI	B
Lees-McRae Coll, NC	B
Limestone Coll, SC	B
Lipscomb U, TN	B
Long Island U, C.W. Post Campus, NY	B
Longwood U, VA	B
Lycoming Coll, PA	B
Lynchburg Coll, VA	B

Manatee Comm Coll, FL	A
Manchester Coll, IN	B
Manhattanville Coll, NY	B
Marian Coll of Fond du Lac, WI	B
Marlboro Coll, VT	B
Marquette U, WI	B
Mesa State Coll, CO	B
Miami U, OH	B
Michigan Technological U, MI	B
Midwestern State U, TX	B
Minnesota State U Mankato, MN	B
Minnesota State U Moorhead, MN	B
Molloy Coll, NY	B
Morningside Coll, IA	B
Mountain State U, WV	B
Mount Mercy Coll, IA	B
Muskingum Coll, OH	B
New Mexico Highlands U, NM	B
New York U, NY	B
Niagara U, NY	B
North Central Coll, IL	B
Northern Arizona U, AZ	B
Northern Kentucky U, KY	B
Northern Michigan U, MI	B
Northern State U, SD	B
Northland Coll, WI	B
Northwestern U, IL	B
Northwest Missouri State U, MO	B
Notre Dame Coll, OH	B
Notre Dame de Namur U, CA	B
Nova Southeastern U, FL	B
Ohio Wesleyan U, OH	B
Oklahoma State U, OK	B
Oklahoma Wesleyan U, OK	B
Oregon State U, OR	B
Otterbein Coll, OH	B
Peru State Coll, NE	B
Philadelphia U, PA	B
Pitzer Coll, CA	B
Quincy U, IL	B
Quinnipiac U, CT	B
Ramapo Coll of New Jersey, NJ	B
Rasmussen Coll Mankato, MN	A
Rensselaer Polytechnic Inst, NY	B
Riverside Comm Coll District, CA	A
Rochester Inst of Technology, NY	B
Roger Williams U, RI	B
Roosevelt U, IL	B
Rose State Coll, OK	A
Sacred Heart U, CT	B
Sage Coll of Albany, NY	A,B
Saint Anselm Coll, NH	B
Saint Francis U, PA	B
St. Gregory's U, OK	B
St. John's Coll, NM	B
Saint John's U, MN	B
St. Louis Comm Coll at Florissant Valley, MO	A
Saint Mary-of-the-Woods Coll, IN	B
St. Mary's U of San Antonio, TX	B
Saint Michael's Coll, VT	B
St. Thomas U, FL	B
Sam Houston State U, TX	B
Santa Barbara City Coll, CA	A
Santa Rosa Jr Coll, CA	A
Sarah Lawrence Coll, NY	B
Sauk Valley Comm Coll, IL	A
Schreiner U, TX	B
Scripps Coll, CA	B
Siena Coll, NY	B
Simmons Coll, MA	B
Simpson Coll, IA	B
South Dakota State U, SD	B
Southern Oregon U, OR	B
Southwest Minnesota State U, MN	B
State U of New York at Oswego, NY	B
State U of New York Coll at Geneseo, NY	B
State U of New York Coll at Oneonta, NY	B
Suffolk County Comm Coll, NY	A
Suffolk U, MA	B

A=Associate; B=Bachelor's Degree

Susquehanna U, PA — B
Syracuse U, NY — B
Tabor Coll, KS — B
Taylor U, IN — B
Tennessee Technological U, TN — B
Texas A&M U–Corpus Christi, TX — B
Texas A&M U–Kingsville, TX — B
Texas Wesleyan U, TX — B
Trinity U, TX — B
Trinity (Washington) U, DC — B
Troy U, AL — R
Truman State U, MO — B
Tusculum Coll, TN — B
U of Arkansas at Pine Bluff, AR — B
U of Baltimore, MD — B
U of California, Santa Cruz, CA — B
U of Central Missouri, MO — B
U of Charleston, WV — B
U of Cincinnati, OH — B
U of Colorado at Colorado Springs, CO — B
U of Dayton, OH — B
U of Detroit Mercy, MI — A,B
The U of Findlay, OH — B
U of Hartford, CT — B
U of Illinois at Springfield, IL — B
U of Indianapolis, IN — B
The U of Iowa, IA — B
U of Maryland, Baltimore County, MD — B
U of Mary Washington, VA — B
U of Miami, FL — B
U of Minnesota, Morris, MN — B
U of Missouri–St. Louis, MO — B
U of Nebraska–Lincoln, NE — B
U of Nevada, Reno, NV — B
U of Oregon, OR — B
U of Pittsburgh, PA — B
U of Puget Sound, WA — B
U of Saint Francis, IN — B
U of San Diego, CA — B
U of San Francisco, CA — B
U of Sioux Falls, SD — B
The U of Tampa, FL — B
The U of Tennessee at Martin, TN — R
U of the Incarnate Word, TX — B
U of Utah, UT — B
U of Wisconsin–Oshkosh, WI — B
U of Wisconsin–Superior, WI — B
Upper Iowa U, IA — B
Utah State U, UT — B
Utah Valley State Coll, UT — A,B
Utica Coll, NY — B
Wabash Coll, IN — B
Washington Coll, MD — B
Washington State U, WA — B
Washington U in St. Louis, MO — B
Waynesburg Coll, PA — B
Wayne State Coll, NE — B
Wells Coll, NY — B
Western New Mexico U, NM — B
Western Wyoming Comm Coll, WY — A
Westmont Coll, CA — B
Widener U, PA — B
Wilmington Coll, OH — R
Winona State U, MN — B
York Coll of Pennsylvania, PA — B

Psychology and Social Work

Adelphi U, NY — B
Adrian Coll, MI — A,B
Agnes Scott Coll, GA — B
Alamance Comm Coll, NC — A
Alaska Pacific U, AK — B
Albertus Magnus Coll, CT — B
Albion Coll, MI — B
Alderson-Broaddus Coll, WV — B
Allegheny Coll, PA — B
Alvernia Coll, PA — B
Alverno Coll, WI — B
American U, DC — B
Anna Maria Coll, MA — B
Antioch Coll, OH — B
Aquinas Coll, MI — B
Arcadia U, PA — B
Arizona State U, AZ — B
Ashford U, IA — B
Ashland U, OH — B
Assumption Coll, MA — B

Austin Peay State U, TN — B
Averett U, VA — B
Baker U, KS — B
Baldwin-Wallace Coll, OH — B
Ball State U, IN — B
Bard Coll, NY — B
Barnard Coll, NY — B
Barry U, FL — B
Bastyr U, WA — B
Bates Coll, ME — B
Bay Path Coll, MA — B
Beacon U, GA — B
Belmont U, TN — B
Beloit Coll, WI — B
Bemidji State U, MN — B
Benedict Coll, SC — B
Bennington Coll, VT — B
Berea Coll, KY — B
Berkshire Comm Coll, MA — A
Bethany Coll, KS — B
Bethel Coll, KS — B
Bethel U, MN — B
Black Hills State U, SD — B
Bluefield State Coll, WV — A
Blue Mountain Coll, MS — B
Boise State U, ID — B
Boston U, MA — B
Bowdoin Coll, ME — B
Brescia U, KY — B
Bronx Comm Coll of the City U of New York, NY — A
Bryant U, RI — B
Bryn Mawr Coll, PA — B
Bucknell U, PA — B
Bunker Hill Comm Coll, MA — A
Butler U, IN — B
Caldwell Coll, NJ — B
California Lutheran U, CA — B
California Polytechnic State U, San Luis Obispo, CA — B
California State Polytechnic U, Pomona, CA — B
California State U, Long Beach, CA — B
California State U, Sacramento, CA — B
California State U, Stanislaus, CA — B
Calvin Coll, MI — B
Cameron U, OK — B
Cañada Coll, CA — A
Capital U, OH — B
Cardinal Stritch U, WI — B
Carleton Coll, MN — B
Carlow U, PA — B
Carroll Coll, MT — B
Carroll Coll, WI — B
Carson-Newman Coll, TN — B
Carthage Coll, WI — B
The Catholic U of America, DC — B
Cazenovia Coll, NY — B
Centenary Coll, NJ — B
Central Christian Coll of Kansas, KS — A
Centralia Coll, WA — A
Central Lakes Coll, MN — A
Central Michigan U, MI — B
Central Piedmont Comm Coll, NC — A
Central Wyoming Coll, WY — A
Centre Coll, KY — B
Century Coll, MN — A
Chabot Coll, CA — A
Chaffey Coll, CA — A
Chapman U, CA — B
Chatham U, PA — B
City Coll of San Francisco, CA — A
City Coll of the City U of New York, NY — B
City Colls of Chicago, Harold Washington Coll, IL — B
City Colls of Chicago, Kennedy-King Coll, IL — A
City U, WA — B
Clarendon Coll, TX — A
Clarion U of Pennsylvania, PA — B
Clarke Coll, IA — B
Clarkson U, NY — B
Clark U, MA — B
Clearwater Christian Coll, FL — B
Cleveland State U, OH — B
Coastal Carolina U, SC — B
Coastal Georgia Comm Coll, GA — A

Cochise Coll, Sierra Vista, AZ — A
Coe Coll, IA — B
Coffeyville Comm Coll, KS — A
Colby Coll, ME — B
Colby Comm Coll, KS — A
Colby-Sawyer Coll, NH — B
Coll Misericordia, PA — B
Coll of Lake County, IL — A
Coll of Saint Benedict, MN — B
Coll of St. Catherine, MN — B
Coll of the Atlantic, ME — B
Coll of the Canyons, CA — A
Coll of the Desert, CA — A
Coll of the Holy Cross, MA — B
Coll of the Ozarks, MO — B
The Colorado Coll, CO — B
Colorado State U, CO — B
Columbia Coll, MO — B
Columbia Union Coll, MD — B
Columbia U, School of General Studies, NY — B
Concordia Coll, MN — B
Concordia Coll, NY — B
Concordia U, IL — B
Connecticut Coll, CT — B
Connors State Coll, OK — A
Cornell Coll, IA — B
Cosumnes River Coll, Sacramento, CA — A
Culver-Stockton Coll, MO — B
Cumberland U, TN — B
Daemen Coll, NY — B
Dakota Wesleyan U, SD — B
Dana Coll, NE — B
Davidson Coll, NC — B
De Anza Coll, CA — A
Defiance Coll, OH — B
Del Mar Coll, TX — A
Delta Coll, MI — A
Denison U, OH — B
DePaul U, IL — B
DePauw U, IN — B
DeSales U, PA — B
Dominican U of California, CA — B
Dordt Coll, IA — B
Drake U, IA — B
Drew U, NJ — B
Drury U, MO — B
Duquesne U, PA — B
D'Youville Coll, NY — B
East Carolina U, NC — B
East Central U, OK — A
Eastern Connecticut State U, CT — B
Eastern Mennonite U, VA — B
Eastern U, PA — B
Eastern Wyoming Coll, WY — A
East Los Angeles Coll, CA — A
East Tennessee State U, TN — B
East Texas Baptist U, TX — B
Eckerd Coll, FL — B
Edgewood Coll, WI — B
Edinboro U of Pennsylvania, PA — A,B
El Camino Coll, CA — A
Elizabethtown Coll, PA — B
Elmira Coll, NY — B
Elms Coll, MA — B
Elon U, NC — B
Emmanuel Coll, MA — B
Emory U, GA — B
Emporia State U, KS — B
Fairfield U, CT — B
Fairleigh Dickinson U, Coll at Florham, NJ — B
Fairleigh Dickinson U, Metropolitan Campus, NJ — B
Ferris State U, MI — B
Flagler Coll, FL — B
Florida Atlantic U, FL — B
Florida Gulf Coast U, FL — B
Florida Inst of Technology, FL — B
Florida International U, FL — B
Florida State U, FL — B
Foothill Coll, CA — A
Fordham U, NY — B
Fort Lewis Coll, CO — B
Fresno Pacific U, CA — A,B
Frostburg State U, MD — B
Fullerton Coll, CA — A
Fulton-Montgomery Comm Coll, NY — A
Furman U, SC — B
Gannon U, PA — B

Garden City Comm Coll, KS — A
Gardner-Webb U, NC — B
GateWay Comm Coll, AZ — A
Genesee Comm Coll, NY — A
George Fox U, OR — B
Georgetown Coll, KY — B
Georgia Coll & State U, GA — B
Georgia Highlands Coll, GA — A
Georgia Southern U, GA — B
Georgia State U, GA — B
Gettysburg Coll, PA — B
Gonzaga U, WA — B
Goshen Coll, IN — B
Grambling State U, LA — B
Grand Valley State U, MI — B
Grand View Coll, IA — B
Green Mountain Coll, VT — B
Greenville Coll, IL — B
Grinnell Coll, IA — B
Gulf Coast Comm Coll, FL — A
Gustavus Adolphus Coll, MN — B
Hamilton Coll, NY — B
Hampden-Sydney Coll, VA — B
Hampshire Coll, MA — B
Harding U, AR — B
Hardin-Simmons U, TX — B
Harrisburg Area Comm Coll, PA — A
Hartwick Coll, NY — B
Harvard U, MA — B
Haverford Coll, PA — B
Hawai'i Pacific U, HI — B
Hilbert Coll, NY — B
Hill Coll of the Hill Jr Coll District, TX — A
Hillsdale Coll, MI — B
Hillsdale Free Will Baptist Coll, OK — A
Hiram Coll, OH — B
Hofstra U, NY — B
Holy Family U, PA — B
Hope Coll, MI — B
Hope International U, CA — B
Howard Payne U, TX — B
Huntingdon Coll, AL — B
Huntington U, IN — B
Idaho State U, ID — B
Illinois Coll, IL — B
Illinois Inst of Technology, IL — B
Illinois Wesleyan U, IL — B
Indiana Tech, IN — B
Indiana U Bloomington, IN — B
Indiana U of Pennsylvania, PA — B
Indiana U South Bend, IN — B
Indiana U Southeast, IN — B
Indiana Wesleyan U, IN — B
Iowa State U of Science and Technology, IA — B
Itasca Comm Coll, MN — A
Jacksonville State U, AL — B
Jacksonville U, FL — B
James Madison U, VA — B
John Carroll U, OH — B
John F. Kennedy U, CA — B
The Johns Hopkins U, MD — B
Johnson State Coll, VT — B
Judson Coll, IL — B
Juniata Coll, PA — B
Kankakee Comm Coll, IL — B
Kansas State U, KS — B
Kansas Wesleyan U, KS — B
Kean U, NJ — B
Kennesaw State U, GA — B
Kent State U, OH — B
Kentucky Wesleyan Coll, KY — B
Kenyon Coll, OH — B
Kilgore Coll, TX — A
Kingwood Coll, TX — A
Kirkwood Comm Coll, IA — A
Knox Coll, IL — B
Lafayette Coll, PA — B
Lake Land Coll, IL — A
Lakeland Coll, WI — B
Lancaster Bible Coll, PA — B
Lander U, SC — B
Langston U, OK — B
Lansing Comm Coll, MI — A
Laramie County Comm Coll, WY — A
Lawrence U, WI — B
Lees-McRae Coll, NC — B
LeMoyne-Owen Coll, TN — B
Lewis & Clark Coll, OR — B
Lewis-Clark State Coll, ID — B

Liberty U, VA — B
Limestone Coll, SC — B
Linfield Coll, OR — B
Lipscomb U, TN — B
Long Beach City Coll, CA — A
Long Island U, C.W. Post Campus, NY — B
Longwood U, VA — B
Los Angeles Harbor Coll, CA — A
Los Angeles Mission Coll, CA — A
Los Angeles Southwest Coll, CA — A
Louisiana State U at Alexandria, LA — A
Loyola U Chicago, IL — B
Luther Coll, IA — B
Lycoming Coll, PA — B
Lynchburg Coll, VA — B
Lyndon State Coll, VT — B
Lynn U, FL — B
Manatee Comm Coll, FL — A
Manchester Coll, IN — A
Manhattan Coll, NY — B
Manhattanville Coll, NY — B
Marian Coll of Fond du Lac, WI — B
Marlboro Coll, VT — B
Marquette U, WI — B
Marshall U, WV — B
Mary Baldwin Coll, VA — B
Marylhurst U, OR — B
Marymount Manhattan Coll, NY — B
Maryville Coll, TN — B
Maryville U of Saint Louis, MO — B
Marywood U, PA — B
Massachusetts Inst of Technology, MA — B
McDaniel Coll, MD — B
McMurry U, TX — B
McNeese State U, LA — B
Mercy Coll, NY — B
Merritt Coll, CA — A
Mesa State Coll, CO — B
Miami Dade Coll, FL — A
Miami U, OH — B
Michigan Technological U, MI — B
MidAmerica Nazarene U, KS — B
Middlebury Coll, VT — B
Middle Tennessee State U, TN — B
Midland Coll, TX — A
Midwestern State U, TX — B
Millersville U of Pennsylvania, PA — A
Milligan Coll, TN — B
Millsaps Coll, MS — B
Mills Coll, CA — B
Minnesota State U Mankato, MN — B
Minnesota State U Moorhead, MN — B
Minot State U, ND — B
MiraCosta Coll, CA — A
Mississippi U for Women, MS — B
Missouri Baptist U, MO — B
Mitchell Coll, CT — A
Molloy Coll, NY — B
Monmouth U, NJ — B
Montclair State U, NJ — B
Monterey Peninsula Coll, CA — A
Moravian Coll, PA — B
Morehead State U, KY — B
Morningside Coll, IA — B
Mountain State U, WV — B
Mount Holyoke Coll, MA — B
Mount Ida Coll, MA — B
Mount Mercy Coll, IA — B
Muskingum Coll, OH — B
Nebraska Wesleyan U, NE — B
New Coll of California, CA — B
New Coll of Florida, FL — B
New England Coll, NH — B
New Mexico Highlands U, NM — B
New Mexico Inst of Mining and Technology, NM — B
New Mexico State U, NM — B
New Mexico State U–Alamogordo, NM — A
New River Comm Coll, VA — A
New York U, NY — B
Niagara U, NY — B
Nichols Coll, MA — B
Northampton County Area Comm Coll, PA — A

North Carolina State U, NC — B
North Central Coll, IL — B
North Central U, MN — A,B
North Dakota State U, ND — B
Northeastern U, MA — B
Northern Arizona U, AZ — B
Northern Kentucky U, KY — B
Northern Michigan U, MI — B
Northern State U, SD — A
Northland Coll, WI — B
Northwest Coll, WY — A
Northwestern State U of Louisiana, LA — B
Northwestern U, IL — B
Northwest Missouri State U, MO — B
Northwest U, WA — B
Notre Dame Coll, OH — B
Notre Dame de Namur U, CA — B
Nova Southeastern U, FL — B
Oakland U, MI — B
Ohio Wesleyan U, OH — B
Oklahoma Panhandle State U, OK — B
Oklahoma State U, OK — B
Old Dominion U, VA — B
Oregon State U, OR — B
Ottawa U, KS — B
Otterbein Coll, OH — B
Pace U, NY — B
Palomar Coll, CA — A
Park U, MO — A,B
Peace Coll, NC — B
Peru State Coll, NE — B
Philadelphia Biblical U, PA — B
Philadelphia U, PA — B
Pittsburg State U, KS — B
Pitzer Coll, CA — B
Plymouth State U, NH — B
Portland Comm Coll, OR — A
Portland State U, OR — B
Prescott Coll, AZ — B
Presentation Coll, SD — B
Purdue U, IN — B
Quincy U, IL — B
Quinnipiac U, CT — B
Radford U, VA — B
Ramapo Coll of New Jersey, NJ — B
Randolph Coll, VA — B
Randolph-Macon Coll, VA — B
Redlands Comm Coll, OK — A
Reed Coll, OR — B
Rensselaer Polytechnic Inst, NY — B
Rhodes Coll, TN — B
Rider U, NJ — B
Ridgewater Coll, MN — A
Rochester Inst of Technology, NY — B
Rocky Mountain Coll, MT — B
Roger Williams U, RI — B
Roosevelt U, IL — B
Rose State Coll, OK — A
Sacramento City Coll, CA — A
Sacred Heart U, CT — A,B
Sage Coll of Albany, NY — B
St. Ambrose U, IA — B
Saint Anselm Coll, NH — B
Saint Francis U, PA — B
St. Gregory's U, OK — B
Saint John's U, MN — B
Saint Joseph's Coll, IN — B
Saint Leo U, FL — B
Saint Louis U, MO — B
Saint Mary-of-the-Woods Coll, IN — B
Saint Mary's Coll, IN — B
Saint Mary's Coll of California, CA — B
St. Mary's Coll of Maryland, MD — B
Saint Mary's U of Minnesota, MN — B
St. Mary's U of San Antonio, TX — B
Saint Michael's Coll, VT — B
St. Olaf Coll, MN — B
St. Thomas U, FL — B
Saint Vincent Coll, PA — B
Sam Houston State U, TX — B
San Bernardino Valley Coll, CA — A
San Diego City Coll, CA — A

San Diego State U, CA — B
San Francisco State U, CA — B
San Jacinto Coll Central Campus, TX — A
San Jacinto Coll North Campus, TX — A
San Jacinto Coll South Campus, TX — A
Santa Barbara City Coll, CA — A
Santa Fe Comm Coll, NM — A
Santa Monica Coll, CA — A
Santa Rosa Jr Coll, CA — A
Sarah Lawrence Coll, NY — B
Sauk Valley Comm Coll, IL — A
Savannah State U, GA — B
Schreiner U, TX — B
Scripps Coll, CA — B
Seattle U, WA — B
Seton Hall U, NJ — B
Shenandoah U, VA — B
Shepherd U, WV — B
Shorter Coll, GA — B
Siena Coll, NY — B
Simmons Coll, MA — B
Simpson Coll, IA — B
Skagit Valley Coll, WA — A
Skidmore Coll, NY — B
Slippery Rock U of Pennsylvania, PA — B
South Dakota State U, SD — B
Southeast Missouri State U, MO — B
Southern Arkansas U–Magnolia, AR — B
Southern Illinois U Carbondale, IL — B
Southern Illinois U Edwardsville, IL — B
Southern New Hampshire U, NH — B
Southern Oregon U, OR — B
Southern Utah U, UT — B
South Georgia Coll, GA — A
Southwestern Coll, KS — B
Southwest Minnesota State U, MN — B
Spokane Falls Comm Coll, WA — A
Spring Arbor U, MI — B
Stanford U, CA — B
State U of New York at Oswego, NY — B
State U of New York at Plattsburgh, NY — B
State U of New York Coll at Geneseo, NY — B
State U of New York Coll at Oneonta, NY — B
Stony Brook U, State U of New York, NY — B
Suffolk County Comm Coll, NY — A
Suffolk U, MA — A,B
Susquehanna U, PA — B
Swarthmore Coll, PA — B
Syracuse U, NY — B
Tabor Coll, KS — B
Taylor U, IN — B
Tennessee Technological U, TN — B
Texas A&M U–Corpus Christi, TX — B
Texas A&M U–Kingsville, TX — B
Texas A&M U–Texarkana, TX — B
Texas Christian U, TX — B
Texas State U–San Marcos, TX — B
Texas Wesleyan U, TX — B
Thomas More Coll, KY — A,B
Trevecca Nazarene U, TN — B
Trinity Coll, CT — B
Trinity Coll of Florida, FL — B
Trinity U, TX — B
Trinity (Washington) U, DC — B
Troy U, AL — B
Truman State U, MO — B
Tusculum Coll, TN — B
Union Coll, NY — B
U at Buffalo, the State U of New York, NY — B
The U of Alabama, AL — B
The U of Alabama in Huntsville, AL — B
U of Arkansas, AR — B
U of Arkansas at Fort Smith, AR — B

U of Arkansas at Pine Bluff, AR — B
U of Baltimore, MD — B
U of California, Santa Cruz, CA — B
U of Central Florida, FL — B
U of Central Missouri, MO — B
U of Charleston, WV — B
U of Cincinnati, OH — A,B
U of Cincinnati Raymond Walters Coll, OH — A
U of Colorado at Boulder, CO — B
U of Colorado at Colorado Springs, CO — B
U of Dayton, OH — B
U of Denver, CO — B
U of Detroit Mercy, MI — B
U of Dubuque, IA — B
The U of Findlay, OH — A
U of Guam, GU — B
U of Hartford, CT — B
U of Hawaii at Manoa, HI — B
U of Illinois at Springfield, IL — B
U of Indianapolis, IN — B
The U of Iowa, IA — B
U of Kansas, KS — B
U of La Verne, CA — B
U of Maine at Farmington, ME — B
U of Maine at Presque Isle, ME — B
U of Mary Hardin-Baylor, TX — B
U of Maryland, Baltimore County, MD — B
U of Maryland, Coll Park, MD — B
U of Mary Washington, VA — B
U of Miami, FL — B
U of Michigan–Flint, MI — B
U of Minnesota, Morris, MN — B
U of Missouri–Columbia, MO — B
U of Missouri–St. Louis, MO — B
U of Nebraska–Lincoln, NE — B
U of Nevada, Reno, NV — B
U of New Mexico, NM — A
U of New Orleans, LA — B
U of North Alabama, AL — B
The U of North Carolina at Asheville, NC — B
The U of North Carolina at Pembroke, NC — B
U of Northern Iowa, IA — B
U of North Texas, TX — B
U of Oregon, OR — B
U of Pittsburgh, PA — B
U of Pittsburgh at Bradford, PA — B
U of Puget Sound, WA — B
U of Rhode Island, RI — B
U of Rochester, NY — B
U of Saint Francis, IN — B
U of San Diego, CA — B
U of San Francisco, CA — B
U of Sioux Falls, SD — A
U of South Carolina, SC — B
U of South Carolina Upstate, SC — B
U of Southern Indiana, IN — B
U of Southern Maine, ME — B
U of South Florida, FL — B
The U of Tampa, FL — A,B
The U of Tennessee at Martin, TN — B
The U of Texas at San Antonio, TX — B
U of the Incarnate Word, TX — B
U of Tulsa, OK — B
U of Utah, UT — B
U of Virginia, VA — B
U of Washington, WA — B
U of West Florida, FL — B
U of Wisconsin–Eau Claire, WI — B
U of Wisconsin–La Crosse, WI — B
U of Wisconsin–Oshkosh, WI — B
U of Wisconsin–Stevens Point, WI — B
U of Wisconsin–Stout, WI — B
U of Wisconsin–Superior, WI — B
U of Wisconsin–Whitewater, WI — B
U of Wyoming, WY — B
Upper Iowa U, IA — B
Utah State U, UT — B
Utica Coll, NY — B
Valparaiso U, IN — B
Vanderbilt U, TN — B
Vanguard U of Southern California, CA — B

A=Associate; B=Bachelor's Degree

Villanova U, PA — B
Virginia Commonwealth U, VA — B
Virginia Polytechnic Inst and State U, VA — B
Viterbo U, WI — B
Wabash Coll, IN — B
Wake Forest U, NC — B
Waldorf Coll, IA — B
Warren Wilson Coll, NC — B
Wartburg Coll, IA — B
Washington & Jefferson Coll, PA — B
Washington Coll, MD — B
Washington State U, WA — B
Washington U in St. Louis, MO — B
Waynesburg Coll, PA — B
Wayne State Coll, NE — B
Wells Coll, NY — B
Wesleyan U, CT — B
Western Illinois U, IL — B
Western Kentucky U, KY — B
Western New England Coll, MA — B
Western New Mexico U, NM — B
Western Washington U, WA — B
Western Wyoming Comm Coll, WY — A
Westmont Coll, CA — B
West Texas A&M U, TX — B
West Valley Coll, CA — A
Wichita State U, KS — B
Widener U, PA — B
Wilkes U, PA — B
Williams Coll, MA — B
Wilmington Coll, OH — B
Wilson Coll, PA — B
Winona State U, MN — B
Woodbury U, CA — B
Worcester State Coll, MA — B
York Coll, NE — B
York Coll of Pennsylvania, PA — B
York Coll of the City U of New York, NY — B
Young Harris Coll, GA — A

Social Sciences and History

Adelphi U, NY — B
Adrian Coll, MI — A,B
Agnes Scott Coll, GA — B
Albertus Magnus Coll, CT — B
Albion Coll, MI — B
Alderson-Broaddus Coll, WV — B
Allegheny Coll, PA — B
Alvernia Coll, PA — B
Alverno Coll, WI — B
American U, DC — B
Ancilla Coll, IN — A
Anna Maria Coll, MA — B
Antioch Coll, OH — B
Aquinas Coll, MI — B
Arcadia U, PA — B
Arizona State U, AZ — B
Ashford U, IA — B
Ashland U, OH — B
Assumption Coll, MA — B
Austin Peay State U, TN — B
Averett U, VA — B
Babson Coll, MA — B
Baker U, KS — B
Baldwin-Wallace Coll, OH — B
Ball State U, IN — A,B
Bard Coll, NY — B
Barnard Coll, NY — B
Barry U, FL — B
Bates Coll, ME — B
Belmont U, TN — B
Beloit Coll, WI — B
Bemidji State U, MN — B
Benedict Coll, SC — B
Bennington Coll, VT — B
Bentley Coll, MA — B
Berea Coll, KY — B
Berkshire Comm Coll, MA — A
Bethany Coll, KS — B
Bethel Coll, KS — B
Bethel U, MN — B
Black Hills State U, SD — B
Bluefield State Coll, WV — B
Blue Mountain Coll, MS — B
Boise State U, ID — B
Boston U, MA — B
Bowdoin Coll, ME — B
Bowling Green State U–Firelands Coll, OH — A

Brescia U, KY — B
Bronx Comm Coll of the City U of New York, NY — B
Bryant U, RI — B
Bryn Mawr Coll, PA — B
Bucknell U, PA — B
Bunker Hill Comm Coll, MA — A
Butler U, IN — B
Caldwell Coll, NJ — B
California Lutheran U, CA — B
California Polytechnic State U, San Luis Obispo, CA — B
California State Polytechnic U, Pomona, CA — B
California State U, Long Beach, CA — B
California State U, Sacramento, CA — B
California State U, Stanislaus, CA — B
Calvin Coll, MI — B
Cameron U, OK — B
Cañada Coll, CA — A
Capital U, OH — B
Cardinal Stritch U, WI — B
Carleton Coll, MN — B
Carlow U, PA — B
Carroll Coll, MT — B
Carroll Coll, WI — B
Carson-Newman Coll, TN — B
Carthage Coll, WI — B
The Catholic U of America, DC — B
Cazenovia Coll, NY — B
Centenary Coll, NJ — B
Central Christian Coll of Kansas, KS — A
Centralia Coll, WA — A
Central Michigan U, MI — B
Central Wyoming Coll, WY — A
Centre Coll, KY — B
Chabot Coll, CA — A
Chaffey Coll, CA — A
Chapman U, CA — B
Chatham U, PA — B
Chemeketa Comm Coll, OR — A
Christendom Coll, VA — B
City Coll of San Francisco, CA — A
City Coll of the City U of New York, NY — B
City Colls of Chicago, Harold Washington Coll, IL — A
Claflin U, SC — B
Clarendon Coll, TX — A
Clarion U of Pennsylvania, PA — B
Clarke Coll, IA — B
Clarkson U, NY — B
Clark U, MA — B
Cleveland State U, OH — B
Coastal Carolina U, SC — B
Coastal Georgia Comm Coll, GA — A
Cochise Coll, Sierra Vista, AZ — A
Coe Coll, IA — B
Coffeyville Comm Coll, KS — A
Colby Coll, ME — B
Colby Comm Coll, KS — A
Coll of Saint Benedict, MN — B
Coll of St. Catherine, MN — B
Coll of Southern Maryland, MD — A
Coll of the Atlantic, ME — B
Coll of the Canyons, CA — A
Coll of the Desert, CA — A
Coll of the Holy Cross, MA — B
Coll of the Ozarks, MO — B
The Colorado Coll, CO — B
Colorado State U, CO — B
Columbia Coll, MO — B
Columbia Union Coll, MD — B
Columbia U, School of General Studies, NY — B
Concordia Coll, MN — B
Concordia Coll, NY — B
Concordia U, IL — B
Connecticut Coll, CT — B
Connors State Coll, OK — A
Cornell Coll, IA — B
Cosumnes River Coll, Sacramento, CA — A
County Coll of Morris, NJ — A
Cumberland U, TN — B
Daemen Coll, NY — B
Dakota Wesleyan U, SD — B
Dana Coll, NE — B
Davidson Coll, NC — B

De Anza Coll, CA — A
Defiance Coll, OH — A
Del Mar Coll, TX — A
Denison U, OH — B
DePaul U, IL — B
DePauw U, IN — B
DeSales U, PA — B
Dominican U of California, CA — B
Dordt Coll, IA — B
Drake U, IA — B
Drew U, NJ — B
Drury U, MO — B
Duquesne U, PA — B
D'Youville Coll, NY — B
East Carolina U, NC — B
East Central Coll, MO — A
Eastern Connecticut State U, CT — B
Eastern Mennonite U, VA — B
Eastern U, PA — B
Eastern Wyoming Coll, WY — A
East Los Angeles Coll, CA — A
East Tennessee State U, TN — B
East Texas Baptist U, TX — B
Eckerd Coll, FL — B
Edgewood Coll, WI — B
Edinboro U of Pennsylvania, PA — B
Edison Coll, FL — A
El Camino Coll, CA — A
Elizabethtown Coll, PA — B
Elmira Coll, NY — B
Elms Coll, MA — B
Elon U, NC — B
Emmanuel Coll, MA — B
Emory U, GA — B
Emporia State U, KS — B
The Evergreen State Coll, WA — B
Fairfield U, CT — B
Fairleigh Dickinson U, Coll at Florham, NJ — B
Fairleigh Dickinson U, Metropolitan Campus, NJ — B
Ferris State U, MI — B
Flagler Coll, FL — B
Florida Atlantic U, FL — B
Florida Gulf Coast U, FL — B
Florida International U, FL — B
Florida State U, FL — B
Foothill Coll, CA — A
Fordham U, NY — B
Fort Lewis Coll, CO — B
Fresno City Coll, CA — A
Fresno Pacific U, CA — A,B
Frostburg State U, MD — B
Fullerton Coll, CA — A
Fulton-Montgomery Comm Coll, NY — A
Furman U, SC — B
Gannon U, PA — B
Garden City Comm Coll, KS — A
GateWay Comm Coll, AZ — A
George Fox U, OR — B
Georgetown Coll, KY — B
Georgia Coll & State U, GA — B
Georgia Highlands Coll, GA — A
Georgia Southern U, GA — B
Georgia State U, GA — B
Gettysburg Coll, PA — B
Glendale Comm Coll, CA — A
Gonzaga U, WA — B
Goshen Coll, IN — B
Grambling State U, LA — B
Grand Valley State U, MI — B
Grand View Coll, IA — A
Green Mountain Coll, VT — B
Greenville Coll, IL — B
Grinnell Coll, IA — B
Gulf Coast Comm Coll, FL — A
Gustavus Adolphus Coll, MN — B
Hamilton Coll, NY — B
Hampden-Sydney Coll, VA — B
Hampshire Coll, MA — B
Harding U, AR — B
Hardin-Simmons U, TX — B
Harper Coll, IL — A
Harrisburg Area Comm Coll, PA — A
Hartwick Coll, NY — B
Harvard U, MA — B
Haverford Coll, PA — B
Hawai'i Pacific U, HI — B

Hill Coll of the Hill Jr Coll District, TX — A
Hillsdale Coll, MI — B
Hiram Coll, OH — B
Hofstra U, NY — B
Holy Apostles Coll and Seminary, CT — B
Holy Family U, PA — B
Hope Coll, MI — B
Hope International U, CA — B
Houston Comm Coll System, TX — A
Howard Coll, TX — A
Howard Payne U, TX — B
Hudson Valley Comm Coll, NY — A
Huntingdon Coll, AL — B
Huntington U, IN — B
Idaho State U, ID — A,B
Illinois Coll, IL — B
Illinois Inst of Technology, IL — B
Illinois Wesleyan U, IL — B
Indiana U Bloomington, IN — A,B
Indiana U of Pennsylvania, PA — A,B
Indiana U South Bend, IN — A,B
Indiana U Southeast, IN — B
Indiana Wesleyan U, IN — A,B
Iowa State U of Science and Technology, IA — B
Itasca Comm Coll, MN — A
Jacksonville State U, AL — B
Jacksonville U, FL — B
James Madison U, VA — B
John Carroll U, OH — B
John Jay Coll of Criminal Justice of the City U of New York, NY — B
The Johns Hopkins U, MD — B
Johnson State Coll, VT — B
Joliet Jr Coll, IL — A
Judson Coll, IL — B
Juniata Coll, PA — B
Kansas State U, KS — B
Kansas Wesleyan U, KS — B
Kean U, NJ — B
Kennesaw State U, GA — B
Kent State U, OH — B
Kentucky Wesleyan Coll, KY — B
Kenyon Coll, OH — B
Kilgore Coll, TX — A
Kingwood Coll, TX — A
Kirkwood Comm Coll, IA — A
Knox Coll, IL — B
Lafayette Coll, PA — B
Lakeland Coll, WI — B
Lamar State Coll–Port Arthur, TX — A
Lander U, SC — B
Laney Coll, CA — A
Langston U, OK — B
Lansing Comm Coll, MI — A
Laramie County Comm Coll, WY — A
Lawrence U, WI — B
Lees-McRae Coll, NC — B
LeMoyne-Owen Coll, TN — B
Lewis & Clark Coll, OR — B
Lewis-Clark State Coll, ID — B
Liberty U, VA — B
Lincoln U, CA — B
Linfield Coll, OR — B
Lipscomb U, TN — B
Long Beach City Coll, CA — A
Long Island U, C.W. Post Campus, NY — B
Longwood U, VA — B
Los Angeles Mission Coll, CA — A
Los Angeles Southwest Coll, CA — A
Loyola U Chicago, IL — B
Luther Coll, IA — B
Lycoming Coll, PA — B
Lynchburg Coll, VA — B
Lyndon State Coll, VT — B
Lynn U, FL — B
Manatee Comm Coll, FL — A
Manchester Coll, IN — B
Manhattan Coll, NY — B
Manhattanville Coll, NY — B
Marian Coll of Fond du Lac, WI — B
Marlboro Coll, VT — B
Marquette U, WI — A,B
Marshall U, WV — B
Mary Baldwin Coll, VA — B
Marylhurst U, OR — B

Marymount Manhattan Coll, NY	A	Peru State Coll, NE		Southeast Missouri State U, MO	B	U of Minnesota, Morris, MN	B
Maryville Coll, TN	B	Piedmont Comm Coll, NC	A	Southern Arkansas U–Magnolia, AR	B	U of Missouri–Columbia, MO	B
Maryville U of Saint Louis, MO	B	Pittsburg State U, KS	B	Southern Illinois U Carbondale, IL	B	U of Missouri–St. Louis, MO	B

Marymount Manhattan Coll, NY — A
Maryville Coll, TN — B
Maryville U of Saint Louis, MO — B
Marywood U, PA — B
Massachusetts Bay Comm Coll, MA — A
Massachusetts Inst of Technology, MA — B
McDaniel Coll, MD — B
McMurry U, TX — B
McNeese State U, LA — B
Mercy Coll, NY — B
Merritt Coll, CA — A
Mesa State Coll, CO — A,B
Miami Dade Coll, FL — A
Miami U, OH — B
Michigan Technological U, MI — B
MidAmerica Nazarene U, KS — B
Middlebury Coll, VT — B
Middle Tennessee State U, TN — B
Midland Coll, TX — A
Midwestern State U, TX — B
Millersville U of Pennsylvania, PA — B
Milligan Coll, TN — B
Millsaps Coll, MS — B
Mills Coll, CA — B
Minnesota State U Mankato, MN — B
Minnesota State U Moorhead, MN — B
Minot State U, ND — B
MiraCosta Coll, CA — A
Mississippi U for Women, MS — B
Missouri Baptist U, MO — B
Modesto Jr Coll, CA — A
Molloy Coll, NY — B
Monmouth U, NJ — B
Montclair State U, NJ — B
Monterey Peninsula Coll, CA — A
Moravian Coll, PA — B
Morehead State U, KY — B
Morningside Coll, IA — B
Mount Holyoke Coll, MA — B
Mount Mercy Coll, IA — B
Muskingum Coll, OH — B
Nebraska Wesleyan U, NE — B
New Coll of California, CA — B
New Coll of Florida, FL — B
New England Coll, NH — B
New Mexico Highlands U, NM — B
New Mexico Military Inst, NM — A
New Mexico State U, NM — B
New York U, NY — B
Niagara U, NY — B
Nichols Coll, MA — B
North Carolina State U, NC — B
North Central Coll, IL — B
North Dakota State U, ND — B
Northeast Comm Coll, NE — A
Northeastern U, MA — B
Northern Arizona U, AZ — B
Northern Kentucky U, KY — B
Northern Michigan U, MI — B
Northern State U, SD — B
Northland Coll, WI — B
Northwest Coll, WY — A
Northwestern State U of Louisiana, LA — B
Northwestern U, IL — B
Northwest Missouri State U, MO — B
Northwest U, WA — B
Notre Dame Coll, OH — B
Notre Dame de Namur U, CA — B
Oakland U, MI — B
Ohio Wesleyan U, OH — B
Oklahoma Panhandle State U, OK — B
Oklahoma State U, OK — B
Oklahoma Wesleyan U, OK — B
Old Dominion U, VA — B
Orange Coast Coll, CA — A
Oregon State U, OR — B
Ottawa U, KS — B
Otterbein Coll, OH — B
Pace U, NY — B
Palomar Coll, CA — A
Park U, MO — B
Pellissippi State Tech Comm Coll, TN — A

Peru State Coll, NE
Piedmont Comm Coll, NC — A
Pittsburg State U, KS — B
Pitzer Coll, CA — B
Plymouth State U, NH — B
Portland State U, OR — B
Prescott Coll, AZ — B
Principia Coll, IL — B
Purdue U, IN — B
Quincy U, IL — B
Quinnipiac U, CT — B
Radford U, VA — B
Ramapo Coll of New Jersey, NJ — B
Randolph Coll, VA — B
Randolph-Macon Coll, VA — B
Raritan Valley Comm Coll, NJ — A
Redlands Comm Coll, OK — A
Reed Coll, OR — B
Rensselaer Polytechnic Inst, NY — B
Rhodes Coll, TN — B
Rider U, NJ — B
Ridgewater Coll, MN — A
Rochester Inst of Technology, NY — B
Rocky Mountain Coll, MT — B
Roger Williams U, RI — B
Roosevelt U, IL — B
Rose State Coll, OK — A
Sacramento City Coll, CA — A
Sacred Heart U, CT — A,B
Sage Coll of Albany, NY — A
St. Ambrose U, IA — B
Saint Anselm Coll, NH — B
Saint Francis U, PA — B
St. Gregory's U, OK — B
St. John's Coll, MD — B
St. John's Coll, NM — B
Saint John's U, MN — B
Saint Joseph's Coll, IN — B
Saint Leo U, FL — B
Saint Louis U, MO — B
Saint Mary-of-the-Woods Coll, IN — B
Saint Mary's Coll, IN — B
Saint Mary's Coll of California, CA — B
St. Mary's Coll of Maryland, MD — B
Saint Mary's U of Minnesota, MN — B
St. Mary's U of San Antonio, TX — B
Saint Michael's Coll, VT — B
St. Olaf Coll, MN — B
St. Thomas U, FL — B
Saint Vincent Coll, PA — B
Sam Houston State U, TX — B
San Bernardino Valley Coll, CA — A
San Diego City Coll, CA — A
San Diego State U, CA — B
San Francisco State U, CA — B
San Jacinto Coll Central Campus, TX — A
San Jacinto Coll North Campus, TX — A
San Jacinto Coll South Campus, TX — A
Santa Barbara City Coll, CA — A
Santa Monica Coll, CA — A
Santa Rosa Jr Coll, CA — A
Sarah Lawrence Coll, NY — B
Sauk Valley Comm Coll, IL — A
Savannah State U, GA — B
Schiller International U, FL — B
Schreiner U, TX — B
Scripps Coll, CA — B
Seattle U, WA — B
Seton Hall U, NJ — B
Shenandoah U, VA — B
Shepherd U, WV — B
Sheridan Coll–Sheridan and Gillette, WY — A
Shorter Coll, GA — B
Siena Coll, NY — B
Simmons Coll, MA — B
Simpson Coll, IA — B
Skagit Valley Coll, WA — A
Skidmore Coll, NY — B
Slippery Rock U of Pennsylvania, PA — B
South Dakota State U, SD — B

Southeast Missouri State U, MO — B
Southern Arkansas U–Magnolia, AR — B
Southern Illinois U Carbondale, IL — B
Southern Illinois U Edwardsville, IL — B
Southern New Hampshire U, NH — B
Southern Oregon U, OR — B
Southern Utah U, UT — B
South Georgia Coll, GA — A
Southwest Minnesota State U, MN — B
Spring Arbor U, MI — B
Stanford U, CA — B
State U of New York at Oswego, NY — B
State U of New York at Plattsburgh, NY — B
State U of New York Coll at Geneseo, NY — B
State U of New York Coll at Oneonta, NY — B
Stony Brook U, State U of New York, NY — B
Suffolk County Comm Coll, NY — A
Suffolk U, MA — B
Susquehanna U, PA — B
Swarthmore Coll, PA — B
Syracuse U, NY — B
Tabor Coll, KS — B
Taylor U, IN — B
Tennessee Technological U, TN — B
Texas A&M U–Corpus Christi, TX — B
Texas A&M U–Kingsville, TX — B
Texas Christian U, TX — B
Texas State U-San Marcos, TX — B
Texas Wesleyan U, TX — B
Thomas Aquinas Coll, CA — B
Thomas More Coll, KY — A,B
Trevecca Nazarene U, TN — B
Trinity Coll, CT — B
Trinity U, TX — B
Trinity (Washington) U, DC — B
Troy U, AL — B
Truman State U, MO — B
Union Coll, NY — B
U at Buffalo, the State U of New York, NY — B
The U of Alabama, AL — B
The U of Alabama in Huntsville, AL — B
U of Arkansas, AR — B
U of Arkansas at Pine Bluff, AR — B
U of Baltimore, MD — B
U of California, Santa Cruz, CA — B
U of Central Florida, FL — B
U of Central Missouri, MO — B
U of Charleston, WV — B
U of Cincinnati, OH — A,B
U of Cincinnati Raymond Walters Coll, OH — A
U of Colorado at Boulder, CO — B
U of Colorado at Colorado Springs, CO — B
U of Dayton, OH — B
U of Denver, CO — B
U of Detroit Mercy, MI — B
U of Dubuque, IA — A,B
The U of Findlay, OH — A,B
U of Guam, GU — B
U of Hartford, CT — B
U of Hawaii at Manoa, HI — B
U of Illinois at Springfield, IL — B
U of Indianapolis, IN — B
The U of Iowa, IA — B
U of Kansas, KS — B
U of La Verne, CA — B
U of Maine at Farmington, ME — B
U of Maine at Fort Kent, ME — B
U of Maine at Presque Isle, ME — B
U of Mary Hardin-Baylor, TX — B
U of Maryland, Baltimore County, MD — B
U of Maryland, Coll Park, MD — B
U of Mary Washington, VA — B
U of Miami, FL — B
U of Michigan–Flint, MI — B

U of Minnesota, Morris, MN — B
U of Missouri–Columbia, MO — B
U of Missouri–St. Louis, MO — B
U of Nebraska–Lincoln, NE — B
U of Nevada, Reno, NV — B
U of New Mexico, NM — B
U of New Orleans, LA — B
U of North Alabama, AL — B
The U of North Carolina at Asheville, NC — B
The U of North Carolina at Pembroke, NC — B
U of Northern Iowa, IA — B
U of North Texas, TX — B
U of Oregon, OR — B
U of Pittsburgh, PA — B
U of Pittsburgh at Bradford, PA — B
U of Puget Sound, WA — B
U of Rhode Island, RI — B
U of Rochester, NY — B
U of San Diego, CA — B
U of San Francisco, CA — B
U of Sioux Falls, SD — A,B
U of South Carolina, SC — B
U of South Carolina Upstate, SC — B
U of Southern Indiana, IN — A,B
U of Southern Maine, ME — B
U of South Florida, FL — B
The U of Tampa, FL — A,B
The U of Tennessee at Martin, TN — B
The U of Texas at San Antonio, TX — B
U of the Incarnate Word, TX — B
U of Tulsa, OK — B
U of Utah, UT — B
U of Virginia, VA — B
U of Washington, WA — B
U of West Florida, FL — B
U of Wisconsin–Eau Claire, WI — B
U of Wisconsin–La Crosse, WI — B
U of Wisconsin–Oshkosh, WI — B
U of Wisconsin–Stevens Point, WI — B
U of Wisconsin–Superior, WI — B
U of Wisconsin–Whitewater, WI — B
U of Wyoming, WY — B
Upper Iowa U, IA — B
Utah State U, UT — B
Utah Valley State Coll, UT — B
Utica Coll, NY — B
Valparaiso U, IN — A
Vanderbilt U, TN — B
Vanguard U of Southern California, CA — B
Villanova U, PA — B
Virginia Commonwealth U, VA — B
Virginia Polytechnic Inst and State U, VA — B
Viterbo U, WI — B
Wabash Coll, IN — B
Wake Forest U, NC — B
Warren Wilson Coll, NC — B
Wartburg Coll, IA — B
Washington & Jefferson Coll, PA — B
Washington Coll, MD — B
Washington State U, WA — B
Washington U in St. Louis, MO — B
Waynesburg Coll, PA — B
Wayne State Coll, NE — B
Wells Coll, NY — B
Wesleyan U, CT — B
Western Illinois U, IL — B
Western Kentucky U, KY — B
Western New England Coll, MA — B
Western New Mexico U, NM — B
Western Washington U, WA — B
Western Wyoming Comm Coll, WY — A
Westmont Coll, CA — B
West Texas A&M U, TX — B
West Valley Coll, CA — A
Wichita State U, KS — B
Widener U, PA — B
Wilkes U, PA — B
Williams Coll, MA — B
Wilmington Coll, OH — B
Wilson Coll, PA — B
Winona State U, MN — B
Woodbury U, CA — B

A=Associate; B=Bachelor's Degree

Worcester Polytechnic Inst, MA	B
Worcester State Coll, MA	B
York Coll of Pennsylvania, PA	A,B
York Coll of the City U of New York, NY	B
Young Harris Coll, GA	A

Technical Trades, Crafts, and Aviation

Aims Comm Coll, CO	A
Alamance Comm Coll, NC	A
Averett U, VA	B
Baker Coll of Flint, MI	A
Boise State U, ID	A
Calhoun Comm Coll, AL	A
California State U, Long Beach, CA	B
Cameron U, OK	A
Central Comm Coll–Columbus Campus, NE	A
Central Comm Coll–Grand Island Campus, NE	A
Central Comm Coll–Hastings Campus, NE	A
Centralia Coll, WA	A
Central Piedmont Comm Coll, NC	A
Central Wyoming Coll, WY	A
Century Coll, MN	A
Cerro Coso Comm Coll, CA	A
Chabot Coll, CA	A
Chattanooga State Tech Comm Coll, TN	A
Chemeketa Comm Coll, OR	A
City Coll of San Francisco, CA	A
Clinton Comm Coll, IA	A
Cochise Coll, Sierra Vista, AZ	A
Coffeyville Comm Coll, KS	A
Coll of DuPage, IL	A
Coll of Eastern Utah, UT	A
Coll of Lake County, IL	A
Coll of the Canyons, CA	A
Coll of the Desert, CA	A
Coll of the Ozarks, MO	B
Cosumnes River Coll, Sacramento, CA	A
Dakota County Tech Coll, MN	A
Davenport U, Midland, MI	A
De Anza Coll, CA	A
DeKalb Tech Coll, GA	A
Delaware Tech & Comm Coll, Jack F. Owens Campus, DE	A
Del Mar Coll, TX	A
Delta Coll, MI	A
East Central Coll, MO	A
Eastern Wyoming Coll, WY	A
El Camino Coll, CA	A
Ferris State U, MI	A,B
Foothill Coll, CA	A
Fox Valley Tech Coll, WI	A
Fresno City Coll, CA	A
Fullerton Coll, CA	A
Fulton-Montgomery Comm Coll, NY	A
Garden City Comm Coll, KS	A
GateWay Comm Coll, AZ	A
Glendale Comm Coll, CA	A
Grays Harbor Coll, WA	A
Harper Coll, IL	A
Hawaii Comm Coll, HI	A
Hill Coll of the Hill Jr Coll District, TX	A
Idaho State U, ID	A
Iowa Western Comm Coll, IA	A
Isothermal Comm Coll, NC	A
Johnson County Comm Coll, KS	A
Joliet Jr Coll, IL	A
Kankakee Comm Coll, IL	A
Kilgore Coll, TX	A
Kirkwood Comm Coll, IA	A
Lake Region State Coll, ND	A
Laney Coll, CA	A
Lansing Comm Coll, MI	A
Laramie County Comm Coll, WY	A
Las Positas Coll, CA	A
Lewis-Clark State Coll, ID	A,B
Long Beach City Coll, CA	A
Los Angeles Mission Coll, CA	A
Los Angeles Pierce Coll, CA	A
Maui Comm Coll, HI	A
Mesa State Coll, CO	A
Midland Coll, TX	A
Minnesota State Coll–Southeast Tech, MN	A
Minnesota State U Mankato, MN	B
MiraCosta Coll, CA	A
Mitchell Tech Inst, SD	A
Modesto Jr Coll, CA	A
Montana Tech of The U of Montana, MT	B
New River Comm Coll, VA	A
North Dakota State Coll of Science, ND	A
Northeast Comm Coll, NE	A
Northeast State Tech Comm Coll, TN	A
Northern Michigan U, MI	A
North Lake Coll, TX	A
Northwest Coll, WY	A
Orange Coast Coll, CA	A
Oregon State U, OR	B
Palomar Coll, CA	A
Pellissippi State Tech Comm Coll, TN	A
Pikes Peak Comm Coll, CO	A
Pittsburg State U, KS	B
Portland Comm Coll, OR	A
Pratt Inst, NY	A,B
Renton Tech Coll, WA	A
Richmond Comm Coll, NC	A
Riverside Comm Coll District, CA	A
Roger Williams U, RI	B
Rose State Coll, OK	A
Sacramento City Coll, CA	A
Sam Houston State U, TX	B
San Bernardino Valley Coll, CA	A
San Diego City Coll, CA	A
San Jacinto Coll Central Campus, TX	A
San Jacinto Coll North Campus, TX	A
Santa Monica Coll, CA	A
Santa Rosa Jr Coll, CA	A
Scott Comm Coll, IA	A
Seattle Central Comm Coll, WA	A
Sheridan Coll–Sheridan and Gillette, WY	A
Sierra Coll, CA	A
Skagit Valley Coll, WA	A
Southern Illinois U Carbondale, IL	B
Southern Utah U, UT	A
South Puget Sound Comm Coll, WA	A
Southwestern Comm Coll, IA	A
Spokane Comm Coll, WA	A
Spokane Falls Comm Coll, WA	A
Texas State Tech Coll Waco, TX	A
Texas State Tech Coll West Texas, TX	A
U of Cincinnati, OH	B
U of Denver, CO	B
U of Minnesota, Crookston, MN	A
U of Washington, WA	B
Utah State U, UT	B
Utah Valley State Coll, UT	A
Wentworth Inst of Technology, MA	A,B
Western New Mexico U, NM	A
Western Wyoming Comm Coll, WY	A
Wytheville Comm Coll, VA	A

Geographical Listing of In-Depth Descriptions

Alphabetical Listing of Colleges and Universities